Strawfield

RAND McNALLY

WORLD
ATLAS

1970 EDITION

RAND McNALLY & COMPANY
Chicago   New York   San Francisco

CONTENTS

MAP PROJECTIONS. . . . . vi-vii
THE WESTERN HEMISPHERE viii
THE EASTERN HEMISPHERE ix

SAGA OF SPACE—*pages x to xxix*

MEMBERS OF THE UNIVERSE x
THE MILKY WAY. xi
STAR CHART FOR THE NORTHERN SKIES xii
STAR CHART FOR THE SOUTHERN SKIES xiii
SOLAR SYSTEM CHART . . . . xiv-xv
THE SOLAR SYSTEM—PLANET INFORMATION TABLE xvi
VENUS, MARS, JUPITER AND SATURN xvii
THE SAGA OF SPACE EXPLORATION xviii
THE FIRST STEPS UPWARD xix
AMERICA'S FIRST DAY IN ORBIT xx
PROJECT GEMINI xxi
APOLLO 11—THE FLIGHT OF THE EAGLE. . . . . xxii-xxiii
THE MOON . . . . xxiv-xxv
THE FARSIDE OF THE MOON xxvi
MARS AND THE MARINER PROBES. xxvii
COMMUNICATIONS SATELLITE xxviii
SPACE AGE GLOSSARY xxix

THE POLITICAL WORLD IN MAPS—*pages xxx to 89*

THE WORLD—*pages xxx to 2*

PAGES

Introduction to the Political Maps xxx
Polar Map of the World 1
The World 2

EUROPE—*pages 3 to 14*

Europe 3
British Isles 4
France and the Low Countries 5

Germany, Austria and Switzerland 6
Poland and Czechoslovakia 7
Spain and Portugal 8
Italy 9
Yugoslavia, Hungary, Romania and Bulgaria . . 10
Norway, Sweden and Finland 11
Western Soviet Union 12
Soviet Union 13
Eastern Mediterranean 14

CONTENTS—*continued*

ASIA—*pages 15 to 20*	PAGES	NORTH AMERICA—*continued*	PAGES
Israel and Arabia	15	Delaware	53
Eurasia	16	Florida	54
China, Mongolia, Korea, Japan and Taiwan	17	Georgia	55
Japan and Korea	18	Hawaii	56
Indonesia and the Philippines	19	Idaho	57
India, Pakistan, Burma and Ceylon	20	Illinois	58
AFRICA—*pages 21 to 24*		Indiana	59
Africa	21	Iowa	60
Northwestern Africa	22	Kansas	61
Northeastern Africa	23	Kentucky	62
Central and Southern Africa	24	Louisiana	63
AUSTRALIA AND NEW ZEALAND—*pages 25 to 26*		Maine	64
Australia	25	Maryland	53
Southeastern Australia and New Zealand	26	Massachusetts	65
SOUTH AMERICA—*pages 27 to 32*		Michigan	66
South America	27	Minnesota	67
Central and Southern Argentina and Chile	28	Mississippi	68
Bolivia, Paraguay, Northern Argentina and Chile	29	Missouri	69
Uruguay and Southern Brazil	30	Montana	70
Peru and Ecuador	31	Nebraska	71
Colombia and Venezuela	32	Nevada	72
NORTH AMERICA—*pages 33 to 89*		New Hampshire	73
North America	33	New Jersey	74
Mexico	34	New Mexico	48
West Indies	35	New York	75
Canada	36	North Carolina	76
British Columbia	37	North Dakota	77
Alberta	38	Ohio	78
Saskatchewan	39	Oklahoma	79
Manitoba	40	Oregon	80
Ontario	41	Pennsylvania	81
Quebec	42	Rhode Island	52
Maritime Provinces	43	South Carolina	82
Newfoundland	44	South Dakota	77
United States	45	Tennessee	83
Alabama	46	Texas	84
Alaska	47	Utah	72
Arizona	48	Vermont	73
Arkansas	49	Virginia	85
California	50	Washington	86
Colorado	51	West Virginia	87
Connecticut	52	Wisconsin	88
		Wyoming	89

CONTENTS—*continued*

EXPLANATION OF THE INDEX REFERENCE SYSTEM—*page 90*

SELECTED UNITED STATES INFORMATION—*pages 91 to 92*

PAGE

GEOGRAPHICAL FACTS ABOUT
THE UNITED STATES 91

PAGE

UNITED STATES
STATE GENERAL INFORMATION TABLE. . 92

PAGES

LIST OF ABBREVIATIONS 93

EXPLANATION OF THE MAP INDEX 94

INDEX 94-189

GLOSSARY OF FOREIGN GEOGRAPHICAL TERMS 190-191

SELECTED WORLD INFORMATION—*pages 192 to 207*

PAGES

WORLD POLITICAL INFORMATION TABLE 192-196

WORLD FACTS AND COMPARISONS . . 197-199

MOVEMENTS, MEASUREMENTS, INHABITANTS, SURFACE
AND EXTREMES OF TEMPERATURE AND RAINFALL OF THE
EARTH; THE CONTINENTS; APPROXIMATE POPULATION
OF THE WORLD 1650-1965; LARGEST COUNTRIES OF THE
WORLD IN POPULATION; LARGEST COUNTRIES OF THE
WORLD IN AREA 197
PRINCIPAL MOUNTAINS OF THE WORLD 198
GREAT OCEANS AND SEAS OF THE WORLD 199
PRINCIPAL LAKES OF THE WORLD 199

PAGES

PRINCIPAL RIVERS OF THE WORLD 199
PRINCIPAL ISLANDS OF THE WORLD 199

LARGEST METROPOLITAN AREAS
AND CITIES OF THE WORLD, 1964 200

PRINCIPAL WORLD CITIES AND
POPULATIONS 201

PRINCIPAL DISCOVERIES
AND EXPLORATIONS 202-205

WORLD AIR AND STEAMSHIP
DISTANCE TABLES 206-207

WORLD HISTORY IN MAPS—*pages 208 to 233*

THE WORLD IN FOCUS—MAPS, TEXT, AND PICTURES—*pages 234 to 294*

PAGES

WORLD POPULATION 234-241

WORLD TRANSPORTATION 242-253

WORLD LANGUAGES 254-259

WORLD RACES 260-267

PAGES

WORLD RELIGIONS 268-275

NATURAL VEGETATION 276-283

WORLD CLIMATES 284-289

WORLD LANDFORMS. 290-294

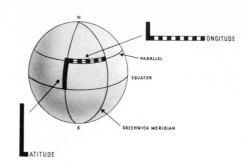

A map projection is merely an orderly system of parallels and meridians on which a flat map can be drawn. There are hundreds of projections, but no one represents the earth's spherical surface without some distortion. The distortion is relatively small for most practical purposes when a small part of the sphere is projected. For larger areas, a sacrifice of some property is necessary.

Most projections are designed to preserve on the flat map some particular property of the sphere. By varying the systematic arrangement or spacing of the latitude and longitude lines, a projection may be made either equal-area or conformal. Although most projections are derived from mathematical formulas, some are easier to visualize if thought of as projected upon a plane, or upon a cone or cylinder which is then unrolled into a plane surface. Thus, many projections are classified as plane (azimuthal), conic, or cylindrical.

SIMPLE CONIC PROJECTIONS

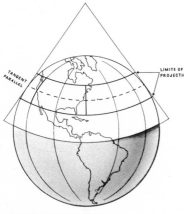

A perspective projection on a tangent cone with the origin point at the center of the globe. At the parallel of tangency, all elements of the map are true angles, distances, shapes, areas. Away from the tangent parallel, distances increase rapidly, giving bad distortion of shapes and areas.

EARTH PROJECTED UPON
A TANGENT CONE

CONE CUT FROM BASE TO APEX

CONE DEVELOPED INTO
A PLANE SURFACE

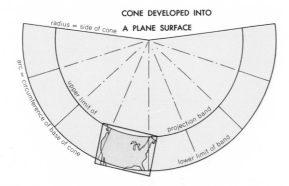

MODIFIED CONIC PROJECTION

EARTH PROJECTED UPON AN INTERSECTING CONE

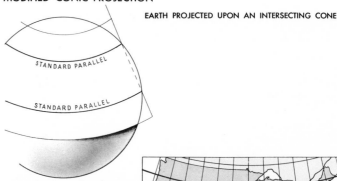

This modification of the conic has two standard parallels, or lines of intersection. It is not an equal-area projection, the space being reduced in size between the standard parallels and progressively enlarged beyond the standard parallels. Careful selection of the standard parallels provides however, good representation for areas of limited latitudinal extent.

CONIC PROJECTION WITH TWO STANDARD PARALLELS

BONNE PROJECTION

An equal-area modification of the conic principle. Distances are true along all parallels and the central meridian; but away from it, increasing obliqueness of intersections and longitudinal distances, with their attendant distortion of shapes, limits the satisfactory area.

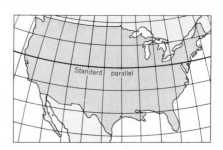

POLYCONIC PROJECTION

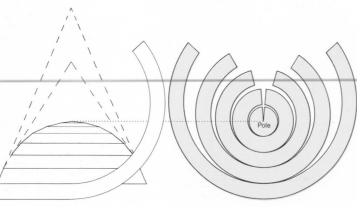

EARTH CONSIDERED AS FORMED
BY BASES OF CONES

DEVELOPMENT OF THE CONICAL BASES

POLYCONIC PROJECTION

This variation is not equal-area. Parallels are nonconcentric circles truly divided. Distances along the straight central meridian are also true, but along the curving meridians are increasingly exaggerated. Representation is good near the central meridian, but away from it there is marked distortion.

TYPICAL PLANE PROJECTIONS

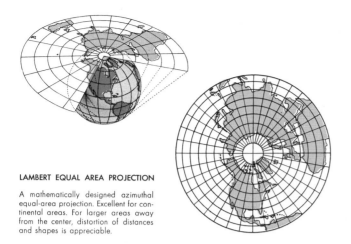

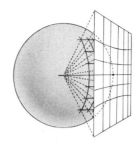

LAMBERT EQUAL AREA PROJECTION

A mathematically designed azimuthal equal-area projection. Excellent for continental areas. For larger areas away from the center, distortion of distances and shapes is appreciable.

GNOMONIC PROJECTION

A geometric or perspective projection on a tangent plane with the origin point at the center of the globe. Shapes and distances rapidly become increasingly distorted away from the center of the projection. Important in navigation, because all straight lines are great circles.

CYLINDRICAL PROJECTIONS

EARTH PROJECTED UPON A CYLINDER

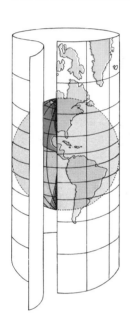

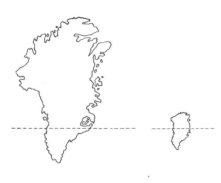

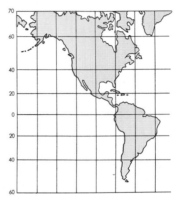

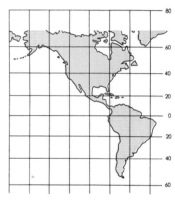

PERSPECTIVE PROJECTION

A perspective projection on a tangent cylinder. Because of rapidly increasing distortion away from the line of tangency and the lack of any special advantage, it is rarely used.

Note the increasing distortion of Greenland (above left) compared to an equal area projection (above right).

MERCATOR CONFORMAL PROJECTION

Mercator's modification increases the longitudinal distances in the same proportion as latitudinal distances are increased. Thus, at any point shapes are true, but areas become increasingly exaggerated. Of value in navigation, because a line connecting any two points gives the true direction between them.

MILLER PROJECTION

This recent modification is neither conformal nor equal-area. Whereas shapes are less accurate than on the Mercator, the exaggeration of areas has been reduced somewhat.

EQUAL AREA PROJECTIONS OF THE WORLD

The earth's surface peeled like the skin from an orange.

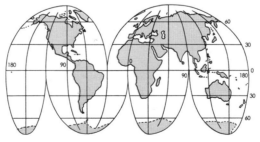

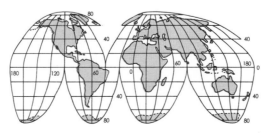

MOLLWEIDE'S HOMOLOGRAPHIC PROJECTION

GOODE'S INTERRUPTED HOMOLOGRAPHIC PROJECTION

SINUSOIDAL PROJECTION

GOODE'S INTERRUPTED HOMOLOSINE PROJECTION

Although each of these projections is equal-area, differences in the spacing and arrangement of latitude and longitude lines result in differences in the distribution and relative degree of the shape and distance distortion within each grid. On the homolographic, there is no uniformity in scale. It is different on each parallel and each meridian. On the sinusoidal, only distances along all latitudes and the central meridian are true. The homolosine combines the homolographic, for areas poleward of 40°, with the sinusoidal. The principle of interruption permits each continent in turn the advantage of being in the center of the projection, resulting in better shapes.

This distinctive relief interpretation shows the New World as it might be seen from outer space if all hindrances to vision were removed. You can see how the mountain backbone of the Rockies and the Andes stretches nearly from pole to pole, and how the major river systems of the Mississippi-Missouri and the Amazon each drain half a continent.

The face of the land is shown from the ice pack of Greenland and the tundra region of Northern Canada to the great plains of the Midwest and the deserts of southwestern United States and Mexico. The vegetation of South America is depicted from the highlands of Venezuela and the tropical rain forest of the Amazon Valley to the Pampas and Patagonia.

A realistic picture of the Old World is afforded by precise and accurate shaded relief combined with subtly blended colors portraying the face of the land. You can see how the mighty Sahara and the deserts of Arabia confined early civilizations in the Nile and Tigris-Euphrates river valleys.

The topography and vegetation of the earth as shown here reveal something of how such great barriers as the Himalayas, the dense jungles of Africa, and the vast deserts have affected and controlled man's efforts in transportation, communication, and broad cultural interchange.

FIGURE 1

COURTESY LICK OBSERVATORY

Members of the Universe

The Universe consists of a vast Space, within which are contained untold numbers of galaxies, billions of stars, planets, asteroids, and other celestial objects of varying sizes, shapes and characteristics.

Among the important members of the Universe are the galaxies, known also as "Universe Islands."

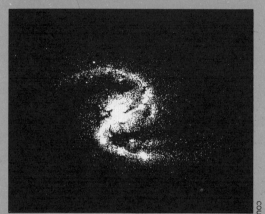

FIGURE 2

FIGURE 3

COURTESY MT. WILSON & MT. PALOMAR OBSERVATORIES

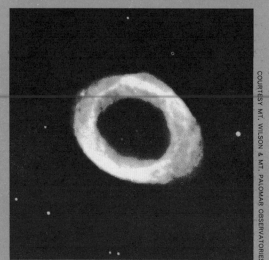

FIGURE 4

FIGURE 5

COURTESY MT. WILSON & MT. PALOMAR OBSERVATORIES

A Galaxy is a large community of stars. Several types of Galaxies can be classified by their shape and structure. Thus, our "Milky Way" is a Spiral Galaxy (Figure No. 1). The Sun is a star in the Milky Way and is located over half way out from the center of the Galaxy. In Figure No. 2 the Milky Way is shown as a side view; its diameter approximates 100,000 light years.

There are other types of Galaxies, among them, Barred Spirals (Fig. 3), which have straighter spiral arms than the normal spirals. Also Elliptical galaxies, such as M32, which is located in the region of Andromeda. And, Irregular galaxies, such as the Magellanic Clouds, characterized by having no particular shape. Stars are also grouped close together in Star Clusters (Fig. 4), such as that of Hercules.

In Space, there are also clouds of gases and dust. Any of these clouds are termed Nebula. There are two kinds of them: Diffuse Nebulae and Dark Nebulae. The former are located near a star, which is their source of light (Fig. 5), such as the Ring Nebula in Lyra. Dark Nebulae are those which have no star nearby from which to draw light, (Fig. 6), such as the Horsehead Nebula in Orion.

Our Sun is a smaller than average star. It is completely gaseous and rotates irregularly. The two major portions of the Sun are: its Atmosphere composed of 3 layers, and the Nucleus, or Sun proper. The atmosphere is separated from the Nucleus by the Photosphere, an opaque layer, which does not permit the observer to see under it, (Fig. 7). The effective temperature of the Sun approximates 10,000° F. The amount of energy received from it at the earth's surface is of 1.94 calories per square centimeter per minute.

The upper layer of the Sun's atmosphere registers some very turbulent phenomena known as solar prominences, which resemble flame tongues, streaking upward to tremendous heights dwarfing the size of earth to a mere dot, (Fig. 8).

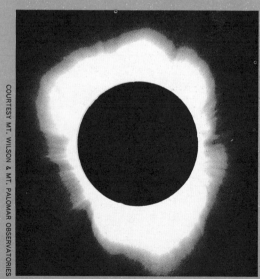

FIGURE 6

COURTESY MT. WILSON & MT. PALOMAR OBSERVATORIES

FIGURE 7

COURTESY MT. WILSON & MT. PALOMAR OBSERVATORIES

FIGURE 8

COURTESY MT. WILSON OBSERVATORY

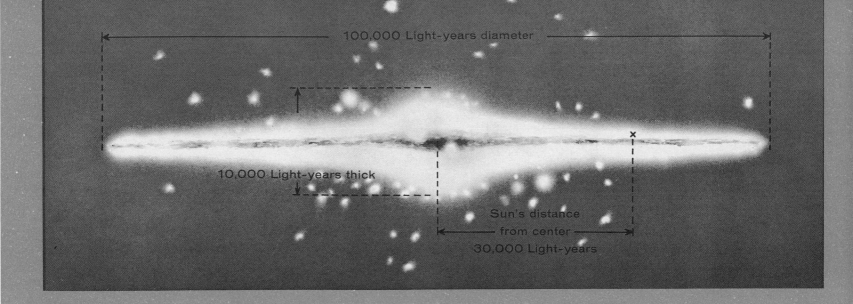

100,000 Light-years diameter

10,000 Light-years thick

Sun's distance from center 30,000 Light-years

The Milky Way

Above is shown a side view of the Milky Way, as conceived today. In it, the Sun is only one of about 100 billion stars. Below is a "top view" of the Whirlpool galaxy in Canes Venatici, which is very similar to our Milky Way. The Milky Way resembles a huge cartwheel revolving through the intergallactic Space at ponderous velocities. Our Galaxy has enormous quantities of interstellar gas clouds which occur in varying densities and cause the lack of temporary clear vision. (Distances are given in light years. One light year is about six million million miles.)

Photo from Mt. Wilson & Palomar Observatories

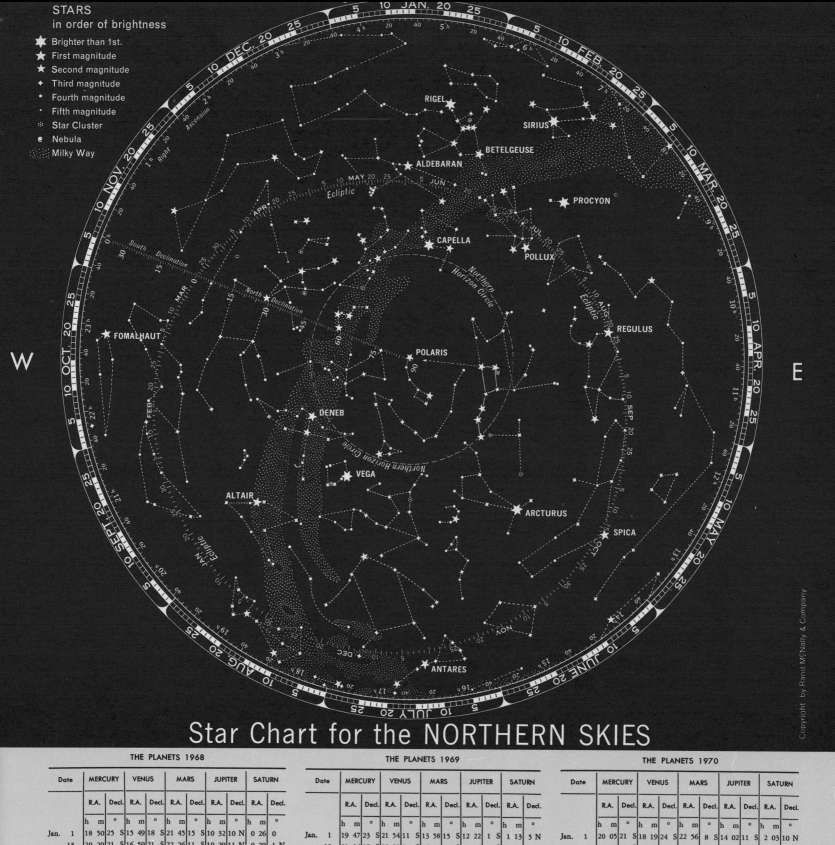

Star Chart for the NORTHERN SKIES

THE PLANETS 1968

Date	MERCURY R.A.	MERCURY Decl.	VENUS R.A.	VENUS Decl.	MARS R.A.	MARS Decl.	JUPITER R.A.	JUPITER Decl.	SATURN R.A.	SATURN Decl.
	h m	°	h m	°	h m	°	h m	°	h m	°
Jan. 1	18 50	25 S	15 49	18 S	21 45	15 S	10 32	10 N	0 26	0
15	20 29	21 S	16 59	21 S	22 26	11 S	10 29	11 N	0 29	1 N
Feb. 1	22 06	11 S	18 28	22 S	23 15	6 S	10 23	11 N	0 33	1 N
15	21 51	9 S	19 42	21 S	23 55	1 S	10 16	12 N	0 38	2 N
Mar. 1	21 17	14 S	20 59	18 S	0 37	4 N	10 09	13 N	0 44	2 N
15	21 59	14 S	22 07	13 S	1 16	8 N	10 00	13 N	0 50	3 N
Apr. 1	23 27	6 S	23 26	5 S	2 03	12 N	9 57	14 N	0 50	3 N
15	0 56	4 N	0 30	2 N	2 43	16 N	9 54	14 N	0 58	4 N
May 1	3 00	18 N	1 43	9 N	3 29	19 N	9 54	14 N	1 05	4 N
15	4 50	25 N	2 49	15 N	4 10	21 N	9 57	14 N	1 12	5 N
June 1	6 04	24 N	4 14	21 N	5 00	23 N	10 03	13 N	1 18	6 N
15	5 58	21 N	5 27	23 N	5 42	24 N	10 10	12 N	1 25	6 N
July 1	5 32	19 N	6 53	24 N	6 29	24 N	10 19	12 N	1 30	7 N
15	6 09	21 N	8 07	21 N	7 09	23 N	10 28	11 N	1 34	7 N
Aug. 1	8 16	21 N	9 33	16 N	7 57	22 N	10 41	9 N	1 38	7 N
15	10 10	13 N	10 39	10 N	8 35	20 N	10 51	8 N	1 38	7 N
Sept. 1	11 56	0	11 56	2 N	9 19	17 N	11 05	7 N	1 37	7 N
15	13 03	9 S	12 59	5 S	9 54	14 N	11 16	6 N	1 34	7 N
Oct. 1	13 50	15 S	14 12	13 S	10 32	11 N	11 29	4 N	1 30	6 N
15	13 23	11 S	15 19	18 S	11 05	7 N	11 40	3 N	1 26	6 N
Nov. 1	13 08	6 S	16 46	24 S	11 44	3 N	11 52	2 N	1 22	6 N
15	14 33	14 S	18 00	25 S	12 15	0	12 10	1 N	1 18	5 N
Dec. 1	16 14	22 S	19 25	24 S	12 50	4 S	12 10	0	1 14	9 N
15	17 49	25 S	20 36	21 S	13 21	7 S	12 10	0	1 13	5 N

THE PLANETS 1969

Date	MERCURY R.A.	MERCURY Decl.	VENUS R.A.	VENUS Decl.	MARS R.A.	MARS Decl.	JUPITER R.A.	JUPITER Decl.	SATURN R.A.	SATURN Decl.
	h m	°	h m	°	h m	°	h m	°	h m	°
Jan. 1	19 47	23 S	21 54	11 S	13 58	15 S	12 22	1 S	1 13	5 N
15	21 04	17 S	22 52	8 S	14 28	13 S	12 24	1 S	1 15	5 N
Feb. 1	20 30	15 S	23 54	0	15 04	16 S	12 24	1 S	1 18	6 N
15	20 13	18 S	0 38	7 N	15 33	18 S	12 21	1 S	1 23	6 N
Mar. 1	21 07	17 S	1 12	3 N	15 59	19 S	12 16	0	1 28	7 N
15	22 25	12 S	1 29	17 N	16 23	21 S	12 10	1 N	1 33	7 N
Apr. 1	0 14	0	1 13	16 N	16 46	22 S	12 02	2 N	1 41	8 N
15	1 57	12 N	0 45	20 N	16 59	22 S	11 56	2 N	1 48	9 N
May 1	3 51	23 N	0 35	7 N	17 02	23 S	11 51	3 N	1 55	9 N
15	4 40	24 N	0 54	6 N	16 54	24 S	11 48	3 N	2 02	10 N
June 1	4 20	19 N	1 39	8 N	16 32	24 S	11 48	3 N	2 10	11 N
15	4 12	17 N	2 26	12 N	16 11	24 S	11 51	3 N	2 15	11 N
July 1	5 10	21 N	3 29	16 N	15 57	24 S	11 56	3 N	2 21	12 N
15	5 59	23 N	4 29	19 N	16 02	24 S	12 02	2 N	2 25	12 N
Aug. 1	9 27	17 N	5 58	21 N	16 33	25 S	12 20	0	2 28	12 N
15	10 58	7 N	6 58	21 N	16 35	25 S	12 11	0	2 28	12 N
Sept. 1	12 16	4 S	8 23	19 N	17 08	25 S	12 32	2 S	2 28	12 N
15	12 48	9 S	9 31	15 N	17 26	24 S	12 42	3 S	2 28	12 N
Oct. 1	12 13	5 S	10 46	9 N	17 27	24 S	12 55	5 S	2 24	11 N
15	12 15	0	11 51	4 N	19 08	24 S	13 06	6 S	2 21	11 N
Nov. 1	13 49	10 S	13 08	6 S	19 59	24 S	13 19	7 S	2 15	11 N
15	15 17	18 S	14 14	13 S	20 41	20 S	13 31	8 S	2 11	10 N
Dec. 1	17 02	24 S	15 33	18 S	21 28	15 S	13 43	9 S	2 07	10 N
15	18 37	25 S	16 47	22 S	22 08	12 S	13 52	10 S	2 05	10 N

THE PLANETS 1970

Date	MERCURY R.A.	MERCURY Decl.	VENUS R.A.	VENUS Decl.	MARS R.A.	MARS Decl.	JUPITER R.A.	JUPITER Decl.	SATURN R.A.	SATURN Decl.
	h m	°	h m	°	h m	°	h m	°	h m	°
Jan. 1	20 05	21 S	18 19	24 S	22 56	8 S	14 02	11 S	2 03	10 N
15	19 27	19 S	19 36	22 S	23 34	3 S	14 09	12 S	2 03	10 N
Feb. 1	19 12	21 S	21 05	18 S	0 20	2 N	14 14	12 S	2 06	10 N
15	20 17	20 S	22 14	12 S	0 57	6 N	14 16	12 S	2 09	11 N
Mar. 1	21 41	16 S	23 20	6 S	1 35	10 N	14 16	12 S	2 13	11 N
15	23 12	7 S	0 24	1 N	2 13	14 N	14 13	12 S	2 18	12 N
Apr. 1	1 12	8 N	1 41	10 N	3 00	18 N	14 08	11 S	2 26	12 N
15	2 43	18 N	2 47	16 N	3 40	20 N	14 01	11 S	2 32	13 N
May 1	3 17	20 N	4 07	22 N	4 26	22 N	13 53	10 S	2 40	13 N
15	2 52	15 N	5 20	24 N	5 07	24 N	13 47	10 S	2 47	14 N
June 1	3 01	13 N	6 50	25 N	5 56	24 N	13 42	9 S	2 56	15 N
15	4 02	18 N	8 02	24 N	6 37	24 N	13 39	9 S	3 02	15 N
July 1	6 07	24 N	9 19	18 N	7 22	23 N	13 39	9 S	3 09	15 N
15	8 16	19 N	10 09	11 N	8 01	22 N	13 41	9 S	3 14	16 N
Aug. 1	10 14	12 N	11 31	4 N	8 46	20 N	13 48	9 S	3 19	16 N
15	11 13	3 N	12 25	3 S	9 15	18 N	13 53	10 S	3 22	16 N
Sept. 1	11 45	3 S	13 33	10 S	10 05	13 N	14 03	11 S	3 23	16 N
15	11 09	2 N	14 41	17 S	10 38	10 N	14 12	12 S	3 23	16 N
Oct. 1	11 25	5 N	14 59	23 S	11 16	6 N	14 23	13 S	3 21	16 N
15	12 48	3 S	15 47	25 S	11 49	2 N	14 34	14 S	3 18	16 N
Nov. 1	14 35	14 S	16 53	25 S	12 24	2 S	14 50	15 S	3 13	15 N
15	16 03	22 S	17 48	24 S	13 01	5 S	15 02	16 S	3 09	15 N
Dec. 1	17 45	26 S	14 30	14 S	13 39	9 S	15 16	17 S	3 04	15 N
15	18 55	24 S	14 47	15 S	14 13	13 S	15 28	18 S	2 60	14 N

STARS
in order of brightness

- ★ Brighter than 1st.
- ★ First magnitude
- ★ Second magnitude
- ✦ Third magnitude
- • Fourth magnitude
- · Fifth magnitude
- ⁂ Star Cluster
- ⊚ Nebula
- ░ Milky Way

Star Chart for the SOUTHERN SKIES

A LIST OF THE BRIGHTER STARS

NAME	R.A.*	DECL.**	MAGNITUDE***
Achernar	1 h. 35 m.	S 57° 35′	+1
Acrux	12 h. 22 m.	S 62° 42′	+1
Agena	13 h. 58 m.	S 60° 2′	+1
Aldebaran	4 h. 31 m.	N 16° 22′	+1
Altair	19 h. 47 m.	N 8° 40′	+1
Antares	16 h. 25 m.	S 26° 16′	+1
Arcturus	14 h. 12 m.	N 19° 32′	0
Betelgeuse	5 h. 51 m.	N 7° 23′	+1
Canopus	6 h. 22 m.	S 52° 39′	−1
Capella	5 h. 11 m.	N 45° 55′	0
Deneb	20 h. 39 m.	N 45° 1′	+1
Fomalhaut	22 h. 53 m.	S 29° 59′	+1
Pollux	7 h. 39 m.	N 32° 2′	+1
Procyon	7 h. 37 m.	N 5° 20′	0
Regulus	10 h. 4 m.	N 12° 18′	+1
Rigel	5 h. 11 m.	S 8° 16′	0
Rigil Kentaurus	14 h. 34 m.	S 60° 32′	0
Spica	13 h. 21 m.	S 10° 47′	+1
Sirius	6 h. 42 m.	S 16° 37′	−1.6
Vega	18 h. 34 m.	N 38° 43′	0

*Right Ascension—The distance, in time units, eastward along the Celestial Equator, from the Spring Equinox (Mar. 21 in Ecliptic) to the meridian passing through any given celestial body.

**Declination—The distance, in degrees, northward and southward from the celestial Equator, to any given celestial body. This concept is similar to latitude on earth.

***Magnitude—The relative brightness of celestial bodies, as indicated by a scale of stellar light intensity. The brightest is indicated by a negative number.

DIRECTIONS FOR THE USE OF THE STAR CHARTS

For anyone living in North America, the Star Chart for the NORTHERN SKIES will be most useful. Face north and hold the atlas in a vertical position. Rotate the book until the current date is at the top of the chart. The stars and constellations in the upper two-thirds of the chart are those visible in the sky at about 9 P.M. that night.

The star nearly at the center of the chart is Polaris, the North Star. The stars within the Northern Horizon Circle correspond to the stars that rotate anticlockwise around the North Star, and are always above the horizon for anyone living at 40° North Latitude. The stars to the right of center will be visible in the eastern sky; those to the left of center in the western sky. Stars near the upper edges of the chart will be close to the southern horizon. To visualize the positions of the stars directly overhead and in the southern sky, hold the star chart of the Northern skies overhead with the current date pointing south.

The Star Chart for the SOUTHERN SKIES would be used in similar fashion by anyone living south of the equator.

The positions of the sun and the major planets among the stars for any given date may be added to the charts. Lay a piece of acetate or tracing paper over the chart to be used. Find the sun's position for the day according to the calendar scale along the Ecliptic and mark it with a crayon or wax pencil. Then locate each of the planets along or near the Ecliptic according to its Right Ascension and Declination as given for the nearest date in the table for the current year. Note that Right Ascension is measured eastward from the Declination Scale in hours and minutes from 0 to 24; while Declination is measured in degrees north or south of the celestial equator, 0° on the Declination Scale. Thus Right Ascension on a star chart corresponds to longitude on a map; while Declination corresponds to latitude.

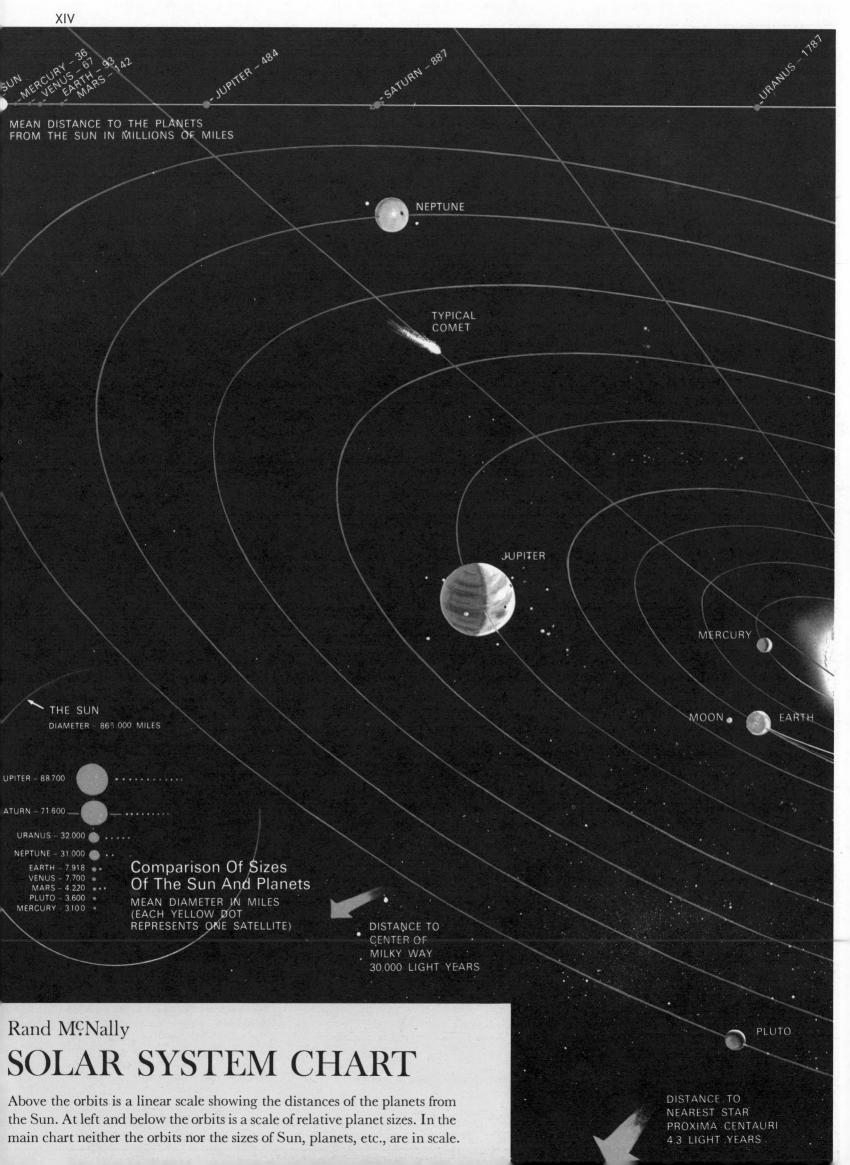

SUN MERCURY – 36
VENUS – 67
EARTH – 93
MARS – 142
JUPITER – 484
SATURN – 887
URANUS – 1787

MEAN DISTANCE TO THE PLANETS
FROM THE SUN IN MILLIONS OF MILES

NEPTUNE

TYPICAL
COMET

JUPITER

MERCURY

MOON   EARTH

THE SUN
DIAMETER – 865,000 MILES

JUPITER – 88,700

SATURN – 71,600

URANUS – 32,000

NEPTUNE – 31,000

EARTH – 7,918
VENUS – 7,700
MARS – 4,220
PLUTO – 3,600
MERCURY – 3,100

Comparison Of Sizes
Of The Sun And Planets

MEAN DIAMETER IN MILES
(EACH YELLOW DOT
REPRESENTS ONE SATELLITE)

DISTANCE TO
CENTER OF
MILKY WAY
30,000 LIGHT YEARS

PLUTO

Rand McNally

SOLAR SYSTEM CHART

Above the orbits is a linear scale showing the distances of the planets from
the Sun. At left and below the orbits is a scale of relative planet sizes. In the
main chart neither the orbits nor the sizes of Sun, planets, etc., are in scale.

DISTANCE TO
NEAREST STAR
PROXIMA CENTAURI
4.3 LIGHT YEARS

NEPTUNE – 2797

PLUTO 3675

ANDROMEDA
GALAXY

2,000,000 LIGHT
YEARS DISTANCE

URANUS

MARS

VENUS

ASTEROIDS

SATURN

THE SOLAR SYSTEM

The Solar System, of which the Earth is a part, is depicted graphically on the preceding two pages. This chart simulates the view an observer might expect if situated at a point in space. The system consists of a central star, the Sun, about which moves a family of nine planets, thirty-two moons, thousands of asteroids (or planetoids), and numerous comets and meteor clusters. The planets move around the Sun in nearly circular orbits, lying in approximately the same plane. All revolve in the same direction which is also the direction in which the Sun rotates on its own axis. As the planets' distances from the Sun increase, their respective orbital velocities proportionately decrease. Nearly all of the moons revolve in almost circular orbits along the equatorial planes of their respective planets. One of the exceptions to this rule is the Earth's Moon.

The Planet Information Table below, showing the planets' significant characteristics, will aid in making comparisons between them. The following text sets down further distinguishing characteristics of each. There is one omission, the Earth, which is amply described through the maps of this atlas.

MERCURY: Owing to its small size and consequent low surface gravity, most of its atmosphere escaped into space eons ago. This factor, coupled with a relatively short mean distance from the Sun, has turned Mercury into an arid, Sun-drenched, and most inhospitable world of extremes. On the illuminated side the surface temperature reaches 650° F.

VENUS: It is often called the Earth's "twin sister" because it is so nearly the same size. Venus is shrouded by so dense an atmosphere that its surface has never been seen through telescopes. In 1962, Mariner II spacecraft flew past Venus at a distance of 21,648 miles, and probed the environment of the planet. Thus, it was tentatively determined that the surface temperature might be 800° F., a much higher figure than had been anticipated. It was also ascertained that the dense cloud masses begin at an altitude of 45 miles above the planet's surface, reaching upward to an altitude of 60 miles. Earth-based radar analyses indicate that the surface of Venus might be sandy; alternately some scientists believe that the surface might have oceans and swamps as well as rocky landmasses. Other scientists maintain that the surface might be rocky and wind beaten.

MARS: Mars is the fourth planet in distance from the Sun, and the first located past the Earth. It has several Earth-like features, among them climatic seasons, seasonal water cycles, a surface temperature believed to range from a high of 80° F. to a low of −100° F. Its bright regions suggest the presence of vegetation which changes according to the seasons. Its atmosphere is believed to be thin, yet it is dense enough for clouds to form. Mars has two moons, each less than 10 miles in diameter and located rather near the planet.

JUPITER: Largest of the planets, it is a world of turmoil and change. It rotates so fast that the gases at its surface are forced into bands of turbulent motion. It is believed that it has a small rocky interior surrounded by a huge shell of ice, which in turn is surrounded by layers of solid, then liquid, then gaseous hydrogen topped with clouds of deadly methane and ammonia. The average surface temperature might be about −190° F. Jupiter has twelve moons, three of which are larger than our own.

SATURN: Physically similar to Jupiter, it has a family of nine moons. Due to its greater distance from the Sun, its surface temperature is lower yet, −235° F. Surrounding the planet along its equatorial plane is a ring system with an outside diameter of 175,000 miles. The rings are made up of small solid particles.

URANUS, NEPTUNE, and PLUTO: These are the outer planets of the Solar System. They are also the least-known ones. It is estimated that their surface temperatures drop considerably below −300° F.

PLANET INFORMATION TABLE

PLANET	Mercury	Venus	Earth*	Mars	Jupiter†	Saturn	Uranus	Neptune	Pluto
Number of Natural Satellites per Planet	0	0	1	2	12	9	5	2	0
Mean Diameter (in Miles)	3,100	7,700	7,918	4,220	88,700	71,600	32,000	31,000	3,600
Mean Distance to the Sun (in millions of miles)	36.0	67.25	93.0	141.7	484.0	887.0	1,787.0	2,797.0	3,675.0
Comparative Volume (Earth = 1.00)	0.06	0.92	1.00	0.15	1,318	736	64	60	0.09
Comparative Mass (Earth = 1.00)	0.04	0.81	1.00	0.11	316.94	94.9	14.7	17.2	0.1
Necessary Escape Velocity	2.66	6.38	6.95	3.16	37.0	22.10	13.70	15.40	3.30(?)
Mean Surface Gravity (Earth = 1.00)	0.29	0.86	1.00	0.37	2.64	1.17	0.91	1.12	<0.5
Weight of a Human Being (in pounds)	38	88	100	39	265	117	105	123	55
Rotation on Planet's Own Axis	88.0 days	Unknown	23^{h}56^m	24^{h}37^m	9^{h}50^m	10^{h}14^m	10^{h}45^m	15^{h}48^m	6.39 days
Revolution Around the Sun	88.0 days	224.7 days	365.2 days	687.0 days	11.9 years	29.5 years	84.0 years	164.8 years	248.4 years
Mean Orbital Velocity (in miles per second)	29.76	21.78	18.52	15.00	8.12	6.00	4.23	3.37	2.95
Inclination of Planet's Orbit to the Ecliptic	7°00′	3°24′	0°00′	1°51′	1°18′	2°29′	0°46′	1°47′	17°09′
Inclination of Planet's Equator	0°(?)	32°(?)	23°27′	25°10′	3°07′	26°45′	97°53′	29°	Unknown

*EARTH   †LARGEST PLANET

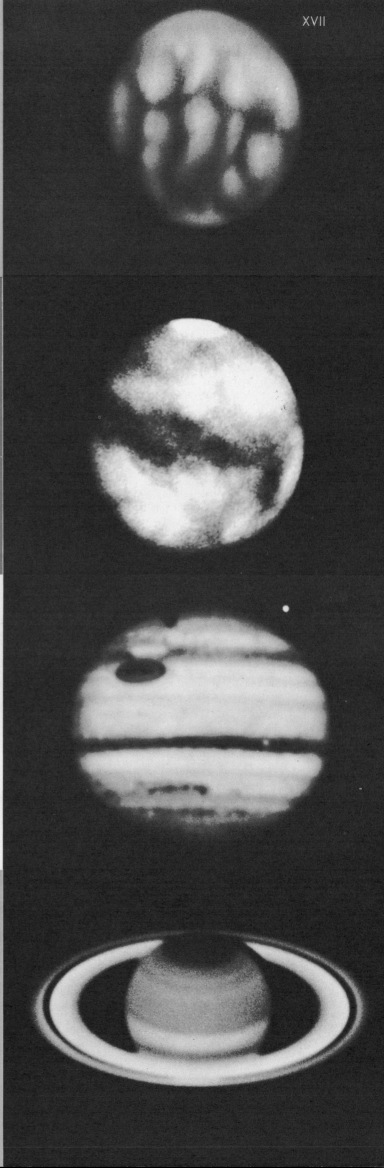

VENUS

The surface of Venus has never been seen due to the obstructive nature of its upper atmosphere. However, it is believed to have a rugged topography, mostly covered with water. Its upper atmosphere is rich in carbon dioxide, with the occurrence of frequent underlying clouds of formaldehyde droplets. The possibility of organic life is extremely limited. Perhaps there might exist some forms of primitive organic life in association with its extensive water bodies. The Venusian year is composed of 224.7 days. The planet has an orbital velocity of 21.78 miles per second, and any given object would require an escape velocity of 6.4 miles per second to leave the planet as compared with the Earth's 18.5 miles per second and 7.0 miles per second respectively. Venus has no moons.

MARS

The surface of Mars has been the object of extensive studies which seem to indicate the existence of vegetation in both hemispheres. Mars has similar climatic seasons to those of Earth. The Polar caps are easily distinguishable as are their seasonal changes. The surface configurations can be summarized as "debatable in nature." These include a large network of visible lines which at one time were thought to be canals, and regions of four different colors which vary with the seasons. The atmosphere is thinner than that of Earth, nevertheless, it is sufficiently dense to eliminate the need for pressurized suits, although a breathing helmet would still be required. The Martian year consists of 687 days. The planet has an orbital velocity of 15 miles per second and an escape velocity of 3.1 miles per second. This planet has two very small moons.

COURTESY MT. WILSON & MT. PALOMAR OBSERVATORIES

JUPITER

The surface of this planet has never been seen. Consequently, its visible upper atmosphere has been the object of intensive study. That region of the atmosphere is rich in ammonia, methane and hydrogen. Jupiter rotates more rapidly than Earth and, therefore, its day is only 9.8 hours in length. As a contrast, it takes 11.9 Earth years for Jupiter to travel once around the Sun, with an orbital velocity of about 8 miles per second. The planet requires an escape velocity of 37 miles per second, or over 5 times that required to escape Earth. Jupiter has 12 moons.

COURTESY MT. WILSON & MT. PALOMAR OBSERVATORIES

SATURN

Saturn's most distinguishing characteristic consists of the three concentric rings that revolve around it. The nearest of these is located a little over 6,000 miles above the planet itself. The rings are extremely thin and are made up of drifting material of varying sizes. Saturn has nine moons. The atmosphere is deep and shows evidence of some turbulence; it does not permit the observation of the actual surface of the planet. It revolves around the Sun once in 29.5 Earth years, with an orbital velocity of 6 miles per second. The escape velocity is 22 miles per second.

COURTESY MT. WILSON & MT. PALOMAR OBSERVATORIES

THE SAGA OF SPACE EXPLORATION

Man's exploration of the space above the surface of the Earth, first in and then beyond the life-giving atmosphere, has been a dramatic experience. In the scientific era in which we live, fundamental knowledge of the Earth's relationship to space will increasingly determine the destiny of man. Already the exploration of space has provided important information concerning the true nature of matter, time, motion, and even life itself. Vast scopes of basic data about many terrestrial as well as extraterrestrial realities are being gathered and processed. Unpredictable benefits for men on Earth will inevitably result from this complex effort.

Man is, now, capable of producing the enormous force required to place a human being in space. Nevertheless, to achieve this goal adequately and safely, it has been necessary first to start with instrumented probes and satellites to gather data helpful in developing the technological ability and equipment. These instrumented probes and satellites have come to number in the hundreds. It is appropriate here to note only the major efforts so far, and their practical returns to man.

Satellites equipped with television cameras and infrared sensors, by observing changing atmospheric conditions which man has no other way of knowing, have made possible vastly improved weather forecasts. These meteorological satellites provide advance warnings of tornadoes, floods, blizzards, and hurricanes, thus enabling people to minimize material loss. Below are examples of the Nimbus and Tiros satellites' photography, which is useful to a great number of Earth scientists in furthering man's understanding of his own planet.

Another example of the practical application of space technology are the communications satellites which have greatly augmented the world's radio and telecommunications facilities. Such satellites as Telstar, Relay, Syncom, and Early Bird have made possible global telecasts which measurably improve the degree of understanding between nations and peoples.

Other applications are navigation satellites which will provide accurate information to any of the hundreds of aircraft that crowd the world's skies, or to the 20,000 surface ships that are estimated to be on the Atlantic Ocean alone at certain times.

There are numerous other benefits which are not of direct application to everyday life, but which are just as important to research in other fields. For example, the astronomical satellites help astronomers overcome the distorting and obscuring effects of the Earth's atmosphere while studying the heavens. And satellites in general assist in determining exact distances, locations, and precise shapes of land and sea areas on Earth, a boon to the mapmakers.

Beside satellites, there are the space probes through which much information has been gathered. These probes differ from satellites in that they are not intended to achieve Moon or planetary orbit. Their purpose is to obtain new data via their instruments. In late 1962, Mariner II was launched and guided toward Venus. As it flew by that planet, Mariner II probed the Venusian environment for new data, and transmitted it back to Earth through 48,000,000 miles of interplanetary space. In 1964, Mariner IV scanned photographically a small portion of the Martian surface. In 1969, Mariners VI and VII flew by Mars, providing our most detailed views of the surface of that planet to date. The photographs shown on a later page attest to the success of the Mariner missions to Mars. These

first fly-bys will be followed in 1971 by Mars orbiter missions, and several years later Mars landers will search for microbe life on Mars.

The 1960's will certainly be remembered as the decade in which man first set foot on the Moon. Almost more remarkable than man on the Moon, however, is the fact that this one decade spans the entire history of manned space flight prior to and including man's first visit to the Moon. This ten year period saw lone men thrust into orbit (Projects Mercury and Vostok), later followed by flights of pairs of astronauts, flights during which men left their spacecraft and drifted in space (Projects Gemini and Voskhod). During these first flights into space, man learned that he could function effectively under these new conditions. Perhaps the most fascinating aspect of the first decade of space travel, however, is the fact that for the first time in history millions of people were able to know what their explorers were doing on a minute by minute basis; and the peoples of the world have undeniably been brought a little closer by this vibrant new bond of mutual interest.

Project Apollo, based on lessons learned in a few short years and in the centuries of human endeavor and achievement that went before, resulted in man's first step on the lunar surface at 10:56 p.m. (EDT), July 20, 1969. Again the world watched as man learned first to walk, then to run, and finally, over the brief span of a few minutes, to work effectively for the first time on the surface of another astronomical body.

Now we look ahead to a continuing program of space exploration, including many more flights to the Moon, astronomical telescopes in orbit and on the Moon, and the excitement of man on Mars. The saga of space exploration is truly man's quest for knowledge and understanding of his real home, the entire universe.

Nimbus I took this clear picture of the Italian Peninsula and Sicily. Clouds on the right obscure the view of Yugoslavia, Albania, and Greece.

NASA

A photograph of the Red Sea area taken by Tiros I. Major features have been labeled for reference.

A reference map showing the same area photographed by Tiros I.

NASA

TITAN
N.A.S.A.
Type / Intercontinental Ballistic Missile.
Range / 5,500 nautical miles

THOR
U.S. Air Force Photo
Type / Intermediate Ballistic Missile.
Range / 1,500 nautical miles

POLARIS
Official U.S. Navy Photo
Type / Intermediate Ballistic Missile.
Range / 1,200 — 1,500 nautical

REDSTONE
N.A.S.A.
Type/Intercontinental Ballistic Missile and Spacecraft.
Range/Restricted information.

THE FIRST STEPS UPWARD

The rocket is, at this time, the only usable means of providing propulsion in the vacuum of space. It needs neither ground, nor water, nor air to push against, as do other vehicles that move by such resistance (such as wheels turning on a roadway or propeller blades churning air or water). The rocket's movement forward is an illustration of the law of reaction; in this case, reaction to the gases which are expelled from the rocket's exhaust. Out in space the rocket is even more efficient than inside a planet's atmosphere.

In space, a rocket engine operates only during part of its journey; the rest of the time the space vehicle keeps moving because it has achieved momentum and there is no air resistance to slow it down. When this stage of flight, the rocket and its contents are in a state of "free fall" and weightlessness.

Traveling through space, man must carry with him absolutely everything he needs—even the air he breathes. He will also need to conserve sufficient fuel for his eventual return to Earth.

JUNO–II
Type/Spacecraft
Range/Restricted information.
N.A.S.A.

VANGUARD
Type / Spacecraft.
Range / Restricted information
Official U.S. Navy Photo

JUPITER-C
Type / Intercontinental Ballistic Missile and Spacecraft.
Range / 3,300 nautical miles
U.S. Army Photo

ATLAS
Type / Intercontinental Ballistic Missile.
Range / 5,500 nautical miles.
U.S. Air Force Photo

AMERICA'S FIRST DAY IN ORBIT

An Atlas-D rocket (360,000 pounds of thrust) launched Lt. Col. J. H. Glenn, aboard spacecraft "Friendship 7", into orbit on February 20, 1962. The principal orbital characteristics of the manned capsule were: perigee, 97.6 miles; apogee, 159.5 miles; average velocity, 17,545 m.p.h.; and inclination, 32.5°.

The capsule afforded a maximum degree of protection for its astronaut against the effects of heat, acceleration changes, and various aerodynamic forces. Within the 9 ft. 6 in. long capsule the temperature averaged about 90°F while traversing over the "night" regions of the Earth and over 100°F while traversing over the "daylight" regions. The separately controlled suit, however, kept astronaut Glenn at a more comfortable 67°F, approximately, while he made valuable observations, performed preassigned experiments on human reaction and adaptation, and took photographs through the porthole. One of the most interesting observations was the phenomenon of numerous small particles of metal-like texture moving at approximately the same velocity as the spacecraft which Glenn encountered in those regions undergoing the process of sunrise.

The re-entry of the capsule began during the end of the third orbit, over the Pacific Ocean, while approaching the West Coast of the United States. This was achieved with the help of the retro-rockets which slowed down the capsule. During re-entry, the temperature rose to about 3,000°F. Subsequently, the spacecraft deployed a parachute for the final descent.

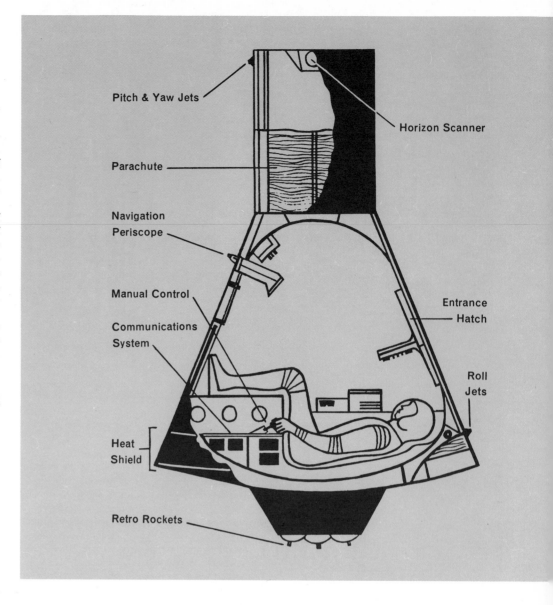

Pitch & Yaw Jets

Horizon Scanner

Parachute

Navigation Periscope

Manual Control

Communications System

Entrance Hatch

Roll Jets

Heat Shield

Retro Rockets

TOP—*Astronaut J. H. Glenn boards "Friendship 7"*

BOTTOM—*Instrument panel of the Mercury capsule*

The beginning of the voyage: lift-off!

TOP—*View of a sunset, taken by J. H. Glenn, from "Friendship 7"*

BOTTOM—*View of the Florida coast taken by J. H. Glenn, at the beginning of his second orbit*

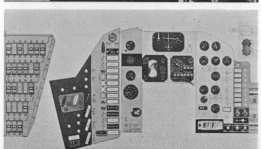

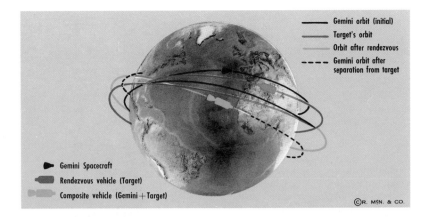

Legend:
- Gemini orbit (initial)
- Target's orbit
- Orbit after rendezvous
- Gemini orbit after separation from target

◄ Gemini Spacecraft
◄ Rendezvous vehicle (Target)
◄ Composite vehicle (Gemini + Target)

©R. MᴄN. & CO.

The surface details of a small portion of
the Earth, photographed by U.S. astronauts

N.A.S.A.

N.A.S.A.

PROJECT GEMINI

Project Gemini was the nation's second major step into manned exploration of space. It employed a two-man spacecraft known as Gemini, which was designed for long duration flights. The principal objectives of the project were: to provide manned rendezvous capability and experience, to provide long duration manned flight experience and its technology, to develop space navigation capability, and to collect data on the biological factors involved in prolonged space travel.

The spacecraft is similar to the Mercury capsule, although twice as heavy. It contains 50% more volume, and is about 20% longer. One of the experiments called for an astronaut to step out of the spacecraft, although safely anchored to it.

In 1965, Astronaut Edward White executed his now famous 20 minute "walk in space." Connected to the Gemini spacecraft by a 25-foot "umbilical cord," he floated freely, and performed several maneuvering experiments. He also photographed the view shown on this page. Although the view was taken from an altitude of just over 100 miles, it is not possible to readily identify any cultural features. Nevertheless, the view clearly shows the characteristics of the Earth's surface and its principal features, such as mountains, rivers, etc.

In revolving about the Earth, a manned satellite has to obey the same physical laws that a natural satellite must. Consequently, man is being exposed to these new conditions and is, through these orbital missions, in the process of learning how to maneuver and behave effectively while in space.

As the intermediate step between Projects Mercury and Apollo, the objectives of Project Gemini were designed to contribute toward the lunar efforts, with experience and knowledge. This combination of objectives successfully provided the United States with the necessary experience to make the first voyages to the Moon.

Astronaut Edward White, the first American to "walk in space." Behind, the Earth partially covered by clouds.

APOLLO 11
THE FLIGHT
OF THE EAGLE

On July 16, 1969, a huge Saturn V thundered off the launch pad with the job of transporting three Americans to the Moon. After four days of coasting over the 239,000 miles to the Moon, Astronauts Neil A. Armstrong and Edwin E. Aldrin, Jr. crawled from the Command Service Module, named Columbia, into the Lunar Module, named Eagle, and parted company from their companion, Michael Collins, as they began their descent to the lunar surface.

Their flight followed earlier Apollo flights which had orbited men around the Moon in December 1968, Apollo 8; tested the Lunar Module in Earth orbit in March 1969, Apollo 9; and flown men to within 50,000 feet of the lunar surface in May 1969, Apollo 10, to test all systems prior to an actual lunar landing.

After a near perfect descent-orbit-injection burn, Eagle coasted halfway around the Moon, and down to an altitude of 50,000 feet. Here the powered descent phase began. With no atmosphere to slow the orbiting spacecraft, the descent engines were fired continuously, slowly counteracting the orbital momentum of the Eagle and lowering it to an altitude of a few hundred feet. At this point, Armstrong switched from the automatic landing sequence to manual control in order to avoid a rock-strewn crater "about the size of a football field." Then, when the lunar surface contact lights lit up on the control panel, Armstrong shut down the descent engines and announced, "Houston. Tranquility Base here. The Eagle has landed on the Moon." The sentiment of millions on Earth went back to the Moon with the response, "Roger . . . we're breathing again."

Mindful that the astronauts safe return to Earth was the most important factor of the mission, the flight plan called for immediate preparation of the spacecraft for the return trip to the orbiting Command Service Module. Finally, the astronauts were ready, the hatch was opened, Armstrong carefully lowered himself down the ladder, and at 10:56 p.m. (EDT), July 20, 1969, as Earth-bound people watched with a single-minded fascination, Neil Armstrong took ". . . one small step for a man; one giant leap for mankind."

Even as the first men to visit the Moon returned to their spacecraft to begin the return voyage to Earth, men on Earth were planning more manned flights to the Moon and beyond. Certainly, the splashdown of Apollo 11 in the Pacific Ocean marked the accomplishment of an age-old dream of man, and just as surely it marked the beginning of an amazing new era of exploration that will in some degree enrich the minds of all mankind.

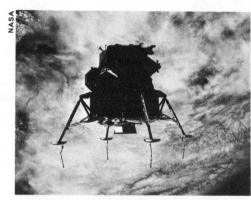

Apollo 9 Lunar Module undergoing first flight test in earth orbit, with James McDivitt and Russell Schweickart at the controls. The picture was taken by David Scott in the Command Module.

Apollo 11 crew (from left): Neil A. Armstrong, Commander, Michael Collins, Command Module Pilot, and Edwin A. Aldrin, Jr., Lunar Module Pilot. All mankind will forever remember the first men on the Moon.

The 363-foot-high Saturn V being moved to the launch site for the Apollo 9 flight.　　NASA

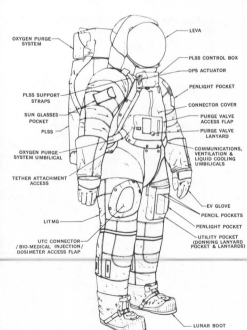

Extra vehicular suit. Most of the items described are visible in the picture to the right, showing Edwin Aldrin at Tranquility Base.

A.

C.

B.

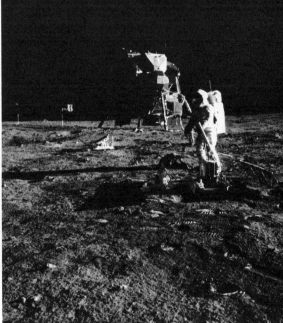

D.

A.   Edwin Aldrin descending to the lunar surface from the Lunar Module "Eagle."

B.   Aldrin, looking like some strange visitor from another planet, is exactly that as he stands on the Sea of Tranquility, some 240,000 miles from home. Armstrong, who took the picture, is visible as a bright reflection in the center of the gold-coated visor of Aldrin's helmet. Also visible in the visor are Aldrin's shadow, and the Lunar Module.

C.   The Stars and Stripes are unfurled by the first human beings ever to set foot on another astronomical body.

D.   Tranquility Base. Aldrin is shown standing near the passive seismometer. The Reflector is to the left. The American flag waves proudly in an airless "breeze." The TV camera, which transmitted live pictures back to Earth, is visible on the horizon, at the extreme left.

NASA

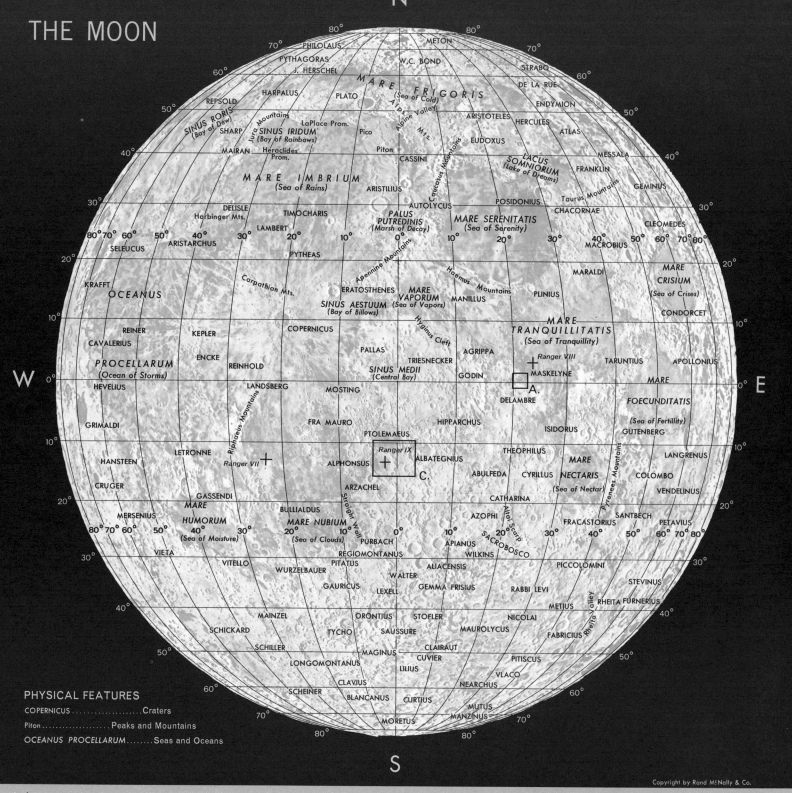

THE MOON

N

80° 80°
70° 70°
60° 60°

PHILOLAUS METON
PYTHAGORAS W.C. BOND STRABO
J. HERSCHEL DE LA RUE
MARE FRIGORIS
REPSOLD HARPALUS (Sea of Cold) ENDYMION
PLATO ARISTOTELES HERCULES
SINUS RORIS Alpine Valley EUDOXUS ATLAS MESSALA
(Bay of Dew) SHARP *SINUS IRIDUM* Alps Mts. *LACUS*
MAIRAN (Bay of Rainbows) Pico *SOMNIORUM* FRANKLIN
Heraclides Piton (Lake of Dreams) GEMINUS
Prom. CASSINI
MARE IMBRIUM AUTOLYCUS POSIDONIUS *MARE SERENITATIS* CHACORNAE
(Sea of Rains) ARISTILLIUS Taurus Mountains
DELISLE *PALUS* MARE SERENITATIS CLEOMEDES
Harbinger Mts. TIMOCHARIS *PUTREDINIS* (Sea of Serenity) MACROBIUS
LAMBERT (Marsh of Decay)
ARISTARCHUS PYTHEAS

PHYSICAL FEATURES

COPERNICUS . . . . Craters

Piton . . . . Peaks and Mountains

OCEANUS PROCELLARUM . . . . Seas and Oceans

Copyright by Rand McNally & Co.

S

+ = Impact sites of Ranger Spacecraft

The Moon is the only natural satellite of the Earth. In comparison to our planet, the Moon is considerably smaller; its diameter is only 2,160 miles. It travels around the Earth once every 27⅓ days, at an average distance of 238,862 miles. Due to the nature of its orbital behavior, only one half of its surface can be seen from Earth. This half is commonly known as the faceside or nearside. The relatively short distance to it has made it possible to study its surface details through telescopes. The above map was made from numerous photographs taken through various telescopes.

The Moon is a compact world of steep moun-

tain peaks, mountain ranges, craters of all sizes, barren plains, valleys, clefts, and rilles. Among these, the plains are commonly but erroneously called seas and oceans, since Galileo thought these plains to be oceans. As part of its environment, the Moon has a very thin atmosphere consisting of rare gases such as argon and krypton. Therefore, there is no weather, no wind. Sound does not propagate. Due to the absence of wind and weather, its surface features have not eroded and consequently have remained unchanged through the ages except for the damage done by meteoroids falling on its surface. Water, which is fundamental to life as we con-

ceive it, is thought to be almost nonexistent. Therefore, astronauts on exploratory ventures, will have to carry their own water, air, and other elements necessary for man's existence.

In recent years some inconclusive evidence shows that the Moon is still undergoing some of its distant-past volcanic activity.

The farside of the moon was extensively mapped by NASA's lunar Orbiter missions which followed the first lunar close-up photographs recorded by Ranger spacecraft in 1965. The NASA Orbiter spacecraft revealed a surface rather different from the nearside, in that very few maria are found on the lunar farside.

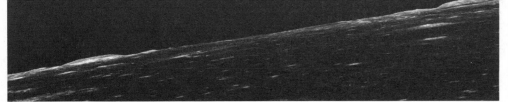

A. The earthrise seen by Apollo 10.

NASA

B. Apollo 10 photograph of crater Schmidt.

NASA

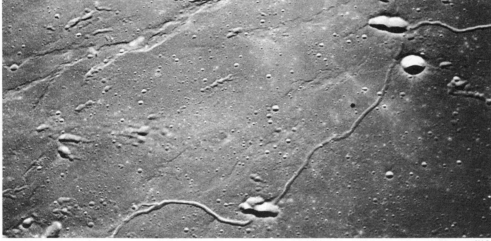

C. A view of the Sea of Tranquility by Apollo 10.

NASA

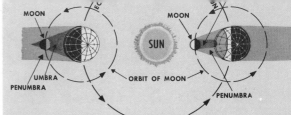

TOTAL ECLIPSE OF THE MOON
Eclipse of the moon occurs only when moon is full. Moon usually appears dull red during the eclipse due to the refraction of the red rays of the sun by the atmosphere of the earth.

TOTAL ECLIPSE OF THE SUN
Eclipse of the sun occurs only during new moon. Sun is invisible in *umbra* and partly invisible in *penumbra*. Total eclipse is visible only in portion of earth touched by shadow of moon (umbra).

THE TIDES

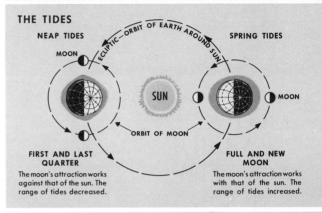

NEAP TIDES

SPRING TIDES

FIRST AND LAST QUARTER
The moon's attraction works against that of the sun. The range of tides decreased.

FULL AND NEW MOON
The moon's attraction works with that of the sun. The range of tides increased.

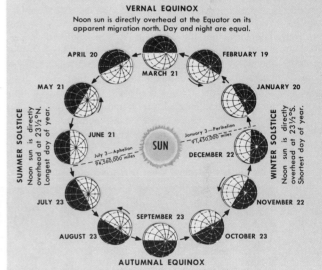

VERNAL EQUINOX
Noon sun is directly overhead at the Equator on its apparent migration north. Day and night are equal.

SUMMER SOLSTICE Noon sun is directly overhead at 23½°N. Longest day of year.

WINTER SOLSTICE Noon sun is directly overhead at 23½°S. Shortest day of year.

July 3 — Aphelion 94,560,000 miles
January 3 — Perihelion 91,430,000 miles

AUTUMNAL EQUINOX
Noon sun is directly overhead at the Equator on its apparent migration south. Day and night are equal.

THE SEASONS Northern Hemisphere

The prime objective of NASA's Project Apollo was the landing of men on the Moon prior to 1970. A series of unmanned projects blazed the trail toward the goal: the Ranger series took the first close-up photographs of the Moon; the Surveyor series, with soft landings on the Moon by instrumented vehicles, returned photographs of the lunar surface, dug into the soil, and tested its chemical composition; the Orbiter series provided the first detailed mapping of the entire lunar surface.

Project Mercury orbited a single man about the Earth on each flight. Project Gemini followed with two-man spacecraft orbiting Earth for long periods, during which rendezvousing, docking, and space-walk techniques were developed to a faultless degree of competence.

On the flight of Apollo 8 three men orbited the Moon, December 25, 1968. Apollo 9 tested the lunar landing vehicle in orbit around the Earth. Apollo 10 carried three men again to the Moon for a dress rehearsal without landing. While orbiting the Moon, the crew took the photographs you see here. The first view, photograph A, is looking back on the Earth as it rises over the lunar horizon. The crater Schmidt, in the Sea of Tranquility, not far from the Apollo 11 landing site, is shown in photograph B.

Photograph C shows "Sidewinder" rille near the planned landing site of Apollo 11 in the Sea of Tranquility.

Thus the stage was set for man's epic odyssey, the flight of Apollo 11. Neil Armstrong, Michael Collins, and Edwin Aldrin, Jr. blasted off from Cape Kennedy on July 16, 1969, atop a huge Saturn V rocket. In orbit around the Moon, Armstrong and Aldrin in the Lunar Module, Eagle, separated from the Command Module, Columbia, and began man's first descent to the lunar surface. Then on July 20, 1969, when Neil Armstrong took that first long step onto the Moon NASA fulfilled its founding objective.

Apollo 8 crew (from left): Frank Borman, Commander; William A. Anders, Lunar Module Pilot; James A. Lovell, Jr., Command Module Pilot. First men to actually see the farside of the Moon.

NASA

Apollo 10 crew (from left): Eugene A. Cernan, Lunar Module Pilot; John W. Young, Command Module Pilot; Thomas P. Stafford, Commander. The second crew to orbit the Moon.

NASA

THE FARSIDE OF THE MOON

The farside of the Moon is hidden from our direct view, because of tidal forces that hold the Moon to one rotation on its axis, which takes place in the amount of time that the Moon revolves around the Earth. In the distant past, millions of years ago, the Moon rotated faster than it does now, completing one rotation in a few hours. The force of tidal friction, caused by the gravitational pull of the Sun and Earth, has slowed down the Moon and lengthened its period of rotation to its present $27\frac{1}{3}$ days. Efforts have already been made to discover the nature of the farside of the Moon. In October 1959, Lunik III, a 614-pound Soviet lunar probe, is claimed to have photographed a major portion of the hidden side, using two cameras, as it moved around the Moon. The closest point of approach was at 4,350 miles above the lunar surface. At the time of photography, Lunik III moved along at an altitude which ranged between 37,300 and 43,500 miles above the Moon. The probe took some thirty-two photographs in a 40-minute period. During this time, the cameras were in a line connecting the Sun and the Moon. Thus, the Moon was almost completely illuminated. These photographs were successfully transmitted to Earth a few hours later. The resulting photographs recorded about two-thirds of the farside of the Moon, plus a narrow marginal area of the visible or nearside of the lunar surface. Below is one of the best known views taken by Lunik III.

NASA's lunar Orbiter series provided detailed coverage of the farside. High resolution photographs recorded features as small as a few feet in diameter. Medium resolution photographs, such as the one of the area around the crater Tsiolkovsky shown below, clearly revealed that the lunar farside is remarkably different from the nearside.

Huge maria, like those on the nearside are essentially nonexistent on the lunar farside which is nearly everywhere rough and cratered.

The answer to why the two sides should be so different, as well as the answers to many other questions about the moon's surface will probably not be known until man systematically explores much of the lunar surface.

Orbiter III photograph of crater Tsiolkovsky on the farside.

NASA

Farside of the Moon, taken by Lunik III.

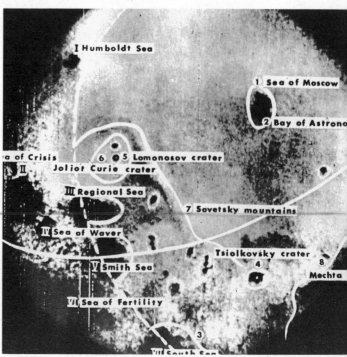

United Press International Photo.

MARS AND THE MARINER PROBES

The Mariner space probe program, begun in the early 1960's, has provided some spectacular and unexpected information about our neighbor planets Mars and Venus. On this page are photographs of Mars taken in a few minutes by three different spacecraft that tell us enormously more about Mars than man has ever been able to learn from the Earth, even with much larger telescopes. These pictures illustrate the very real fact that the most expedient way to learn about a remote but accessible place is to go there. No conceivable Earth telescope can come close to matching the effectiveness of the capability man now has to explore the Solar System with space probes like the Mariners. In addition to telling us much about the planets themselves, these unmanned probes pave the way for further manned exploration of the Solar System.

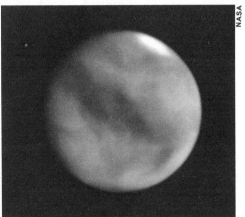

An example of the best photographs of Mars that can be taken from the Earth. The great distance, some 40 million miles, and the blurring caused by the Earth's atmosphere limit the detail.

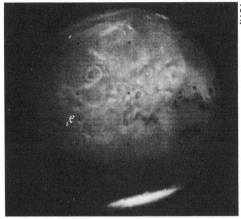

At a distance of about 300,000 miles, Mariner VII in August, 1969, recorded details which are completely invisible from the Earth's surface. The south polar cap is prominent.

In 1965, Mariner IV recorded this view of Mars from a distance of 7,800 miles. This and other Mariner IV photographs revealed for the first time that Mars has a heavily cratered surface.

The south polar cap region photographed by Mariner VII from a distance of 3,100 miles. The picture covers an area 550 by 1,100 miles. The largest crater-like features are nearly 100 miles in diameter. The "snow" persists at the higher elevations on mountains and crater rims for a considerable distance from the main polar cap region. The exact nature of the "snow" is still unknown, the best probabilities being frozen water or frozen carbon dioxide (dry ice).   NASA

The Mariner spacecraft which carried a scant 50 pounds of payload, including the television cameras to record and transmit back to Earth the photographs on this page.

The Martian surface recorded by Mariner VI at a distance of 2,100 miles. The large crater is about 8 miles in diameter.

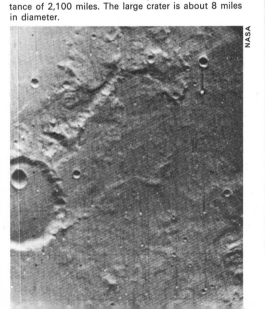

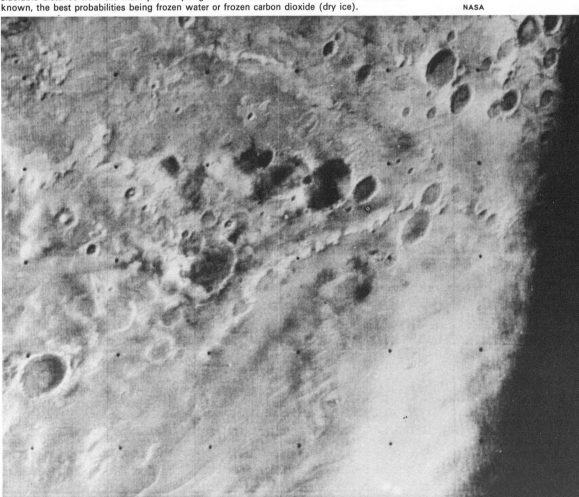

COMMUNICATIONS SATELLITE

Burgeoning telephone and television traffic requirements on overland routes have been met through the use of microwave repeater systems, whose towers are now a familiar site throughout the United States. Microwaves travel in a straight line, and repeaters must be located at intervals of 20 to 30 miles.

Placing a repeater in a satellite, therefore, becomes an economic asset as well as an enormous technical advantage. The horizons, as "seen" from a communications satellite located several thousands of miles above the Earth, spans whole continents and oceans.

The communications satellite era began in 1958, when the Project Score satellite transmitted to the world the now famous Presidential Christmas message. In 1960 Echo I, became the first "passive" communications satellite, and Courier became the first "active" one. Passive satellites merely reflect radio signals, they do not amplify them.

On the other hand, the active communications satellite is equipped with receivers and transmitters for amplifying and retransmitting the received signals. It also has other electronic equipment for control, telemetry and power.

Since the Courier "delayed repeater" satellite, several experimental communications satellites have been orbited, achieving promising degrees of efficiency. Telstar and Relay in 1962, Syncom in 1963 and Early Bird in 1964. Syncom became the first successful attempt at synchronous communications systems.

The development of advanced communications satellites, calls for a system of synchronous satellites such as the one shown on the adjacent diagram. Synchronous or stationary, satellites are those which remain at a designated altitude while completing one revolution around the Earth in 24 hours. In effect, it appears to hover when such a system of satellites is located in an equatorial orbit, at 22,300 miles.

The advantages of the synchronous orbit are that, with only 3 satellites, placed equidistantly, it is theroetically possible to provide almost world coverage. The map below shows the scope of world coverage that an advanced synchronous system is envisaged to provide.

The economics of operational communications satellite system will be dictated by their ability to remain operable for as long as possible. The lifetime of a satellite, in turn, depends on the behavior of its components and on its resistance to hazards such as micrometeorites, etc.

N.A.S.A.

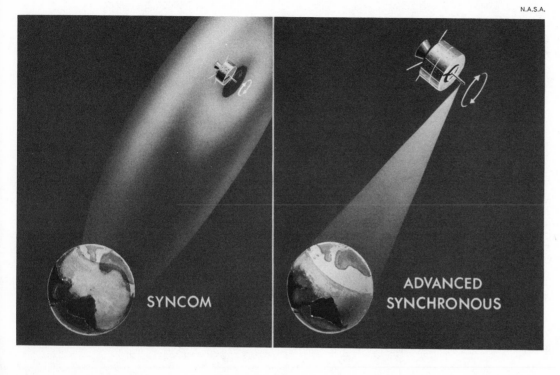

SYNCOM

ADVANCED SYNCHRONOUS

Syncom, on the left, in spin-stabilized. Its antenna radiates uniformly. The Advanced Synchronous satellite, larger and heavier than Syncom, will have a contrarotating antenna that will orient to Earth when transmitting without disturbing the attitude of the satellite.

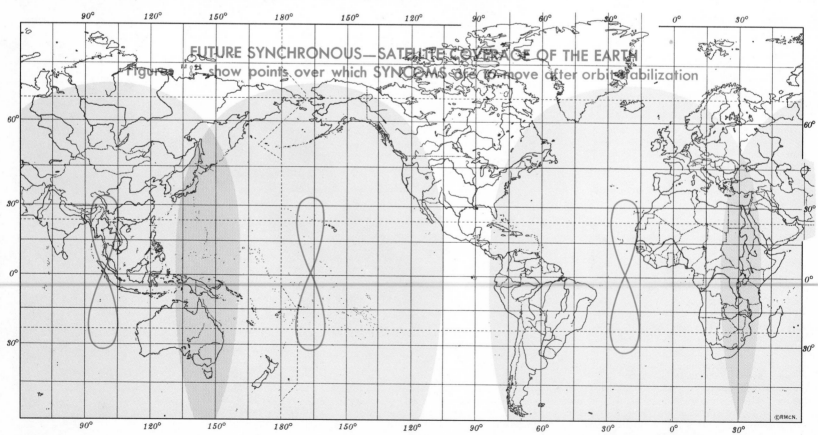

FUTURE SYNCHRONOUS—SATELLITE COVERAGE OF THE EARTH
Figure "8" show points over which SYNCOMS are to move after orbit stabilization

©RMCN.

Space Age Glossary

ACCELERATION: Rate of change of velocity. It may be positive, representing a speeding up, or negative, representing a slowing down.

ALBEDO: The ratio between the light reflected from a surface and the light received by it. Thus the Moon, with an albedo of .07, reflects 7 per cent of the sunlight received.

APHELION: That point, in an orbit around the Sun, where a planet, comet, asteroid, etc., is most distant from the Sun. Opposite term: Perihelion.

APOGEE: That point, in an orbit around the Earth, where a satellite is most distant from the Earth. *Opposite term* Perigee.

ARTIFICIAL EARTH SATELLITE: Any one of the man-made objects placed into orbit around the Earth—Sputnik, Explorer, Vanguard, Discoverer, Tiros, etc.

ASTEROID: A small body, larger than a meteoroid, orbiting around the sun. Its name refers to its star-like appearance from Earth.

ASTRONAUTICS: The science of space flight.

ASTRONOMICAL UNIT: The mean distance between Earth and Sun, about 92,900,000 miles.

ASTRONOMY: The study of all celestial bodies; their behavior, composition, relative distances, motion, etc.

ASTROPHYSICS: The science dealing with the principles and applications of physics to problems in astronomy, especially the analysis of light.

ATMOSPHERE: The envelope of gas surrounding a planet, satellite, or a star.

ATMOSPHERE OF THE EARTH: The thin envelope of gases surrounding the Earth.

AURORA (Polaris, Borealis, and Australis): Streams of glowing light in the sky, usually around the polar regions; caused by the symmetrical deflection, toward the poles, of electrically-charged particles received from the Sun.

BALLISTICS: The science dealing with the motions and trajectories of projectiles.

BALLISTIC MISSILE: A missile that progresses in its trajectory with no guidance or propulsion other than that imparted during launching.

BOLIDE: A fireball that explodes in midair. *See* Fireball.

CELESTIAL EQUATOR: The line constituting the perimeter of the plane of the Earth's equator, as it cuts the Celestial Sphere.

CELESTIAL SPHERE: The apparent sphere of infinite radius on which all celestial objects are assumed to be located for purposes of mapping and identification.

CEPHEID VARIABLE: A giant-type star that undergoes regular periodic changes in brightness due to internal pulsations. It is used in determination of distances.

COMET: A luminous body which moves in an elongated orbit around the sun. Usually it has a long tail which always points away from the Sun.

CONSTELLATION: A configuration of stars associated by patterns in the sky. Constellations can be used to identify areas in the sky like states are used to designate areas in the United States.

COSMIC RAYS: Streams of extremely penetrating and fast electrically-charged particles, which originate in interstellar space.

CRATER: *See* Lunar Crater.

DECELERATION: Negative acceleration—a slowing down or retardation.

DECLINATION: The distance, in degrees, northward and southward from the celestial equator, to any given celestial body. This concept is similar to latitude on Earth.

DISCOVERER: The name given to the series of U. S. data-gathering Earth satellites having polar orbits.

ECHO: The name given to the series of U. S. Earth satellites designed for use as reflectors in radio communications.

ECLIPTIC: The apparent annual path of the Sun among the stars, defining the center of the zodiac.

ELLIPSE: The geometrical form of the orbit of one celestial body revolving around another. The Earth's orbit around the Sun is an ellipse distorted by the presence of other planets.

ESCAPE VELOCITY: The minimum velocity required by an object (space ship, rocket, etc.) to escape the gravitational attraction of a planet thus leaving its surface.

EXOSPHERE: The outermost region of the Earth's atmosphere. It begins at approximately 625 miles above the Earth's surface.

EXOTIC FUELS: Any of several types of rocket fuels, recently developed, that have components not hitherto used for such purposes.

EXPLORER: The name given to a series of U. S. data-gathering Earth satellites. The Explorer satellites have an equatorial orbit.

FIREBALL: An extremely bright meteor.
See Bolide.

FREE FALL: The condition of unrestricted motion of an object as it travels through space with its propelling force shut off.

GALAXY: An aggregation of millions of stars, gas, and dust. The Milky Way is an example.

GRAVITATION: The force of mutual attraction existing between all objects or matter in the universe. The amount of force depends on the mass of the objects and distance between them.

GRAVITY: The gravitational acceleration of objects toward the Earth, slightly modified by centrifugal force, the shape of the Earth, etc. The term is also applied to a similar force on other bodies (planets, etc.) in space.

GUIDED MISSILE: A self-propelled projectile with a controlled path. The control may be internal or external, and the missile may or may not have a warhead.

INFERIOR PLANETS: Mercury and Venus, between the Earth and the Sun. *See* Superior Planets.

INTERNATIONAL GEOPHYSICAL YEAR: The eighteen-month interval ending Dec. 31, 1958, during which scientists from many nations cooperated in research activity in geophysics and related fields.

IONOSPHERE: That layer-region of the Earth's atmosphere, consisting mainly of varying layers of ionized gases. It is located between 35 and 235 miles above the Earth's surface.

JET PROPULSION: Propulsion by reaction where the exhaust jet contains matter, such as air, which has not been carried aboard the vehicle. Can be used only in the atmosphere.

LIGHT-YEAR: A measure of distance based on the speed of light. It is about 6 million million miles, the product of 186,000 miles per second (the speed of light) times the number of seconds in a year.

LUNAR CRATER: Generally a circular walled formation, of which there are thousands on the Moon, varying in diameters and depth.

LUNIK: The name given to the Soviet series of lunar probes.

MAGNITUDE: The relative brightness of celestial bodies, as indicated by a scale of stellar light intensity.

MASS: The quantity of matter within an object.

MESOSPHERE: That layer-region of the Earth's atmosphere located between 235 and 630 miles above the Earth's surface.

METEOR: A meteoroid that enters the Earth's atmosphere. It is made luminous by air resistance and may be seen from the Earth's surface momentarily as a streak of light. *See* Fireball and Bolide.

METEORITE: A meteoroid that has survived a journey through the Earth's atmosphere and has landed on the surface. The largest on display weighs about 34 tons. It is in the American Museum—Hayden Planetarium.

METEOROID: A small solid object in space.

MIDAS: The name given to the U. S. series of Earth satellites designed to detect missile launchings by means of infrared sensors.

MILKY WAY: The luminous belt stretching across the heavens consisting mostly of stars so faint that they cannot be seen individually. This belt defines the central plane of our Galaxy. The Galaxy itself is often loosely referred to as the Milky Way.

NEBULA: A true nebula is a mass of gas in space; it may be bright or dark. Exterior galaxies were thought to be nebulae before modern large telescopes showed them to consist of billions of stars at a great distance. They are still sometimes called "spiral nebulae."

NORTH STAR: Polaris, the star which happens to be nearly over the Earth's north pole at this time in history.

ORBIT: The path described by a celestial body revolving around another; or by an artificial satellite revolving around a celestial body.

PAYLOAD: The weight of all such components, as scientific instruments, radio transmitter, etc., which together will perform a predetermined controllable task. Generally the payload is part of a rocket's last stage, or part of an artificial satellite.

PERIGEE: The point in an orbit around the Earth where a satellite is nearest the Earth. *Opposite term* Apogee.

PERIHELION: The point in an orbit around the Sun where a planet, comet, etc., is nearest the Sun. *Opposite term* Aphelion.

PIONEER: The name given to the U. S. series of lunar probes.

PLANET: One of the dark, mostly solid objects revolving around the Sun, and shining by reflected light. The Earth is a planet.

PROXIMA CENTAURI: Name of the star nearest the Earth, other than the Sun. It is 4.25 light-years away.

RADIATION PRESSURE: The force exerted by light or other electromagnetic radiation in a direction opposite the source.

REVOLUTION: The movement of an object around an external point or object. The Earth revolves around the Sun.

RIGHT ASCENSION: The distance, in time units, counter-clockwise (due east) along the Celestial Equator, from the first point of Aries to the meridian passing through any given celestial body.

ROCKET: A device or vehicle with self-contained material for the production of the jet, which causes the rocket to recoil in the opposite direction of the jet. It does not depend on air or any other exterior medium for its operation.

ROTATION: The motion of an object about an axis through its center of gravity.
Example: The Earth rotates on its axis.

SATELLITE: A body in orbit around a planet. The Moon is the Earth's satellite.

SPACE SHIP: A manned vehicle to be used for interplanetary travel and exploration.

SPACE STATION SATELLITE: A large artificial satellite of the Earth designed for human occupancy.

SPUTNIK: The Russian name for the Soviet series of artificial Earth satellites.

STAR: A self-luminous celestial body, as distinguished from planets which shine by reflected light, and excluding comparatively small objects such as comets and meteors. The Sun is a typical star.

STRATOSPHERE: That layer-region of the Earth's atmosphere located between 13 and 35 miles above the Earth's surface.

SUN, THE: Nearest star to the Earth.

SUPERIOR PLANETS: Those beyond the Earth with respect to distance from the Sun. *See* Inferior Planets.

THRUST: The recoil of a rocket in one direction caused by expulsion of the jet.

TIROS: The name given to the series of U. S. Meteorological Earth satellites; forerunner of forthcoming geodetic satellites.

TRANSIT: The name given to the series of U. S. Navigational Earth satellites; to be used by ships and aircraft as navigational aids.

TROPOSPHERE: That layer-region of the atmosphere which is in contact with the Earth's surface. It is located between ground level and 6 miles (at the poles) to 13 miles (at the equator) above the Earth's surface.

VANGUARD: The name given to the U. S. Navy's program for launching a series of data-gathering Earth satellites as part of the International Geophysical Year. The name also applies to the rockets used.

ZODIAC: The belt in the sky through which the planets appear to move, as viewed from the Earth. It extends 8° on each side of the Ecliptic.

INTRODUCTION TO THE POLITICAL MAPS

The political maps in this Atlas have been arranged on a regional basis instead of country by country. Each regional map is centered around a major country or an important grouping of countries.

Each of the great land masses of the earth is shown as a whole and then broken down into major regions. All the regional maps for each continent are drawn on the same scale. Thus it is possible to make direct visual comparisons of the sizes of countries and the distances between places, simply by turning from one map to another.

City names on the maps are usually shown with the local or official spelling. Sometimes this official name differs from the form of the name commonly used in English-speaking countries. Whenever the anglicized form of the name of a capital city differs from the official spelling, the official name is included on the maps in parentheses. For other cities, the local official form is given first on the map, with the customary English form in parentheses. Often, where two forms of a name are in common use because of a recent change in sovereignty, an official change in name, or for any other reason, both forms are given on the map.

In general, spellings follow the recommendations of the United States Board on Geographic Names of the Department of the Interior, which determines the official spelling of foreign geographical names for U.S. Government use. For the spelling of place names in the United States, the United States Postal Guide is the authority that is followed.

The political maps carry as many political subdivisions as space will permit. Counties are shown on all state maps in the United States and on most of the maps of Canadian provinces. Other countries may not be mapped on a large enough scale to permit showing present administrative subdivisions. For some of these countries, the names of larger administrative subdivisions appear without the boundaries. In others, regions with historical significance are shown instead of present subdivisions.

The names of physical features on the maps are distinguished by two styles of *italic* type. The type for topographic features, such as mountains, passes, etc., appears in all capital italic letters. Hydrographic features, such as rivers, bays, gulfs, etc., appear in capital and lower case italic letters.

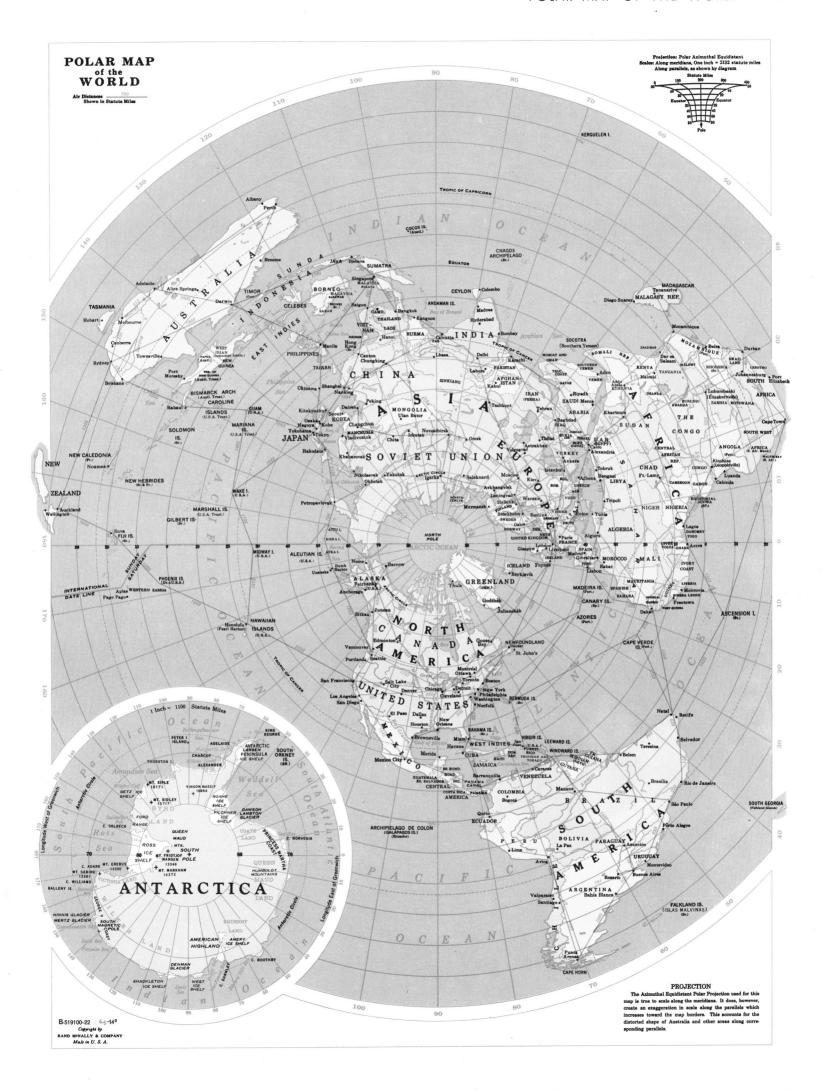

POLAR MAP
of the
WORLD

Air Distances ─── 700 ───
Shown in Statute Miles

Projection: Polar Azimuthal Equidistant
Scales: Along meridians, One inch = 2182 statute miles
Along parallels, as shown by diagram

PROJECTION

The Azimuthal Equidistant Polar Projection used for this map is true to scale along the meridians. It does, however, create an exaggeration in scale along the parallels which increases toward the map borders. This accounts for the distorted shape of Australia and other areas along corresponding parallels.

ANTARCTICA

1 Inch = 1100 Statute Miles

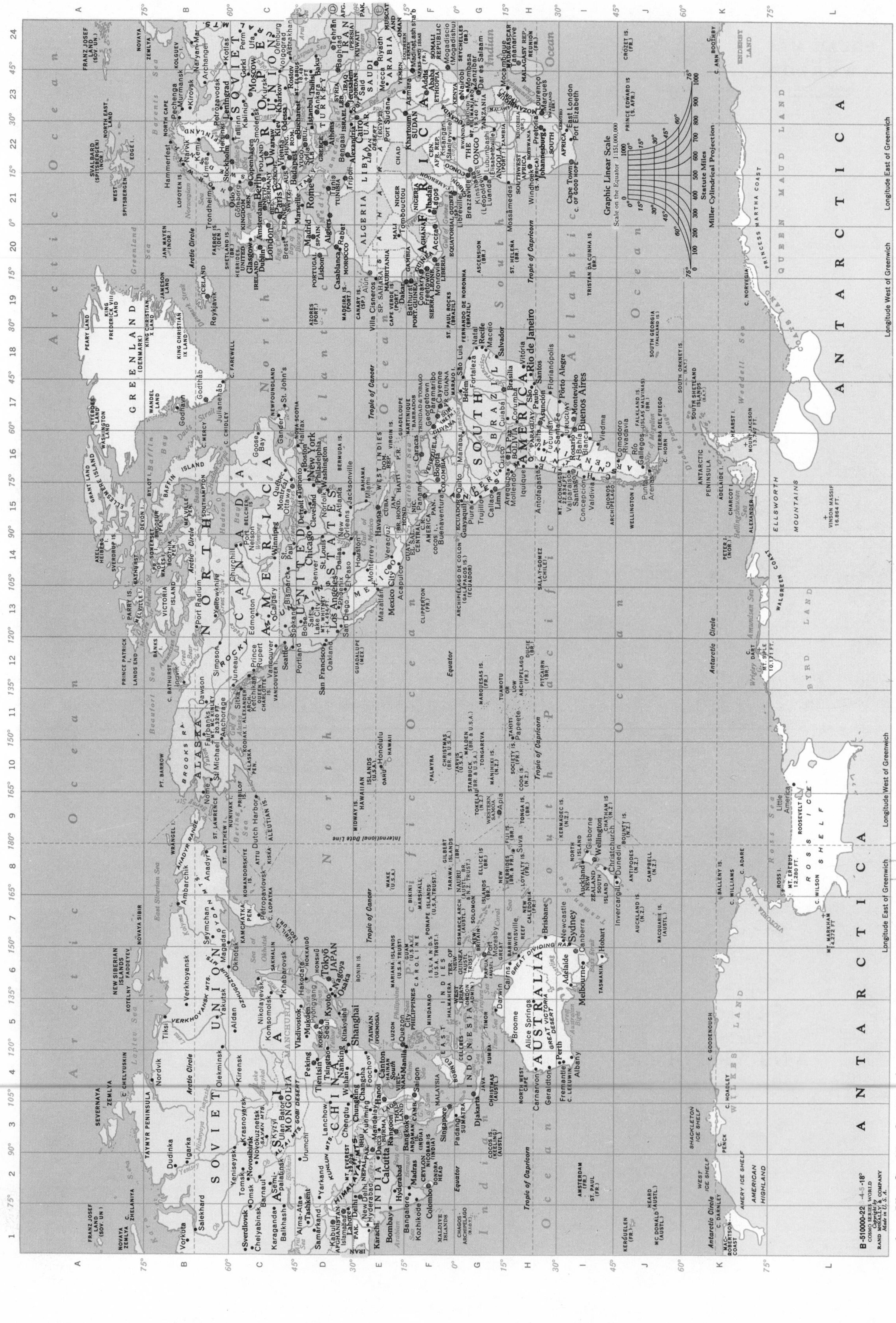
Arctic Ocean
NORTH AMERICA
SOUTH AMERICA
AFRICA
AUSTRALIA
ANTARCTICA
SOVIET UNION
North Atlantic Ocean
South Atlantic Ocean
North Pacific Ocean
South Pacific Ocean
Indian Ocean
Tropic of Cancer
Equator
Tropic of Capricorn
Arctic Circle
Antarctic Circle
International Date Line
Graphic Linear Scale
Scale on the Equator 1:151,000,000
Statute Miles
Miller Cylindrical Projection
Longitude West of Greenwich
Longitude East of Greenwich
B-510000-22 -4-5-18
COSMO SERIES WORLD
Copyright by
RAND McNALLY & COMPANY
Made in U.S.A.

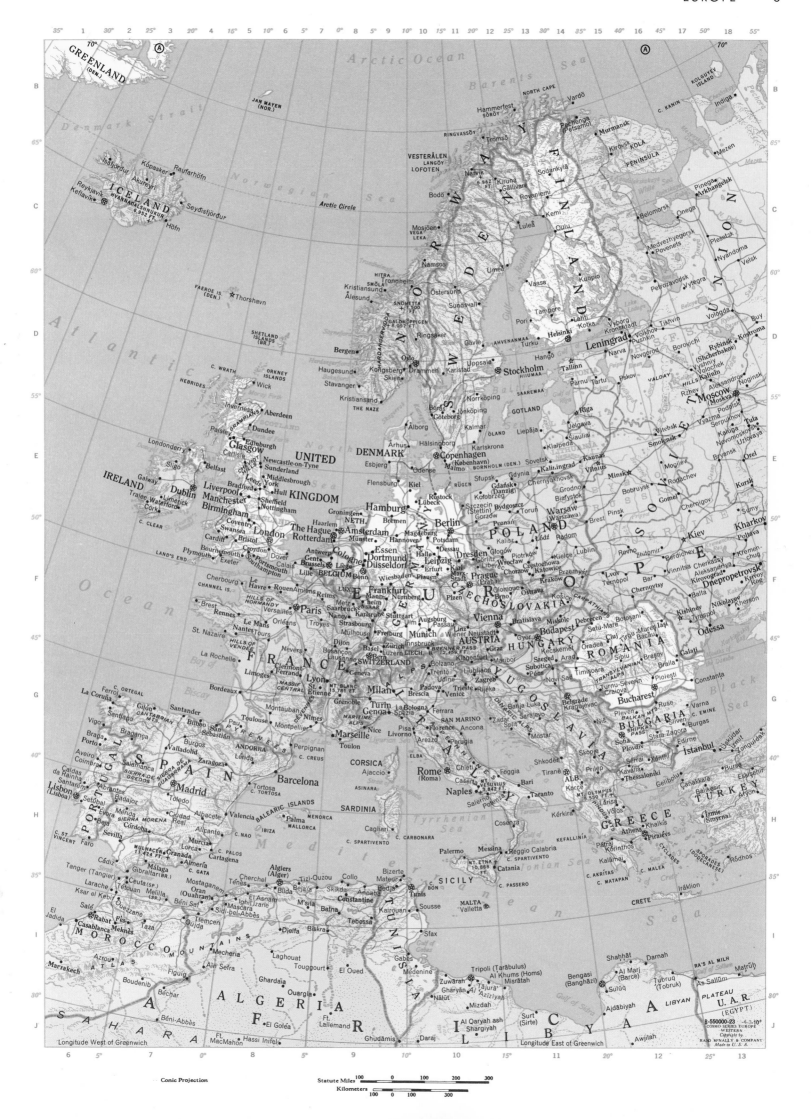

GREENLAND (DEN.)

Arctic Ocean

Barents Sea

JAN MAYEN (NOR.)

KOLGUYEV ISLAND

C. KANIN

Indiga

Pechora

Mezen

Denmark Strait

NORTH CAPE

SÖRÖY

Vardö

C. NORTH CAPE

Hammerfest

RINGVASSÖY

Tromsö

Pechenga (Petsamo)

Murmansk

Kirovsk

KOLA PENINSULA

Belomorsk

Onega

Pinega

Arkhangelsk

Reykjavík
Keflavík
Ísafjördur   Kópasker
Akureyri   Raufarhöfn
ICELAND
HVANNADALSHNUKUR 6,952 FT.
Seydisfjördur
Höfn

Arctic Circle

Norwegian Sea

VESTERÅLEN
LANGÖY
LOFOTEN

Narvik
Bodö

6,962 FT.
Kiruna
Gällivare

Sodankylä
Rovaniemi

Kemi

Kirovsk

Medvezhyegorsk
Povenets

Nyandoma

Velsk

FAEROE IS. (DEN.)   Thorshavn

SHETLAND ISLANDS (BR.)

ORKNEY ISLANDS

Mosjöen
VEGA
LEKA

Namsos

Östersund

HITRA
SMÖLA
Kristiansund

Trondheim

Luleå

Oulu

Umeå

Vaasa

Tampere

Kuopio

Lahti

Petrozavodsk

Vytegra

Belozersk

U.

N.

I.

O.

S.

S.

R.

Vologda
Buy
Kostroma

GALDHÖPPIGEN 8,097 FT.
SNÖHETTA 7,500 FT.

Ringsaker

Ålesund

SNÖHETTA

Pori

Helsinki

Kotka

Vyborg
Kronstadt

Tikhvin

Borovichi

C. WRATH
HEBRIDES
Wick

Inverness

Aberdeen
Dundee

GRAMPIANS

Bergen

Haugesund
Stavanger

Oslo
Kongsberg
Drammen
Skien

Gävle

Uppsala

Norrköping

Hangö

AHVENANMAA
Turku

Helsinki

Tallinn

HIIUMAA

Narva

Pskov

Novgorod

VALDAY HILLS

Rybinsk
(Shcherbakov)
Vyshniy Volochek

Rzhev

Kalinin

Aleksandrov

Kostroma

Moscow
(Moskva)

Moskva

N

O

R

W

A

Y

S

W

E

D

E

N

F

I

N

L

A

N

D

Kristiansand

Skagen

Ålborg

Hälsingborg

Kalmar

Göteborg
Borås
Jönköping

ÖLAND

GOTLAND

Karlstad

Stockholm

Leningrad

Podolsk

Volkhov
Pushkin

Kaluga

Novomoskovsk

Uzlovaya

Orel

Sligo
Londonderry
Belfast

Galway

IRELAND

Dublin

Limerick
Tralee
Waterford
Cork

C. CLEAR

Paisley
Glasgow
Edinburgh
Carlisle
Newcastle-on-Tyne
Sunderland

CHEVIOT HILLS

SCOTLAND

UNITED

Middlesbrough

York
Leeds
Hull

Bradford
Manchester
Liverpool
Sheffield
Nottingham

KINGDOM

Birmingham
Coventry

NORTH CAPE

Esbjerg

DENMARK

Odense

Kiel
Flensburg

Lübeck
Rostock

RÜGEN

Stralsund

Szczecin
(Stettin)

Gdynia

Gdańsk
(Danzig)

Kołobrzeg

Sovetsk

Klaipėda

Liepāja

SAAREMAA

Pärnu   Tartu

Riga

Jelgava

Siauliai

Kaliningrad

Chernyakhovsk

Vilnius

Grodno

Minsk

Vitebsk

Smolensk

Bryansk

Vyazma
Serpukhov
Tula

Kaluga

Roslavl

Gomel

Chernigov

Kursk

Copenhagen
(København)
Malmö
BORNHOLM (DEN.)

Karlskrona

Hamburg

Bremen

Groningen

NETH.

Haarlem

Amsterdam

The Hague
Rotterdam

Münster

Hannover

Magdeburg

Berlin

Potsdam

Dessau

Halle

Leipzig

Dresden

Görlitz

Poznań

Gorzów

Bydgoszcz
Toruń

Warsaw
(Warszawa)

Łódź

Radom

Lublin

Białystok

Brest

Pinsk

Rovno

Zhitomir

Kiev

Poltava

Kharkov

Dnepropetrovsk

Swansea
Cardiff
Bristol

London

Croydon

Dover
Calais

Lille

Amiens

Antwerp
Gent
Brussels
Liège

BELGIUM

Bonn

Cologne
Dortmund
Düsseldorf
Essen

LUX.

Wiesbaden

Frankfurt

Mainz

Plauen

Karl-Marx-Stadt

Prague
(Praha)

Plzeň

Olomouc

Brno

Ostrava

Wrocław

Głogów

Piotrków

Częstochowa

Chorzów

Katowice

Kraków

Przemyśl

Lvov

Ternopol

Chernovtsy

Balta

Kishinev

Nikolayev

Kremenchug

Kirovograd

Kirov
Rog

Plymouth
Exeter
Bournemouth
Southampton
Portsmouth

LAND'S END

Cherbourg
Le Havre

CHANNEL IS.

Brest

Rennes

Rouen

Reims

Metz

Saarbrücken

Nancy

Strasbourg

Karlsruhe
Stuttgart

Nürnberg

Erfurt

GERMANY

Linz

Wiener Neustadt

Vienna

Bratislava

CZECHOSLOVAKIA

Košice

Miskolc
Debrecen

Satu-Mare

Botoşani

Iaşi

Nantes
Tours

Le Mans

Orléans

Troyes

Paris

Versailles

Dijon

Besançon

Basel

Mulhouse

Freiburg

Augsburg

Ulm

Passau

Munich

Innsbruck

BRENNER PASS 4,495 FT.

Salzburg

Graz

Klagenfurt

Maribor

AUSTRIA

Győr

Budapest

Kecskemét

Szeged

Arad

Oradea

Timişoara

HUNGARY

Cluj

Tîrgu Mureş

Bacău

ROMANIA

Galaţi

Braila

St. Nazaire

La Rochelle

HILLS OF VENDÉE

Nevers

Clermont-Ferrand

MASSIF CENTRAL

Lyon

St. Etienne

MT. BLANC 15,781 FT.

Geneva

Bern

SWITZERLAND

LIECH.

Zürich

Luzern

Lausanne

Bolzano

Trento

Udine

Ljubljana

Zagreb

Novi Sad

Subotica

Pécs

JUGOSLAVIA

Turnu-Severin

Craiova

Pioieşti

Ploieşti

Bucharest

Constanţa

Bay of Biscay

Bordeaux

Montauban

Toulouse

Montpellier

Nîmes

Grenoble

Turin

Milan

Brescia

Padova

Venice

Trieste

Rijeka

Zadar

Zagreb

MARITIME ALPS

Nice

Genoa

La Spezia

Bologna

Ferrara

SAN MARINO

Split

Mostar

Sarajevo

Banja Luka

DINARIC ALPS

Belgrade

Kragujevac

Niš

Plevna

Sofia

Ruse

Varna

C. EMINE

Burgas

BALKAN MTS.

Stara Zagora

Sliven

BULGARIA

Plovdiv

Edirne

İstanbul

Zonguldak

C. ORTEGAL

La Coruña

Ferrol

Gijón
Santander

Santiago

Vigo

Braga
Rainha

Porto

Aveiro

Coimbra

Bragança

Bilbao

San Sebastián

PYRENEES

Pau

Perpignan

C. CREUS

ANDORRA

Lérida

CANTABRIAN MTS.

Burgos

Valladolid

Zaragoza

SIERRA DE GUADARRAMA

CORSICA

Ajaccio

ASINARA

Rome
(Roma)

Chieti

Foggia

SARDINIA

Cagliari

C. CARBONARA

Naples

Caserta

Salerno

Potenza

VESUVIUS 3,842 FT.

Bari

Taranto

Brindisi

ALB.

Tiranë

Shkodër

Korçë

Prilep

Skopje

Kavalla

Thessaloniki

Sérrai

Xánthi

Kírklareli

Çanakkale

Gelibolu

Bursa

İzmit

Eskişehir

Afyon

TURKEY

İzmir (Smyrna)

Lisbon
(Lisboa)

Setúbal

Santarém

Abrantes

Évora

Beja

PORTUGAL

C. ST. VINCENT

Faro

Cádiz

SPAIN

Madrid

Toledo

Ciudad Real

Albacete

Valencia

Alicante

Murcia

Cartagena

SIERRA MORENA

Córdoba

Sevilla

Badajoz

Mérida

Salamanca

Lorca

Almería

C. GATA

Granada

MULHACÉN 11,424 FT.

Málaga

Gibraltar (BR.)

Ceuta (SP.)

Melilla (SP.)

Tétouan

Tangier (Tanger)

Larache

Ksar el Kebir

Barcelona

Tortosa

C. TORTOSA

BALEARIC ISLANDS

IBIZA

MENORCA

MALLORCA

Palma

C. NAO

C. PALOS

Mediterranean

GREECE

Athens
(Athinai)

Piraiévs

Kórinthos

Pátrai

Kalámai

KEFALLINÍA

Kérkira

Lárisa

Vólos

Khalkís

CYCLADES

OLYMPUS 9,550 FT.

SPORADES (DODECANESE)

Ródhos

Iráklion

CRETE

C. MALEA

C. MATAPAN

C. AKRITAS

Palermo

Messina

Reggio Calabria

C. SPARTIVENTO

SICILY

Catania

MT. ETNA 10,868 FT.

C. PASSERO

MALTA

Valletta

Marrakech

Azrou

ATLAS

MOROCCO

Casablanca

Rabat

Meknès

Fès

Taza

Oujda

Salé

El Jadida

Oued Zem

MOUNTAINS

Figuig

Béchar

Boudenib

Béni-Abbès

SAHARA

Ft. MacMahon

Ghudāmis

Daraj

Ghardaïa

Ouargla

El Oued

Touggourt

Laghouat

Biskra

Batna

Tébessa

Sfax

Gafsa

ALGERIA

Ft. Lallemand

Hassi Inifel

El Goléa

Tamanrasset

Mecheria

Aïn Sefra

Djelfa

Oran
(Ouahran)

Mostaganem

Sidi-bel-Abbès

Tlemcen

Mascara

Ighil Izane

Ténès

Cherchel

Blida

Algiers
(Alger)

Tizi-Ouzou

Bejaïa

El Asnam

Skikda

Béja

Collo

Constantine

Bône

Annaba

Bizerte

Mateur

Tunis

Souse

Kairouan

Medjez

TUNISIA

M'sila

Gabes

Gulf of Gabes

Médenine

Zuwārah

Al Khums (Homs)

Tripoli (Tarābulus)

Al Jufrah

Aţ Ţājūrā

Al 'Aziziyah

Gharyān

Mizdah

Nālūt

Al Qaryah ash Sharqiyah

Surt (Sirte)

Gulf of Sidra

Ajdābiyah

Awjilah

Bengasi (Banghāzī)

Al Marj (Barce)

Shahhāt

Darnah

Tubruq (Tobruk)

Sulūq

As Sallūm

RA'S AL MILH

Maţrūḩ

LIBYAN PLATEAU

U.A.R. (EGYPT)

LIBYA

Black Sea

Kerch

Sevastopol

Simferopol

Odessa

Tiraspol

Kherson

Melitopol

Gulf of Karkinit

Sulina

Atlantic Ocean

Tyrrhenian Sea

Ionian Sea

Aegean Sea

Adriatic Sea

Ligurian Sea

Gulf of Bothnia

Baltic Sea

North Sea

Longitude West of Greenwich   Longitude East of Greenwich   B-550000-23
COSMO SERIES EUROPE
WESTERN
Copyright by
RAND McNALLY & COMPANY
Made in U. S. A.

Conic Projection

Statute Miles

Kilometers

100   0   100   200   300

100   0   100   300

Longitude West of Greenwich   Longitude East of Greenwich

Inset: Shetland
Same Scale as Main Map

Atlantic
UNST
YELL
SHETLAND
St. Magnus Bay
ISLANDS   MAINLAND
(SCOTLAND)
FOULA   Lerwick
SUMBURGH PT.
Ocean

Main Map

Atlantic Ocean

North Sea

N. RONALDSAY
WESTRAY
ROUSAY   SANDAY
MAINLAND   STRONSAY
Kirkwall   ORKNEY
HOY   S. RONALDSAY
ISLANDS
Scapa Flow
Pentland   DUNCANSBY HEAD

FLANNAN IS.
BUTT OF LEWIS
CAPE WRATH   Durness   Bettyhill   Thurso
Scourie   BEN HOPE 3042   Wick
LEWIS   Barvas   Kinbrace
Stornoway   BEN MORE ASSYNT 3273   Laird   Helmsdale
Ullapool   Golspie
OUTER HEBRIDES   Gairloch   Tain   TARBAT NESS
NORTH UIST   BEINN DEARG 3547   Cromarty   Buckie   Banff   KINNAIRDS HEAD
Uig   Dingwall   Nairn   Elgin   Keith   Fraserburgh
SKYE   Inverness   Forres   Huntly   Peterhead
SOUTH UIST   BEINN FHADA 3383   BEN MACDHUI 4300   Maud   Cruden Bay
Ellon
CANNA   Mallaig   Kingussie   GRAMPIAN MTS.   Ballater   Aberdeen
RHUM   Kilmallie   Stonehaven
BARRA   EIGG   BEN NEVIS 4406   SCOTLAND
MUCK   Fort William   Pitlochry   Brechin
BARRA HEAD   COLL   Aberfeldy   Blairgowrie   Forfar   Montrose
TIREE   Oban   Killin   Coupar Angus   Arbroath
MULL   Inveraray   Crieff   Perth   Broughty Ferry
Callander   St. Andrews   Dundee   Firth of Tay
Helensburgh   Stirling   Leven   FIFE NESS
COLONSAY   Dunoon   Alloa   Kirkcaldy   Buckhaven
JURA   Rothesay   Paisley   Falkirk   Dunfermline   Firth of Forth
ISLAY   Glasgow   Coatbridge   Musselburgh   Dunbar
Ardrossan   Motherwell   Edinburgh   Eyemouth
Irvine   Hamilton and Wishaw   Peebles   Berwick-upon-Tweed
Kilmarnock   Lanark   Galashiels   HOLY I.
Ayr   Selkirk   Jedburgh   FARNE IS.
INISHTRAHULL   Maybole   New Cumnock   Hawick   Kelso   Alnwick
MALIN HEAD   Dalmellington   WHITE COOMB 2696
TORY I.   Carndonagh   Girvan   CHEVIOT HILLS   Bedlington   Blyth
RATHLIN I.   Ballantrae   Dumfries   Annan   Newcastle-on-Tyne   Tynemouth
ARAN I.   Coleraine   Ballycastle   New Galloway   South Shields
ERRIGAL 2466   Letterkenny   Ballymena   Castle Douglas   Carlisle   Gateshead   Sunderland
Lifford   Larne   Kirkcudbright   Durham
Londonderry   SPERRIN MTS.   Wigtown   Stockton-on-Tees   Hartlepool
MALINMORE HEAD   Donegal   Omagh   NORTHERN   Portpatrick   Maryport   West Hartlepool
Dungannon   IRELAND   Bangor   Workington   Darlington   Middlesbrough
Ballyshannon   Monaghan   Lisburn   Donaghadee   Whitehaven   Thornaby-on-Tees   Whitby
Killala   Enniskillen   Lurgan   Belfast   Newtownards   ST. BEES HD.   LAKE DISTRICT   Windermere   Kendal   NORTH YORK MOORS
ERRIS HEAD   Ballina   Boyle   Banbridge   Ramsey   Scarborough
MULLET PEN.   Cavan   MOURNE   Downpatrick   ISLE OF MAN   Ulverston   Malton   FLAMBOROUGH HEAD
ACHILL IS.   Sligo   MTS. SLIEVE DONARD 2796   Douglas   Barrow-in-Furness   Lancaster   Ripon   Bridlington
Achill Sound   Dundalk   CALF OF MAN   WALNEY I.   Harrogate   YORK WOLDS
INISHTURK   Westport   Ardee   Morecambe   York   Beverley   Hornsea
INISHBOFIN   Castlebar   L. Boderg   Drogheda   *Irish Sea*   Blackpool   Preston   Keighley   Leeds   Hull   Withernsea
Claremorris   Longford   An Uaimh   Burnley   Bradford
Roscommon   Mullingar   Rush   Blackburn   Halifax   Huddersfield   Scunthorpe   Grimsby
SLYNE HEAD   Tuam   Athlone   Edenderry   Southport   Bolton   Rochdale   Oldham   Doncaster   Gainsborough   Louth
Clifden   Galway   Ballinasloe   Dublin   Liverpool   ANGLESEY   Wallasey   Salford   Manchester   Sheffield   LINCOLN WOLDS
ARAN IS.   Loughrea   (Baile Atha Cliath)   Holyhead   Birkenhead   Stockport   Lincoln   Skegness
Ennistymon   Portarlington   Dun Laoghaire   HOLY I.   Rhyl   Warrington   Chesterfield   Newark
Ennis   Portlaoise   Naas   Bray   Llandudno   Chester   Crewe   Macclesfield   Spilsby
Kilkee   Nenagh   Birr   WICKLOW   Caernarvon   Bangor   Denbigh   Sutton-in-Ashfield   THE WASH
Kilrush   Roscrea   Kildare   MTS.   Wrexham   Stoke-on-Trent   Nottingham   Boston
LOOP HEAD   Thurles   Carlow   LUGNAQUILLA MTN. 3039   CAERNARVON BAY   SNOWDON 3560   Derby   Grantham   Spalding
Limerick   Kilkenny   Wicklow   Ffestiniog   Oswestry   Burton-on-Trent   Loughborough   Wisbech   King's Lynn   Great Yarmouth
BRANDON MTN. 3127   Foynes   Tipperary   Arklow   PWLLHELI   Stafford   Walsall   Leicester   Peterborough   Norwich   Lowestoft
Listowel   Cashel   Clonmel   Gorey   LLEYN PENINSULA   Shrewsbury   Wolverhampton   Kettering   Ely   Thetford   Bury St. Edmunds
Dingle   Newcastle   Carrick   Enniscorthy   Barmouth   Welshpool   WALES   Dudley   Birmingham   Northampton   Cambridge   Ipswich
CARRANTUOHILL 3414   Tralee   GALTY MTS.   Mitchelstown   New Ross   Wexford   Aberystwyth   Smethwick   Coventry   Bedford   Bishop's Stortford   Harwich
MACGILLICUDDY'S REEKS   Killarney   KNOCKMEALDOWN MTS.   Waterford   CARNSORE PT.   CARDIGAN BAY   Ludlow   Kidderminster   Warwick   Leamington   Wolverton   Colchester
VALENCIA I.   Mallow   Fermoy   Dungarvan   Tregaron   Llandrindod Wells   Worcester   Stratford-upon-Avon   Luton
Macroom   Youghal   YOUGHAL BAY   Cardigan   Hereford   Banbury   Hertford   Chelmsford
Kenmare   Midleton   ST. DAVID'S HEAD   Fishguard   BRECON BEACONS 2906   Brecon   Cheltenham   Aylesbury   London   Southend-on-Sea
Bantry   Kinsale   Cobh   Carmarthen   Merthyr Tydfil   Abergavenny   Cirencester   High Wycombe   Slough   Sheerness   Margate
Clonakilty   Cork   Milford Haven   Llanelly   Neath   Aberdare   Chepstow   Gloucester   Reading   Croydon   Gravesend   NORTH FORELAND
Skibbereen   OLD HEAD OF KINSALE   Pembroke   Swansea   Rhondda   Newport   Bristol   Swindon   Newbury   Guildford   Gillingham   Ramsgate
C. CLEAR   BANTRY BAY   *St. George's Channel*   Cardiff   Bath   Trowbridge   Basingstoke   Reigate   Maidstone   Canterbury
ILFRACOMBE   Weston-super-Mare   Aldershot   Tunbridge Wells   Dover
Bristol Channel   Minehead   Bridgwater   Salisbury   Winchester   SOUTH DOWNS   Folkestone   Calais
LUNDY I.   EXMOOR   Taunton   Yeovil   Southampton   Chichester   Hove   Hastings   Boulogne-sur-Mer
HARTLAND PT.   Barnstaple   BLACKDOWN HILLS   Dorchester   Cowes   Portsmouth   Brighton   Eastbourne   Outreau
Bideford   Tiverton   Weymouth and Melcombe Regis   ISLE OF WIGHT   Worthing   Étaples
Bude   Okehampton   Exeter   Poole   Newport   Ryde   Bournemouth   Berck
Launceston   BODMIN MOOR   DARTMOOR   Torquay   BILL OF PORTLAND   ST. ALBAN'S HEAD   St. Valery-sur-Somme
Camborne   Bodmin   Dartmouth   Abbeville
Newquay   START PT.   PICARDY   Le Tréport   Eu
Penzance   Truro   EDDYSTONE ROCKS   Dieppe
SCILLY IS.   Falmouth   Plymouth   Neufchâtel-en-Bray
LAND'S END   LIZARD PT.   *English Channel*

UNITED KINGDOM

IRELAND (EIRE)

ENGLAND

North Channel

ARTOIS

C. DE LA HAGUE   PTE. DE BARFLEUR   Fécamp   Bolbec   Barentin
ALDERNEY   Tourlaville   PTE. DE BARFLEUR   Yvetot
Équeurdreville   Cherbourg   Valognes   Le Havre   Rouen   Sotteville-lès-Rouen
Octeville   Barneville-sur-Mer   Isigny-sur-Mer   Trouville   Honfleur   Pavilly   Louviers   Gisors
GUERNSEY   St. Peter Port   Bayeux   Deauville   Dives-sur-Mer   Vernon
SARK   Carentan   St. Lô   Caen   Lisieux   Évreux
CHANNEL ISLANDS (BR.)   JERSEY   Coutances   Condé-sur-Noireau   Argentan   Verneuil   Dreux
St. Helier   Granville   Vire   Paris
Tréguier   Gulf of St. Malo   Mont-St-Michel   Avranches   Flers   HILLS OF NORMANDY   Mortagne   Chartres
St. Pol-de-Léon   Lannion   Paramé   St. Malo   NORMANDY
Morlaix   Guingamp   *BRITTANY*

FRANCE

Inset: London

1   10°   2   8°   3
Welwyn Garden City   Hertford   Harlow
Hemel Hempstead   St. Albans   Hoddesdon
Chesham   Cheshunt   Epping
Rickmansworth   Watford   Enfield   Chigwell   Brentwood
London   Barnet   Romford
Uxbridge   Hendon   Tottenham   Hackney   Dagenham
Slough   Harrow   Hampstead   CITY OF LONDON
Ealing   Kensington   Westminster   Woolwich   Grays
Windsor (New Windsor)   London Heathrow Airport   Wandsworth   Chelsea   Greenwich   Tilbury
Staines   RICHMOND PARK   Lambeth   Gravesend
Weybridge   Wimbledon   Bromley
Kingston-upon-Thames   Orpington
Woking   Esher   Cheam   Croydon
Cobham   Epsom   Coulsdon
Dorking   Leatherhead   Sevenoaks
Guildford   Redhill   Reigate

1 Inch = 18.2 Statute Miles

B-553600-21 -4-4-7°
COSMO SERIES BRITISH ISLES
Copyright by
RAND McNALLY & COMPANY
Made in U.S.A.

Statute Miles   25 0 25 50 75
Kilometers   25 0 25 50 100

Conic Projection

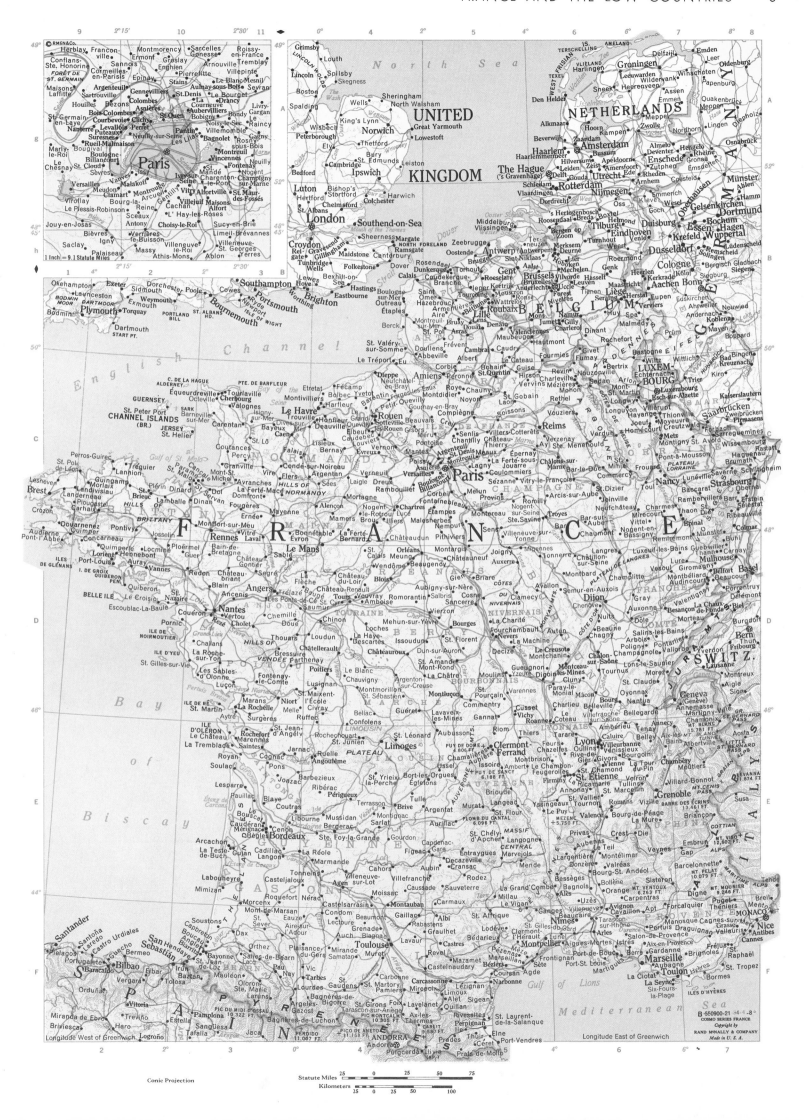

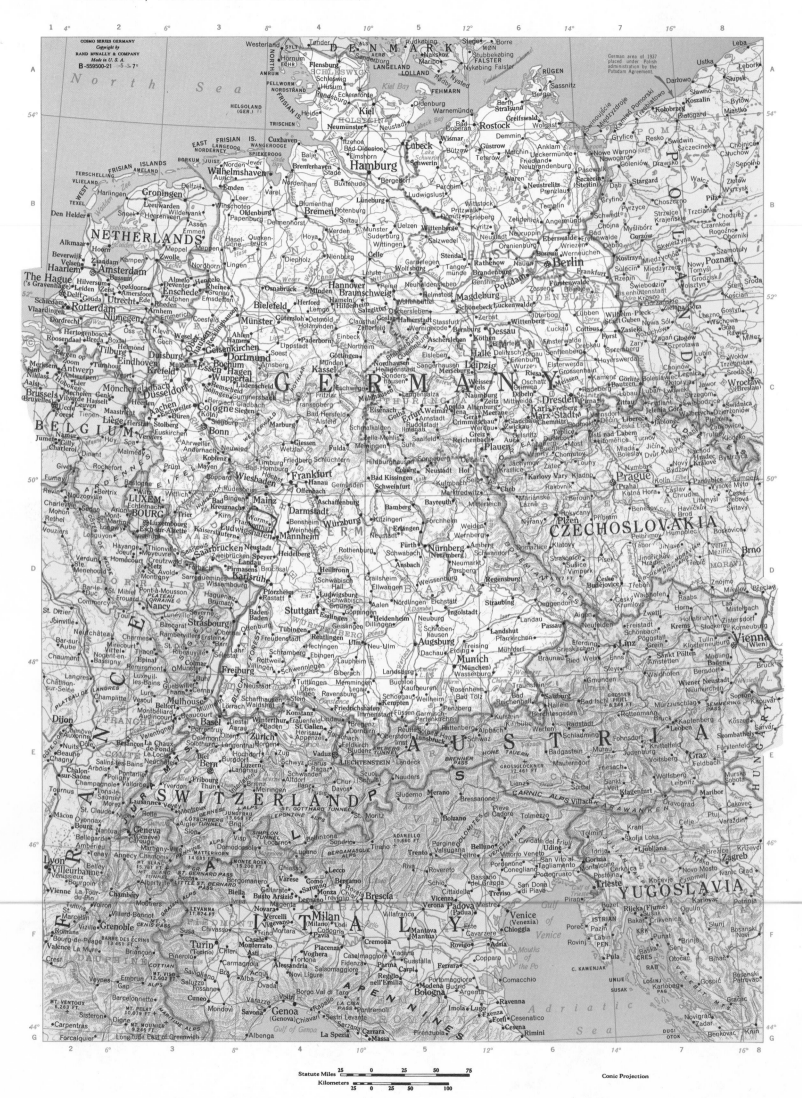

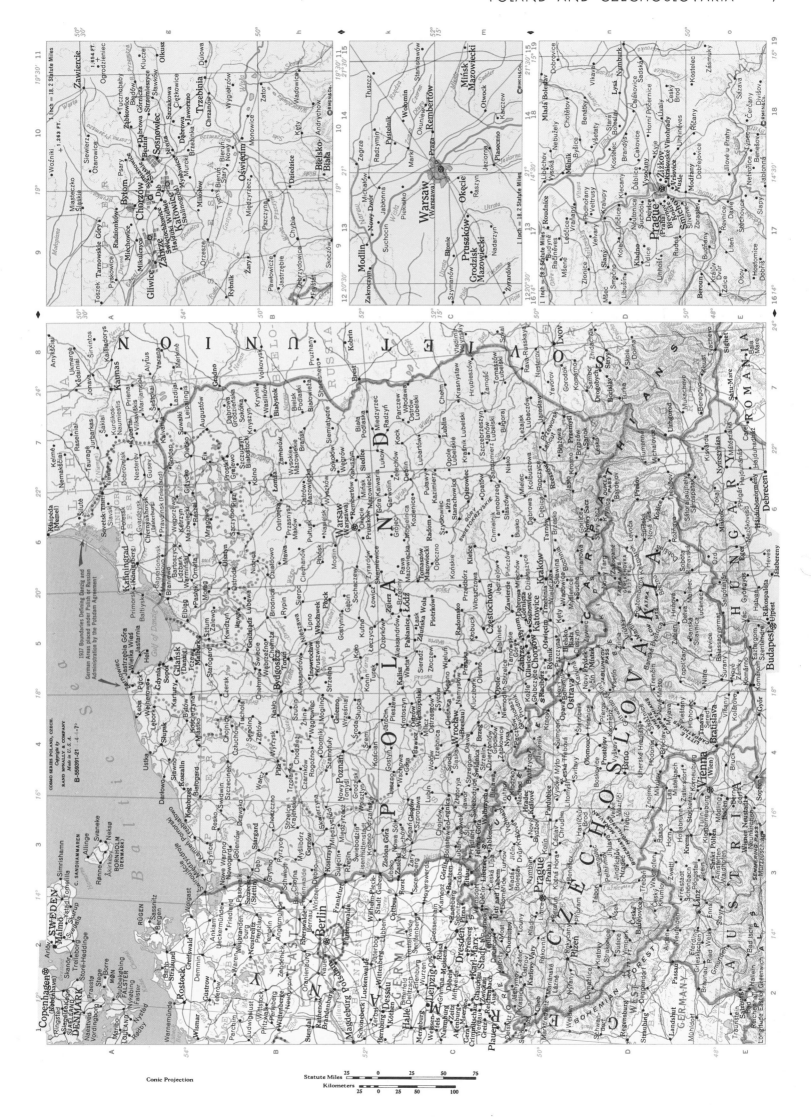

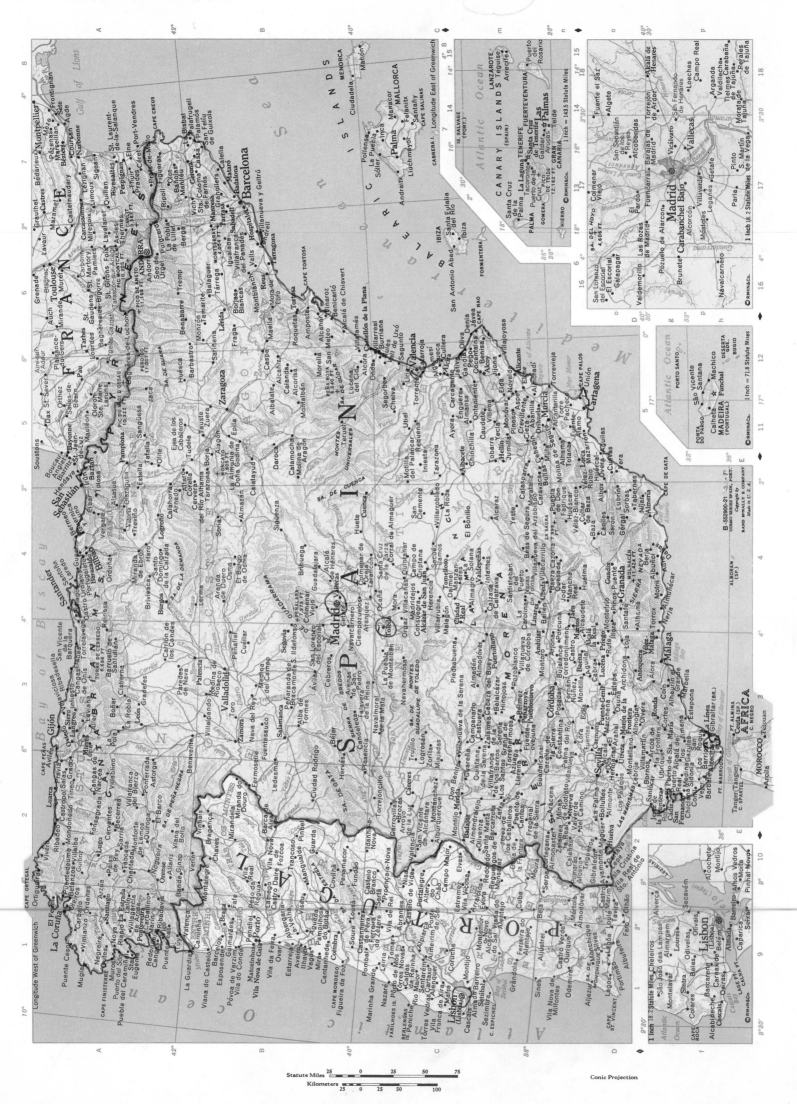

Statute Miles 25 0 25 50 75
Kilometers 25 0 25 50 100

Conic Projection

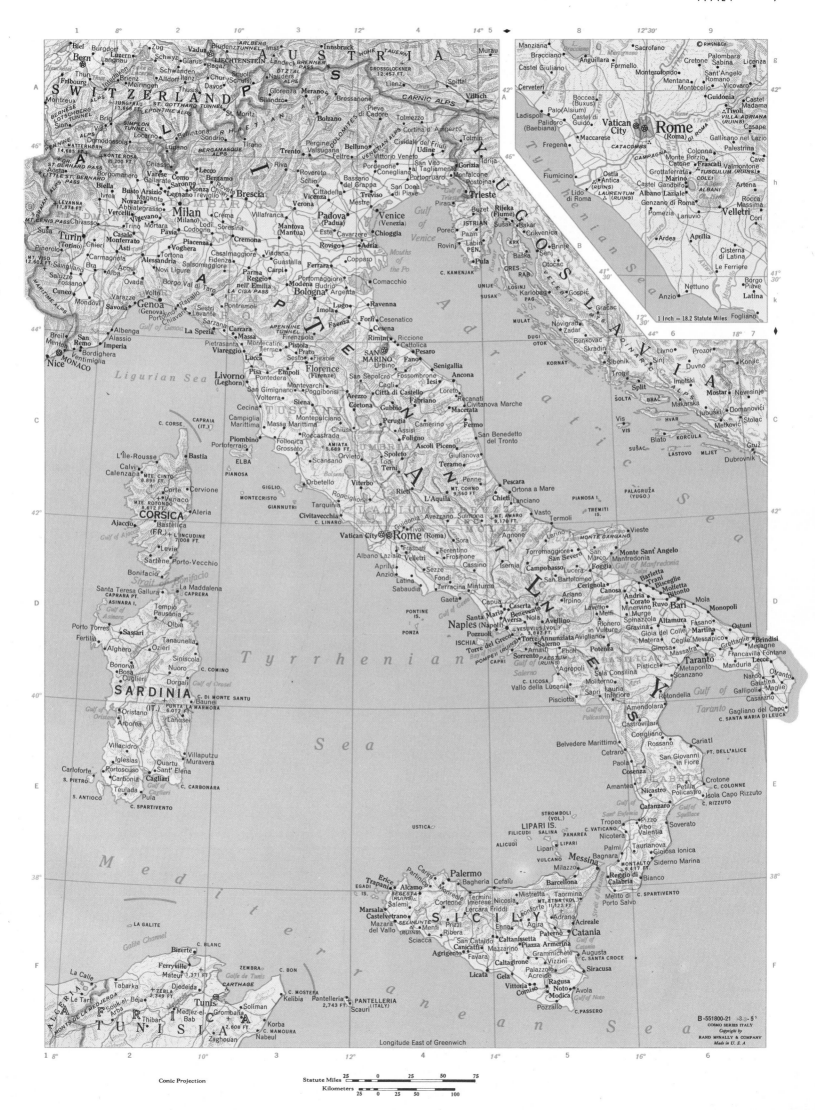

Statute Miles
Kilometers

Conic Projection

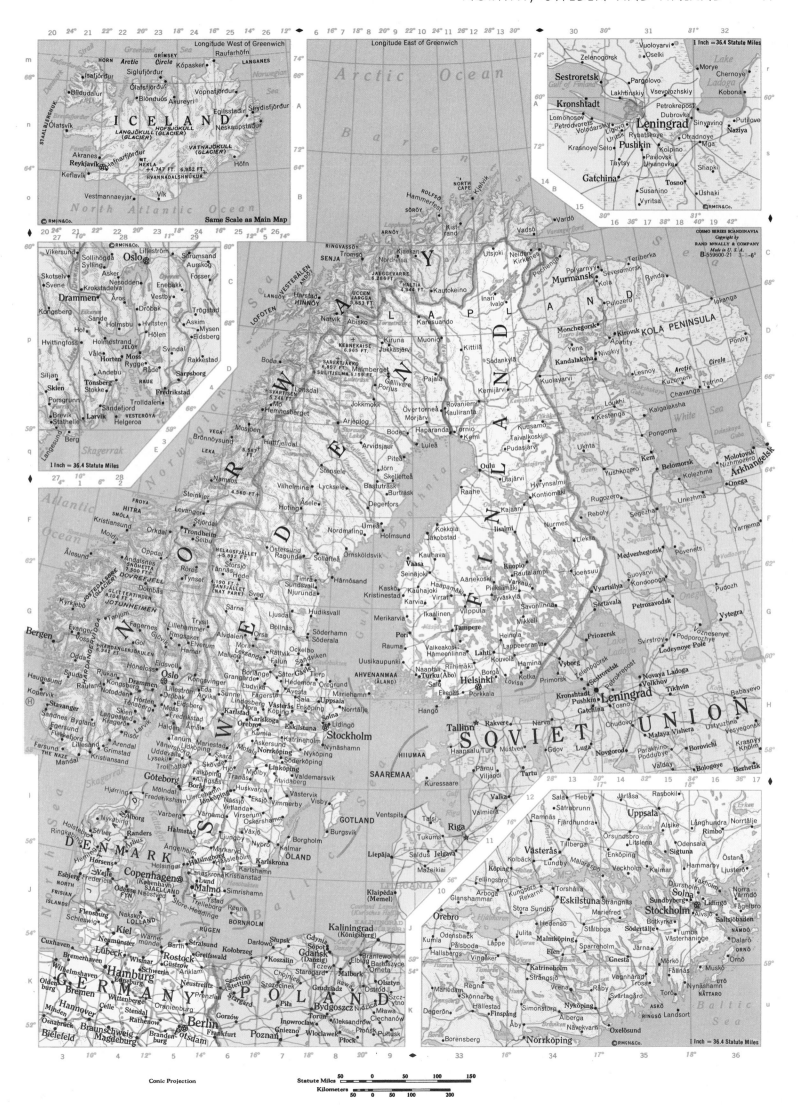

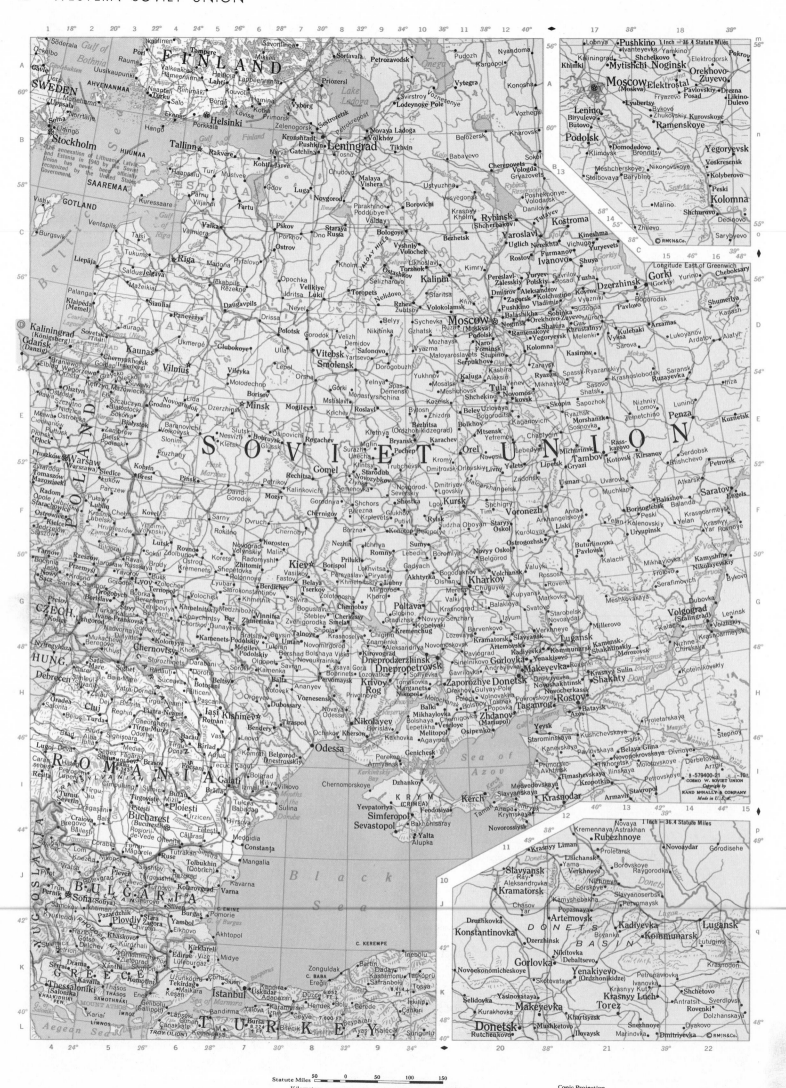

Lambert Azimuthal Equal Area Projection

Statute Miles
100 0 100 200 300 400 500

Kilometers
100 0 100 300 500 700

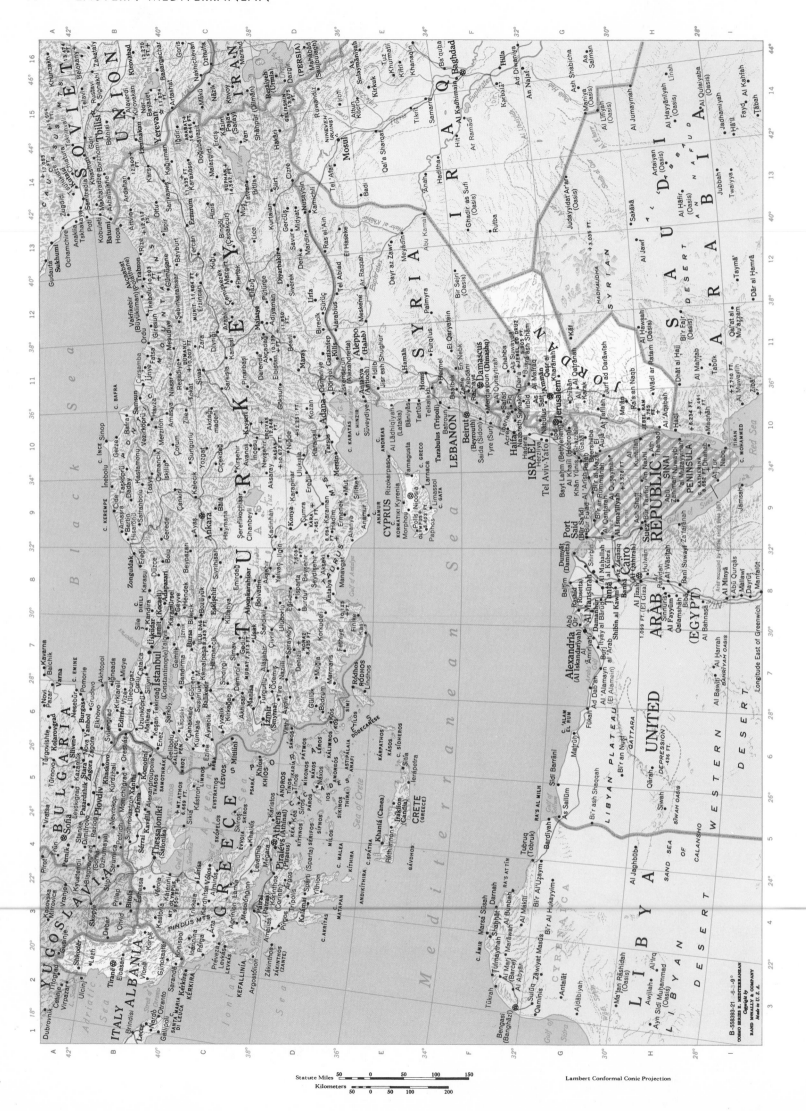

Statute Miles 50 0 50 100 150
Kilometers 50 0 50 100 200

Lambert Conformal Conic Projection

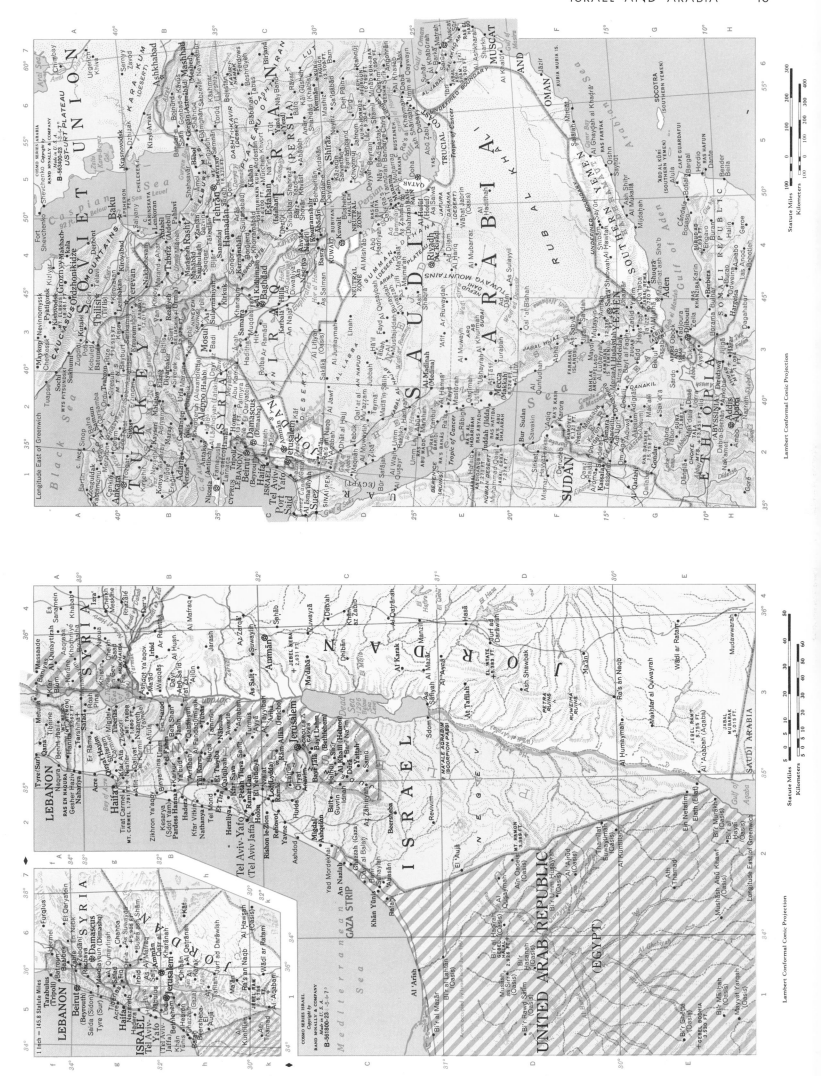

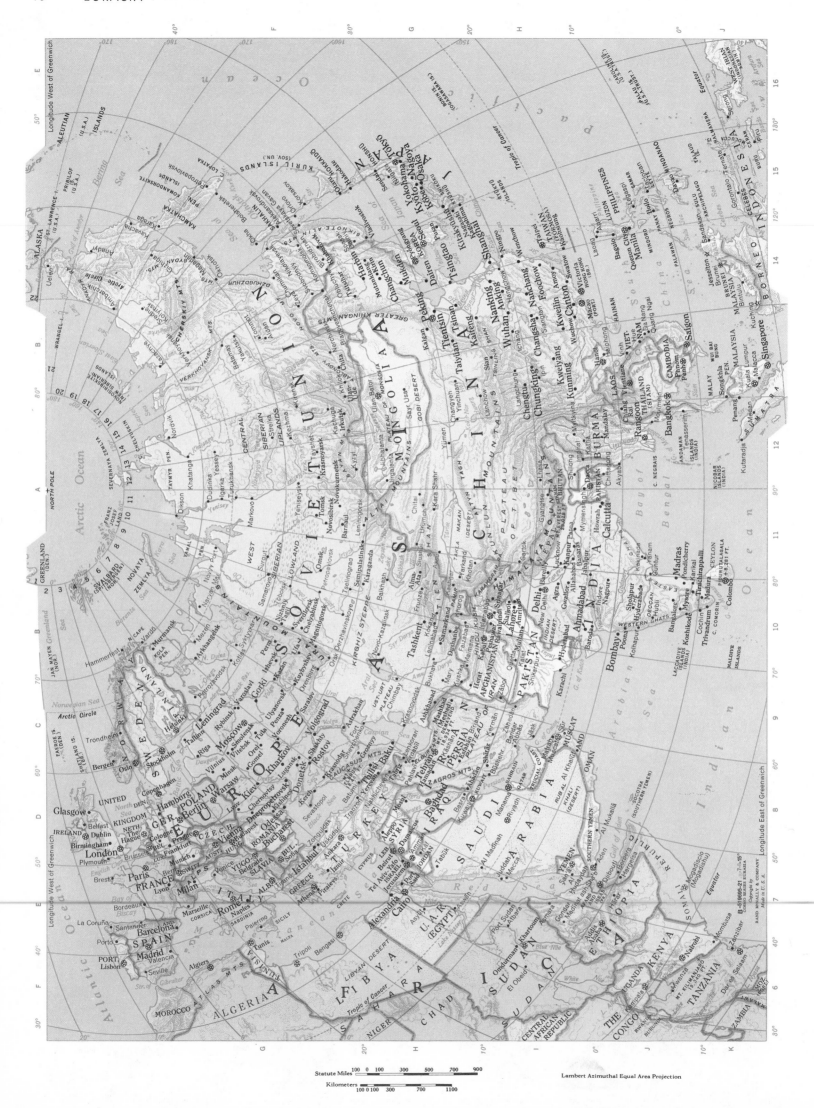

Statute Miles 100 0 100 300 500 700 900

Kilometers 100 0 100 300 700 1100

Lambert Azimuthal Equal Area Projection

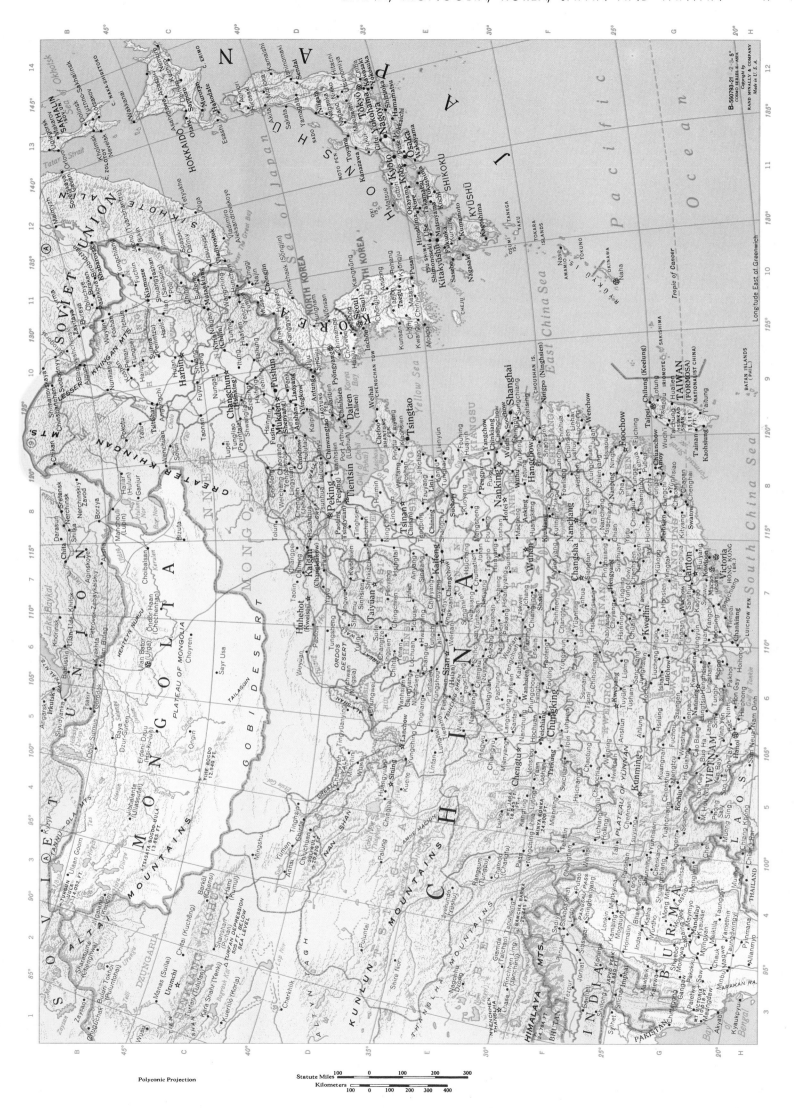

Polyconic Projection

Statute Miles
100   0   100   200   300

Kilometers
100   0   100   200   300   400

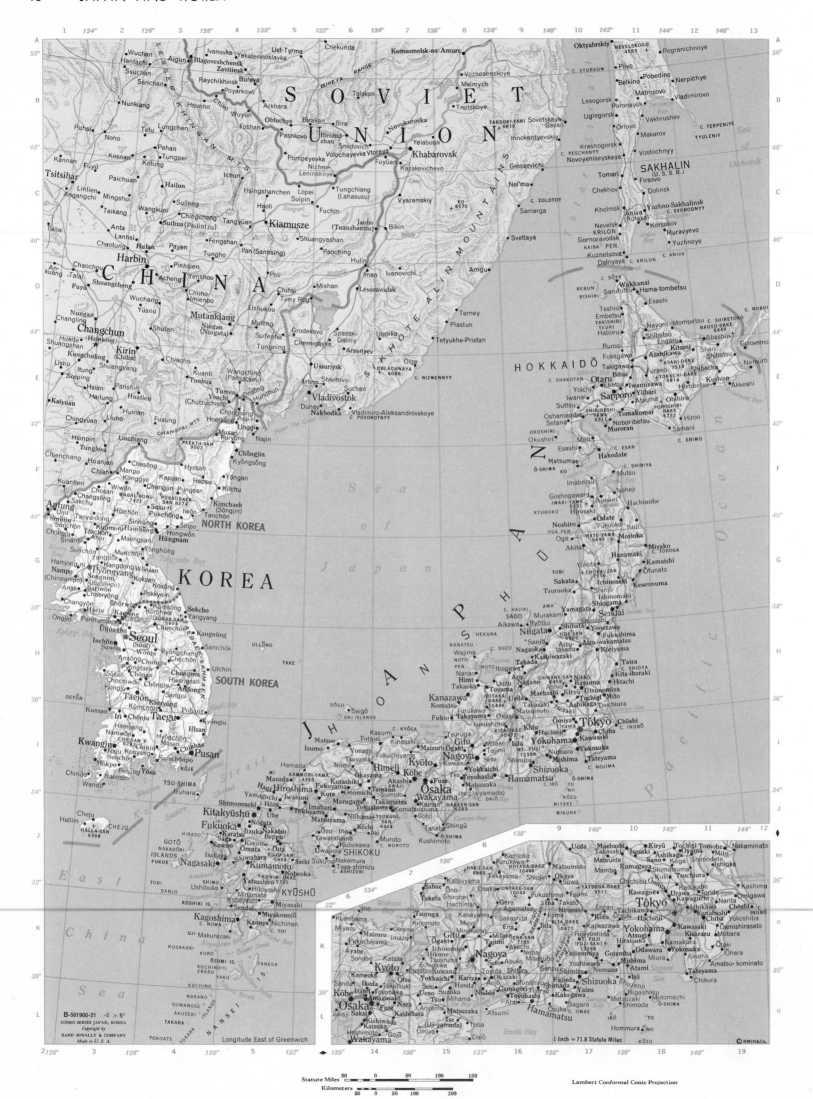

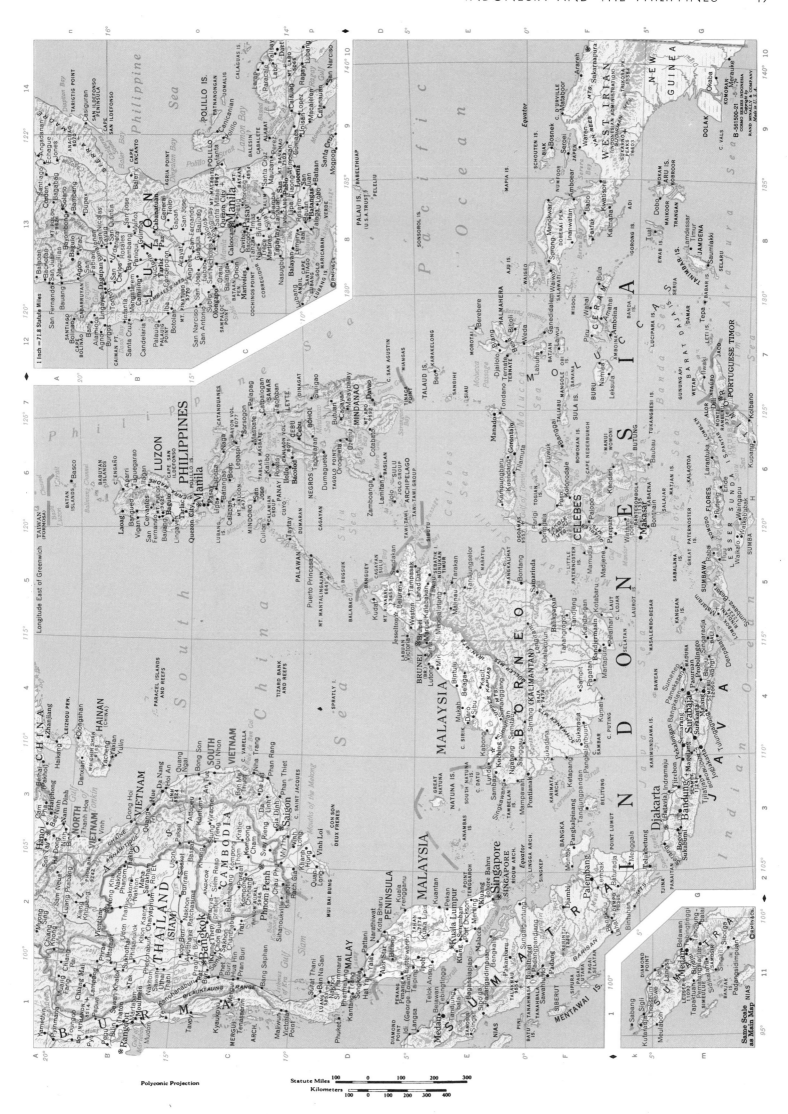

Statute Miles   100   0   100   200   300

Kilometers   100   0   100   200   300   400

Polyconic Projection

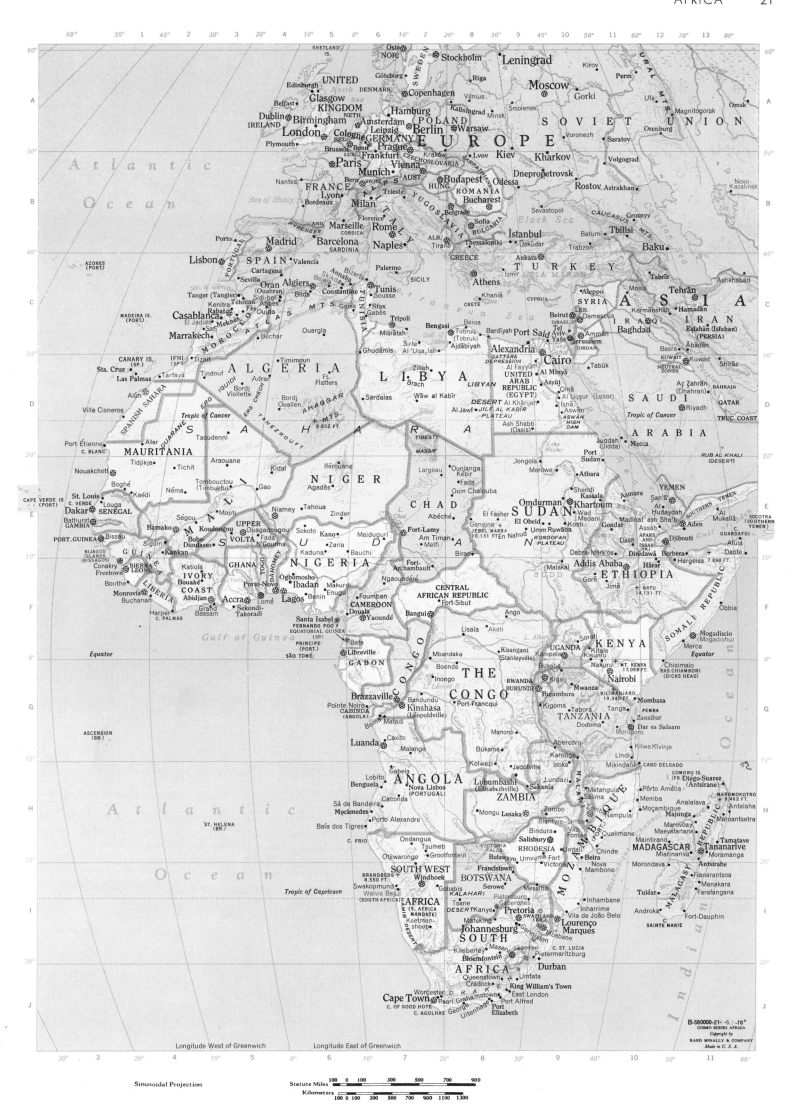

Sinusoidal Projection

Statute Miles
Kilometers

Longitude West of Greenwich   Longitude East of Greenwich

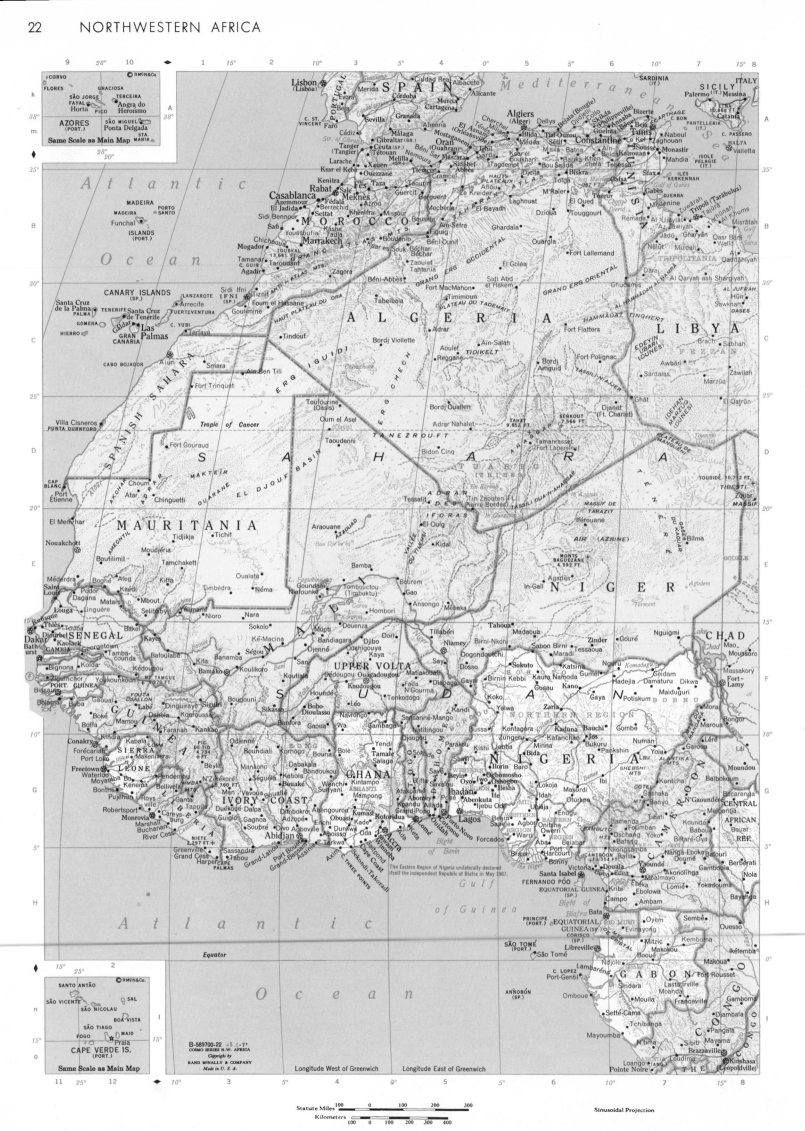

Longitude West of Greenwich   Longitude East of Greenwich

Statute Miles 100   0   100   200   300
Kilometers 100   0   100   200   300   400

Sinusoidal Projection

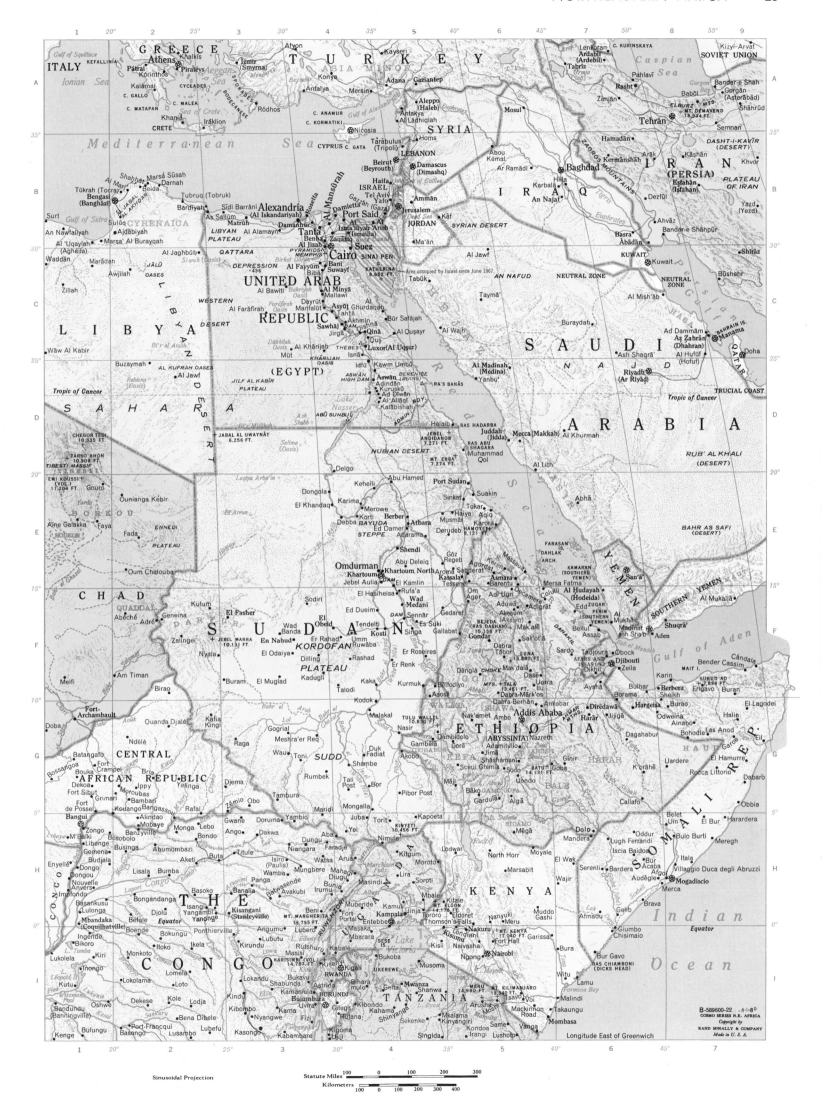

Sinusoidal Projection

Statute Miles 100 0 100 200 300
Kilometers 100 0 100 200 300 400

B-589600-22 -4-4-8 D
COSMO SERIES N.E. AFRICA
Copyright by
RAND McNALLY & COMPANY
Made in U.S.A.

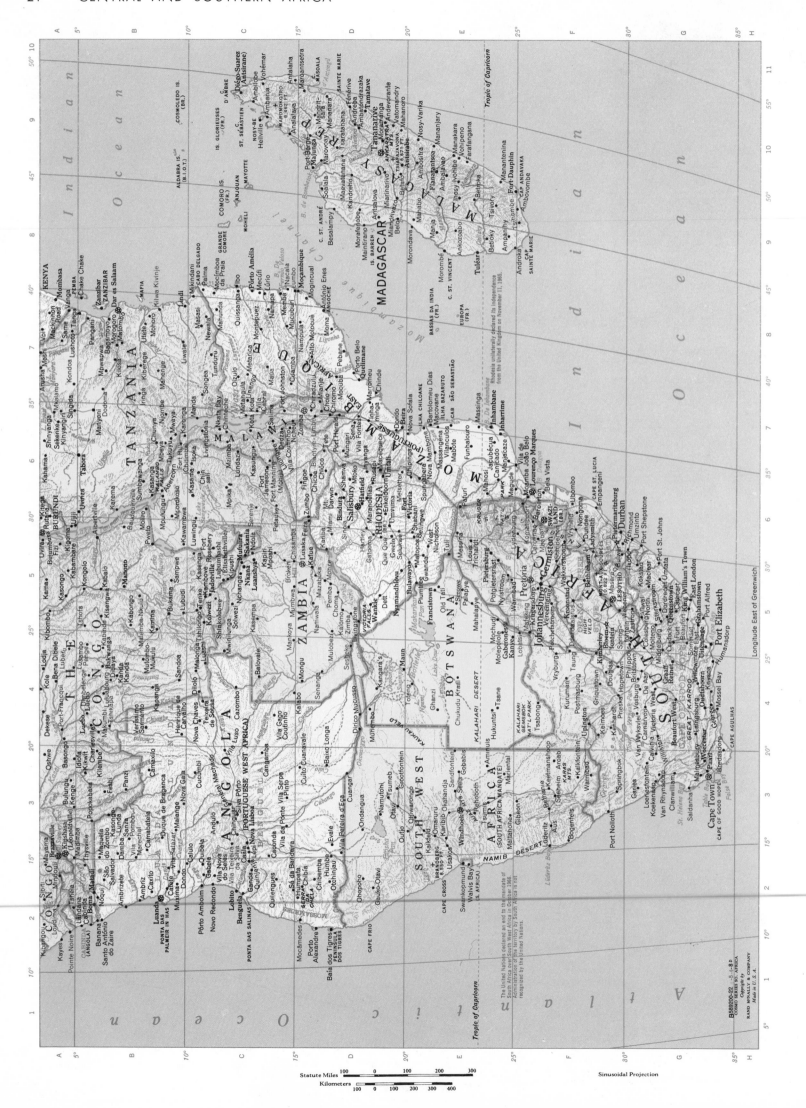

Statute Miles
Kilometers

Sinusoidal Projection

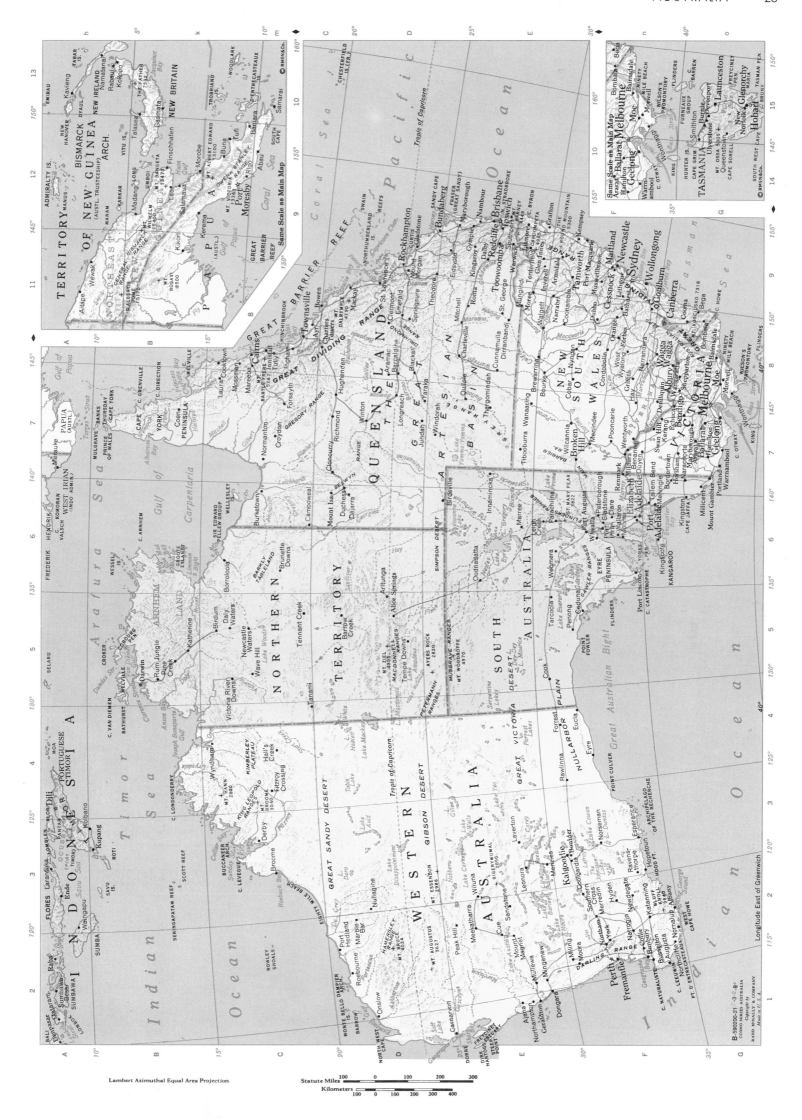

TERRITORY OF NEW GUINEA
(AUSTL. TRUSTEESHIP)

BISMARCK ARCH.

NEW BRITAIN

PAPUA
(AUSTL.)

Port Moresby

Same Scale as Main Map

Same Scale as Main Map

TASMANIA

Launceston

Hobart

New Glenorchy

WESTERN AUSTRALIA

NORTHERN TERRITORY

SOUTH AUSTRALIA

QUEENSLAND

NEW SOUTH WALES

VICTORIA

Pacific Ocean

Indian Ocean

Arafura Sea

Timor Sea

Coral Sea

Tasman Sea

Great Australian Bight

Gulf of Carpentaria

INDONESIA

PORTUGUESE TIMOR

WEST IRIAN (INDO ADMIN.)

Lambert Azimuthal Equal Area Projection

Statute Miles   100   0   100   200   300

Kilometers   100   0   100   200   300   400

B-593200-21
COSMO SERIES AUSTRALIA
Copyright by
RAND MCNALLY & COMPANY
Made in U.S.A.

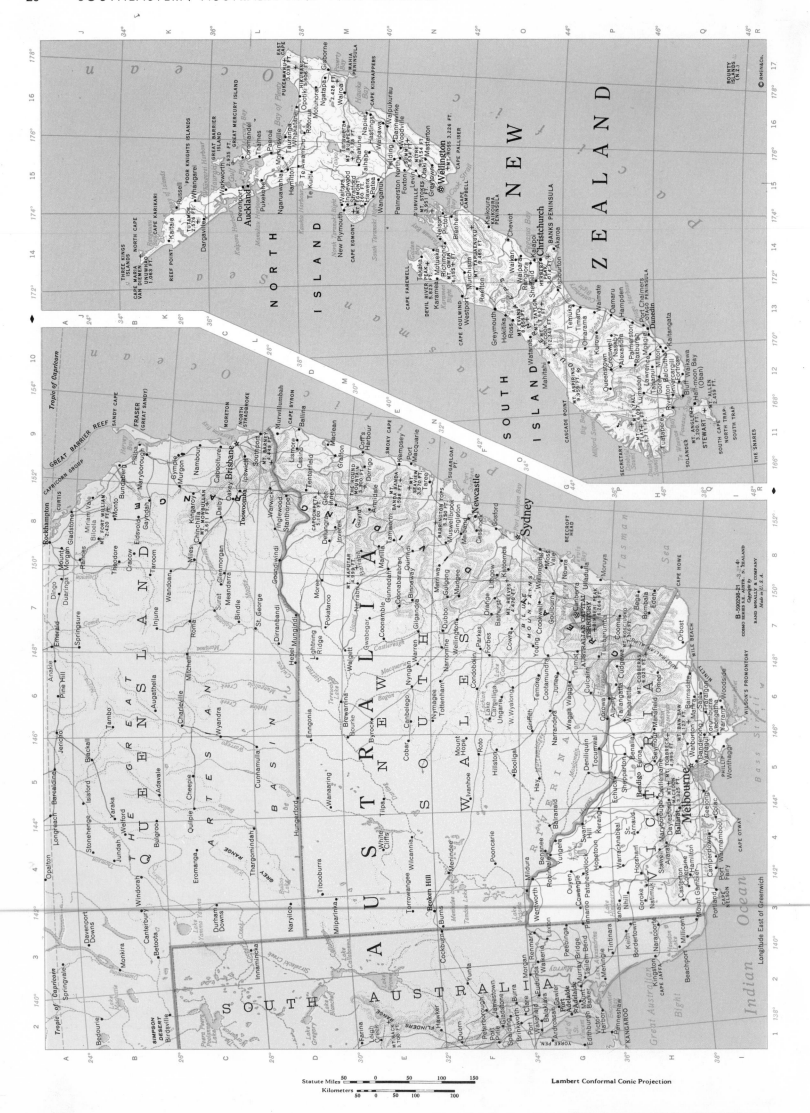

Statute Miles 50 0 50 100 150

Kilometers 50 0 50 100 200

Lambert Conformal Conic Projection

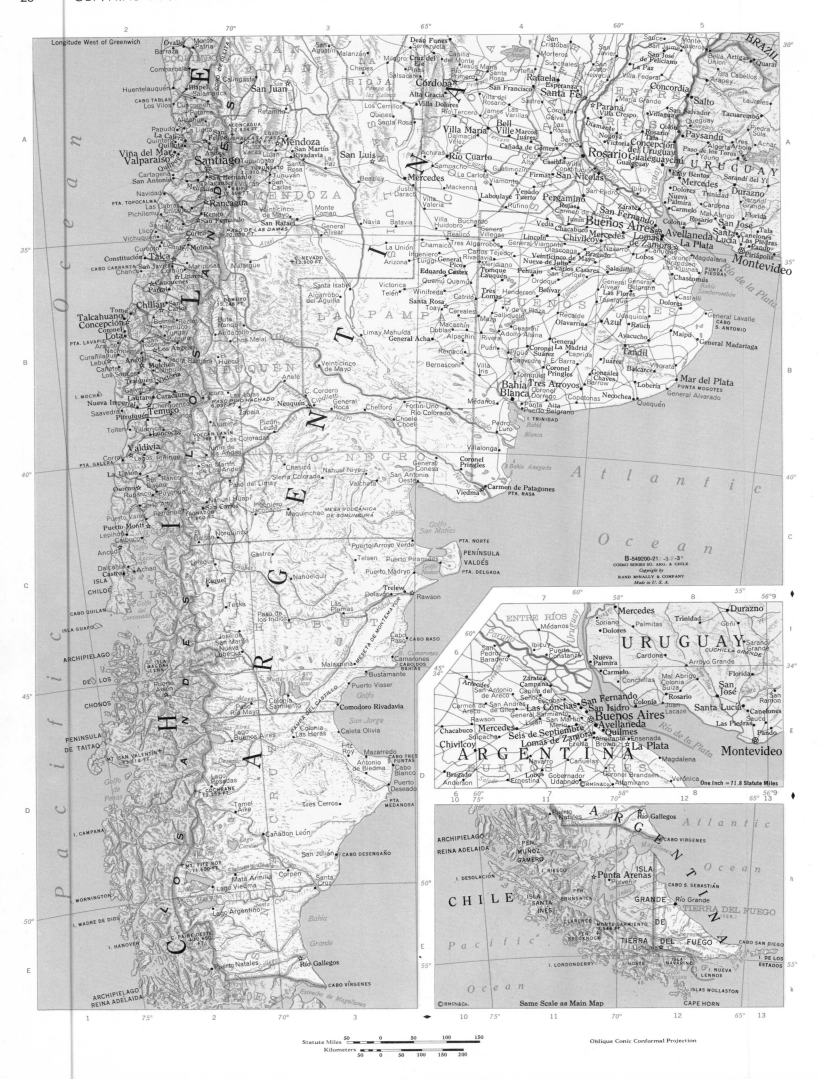

Statute Miles

Kilometers

Oblique Conic Conformal Projection

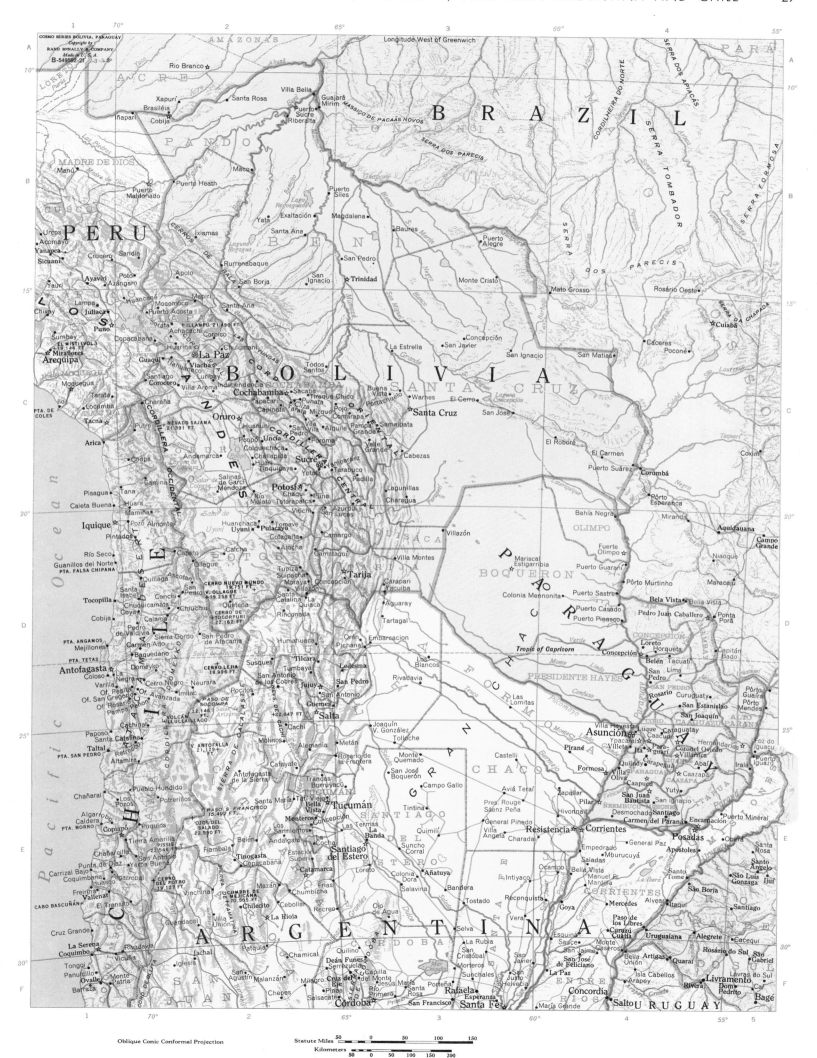

Statute Miles
50   0   50   100   150

Kilometers
50   0   50   100   150   200

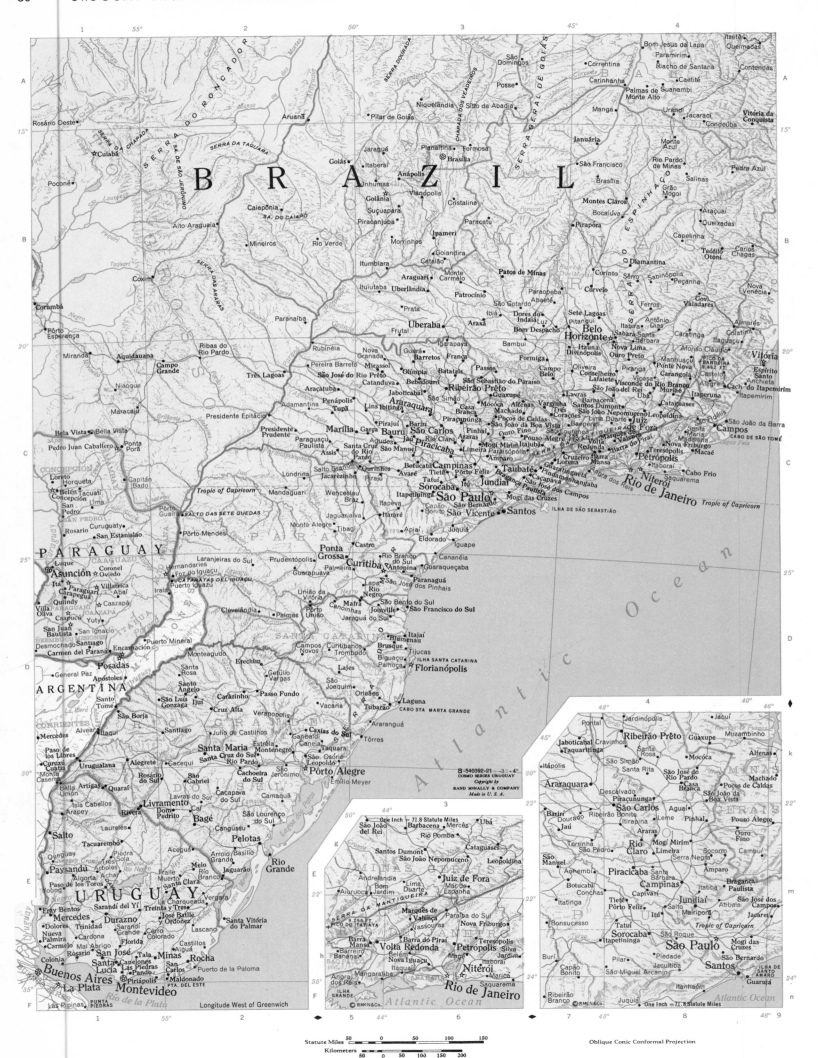

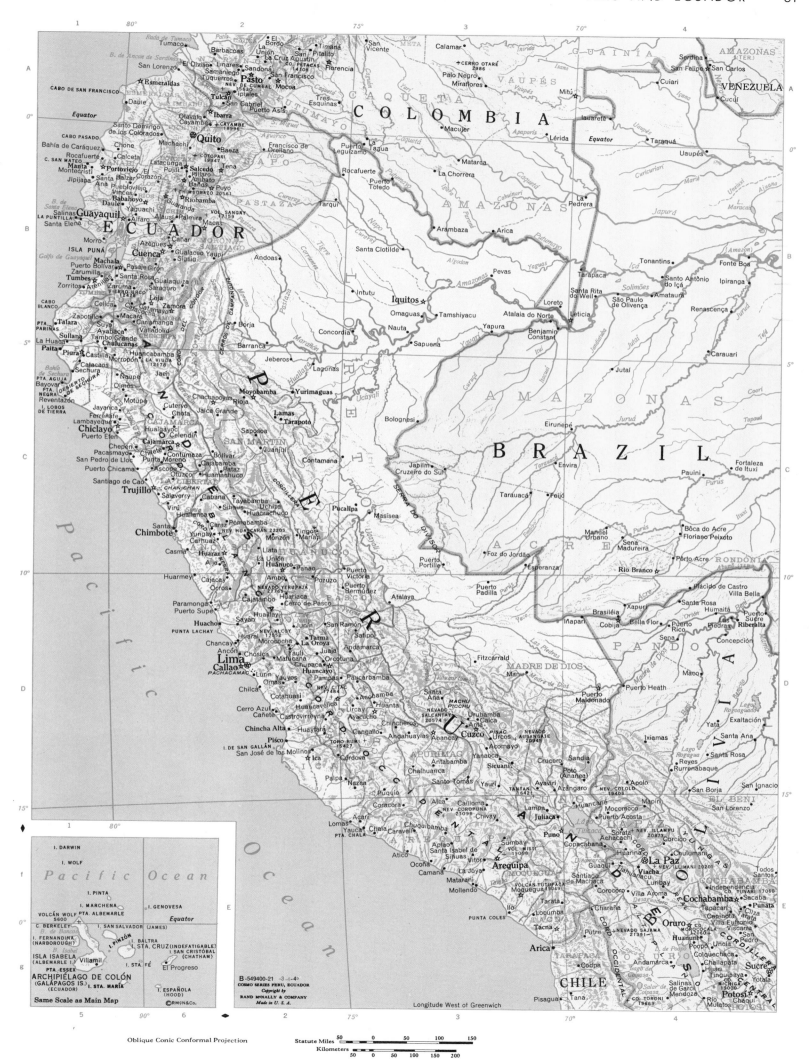

Oblique Conic Conformal Projection

Statute Miles
50   0   50   100   150

Kilometers
50   0   50   100   150   200

ARCHIPIÉLAGO DE COLÓN
(GALÁPAGOS IS.)
(ECUADOR)

Same Scale as Main Map

B-549400-21 -3-4-4ᵒ
COSMO SERIES PERU, ECUADOR
Copyright by
RAND McNALLY & COMPANY
Made in U.S.A.

Longitude West of Greenwich

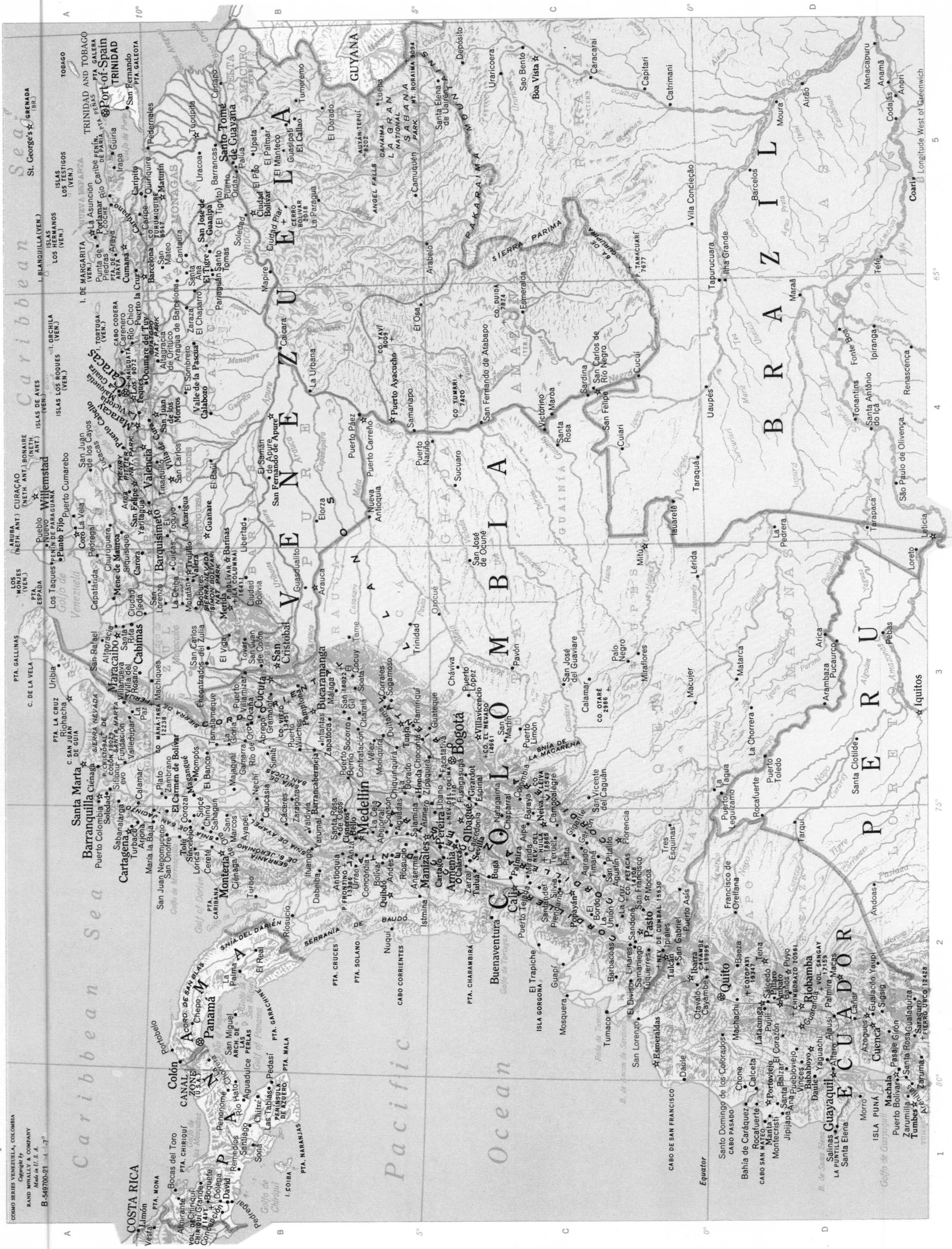

Caribbean Sea

Pacific Ocean

VENEZUELA

COLOMBIA

BRAZIL

PERU

ECUADOR

PANAMA

COSTA RICA

GUYANA

TRINIDAD AND TOBAGO

Caracas

Bogotá

Maracaibo

Medellín

Cali

Barranquilla

Cartagena

Santa Marta

Valencia

Barquisimeto

Ciudad Bolívar

Santo Tomé de Guayana

Port-of-Spain

Willemstad

CURAÇAO (NETH. ANT.)

ARUBA (NETH. ANT.)

BONAIRE (NETH. ANT.)

Panamá

Colón

CANAL ZONE U.S.A.

Quito

Guayaquil

Cuenca

Riobamba

Iquitos

Leticia

Bucaramanga

Cúcuta

Manizales

Armenia

Pasto

Buenaventura

Tumaco

San Cristóbal

Mérida

Puerto Ayacucho

San Fernando de Apure

Cumaná

Maturín

Angel Falls

MT. RORAIMA 2810

SIERRA PARIMA

LA GRAN SABANA

GAVIANA NATIONAL PARK

Statute Miles 50 0 50 100 150

Kilometers 50 0 50 100 150 200

Oblique Conic Conformal Projection

COSMO SERIES VENEZUELA, COLOMBIA
Copyright by
RAND M°NALLY & COMPANY
Made in U.S.A.
B-549700-21

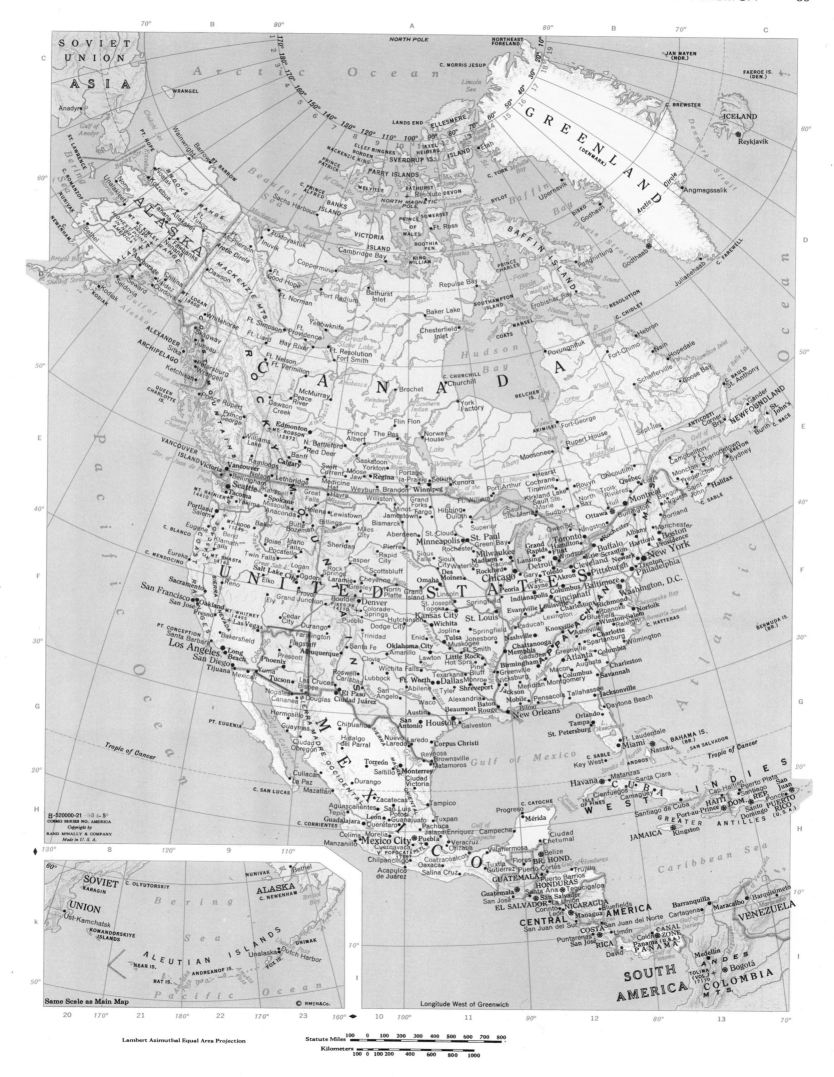

SOVIET UNION
ASIA

Arctic Ocean

NORTH POLE

NORTHEAST FORELAND

JAN MAYEN (NOR.)

FAEROE IS. (DEN.)

ICELAND
Reykjavík

GREENLAND (DENMARK)

ALASKA

MACKENZIE MTS.

C A N A D A

Hudson Bay

BAFFIN ISLAND

Baffin Bay

NEWFOUNDLAND

VANCOUVER ISLAND

U N I T E D   S T A T E S

Seattle
Portland

San Francisco
Los Angeles
San Diego

Denver

Chicago

New York
Washington, D.C.

APPALACHIAN

Atlanta

New Orleans
Houston

Miami

Gulf of Mexico

M E X I C O

Mexico City

Atlantic Ocean

BERMUDA IS. (BR.)

BAHAMA IS. (BR.)
SAN SALVADOR

CUBA
Havana

WEST INDIES

HAITI
PUERTO RICO (U.S.A.)
DOM. REP.

JAMAICA

Caribbean Sea

GUATEMALA
BR. HOND.
HONDURAS
EL SALVADOR
NICARAGUA
COSTA RICA
PANAMA

CENTRAL AMERICA

VENEZUELA
COLOMBIA

SOUTH AMERICA

Pacific Ocean

Tropic of Cancer

B-520000-21 -3 & -5°
COSMO SERIES NO. AMERICA
Copyright by
RAND McNALLY & COMPANY
Made in U.S.A.

SOVIET UNION
ALASKA
ALEUTIAN ISLANDS
Bering Sea
Pacific Ocean

Same Scale as Main Map

Longitude West of Greenwich

Lambert Azimuthal Equal Area Projection

Statute Miles   100 0 100 200 300 400 500 600 700 800
Kilometers   100 0 100 200 400 600 800 1000

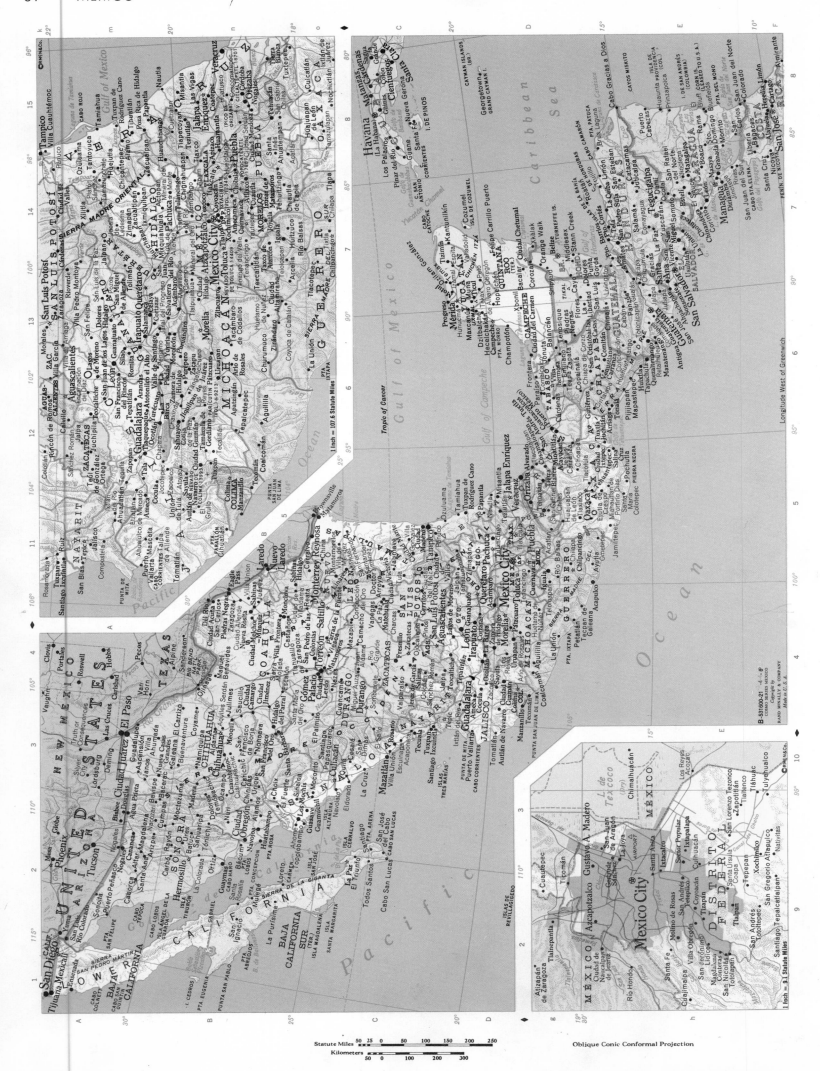

Statute Miles 50 25 0 50 100 150 200 250
Kilometers 50 0 100 200 300

Oblique Conic Conformal Projection

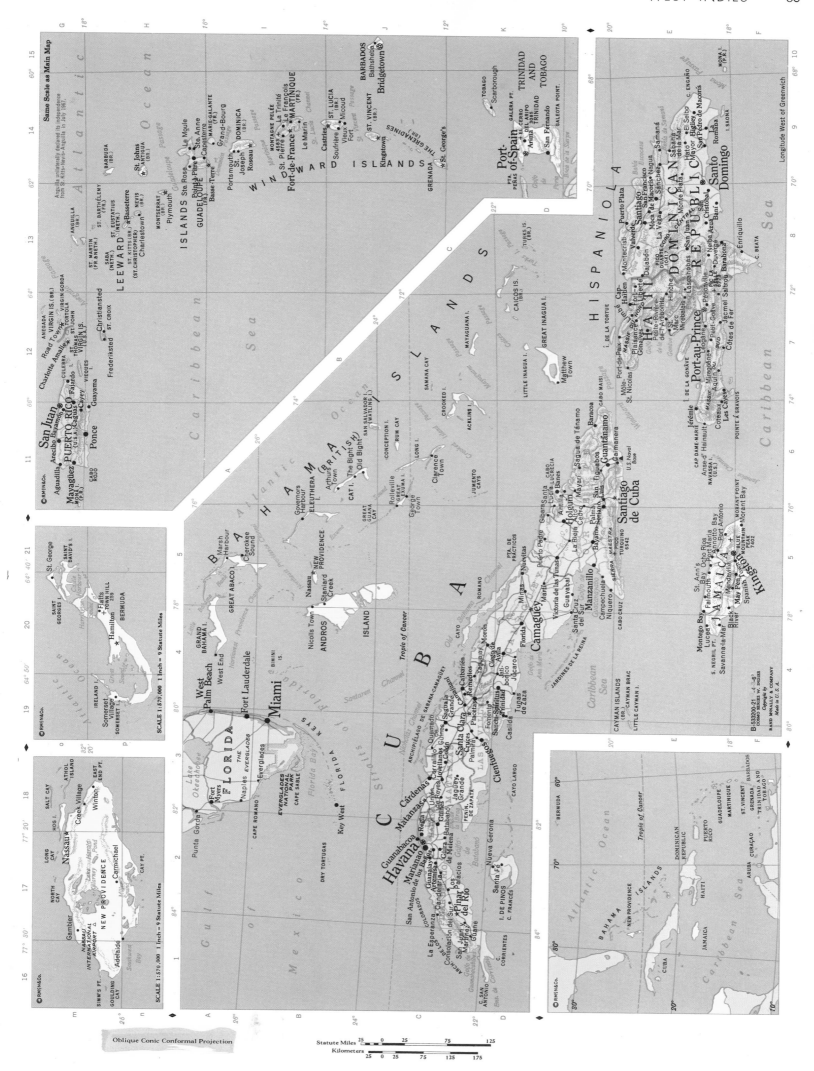

Same Scale as Main Map

Anguilla unilaterally declared its independence
from St. Kitts-Nevis-Anguilla in July 1967.

Atlantic Ocean

VIRGIN IS. (BR.)
Road Town
Charlotte Amalie
ANEGADA
CULEBRA
VIRGIN GORDA
ST. THOMAS
ST. JOHN (U.S.)
VIRGIN IS.
Fajardo
Vieques
Guayama
Christiansted
ST. CROIX
Frederiksted

San Juan
Aguadilla
Arecibo Bayamón
PUERTO RICO
(U.S.A.)
Mayagüez
MONA I.
(P.R.)
CABO ROJO
Ponce

ANGUILLA (BR.)
ST. MARTIN (FR. & NETH.)
ST. BARTHÉLEMY (FR.)
SABA (NETH.)
ST. EUSTATIUS (NETH.)
ST. KITTS (BR.)
ST. CHRISTOPHER
Basseterre
NEVIS (BR.)
Charlestown
MONTSERRAT (BR.)
Plymouth

BARBUDA (BR.)
ANTIGUA (BR.)
St. Johns

LEEWARD ISLANDS

Le Moule
Ste. Anne
GUADELOUPE (FR.)
Basse-Terre
MARIE-GALANTE (FR.)
Grand-Bourg

St. Joseph
DOMINICA (BR.)
Roseau
Portsmouth

MONTAGNE PELÉE
St. Pierre
Le François
La Trinité
MARTINIQUE (FR.)
Fort-de-France
Le Marin

ST. LUCIA (BR.)
Castries
Soufrière
Vieux Fort

ST. VINCENT (BR.)
Kingstown

THE GRENADINES (BR.)

GRENADA
St. George's

WINDWARD ISLANDS

BARBADOS
Bathsheba
Bridgetown

TOBAGO
Scarborough

TRINIDAD AND TOBAGO
GALERA PT.
EL CERRO DEL ARIPO
Arima TRINIDAD
Port-of-Spain
San Fernando
GALEOTA POINT.
PTA. DE PEÑAS

Atlantic Ocean

Caribbean Sea

Longitude West of Greenwich

HISPANIOLA

DOMINICAN REPUBLIC
Puerto Plata
Monte Cristi
Valverde
Dajabón
Santiago
Moca
San Francisco de Macorís
Sánchez
Samaná
SABANA DE LA MAR
El Seibo
C. ENGAÑO
San Pedro de Macorís
Higüey
La Vega
C. MAYOR
La Romana
Cotuí
Bonao
San
S. I. SAONA
Baní
San Cristóbal
Santo Domingo
Azua
Barahona
C. BEATA
Enriquillo

HAITI
Cap-Haïtien
I. DE LA TORTUE
Fort-Liberté
Mole-St. Nicolas
St. Nicolas
Plaisance
Gonaïves
MASSIF DU NORD
Hinche
Marc
Mirebalais
St. Marc
I. DE LA GONÂVE
Port-au-Prince
Pétionville
CAP DAME-MARIE
Jérémie
Anse-d' Hainault
Miragoâne
Petit-Goâve
Aquin
Les Cayes
Coteaux
POINTE À GRAVOIS
Côtes de Fer
Petit-Trou
Jacmel
Saltou

Caribbean Sea

BAHAMA
GRAND BAHAMA I.
West End
Marsh Harbour
Cherokee Sound
GREAT ABACO I.
BIMINI IS.
NEW PROVIDENCE
Nassau
Nicolls Town
ANDROS
Staniard Creek
ISLAND
Governors Harbour
ELEUTHERA I.
CAT I.
The Bight
Old Bight
Rolleville
GREAT EXUMA I.
George Town
SAN SALVADOR
(WATLING) I.
CONCEPTION I.
RUM CAY
Clarence Town
LONG I.
JUMENTO CAYS
CROOKED I.
ACKLINS I.
SAMANA CAY

Atlantic Ocean

MAYAGUANA I.
CAICOS IS. (BR.)
TURKS IS. (BR.)
GREAT INAGUA I.
LITTLE INAGUA I.
Matthew Town

BAHAMA ISLANDS

CUBA
Nuevitas
PTA. DE PRÁCTICOS
Puerto Padre
Gibara
Holguín
Banes
CABO LUCRECIA
Antilla
Mayarí
Sagua de Tánamo
Baracoa
CABO MAISÍ
Guantánamo
Santiago de Cuba
U.S. Naval Base
Caimanera
PICO TURQUINO 6542
SIERRA MAESTRA
Niquero
Manzanillo
Campechuela
CABO CRUZ
Bayamo
Palma Sto.
San Luis
Jiguaní
Contramaestre
Victoria de las Tunas
Guayabal
La Riola
Ciego de Ávila
Morón
Florida
Martí
Camagüey
ROMANO
CAYO SABANA-CAMAGÜEY
ARCHIPIÉLAGO DE SABANA-CAMAGÜEY
Santa Cruz del Sur
Jardines de la Reina
Nuevitas
Minas

Santa Clara
Cienfuegos
Sagua la Grande
Caibarién
Remedios
Placetas
Sancti-Spíritus
Trinidad
Casilda
Colón
Cárdenas
Matanzas
Cruces
Palmira
CAYO LARGO
Jatibonico
Morón
Ciego
Fomento
Tunas de Zaza

Havana
Regla
Marianao
Guanabacoa
Güines
San José de las Lajas
Güira de Melena
Batabanó
Jagüey Grande
Unión de Reyes
LAS VILLAS
PEN. DE ZAPATA
ISLA DE PINOS
(I. DE PINOS)
Nueva Gerona
Santa Fe
La Coloma
Pinar del Río
San Juan y Martínez
Consolación del Sur
Artemisa
Candelaria
Guanajay
La Esperanza
Guane
ARCH. DE LOS CANARREOS
C. SAN ANTONIO
COLORADOS
ARCHIPIÉLAGO DE LOS COLORADOS
Guayabal
C. CORRIENTES

Gulf of Mexico

Straits of Florida

FLORIDA
West Palm Beach
Port Lauderdale
Miami
West End
Key West
DRY TORTUGAS
CAPE SABLE
CAPE ROMANO
Naples
Fort Myers
Punta Gorda
Port Charlotte
THE EVERGLADES
EVERGLADES NATIONAL PARK
Everglades
Lake Okeechobee
FLORIDA KEYS
Florida Bay

Tropic of Cancer

Old Bahama Channel

Nicholas Channel

Santaren Channel

Tropic of Cancer

JAMAICA
Montego Bay
Lucea
S. NEGRIL PT.
Savanna-la-Mar
Black River
Mandeville
May Pen
Spanish Town
Kingston
Port Antonio
Annotto Bay
Ocho Rios
St. Ann's Bay
Falmouth
Port Maria
BLUE MOUNTAIN 7402
MORANT POINT
Morant Bay
Port Royal
C. CHRISTOBAL

Caribbean Sea

BERMUDA
St. George
SAINT GEORGE'S
SAINT DAVID'S I.
Flatts TOWN HILL 259
Hamilton
Somerset Village
Somerset I.
IRELAND I.
BERMUDA

SCALE 1:570,000   1 Inch = 9 Statute Miles

Atlantic Ocean

LONG CAY
HOG I.
NORTH CAY
SALT CAY
ATHOL ISLAND
EAST END PT.
Creek Village
Wimbot
EAST END PT.
CAY PT.
Nassau
Gambier
Carmichael
NEW PROVIDENCE
Adelaide
Lake Killarney
SIMM'S PT.
GOULDING CAY
C. SAN ANTONIO

SCALE 1:570,000   1 Inch = 9 Statute Miles

BERMUDA
BAHAMA
NEW PROVIDENCE
CUBA
JAMAICA
HAITI
DOMINICAN REPUBLIC
PUERTO RICO
VIRGIN ISLANDS
GUADELOUPE
DOMINICA
MARTINIQUE
ST. LUCIA
ST. VINCENT
GRENADA
BARBADOS
TRINIDAD AND TOBAGO
ARUBA
CURAÇAO
Tropic of Cancer

Oblique Conic Conformal Projection

Statute Miles   25 0   25   75   125
Kilometers   25 0   25   75   125   175

B-533200-21   -4--6°
COSMO SERIES W. INDIES
Copyright by
RAND McNALLY & COMPANY
Made in U.S.A.

CAYMAN ISLANDS (BR.)
GRAND CAYMAN I.
CAYMAN BRAC
LITTLE CAYMAN I.

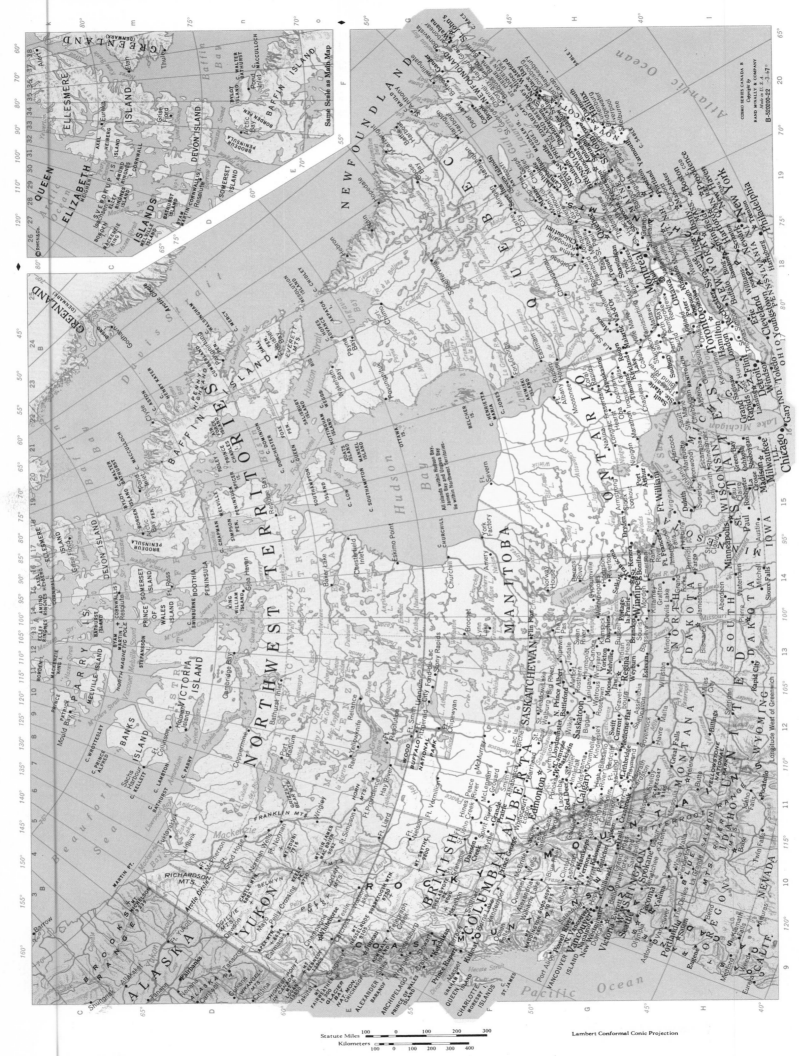

Same Scale as Main Map

Statute Miles 100 0 100 200 300
Kilometers 100 0 100 200 300 400

Lambert Conformal Conic Projection

Oblique Cylindrical Projection

Statute Miles 10 0 10 20 30 40 50 60 70 80 90 100

Kilometers 10 0 10 20 40 60 80 100 120 140

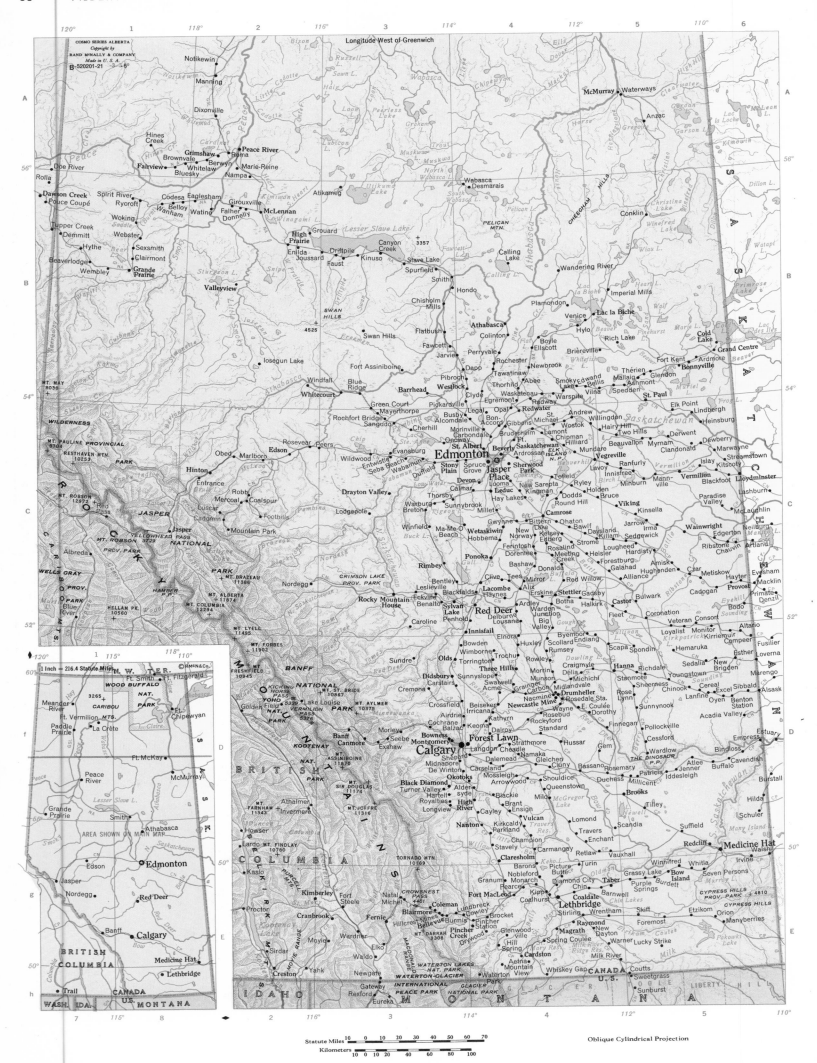

Longitude West of Greenwich

Statute Miles 10 0 10 20 30 40 50 60 70

Kilometers 10 0 10 20 40 60 80 100

Oblique Cylindrical Projection

1 Inch = 216.4 Statute Miles

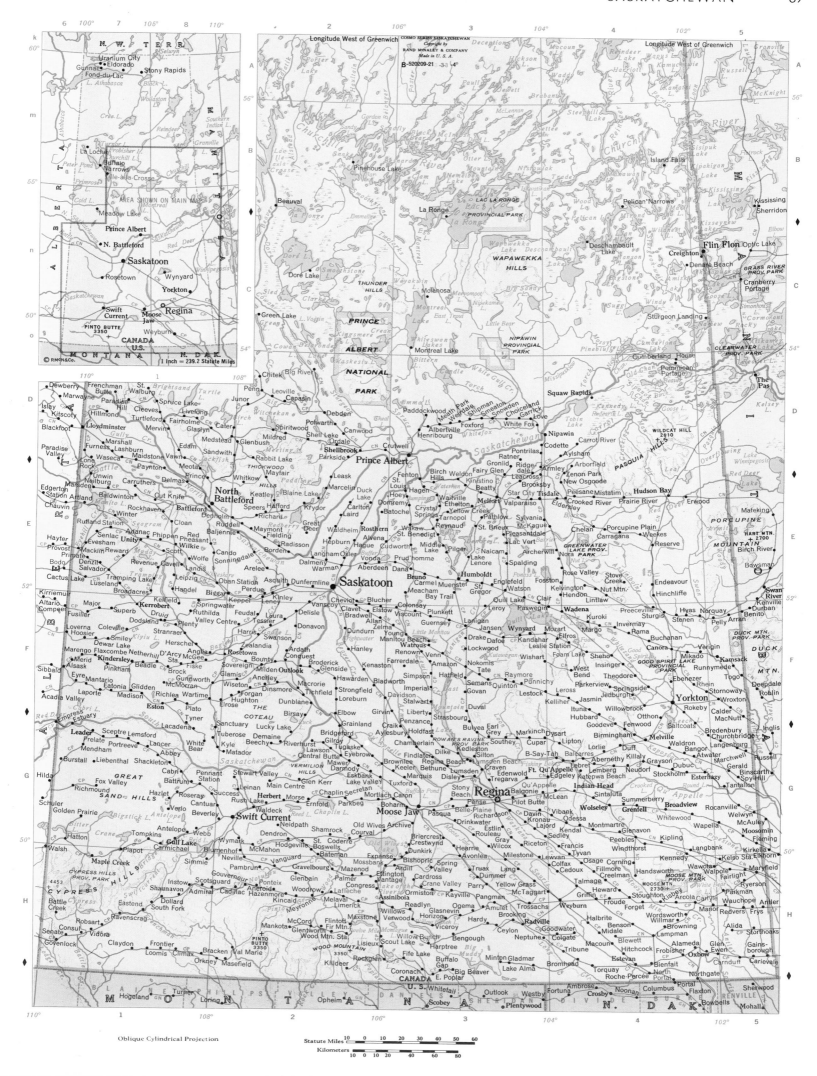

Oblique Cylindrical Projection

Statute Miles 10 0 10 20 30 40 50 60

Kilometers 10 0 10 20 40 60 80

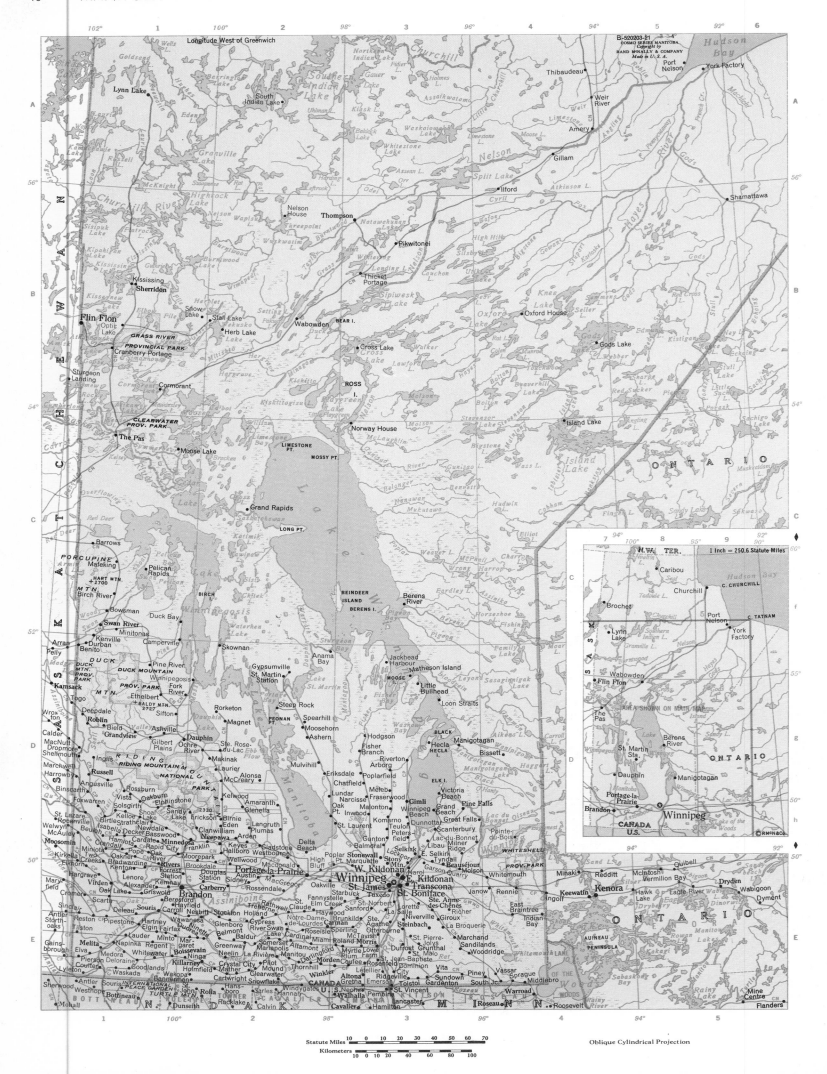

Longitude West of Greenwich

B-520203-21   -4°
COSMO SERIES MANITOBA
Copyright by
RAND McNALLY & COMPANY
Made in U.S.A.

Oblique Cylindrical Projection

Statute Miles 10 0 10 20 30 40 50 60 70
Kilometers 10 0 10 20 40 60 80 100

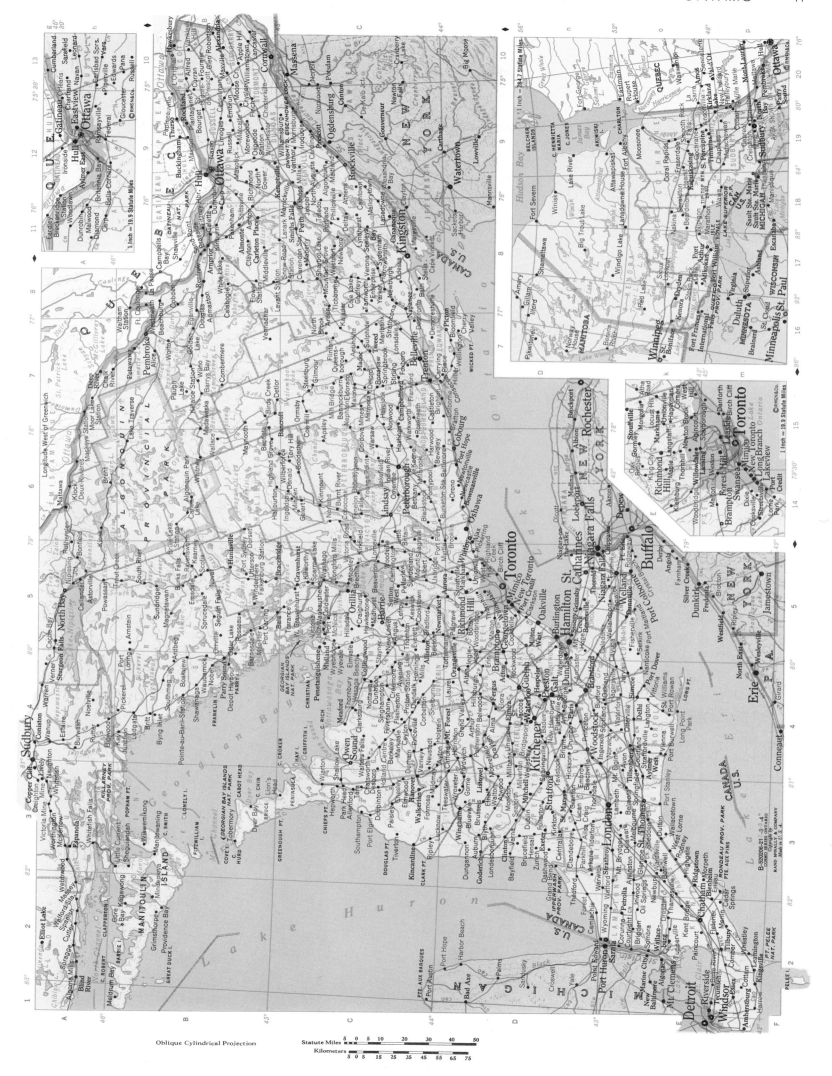

Oblique Cylindrical Projection

Statute Miles 5 0 5 10 20 30 40 50

Kilometers 5 0 5 15 25 35 45 55 65 75

Statute Miles 5 0 5 10 20 30 40
Kilometers 5 0 5 15 25 35 45 55

Oblique Cylindrical Projection

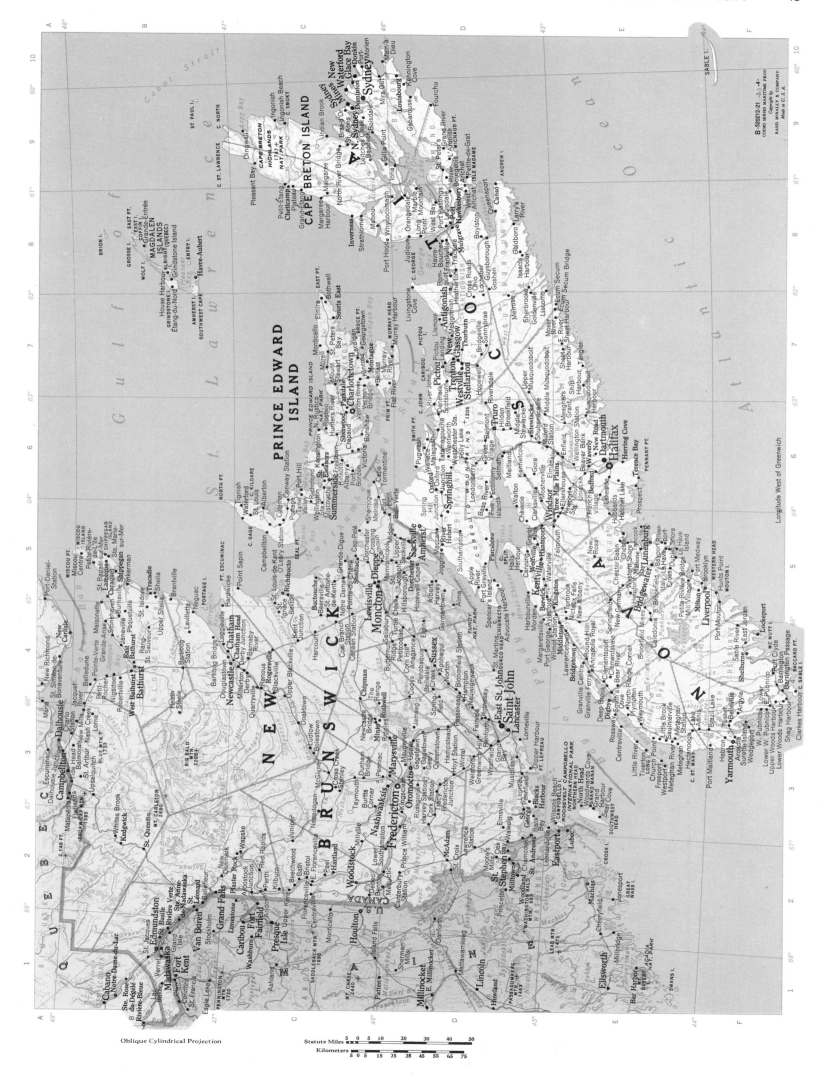

PRINCE EDWARD ISLAND

CAPE BRETON ISLAND

NEW BRUNSWICK

QUEBEC

NOVA SCOTIA

CANADA
U.S.

Gulf of St. Lawrence

Atlantic Ocean

Oblique Cylindrical Projection

Statute Miles
Kilometers

Longitude West of Greenwich

NEWFOUNDLAND

Main map

Labrador Sea

LABRADOR (PART OF NEWFOUNDLAND)

QUEBEC

Goose Bay
Happy Valley
North West River
Montagnais Pt.
Rigolet
Cartwright
Paradise River
Lake Melville
Groswater Bay
Hamilton Inlet
Mealy Mountains

BRIG HARBOUR I.
CUT THROAT I.
WHITE BEAR IS.
GEORGE I.
FISH COVE PT.
C. PORCUPINE
GANNET IS.
HUNTINGDON
EARL
S. WOLF I.
SPOTTED I.
I. OF PONDS
Frenchman's Island
HAWKE I.
STONY I.
Square Islands
St. Michael's Bay
Port Hope Simpson
GRANDY I.
Fox Harbour
Mary's Harbour
Battle Harbour
Cape Charles
C. ST. CHARLES
Henley Harbour
TABLE HD.
NORTHEAST
YORK PT. BELLE ISLE
SOUTH PT.
Red Bay
West St. Modeste
Cook's Harbour
C. BAULD
QUIRPON
L'Anse-au-Loup
L'Anse-au-Meadow
Salmon Bay
BRADORE HILLS
Raleigh
Forteau
L'Anse-au-Clair
St. Anthony
Old Fort Bay
Blanc-Sablon
Flower's Cove
St. Augustin Saguenay
OUTER I.
FISHOT I.
Bartlett's Harbour
Brig Bay
WINDY PT.
GROAIS I.
GREY ISLANDS
La Tabatière
GREAT MECATINA I.
FLAT I.
ST. JOHN
Roddickton
Conche
BELL I.
Mutton Bay
Tête-à-la-Baleine
PT. RICHE
Port Saunders
LITTLE MECATINA I.
Hooping Harbour
Williamsport
GRANITE PT.
River of Ponds
BLUE MTN. 2126
Harbour Deep
ST. MARY IS.
Daniel's Harbour
Little Harbour Deep
Great Harbour Deep
Parson's Pond
WESTERN EASTERN I.
PARTRIDGE PT.
Horse Islands
Fleur-de-Lys
Cow Head
Seal Cove Pacquet
C. ST. JOHN
Jackson's Arm
Shoe Cove
Round Harbour
Pollards Point
Westport
Burlington
Baie Verte
Nippers Harbour
Rocky Harbour
GROS MORNE 2644
Rattling Brook
Little Bay Island
Beaumont
Notre Dame Bay
FOGO ISLAND
Fogo
Joe Batt's Arm
Tilting
FUNK I.
WESTERN HEAD
Woody Point
Norris Point
Hampden
King's Point
Port Anson
TWILLINGATE
Twillingate
C. FOGO
Trout River
LOMOND
Springdale
Pilley's Island
Summerford
NEW WORLD I.
WADHAM IS.
Durrells
Change Islands
BEVERLY HD.
MT. ST. GREGORY 2251
Robert's Arm
Point Leamington
Musgrave Harbour
Doting Cove
Lumsden
Deer Lake
OLD MAN MTN. 1628
Boyd's Cove
Birchy Cove
Carmanville
C. FREELS
Howley
MAIN TOPSAIL 1822
HODGES HILL 1870
Campbellton
Loon Bay
Gander Bay
Newtown
Lark Harbour
Wood's Island
Frenchman's Cove
Cox's Cove
Pasadena
Millertown Jct.
Botwood
Lewisporte
Valleyfield
Wesleyville
Greenspond
SERPENTINE PROV. PARK
Humbermouth
Badger
Windsor
Norris Arm
Northern Arm
LONG PT.
LEWIS HILLS 2670
Spruce Brook
Corner Brook
Buchans
Bishop's Falls
Grand Falls
Glenwood
Gander
Hare Bay
Trinity
ST. BRENDAN'S
Three Rock Cove
Lourdes
Boswarlos
Millertown
Gambo
Middle Brook
BONAVISTA
COTTEL'S I.
WILLIS I.
Piccadilly
Port-au-Port
Glovertown
Salvage
Keels
Bonavista
Eastport
Elliston
Little Catalina
PORT AU PORT PENINSULA
Stephenville
St. George's
NEWFOUNDLAND
TERRA NOVA NAT'L PARK
Plate Cove West
Catalina
Port Union
C. ST. GEORGE
Flat Bay
Stephenville Crossing
Terra Nova
Princeton
Champney's West
St. George's Bay
Robinsons
BARACHOIS POND PROV. PARK
Musgravetown
Port Blandford
Lethbridge
Trinity
Pt. Rexton
St. David's
ST. FINTAN
MT. HOWLEY 1475
Shoal Harbour
Clarenville
Grates Cove
GRATES PT.
Codroy Pond
ANNIEOPSQUOTCH MTS.
MT. SYLVESTER 1234
RANDOM I.
Old Perlican
Bay de Verde
BACCALIEU I.
LONG RANGE MTS.
Victoria L.
Meelpaeg L.
Winterton
New Perlican
Hearts Content
Lower Island Cove
C. ANGUILLE
Codroy
Searston
St. Andrew's
Doyles
Tompkins
BLUE HILLS OF COTEAU 2090
Head Bay D'Espoir
St. Alban's
Milltown
Round Pond
Sunnyside
Hant's Harbour
Victoria
C. ST. FRANCIS
Pouch Cove
C. RAY
Cape Ray
South Branch
BURNT MTN. 1925
Rose Blanche
Rencontre East
Terrenceville
Carbonear
Harbour Grace
Spaniard's Bay
Upper I. Cove
Torbay
Wabana (Bell Island)
Mouse Island
Channel-Port-aux-Basques
Isle-aux-Morts
Grand Bruit
Richard's Harbour
Pushthrough
Hermitage
Belleoram
Harbour Mille
Bay l'Argent
Harbour Buffett
MERASHEEN RED
New Harbour
Bay Roberts
St. John's
C. SPEAR
Burgeo
Cape La Hune
Ramea
PENGUIN IS.
Harbour Breton
English Harbour West
Garnish
Long Harbour
Whitbourne
Harbour Main
BUTTERPOT PROV. PARK
Bay Bulls
RAMEA
BRUNETTE I.
Frenchman's Cove
Marystown
JUDE I.
Fox Harbour
Dunville
Placentia
AVALON PENINSULA
Witless Bay
Tors Cove
Mobile
Grand Bank
Fortune
Creston
Burin
Ship Cove
SAWYER'S HILL 902
Admiral's Beach
MT. CARMEL
St. Joseph's
Colinet
Cape Broyle
CAP MIQUELON
MIQUELON
BURIN PEN.
Lawn
Lamaline
St. Lawrence
Mosquito
Branch
St. Bride's
C. ST. MARY'S
St. Mary's
St. Vincent's
Ferryland
Fermeuse
Renews
ST. PIERRE AND MIQUELON (FRANCE)
LANGLADE
Placentia Bay
Trepassey
Portugal Cove South
CAP COUPÉ
ST. PIERRE
St. Pierre
St. Shotts
PT. LANCE
C. PINE
C. RACE
MISTAKEN PT.

Gulf of St. Lawrence

Atlantic Ocean

Longitude West of Greenwich

Inset map (upper right)

Ungava Bay
QUEBEC
TORNGAT MOUNTAINS
Atlantic Ocean
Labrador Sea

BUTTON IS.
AKPATOK I.
KILLINEK I.
C. CHIDLEY
N. AULATSIVIK I.
Seven Islands Bay
CIRQUE MTN. 5160
C. UIVAK
BIG
George River
Hebron
Fort Chimo
COD I.
OKAK IS.
S. AULATSIVIK I.
Nain
PAUL I.
Schefferville
TUNUNGAYUALOK I.
Davis Inlet
Hopedale
MT. BENEDICT 2720
Makkovik
ADLAVIK IS.
C. HARRISON
Rigolet
Hamilton Inlet
LABRADOR (PART OF NEWFOUNDLAND)
CHURCHILL FALLS
North West River
Cartwright
Labrador City
Goose Bay
Happy Valley
Wabush
MEALY MOUNTAINS 3700
Square Islands
Battle Harbour
Red Bay
Salmon Bay
Blanc Sablon
Sept-Îles (Seven Islands)
Magpie
Havre St. Pierre
Baie Johan Beetz
Aguanish
Port Saunders
Mutton Bay
Roddickton
Englee
Clarke City
Moisie
Minpan
Natashquan
Kegaska
Gethsémani
NEWFOUNDLAND
Parson's Pond
Fleur-de-Lys
Port-Cartier
Port-Menier
WEST PT.
ANTICOSTI I.
Gulf of St. Lawrence
Cow Head
Westport

QUEBEC

1 Inch = 143.5 Statute Miles

Labrador

COSMO SERIES NEWFOUNDLAND
Copyright by
RAND McNALLY & COMPANY
Made in U.S.A.
B-520204-21 -3-4-5°
© RMcN & Co.

Statute Miles 5 0 5 10 20 30 40 50 60
Kilometers 5 0 5 10 20 30 40 50 60 70 80

Lambert Conformal Conic Projection

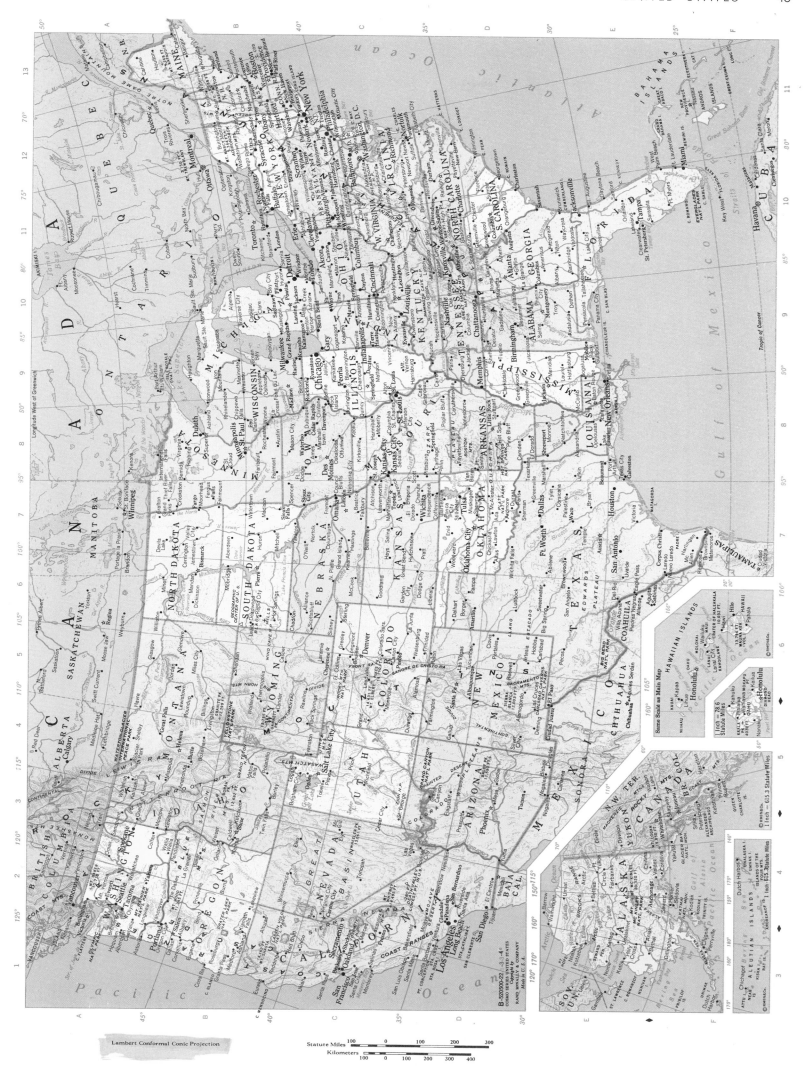

Lambert Conformal Conic Projection

Statute Miles
100   0   100   200   300

Kilometers
100   0   100   200   300   400

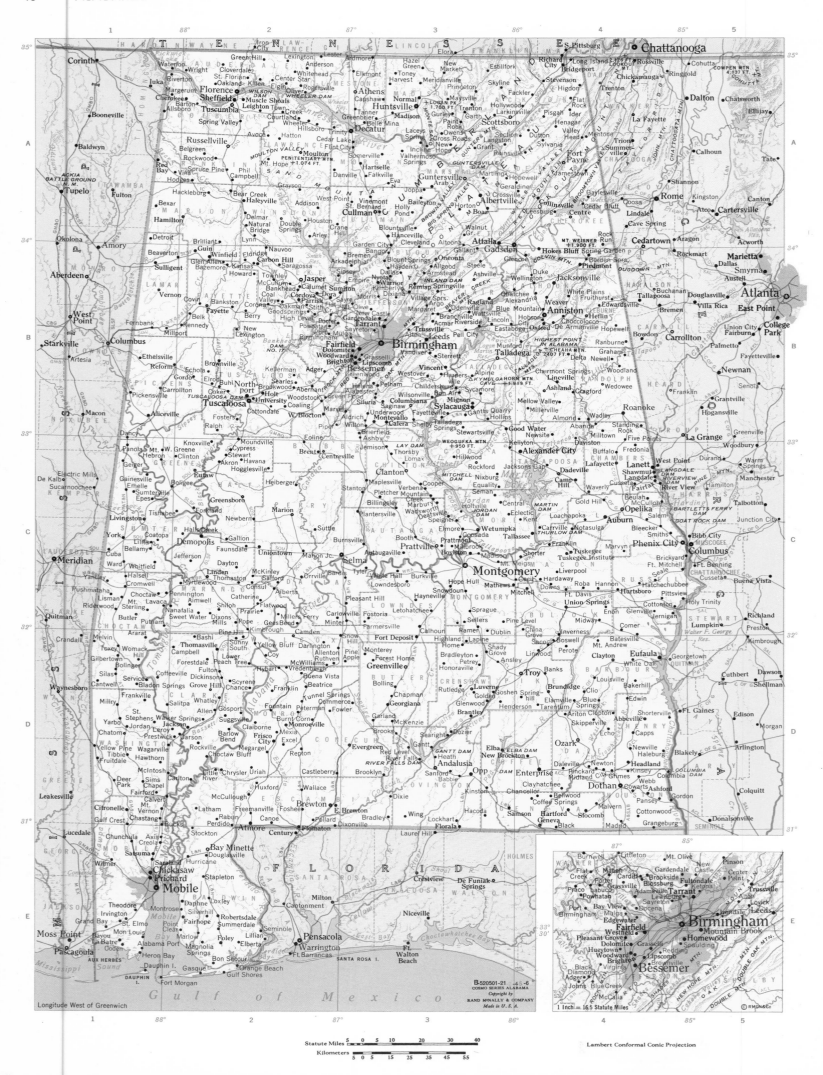

Statute Miles 5 0 5 10 20 30 40
Kilometers 5 0 5 15 25 35 45 55

Longitude West of Greenwich

B-520501-21 44-6
COSMO SERIES ALABAMA
Copyright by
RAND McNALLY & COMPANY
Made in U. S. A.

1 Inch = 16.5 Statute Miles

Lambert Conformal Conic Projection

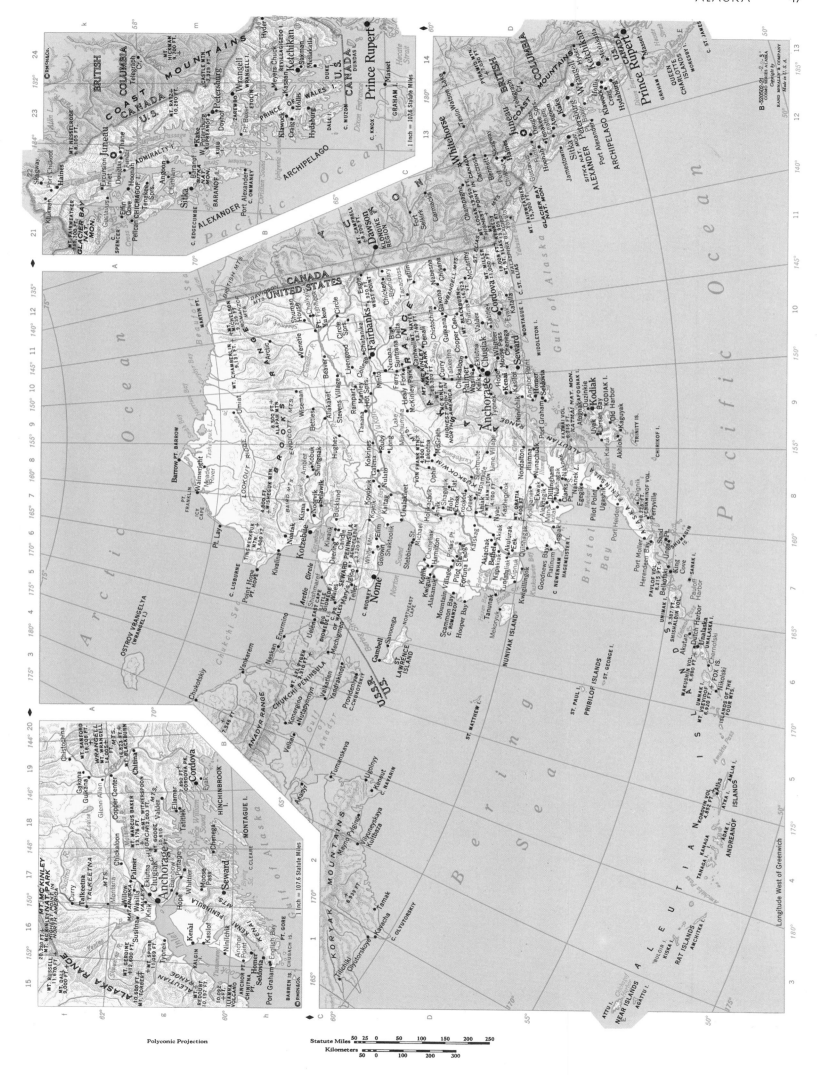

Polyconic Projection

Statute Miles 50 25 0 50 100 150 200 250

Kilometers 50 0 100 200 300

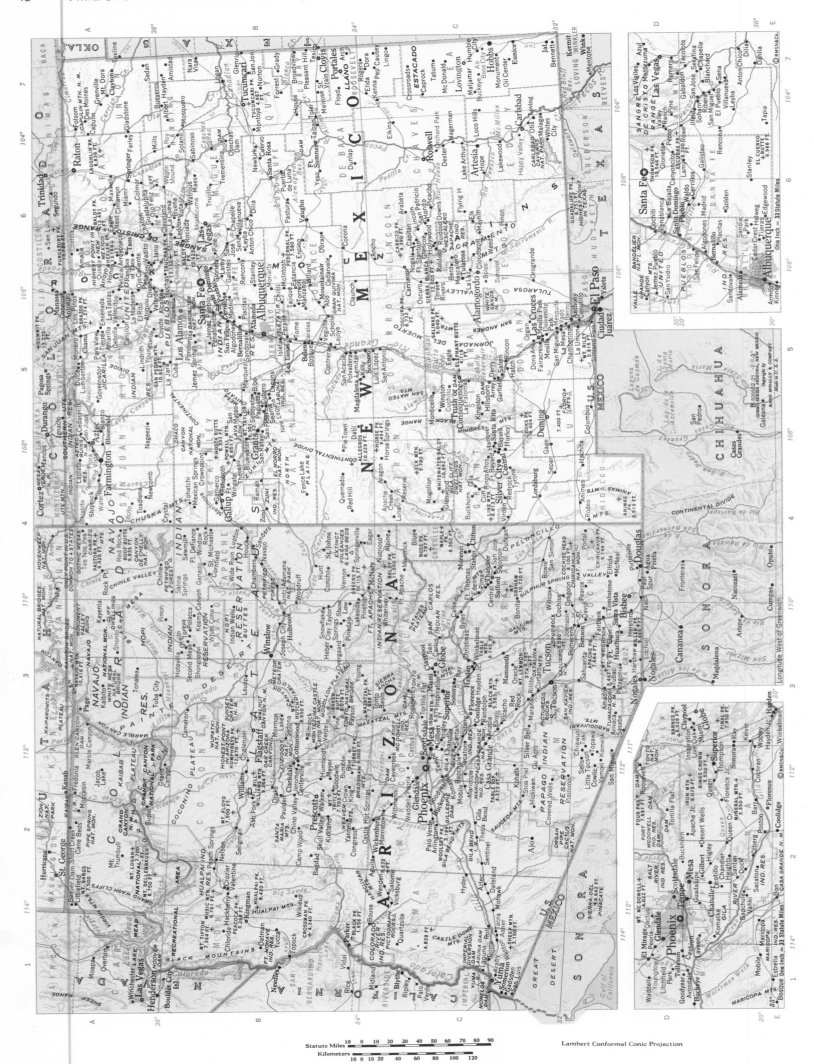

Statute Miles 10 0 10 20 30 40 50 60 70 80 90

Kilometers 10 0 10 20 30 40 50 60 70 80 90 100 110 120

Lambert Conformal Conic Projection

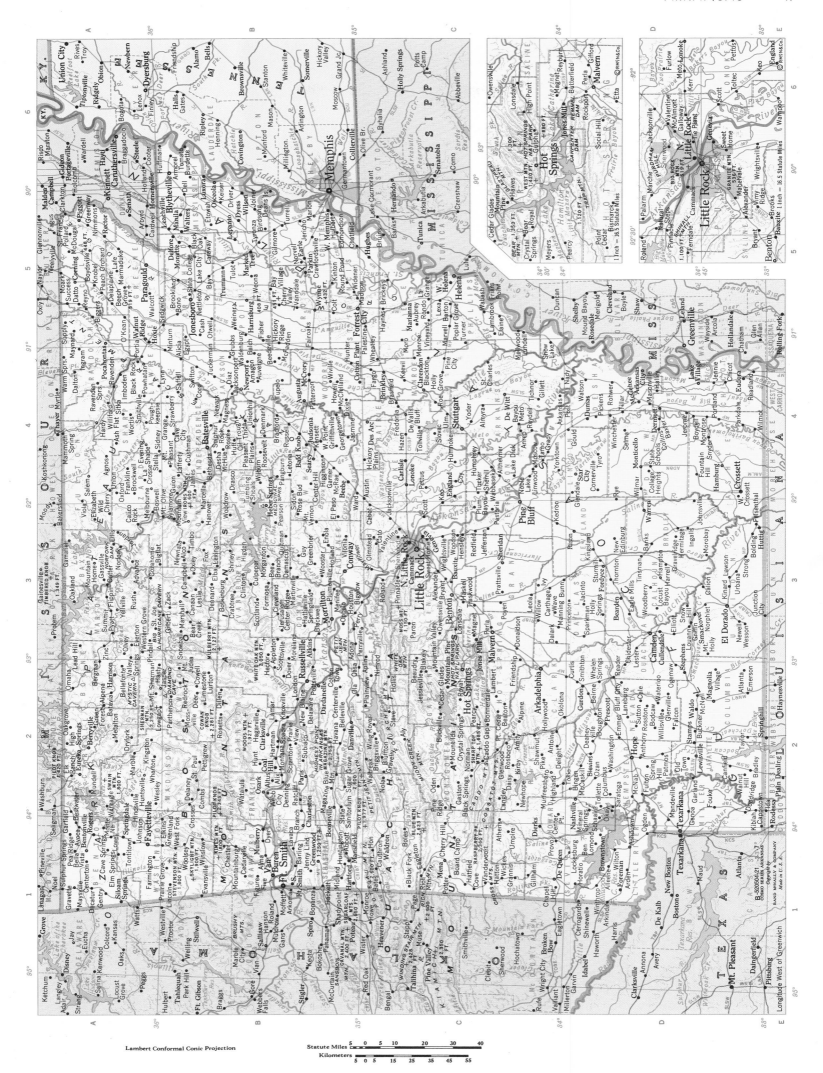

Lambert Conformal Conic Projection

Statute Miles 5 0 5 10 20 30 40
Kilometers 5 0 5 15 25 35 45 55

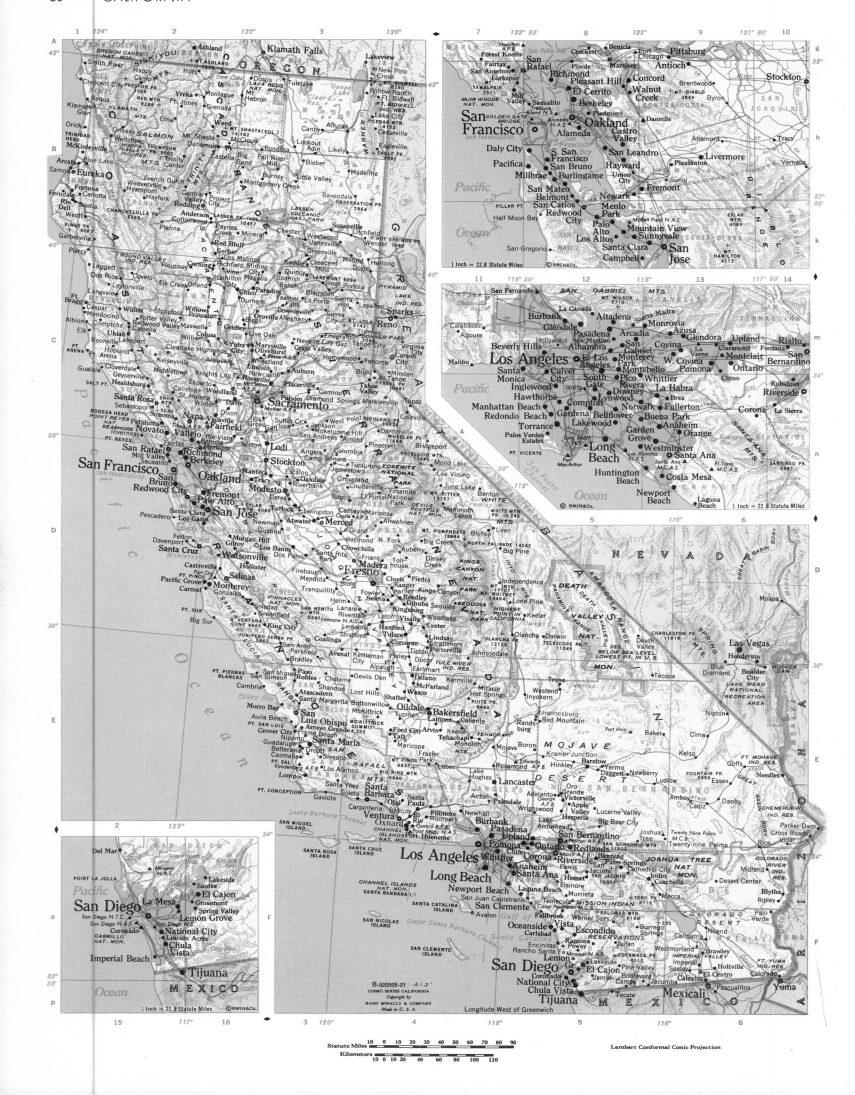

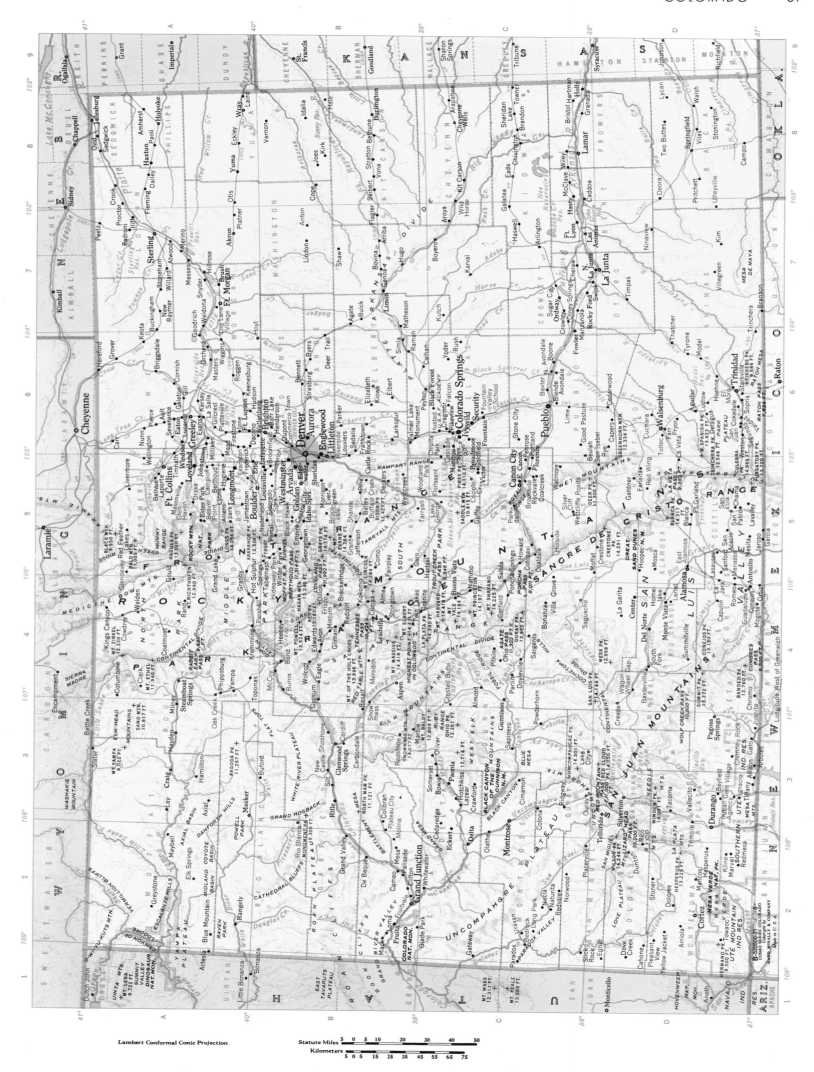

Lambert Conformal Conic Projection

Statute Miles 5 0 5 10 20 30 40 50
Kilometers 5 0 5 15 25 35 45 55 65 75

B-320606-21
COSMO SERIES COLORADO
Copyright by
RAND McNALLY & COMPANY
Made in U.S.A.

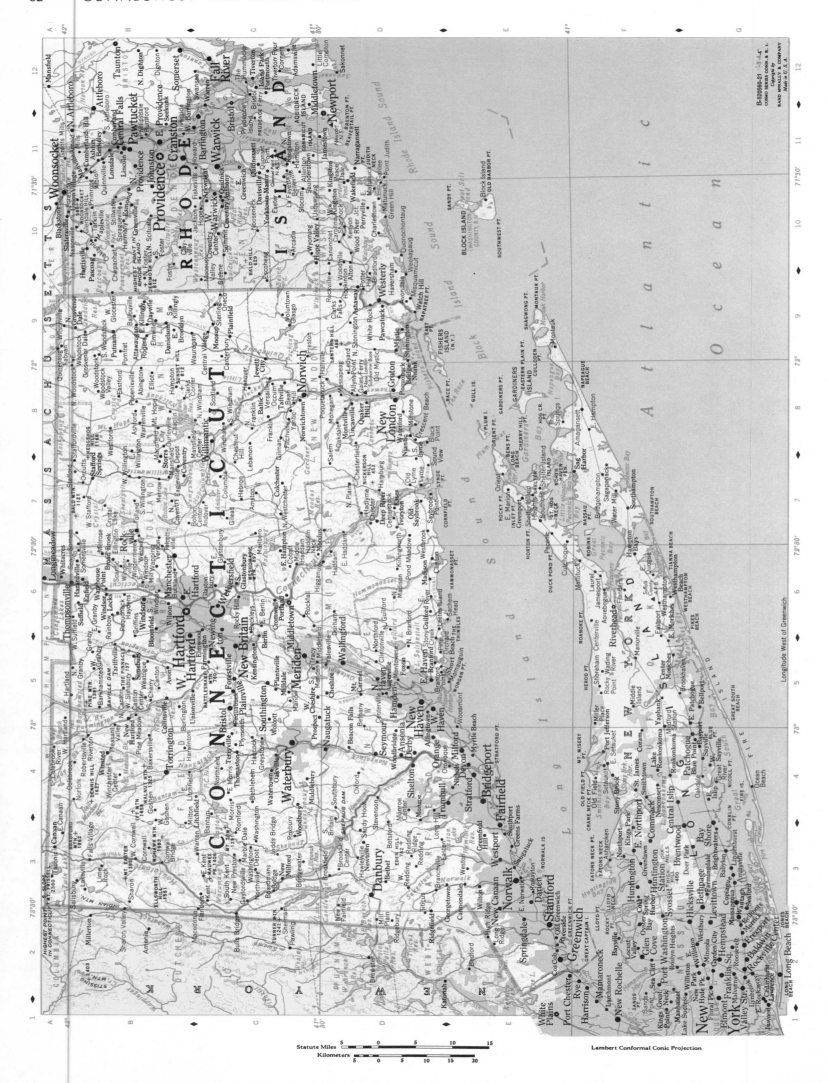

Statute Miles

Kilometers

Lambert Conformal Conic Projection

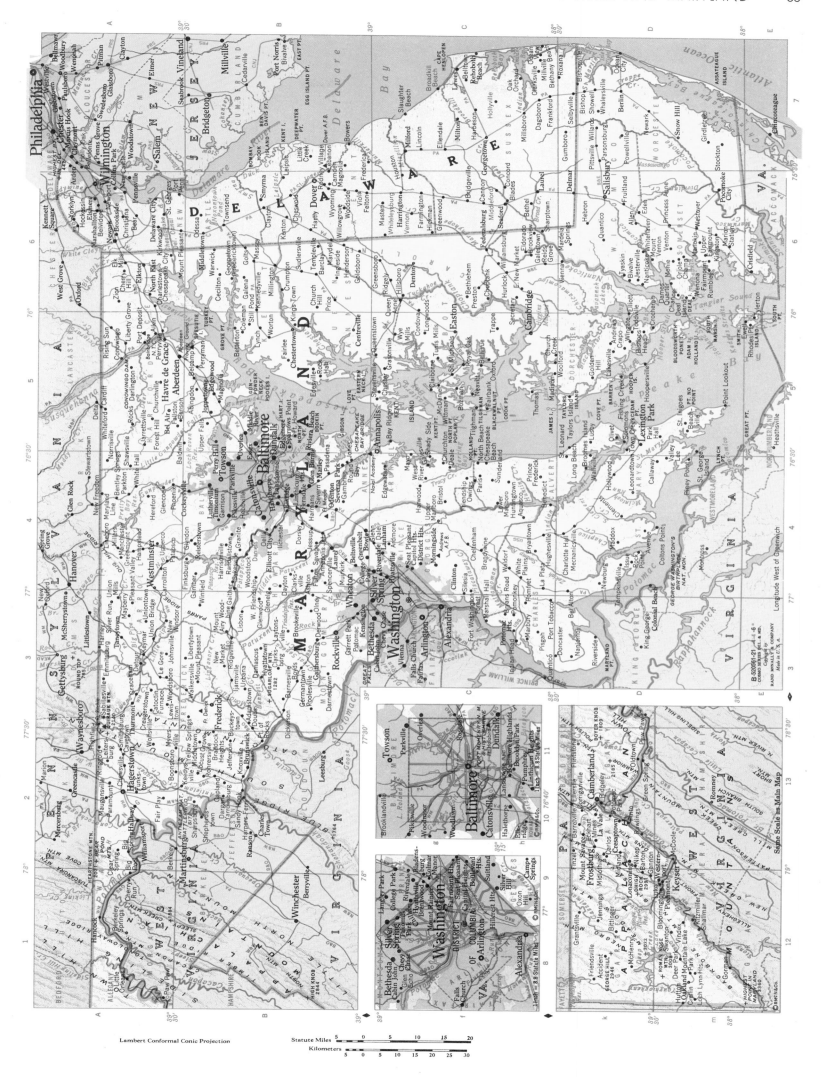

Lambert Conformal Conic Projection

Statute Miles

Kilometers

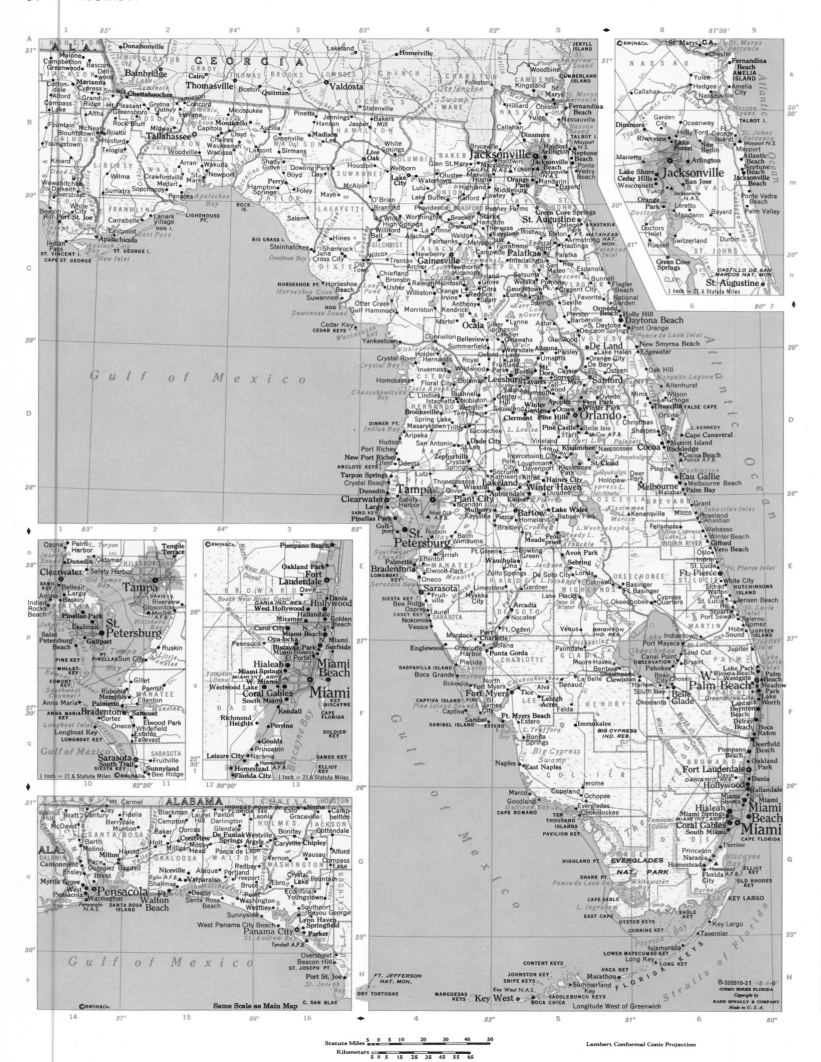

Statute Miles 5 0 5 10   20   30   40   50
Kilometers 5 0 5 15 25 35 45 55 65

Lambert Conformal Conic Projection

B-520510-21 -3-4-5
COMMO SERIES FLORIDA
Copyright by
RAND McNALLY & COMPANY
Made in U.S.A.

1 Inch = 21.6 Statute Miles

Longitude West of Greenwich

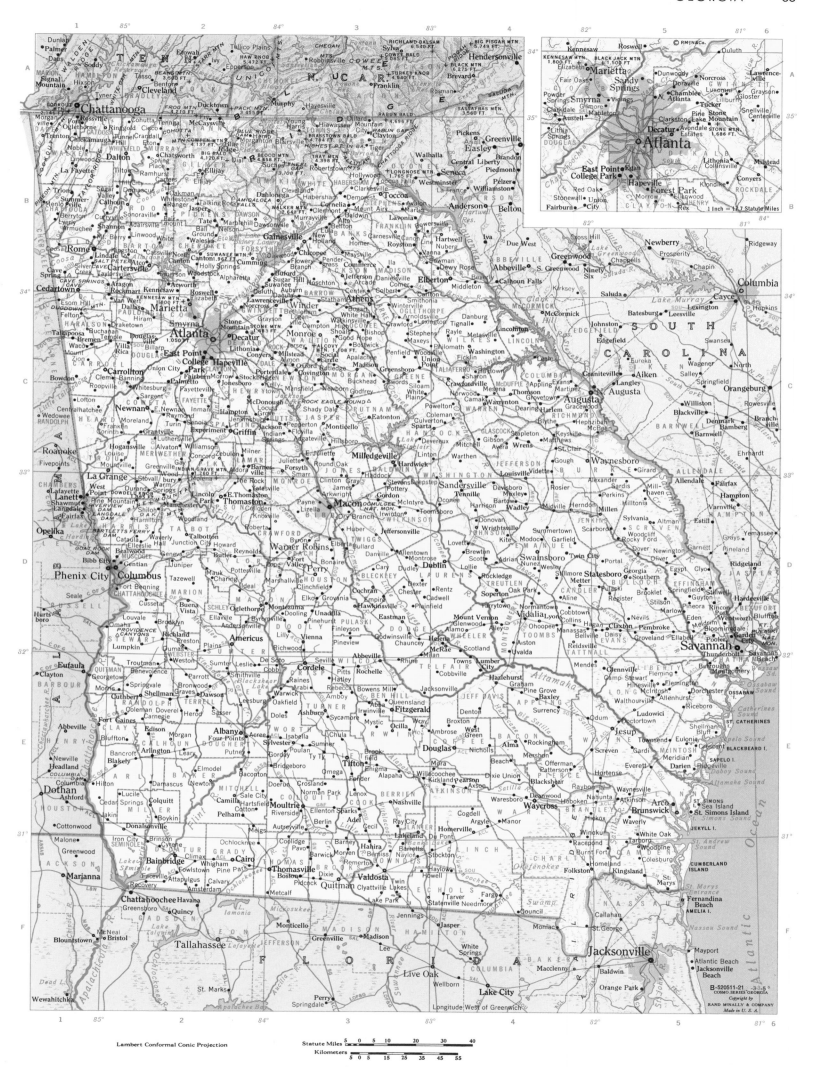

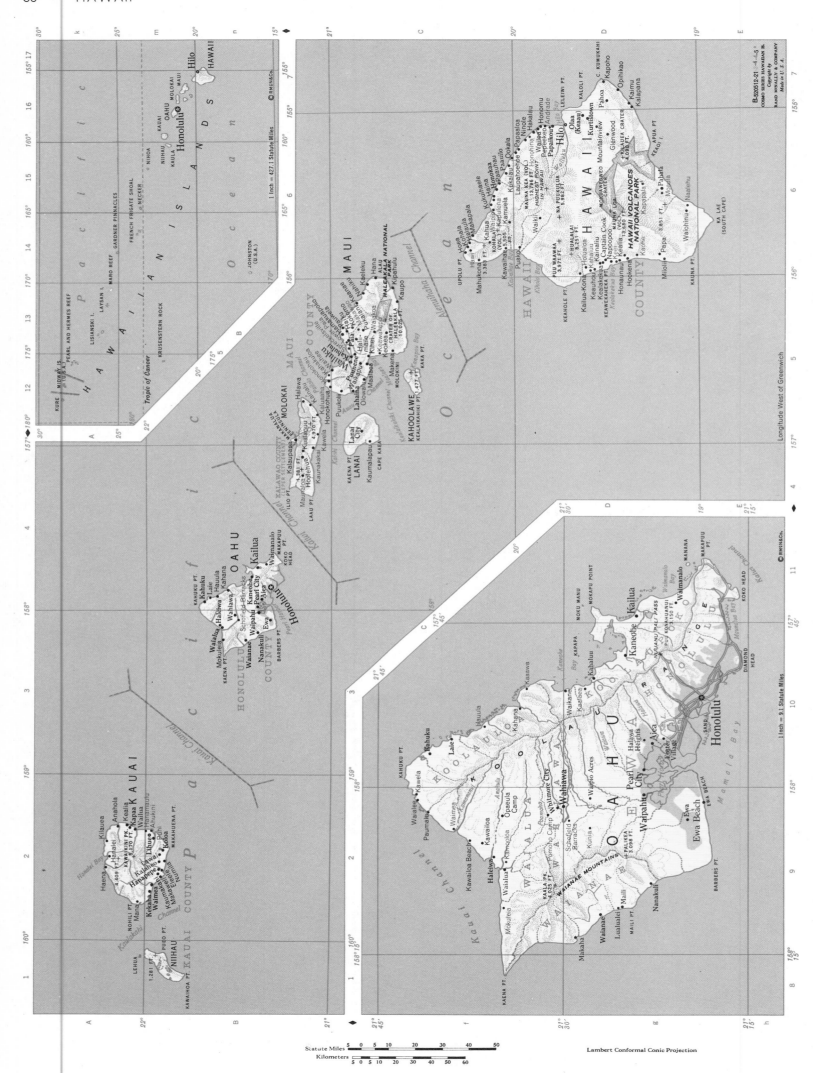

Statute Miles 5 0 5 10   20   30   40   50
Kilometers 5 0 5 10 20   30   40   50 60

Lambert Conformal Conic Projection

B.520512-21 -4-.5°
COSMO SERIES: HAWAIIAN IS.
Copyright by
RAND McNALLY & COMPANY
Made in U.S.A.

Statute Miles
Kilometers

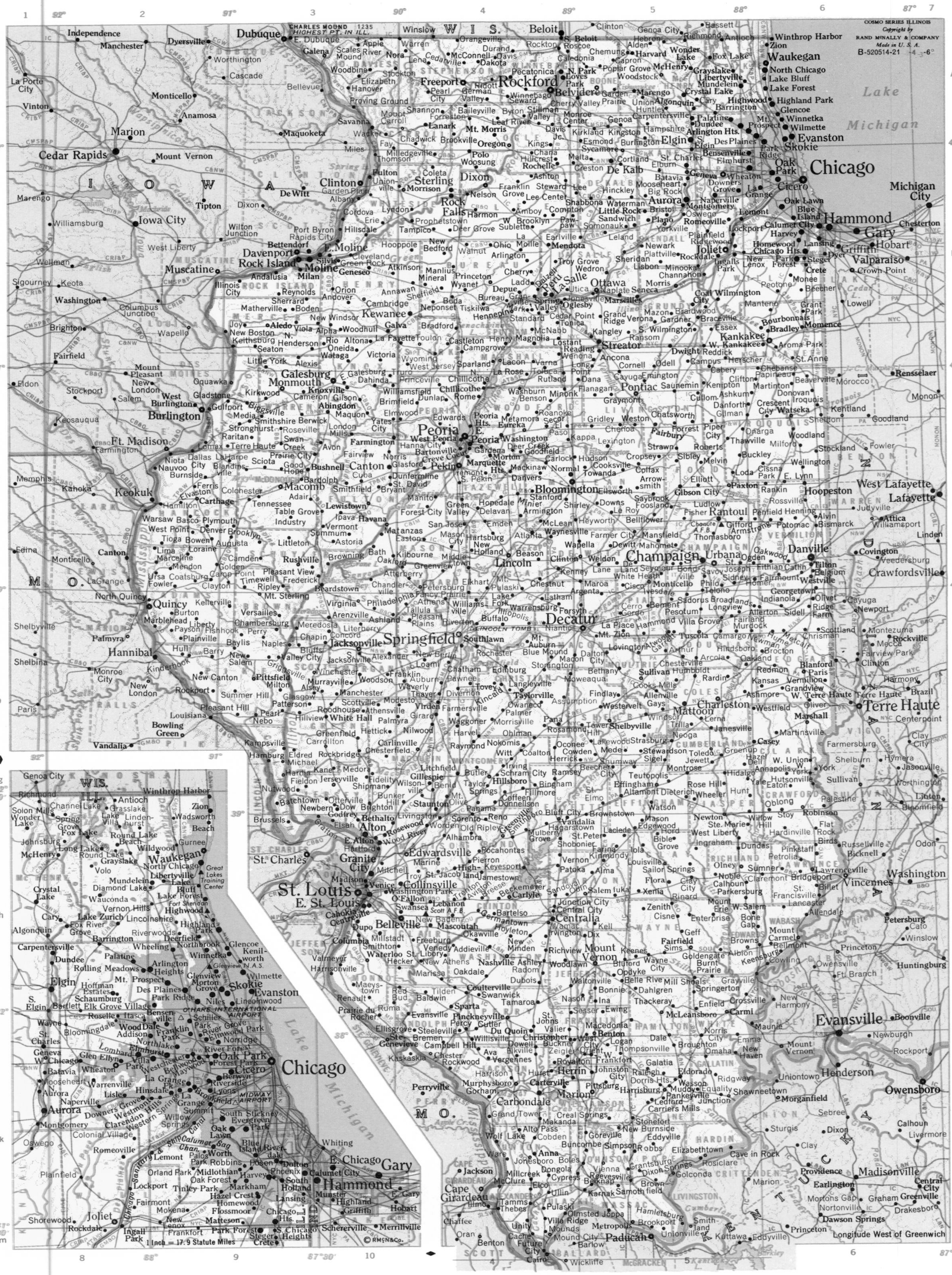
COSMO SERIES ILLINOIS
Copyright by RAND McNALLY & COMPANY
Made in U. S. A.
B-520514-21
CHARLES MOUND 1235 HIGHEST PT. IN ILL.
W I S.
I O W A
M O.
Lake Michigan
Chicago
Rockford
Peoria
Springfield
Decatur
Champaign
Bloomington
St. Louis
E. St. Louis
Evansville
Terre Haute
Hammond
Gary
Waukegan
Aurora
Joliet
Davenport
Rock Island
Moline
Galesburg
Quincy
Danville
Kankakee
Carbondale
Cairo
Paducah
Statute Miles 5 0 5 10 20 30 40
Kilometers 5 0 5 15 25 35 45 55
Lambert Conformal Conic Projection
Longitude West of Greenwich
1 Inch = 17.9 Statute Miles

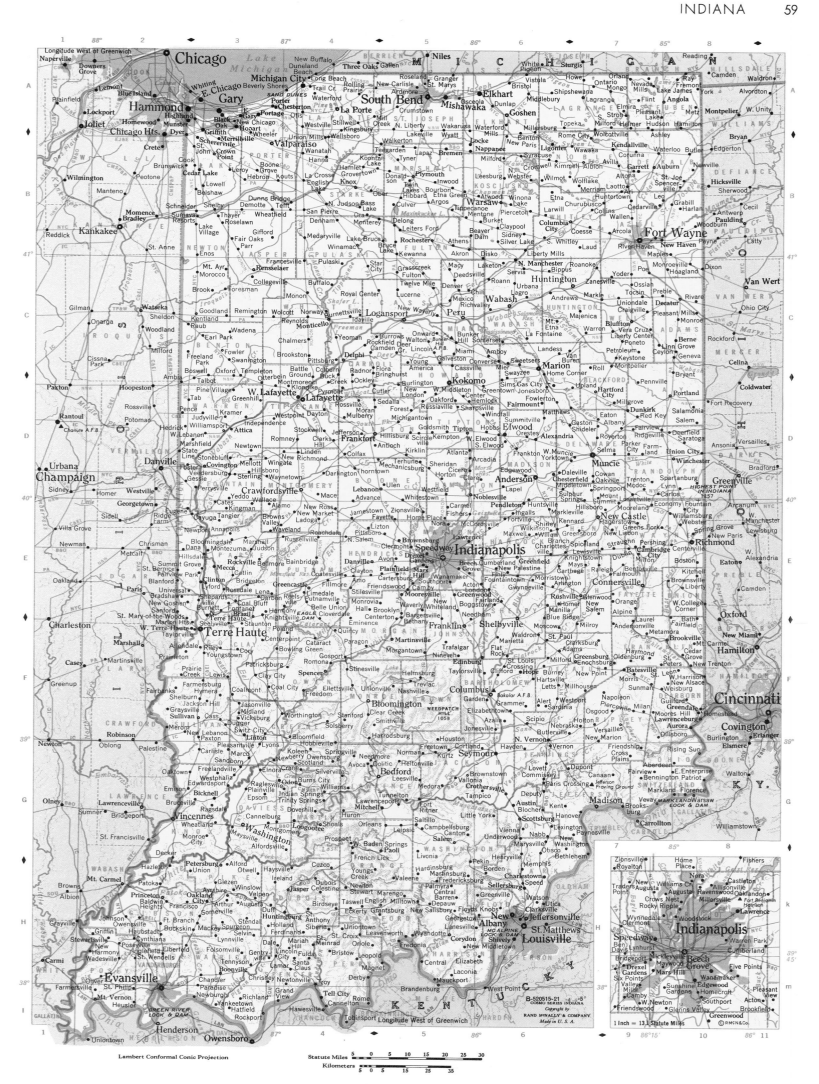

Lambert Conformal Conic Projection

B-520515-21

Cosmo Series Indiana
Copyright by
RAND McNALLY & COMPANY
Made in U.S.A.

Statute Miles 5 0 5 10 15 20 25 30
Kilometers 5 0 5 15 25 35

1 Inch = 13.1 Statute Miles

©RMcN&Co.

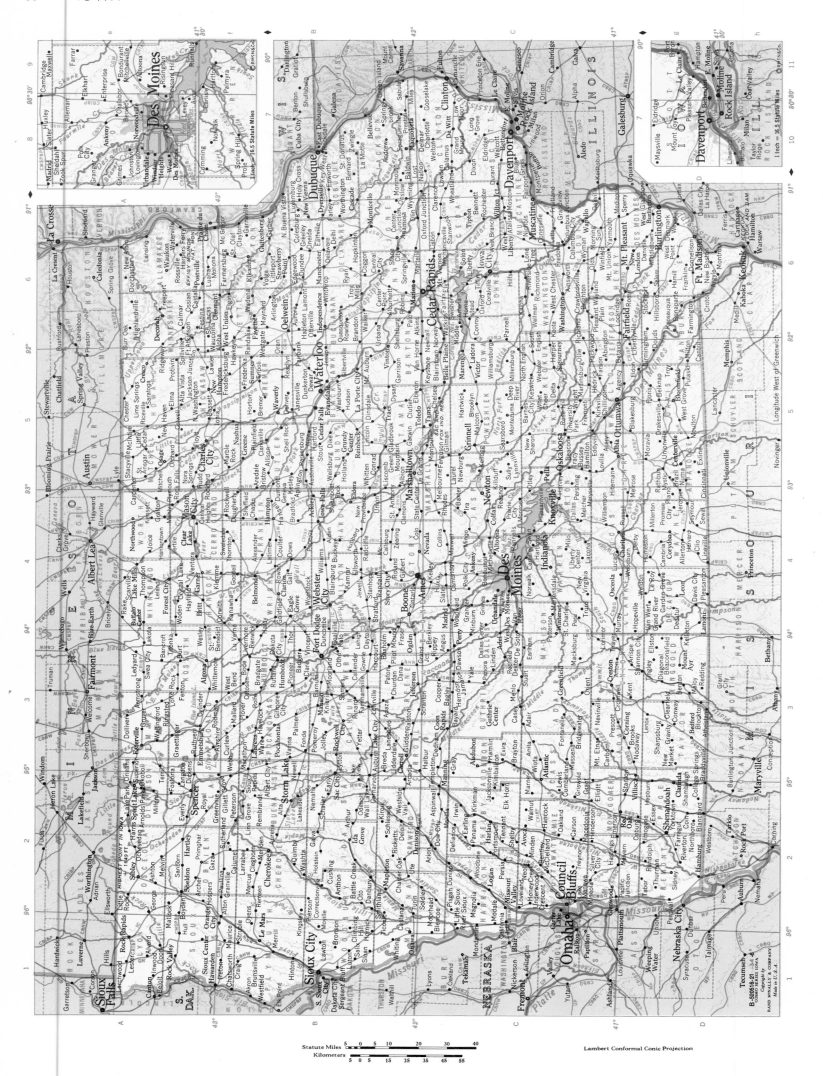

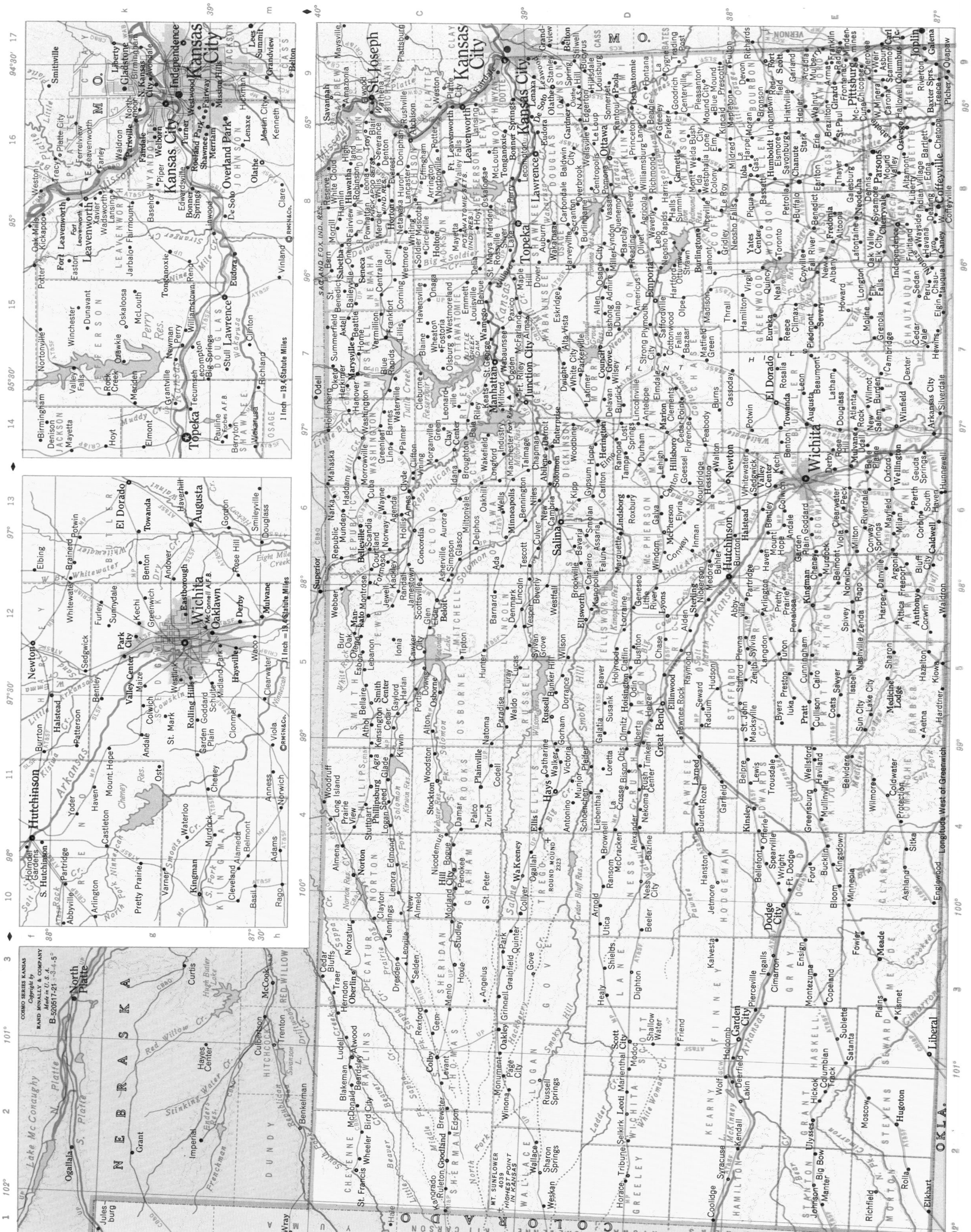

Lambert Conformal Conic Projection

Statute Miles
Kilometers

COSMO BERGES KANSAS
Copyright
RAND M9NALLY & COMPANY
Made in U.S.A.
B-520517-21-1-2-3-4-5

1 Inch = 19.6 Statute Miles

NEBRASKA

COLORADO

OKLA.

MO.

Kansas City
Topeka
Wichita
Hutchinson
El Dorado
Augusta
Leavenworth
Overland Park
St. Joseph
Salina
Dodge City
Liberal

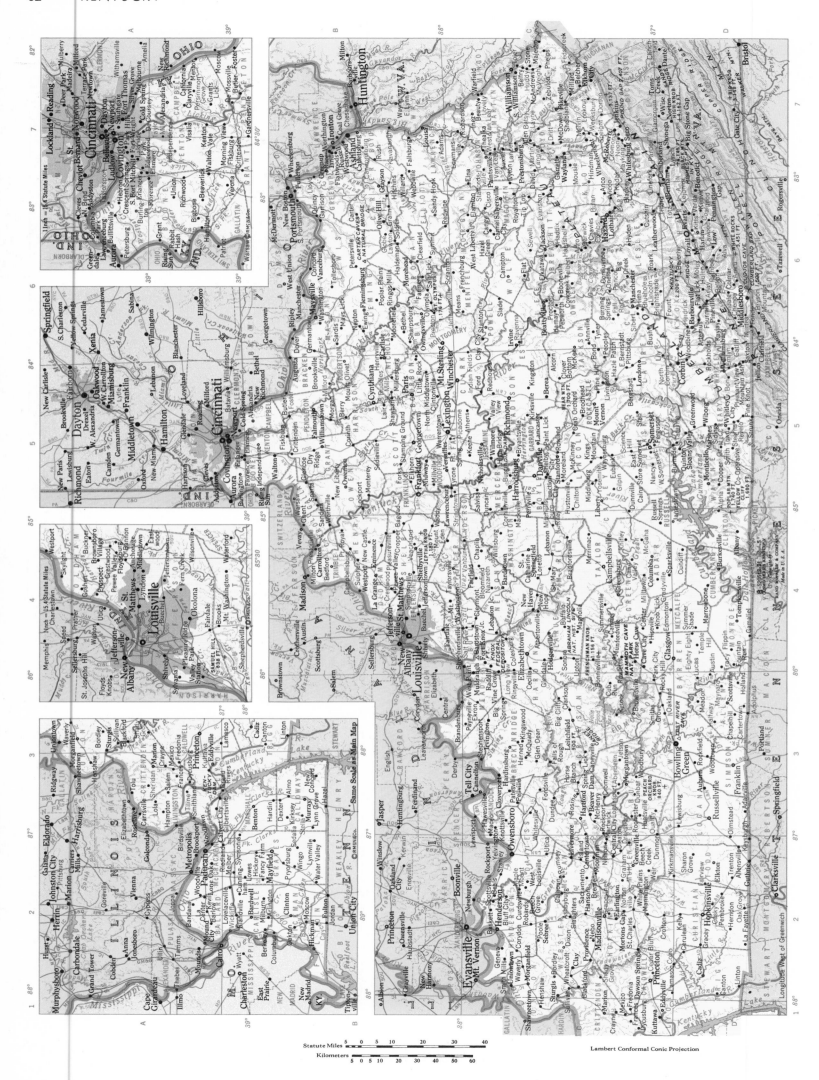

Statute Miles

Kilometers

Lambert Conformal Conic Projection

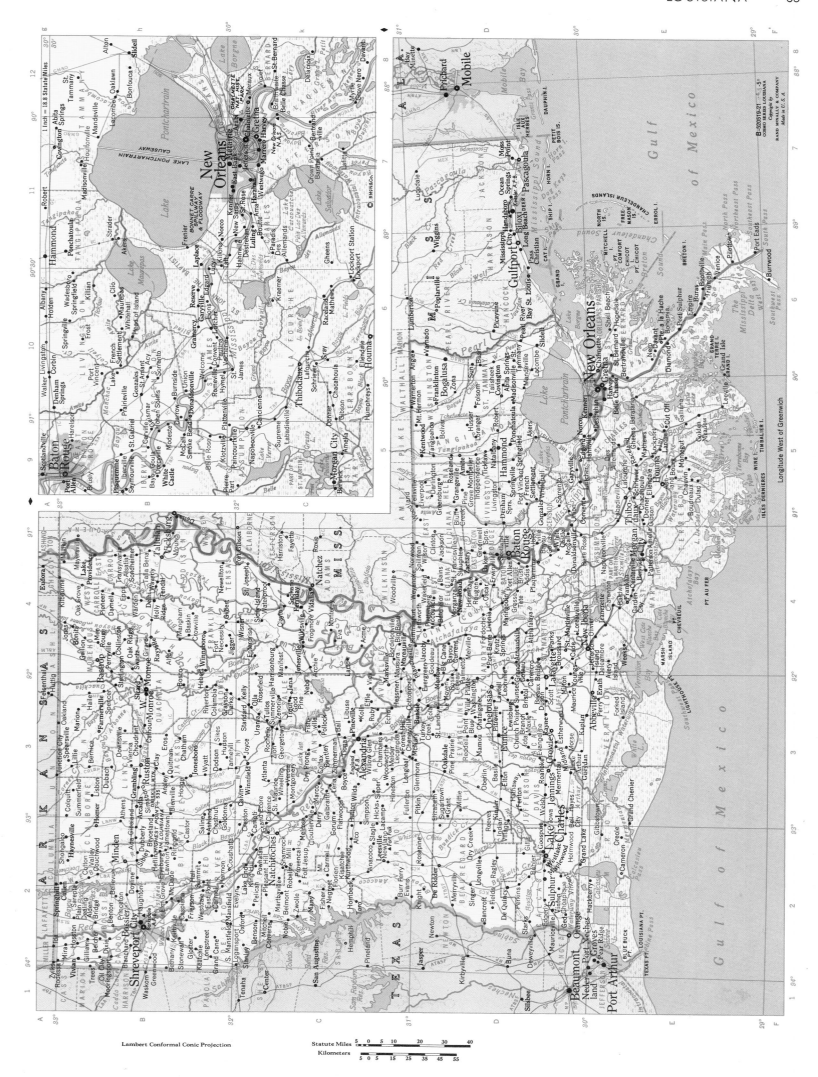

Lambert Conformal Conic Projection

Statute Miles 5 0 5 10   20   30   40

Kilometers 5 0 5 15   25   35   45   55

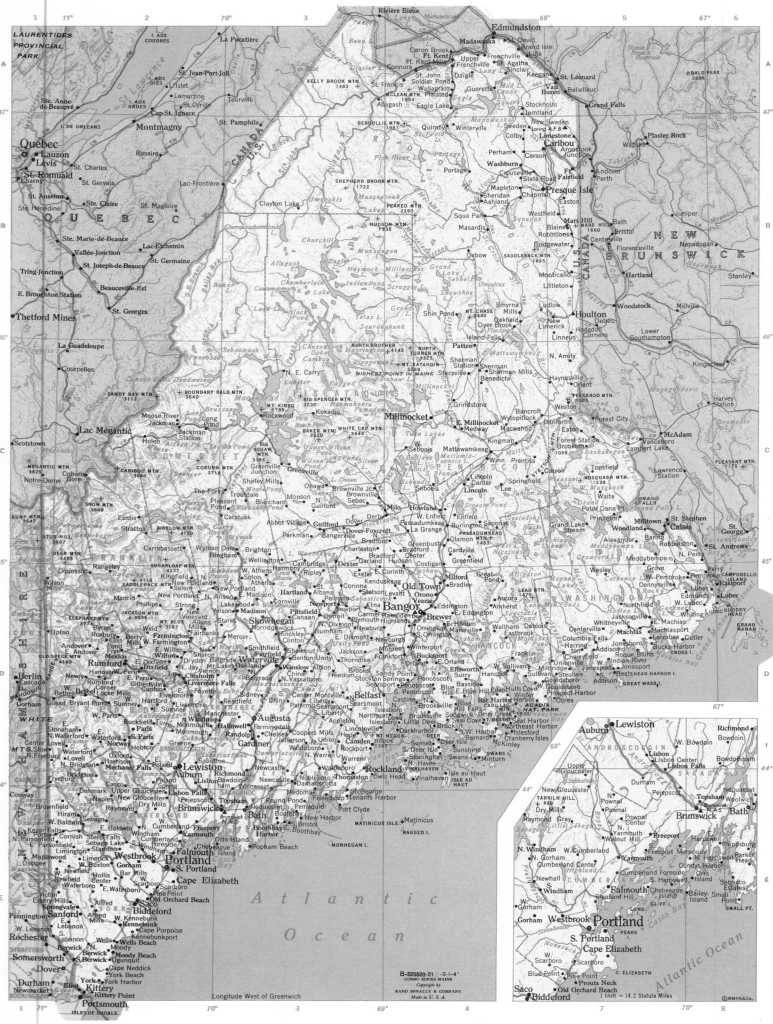

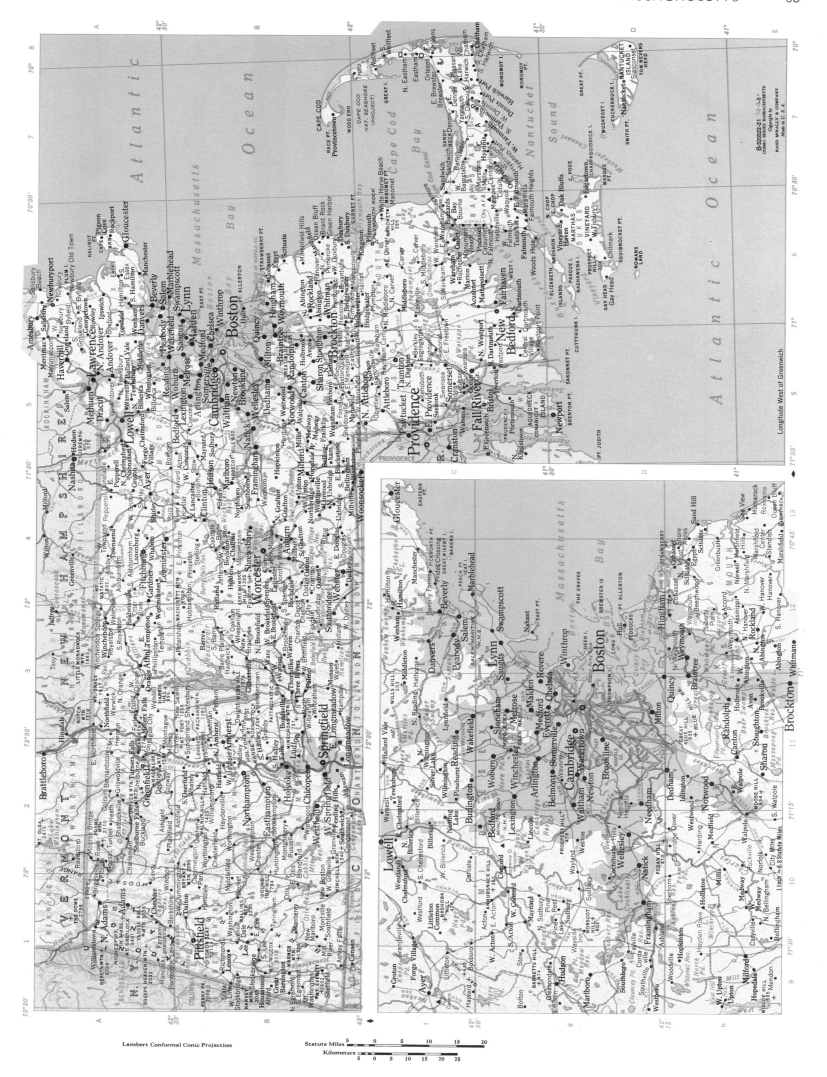

Lambert Conformal Conic Projection

Statute Miles

Kilometers

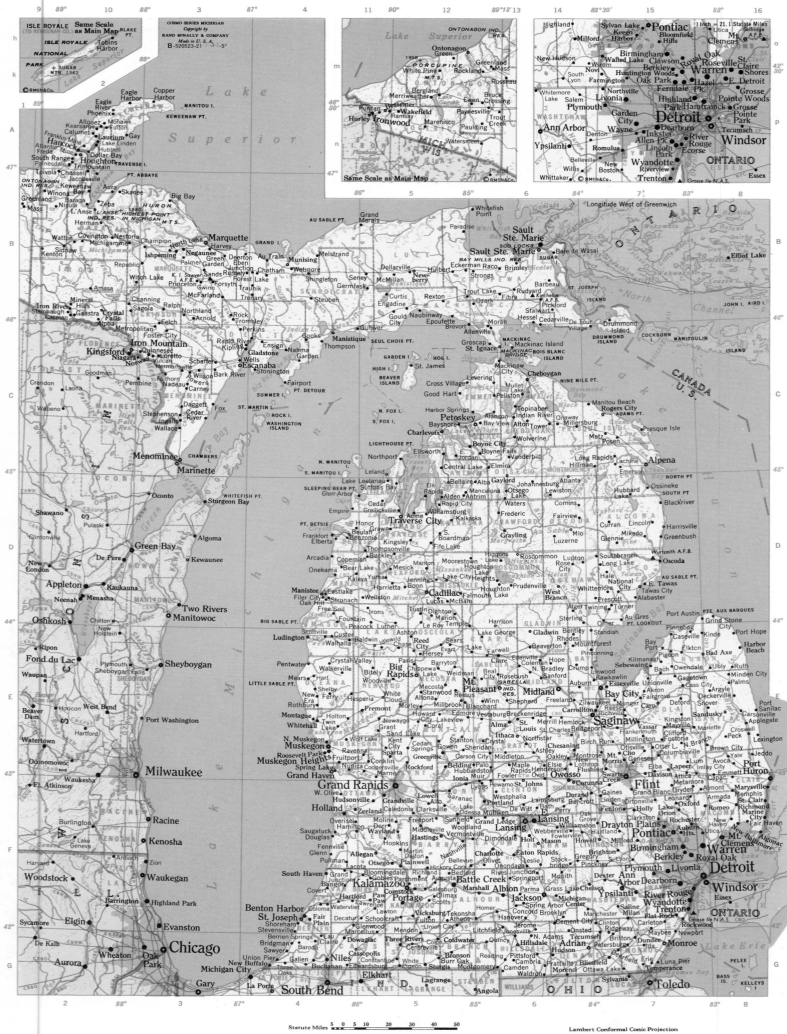

Statute Miles   5 0 5 10   20   30   40   50

Kilometers   5 0 5 15   25   35   45 55 65 75

Lambert Conformal Conic Projection

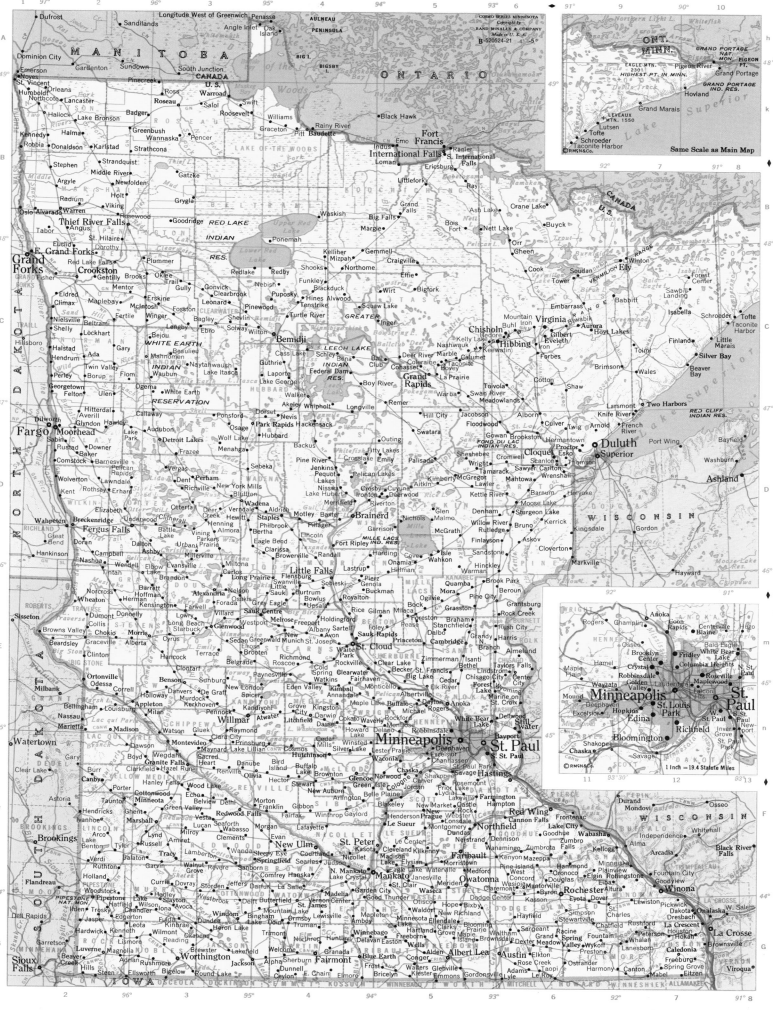

Longitude West of Greenwich

MANITOBA

CANADA
U.S.

ONTARIO

ONT.
MINN.

GRAND PORTAGE
NAT. MON.

EAGLE MTN.
2301
HIGHEST PT. IN MINN.

+ LEVEAUX
MTN. 1550

Same Scale as Main Map

LAKE OF THE WOODS

RED LAKE
INDIAN
RES.

Grand
Forks

E. Grand Forks

WHITE EARTH
INDIAN
RESERVATION

Bemidji

LEECH LAKE
INDIAN
RES.

Virginia

Chisholm

Hibbing

Grand
Rapids

Fargo Moorhead

Fergus Falls

Brainerd

MILLE LACS
IND. RES.

Duluth
Superior

Ashland

WISCONSIN

Little Falls

St. Cloud

Alexandria

Willmar

Minneapolis

St. Paul

Hastings

Red Wing

Northfield

Brookings

New Ulm

St. Peter

Faribault

Owatonna

Winona

Mankato

Rochester

La Crosse

Sioux
Falls

Worthington

Fairmont

Albert Lea

Austin

WISCONSIN

IOWA

Minneapolis

St. Paul

1 Inch = 19.4 Statute Miles

Lambert Conformal Conic Projection

Statute Miles 5 0 5 10   20   30   40   50

Kilometers 5 0 5 15 25 35 45 55 65

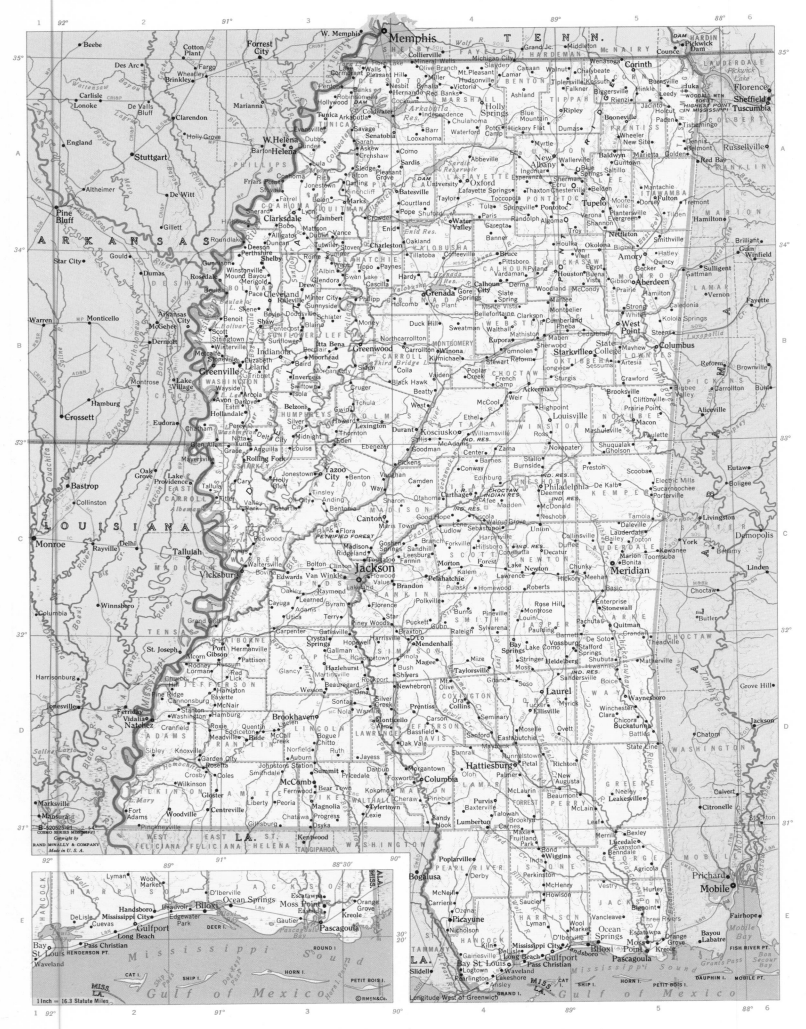

Lambert Conformal Conic Projection

Statute Miles

Kilometers

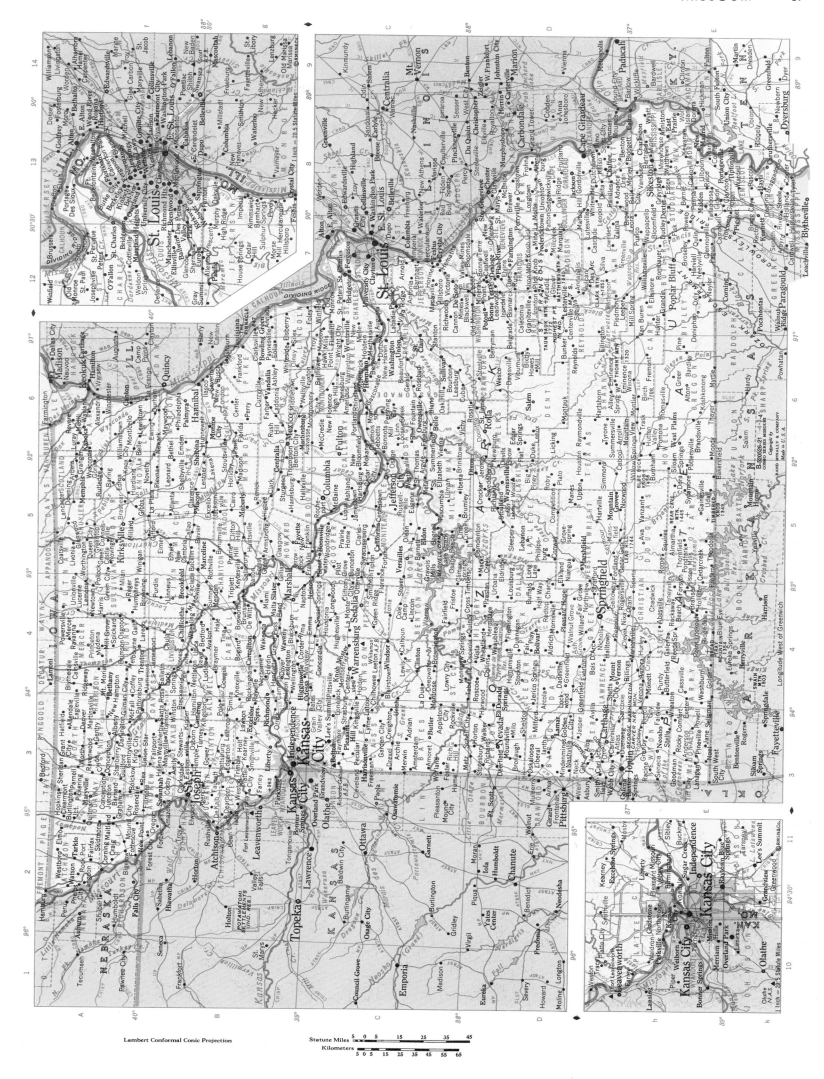

Lambert Conformal Conic Projection

Statute Miles
5 0 5   15   25   35   45

Kilometers
5 0 5 15 25 35 45 55 65

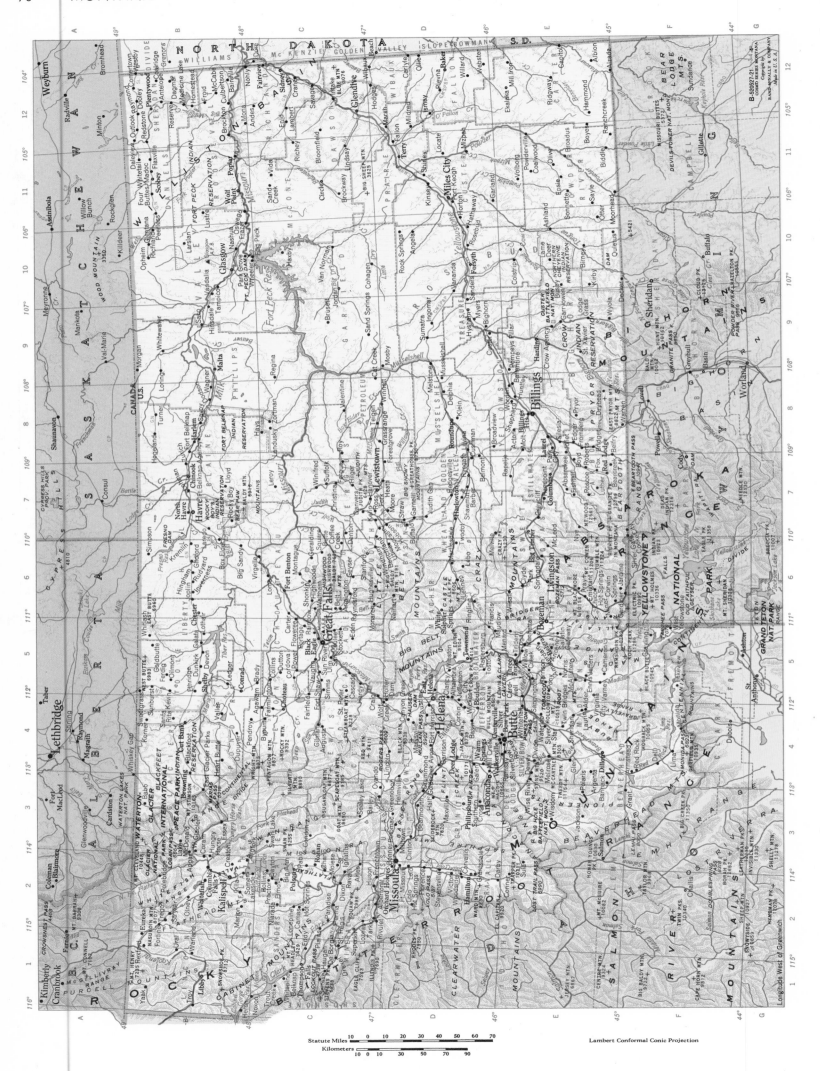

Statute Miles 10 0 10 20 30 40 50 60 70

Kilometers 10 0 10 30 50 70 90

Lambert Conformal Conic Projection

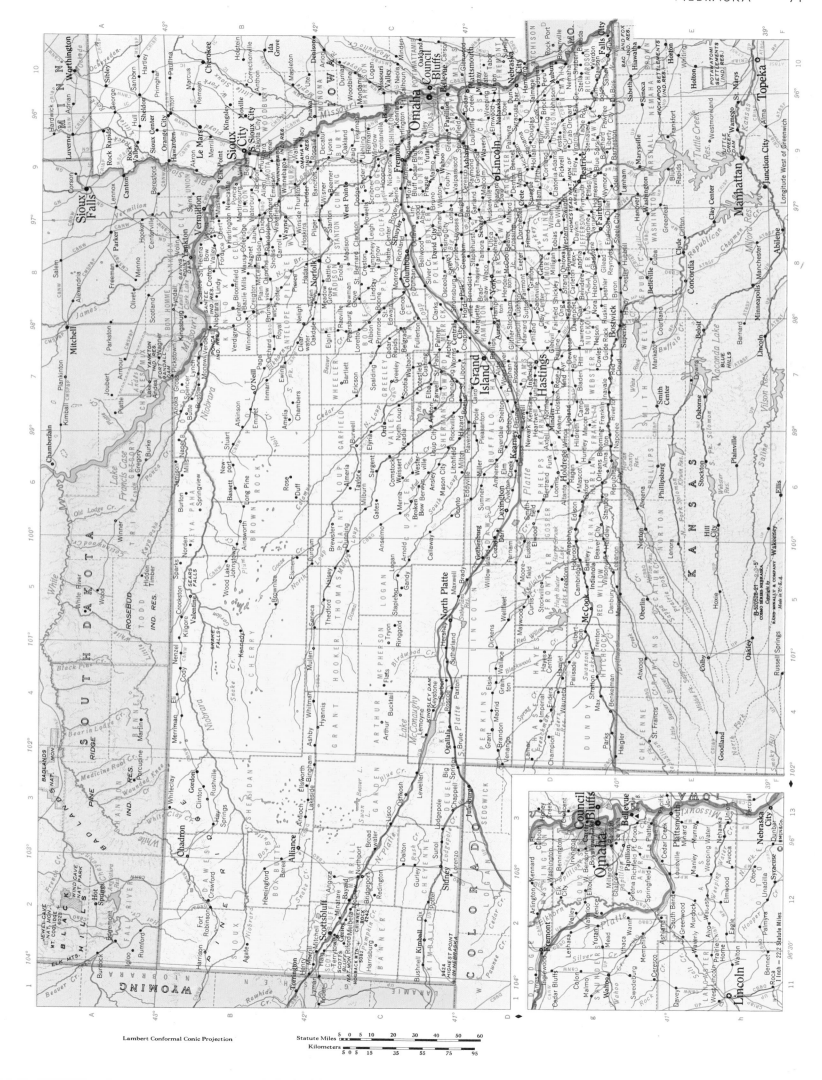

Lambert Conformal Conic Projection

Statute Miles

Kilometers

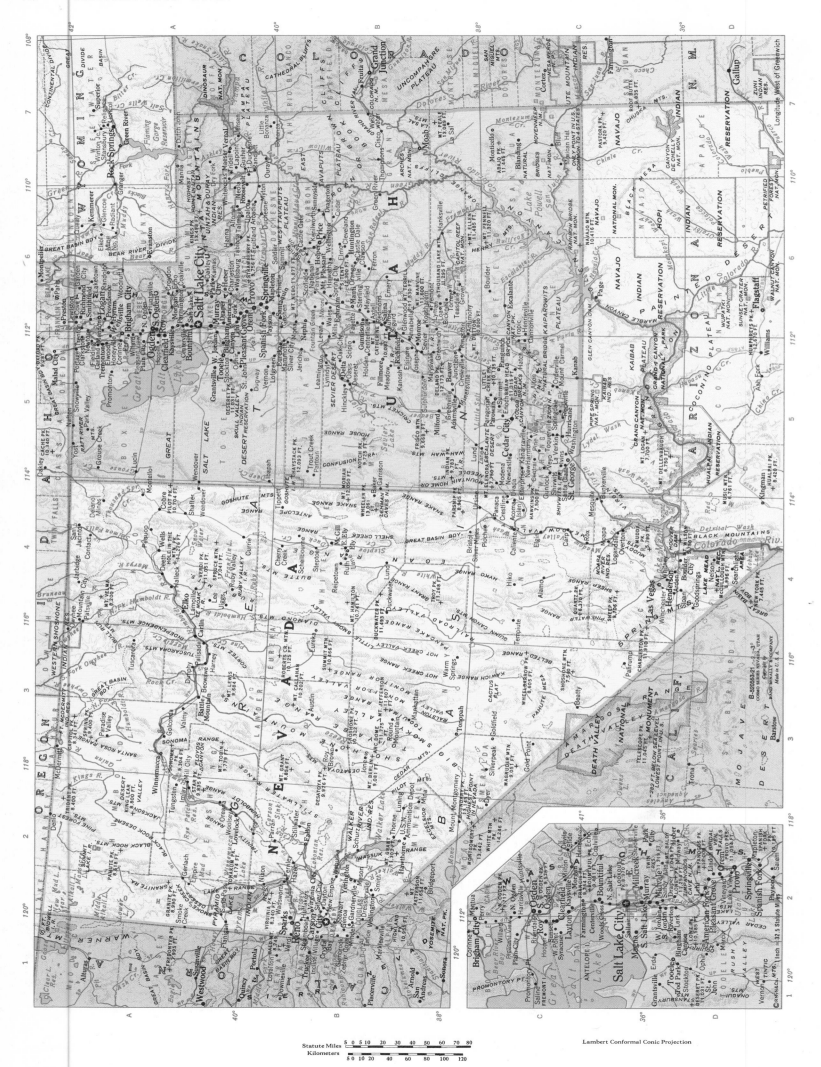

Statute Miles   5 0 5 10   20   30   40   50   60   70   80
Kilometers   5 0 10 20   40   60   80   100   120

Lambert Conformal Conic Projection

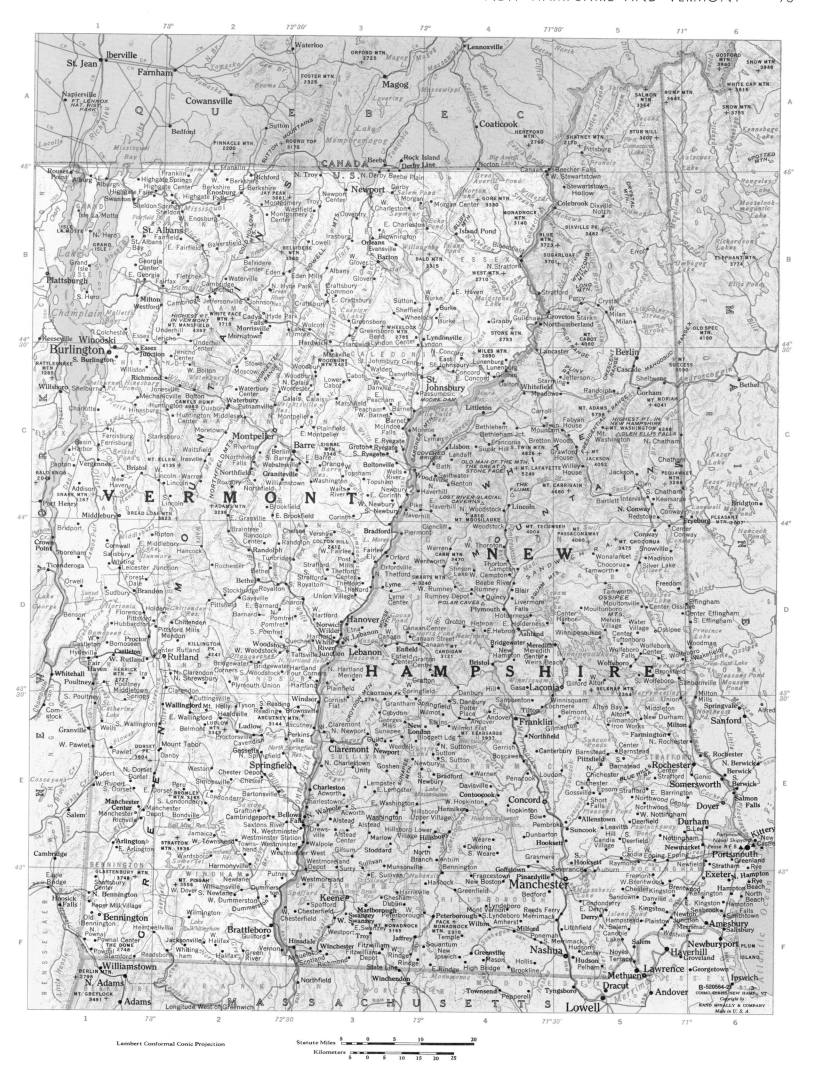

Lambert Conformal Conic Projection

Statute Miles

Kilometers

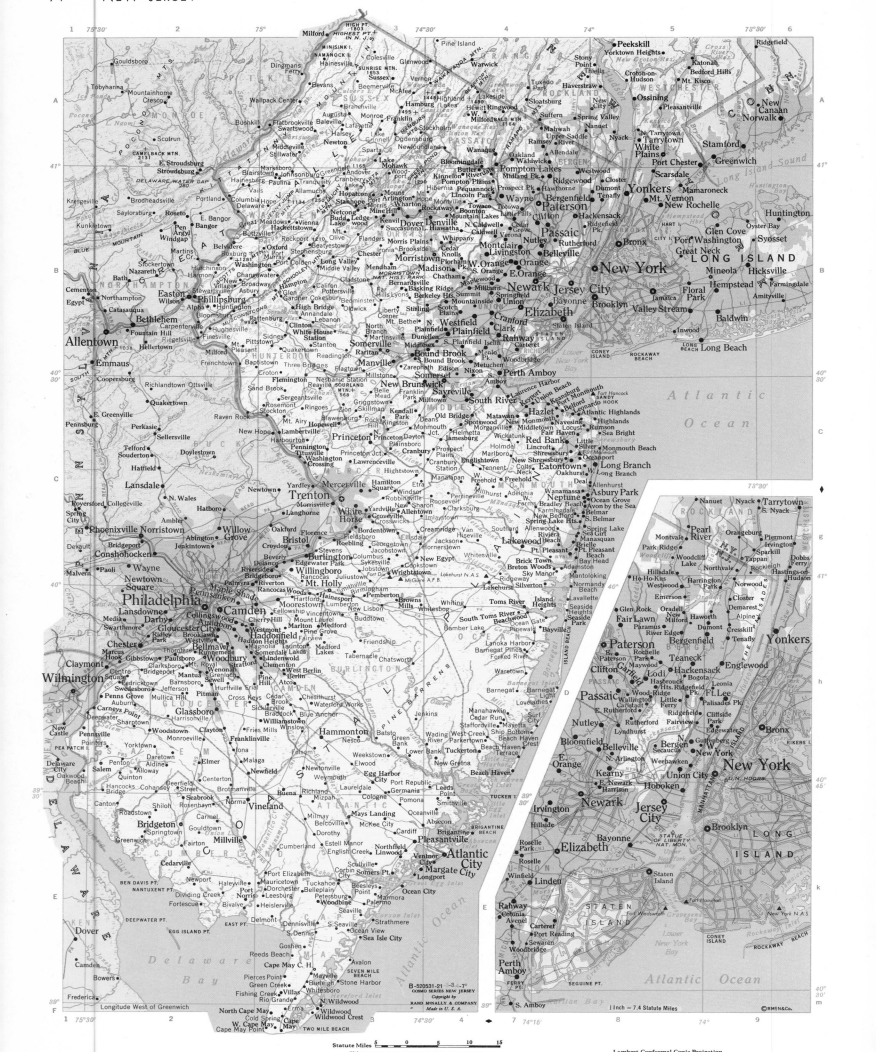

Statute Miles
Kilometers

Lambert Conformal Conic Projection

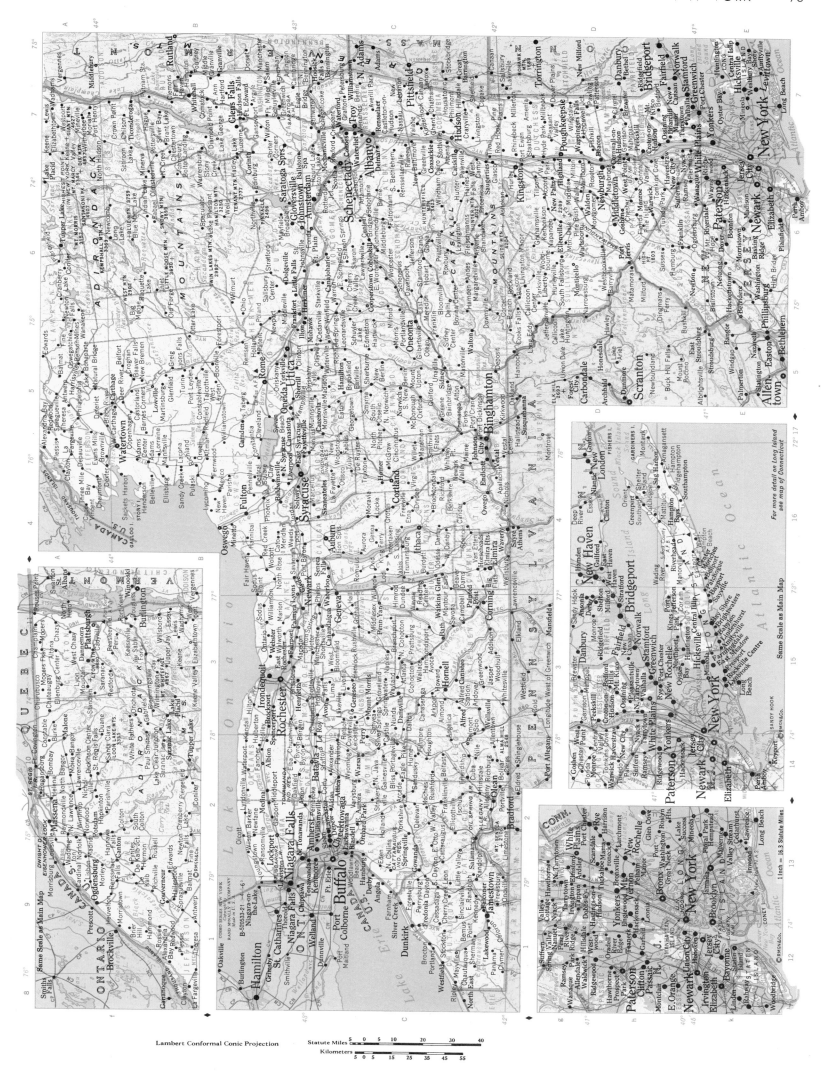

Lambert Conformal Conic Projection

Statute Miles 5 0 5 10 20 30 40

Kilometers 5 0 5 15 25 35 45 55

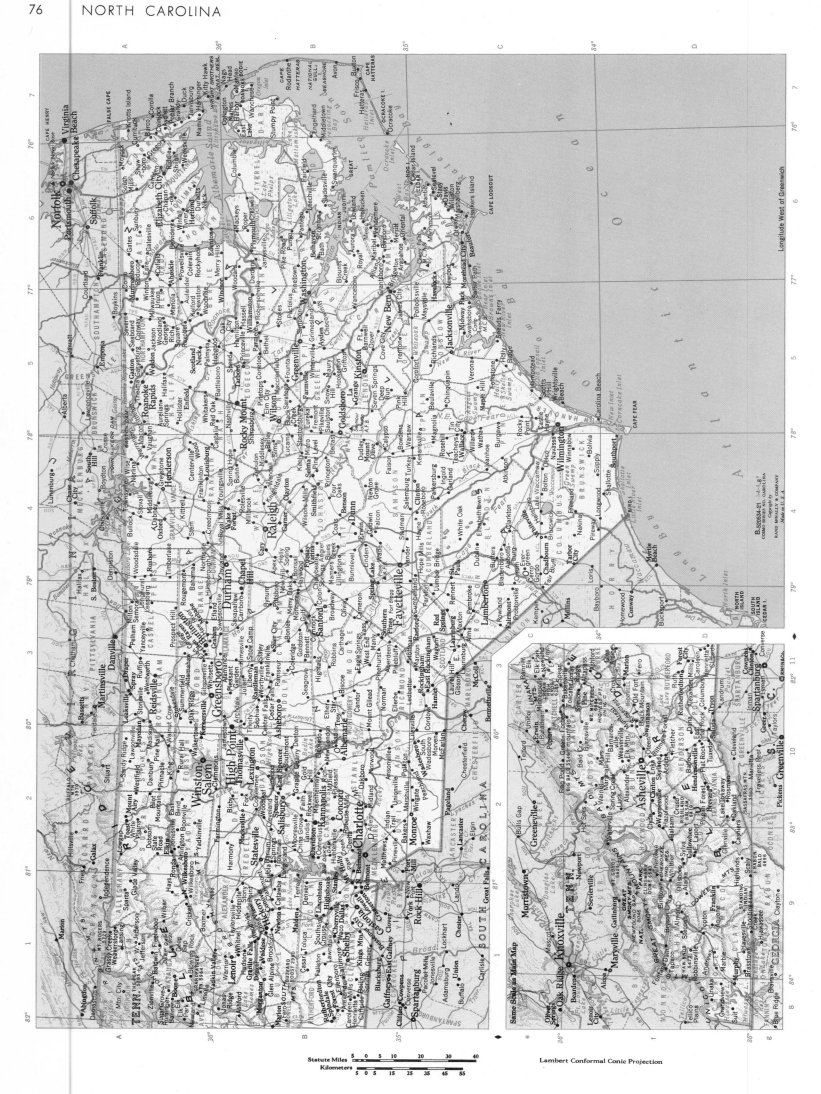

Statute Miles
Kilometers

Lambert Conformal Conic Projection

Same Scale as Main Map

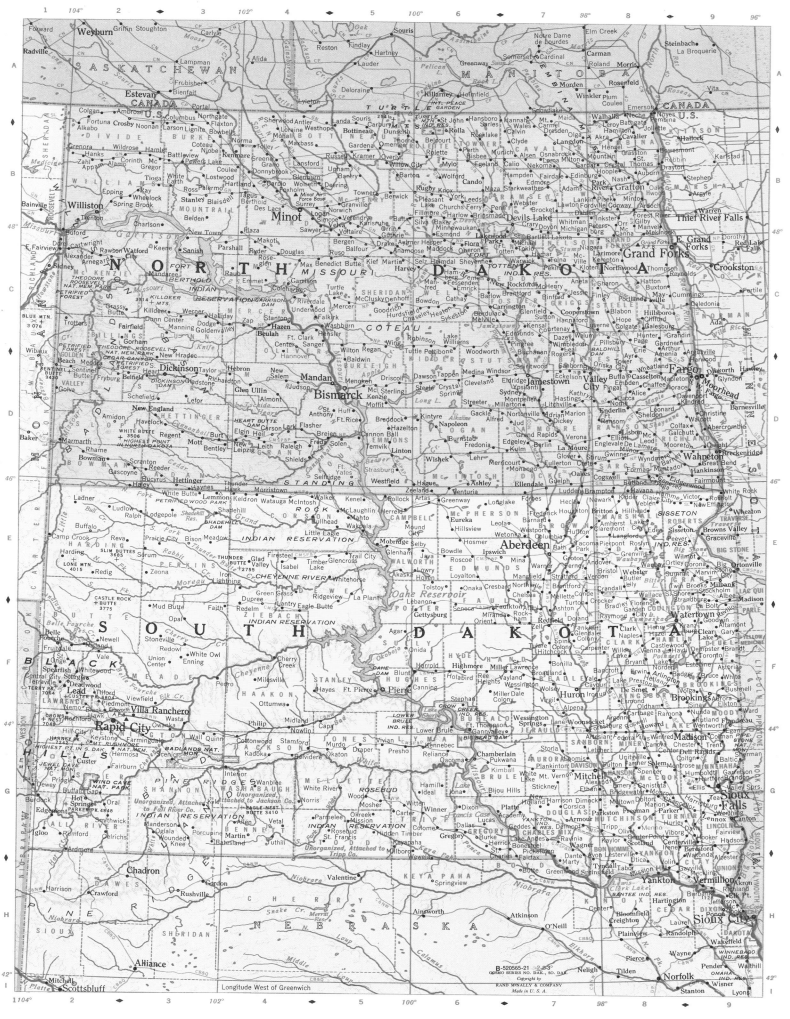

B-520565-21
COSMO SERIES NO. DAK., SO. DAK.
Copyright by
RAND McNALLY & COMPANY
Made in U.S.A.

Longitude West of Greenwich

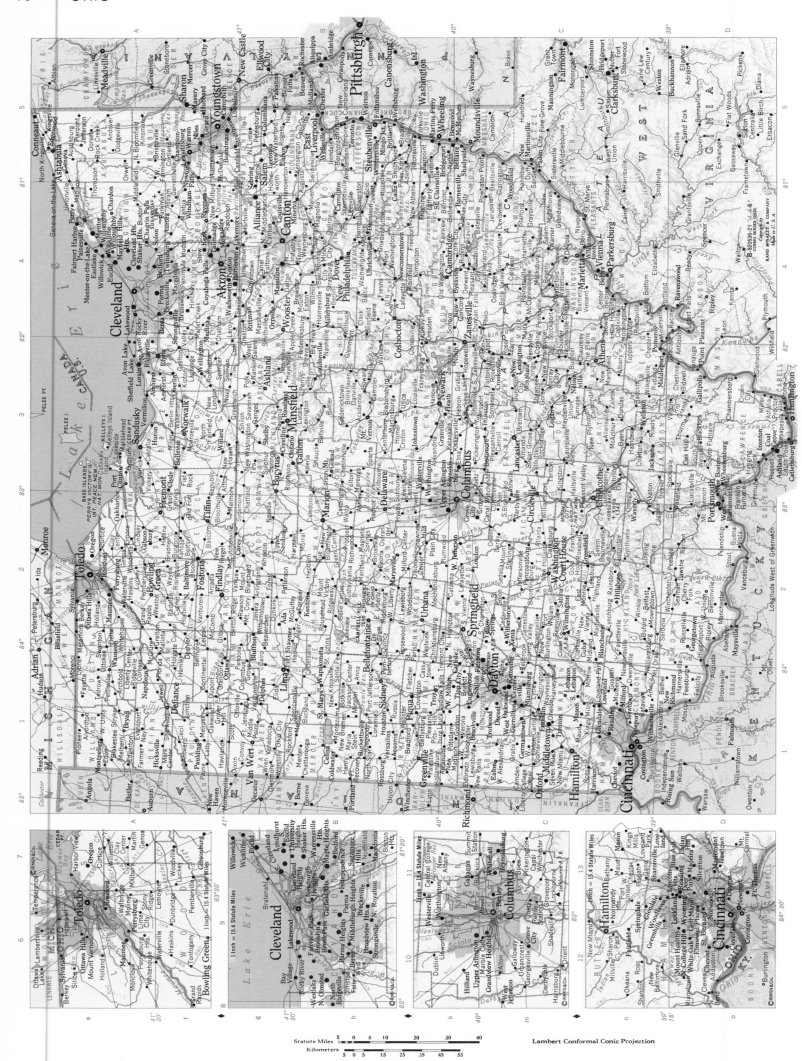

Statute Miles 5 0 5 10 20 30 40
Kilometers 5 0 5 15 25 35 45 55

Lambert Conformal Conic Projection

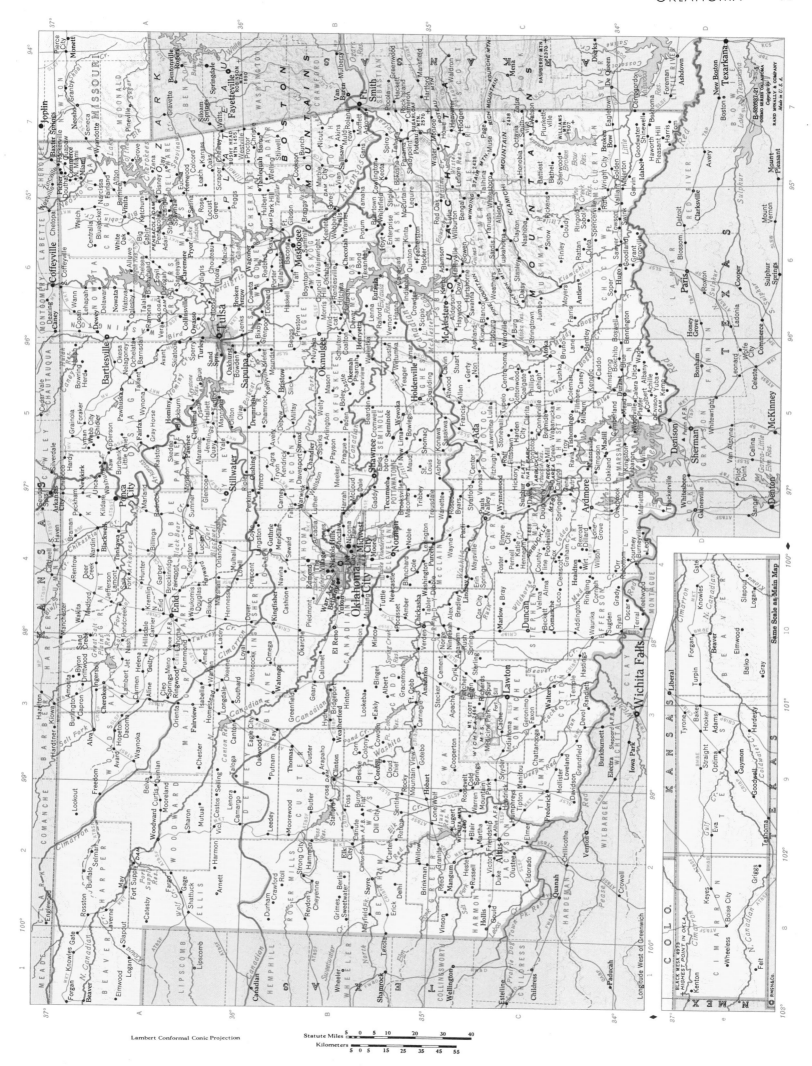

Lambert Conformal Conic Projection

Statute Miles 5 0 5 10 20 30 40

Kilometers 5 0 5 15 25 35 45 55

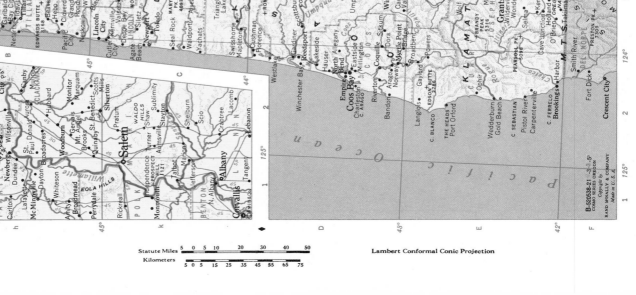

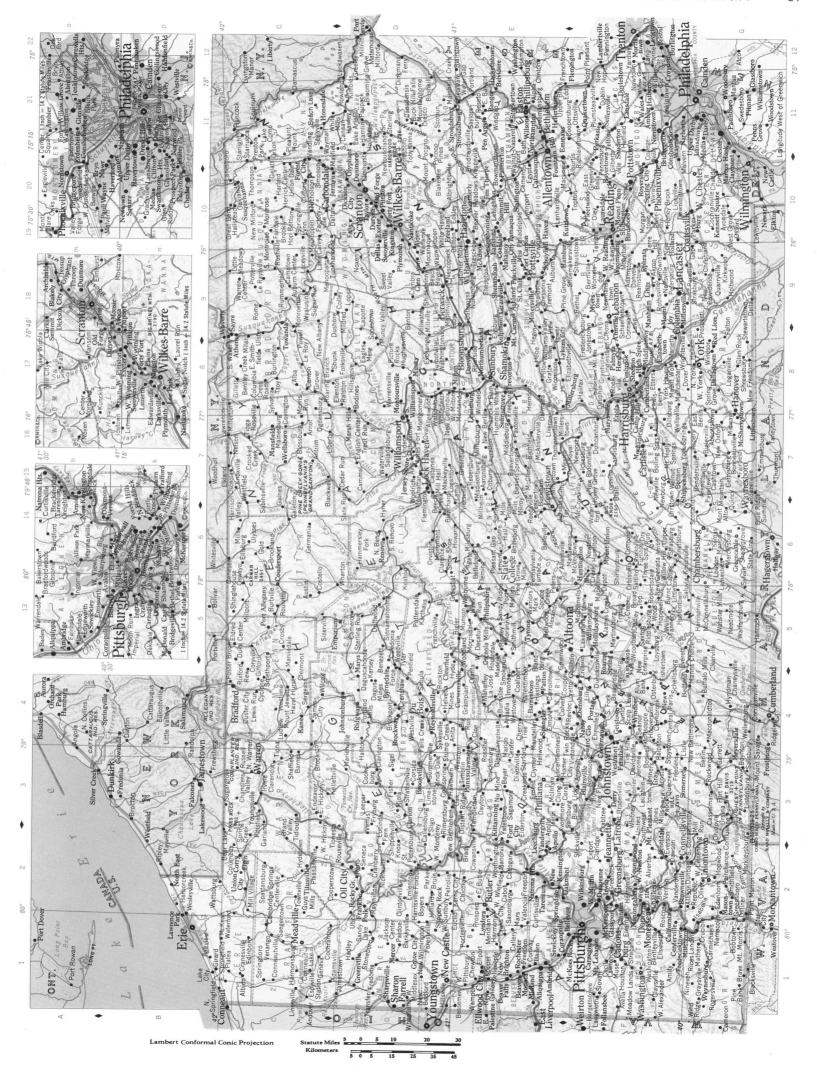

Lambert Conformal Conic Projection

Statute Miles

Kilometers

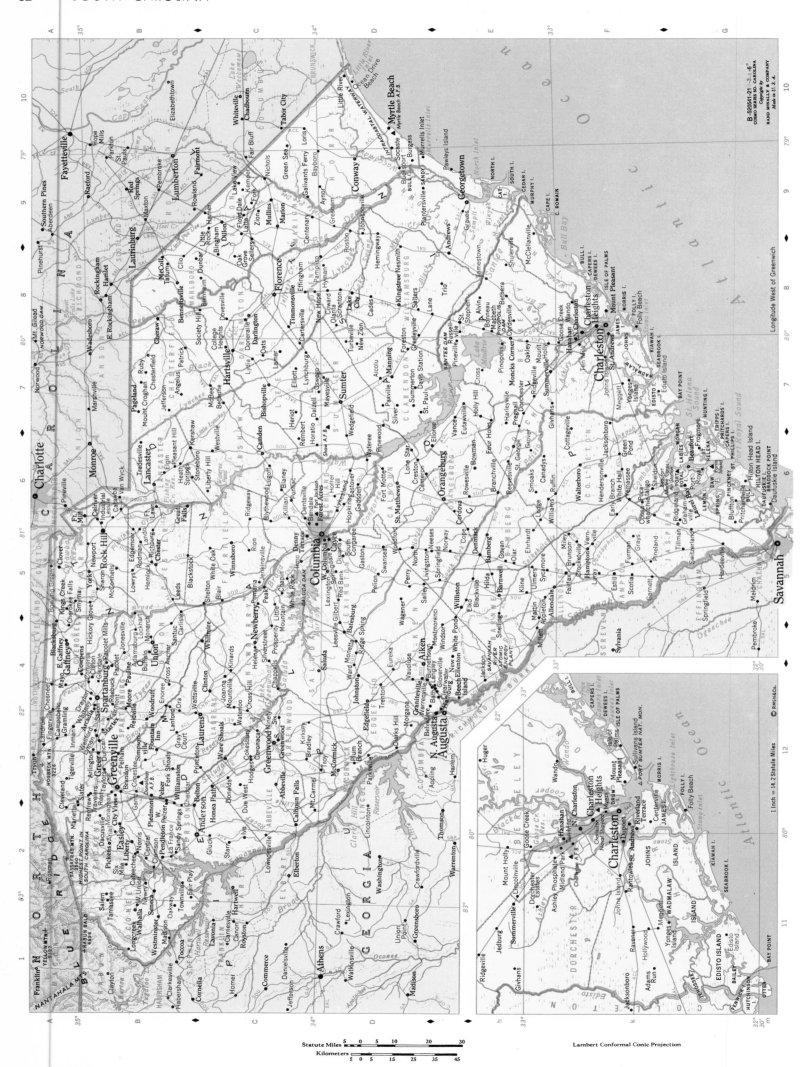

Statute Miles
Kilometers

Lambert Conformal Conic Projection

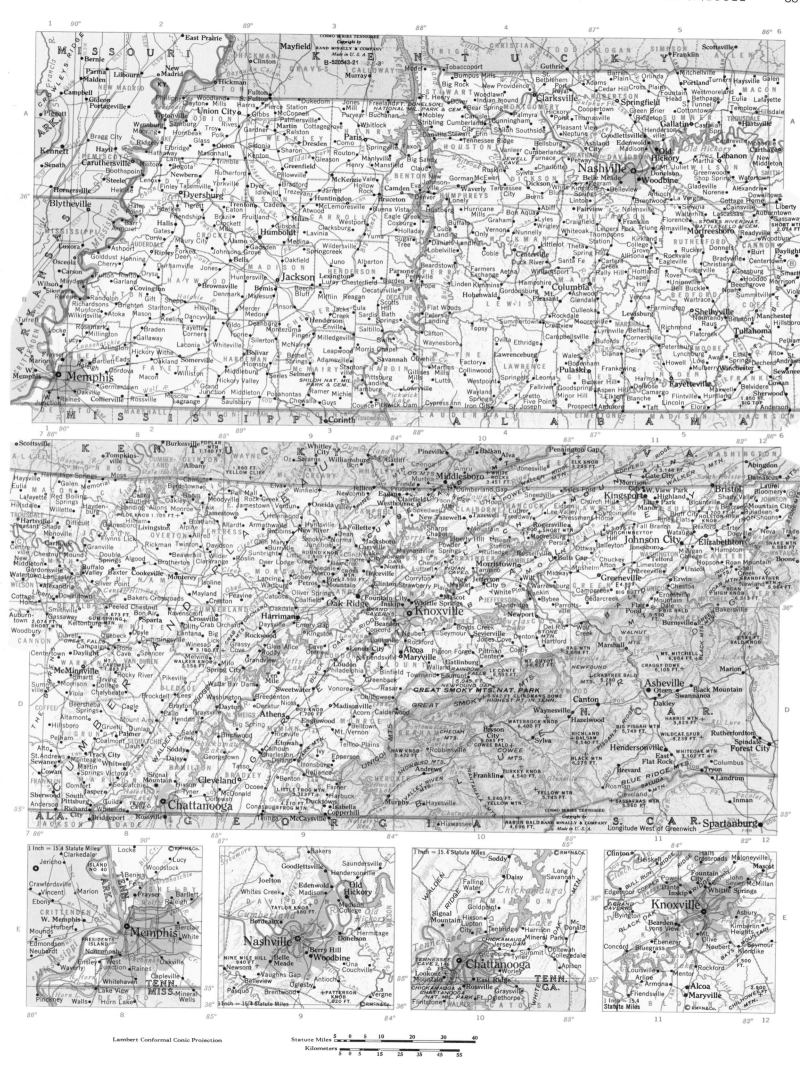

Lambert Conformal Conic Projection

Statute Miles 5 0 5 10 20 30 40

Kilometers 5 0 5 15 25 35 45 55

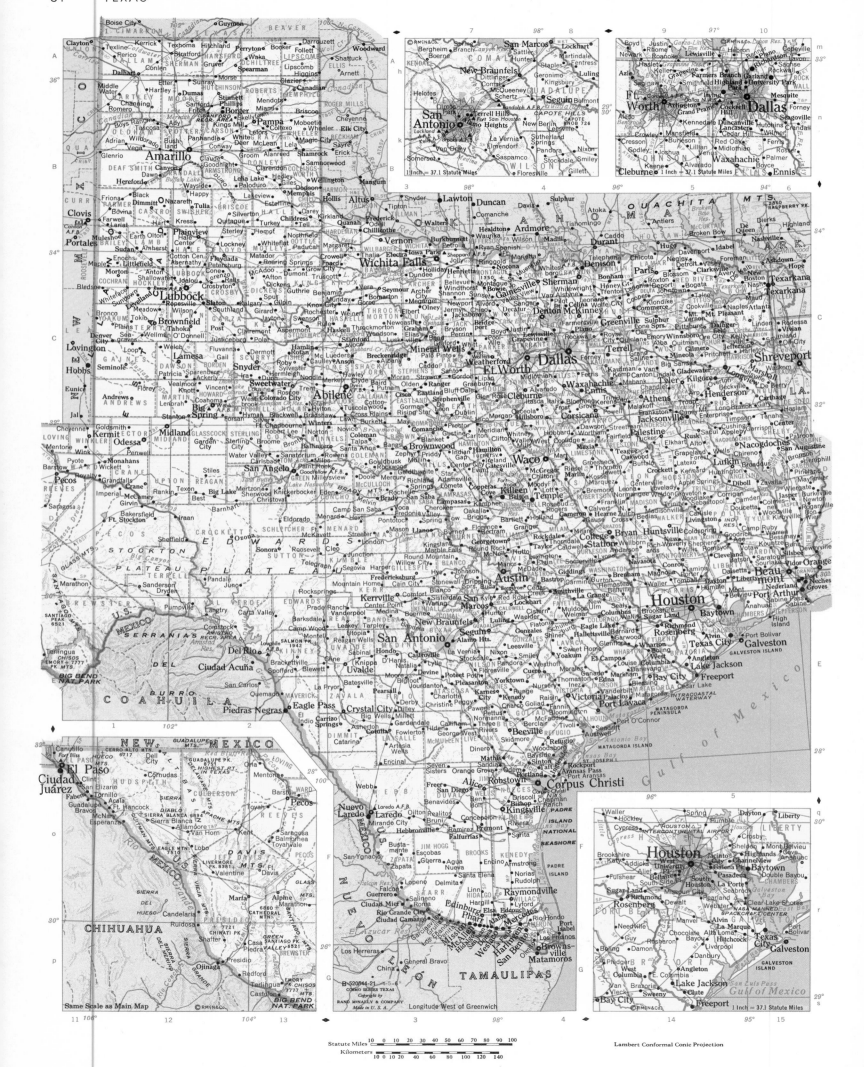

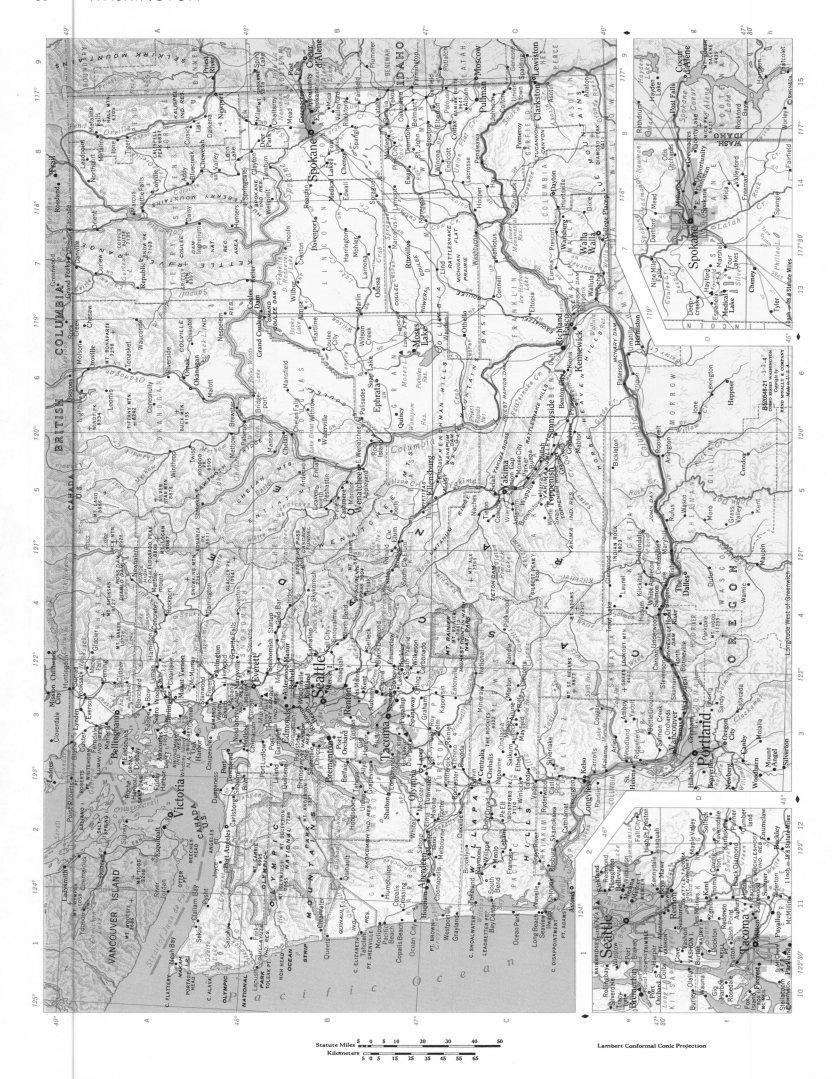

Statute Miles 5 0 5 10   20   30   40   50
Kilometers 5 0 5 15 25 35 45 55 65

Lambert Conformal Conic Projection

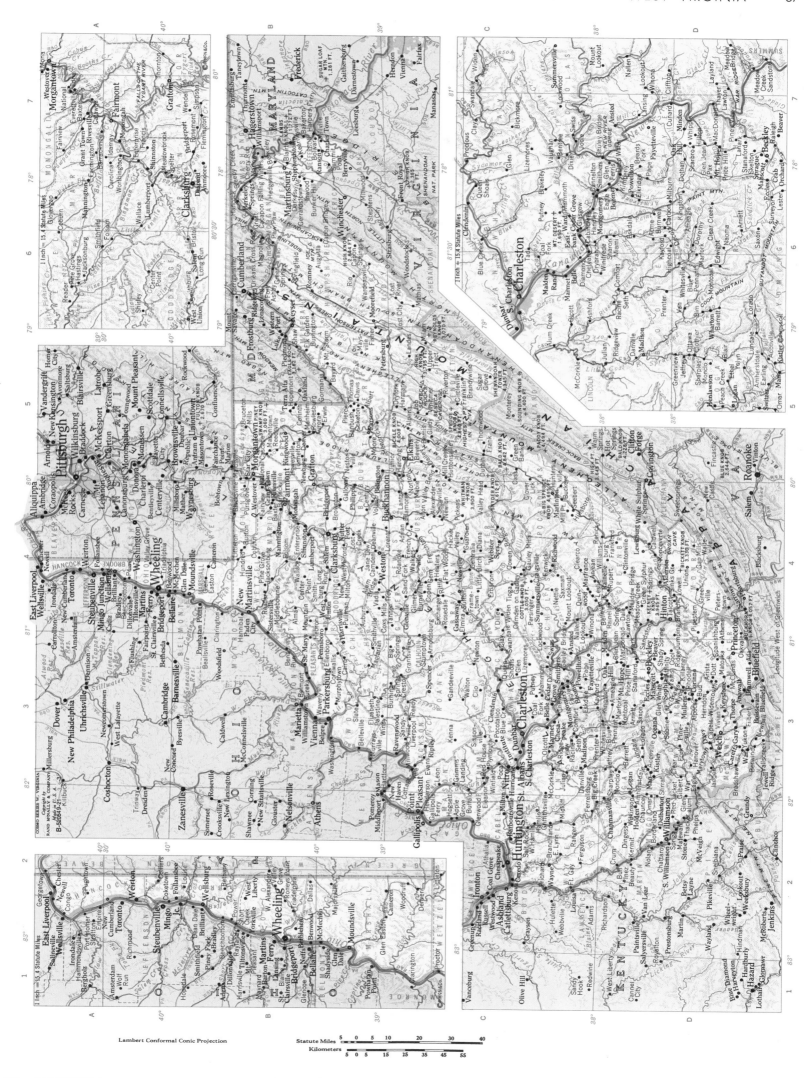

Lambert Conformal Conic Projection

Statute Miles   5 0 5 10   20   30   40

Kilometers   5 0 5   15   25   35   45   55

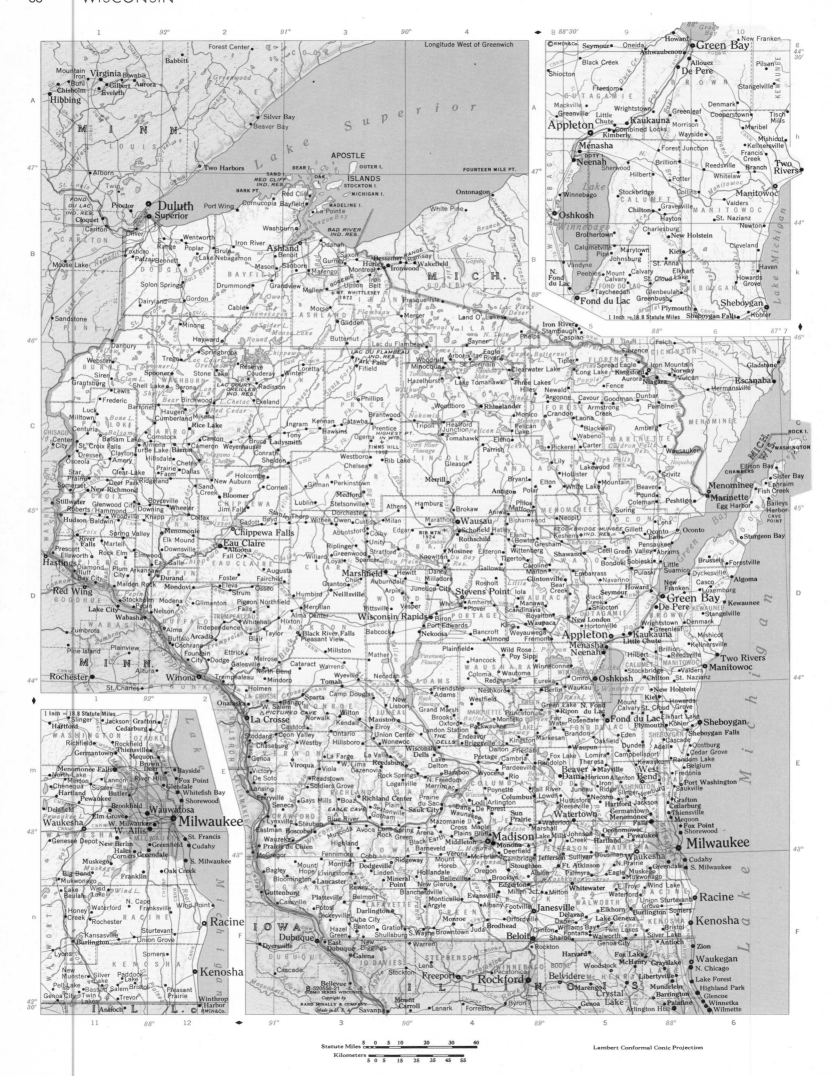

Longitude West of Greenwich

Lake Superior

APOSTLE ISLANDS

FOURTEEN MILE PT.

1 Inch = 18.8 Statute Miles

Statute Miles
Kilometers

Lambert Conformal Conic Projection

Copyright by
RAND McNALLY & COMPANY
Made in U.S.A.

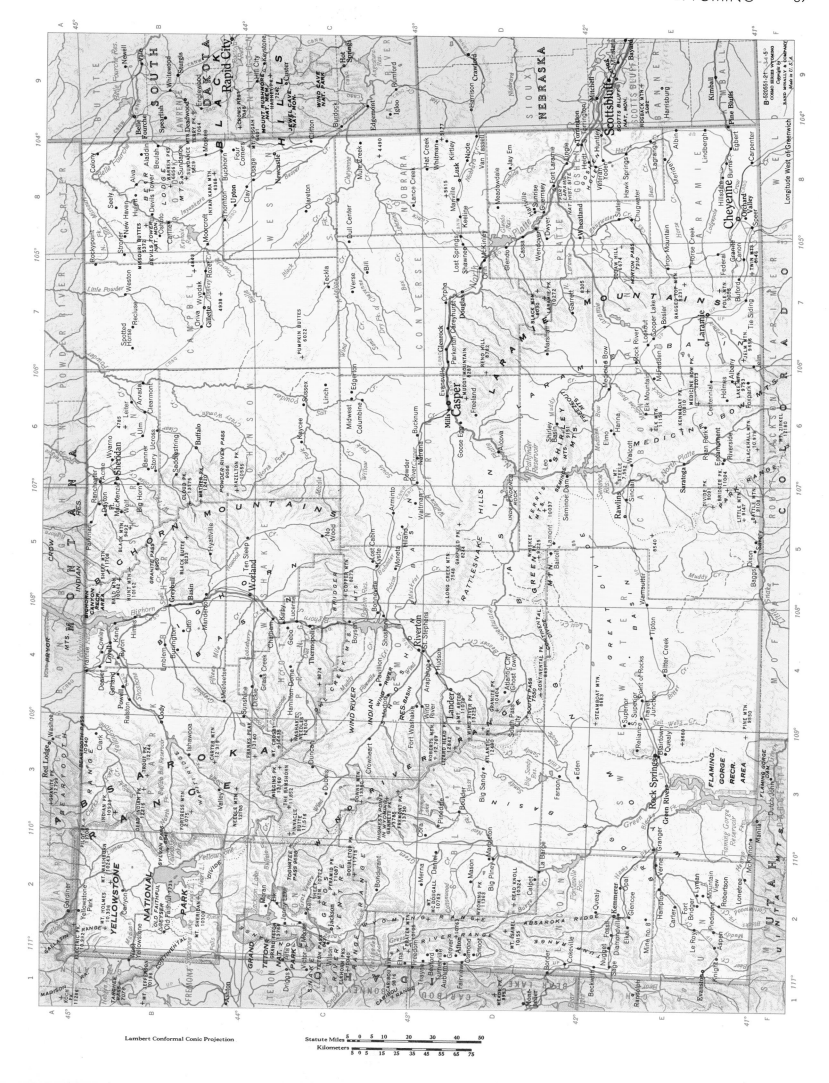

Lambert Conformal Conic Projection

Statute Miles
5 0 10   20   30   40   50

Kilometers
5 0 5 15 25 35 45 55 65 75

MAP SYMBOL

CULTURAL FEATURES

Political Boundaries

—————— International

—————— Secondary (State, province, etc.)

—————— County

Populated Places

Cities, towns, and villages

•••••● Symbol size represents population of the place

Chicago
Gary
Racine
Glenview
Edgewood

Type size represents relative importance of the place.

Corporate area of large U.S. and Canadian cities and urban area of other foreign cities

Major Urban Area
Area of continuous commercial, industrial, and residential development in and around a major city

○ Community within a city

⊗ Capital of major political unit

☆ Capital of secondary political unit

◉ Capital of U.S. state or Canadian province

○ County Seat

▲ Military Installation

⊙ Scientific Station

Miscellaneous

National Park

National Monument

Provincial Park

Indian Reservation

△ Point of Interest

∴ Ruins

■ ■ Buildings

Race Track

NYC Railroad (Initialed in U.S. and Canada)

Tunnel

Underground or Subway

Dam

Bridge

Dike

LAND FEATURES

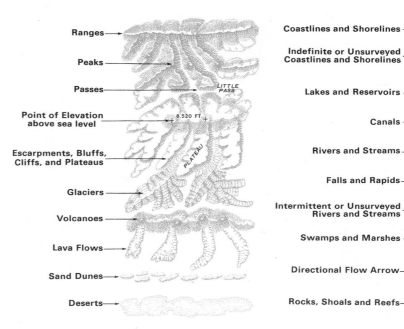

Ranges

Peaks

Passes — LITTLE PASS

Point of Elevation above sea level — 8,520 FT.

Escarpments, Bluffs, Cliffs, and Plateaus — PLATEAU

Glaciers

Volcanoes

Lava Flows

Sand Dunes

Deserts

WATER FEATURES

Coastlines and Shorelines

Indefinite or Unsurveyed Coastlines and Shorelines

Lakes and Reservoirs

Canals

Rivers and Streams

Falls and Rapids

Intermittent or Unsurveyed Rivers and Streams

Swamps and Marshes

Directional Flow Arrow

Rocks, Shoals and Reefs

TYPE STYLES USED TO NAME FEATURES

A S I A	Continent	PANTELLERIA (ITALY)	Country of which unit is a dependency in parentheses	UINTA DESERT — Major Terrain Features
DENMARK CANADA	Country, State, or Province	MALAWI (NYASALAND)	Former or alternate name	MT. MORIAH — Individual Mountain
		Rome (Roma)	Local or alternate city name	STROMBOLI NUNIVAK — Island or Coastal Featu
BÉARN	Region, Province, or Historical Region	Naval Air Station	Military Installation	Ocean Lake River Canal — Hydrographic Features
CROCKETT	County	MESA VERDE SAN XAVIER	National Park or Monument, Provincial Park, Indian Res.,	

Note: Size of type varies according to importance and available space. Letters for names of major features are spread across the extent of the feature.

THE INDEX REFERENCE SYSTEM

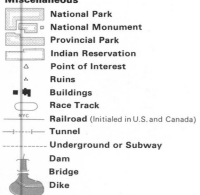

	Index
Place Location Pop.	Key Page
Cadillac, Que., Can., 1,077.	*E9 72
Cadillac, Sask., Can., 245.	H2 70
Cadillac, Fr., 2,324.	E3 14
Cadillac, Wexford, Mich., 10,112.	B4 98
Cadiz, San Bernardino, Calif., 50.	E6 79
Cadiz, Trigg, Ky., 1,980.	D2 94
Cadron, creek, Ark.	B3 81
Caen, Fr., 91,336 (*120,000).	C3 14
Caetité, Braz., 4,823.	D2 57
Chamblee, DeKalb, Ga., 6,635.	A5 87
Chambly Canton, Que., Can., 1,885.	*D4 73
Chamdo (Changtu), China.	E4 34
Champagne, former prov., Fr., 1,504,000.	C5 14
Champaign, Champaign, Ill., 49,583.	B4 90
Champdore, lake, Que., Can.	g8 75
Champerico, Guat., 982.	C2 62
Champéry, Switz., 810.	D2 19
Champex, Switz.	D3 19
Champigneulles, Fr., 5,854.	F6 15
Champion, Chase, Nebr., 140.	D4 103
Champlain, co., Que., Can., 111,953.	B4 73
Champlain, lake, Que., Can.	E4 73
Champlain, lake, N.Y., Vt.	B2 120
Chiapa de Corzo, Mex., 6,972.	D6 63
Chiapas, state, Mex., 1,215,475.	D6 63
Chiba, Jap., 241,615.	I10, n19 37
Chiba, pref., Jap., 2,306,010.	*I10 37
Chibemba, Ang., 354.	E1 48
Chibougamau, Que., Can., 4,765.	G18 61, B2 73
Chicago, Cook, Ill., 3,550,404 (*6,517,600).	B4, F3 90
Chichaoua, Mor.	C3 44
Chichen-Itzá, ruins, Mex.	C7 63
Chichester, Eng., 20,118.	D7 12
Chickasaw, co., Iowa, 15,034.	A5 92
Chiclana, Sp., 21,524.	D2 20
Chiclayo, Peru, 38,517.	C2 58

The indexing system used in this atlas based upon the conventional pattern of pa allels and meridians used to indicate latitu and longitude. The index samples beside t map indicate that the cities of *Chicago*, *Caa lac*, and *Champaign* are all located in *B4*. Ea index key letter, in this case "*B*," is place between corresponding degree numbers latitude in the vertical borders of the ma Each index key number, in this case "*4*," placed between corresponding degree nu bers of longitude in the horizontal borders the map. Crossing of the parallels above a below the index letter with the meridians each side of the index number forms a co fining "box" in which the given place certain to be located. It is important to no that location of the place may be anywhe in this confining "box."

Insets on many foreign maps are index independently of the main maps by separa index key letters and figures. All places i dexed to these insets are identified by t lower case reference letter in the index ke A diamond-shaped symbol in the margin the map is used to separate the insets fro the main map and also to separate key lette and numbers where the spacing of the para lels and meridians is great.

Place-names are indexed to the locati of the city symbol. Political divisions a physical features are indexed to the locati of their names on the map.

GEOGRAPHICAL FACTS ABOUT THE UNITED STATES

ELEVATION

The highest elevation in the United States is Mount McKinley, Alaska, 20,320 feet.
The lowest elevation in the United States is in Death Valley, California, 282 feet below sea level.
The average elevation of the United States is 2,500 feet.

EXTREMITIES

Direction	Location	Latitude	Longitude
North	Point Barrow, Alaska	71°23′N.	156°29′W.
South	South Cape, Hawaii	18°56′N.	155°41′W.
East	West Quoddy Head, Maine	44°49′N.	66°57′W.
West	Cape Wrangell, Alaska	52°55′N.	172°27′E.

The two places in the United States separated by the greatest distance are Kure Island, Hawaii, and Mangrove Point, Florida. These points are 5,848 miles apart.

LENGTH OF BOUNDARIES

The total length of the Canadian boundary of the United States is 5,525 miles.
The total length of the Mexican boundary of the United States is 2,013 miles.

The total length of the Atlantic coastline of the United States is 2,069 miles.
The total length of the Pacific and Arctic coastline of the United States is 8,683 miles.
The total length of the Gulf of Mexico coastline of the United States is 1,631 miles.
The total length of all coastlines and land boundaries of the United States is 19,921 miles.
The total length of the tidal shoreline and land boundaries of the United States is 96,171 miles.

GEOGRAPHIC CENTERS

The geographic center of the United States (including Alaska and Hawaii) is in Butte County, South Dakota at 44°58′N., 103°46′W.
The geographic center of North America is in North Dakota, a few miles west of Devils Lake, at 48°10′N., 100°10′W.

EXTREMES OF TEMPERATURE

The highest temperature ever recorded in the United States was 134°F., at Greenland Ranch, Death Valley, California, on July 10, 1913.

The lowest temperature ever recorded in the United States was —76°F., at Tanana, Alaska, in January, 1886.

PRECIPITATION

The average annual precipitation for the United States is approximately 29 inches.
Hawaii is the wettest state, with an average annual rainfall of 82.48 inches. Nevada, with an average annual rainfall of 8.81 inches, is the driest state.
The greatest local average annual rainfall in the United States is at Mt. Waialeale, Kauai, Hawaii, 460 inches.
Greatest 24-hour rainfall in the United States, 23.22 inches at New Smyrna, Florida, October 10–11, 1924.
Extreme minimum rainfall records in the United States include a total fall of only 3.93 inches at Bagdad, California, for a period of 5 years, 1909–13, and an annual average of 1.78 inches at Death Valley, California.
Heavy snowfall records include 60 inches at Giant Forest, California, in 1 day; 42 inches at Angola, New York, in 2 days; 87 inches at Giant Forest, California, in 3 days; and 108 inches at Tahoe, California, in 4 days.
Greatest seasonal snowfall, 1,000.3 inches, more than 83 feet, at Paradise Ranger Station, Washington, during the winter of 1955–56.

HISTORICAL FACTS ABOUT THE UNITED STATES

TERRITORIAL ACQUISITIONS

Accession	Date	Area (sq. mi.)	Cost in Dollars
Original territory of the Thirteen States	1790	888,811	....
Purchase of Louisiana Territory, from France	1803	827,192	$11,250,000.00
By treaty with Spain: Florida	1819	58,560	$ 5,000,000.00
Other areas	1819	13,443	
Annexation of Texas	1845	390,144	....
Oregon Territory, by treaty with Great Britain	1846	285,580	....
Mexican Cession	1848	529,017	$15,000,000.00
Gadsden Purchase, from Mexico	1853	29,640	$10,000,000.00
Purchase of Alaska, from Russia	1867	586,400	7,200,000.00
Annexation of Hawaiian Islands	1898	6,424	....
Puerto Rico, by treaty with Spain	1899	3,435	....
Guam, by treaty with Spain	1899	212	....
American Samoa, by treaty with Great Britain and Germany	1900	76	....
Panama Canal Zone, by treaty with Panama	1904	553	*$10,000,000.00
Virgin Islands, by purchase from Denmark	1917	133	$25,000,000.00
Total		3,619,620	$83,450,000.00

Note: The Philippines, ceded by Spain in 1898 for $20,000,000.00, were a territorial possession of the United States from 1898 to 1946. On July 4, 1946 they became the independent republic of the Philippines.

* $25,000,000.00 was also paid to the republic of Colombia, out of whose territory the republic of Panama was created. In addition, an annual payment of $1,930,000 is made to the republic of Panama.

WESTWARD MOVEMENT OF CENTER OF POPULATION

Year	U.S. Population Total at Census	Approximate Location
1790	3,929,214	23 miles east of Baltimore, Md.
1800	5,308,483	18 miles west of Baltimore, Md.
1810	7,239,881	40 miles northwest of Washington, D.C.
1820	9,638,453	16 miles east of Moorefield, W. Va.
1830	12,866,020	19 miles southwest of Moorefield, W. Va.
1840	17,069,453	16 miles south of Clarksburg, W. Va.
1850	23,191,876	23 miles southeast of Parkersburg, W. Va.
1860	31,443,321	20 miles southeast of Chillicothe, Ohio
1870	39,818,449	48 miles northeast of Cincinnati, Ohio
1880	50,155,783	8 miles southwest of Cincinnati, Ohio
1890	62,947,714	20 miles east of Columbus, Ind.
1900	75,994,575	6 miles southeast of Columbus, Ind.
1910	91,972,266	Bloomington, Ind.
1920	105,710,620	8 miles southeast of Spencer, Ind.
1930	122,775,046	3 miles southwest of Linton, Ind.
1940	131,669,275	2 miles southeast of Carlisle, Ind.
1950	150,697,361	8 miles northwest of Olney, Ill.
1960	179,323,175	6 miles northwest of Centralia, Ill.

STATE AREAS AND POPULATIONS

STATE	Land Area (square miles) in 1960	Water Area (square miles) in 1960	Total Area (square miles) in 1960	Rank in Area	Population in 1960	Population Per Square Mile in 1960	Rank in Population in 1960	Population in 1950	Rank in Population in 1950	Population 1940
Alabama	51,060	549	51,609	29	3,266,740	63	19	3,061,743	17	2,832,961
Alaska	571,065	15,335	586,400	1	226,167	0.4	50	128,643	50	72,524‡
Arizona	113,575	334	113,909	6	1,302,161	11	35	749,587	37	499,261
Arkansas	52,499	605	53,104	27	1,786,272	34	31	1,909,511	30	1,949,387
California	156,573	2,120	158,693	3	15,717,204	99	2	10,586,223	2	6,907,387
Colorado	103,884	363	104,247	8	1,753,947	17	33	1,325,089	34	1,123,296
Connecticut	4,899	110	5,009	48	2,535,234	506	25	2,007,280	28	1,709,242
Delaware	1,978	79	2,057	49	446,292	217	46	318,085	47	266,505
District of Columbia†	61	8	69	..	763,956	11,072	..	802,178	..	663,091
Florida	54,252	4,308	58,560	22	4,951,560	85	10	2,771,305	20	1,897,414
Georgia	58,274	602	58,876	21	3,943,116	67	16	3,444,578	13	3,123,723
Hawaii	6,415	9	6,424	47	632,772	99	43	499,794	45	423,330
Idaho	82,708	849	83,557	13	667,191	8.0	42	588,637	43	524,873
Illinois	55,930	470	56,400	24	10,081,158	179	4	8,712,176	4	7,897,241
Indiana	36,185	106	36,291	38	4,662,498	128	11	3,934,224	12	3,427,796
Iowa	56,032	258	56,290	25	2,757,537	49	24	2,621,073	22	2,538,268
Kansas	82,048	216	82,264	14	2,178,611	26	28	1,905,299	31	1,801,028
Kentucky	39,863	532	40,395	37	3,038,156	75	22	2,944,806	19	2,845,627
Louisiana	45,106	3,417	48,523	31	3,257,022	67	20	2,683,516	21	2,363,880
Maine	31,012	2,203	33,215	39	969,265	29	36	913,774	35	847,226
Maryland	9,874	703	10,577	42	3,100,689	293	21	2,343,001	23	1,821,244
Massachusetts	7,867	390	8,257	45	5,148,578	624	9	4,690,514	9	4,316,721
Michigan	57,019	1,197	58,216	23	7,823,194	134	7	6,371,766	7	5,256,106
Minnesota	80,009	4,059	84,068	12	3,413,864	41	18	2,982,483	18	2,792,300
Mississippi	47,223	493	47,716	32	2,178,141	46	29	2,178,914	26	2,183,796
Missouri	69,138	548	69,686	19	4,319,813	62	13	3,954,653	11	3,784,664
Montana	145,736	1,402	147,138	4	674,767	4.6	41	591,024	42	559,456
Nebraska	76,612	615	77,227	15	1,411,330	18	34	1,325,510	33	1,315,834
Nevada	109,788	752	110,540	7	285,278	2.6	49	160,083	49	110,247
New Hampshire	9,014	290	9,304	44	606,921	65	45	533,242	44	491,524
New Jersey	7,521	315	7,836	46	6,066,782	774	8	4,835,329	8	4,160,165
New Mexico	121,510	156	121,666	5	951,023	7.8	37	681,187	39	531,818
New York	47,939	1,637	49,576	30	16,782,304	339	1	14,830,192	1	13,479,142
North Carolina	49,067	3,645	52,712	28	4,556,155	86	12	4,061,929	10	3,571,623
North Dakota	69,457	1,208	70,665	17	632,446	8.9	44	619,636	41	641,935
Ohio	40,972	250	41,222	35	9,706,397	235	5	7,946,627	5	6,907,612
Oklahoma	68,887	1,032	69,919	18	2,328,284	33	27	2,233,351	25	2,336,434
Oregon	96,248	733	96,981	10	1,768,687	18	32	1,521,341	32	1,089,684
Pennsylvania	45,007	326	45,333	33	11,319,366	250	3	10,498,012	3	9,900,180
Rhode Island	1,058	156	1,214	50	859,488	708	39	791,896	36	713,346
South Carolina	30,272	783	31,055	40	2,382,594	77	26	2,117,027	27	1,899,804
South Dakota	76,378	669	77,047	16	680,514	8.8	40	652,740	40	642,961
Tennessee	41,762	482	42,244	34	3,567,089	84	17	3,291,718	16	2,915,841
Texas	262,840	4,499	267,339	2	9,579,677	36	6	7,711,194	6	6,414,824
Utah	82,339	2,577	84,916	11	890,627	10	38	688,862	38	550,310
Vermont	9,276	333	9,609	43	389,881	41	47	377,747	46	359,231
Virginia	39,838	977	40,815	36	3,966,949	97	14	3,318,680	15	2,677,773
Washington	66,709	1,483	68,192	20	2,853,214	42	23	2,378,963	24	1,736,191
West Virginia	24,079	102	24,181	41	1,860,421	77	30	2,005,552	29	1,901,974
Wisconsin	54,705	1,449	56,154	26	3,951,777	70	15	3,434,575	14	3,137,587
Wyoming	97,411	503	97,914	9	330,066	3.4	48	290,529	48	250,742
United States	3,548,974	66,237	3,675,633*	..	179,323,175	49	..	151,325,798	..	132,165,129

† District.   * Includes the United States parts of the Great Lakes (60,422 square miles). These are not included in state figures.   ‡ Census taken in 1939.

U. S. STATE GENERAL INFORMATION TABLE

STATE	CAPITAL	LARGEST CITY	ENTERED UNION AS STATE — Date of Entry	Rank of Entry	Greatest N-S Measurement (miles)	Greatest E-W Measurement (miles)	HIGHEST POINT — Location	Altitude (feet)	STATE FLOWER	STATE BIRD	STATE NICKNAME
Alabama	Montgomery	Birmingham	Dec. 14, 1819	22	330	200	Cheaha Mountain	2,407	Camellia	Yellowhammer	Yellowhammer
Alaska	Juneau	Anchorage	Jan. 3, 1959	49	1,332	2,250	Mt. McKinley	20,320	Forget-me-not	Willow Ptarmigan	Last Frontier
Arizona	Phoenix	Phoenix	Feb. 14, 1912	48	390	335	Humphreys Peak	12,670	Saguaro Cactus	Cactus Wren	Grand Canyon
Arkansas	Little Rock	Little Rock	June 15, 1836	25	240	275	Magazine Mtn.	2,823	Apple Blossom	Mockingbird	Land of Opportunity
California	Sacramento	Los Angeles	Sept. 9, 1850	31	800	375	Mt. Whitney	14,495	Golden Poppy	California Valley Quail	Golden
Colorado	Denver	Denver	Aug. 1, 1876	38	270	380	Mt. Elbert	14,431	Rocky Mountain Columbine	Lark Bunting	Centennial
Connecticut*	Hartford	Hartford	Jan. 9, 1788	5	75	90	S. slope of Mt. Frissell	2,380	Mountain Laurel	American Robin	Constitution
Delaware*	Dover	Wilmington	Dec. 7, 1787	1	95	35	Ebright Road, New Castle Co.	442	Peach Blossom	Blue Hen Chicken	First
District of Columbia†	Washington	Washington	March 3, 1791	..	15	15	Tenleytown	410	American Beauty Rose	...	...
Florida	Tallahassee	Miami	March 3, 1845	27	460	400	N. boundary, Walton Co.	345	Orange Blossom	Mockingbird	Sunshine
Georgia*	Atlanta	Atlanta	Jan. 2, 1788	4	315	250	Brasstown Bald (mtn.)	4,784	Cherokee Rose	Brown Thrasher	Peach State
Hawaii	Honolulu	Honolulu	Aug. 21, 1959	50	...	1,600	Mauna Kea	13,796	Red Hibiscus	Nene (Hawaiian Goose)	The Aloha
Idaho	Boise	Boise	July 3, 1890	43	480	305	Borah Peak	12,662	Syringa	Mountain Bluebird	Gem
Illinois	Springfield	Chicago	Dec. 3, 1818	21	380	205	Charles Mound	1,241	Native Violet	Cardinal	Prairie
Indiana	Indianapolis	Indianapolis	Dec. 11, 1816	19	265	160	Near Spartanburg	1,253	Peony	Cardinal	Hoosier
Iowa	Des Moines	Des Moines	Dec. 28, 1846	29	205	310	Ocheyedan Mound	1,675	Wild Rose	Eastern Goldfinch	Hawkeye
Kansas	Topeka	Wichita	Jan. 29, 1861	34	205	410	Mt. Sunflower	4,026	Sunflower	Western Meadowlark	Sunflower
Kentucky	Frankfort	Louisville	June 1, 1792	15	175	350	Black Mountain	4,145	Goldenrod	Kentucky Cardinal	Bluegrass
Louisiana	Baton Rouge	New Orleans	April 30, 1812	18	275	300	Driskill Mountain	535	Magnolia	Eastern Brown Pelican**	Pelican
Maine	Augusta	Portland	March 15, 1820	23	310	210	Mt. Katahdin	5,268	White Pine Cone and Tassel	Chickadee	Pine Tree
Maryland*	Annapolis	Baltimore	April 28, 1788	7	120	200	Backbone Mountain	3,360	Black-eyed Susan	Baltimore Oriole	Free
Massachusetts*	Boston	Boston	Feb. 6, 1788	6	110	190	Mt. Greylock	3,491	Mayflower	Chickadee	Bay
Michigan	Lansing	Detroit	Jan. 26, 1837	26	400	310	N.E. Baraga Co.	1,980	Apple Blossom	Robin	Wolverine
Minnesota	St. Paul	Minneapolis	May 11, 1858	32	400	350	Eagle Mtn.	2,301	Showy Lady's-slipper	Loon	Gopher
Mississippi	Jackson	Jackson	Dec. 10, 1817	20	340	180	Woodall Mountain	806	Magnolia	Mockingbird	Magnolia
Missouri	Jefferson City	St. Louis	Aug. 10, 1821	24	280	300	Taum Sauk Mountain	1,772	Hawthorne	Bluebird	Show Me
Montana	Helena	Great Falls	Nov. 8, 1889	41	315	570	Granite Peak	12,799	Bitterroot	Western Meadowlark	Treasure
Nebraska	Lincoln	Omaha	March 1, 1867	37	210	415	S.W. corner Kimball Co.	5,424	Goldenrod	Western Meadowlark	Cornhusker
Nevada	Carson City	Las Vegas	Oct. 31, 1864	36	485	315	Boundary Peak	13,145	Sagebrush	Mountain Bluebird**	Battle Born
New Hampshire*	Concord	Manchester	June 21, 1788	9	185	90	Mt. Washington	6,288	Purple Lilac	Purple Finch	Granite
New Jersey*	Trenton	Newark	Dec. 18, 1787	3	166	70	High Point	1,803	Purple Violet	Eastern Goldfinch	Garden
New Mexico	Santa Fe	Albuquerque	Jan. 6, 1912	47	390	350	Wheeler Peak	13,160	Yucca	Road Runner	Land of Enchantment
New York*	Albany	New York	July 26, 1788	11	310	330	Mt. Marcy	5,344	Rose	Bluebird**	Empire
North Carolina*	Raleigh	Charlotte	Nov. 21, 1789	12	200	520	Mt. Mitchell	6,684	Dogwood	Cardinal	Tar Heel
North Dakota	Bismarck	Fargo	Nov. 2, 1889	39	210	360	White Butte	3,530	Wild Prairie Rose	Western Meadowlark	Flickertail
Ohio	Columbus	Cleveland	March 1, 1803	17	230	205	Campbell Hill	1,550	Scarlet Carnation	Cardinal	Buckeye
Oklahoma	Oklahoma City	Oklahoma City	Nov. 16, 1907	46	210	460	Black Mesa	4,978	Mistletoe	Scissor-tailed Flycatcher	Sooner
Oregon	Salem	Portland	Feb. 14, 1859	33	290	375	Mt. Hood	11,245	Oregon Grape	Western Meadowlark	Beaver
Pennsylvania*	Harrisburg	Philadelphia	Dec. 12, 1787	2	180	310	Mt. Davis	3,213	Mountain Laurel	Ruffed Grouse	Keystone
Rhode Island*	Providence	Providence	May 29, 1790	13	50	35	Jerimoth Hill	812	Violet**	Rhode Island Red	Little Rhody
South Carolina*	Columbia	Columbia	May 23, 1788	8	215	285	Sassafras Mountain	3,560	Carolina Jessamine	Carolina Wren	Palmetto
South Dakota	Pierre	Sioux Falls	Nov. 2, 1889	40	240	360	Harney Peak	7,242	Pasque	Ringnecked Pheasant	Coyote
Tennessee	Nashville	Memphis	June 1, 1796	16	120	430	Clingmans Dome	6,642	Iris	Mockingbird	Volunteer
Texas	Austin	Houston	Dec. 29, 1845	28	710	760	Guadalupe Peak	8,751	Bluebonnet	Mockingbird	Lone Star
Utah	Salt Lake City	Salt Lake City	Jan. 4, 1896	45	345	275	Kings Peak	13,498	Sego Lily	Seagull	Beehive
Vermont	Montpelier	Burlington	March 4, 1791	14	155	90	Mt. Mansfield	4,393	Red Clover	Hermit Thrush	Green Mountain
Virginia*	Richmond	Norfolk	June 25, 1788	10	205	425	Mt. Rogers	5,720	American Dogwood	Cardinal	Old Dominion
Washington	Olympia	Seattle	Nov. 11, 1889	42	230	340	Mt. Rainier	14,410	Rhododendron	Willow Goldfinch	Evergreen
West Virginia	Charleston	Charleston	June 20, 1863	35	200	225	Spruce Knob	4,860	Rhododendron	Cardinal	Mountain
Wisconsin	Madison	Milwaukee	May 29, 1848	30	300	290	Timms Hill	1,952	Violet	Robin	Badger
Wyoming	Cheyenne	Cheyenne	July 10, 1890	44	275	365	Gannett Peak	13,785	Indian Paint Brush	Meadowlark	Equality
United States	Washington, D.C.	New York	...	..	...	...	Mt. McKinley, Alaska	20,320	...	Bald Eagle	...

*One of the Thirteen Original States.   **Unofficial.   †District.

ABBREVIATIONS

admin	administered
Afg	Afghanistan
Afr	Africa
A. & I.	Afars & Issas
Ala	Alabama
Alb	Albania
Alg	Algeria
Alsk	Alaska
Alta	Alberta
Am	American
Am. Sam.	American Samoa
And	Andorra
Ang	Angola
Ant	Antarctica
Arc	Arctic
arch	archipelago
Arg	Argentina
Ariz	Arizona
Ark	Arkansas
Atl. O.	Atlantic Ocean
Aus	Austria
Austl	Australia, Australian
auton	autonomous
Az. Is.	Azores Islands
Ba. Is.	Bahama Islands
Barb	Barbados
B. C.	British Columbia
Bel	Belgium, Belgian
Bhu	Bhutan
Bis. Arch.	Bismarck Archipelago
Bol	Bolivia
Bots	Botswana
Br	British
Braz	Brazil
Br. Hond.	British Honduras
Bru	Brunei
Bul	Bulgaria
Bur	Burma
Calif	California
Cam	Cameroon
Camb	Cambodia
Can	Canada
Can. Is.	Canary Islands
Cen. Afr. Rep.	Central African Republic
Cen. Am.	Central America
Cey	Ceylon
co	county
Col	Colombia
Colo	Colorado
Con. B.	Congo; Capital: Brazzaville
Con. K.	Congo, The; Capital: Kinshasa
Conn	Connecticut
cont	continent
C. R.	Costa Rica
C. V. Is.	Cape Verde Islands
Cyp	Cyprus
C.Z.	Canal Zone
Czech	Czechoslovakia
Dah	Dahomey
Dan	Danish
D.C.	District of Columbia
Del	Delaware
Den	Denmark
dep	dependency, dependencies
dept	department
dist	district
div	division
Dom. Rep.	Dominican Republic
Ec	Ecuador
Eg	Egypt
Eng	England
Equat. Gui.	Equatorial Guinea
Eth	Ethiopia
Eur	Europe
Falk. Is.	Falkland Islands
Fed	Federation
Fin	Finland
Fla	Florida
Fr	France, French
Fr. Gu.	French Guiana
Ga	Georgia
Gam	Gambia
Ger	Germany
Gib	Gibraltar
Grc	Greece
Grnld	Greenland
Guad	Guadeloupe
Guat	Guatemala
Guy	Guyana
Hai	Haiti
Haw	Hawaii
Hond	Honduras
Hung	Hungary
I.	Island
I.C.	Ivory Coast
Ice	Iceland
Ill.	Illinois
incl	includes, including
Ind	Indiana
Indian res.	Indian reservation
Indon	Indonesia
I. of Man	Isle of Man
Ire	Ireland
is	islands
isl	island
Isr	Israel
It	Italy
Jam	Jamaica
Jap	Japan
Kans	Kansas
Ken	Keyna
Kor	Korea
Kuw	Kuwait
Ky	Kentucky
La	Louisiana
Leb	Lebanon
Le. Is.	Leeward Islands
Leso	Lesotho
Lib	Liberia
Liech	Liechtenstein
Lux	Luxembourg
Mad. Is.	Madeira Islands
Mala	Malaysia
Malag	Malagasy Republic
Man	Manitoba
Mart	Martinique
Mass	Massachusetts
Maur	Mauritania
Md	Maryland
Medit	Mediterranean
Mex	Mexico
Mich	Michigan
Minn	Minnesota
Miss	Mississippi
Mo	Missouri
Mong	Mongolia
Mont	Montana
Mor	Morocco
Moz	Mozambique
mtn	mount, mountain
mts	mountains
mun	municipality
Mus. & Om.	Muscat & Oman
N.A.	North America
nat. mon.	national monument
nat. park	national park
N.B.	New Brunswick
N.C.	North Carolina
N. Cal.	New Caledonia
N. Dak.	North Dakota
Nebr	Nebraska
Nep	Nepal
Neth	Netherlands
Nev	Nevada
Newf	Newfoundland
New Hebr.	New Hebrides
N. Gui.	New Guinea Territory
N.H.	New Hampshire
Nic	Nicaragua
Nig	Nigeria
N. Ire.	Northern Ireland
N.J.	New Jersey
N. Mex.	New Mexico
Nor	Norway, Norwegian
N.S.	Nova Scotia
N.W. Ter.	Northwest Territories
N.Y.	New York
N.Z.	New Zealand
occ	occupied area
Okla	Oklahoma
Ont	Ontario
Oreg	Oregon
Pa	Pennsylvania
Pac. O.	Pacific Ocean
Pak	Pakistan
Pan	Panama
Pap	Papua
Par	Paraguay
par	parish
P.E.I.	Prince Edward Island
pen	peninsula
Phil	Philippines
Pol	Poland
pol. dist.	political district
pop	population
Port	Portugal, Portuguese
Port. Gui.	Portuguese Guinea
Port. Timor	Portuguese Timor
poss	possession
P.R.	Puerto Rico
pref	prefecture
prot	protectorate
prov	province, provincial
pt	point
Que	Quebec
reg	region
rep	republic
res	reservation, reservoir
Rh	Rhodesia
R.I.	Rhode Island
riv	river
Rom	Romania
S. A.	South America
S. Afr.	South Africa
Sal	El Salvador
Sask	Saskatchewan
Sau. Ar.	Saudi Arabia
S.C.	South Carolina
Scot	Scotland
S. Dak.	South Dakota
Sen	Senegal
S.L.	Sierra Leone
Sol. Is.	Solomon Islands
Som	Somali Republic
Sov. Un.	Soviet Union
Sp	Spain, Spanish
St., Ste.	Saint, Sainte
Sud	Sudan
Sur	Surinam
S. W. Afr.	South West Africa
Swaz	Swaziland
Swe	Sweden
Switz	Switzerland
S. Yem.	Southern Yemen
Syr	Syria
Tan	Tanzania
Tenn	Tennessee
ter	territories, territory
Tex	Texas
Thai	Thailand
Tr. Coast	Trucial Coast
Trin	Trinidad & Tobago
trust	trusteeship
Tun	Tunisia
Tur	Turkey
U.A.R.	United Arab Republic
Ug	Uganda
U.K.	United Kingdom
Ur	Uruguay
U.S.	United States
Va	Virginia
Ven	Venezuela
Viet	Vietnam
Vir. Is.	Virgin Islands
vol	volcano
Vt	Vermont
Wash	Washington
W.I.	West Indies
Win. Is.	Windward Islands
Wis	Wisconsin
W. Sam.	Western Samoa
W. Va.	West Virginia
Wyo	Wyoming
Yugo	Yugoslavia

EXPLANATION OF THE MAP INDEX

This universal index includes in a single alphabetical list all important names that appear on the reference maps. Each place name is followed by its location; the population figure, when available; the map index key; and the page number of the map.

State locations are given for all places in the United States. Province and country locations are given for all places in Canada. All other place name entries show only country locations.

Populations are based upon latest available official census figures and estimates. For some larger cities a second population figure is given accompanied by a star (*). The second figure indicates the population of the city's entire metropolitan area including suburbs, as: Chicago, 3,460,000 (*7,435,000). A triangular symbol (▲) denotes a population figure for an *entire* township, district, or other minor civil division.

The index reference key, always a letter and figure combination, and the map page are the last items in each entry. Because some places are shown on both a main map and an inset map, more than one index key may be given for a single map page. Reference also may be made to more than a single map. In each case, however, the index key *letter and figure* precede the map *page number* to which reference is made. A lower case key letter indicates reference to an inset map which has been keyed separately.

All major and minor political divisions are followed by both a descriptive term (co., dist., region, prov., dept., state, etc.), indicating political status, and by the country in which they are located. U. S. counties are listed with state locations; all others are given with county references.

The more important physical names that are shown on the maps are listed in the index. Each entry is followed by a descriptive term (bay, hill, range, riv., mtn., isl., etc.), to indicate its nature.

Country locations are given for each name, except for features entirely within States of the United States or provinces of Canada, in which case these divisions are also given.

Some names are included in the index that were omitted from the maps because of scale size or lack of space. These entries may be identified by an asterisk (*) and reference is given to the approximate location on the map.

A long name may appear on the map in a shortened form, with the full name given in the index. The part of the name not on the map then appears in brackets, thus: St. Gabriel [-de-Brandon].

The system of alphabetizing used in the index is standard. When more than one name with the same spelling is shown, place names are listed *first* and political divisions *second*.

INDEX

A

Aachen, Ger., 174,700.....C3 6
Aalen, Ger., 31,800.......D5 6
Aalst, Bel., 45,092........B6 5
Äänekoski, Fin., 7,200...F11 11
Aarau, Switz., 16,900.... E4 6
Aargua, canton, Switz.,
  390,000..............*E3 6
Ābādān, Iran, 226,083.....B7 23
Abaetetuba, Braz.,
  11,196.................*D6 27
Abakan, Sov. Un.,
  66,000................D12 13
Abancay, Peru, 8,100.....D3 31
Abashiri, Jap., 30,100....D12 18
Abbeville, Ala., 2,524....D4 46
Abbeville, Fr., 22,005.....B4 5
Abbeville, La., 10,414.....E3 63
Abbeville, S.C. 5,436......C3 82
Abbeville, co., S.C.,
  21,417................C2 82
Abbiategrasso, It., 21,652..C2 82
Abbot Butte, Oreg........E4 80
Abbotsford, B.C., Can.,
  888...................f13 37
Abbotsford, Wis., 1,171....D3 88
Åbenrå, co., Den.,
  49,769...............*J3 11
Abeokuta, Nig., 187,292...G5 22
Aberdare, Wales, 39,000...E5 4
Aberdeen, Idaho, 1,484....G6 57
Aberdeen, Md., 9,679......A5 53
Aberdeen, Miss., 6,450.....B5 68
Aberdeen, N.C., 1,531.....B3 76
Aberdeen, S. Dak., 23,073..E7 77
Aberdeen, Scot., 186,000...B5 4
Aberdeen, Wash., 18,741...C2 86
Aberdeen, co., Scot.,
  320,600...............*B5 4
Abergavenny, Wales.,
  9,700.................E5 4
Abernathy, Tex., 2,491...C2 84
Aberystwyth, Wales.,
  10,400................D4 4
Abidjan, I.C., 180,000.... G4 22
Abilene, Kans., 6,746.....D6 61
Abilene, Tex., 90,368.....C3 84
Abingdon, Ill., 3,469......C3 58
Abingdon, Va., 4,758.....f10 85
Abington, Mass.,
  4,700.............B6, h12 65
Abington, Pa., 9,500......o21 81
Abitibi, co., Que., Can.,
  108,313..............*H12 42
Abomey, Dah., 18,900.....G5 22
Abony, Hung., 12,633......B5 10
Åbo, see Turku, Fin.
Abra, prov., Phil.,
  115,193..............*B6 19
Abruzzi and Molise,
  reg., It...............C4 9
Abruzzi e Molise, pol. dist.,
  It., 1,564,318..........C4 9

Absecon, N.J., 4,320......E3 74
Abu Kamal, Syr., 8,266...E13 14
Aby, Swe., 2,795.........u34 11
Acadia, par., La., 49,931..D3 63
Acámbaro, Mex.,
  26,187............C4, m13 34
Acaponeta, Mex.,8,462....C4 34
Acapulco [de Juárez],
  Mex., 49,149...........D5 34
Acarigua, Ven., 30,683....B4 32
Acatlán [de Osorio], Mex.,
  7,268..............D5, m14 34
Acayucan, Mex., 12,831...D6 34
Accomack, co., Va.,
  30,635................C7 85
Accoville, W. Va.,
  800...............D3, D5 87
Accra, Ghana, 337,800....G4 22
Achinsk, Sov. Un.,
  60,000...............D12 13
Acireale, It., 26,600......F5 9
Ackerman, Miss., 1,382...B4 68
Ackley, Iowa, 1,731.......B4 60
Acmetonia, Pa., 1,500....*E1 81
Aconcagua, prov., Chile,
  140,528...............A2 28
Aconcagua, peak, Arg.....A3 28
Acqui, It., 12,200.........B2 9
Acre, riv., Braz..........D4 31
Acre, Isr. 28,100......B3, g5 15
Acres Homes, Tex.,
  5,000................*E5 84
Acton, Ont., Can., 4,144..D4 41
Acton, Eng., 65,274.....k11 4
Acton Vale, Que., Can.,
  3,957.................D5 42
Açu, Braz., 8,158........*D7 27
Acushnet, Mass., 3,200...C6 65
Acworth, Ga., 2,359......B2 55
Ada, Minn., 2,064........C2 67
Ada, Ohio, 5,916.........B2 78
Ada, Okla., 14,347.......C5 79
Ada, Yugo., 11,534.......C5 10
Ada, co., Idaho, 93,460...F2 57
Adair, co., Iowa, 10,893...C3 60
Adair, co., Ky., 14,699....C4 62
Adair, co., Mo., 20,105...A5 69
Adair, co., Okla., 13,112...B7 79
Adairsville, Ga., 1,026....B2 55
Adam, mtn., Wash........C4 86
Adamantina, Braz.,
  18,164................C2 30
Adams, Mass., 12,391.....A1 65
Adams, Minn., 806........G6 67
Adams, N.Y., 1,914.......B4 75
Adams, Wis., 1,301.......E4 88
Adams, co., Colo.,
  120,296...............B6 51
Adams, co., Idaho, 2,978..E2 57
Adams, co., Ill., 68,467...D2 58
Adams, co., Ind., 24,643...C8 59
Adams, co., Iowa, 7,468...C3 60

Adams, co., Miss., 37,730..D2 68
Adams, co., Nebr.,
  28,944................D7 71
Adams, co., N. Dak.,
  4,449.................D3 77
Adams, co., Ohio, 19,982..D2 78
Adams, co., Pa., 51,906...G7 81
Adams, co., Wash., 9,929..B7 86
Adams, co., Wis., 7,566...D4 88
Adams, mtn., Mass.......A2 65
Adams, mtn., Wash.......C4 86
Adams Center, N.Y., 800..B5 75
Adamston, N.J., 900......C4 74
Adamstown, Pa., 1,190...F9 81
Adamsville, Ala., 11,408...E4 46
Adamsville, Tenn., 1,046..B3 83
Adana, Tur., 231,548.....D10 14
Addison, co., Vt., 20,076..C1 73
Addyston, Ohio, 1,376....o12 78
Adel, Iowa, 2,295........C3 60
Adelaide, Austl., 18,580
  (*770,628) F6 25
Adelphi, Md., 8,000......*C4 53
Aden, S. Yem., 99,285....G4 15
Adena, Ohio, 1,317.......B5 78
Adigrāt, Eth., 5,000......F5 23
Adirondack, mts.,
  N.Y...............A6, f10 75
Adi Ugri, Eth., 5,000.....F5 23
Adiyaman, Tur., 17,000..C12 14
Adjuntas, P.R., 5,318....*G11 35
Adle, Ga., 4,321.........E3 55
Admiralty, is., N. Gui....h12 25
Adrano, It., 31,532.......F5 9
Adria, It., 12,100.........B4 9
Adrian, Mich., 20,347.....G6 66
Adrian, Minn., 1,215......G3 67
Adrian, Mo., 1,082.......C3 69
Adrianople, see Edirne, Tur.
Aduwā, Eth., 5,000.......F5 23
Afars & Issas
  (Fr. Somaliland),
  Fr. dep., Afr., 80,000....F6 23
Afghanistan, country,
  Asia, 15,200,000.......B4 20
Africa, cont., 310,000,000.... 21
Afton, Iowa, 773.........C3 60
Afton, N.Y., 956.........C5 75
Afton, Okla., 1,111.......A7 79
Afton, Wyo., 1,337.......D2 89
Afula, Isr., 15,000.......B3 15
Afyonkarahisar, Tur.,
  38,394................C8 14
Agadès, Niger, 4,700.....E6 22
Agadir, Mor., 16,695.....B3 22
Agana, Guam, 1,642....*F6 2
Agartala, India, 54,878...D9 20
Agate Beach, Oreg., 800..C2 80
Agawam, Mass., 7,000....B2 65

Agboville, I.C., 13,000... G4 22
Agde, Fr., 7,696..........F5 5
Agematsu, Jap., 4,900....n16 18
Agen, Fr., 32,800.........E4 5
Agira, It., 14,079........F5 9
Agnone, It., 9,888........D5 9
Agra, India, 462,020......C6 20
Agrinion, Grc., 24,763....C3 14
Agrigento, It., 41,300.....F4 9
Aguada, P.R., 3,759.....*G11 35
Aguadas, Col., 10,822.....B2 32
Aguadilla, P.R., 15,943...G11 35
Aguascalientes, Mex.,
  126,617...........C4, m12 34
Aguascalientes, state,
  Mex., 243,363.....C4, K12 34
Aguilar, Colo., 777.......D6 51
Agujita, Mex., 5,463.....*B4 34
Agusan prov., Phil.,
  271,010..............*D7 19
Ahlen, Ger., 44,500.......C3 6
Ahmadabad, India,
  1,149,918.............D5 20
Ahmadnagar
  (Ahmednagar),
  India, 119,020.........E5 20
Ahmadpur, Pak., 20,423...C5 20
Aho, Jap., 3,210........*o15 18
Ahoskie, N.C., 4,583......A6 76
Ahrweiler, Ger., 8,700.....C3 6
Ahuachapan, Sal.,
  13,261..............*H12 33
Ahualulco de Mercado,
  Mex., 8,292..........m12 34
Ahvāz Iran,
  120,096...............B7 23
Ahvenanmaa (Åland),
  prov., Fin., 21,100......G8 11
Aibonito, P.R., 5,477....*G11 35
Aichi, pref., Jap.,
  4,798,653.............*I8 18
Aiea, Haw., 14,000..B4, G10 56
Aigun, China, 25,000.....A10 17
Aikawa, Jap., 5,800.......G9 18
Aiken, S.C., 11,243.......D4 82
Aiken, co., S.C.,81,038....D4 82
Aiken South, S.C., 2,980..*D4 82
Aiken West, S.C., 2,602..*D4 82
Aimorés, Braz., 11,448....B4 30
Ain, dept., Fr., 327,146...*D6 5
Ain-Sefra, Alg., 7,971....B4 22
Ainsworth, Nebr., 1,982...B6 71
Aire-sur-la-Lys, Fr.,
  5,528.................B5 5
Aisén, prov., Chile,
  37,803................D2 28
Aitkin, Minn., 1,829......D5 67
Aitkin, co., Minn.,
  12,162................D5 67
Aitolia kai Akarnania,
  prov., Grc., 237,738...*C3 14
Aitolikon, Grc., 3,459....*C3 24

Aiud, Rom., 11,886......B6 10
Aix-[en-Provence], Fr.,
  67,943..................F6 5
Aix-la-Chapelle, see
  Aachen, Ger.
Aix-les-Bains, Fr.,18,132...E6 5
Aiyina, Grc., 4,989......*D4 14
Aiyion, Grc., 17,762......*C4 14
Ajaccio, Fr., 41,006........D2 9
Ajax, Ont., Can., 7,755...D6 41
Ajigasawa, Jap., 8,100...F10 18
Ajmer, India, 231,240.....C5 20
Ajo, Ariz., 7,100..........C2 48
Akashi, Jap., 159,299......I7 18
Akcaabat, Tur., 4,414.....B12 14
Akershus, co., Nor.,
  266,400...............*H4 11
Aketi, Con. K., 12,100.....H2 23
Akhaia (Achaea), prov.,
  Grc., 239,206..........*C3 14
Akharnai, Grc., 11,290...*C4 14
Akhisar, Tur., 40,000.....C6 14
Akhtyrka, Sov. Un.,
  55,200................F10 12
Aki, Jap., 14,900..........J6 18
Akita, Jap., 216,607......G10 18
Akita, pref., Jap.,
  1,279,835.............*G1 18
Akkeshi, Jap., 16,000.....E12 18
Akola, India, 115,760......D6 20
Akron, Colo., 1,890........A7 51
Akron, Ind., 958..........B5 59
Akron, Iowa, 1,351........B1 60
Akron, N.Y., 2,841........B2 75
Akron, Ohio, 293,000
  (*620,000)............A4 78
Akron, Pa., 2,167.........F9 81
Aksaray, Tur., 20,000....C10 14
Aksehir, Tur., 20,600.....C8 14
Aksenovo-Zilovskoye,
  Sov. Un., 10,000....D14 13
Aktyubinsk, Sov. Un.,
  116,000...............D8 13
Akureyri, Ice., 8,957.....n23 11
Akyab, Bur., 42,329......D9 20
Alabama, state, U.S.,
  3,266,740.................. 46
Alabaster, Ala., 1,623....B3 46
Alachua, Fla., 1,974......C4 54
Alachua, co., Fla., 74,074..C4 54
Alagoa Grande, Braz.,
  12,115...............*D7 27
Alagôas, state, Braz.,
  1,271,062............*D7 27
Alagoinhas, Braz.,
  38,246...............*E7 27
Al 'Ajamiyin, Eg.,
  U.A.R., 2,000.........G7 14
Alajuela, C.R., 19,620....E8 34
Alajuela, C.R., 232,000...*E8 34
Al 'Alamayn (El Alamein),
  Eg., U.A.R...........G7 14
Alamance, co., N.C.,
  85,674...............B3 76
Alameda, Calif., 63,855...h8 50
Alameda, N. Mex.,
  3,500..............B5, D5 48
Alameda, co., Calif.,
  908,209...............D3 50
Alamo, Calif., 1,791.....*D3 50
Alamo, Tenn., 1,665......B2 83
Alamo, Tex., 4,121........F3 84
Alamogordo, N. Mex.,
  21,723................C6 48
Alamo Heights, Tex.,
  7,552..............E3, k7 84
Alamosa, Colo., 6,205....D5 51
Alamosa, co., Colo.,
  10,000................D5 51
Alanya, Tur., 10,100......D9 14
Alasehir, Tur., 13,900....C7 14
Al Ashkharah,
  Mus. & Om............G9 14
Alava, prov., Sp.,
  138,934...............*A4 8
Alaska, State, U.S.,
  226,167.................. 47
Alassio, It., 8,544........C2 9
Alatyr, Sov. Un., 34,700..D16 12
Alba, It., 12,000..........B2 9
Albacete, Sp., 61,635.....C5 8
Alba Iulia, Rom., 14,776..B6 10
Albania, country, Eur.,
  1,814,000.............B2 14
Albano Laziale, It.,
  15.300..............D4, H9
Albany, Ga., 55,890......E2 55
Albany, Ind., 2,132.......D7 59
Albany, Ky., 1,887.......D4 62
Albany, Minn., 1,375.....E4 67
Albany, Mo., 1,662.......A3 69
Albany, N.Y., 129,726....C7 75
Albany, Oreg.,
  12,926.............C3, k11 80
Albany, Tex., 2,174......C3 84
Albany, Wis., 892........F4 88
Albany, co., N.Y.,
  272,926...............C6 75

Albany, Co., Wyo.,21,290..E6 89
Albany, riv., Ont........o18 41
Albany South, Ga., 800...*E2 55
Albay, prov., Phil.,
  514,980..............*C6 19
Albemarle, N.C., 12,261...B2 76
Albemarle, co., Va.,
  30,969................C4 85
Albenga, It., 8,700.......B2 9
Alberni, B.C., Can.,
  4,916................E5 37
Albert, Fr., 10,247.......B5 5
Albert, co., N.B., Can.,
  12,485................D5 43
Albert, lake, Con. K.,
  Ug....................H4 23
Alberta, prov., Can.,
  1,331,944................ 38
Alberta, mtn., Alta.,
  Can...................C2 38
Albert Edward, mtn.,
  Austl................k12 25
Albert Lea, Minn.,
  18,454................G5 67
Albertson, N.Y.,
  12,200...............*G2 52
Albertville, Ala., 8,250....A3 46
Albertville, Con. K.,
  29,500................B5 24
Albertville, Fr., 12,159....E7 5
Albi, Fr., 38,709.........F5 5
Albia, Iowa, 4,582.......C5 60
Albion, Ill., 2,025.......E5 58
Albion, Ind., 1,325.......B7 59
Albion, Mich., 12,749....F6 66
Albion, Nebr., 1,982......C7 71
Albion, N.Y., 5,182......B2 75
Albion, R.I., 700.........B11 52
Ålborg, Den., 85,800......I3 11
Albuñol, Sp., 7,989......D4 8
Albuquerque, N. Mex.,
  244,000
  (*322,000)........B5, D5 48
Alburquerque, Sp., 9,756..C2 8
Alburtis, Pa., 1,086......F10 81
Albury, Austl., 25,212....G8 25
Alcalá [de Guadiara], Sp.,
  25,000................D3 8
Alaclá de Henares, Sp.,
  25,123.............B4, p18 8
Alcalá de los Gazules,
  Sp., 9,693............D3 8
Alcamo, It., 43,000......F4 9
Alcanar, Sp., 6,944......B6 8
Alcañiz, Sp., 10,035......B5 8
Alcaraz, Sp., 5,864......C4 8
Alcaudete, Sp., 18,442...D3 8
Alcázar de San Juan, Sp.,
  24,963................C4 8
Alcazarquivir, see Ksarel
  Kebir, Mor.
Alcira, Sp., 26,669.......C5 8
Alco, La., 40.............C2 63
Alcoa, Tenn.,
  6,395............D10, E11 83
Alcona, co., Mich., 6,352..D7 66
Alcorn, co., Miss., 25,282..A5 68
Alcoy, Sp., 51,096.......C5 8
Alcoy, Nevado, mtn.,
  Peru..................D2 31
Aldan, Pa., 4,324.......*G11 81
Aldan, Sov. Un.,
  121,000..............D15 13
Aldan, riv., Sov. Un....C16 13
Alden, Iowa, 838........B4 60
Alden, N.Y., 2,694......C2 75
Alden, Pa., 1,000.......D9 81
Aldershot, Eng., 32,900...E6 4
Alderson, W. Va., 1,225..D4 87
Alderwood Manor, Wash.,
  4,000.................B3 86
Aledo, Ill., 3,080........B3 58
Alegre, Braz., 7,487......C4 30
Alegrete, Braz., 33,735...D1 30
Aleksandriya, Sov. Un.,
  43,300................G9 12
Aleksandrov, Sov. Un.,
  30,600...............C12 12
Aleksandrovsk
  [-Sakhalinskiy],
  Sov. Un., 39,400......D17 13
Aleksandrow, Pol., 7,577...B5 7
Aleksinac, Yugo., 8,741...D5 10
Alençon, Fr., 25,584.....C4 5
Aleppo (Halab), Syr.,
  425,467..............D11 14
Alert Bay, B.C., Can.,
  825...................D4 37
Alès, Fr., 41,360.........E6 5
Alessandri, It., 96,100....B2 9
Ålesund, Nor., 19,200....F2 11
Alexander, co., Ill.,16,061..F4 58
Alexander, co., N.C.,
  15,625................B1 76
Alexander City, Ala.,
  13,140................C4 46
Alexander Mills, N.C.,
  947.............B1, f11 76

Alexandria, Ont., Can.,
  2,597................B10 41
Alexandria, Ind., 5,582...D6 59
Alexandria, Ky.,
  1,318..............A7, B5 62
Alexandria, La., 40,279....C3 63
Alexandria, Minn.,
  6,713.................E3 67
Alexandria, Rom., 19,294..D7 10
Alexandria
  (Al Iskandariyah), Eg.,
  U.A.R., 1,587,700.....G7 14
Alexandria Bay, N.Y.,
  1,583..............A5, f9 75
Alexandria
  (Independent City),
  Va., 91,023........B5, g12 85
Alexandria Southwest,
  La., 2,782............*C3 63
Alexandroupolis, Grc.,
  18,712................B5 14
Alexis, Ill., 878.........B3 58
Alfalfa, co., Okla., 8,445...A3 79
Al Farâfirah, Eg.,
  U.A.R., 749...........C3 23
Alfaro, Sp., 8,570........A5 8
Al Fayyûm (El Faiyûm),
  Eg., U.A.R., 117,800...H8 14
Alfenas, Braz., 16,051..C3, k9 30
Alfortville, Fr., 32,332....g10 5
Alfred, Ont., Can.,
  1,195................B10 41
Alfred, N.Y., 3,383.......C3 75
Algarve, prov., Port.,
  328,231...............D1 8
Algarve, reg., Port.,
  314,800..............*D2 8
Algeciras, Sp., 66,317....D3 8
Algemesí, Sp., 19,057....C5 8
Alger, Ohio, 1,068.......B2 78
Alger, co., Mich., 9,250...B4 66
Algeria, country, Afr.,
  10,670,000............C3 22
Alghero, It., 24,000......D2 9
Al Ghurdaqah, Eg.,
  U.A.R., 2,727.........C4 23
Algiers (Alger), Alg.,
  883,879 (*995,000)....A5 22
Algoma, dist., Ont., Can...A2 41
Algoma, Wis., 3,855......D6 88
Algona, Iowa, 5,977......A3 60
Algona, Wash., 1,311..B3, f11 86
Algonac, Mich., 3,190....F8 66
Algonquin, Ill., 2,692..A5, h8 58
Alhama, Sp., 9,849.......D5 8
Alhambra, Calif.,
  54,807...............m12 50
Alhaurín el Grande, Sp.,
  11,525................D3 8
Al Hudaydah, Yemen,
  40,000................F6 23
Al Hufûf (Hofuf), Sau. Ar.,
  85,000................D4 15
Alicante, Sp., 121,527....C5 8
Alice, Tex., 20,861......F3 84
Alice Southwest, Tex.,
  1,813................*F3 84
Aliceville, Ala., 65.......D8 61
Aligarh, India, 185,020...C6 20
Alingsås, Swe., 17,500.....I5 11
Aliquippa, Pa.,
  26,369.............E1, h13 81
Al Isma 'Iliyah,
  Eg., U.A.R., 156,300...G9 14
Alistrati, Grc., 3,536.....B4 14
Aliwal North, S. Afr.,
  10,762................G5 24
Al Jawf (Jauf), Sau. Ar.,
  20,000................D2 15
Al Jizah (El Gizeh)
  (El Gîza), Eg.,
  U.A.R., 276,200.......H8 14
Aljustrel, Port., 5,844....D1 8
Al Kadhimain, Iraq,
  126,443...............C3 15
Al Karak, Jordan,
  5,539..............C3, h5 15
Al Khalîl (Hebron),
  Jordan, 37,868.....C3, h5 15
Al Khârijah, Eg., U.A.R.,
  11,155................C4 23
Allahabad, India, 411,955
  (*430,730)............C7 20
Allamakee, co., Iowa,
  15,982................A6 60
Allamuchy, mtn., N.J.....B3 74
Allanmyo, Bur., 15,580....E10 20
Allariz, Sp., 9,403.......A2 8
Allaykha, Sov. Un., 800..B17 13
Allegany, N.Y., 2,064.....C2 75

Allegany, co., Md.,
  84,169................A1 53
Allegany, co., N.Y.,
  43,978................C2 75
Allegany, co., N.C., 7,734..A1 76
Alleghany, co., Pa.,
  1,628,587.............E1 81
Allegany, co., Va., 12,128..C3 85
Allegheny, mts., U.S.....C10 45
Allen, Okla., 1,005.......C5 79
Allen, co., Ind., 232,196...B7 59
Allen, co., Kans., 16,369..E8 61
Allen, co., Ky., 12,269....D3 62
Allen, co., Ohio, 103,691..B1 78
Allen, par., La., 19,867...D3 63
Allendale, N.J., 4,092....A4 74
Allendale, S.C., 3,114....E5 82
Allendale, co., S.C.,
  11,362................F5 82
Allen Park, Mich.,
  37,494...............p15 66
Allenport, Pa., 981.......F1 81
Allenstein, see Olsztyn,
  Pol.
Allentown, N.J., 1,393....C3 74
Allentown, Pa., 105,000
  (*308,000)...........E11 81
Alleppey, India, 138,834...G6 20
Aller (Cabañaquinta),
  Sp., 828..............A3 8
Alliance, Nebr., 7,845....B3 71
Alliance, Ohio, 28,362....B4 78
Allier, dept., Fr., 380,221 D5 5
Allinge, Den., 2,114......A3 7
Allison, Iowa, 952.......B5 60
Allison, Pa., 1,285.......G2 81
Allison Park, Pa., 6,000...h14 81
Alliston, Ont., Can.,
  2,884................C5 41
Al Lith, Sau. Ar., 10,000..D6 23
Alloa, Scot., 14,900......B5 4
Allouez, Wis., 9,557......h9 88
Al Luhayyah, Yemen,
  5,000.................F3 15
Alma, Ark., 1,370........B1 49
Alma, Ga., 3,515.........E4 55
Alma, Kans., 838.........C7 61
Alma, Mich., 8,978.......E6 66
Alma, Nebr., 1,342.......D6 71
Alma, Wis., 1,008........D2 88
Alma-Ata, Sov. Un.,
  617,000..............E10 13
Almada, Port., 11,995....f9 8
Almadén, Sp., 13,443....C3 8
Al Madînah (Medina),
  Sau. Ar., 60,000......E2 15
Almagro, Sp., 9,681.....C4 8
Al Mahallah al Kubrá, Eg.,
  U.A.R., 198,900.......G8 14
Almansa, Sp., 15,391.....C5 8
Al Mansûrah, Eg., U.A.R.,
  172,000...............G8 14
Al Marj (Barce), Libya,
  10,600................B2 23
Almeirim, Port., 7,104....C1 8
Almelo, Neth., 54,600.....A7 5
Almendralejo, Sp.,
  21,884................C2 8
Almería Sp., 86,808......D4 8
Al Minyâ, Eg., U.A.R.,
  104,800...............C4 23
Almiros, Grc., 6,010......C4 14
Almodóvar, Sp., 14,633...C3 8
Almogía, Sp., 8,341......D3 8
Almon, Ga., 300.........C3 55
Almonesson, N.J., 2,000...D2 74
Almont, Mich., 1,279.....F7 66
Almonte, Ont., Can.,
  3,267................*B8 41
Almora, Minn., 100.....*D3 67
Almoradí, Sp., 3,998.....C5 8
Al Mukallá, S. Yem.,
  25,000...............G4 15
Al Mukhâ, Yemen, 5,000..G3 15
Almuñécar, Sp., 6,235....D4 8
Alnwick, Eng., 7,600.....C6 4
Aloha, Oreg., 4,000......h12 80
Álora, Sp., 5,960........D3 8
Alor Star, Mala., 52,915...D2 19
Alorton (Fireworks), Ill.,
  3,282................*E3 58
Alosno, Sp., 5,814.......D2 8
Alpaugh, Calif., 800......E4 50
Alpena, Mich., 14,682....C7 66
Alpena, co., Mich., 28,556..C7 66
Alpes-Maritimes, dept.,
  Fr., 618,265..........*F7 5
Alpha, N.J., 2,406.......B2 74
Alpharetta, Ga., 1,349....B2 55
Alpiarça, Port., 6,680....C1 8
Alpine, Calif., 1,044.....*F5 50
Alpine, N.J., 921........h9 74
Alpine, Tex., 4,740......o13 84
Alpine, co., Calif., 397...C4 50
Alpoca, W. Va., 400.....D3 87
Al Qâhirah, see Cairo,
  Eg., U.A.R.

Al Qanṭarah, Eg., U.A.R., 2,000.........G9 14
Al Qaṭīf, Sau. Ar., 30,000.........D4 15
Al Quanayṭirah, Syr., 17,080.........F10 14
Alsfeld, Ger., 10,300.....C4 6
Alsip, Ill., 3,770.........B6 58
Alta, Iowa, 1,605.......B2 6
Altadena, Calif., 42,800.........m12 50
Alta Gracia, Arg., 19,366....A4 28
Al Tahoe, Calif., 1,500....C4 50
Alta Loma, Tex., 1,020...r14 84
Altamont, Ill., 1,656.....D5 58
Altamont, N.Y., 1,365.....C6 75
Altamont, Oreg., 11,500...E5 80
Altamonte Springs, Fla., 1,212.........*D5 54
Altamura, It., 43,700......D6 9
Altavista, Va., 3,229......C3 85
Altdorf, Switz., 7,477....E4 6
Alto, Tex., 869........D5 84
Alto Alentejo, prov., Port., 400,374........*C2 8
Alton, Ill., 43,047.......E3 58
Alton, Iowa, 1,048.......B1 60
Altona, Man., Can., 2,026.........E3 40
Altoona, Ala., 744.......A3 46
Altoona, Iowa, 1,424.....C4 6
Altoona, Pa., 66,000 (*108,000).........F5 81
Altoona, Wis., 2,114.....D2 88
Alto Paraná, dept., Par., 26,700.........D4 29
Alturas, Calif., 2,819.....B3 50
Altus, Okla., 21,225......C2 79
Alula, Som., 1,300.......F8 23
Alva, Ky., 700.........D6 62
Alva, Okla., 6,258.......A3 79
Alvarado, Tex., 1,907..C4, n9 84
Alvin, Tex., 5,643.....E5, r14 84
Alviso, Calif., 1,174......*D3 50
Älvsborg, co., Swe., 375,000.........*H5 11
Alwar, India, 72,707.....C6 20
Al Wāsiṭah, Eg., U.A.R., 4,000.........H8 14
Alx, mtn., Wash.........C4 86
Alytus, Sov. Un., 9,084....A8 7
Amador, co., Calif., 9,990..C3 50
Amagansett, N.Y., 1,300..n16 75
Amagasaki, Jap., 500,990..o14 18
Amål, Swe., 9,200.......H5 11
Amalias, Grc., 15,468.....D3 14
Amambay, dept., Par., 33,800.........D4 29
Amantea, It., 5,822......E6 9
Amapá, Braz., 1,591.....C5 27
Amarillo, Tex., 159,000 (*165,000).........B2 84
Amarousion, Grc., 20,135..C4 14
Amasya (Amasia), Tur., 28,200.........B10 14
Amazonas, comisaría, Col., 12,962.........D3 32
Amazonas, dept., Peru, 129,003.........B2 31
Amazonas, state, Braz., 721,215.........C3 31
Amazonas, (Amazon), riv., Braz., Peru.........D5 27
Amazon, see Amazonas, riv., Braz., Peru
Ambala, India, 76,204.....B6 20
Ambarchik, Sov. Un., 800.........C19 13
Ambato, Ec., 53,372......B2 31
Amberg, Ger., 42,100.....D5 6
Ambérieu [-en-Bugey], Fr., 7,748.........E6 5
Amberley, Ohio, 2,951...*C1 78
Ambikapur, India, 15,240.........D7 20
Ambler, Pa., 6,765...F11, o21 81
Amboina, Indon., 55,263..F7 19
Amboise, Fr., 7,953......C4 5
Amboy, Ill., 2,067.......B4 58
Ambridge, Pa., 13,865.........E1, h13 81
Ambridge Heights, Pa., 5,106.........*E1 81
Amderma, Sov. Un., 10,000.........C9 13
Ameca, Mex., 17,588.........C4, m11 34
Amecameca [de Juárez], Mex., 12,291.........n14 34
Amelia, La., 950.....E4, k9 63
Amelia, Ohio, 913.......C1 78
Amelia, co., Va., 7,815....C4 85
Amelia Court House, Va., 800.........C5 85
Amenia, N. Dak., 117.....D8 77
Amenia, N.Y., 900.......D7 75

American Falls, Idaho, 2,602.........G6 57
American Fork, Utah, 6,373.........A6, D2 72
American Samoa, U.S. dep., Oceania, 21,000..*G9 2
Americus, Ga., 13,472.....D2 55
Amersfoort, Neth., 72,600..A6 5
Amery, Wis., 1,769......C1 88
Ames, Iowa, 34,826......B4 60
Amesbury, Mass., 10,787..A6 65
Amfissa, Grc., 6,076......C4 14
Amga, Sov. Un., 800.....C16 13
Amherst, N.S., Can., 10,788.........D5 43
Amherst, Mass., 14,500...B2 65
Amherst (Eggertsville), N.Y., 52,000.........*C2 75
Amherst, Ohio, 6,750.....A3 78
Amherst, Tex., 883.......B1 84
Amherst, Va., 1,200......C3 85
Amherst, co., Va., 22,953..C3 85
Amherstburg, Ont., Can., 4,452.........E1 41
Amherstdale, W. Va., 900.........D3, D5 87
Amiens, Fr., 105,433......C5 5
Amite, La., 3,316.......D5 63
Amite, co., Miss., 15,573..D3 68
Amityville, N.Y., 8,890.........E7, n15 75
'Ammān, Jordan., 224,974.........C3, h5 15
Ammon, Idaho, 1,882.....F7 57
Amory, Miss., 6,474......B5 68
Amos, Que., Can., 6,080..o20 41
Amoy (Hsiamen), China, 224,300.........G8 17
Amparo, Braz., 14,382.........C3, m8 30
Amqui, Que., Can., 3,659.........*k13 42
'Amrān, Yemen, 20,000....F3 15
Amraoti, India, 137,875...D6 20
Amritsar, India, 376,295...B5 20
Amsterdam, Neth., 868,400.........A6 5
Amsterdam, N.Y., 28,772..C6 75
Amsterdam, Ohio, 931.....B5 78
Amstetten, Aus., 12,086...D7 6
Amu Darya, riv. Sov. Un.........F9 13
Amur, riv., China, Sov. Un...D15, E16 13
'Ana, Iraq, 5,860.........C3 15
Anaconda, Mont., 12,054..D4 70
Anacortes, Wash., 8,414...A3 86
Anadarko, Okla., 6,299....B3 79
Anadyr, Sov. Un., 5,000..C20 13
Anaheim, Calif., 104,184.........F5, n13 50
Anahuac, Tex., 1,985..E5, r15 84
Anakapalle, India, 46,402..E7 20
Analalava, Malag., 1,900..C9 24
Anamosa, Iowa, 4,616.....B6 60
Anandale, La., 2,827......*C3 63
Anantapur, India, 52,280..F6 20
Anantnag, India, 21,087...B6 20
Ananyev, Sov. Un., 5,000..H7 12
Anápolis, Braz., 48,847....B3 30
Añatuya, Arg., 9,310......E3 29
Anawalt, W. Va., 1,062...D3 87
Ancash, dept., Peru, 605,548.........C2 31
Anchorage, Alsk., 51,000 (*104,000)....C10, g17 47
Anchorage, Ky., 1,170.....A4 62
Anchor Bay Gardens, Mich., 1,830.........*F8 66
Ancienne Lorette, Que., Can., 3,961.....C6, n17 42
Ancon, C.Z., 1,151.......B2 32
Ancona, It., 103,300......C4 9
Andalusia, Ill., 10,263....D3 46
Andalusia, reg., Sp., 5,893,396.........D3 8
Anderlecht, Bel., 94,677...B6 5
Andernach, Ger., 20,800...C3 6
Anderson, Calif., 4,492....B2 50
Anderson, Ind., 49,061....D6 59
Anderson, Mo., 992......E3 69
Anderson, S.C., 41,316....B2 82
Anderson, co., Kans., 9,035.........D8 61
Anderson, co., Ky., 8,618..C4 62
Anderson, co., S.C., 98,478.........B2 82
Anderson, co,. Tenn., 60,032.........C9 83
Anderson, co., Tex., 28,162.........D5 84
Anderson, mtn., Wash.....B2 86
Anderson East Side, Ind., 3,378.........*D6 59
Andes, Col., 11,135......B2 32
Andhra Pradesh, India, 35,983,447.........E6 20

Andizhan, Sov. Un., 150,000.........E10 13
Andkhui, Afg., 18,438.....A4 20
Andong, Kor., 52,200.....H4 18
Andorra, And., 600......A6 8
Andorra, country, Eur., 12,000.........A6 8
Andover, Mass., 10,800 (17,134▲).........A5 65
Andover, N.B., Can., 848..C2 43
Andover, N.Y., 1,247.....C3 75
Andover, Ohio, 1,116.....A5 78
Andraitx, Sp., 5,077......C7 68
Andrew, co., Mo., 11,062..B3 69
Andrew Jackson, mtn., Ant.........K16 2
Andrews, Ind., 1,132.....C6 59
Andrews, N.C., 1,404.....f9 76
Andrews, S.C., 2,995.....E8 82
Andrews, Tex., 11,135....C1 84
Andrews, co., Tex., 13,450.........C1 84
Andreyevka, Sov. Un., 10,000.........G11 12
Andria, It., 72,400.......D6 9
Androscoggin, co., Maine, 86,312.........D2 64
Andros, Isl., Ba. Is.......B4 35
Andrychow, Pol., 5,055...h10 7
Andújar, Sp., 26,100.....C3 8
Aneto, mtn., Sp.........A6 8
Angara, riv., Sov. Un....D13 13
Angelholm, Swe., 12,600..I5 11
Angelica, N.Y., 898......C2 75
Angelina, co., Tex., 39,814.........D5 84
Angels Camp, Calif., 1,489.........C3 50
Angermunde, Ger., 11,700.........B7 6
Angers, Fr., 115,252.....D3 5
Angier, N.C., 1,344......B4 76
Anglesey, is., Wales......D4 4
Anglet, Fr., 16,150......F3 5
Angleton, Tex., 7,312.........E5, r14 84
Ango, Con. K.........H3 23
Angol, Chile, 18,600.....B2 28
Angola, Ind., 5,234......A8 59
Angola, N.Y., 2,550......C1 75
Angola, Port. dep., Afr., 4,832,677.........C3 24
Angoulême, Fr., 48,190...E4 5
Angra do Heroísmo, Port., 10,296.........k10 22
Angra dos Reis, Braz., 10,634.........C4, h5 30
Angus, co., Scot., 279,700.........*B5 4
Angwin, Calif., 1,400.....*C2 50
Anhwei, prov., China, 33,560,000.........E8 17
Anina, Rom., 11,837.....C5 10
Anita, Iowa, 1,233......C3 60
Anita, Pa., 550.........D4 81
Aniva (Rutaka), Sov. Un., 10,000.........C11 18
Anjo, Jap., 66,088......o16 18
Anjou, former prov. Fr., 631,000.........D3 5
Anju, Kor., 21,861......G2 18
Ankang, China,.........E6 17
Ankara, Tur., 650,067....C9 14
Ankeny, Iowa, 2,964..C4, e8 60
Anklam, Ger., 19,400.....B6 6
Ankuang, China, 5,000...D1 18
Anmoore, W. Va., 1,050..B7 87
Annaba (Bône), Alg., 137,716.........A6 22
An Najaf, Iraq, 74,089....C3 15
Annalee Heights, Va., 2,000.........*B5 85
Annam, reg., Viet., 8,000,000.........*B3 19
Annandale, Minn., 984....E4 67
Annandale, Va., 21,000...g12 85
Annapolis, Md., 23,385...C5 53
Annapolis Royal, N.S., Can., 800.........E4 43
Annapurna 1, peak, Nep.........C7 20
Ann Arbor, Mich., 67,340.........F7, p14 66
An Nasiriya, Iraq, 25,515..C4 15
Anne Arundel, co., Md., 206,634.........B4 53
Annecy, Fr., 43,255......E7 5
Annemasse, Fr., 13,814...D7 5
Anniston, Ala., 33,657....B4 46
Annonay, Fr., 18,434.....E6 5
Annville, Pa., 4,264......F8 81
Anoka, Minn., 11,529.........E5, m12 67
Anoka, co., Minn., 85,916.........E5 67
Anona, Fla., 900.........p10 54
Ansbach, Ger., 32,900....D5 6
Anserma, Col., 14,129....B2 32

Anshan, China, 805,000...C9 17
Anson, Maine, 870 (2,252▲).........D3 64
Anson, Tex., 2,890......C3 84
Anson, co., N.C., 24,962..B2 76
Ansŏng, Kor., 15,800.....H3 18
Ansonia, Conn., 19,819...D4 52
Ansonia, Ohio, 1,002.....B1 78
Ansted, W. Va., 1,511.........C3, D7 87
Anta, China, 5,000......C2 18
Anta, Peru, 1,542.......D3 31
Antakya (Antioch), Tur., 45,674.........D11 14
Antalaha, Malag., 12,100.........C10 24
Antalya (Adalia), Tur., 50,908.........D8 14
Antarctic, pen., Ant.,....K16 2
Antartica, cont.,.........5 71
Antelope, co., Nebr., 10,176.........B7 71
Antequera, Sp., 28,400...D3 8
Anthon, Iowa, 681.......B2 60
Anthony, Kans., 2,744....E5 61
Anthony, N. Mex., 1,000..D5 48
Anthony, R. I., 3,000....C10 52
Anthony Wayne Village, Ind., 3,000.........*B7 59
Antibes, Fr., 35,439......F7 5
Antigo, Wis., 9,691......C4 88
Antigonish, N.S., Can., 4,344.........D8 43
Antigonish, co., N.S., Can., 14,360.........D8 43
Antigua, Br. dep., N.A., 54,304.........H14 35
Antigua Guatemala, Guat., 10,996.........E6 34
Antilla, Cuba, 7,500.....D6 35
Antioch, Calif., 17,305....h9 50
Antioch, Ill., 2,778...A5, h8 58
Antioch, see Antakya, Tur.
Antioquia, Col., 3,998....B2 32
Antioquia, dept., Col., 2,477,299.........B2 32
Antique, prov., Phil., 238,405.........*C6 19
Antlers, Okla., 2,085.....C6 79
Antofagasta, Chile, 87,900.........D1 29
Antofagasta, prov., Chile, 215,376.........D1 29
Anton, Tex., 1,068......C1 84
Antonina, Braz., 8,520....D3 30
António Enes, Moz., 11,628.........D7 24
Antonito, Colo., 1,045....D5 51
Antony, Fr., 46,483......g10 5
Antratsit, Sov. Un., 60,000.........g22 12
Antrim, co., Mich., 10,373.........C5 66
Antrim, co., N. Ire., 283,400.........*C3 4
Antsirabe, Malag., 23,129.........D9 24
Antung, China, 360,000.........C9 17
Antwerp, N.Y., 881...A5, f9 75
Antwerp, Ohio, 1,465....A1 78
Antwerpen, prov., Bel., 1,443,355.........*B6 5
Antwerpen (Antwerp) (Anvers), Bel., 253,295..B6 5
Antwerp, see Antwerpen, Bel.
Anuradhapura, Cey., 18,390.........G7 20
Anvers, see Antwerpen, Bel.
Anyang, China, 124,900...D7 17
Anzhero-Sudzhensk, Sov. Un., 120,000....D11 13
Anzio, It., 14,300....D4, k7 9
Anzoátegui, state., Ven., 382,002.........B5 32
Aomori, Jap., 224,433...*F10 18
Aomori, pref., Jap., 1,416,591.........F10 18
Aosta, It., 32,500.......B1 9
Apache, Okla., 1,455.....C3 79
Apache, co., Ariz., 30,438..B4 48
Apache, mts., Tex.......o12 84
Apache Junction, Ariz., 3,000.........D2 48
Apalachicola, Fla., 3,099..C2 54
Apalachin, N.Y., 900.....C4 75
Apam, Mex., 8,640.......n14 34
Aparri, Phil., 14,315.....B6 19
Apatin, Yugo., 17,203....C4 10
Apeldoorn, Neth., 110,000.........A6 5
Apex, N.C., 1,573......B4 76
Apia, W. Sam., 21,699....G9 2
Apizaco, Mex., 15,705...n14 34
Aplao, Peru, 840.......E3 31
Aplington, Iowa, 840.....B5 60
Apo, vol., Phil.........D7 19

Apolda, Ger., 29,300......C5   6
Apollo, Pa., 2,694.........E2   8
Apopka, Fla., 3,578.......D5   54
Appalachia, Va., 2,456....f9   85
Appalachian, mts., U.S...F12   33
Appanoose, co., Iowa,
  16,015................D5   60
Appenzell, canton, Switz.,
  63,800................*B7   6
Apple Orchard, mtn., Va..C3   85
Appleton, Minn., 2,172....E2   67
Appleton, Wis., 54,000
  (*142,000).........D5, h9   88
Appleton City, Mo.,
  1,075.................C3   69
Appleyard, Wash., 950....B5   86
Appling, co., Ga., 13,246...E4   55
Appomattox, Va., 1,184....C4   85
Appomattox, co., Va.,
  9,148.................C4   85
Aprelsk, Sov. Un., 800...D14   13
Apt, Fr., 5,521............F6   5
Apulia, reg., It...........D6   9
Apure, riv., Ven..........B4   32
Apurímac, riv., Peru......D3   31
Aquidauana, Braz.,
  11,997................C1   30
Arab, Ala., 2,989.........A3   46
Arabi, La., 12,000.......k11   63
Arabia, see Saudi Arabia,
  Asia
Aracaju, Braz., 112,516....E7   27
Aracati, Braz., 11,016.....D7   27
Araçatuba, Braz., 53,563...C2   30
Arad, Rom., 113,500.....B5   10
Aragon, Ga., 1,023........B1   55
Aragua, state, Ven.,
  313,274...............A4   32
Araguaia, riv., Braz.......D6   27
Araguari, Braz., 35,520...*E5   27
Arai, Jap., 14,019.......o16   18
Arāk (Sultanabad), Iran,
  58,998................B7   23
Aral, sea, Sov. Un........E8   13
Aranda de Duero, Sp.,
  13,454................B4   8
Arandas, Mex., 17,071...m12   34
Aranjuez, Sp., 27,251.....B4   8
Aransas, co., Tex., 7,006...E4   84
Aransas Pass, Tex., 6,956..F4   84
Aranyaprathet, Thai.,
  11,078................C2   19
Arapahoe, Nebr., 1,084...D6   71
Arapkir, Tur., 6,900.....C12   14
Arapohoe, co., Colo.,
  113,426...............B6   51
Araraquara, Braz.,
  58,076.............C3, k7   30
Araras, Braz., 23,898..C3, m8   30
Ararat, Ala., 30..........D1   46
Ararat, Austl., 8,237..G7, n14   25
Ararat, mtn., Tur.........C1   14
Arauca, Col., 4,280.......B3   32
Arauca, intendencia, Col.,
  24,148................B3   32
Arauco, prov., Chile
  89,554................B2   28
Araxá, Braz., 24,041......B3   30
Arboga, Swe., 11,100.....t33   11
Arbor, N.J., 2,800.......*B4   74
Arborg, Man., Can., 811...D3   40
Arbor Terrace, Mo.,
  1,225................*C7   69
Arbroath, Scot., 19,700...B5   4
Arbuckle, Calif., 950.....C2   50
Arcachon, Fr., 14,862.....E3   5
Arcade, N.Y., 1,930......C2   75
Arcadia, Calif., 41,005...m12   50
Arcadia, Fla., 5,889......E5   54
Arcadia, Ind., 1,271......D5   59
Arcadia, La., 2,547.......B3   63
Arcadia, S.C., 2,000......B3   82
Arcadia, Wis., 2,084......D2   88
Arcanum, Ohio, 1,678.....C1   78
Arcata, Calif., 5,235......B1   50
Archangel, see
  Arkhangelsk, Sov. Un.
Archbald, Pa., 5,471.....m18   81
Archbold, Ohio, 2,348....A1   78
Archdale, N.C., 1,520....B3   76
Archer, co., Tex., 6,110...C3   84
Archer City, Tex., 1,974...C3   84
Archidona, Sp. 7,962.....D3   8
Archuleta, co., Colo.,
  2,629.................D3   51
Arcila, Mor., 10,839......E2   8
Arco, Ga., 5,417..........E5   55
Arco, Idaho, 1,562........F5   57
Arcola, Ill., 2,273........D5   58
Arcoverde, Braz., 18,008..*D6   27
Arctic, ocean............A6   2
Arcueil, Fr., 20,224......g10   5
Ardabil (Ardebil), Iran,
  65,742................B4   15
Ardatov, Sov. Un., 5,000.D16   12
Ardèche, dept., Fr.,
  248,516...............*E6   5

Arden (Ardentown), Del.,
  1,500.................A7   53
Arden Hills, Minn.,
  3,930................*E7   67
Ardennes, dept., Fr.,
  300,247..............*C6   5
Ardmore, Okla., 20,184....C4   79
Ardmore, Pa., 16,500.....g20   81
Ardrossan, Scot., 9,700...C4   4
Ardsley, N.Y., 4,486.....g13   75
Arecibo, P.R., 28,826....g11   35
Areia Branca, Braz.,
  8,904................*D7   27
Arenac, co., Mich., 9,860..D7   66
Arendal, Nor., 11,300.....H3   11
Arequipa, Peru, 156,700...E3   31
Arequipa, dept., Peru,
  407,163...............E3   31
Arezzo, It., 40,800.......C3   9
Argenta, Ill., 860........D5   58
Argenta, It., 4,600.......B3   8
Aggentan, Fr., 12,757.....C4   5
Argenteuil, Fr.,
  82,321.............C5, g10   5
Argenteuil, co., Que.,
  Can., 31,830..........D3   42
Argentina, country, S.A.,
  22,691,000............G4   27
Argenton-sur-Creuse, Fr.,
  6,344.................D4   5
Argolis, prov., Grc.,
  90,145...............*D4   14
Argos, Grc., 16,712......D4   14
Argos, Ind., 1,339........B5   59
Argostolion, Grc., 7,322...C3   14
Argyll, co., Scot., 60,400..*B4   4
Århus, Den., 119,568......I4   11
Århus, co., Den., 221,895..*I4   11
Ariail, S.C., 950.........B2   82
Ariano Irpino, It., 11,300..D5   9
Arica, Chile, 43,300......C1   29
Ariège, dept., Fr.,
  137,192..............*F4   5
Arīhā (Jericho), Jordan,
  10,166................C3   15
Ario de Rosales, Mex.,
  9,261............D4, n13   34
Aripo, El Cerro del, mtn.,
  Trin.................K14   35
Arizona, state, U.S.,
  1,302,161..............   48
Arjay, Ky., 500..........D6   62
Arjona, Col., 16,510......A2   32
Arjona, Sp., 8,154........D3   8
Arkadelphia, Ark., 8,069...C2   49
Arkadhia (Arcadia), prov.,
  Grc., 135,042.........*D4   14
Arkansas, state, U.S.,
  1,786,272..............   49
Arkansas, co., Ark.,
  23,355................C4   49
Arkansas, riv., U.S.......C8   45
Arkansas City, Ark., 783..D4   49
Arkansas City, Kans.,
  14,262................E6   61
Arkhangelsk (Archangel),
  Sov. Un., 303,000......C7   13
Arkoma, Okla., 1,862.....B7   79
Arkonam, India, 30,658...F6   20
Arkport, N.Y., 837........C3   75
Arkwright, R.I., 1,500....C10   52
Arkwright, S.C., 1,656...*B4   82
Arles, Fr., 29,362........F6   5
Arlington, Fla.,
  24,000.............B5, m8   54
Arlington, Ga., 1,462.....F2   55
Arlington, Mass.,
  49,953.............B5, g11   65
Arlington, Minn., 1,601...F4   67
Arlington, N.Y., 8,400...*D7   75
Arlington, Ohio 955......B2   78
Arlington, S.C., 800......B3   82
Arlington, S. Dak., 996...F8   77
Arlington, Tex., 44,775...n9   84
Arlington, Vt., 700.......E1   73
Arlington, Va.,
  163,401............B5, g12   85
Arlington, Wash., 2,025...A3   86
Arlington, co., Va.,
  163,401............B5, g12   85
Arlington Heights, Ill.,
  40,622.............A5, a9   58
Arlington Heights, Ohio,
  1,355................*C1   78
Arlon, Bel., 13,272.......C6   5
Arma, Kans., 1,296.......E9   61
Armada, Mich., 1,111.....F8   66
Armagh, N. Ire., 10,062...C3   4
Armagh, Que., Can., 914..C7   42
Armagh, co., N. Ire.,
  118,600..............*C3   4
Armavir, Sov. Un.,
  123,000...............I13   12
Armenia, Col., 137,222....C2   32
Armenia (S.S.R.), rep.,
  Sov. Un., 2,134,000.....A4   15
Armentières, Fr., 25,248..B5   5
Armero, Col., 17,495......C3   32

Armidale, Austl., 14,990...F9   25
Armijo, N. Mex., 9,000....E5   48
Armona, Calif., 1,302.....*D4   50
Armonk, N.Y., 1,100.....*D7   75
Armour, S. Dak., 875.....G7   77
Armstrong, B.C., Can.,
  1,288.................D8   37
Armstrong, Iowa, 1,070...A3   60
Armstrong, co., Pa.,
  79,524................E3   81
Armstrong, co., Tex.,
  1,966.................B2   84
Arnaudville, La., 1,184...D4   63
Arnedo, Sp., 7,958........A4   8
Arnhem, Neth., 129,100...B6   5
Arnissa, Grc., 2,915......E5   10
Arnold, Mo., 550.........C7   69
Arnold, Nebr., 844.......C5   71
Arnold, Pa., 9,437.......h14   81
Arnolds Park, Iowa, 953...A2   60
Arnouville [-les-Gonesse],
  Fr., 10,227...........g10   5
Arnprior, Ont., Can.,
  5,474.................B8   41
Arnsberg, Ger., 21,300.....C4   6
Arnstadt, Ger., 26,400....C5   6
Aroostook, co., Maine,
  106,064...............B4   64
Arp, Tex., 812...........C5   84
Arrah, India, 76,766......C7   20
Ar Ramādī, Iraq, 67,395..F14   14
Ar Raqqah, Syr., 14,554..E12   14
Arras, Fr., 41,761........B5   5
Arrecife, Sp., 12,886....m15   8
Arrecifes, Arg., 7,635....g6   28
Arroyo, P.R., 3,741.....*G11   35
Arroyo Grande, Calif.,
  6,862.................E3   50
Arsenal, Ark., 950......*C3   49
Arta, Grc., 16,899........C3   14
Arta, prov., Grc., 82,630..*C3   14
Artem, Sov. Un., 61,000..E16   13
Artemisa, Cuba, 20,100...C2   35
Artemovsk, Sov. Un.,
  66,000............G12, o21   12
Artena, It., 7,707........h9   9
Arter, mtn., Wyo.........D4   89
Artesia, Calif., 9,993....*F4   50
Artesia, N. Mex., 12,000...C6   48
Arthabaska, Que.,
  Can., 2,977...........C6   42
Arthabaska, co., Que., Can.,
  2,977.................C5   42
Arthabaska, co., Que.,
  Can., 2,977...........C5   42
Arthur, Ill., 2,120.......D5   58
Arthur, co., Nebr., 680...C4   71
Artigas, Ur., 23,429......E1   30
Artigas, dept., Ur.,
  52,100...............*E1   30
Artois, former prov., Fr.,
  1,010,000.............B5   5
Arundel Village, Md.,
  1,600................*B4   53
Arusha, Tan., 10,038......I5   23
Arvada, Colo., 19,242....B5   51
Arvida, Que., Can.,
  14,460................A6   42
Arvidsjaur, Swe., 2,900...E8   11
Arvika, Swe., 15,800......H5   11
Arvin, Calif., 5,440......E4   50
Arzamas, Sov. Un.,
  39,000...............D14   12
Arzúa, Sp., 1,368.........A1   8
Ås, Czech., 9,600........C2   7
Asahi-Dake, mtn., Jap....E11   18
Asahikawa, Jap.,
  245,246..............E11   18
Asan, Guam, 543........*F6   2
Asansol, India, 103,405...D8   20
Asbest, Sov. Un., 65,000...D9   13
Asbestos, Que., Can.,
  11,083................D6   42
Asbury Park, N.J., 17,366..C4   74
Ascension, par., La.,
  27,927................D5   63
Ascension Isl., Br. dep.,
  Atl. O., 400.........G20   2
Aschaffenburg, Ger.,
  55,600................D4   6
Aschersleben, Ger.,
  34,400................C5   6
Ascoli Piceno, It., 40,300...C4   9
Asenovgrad, Bul., 20,920...E7   10
Ashaway, R.I., 1,298......D9   52
Ashburn, Ga., 3,291......E3   55
Ashburnham, Mass.,
  900 (3,042 ▲).........A4   65
Ashburton, N.Z., 12,672..O13   26
Ashby, Ala., 65..........D2   46
Ashcroft, B.C., Can., 886..D7   37
Ashdown, Ark., 2,725.....D1   49
Ashe, co., N.C., 19,768....A1   76
Asheboro, N.C., 9,449....B3   76
Asheboro South, N.C.,
  1,515................*B3   76
Asheboro West, N.C.,
  1,228................*B3   76

Asherton, Tex., 1,890.....E3   84
Asheville, N.C., 60,192...f10   76
Ashford, Ala., 1,511......D4   46
Ash Grove, Mo., 886......D4   69
Ashikaga, Jap.,
  150,259...........H9, m18   18
Ashio, Jap., 14,470.......H9   18
Ashkhabad, Sov. Un.,
  224,000...............F8   13
Ashland, Ala., 1,610......B4   46
Ashland, Ill., 1,064......D3   58
Ashland, Kans., 1,312.....E4   61
Ashland, Ky., 31,283......B7   62
Ashland, Maine, 800
  (1,980 ▲).............B4   64
Ashland, Mass., 7,779....g10   65
Ashland, Nebr.,
  1,989.............C9, g12   71
Ashland, N.H., 1,237......D4   73
Ashland, Ohio, 17,419.....B3   78
Ashland, Oreg., 9,119.....E4   80
Ashland, Pa., 5,237.......E9   81
Ashland, Va., 2,773.......C5   85
Ashland, Wis., 10,132.....B3   88
Ashland, co., Ohio,
  38,771................B3   78
Ashland, co., Wis., 17,375..B3   88
Ashland, mtn., Oreg......E4   80
Ashland City, Tenn.,
  1,400.................A4   83
Ashley, N. Dak., 1,419....D6   77
Ashley, Ohio, 907........B5   78
Ashley, Pa., 4,258.......n17   81
Ashley, co., Ark., 24,220..D4   49
Ashmūn, Eg., U.A.R.,
  26,100...............*G8   14
Ash Shaṭṭ, Eg., U.A.R.,
  2,000.................H9   14
Ashtabula, Ohio, 24,559...A5   78
Ashtabula, co., Ohio,
  93,067................A5   78
Ashton, Idaho, 1,242......E7   57
Ashton, Ill., 1,024.......B4   58
Ashton, R.I., 2,000.......B11   52
Ashville, Ala., 973.......B3   46
Ashville, Ohio, 1,639......C3   78
Ashwaubenon, Wis.,
  2,657.................g9   88
Asia, cont., 1,877,000,000..F9   16
Asir, reg., Sau. Ar........E6   23
Asmara, Eth., 131,800.....E5   23
Asnières [-sur-Seine], Fr.,
  81,768...............g10   5
Asotin, co., Wash., 12,909..C8   86
Aspe, Sp., 10,279.........C5   8
Aspen, Colo., 1,101.......B4   51
Aspen Butte, Oreg........E4   80
Aspermont, Tex., 1,286....C2   84
Aspinwall, Pa., 3,727....k14   81
As Salt, Jordan,
  16,176.............B3, g5   15
Assam, state, India,
  11,872,772............C9   20
Assateague, isl., Va.......C7   85
Assen, Neth., 31,800......A7   5
Assens, co., Den., 57,472..*J3   11
Assiniboia, Sask., Can.,
  2,491................H3   39
Assiniboine, mtn., Alta.,
  Can..................D3   38
Assinie, I.C., 1,000.......G4   22
Assis, Braz., 30,207......C2   30
Assisi, It., 5,200.........C4   9
As Sulaymānīyah, Iraq,
  35,352................B3   15
Assumption, Ill., 1,439....D4   58
Assumption, par., La.,
  17,991................E4   63
As Suwaydā, Syr., 18,154..F11   14
Asti, It., 48,200.........B2   9
Aston, Pa., 1,200.......*G11   81
Astorga, Sp., 10,101......A2   8
Astoria, Ill., 1,026.......C3   58
Astoria, Oreg., 11,239....A3   80
Astrakhan, Sov. Un.,
  342,000...............E7   13
Asturias, reg., Sp.,
  989,344...............A2   8
Asuncion, Par., 305,300....E4   29
Aswan, Eg., U.A.R.,
  28,400................D4   23
Asyut, Eg., U.A.R.,
  133,500...............C4   23
Atacama, prov., Chile
  116,309...............E1   29
Atami, Jap., 54,540......n18   18
Atascadero, Calif., 7,000..E3   50
Atascosa, co., Tex.,
  18,828................E3   84
Atbara, Sud., 36,298......E4   23
Atbasar, Sov. Un.,
  22,300................D9   13
Atchison, Kans., 12,529...C8   61
Atchison, co., Kans.,
  20,898................C8   61
Atchison, co., Mo., 9,213..A2   69
Atco, N.J., 1,900.........D3   74

Athabasca, Alta, Can., 1,487...........B4, D1 38
Athabasca, lake, Alta., Sask., Can............m6 39
Athabasca, riv., Can.....E11 36
Athena, Oreg., 950.......B8 80
Athens, Ala., 9,330......A3 46
Athens, Ont., Can., 1,015...C9 41
Athens, Ga., 31,355......C3 55
Athens (Athínai), Grc., 627,564 (*1,852,709)..........D4 14
Athens, Ill., 1,035.......D4 58
Athens, Mich., 966.......F5 66
Athens, N.Y., 1,754......C7 75
Athens, Ohio, 16,470.....C3 78
Athens, Pa., 4,515.......C9 81
Athens, Tenn., 12,103....D9 83
Athens, Tex., 7,086......C5 84
Athens, W. Va., 1,086....D3 87
Athens, co., Ohio, 46,998..C3 78
Atherton, Calif., 7,717....*D2 60
Athis-Mons, Fr., 24,004...h10 5
Athleague, Ire., 132......D3 4
Athok, Bur., 4,770......E10 20
Athol, Mass., 11,637......A3 65
Atibaia, Braz, 8,957......m8 30
Atikokan, Ont., Can., 6,674...........E8 41
Atkarsk, Sov. Un., 39,800............F15 12
Atkins, Ark., 1,391......B3 49
Atkinson, Ill., 944.......B3 58
Atkinson, Nebr., 1,324....B7 71
Atkinson, co., Ga., 6,188..E4 55
Atlanta, Ga., 500,000 (*1,285,000).........B5, C2 55
Atlanta, Ill., 1,568.......C4 58
Atlanta, Tex., 4,076......C5 84
Atlantic, Iowa, 6,890.....C2 60
Atlantic, N.C., 850.......C6 76
Atlantic, co., N.J., 160,880............E3 74
Atlantic, ocean...........D17 2
Atlantic, peak, Wyo......D3 89
Atlantic Beach, Fla., 3,125...........m9 54
Atlantic Beach, N.Y., 1,025...........n15 75
Atlantic City, N.J., 59,000 (*145,000)..........E4 74
Atlantic Highlands, N.J., 4,119............C4 74
Atlántico, dept., Col., 717,406............A2 32
Atlas, Pa., 1,574.........*D8 81
Atlixco, Mex., 30,650.....n14 34
Atmore, Ala., 8,173......D2 46
Atna, peak, B.C., Can.....C3 37
Atoka, Okla., 2,877......C5 79
Atoka, co., Okla., 10,352...C5 79
Atotonilco el Alto, Mex., 14,430............m12 34
Atrisco, N. Mex., 4,000...*B5 48
Atsugi, Jap., 37,000......n18 18
At Tafilah, Jordan, 4,506............D3, h5 15
At Ṭāif, Sau. Ar., 30,000..E3 15
Attala, co., Miss., 21,335..B4 68
Attalla, Ala., 8,257.......A3 46
At Ṭayyibah, Jordan, 1,677............C3 15
Attica, Ind., 4,341.......D3 59
Attica, Kans., 845.......E5 61

Attica, N.Y., 2,758.......C2 75
Attica, Ohio, 965........A3 78
Attika (Attica) prov., Grc., 2,057,974........*C4 14
Attleboro, Mass., 27,118...C5 65
Atvidaberg, Swe., 7,800...H6 11
Atwater, Calif., 11,105....D3 50
Atwater, Minn., 899......E4 67
Atwood, Ill., 1,258.......D5 58
Atwood, Kans., 1,906.....C2 61
Atzcapotzalco (Azcapotzalco), Mex., 63,857.......h9, n14 34
Atzmon, mtn., Isr.........A3 15
Aubagne, Fr., 12,612......F3 5
Aube, dept., Fr., 255,099. *C6 5
Aubenas, Fr., 5,754......E6 5
Aubervilliers, Fr., 70,632..g10 5
Aubin, Fr., 7,821.........E5 5
Auburn, Ala., 16,261.....C4 46
Auburn, Ill., 2,441.......D4 58
Auburn, Ind., 6,350......B7 59
Auburn, Kans., 228......D8 61
Auburn, Ky., 1,013.......D3 62
Auburn, Maine, 24,449...........D2, f7 64
Auburn, Mass., 14,047....B4 65
Auburn, Mich., 1,497.....E6 66
Auburn, Nebr., 3,229.....D10 71
Auburn, N.Y., 35,249.....C4 75
Auburn, Pa., 936.........E9 81
Auburn, Wash., 11,933...........B3, f11 86
Auburndale, Fla., 5,595...D5 54
Auburn Heights, Mich., 4,500...........F7 66
Aubusson, Fr., 5,669......E5 5
Auch, Fr., 18,918........F4 5
Auckland, N.Z., 149,989 (*548,293)..........L15 26
Aude, dept., Fr., 269,782............*C6 5
Audincourt, Fr., 12,433....D7 5
Audrain, co., Mo., 26,079..B6 69
Audubon, Iowa, 2,928.....C3 60
Audubon, N.J., 10,440....D2 74
Audubon, co., Iowa, 10,919............C3 60
Audubon Park, Ky., 1,867............*A4 62
Audubon Park, N.J., 1,713............*C3 74
Aue, Ger., 31,200........C6 6
Auglaize, co., Ohio, 36,147............B1 78
Augsburg, Ger., 209,600...D5 6
Augusta, Ark., 2,272......B4 49
Augusta, Ga., 68,000 (*198,000)...........C5 55
Augusta, Ill., 915........C3 58
Augusta, It., 27,950......F6 9
Augusta, Kans., 6,434............E6, g13 61
Augusta, Ky., 1,458......B6 62
Augusta, Maine, 21,680...D3 64
Augusta, Mich., 972......F5 66
Augusta, Wis., 1,338.....D2 88
Augusta, co., Va., 37,363............B3 85
Augustow, Pol., 16,100...B7 7
Augustus, mtn., Austl.....D2 25
Aulander, N.C., 1,083.....A5 76
Aulnay-sous-Bois, Fr., 47,507............g11 5

Aurangabad, India, 87,579............F6 20
Auray, Fr., 8,118.........D2 5
Aurelia, Iowa, 1,127......B2 60
Aurich, Ger., 13,000......B3 6
Aurillac, Fr., 24,563......E5 5
Aurora, Ont., Can., 8,791............D5 42
Aurora, Colo., 48,548.....B6 51
Aurora, Ill., 63,715.......B5, k8 58
Aurora, Ind., 4,756.......F8 59
Aurora, Minn., 2,799.....C6 67
Aurora, Mo., 4,683......E4 69
Aurora, Nebr., 2,576.....D7 71
Aurora, Ohio, 4,049......A4 78
Aurora, co., S. Dak., 4,749............G7 77
Au Sable Forks, N.Y., 2,100............f11 75
Aust-Agder, co., Nor., 77,700............*H3 11
Austell, Ga., 1,867.......B4 55
Austin, Ind., 4,000.......G6 59
Austin, Minn., 27,908....C6 67
Austin, Tex., 232,000 (*263,000)...........D4 84
Austin, co., Tex., 13,777...E4 84
Austin lake, Mich., 3,520............*F5 66
Austintown, Ohio, 5,000...A5 78
Australia, country, Oceania, 11,540,764....... 25
Australian Capital Territory, Austl., 95,913............*G8 25
Austria, country, Eur., 7,215,000............E6 6
Autauga, co., Ala., 18,739............C3 46
Autlán de Navarro, Mex., 17,017......D4, n11 34
Autun, Fr., 15,305........D6 5
Auvergne, former prov., Fr., 838,000..........E5 5
Auxerre, Fr., 31,178......D5 5
Auxier, Ky., 800.........C7 62
Ava, Mo., 1,581.........E5 69
Avalon, Calif., 1,536.....F4 50
Avalon, Pa., 6,859.......h13 81
Avanos, Tur., 5,700......C10 14
Avaré, Braz., 20,334......C3 30
Aveiro, Port., 13,423.....B1 8
Avella, Pa., 1,310........F1 81
Avellaneda, Arg., 329,056............A5, g7 28
Avellino, It., 35,600......D5 9
Avenal, Calif., 3,147......E3 50
Avenel, N.J., 10,000......k7 74
Aversa, It., 42,300.......D5 9
Avery, co., N.C., 12,009............e11 76
Avesta, Swe., 10,900.....G7 11
Aveyron, dept., Fr., 290,442............*E5 5
Avezzano, It., 25,000.....C4 9
Avigliano, It., 4,554......D5 9
Avignon, Fr., 72,717......F6 5
Ávila, Sp., 26,807........B3 8
Avilés, Sp., 48,503.......A3 8
Avilla, Ind., 919.........B7 59
Avis, Pa., 1,262.........D7 81
Avoca, Ala., 400.........A2 46
Avoca, Iowa, 1,540.......C2 60
Avoca, N.Y., 1,086.......C3 75

Avoca, Pa., 3,562........m18 81
Avola, It., 27,453........F5 9
Avon, Conn., 2,500......B5 52
Avon, Ill., 996..........C3 58
Avon, Mass., 4,301...B5, a11 65
Avon, N.Y., 2,772.......C3 75
Avon, Ohio, 6,002.......A3 78
Avon, Pa., 1,212........*F9 81
Avon by the Sea, N.J., 1,707............C4 74
Avondale, Ariz., 6,581....D1 48
Avondale, Pa., 1,016.....G10 81
Avondale Estates, Ga., 1,646............B5 55
Avon Lake, Ohio, 9,403...A3 78
Avonmore, Pa., 1,351....E3 81
Avon Park, Fla., 6,073....E5 54
Avoyelles, par., La., 37,606............C3 63
Avranches, Fr., 8,854.....C3 5
Axim, Ghana, 5,600......H4 22
Axis, Ala., 300..........E1 46
Ay, Fr., 6,806...........C5 5
Ayabe, Jap., 25,500......n14 18
Ayacucho, Arg., 9,220....B5 28
Ayacucho, Peru, 24,300...D3 31
Ayacucho, dept., Peru, 430,289............D3 31
Ayaguz, Sov. Un., 52,400............E11 13
Ayamonte, Sp., 8,908....D2 8
Ayan, Sov. Un., 9,300....D16 13
Ayaviri, Peru, 7,500......D3 31
Ayden, N.C., 3,108......B5 76
Aydin (Aidin), Tur., 35,700............D6 14
Ayer, Mass., 14,927....A4, f9 65
Ayion Oros (Mount Athos), prov., Grc., 2,687......B5 14
Ayios Dhimitrios, Grc., 21,365............*C4 14
Aylesbury, Eng., 31,000...E6 4
Aylesford, N.S., Can., 964..D5 43
Aylmer East, Que., Can., 6,286............D2 42
Aylmer West, Ont., Can., 4,705............E4 41
Ayora, Sp., 6,067........C5 8
Ayr, Scot., 45,200.......C4 4
Ayr, co., Scot., 345,900...*C4 4
Aytos, Bul., 13,914......D8 10
Ayutthaya, Thai., 32,368..C2 19
Ayvalik, Tur., 16,100....C6 14
Azalea Park, Fla., 6,500. *D5 54
Azemmour, Mor., 12,449..B3 22
Azerbaidzhan, (S.S.R.), rep., Sov. Un., 4,400,000............*E7 16
Azle, Tex., 2,969........n9 84
Azogues, Ec., 8,075......B2 31
Azores Islands, reg., Port., 327,500..........C3 21
Azov, Sov. Un., 39,931...H12 12
Azrou, Mor., 14,143......B3 22
Aztec, N. Mex., 4,137.....A5 48
Azua, Dom. Rep., 12,600..E8 35
Azuay, prov., Ec., 274,642............B2 31
Azul, Arg., 32,886.......B5 28
Azusa, Calif., 20,497.....m13 50
'Az Ẓahrān (Dhahran), Sau. Ar., 12,500......D5 15
Az Zaqazīg, Eg., U.A.R., 131,200............B4 23

B

Baalbek, Leb., 9,600......f6 15
Babaeski, Tur., 11,700....E8 10
Babahoyo, Ec., 16,444....B2 31
Babayevo, Sov. Un., 10,000............B11 12
Babbitt, Minn., 2,587.....C7 67
Babbitt, Nev., 2,159......*B2 72
Bābol, Iran, 36,194......A8 23
Babson Park, Fla., 950....E5 54
Babyak, Bul., 6,211......E6 10
Babylon, N.Y., 12,299....n15 75
Baca, co., Colo., 6,310....D8 51
Bacalar, Mex., 939.......D7 34
Bacău, Rom., 62,900.....B8 10
Baccarat, Fr., 6,067......C7 5
Back, riv., Can..........C12 36
Bac Kan, Viet., 10,000...*G5 17

Backa Palanka, Yugo., 16,487............C4 10
Backa Topola, Yugo., 15,057............C4 10
Backbay, Va., 500.......D6 85
Bac Lieu, Viet., 58,920...*D3 19
Bacliff, Tex., 1,707......*E5 84
Bac Ninh, Viet., 25,000...G6 17
Bacolod, Phil., 88,854....C6 19
Bacon, co., Ga., 8,359....E4 55
Bacsalmas, Hung., 7,344..B4 10
Bács-Kiskun, co., Hung., 568,600............*B4 10
Badajoz, Sp., 80,000.....C2 8
Badalona, Sp., 92,257....B7 8
Bad Axe, Mich., 2,998....E8 66
Baddeck, N.S., Can., 825..C9 43

Bad Doberan, Ger., 12,600............A5 6
Baden, Aus., 22,484.....D8 6
Baden, Ont., Can., 977...D4 41
Baden, Pa., 6,109.......E1 81
Baden, Switz., 14,900....E4 6
Baden, reg., Ger.........D4 6
Baden-Baden, Ger., 39,800............D4 6
Baden-Württemberg, state, Ger., 8,426,200.......*D4 6
Bad Freienwalde, Ger., 12,200............B7 6
Badger, Newf., Can., 1,036............D3 44
Bad Hersfeld, Ger., 23,000..C4 6
Badin, N.C., 1,905......B2 76

Bad Ischl, Aus., 12,703....E6 6
Bad Kissingen, Ger., 12,900............C5 6
Bad Kreuznach, Ger., 36,000............D3 6
Bad Oldesloe, Ger., 16,000............B5 6
Bad Reichenhall, Ger., 13,100............E6 6
Bad Tölz, Ger., 11,700....E5 6
Badulla, Cey., 17,323....G7 20
Baffin, isl., Can........B19 36
Bafra, Tur., 20,759......B10 14
Bagdad, Ariz., 1,800.....D2 48
Bagé, Braz., 47,930......E2 30
Baghdad, Iraq, 355,958...C3 15

Bagheria, It., 35,100......E4 9
Baghlan, Afg., 24,410.....A4 20
Bagley, Minn., 1,385......C3 67
Bagnara [Calabra], It.,
10,000................F5 9
Bagnères-de-Bigorre, Fr.,
8,996................F4 5
Bagnolet, Fr., 31,576.....g10 5
Bagnols [-sur-Cèze], Fr.,
12,905................E6 5
Bagot, co., Que., Can.,
21,390................D5 42
Bagotville, Que., Can.,
5,629................A7 42
Bahama Islands, Br. dep.,
N.A., 130,700........B11 35
Bahawalpur, Pak., 84,377..C5 20
Bahia, state, Braz.,
5,990,605............A4 30
Bahía Blanca, Arg.,
136,137..............B4 28
Bahia de Caráquez, Ec.,
8,845................B1 31
Bahia, see Salvador, Braz.
Bahrain (Bahrein), country,
Asia, 143,135........C8 23
Baia-Mare, Rom., 43,100..B6 10
Baie-Comeau, Que., Can.,
7,956................k13 42
Baie-St. Paul, Que., Can.,
4,674................B7 42
Baie Verte, Newf., Can.,
958.................D3 44
Baile Atha Cliath, see
Dublin, Ire.
Bailén, Sp., 11,245.......C4 8
Băilești, Rom., 15,932.....C6 10
Bailey, co., Tex., 9,090...B1 84
Bainbridge, Ga., 12,714...F2 55
Bainbridge, N.Y., 1,712...C5 75
Bainbridge, Ohio, 1,001...C2 78
Baird, Tex., 1,633........C3 84
Bairdford, Pa., 950......h14 81
Baixo Alentejo, prov.,
Port.................*C2 8
Baja, Hung., 30,355.......B4 10
Baja California, state,
Mex., 520,165..........A1 34
Baja California Sur, ter.,
Mex., 81,594..........C2 34
Baker, La., 4,823........*D4 63
Baker, Mont., 2,365......D12 70
Baker, Oreg., 9,986.......C9 80
Baker, co., Fla., 7,363....B4 54
Baker, co., Ga., 4,543....F2 55
Baker, co., Oreg., 17,295..C9 80
Bakersfield, Calif., 70,000
(*185,000)............E4 50
Bakerton, see Elmora, Pa.
Baku, Sov. Un., 730,000...E7 13
Bala-Cynwyd, Pa.,
8,000................*F11 81
Balaguer, Sp., 8,342......B6 8
Balakleya, Sov. Un.,
5,000................G11 12
Balanda, Sov. Un.,
10,000................F15 12
Balanga, Phil., 1,466.....*C6 19
Balashov, Sov. Un.,
62,000................F14 12
Balasore, India, 33,931...D8 20
Balassagyarmat, Hung.,
12,457................A4 10
Balboa, C.Z., 3,139......*B2 32
Balcarce, Arg., 15,210....B5 28
Balch, Ark., 100.........B4 49
Balcones Heights, Tex.,
950.................*E3 84
Bald Eagle, Minn., 1,700..E7 67
Bald Knob, Ark., 1,705...B4 49
Baldwin, Fla., 1,272......B5 54
Baldwin, La., 1,548.......E4 63
Baldwin, Mich., 835......E5 66
Baldwin, N.Y., 34,500....G2 52
Baldwin, Wis., 1,184.....D1 88
Baldwin, co., Ala.,
49,088................E2 46
Baldwin, co., Ga., 34,064..C3 55
Baldwin City, Kans.,
1,877................D8 61
Baldwin Park, Calif.,
33,951...............*F4 50
Baldwinsville, N.Y., 6,076.B4 75
Baldwinville, Mass.,
1,700................A3 65
Baldwyn, Miss., 2,023.....A5 68
Balearic, is., Sp.........C6 9
Baler, Phil., 3,081.......B6 19
Balfour, N.C., 1,106......f10 76
Balikesir (Balikisri), Tur.,
61,145................C6 14
Balikpapan, Indon.,
88,534................F5 19
Balkh, Afg., 12,466.......A4 20
Balkhash, Sov. Un.,
65,000................E10 13
Balkhash, lake, Sov. Un...E10 13
Balki, Sov. Un., 25,000...H10 12

Ballarat, Austl.,
41,650.............G7, n14 25
Ballard, co., Ky., 8,291...A2 62
Ballard Vale, Mass.,
1,000..............A5, f11 65
Ballina, Ire., 273........C2 4
Ballinasloe, Ire., 5,800...D2 4
Ballinger, Tex., 5,043.....D3 84
Ballston Lake, N.Y., 930...C7 75
Ballston Spa, N.Y., 4,814..B7 75
Ballville, Ohio, 1,424....*A2 78
Ballwin, Mo., 5,710......g12 69
Bally, Pa., 1,033........F10 81
Ballymena, N. Ire.,
14,800................C3 4
Balm, Fla., 250..........E4 54
Balmazujvaros, Hung.,
16,312................B5 10
Balmville, N.Y., 1,538....*D6 75
Balotra, India, 12,110....C5 20
Balș, Rom., 6,956........C7 10
Balta, Sov. Un., 47,400...H7 12
Baltic, Conn., 1,400......C8 52
Baltic, sea, Eur..........I8 11
Baltimore, Ohio, 2,116....C3 78
Baltimore, co., Md.,
939,024..............B4 53
Baltimore (Independent City),
Md., 915,000
(*1,785,000)......B4, g11 53
Baluchistan, reg., Pak....C4 20
Bamako, Mali, 135,000....F3 22
Bamberg, Ger., 73,400....D5 6
Bamberg, S.C., 3,081.....E5 82
Bamberg, co., S.C.,
16,274................E5 82
Banaras (Benares), India,
471,258..............C7 20
Banat, prov., Rom.,
1,234,300............*C5 10
Banat, reg., Yugo.,
948,596..............C5 10
Banbridge, N. Ire., 6,115..C3 4
Banbury, Eng., 22,100....D6 4
Bancroft, Ont., Can.,
2,615................B7 41
Bancroft, Iowa, 1,000.....A3 6
Banda, India, 37,744......C7 20
Bandar 'Abbās, Iran,
14,278...............*D6 15
Bande, Sp., 6,275........A2 8
Bandeira, peak,
Braz.................C4 30
Bandera, Tex., 950.......E3 84
Bandera, co., Tex., 3,892..E3 84
Bandirma, Tur., 28,880....B6 14
Bandjermasin, Indon.,
212,683..............F4 19
Bandon, Oreg., 1,653.....D2 80
Bandung (Bandoeng),
Indon., 966,359........G3 19
Banes, Cuba, 26,700......D6 35
Banff, Alta., Can......D3, g7 38
Banff, co., Scot., 45,600..*B5 4
Bangalore, India, 905,134..F6 20
Banggai, Indon...........F6 19
Bangkok (Krung Thep),
Thai., 1,299,528........C2 19
Bangor, Maine, 38,912....D4 64
Bangor, Mich., 2,109.....F4 66
Bangor, N. Ire., 24,900...C4 4
Bangor, Pa., 5,766......E11 81
Bangor, Wales, 14,500....D4 4
Bangor, Wis., 928........E3 88
Bangs, Tex., 967.........D3 84
Bangued, Phil., 7,602.....B6 19
Bangui, Cen. Afr. Rep.,
11,266................H1 23
Bangweulu, lake, Zambia..C6 24
Banhã, Eg., U.A.R.,
42,600................G8 14
Baní, Dom. Rep., 14,570..E8 35
Bani Suwayf, Eg., U.A.R.,
65,600................C4 23
Banja Luka, Yugo.,
50,463................C3 10
Banjuwangi, Indon.,
25,185................G4 19
Banks, co., Ga., 6,497....B3 55
Banks, isl., Can.........B9 36
Bankura, India, 62,833...D8 20
Banner, co., Nebr., 1,269..C2 71
Banner Hill, Tenn.,
1,100...............*C11 83
Bannertown, N.C., 1,096..*A2 76
Bannock, co., Idaho,
49,342................G6 57
Bannu, Pak., 20,509......B5 20
Bañolas, Sp., 8,075.......A7 8
Banska Bystrica, Czech.,
25,000................D5 7
Banska Stiavnica, Czech.,
9,500................D5 7
Bansko, Bul., 6,161......E6 10
Bantam, Conn., 833......C4 52
Bar, Sov. Un., 22,100....G6 12
Barabinsk, Sov. Un.,
38,900...............D10 13

Baraboo, Wis., 7,660.....E4 88
Baracaldo, Sp., 77,802....A4 8
Baracoa, Cuba, 13,000....D6 35
Baradero, Arg., 10,194....F7 28
Baraga, Mich., 991.......B2 66
Baraga, co., Mich., 7,151..B2 66
Barahona, Dom. Rep.,
20,270................E8 35
Baramula, India, 19,854...B5 20
Baranovichi, Sov. Un.,
64,000................E3 12
Baranya, co., Hung.,
280,600..............*B4 10
Barataria, La., 900....E5, k11 63
Barbacena, Braz.,
41,931.............C4, G6 30
Barbados, country, N.A.,
235,000..............J15 35
Barbastro, Sp., 10,227....A6 8
Barbate, Sp., 10,720......D3 8
Barber, co., Kans., 8,713..E5 61
Barberton, Ohio, 33,805...A4 78
Barberton, S. Afr., 11,075..F6 24
Barbour, co., Ala., 24,700..D4 46
Barbour, co., W. Va.,
15,474................B4 87
Barboursville, W. Va.,
2,331................C2 87
Barbourville, Ky., 3,211...D6 62
Barbuda, isl., Antigua....H14 35
Barcarrota, Sp., 7,898....C2 8
Barcelona, Sp., 1,655,600
(*2,375,000)..........B7 8
Barcelona, Ven., 42,379...A5 32
Barcelos, Port., 7,875.....B1 8
Bardejov, Czech., 6,572...D6 7
Bardstown, Ky., 4,798....C4 62
Bardwell, Ky., 1,067......A2 62
Bareilly, India, 254,409...C6 2
Baresville, Pa., 1,700....*G8 81
Barguzin, Sov. Un.,
5,600................D13 13
Bar Harbor, Maine,
2,500 (3,807▲).........D4 64
Bari, It., 323,100........D6 9
Barinas, state, Ven.,
139,271..............B3 32
Baripada, India, 20,301...D8 20
Bariri, Braz., 8,403....C3, m7 30
Barking, Eng., 72,282....k13 4
Barkol (Chensi), China,
10,000................C3 17
Bar-le-Duc, Fr., 18,346...C6 5
Barletta, It., 69,300.....D6 9
Barling, Ark., 770........B1 49
Barmer, India, 27,600....C5 20
Barnaul, Sov. Un.,
382,000..............D11 13
Barnegat, N.J., 900......D4 74
Barnes, Oreg., 5,076.....*D3 80
Barnes, co., N. Dak.,
16,719................C7 77
Barnesboro, N.J., 900....D2 74
Barnesboro, Pa., 3,035....E4 81
Barnesville, Ga., 4,919....C2 55
Barnesville, Minn., 1,632..D2 67
Barnesville, Ohio, 4,425...C4 78
Barnhill, Ohio, 350......B4 78
Barnsdall, Okla., 1,663...A5 79
Barnstable, Mass., 900
(13,465▲)............C7 65
Barnstable, co., Mass.,
70,286................C7 65
Barnstaple, Eng., 15,900..E4 4
Barnwell, S.C., 4,568.....E5 82
Barnwell, co., S.C.,
17,266................E4 82
Baroda, India, 295,144....D5 20
Barquisimeto, Ven.,
227,400..............A4 32
Barra, Braz., 7,237......*E5 27
Barraba, Austl., 1,469....E8 26
Barrackville, W. Va.,
950..............A7, B4 87
Barra do Piraí, Braz.,
29,398.............C4, H6 30
Barra Mansa, Braz.,
47,398.............C4, h6 30
Barrancabermeja, Col.,
59,625................B3 32
Barranquilla, Col.,
498,301..............A3 32
Barre, Mass., 1,100
(3,479▲).............B3 65
Barre, Vt., 10,387.......C3 73
Barreiras, Braz., 7,175...*E5 27
Barreiro, Port., 22,190..C1, f9 8
Barreiros, Braz., 10,402..*D7 27
Barren, co., Ky., 28,303..D4 62
Barretos, Braz., 39,950...C3 30
Barrett, Tex., 1,200.....*E5 84
Barrhead, Alta., Can.,
2,286................B3 38
Barrie, Ont., Can., 21,169..C5 41
Barrigada, Guam, 1,729...*F6 2
Barrington, Ill., 6,525..A5, h8 58

Barrington, N.J., 7,943...*D2 74
Barrington, R.I.,
11,200 (16,390▲).......C11 52
Barrington Hills, Ill.,
1,726................*A5 58
Barron, Wis., 2,338......C2 88
Barron, co., Wis., 34,270..C2 88
Barrow, Alsk., 1,314.....A8 47
Barrow, co., Ga., 14,485..B3 55
Barrow-in-Furness, Eng.,
65,300................C5 4
Barruelo de Santullán, Sp.,
7,770................A3 8
Barry, Ill., 1,422........D2 58
Barry, co., Mich., 31,738..F5 66
Barry, co., Mo., 18,921...E4 69
Barrys Bay, Ont., Can.,
1,439................B7 41
Barsi, India, 50,389......E6 20
Barstow, Calif., 11,644...E5 50
Barth, Fla., 200........u14 54
Barth, Ger., 12,200......A6 6
Bartholomew, co., Ind.,
48,198................F6 59
Bartin, Tur., 11,506.....B9 14
Bartle Frere, mtn., Austl..C8 25
Bartlesville, Okla., 27,893..A6 79
Bartlett, Ill., 2,291......h8 58
Bartlett, Tex., 1,540.....D4 84
Barton, Ala., 300.......A2 46
Barton, Ohio, 975.......B5 78
Barton, Vt., 1,169.......B3 73
Barton, co., Kans., 32,368..D5 61
Barton, co., Mo., 11,113..D3 69
Bartonville, Ill., 7,253....C4 58
Bartonwoods, Ga., 3,000..*C2 55
Bartow, Fla., 12,849.....E5 54
Bartow, co., Ga., 28,267..B2 55
Barvas, Scot............A3 4
Barvenkovo, Sov. Un.,
10,000................G11 12
Barwick, Ky., 300.......C6 62
Basel, Switz., 211,500....E3 6
Basel-Land, sub canton,
Switz...............*E3 6
Basel-Stadt, sub canton,
Switz., 233,500.......*E3 6
Basile, La., 1,932.......D3 63
Basilicata, pol. dist., It...*D5 9
Basin, Wyo., 1,319......B4 89
Basingstoke, Eng., 28,300..E6 4
Baskin, Fla., 500.......P10 54
Basking Ridge, N.J.,
2,600................B3 74
Basque Provinces, reg.,
Sp., 1,371,654.........A4 8
Basra, Iraq, 164,623.....B7 23
Bas-Rhin, dept., Fr.,
770,150..............*C7 5
Bassac, Laos, 5,000......C3 19
Bassano, Alta., Can., 815..D4 38
Bassano del Grappa, It.,
23,800................B3 9
Bassein, Bur., 77,905....E9 20
Basses-Alpes, dept., Fr.,
91,843...............*E7 5
Basses-Pyrénées, dept., Fr.,
466,038..............*F3 5
Basse-Terre, Guad.,
13,978...............I14 35
Basseterre, St. Kitts,
15,579...............H13 35
Bassett, Calif., 2,000....*E5 50
Bassett, Nebr., 1,023.....B6 71
Bassett, Va., 3,700......D3 85
Bastia, Fr., 50,117......C2 9
Bastogne, Bel., 5,927.....B6 5
Bastrop, La., 15,193.....B4 63
Bastrop, co., Tex., 16,925..D4 84
Basutoland, see Lesotho,
country, Afr.
Bata, Equat. Gui., 4,000..H6 22
Bataan, prov., Phil.,
145,323..............*C6 19
Batala, India, 51,300.....B6 20
Batanes, prov., Phil.,
10,309...............*A6 19
Batangas, Phil., 34,496...p13 19
Batangas, prov., Phil.,
681,414..............*C6 19
Bataszek, Hung., 6,235....B4 10
Batatais, Braz., 15,266...C3 30
Batavia, Ill., 7,496.....B5, k8 58
Batavia, N.Y., 18,210....C2 75
Batavia, Ohio, 1,729......C1 78
Batavia, see Djakarta,
Indon.
Bataysk, Sov. Un.,
72,000...............H12 12
Bates, co., Mo., 15,905...C3 69
Batesburg, S.C., 3,806....D4 82
Batesville, Ark., 6,207....B4 49
Batesville, Ind., 3,349....F7 59
Batesville, Miss., 3,284...A4 68
Bath, Eng., 82,600.......E5 4
Bath, Maine, 10,717...E3, g8 64
Bath, N.Y., 6,166.......C3 75
Bath, Pa., 1,736.......E11 81

Bath, S.C., 1,419........D4 82
Bath, co., Ky., 9,114.....B6 62
Bath, co., Va., 5,335.....B3 85
Bathurst, Austl., 17,220...F8 25
Bathurst, N.B., Can.,
  5,494................B4 43
Bathurst, Gam., 28,900...F1 22
Batna, Alg., 19,255......H6 22
Baton Rouge, La., 173,000
  (*295,000).........D4, h9 63
Batouri, Cam H7 22
Batroun, Leb., 2,500......f5 15
Battambang, Camb.,
  38,800...............C2 19
Batticaloa, Cey., 17,662...G7 20
Battle Creek, Mich., 41,000,
  (*109,000)..........F5 66
Battleford, Sask., Can.,
  1,627................E1 39
Battle Ground, Ind., 804...C4 59
Battle Ground, Wash.,
  888.................D3 86
Battonya, Hung., 9,216...B5 10
Batumi, Sov. Un., 91,000..E7 13
Batu Pahat, Mala.,
  39,294..............*E2 19
Baturité, Braz., 7,198....D7 27
Bauchi, Nig., 13,440.....F6 22
Baudette, Minn., 1,597...B4 67
Bauru, Braz., 85,237....C3 30
Bautzen, Ger., 42,300...C7   6
Bauxite, Ark., 950.....E5 49
Bavaria, reg., Ger.....D5   6
Bavispe, Mex., 915......A3 34
Bawcomville, La., 1,500..*B3 63
Baxley, Ga., 4,268......E4 55
Baxter, Minn., 1,037....D4 67
Baxter, co., Ark., 9,943...A3 49
Baxter Estates, N.Y., 932..*E7 75
Baxter Springs, Kans.,
  4,498................E9 61
Bay, co., Fla.,
  67,131............B1, u16 54
Bay, co., Mich., 107,042...E6 66
Baya Dzur-Gunen, Mong.,
  5,000................B5 17
Bayamo, Cuba, 30,200...D5 35
Bayamón, P.R., 15,109...G11 35
Bayanovka, Sov. Un.......C8 13
Bayard, Nebr., 1,519....C2 71
Bayard, N. Mex., 2,327...C4 48
Baybay, Phil., 10,021....*C6 19
Bayburt, Tur., 11,937....B13 14
Bay City, Mich., 53,604...E7 66
Bay City, Oreg., 996.....B3 80
Bay City, Tex.,
  11,656...........E5, s14 84
Bay de Verde, Newf.,
  Can., 884...........D5 44
Bayern, state, Ger.,
  10,100,900.........*D5   6
Bayeux, Fr., 9,678......C3   5
Bayfield, Wis., 969......B3 88
Bayfield, co., Wis., 11,910.B2 88
Bay Harbor Island, Fla.,
  3,249..............*F3 54
Bay Head, N.J., 824.....C4 74
Bayindir, Tur., 11,300...*C6 14
Baykal, lake, Sov. Un.....D13 13
Baylor, co., Tex., 5,893...C3 84
Bay Minette, Ala., 5,197...E2 46
Bayombong, Phil., 8,312..*B6 19
Bayonne, Fr., 36,941....F3   5
Bayonne, N.J., 72,215..B4, k8 74
Bayou Cane, La., 3,173...*E5 63
Bayou LaBatre, Ala.,
  2,572................E1 46
Bay Park, N.Y., 2,500...*E7 75
Bayport, Minn.,
  3,205................E6 67
Bayport, N.Y., 5,800....n15 75
Bayreuth, Ger., 61,600...D5   6
Bay Roberts, Newf., Can.,
  1,328................E5 44
Bayshore, Calif., 1,500..*D2 50
Bay Shore, N.Y.,
  32,000..........E7, n15 75
Bayshore Gardens, Fla.,
  2,297..............*E4 54
Bayside, Wis., 3,181....m12 88
Bay Springs, Miss., 1,544..D4 68
Bay St. Louis, Miss.,
  5,073............E2, E4 68
Bayt Lahm (Bethlehem),
  Jordan, 22,453.....C3, h5 15
Baytown, Tex.,
  28,159...........E5, r15 84
Bay View, Ala., 1,081....E4 46
Bayview, Calif., 1,800...*B1 50
Bayview, Mass., 100.....A6 65
Bay Village, Ohio, 14,489..h9 78
Bayville, N.Y., 3,962....F2 52
Baztán, Sp., 1,534......A5   8
Beach, N. Dak., 1,460...D2 77
Beach City, Ohio, 1,151...B4 78
Beach (Dunes Park), Ill.,
  1,800..............*A6 58
Beach Haven, N.J., 1,041..D4 74

Beachville, Ont., Can.,
  849.................D4 41
Beachwood, N.J., 2,765...D4 74
Beachwood, Ohio, 6,089..*A4 78
Beacon, N.Y., 13,922.....D7 75
Beacon Falls, Conn.,
  1,500................D4 52
Beacon Hill, Wash.,
  1,019..............*C3 86
Beaconsfield, Que., Can.,
  10,064...............D8 42
Beadle, co., S. Dak.,
  21,682...............F7 77
Beadling, Pa., 1,500....*E1 81
Beamsville, Ont., Can.,
  2,537................D5 41
Bearden, Ark., 1,268.....D3 49
Bearden, Tenn.,
  14,000.........D9, E11 83
Beardstown, Ill., 6,294....C3 58
Bear Lake, co., Idaho,
  7,148................G7 57
Béarn, former prov., Fr.,
  275,000..............F3   5
Bear River, N.S., Can.,
  830.................E4 43
Bear Town, Miss., 1,865...D3 68
Beas de Segura, Sp.,
  9,251................C4   8
Beatrice, Nebr., 12,132...D9 71
Beattyville, Ky., 1,048...C6 62
Beaucaire, Fr., 8,243....F6   5
Beauce, co., Que., Can.,
  62,264...............C7 42
Beauceville Est, Que., Can.,
  1,920................C7 42
Beauceville, Ouest, Que.,
  Can., 1,645.........*C7 42
Beaufort, N.C., 2,922....C6 76
Beaufort, S.C., 6,298....G6 82
Beaufort, co., N.C.,
  36,134...............B5 76
Beaufort, co., S.C.,
  44,187...............G6 82
Beaufort West, S. Afr.,
  16,467...............G4 24
Beauharnois, Que., Can.,
  8,704...........D4, q19 42
Beauharnois, co., Que.,
  Can., 49,667.........D3 42
Beaumont, Calif., 4,432..*F5 50
Beaumont, Tex., 123,000,
  (*280,000)..........D5 84
Beaumont Place, Tex.,
  1,500..............*E5 84
Beaune, Fr., 15,367.....D6   5
Beaupré, Que., Can.,
  2,587................B7 42
Beauregard, par., La.,
  19,191...............D2 63
Beaurepaire, Que., Can.,
  2,400................D8 42
Beauséjour, Man., Can.,
  1,770................D3 40
Beauvais, Fr., 33,995....C5   5
Beaver, Okla., 2,087..A1, e10 79
Beaver, Pa., 6,160......E1 81
Beaver, Utah, 1,548.....B5 72
Beaver, co., Pa., 206,948..E1 81
Beaver, co., Utah, 4,331..B5 72
Beaver Bank, N.S., Can.,
  870.................E6 43
Beaver City, Nebr., 818...D6 71
Beaverdale, Pa., 1,400....F4 81
Beaver Dam, Ky., 1,648...C3 62
Beaver Dam, Wis.,
  13,118...............E5 88
Beaver Falls, Pa., 16,240..E1 81
Beaver (Glen Hedrick),
  W. Va., 1,230......D3, D7 87
Beaverhead, Mont., 7,194..E3 70
Beaverlodge, Alta., Can.,
  897.................B1 38
Beaver Meadows, Pa.,
  1,392...............E10 81
Beaverton, Ont., Can.,
  1,217................C5 42
Beaverton, Mich., 926....E6 66
Beaverton, Oreg.,
  5,937............B4, h12 80
Beawar, India, 53,931....C1 20
Bebedouro, Braz., 18,249..C3 30
Bečej, Yugo., 24,853....C5 10
Béchar, Alg., 16,408.....B4 22
Bechuanaland, see Botswana,
  country, Afr.
Beckenham, Eng.,
  77,265..............m12   4
Becker, co., Minn.,
  23,959...............D3 67
Beckham, co., Okla.,
  17,782...............B2 79
Beckley, W. Va.,
  18,642.........D3, D7 87
Bédarieux, Fr., 7,263....F5   5
Bedford, N.S., Can E6 43
Bedford, Que., Can.,
  2,855................D5 42

Bedford, Eng., 65,400....D6   4
Bedford, Ind., 13,479....G5 59
Bedford, Iowa, 1,807....D3 60
Bedford, Mass.,
  10,969...........B5, g10 65
Bedford, Ohio,
  15,223...........A4, h9 78
Bedford, Pa., 3,696.....F4 81
Bedford, Tex., 2,706....*C4 84
Bedford, Va., 5,921.....C3 85
Bedford, co., Eng.,
  403,800............*D6   4
Bedford, co., Pa., 42,451...G4 81
Bedford, co., Tenn.,
  23,150...............B5 83
Bedford, co., Va., 31,028..C3 85
Bedford Heights, Ohio,
  5,275..............*A4 78
Bedford Hills, N.Y.,
  3,000...............m15 75
Bedja, see Beja, Tun.
Bedlington, Eng., 30,600...C6   4
Bedminster, N.J., 800.....B3 74
Bedzin, Pol., 41,200.....g10   7
Bee, co., Tex., 23,755....E4 84
Beebe, Ark., 1,697.....B4 49
Beebe, Que., Can., 1,363...D5 42
Beecher, Ill., 1,367.....B6 58
Beech Grove, Ind.,
  12,632...........E5, m10 59
Beechwood Village, Ky.,
  1,903..............*A4 62
Bee Ridge, Fla.,
  1,000...........E4, q11 54
Beersheba, Isr.,
  51,600...........C2, h5 15
Beeskow, Ger., 7,571....B7   6
Beeton, Ont., Can., 810...C5 41
Beeville, Tex., 13,811.....E4 84
Bègles, Fr., 24,388......E3   5
Beida, Libya, 12,800....B2 23
Beira, Moz., 40,000.....D6 24
Beira, reg., Port.........B2   8
Beira Alta, Prov., Port...*B2   8
Beira Baixa, prov., Port...*C2   8
Beira Litoral, prov., Port..*B1   8
Beirut (Beyrouth), Leb.,
  400,000.............g5 15
Beja (Bedja), Tun., 34,645..A6 22
Bejaïa (Bougie), Alg.,
  62,921...............A5 22
Bejeda (Ras Dashan), mtn.,
  Eth................F5 23
Békés, Hung., 17,661....B5 10
Békés, co., Hung.,
  452,400............*B5 10
Bekescsaba, Hung.,
  42,500...............B5 10
Bela, India, 21,397.....C7 20
Bela Crkva, Yugo., 10,749..C5 10
Bel Air, Md., 4,300......A5 53
Belalcázar, Sp., 8,793....C3   8
Bela Vista, Braz., 8,878...C1 30
Belaya Tserkov, Sov. Un.,
  77,000...............G8 12
Belchertown, Mass.,
  950 (5,186 ▲).......B3 65
Belding, Mich., 4,887.....E5 66
Belém, Braz., 359,988....D6 27
Belen, N. Mex., 5,031....B5 48
Belén, Par., 6,647......D4 29
Belev, Sov. Un., 10,000...E11 12
Belfair, Wash., 400.....B3 86
Belfast, Maine, 6,140....D3 64
Belfast, N.Y., 900.....C2 75
Belfast, N. Ire., 412,500...C4   4
Belfest, N.C., 900.......B5 76
Belfield, N. Dak., 1,064...D3 77
Belford, N.J., 6,000....C4 74
Belfort, Fr., 48,070.....D7   5
Belfort, dept., Fr.,
  109,371............*D7   5
Belfry, Ky., 950.........C7 62
Belgaum, India, 127,885...E5 20
Belgium, country, Eur.,
  9,189,741............B6   5
Belgorod, Sov. Un.,
  92,000...............F11 12
Belgorod-Dnestrovskiy,
  Sov. Un., 38,600......H8 12
Belgrade, Mont., 1,057...E5 70
Belgrade (Beograd), Yugo.,
  585,234.............C5 10
Belhaven, N.C., 2,395....B6 76
Belington, W. Va., 1,528...B5 87
Belize, Br. Hond., 32,690..D7 34
Belknap, co., N.H.,
  28,912...............D5 73
Bell, Calif., 19,450....*F4 50
Bell, co., Ky., 35,336.....D6 62
Bell, co., Tex., 94,097....D4 84
Bell Acres, Pa., 1,283...*E1 81
Bellaire, Ohio, 11,502....C5 78
Bellaire, Tex., 19,872....r14 84
Bellary, India, 85,673....E6 20
Bella Unión, Ur., 2,519...E1 30
Bella Vista, Arg., 8,352...E2 29
Bella Vista, Arg., 7,922...E4 29

Bella Vista, Par., 5,762....D4 29
Bellbrook, Ohio, 941.....C1 78
Belle, Mo., 1,016.......C6 69
Belle, W. Va., 2,559.....C6 87
Belleair, Fla., 2,456....p10 54
Belle Center, Ohio, 949...B2 78
Bellechasse, co., Que., Can.,
  26,054...............C7 42
Bellefontaine, Ohio, 11,424..B2 78
Bellefontaine Neighbors,
  Mo., 13,650........*C7 69
Bellefonte, Del., 1,536...*A7 53
Bellefonte, Pa., 6,088....E6 81
Belle Fourche, S. Dak.,
  4,087................F2 77
Bellegarde-sur-Valserine,
  Fr., 6,588...........D6   5
Belle Glade, Fla., 11,273...F6 54
Belle Isle, Fla., 2,344....D5 54
Bellemead, Md., 1,400...*C4 53
Belle Meade, Tenn.,
  3,082................A5 83
Belle Plaine, Iowa, 2,923..C5 60
Belle Plaine, Kans., 1,579..E6 61
Belle Plaine, Minn., 1,931..F5 67
Belle River, Ont., Can.,
  1,854..............*E2 41
Belle Rose, La., 800...D4, h9 63
Bellerose, N.Y., 1,083...*E7 75
Belleterre, Que., Can.,
  638...............*o20 41
Belle Vernon, Pa., 1,784...F2 81
Belleview, Fla., 864.....C4 54
Belleville, Ont., Can.,
  30,655...............C7 41
Belleville, Ill., 37,264....E4 58
Belleville, Kans., 2,940...C6 61
Belleville, Mich., 1,921...p15 66
Belleville, N.J., 35,005..B4, h8 74
Belleville, Pa., 1,539....E6 81
Belleville, Wis., 844.....F4 88
Bellevue, Ill., 1,561....*C4 58
Bellevue, Iowa, 2,181....B7 60
Bellevue, Ky., 9,336.....A7 62
Bellevue, Mich., 1,277...F5 66
Bellevue, Nebr.,
  17,496...........C10, g3 71
Bellevue, Ohio, 8,286....A3 78
Bellevue, Wash., 12,809..e11 86
Belley, Fr., 4,609......E6   5
Bellflower, Calif., 45,909..n12 50
Bell Gardens, Calif.,
  26,467.............*F4 50
Bellingham, Mass., 1,000
  (6,774 ▲).........B5, h10 65
Bellingham, Wash.,
  34,688...............A3 86
Bellinzona, Switz., 13,435..E4   6
Bell Island, see Wabana,
  Newf., Can.
Bellmawr, N.J., 11,853...D2 74
Bellmead, Tex., 5,127...*D4 84
Bellmore, N.Y., 14,100...G2 52
Bello, Col., 93,207.....B2 32
Bellows Falls, Vt., 3,831..E3 73
Bellport, N.Y., 2,707....G5 52
Bells, Tenn., 1,232.....B2 83
Belluno, It., 23,000.....A4   9
Bell Ville, Arg., 19,342...A4 28
Bellville, Ohio, 1,621....B3 78
Bellville, Tex., 2,218....E4 84
Bellwood, Ill., 22,821....k9 58
Bellwood, Pa., 2,330....E5 81
Belmar, N.J., 5,190.....C4 74
Bélmez, Sp., 8,068.....C3   8
Belmond, Iowa, 2,506....B4 60
Belmont, Calif., 15,996...h8 50
Belmont, Fla., 2,000...*E4 54
Belmont, Mass., 28,715...g11 65
Belmont, Miss., 901.....A5 68
Belmont, N.Y., 1,146....C2 75
Belmont, N.C., 4,718....B1 76
Belmont, co., Ohio,
  83,864...............C4 78
Belmonte, Braz., 7,897..*E7 27
Bel-Nor, Mo., 2,388....f13 69
Beloeil, Que., Can., 6,283..D4 42
Belo Horizonte, Braz.,
  642,912.............B4 30
Beloit, Kans., 4,302....C5 61
Beloit, Ohio, 877......B5 78
Beloit, Wis., 35,199....F4 88
Beloit West, Wis., 2,162..*F4 88
Belomorsk, Sov. Un.,
  17,400...............C6 13
Belopolye, Sov. Un.,
  10,000...............F10 12
Beloretsk, Sov. Un.,
  62,000...............D8 13
Belovo, Sov. Un.,
  118,000............*D11 13
Belpre, Ohio, 5,418.....C4 78
Bel-Ridge, Mo., 4,878...*C7 69
Belton, Mo., 4,897.....C3 69
Belton, S.C., 5,106.....B3 82
Belton, Tex., 8,163.....D4 84
Beltrami, co., Minn.,
  23,425...............B3 67

Beltsville, Md., 6,500......B4 53
Beltsy, Sov. Un., 73,000...H6 12
Belukha, mtn., Sov. Un. ..E11 13
Belvedere, Calif., 2,148...*C2 50
Belvedere, Va., 1,100....*B5 85
Belvedere Marittimo, It....E5 9
Belvidere, Del., 1,000.....A6 53
Belvidere, Ill., 13,049.....A5 58
Belvidere, N.J., 2,636.....B2 74
Belzoni, Miss., 4,142......B3 68
Bement, Ill., 1,558.......D5 58
Bemidji, Minn., 9,958....C4 67
Bemis, Tenn., 3,127.......B3 83
Benavente, Sp., 11,080....A3 8
Ben Avon, Pa., 2,553.....*E1 81
Benbrook, Tex., 3,254.....*C4 84
Bend, Oreg., 11,936......C5 80
Bendale, S.C., 1,544......C6 82
Ben Davis, Ind., 1,600....k9 59
Bendery, Sov. Un.,
 38,000.............H7 12
Bendigo, Austl., 30,792....G7 25
Benesov, Czech.,
 9,000.............D3, o18 7
Benevento, It., 40,800.....D5 9
Benewah, Idaho 6,036....B2 57
Bengal, Pak.,.............D8 20
Bengasi (Banghazi), Libya
 136,600............B2 23
Bengkulu, Indon., 16,800...F2 19
Benguela, Ang., 23,256....C2 24
Benguela, dist., Ang.,.....C3 24
Benham, Ky., 1,874......D7 62
Benicarló, Sp., 10,627.....B6 8
Benicia, Calif., 6,070...C2, g8 50
Benin, Nig., 100,694......G6 22
Benisa, Sp., 6,036........C6 8
Benkelman, Nebr., 1,400...D4 71
Benld, Ill., 1,848........D4 58
Ben Lomond, Calif.,
 1,814.............*D2 50
Bennett, co., S. Dak.,
 3,053.............G4 77
Bennettsville, S.C., 6,963..B8 82
Bennettsville Southwest, S.C.,
 1,022.............*B8 82
Ben Nevis, mtn., Scot.....B4 4
Bennington, Vt., 8,023....F1 73
Bennington, co., Vt.,
 25,088.............E1 73
Bensenville, Ill.,
 12,212.........B6, k9 58
Bensheim, Ger., 24,100...D4 6
Benson, Ariz., 2,494......D3 48
Benson, Minn., 3,678.....E3 67
Benson, N.C., 2,369......B4 76
Benson, co., N. Dak.,
 9,435.............B6 77
Bent, co., Colo., 7,419.....D7 51
Bentleyville, Pa., 3,160....F1 81
Benton, Ark., 10,399......C3 49
Benton, Ill., 7,023........E5 58
Benton, Ky., 3,074.......B3 62
Benton, La., 1,336........B2 63
Benton, Pa., 981.........D9 81
Benton, Tenn., 638.......D9 83
Benton, Wis., 837........F3 88
Benton, co., Ark., 36,272...A1 49
Benton, co., Ind., 11,912...C3 59
Benton, co., Iowa, 23,422..B5 60
Benton, co., Minn.,
 17,287.............E4 67
Benton, co., Miss., 7,723...A4 68
Benton, co., Mo., 8,737....C4 69
Benton, co., Oreg., 39,165..C3 80
Benton, co., Tenn., 10,662..A3 83
Benton, co., Wash.,
 62,070.............C6 86
Benton City, Wash., 1,210..C6 86
Benton Harbor, Mich.,
 19,136.............F4 66
Benton Heights, Mich.,
 6,112.............*F4 66
Bentonville, Ark., 3,649....A1 49
Benwood, W. Va.,
 2,850..........A4, B2 87
Benzie, co., Mich., 7,834...D4 66
Beograd, see Belgrade,
 Yugo.
Beppu, Jap., 118,938.....J5 18
Berat, Alb., 15,700......*B2 14
Berat, pref., Alb.,
 176,000...........*B2 14
Berber, Sud., 10,977......E4 23
Berbera, Som., 20,000....F7 23
Berchtesgaden, Ger.,
 4,800.............E6 6
Berck-Sur-Mer, Fr.,
 12,877.............B4 5
Berdichev, Sov. Un.,
 57,000.............G7 12
Berea, Ky., 4,302........C5 62
Berea, Ohio, 16,592....A4, h9 78
Beregovo, Sov. Un.,
 5,000.............G4 12
Beresford, S. Dak., 1,794..G9 77
Berettyoujfalu, Hung.,
 11,377.............B5 10

Berezhany, Sov. Un.,
 5,000.............G5 12
Berezna, Sov. Un., 10,000..F8 12
Berezniki, Sov. Un.,
 120,000............D8 13
Berg, Nor................q27 11
Berga, Sp., 9,822........A6 8
Bergama, Tur., 21,689...*C6 14
Bergamo, It., 118,700.....B2 9
Bergen, Ger., 10,500.....A2 7
Bergen, N.Y., 964........B3 75
Bergen, Nor., 117,300.....G1 11
Bergen, co., N.J., 780,255..A4 74
Bergen, co., Nor.,
 117,300...........*G1 11
Bergenfield, N.J.,
 27,203.........B5, h8 74
Bergen op Zoom, Neth.,
 35,500.............B6 5
Bergen, see Mons, Bel.
Bergerac, Fr., 21,236.....E4 5
Bergholz, Ohio, 955......B5 78
Bergisch Gladback, Ger.,
 47,000.............C3 6
Berhampore, India,
 76,931.............D8 20
Berhampur, India, 62,317..E7 20
Bering, sea, Pac. O.......D21 16
Berislav, Sov. Un., 10,000..H9 12
Berja, Sp., 6,425........D4 8
Berkeley, Ill., 5,729.....*B6 58
Berkeley, Mo., 18,676....f13 69
Berkely, R.I., 20,000.....B11 52
Berkeley, co., S.C., 38,196..E7 82
Berkeley, co., W. Va.,
 33,791.............B6 87
Berkeley Heights, N.J.,
 8,721.............B4 74
Berkeley Springs (Bath),
 W. Va., 1,138........B6 87
Berkley, Mich.,
 23,275.........F7, o15 66
Berkovitsa, Bul., 6,870....D6 10
Berks, co., Pa., 275,414...F9 81
Berkshire, Md., 1,200....*C4 53
Berkshire, co., Eng.,
 538,800...........*E6 4
Berksire, co., Mass.,
 142,135............B1 65
Berlin, Ger., 3,247,400....B6 6
Berlin, Md., 2,046.......D7 53
Berlin, N.H., 17,821......C5 73
Berlin, N.J., 3,578.......D3 74
Berlin, N.Y., 800........C7 75
Berlin, Pa., 1,660........G4 81
Berlin, Wis., 4,838.......E5 88
Berlin East, Ger.,
 1,061,200..........*B6 6
Berlin West, Ger.,
 2,186,200..........*B6 6
Bermeo, Sp., 13,781......A4 8
Bermuda, Br. dep., N.A.,
 48,000.............p20 35
Bern, Switz., 166,600.....E3 6
Bern, canton, Switz.,
 935,000...........*E3 6
Bernalillo, N. Mex.,
 2,574.........B5, D6 48
Bernalillo, co., N. Mex.,
 262,199............B5 48
Bernardsville, N.J., 5,515..B3 74
Bernau, Ger., 13,600.....B6 6
Bernay, Fr., 7,418........C4 5
Bernberg, Ger., 44,800....C5 6
Berndorf, Aus., 8,992.....E8 6
Berne, Ind., 2,644........C8 59
Bernice, La., 1,641.......B3 63
Bernie, Mo., 1,578.......E8 69
Bernville, Pa., 884.......F9 81
Beroun, Czech.,
 15,600.........D3, o17 7
Berrien, co., Ga., 12,038...E3 55
Berrien, co., Mich.,
 149,865............F4 66
Berrien Springs, Mich.,
 1,953.............G4 66
Berry, former prov., Fr.,
 464,000............D4 5
Berry Hill, Tenn., 1,551...E9 83
Berryville, Ark., 1,999....A2 49
Berryville, Va., 1,645.....A5 85
Bershad, Sov. Un., 10,000.G7 12
Berthier, Que., Can.,
 27,325.............C3 42
Berthierville, Que., Can.,
 3,708.............C4 42
Berthoud, Colo., 1,014....A5 51
Bertie, N.C., 24,350......A5 76
Bertram, Tex., 900.......D4 84
Bertrand, Mich., 3,500...*G4 66
Berwick, N.S., Can.,
 1,282.............D5 43
Berwick, La., 3,880.......E4 63
Berwick, Maine, 1,800
 (2,738▲)...........F2 64
Berwick, Pa., 13,353......D9 81
Berwick, co., Scot.,
 21,900...........*C5 4

Berwick-upon-Tweed, Eng.,
 12,100............C6 4
Berwind, W. Va., 950.....D3 87
Berwyn, Ill., 54,224,......k9 58
Berwyn, Pa., 8000.......o20 81
Berwyn Heights, Md.,
 2,376............*B4 53
Besa, Indon.............E7 19
Besançon, Fr., 95,642.....D7 5
Besni, Tur., 11,194.......D11 14
Bessèges, Fr., 5,770......E6 5
Bessemer, Ala., 33,054..B3, E4 46
Bessemer, Mich., 3,304....n11 66
Bessemer, Pa., 1,491......E1 81
Bessemer City, N.C.,
 4,271.............B1 76
Bethalto, Ill., 5,404......E3 58
Bethany, Conn., 800......D5 52
Bethany, Ill., 1,118.......D5 58
Bethany, Mo., 2,771......A3 69
Bethany, Okla., 12,342....B4 79
Bethany, W. Va., 992.....B2 87
Bethayres-Huntingdon
 Valley, Pa., 2,500....*F11 81
Bethel, Alsk., 1,258......C7 47
Bethel, Conn., 8,200......D3 52
Bethel, Maine, 1,150
 (2,408▲)...........D2 64
Bethel, N.C., 1,578.......B6 76
Bethel, Ohio, 2,019.......D1 78
Bethel, Oreg., 1,500.....*C3 80
Bethel (Bethel Park), Pa.,
 23,650...........*k13 81
Bethesda, Md., 76,000..C3, f8 53
Bethesda, Ohio, 1,178.....B4 78
Bethlehem, Pa., 754,008..E11 81
Bethlehem, S. Afr., 24,125..F5 24
Bethlehem, W. Va., 2,308..B2 87
Bethpage, N.Y., 28,500...G3 52
Bettendorf, Iowa,
 17,264.........C7, g11 60
Betul, India, 19,860......D6 20
Beulah, N. Dak., 1,318....C4 77
Beulaville, N.C., 1,131....C5 76
Beverley, Eng., 16,300....D6 4
Beverly, Alta., Can.,
 9,041.............C4 38
Beverly, Mass.,
 36,108.........A6, f12 65
Beverly, N.J., 3,400......C3 74
Beverly, Ohio, 1,194......C4 78
Beverly Gardens, Ohio,
 2,200.............*C1 78
Beverly Hills, Calif.,
 30,817............m12 50
Beverly Hills, Mich.,
 8,633............*F7 66
Beverwijk, Neth., 40,900..A6 5
Bexar, co., Tex., 687,151...E3 84
Bexhill-on-Sea, Eng.,
 30,900.............E7 4
Bexley, Ohio, 14,319.....m11 78
Beypazari, Tur., 8,854....B8 14
Beyrouth, see Beirut, Leb.
Bezerros, Braz., 7,737....*D7 27
Bezhetsk, Sov. Un.,
 25,000............C11 12
Bezhitsa, Sov. Un.,
 85,000............E10 12
Béziers, Fr., 73,538......F5 5
Bezons, Fr., 22,061.......g9 5
Bhagalpur, India,
 143,850............C8 20
Bhakkar, Pak., 12,397....B5 20
Bhamo, Bur., 9,817......D10 20
Bharatpur, India, 49,776...C6 20
Bhatpara, India, 147,630..D8 20
Bhavnagar, India,
 171,039............D5 20
Bhind, India, 28,208......C6 20
Bhopal, India, 185,374....D6 20
Bhor, India, 8,627.......E5 20
Bhuj, India, 40,180......D4 20
Bhutan, country, Asia,
 640,000............C9 20
Biala Podlaska, Pol.,
 22,200.............B7 7
Białogard, Pol., 19,000....A4 7
Białystok, Pol., 132,100...B7 7
Bianco, It., 5,057........E6 9
Biarritz, Fr., 25,231......F3 5
Bibai, Jap., 63,051.......E10 18
Bibb, co., Ala., 14,357....C2 46
Bibb, co., Ga., 141,249....D3 55
Bibb City, Ga., 1,213.....D2 55
Biberach, Ger., 21,500....D4 6
Bic, Que., Can., 1,177....A9 42
Bicknell, Ind., 3,878......G3 59
Bicske, Hung., 8,148......B4 10
Bida, Nig., 19,346.......G6 22
Bidar, India, 32,420......E6 20
Biddeford, Maine,
 19,255.........E2, g7 64
Bideford, Eng., 10,800....E4 4
Biel, Switz., 65,300......E3 6
Bielawa, Pol., 30,000.....C4 7
Bielefeld, Ger., 171,700...B4 6
Biella, It., 52,000........B2 9

Bielsko-Biała, Pol.,
 80,500..........D5, h10 7
Bielsk Podlaski, Pol.,
 11,800.............B7 7
Bienfait, Sask., Can., 842..H4 39
Bienville, par., La.,
 16,726.............C2 63
Biga, Tur., 10.800......*B7 14
Big Bear City, Calif., 800...E5 50
Big Bear Lake, Calif.,
 1,562............*E5 50
Big Beaver, Pa., 2,381....*E1 81
Big Flats, N.Y., 900......C4 75
Bigger, Sask., Can., 2,702..E1 39
Biggs, Calif., 831........C3 50
Big Horn, co., Mont.,
 10,007............E9 70
Big Horn, co., Wyo.,
 11,898............B4 89
Big Lake, Tex., 2,668.....D2 84
Biglerville, Pa., 923......G7 81
Big Pine, Calif., 800......D4 50
Big Rapids, Mich., 8,686..E5 66
Big River, Sask., Can.,
 896..............D2 39
Big Run, Pa., 857........E4 81
Big Sandy, Mont., 954....B6 70
Big Spring, Tex., 31,230...C2 84
Big Stone, co., Minn.,
 8,954.............E2 67
Big Stone Gap, Va., 4,688..f9 85
Big Timber, Mont., 1,660..E7 70
Big Wells, Tex., 801......E3 84
Bihać, Yugo., 15,552.....C2 10
Bihar, India, 78,581......C8 20
Bihar, state, India,
 46,455,610.........D8 20
Bijapur, India, 78,854.....E6 20
Bijeljina, Yugo., 15,682...C4 10
Bijou, Calif., 2,000......C4 50
Bikaner, India, 150,634...C5 20
Bikin, Sov. Un., 10,000...C7 18
Bilaspur, India, 86,706....D7 20
Bilbad, Sp., 297,942.....A4 8
Bileća, Yugo., 2,489......D4 10
Bilin, Bur., 5,265........E10 20
Billerica, Mass.,
 3,000 (17,867▲)...A5, F10 65
Billings, Mont., 52,851....E8 70
Billings, co., N. Dak.,
 1,513.............C2 77
Billings Heights, Mont.,
 2,500.............E8 70
Biloela, Austl., 2,048.....B8 26
Biloxi, Miss., 44,053..E2, E5 68
Bilqas Qism Awwal,
 Eg., U.A.R., 43,200...*G8 14
Biltmore Forest, N.C.,
 1,004.............f10 76
Binalbagan, Phil., 13,545.*C6 19
Bindura, Rh., 5,530......D6 24
Bingen, Ger., 20,200.....D3 6
Bingham, Maine, 1,180
 (1,308▲)...........C3 64
Bingham, co., Idaho,
 28,218............F6 57
Bingham Canyon, Utah,
 1,516.........A5, D2 72
Binghamton, N.Y.,
 69,435............C5 75
Bintulu, Mala., 5,307....E4 19
Bío-Bío, prov., Chile,
 168,837............B2 28
Birakan, Sov. Un., 5,000..B5 18
Bi'r Ar Rummānah, Eg.,
 U.A.R., 1,000.......G9 14
Birch Cliff, Ont.,
 Can.............D5, E7 41
Birch Run, Mich., 844.....E7 66
Bird Island, Minn., 1,384..F4 67
Birdsboro, Pa., 3,025.....F10 81
Birecik, Tur., 13,110......D11 14
Bir Hasanah (Oasis),
 Eg., U.A.R..........*G8 14
Birkenhead, Eng.,
 143,700............D5 4
Birlad, Rom., 35,400......B8 10
Birmingham, Ala.,
 340,887.........B3, E4 46
Birmingham, Eng.,
 1,115,600..........D6 4
Birmingham, Mich.,
 25,525..........F7, o15 66
Birobidzhan, Sov. Un.,
 42,000............E16 12
Birtle, Man., Can., 846....D1 40
Bisbee, Ariz., 9,914......D4 48
Biscayne Park, Fla.,
 2,911.............s13 54
Bisceglie, It., 42,000.....D6 9
Biscoe, N.C., 1,053......B3 76
Bishop, Calif., 2,958.....D4 50
Bishop, Tex., 3,772......F4 84
Bishop's Falls, Newf., Can.,
 4,099.............D4 44
Bishop's Stortford, Eng.,
 20,100.............E7 4
Bishopville, S.C., 3,586...C7 82

Biskra, Alg., 55,372......B6 22
Bismarck, Mo., 1,237......D7 69
Bismarck, N. Dak., 30,584..D5 77
Bissett, Man., Can., 857..D4 40
Bistrita, Rom., 20,292....B7 10
Bitlis, Tur., 16,636......C14 14
Bitola, Yugo., 49,101.....E5 10
Bitonto, It., 33,300......D6 9
Bitterfeld, Ger., 30,900..C6 6
Biwabik, Minn., 1,836....C6 67
Bixby, Okla., 1,711......B6 79
Biysk, Sov. Un., 165,000..D11 12
Bizerte, Tun., 44,721....A6 22
Bizuta, Mong., 10,000....B8 17
Bjelovar, Yugo., 15,637...C3 10
Black, mtn., Ky.,........D7 62
Black, sea., Eur.,.......G14 3
Blackburn, Eng., 105,000..D5 4
Black Diamond, Alta.,
  Can., 1,043...........D3 38
Black Diamond, Wash.,
  1,026............B4, f11 86
Black Eagle, Mont., 2,200..C5 70
Blackford, co., Ind.,
  14,792..............D7 59
Black Forest, Colo., 1,000..C6 51
Black Hawk, co., Iowa,
  122,482.............B5 60
Black Lake, Que., Can.,
  4,180...............C6 42
Black Mountain, N.C.,
  1,313...............f10 76
Black Oak, Ind., 16,500...*A3 59
Black Point, Calif., 650..*C2 50
Blackpool, Eng., 151,000..D5 4
Black River, N.Y., 1,237..A5 75
Black River Falls, Wis.,
  3,195...............D3 88
Blacksburg, S.C., 2,174...A4 82
Blacksburg, Va., 7,070....C2 85
Blackshear, Ga., 2,482....E4 55
Blackstone, Mass., 2,500
  (5,130▲)............B4 65
Blackstone, Va., 3,659....C5 85
Blackville, S.C., 1,901...E5 82
Blackwell, Okla., 9,588...A4 79
Blackwood, N.J., 3,500...*D2 74
Bladen, co., N.C., 26,605..C4 76
Bladenboro, N.C., 805....C4 76
Bladensburg, Md., 3,103...f9 53
Blagoevgrad (Gorna-
  Dzhumaya), Bul.,
  32,744..............D6 10
Blagoveshchensk, Sov.
  Un., 114,000.........D15 13
Blain, Fr., 2,009.........D3 5
Blaine, Minn., 15,544....m12 67
Blaine, Wash., 1,735.....A3 86
Blaine, co., Idaho, 4,598..F4 57
Blaine, co., Mont., 8,091..B7 70
Blaine, co., Nebr., 1,016..C5 71
Blaine, Okla., 12,077....B3 79
Blair, Nebr., 4,931......C9 71
Blair, Okla., 893........C2 79
Blair, Wis., 909.........D2 88
Blair, co., Pa., 137,270..E5 81
Blairgowrie [& Rattray],
  Scot., 5,100.........B5 4
Blairmore, Alta., Can.,
  1,980...............E3 38
Blairsville, Pa., 4,930...F3 81
Blaj, Rom., 8,731.......B7 10
Blakely, Ga., 3,580......E2 55
Blanc, mtn., Fr.,........E7 5
Blanca, pk., Colo.........D5 51
Blanchard, Okla., 1,377..B4 79
Blanchester, Ohio, 2,944..C2 78
Blanco, co., Tex., 3,657..D3 84
Bland, co., Va., 5,982....C1 85
Blanding, Utah, 1,805....C7 72
Blandinsville, Ill., 853..C3 58
Blankenburg, Ger.,
  19,500..............C5 6
Blasdell, N.Y., 3,786.....C2 75
Blato, Yugo., 5,140......D3 10
Blauvelt, N.Y., 3,500....*D6 75
Blawnox, Pa., 2,085......k14 81
Bled-Grad, Yugo., 4,120..B2 10
Bledsoe, co., Tenn., 7,811..D8 83
Blekinge, co., Swe.,
  144,500.............*I6 11
Blenheim, Ont., Can.,
  3,151...............E2 41
Blenheim, N.Z., 13,242...N14 26
Blida, Alg., 79,223......A5 22
Blind River, Ont., Can.,
  4,093...............A2 41
Blissfield, Mich., 2,653...G7 66
Bloemfontein, S. Afr., 112,606
  (*145,273)..........F5 24
Blois, Fr., 33,838.......D4 5
Blonie, Pol., 11,200.....m13 7
Bloomer, Wis., 2,834.....C2 88
Bloomfield, Ont., Can.,
  803................D7 41
Bloomfield, Conn., 4,000..B6 52
Bloomfield, Ind., 2,224...F4 59
Bloomfield, Iowa, 2,771...D5 60

Bloomfield, Ky., 916.....C4 62
Bloomfield, Mo., 1,330...E8 69
Bloomfield, Nebr., 1,349..B8 71
Bloomfield, N.J., 51,867..h8 74
Bloomfield, N. Mex.,
  1,292...............A5 48
Bloomfield Hills, Mich.,
  2,378...............o15 66
Bloomfield Village, Mich.,
  3,500...............*F7 66
Bloomingdale, Ga., 900...D5 55
Bloomingdale, Ill., 1,262..*B5 58
Bloomingdale, N.J., 5,293..A4 74
Blooming Prairie, Minn.,
  1,778...............G5 67
Bloomington, Calif.,
  11,800..............*F5 50
Bloomington, Ill., 37,791..C4 58
Bloomington, Ind., 42,058..F4 59
Bloomington, Minn.,
  66,542..............n12 67
Bloomington, Tex., 1,800..E4 84
Bloomsburg, Pa., 10,655..E9 81
Bloomsbury, N.J., 838....B2 74
Bloomville, Ohio, 836....A2 78
Blossburg, Pa., 1,956....C7 81
Blossom Hill, Pa., 1,000..*G9 81
Blount, co., Ala., 25,449..B3 46
Blount, co., Tenn.,
  57,525..............D10 83
Blountstown, Fla., 2,375..B1 54
Bludenz, Aus., 11,127....E4 6
Blue Ash, Ohio, 8,341....o13 78
Blue Bell, Pa., 1,000....*F11 81
Blue Earth, Minn., 4,200..G4 67
Blue Earth, co., Minn.,
  44,385..............F4 67
Bluefield, Va., 4,235....e10 85
Bluefield, W. Va., 19,256..D3 87
Bluefields, Nic., 9,292...E8 34
Blue Hills, Conn., 6,500..*B6 52
Blue Island, Ill.,
  21,986..............B6, k9 58
Blue Lake, Calif., 1,234..B2 50
Blue Mound, Ill., 1,038..D4 58
Blue Mountain, pk.,
  Jam................F5 35
Blue Point, N.Y., 2,600..G4 52
Blue Rapids, Kans.,
  1,426...............C7 61
Blue Ridge, Ga., 1,406...B2 55
Blue Ridge, Va., 900.....C3 85
Blue Ridge, mts.,
  Tenn...............D11 83
Blue Springs, Mo., 2,555..h11 69
Bluff City, Tenn., 948...C11 83
Bluff Park, Ala., 3,000...*B3 46
Bluffton, Ind., 6,238....C7 59
Bluffton, Ohio, 2,591....B2 78
Blumenau, Braz., 46,591..D3 30
Bly, Calif., 1,554.......*F5 50
Blyth, Eng., 36,400......C6 4
Blythe, Calif., 6,023....F6 50
Blytheville, Ark., 20,796..B6 49
Bnei Braq, Isr., 51,700...*B2 15
Boac, Phil., 3,934.......C6 19
Boalsburg, Pa., 800.....E6 81
Boardman, Ohio, 27,000..A5 78
Boaz, Ala., 4,654.......A3 46
Bobbili, India, 25,592....E7 20
Bobcaygeon, Ont., Can.,
  1,210...............C6 41
Bobigny, Fr., 37,010.....g10 5
Bobo-Dioulasso, Upper Volta,
  45,000..............F4 22
Bobrinets, Sov. Un.,
  10,000..............G9 12
Bobrka, Sov. Un., 10,000..G5 12
Bobruysk, Sov. Un.,
  108,000.............E7 12
Bobtown, Pa., 1,167.....G2 81
Bobures, Ven., 2,159....B3 32
Boca Raton, Fla., 6,961..F6 54
Bochnia, Pol., 13,000....D6 7
Bochum, Ger., 360,000..C3 6
Bodaybo, Sov. Un.,
  14,700..............D14 13
Boden, Swe., 13,700.....E9 11
Bodmin, Eng., 6,300.....E4 4
Bodö, Nor., 12,700......D6 11
Boerne, Tex., 2,169.....E3, h7 84
Bogalusa, La., 21,423....D6 63
Bogata, Tex., 1,112.....C5 84
Boger City, N.C., 2,200...B1 76
Bogo, Phil., 6,786.......C6 19
Bogodukhov, Sov. Un.,
  10,000..............F10 12
Bogor Buitenzorg, Indon.,
  146,907.............G3 19
Bogoroditsk, Sov. Un.,
  10,000..............E12 12
Bogorodsk, Sov. Un.,
  36,200..............C14 12
Bogotá, Col., 1,697,311..C3 32
Bogota, N.J., 7,965.....h8 74
Bogra, Pak., 25,303.....D8 20
Boguslav, Sov. Un.,
  10,000..............G8 12

Bohain [-en-Vermandois],
  Fr., 6,726..........C5 5
Bohemia, N.Y., 3,000....n15 75
Bohemia (Čěchy), reg.,
  Czech., 6,039,087....D3 7
Bohol, prov., Phil.,
  592,194.............D6 19
Boiling Springs, N.C.,
  1,771...............B1 76
Boiling Springs, Pa., 1,182..F7 81
Boischatel, Que., Can.,
  1,576...............C6, n17 42
Bois-Colombes, Fr.,
  29,938..............G10 5
Bois-des-Filion, Que., Can.,
  2,499...............p19 42
Boise, Idaho, 72,090....F2 57
Boise, co., Idaho, 1,646..F3 57
Boise City, Okla., 1,978..e8 79
Boissevain, Man., Can.,
  1,303...............E1 40
Boissevain, Va., 600....e10 85
Bolbec, Fr., 12,212.....C4 5
Bolgrad, Sov. Un., 10,000..I7 12
Boling, Tex., 950.......E5, r14 84
Bolívar, Arg., 14,010....B4 28
Bolivar, Mo., 3,512.....D4 69
Bolivar, N.Y., 1,450....C2 75
Bolivar, Ohio, 932......B4 78
Bolivar, Tenn., 3,338....B3 83
Bolivar, co., Miss., 54,464..B3 68
Bolívar, dept., Col.,
  1,006,347...........B2 32
Bolívar, prov., Ec.,
  131,651.............B2 31
Bolívar, state, Ven.,
  213,543.............B4 32
Bolivar (La Columna), pk.,
  Ven................B3 32
Bolivia, country, S.A.,
  3,462,000...........C2 29
Bolkhov, Sov. Un.,
  10,000..............E11 12
olling, Tex., 950......E5, r14 84
Bollinger, co., Mo., 9,167..D7 69
Bollnäs, Swe., 10,679....G7 11
Bollullos, Sp., 10,947...D2 8
Bologna, It., 475,700....B3 9
Bologoye, Sov. Un.,
  22,000..............C10 12
Bolshaya Lepetikha,
  Sov. Un., 5,000......H9 12
Bolshaya Viska, Sov. Un.,
  10,000..............G8 12
Bolshoy Tokmak,
  Sov. Un., 10,000.....H10 12
Bolton, Ont., Can., 2,104..D5 41
Bolton, Eng., 159,800....D5 4
Bolton Landing, N.Y.,
  900................B7 75
Bolu, Tur., 13,745......B8 14
Bolvadin, Tur., 16,026...C8 14
Bolzano, It., 93,700.....A3 9
Boma, Con. K., 31,500...B2 24
Bombay, India, 4,152,056..E5 20
Bom Conselho, Braz.,
  6,840...............*D7 27
Bom Despacho, Braz.
  13,568..............B3 30
Bon Air, Pa., 1,000.....*G11 81
Bon Air, Va., 2,000.....m17 85
Bonaventure, Que., Can.,
  804................*k13 42
Bonaventure, co., Que.,
  Can., 42,962........A3 43
Bonavista, Newf., Can.
  4,186...............D5 44
Bond, co., Ill., 14,060...E4 58
Bondy, Fr., 38,039......G10 5
Bone, see Annaba, Alg.
Bonham, Tex., 7,357....C4 84
Bon Homme, Co., S. Dak.,
  9,229...............G8 77
Bonifay, Fla., 2,222....G3 54
Bonin Islands, U.S. occ.,
  Asia...............E6 2
Bonita, Calif., 2,000....*E5 50
Bonita Springs, Fla., 900..F5 54
Bonn, Ger., 143,000....C3 6
Bonner, co., Idaho,
  15,587..............A2 57
Bonners Ferry, Idaho,
  1,921...............A2 57
Bonner Springs, Kans.,
  3,171...............C9, K16 61
Bonne Terre, Mo., 3,219..D7 69
Bonneville, co., Idaho,
  46,906..............F7 57
Bonnyville, Alta., Can.,
  1,736...............B5 38
Bonorva, It., 6,669.....D2 9
Bonthain, Indon., 6,711..G5 19
Bontoc, Phil., 5,472....*B6 19
Boomer, W. Va.,
  1,657...............C3, D6 87
Boone, Iowa, 12,468....B4 60
Boone, N.C., 3,686......A1 76
Boone, co., Ark., 16,116..A2 49

Boone, co., Ill., 20,326...A5 58
Boone, co., Ind., 27,543..D4 59
Boone, co., Iowa, 28,037..B4 60
Boone, co., Ky., 21,940...B5 62
Boone, co., Mo., 55,202..B5 69
Boone, co., Nebr., 9,134..C7 71
Boone, co., W. Va.,
  28,764..............C3 87
Booneville, Ark., 2,690...B2 49
Booneville, Miss., 3,480..A5 68
Boonsboro, Md., 1,211...A2 53
Boon Terrace, Pa., 1,100..*F1 81
Boonton, N.J., 7,981....B4 74
Boonville, Calif., 950....C2 50
Boonville, Ind., 4,801....H3 59
Boonville, Mo., 7,090....C5 69
Boonville, N.Y., 2,403....B5 75
Boothbay Harbor, Maine,
  1,800 (2,252▲)......E3 64
Boothwyn, Pa., 5,000....*G11 81
Boppard, Ger., 8,600....C3 6
Boqueron, dept., Par.,
  42,200..............D3 29
Borah, pk., Idaho.......E3 57
Borås, Swe., 68,000.....I5 11
Bordeaux, Fr., 249,688..E3 5
Borden, co., Tex., 1,076..C2 84
Borden Springs, Ala., 500..B4 46
Bordentown, N.J., 4,974..C3 74
Bordighera, It., 8,621...C1 9
Borgå, Fin., 11,800.....G11 11
Borger, Tex., 20,911....B2 84
Borgomanero, It., 7,900..B2 9
Borgo Val di Taro, It.,
  11,809..............B2 9
Borislav, Sov. Un., 47,500..G7 12
Borisoglebsk, Sov. Un.,
  57,000..............F13 12
Borisov, Sov. Un., 65,000..D7 12
Borispol, Sov. Un.,
  25,000..............F8 12
Borja, Sp., 4,381.......B5 8
Borkou, reg., Chad......E1 23
Borlänge, Swe., 26,700...G6 11
Borneo (Kalimantan), isl.
  Asia...............E4 19
Bornholm, co., Den.,
  48,373..............*A3 7
Bornos, Sp., 8,697......D3 8
Boromlya, Sov. Un.,
  10,000..............F10 12
Borovan, Bul., 5,905....D6 10
Borovichi, Sov. Un.,
  47,100..............B9 12
Borovskoye, Sov. Un.,
  5,000...............q21 12
Borsod-Abauj-Zemplen, co.,
  Hung., 588,900......*A5 10
Bort-les-Orgues, Fr.,
  5,115...............E5 5
Borzna, Sov. Un., 10,000..F9 12
Bosa, It., 8,169........D2 9
Bosanska Gradiska, Yugo.,
  6,373...............C3 10
Bosanska Kostajnica, Yugo.,
  2,037...............C3 10
Bosanski Novi, Yugo.,
  7,082...............C3 10
Boscobel, Wis., 2,608....E3 88
Boskovice, Czech., 6,396..D4 7
Bosnia, reg., Yugo.......C3 10
Bosnia-Hercegovina, rep.
  Yugo., 3,277,948....*C3 10
Bosque, co., Tex. 10,809..D4 84
Bossier, par. La., 57,622..B2 63
Bossier City, La., 32,776..B2 63
Boston, Eng., 25,000....D6 4
Boston, Ga., 1,357......F3 55
Boston, Mass., 590,000
  (*3,575,000).........B5, g11 65
Boston, Pa., 2,300......*E1 81
Boswell, Ind., 957......B3 59
Botetourt, co., Va. 16,715..C3 85
Botevgrad, Bul., 5,925...D6 10
Bothwell, Ont., Can., 819..E3 41
Botkins, Ohio, 853......B1 78
Botoşani, Rom., 29,569..E8 10
Botswana, Br. dep., Afr.,
  559,000.............E4 24
Bottineau, N. Dak., 2,613..A5 77
Bottineau, co., N. Dak.,
  11,315..............B5 77
Botucatu, Braz.,
  33,878..............C3, m7 30
Botwood, Newf., Can.,
  3,680...............D4 44
Bouaké, I.C., 45,000....G3 22
Boucherville, Que., Can.
  8,182...............D4, p20 42
Bouches-du-Rhône, dept.,
  Fr., 1,248,355.......*F6 5
Bougie, see Bejaïa, Alg.
Boulder, Austl., 5,230...F3 25
Boulder, Colo., 37,718..A5 51
Boulder, Mont., 1,394...D4 70
Boulder, co., Colo.,
  74,254..............A5 51
Boulder City, Nev., 4,059..D4 72

Boulder Creek, Calif., 1,306................*D2 50
Boulogne-sur-Mer, Fr., 49,281 (*98,000).......B4 5
Boulogne-sur-Mer, Fr., 49,281 (*98,000).......B4 5
Boundary, co., Idaho, 5,809................A2 57
Boundary, pk., Nev., ...C2 72
Bound Brook, N.J., 10,263..B3 74
Bountiful, Utah, 17,039.............A6, C2 72
Bourbon, Ind., 1,522.....B5 59
Bourbon, co., Kans., 16,090................E9 61
Bourbon, co., Ky, 18,178..B5 62
Bourbonnais, Ill, 3,336...B6 58
Bourbonnais, former prov., Fr., 318,000........D5 5
Bourg, La., 900.........E5 63
Bourg-de-Péage, Fr., 7,804................E6 5
Bourg-[en-Bresse], Fr., 32,596.............D6 5
Bourges, Fr., 60,632......D5 5
Bourg-la-Reine, Fr., 17,694.............g10 5
Bourgoin, Fr., 9,240......E6 5
Bournemouth, Eng., 150,700.............E6 4
Bovey, Minn., 1,086......C5 67
Bovina, Tex., 1,029......B1 84
Bowdon, Ga., 1,548......C1 55
Bowie, Md., 1,072.......B4 53
Bowie, Tex., 4,566......C4 84
Bowie, co., Tex., 59,971..C5 84
Bow Island, Alta., Can., 1,122................E5 38
Bowling Green, Fla., 1,171................E5 54
Bowling Green, Ky., 28,338.............D3 62
Bowling Green, Mo., 2,650................B6 69
Bowling Green, Ohio, 13,574.............A2, F6 78
Bowling Green, S.C., 700..A5 82
Bowman, N. Dak., 1,730..D2 77
Bowman, S.C., 1,106.....E6 82
Bowman, co., N. Dak., 4,154................D2 77
Bowmanstown, Pa., 888...E10 81
Bowmanville, Ont., Can., 7,397................D6 41
Bowness, Alta., Can., 9,184................D3 38
Box Butte, co., Nebr., 11,688................B2 71
Box Elder, co., Utah, 25,061................A5 72
Boxtel, Neth., 11,000.....B6 5
Boyacá, dept., Col., 1,058,152............B3 32
Boyce, La., 1,094.......C3 63
Boyd, co., Ky., 52,163.....B7 62
Boyd, co., Nebr., 4,513....B7 71
Boyertown, Pa., 4,067....F10 81
Boyes Hot Springs, Calif., 2,462................*C2 50
Boyle, co., Ky., 21,257.....C5 62
Boylston, Ala., 1,300......C3 46
Boyne City, Mich., 2,797..C5 66
Boynton Beach, Fla., 10,467.............F6 54
Boys Town, Nebr., 997....g12 71
Bozeman, Mont., 13,361..E5 70
Bozuyuk, Tur., 9,101.....C8 14
Bra, It., 16,400.........B1 9
Brabant, prov., Bel., 1,992,139...........*B6 5
Bracciano, It., 6,460......g8 9
Bracebridge, Ont., Can., 2,927................B5 41
Bracken, co., Ky., 7,422...B5 62
Brackenridge, Pa., 5,697.h15 81
Brackettville, Tex., 1,662..E2 84
Brad, Sov. Un., 9,963.....B6 10
Bradbury Heights, Md., 1,100................*C3 53
Braddock, Pa., 12,337....k14 81
Braddock Heights, Md., 800................B2 53
Braddock Hills, Pa., 2,414................*E1 81
Bradenton, Fla., 19,380.............E4, q10 54
Bradenton Beach, Fla., 1,124................*E4 54
Bradenville, Pa., 1,100.....F3 81
Bradford, Ont., Can., 2,342................C5 41
Bradford, Eng., 297,000...D6 4
Bradford, Ill., 857.......B4 58
Bradford, Ohio, 2,148.....B1 78
Bradford, Pa., 15,061.....C4 81
Bradford, R.I., 950......D10 52
Bradford, co., Fla., 12,446..C4 54
Bradford, co., Pa., 54,925..C8 81

Bradfordwoods, Pa., 866..h13 81
Bradley, Fla., 1,035.......E5 54
Bradley, Ill., 9,381.......B6 58
Bradley, co., Ark., 14,029..D3 49
Bradley, co., Tenn., 38,324................D9 83
Bradley Beach, N.J., 4,204................C4 74
Bradley Gardens, N.J., 1,500................*B3 74
Bradner, Ohio, 994......A2 78
Bradshaw, W. Va., 950...D3 87
Brady, Tex., 5,338.......D3 84
Braga, Port., 40,977......B1 8
Bragado, Arg., 16,104..B4, g6 28
Bragança, Braz., 12,848..*D6 27
Bragança, Port., 8,075....B2 8
Bragança Paulista, Braz., 27,328........C3, m8 30
Brahmaputra, riv, Asia....C9 20
Braidwood, Ill., 1,944....B5 58
Brăila, Rom., 113,200....C8 10
Brainerd, Minn., 12,898..D4 67
Braintree, Mass., 31,069.............B5, h11 65
Brampton, Ont., Can., 18,467.............D9, E6 41
Bramwell, W. Va., 1,195...D3 87
Branch, co., Mich., 34,903................G5 66
Branchville, N.J., 963.....A3 74
Branchville, S.C., 1,182...E6 82
Branco, riv., Braz.,......C5 32
Brandenburg, Ger., 89,800................B6 6
Brandenburg, Ky., 1,542..C3 62
Brandenburg, former state, Ger., 2,527,492.......B6 6
Brandenburg, reg., Ger.,..B6 6
Brandon, Man., Can., 28,166.............E2, h7 40
Brandon, Fla., 3,000......E4 54
Brandon, Miss., 2,139....C4 68
Brandon, S.C., 2,200.....B3 82
Brandon, Vt., 1,675......D1 73
Brandys nad Labem, Czech., 13,300........n18 7
Branford, Conn., 2,371...D5 52
Branson, Mo., 1,887......E4 69
Brant, co., Ont., Can., 83,839................D4 41
Brantford, Ont., Can., 55,201................D4 41
Brant Lake, N.Y., 800....B7 75
Brantley, Ala., 1,014.....D3 46
Brantley, co., Ga., 5,891..E4 55
Bras-d'or, N.S., Can., 947..C9 43
Brasília, Braz., 150,000...B3 30
Braşov, Rom., 129,600....C7 10
Bratenahl, Ohio, 1,332....g9 78
Bratislava, Czech., 252,800.............D4 7
Bratslav, Sov. Un., 10,000................G7 12
Brattleboro, Vt., 11,734...F2 73
Braunau [am Inn], Aus., 14,449.............D6 6
Braunschweig (Brunswick), Ger., 240,400.......B5 6
Brawley, Calif., 14,467....F6 50
Braxton, co., W. Va., 15,152................C4 87
Bray, Ire., 12,700........D3 4
Braymer, Mo., 874.......B4 69
Brazil, Ind., 8,853.......E3 59
Brazil, country, S.A., 81,301,000...........C3 30
Brazoria, Tex., 1,291......r14 84
Brazoria, co., Tex., 76,204..E5 84
Brazos, co., Tex., 44,895..D4 84
Brazzaville, Con. B., 133,700.............A3 24
Brčko, Yugo., 17,834.....C4 10
Brea, Calif., 12,350......n13 50
Breathitt, co., Ky., 15,490................C6 62
Breaux Bridge, La., 3,303..D4 63
Brechin, Scot., 7,100.....B5 4
Breckenridge, Mich., 1,131................E6 66
Breckenridge, Minn., 4,335................D2 67
Breckenridge, Tex., 6,273..C3 84
Breckenridge Hills, Mo., 6,299................*C7 69
Breckinridge, co., Ky., 14,734................C3 62
Brecknock, co., Wales, 54,400................*E5 4
Brecksville, Ohio, 5,435................A4, h9 78
Břeclav, Czech., 11,800....D4 7
Brecon, Wales, 5,800.....E5 4
Breda, Neth., 114,900.....B6 5
Breese, Ill., 2,810........E4 58
Bregenz, Aus., 21,428....E4 6
Bregovo, Bul., 5,271......C6 10
Bremen, Ga., 3,132......C1 55

Bremen, Ger., 581,000....B4 6
Bremen, Ind., 3,062......B5 59
Bremen, Ohio, 1,417.....C3 78
Bremen, state, Ger., 742,500.............*B4 6
Bremer, co., Iowa, 21,108..B5 60
Bremerhaven, Ger., 143,900.............B4 6
Bremerton, Wash., 28,922.............B3, e10 86
Bremerton East (Enetai), Wash., 2,539.......*B3 86
Bremond, Tex., 803......D4 84
Brenham, Tex., 7,740....D4 84
Brent, Ala., 1,879.......C2 46
Brent, Fla., 7,000.......u14 54
Brentford [& Chiswick], Eng., 54,832........m11 4
Brenton, W. Va., 500.....D3 87
Brentwood, Calif., 2,415...h9 50
Brentwood, Md., 3,693....F9 53
Brentwood, Mo., 12,250..f13 69
Brentwood, N.Y., 28,500..F4 52
Brentwood, Pa., 13,706..k14 81
Brescia, It., 185,000......B3 9
Breslau, see Wrocław, Pol.
Bressanone, It., 9,100.....A3 9
Bressler, Pa., 1,000......*F8 81
Bressuire, Fr., 6,528......D3 5
Brest, Fr., 136,104.......C1 5
Brest, Sov. Un., 82,000...E4 12
Breton Woods, N.J., 1,200................C4 74
Bretton Woods, Mich., 1,500................*F6 66
Brevard, co., Fla., 111,435.............E6 54
Brevard, N.C., 4,857......f10 76
Brewer, Maine, 9,009....D4 64
Brewster, N.Y., 1,574................D7, m15 75
Brewster, Ohio, 2,025....B4 78
Brewster, Wash., 940....A6 86
Brewster, co., Tex., 6,434..E1 84
Brewton, Ala., 6,309.....D2 46
Brezno [nad Hronom], Czech., 9,900........D5 7
Briançon, Fr., 7,570......E7 5
Briarcliff, Pa., 9,000.....*G11 81
Briarcliff Manor, N.Y., 6,788................D7 75
Briceville, Tenn., 1,217...C9 83
Bridge City, Mich., 1,326...E7 66
Bridge City, Tex., 4,677..*D6 84
Bridgehampton, N.Y., 900................n16 75
Bridgeport, Ala., 2,906....A4 46
Bridgeport, Ont., Can., 1,672................*D4 41
Bridgeport, Conn., 156,748 (*420,000)..........E4 52
Bridgeport, Ill., 2,260.....E6 58
Bridgeport, Ind., 900.....m9 59
Bridgeport, Nebr., 1,645..C2 71
Bridgeport, Ohio, 3,824...B5 78
Bridgeport, Pa., 5,306................F11, o20 81
Bridgeport, Tex., 3,218....C4 84
Bridgeport, Wash., 876...B6 86
Bridgeport, W. Va., 2,414................B4, B7 87
Bridgeton, Mo., 7,820................C7, f13 69
Bridgeton, N.J., 20,966...E2 74
Bridgetown, Barb., 11,452 (*110,000)..........J15 35
Bridgetown, N.S., Can., 1,043................E4 43
Bridgetown, Ohio, 5,000..*C1 78
Bridgeview, Ill., 7,334...*B6 58
Bridgeville, Del., 1,469....C6 53
Bridgeville, Pa., 7,112....k13 81
Bridgewater, N.S., Can., 4,497................E5 43
Bridgewater, Mass., 4,500 (10,276▲)..........C6 65
Bridgewater, Va., 1,815...B4 85
Bridgman, Mich., 1,454...G4 66
Bridgton, Maine, 1,750 (2,707▲)............D2 64
Bridgwater, Eng., 26,100..E5 4
Bridlington, Eng., 26,000..C6 4
Brielle, N.J., 2,619.......C4 74
Brigantine, N.J., 4,201...E4 74
Brigham City, Utah, 11,728.............A5, C2 72
Brighton, Ala., 2,884..B3, E4 46
Brighton, Colo., 7,055....B6 51
Brighton, Eng., 162,900 (*405,000)..........E6 4
Brighton, Ill., 1,502......D3 58
Brighton, Mich., 2,282...F7 66
Brighton, N.Y., 29,898....*B3 75
Brightwaters, N.Y., 3,389..n15 75
Brignoles, Fr., 5,347......F7 5
Brilliant, Ohio, 2,174.....B5 78
Brillion, Wis., 1,783..D5, H9 88
Brindisi, It., 74,100......D6 9

Brinkley, Ark., 4,636......C4 49
Brioude, Fr., 6,184.......E5 5
Brisbane, Austl., 656,540..E9 25
Brisbane, Calif., 5,000....*D2 50
Briscoe, co., Tex., 3,577..B2 84
Bristol, Conn., 45,499....C5 52
Bristol, Eng., 433,900....E5 4
Bristol, Ind., 991........A6 59
Bristol, N.H., 1,054......C3 73
Bristol, Pa., 12,364.......F12 81
Bristol, R.I., 15,716......C11 52
Bristol, Tenn., 17,582....C11 83
Bristol, Vt., 1,421.......C1 73
Bristol (Independent City), Va., 17,144..........f9 85
Bristol, co., Mass., 398,488.............C5 65
Bristol, co., R.I., 37,146..C11 52
Bristol Terrace No. 2, Pa., 1,300................*F11 81
Bristow, Okla., 4,795.....B5 79
Brittania Beach, B.C., Can., 775................E6 37
British Antarctic Territory, ter., S.A., 100........*K17 2
British Columbia, prov., Can., 1,629,082............37
British Guiana, see Guyana, country, S.A.
British Indian Ocean Territory, ter., Ind. O., 2,000...............*B9 24
British Honduras, dep., N.A., 106,000.......D7 34
British North Borneo, see Sabah, reg., Mala.
Britt, Iowa, 2,042........A4 60
Brittany (Bretagne), former prov., Fr., 3,072,000....C2 5
Britton, S. Dak., 1,442....E8 77
Brive [-la-Gaillarde], Fr., 40,175.............E4 5
Brno, Czech., 319,900....D4 7
Broach, India, 73,639....D5 20
Broadalbin, N.Y., 1,438..B6 75
Broad Brook, Conn., 1,500..B6 52
Broadmoor, Colo., 1,700..C6 51
Broadview, Sask., Can., 1,008................G4 39
Broadview, Ill., 8,588....*B6 58
Broadview, Ind., 1,856...*F4 59
Broadview Heights, Ohio, 6,209................B2 78
Broadwater, co., Mont., 2,804................D5 70
Brockport, N.Y., 6,058....B3 75
Brockton, Mass., 72,813.............B5, h11 65
Brockville, Ont., Can., 17,744.............C9 41
Brockway, Pa., 2,563.....D4 81
Brocton, Ill., 380........D6 58
Brod, Yugo., 28,729......C4 10
Broderick, Calif., 5,000...*C3 50
Brodhead, Wis., 2,444....F4 88
Brodnica, Pol., 15,500....B5 7
Brody, Sov. Un., 10,000...F5 12
Broken Arrow, Okla., 5,928................A6 79
Broken Bow, Nebr., 3,482..C6 71
Broken Bow, Okla., 2,087..C7 79
Broken Hill, Austl., 30,023................F7 25
Broken Hill, Zambia, 44,600.............C5 24
Brome, co., Que., Can., 13,691.............D5 42
Bromley, Eng., 68,169....m13 4
Bromptonville, Que., Can., 2,726................D6 42
Bronson, Mich., 2,267....G5 66
Bronte, Tex., 999........D2 84
Bronx, borough and co., N.Y., 1,424,815........E7 75
Bronxville, N.Y., 6,735..h13 75
Brook, Ind., 845........C3 59
Brooke, co., W. Va., 28,940................A4 87
Brookfield, Ill., 20,429...k9 58
Brookfield, Mass., 950 (1,751▲)...........B3 65
Brookfield, Mo., 5,694....B4 69
Brookfield, Wis., 19,812..m11 88
Brookhaven, Miss., 9,885..D3 68
Brookhaven, Pa., 5,280.*G11 81
Brookings, Oreg., 2,627..E2 80
Brookings, S. Dak., 10,558.............F9 77
Brookings, co., S. Dak., 20,046.............F9 77
Brooklands, Man., Can., 4,369................*E3 40
Brooklands, Mich., 1,800.*F7 66
Brooklawn, N.J., 2,504...D2 74
Brookline, Mass., 54,044.............B5, g11 65
Brookline, Mich., 1,600..*F6 66
Brooklyn, Conn., 800.....B9 52

Brooklyn, Ind., 866.......E5 59
Brooklyn, Iowa, 1,415.....C5 60
Brooklyn, Mich., 986.....F6 66
Brooklyn, Ohio, 10,733...h9 78
Brooklyn (Lovejoy), Ill.,
  1,922............g13 69
Brooklyn, borough, N.Y.,
  2,627,319............k13 75
Brooklyn Center, Minn.,
  24,356............E6 67
Brooklyn Park, Md.,
  4,000............*B4 53
Brooklyn Park, Minn.,
  10,197............*E6 67
Brookneal, Va., 1,070.....C4 85
Brook Park, Ohio, 12,856..h9 78
Brookport, Ill., 1,154.....F5 58
Brooks, Alta., Can., 2,827..D5 38
Brooks, co., Ga., 15,292...F3 55
Brooks, co., Tex., 8,609...F3 84
Brookshire, Tex.,
  1,339............E5, r14 84
Brookside, Ala., 999......E4 46
Brookside, Del., 4,000....A6 53
Brookside, N.J., 800......B3 74
Brookston, Ind., 1,202....C4 59
Brooksville, Fla., 3,301...D4 54
Brookview, Fla., 1,500....*B5 54
Brookville, Ind., 2,603....F7 59
Brookville, Mass., 2,500...h11 65
Brookville, N.Y., 1,468...*G2 52
Brookville, Ohio, 3,184...C1 78
Brookville, Pa., 4,620....D3 81
Broomall, Pa., 19,722....*G11 81
Broome, co., N.Y.,
  222,122............C5 75
Broomfield, Colo., 4,535..B5 51
Broughton, Pa., 3,500....*E1 81
Broussard, La., 1,600.....D4 63
Broward, co., Fla., 333,946.F6 54
Brown, co., Ill., 6,210....D3 58
Brown, co., Ind., 7,024...F5 59
Brown, co., Kans., 13,229..C8 61
Brown, co., Minn., 27,676.F4 67
Brown, co., Nebr., 4,436..B6 71
Brown, co., Ohio, 25,178..D2 78
Brown, co., S. Dak.,
  34,106............E7 77
Brown, co., Tex., 24,728..D3 84
Brown, co., Wis., 125,082.D6 88
Brown City, Mich., 993...E8 66
Brown Deer, Wis.,
  11,280............m12 88
Brownfield, Tex., 10,286..C1 84
Browning, Mont., 2,011...B3 70
Brownlee Park, Mich.,
  3,307............*F5 66
Brownsburg, Que., Can.,
  3,617............D3 42
Brownsburg, Ind., 5,121..E5 59
Browns Mills, N.J., 1,000.D3 74
Brownstown, Ind., 2,158..G5 59
Brownstown, Pa., 1,379..*E4 81
Browns Valley, Minn.,
  1,033............E2 67
Brownsville, La., 3,000...*B3 63
Brownsville, Oreg., 875...C4 80
Brownsville, Pa., 6,055...F2 81
Brownsville, Tenn., 5,424.B2 83
Brownsville, Tex., 49,000
  (*51,500)............G4 84
Brownville, Ala., 534.....E4 46
Brownville, N.Y., 1,082..A5 75
Brownville Junction, Maine,
  800................C3 64
Brownwood, Tex., 16,974..D3 84
Broxton, Ga., 907........E4 55
Brozas, Sp., 5,634........C2 8
Bruay-en-Artois, Fr.,
  30,902............B5 5
Bruce, mtn., Austl.......D2 25
Bruce, Miss., 1,698......B4 68
Bruceton, Tenn., 1,158...A3 83
Bruchsal, Ger., 22,600...D4 6
Bruck (Ander Leitha),
  Aus., 6,791..........D8 6
Bruck (Ander Mur), Aus.,
  16,087............E7 6
Brugge (Bruges), Bel.,
  52,220............B5 5
Brule, co., S. Dak., 6,319.G6 77
Brumath, Fr., 6,801......C7 5
Brundidge, Ala., 2,523...D4 46
Brunei, Br. dep., Asia,
  83,877............E4 19
Brunei, Bru., 9,702......E4 19
Brunswick, Ga., 21,703...E5 55
Brunswick, Maine,
  13,000 (15,797▲)...E3, g8 64
Brunswick, Md., 3,555...B2 53

Brunswick, Mo., 1,493....B4 69
Brunswick, Ohio, 11,725..A4 78
Brunswick, co., N.C.,
  20,278............C4 76
Brunswick, co., Va.,
  17,779............D5 85
Brush, Colo., 3,631......A7 51
Brusly, La., 544......D4, h9 63
Brusque, Braz., 16,127...D3 30
Brussels (Bruxelles), Bel.,
  170,489 (*1,930,000)...B6 5
Brussels, Ont., Can., 844..D3 41
Bruxelles, see Brussels, Bel.
Bryan, Ohio, 7,361......A1 78
Bryan, Tex., 27,542.....D4 84
Bryan, co., Ga., 6,226...D5 55
Bryan, co., Okla., 24,252.D5 79
Bryansk, Sov. Un.,
  249,000............E10 12
Bryant, Fla., 400........F6 54
Bryantville, Mass., 800...B6 65
Bryn Athyn, Pa., 1,057...o21 81
Bryn Mawr, Pa., 11,000..o20 81
Bryn Mawr, Wash., 8,000.D2 86
Bryson City, N.C., 1,084..f9 76
Bryte, Calif., 3,000......*C3 50
Brzeg, Pol., 26,900......C4 7
Brzeziny, Pol., 6,008....C5 7
Bsa, It., 16,400.........B1 9
Bucaramanga, Col.,
  229,748............B3 32
Buchanan, Mich., 5,341..G4 66
Buchanan, N.Y., 2,019...*D7 75
Buchanan, Va., 1,349....C3 85
Buchanan, co., Iowa,
  22,293............B6 60
Buchanan, co., Mo.,
  90,581............B3 69
Buchanan, co., Va., 36,724.e9 85
Buchans, Newf., Can.,
  2,463............D3 44
Bucharest (Bucureşti),
  Rom., 1,229,100
  (*1,354,000)........C8 10
Buchloe, Ger., 5,700....D5 6
Buckeye, Ariz., 2,286.C2, D1 48
Buckeye Lake, Ohio, 2,129.C3 78
Buckhannon, W. Va.,
  6,386............C4 87
Buckhaven [& Methil],
  Scot., 20,900........B5 4
Buckhorn, Ariz., 1,400...D2 48
Buckie, Scot., 7,600.....B5 4
Buckingham, Que., Can.,
  7,421............D2 42
Buckingham, co., Eng.,
  515,900............*E6 4
Buckingham, co., Va.,
  10,877............C4 85
Buckley, Wash., 3,538..B3, f11 86
Bucknell Manor, Va.,
  2,000............*B5 85
Buckner, Mo., 1,198.....*B3 69
Bucks, co., Pa., 308,567..F11 81
Bucksport, Maine, 2,500
  (3,466▲)............D4 64
Bucksport, S.C., 600.....D9 82
Bucovina, reg., Rom.....B7 10
Bucovina, reg., Sov. Un...B7 10
Bucuresti, see Bucharest,
  Rom.
Bucyrus, Ohio, 12,276...B3 78
Budapest, Hung.,
  1,899,700............B4 10
Budd Lake, N.J., 1,700...B3 74
Bude, Eng., 4,900.......E4 4
Bude, Miss., 1,185......D3 68
Budrio, It., 16,364......B3 9
Buechel, Ky., 8,000...A4, B4 62
Buena, N.J., 3,243......D3 74
Buena Park, Calif.,
  46,401............n13 50
Buenaventura, Col.,
  70,079............C2 32
Buena Vista, Colo., 1,806.C4 51
Buena Vista, Ga., 1,574..D2 55
Buena Vista (Independent
  City), Va., 6,300......C3 85
Buena Vista, co., Iowa,
  21,189............B2 60
Buenos Aires, Arg.,
  2,966,816
  (*6,975,000)........A5, g7 28
Buenos Aires, prov.,
  Arg., 6,734,548....B4, g7 28
Buffalo, Iowa, 1,088..C7, h10 60
Buffalo, Minn., 2,322....E5 67
Buffalo, Mo., 1,477......D4 69
Buffalo, N.Y., 465,000
  (*1,280,000)........C2 75

Buffalo, Ohio, 800.......C4 78
Buffalo, Okla., 1,618....A2 79
Buffalo, S.C., 1,209.....B4 82
Buffalo, Tex., 1,108.....D4 84
Buffalo, Wyo., 2,907....B6 89
Buffalo, co., Nebr.,
  26,236............D6 71
Buffalo, co., S. Dak.,
  1,547............F6 77
Buffalo, co., Wis., 14,202.D2 88
Buffalo Center, Iowa,
  1,140............A4 60
Buffalo Grove, Ill.,
  1,497............*A6 58
Buford, Ga., 4,168......B2 55
Buga, Col., 65,535......C2 32
Bugojno, Yugo., 5,411...C3 10
Buhl, Idaho, 3,059......G4 57
Buhl, Minn., 1,526......C6 67
Buhler, Kans., 888......D6 61
Buhuşi, Rom., 12,382...B8 10
Bujalance, Sp., 11,475..D3 8
Bujumbura, Burundi,
  50,000............I3 23
Bukama, Con. K.......B5 24
Bukavu, Con. K., 33,500..I3 23
Bukhara, Sov. Un.,
  88,000............F9 13
Bukidnon, prov., Phil.,
  194,368............*D6 19
Bukoba, Tan., 5,297....I4 23
Bulacan, prov., Phil.,
  555,819............*C6 19
Bulan, Ky., 500........C6 62
Bulan, Phil., 16,042....*C6 19
Bulawayo, Rh., 180,000..E5 24
Bulgaria, country, Eur.,
  8,226,564............D7 10
Bullas, Sp., 8,936......C5 8
Bullitt, co., Ky., 15,726..C4 62
Bulloch, co., Ga., 24,263.D11 55
Bullock, co., Ala., 13,462.C4 46
Bulun, Sov. Un., 800....B15 13
Bulun Tukhoi (Puluntohai),
  China, 10,000........B2 17
Bunbury, Austl., 15,453..F2 25
Buncombe, co., N.C.,
  130,074............f10 76
Bundaberg, Austl., 25,404.D9 25
Bunia, Con. K., 5,000...H4 23
Bunker Hill, Ill., 1,684...D4 58
Bunker Hill, Ind., 1,049..C5 59
Bunker Hill, Oreg.,
  1,655............*D2 80
Bunker Hill, Tex., 2,216..*E5 84
Bunkie, La., 5,188......D3 63
Bunnell, Fla., 1,860.....C5 54
Bunny Run, Mich.,
  1,058............*F7 66
Buo Ha, Viet., 10,000...*G5 17
Burao, Som., 10,000....G7 23
Buras, La., 3,000.......E6 63
Buraydah, Sau. Ar.,
  50,000............D3 15
Burbank, Calif.,
  90,155............E4, m12 50
Burdur, Tur., 25,271....D8 14
Burdwan, India, 108,224..D8 20
Bureau, co., Ill., 37,594..B4 58
Bureya, Sov. Un., 5,000...B4 18
Burgas, Bul., 106,127....D8 10
Burgas, co., Bul.,
  629,593............*D8 10
Burgaw, N.C., 1,773....C5 76
Burgdorf, Switz., 15,300
  (*18,600)............E3 6
Burgeo, Newf., Can.,
  1,454............E3 44
Burgettstown, Pa., 2,383..F1 81
Burgos, Sp., 82,177....A4 8
Burgos, prov., Sp.,
  380,791............*A4 8
Burgundy (Bourgogne),
  former prov., Fr.,
  1,264,000............D6 5
Burhanpur, India, 82,090.D6 20
Burien, Wash., 10,000...*B3 86
Burin, Newf., Can., 1,144.E4 44
Buriram, Thai., 12,579...*C2 19
Burkburnett, Tex., 7,621..B3 84
Burke, co., Ga., 20,596...C4 55
Burke, co., N.C., 52,701..B1 76
Burke, co., N. Dak., 5,886.B3 77
Burke City, Mo., 1,800...f13 69
Burkesville, Ky., 1,688...D4 62
Burks Falls, Ont., Can.,
  926................B5 41
Burleigh, co., N. Dak.,
  34,016............D5 77
Burleson, Tex., 2,345....n9 84

Burleson, co., Tex.,
  11,177............D4 84
Burlingame, Calif., 24,036..h8 50
Burlingame, Kans., 1,151.D8 61
Burlington, Ont., Can.,
  47,008............D5 41
Burlington, Colo., 2,090..B8 51
Burlington, Iowa, 33,285..D6 60
Burlington, Kans., 2,113..D8 61
Burlington, Mass., 12,852.f11 65
Burlington, N.J., 12,687..C3 74
Burlington, N.C., 33,199..A3 76
Burlington, Vt., 35,531...C1 73
Burlington, Wash., 2,968..A3 86
Burlington, Wis.,
  5,856............F5, n11 88
Burlington, co., N.J.,
  224,499............D3 74
Burma, country, Asia,
  24,500,000............D10 20
Burnet, Tex., 2,214......D3 84
Burnet, co., Tex., 9,265...D3 84
Burnett, co., Wis., 9,214..C1 88
Burney, Calif., 1,294....B3 50
Burnham, Ill., 2,478....*B6 58
Burnham, Pa., 2,755.....E6 81
Burnie, Austl., 18,028...o15 25
Burnley, Eng., 80,200...D5 4
Burns, Oreg., 3,523......D7 80
Burns Flat, Okla., 2,280..B2 79
Burns Lake, B.C., Can.,
  1,041............B5 37
Burnsville, N.C., 1,388...f10 76
Burnwell, Ala., 200.....E4 46
Burr Oak, Mich., 867....G5 66
Bursa, Tur., 153,866....B7 14
Burt, co., Nebr., 10,192..C9 71
Burton, Ohio, 1,085.....A4 78
Burton-on-Trent, Eng.,
  50,600............D6 4
Burton Porterville West,
  Calif., 4,635.........*D4 50
Burundi, country, Afr.,
  2,300,000............I3 23
Büshehr, Iran, 27,317....G8 16
Buskerud, co., Nor.,
  189,200............*H4 11
Busko, Pol., 5,975......C6 7
Bussum, Neth., 41,500...A6 5
Busto Arsizio, It., 68,600..B2 9
Buta, Con. K., 11,200...H2 23
Bute, co., Scot., 13,900..*C4 4
Butler, Ala., 1,765......C1 46
Butler, Ga., 1,346......D2 55
Butler, Ind., 2,176......B8 59
Butler, Mo., 3,791......C3 69
Butler, N.J., 5,414......B4 74
Butler, Ohio, 976.......B3 78
Butler, Pa., 20,975.....E2 81
Butler, Wis., 2,274.....m11 88
Butler, co., Ala., 24,560..D3 46
Butler, co., Iowa, 17,467..B5 60
Butler, co., Kans., 38,395.E7 61
Butler, co., Ky., 9,586...C3 62
Butler, co., Mo., 34,656..E7 69
Butler, co., Nebr., 10,312.C8 71
Butler, co., Ohio, 199,076.C1 78
Butler, co., Pa., 114,639..E2 81
Butner, N.C., 1,000.....*A4 76
Butte, Mont., 27,877....D4 70
Butte, co., Calif., 82,030..C3 50
Butte, co., Idaho, 3,498..F5 57
Butte, co., S. Dak., 8,592.F2 77
Butterworth, Mala.,
  42,504............D2 19
Buttonwillow, Calif., 950..E4 50
Butts, co., Ga., 8,976...C3 55
Butuan, Phil., 34,443...D7 19
Buturlinovka, Sov. Un.,
  39,800............F13 12
Bützow, Ger., 10,900...B5 6
Buxtehude, Ger., 15,700..B4 6
Buxton, Guy., 3,800....C5 27
Buzău, Rom., 52,300...C8 10
Buzet, Yugo., 444......C1 10
Buzzards Bay, Mass.,
  2,500............C6 65
Byala Slatina, Bul., 9,357.D6 10
Bydgoszcz, Pol., 248,300..B5 7
Byelorussia (S.S.R.), rep.,
  Sov. Un., 8,500,000...E5 12
Byesville, Ohio, 2,447...C4 78
Byfield, Mass., 850.....A6 65
Bykovo, Sov. Un.,
  10,000............G15 12
Byron, Ga., 1,138......D3 55
Byron, Ill., 1,578......A4 58
Bystrzyca, Pol., 9,564...C4 7
Bytom, Pol., 191,400..C5, G9 7
Bytosh, Sov. Un., 10,000..E10 12

C

Caacupé, Par., 15,834.....E4 29
Caaguazú, dept., Par., 2,610................D4 29
Caapucú, Par., 6,608......E4 29
Caazapá, Par., 16,588....E4 29
Caazapá, dept., Par., 3,003................E4 29
Cabaceiras, Braz., 581....*D4 27
Cabana, Peru, 2,560......C2 31
Cabanatuan, Phil., 38,379...............o13 19
Cabano, Que., Can., 2,695................B9 42
Cabarrus, co., N.C., 68,137................B2 76
Cabedelo, Braz., 10,738..*D7 27
Cabell, Ky...............C2 87
Cabeza del Buey, Sp., 11,737................C3 8
Cabimas, Ven., 111,400...A3 32
Cabinda, Ang., 1,554.....B2 24
Cabinda, dist., Ang., 58,453................B2 24
Cabin John, Md., 2,500...............C3, f8 53
Cabo, Braz., 6,029.......*D7 27
Cabo Frio, Braz., 13,117...C4 30
Cabool, Mo., 1,284.......D5 69
Caborca, Mex., 9,338.....A2 34
Cabo Rojo, P.R., 3,086..*G11 35
Cabo San Lucas, Mex., 1,859................C3 34
Cabot, Ark., 1,321.......C3 49
Cache, co., Utah, 35,788..A6 72
Cache, peak, Idaho......G5 57
Cache Bay, Ont., Can., 810...............A5 41
Cachi, Arg.............E2 29
Cachoeira, Braz., 11,415..*E7 27
Cachoeira do Sul, Braz., 38,661...............E2 30
Cachoeiro do Itapemirim, Braz., 39,470.........C4 30
Cacouna, Que., Can., 834.................B8 42
Caddo, Okla., 814.......C5 79
Caddo, co., Okla., 28,621..B3 79
Caddo, par., La., 223,859..B2 63
Cadillac, Que., Can., 1,077................o20 41
Cadillac, Mich., 10,112...D5 66
Cadiz, Ky., 1,980........D2 62
Cadiz, Ohio, 3,259.......B4 78
Cádiz, Sp., 117,871......D2 8
Cádiz, prov., Sp., 818,847...............*D2 8
Cadott, Wis., 881........D2 88
Cadyville, N.Y., 800.....f11 75
Caen, Fr., 91,336 (*120,000)...........C3 5
Caernarvon, Wales, 9,100..D4 4
Caernarvon, co., Wales, 120,600..............*D4 4
Cagayan, Phil., 34,672....D6 19
Cagayan, prov., Phil., 445,289..............*B6 19
Cagli, It., 3,235.........C4 9
Cagliari, It., 194,000.....E2 9
Cagnes-sur-Mer, Fr., 15,392................F7 5
Caguas, P.R., 32,015....G12 35
Cahaba Heights, Ala., 3,500................*B3 46
Cahokia, Ill., 15,829.....E3 58
Cahors, Fr., 17,046.......E4 5
Caibarién, Cuba, 22,900...C4 35
Caicedonia, Col., 16,327...C2 32
Caicó, Braz., 15,826.....*D7 27
Cailloma, Peru, 923......E3 31
Cairnbrook, Pa., 1,100....F4 81
Cairns, Austl., 26,555....C8 25
Cairo, Ga., 7,427........F2 55
Cairo, Ill., 9,348........F4 58
Cairo (Al Qāhirah), Eg., U.A.R., 3,518,200.......B4 23
Caithness, co., Scot., 28,400...............*A5 4
Cajabamba, Peru, 10,500..C2 31
Cajacay, Peru 1,094......D2 31
Cajamarca, Peru, 23,000...C2 31
Cajamarca, dept., Peru, 786,599..............C2 31

Cajatambo, Peru, 2,561....D2 31
Cajázeiras, Braz., 15,884..*D7 27
Cakovec, Yugo., 9,647.....B3 10
Calabria, pol. dist., It., 2,045,047.............*E5 9
Calabria, reg., It........E6 9
Calafat, Rom., 8,069......D6 10
Calahorra, Sp., 14,462....A5 8
Calais, Fr., 70,372.......B4 5
Calais, Maine, 4,223......C5 64
Calamar, Col., 6,055......A3 32
Calamba, Phil., 11,868....C6 19
Calañas, Sp., 4,059.......D2 8
Calapan, Phil., 4,180.....C6 19
Călărasi, Rom., 25,555...C8 10
Calarcá, Col., 15,707.....C2 32
Calasparra, Sp., 8,155....C5 8
Calauag, Phil., 3,981.....P14 19
Calaveras, co., Calif., 10,289................C3 50
Calca, Peru, 3,037.......D3 31
Calcasieu, par., La., 145,475...............D2 63
Calceta, Ec., 4,946........B1 31
Calcutta, India, 2,927,289 (*6,350,000)...........D8 20
Calcutta, Ohio, 1,500.....B5 78
Caldas, dept., Col., 1,455,872.............B2 32
Caldas da Rainha, Port., 10,635................C1 8
Caldwell, Idaho, 12,230....F2 57
Caldwell, Kans., 1,788....E6 61
Caldwell, N.J., 6,942.....B4 74
Caldwell, Ohio, 1,999.....C4 78
Caldwell, Tex., 2,204.....D4 84
Caldwell, co., Ky., 13,073..C2 62
Caldwell, co., Mo., 8,830..B3 69
Caldwell, co., N.C., 49,552................B1 76
Caldwell, co., Tex., 17,222................E4 84
Caldwell, par., La., 9,004..B3 63
Caledonia, Ont., Can., 2,198................D5 41
Caledonia, Minn., 2,567...G7 67
Caledonia, N.Y., 1,917....C3 75
Caledonia, Ohio, 673......B3 78
Caledonia, co., Vt., 22,786................C3 73
Calella, Sp., 7,947.......B7 8
Calera, Ala., 1,928.......B3 46
Calera, Chile, 13,047.....A2 28
Calexico, Calif., 9,850....F6 50
Calgary, Alta., Can., 249,641, (*279,062)..D3, g8 38
Calhoun, Ga., 3,587.......B2 55
Calhoun, co., Ala., 95,878..B4 46
Calhoun, co., Ark., 5,991..D3 49
Calhoun, co., Fla., 7,422..B1 54
Calhoun, co., Ga., 7,341...E2 55
Calhoun, co., Ill., 5,933...D3 58
Calhoun, co., Iowa, 15,923................B4 60
Calhoun, co., Mich., 138,858..............F5 66
Calhoun, co., Miss., 15,941................B4 68
Calhoun, co., S.C., 12,256................D6 82
Calhoun, co., Tex., 16,592................E4 84
Calhoun, co., W. Va., 7,948................C3 87
Calhoun City, Miss., 1,714................B4 68
Calhoun Falls, S.C., 2,525..C2 82
Cali, Col., 637,929.......C2 32
Calico Rock, Ark., 773....A3 49
Calicut, see Kozhikode, India
Caliente, Nev., 792.......C4 72
California, Mo., 2,788.....C5 69
California, Pa., 5,978.....F2 81
California, state, U.S., 15,717,204...........C2 50
Calipatria, Calif., 1,953...F6 50
Calispell, peak, Wash.....A8 86
Calistoga, Calif., 1,514...C2 50
Callahan, co., Tex., 7,929..C3 84
Callander, Ont., Can., 1,236................A5 41
Callander, Scot., 1,700....B4 4
Callao, Peru, 161,300.....D2 31
Callao, prov., Peru, 219,420...............D2 31
Callaway, co., Mo., 23,858................C6 69
Callicoon, N.Y., 800......D5 75
Calloway, co., Ky., 20,972................B3 62

Calmar, Alta., Can., 700...C4 38
Calmar, Iowa, 954........A6 60
Caltagirone, It., 35,000...F5 9
Caltanissetta, It., 49,000...F5 9
Caluire [-et-Cuire], Fr., 25,754................E6 5
Calumet, Que., Can., 889.................D3 42
Calumet, Mich., 1,139....A2 66
Calumet, Pa., 1,241.....*F2 81
Calumet, co., Wis., 22,268..D5 88
Calumet City, Ill., 27,420..............B6, k9 58
Calumet Park, Ill., 8,448..*B6 58
Calvados, dept., Fr., 480,686..............*C3 5
Calvert, Tex., 2,073......D4 84
Calvert, co., Md., 15,826..C4 53
Calvert City, Ky., 1,505...A3 62
Calverton Park, Mo., 1,714................A8 69
Calvillo, Mex., 5,735....m12 34
Calwa, Calif., 8,000.....*D4 50
Camacho, Mex., 1,495....C4 34
Camagüey, Cuba, 141,900...............D5 35
Camagüey, prov., Cuba, 618,256..............D5 35
Camaná, Peru, 5,100......E2 31
Camanche, Iowa, 3,055....C7 60
Camargo, see Ciudad Camargo, Mex.
Camarillo, Calif., 2,359..*E4 50
Camarines Norte, prov., Phil., 188,091.........*C6 19
Camarines Sur, prov., Phil., 819,565.........*C6 19
Camas, Wash., 5,666,....D3 86
Camas, co., Idaho, 917....F4 57
Cambodia, country, Asia, 69,898................C2 19
Camborne [-Redruth], Eng., 36,200...........E4 4
Cambrai, Fr., 32,897......B5 5
Cambria, Calif., 700......E3 50
Cambria, co., Pa., 203,283...............E4 81
Cambrian Park, Calif., 4,000................*D3 50
Cambridge, Eng., 96,000...D7 4
Cambridge, Ill., 1,665....B3 58
Cambridge, Md., 12,239...C5 53
Cambridge, Mass., 107,716.............B5, g11 65
Cambridge, Minn., 2,728...E5 67
Cambridge, Nebr., 1,090...D5 71
Cambridge, N.J., 1,000...*C3 74
Cambridge, N.Y., 1,748....B7 75
Cambridge, Ohio, 14,562..B4 78
Cambridge, co., Eng., 189,913..............*D7 4
Cambridge City, Ind., 2,569................E7 59
Cambridge Springs, Pa., 2,031................C1 81
Camden, Ala., 1,121......D2 46
Camden, Ark., 15,823.....D3 49
Camden, Del., 1,125......B6 53
Camden, Maine, 3,523....D3 64
Camden, N.J., 117,159....D2 74
Camden, N.Y., 2,694......B5 75
Camden, Ohio, 1,308......C1 78
Camden, S.C., 6,842......C6 82
Camden, Tenn., 2,774.....A3 83
Camden, Tex., 1,100......D5 84
Camden, co., Ga., 9,975...F5 55
Camden, co., Mo., 9,116...C5 69
Camden, co., N.J., 392,035...............D3 74
Camden, co., N.C., 5,407..A6 76
Camdenton, Mo., 1,405....D5 69
Cameron, La., 950........E2 63
Cameron, Mo., 3,674......B3 69
Cameron, Tex., 5,640.....D4 84
Cameron, W. Va., 1,652.............B4, C2 87
Cameron, Wis., 982.......C2 88
Cameron, co., Pa., 7,586..D5 81
Cameron, co., Tex., 151,098..............F4 84
Cameron, par., La., 6,909..E2 63
Cameroon, country, Afr., 5,150,000............G7 22
Cameroon, mtn., Cam....H6 22
Camiling, Phil., 9,799....o13 19
Camilla, Ga., 4,753......E2 55
Camillus, N.Y., 1,401....*B4 75
Camino, Calif., 800......C3 50
Cammack, Ark., 1,355..............C3, D5 49

Camocim, Braz., 10,788 *D6 27
Camp, co., Tex., 7,849....C5 84
Campagna di Roma, reg., It.,.................h9 9
Campana, Arg., 14,452....g7 28
Campanario, Sp., 9,660....C3 8
Campania, pol. dist., It., 4,760,759.............*D5 9
Campania, reg., It.,......D5 9
Campbell, Calif., 11,863...k8 50
Campbell, Mo., 1,964.....E7 69
Campbell, Ohio, 13,406...A5 78
Campbell, co., Ky., 86,803................B5 62
Campbell, co., S. Dak., 3,531................E5 77
Campbell, co., Tenn., 27,936................C9 83
Campbell, co., Va., 32,958................C3 85
Campbell, co., Wyo., 5,861................B7 89
Campbell, hill, Ohio......B2 78
Campbellford, Ont., Can., 3,478................C7 41
Campbellpur, Pak., 14,892 (*19,041)............B5 20
Campbell River, B.C., Can., 3,737............D5 37
Campbells Bay, Que., Can., 1,024................B8 41
Campbellsport, Wis., 1,472................E5 88
Campbellsville, Ky., 6,966................C4 62
Campbellton, N.B., Can., 9,873................A3 43
Campbelltown, Pa., 1,061...............*F9 81
Campbeltown, Scot., 6,400................C4 4
Campeche, Mex., 43,874...D6 34
Camp Hill, Ala., 1,270....C4 46
Camp Hill, Pa., 8,559....F8 81
Campiglia Marittima, It., 2,716................C3 9
Campina Grande, Braz., 116,226..............D7 27
Campinas, Braz., 179,797.............C3, m8 30
Campoalegre, Col., 9,768................C2 32
Campobasso, It., 27,400...D5 9
Campo Belo, Braz., 15,742................C3 30
Campo de Criptana, Sp., 14,608................C4 8
Campo Grande, Braz., 64,477................C2 30
Campo Maior, Braz., 13,939...............*D6 27
Campo Maior, Port., 8,086................C2 8
Campos, Braz., 90,601.....C4 30
Camp Point, Ill., 1,092....C2 58
Camp Springs, Md., 2,000................f9 53
Campti, La., 1,045.......C2 63
Campton Heights, Calif., 1,200...............*B1 50
Camrose, Alta., Can., 6,939................C4 38
Canaan, Conn., 1,200.....A3 52
Canada, Ky., 500........C7 62
Canada, country, N.A., 20,400,000..........D10 33
Cañada de Gómez, Arg., 16,874................A4 28
Canadensis, Pa., 800.....D11 81
Canadian, Tex., 2,239.....B2 84
Canadian, co., Okla., 24,727................B3 79
Canadian, riv., U.S......C6 45
Canajoharie, N.Y., 2,681..C6 75
Canakkale, Tur., 19,500..B6 29
Canal Fulton, Ohio, 1,555................B4 78
Canal Point, Fla., 700.....F6 54
Canal Winchester, Ohio, 1,976.............C3, m11 78
Canal Zone, U.S. dep., N.A., 42,122..........B2 32
Canandaigua, N.Y., 10,058................C3 75
Cananea, Mex., 19,683....A2 34
Cañar, prov., Ec., 112,733...............B2 31
Canary Islands, reg., Sp., 1,005,000............C1 22
Cañas, C.R., 2,991......*E7 34
Canastota, N.Y., 4,971...B5 75

Canavieiras, Braz.,
 10,264...............*E7 27
Canberra, Austl., 93,311...G8 25
Canby, Minn., 2,146.......F2 67
Canby, Oreg.,
 2,168.............B4, h12 80
Candeleda, Sp., 6,983.....B3   8
Candia, see Iraklion, Grc.
Candiac, Que., Can.,
 71,050...............q19 42
Candler, co., Ga., 6,672..D4 55
Cando, N. Dak., 1,566....B6 77
Candor, N.Y., 912........C4 75
Canea, see Khaniá, Grc.
Canelones, Ur., 8,041.....E1 30
Canelones, dept., Ur.,
 255,300..............*E1 30
Cañete, Peru, 7,100......D2 31
Caney, Kans., 2,682......E8 61
Canfield, Ohio, 3,252.....A5 78
Cangallo, Peru, 902......D3 31
Cangas, Sp., 4,008.......A1   8
Cangas de Onís, Sp.,
 9,936................A3   8
Canicatti, It., 31,800.....F4   9
Caniles, Sp., 8,040.......D4   8
Canisteo, N.Y., 2,731.....C3 75
Cankiri (Changra), Tur.,
 20,047...............B9 14
Canmore, Alta, Can.,
 1,736................D3 38
Cannelton, Ind., 2,467....I4 59
Cannes, Fr., 58,079.......F7   5
Canning, N.S., Can.,
 850.................D5 43
Cannington, Ont., Can.,
 1,024................C5 41
Cannon, co., Tenn., 8,537.B5 83
Cannon Falls, Minn.,
 2,055................F6 67
Canoinhas, Braz., 9,252...D2 30
Canon City, Colo., 8,973..C5 51
Canonsburg, Pa., 12,910..F1 81
Canora, Sask., Can.,
 2,117................F4 39
Canosa, It., 34,015.......D6   9
Canso, N.S., Can., 1,151..D8 43
Cantal, dept., Fr.,
 172,977..............*E5   5
Canterbury, Eng., 31,000..E7   4
Can Tho, Viet., 49,310...*C3 19
Cantilan, Phil., 2,048....*D7 19
Canton, China, 1,840,000..G7 17
Canton, Ga., 2,411.......B2 55
Canton, Ill., 13,588......C3 58
Canton, Mass.,
 12,771............B5, h11 65
Canton, Miss., 9,707.....C3 68
Canton, Mo., 2,562.......A6 69
Canton, N.Y., 5,046......F9 75
Canton, N.C., 5,068......D3 76
Canton, Ohio, 110,000
 (*300,000)...........B4 78
Canton, Okla., 887.......A3 79
Canton, Pa., 2,102.......C8 81
Canton, S. Dak., 2,511...G9 77
Canton, Tex., 1,114......C5 84
Cantonment, Fla., 2,600..u14 54
Cantwell, Mo., 950.......D7 69
Canutillo, Tex., 1,400...o11 84
Canyon, Tex., 5,864......B2 84
Canyon, co., Idaho,
 57,662...............F2 57
Canyonville, Oreg.,
 1,089................E3 80
Cao Bang, Viet., 25,000..G6 17
Capac, Mich., 1,235......F8 66
Cap Chat, Que., Can.,
 2,035...............G20 36
Cap-de-la-Madeleine,
 Que., Can., 26,925.....C5 42
Cape Breton, Can.,......G21 36
Cape Breton, co., N.S.,
 Can., 131,507.........D9 43
Cape Canaveral, Fla.,
 3,500................D6 54
Cape Charles, Va., 2,041..C6 85
Cape Coast, Ghana,
 41,200...............G4 22
Cape Elizabeth, Maine,
 5,505.............E2, g7 64
Cape Girardeau, Mo.,
 24,947...............D8 69
Cape Girardeau, co., Mo.,
 42,020...............D8 69
Cape Horn, mtn., Idaho...E3 57
Capels, W. Va., 800.......D3 87
Cape May, N.J., 4,477....F3 74
Cape May, co., N.J.,
 48,555...............E3 74
Cape May Court House,
 N.J., 1,900...........E3 74
Cape of Good Hope, prov.,
 S. Afr., 5,355,368......G4 24
Capesterre, Guad.,
 6,255...............H14 35
Cape Town, S. Afr.,
 508,341 (*807,211)......G3 24

Cape Verde Island, Port.
 dep., Afr., 201,549....o12 22
Cape Vincent, N.Y., 770...A4 75
Cap-Haïtien, Hai., 24,423..E7 35
Capiata, Par., 1,900.....*E4 29
Capistrano Beach, Calif.,
 2,026...............*F5 50
Capitan, N. Mex., 552....C6 48
Capitola, Calif., 2,021...*D2 50
Capitol Heights, Md.,
 3,138.............C4, f9 53
Capivarí, Braz., 10,961...m8 30
Capiz, prov., Phil.,
 315,079.............*C6 19
Capoompeta, mtn.,
 Austl................E9 25
Cap-Pelé, N.B., Can., 859..C5 43
Caperol, Ont., Can.,
 3,003...............p19 41
Cap-St. Ignace, Que.,
 Can., 1,247..........B7 42
Captain Cook, Haw.,
 1,300................D6 56
Capua, It., 14,800.......D5   9
Caquetá, intendencia, Col.,
 103,718.............C3 32
Carabobo, state, Ven.,
 381,636.............A4 32
Caracal, Rom., 19,082....C7 10
Caracas, Ven., 1,250,000..A4 32
Caraguatay, Par., 1,900...E4 29
Carangola, Braz., 11,896..C4 30
Caransebes, Rom., 15,195..C6 10
Carapeguá, Par., 23,675...E4 29
Caraquet, N.B., Can.,
 1,214................B5 43
Caratinga, Braz., 22,275..B4 30
Caravelí, Peru, 1,177.....E3 31
Caraway, Ark., 821.......B5 49
Caraz, Peru, 3,065.......C2 31
Caràzinho, Braz., 18,163..D2 30
Carballino, Sp., 9,639....A1   8
Carballo, Sp., 3,110......A1   8
Carberry, Man., Can.,
 1,113................E2 40
Carbó, Mex., 2,428.......B2 34
Carbon, co., Mont., 8,317..E7 70
Carbon, co., Pa., 52,889..E10 81
Carbon, co., Utah, 21,135..B6 72
Carbon, co., Wyo., 14,937..E5 89
Carbondale, Ill., 18,531...F4 58
Carbondale, Pa., 13,595..C10 81
Carbonear, Newf., Can.,
 4,234................E5 44
Carbon Hill, Ala., 1,944..B2 46
Carbonia, It., 34,700.....E2   9
Carcagente, Sp., 17,937...C5   8
Carcar, Phil., 6,657.....*C6 19
Carcassonne, Fr., 40,897..F5   5
Carchi, prov., Ec., 94,649..A2 31
Cardale, Pa., 900.......*G2 81
Cárdenas, Cuba, 54,600...C3 35
Cárdenas, Mex., 4,583....D6 34
Cárdenas, Mex., 12,461..m14 34
Cardiff, Wales, 260,600...E5   4
Cardiff-by-the-Sea, Calif.,
 1,500...............*F5 50
Cardigan, Wales, 3,700...D4   4
Cardigan, co., Wales,
 53,300..............*D4   4
Cardinal, Ont., Can.,
 1,944................C9 41
Cardington, Ohio, 1,613..B3 78
Cardston, Alta., Can.,
 2,801................E4 38
Cardwell, Mo., 816.......E7 69
Carei, Rom., 16,780......B6 10
Carencro, La., 1,519......D3 63
Carenero, Ven., 312......A4 32
Caretta, W. V., 1,092.....D3 87
Carey, Ohio, 3,722.......B2 78
Carhuaz, Peru, 2,359.....C2 31
Cariati, It., 5,204.......E6   9
Caribbean, sea, N.A......H13 33
Cariboo mts., B.C.,
 Can..................C7 37
Caribou, Maine, 12,464....B5 64
Caribou, mtn., Idaho......F7 57
Caribou, mtn., Maine.....C2 64
Carichic, Mex., 1,237.....B3 34
Carini, It., 16,723.......E4   9
Carinthia, reg., Aus.,
 2,178,141............E6   6
Caripito, Ven., 21,598....A5 32
Carle Place, N.Y., 7,300..*G2 52
Carleton, Mich., 1,379....F7 66
Carleton, co., N.B., Can.,
 23,507...............C2 43
Carleton, co., Ont., Can.,
 352,932.............B9 41
Carleton, mtn., N.B.,
 Can..................B3 43
Carleton Place, Ont., Can.,
 4,796................B8 41
Carlin, Nev., 1,023.......A3 72
Carlinville, Ill., 5,440....D4 58
Carlisle, Ark., 1,514.....C4 49
Carlisle, Eng., 71,000.....C5   4

Carlisle, Iowa, 1,930.....C4 60
Carlisle, Ky., 1,601......B5 62
Carlisle, Pa., 16,623.....F7 81
Carlisle, co., Ky., 5,608..B2 62
Carl Junction, Mo., 1,220..D3 69
Carloforte, It., 7,275.....E2   9
Carlos Casares, Arg.,
 7,558................B4 28
Carlow, Ire., 7,800.......D3   4
Carlow, co., Ire., 33,500..*D3   4
Carlsbad, Calif., 9,253...F5 50
Carlsbad, N. Mex.,
 25,541...............C6 48
Carlstadt, N.J., 6,042....h8 74
Carlton, Oreg., 959...B3, h11 80
Carlton, co., Minn.,
 27,932...............D6 67
Carlyle, Sask., Can.,
 982.................H4 39
Carlyle, Ill., 3,193.......E4 58
Carmagnola, It., 4,800....B1   9
Carman, Man., Can.,
 1,930................E2 40
Carman, N.Y., 1,500....*C6 75
Carman, hill, Pa.........C6 81
Carmanville, Newf., Can.,
 855.................D4 44
Carmarthen, Wales,
 12,900...............E4   4
Carmarthen, co., Wales,
 166,600.............*E4   4
Carmaux, Fr., 14,565.....E5   5
Carmel, Calif., 4,136.....D3 50
Carmel, Ind., 3,023......E5 59
Carmel, N.Y., 800.......D7 75
Carmel, mtn., Isr........B3 15
Carmel Valley, Calif.,
 1,143...............*D3 50
Carmel Woods, Calif.,
 1,043...............*D3 50
Carmen del Paraná, Par.,
 10,699...............E4 29
Carmen de Patagones,
 Arg., 5,423..........C4 28
Carmi, Ill., 6,152.......E5 58
Carmichael, Calif.,
 20,455..............*C3 50
Carmichaels, Pa., 788....G2 81
Carmona, Sp., 28,216....D3   8
Carnarvon, Austl.,
 2,957................D1 25
Carnduff, Sask., Can.,
 957.................H5 39
Carnegie, Okla., 1,500...B3 79
Carnegie, Pa., 11,887.F1, k13 81
Carneys Point, N.J.,
 3,000................D2 74
Caro, Mich., 3,534.......E7 66
Carol City, Fla., 28,500..s13 54
Caroleen, N.C., 1,168.B1, f11 76
Carolina, P.R., 3,075....*G11 35
Carolina Beach, N.C.,
 1,192................C5 76
Caroline, co., Md.,
 19,462...............C6 53
Caroline, co., Va., 12,725..C5 85
Caroline, arch., Pac. O....F6   2
Carora, Ven., 23,227.....A3 32
Carouge, Switz., 12,760...E3   6
Carpentersville, Ill.,
 17,424............A5, h8 58
Carpentras, Fr., 14,169...E6   5
Carpi, It., 21,000.......B3   9
Carpinteria, Calif., 5,500..E4 50
Carrabelle, Fla., 1,146...C2 54
Carrantuohill, mtn., Ire...D1   4
Carrara, It., 65,900......B3   9
Carrboro, N.C., 1,997....B3 76
Carrickfergus, N. Ire.,
 10,211...............C4   4
Carrie, mtn., Wash......B2 86
Carriers Mills, Ill., 2,006..F5 58
Carrington, N. Dak.,
 2,438................C6 77
Carrizo, see El Carrizo,
 Mex.
Carrizo Springs, Tex.,
 5,699................E3 84
Carrizozo, N. Mex., 1,546..C6 48
Carroll, Iowa, 8,481.....B3 60
Carroll, co., Ark., 11,284..A2 49
Carroll, co., Ga., 36,451..C1 55
Carroll, co., Ill., 19,507..A4 58
Carroll, co., Ind., 16,934..C4 59
Carroll, co., Iowa, 23,431..B3 60
Carroll, co., Ky., 7,978...B4 62
Carroll, co., Md., 52,785..A3 53
Carroll, co., Miss., 11,177..B4 68
Carroll, co., Mo., 13,847..B4 69
Carroll, co., N.H., 15,829..D5 73
Carroll, co., Ohio, 20,857..B4 78
Carroll, co., Tenn., 23,476..B3 83
Carroll, co., Va., 23,178..D2 85
Carrollton, Ga., 10,973...C1 55
Carrollton, Ill., 2,558....D3 58
Carrollton, Ky., 3,218....B4 62
Carrollton, Md., 3,385...A4 53

Carrollton, Mich., 6,718...E7 66
Carrollton, Mo., 4,554....B4 69
Carrollton, Ohio, 2,786...B4 78
Carrollton, Tex., 4,242...*C4 84
Carrolltown, Pa., 1,525...E4 81
Carrot River, Sask.,
 Can., 930............D4 39
Carrville, Ala., 1,081.....C4 46
Carşamba, Tur., 14,877...B11 14
Carshalton, Eng.,
 61,000..............m12   4
Carson, Iowa, 583.......C10 71
Carson, co., Tex., 7,781...B2 84
Carson City, Mich., 1,201..E6 66
Carson City, Nev., 5,163..B2 72
Carsonville, Mo., 4,500..*C7 69
Carswell, W. Va., 500...*D3 87
Cartagena, Col., 242,085..A2 32
Cartagena, Sp., 100,000..D5   8
Cartago, Col., 55,682....C2 32
Cartago, C.R., 18,084....F8 34
Cartago, prov., C.R.,
 154,200.............*I12 33
Cartaxo, Port., 5,920....C1   8
Cartaya, Sp., 9,002......D2   8
Carter, co., Ky., 20,817...B6 62
Carter, co., Mo., 3,973...E7 69
Carter, co., Mont., 2,493..E12 70
Carter, co., Okla., 39,044..C4 79
Carter, co., Tenn.,
 41,578..............C11 83
Carteret, N.J., 20,502.B4, k8 74
Carteret, co., N.C.,
 30,940..............C6 76
Carter Lake, Iowa, 2,287..C2 60
Cartersville, Ga., 8,668..B2 55
Carterville, Ill., 2,643...F4 58
Carterville, Mo., 1,443...D3 69
Carthage, Ill., 3,325.....C2 58
Carthage, Ind., 1,043....E6 59
Carthage, Miss., 2,442...C4 68
Carthage, Mo., 11,264...D3 69
Carthage, N.Y., 4,216....B5 75
Carthage, N.C., 1,190....B3 76
Carthage, Tenn., 2,021...C8 83
Carthage, Tex., 5,262....C5 84
Caruaru, Braz., 64,471...D7 27
Carúpano, Ven., 38,197..A5 32
Caruthersville, Mo., 8,643..E8 69
Carver, Minn., 467......F5 67
Carver, co., Minn.,
 21,358..............F5 67
Carville, La., 950.......H9 63
Cary, Ill., 3,839.....A5, h8 58
Cary, N.C., 5,331.......B4 76
Caryville, Tenn., 950....C9 83
Casablanca, Mor.,
 965,277.............B3 22
Casa Branca, Braz.,
 8,980.............C3, k8 30
Casa de Oro, Calif.,
 1,500...............*F5 50
Casa Grande, Ariz., 8,311..C3 48
Casale Monferrato, It.,
 33,200..............B2   9
Casalmaggiore, It., 5,656..B3   9
Casarano, It., 14,744....D7   9
Casas Adobes, Ariz.,
 5,000...............*C3 48
Cascade, Idaho, 923.....E2 57
Cascade, Iowa, 1,732.....B6 60
Cascade, co., Mont.,
 73,418..............C5 70
Cascade, range, Can.,
 U.S.................B2 45
Cascais, Port., 10,861...C1, f9   8
Caserta, It., 39,200......D5   9
Casey, Ill., 2,890.......D6 58
Casey, co., Ky., 14,327...C5 62
Casey, mtn., Idaho.......A2 57
Caseyville, Ill., 2,455...*E3 58
Cashion, Ariz., 1,000....D1 48
Cashmere, Wash., 1,891..B5 86
Cashton, Wis., 828......E3 88
Casilda, Arg., 16,076....A4 28
Casino, Austl., 8,091....D9 26
Caslav, Czech., 10,100...D3   7
Casma, Peru, 5,300......C2 31
Caspe, Sp., 9,033.......B5   8
Casper, Wyo., 38,930....D6 89
Caspian, Mich., 1,493....B2 66
Caspian, sea, Asia.......E7 13
Cassadaga, N.Y., 820....C1 75
Cass, co., Ill., 14,539....D3 58
Cass, co., Ind., 40,931...C5 59
Cass, co., Iowa, 17,919...C3 60
Cass, co., Mich., 36,932..G4 66
Cass, co., Minn., 16,720..D4 67
Cass, co., Mo., 29,702...C3 69
Cass, co., Nebr., 17,821..D9 71
Cass, co., N. Dak., 66,947..C8 77
Cass, co., Tex., 23,496...C5 84
Cass City, Mich., 1,945...E7 66
Casselberry, Fla., 2,463..*D5 54
Casselman, Ont., Can.,
 1,277................B9 41
Casselton, N. Dak., 1,394..D8 77
Cassia, co., Idaho, 16,121..G5 57

Cassino, It., 8,700......D4 9
Cass Lake, Minn., 1,586...C4 67
Cassopolis, Mich., 2,027...G4 66
Cassville, Mo., 1,451.....E4 69
Cassville, Wis., 1,290.....F3 88
Castalia, Ohio, 954......A3 78
Castanea, Pa., 1,218.....D7 81
Castaños, Mex., 4,999....B4 34
Castellón (Castellón
  de la Plana), prov.,
  Sp., 339,229.......*C5 8
Castellón de la Plana, Sp.,
  62,493.............C5 8
Castelnaudary, Fr., 8,071..F4 5
Castelo Branco, Port.,
  14,838.............C2 8
Castelvetrano, It., 31,282..F4 9
Castile, N.Y., 1,146......C2 75
Castilla, Peru, 8,892.....C1 31
Castle, peak, Idaho......E4 57
Castle Douglas, Scot.,
  3,200.............C5 4
Castlegar, B.C., Can.,
  2,253.............E9 37
Castle Hills, Tex., 2,622..*E3 84
Castlemaine, Austl.,
  7,217.............H5 26
Castle Park, Calif., 1,800.*F5 50
Castle Rock, Colo., 1,152..B6 51
Castle Rock, Wash., 1,424.C3 86
Castle Rock, mtn., Oreg....C8 80
Castle Rock, mtn., Va.....C4 85
Castle Shannon, Pa.,
  11,836............k13 81
Castleton-on-Hudson,
  N.Y., 1,837.........C7 75
Castor, Alta., Can., 1,025..C5 38
Castres, Fr., 36,978......F5 5
Castries, St. Lucia, 4,353..J14 35
Castro, Braz., 9,249......C3 30
Castro, Sp., 11,842.......D3 8
Castro, co., Tex., 8,923...B1 84
Castro Alves, Braz.,
  7,388............*E7 27
Castropol, Sp., 7,368.....A2 8
Castro Valley, Calif.,
  44,000............h8 50
Castrovillari, It., 12,500..E6 9
Castroville, Calif., 3,000..D3 50
Castroville, Tex., 1,508...E3 84
Castrovirreyna, Peru, 872..D2 31
Castuera, Sp., 10,166.....C3 8
Caswell, co., N.C., 19,912..A3 76
Catacaos, Peru, 8,526.....C1 31
Catacocha, Ec., 3,796.....B2 31
Cataguases, Braz.,
  21,476...........C4, g6 30
Catahoula, par., La.,
  11,421............C4 63
Cataiñgan, Phil., 2,669...*C6 19
Catalao, Braz., 11,471....B3 30
Catalca, Tur., 5,674......B7 14
Catalina, Newf., Can.,
  1,110.............D5 44
Catamarca, Arg., 31,067...E2 29
Catamarca, prov., Arg.,
  172,407...........E2 29
Catanduva, Braz., 37,307..C3 30
Cantania, It., 380,000.....F5 9
Cataño, P.R., 8,276.....*G11 35
Catanzaro, It., 76,000.....E6 9
Catarman, Phil., 8,248....C6 19
Catarroja, Sp., 11,680....C5 8
Catasauqua, Pa., 5,062...E11 81
Catawba, co., N.C.,
  73,191............B1 76
Catawissa, Pa., 1,824.....E9 81
Catbalogan, Phil., 19,360..C6 19
Cathedral, mtn., Tex....o13 84
Cathedral City, Calif.,
  2,600.............F5 50
Catlettsburg, Ky., 3,874...B7 62
Catlin, Ill., 1,600........C6 58
Catonsville, Md.,
  44,500..........B4, g10 53
Catoosa, co., Ga., 21,101..B1 55
Catron, co., N. Mex.,
  2,773.............C4 48
Catskill, N.Y., 5,825......C7 75
Catskill, mtns., N.Y......C6 75
Catt, mtn., B.C., Can......B3 37
Cattaraugus, N.Y., 1,258...C2 75
Cattaraugus, co., N.Y.,
  80,187............C2 75
Cattolica, It., 12,969.....C4 9
Cauca, dept., Col.,
  607,197...........C2 32
Caucasia, Col., 5,616.....B2 32
Caudebec [-lès-Elbeuf],
  Fr., 9,270.........C4 5
Caudéran, Fr., 28,715.....E3 5
Caudete, Sp., 7,544......C5 8
Caudry, Fr., 13,207......B5 5
Caughnawaga, Que.,
  Can...........D4, q19 42
Cauquenes, Chile, 17,800..B2 28
Causapscal, Que., Can.,
  3,463............*h14 42

Cautín, prov., Chile,
  394,785...........B2 28
Cavadas, Mex., 24,377...m12 34
Cavaillon, Fr., 12,067.....F6 5
Cavalier, N. Dak., 1,404...B8 77
Cavalier, co., N. Dak.,
  10,064............B7 77
Cavan, co., Ire., 53,800...*D3 4
Cavarzere, It., 5,600......B4 9
Cave, It., 5,856.........h9 9
Cave City, Ky., 1,418.....C4 62
Cave Junction, Oreg.,
  248..............E3 80
Cave Spring, Ga., 1,153....B1 55
Cavite, Phil., 54,891.....o13 19
Cavite, prov., Phil.,
  378,138..........*C6 19
Cawnpore, see Kanpur,
  India
Cawood, Ky., 900.......D6 62
Caxias, Braz., 19,092....*D6 27
Caxias do Sul., Braz.,
  60,607............D2 30
Caxito, Ang., 8,690......B2 24
Cayambe, Ec., 8,101.....A2 31
Cayce, S.C., 8,517.......D5 82
Cayenne, Fr. Gu., 18,615..C5 27
Cayey, P.R., 19,738.....G11 35
Cayman Islands, Br. dep.,
  N.A., 7,622........F3 35
Cayuga, Ont., Can., 897...E5 41
Cayuga, Ind., 904.......E3 59
Cayuga, co., N.Y., 73,942..C4 75
Cayuga Heights, N.Y.,
  3,128............*C4 75
Cazalla de la Sierra, Sp.,
  9,284.............D3 8
Cazenovia, N.Y., 2,676....C5 75
Cazorla, Sp., 8,699......D4 8
Ceará, state, Braz.,
  3,337,856.........*D7 27
Ceará Mirim, Braz.,
  8,290............*D7 27
Cebu, Phil., 251,146......C6 19
Cebu, prov., Phil.,
  1,332,847.........*C6 19
Cecil, Pa., 900.........F1 81
Cecil, co., Md., 48,408....A6 53
Cecina, It., 6,741.......C3 9
Cedar, co., Iowa, 17,791...C6 60
Cedar, co., Mo., 9,185....D4 69
Cedar, co., Nebr., 13,368..B8 71
Cedar, mtn., Cal.......B3 50
Cedar Bluff, Va., 995.....e10 85
Cedarburg, Wis.,
  5,191...........E5, m12 88
Cedar City, Utah, 7,543....C5 72
Cedar Falls, Iowa, 26,016..B5 60
Cedar Grove, N.J.,
  14,603...........*B4 74
Cedar Grove, W. Va.,
  1,569..........C3, C6 87
Cedar Grove, Wis., 1,175..E6 88
Cedar Hammock, Fla.,
  3,089............*E4 54
Cedar Heights, Md.,
  1,900............*C4 53
Cedar Hill, Tex., 1,848...n10 84
Cedar Hills, Fla., 8,000...m8 54
Cedar Hills, Oreg.,
  7,000............*B4 80
Cedarhurst, N.Y., 6,824...k13 75
Cedar Key, Fla., 668......C3 54
Cedar Knolls, N.J., 3,300..B4 74
Cedar Lake, Ind., 7,494...B3 59
Cedar Rapids, Iowa, 107,000
  (*140,000)........C6 60
Cedar Springs, Mich.,
  1,768.............E5 66
Cedar Terrace, S.C.,
  1,000............*D5 82
Cedartown, Ga., 9,340....B1 55
Cedar Vale, Kans., 859....E7 61
Cedarville, Calif., 800....B3 50
Cedarville, N.J., 1,130....E2 74
Cedarville, Ohio, 1,702...C2 78
Cedarwood Park, N.J.,
  1,300............*C4 74
Ceduna, Austl., 1,405.....F5 25
Cefalù, It., 10,700.......E5 9
Cegled, Hung., 30,310....B4 10
Ceglie Messapico, It.,
  16,500............D6 9
Celakovice, Czech., 6,041..n18 7
Celanese Village, Ga.,
  1,500............*B1 55
Celaya, Mex., 58,851.....m13 34
Celebes (Sulawesi), isl.,
  Indon.............F6 19
Celendín, Peru, 5,800.....C2 31
Celina, Ohio, 7,659......B1 78
Celina, Tenn., 1,228.....C8 83
Celina, Tex., 1,204......C4 84
Celje, Yugo., 16,487......B2 10
Celoron, N.Y., 1,507......C1 75
Cement, Okla., 959......C3 79
Cementon, Pa., 1,800.....E10 81

Cenon, Fr., 13,821.......E3 5
Centennial, mts., Mont....F4 70
Center, Colo., 1,600......D4 51
Center, Tex., 4,510......D5 84
Centerburg, Ohio, 963....B3 78
Centereach, N.Y., 8,524...E3 75
Center Line, Mich.,
  10,164...........*F8 66
Center Moriches, N.Y.,
  3,300............n16 75
Center Point, Ala., 9,500..E5 46
Center Point, Iowa, 1,236..B6 60
Centerport, N.Y., 4,600...*n15 75
Centerville, Ind., 2,378...E8 59
Centerville, Iowa, 6,629...D5 60
Centerville, Mont., 1,800..D4 70
Centerville, Ohio, 3,490...C1 78
Centerville, Pa., 5,088....F2 81
Centerville, S. Dak., 887..G9 77
Centerville, Tenn., 1,678..B4 83
Centerville, Tex., 836.....D5 84
Centerville, Utah,
  2,361...........A6, C2 72
Central, N. Mex., 1,075...C4 48
Central, S.C., 1,473......B2 82
Central, mts., Dom. Rep...E8 35
Central African Republic,
  country, Afr.,
  1,352,000.........G2 23
Central America, reg.,
  N.A., 13,800,000......E6 34
Central Avenue Park,
  Ohio, 2,500.......*A2 78
Central City, Ill., 1,422...E4 58
Central City, Iowa,
  1,087.............B6 60
Central City, Ky., 3,694...C2 62
Central City, Nebr.,
  2,406.............C7 71
Central City, Pa., 1,604...F4 81
Central Falls, R.I.,
  18,677............B11 52
Central Heights, Ariz.,
  1,800............*C3 48
Central Heights, Iowa,
  900..............A4 60
Centralia, Ill., 13,904.....E4 58
Centralia, Mo., 3,200.....B5 69
Centralia, Pa., 1,435....*D8 81
Centralia, Wash., 8,586...C3 86
Central Islip, N.Y.,
  24,000...........E7, n15 75
Central Nyack, N.Y.,
  1,300............*D7 75
Central Park, Ill., 2,676..*C6 58
Central Park, Wash.,
  1,622............*C2 86
Central Point, Oreg.,
  2,289.............E4 80
Central Square, N.Y.,
  935..............B4 75
Central Valley, Calif.,
  2,000.............B2 50
Central Valley, N.Y.,
  900............D6, m14 75
Centre, Ala., 2,392......A4 46
Centre, co., Pa., 78,580...E6 81
Centre, mtn., Idaho......D3 57
Centre, peak, B.C., Can....B4 37
Centre Hall, Pa., 1,109...E6 81
Centreville, Ala., 1,981...C2 46
Centreville, Ill., 12,769...E3 58
Centreville, Md., 1,863....B5 53
Centreville, Mich., 971....G5 66
Centreville, Miss., 1,737..D2 68
Century, Fla., 2,046.....u14 54
Ceram, isl., Indon.......F7 19
Ceredo, W. Va., 1,387....C2 87
Ceres, Calif., 5,573......D3 50
Ceres Northwest, Calif.,
  1,126.............D3 50
Cereté, Col., 11,849......B2 32
Cerignola, It., 47,400.....D5 9
Cernavoda, Rom., 8,802...C9 10
Cerralvo, Mex., 4,057.....B5 34
Cerritos, Mex., 9,989.....C4 34
Cerro Alto, mtn., Tex....o12 84
Cerro Azul, Peru, 1,372...D2 31
Cerro de Pasco, Peru,
  5,700.............D2 31
Cerro Gordo, Ill., 1,067...D5 58
Cerro Gordo, co., Iowa,
  49,894............A4 60
Cerro Largo, dept., Ur.,
  71,200...........*E2 30
Cervantes, Sp., 7,011.....A2 8
Cervera del Río Alhama,
  Sp., 7,101.........A2 8
Cesena, It., 39,000......B4 9
Cesenatico, It., 5,935.....B4 9
Ceska Lipa, Czech.,
  14,000............D4 7
Ceska Trebova, Czech.,
  13,000............C3 7
Ceské Budejovice, Czech.,
  65,000............D3 7
Cesky Brod, Czech.,
  5,754.............n8 7

Cesky Krumlov, Czech.,
  8,900.............D3 7
Cessnock, Austl., 34,517...F9 25
Cetinje, Yugo., 9,345.....D4 10
Cetraro, It., 9,366.......E5 9
Ceuta, Sp. dep., Afr.,
  73,182............A3 22
Ceylon, country, Asia,
  11,000,000.........G7 20
Chacabuco, Arg.,
  12,530..........A4, m9 28
Chachapoyas, Peru,
  6,900.............C2 31
Chaco, prov., Arg.,
  62,377............E3 29
Chad, country, Afr.,
  3,300,000..........F1 23
Chad, lake, Cam., Nig....E7 22
Chadbourn, N.C., 2,323...C4 76
Chadron, Nebr., 5,079....B3 71
Chadwicks, N.Y., 1,000...*B5 75
Chaffee, Mo., 2,862......D8 69
Chaffee, co., Colo., 8,298..C4 51
Chaffins, Mass., 3,000....*B4 65
Chagrin Falls, Ohio,
  3,458.............A4 78
Chahar Burjak, Afg.,
  5,000.............B3 20
Chaibasa, India, 22,019...D8 20
Chakradharpur, India,
  20,260............D8 20
Chakwal, Pak., 13,319....B5 20
Chalchuapa, Sal., 13,339..*E7 34
Chalfant, Pa., 1,414.....*E1 81
Chalhuanca, Peru, 2,538...D3 31
Chalk River, Ont., Can.,
  1,135.............A7 41
Chalkville, Ala., 2,000...*E4 46
Chalmette, La.,
  16,000..........E6, k11 63
Châlons-sur-Marne, Fr.,
  41,705............C6 5
Chalon-sur-Saône, Fr.,
  43,655............D6 5
Chama, N. Mex., 1,000...A5 48
Chamalières, Fr., 14,700..E5 5
Chaman, Pak., 7,161.....B4 20
Chamberlain, S. Dak.,
  2,598.............G6 77
Chamberlayne Heights,
  Va., 1,000........*C5 85
Chambers, co., Ala.,
  37,828............C4 46
Chambers, co., Tex.,
  10,379............E5 84
Chambersburg, Pa.,
  17,670............G6 81
Chambéry, Fr., 44,246....E6 5
Chamblee, Ga., 6,635....A5 55
Chambly, Que., Can.,
  3,737.............D4 42
Chambly, co., Que., Can.,
  146,745...........D4 42
Chambord, Que., Can.,
  1,188.............A5 42
Chancelulla, peak,
  Cal..............B2 50
Champaign, Ill., 49,583...C5 58
Champaign, co., Ill.,
  132,436...........C5 58
Champaign, co., Ohio,
  29,714............B2 78
Champigny-sur-Marne,
  Fr., 57,876.......g11 5
Champion, Ohio, 2,500...A5 78
Champlain, N.Y., 1,549...f11 75
Champlain, co., Que.,
  Can., 750.........B4 42
Champlin, Minn., 1,724..m12 67
Champotán, Mex., 4,694..D6 34
Chañaral, Chile, 5,200....F3 27
Chancay, Peru, 2,761.....D2 31
Chanda, India, 51,484....E6 20
Chandigarh, India,
  89,321............B6 20
Chandler, Ariz.,
  12,181..........C3, D2 48
Chandler, Que., Can.,
  3,406............k14 42
Chandler, Ind., 1,784....H3 59
Chandler, Okla., 2,524...B5 79
Chandpur, Pak., 32,048...D9 20
Changchow, China,
  296,500...........E8 17
Changchun (Hsinking),
  China, 975,000....C10 17
Changhua, Taiwan,
  52,340...........*G9 17
Changjin, Kor., 5,000.....F3 18
Changsha, China,
  703,000...........F7 17
Changte, China, 94,800...F7 17
Changting, China, 27,000..F8 17
Changyon, Kor., 18,072...G2 18
Chankiang, China,
  166,000...........G7 17
Channel, is., Eur........F5 4
Channel Lake, Ill., 1,969..H8 58

Channel-Port-aux-Basques,
    Newf., Can., 4,141......E2   44
Channelview, Tex.,
    11,000...............r14   84
Chantada, Sp., 2,262......A2   8
Chanthaburi, Thai.,
    10,795...............C2   19
Chantilly, Fr., 8,197......C5   5
Chanute, Kans., 10,849...E8   61
Chaoah (Chaochow),
    China, 101,300........G8   17
Chaochou, China, 5,000..D2   18
Chaoyang, China,
    16,000.............*G8   17
Chaoyang, China, 66,000..C9   17
Chapala, Mex., 7,216....m12   34
Chaparral, Col., 13,261...C2   32
Chapayevsk, Sov. Un.,
    85,000.............*D7   13
Chapel Hill, N.C., 12,573..B3   76
Chapleau, Ont., Can.,
    3,350...............p19   41
Chaplygin, Sov. Un.,
    10,000...............E12   12
Chapman, Ala., 617......D3   46
Chapman, Kans., 1,095...D7   61
Chapmanville, W. Va.,
    1,241...............D2   87
Chappaqua, N.Y., 4,500..*D7   75
Chappell, Nebr., 1,280...C3   71
Chapra, India, 75,580...C7   20
Charala, Col., 5,458.....B2   32
Charcas, Mex., 9,105....C4   34
Chardon, Ohio, 3,154.....A4   78
Chardzhou, Sov. Un.,
    75,000...............F9   13
Charente, dept., Fr.,
    327,658............*E4   5
Charente-Maritime, dept.,
    Fr., 470,897........*D3   5
Charenton-le-Pont, Fr.,
    22,530..............g10   5
Charikar, Afg., 21,070....A4   20
Chariton, Iowa, 5,042....C4   60
Chariton, co., Mo., 12,720..B4   69
Charlack, Mo., 1,493....*C7   69
Charlemagne, Que., Can.,
    3,068............D4, p19   42
Charleroi, Bel., 26,175....B6   5
Charleroi, Pa., 8,148.....F2   81
Charleroix West, co., Que.,
    Can., 16,450.........B7   42
Charles, co., Md., 32,572..C3   53
Charlesbourg, Que., Can.,
    14,308..............n17   42
Charles City, Iowa,
    10,419..............A5   60
Charles City, co., Va.,
    5,492...............C5   85
Charles Mix, co., S. Dak.,
    11,785..............G7   77
Charleston, Ark., 1,036...B1   49
Charleston, Ill., 13,611...D5   58
Charleston, Miss., 2,528...A3   68
Charleston, Mo., 5,911...E8   69
Charleston, S.C., 81,000
    (*240,000)......F8, k12   82
Charleston, W. Va.,
    83,000
    (*208,000)......C3, C5   87
Charleston, Utah, 223....C4   72
Charleston, co., S.C.,
    216,382.............F8   82
Charleston Heights, S.C.,
    24,000..........F8, k12   82
Charlestown, Ind., 5,571..H6   59
Charlestown, N.H., 1,200..E3   73
Charlestown, St. Kitts-
    Nevis-Anguilla,
    1,852..............H13   35
Charles Town, W. Va.,
    3,329..............B7   87
Charleville, Austl., 4,799..E8   25
Charleville, Fr., 24,668...C6   5
Charlevoix, Mich., 2,751..C5   66
Charlevoix, co., Mich.,
    13,421..............C5   66
Charlieu, Fr., 4,911......D6   5
Charlotte, Mich., 7,657...F6   66
Charlotte, N.C., 256,000
    (*335,000)..........B2   76
Charlotte, Tex., 1,465....E3   84
Charlotte, co., N.B., Can.,
    23,285..............D3   43
Charlotte, co., Fla.,
    12,594..............F5   54
Charlotte, co., Va.,
    13,368..............D4   85
Charlotte Amalie, Vir. Is.
    (U.S.), 12,880.......G12   35
Charlotte Harbor, Fla.,
    1,000...............F4   54
Charlottesville
    (Independent City),
    Va., 29,427.........B4   85
Charlottetown, P.E.I., Can.,
    18,318..............C6   43
Charlton City, Mass., 900..B4   65

Charlton, co., Ga., 5,313...F4   55
Charmco, W. Va., 700....D4   87
Charny, Que., Can.,
    4,189...........C6, o17   42
Charter Oak., Calif.,
    4,000..............*E4   50
Charters Towers, Austl.,
    7,533...............D8   25
Chartres, Fr., 31,495.....C4   5
Chascomús, Arg., 9,105...B5   28
Chase, B.C., Can., 990...D8   37
Chase, Kans., 3,921.....D5   61
Chase, co., Kans., 3,921...D7   61
Chase, co., Nebr., 4,317...D4   71
Chase City, Va., 3,207...D4   85
Chase, mtn., Maine......B4   64
Chaska, Minn.,
    3,268...........F5, n11   67
Chasong, Kor., 5,000....F3   18
Chasov Yar, Sov. Un.,
    10,000..............q20   12
Chataignier, La., 550....D3   63
Châteaubriant, Fr.,
    10,852..............C4   5
Châteaudun, Fr., 11,982..C4   5
Chateaugay, N.Y., 1,097..f11   10
Château-Gontier, Fr.,
    7,065...............D3   5
Châteauguay, Que., Can.,
    7,570...........D4, q19   42
Châteauguay, co., Que.,
    Can., 34,042........D4   42
Châteauguay Heights,
    Que., Can., 1,231....q19   42
Château-Richer, Que.,
    Can., 1,837.........C6   42
Châteauroux, Fr., 45,063..D4   5
Château-Theirry, Fr.,
    10,006..............C5   5
Châtellerault, Fr., 27,079..D4   5
Chatfield, Minn., 1,841...G6   67
Chatham, N.B., Can.,
    7,109...............B4   43
Chatham, Ont., Can.,
    29,826..............E2   41
Chatham, Ill., 2,023.....D4   58
Chatham, Mass., 1,580...C8   65
Chatham, N.J., 9,517....B4·   74
Chatham, N.Y., 2,426...C7   75
Chatham, Va., 1,822....D3   85
Chatham, co., Ga.,
    188,299.............E5   55
Chatham, co., N.C., ...
    26,785..............B3   76
Chatom, Ala., 993.......D1   46
Chatsworth, Ga., 1,184...B2   55
Chatsworth, Ill., 1,330...C5   58
Chattahoochee, Fla.,
    9,699...............B2   54
Chattahoochee, co., Ga.,
    13,011..............D2   55
Chattanooga, Tenn.,
    125,000
    (*305,000)......D8, E10   83
Chattaroy, W. Va., 950...D2   87
Chattooga, co., Ga.,
    19,954..............B1   55
Chatwood, Pa., 3,621...*G10   81
Chau Doc, Viet., 5,000...*C3   19
Chauk, Bur., 24,466.....D9   20
Chaumont, Fr., 21,717...C6   5
Chauncey, Ohio, 996....C3   78
Chauny, Fr., 12,626.....C5   5
Chautauqua, co., Kans.,
    5,956...............E7   61
Chautauqua, co., N.Y.,
    145,377.............C1   75
Chauvin, La., 950.......E5   63
Chaves, Port., 13,156....B2   8
Chaves, co., N. Mex.,
    57,649..............C6   48
Chavinda, Mex., 7,202...m12   34
Chazelles [sur-Lyon], Fr.,
    5,076...............E6   5
Chazy, N.Y., 800.......f11   75
Cheatham, co., Tenn.,
    9,428...............A4   83
Cheb, Czech., 22,300....C2   7
Chebanse, Ill., 995.....C6   58
Cheboksary, Sov. Un.,
    142,000.............C16   12
Cheboygan, Mich., 5,859..C6   66
Cheboygan, co., Mich.,
    14,550..............C6   66
Checotah, Okla., 2,614...B6   79
Cheddar, S.C., 500......B3   82
Cheektowaga, N.Y.,
    80,500..............C2   75
Cheektowaga-Southwest,
    N.Y., 12,766.........*C2   75
Chefoo, China, 116,000...D9   17
Chehalis, Wash., 5,199...C3   86
Cheju, Kor., 37,000......J3   18
Chekhov, Sov. Un.,
    10,000..............C10   18
Chekiang, prov., China,
    25,280,000..........F9   17
Chelan, Wash., 2,402....B5   86

Chelan, co., Wash.,
    40,744..............B4   86
Chelan, mts., Wash......A5   86
Chelkar, Sov. Un., 19,300..E3   13
Chelm [Lubelski], Pol.,
    33,500..............C7   7
Chelmno, Pol., 17,100....B5   7
Chelmsford, Ont., Can.,
    2,559..............*A3   41
Chelmsford, Eng., 52200..E7   4
Chelmsford, Mass.,
    4,000...........A5, f10   65
Chelmza, Pol., 14,400....B5   7
Chelsea, Mass.,
    33,749...........B5, g11   65
Chelsea, Mich., 3,355...F6   66
Chelsea, Okla., 1,514...A6   79
Chelsea Park, Wash.,
    2,000..............*B3   86
Cheltenham, Eng., 74,300..E5   4
Cheltenham, Md., 500...C4   53
Cheltenham, Pa., 7,000..*F11   81
Chelyabinsk, Sov. Un.,
    805,000.............D9   13
Chemainus, B.C., Can.,
    1,518...........E6, g12   37
Chemnitz, see Karl-Marx-
    Stadt, Ger.
Chemung, co., N.Y.,
    98,706..............C4   75
Chenango, co., N.Y.,
    43,243..............C5   75
Chenango Bridge, N.Y.,
    3,500..............*C5   75
Cheney, Kans.,
    1,101...........E6, g11   61
Cheney, Wash.,
    3,173...........B8, h13   86
Cheneyville, La., 1,037...C3   63
Chengchow, China,
    766,000.............E7   17
Chenghwa, see Sharasume,
    China
Chengteh (Jehol),
    China, 92,900........C8   17
Chengtu, China,
    1,107,000...........E5   17
Chenoa, Ill., 1,523.....C5   58
Chepén, Peru, 8,214....C2   31
Chepstow, Wales, 7,400...E5   4
Cher, dept., Fr.,
    293,514............*D5   5
Cheraw, S.C., 5,171....B8   82
Cherbourg, Fr., 37,486...C3   5
Cheremkhovo, Sov. Un.,
    140,000.............D13   13
Cherepovets, Sov. Un.,
    124,000.............B11   12
Cherkassy, Sov. Un.,
    103,000.............G9   12
Chernigov, Sov. Un.,
    113,000.............F8   12
Chernobay, Sov. Un.,
    25,000..............G9   12
Chernobyl, Sov. Un.,
    10,000..............F8   12
Chernovtsy, Sov. Un.,
    152,000.............G5   12
Chernyakhovsk
    (Insterburg),
    Sov. Un., 33,000.......D3   12
Cherokee, Ala., 1,349...A2   46
Cherokee, Iowa, 7,724...B2   60
Cherokee, Kans., 797....E9   61
Cherokee, Okla., 2,410...A3   79
Cherokee, co., Ala.,
    16,303..............A4   46
Cherokee, co., Ga.,
    23,001..............B2   55
Cherokee, co., Iowa,
    18,598..............B2   60
Cherokee, co., Kans.,
    22,279..............E9   61
Cherokee, co., N.C.,
    16,335..............f8   76
Cherokee, co., Okla.,
    17,762..............B6   79
Cherokee, co., S.C.,
    35,205..............A4   82
Cherokee, co., Tex.,
    33,120..............D5   84
Cherokee Forest, S.C.,
    2,000..............*B3   82
Cherokee Ranch, Pa.,
    1,200..............*F9   81
Cherry, co., Nebr., 8,218..B4   71
Cherry Grove, Ohio,
    2,000..............*C1   78
Cherry Hill, N.J., 31,522..D2   74
Cherry Hills Village,
    Colo., 1,931........*B6   51
Cherryvale, Kans., 2,783..E8   61
Cherry Valley, Ill., 875...A5   58
Cherry Valley, Mass.,
    1,800...............B4   65
Cherryville, N.C., 4,056...B1   76
Chesaning, Mich., 2,770...E6   66
Chesapeake, Ohio, 1,396..D3   78

Chesapeake (Independent
    City), Va., 73,647..D6, k15   85
Chesapeake, W. Va., 150..C3   87
Chesapeake City, Md.,
    1,104...............A6   53
Chesham, Eng., 18,300...k11   4
Cheshire, Conn., 3,500...D5   52
Cheshire, Mass., 1,150...A1   65
Cheshire, co., Eng.,
    1,410,100..........*D5   4
Cheshire, co., N.H.,
    43,342..............F3   73
Cheshunt, Eng., 37,500...k12   4
Chesley, Ont., Can.,
    1,697...............C3   41
Chesnee, S.C., 1,045....A4   82
Chester, Calif., 1,553....B3   50
Chester, N.S., Can., 990..E5   43
Chester, Conn., 1,500...D7   52
Chester, Eng., 59,400...D5   4
Chester, Ill., 5,300.....F4   58
Chester, Md., 900......C5   53
Chester, Mass., 750.....B2   65
Chester, Mont., 1,158...B6   70
Chester, N.J., 1.074....B3   74
Chester, N.S., Can., 990..E5   43
Chester, N.Y.,
    1,650...........D6, m14   75
Chester, Pa.,
    63,658.........G11, p10   81
Chester, S.C., 6,906....B5   82
Chester, Vt., 923.......E3   73
Chester, Va., 2,000....C5, n18   85
Chester, W. Va.,
    3,787...........A2, A4   87
Chester, co., Pa.,
    210,608.............G10   81
Chester, co., S.C., 30,888..B5   82
Chester, co., Tenn.,
    9,569...............B3   83
Chesterfield, Eng., 68,200..D6   4
Chesterfield, Ind., 2,588...D6   59
Chesterfield, S.C., 1,532...B7   82
Chesterfield, co., S.C.,
    33,717..............B7   82
Chesterfield, co., Va.,
    71,197..............C5   85
Chesterhill, Ohio, 876....C4   78
Chesterton, Ind., 5,058...A3   59
Chesterville, Ont., Can.,
    1,248...............B9   41
Cheswick, Pa., 2,734....h14   81
Cheticamp, N.S., Can.,
    1,223...............C8   43
Chetopa, Kans., 1,538...E8   61
Chetumal, see Ciudad
    Chetumal, Mex.
Chetwynd, B.C., Can.,
    1,020...............B7   37
Cheverly, Md., 5,223....*C4   53
Cheviot, Ohio,
    10,701..........C1, o12   78
Chevy Chase, Md.,
    10,600...........C3, f8   53
Chevy Chase Heights, Pa.,
    1,160..............*E3   81
Chevy Chase Lake, Md.,
    2,500..............*C3   53
Chevy Chase Section
    Four, Md., 2,243....*C3   53
Chevy Chase View, Md.,
    1,000..............*C3   53
Chewelah, Wash., 1,525..A8   86
Chews (Chews Landing),
    N.J., 1,500.........*C4   74
Cheyenne, Okla., 930....B2   79
Cheyenne, Wyo., 43,505..E8   89
Cheyenne, co., Colo.,
    2,789...............C8   51
Cheyenne, co., Kans.,
    4,708...............C2   61
Cheyenne, co., Nebr.,
    14,828..............C2   71
Cheyenne Wells, Colo.,
    1,020...............C8   51
Chiahsing, China, 78,300..E9   17
Chiai, Taiwan, 96,500...*G9   17
Chiamussu, see Kiamusze,
    China
Chian, China, 52,800.....F3   18
Chiang Khong, Thai.,
    3,320...............A2   19
Chiangling, China, 15,000..E7   17
Chiang Mai, Thai.,
    65,736..............B1   19
Chiang Rai, Thai., 11,659..B1   19
Chiapa de Corzo, Mex.,
    6,960...............D6   34
Chiapas, state, Mex.,
    1,210,870...........D6   34
Chiari, It., 9,000........B2   9
Chiautla de Tapia, Mex.,
    3,957..............n14   34
Chiavari, It., 24,603.....B2   9
Chiba, Jap.,
    332,188........I10, n19   18

Chiba, pref., Jap., 2,701,770 . . . . *I10 18
Chicago, Ill., 3,460,000 (*7,435,000) B6, k9 58
Chicago Heights, Ill., 34,331 . . . . B6, k9 58
Chicago Ridge, Ill., 5,748 . . . . *B6 58
Chichester, Eng., 19,600 . . . E6 4
Chichibu, Jap., 60,330 . . . . n18 18
Chickamauga, Ga., 1,824 . . B1 55
Chickasaw, Ala., 10,002 . . . E1 46
Chickasaw, co., Iowa, 15,034 . . . . A5 60
Chickasaw, co., Miss., 16,891 . . . . B5 68
Chickasha, Okla., 14,866 . . . B4 79
Chiclana, Sp., 21,524 . . . . . . D2 8
Chiclayo, Peru, 86,900 . . . . C2 31
Chico, Calif., 14,757 . . . . . . C3 50
Chico, Tex., 654 . . . . C4 84
Chico, Wash., 300 . . . . B3 86
Chicontepec, Mex., 3,287 . . . . m14 34
Chicopee, Ga., 900 . . . . B3 55
Chicopee, Mass., 61,553 . . B2 65
Chicora, Pa., 1,156 . . . . E2 81
Chicot, co., Ark., 18,990 . . D4 49
Chicoutimi, Que., Can., 31,657 . . . . A6, k12 42
Chicoutimi-Nord, Que., Can., 11,229 . . . . A6 42
Chicoutimi, co., Que., Can., 157,196 . . . . A6 42
Chico Vecino, Calif., 4,688 . . . . *C3 50
Chiefland, Fla., 1,459 . . . . C4 54
Chieri, It., 11,900 . . . . B1 9
Chieti, It., 36,800 . . . . C5 9
Chigirin, Sov. Un., 10,000 . . . . G9 12
Chignahuapan, Mex., 3,081 . . . . n14 34
Chigwell, Eng., 62,200 . . . . k13 4
Chihchiang, China, 19,000 . . . . F6 17
Chihfeng, China, 40,000 . . . C8 17
Chihuahua, Mex., 150,430 . . . . B3 34
Chihuahua, state, Mex., 1,226,793 . . . . B3 34
Chii-san, mtn., Korea I3 18
Chikura, Jap., 11,300 . . . . o18 18
Chilapa de Alvarez, Mex., 7,368 . . . . D5, o14 34
Childersburg, Ala., 4,884 . . B3 46
Chilca, Peru, 1,341 . . . . D2 31
Childress, Tex., 6,399 . . . . . B2 84
Childress, co., Tex., 8,421 . B2 84
Chile, country, S.A., 8,450,000 . . . . E2 29
Chilecito, Arg., 6,121 . . . . . E2 29
Chilhowie, Va., 1,169 . . . . f10 85
Chillán, Chile, 59,100 . . . . B2 28
Chillicothe, Ill., 3,054 . . . . C4 58
Chillicothe, Mo., 9,236 . . . . B4 69
Chillicothe, Ohio, 24,957 . . C3 78
Chillicothe, Tex., 1,161 . . . B3 84
Chilliwack, B.C., Can., 8,259 . . . . E7, f14 37
Chillum, Md., 13,800 . . . . *C3 53
Chiloé, prov., Chile, 99,205 . . . . C2 28
Chiloquin, Oreg., 945 . . . . . E5 80
Chilpancingo [de los Bravos], Mex., 18,022 . . . . D5, o14 34
Chilton, Tex., 400 . . . . D4 84
Chilton, Wis., 2,578 . . D5, h10 88
Chilton, co., Ala., 25,693 . . C3 46
Chilung (Keelung), Taiwan, 201,000 . . . . . . F9 17
Chimalhuacán, Mex., 2,495 . . . . h10 34
Chimayo, N. Mex., 600 . . . B6 48
Chimbay, Sov. Un., 16,100 . . . . E8 13
Chimborazo, prov., Ec., 276,668 . . . . B2 31
Chimborazo, vol., Ec. B2 31
Chimbote, Peru, 64,000 . . . C2 31
Chimney Rock, Neb. C2 71
China, Mex., 2,463 . . . . B5 34
China (Excl. Taiwan), country, Asia, 86,400,000 . . . . E4 17
Chinati, peak, Tex. p12 84
China Grove, N.C., 1,500 . . B2 76
Chinandega, Nic., 22,409 . . E7 34
Chincha Alta, Peru, 19,600 . . . . D2 31
Chincheros, Peru, 1,300 . . . D3 31
Chinchilla, Pa., 1,100 . . . *D10 81
Chinchow (Chinhsien), China, 352,200 . . . . C9 17
Chincoteague, Va., 2,131 . . C7 85
Chingford, Eng., 45,777 . . . k13 4
Chindo, Kor., 4,100 . . . . . . I3 18

Chinhae, Kor., 68,500 . . . . I4 18
Chining, China, 86,200 . . . . D8 17
Chiniot, Pak., 47,099 . . . . . B5 20
Chinju, Kor., 82,800 . . . . . . I4 18
Chinkiang, China, 207,600 . . . . E8 17
Chinnampo (Nampo), Kor., 82,162 . . . . G2 18
Chino, Calif., 14,246 . . F5, m13 50
Chinook, Mont., 2,326 . . . . B7 70
Chinquapin, N.C., 800 . . . . C5 76
Chinú, Col., 7,552 . . . . B3 32
Chinwangtao, China, 186,800 . . . . D8 17
Chioggia, It., 46,800 . . . . . B4 9
Chipley, Fla., 3,159 . . . . . . u16 54
Chipman, N.B., Can., 1,490 . . . . C4 43
Chippawa, Ont., Can., 3,256 . . . . D5 41
Chippewa, co., Mich., 32,655 . . . . B6 66
Chippewa, co., Minn., 16,320 . . . . E3 67
Chippewa, co., Wis., 45,096 . . . . C2 88
Chippewa Falls, Wis., 11,708 . . . . D2 88
Chiquimula, Guat., 8,840 . . E7 34
Chiquinquirá, Col., 16,926 . . . . B3 32
Chiriqui Grande, Pan., 98 . . B1 32
Chirpan, Bul., 13,231 . . . . . D7 10
Chisago, co., Minn., 13,419 . . . . E6 67
Chisholm, Ala., 1,500 . . . . . C3 46
Chisholm, Maine, 1,240 . . . D2 64
Chisholm, Minn., 7,144 . . . C6 67
Chişineu-Criş, Rom., 6,124 . . . . B5 10
Chislehurst [& Sidcup], Eng., 86,907 . . . . m13 4
Chisos, mts., Tex. p13 84
Chistyakovo, Sov. Un., 90,000 . . . . q12 12
Chita, Sov. Un., 198,000 . . D14 13
Chitai (Kuchêng), China, 25,000 . . . . C2 17
Chitaldroog, India, 33,336 . . F6 20
Chitré, Pan., 9,120 . . . . B1 32
Chittagong, Pak., 364,205 . . D9 20
Chittenango, N.Y., 3,180 . . *B5 75
Chittenden, co., Vt., 74,425 . . . . C1 73
Chittoor, India, 47,876 . . . . F6 20
Chiusi, It., 8,498 . . . . C3 9
Chivasso, It., 8,800 . . . . . . B1 9
Chivay, Peru, 2,027 . . . . . . E3 31
Chivilcoy, Arg., 23,386 . . . . A4, g6 28
Chochiwon, Kor., 16,700 . . H3 18
Chocó, dept., Col., 181,863 . . . . C2 32
Chocontá, Col., 3,379 . . . . . B3 32
Choctaw, co., Ala., 17,870 . . . . C1 46
Choctaw, co., Miss., 8,423 . . . . B4 68
Choctaw, co., Okla., 15,637 . . . . C6 79
Chodziez, Pol., 12,200 . . . . B4 7
Choisy-le-Roi, Fr., 40,950 . . . . g10 5
Choix, Mex., 2,050 . . . . B3 34
Chojna, Pol., 1,484 . . . . . . B3 7
Chojnice, Pol., 21,700 . . . . B4 7
Chojnow, Pol., 10,300 . . . . C3 7
Chōkai-zan mtn., Jap. . . . G10 18
Cholet, Fr., 36,565 . . . . D3 5
Cholula [de Rivadabia, Mex., 12,833 . . . . n14 34
Choluteca, Hond., 11,483 . . E7 34
Chomutov, Czech., 34,000 . . . . C2 7
Chonan, Kor., 46,200 . . . . . H3 18
Chon Buri, Thai., 32,498 . . C2 19
Chone, Ec., 12,832 . . . . B1 31
Chŏngjin, Kor., 184,301 . . . F4 18
Chŏngju, Kor., 98,500 . . . . H3 18
Chonju, Kor., 174,500 . . . . I3 18
Chorrillos, Peru, 6,996 . . . . D2 31
Chorwon, Kor., 30,085 . . . . G3 18
Chorzów, Pol., 153,200 . . . . g9 7
Chosen, Fla., 1,858 . . . . . . F6 54
Chosen, see Korea, Asia
Chōshi, Jap., 73,000 . . I10, n19 18
Chosica, Peru, 4,160 . . . . . D2 31
Chota, Peru, 2,705 . . . . C2 31
Choteau, Mont., 1,966 . . . . C4 70
Chouchiakou, China, 85,500 . . . . *E7 17
Choum, Maur. D2 22
Chouteau, Okla., 958 . . . . . A6 79
Chouteau, co., Mont., 7,348 . . . . C6 70
Chowan, co., N.C., 11,729 . . . . A6 76

Chowchilla, Calif., 4,611 . . D3 50
Chrisman, Ill., 1,221 . . . . . . D6 58
Christchurch, N.Z., 161,566, (*247,248) O14 26
Christian, co., Ill., 37,207 . . D4 58
Christian, co., Ky., 56,904 . . . . D2 62
Christian, co., Mo., 12,359 . . . . E4 69
Christiana, Pa., 1,069 . . . . . G9 81
Christiansburg, Va., 3,653 . . . . C2 85
Christiansted, Vir. Is., (U.S.), 5,137 . . . . H12 35
Christmas Island, Austl. dep., Oceania, 3,500 . . . G4 2
Christopher, Ill., 2,854 . . . . F4 58
Chrudim, Czech., 15,500 . . D3 7
Chrzanow, Pol., 22,500 . . . g10 7
Chüanchow (Chinchiang), China, 107,700 . . . . . . G8 17
Chubbuck, Idaho, 1,590 . . . G6 57
Chubut, prov., Arg., 142,195 . . . . C3 28
Chugiak, Alsk., 1,500 . . . . C10, g17 47
Chuguyev, Sov. Un., 10,000 . . . . G11 12
Chuho, China, 5,000 . . . . . . D3 18
Chuhsien, China, 32,000 . . . F8 17
Chuius, mtn., B.C., Can. . . B5 37
Chula Vista, Calif., 42,034 . . . . F5, o15 50
Chulucanas, Peru, 19,700 . . B1 31
Chumikan, Sov. Un., 1,100 . . . . D16 13
Chunchŏn, Kor., 101,300 . . H3 18
Chungju, Kor., 54,100 . . . . H3 18
Chungking (Chungching), China, 1,800,000 . . . . . F6 17
Chupaca, Peru, 4,482 . . . . . D2 31
Chuquibamba, Peru, 2,480 . . . . E3 31
Chuquisaca, dept., Bol., 282,980 . . . . D3 29
Chur, Switz., 24,825 . . . . . . E4 6
Church, mtn., B.C., Can. . . f14 37
Church Hill, Tenn., 769 . . C11 83
Churchill, Man., Can., 1,878 . . . . f9 40
Churchill, Pa., 3,428 . . . . . *E1 81
Churchill, co., Nev., 8,452 . . B2 72
Churchill, mtn., B.C., Can. E6 37
Churchill, riv., Man., Sask., Can. B2 39
Churchville, Pa., 1,500 . . . *F11 81
Churubusco, Ind., 1,284 . . . B7 59
Churchs Ferry, N. Dak., 161 . . . . B6 77
Churumuco, Mex., 1,502 . . . . n13 34
Chusovoy, Sov. Un., 63,000 . . . . *D8 13
Cicero, Ill., 69,130 . . . B6, k9 58
Cicero, Ind., 1,284 . . . . D5 59
Ciechanow, Pol., 20,900 . . . B6 7
Ciego de Avila, Cuba, 52,800 . . . . D4 35
Ciénaga, Col., 47,719 . . . . . A3 32
Ciénaga de Oro, Col., 8,047 . . . . B2 32
Cienfuegos, Cuba, 70,200 . . C3 35
Cieszyn, Pol., 23,800 . . . . . D5 7
Cihuatlán, Mex., 4,125 . . . n11 34
Cimarron, Kans., 1,293 . . . E3 61
Cimarron, N. Mex., 997 . . . A6 48
Cimarron, co., Okla., 4,496 . . . . e8 79
Cimarron, riv., U.S. C7 45
Cîmpina, Rom., 20,700 . . . . C7 10
Cîmpulung, Rom., 21,500 . . C7 10
Cîmpulung Moldovenesc, Rom. B7 10
Cincinnati, Ohio, 495,000 (*1,325,000) C1, o12 78
Cinnaminson Township, N.J., 8,302 . . . . *C2 74
Cintalapa [de Figueroa], Mex., 8,150 . . . . D6 34
Cinto, mtn., Fr. C2 9
Circle, Mont., 1,117 . . . . . C11 70
Circle Pines, Minn., 2,789 . . . . *E5 67
Circleville, Ohio, 11,059 . . C3 78
Cirencester, Eng., 12,600 . . E6 4
Cirque, mtn., Newf., Can. f9 44
Cisco, Tex., 4,499 . . . . C3 84
Cisneros, Col., 7,554 . . . . . B2 32
Cissna Park, Ill., 803 . . . . . C6 58
Cisterna di Latina, It., 8,000 . . . . h9 9
Citac, mtn., Peru D2 31
Citlaltépet (Pico de Orizaba), vol., Mex. . . . n15 34
Citronelle, Ala., 1,918 . . . . D1 46

Citrus, co., Fla., 9,268 . . . . D4 54
Citrus Heights, Calif., 24,000 . . . . *C3 50
Cittadella, It., 5,002 . . . . . . B3 9
Città di Castello, It., 11,300 . . . . C4 9
City Park, Ill., 1,133 . . . . . *D4 58
City Terrace, Calif., 6,000 . . . . *F4 50
City View, S.C., 2,475 . . . . B3 82
Ciudad Acuña, Mex., 20,048 . . . . B4 34
Ciudad Allende, Mex., 9,418 . . . . B4 34
Ciudad Altamirano, Mex., 6,014 . . . . n13 34
Ciudad Bolívar, Ven., 63,266 . . . . B5 32
Ciudad Camargo, Mex., 18,951 . . . . B3 34
Ciudad Chetumal, Mex., 12,855 . . . . D7 34
Ciudad del Carmen, Mex., 21,164 . . . . D6 34
Ciudad del Maíz, Mex., 4,767 . . . . C5 34
Ciudadde Naucalpan de Juárez, Mex., 10,365 . . h9 34
Ciudad de Valles, Mex., 23,823 . . . . C5, m14 34
Ciudad de Villaldama, Mex., 2,277 . . . . B4 34
Ciudad Dr. Hernández Alvarez, Mex., 8,553 . . *m13 34
Ciudad Guzmán, Mex., 30,941 . . . . D4, n12 34
Ciudad Hidalgo, Mex., 17,155 . . . . n13 34
Ciudad Ixtepec, Mex., 12,087 . . . . D5 34
Ciudad Jiménez, Mex., 14,922 . . . . B4 34
Ciudad Juárez, Mex., 262,119 . . . . A3 34
Ciudad Lerdo, Mex., 17,682 . . . . B4 34
Ciudad Madero, Mex., 53,628 . . . . C5 34
Ciudad Mante, Mex., 22,919 . . . . C5 34
Ciudad Melchor Múzquiz, Mex., 12,971 . . . . B4 34
Ciudad Mendoza, Mex., 16,051 . . . . n15 34
Ciudad Obregón, Mex., 67,956 . . . . B3 34
Ciudad Real, Sp., 37,081 . . C4 8
Ciudad Real, prov., Sp., 583,948 . . . . *C4 8
Ciudad Serdán, Mex., 9,942 . . . . n15 34
Ciudad Victoria, Mex., 50,797 . . . . C5 34
Cividale de Friuli, It., 7,074 . . . . A4 9
Civitanova Marche, It., 12,300 . . . . C4 9
Civitavecchia, It., 40,000 . . . . C3 9
Cizre, Tur., 6,473 . . . . D14 14
Clackamas, Oreg., 900 . . . h12 80
Clackamas, co., Oreg., 113,038 . . . . B4 80
Clackmannan, co., Scot., 41,900 . . . . *B5 4
Claflin, Kans., 891 . . . . D5 61
Claiborne, co., Miss., 10,845 . . . . D3 68
Claiborne, co., Tenn., 19,067 . . . . C10 83
Claiborne, par., La., 19,407 . . . . B2 63
Clairfield, Tenn., 500 . . . . C10 83
Clair Haven, Mich., 1,365 . . . . *F8 66
Clairton, Pa., 18,389 . . . . . F2 81
Clallam, co., Wash., 30,022 . . . . A1 86
Clamart, Fr., 47,991 . . . . . g10 5
Clamecy, Fr., 5,520 . . . . . . D5 5
Clanton, Ala., 5,683 . . . . . . C3 46
Clara Barton, N.J., 6,500 . . . . *B4 74
Clara City, Minn., 1,358 . . F3 67
Clare, Austl., 1,584 . . . . . . F6 25
Clare, Mich., 2,442 . . . . . . E6 66
Clare, co., Ire., 73,500 . . . *D2 4
Clare, co., Mich., 11,647 . . E6 66
Claremont, Calif., 12,633 . . . . m13 50
Claremont, N.H., 13,564 . . E3 73
Claremont, mtn., Cal. C3 50
Claremore, Okla., 6,639 . . . A6 79
Clarence, Iowa, 859 . . . . . . C6 60
Clarence, Mo., 1,103 . . . . . B5 69
Clarence, N.Y., 1,600 . . . . *C2 75
Clarendon, Ark., 2,293 . . . . C4 49
Clarendon, Tex., 2,172 . . . . B2 84

Clarendon, co., S.C., 29,490.............D7 82
Clarendon Hills, Ill., 5,885...............k9 58
Clarenville, Newf., Can., 1,541..............D4 44
Claresholm, Alta., Can., 2,143..............D4 38
Claridge, Pa., 1,100......F2 81
Clarinda, Iowa, 5,714.....D2 60
Clarion, Iowa, 3,232.....B4 60
Clarion, Pa., 4,958......D3 81
Clarion, co., Pa., 37,408..D2 81
Clark, N.J., 12,195......B4 74
Clark, S. Dak., 1,484......F8 77
Clark, co., Ark., 20,950....C2 49
Clark, co., Idaho, 915....E6 57
Clark, co., Ill., 16,546.....D6 58
Clark, co., Ind., 66,453....H6 59
Clark, co., Kans., 3,396....E4 61
Clark, co., Ky., 21,075....C5 62
Clark, co., Mo., 8,725.....A6 69
Clark, co., Nev., 127,016..C4 72
Clark, co., Ohio, 131,440..C2 78
Clark, co., S. Dak., 7,134..F8 77
Clark, co., Wash., 93,809..D3 86
Clark, co., Wis., 31,527...D3 88
Clark, mtn., Mo..........D7 69
Clarkdale, Ariz., 1,095....B2 48
Clarke, co., Ala., 25,738..D2 46
Clarke, co., Ga., 45,363....C3 55
Clarke, co., Iowa, 8,222...D4 60
Clarke, co., Miss., 16,493..C5 68
Clarke, co., Va., 7,942.....A4 85
Clarkes Harbour, N.S., Can., 945..........F4 43
Clarkfield, Minn., 1,100...F3 67
Clark Mills, N.Y., 1,148..*B5 75
Clarks, La., 940.........B3 63
Clarksburg, W. Va., 28,112............B4, B6 87
Clarksdale, Miss., 21,105..A3 68
Clarks Green, Pa., 1,256..............*D10 75
Clarks Harbour, N.S., Can., 945..........F4 43
Clarkson, Ont., Can.,.....D5 41
Clarks Summit, Pa., 3,693.............m18 81
Clarkston, Ga., 1,524....B5 55
Clarkston, Wash., 6,209...C8 86
Clarksville, Ark., 3,919...B2 49
Clarksville, Ind., 9,089...H6 59
Clarksville, Iowa, 1,328...B5 60
Clarksville, Tenn., 22,021..A4 83
Clarksville, Tex., 3,851...C5 84
Clarksville, Va., 1,530...D4 85
Clarkton, Mo., 1,049......E8 69
Clatskanie, Oreg., 797...A3 80
Clatsop, co., Oreg., 27,380...........A3 80
Claude, Tex., 895......B2 84
Clausthal-Zellerfeld, Ger., 15,200...........C5 6
Clawson, Mich., 14,795...o15 66
Claxton, Ga., 2,672.....D5 55
Clay, Ky., 1,343.......C2 62
Clay, co., Ala., 12,400....B4 46
Clay, co., Ark., 21,258...A5 49
Clay, co., Fla., 19,535...B5 54
Clay, co., Ga., 4,551....E2 55
Clay, co., Ill., 15,815....E5 58
Clay, co., Ind., 24,207...F3 59
Clay, co., Iowa, 18,504...A2 60
Clay, co., Kans., 10,675...C6 61
Clay, co., Ky., 20,748....C6 62
Clay, co., Minn., 39,080..D2 67
Clay, co., Miss., 18,933...B5 68
Clay, co., Mo., 87,474....B3 69
Clay, co., Nebr., 8,717....D7 71
Clay, co., N.C., 5,526....f9 76
Clay, co., S. Dak., 10,810..H9 77
Clay, co., Tenn., 7,289...C8 83
Clay, co., Tex., 8,351....C3 84
Clay, co., W. Va., 11,942..C3 87
Clay Center, Kans., 4,613.............C6 61
Clay City, Ill., 1,144.....E5 58
Clay City, Ind., 950.....F3 59
Claycomo, Mo., 1,423...*B3 69
Claymont, Del., 12,500...A7 53
Claypool, Ariz., 2,000.............C3, D3 48
Claysburg, Pa., 1,439....F5 81
Claysville, Pa., 986.....F1 81
Clayton, Ala., 1,313......D4 46
Clayton, Del., 1,028......B6 53
Clayton, Ga., 1,507......B3 55
Clayton, Ill., 774.......C3 58
Clayton, La., 882.......C4 63
Clayton, Mo., 15,245..C7, f13 69
Clayton, N.J., 4,711.....D2 74
Clayton, N. Mex., 3,314..A7 48
Clayton, N.Y., 1,996..A4, f8 75
Clayton, N.C., 2,965.....B4 76
Clayton, Okla., 615.....C6 79
Clayton, co., Ga., 46,365...........C2 55

Clayton, co., Iowa, 21,962............B6 60
Clearbrook, B.C., Can., 1,964.............f13 37
Clear Creek, co., Colo., 2,793.............B5 51
Clearfield, Pa., 9,270.....D5 81
Clearfield, Utah, 8,833..A5 72
Clearfield, co., Pa., 81,534............D4 81
Clear Lake, Iowa, 6,301..A4 60
Clear Lake, S. Dak., 1,137..............F9 77
Clearlake Highlands, Calif., 800............C2 50
Clear Lake Shores, Tex., 700.............r14 84
Clearwater, Fla., 34,653.........E4, p10 54
Clearwater, Kans., 1,073..E6 61
Clearwater, S. C., 1,450..E4 82
Clearwater, co., Idaho, 8,548............C3 57
Clearwater, co., Minn., 8,864............C3 67
Clearwater, mts., Idaho....C2 57
Cleburne, Tex., 15,381..........C4, n9 84
Cleburne, co., Ala., 10,911............B4 46
Cleburne, co., Ark., 9,059..B3 49
Cle Elum, Wash., 1,816...B5 86
Clementon, N.J., 3,766...D3 74
Clemmons, N.C., 1,000..A2 76
Clemson, S.C., 1,587....B2 82
Clemson College, S.C., 3,500............*B2 82
Clendenin, W. Va., 1,510..........C3, C6 87
Cleona, Pa., 1,988......F9 81
Clermont, Austl., 1,648...D8 25
Clermont, Que., Can., 3,114.............B7 42
Clermont, Fla., 3,313.....D5 54
Clermont, Ind., 1,058..E5, k9 59
Clermont, co., Ohio, 80,530............C1 78
Clermont-Ferrand, Fr., 127,684............E5 5
Clermont-l'Hérault, Fr., 5,538.............F5 5
Cleveland, Miss., 10,172..B3 68
Cleveland, Ohio, 790,000 (*2,250,000).....A4, h9 78
Cleveland, Okla., 2,519...A5 79
Cleveland, Tenn., 16,196..D9 83
Cleveland, Tex., 5,838...D5 84
Cleveland, co., Ark., 6,944.............D3 49
Cleveland, co., N.C., 69,372............B1 76
Cleveland, co., Okla., 47,600............B4 79
Cleveland, mtn., Mont....B3 70
Cleveland Heights, Ohio, 61,813.........A4, g9 78
Cleves, Ohio, 2,076....o12 78
Clewiston, Fla., 3,114....F6 54
Clichy [-la-Garenne], Fr., 56,316.........C5, g10 5
Cliffside, N.C., 1,275..B1, f11 76
Cliffside Park, N.J., 17,642...........h9 74
Cliffwood, N.J., 1,500..*C4 74
Cliffwood Beach, N.J., 3,500...........*C4 74
Clifton, Ariz., 4,191.....C4 48
Clifton, Ill., 1,018......C6 58
Clifton, N.J., 82,084..B4, H8 74
Clifton, S.C., 1,249.....B4 82
Clifton, Tex., 2,335.....D4 84
Clifton Forge, (Independent City), Va., 5,268...........C3 85
Clifton Heights, Pa., 8,005..............p20 81
Clifton Springs, N.Y., 1,953.............C3 75
Climax, Colo., 500......B4 51
Clinch, co., Ga., 6,545...F4 55
Clinch, mtn., Va........f9 85
Clinchco, Va., 975......e10 85
Clinchfield, N.C., 950..*F10 76
Clingmans Dome, mtn...f9 76
Clint, Tex., 900........o11 84
Clinton, Ark., 744......B3 49
Clinton, B.C., Can., 1,011.............D7 37
Clinton, Ont., Can., 3,491.............D3 41
Clinton, Conn., 4,166...D6 52
Clinton, Ill., 7,355.....C5 58
Clinton, Ind., 5,843.....E3 59
Clinton, Iowa, 33,589...C7 60
Clinton, Ky., 1,647.....B2 62
Clinton, La., 1,568.......D4 63
Clinton, Maine, 800 (1,729▲)............D3 64

Clinton, Md., 4,000......C4 53
Clinton, Mass., 12,848...B4 65
Clinton, Mich., 1,481....F7 66
Clinton, Miss., 3,438....C3 68
Clinton, Mo., 6,925.....C4 69
Clinton, N.J., 1,158.....B3 74
Clinton, N.Y., 2,029.....B5 75
Clinton, N.C., 7,461.....C4 76
Clinton, Ohio, 924......*A4 78
Clinton, Okla., 9,617....B3 79
Clinton, S.C., 7,937.....C4 82
Clinton, Tenn., 4,943.........C9, E11 83
Clinton, Utah, 1,025.....B3 72
Clinton, Wash., 800.....B3 86
Clinton, Wis., 1,274.....F5 88
Clinton, co., Ill., 24,029..E4 58
Clinton, co., Ind., 30,765..D4 59
Clinton, co., Iowa, 55,060............C7 60
Clinton, co., Ky., 8,886...D4 62
Clinton, co., Mich., 37,969............F6 66
Clinton, co., Mo., 11,588..B3 69
Clinton, co., N.Y., 72,722..f11 75
Clinton, co., Ohio, 30,004..C2 78
Clinton, co., Pa., 37,619..D6 81
Clintonville, Wis., 4,778..D5 88
Clintwood, Va., 1,400...e9 85
Clio, Ala., 929.........D4 46
Clio, Mich., 2,212......E7 66
Clio, S.C., 847.........B8 82
Cloncurry, Austl., 2,174..D7 25
Clonmel, Ire., 11,000...D3 4
Cloquet, Minn., 9,013...D6 67
Closter, N.J., 7,767....B5, h9 74
Clothier, W. Va., 500....D5 87
Cloud, co., Kans., 14,407..C6 61
Cloud, peak, Wyo.......A5 89
Clover, S.C., 3,500......A5 82
Cloverdale, Calif., 3,201..C2 50
Cloverdale, B.C., Can., 650..............f13 37
Cloverleaf, Tex., 3,000..*E5 84
Cloverport, Ky., 1,334...C3 62
Clovis, Calif., 11,461....D4 50
Clovis, N. Mex., 23,713..B7 48
Cluj, Rom., 163,200.....B6 10
Clute, Tex., 4,001.....r14 84
Clyde, Kans., 1,025.....C6 61
Clyde, N.Y., 2,735.....B4 75
Clyde, Ohio, 4,826......A3 78
Clyde, Tex., 1,116......C3 84
Clydebank, Scot., 50,200..C4 4
Clyde Hill, Wash., 1,871..*B3 86
Clymer, Pa., 2,251......E3 81
Coachella, Calif., 7,502..F5 50
Coahoma, Tex., 1,239...C2 84
Coahoma, co., Miss., 46,212............A3 68
Coahuila, state, Mex., 907,734............B4 34
Coal, co., Okla., 5,546...C5 79
Coal City, Ill., 2,852....B5 58
Coalcomán [de Matamoros], Mex., 7,695..........D4, n12 34
Coaldale, Alta., Can., 2,592..............E4 38
Coaldale, Pa., 3,949.....E10 81
Coal Fork, W. Va., 900...C6 87
Coalgate, Okla., 1,689...C5 79
Coalgood, Ky., 800.....D6 62
Coal Grove, Ohio, 2,961..D3 78
Coal Hill, Ark., 704.....B2 49
Coalinga, Calif., 5,965...D3 50
Coalport, Pa., 821......E4 81
Coaltown, Pa., 1,033...*E1 81
Coalville, Utah, 907..A6, C2 72
Coalwood, W. Va., 1,199..D3 87
Coast, mts., B.C., Can............B3, m16 37
Coast, ranges, Cal.......B2 50
Coamo, P.R., 12,146...*G11 35
Coatbridge, Scot., 54,800..C5 4
Coatepec, Mex., 18,022..n15 34
Coatepeque, Guat., 6,281............*E6 34
Coatesville, Pa., 12,971..G10 81
Coaticook, Que., Can., 6,906.............D6 42
Coats, N.C., 1,066......B4 76
Coatzacoalcos (Puerto México), Mex., 37,300......D6 34
Cobalt, Ont., Can., 2,209..p19 41
Cobán, Guat., 7,911....D6 34
Cobb, co., Ga., 114,174..C2 55
Cobden, Ont., Can., 942..B8 41
Cobden, Ill., 918.......F4 58
Cobequid, mts., N.S., Can..............D5 43
Cobh, Ire., 5,600......E2 4
Cobija, Bol., 1,726.....E4 27
Cobleskill, N.Y., 3,471..C6 75
Cobourg, Ont., Can., 10,646............D6 41
Coburg, Ger., 42,900...C5 6

Coburn, mtn., Maine.....C2 64
Cocentaina, Sp., 8,108...C5 8
Cochabamba, Bol., 90,000..C2 29
Cochabamba, dept., Bol., 490,475............C2 29
Cochin, India, 35,076.....G6 20
Cochin China, reg., Viet., 6,500,000..........*D3 19
Cochise, co., Ariz., 55,039............D4 48
Cochituate, Mass., 5,200..g10 65
Cochran, Ga., 4,714.....D3 55
Cochran, co., Tex., 6,417..C1 84
Cochrane, Alta., Can., 857.............D3 38
Cochrane, Ont., Can., 4,521............o19 41
Cochrane, dist., Ont., Can., 4,521..........e9 41
Cochranton, Pa., 1,139..C1 81
Cocke, co., Tenn., 23,390............D10 83
Cockeysville, Md., 3,500..B4 53
Cockrell Hill, Tex., 3,104.............n10 84
Cocoa, Fla., 12,294.....D6 54
Cocoa Beach, Fla., 3,475..D6 54
Cocoa West, Fla., 3,975..*D6 54
Coconino, co., Ariz., 41,857............B2 48
Cocula, Mex., 10,119..........C4, m12 34
Codington, co., S. Dak., 20,220............F8 77
Codogno, It., 10,500....B2 9
Cody, Wyo., 4,838......B3 89
Coeburn, Va., 2,471.....f9 85
Coesfeld, Ger., 20,300...C3 6
Coeur d'Alene, Idaho, 14,291............B2 57
Coeur d'Alene, mts., Idaho............B2 57
Coffee, co., Ala., 30,583..D3 46
Coffee, co., Ga., 21,953..E4 55
Coffee, co., Tenn., 28,603..B5 83
Coffey, co., Kans., 8,403..D8 61
Coffeyville, Kans., 17,382..E8 61
Coff's Harbour, Austl., 7,185............E9 26
Cognac, Fr., 20,798.....E3 5
Cohasset, Mass., 3,000.........B6, h12 65
Cohocton, N.Y., 929....C3 75
Cohoes, N.Y., 20,129...C7 75
Coimbatore, India, 286,305............F6 20
Coimbra, Port., 46,313...B1 8
Coín, Sp., 11,828.......D3 8
Cojedes, state, Ven., 72,652............B4 32
Cojutepeque, Sal., 11,415............*E7 34
Cokato, Minn., 1,356...E4 67
Coke, co., Tex., 3,589...D2 84
Cokeburg, Pa., 989....*F1 81
Colac, Austl., 9,257....I4 26
Colbert, co., Ala., 46,506..A2 46
Colborne, Ont., Can., 1,336.............C7 41
Colby, Kans., 4,210.....C2 61
Colby, Wis., 1,085......D3 88
Colchagua, prov., Chile, 158,543............A2 28
Colchester, co., N.S., Can., 34,307............D6 43
Colchester, Conn., 2,260..C7 52
Colchester, Eng., 67,400..E7 4
Colchester, Ill., 1,495...C3 58
Cold Lake, Alta., Can., 1,307.............B5 38
Cold Spring, Ky., 1,095............A7, B5 62
Cold Spring, Minn., 1,760..E4 67
Cold Spring, N.Y., 2,083..*D7 75
Cold Spring Harbor, N.Y., 1,800.............F3 52
Coldwater, Kans., 1,164..E4 61
Coldwater, Mich., 8,880..G5 66
Coldwater, Miss., 1,264..A4 68
Coldwater, Ohio, 2,766...B1 78
Cole, co., Mo., 40,761...C5 69
Colebrook, N.H., 1,600..B5 73
Cole Camp, Mo., 853...C4 69
Coleman, Alta., Can., 1,713.............E3 38
Coleman, Fla., 921......D4 54
Coleman, Mich., 1,264...E6 66
Coleman, Tex., 6,371...D3 84
Coleman, co., Tex., 12,458............D3 84
Coleraine, Minn., 1,346..C5 67
Coleraine, N. Ire., 12,600..C3 4
Coles, co., Ill., 42,860...D5 58
Colfax, Calif., 915......C3 50
Colfax, Ill., 894........C5 58
Colfax, Iowa, 2,331.....C4 60
Colfax, La., 1,934......C3 63
Colfax, Wash., 2,860...C8 86

Colfax, Wis., 885........D1 88
Colfax, co., Nebr., 9,595...C8 71
Colfax, co., N. Mex.,
  13,806................A6 48
Colima, Mex.,
  43,518.............D4, n12 34
Colima, state, Mex.,
  164,450.............D4, n12 34
College, Alsk., 1,755.....C10 47
Collegedale, Tenn.,
  1,500................E10 83
College Heights, Ark.,
  1,200................D4 49
College Heights, S.C.,
  1,330................C7 82
College Park, Fla., 950....C5 54
College Park, Ga.,
  23,469...........B5, C2 55
College Park, Md., 18,482..f9 53
College Place, Wash.,
  4,031................C7 86
College Station, Tex.,
  11,396...............D4 84
College View, Colo.,
  1,800................*B6 51
Collegeville, Ind., 2,100...C3 59
Collegeville (P.O.), Minn.,
  1,600................*E4 67
Collegeville, Pa., 2,254....F11 81
Colleton, co., S.C., 27,816..F6 82
Colleyville, Tex., 1,491...*C4 84
Collie, Austl., 7,616........F2 25
Collier, co., Fla., 15,753...F5 54
Collierville, Tenn., 2,020...B2 83
Collin, co., Tex., 41,247...C4 84
Collingdale, Pa., 10,268...p20 81
Collingswood, N.J.,
  17,370...............D2 74
Collingsworth, co., Tex.,
  6,276................B2 84
Collingwood, Ont., Can.,
  8,385................C4 41
Collins, Miss., 1,537......D4 68
Collins Park, Del., 2,600..*A6 53
Collins View, Oreg.,
  1,500................*B4 80
Collinsville, Ala., 1,199....A4 46
Collinsville, Conn., 1,700..B5 52
Collinsville, Ill., 14,217...E4 58
Collinsville, Okla., 2,526..A6 79
Collinsville, Va., 3,586...*D3 85
Collister, Idaho, 5,750.....F2 57
Colmar, Fr., 52,355........C7 5
Colmar Manor, Md.,
  1,772................f9 53
Colmenar Viejo, Sp.,
  8,375.............B4, o17 8
Cologne, see Köln, Ger.
Coloma, Mich., 1,473.....F4 66
Colomb-Bechar, see
  Bechar, Alg.
Colombes, Fr., 76,918.....g10 5
Colombia, Col., 1,599....C3 32
Colombia, country, S.A.,
  17,484,508...........C3 32
Colombo, Cey., 510,947...G6 20
Colón, Arg., 6,813.......A5 28
Colón, Cuba, 22,900......C3 35
Colon, Mich., 1,055......G5 66
Colón, Pan., 59,598......B2 32
Colón, Archipiélago de,
  ter., Ec., 2,391........g5 31
Colón, Archipiélago de
  (Galápagos Islands), is.,
  Ec.................g5 31
Colonia, N.J., 18,500...*k7 74
Colonia, Ur., 7,500.......E1 30
Colonia, dept., Ur.,
  104,800..............*E1 30
Colonia Gustavo A Madero,
  Mex., 102,602..........h9 34
Colonial Beach, Va., 1,769..B6 85
Colonial Heights,
  (Independent City),
  Va., 9,587........C5, n18 85
Colonial Manor, N.J.,
  1,000................*D2 74
Colonial Park, Pa., 2,500..*F8 81
Colonia Suiza, Ur., 4,307..g8 28
Colonie, N.Y., 6,992......*C7 75
Colorado, co., Tex.,
  18,463...............E4 84
Colorado, state, U.S.,
  1,753,947............51
Colorado, riv., Mex., U.S..C5 45
Colorado, riv., Tex........D3 84
Colorado City, Tex.,
  6,457................C2 84
Colorado Springs, Colo.,
  93,000 (*188,000)......C6 51
Colored Hill, W. Va.,
  1,115................*D3 87
Colotlán, Mex.,
  6,337.............C4, k12 34
Colquitt, Ga., 1,556......E2 55
Colquitt, co., Ga., 34,048..E3 55
Colton, Calif., 18,666.....*E5 50
Columbia, Ill., 3,174......E3 58

Columbia, Ky., 2,255....C4 62
Columbia, La., 1,021.....B3 63
Columbia, Miss., 7,117....D4 68
Columbia, Mo., 36,650....C5 69
Columbia, N.C., 1,099....B6 76
Columbia, Pa., 12,075....F9 81
Columbia, S.C., 100,000
  (*260,000)..........C5 82
Columbia, Tenn., 17,624..B4 83
Columbia, co., Ark.,
  26,400...............D2 49
Columbia, co., Fla.,
  20,077...............B4 54
Columbia, co., Ga.,
  13,423...............C4 55
Columbia, co., N.Y.,
  47,322...............C7 75
Columbia, co., Oreg.,
  22,379...............B3 80
Columbia, co., Pa.,
  53,489...............D8 81
Columbia, co., Wash.,
  4,569................C7 86
Columbia, co., Wis.,
  36,708...............E4 88
Columbia, mtn., Alta.,
  Can.................C2 38
Columbia, riv., Can., U.S..G9 36
Columbia City, Ind.,
  4,803................B7 59
Columbia Falls, Mont.,
  2,132................B2 70
Columbia Heights, Minn.,
  23,283..............m12 67
Columbia Heights, Wash.,
  2,227................*C3 86
Columbiana, Ala., 2,264...B3 46
Columbiana, Ohio, 4,164..B5 78
Columbiana, co., Ohio,
  107,004..............B5 78
Columbia Station, Ohio,
  1,000................*A3 78
Columbiaville, Mich.,
  878.................E7 66
Columbus, Ga., 123,000
  (*254,000)...........D2 55
Columbus, Ind., 24,782...F6 59
Columbus, Kans., 3,395...E9 61
Columbus, Miss., 24,771..B5 68
Columbus, Mont., 1,281..E7 70
Columbus, Nebr., 12,476..C8 71
Columbus, Ohio, 540,000
  (*850,000).......C3, m11 78
Columbus, Tex., 3,656.....E4 84
Columbus, Wis., 3,467....E4 88
Columbus, co., N.C.,
  48,973...............C4 76
Columbus Grove, Ohio,
  2,104................B1 78
Columbus Junction, Iowa,
  1,160................C6 60
Colusa, Calif., 3,518......C2 50
Colusa, co., Calif., 12,075..C2 50
Colver, Pa., 1,261........E4 81
Colville, Wash., 3,806.....A8 86
Colwood, B.C., Can.,
  863.................h12 37
Colwyn, Pa., 3,074......*G11 81
Comacchio, It., 10,200....B4 9
Comal, co., Tex., 19,844...E3 84
Comalapa, Guat., 7,404...E6 34
Comalcalco, Mex.,
  7,745................D6 34
Comanche, Okla., 2,082...C4 79
Comanche, Tex., 3,415....D3 84
Comanche, co., Kans.,
  3,271................E4 61
Comanche, co., Okla.,
  90,803...............C3 79
Comanche, co., Tex.,
  11,865...............D3 84
Combined Locks, Wis.,
  1,421................h9 88
Combs, Ky., 900.........C6 62
Comerío, P.R., 5,232....*G11 35
Comfort, Tex., 950.......E3 84
Comilla, Pak., 54,504.....D9 20
Comiso, It., 25,904.......F5 9
Comitán [de Dominguez],
  Mex., 15,409..........D6 34
Commack, N.Y., 19,200..*n15 75
Commentry, Fr., 9,711....D5 5
Commerce, Calif., 9,555..*E4 50
Commerce, Ga., 3,551....B3 55
Commerce, Mich.,
  1,200................*F7 66
Commerce, Okla., 2,378...A7 79
Commerce, Tex., 5,789....C5 84
Commerce Town, Colo.,
  8,970................B6 51
Commercy, Fr., 7,043.....C6 5
Communism, peak
  Sov. Un............F10 13
Como, Que., Can., 807...q18 42
Como, Colo., 35.........e11 86
Como, It., 85,100........B2 9
Comodoro Rivadavia, Arg.,
  35,966...............D3 28

Comoro Island, Fr. dep.,
  Afr., 210,000........C8 24
Comox, B.C., Can., 1,756..E5 37
Compiègne, Fr., 24,427....C5 5
Compostela, Mex.,
  7,658...............m11 34
Compton, Calif., 71,812...n12 50
Compton, co., Que., Can.,
  24,410...............D6 42
Comstock, Mich., 4,500....F5 66
Comstock Park, Mich.,
  2,500................*E5 66
Conakry, Guinea, 43,000..G2 22
Concarneau, Fr., 11,691...D2 5
Concepción, Arg., 12,479..E2 29
Concepción, Chile,
  148,100..............B2 28
Concepción, prov., Chile,
  539,450..............B2 28
Concepción, Par., 18,000..D4 29
Concepción, dept., Par.,
  14,640...............D4 29
Concepción del Oro, Mex.,
  8,452................C4 34
Concepción del Uruguay,
  Arg., 36,486..........A5 28
Concho, co., Tex., 3,672...D3 84
Corcoran, Calif., 4,976....D4 50
Concord, Calif., 36,208....h8 50
Concord, Mass.,
  5,000.............B5, g10 65
Concord, Mich., 990......F6 66
Concord, N.H., 28,991....E4 73
Concord, N.C., 17,799....B2 76
Concordia, Arg., 56,654...A5 28
Concordia, Col., 5,187....B2 32
Concordia, Kans., 7,022...C6 61
Concordia, Mo., 1,471....C4 69
Concordia, par., La.,
  20,467...............C4 63
Concord North, N.C.,
  2,199................*B2 76
Concrete, Wash., 840.....A4 86
Condobolin, Austl., 3,569..F8 25
Condon, Oreg., 1,149.....B6 80
Conecuh, co., Ala.,
  17,762...............D2 46
Conegliano, It., 11,300....B4 9
Conejos, co., Colo., 8,428..D4 51
Conemaugh, Pa., 3,334...F4 81
Conflans-Ste. Honorine, Fr.,
  21,874...............g9 5
Confluence, Pa., 938......G3 81
Congamond, Mass., 800..B2 65
Congers, N.Y., 3,500.....*D7 75
Congo (Brazzaville), country,
  Afr., 826,000.........I7 22
Congo, The (Kinshasa),
  country, Afr.,
  15,627,000...........B4 24
Congo, riv., Afr..........G7 21
Conil, Sp., 9,002........D2 8
Coniston, Ont., Can.,
  2,692.............A4, p19 41
Conjeeveram, see
  Kancheepuram, India
Connacht, prov., Ire.,
  401,500..............*D2 4
Conneaut, Ohio, 10,557...A5 78
Conneautville, Pa., 1,100..C1 81
Connecticut, state, U.S.,
  2,535,234.............52
Connell, Wash., 900......C7 86
Connellsville, Pa., 12,814..F2 81
Connersville, Ind., 17,698..E7 59
Conning Towers, Conn.,
  3,457...............*D8 52
Conover, N.C., 2,281.....B1 76
Conrad, Iowa, 799.......B5 60
Conrad, Mont., 2,665....B5 70
Conroe, Tex., 9,192......D5 84
Conselheiro Lafaiete, Braz.,
  29,208...............C4 30
Conshohocken, Pa.,
  10,259............F11, o20 81
Consolación del Sur, Cuba,
  7,300................C2 35
Constanța, Rom., 115,100..C9 10
Constantia, N.Y., 900.....B5 75
Constantina, Sp., 11,910...D3 8
Constantine, Alg.,
  171,481..............A6 22
Constantine, Mich., 1,710..G5 66
Constantinople, see Istanbul,
  Tur.
Continental, peak, Wyo....D4 89
Constitución, Chile, 9,500..B2 28
Constitution, Ga., 900....*B5 55
Consuegra, Sp., 10,572...C4 8
Contamana, Peru, 2,860...C2 31
Continental, Ohio, 1,147...A1 78
Contra Costa, co., Calif.,
  409,030..............D2 50
Contratación, Col.,
  3,117................B3 32
Contrecoeur, Que., Can.,
  2,007................D4 42
Contreras, Mex., 10,112...h9 34

Contumaza, Peru, 1,911...C2 31
Convent, La., 400....D5, h10 63
Converse, Ind., 1,044.....C6 59
Converse, S.C., 700......B4 82
Converse, co., Wyo.,
  6,366................C7 89
Convoy, Ohio, 976.......B1 78
Conway, Ark., 9,791......B3 49
Conway, Fla., 3,000.....*D5 54
Conway, N.H., 1,143.....D5 73
Conway, Pa., 1,926.......E1 81
Conway, S.C., 8,563......D9 82
Conway, co., Ark., 15,430..B3 49
Conway Springs, Kans.,
  1,057................E6 61
Conyers, Ga., 2,881...B6, C2 55
Conyngham, Pa., 1,163...*D9 81
Cooch-Behār, India,
  41,922...............C8 20
Cook, co., Ga., 11,822....E3 55
Cook, co., Ill., 5,129,725..B6 58
Cook, co., Minn., 3,377....C8 67
Cooke, co., Tex., 22,560...C4 84
Cook, mtn., N.Z.,........O13 26
Cookeville, Tenn., 7,800...C8 83
Cookshire, Que., Can.,
  1,412................D6 42
Cookstown, Ont., Can.,
  1,025................C5 41
Cooksville, Ont.,
  Can.,............D5, m14 41
Cooleemee, N.C., 1,609...B2 76
Coolidge, Ariz., 4,990...C3, E2 48
Coolidge, Tex., 913......D4 84
Cool Ridge, W. Va., 400...D3 87
Cool Valley, Mo., 1,492...*C7 69
Cooma, Austl., 9,101......G8 25
Coon Rapids, Iowa, 1,560..C3 60
Coon Rapids, Minn.,
  26,412..............m12 67
Cooper, Tex., 2,213......C5 84
Cooper, co., Mo., 15,448...C5 69
Coopersburg, Pa., 1,800..E11 81
Cooperstown, N.Y., 2,553..C6 75
Cooperstown, N. Dak.,
  1,424................C7 77
Coopersville, Mich., 1,584..E5 66
Coos, co., N.H., 37,140...B5 73
Coos, co., Oreg., 54,955...D2 80
Coosa, co., Ala., 10,726...C3 46
Coos Bay, Oreg., 7,084....D2 80
Cootamundra, Austl.,
  5,938................G7 26
Copainalá, Mex., 2,463...D6 34
Copenhagen, (København),
  Den., 721,381.........J5 11
Copiague, N.Y., 17,500...G3 52
Copiah, co., Miss., 27,051..D3 68
Copiapó, Chile, 28,000....E1 29
Coplay, Pa., 3,701......*E10 81
Copley, Ohio, 4,000.....*A4 78
Copparo, It., 5,800.......B3 9
Copper, mtn., Wyo........C5 89
Copperas Cove, Tex.,
  4,567................D4 84
Copper Cliff, Ont., Can.,
  3,600................A3 41
Copperhill, Tenn., 631.....D9 83
Coquille, Oreg., 4,730....D2 80
Coquimbo, Chile, 31,000..E1 29
Coquimbo, prov., Chile
  309,177..............A2 28
Cora, W. Va., 500.......*D2 87
Corabia, Rom., 11,502....D7 10
Coracora, Peru, 6,500....E3 31
Coral Gables, Fla.,
  34,793...........G6, s13 54
Coralville, Iowa, 3,390....C6 60
Coram, N.Y., 1,000......n15 75
Coraopolis, Pa.,
  9,643.............E1, h13 81
Corato, It., 38,800.......D6 9
Corbeil, Fr., 26,804.......C5 5
Corbin, Ky., 7,119........D5 62
Corcoran, Calif., 4,976....D4 50
Corcoran, Minn., 1,237...*E5 67
Cordele, Ga., 10,609......E3 55
Cordell, Okla., 3,589......B3 79
Cordillera, dept., Par.,
  145,232..............D4 29
Córdoba, Arg., 589,153...A4 28
Córdoba, Mex., 47,448...n15 34
Córdoba, Sp., 198,148...D3 8
Córdoba, dept., Sp.,
  798,437..............*D3 8
Córdoba, prov., Arg.,
  1,759,997............A4 28
Cordova, Ala., 3,184......B2 46
Cordova, Alsk.,
  1,128...........C10, g19 47
Cordova, N.C., 950.......C3 76
Córdova, Peru, 534.......D2 31
Cori, It., 9,681.........h9 9
Corigliano, It., 16,300.....E6 9
Corinna, Maine, 900
  (1,895 ▲)............D3 64

Corinne, W. Va., 1,273....D3 87
Corinth, Miss., 11,453.....A5 68
Corinth, N.Y., 3,184......B7 75
Corinth, see Kórinthos, Grc.
Corinto, Braz., 12,247.....B4 30
Corinto, Nic., 9,177......H12 33
Cork, Ire., 122,100........E2 4
Cork, co., Ire., 339,500...*E2 4
Corleone, It., 14,682......F4 9
Corlu, Tur., 21,983........B6 14
Cormeilles-en-Parisis, Fr.,
 11,486..................g9 5
Cornelia, Ga., 2,936.......B3 55
Cornelius, N.C., 1,444.....B2 76
Cornelius, Oreg., 1,146...g11 80
Cornell, Wis., 1,685.......C2 88
Corner Brook, Newf., Can.,
 25,185..................D3 44
Corning, Ark., 2,192.......A5 49
Corning, Calif., 3,006.....C2 50
Corning, Iowa, 2,041.......D3 60
Corning, N.Y., 17,085......C3 75
Corning, Ohio, 1,065.......C3 78
Corno, mtn., It.,..........C4 9
Cornwall, Ont., Can.,
 43,639.................B10 41
Cornwall, N.Y., 2,824......D6 75
Cornwall, Pa., 1,934......F9 81
Cornwall, see Cornwall-on
 the-Hudson, N.Y.
Cornwall, co., Eng.,
 342,900.................*E4 4
Cornwall-on-the-Hudson
 (Cornwall),
 N.Y., 3,127.............D6 75
Cornwells Heights, Pa.,
 10,000.................o22 81
Coro, Ven., 45,506.........A4 32
Corona, Calif.,
 13,336............F5, n13 50
Coronado, Calif.,
 18,039............F5, o15 50
Coronation, Alta., Can.,
 864....................C5 38
Coronel, Chile, 33,900.....B2 28
Coronel Dorrego, Arg.,
 7,245..................B4 28
Coronel Oviedo, Par.,
 34,442.................E4 29
Coronel Pringles, Arg.,
 12,844.................B4 28
Coronel Suárez, Arg.,
 11,133.................B4 28
Coropuna, mtn., Peru....E3 31
Corozal, Col., 14,000.....B2 32
Corpus Christi, Tex., 202,000
 (*215,000)............F4 84
Corral de Almaguer, Sp.,
 8,261..................C4 8
Corrales, Col., 1,378......B3 32
Corralillo, Cuba, 1,123....C3 35
Correctionville, Iowa, 912..B2 60
Corrèze, dept., Fr.,
 237,926................*E4 5
Corrientes, Arg., 104,000...E4 29
Corrigan, Tex., 986........D5 84
Corry, Pa., 7,744..........C2 81
Corse, dept., Fr.,
 275,465................*C2 9
Corsica, isl., Eur.........C2 9
Corsicana, Tex., 20,344....C4 84
Corson, co., S.Dak.,
 5,798..................E4 77
Cortazar, Mex.,
 17,925............C4, m13 34
Cortegana, Sp., 7,179......D2 8
Corte Madera, Calif.,
 5,962..................*C2 50
Cortez, Colo., 6,764.......D1 51
Cortez, Fla., 900.........q10 54
Cortland, N.Y., 19,523.....C4 75
Cortland, Ohio, 1,957......A5 78
Cortland, co., N.Y.,
 41,113.................C4 75
Cortona, It., 4,000........C3 9
Corumbá, Braz., 36,744....B1 30
Çorum (Chorum), Tur.,
 34,726................B10 14
Corunna, Ont., Can.,
 1,942..................E2 41
Corunna, Mich., 2,764.....F6 66
Corvallis, Oreg.,
 20,669.............C3, k11 80
Corydon, Ind., 2,701......H5 59
Corydon, Iowa, 1,687......C4 60
Coryell, co., Tex., 23,961..D4 84
Cosalá, Mex., 2,129.......C3 34
Cosamaloapan [de Carpio],
 Mex., 16,944...........D5 34
Coscomatepec [de Bravo],
 Mex., 5,187...........n15 34
Cosenza, It., 82,900.......E6 9
Coshocton, Ohio, 13,106...B4 78
Coshocton, co., Ohio,
 32,224.................B3 78
Cosmopolis, Wash., 1,312...C2 86
Cosne [-sur-Loire], Fr.,
 8,802..................D5 5

Costa Mesa, Calif.,
 66,396................n13 50
Costa Rica, country, N.A.,
 1,433,000..............E8 34
Costilla, N. Mex., 180.....A6 48
Costilla, co., Colo., 4,219..D5 51
Cotabato, Phil., 27,980....D6 19
Cotabato, prov., Phil.,
 1,029,119.............*D6 19
Cotahuasi, Peru, 1,354....D2 31
Cotati, Calif., 1,852......*C2 50
Coteaux, Hai., 2,893......E6 35
Côte-d'or, dept., Fr.,
 387,869...............*D6 5
Côtes-du-Nord, dept., Fr.,
 501,923...............*C2 5
Côte-St. Luc., Que., Can.,
 13,266................*D4 42
Cotija de la Paz, Mex.,
 8,059.................n12 34
Cotonou, Dah., 109,300...G5 22
Cotopaxi, prov., Ec.,
 154,971................B2 31
Cotopaxi, vol., Ec........A2 31
Cottage City, Md., 1,099..*C4 53
Cottage Grove, Oreg.,
 3,895..................D3 80
Cottage Grove, Wis.,
 413...................*E4 88
Cottage Hills, Ill., 3,976..*E3 58
Cottbus, Ger., 69,500......C7 6
Cotter, Ark., 683..........A3 49
Cottle, co., Tex., 4,207...B2 84
Cotton, co., Okla., 8,031...C3 79
Cottondale, Fla.,
 849................B1, u16 54
Cotton Mills, Tex.,
 950...................*C4 84
Cotton Plant, Ark., 1,707..B4 49
Cottonport, La., 1,581....D3 63
Cotton Valley, La., 1,145..B2 63
Cottonwood, Ala., 953....D4 46
Cottonwood, Ariz., 2,130..B3 48
Cottonwood, Calif., 1,000..B2 50
Cottonwood, Idaho,
 1,081..................C2 57
Cottonwood, co., Minn.,
 16,166.................F3 67
Cottonwood Falls, Kans.,
 971...................D7 61
Cottonwood Heights, Utah,
 8,200.................*D2 72
Cotuit, Mass., 900........C7 65
Cotulla, Tex., 3,960......E3 84
Coudekerque-Branche, Fr.,
 20,757.................B5 5
Coudersport, Pa., 2,889...C5 81
Coulee City, Wash., 654...B6 86
Coulee Dam, Wash.,
 1,344..................B7 86
Coulommiers, Fr., 8,561...C5 5
Coulterville, Ill., 1,022....E4 58
Council, Idaho, 827.......E2 57
Council, mtn., Idaho......E2 57
Council Bluffs, Iowa,
 52,957.................C2 60
Council Grove, Kans.,
 2,664.................D7 61
Country Club Hills, Ill.,
 4,771.................*B6 58
Country Club Hills, Mo.,
 1,763.................*C7 69
Country Homes, Wash.,
 1,600.................*B8 86
Coupar Angus, Scot.,
 2,000..................B5 4
Courbevoie, Fr., 59,491...g10 5
Courtdale, Pa., 845.......*D9 81
Courtenay, B.C., Can.,
 3,485..................E5 37
Courtland, Calif., 550....*C3 50
Courtland, Va., 855.......D5 85
Courtrai, see Kortrijk, Bel.
Courville, Que., Can.,
 4,670.................n17 42
Coushatta, La., 1,663.....B2 63
Coutances, Fr., 7,806.....C3 5
Coutras, Fr., 3,688.......E3 5
Cove City, Tex., 1,749....*D6 84
Covedale, Ohio, 11,000...o12 78
Covelo, Calif., 800.......C2 50
Coventry, Conn., 3,700....B7 52
Coventry, Eng., 313,900...D6 4
Coventry, R.I., 5,000.....C10 52
Covilhã, Port., 23,091....B2 8
Covina, Calif., 20,124...m13 50
Covington, Ga., 8,167.....C3 55
Covington, Ind., 2,759....D3 59
Covington, Ky.,
 60,376.............A5, A7 62
Covington, La.,
 6,754.............D5, h11 63
Covington, Ohio, 2,800....B1 78
Covington, Tenn., 529.....B2 83
Covington (Independent
 City), Va., 11,062......C3 85
Covington, co., Ala.,
 35,631.................D3 46

Covington, co., Miss.,
 13,637.................D4 68
Cowan, Tenn., 1,979......B5 83
Cowen, mtn., Mont......E6 70
Cowansville, Que., Can.,
 7,050..................D5 42
Cowansville, Pa., 400.....E2 81
Cowes, Eng., 17,100......E6 4
Coweta, Okla., 1,858......B6 79
Coweta, co., Ga., 28,893...C2 55
Cowley, co., Kans.,
 37,861.................E7 61
Cowlitz, co., Wash.,
 57,801.................C3 86
Cowpens, S.C., 2,038......A4 82
Cowra, Austl., 6,289......F7 26
Coxsackie, N.Y., 2,849....C7 75
Coyame, Mex., 815........B3 34
Coyoacán, Mex.,
 54,866.............H9, n14 34
Coyuca de Catalán, Mex.,
 3,124.................n13 34
Cozad, Nebr., 3,184.......D6 71
Cozumel, Mex., 2,915.....C7 34
Crab Orchard, W. Va.,
 1,953..................D7 87
Crabtree, Pa., 950........F3 81
Crabtree Mills, Que., Can.,
 1,313..................D4 42
Cradock, S. Afr., 19,561...G5 24
Crafton, Pa., 8,418......k13 81
Craig, Colo., 3,984.......A3 51
Craig, co., Okla., 16,303...A6 79
Craig, co., Va., 3,356.....C2 85
Craig Beach, Ohio,
 1,139.................*B5 78
Craighead, co., Ark.,
 47,253.................B5 49
Craigsville, Va., 978......B3 85
Crailsheim, Ger., 14,400..D5 6
Craiova, Rom., 112,400...C6 10
Cramerton, N.C., 3,200....B1 76
Cranberry Portage, Man.,
 Can., 838............B10 40
Cranbrook, B.C., Can.,
 5,549.................E10 37
Cranbury, N.J., 1,300.....C3 74
Crandon, Wis., 1,679.....C5 88
Crane, Mo., 954..........E4 69
Crane, Tex., 3,796.......D1 84
Crane, co., Tex., 4,699...D1 84
Crane, mtn., Oreg.......E6 80
Cranford, N.J., 26,424....B4 74
Cranston, R.I., 71,913....B11 52
Crateús, Braz., 14,572....*D6 27
Crato, Braz., 27,649......*D7 27
Craven, co., N.C., 58,773..B5 76
Crawford, Nebr., 1,588....B2 71
Crawford, co., Ark.,
 21,318.................B1 49
Crawford, co., Ga., 5,816..D3 55
Crawford, co., Ill., 20,751..D6 58
Crawford, co., Ind.,
 8,379..................H4 59
Crawford, co., Iowa,
 18,569.................B2 60
Crawford, co., Kans.,
 37,032.................E9 61
Crawford, co., Mich.,
 4,971..................D6 66
Crawford, co., Mo.,
 12,647.................D6 69
Crawford, co., Ohio,
 46,775.................B2 78
Crawford, co., Pa.,
 77,956.................C1 81
Crawford, co., Wis.,
 16,351.................E3 88
Crawfordsville, Ind.,
 14,446.................D4 59
Crawfordville, Ga., 786...C4 55
Crazy, peak, Mont......D6 70
Creedmoor, N.C., 1,330...A4 76
Creek, co., Okla, 40,495...B5 79
Creemore, Ont., Can.,
 850...................C4 41
Creighton, Sask., Can.,
 1,729..................C5 39
Creighton, Nebr., 1,388...B8 71
Creighton, Pa., 2,865....h14 81
Creighton Mine, Ont.,
 Can., 1,727........A3, p19 41
Creil, Fr., 19,235.........C5 5
Crema, It., 30,035........B2 9
Cremona, It., 76,900.....B3 9
Crenshaw, Miss., 1,382...A3 68
Crenshaw, co., Ala.,
 14,909.................D3 46
Cresaptown, Md., 1,800..k13 53
Crescent, Okla., 1,264....B4 79
Crescent City, Calif.,
 2,958..................B1 50
Crescent City, Fla., 1,629..C5 54
Crescent City Northwest,
 Calif., 3,086..........*B1 50
Crescent Springs, Ky.,
 946...................A7 62
Cresco, Iowa, 3,878.......A5 60

Cresskill, N.J., 7,290......h9 74
Cresson, Pa., 2,659.......F4 81
Cressona, Pa., 1,854......E9 81
Crest, Fr., 4,494.........E6 5
Crest Hill, Ill., 5,887....*B5 58
Crestline, Calif., 1,290...*E5 50
Crestline, Ohio, 5,521....B3 78
Crestmont, Pa., 2,000...*F11 81
Creston, B.C., Can., 2,460..E9 37
Creston, Newf., Can.,
 837...................E4 44
Creston, Iowa, 8,119......C3 60
Creston, Ohio, 1,521......B4 78
Crestview, Fla., 7,467...u15 54
Crestwood, Ill., 3,918....*B6 58
Crestwood, Mo., 11,106..*C7 69
Crete, Ill., 3,788.....B6, m9 58
Crete, Nebr., 3,546.......D9 71
Crete, isl., Grc..........E5 14
Crete, sea, Grc..........E5 14
Creuse, dept., Fr.,
 163,515...............*D4 5
Creutzwald, Fr., 13,649...C7 5
Creve Coeur, Ill., 6,684...C4 58
Creve Coeur, Mo., 5,122..*C7 69
Crevillente, Sp., 14,047...C5 8
Crewe, Eng., 53,200......D5 4
Crewe, Va., 2,012........C4 85
Cricket, N.C., 950........A1 76
Cridersville, Ohio, 1,053..B1 78
Crieff, Scot., 5,400......B5 4
Crimmitschau, Ger.,
 31,300.................C6 6
Crisana-Maramures, prov.,
 Rom., 1,391,672.......B6 10
Crisfield, Md., 3,540.....E6 53
Crisp, co., Ga., 17,768....E3 55
Cristóbal Colón, mtn., Col..A3 32
Crittenden, co., Ark.,
 47,564.................B5 49
Crittenden, co., Ky.,
 8,648..................A3 62
Croatia, reg., Yugo......*C2 10
Croatia, rep., Yugo.,
 4,159,696..............C2 10
Crocker, Mo., 821........D5 69
Crockett, Calif., 3,500....g8 50
Crockett, Tex., 5,356.....D5 84
Crockett, co., Tenn.,
 14,594.................B2 83
Crockett, co., Tex., 4,209..D2 84
Croghan, N.Y., 821.......B5 75
Cromona, Ky., 950........C7 62
Cromwell, Conn., 6,780...C6 52
Crook, co., Oreg., 9,430...C6 80
Crook, co., Wyo., 4,691...B8 89
Crookston, Minn., 8,546...C2 67
Crooksville, Ohio, 2,958...C3 78
Crosby, Minn., 2,629......D5 67
Crosby, Miss., 705........D2 68
Crosby, N. Dak., 1,759....A2 77
Crosby, Tex., 1,200......q14 84
Crosby, co., Tex., 10,347..C2 84
Crosby, mtn., Wyo.......C3 89
Crosbyton, Tex., 2,088...C2 84
Cross, co., Ark., 19,551...B5 49
Cross City, Fla., 1,857....C3 54
Crossett, Ark., 5,370.....D4 49
Cross Mill, N.C., 700....f10 76
Cross Plains, Tex., 1,168..C3 84
Cross Plains, Wis., 1,066..E4 88
Crossville, Ill., 874.......E5 58
Crossville, Tenn., 4,668...D8 83
Croswell, Mich., 1,817....E8 66
Crothersville, Ind., 1,449.G6 59
Crotone, It., 44,800......E6 9
Croton-on-Hudson, N.Y.,
 7,039.............D7, m15 75
Crouse, N.C., 901........B1 76
Crow, peak, Mont.......D5 70
Crow Agency, Mont., 600..E9 70
Crowell, Tex., 1,703......C3 84
Crowley, La., 15,617.....D3 63
Crowley, co., Colo., 3,978..C7 51
Crown Point, Ind., 8,443..B3 59
Crown Point, N.Y., 800....B7 75
Crow Wing, co., Minn.,
 32,134.................D4 67
Croydon, Pa., 9,500.....F12 81
Crozet, Va., 900.........B4 85
Cruces, Cuba, 15,100.....C3 35
Crucible, Pa., 1,064......G1 81
Cruden Bay, Scot., 2,294..B6 4
Crum Lynne, Pa., 3,500..*E1 81
Cruz Alta, Braz., 33,190..D2 30
Cruz del Eje, Arg.,
 22,024.................A4 28
Cruzeiro, Braz., 27,005...C4 30
Crystal, Minn., 29,089...m12 67
Crystal Beach, Ont., Can.,
 1,886..................E5 41
Crystal Beach, Fla., 1,000..D4 54
Crystal City, Mo.,
 3,678............C7, g13 69
Crystal City, Tex., 9,101..E3 84
Crystal Falls, Mich.,
 2,203..................B2 66
Crystal Lake, Fla., 100...u16 54

Crystal Lake, Ill.,
10,211 . . . . A5, h8   58
Crystal Lakes, Ohio,
1,569 . . . . C1   78
Crystal River, Fla., 1,423 . . D4   54
Crystal Springs, Miss.,
4,496 . . . . D3   68
Csongrad, Hung., 16,801 . . . B5   10
Csongrad, co., Hung.,
335,565 . . . . *B5   10
Csorna, Hung., 9,208 . . . . . B3   10
Cuajimalpa, Mex., 9,111 . . h9   34
Cuauhtémoc, Mex.,
14,686 . . . . B3   34
Cuautepec, Mex.,
4,909 . . . . g9   34
Cuautla [Morelos], Mex.,
12,427 . . . . n14   34
Cuba, Ill., 1,380 . . . . C3   58
Cuba, Mo., 1,672 . . . . C6   69
Cuba, N.Y., 1,949 . . . . C2   75
Cuba, country, N.A.,
7,631,000 . . . . C3   35
Cuba City, Wis., 1,673 . . . . F3   88
Cucamonga, Calif.,
2,500 . . . . *E5   50
Cúcuta, Col., 175,336 . . . . . B3   32
Cudahy, Calif., 12,000 . . . . *F4   50
Cudahy, Wis.,
17,975 . . . . F6, n12   88
Cuddalore, India,
79,168 . . . . F6   20
Cuddapah, India, 49,027 . . F6   20
Cuddy, Pa., 1,400 . . . . *B5   81
Cuenca, Ec., 60,402 . . . . . . B2   31
Cuenca, Sp., 27,007 . . . . . . B4   8
Cuenca, prov., Sp.,
315,433 . . . . *B4   8
Cuencamé [de Ceniceros],
Mex., 2,982 . . . . C4   34
Cuernavaca, Mex.,
37,144 . . . . D5, n14   34
Cuero, Tex., 7,338 . . . . E4   84
Cuetzalan, Mex., 3,528 . . . m15   34
Cuevas, Sp., 9,530 . . . . D5   8

Cuiabá, Braz., 43,112 . . . . . . B1   30
Cuicatlán, Mex., 2,455 . . . . o15   34
Culberson, co., Tex.,
2,794 . . . . o12   84
Culbertson, Mont., 919 . . . . B12   70
Culbertson, Nebr., 803 . . . . D5   71
Culhuacán, Mex., 5,095 . . . h9   34
Culiacán, Mex., 85,024 . . . . C3   34
Cúllar de Baza, Sp.,
9,502 . . . . D4   8
Cullen, La., 2,194 . . . . B2   63
Cullera, Sp., 14,103 . . . . . . C5   8
Cullman, Ala., 10,883 . . . . . A3   46
Cullman, co., Ala.,
45,572 . . . . A3   46
Culloden, W. Va., 700 . . . . C2   87
Cullowhee, N.C., 2,800 . . . . f9   76
Culmore, Va., 1,700 . . . . . . *B5   85
Culpeper, Va., 2,412 . . . . . . B4   85
Culpeper, co., Va., 15,088 . . B5   85
Culver, Ind., 1,558 . . . . B5   59
Culver City, Calif.,
32,163 . . . . m12   50
Cumaná, Ven., 69,937 . . . . . A5   32
Cumberland, B.C., Can.,
1,303 . . . . E5   37
Cumberland, Ind.,
1,124 . . . . E6, k11   59
Cumberland, Ky., 4,271 . . . D7   62
Cumberland, Md.,
33,415 . . . . k13   53
Cumberland, R.I., 5,800 . . . B11   52
Cumberland, Wis., 1,860 . . . C2   88
Cumberland, co., N.S., Can.,
37,767 . . . . D5   43
Cumberland, co., Eng.,
295,600 . . . . *C5   4
Cumberland, co., Ill.,
9,936 . . . . D5   58
Cumberland, co., Ky.,
7,835 . . . . D4   62
Cumberland, co., Maine,
182,751 . . . . E2   64
Cumberland, co., N.J.,
106,850 . . . . E2   74

Cumberland, co., N.C.,
148,418 . . . . C4   76
Cumberland, co., Pa.,
124,816 . . . . F7   81
Cumberland, co., Tenn.,
19,135 . . . . D8   83
Cumberland, co., Va.,
6,360 . . . . C4   85
Cumberland, mts., Ky.,
Tenn. C9   83
Cumberland, riv., U.S. C10   45
Cuming, co., Nebr.,
12,435 . . . . C9   71
Cumming, Ga., 1,561 . . . . . B2   55
Cumpas, Mex., 2,181 . . . . . A3   34
Cumra, Tur., 7,052 . . . . D9   14
Cundinamarca, dept., Col.,
2,819,524 . . . . C3   32
Cuneo, It., 35,800 . . . . B1   9
Cunnamulla, Austl., 1,992 . . E8   25
Cupertino, Calif., 3,664 . . . *D2   50
Curaçao, isl., Neth.
Antilles A4   32
Curacautín, Chile, 9,600 . . . B2   28
Curicó, Chile, 32,600 . . . . . A2   28
Curicó, prov., Chile,
105,839 . . . . A2   28
Curitiba, Braz., 344,560 . . . D3   30
Currais Novos, Braz.,
7,782 . . . . *D7   27
Currituck, co., N.C.,
6,601 . . . . A6   76
Curry, co., N. Mex.,
32,691 . . . . B7   48
Curry, co., Oreg., 13,983 . . . E2   80
Curtea-de-Arges, Rom.,
10,764 . . . . C7   10
Curtici, Rom., 8,050 . . . . . . B5   10
Curtis, Nebr., 868 . . . . D5   71
Curtisville, Pa.,
1,376 . . . . E1, h14   81
Curug, Yugo., 9,457 . . . . . . C5   10
Curuzú Cuatia, Arg.,
15,440 . . . . E4   29
Curvelo, Braz., 21,772 . . . . B4   30

Curwensville, Pa., 3,231 . . . E4   81
Cushing, Okla., 8,619 . . . . . B5   79
Cusset, Fr., 11,468 . . . . D5   5
Custer, S. Dak., 2,105 . . . . . G2   77
Custer, co., Colo., 1,305 . . . C5   51
Custer, co., Idaho,
2,996 . . . . E4   57
Custer, co., Mont.,
13,227 . . . . D11   70
Custer, co., Nebr., 16,517 . . C6   79
Custer, co., Okla., 21,040 . . B2   7l
Custer, co., S. Dak.,
4,906 . . . . G2   77
Cut Bank, Mont., 4,539 . . . B4   70
Cutchogue, N.Y., 350 . . . . m16   75
Cutervo, Peru, 3,481 . . . . . C2   31
Cuthbert, Ga., 4,300 . . . . . . E2   55
Cutler, Calif., 2,191 . . . . . . *D4   50
Cutler Ridge, Fla.,
7,005 . . . . *G6   54
Cuttack, India, 146,308 . . . D8   20
Cutten, Calif., 1,572 . . . . . . *B1   50
Cuxhaven, Ger., 45,400 . . . B4   6
Cuyahoga, co., Ohio,
1,647,895 . . . . A4   78
Cuyahoga Falls, Ohio,
47,922 . . . . A4   78
Cuzco, Peru, 78,300 . . . . . . D3   31
Cuzco, dept., Peru
648,168 . . . . D3   31
Cynthiana, Ky., 5,641 . . . . . B5   62
Cypress, Calif., 1,753 . . . . . *F4   50
Cypress Quarters, Fla.,
800 . . . . E6   54
Cyprus, country, Asia,
580,000 . . . . B4   23
Cyprus, isl., Asia E9   14
Cyrenaica, prov., Libya,
291,328 . . . . B2   23
Cyril, Okla., 1,284 . . . . C3   79
Czechoslovakia, country,
Eur., 14,100,000 . . . . D4   7
Czersk, Pol., 7,092 . . . . B4   7
Częstochowa, Pol.,
171,800 . . . . C5   7

D

Dab, Pol., 9,096 . . . . g9   7
Dab, Pol., 13,666 . . . . B3   7
Dabeiba, Col., 4,218 . . . . . . B2   32
Dablice, Czech., 5,378 . . . . n18   7
Dabrowa, Pol., 4,520 . . . . . C6   7
Dabrowa Gornicza, Pol.,
59,500 . . . . C5, g10   7
Dacca, Pak., 362,006
(*750,000) D9   20
Dachau, Ger., 29,100 . . . . D5   6
Dade, co., Fla., 935,047 . . . G6   54
Dade, co., Ga., 8,666 . . . . . B1   55
Dade, co., Mo., 7,577 . . . . . D4   69
Dade City, Fla., 4,759 . . . . D4   54
Dadeville, Ala., 2,940 . . . . . C4   46
Dadu, Pak., 13,716 . . . . . . C4   20
Daet, Phil., 20,956 . . . . *C6   19
Daggett, co., Utah,
1,164 . . . . A7   72
Dagupan, Phil., 34,484 . . . n13   19
Dahlgren, Va., 475 . . . . B5   85
Dahlonega, Ga., 2,604 . . . . B3   55
Dahomey, country, Afr.,
2,300,000 . . . . G5   22
Daigleville, La., 5,906 . . . . *E5   63
Dailey, W. Va., 800 . . . . . . C5   87
Daimiel, Sp., 19,625 . . . . . . C4   8
Daingerfield, Tex., 3,133 . . C5   84
Daiō, Jap., 7,800 . . . . o15   18
Dairen (Talien) China,
950,000 . . . . D9   17
Dairy Valley, Calif.,
3,508 . . . . *F4   50
Daisetta, Tex., 1,400 . . . . . D5   84
Daisy, Tenn., 1,508 . . D8, E10   83
Daisytown, Pa.,
1,396 . . . . *F1   81
Dajabón, Dom. Rep.,
3,430 . . . . E8   35
Dakar, Sen., 374,700 . . . . . F1   22
Dakota, co., Minn.,
78,303 . . . . F5   67
Dakota, co., Nebr.,
12,168 . . . . B9   71
Dakota City, Nebr., 928 . . . B9   71
Da Lat, Viet., 48,840 . . . . . C3   19

D'Albertis Dome, mtn.,
Austl. k11   25
Dalby, Austl., 8,870 . . . . . . E9   25
Dale, Ind., 900 . . . . H4   59
Dale, Pa., 2,807 . . . . *E4   81
Dale, co., Ala., 31,066 . . . . D4   46
Daleville, Ind., 1,548 . . . . . D6   59
Dalhart, Tex., 5,160 . . . . . . A1   84
Dalhousie, N.B., Can.,
5,856 . . . . A3   43
Dall, mtn., Alsk. f15   47
Dallam, co., Tex., 6,302 . . . A1   84
Dallas, Ga., 2,065 . . . . C2   55
Dallas, N.C., 3,591 . . . . B1   76
Dallas, Oreg., 5,072 . . . . . . C3   80
Dallas, Tex., 2,586 . . D10, m17   81
Dallas, Tex., 795,000
(*1,022,300) C4, n10   84
Dallas, co., Ala., 56,667 . . . C2   46
Dallas, co., Ark., 10,522 . . . D3   49
Dallas, co., Iowa, 24,123 . . C3   60
Dallas, co., Mo., 9,314 . . . . D4   69
Dallas, co., Tex., 951,527 . . C4   84
Dallas Center, Iowa,
1,083 . . . . C4   60
Dallas City, Ill., 1,276 . . . . C2   58
Dallastown, Pa., 3,615 . . . . G8   81
Dalmatia, reg., Yugo. D3   10
Dalmellington, Scot.,
4,702 . . . . C4   4
Dalnyaya, Sov. Un.,
10,000 . . . . D11   18
Dalrymple, mtn., Austl. . . . D8   25
Dalton, Ga., 17,868 . . . . . . B2   55
Dalton, Mass., 6,436 . . . . . B1   65
Dalton, Ohio, 1,067 . . . . . . B4   78
Dalton, Pa., 1,227 . . . . C10   81
Daltonganj, India, 25,270 . . D7   20
Dalton Gardens, Idaho,
1,083 . . . . B2   57
Daly City, Calif., 44,791 . . . h8   50
Damanhûr, Eg., U.A.R.,
133,200 . . . . G8   14
Damão, India, 13,265 . . . . . D5   20
Damariscotta, Maine,
800, (1,093 ▲) D3   64

Damascus, Md., 1,200 . . . . . B3   53
Damascus, Va., 1,485 . . . . . f10   85
Damascus (Dimashq), Syr.,
529,963 . . . . C2   15
Da Nang (Tourane),
Viet, 110,800 . . . . B3   19
Dana Point, Calif., 1,186 . . *F5   50
Danbury, Conn., 22,928 . . . D3   52
Dandenong, Austl.,
24,914 . . . . H5   26
Dane, co., Wis., 222,095 . . . E4   88
Dania, Fla., 7,065 . . . . . F6, r13   54
Daniels, co., Mont.,
3,755 . . . . B11   70
Danielson, Conn., 4,642 . . . B9   52
Dannemora, N.Y., 4,835 . . . f11   75
Dannevirke, N.Z., 5,508 . . . N16   26
Dans, mtn., Md. k13   53
Dansalan, Phil., 4,882 . . . . *D6   19
Dansville, N.Y., 5,460 . . . . C3   75
Dante, Som. F8   23
Dante, Va., 1,436 . . . . f9   85
Danube, riv., Eur. F10   3
Danubyu, Bur., 10,000 . . . *E10   20
Danvers, Mass.,
21,926 . . . . A6, f12   65
Danville, Ark., 955 . . . . B2   49
Danville, Calif., 5,000 . . . . . h9   50
Danville, Ill., 41,856 . . . . . C6   58
Danville, Ind., 3,287 . . . . . E4   59
Danville, Ky., 9,010 . . . . . . C5   62
Danville, Ohio, 926 . . . . . . B3   78
Danville, Pa., 6,889 . . . . . . E8   81
Danville (Independent
City), Va., 46,577 . . . . . . D3   85
Danville East, Pa., 1,758 . . *D8   81
Danzig see Gdańsk, Pol.
Daphne, Ala., 1,527 . . . . . . E2   46
Darabani, Rom., 11,379 . . . A8   10
Darasun, Sov. Un.,
18,000 . . . . D14   13
Darbhanga, India,
103,016 . . . . C8   20
Darby, Pa., 14,059 . . G11, p20   81

Dardanelle, Ark., 2,098 . . . B2   49
Dare, co., N.C., 5,936 . . . . . B7   76
Darende, Tur., 6,930 . . . . . C11   14
Dar es Salaam, Tan.,
128,742 . . . . B7   24
Darien, Conn., 18,437 . . . . E3   52
Darien, Ga., 1,569 . . . . E5   55
Darien, Wis., 805 . . . . F5   88
Darjeeling, India, 40,651 . . C8   20
Dark Cove, Newf., Can.,
955 . . . . *D4   44
Darke, co., Ohio, 45,612 . . . B1   78
Darling Range, mts.,
Austl F2   25
Darling, riv., Austl. E5   26
Darlington, Eng., 84,200 . . C6   4
Darlington, S.C., 6,710 . . . . C8   82
Darlington, Wis., 2,349 . . . F3   88
Darlington, co., S.C.,
52,928 . . . . C7   82
Darłowo, Pol., 5,262 . . . . . A4   7
Darmstadt, Ger., 139,100 . . D4   6
Darnah (Derna), Libya,
21,400 . . . . B2   23
Darrah, mtn., Alta.,
Can. E3   38
Darrington, Wash., 1,272 . . A4   86
Darrow, La., 400 . . . . h10   63
Dartmouth, N.S., Can.,
46,966 . . . . E6   43
Dartmouth, Eng., 6,400 . . . E5   4
Daruvar, Yugo., 6,280 . . . . C3   10
Darwin, Austl., 17,910 . . . . B5   25
Dasē, Eth., 40,000 . . . . F5   23
Dassel, Minn., 863 . . . . E4   67
Daugavpils, Sov. Un.,
74,000 . . . . D6   12
Dauphin, Man., Can
7,374 . . . . D1, g7   40
Dauphin, co., Pa.,
220,255 . . . . F8   81
Dauphiné, former prov.,
Fr., 1,016,000 . . . . E6   5
Davao, Phil., 93,104 . . . . . D7   19
Davao, prov., Phil.,
893,023 . . . . *D7   19

Davenport, Fla., 1,209.....D5 54
Davenport, Iowa, 97,500
  (*289,000).........C7, g10 60
Davenport, Okla., 813.....B5 79
Davenport, Wash., 1,494..B7 86
David, Pan., 22,924.......B1 32
David City, Nebr., 2,304...C8 71
Davidson, Sask., Can.,
  928.....................F3 39
Davidson, N.C., 2,573....B2 76
Davidson, co., N.C.,
  79,493.................B2 76
Davidson, co., Tenn.,
  399,743................A5 83
Davie, Fla., 1,500....F6, r13 54
Davie, co., N.C., 16,728...B2 76
Daviess, co., Ind., 26,636..G3 59
Daviess, co., Ky., 70,588...C3 62
Daviess, co., Mo., 9,502...B3 69
Davis, Calif., 8,910....A6, C3 50
Davis, Okla., 2,203.......C4 79
Davis, W. Va., 898........B5 87
Davis, co., Iowa, 9,199...D4 60
Davis, co., Utah, 64,760...A5 72
Davis, mtn., Pa...........G3 81
Davison, Mich., 3,761....E7 66
Davison, co., S. Dak.,
  16,681.................G7 77
Davisville, R.I., 1,800...C11 52
Davos, Switz., 11,400.....E4 6
Davy, W. Va., 1,331......D3 87
Dawes, co., Nebr., 9,536..B2 71
Dawson, Yukon, Can.,
  881....................D6 36
Dawson, Ga., 5,062.......E2 55
Dawson, Minn., 1,766.....F2 67
Dawson, Tex., 911.........D4 84
Dawson, co., Ga., 3,590...B2 55
Dawson, co., Mont.,
  12,314................C11 70
Dawson, co., Nebr.,
  19,405.................D6 71
Dawson, co., Tex., 19,185..C1 84
Dawson, mtn., B.C.,
  Can....................D9 37
Dawson Creek, B.C., Can.,
  10,946.............B7, m8 37
Dawson Springs, Ky.,
  3,002.................*C2 62
Dax, Fr., 17,051.........F3 5
Day, co., S. Dak., 10,516..E8 77
Daylight, Tenn., 20.......D8 83
Dayrut, Eg., U.A.R.......C4 23
Dayton, Ky., 9,050.......A7 62
Dayton, Ohio, 260,000
  (*648,600)..............C1 78
Dayton, Tenn., 3,500.....D8 83
Dayton, Tex., 3,367..D5, o15 84
Dayton, Va., 930.........B4 85
Dayton, Wash., 2,913.....C8 86
Daytona Beach, Fla.,
  37,395.................C5 54
Dayville, Conn., 950......B9 52
De Aar, S. Afr., 14,510...G4 24
Dead Indian, peak, Wyo..B3 89
Dead Knoll, mtn., Wyo....D2 89
Deadwood, S. Dak., 3,045..F2 77
Deaf Smith, co., Tex.,
  13,187.................B1 84
Deal, N.J., 1,889........C4 74
Deale, Md., 1,000........C4 53
Deán Funes, Arg., 16,311..A4 28
Deanwood, Ga., 2,758.....E4 55
Dearborn, Mich.,
  112,007............F7, p15 66
Dearborn, co., Ind.,
  28,674.................F8 59
Dearborn Heights, Ill.,
  1,300................*B6 58
Death, valley, Calif......D5 50
Deauville, Fr., 5,051.....C4 5
De Baca, co., N. Mex.,
  2,991.................B6 48
Debaltsevo, Sov. Un.,
  33,800...............q21 12
Debar, Yugo., 6,341......E5 10
De Bary, Fla., 2,362.....D5 54
Debica, Pol., 18,300......C6 7
Debno, Pol., 3,341.......B3 7
Deboullie, mtn., Maine....B4 64
Debrecen, Hung., 139,600..B5 10
Decatur, Ala., 29,217....A3 46
Decatur, Ga., 22,026..B5, C2 55
Decatur, Ill., 88,000
  (*120,000)............D5 58
Decatur, Ind., 8,327.....C8 59
Decatur, Mich., 1,827....F5 66
Decatur, Miss., 1,340....C4 68
Decatur, Tex., 3,563.....C4 84
Decatur, co., Ga., 25,203..F2 55
Decatur, co., Ind., 20,019..F6 59
Decatur, co., Iowa,
  10,539.................D5 60
Decatur, co., Kans., 5,778..C3 61
Decatur, co., Tenn., 8,324..B3 83
Decazeville, Fr., 11,855...E5 5

Deccan, reg., India.......E6 20
Deception, mtn., Wash....B2 86
Decherd, Tenn., 1,704....B5 83
Decin, Czech., 40,200....C3 7
Decorah, Iowa, 7,054.....A6 60
Dededo, Guam, 2,247....*F6 2
Dedham, Mass.,
  23,869..............B5, h11 65
Dedinovo, Sov. Un.,
  5,000..................n19 12
Deephaven, Minn.,
  3,286..............F5, n11 67
Deep River, Ont., Can.,
  5,377..................A7 41
Deep River, Conn., 2,200..D7 52
Deepwater, N.J., 700.....D2 74
Deer, mtn., Maine........C2 64
Deerfield, Ill., 17,245....h9 58
Deerfield, Mich., 866....G7 66
Deerfield Beach, Fla.,
  9,573..................F6 54
Deer Lake, Newf., Can.,
  3,998..................D3 44
Deer Lodge, Mont., 4,681..D4 70
Deer Lodge, co., Mont.,
  18,640.................D3 70
Deer Park, N.Y., 23,500..*F3 75
Deer Park, Ohio, 8,423...o13 78
Deer Park, Tex., 4,865...*E5 84
Deer Park, Wash., 1,333..B8 86
Deer River, Minn., 992...C5 67
Defense Highway, Md.,
  1,000.................*C4 53
Defiance, Ohio, 14,553....A1 78
Defiance, co., Ohio
  31,508.................A1 78
Defiance, mtn., Oreg.....B5 80
De Forest, Wis., 1,223....E4 88
De Funiak Springs, Fla.,
  5,282.................u15 54
Degerfors, Swe., 9,500....E8 6
Deggendorf, Ger., 17,100..D6 6
De Graff, Ohio, 996......B2 78
Dehra Dun, India, 126,918
  (*156,341)............B6 20
Dej, Rom., 19,281.......B6 10
De Kalb, Ill., 29,099.....B5 58
De Kalb, Miss., 880......C5 68
De Kalb, Tex., 2,042.....C5 84
De Kalb, co., Ala.,
  41,417.................A4 46
De Kalb, co., Ga.,
  256,182................C2 55
De Kalb, co., Ill., 51,714..B5 58
De Kalb, co., Ind.,
  28,271.................B7 59
De Kalb, co., Mo., 7,226..B3 69
De Kalb, co., Tenn.,
  10,174.................D8 83
Delafield, Wis., 2,334...*E5 88
Del Aire, Calif., 5,000...*F4 50
Delanco, N.J., 4,011.....C3 74
De Land, Fla., 10,775....C5 54
Delano, Calif., 11,913....E4 50
Delano, Minn., 1,612.....E5 67
Delavan, Ill., 1,377......C4 58
Delavan, Wis., 4,846.....F5 88
Delaware, Ohio, 13,282...B2 78
Delaware, co., Ind.,
  110,938................D7 59
Delaware, co., Iowa,
  18,483.................B6 60
Delaware, co., N.Y.,
  43,540.................C5 75
Delaware, co., Ohio,
  36,107.................B2 78
Delaware, co., Okla.,
  13,198.................A7 79
Delaware, co., Pa.,
  553,154...............G11 81
Delaware, state, U.S.,
  446,292...............C11 45
Delaware, bay, Del.......B7 53
Delaware City, Del.,
  1,658..................A6 53
Delbarton, W. Va.,
  1,122..................D2 87
Delcambre, La., 1,857....E4 63
Del City, Okla., 12,934...B4 79
Delémont, Switz., 9,542...E3 6
De Leon, Tex., 2,022.....C3 84
De Leon Springs, Fla.,
  900....................C5 54
De Léry, Que., Can.,
  1,957.................q19 42
Delft, Neth., 76,000......A6 5
Delfzijl, Neth., 16,600....A7 5
Delhi, Calif., 1,175.....*D3 50
Delhi, Ont., Can., 3,427..E4 41
Delhi, India, 2,061,758,
  (*2,658,612)...........C6 20
Delhi, La., 2,514........B4 63
Delhi, N.Y., 2,664.......C6 75
Delhi Hills, Ohio, 5,000..*C1 78
Delisle, Que., Can., 1,302..A6 42
Delitzsch, Ger., 22,900...C6 6
Dellenbaugh, mtn.,
  Ariz...................A2 48

Dell Rapids, S. Dak.,
  1,863..................G9 77
Dellwood, Mo., 4,720...*C7 69
Del Mar, Calif., 3,125...o15 50
Delmar, Del., 2,225......D6 53
Delmar, Md., 1,291......D6 53
Delmar, N.Y., 7,300.....C7 75
Delmenhorst, Ger., 59,900.B4 6
Delmont, Pa., 1,313.....*F2 81
Del Monte Heights, Calif.,
  1,174.................*D3 50
Del Monte Park, Calif.,
  2,177.................*D3 50
Del Norte, Colo., 1,856...D4 51
Del Norte, co., Calif.,
  17,771.................B2 50
Deloraine, Man., Can.,
  916....................E1 40
Delphi, Ind., 2,517......C4 59
Delphos, Ohio, 6,961.....B1 78
Delray Beach, Fla., 12,230..F6 54
Del Rey Oaks, Calif.,
  1,831.................*D3 50
Del Rio, Tex., 18,612.....E2 84
Del Rosa, Calif., 6,000...*E5 50
Delson Village, Que.,
  Can., 2,075...........q19 42
Delta, Colo., 3,832......C2 51
Delta, Ohio, 2,376.......A2 78
Delta, Pa., 822..........G9 81
Delta, Utah, 1,576.......B5 72
Delta, co., Colo., 15,602..C3 51
Delta, co., Mich., 34,298..C3 66
Delta, co., Tex., 5,860...C5 84
Delta, peak, B.C., Can...A3 37
Delta Amacuro, ter., Ven.,
  33,979.................B5 32
Deltaville, Va., 800.....C6 85
Demarest, N.J., 4,231....h9 74
Demavend, mtn., Iran...F8 16
Demidov, Sov., Un.,
  10,000.................D8 12
Deming, N. Mex., 6,764..C5 48
Demirci, Tur., 8,745.....C7 14
Demmin, Ger., 16,400....B6 6
Demopolis, Ala., 7,377...C2 46
Demorest, Ga., 1,029....B3 55
Demotte, Ind., 1,000.....B3 59
Dempo, mtn., Indon.....F2 19
Denain, Fr., 29,467......B5 5
Denbigh, Wales, 8,100...D5 4
Denbigh, co., Wales,
  174,700...............*D5 4
Denham Springs, La.,
  5,991.............D5, h10 63
Den Helder, Neth.,
  52,900.................A6 5
Denia, Sp., 7,876........C6 8
Deniliquit, Austl., 6,269..G7 25
Denison, Iowa, 6,780....B2 60
Denison, Tex., 22,748....C4 84
Denizli, Tur., 48,925....D7 14
Denmark, S.C., 3,221....E5 82
Denmark, Wis.,
  1,100.............D6, h10 88
Denmark, country, Eur.,
  4,654,000..............I3 11
Dennison, Ohio, 4,158....B4 78
Dennis Port, Mass., 1,300..C7 65
Denny Terrace, S.C.,
  3,000..................C5 82
Denpasar, Indon., 16,639..G5 19
Dent, co., Mo., 10,445...D6 69
Denton, Ga., 255.........E4 55
Denton, Md., 1,938......C6 53
Denton, N.C., 852.......B2 76
Denton, Tex., 26,844....C4 84
Denton, co., Tex., 47,432..C4 84
Dentsville, S.C., 1,500...C6 82
Denver, Colo., 500,000,
  (*858,300).............B6 51
Denver, Iowa, 1,046.....B5 60
Denver, Pa., 1,875.......F9 81
Denver, co., Colo.,
  493,887................B6 51
Denver City, Tex., 4,302..C1 84
Denville, N.J., 10,632....B4 74
Departure Bay, B.C.,
  Can., 1,235...........f12 37
De Pere, Wis.,
  10,045............D5, h9 88
Depew, N.Y., 18,309.....C2 75
Deposit, N.Y., 2,025.....C5 75
Depue, Ill., 1,920.......B4 58
De Queen, Ark., 2,859...C1 49
De Quincy, La., 3,928....D2 63
Der'a, Syr., 17,284......F11 14
Dera Ghazi Khan, Pak.,
  47,105.................B5 20
Dera Ismail Khan,
  Pak., 44,319 (*46,140)..B5 20
Derby, Austl., 1,439......C3 25
Derby, Colo., 10,124....*B6 51
Derby, Conn., 12,132....D4 52
Derby, Eng., 131,600....D6 4
Derby, Kans., 6,458......E6 61
Derby, N.Y., 3,000.......C2 75
Derby, co., Eng., 897,700..*D6 4

Derecske, Hung., 9,970...B5 10
De Ridder, La., 7,188....D2 63
Derita, N.C., 1,000......B2 76
Dermott, Ark., 3,665....D4 49
Derry, N.H., 4,500.......F5 73
Derry, Pa., 3,426.......F3 81
Derventa, Yugo., 9,795...C3 10
Derzhavinskoye, Sov.
  Un.....................D9 16
Des Allemands, La.,
  1,167.............E5, k11 63
Des Arc, Ark., 1,482.....C4 49
Debiens, Que., Can.,
  1,970..................A6 42
Deschaillons sur
  St. Lauent, Que.,
  Can., 1,283..........*C5 42
Deschambault, Que., Can.
  1,056..................C6 42
Deschênes, Que., Can.,
  2,090..................D2 42
Deschutes, co., Oreg.,
  23,100.................D5 80
Deseronto, Ont., Can.,
  1,797..................C7 41
Desert Hot Springs, Calif.,
  1,472.................*F5 50
Desha, co., Ark., 20,770..D4 49
Deshler, Nebr., 956......D8 71
Deshler, Ohio, 1,824.....A2 78
Desloge, Mo., 2,308.....D7 69
De Smet, S. Dak., 1,324..F8 77
Des Moines, Iowa, 206,500
  (*280,000).........C4, e8 60
Des Moines, Wash.,
  1,987.............B3, f11 86
Des Moines, co., Iowa
  44,605.................D6 60
De Soto, Kans.,
  1,271.............D9, m16 61
De Soto, Mo., 5,804.....C7 69
De Soto, Tex., 1,969....*C4 84
De Soto, co., Fla.,
  11,683.................E5 54
De Soto, co., Miss.,
  23,891.................A3 68
De Soto, par., La., 24,248..B2 63
Des Peres, Mo., 4,362....f13 69
Des Plaines, Ill.,
  50,789.............A6, h9 58
Dessau, Ger., 95,200....C6 6
Destin, Fla., 900........u15 54
Detmold, Ger., 30,200...C4 6
Detroit, Mich., 1,560,000
  (*4,300,000)......F7, p15 66
Detroit Beach, Mich.,
  1,571.................*G7 66
Detroit Lakes, Minn.,
  5,978..................D3 67
Detva, Czech., 7,786.....D5 7
Deuel, co., Nebr., 3,125..C3 71
Deuel, co., S. Dak., 6,782..F9 77
Deurne, Bel., 68,703.....B6 5
Deux-Montagnes, Que.,
  Can., 7,274...........p19 42
Deux-Sèvres, dept., Fr.,
  321,118..............*D3 5
Deva, Rom., 16,879......C6 10
Devavanya, Hung., 10,828.B5 10
Deventer, Neth., 58,400...A7 5
Devils Lake, N. Dak.,
  6,670..................B7 77
Devine, Tex., 2,522......E3 84
De Vola, Ohio, 900.......C4 78
Devon, Alta., Can., 1,418..C4 38
Devon, Pa., 1,500......*G10 81
Devon, co., Eng.,
  833,100..............*E5 4
Devon, isl., Can.......*A15 36
Devonport, Austl.,
  14,848................o15 25
Devonport, N.Z., 11,092..L15 26
Dewar, Okla., 817.......B6 79
Dewey, Okla., 3,994.....A6 79
Dewey, co., Okla., 6,051..B2 79
Dewey, co., S. Dak.,
  5,257..................E5 77
De Witt, Ark., 3,019.....C4 49
De Witt, Iowa, 3,680....C7 60
De Witt, Mich., 1,238....F6 66
De Witt, N.Y., 7,000....*B4 75
De Witt, co., Ill.,
  17,253.................C5 58
De Witt, co., Tex., 20,638..E4 84
Dewsbury, Eng., 53,800..A6 4
Dexter, Maine, 2,720,
  (3,951▲)..............C3 64
Dexter, Mich., 1,702....F7 66
Dexter, Mo., 5,519......E8 69
Dexter, N.Y., 1,009.....A4 75
Dhamar, Yemen, 20,000..G3 15
Dharamjaygarh, India,
  5,000..................D7 20
Dharmapuri, India,
  28,031.................F6 20
Dharmsala, India, 10,255..B6 20
Dharwar, India, 77,163...E6 20
Dhaulagiri, peak, Nep...C7 20

Dhidhimotikhon, Grc.,
8,111..................E8 10
Dhulia, India, 98,893.....D5 20
Diablo, Calif., 2,096.....*D2 50
Diablo, mtn., Calif......h9 50
Diablo Heights, C.Z.,
1,075..................*B2 32
Diamante, Arg., 13,600....A4 28
Diamantina, Braz.,
14,252.................E6 27
Diamantina, Braz., 14,252..B4 30
Diamond, peak, Oreg......D4 80
Diamond Springs, Calif.,
900....................C3 50
Diber (Dibra), pref., Alb.,
96,000.................*E5 10
D'Iberville, Miss.,
3,005..............E2, E5 68
Diboll, Tex., 2,506.......D5 84
Dickens, co., Tex., 4,963..C2 84
Dickenson, co., Va.,
20,211.................e9 85
Dickey, co., N. Dak.,
8,147..................D7 77
Dickinson, N. Dak., 9,971..D3 77
Dickinson, Tex., 4,715...*E5 84
Dickinson, co., Iowa,
12,574.................A2 60
Dickinson, co., Kans.,
21,572.................D6 61
Dickinson, co., Mich.,
23,917.................B3 66
Dickson, Tenn., 5,028.....A4 83
Dickson, co., Tenn.,
18,839.................A4 83
Dickson City, Pa.,
7,738.............D10, m18 81
Didsbury, Alta., Can.,
1,254..................D3 38
Diégo-Suarez Antsirane),
Malag., 29,887........C9 24
Dien Bien Phu, Viet.....*A2 19
Diepholz, Ger., 10,900....B4 6
Dieppe, N.B., Can., 4,032..C5 43
Dieppe, Fr., 29,967......C4 5
Dierks, Ark., 1,276.......C1 49
Digboi, India, 18,235.....C10 20
Digby, N.S., Can., 2,308..E4 43
Digby, co., N.S., Can.,
20,216.................E4 43
Dighton, Kans., 1,526.....D3 61
Digne, Fr., 10,299.......E7 5
Digoin, Fr., 8,529.......D5 5
Dijon, Fr., 135,694......D6 5
Dikson, Sov. Un., 10,000..B11 16
Dilley, Tex., 2,118.......E3 84
Dillingen [an der Donau],
Ger., 11,200..........D5 6
Dillon, Mont., 3,690......E4 70
Dillon, S.C., 6,173.......C9 82
Dillon, co., S.C., 30,584..C9 82
Dillonvale, Ohio, 1,232...B5 78
Dillsburg, Pa., 1,322.....F7 81
Dilworth, Minn., 2,102....D2 67
Dimitrovgrad, Bul.,
34,162.................D7 10
Dimmit, co., Tex., 10,095..E3 84
Dimmitt, Tex., 2,935......B1 84
Dimondale, Mich., 866....F6 66
Dinan, Fr., 12,847.......C3 5
Dinant, Bel., 6,851.......B6 5
Dinard [-St. Enogat], Fr.,
9,270..................C2 5
Dindigul, India, 92,947....F6 20
Dingwall, Scot., 3,900....B4 4
Dinh Lap, Viet., 10,000...*G6 17
Dinsmore, Fla., 2,500..B5, m8 54
Dinuba, Calif., 6,103.....D4 50
Dinwiddie, co., Va.,
22,183.................C5 85
Diourbel, Sen., 28,600....F1 22
Dipolog, Phil., 8,770....*D6 19
Dirēdawā, Eth., 30,000...G6 23
Diriamba, Nic., 10,499....E7 34
Dirranbandi, Austl., 889...E8 25
Dishman, Wash., 7,800...g14 86
Dismal, peak, Va........C2 85
Disraëli, Que., Can.,
3,079..................D6 42
District Heights, Md.,
7,524.................*C4 53
District of Columbia,
U.S., 763,965.......C3, f8 53
Distrito Federal, fed. dist.,
Mex., 4,870,876......D5 34
Distrito Federal, fed. dist.,
Ven., 1,257,515......A4 32
Disûq, Eg., U.A.R.,
36,600................*G8 14
Diu, India, 5,215........D5 20
Divernon, Ill., 997......D4 58
Dives-sur-Mer, Fr., 6,258..C3 5
Divide, co., N. Dak.,
5,566..................B2 77
Divide, peak, Wyo.......E5 89
Divinópolis, Braz., 41,544..C4 30
Divnoye, Sov. Un.,
17,300.................I14 12

Dix, mtn., N.Y..........A7 75
Dixfield, Maine, 1,400....D2 64
Dixiana, Ala., 500.......B3 46
Dixie, co., Fla., 4,479....C3 54
Dixmoor, Ill., 3,076.....*B6 58
Dixon, Calif., 2,970......C3 50
Dixon, Ill., 19,565......B4 58
Dixon, Mo., 1,473.......D5 69
Dixon, co., Nebr., 8,106..B9 71
Dixonville, Pa., 900......E3 81
Diyarbakir, Tur., 79,888...D3 14
Djakarta (Jakarta Batavia),
Indon., 2,922,000......G3 19
Djakovica, Yugo., 20,741..D5 10
Djakovo, Yugo., 12,069...C4 10
Djambi, Indon., 108,834...F2 19
Djelfa, Alg., 27,479......B5 22
Djibouti, A. & I., 40,000..F6 23
Djurdjevac, Yugo., 6,408..B3 10
Djursholm, Swe., 7,400...t36 11
Dmitriyevka, Sov. Un.,
10,000............H12, r21 12
Dmitriyev-Lgovskiy,
Sov. Un., 10,000......E10 12
Dmitrov, Sov. Un.,
10,000.................C11 12
Dmitrovsk-Orlovskiy,
Sov. Un., 10,000......E10 12
Dnepr, riv., Sov. Un.....H9 12
Dneprodzerzhinsk,
Sov. Un., 207,000.....G10 12
Dnepropetrovsk, Sov. Un.,
738,000...............G10 12
Dnestr, riv., Sov. Un.....H7 12
Dno, Sov. Un., 10,000....C7 12
Dobbs Ferry, N.Y.,
10,076.................g13 75
Döbeln, Ger., 28,900.....C6 6
Doboj, Yugo., 13,445.....C4 10
Dobrich, see
Tolbukhin, Bul.
Dobrogea, prov., Rom.,
507,900...............*C9 10
Dobruja, reg., Bul........C9 10
Dobruja, reg., Rom.......C9 10
Docena, Ala., 1,100......E4 46
Doddridge, co., W. Va.,
6,970..................B4 87
Dodge, co., Ga., 16,483...D3 55
Dodge, co., Minn.,
13,259.................G6 67
Dodge, co., Nebr., 32,471..C9 71
Dodge, co., Wis., 63,170..E5 88
Dodge Center, Minn.,
1,441..................F6 67
Dodge City, Kans.,
13,520.................E3 61
Dodgeville, Wis., 2,911...F3 88
Dodoma, Tan., 13,435.....B7 24
Doerun, Ga., 1,037.......E3 55
Doe Run, Mo., 800.......D7 69
Doha, Qatar, 35,000......C8 23
Doi Angka, mtn., Thai....E10 20
Dolbeau, Que., Can.,
6,052.................G19 36
Dôle, Fr., 24,525.......D6 5
Dolgeville, N.Y., 3,058...B6 75
Dolina, Sov. Un., 5,000...D8 7
Dolinsk (Ochiai),
Sov. Un., 30,000......C11 18
Dolomite, Ala., 2,500..B3, E4 46
Dolores, Arg., 14,438.....B5 28
Dolores, Ur., 13,300.....E1 30
Dolores, co., Colo., 2,196..D2 51
Dolores Hidalgo, Mex.,
12,311................m13 34
Dolton, Ill., 22,557......k9 58
Dolzhanskaya, Sov. Un.,
5,000.................q22 12
Domažlice, Czech., 8,500..D2 7
Dominguez, Calif., 6,000..*F4 50
Dominica, Br. dep., N.A.,
59,916................I14 35
Dominican Republic,
country,
N.A., 3,573,000......E8 35
Dominion, N.S., Can.,
2,999..................C9 43
Domodossola, It., 16,728...A2 9
Dom Pedrito, Braz.,
15,429.................E2 30
Don, riv., Sov. Un.......H13 12
Dona Ana, co., N. Mex.,
59,948.................C5 48
Donaghadee, N. Ire.,
3,226..................C4 4
Donaldsonville, La.,
6,082.............D4, h10 63
Donalsonville, Ga., 2,621..E2 55
Don Benito, Sp., 25,248...C3 8
Doncaster, Eng., 86,900...D6 4
Donegal, co., Ire.,
108,500...............*C2 4
Doneraile, S.C., 1,043....C8 82
Donets, riv., Sov. Un.....G13 12
Donetsk, Sov. Un.,
774,000...........H11, r20 12
Donggala, Indon., 3,821...F5 19

Dong Hoi, Viet., 10,000...B3 19
Dongola, Sud., 3,350.....E4 23
Doniphan, Mo., 1,421....E7 69
Doniphan, co., Kans.,
9,574..................C8 61
Donkin, N.S., Can.,
1,010.................C10 43
Donley, co., Tex., 4,449...B2 84
Donna, Tex., 7,522.......F3 84
Donnacona, Que.,
Can., 4,812.......C6, o16 42
Donora, Pa., 11,131......F2 81
Donzère, Fr., 1,544......E6 5
Doolittle, Mo., 449.......D6 69
Dooly, co., Ga., 11,474...D3 55
Door, co., Wis., 20,685...D6 88
Dora, Ala., 1,776........B2 46
Doraville, Ga., 4,437.....A5 55
Dorchester, N.B., Can.,
1,779..................D5 43
Dorchester, Eng., 12,900..E5 4
Dorchester, co., Que.,
Can., 34,711..........C7 42
Dorchester, co., Md.,
29,666.................D5 53
Dorchester, co., S.C.,
24,383.................E6 82
Dordogne, Dept., Fr.,
375,455...............*E4 5
Dordrecht, Neth., 85,700
(*138,000)............B6 5
Dores do Indaiá, Braz.,
10,354.................B3 30
Dorgali, It., 7,189.......D2 9
Dorking, Eng., 22,700....m12 4
Dormont, Pa., 13,098....k13 81
Dornbirn, Aus., 28,075...E4 6
Dornoch, Scot., 930......B4 4
Dorohoi, Rom., 14,771...B8 10
Dorris, Calif., 973.......B3 50
Dorset, co., Eng.,
322,100...............*F5 4
Dortmund, Ger., 652,000..C3 6
Dorton, Ky., 700........C7 62
Dortyol, Tur., 10,293....D11 14
Dorval, Que., Can.,
18,592................q19 42
Dos Hermanas, Sp.,
22,700.................D3 8
Dos Palos, Calif., 2,373...D3 50
Dothan, Ala., 31,440.....D4 46
Douai, Fr., 47,639
(*135,000)............B5 5
Douala (Duala), Cam.,
187,000...............H6 22
Douarnenez, Fr., 19,887...C1 5
Doubletop, peak, Wyo....C2 89
Doubs, dept., Fr.,
384,881...............*D7 5
Dougherty, co., Ga.,
75,680.................E2 55
Douglas, Alsk.,
1,042............D13, k22 47
Douglas, Ariz., 12,370....D4 48
Douglas, Ga., 8,736......E4 55
Douglas, I. of Man,
18,837.................C4 4
Douglas, Wyo., 2,822....D7 89
Douglas, co., Colo.,
4,816..................B6 51
Douglas, co., Ga., 16,741..C2 55
Douglas, co., Ill., 19,281..D5 58
Douglas, co., Kans.,
43,720.................D8 61
Douglas, co., Minn.,
21,313.................E3 67
Douglas, co., Mo., 9,653..E5 69
Douglas, co., Nebr.,
343,490...............C9 71
Douglas, co., Nev., 3,481..B2 72
Douglas, co., Oreg.,
68,458.................D3 80
Douglas, co., S. Dak.,
5,113..................G7 77
Douglas, co., Wash.,
14,890.................B6 86
Douglas, co., Wis., 45,008..B1 88
Douglass, Kans., 1,058...E7 61
Douglasville, Ga., 4,462...C2 55
Doullens, Fr., 6,321......B5 5
Douro Litoral, prov., Port.,
1,240,194............*B1 8
Dove Creek, Colo., 986...D2 51
Dover, Del., 7,250.......B6 53
Dover, Eng., 36,200......E7 4
Dover, Fla., 800.........D4 54
Dover, Mass., 600.......h10 65
Dover, N.H., 19,131......E6 73
Dover, N.J., 13,034......B3 74
Dover, Ohio, 11,300......B4 78
Dover, Pa., 975..........F8 81
Dover, Tenn., 736.......A4 83
Dover-Foxcroft, Maine,
2,500 (4,173▲)........C3 64
Dover Plains, N.Y., 1,000..D7 75
Dowagiac, Mich., 7,208...G4 66

Down, co., N. Ire.,
275,800..............*C4 4
Downers Grove, Ill.,
22,612.............B5, k8 58
Downey, Calif., 82,505....n12 50
Downington, Pa., 5,598...F10 81
Downpatrick, N. Ire.,
4,219..................C4 4
Downs, Kans., 1,206.....C5 61
Downs, mtn., Wyo.......C3 89
Downton, mtn., B.C.,
Can...................C5 37
Dows, Iowa, 882........B4 60
Doylestown, Ohio, 1,873..B4 78
Doylestown, Pa., 5,917...F11 81
Doyline, La., 1,061......B2 63
Dracut, Mass., 11,500
(13,674▲)............A5 65
Draganovo, Bul., 5,465...D7 10
Drăgăşani, Rom., 9,963...C7 10
Dragerton, Utah, 2,400..*B6 72
Draguignan, Fr., 11,814...F7 5
Drain, Oreg., 1,052......D3 80
Drake, peak, Oreg.......E6 80
Drakesboro, Ky., 832.....C2 62
Drama, Grc., 32,195.....B5 14
Drama, prov., Grc.,
121,006...............*B5 14
Drammen, Nor.,
31,300.............H4, p28 11
Drancy, Fr., 65,890.....g10 5
Draper, N.C., 3,255......A3 76
Draper, Utah, 1,700...A6, D2 72
Dravosburg, Pa., 3,458..*E1 81
Drayton, N. Dak., 1,278...A8 77
Drayton, S.C., 1,128.....B4 82
Drayton Plains, Mich.,
13,500.................F7 66
Drayton Valley, Alta.,
Can., 3,854...........C3 38
Drenthe, prov., Neth.,
314,400...............*A7 5
Dresden, Ont., Can.,
2,346..................E2 41
Dresden, Ger., 503,900
(*630,000)............C6 6
Dresden, Ohio, 1,338.....B3 78
Dresden, Tenn., 1,510....A3 83
Dresden Village, Mich.,
5,500.................*F7 66
Dreux, Fr., 21,588......C4 5
Drew, Miss., 2,143......B3 68
Drew, co., Ark., 15,213...D4 49
Drexel, N.C., 1,146......B1 76
Drexel, Ohio, 4,000......C1 78
Drexel Gardens, Ind.,
5,200.............E5, m9 59
Drexel Hill, Pa.,
36,000...............*G11 81
Drift, Ky., 800.........C7 62
Drifton, Pa., 1,200.....D10 81
Driggs, Idaho, 824......F7 57
Driskill, mtn., La.......B3 63
Drissa, Sov. Un., 10,000..D6 12
Drogheda, Ire., 17,800...D3 4
Drogobych, Sov. Un.,
42,145.................G4 12
Druid Hills, Ga., 3,000..*C2 55
Druid Hills, N.C., 1,207..*f10 76
Drumheller, Alta., Can.,
2,931..................D4 38
Drummond, co., Que.,
Can., 58,220..........D5 42
Drummond Range, mts.,
Austl.................D8 25
Drummondville, Que.,
Can., 27,909..........D5 42
Drummondville Ouest,
Que., Can., 2,057....*D5 42
Drumright, Okla., 4,190...B5 79
Druzhkovka, Sov. Un.,
39,800................q20 12
Dryden, Ont., Can.,
5,728.................o16 41
Dryden, N.Y., 1,353.....C4 75
Duarte, Calif., 13,962...*E5 50
Duarte, peak, Dom. Rep...E8 35
Dubach, La., 1,013......B3 63
Dubawnt, lake,
N.W. Ter., Can.......D13 36
Dubayy, Tr. Coast,
55,000................D6 15
Dubbo, Austl., 15,568....F8 25
Dublin, Ga., 13,814......D4 55
Dublin, Ind., 1,021......E7 59
Dublin (Baile Átha Cliath),
Ire., 568,300
(*760,000)............D3 4
Dublin, Tex., 2,443......C3 84
Dublin, Va., 1,427......C2 85
Dublin, co., Ire., 793,800..D3 4
Dubois, co., Ind., 27,463..H4 59
Du Bois, Pa., 10,667.....D4 81
Duboistown, Pa., 1,358...D7 81
Dubossary, Sov. Un.,
25,000................H7 12
Dubovka, Sov. Un.,
11,700................G15 12

Dubrovnik, Yugo., 22,961..D4   10
Dubsdread, Fla., 1,400...*D5   54
Dubuque, Iowa, 62,853....B7   60
Dubuque, co., Iowa,
    80,048................B7   60
Duchesne, co., Utah,
    7,179.................A6   72
Duchov, Czech., 8,229....C2   7
Duck, mtn., Man., Can....D1   40
Ducktown, Tenn., 741.....D9   83
Dudinka, Sov. Un.,
    17,000................C11   13
Dudley, Eng., 64,100....D5   4
Dudley, Mass., 3,800
    (6,510▲)..............B4   65
Due West, S.C., 1,166....C3   82
Dufferin, co., Ont., Can.,
    16,095................C4   41
Dugger, Ind., 1,062......F3   59
Duisburg, Ger., 497,500...C3   6
Duitama, Col., 31,865
    (52,537▲)............B3   32
Dukes, co., Mass., 5,829..D6   65
Dulawan, Phil., 16,376...*D6   19
Duluth, Ga., 1,483....A5, B2   55
Duluth, Minn., 103,000
    (*163,000)...........D6   67
Dumaguete, Phil., 24,062..D6   19
Dumas, Ark., 3,540.......D4   49
Dumas, Tex., 8,477.......B2   84
Dumfries, Scot., 27,300...C5   4
Dumfries, Va., 1,368.....B5   85
Dumfries, co., Scot.,
    88,400................*C5   4
Dumont, N.J., 18,882..B5, h9   74
Dumyāṭ (Damietta), Eg.,
    U.A.R., 63,100........G8   14
Dunafoldvar, Hung.,
    11,251................B4   10
Dunapataj, Hung., 4,846..B4   10
Dunaujvaros, Hung.,
    39,200................B4   10
Dunayevsty, Sov. Un.,
    10,000................G6   12
Dunbar, Pa., 1,536.......G2   81
Dunbar, Scot., 4,000.....B5   4
Dunbar, W. Va.,
    11,006.............C3, C6   87
Dunbarton, co., Scot.,
    193,500...............*B4   4

Duncan, Ariz., 862.......C4   48
Duncan, B.C., Can.,
    3,726..............E6, g12   37
Duncan, Okla., 20,009....C4   79
Duncan, S.C., 1,186......B3   82
Duncannon, Pa., 1,800....F7   81
Duncansville, Pa., 1,396..F5   81
Duncanville, Tex., 3,774..n10   34
Dundalk, Ont., Can., 852..C4   41
Dundalk, Ire., 19,800....C3   4
Dundalk, Md.,
    85,000...........B4, g11   53
Dundas, Ont., Can.,
    12,912................D5   41
Dundas, co., Ont., Can.,
    17,162................B9   41
Dundee, Ill., 2,530....A5, h6   58
Dundee, Fla., 1,554......D5   54
Dundee, Mich., 2,377....G7   66
Dundee, N.Y., 1,468......C4   75
Dundee, Scot., 184,100...B5   4
Dundee, S. Afr., 10,939...F6   24
Dundy, co., Nebr., 3,570..D4   71
Dunean, S.C., 3,950......*B3   82
Dunedin, Fla., 8,444..D4, o10   54
Dunedin, N.Z., 77,149
    (*108,734)...........P13   26
Dunellen, N.J., 6,840....B4   74
Dunfermline, Scot.,
    49,900................B5   4
Dungannon, N. Ire.,
    6,494.................C3   4
Dungarvan, Ire., 5,400...D3   4
Dunkerque, Fr., 27,616
    (*122,000)...........B5   5
Dunkirk, Ind., 3,117.....D7   59
Dunkirk, N.Y., 18,205....C1   75
Dunkirk, Ohio, 1,006.....B2   78
Dunkirk, see
    Dunkerque, Fr.
Dunklin, co., Mo.,
    39,139................E7   69
Dún Laoghaire, Ire.,
    51,800................D3   4
Dunlap, Ind., 1,935......A6   59
Dunlap, Iowa, 1,254......C2   60
Dunlap, Tenn., 1,026.....D8   83
Dunlo, Pa., 950..........F4   81
Dunmore, Pa.,
    18,917.........D10, m18   81

Dunn, N.C., 7,487........B4   76
Dunn, co., N. Dak., 6,350..C3   77
Dunn, co., Wis., 26,156...D2   88
Dunnellon, Fla., 1,079...C4   54
Dunn Loring, Va., 1,500..*B5   85
Dunnville, Ont., Can.,
    5,181.................E5   41
Dunoon, Scot., 9,400.....C4   4
Dunseith, N. Dak.,
    1,017.................A5   77
Dunsmuir, Calif., 2,873...B2   50
Dunville, Newf., Can.,
    1,121.................E5   44
Duparquet, Que., Can.,
    978...................*D3   42
Duplin, co., N.C., 37,959..C5   76
Dupnitsa, see Stanke
    Dimitrov, Bul.
Dupo, Ill., 2,937........E3   58
Du Quoin, Ill., 6,558....E4   58
Dura, Jordan, 3,852......C3   15
Durand, Mich., 3,312.....F6   66
Durand, Wis., 2,039......D2   88
Durango, Colo., 10,530...D3   51
Durango, Mex., 97,305....C4   34
Durango, state, Mex.,
    760,836...............C4   34
Durant, Iowa, 1,266......C7   60
Durant, Miss., 2,617.....B4   68
Durant, Okla., 10,467....D5   79
Durazno, Ur., 22,203.....E1   30
Durazno, dept., Ur.,
    56,100................*E1   30
Durban, S. Afr., 560,010
    (*681,492)...........F6   24
Düren, Ger., 52,700......C3   6
Durham, Calif., 700......C3   50
Durham, Maine,
    (1,086▲).............g7   64
Durham, Ont., Can.,
    2,180.................C4   41
Durham, Eng., 22,700....C6   4
Durham, N.H., 5,000.....E6   73
Durham, N.C., 97,000
    (*121,000)...........B4   76
Durham, co., Ont., Can.,
    39,916................C6   41

Durham, co., Eng.,
    1,534,500............*C6   4
Durham, co., N.C.,
    111,995...............A4   76
Durres, Alb., 39,946.....*B2   14
Duryea, Pa., 5,626..D10, m17   81
Dushanbe, Sov. Un.,
    312,000...............F9   13
Duson, La., 1,033........D3   63
Düsseldorf, Ger., 701,700..C3   6
Dutchess, co., N.Y.,
    176,008...............D7   75
Dutton, Ont., Can., 815...E3   41
Duval, co., Fla., 455,411..B5   54
Duval, co., Tex., 13,398...F3   84
Duvergé, Dom. Rep.,
    6,600.................E8   35
Duxbury, Mass., 1,100
    (4,727▲)............B6   65
Duzce, Tur., 18,344......B8   14
Dvůr Králove [nad Labem],
    Czech., 15,000.......C3   7
Dwight, Ill., 3,086......B5   58
Dyer, Ind., 3,993........A2   59
Dyer, Tenn., 1,909.......A3   83
Dyer, co., Tenn., 29,537..A2   83
Dyersburg, Tenn.,
    12,499................A2   83
Dyersville, Iowa, 3,270...B6   60
Dyrlow, see Darlowo, Pol.
Dysart, Iowa, 1,197......B5   60
Dzaudzhikau, see
    Ordzhonikidze, Sov. Un.
Dzerzhinsk, Sov. Un.,
    26,200................q20   12
Dzerzhinsk, Sov. Un.,
    193,000.........C14, d7   12
Dzhambul, Sov. Un.,
    139,000...............E10   13
Dzhankoy, Sov. Un.,
    10,000.................I1   12
Dzialdowo, Pol., 5,139....B6   7
Dzierzlow, see
    Darlowo, Pol.
Dzierzoniow, Pol.,
    29,300................C4   7
Dzilam Gonzáles, Mex.,
    2,324.................C7   34
Dzitbalché, Mex.,
    3,666.................C6   34

E

Eads, Colo., 929.........C8   51
Eagan, Tenn., 500.......C10   83
Eagle, W. Va., 200....C3, D6   87
Eagle, co., Colo., 4,677...B4   51
Eagle, mtn., Tex........o13   84
Eagle, peak, Calif......B3   50
Eagle Grove, Iowa, 4,381..B4   60
Eagle Lake, Fla., 1,364..*E5   54
Eagle Lake, Maine, 900
    (1,138▲).............A4   64
Eagle Lake, Tex., 3,565...E4   84
Eagle Pass, Tex., 12,094..E2   84
Eagle River, Wis., 1,367..C4   88
Eagleton Village, Tenn.,
    5,068................*D10   83
Eagleville, Pa., 800.....o20   81
Ealing, Eng., 183,100....k11   4
Earle, Ark., 2,391.......B5   49
Earlimart, Calif., 2,897...E4   50
Earlington, Ky., 2,786....C2   62
Earlville, Ill., 1,420....B5   58
Earlville, N.Y., 1,004....C5   75
Early, Iowa, 824.........B2   60
Early, co., Ga., 13,151...E2   55
Earth, Tex., 1,104.......B1   84
Easley, S.C., 8,283......B2   82
East, div., Ice., 9,794...*n15 11
East Alamosa, Colo., 800..D5   51
East Alliance, Ohio,
    1,275................*B5   78
East Alton, Ill., 7,630...E3   58
East Angus, Que., Can.,
    4,756.................D6   42
East Aurora, N.Y., 6,796..C2   75
East Bangor, Pa., 970....E11   81
Eastbank, W. Va., 1,023...C6   87
East Barnet, Eng., 40,599..k12   4
East Bathurst, N.B., Can.,
    1,876.................B4   43
East Baton Rouge, par.,
    La., 230,058.........D4   63

East Berlin, Pa., 1,037...G8   81
East Bernstadt, Ky., 600..C5   62
East Berwick, Pa., 1,258.*D9   81
East Bethel, Minn.,
    1,408................*E5   67
East Billerica, Mass., 900..f11 65
East Blackstone, Mass.,
    2,000.................B4   65
Eastborough, Kans.,
    1,001.................B5   61
Eastbourne, Eng., 62,000..E7   4
East Brady, Pa., 1,282....E2   81
East Brewton, Ala.,
    2,511.................D2   46
East Bridgewater, Mass.,
    3,000 (6,139▲)........B6   65
East Brookfield, Mass.,
    1,300 (1,533▲).......B3   65
East Brooklyn, Conn.,
    1,213................*B9   52
East Broughton Station,
    Que., Can., 1,136.....C6   42
East Brunswick, N.J.,
    16,000...............*C4   74
East Butler, Pa., 1,007...E2   81
East Canon, Colo., 1,101..C5   51
East Canton, Ohio,
    1,521................*B4   78
East Carroll, par., La.,
    14,433................B4   63
East Chelmsford, Mass.,
    1,000.................f10   65
Eastchester, N.Y.,
    13,000...............*E7   75
East Chicago, Ind.,
    57,669................A3   59
East Chicago Heights, Ill.,
    4,295................*B6   58
East China, sea, China....F9   17
East Cleveland, Ohio,
    37,991................g9   78

East Cleveland, Tenn.,
    1,452................*D9   83
East Conemaugh
    (Conemaugh)
    Pa., 3,334...........*E4   81
East Coulée, Alta., Can.,
    683...................D4   38
East Detroit, Mich.,
    45,756...............p16   66
East Douglas, Mass.,
    1,695.................B4   65
East Dublin, Ga., 1,667..*D4   55
East Dubuque, Ill.,
    2,312.................A3   58
East Dundee, Ill., 2,221..*A5   58
East Ely, Nev., 1,796.....D7   72
Eastern, reg., Nig.,
    12,394,462...........G6   22
Eastern Valley, Ala.,
    1,000................*E4   46
East Falmouth, Mass.,
    1,700.................C6   65
East Farmington Heights,
    Conn., 1,600.........*B6   52
East Faxon, Pa., 3,641...*D7   81
East Fayetteville, N.C.,
    2,797................*B3   76
East Feliciana, par., La.,
    20,198................D4   63
East Flanders, prov., Bel.,
    1,272,005............*B5   5
East Flat Rock, N.C.,
    1,700.................f10   76
East Gaffney, S.C.,
    4,779.................A4   82
East Gary, Ind., 9,309...A3   59
East Gastonia, N.C.,
    3,326................*B1   76
Eastgate, Wash., 3,000..*B3   86
East Glenville, N.Y.,
    8,000................*C7   75

East Grand Forks, Minn.,
    7,898.................C2   67
East Greenbush, N.Y.,
    1,325................*C7   75
East Greenville, Pa.,
    1,931................F10   81
East Greenwich, R.I.,
    8,228................C11   52
East Griffin, Ga., 1,715.*C2   55
East Ham, Eng., 105,359..k13   4
East Hampden, Maine,
    1,500................*D4   64
East Hampton, Conn.,
    3,200.................C6   52
Easthampton, Mass.,
    12,326................B2   65
East Hampton, N.Y.,
    1,772.................m16   75
East Hartford, Conn.,
    43,977................B6   52
East Haven, Conn.,
    21,388................D5   52
East Hazelcrest, Ill.,
    1,457................*B6   58
East Helena, Mont.,
    1,490.................D5   70
East Herkimer, N.Y.,
    1,068................*B6   75
East Hills, N.Y., 7,184...*E7   75
East Islip, N.Y., 11,000...G4   52
East Jordan, Mich., 1,919..C5   66
East Keansburg, N.J.,
    3,500................*C4   74
East Kildonan, Man.,
    Can., 27,305.........E3   40
East Kingsford, Mich.,
    1,063................*C2   66
Eastlake, Ohio, 12,467....A4   78
Eastland, Tex., 3,292.....C3   84
Eastland, co., Tex.,
    19,526................C3   84

East Lansdowne, Pa., 3,224............*G11 81
East Lansing, Mich., 30,198.................F6 66
Eastlawn, Mich., 2,500...*F7 66
East Liverpool, Ohio, 22,306.................B5 78
East London, S. Afr., 113,746 (*116,056).....G5 24
East Longmeadow, Mass., 10,294.................B2 65
East Los Angeles, Calif., 103,500.............m12 50
East Lothian, co., Scot., 51,900.............*C5 4
Eastman, Ga., 5,118.....D3 55
East Marion, N.C., 2,442............*f10 76
East McKeesport, Pa., 3,470.............*F2 81
East Meadow, N.Y., 47,500.............n15 75
East Millbury, Mass., 1,500.............*B4 65
East Millinocket, Maine 2,392.................C4 64
East Moline, Ill., 16,732...B3 58
East Moriches, N.Y., 1,500.................F5 52
East Naples, Fla., 2,500.....F5 54
East Newark, N.J., 1,872...k8 74
East Newnan, Ga., 500...*C2 55
East Northport, N.Y., 17,500.................F3 52
East Norwich, N.Y., 3,200.............*F2 52
East Omaha, Nebr., 684..*D3 71
Easton, Calif., 2,500...*D4 50
Easton, Maine, 400......B5 64
Easton, Md., 6,337......C5 53
Easton, Pa., 31,955......E11 81
East Orange, N.J., 77,259.............B4, h8 74
East Palatka, Fla., 1,133...C5 54
East Palestine, Ohio, 5,232.................B5 78
East Palo Alto, Calif., 12,000.............*D2 50
East Patchogue, N.Y., 8,800.................G5 52
East Paterson, N.J., 19,344.................h8 74
East Pea Ridge, W. Va., 1,500.............*C2 87
East Peoria, Ill., 12,310....C4 58
East Pepperell, Mass., 2,000.................A4 65
East Petersburg, Pa., 2,053.................F9 81
East Pines, Md., 1,800....*C4 53
East Pittsburgh, Pa., 4,122.............*k14 81
East Point, Ga., 35,633.............B5, C5 55
Eastport, Newf., Can., 438.................D5 44
Eastport, Maine, 2,537...D6 64
Eastport, N.Y., 1,200.....n16 75
East Prairie, Mo., 3,449...E8 69
East Pryor, mtn., Mont...E8 70
East Providence, R.I., 44,828.................B11 52
East Quincy, Calif., 1,020.................*C3 50
East Quogue, N.Y., 800..*n16 75
East Rainelle, W. Va., 1,244.................D4 87
East Richmond, Calif., 4,000.................*D2 50
East Ridge, Tenn., 19,570.................E10 83
East Rochester, N.Y., 8,438.................B3 75
East Rochester, Pa., 1,025.................*E1 81
East Rockaway, N.Y., 10,721.................G2 52
East Rockingham, N.C., 3,211.................C3 76
East Rockwood, Mich., 1,000.................*F7 66
East Rutherford, N.J., 7,769.................h8 74
East St. John, N.B., Can., 4,466.................D3 43
East St. Louis, Ill., 81,712.................E3 58
East Setauket, N.Y., 1,300.................F4 52
Eastside, Miss., 4,318.....E3 68
Eastside, Oreg., 1,380.....D2 80
Eastside Galesburg, Ill., 1,147.................C3 58
East Somerset, Ky., 3,645..C5 62
East Sparta, Ohio, 961....B4 78
East Spencer, N.C., 2,171..B2 76
East Spokane, Wash., 3,500.............B8, g14 86

East Stroudsburg, Pa., 7,674.................D11 81
East Sudbury, Mass., 900.................g10 65
East Syracuse, N.Y., 4,623..B4 75
East Tawas, Mich., 2,462..D7 66
East Templeton, Mass., 1,000.................A3 65
East Thomaston, Ga., 2,237.................D2 55
East Troy, Wis., 1,455.....F5 88
East Tulare, Calif., 1,342.............*D4 50
East Uniontown, Pa., 2,424.............*G2 81
East Vandergrift, Pa., 1,388.............*F2 81
Eastview, Ont., Can., 24,555.................h12 41
East View, W. Va., 1,704.............*B4 87
East Walpole, Mass., 3,000.................D2 65
East Wareham, Mass., 900.................C6 65
East Washington, Pa., 2,483.................F1 81
East Wenatchee, Wash., 383.................B5 86
East Whittier, Calif., 19,884.............*F4 50
East Williston, N.Y., 2,940.............*G2 52
East Wilmington, N.C., 5,520.............*C5 76
Eastwood, Mich., 6,000...*E5 66
East York, Pa., 1,800.....*G8 81
Eaton, Colo., 1,267......A6 51
Eaton, Ind., 1,529.......D7 59
Eaton, Ohio, 5,034.......C1 78
Eaton, co., Mich., 49,684..F6 66
Eaton Rapids, Mich., 4,052.................F6 66
Eatonton, Ga., 3,612......C3 55
Eatontown, N.J., 10,334...C4 74
Eatonville, Wash., 896....C3 86
Eau Claire, Wis., 37,987..D2 88
Eau Claire, co., Wis., 58,300.................D2 88
Eau Gallie, Fla., 12,300...D6 54
Ebensburg, Pa., 4,111.....F4 81
Eberswalde, Ger., 32,100..B6 6
Ebetsu, Jap., 29,800 (44,510▲).............E10 18
Ebingen, Ger., 21,100.....D4 6
Eboli, It., 20,500.........D5 9
Eccles, W. Va., 1,145.................D3, D6 87
Eceabat (Maydos), Tur., 2,800.............*B6 14
Echert, Colo., 1,021......C3 51
Echigawa, Jap., 3,200....n15 18
Echols, co., Ga., 1,876....F4 55
Echuca, Austl., 7,046.....E9 25
Écija, Sp., 29,262........D3 8
Eckernförde, Ger., 19,500..A4 6
Eckhart Mines, Md., 1,100.................k13 53
Eckman, W. Va., 1,125...D3 87
Eclectic, Ala., 926.......C3 46
Economy, Pa., 5,925.....*E1 81
Ecorse, Mich., 17,328....p15 66
Ector, co., Tex., 90,995...D1 84
Ecuador, country, S.A., 5,326,000.............31
Edcouch, Tex., 2,814.....F4 84
Ed Damer, Sud., 5,458....E4 23
Eddiceton, Miss., 300.....D3 68
Ed Dueim, Sud., 12,319...F4 23
Eddy, co., N. Mex., 50,783.................C6 48
Eddy, co., N. Dak., 4,936..C7 77
Eddystone, Pa., 3,006....p20 81
Eddyville, Iowa, 1,014....C5 60
Eddyville, Ky., 1,858.....A3 62
Ede, Neth., 31,800.......A6 5
Edea, Cam., 11,000.......H7 22
Eden, N.Y., 2,400.......C2 75
Eden, Tex., 1,486.......D3 84
Edenborn, Pa., 800.......G2 81
Edenton, N.C., 4,458.....A6 76
Edgar, Wis., 803.........D4 88
Edgar, co., Ill., 22,550.....D6 58
Edgartown, Mass., 1,200 (1,474▲).............D6 65
Edgecombe, co., N.C., 54,226.................B5 76
Edgefield, S.C., 2,876....D4 82
Edgefield, co., S.C., 15,735.................D3 82
Edgeley, N. Dak., 992....D7 77
Edgely, Pa., 950........*F11 81
Edgemere, Md., 2,200...*B5 53
Edgemont, Calif., 1,628...*F5 50
Edgemont, Colo., 4,314...*B5 51
Edgemont, S. Dak., 1,772..G2 77
Edgerton, Minn., 1,019...G2 67
Edgerton, Ohio, 1,566....A1 78

Edgerton, Wis., 4,000.....F4 88
Edgewater, Ala., 1,800....E4 46
Edgewater, Colo., 4,314...B5 51
Edgewater, Fla., 2,051....D6 54
Edgewater, Md., 300......C4 53
Edgewater, N.J., 4,113....h9 74
Edgewater Park, Miss., 750.................E2 68
Edgewater Park, N.J., 2,866.................C3 74
Edgewood, Ind., 11,500...m10 59
Edgewood, Ind., 2,119....D6 59
Edgewood, Ky., 100......A7 62
Edgewood, Md., 3,100....B5 53
Edgewood, Ohio, 5,000....A5 78
Edgewood, Pa., 5,124....k14 81
Edgewood, Pa., 3,399....*D8 81
Edgeworth, Pa., 2,030...h13 81
Edhessa, Grc., 15,534....B4 14
Edina, Minn., 35,302....n12 67
Edina, Mo., 1,457.......A5 69
Edinboro, Pa., 1,703.....C1 98
Edinburg, Ill., 1,003.....D4 58
Edinburg, Ind., 3,664.....F6 59
Edinburg, Miss., 200.....C4 68
Edinburg, Tex., 18,706...F3 84
Edinburgh, Scot., 476,200..C5 4
Edirne, Tur., 39,410......B6 14
Edison, Ga., 1,232.......E2 55
Edison, N.J., 9,500......B4 74
Edisto Island, S.C., 30.................F7, k11 82
Edith, mtn., Mont.......D5 70
Edmeston, N.Y., 800.....C5 75
Edmond, Okla., 8,577....B4 79
Edmonds, Wash., 8,016...B3 86
Edmonson, co., Ky., 8,085.................C3 62
Edmonston, Md., 1,197..*C4 53
Edmonton, Alta., Can., 281,027 (*337,568).......C4, g8 38
Edmonton, Eng., 92,062..K12 4
Edmore, Mich., 1,234.....E5 66
Edmunds, co., S. Dak., 6,079.................E6 77
Edmundson, Mo., 1,428..*C7 69
Edmundston, N.B., Can., 12,791.................B1 43
Edna, Tex., 5,038.......E4 84
Edremit, Tur., 22,388....*C6 14
Edson, Alta., Can., 3,198.................C7, g7 38
Edwards, Miss., 1,206....C3 68
Edwards, co., Ill., 7,940....E5 58
Edwards, co., Kans., 5,118.................E4 61
Edwards, co., Tex., 2,317..E2 84
Edwardsburg, Mich., 902..G4 66
Edwardsville, Ill., 9,996...E4 58
Edwardsville, Pa., 5,711..n17 81
Edwight, W. Va., 70.....D6 87
Eferding, Aus., 3,151.....D7 6
Effingham, Ill., 8,172.....D5 58
Effingham, co., Ga., 10,144.................D5 55
Effingham, co., Ill., 23,107.................D5 58
Eganville, Ont., Can., 1,549.................B7 41
Eger, Hung., 35,375......B5 10
Egg Harbor City, N.J., 4,416.................D3 74
Egmont, mtn., N.Z......M15 26
Egypt, Mass., 1,300...B6, h12 65
Egypt, Pa., 1,500.......E10 81
Egypt, see United Arab Republic, country, Afr.
Ehime, pref., Jap., 1,446,384.............*J6 18
Ehrenfeld, Pa., 566.......F4 81
Éibar, Sp., 31,725.......A4 8
Eichstätt, Ger., 10,600....D5 6
Eidsberg, Nor., 233..H4, p29 11
Eidsvoll, Nor., 1,410.....G4 11
Eilenburg, Ger., 19,400...C6 6
Einbeck, Ger., 18,600....C4 6
Eindhoven, Neth., 175,000.................B6 5
Eire, see Ireland, country, Eur.
Eisenach, Ger., 47,600....C5 6
Eisenhüttenstadt, Ger., 34,600.................B7 6
Eisleben, Ger., 34,500....C5 6
Ekalaka, Mont., 738.....E12 70
Eksjö, Swe., 10,100......I6 11
El Arahal, Sp., 17,361....D3 8
El Asnam (Orléansville), Alg., 44,650.............A5 22
Elazig, Tur., 60,289......C12 14
Elba, Ala., 4,321........D3 46
El Banco, Col., 14,889....B3 32
El Barco, Sp., 7,041......A2 8
Elbasan, Alb., 29,787....B3 14
Elbasan, pref., Alb., 115,000.............*B3 14
Elbe, (Labe), riv., Eur.....B5 6

Elbert, Colo., 250........B4 51
Elbert, W. Va., 950......D3 87
Elbert, co., Colo., 3,708...B6 51
Elbert, co., Ga., 17,835...B4 55
Elberton, Ga., 7,107.....B4 55
Elbeuf, Fr., 18,988.......C4 5
Elbing, see Elblag, Pol.
Elbistan, Tur., 10,282....C11 14
Elblag, Pol., 83,200......A5 7
El Bonillo, Sp., 5,286....C4 8
El Bordo, Col., 1,475.....C2 32
Elbow Lake, Minn., 1,521..E3 67
Elbrus, mtn., Sov. Un.....E7 13
Elburn, Ill., 960.........B5 58
El Cajon, Calif., 37,618.............F5, o16 50
El Campo, Tex., 7,700....E4 84
El Campo North, Tex., 1,086.............*E4 84
El Campo South, Tex., 1,884.............*E4 84
El Capitan, mtn., Mont...D2 70
El Carmen, Col., 19,196..B2 32
El Carrizo (Carrizo), Mex., 149.............B3 34
El Centro, Calif., 19,280..F6 50
El Cerrito, Calif., 25,437..h8 50
El Cocuy, Col., 2,869.....B3 32
Elda, Sp., 28,151........C5 8
Eldon, Iowa, 1,386.......D5 60
Eldon, Mo., 3,158.......C5 69
Eldora, Iowa, 3,225......B4 60
El Dorado, Ark., 25,292...D3 49
Eldorado, Ill., 3,573.....F5 58
El Dorado, Kans., 12,523.............E7, g13 61
Eldorado, Mex., 6,423....C3 34
Eldorado, Tex., 1,815.....D2 84
El Dorado, co., Calif., 43,805.................C3 50
Eldorado, peak, Wash.....A4 86
El Dorado Springs, Mo., 2,864.................D3 69
Eldoret, Ken., 19,605.....H5 23
Eldred, Pa., 1,107.......C5 81
Eldridge, Iowa, 842...C7, g10 60
Eleanor, W. Va., 700.....C3 87
Electra, Tex., 4,759......C3 84
Electric, peak, Mont......D6 70
Eleele, Haw., 617........B2 56
Elephant, mtn., Maine....D2 64
Elevsís (Eleusis), Grc., 15,527.............*C4 14
El Fasher, Sud., 26,161...F3 23
El Ferrol, Sp., 74,799.....A1 8
El Fuerte, Mex., 5,331....B3 34
Elgin, Ill., 49,447.....A5, h8 58
Elgin, Iowa, 644........B6 60
Elgin, N. Dak., 944.......D4 77
Elgin, Oreg., 1,315......B9 80
Elgin, Scot., 12,300......B5 4
Elgin, Tex., 3,511.......D4 84
Elgin, co., Ont., Can., 62,862.................E3 41
Elgon, mtn., Ken., Ug.....H4 23
El Grullo, Mex., 9,105....n11 34
El Hasheisa, Sud., 6,600..F4 23
Elida, Ohio, 1,215.......B1 78
Elim, Pa., 1,000........*E4 81
Eliot, Maine, 2,500......E2 64
Elizabeth, Austl., 32,948..F6 25
Elizabeth, Ga., 1,620..A4, C2 55
Elizabeth, La., 1,030.....D3 63
Elizabeth, N.J., 107,698.............B4, k8 74
Elizabeth, Pa., 2,597....*E1 81
Elizabeth City, N.C., 14,062.................A6 76
Elizabeth Lake Estates, Mich., 3,000.........*F7 66
Elizabethton, Tenn., 10,896.................C11 83
Elizabethtown, Ky., 9,641.................C4 62
Elizabethtown, N.C., 1,486.................C4 76
Elizabethtown, Pa., 6,780..F8 81
Elizabethville, Pa., 1,455..E8 81
El Jadida, Mor., 40,302...B3 22
Elk, Pol., 23,500........B7 7
Elk, co., Kans., 5,048.....E7 61
Elk, co., Pa., 37,328.....D4 81
Elk, mtn., Wyo..........E6 89
Elk, peak, Mont.........D6 70
Elkader, Iowa, 1,526.....B6 60
Elk City, Okla., 8,196.....B2 79
Elk Grove, Calif., 2,800...C3 50
Elk Grove Village, Ill., 13,155.................h9 58
Elkhart, Ind., 40,274.....A6 59
Elkhart, Kans., 1,780.....E2 61
Elkhart, co., Ind., 106,790.................A6 59
Elkhorn, W. Va., 900....D3 87
Elkhorn, Wis., 3,586.....F5 88
Elkhorn City, Ky., 1,085...C7 62
Elkhovo, Bul., 6,749.....D8 10
Elkin, N.C., 2,868.......A2 76

Elkins, W. Va., 8,307.....C5　87
Elkins Park, Pa., 10,500...o21　81
Elkland, Pa., 2,189.......C7　81
Elk Mountain, N.C.,
　1,000.................f10　76
Elko, Nev., 6,298.........A4　72
Elko, co., Nev., 12,011...A4　72
Elk Point, S. Dak., 1,378..H9　77
Elk Rapids, Mich., 1,015...D5　66
Elkridge, Md., 2,000..B4, h10　53
Elkridge, W. Va., 250....D6　87
Elk River, Idaho, 382.....C2　57
Elk River, Minn., 1,763...E5　67
Elk Run Heights, Iowa,
　1,124................*B5　60
Elkton, Ky., 1,448........D2　62
Elkton, Md., 5,989........A6　53
Elkton, Mich., 1,014......E7　66
Elkton, Va., 1,506........B4　85
Elkville, Ill., 743........F4　58
Ellaville, Ga., 905........D2　55
Ellendale, N. Dak., 1,800..E7　77
Ellensburg, Wash., 8,625...C5　86
Ellenton, Fla., 950...E4, p10　54
Ellenville, N.Y., 5,003....D6　75
Ellerbe, N.C., 847........B3　76
Ellesmere, isl., N.W. Ter.,
　Can.................k34　36
Ellettsville, Ind., 1,222...F4　59
Ellicott City, Md., 2,000..B4　53
Ellicottville, N.Y., 1,150..C2　75
Ellijay, Ga., 1,320.......B2　55
Ellington, Mo., 812.......D7　69
Ellinwood, Kans., 2,729...D5　61
Elliott, co., Ky., 6,330....B6　62
Ellis, Kans., 2,218.......D4　61
Ellis, co., Kans., 21,270...D4　61
Ellis, co., Okla., 5,457...A2　79
Ellis, co., Tex., 43,395...C4　84
Ellisville, Miss., 4,592...D4　68
Ellisville, Mo., 2,732....f12　69
Ellon, Scot., 1,500.......B5　4
Elloree, S. C., 1,031......D6　82
Ellport, Pa., 1,458.......E1　81
Ellsworth, Kans., 2,361...D5　61
Ellsworth, Maine, 4,444...D4　64
Ellsworth, Pa., 1,456.....F1　81
Ellsworth, Wis., 1,701....D1　88
Ellsworth, co., Kans.,
　7,677................D5　61
Ellwangen, Ger., 12,500...D5　6
Ellwood City, Pa., 12,413..E1　81
Elma, N.Y., 1,000.......*C2　75
Elma, Wash., 1,811.......C2　86
Elmcrest, Mich., 1,000...*E7　66
Elmali, Tur., 7,800......*D7　14
Elmer, N.J., 1,505.......D2　74
Elm Grove, Wis., 4,994..*m11　88
Elmhurst, Ill., 40,329..B6, k9　58
Elmira, Ont., Can., 3,337..D4　41
Elmira, N.Y., 46,517......C4　75
El Mirage, Ariz., 3,258....D1　48
Elmira Heights, N.Y.,
　5,105................C4　75
El Modeno, Calif., 1,000..*F5　50
Elmont, N.Y., 36,500....*G2　52
El Monte, Calif., 13,163..*E4　50
El Monte, Calif., 4,186...*B5　50
Elmora (Bakerton), Pa.,
　1,057................E4　81
Elmore, Minn., 1,078.....G4　67
Elmore, Ohio, 1,302......A2　78
Elmore, co., Ala., 30,524..C3　46
Elmore, co., Idaho,
　16,719...............F3　57
Elmore City, Okla., 982...C4　79
Elmsford, N.Y., 4,031....g13　75
Elmshorn, Ger., 35,000...B4　6
Elmwood, Ill., 1,882......C4　58
Elmwood Park, Ill.,
　23,866...............k9　58
Elmwood Place, Ohio,
　3,813................o13　78
El Nevado, mtn., Col......C3　32
Elnora, Ind., 824.........G3　59
El Obeid, Sud., 59,000....F4　23
Eloise, Fla., 3,256.......E5　54
Elon College, N.C., 1,284..A3　76
Elora, Ont., Can., 1,486...D4　41
El Oro, prov., Ec.,
　160,650..............B2　31
Eloy, Ariz., 4,899........C3　48
El Paso, Ill., 1,964......C4　58
El Paso, Tex., 312,000
　(*348,000)...........o11　84
El Paso, co., Colo.,
　143,742..............C6　51
El Paso, co., Tex.,
　314,070..............o11　84
El Portal, Fla., 2,079....s13　54
El Porto Beach, Calif.,
　1,200...............*F4　50
El Puerto de Santa María,
　Sp., 35,505..........D2　8
Elrama, Pa., 800.........F2　81
El Reno, Okla., 11,015....B4　79
El Rio, Calif., 7,800......E4　50
Elroy, Wis., 1,505.......E3　88

Elsa, Tex., 3,847.........F3　84
El Salto, Mex., 6,947.....C3　34
El Salvador, country, N.A.,
　2,928,000............E7　34
Elsberry, Mo., 1,491......B6　69
El Segundo, Calif.,
　14,219..............*F4　50
El Seibo, Dom. Rep.,
　4,970................E9　35
Elsie, Mich., 933.........E6　66
Elsinore, Calif., 2,432....F5　50
Elsmere, Del., 7,319......A6　53
Elsmere, Ky., 4,607...A7, B5　62
El Sobrante, Calif.,
　15,000..............*D2　50
Elsterwerda, Ger., 9,749..C6　6
El Tigre, Ven., 41,961....B5　32
El Tocuyo, Ven., 14,560...B4　32
Elton, La., 1,595.........D3　63
Elvas, Port., 11,742......C2　8
El Verano, Calif., 1,236..*C2　50
Elverum, Nor., 3,595.....G4　11
El Viejo, mtn., Col.......B3　32
Elvins, Mo., 1,818.......D7　69
El Vista, Ill., 2,000.....*C4　58
Elwood, Ind., 11,793......D6　59
Elwood, Kans., 1,191......C9　61
Elwood, N.Y., 8,000......n15　75
Elwyn, Pa., 1,500.......*G11　81
Ely, Eng., 9,900.........D7　4
Ely, Minn., 5,438........C7　67
Ely, Nev., 4,018.........B4　72
Elyria, Ohio, 43,782......A3　78
Elysburg, Pa., 1,100......E8　81
Emanuel, co., Ga., 17,815..D4　55
Embetsu, Jap., 29,800....D10　18
Embrun, Ont., Can.,
　1,112................B9　41
Emden, Ger., 46,000......B3　6
Emerson, Man., Can.,
　932.................E3　40
Emerson, Nebr., 803......B9　71
Emerson, N.J., 6,849.....H8　74
Emery, co., Utah, 5,546...B6　72
Emeryville, Calif.,
　2,686...............*D3　50
Emi Koussi, vol., Chad....E1　23
Emilia, reg., It..........B3　9
Emilia-Romagna, pol. dist.,
　It., 3,666,680.........B3　9
Emiliano-Zapata, Mex.,
　3,751................D6　34
Eminence, Ky., 1,958.....B4　62
Emirdag, Tur., 10,069....C8　14
Emlenton, Pa., 844.......D2　81
Emmaus, Pa., 10,262.....E11　81
Emmen, Neth., 17,900.....A7　5
Emmerald, Austl., 2,188...D8　25
Emmerich, Ger., 16,800...C3　6
Emmet, co., Iowa, 14,871..A3　60
Emmet, co., Mich.,
　15,904...............C6　66
Emmetsburg, Iowa, 3,824..A3　60
Emmett, Idaho, 3,769.....F2　57
Emmitsburg, Md., 1,369...A3　53
Emmons, co., N. Dak.,
　8,462................D5　77
Emory University, Ga.,
　7,000...............*B5　55
Empire, Calif., 1,635....*D3　50
Empire, La., 450.........E6　63
Empire, Nev., 650........A2　72
Empire, Oreg., 3,781.....D2　80
Empoli, It., 28,500......C3　9
Emporia, Kans., 18,190...D7　61
Emporia, Va., 5,535......D5　85
Emporium, Pa., 3,397.....D5　81
Emsdetten, Ger., 25,000...B3　6
Emsworth, Pa., 3,341.....h13　81
Ena, Jap., 16,000.......n16　18
Encarnación, Arg., 18,500..E4　29
Encarnación de Díaz,
　Mex., 8,710..........m12　34
Encinal, Tex., 900.......E3　84
Encinitas, Calif., 5,000...F5　50
Ende, Indon., 7,226......G6　19
Enderby, B.C., Can.,
　1,075................D8　37
Enderlin, N. Dak., 1,596...D8　77
Endicott, N.Y., 17,473....C4　75
Endwell, N.Y., 14,000...*C4　75
Enfield, Conn., 3,100.....B6　52
Enfield, Eng., 109,600...k12　4
Enfield, Ill., 791........E5　58
Enfield, N.H., 1,100......D3　73
Enfield, N.C., 2,978......A5　76
Engaru, Jap., 13,400....D11　18
Engels, Sov. Un.,
　106,000..............F16　12
Enghien, Fr., 12,504....g10　5
England, Ark., 2,861..C4, E6　49
England, reg., U.K.,
　41,572,585...........D6　4
Englee, Newf., Can.,
　802...............C3, h10　44
Englewood, Colo., 33,398..B6　51
Englewood, Fla., 5,000...*B5　54
Englewood, Fla., 2,877....F4　54

Englewood, Ind., 1,232...*G5　59
Englewood, N.J., 26,057...h9　74
Englewood, Ohio, 1,515...C1　78
Englewood, Oreg., 1,382..*D2　80
Englewood, Tenn., 1,574..D9　83
Englewood Cliffs, N.J.,
　2,913...............*B5　74
Englishtown, N.J., 1,143...C4　74
Enguera, Sp., 5,663......C5　8
Enhaut, Pa., 2,000......*F8　81
Enid, Okla., 38,859......A4　79
Enka, N.C., 950.........f10　76
Enköping, Swe.,
　13,200.............H7, t35　11
Enna, It., 28,600........F5　9
En Nahud, Sud., 16,499...F3　23
Ennis, Ire., 5,800........D2　4
Ennis, Tex., 9,347....C4, n10　84
Enniscorthy, Ire., 5,800...D3　4
Enniskillen, N. Ire., 7,438..C3　4
Enns, Aus., 8,919........D7　6
Enola, Pa., 5,000........F8　81
Enon, Ohio, 1,227.......C2　78
Enoree, S.C., 825........B4　82
Enosberg Falls, Vt., 1,321..B2　73
Enriquillo, Dom. Rep.,
　3,610................F8　35
Enschede, Neth., 131,800..A7　5
Ensenada, Arg., 24,925...g8　28
Ensenada, Mex., 42,561...A1　34
Ensenada, P.R., 3,299...G11　35
Ensley, Fla., 1,836......u14　54
Entebbe, Ug., 10,941.....H4　23
Enterprise, Calif., 4,946..*B2　50
Enterprise, Kans., 1,015...D6　61
Enterprise, Oreg., 1,932...B9　80
Entiat, mts., Wash.......B5　86
Entre Minho e Douro, reg.,
　Port., 2,067,884.......B1　8
Entre Ríos, prov., Arg.,
　803,505...........A5, f7　28
Enugu, Nig., 138,457....G6　22
Enumclaw, Wash.,
　3,269.............B4, f12　86
Enzan, Jap., 14,800.....n17　18
Épernay, Fr., 21,882.....C5　5
Ephraim, Utah, 1,801.....B6　72
Ephrata, Pa., 7,688......F9　81
Ephrata, Wash., 6,548....B6　86
Épila, Sp., 5,072........B5　8
Epileptic Village, Ind.,..*E7　59
Épinal, Fr., 30,313......C7　5
Épinay [-sur-Seine], Fr.,
　34,167..............g10　5
Epirus, reg., Grc........*C3　14
Epping, Eng., 10,100....k13　4
Epping, N.H., 980.......E5　73
Epsom (& Ewell) Eng.,
　70,700..............m12　4
Epworth, Iowa, 1,173....B7　60
Equatorial Guinea,
　Sp. dep., Afr.,
　245,989.............H6　22
Erath, La., 2,019........E3　63
Erath, co., Tex., 16,236...C3　84
Ercis, Tur., 9,927......C14　14
Erciyas, mtn., Tur.......C10　14
Érd, Hung., 23,177......B4　10
Erdek, Tur., 6,700......*B6　14
Erdenheim, Pa., 3,700...o21　81
Erding, Ger., 11,300.....D5　6
Eregli, Tur., 6,360......B8　14
Eregli, Tur., 31,935.....D10　14
Erfurt, Ger., 188,500....C5　6
Erice, It., 18,021.......E4　9
Erick, Okla., 1,342......B2　79
Erickson, B.C., Can., 912..E9　37
Erie, Colo., 875.........A5　51
Erie, Ill., 1,215........B3　58
Erie, Kans., 1,309.......E8　61
Erie, Pa., 135,000
　(*222,000)...........B1　81
Erie, co., N.Y., 1,087,183..C2　75
Erie, co., Ohio, 68,000...A3　78
Erie, co., Pa., 250,682...C1　81
Erie, lake, Can., U.S.....B10　45
Erin, Tenn., 1,097.......A4　83
Eritrea, prov., Eth.......E5　23
Erlangen, Ger., 74,200...D5　6
Erlanger, Ky., 7,072..A5, A7　62
Erlton, N.J., 1,000.....*D6　74
Ermenek, Tur., 7,553....D6　14
Ermont, Fr., 19,263....g10　5
Ernest, Pa., 950.........E3　81
Errigal, mtn., Ire........C2　4
Errol Heights, Oreg.,
　10,000.............*B4　80
Erstein, Fr., 6,165......C7　5
Erwin, N.C., 3,200......B4　76
Erwin, Tenn., 3,210....C11　83
Erzincan (Erzinjan), Tur.,
　36,420.............C12　14
Erzurum, Tur., 90,069...C13　14
Esashi, Jap., 8,500.....D11　18
Esashi, Jap., 5,200.....F10　18
Esbjerg, Den., 55,171....J3　11

Escada, Braz., 13,761...*D7　27
Escalante, Utah, 702.....C6　72
Escalón, Calif., 1,763....D3　50
Escalón, Mex., 1,227.....B4　34
Escambia, co., Ala.,
　33,511..............D2　46
Escambia, co., Fla.,
　173,829.............u14　54
Escanaba, Mich., 15,391..C3　66
Escatawpa, Miss.,
　1,464.............E3, E5　68
Esch-sur-Alzette, Lux.,
　27,954..............C7　5
Eschwege, Ger., 24,100...C5　6
Eschweiler, Ger., 40,200..C3　6
Escondido, Calif., 16,377..F5　50
Escoublac-La-Baule, Fr.,
　13,004..............D2　5
Escuinapa [de Hidalgo],
　Mex., 9,920..........C3　34
Escuintla, Guat., 9,760..*E6　34
Eṣfahān (Isfahān), Iran,
　254,708.............B8　23
Esher, Eng., 61,000.....m12　4
Eskdale, W. Va.,
　800..............C3, D6　87
Eskilstuna, Swe.,
　60,300...........H7, t34　11
Eskişehir, Tur., 153,096...C8　14
Esmeralda, co., Nev., 619..C3　72
Esmeraldas, Ec., 33,403..A2　31
Esmeraldas, prov., Ec.,
　124,881.............A2　31
Esmond, R.I., 4,500.....B10　52
Espanola, Ont., Can.,
　5,353...............A3　41
Espanola, N. Mex., 1,976..B5　48
Esperanza, Arg., 10,035...A4　28
Espinal, Col., 22,791....C3　32
Espírito Santo, Braz.,
　31,027..............C4　30
Espírito Santo, state, Braz.,
　1,188,665...........C4　30
Espita, Mex., 5,161......C7　34
Espy, Pa., 1,375........D9　81
Esquel, Arg., 9,900......C2　28
Esquimalt, B.C., Can.,
　12,048...........E6, h12　37
Essaouria (Mogador), Mor.,
　26,392..............B3　22
Essen, Ger., 728,800....C3　6
Essendon, mtn., Austl....D3　25
Essex, Ont., Can., 3,428..E2　41
Essex, Conn., 1,600......D7　52
Essex, Md., 38,000......B5　52
Essex, co., Ont., Can.,
　258,218.............E2　41
Essex, co., Eng.,
　1,170,000..........*E7　41
Essex, Md., 38,000......B5　53
Essex, co., Mass., 568,831..A5　65
Essex, co., N.J., 923,545..B4　74
Essex, co., N.Y., 35,300...B4　75
Essex, co., Vt., 6,083....B4　73
Essex, co., Va., 6,690....C6　85
Essex Fells, N.J., 2,174..*B4　74
Essex Junction, Vt., 5,340..C1　73
Essexville, Mich., 4,590...E7　66
Essington, Pa., 3,300...*G11　81
Esslingen, Ger., 82,900...D4　6
Estacada, Oreg., 957.....B4　80
Estância, Braz., 16,106..*E7　27
Estancia, N. Mex., 797...B5　48
Este, It., 10,600........B3　9
Esteli, Nic., 12,700......E7　34
Estepa, Sp., 9,476......D3　8
Esterhazy, Sask., Can.,
　1,114...............G4　39
Estes Park, Colo., 1,175..A5　51
Estevan, Sask., Can.,
　7,728...............H4　39
Esther, Mo., 1,033.....*D7　69
Estherville, Iowa, 8,092...A3　60
Estill, S.C., 1,865.......F5　82
Estill, co., Ky., 12,466....C6　62
Eston, Sask., Can., 1,695..F1　39
Estonia (S.S.R.), rep.,
　Sov. Un., 1,244,000...B5　12
Estremadura, prov., Port.,
　1,592,858..........*C1　8
Estremadura, reg., Port.,
　2,626,352..........*C1　8
Estremoz, Port., 7,057...C2　8
Esztergom, Hung., 24,700..B4　10
Étampes, Fr., 13,515.....C5　5
Étaples, Fr., 8,628......B4　5
Etawah, India, 59,986....C6　20
Ethel, W. Va., 650......D5　87
Ethiopia (Abyssinia),
　country, Afr.,
　2,300,000...........G5　23
Etna, Pa., 5,519........k14　81
Etna, vol., It...........F5　9
Etowah, Tenn., 3,223....D9　83
Etowah, co., Ala., 96,980..A3　46
Ettrick, Va., 3,200...C5, n18　85
Etzatlan, Mex., 8,796....m11　34

Eu, Fr., 7,029 . . . . B4　5
Euclid, Ohio, 62,998 . . . A4, g9　78
Euclid Center, Mich.,
　2,343 . . . . *F4　66
Euclid Heights, Ark.,
　2,030 . . . . *C2　49
Eudora, Ark., 3,598 . . . . . . D4　49
Eudora, Kans.,
　1,526 . . . . D8, m15　61
Eufaula, Ala., 8,357 . . . . . D4　46
Eufaula, Okla., 2,382 . . . . . B6　79
Eugene, Oreg., 78,000
　(*158,000) . . . . C3　80
Euless, Tex., 2,062 . . . . . . *C4　84
Eunice, La., 11,326 . . . . D3　63
Eunice, N. Mex., 3,531 . . . . C7　48
Eupen, Bel., 14,445 . . . . B7　5
Euphrates, see Firat, Asia
Eupora, Miss., 1,468 . . . . . B4　68
Eure, dept., Fr., 361,904 . . *C4　5
Eure-et-Loir, dept., Fr.,
　277,546 . . . . *C4　5
Eureka, Calif., 28,137 . . . . B1　50
Eureka, Ill., 2,538 . . . . C4　58
Eureka, Kans., 4,055 . . . . . . E7　61

Eureka, Mo., 1,134 . . . . . . f12　69
Eureka, Mont., 1,229 . . . . . . B1　70
Eureka, S. Dak., 1,555 . . . . E6　77
Eureka, Utah, 771 . . . . B5　72
Eureka, co., Nev., 767 . . . . . B3　72
Eureka Springs, Ark.,
　1,681 . . . . A2　49
Europe, cont.,
　601,900,000 3
Euskirchen, Ger., 20,300 . . . C3　5
Eustis, Fla., 6,189 . . . . D5　54
Eutaw, Ala., 2,784 . . . . C2　46
Evangeline, La., 800 . . . . . . D3　63
Evangeline, par., La.,
　31,639 . . . . D3　63
Evans, Colo., 1,453 . . . . . . A6　51
Evans, co., Ga., 6,952 . . . . D5　55
Evans, mtn., Colo. . . . . B5　51
Evans City (Evansburg),
　Pa., 1,825 . . . . E1　81
Evansdale, Iowa, 5,738 . . . . B5　60
Evanston, Ill., 79,283 . . A6, h9　58
Evanston, Wyo., 4,901 . . . . . E2　89
Evansville, Ill., 846 . . . . . . E4　58
Evansville, Ind., 144,463 . . . I2　59

Evansville, Wis., 2,858 . . . . . F4　88
Evart, Mich., 1,775 . . . . E5　66
Evarts, Ky., 1,473 . . . . D6　62
Eveleth, Minn., 5,721 . . . . . C6　67
Even Yehuda, Isr.,
　52,49 . . . . *B2　15
Everard, mtn., B.C. . . . . D5　37
Everest, peak, China, Nep. . C8　20
Everett, Mass., 43,544 . . . . g11　65
Everett, Pa., 2,279 . . . . F5　81
Everett, Wash., 40,304 . . . . B3　86
Everett, mtn., Mass. . . . . . . B1　65
Everglades, Fla., 552 . . . . . G5　54
Evergreen, Ala., 3,703 . . . . D3　46
Evergreen Park, Ill.,
　25,284 . . . . k9　58
Everman, Tex., 1,076 . . . . *C4　84
Everson, Pa., 1,304 . . . . F2　81
Évora, Port., 24,144 . . . . . . C2　8
Évreux, Fr., 23,647 . . . . . . C4　5
Évros, prov., Grc.,
　157,760 . . . . *B5　14
Évvoia (Euboea), prov.,
　Grc., 166,097 . . . . *C4　14

Ewa, Haw., 2,500 . . . . . B3, g9　56
Ewa Beach, Haw.,
　6,500 . . . . g9　56
Ewing, Va., 500 . . . . f8　85
Ewing Township, N.J.,
　26,628 . . . . *C3　74
Excelsior, Minn.,
　2,020 . . . . F5, n11　67
Excelsior, mtn., Cal. . . . . . . C4　50
Excelsior Springs, Mo.,
　6,473 . . . . B3, h11　69
Exeter, Calif., 4,264 . . . . . . D4　50
Exeter, Ont., Can., 3,047 . . D3　41
Exeter, Eng., 79,700 . . . . . . E5　4
Exeter, N.H., 7,243 . . . . F6　73
Exeter, Pa., 4,747 . . . D10, n17　81
Exira, Iowa, 1,111 . . . . C3　60
Exmore, Va., 1,566 . . . . C7　85
Exmouth, Eng., 20,300 . . . . E5　4
Experiment, Ga., 2,000 . . . . C2　55
Export, Pa., 1,518 . . . . F2　81
Eyemouth, Scot., 2,100 . . . . C5　4
Eylar, mtn., Calif. . . . . D3　50
Eyre, lake, Austl. . . . . E6　25
Ezine, Tur., 7,536 . . . . C6　14

F

Fabens, Tex., 3,200 . . . . o11　84
Fabriano, It., 12,700 . . . . . . C4　9
Facatativá Col., 20,742 . . . . C3　32
Factoryville, Pa., 991 . . . . . C10　81
Fada-N'Gourma, Upper
　Volta, 5,200 . . . . F5　22
Faenza, It., 27,200 . . . . B3　9
Faeroe Islands, Dan. dep.,
　Eur., 34,596 . . . . C6　3
Fafe, Port., 5,855 . . . . B1　8
Făgăraș, Rom., 17,256 . . . . . C7　10
Fagatogo, Am. Sam.,
　1,344 . . . . *G9　2
Fagersta, Swe., 15,500 . . . . . G6　11
Faifo, Viet., 5,000 . . . . *B3　19
Fairbank, Iowa, 650 . . . . . . B5　60
Fairbanks, Alsk., 13,311 . . C10　47
Fair Bluff, N.C., 1,030 . . . . C3　76
Fairborn, Ohio, 19,453 . . . . C1　78
Fairburn, Ga., 2,470 . . B4, C2　55
Fairbury, Ill., 2,937 . . . . . . C5　58
Fairbury, Nebr., 5,572 . . . . D8　71
Fairchance, Pa., 2,120 . . . . G2　81
Fairdale, Kans.,
　2,100 . . . . C8, k16　61
Fairdale, Ky., 4,000 . . . . . . A4　62
Fairfax, Ala., 3,107 . . . . . . C4　46
Fairfax, Calif., 5,813 . . C2, h7　50
Fairfax, Del., 1,000 . . . . . . *A6　53
Fairfax, Iowa, 642 . . . . C6　60
Fairfax, Minn., 1,498 . . . . . F4　67
Fairfax, Mo., 736 . . . . A2　69
Fairfax, Ohio, 2,430 . . . . . . *C1　78
Fairfax, Okla., 2,076 . . . . . A5　79
Fairfax, S.C., 1,814 . . . . . . F5　82
Fairfax (Independent City),
　Va., 13,585 . . . . B5, g12　85
Fairfax, co., Va., 262,482 . . B5　85
Fairfield, Ala., 50 . . . . B3, E4　46
Fairfield, Calif., 14,968 . . . C2　50
Fairfield, Conn., 46,183 . . . E3　52
Fairfield, Ill., 6,362 . . . . . . E5　58
Fairfield, Iowa, 11,587 . . . . D6　60
Fairfield, Maine, 3,766,
　(5,829 ▲) . . . . D3　64
Fairfield, Mont., 752 . . . . . C5　70
Fairfield, N.J., 3,310 . . . . *B4　74
Fairfield, Ohio, 9,734 . . . . n12　78
Fairfield, Oreg., 2,000 . . . *C3　80
Fairfield, Tex., 1,781 . . . . . D4　84
Fairfield, co., Conn.,
　653,589 . . . . D3　52
Fairfield, co., Ohio,
　63,912 . . . . C3　78
Fairfield, co., S.C., 20,713 . . C5　82
Fairfield Highlands, Ala.,
　5,000 . . . . *B3　46
Fairgrove, Mich., 609 . . . . . E7　66
Fair Grove, N.C., 1,500 . . . *B2　76
Fairhaven, Mass., 14,339 . . C6　65
Fair Haven, Mich., 225 . . . . F8　66
Fair Haven, N.J., 5,678 . . . C4　74
Fair Haven, N.Y., 764 . . . . B4　75
Fair Haven, Vt., 2,378 . . . . D1　73
Fairhope, Ala., 4,858 . . . . . E2　46
Fairhope, Pa., 1,700 . . . . . . *G2　81

Fairland, Ind., 800 . . . . E6　59
Fairland, Okla., 646 . . . . . . A7　79
Fair Lawn, N.J., 36,421 . . . h8　74
Fairlawn, Ohio, 2,000 . . . . *A4　78
Fairless Hills, Pa., 8,000 . . *F11　81
Fairmont, Ill., 1,500 . . . . . . k8　58
Fairmont, Minn., 9,745 . . . G4　67
Fairmont, N.C., 2,286 . . . . C3　76
Fairmont, Wash., 1,227 . . . *B3　86
Fairmont, W. Va.,
　27,477 . . . . A7, B4　87
Fairmont City, Ill., 2,688 . . f13　69
Fairmount, Ill., 725 . . . . . . C6　58
Fairmount, Ind., 3,080 . . . . D6　59
Fairmount, N.Y., 7,000 . . . *B4　75
Fairmount Heights, Md.,
　2,308 . . . . f9　53
Fair Oaks, Calif., 9,000 . . . C3　50
Fair Oaks, Calif., 1,622 . . . *E3　50
Fair Oaks, Ga., 7,969 . . . . *C2　55
Fairoaks, Pa., 1,239 . . . . . h13　81
Fair Plain, Mich., 8,500 . . . F4　66
Fairpoint, Ohio, 600 . . . . . B5　78
Fairport, N.Y., 5,748 . . . . . B3　75
Fairport Harbor, Ohio,
　4,267 . . . . A4　78
Fairton, N.J., 900 . . . . E2　74
Fairvale, N.B., Can., 759 . . D4　43
Fairview, Alta., Can.,
　1,506 . . . . A1　38
Fairview, Ga., 4,500 . . . . . . *B1　55
Fariview, Ill., 544 . . . . C3　58
Fairview, Mont., 1,006 . . . C12　70
Fairview, N.J., 35 . . . . D3　74
Fairview, N.J., 9,399 . . . . . h8　74
Fairview, N.Y., 8,626 . . . . *D7　75
Fairview, Ohio, 166 . . . . . . B4　78
Fairview, Okla., 2,213 . . . . A3　79
Fairview, Pa., 2,100 . . . . . . *D8　81
Fairview, Pa., 1,146 . . . . . . *E11　81
Fairview, Pa., 1,399 . . . . . . B1　81
Fairview, Tenn., 1,017 . . . . B4　83
Fairview, Utah, 655 . . . . . . B6　72
Fairview, Wash., 2,758 . . . *C5　86
Fairview, peak, Oreg. . . . . . D4　80
Fairview Park, Ind.,
　1,039 . . . . E3　59
Fairview Park, Ohio,
　14,624 . . . . h9　78
Fairview Shores, Fla.,
　900 . . . . *D5　54
Fairvilla, Fla., 1,000 . . . . . *D5　54
Fairway, Kans., 5,398 . . . . B9　61
Fairyland, Ga., 600 . . . . . . *B1　55
Faison, N.C., 638 . . . . B4　76
Faizabad, Afg., 30,000 . . . . A5　20
Faizabad, India, 83,717
　(*88,296) . . . . C7　20
Fajardo, P.R., 12,409 . . . . G12　35
Fakfak, W. Irian, 1,800 . . . . F8　19
Fălciu, Rom., 5,124 . . . . . . B9　10
Falcón, state, Ven.,
　340,450 . . . . A3　32
Falconer, N.Y., 3,343 . . . . . C1　75
Falcon Heights, Minn.,
　5,927 . . . . n12　67

Falconwood, N.Y., 2,100 . . *C2　75
Faleshty, Sov. Un., 5,000 . . B8　10
Falfurrias, Tex., 6,515 . . . . F3　84
Falher, Alta., Can., 741 . . . B2　38
Falkirk, Scot., 37,900 . . . . . C5　4
Falkland Islands, br. dep.,
　S.A., 2,172 . . . . I5　27
Falköping, Swe., 14,400 . . . H5　11
Fall Branch, Tenn., 950 . . C11　83
Fallbrook, Calif., 5,100 . . . . F5　50
Fallon, Nev., 2,734 . . . . . . B2　72
Fallon, co., Mont., 3,997 . . D12　70
Fall River, Mass., 97,000
　(*144,500) . . . . C5　65
Fall River, co., S. Dak.,
　10,688 . . . . G2　77
Fall Rock, Ky., 50 . . . . C6　62
Falls, co., Tex., 21,263 . . . . D4　84
Falls Church (Independent
　City), Va., 10,192 . . . . . . g12　85
Falls City, Nebr., 5,598 . . . D10　71
Falls City, Oreg., 653 . . . . . C3　80
Falls Creek, Pa., 1,344 . . . . D4　81
Fallsington, Pa., 1,000 . . . *F11　81
Fallsview, W. Va., 525 . . . *C3　87
Falmouth, Eng., 17,400 . . . E4　4
Falmouth, Jam., 4,126 . . . . E5　35
Falmouth, Ky., 2,568 . . . . . B5　62
Falmouth, Maine, 5,976 . . . E5　64
Falmouth, Mass., 3,500 . . . C6　65
Falmouth, N.S., 831 . . . . . . E5　43
Falmouth, Va., 1,478 . . . . . B5　85
Falmouth Heights, Mass.,
　800 . . . . C6　65
Fălticeni, Rom., 13,305 . . . . B8　10
Falun, Swe., 18,700 . . . . . . G6　11
Fannin, co., Ga., 13,620 . . . B2　55
Fannin, co., Tex., 23,880 . . C4　84
Fanny, mtn., Oreg. . . . . B9　80
Fano, It., 23,600 . . . . C4　9
Fanwood, N.J., 7,963 . . . . *B4　74
Farafangana, Malag.,
　9,500 . . . . E9　24
Farah, Afg., 12,000 . . . . . . B3　20
Faranah, Guinea, 2,250 . . . F2　22
Fargo, N. Dak., 49,572 . . . D9　77
Far Hills, N.J., 702 . . . . . . B3　74
Faribault, Minn., 16,926 . . F5　67
Faribault, co., Minn.,
　23,685 . . . . G5　67
Farina, Ill., 692 . . . . E5　58
Farley, Iowa, 1,000 . . . . . . B6　60
Farmer City, Ill., 1,838 . . . C5　58
Farmers Branch, Tex.,
　13,441 . . . . n10　84
Farmersburg, Ind., 1,027 . . F3　59
Farmersville, Calif.,
　3,101 . . . . *D4　50
Farmersville, Tex., 2,021 . . C4　84
Farmerville, La., 2,727 . . . . B3　63
Farmingdale, Maine, 900
　(1,941 ▲) . . . . D3　64
Farmingdale, N.J., 959 . . . . C4　74
Farmingdale, N.Y., 7,637 . . G3　52
Farmington, Conn., 2,000 . . C5　52
Farmington, Ill., 2,831 . . . . C3　58

Farmington, Iowa, 902 . . . . D6　6
Farmington, Maine, 2,800,
　(5,001 ▲) . . . . D2　64
Farmington, Mich.,
　6,881 . . . . p15　66
Farmington, Minn.,
　2,300 . . . . F5　67
Farmington, Mo., 5,618 . . . D7　69
Farmington, N.H., 600 . . . . E5　73
Farmington, N. Mex.,
　23,786 . . . . A4　48
Farmington, Utah,
　1,951 . . . . A6, C2　72
Farmingville, N.Y.,
　3,000 . . . . n16　75
Farmland, Ind., 1,102 . . . . D7　59
Farmville, N.C., 3,997 . . . . B5　76
Farmville, Va., 4,293 . . . . . C4　85
Farnham, Que., Can.,
　6,354 . . . . D5　42
Farnham, mtn., B.C. . . . . . . D9　37
Faro, Port., 18,909 . . . . . . D2　8
Farrell, Pa., 13,793 . . . . . . D1　81
Farrukhabad, India, 87,793
　(*94,591) . . . . C6　20
Farwell, Mich., 737 . . . . . . E6　66
Farwell, Tex., 1,009 . . . . . . B1　84
Fasano, It., 16,100 . . . . D6　9
Fastov, Sov. Un., 10,000 . . F7　12
Fatehpur, India, 28,232 . . . C7　20
Fatsa, Tur., 16,840 . . . . . . B11　14
Faulk, co., S. Dak., 4,397 . . E6　77
Faulkner, co., Ark.,
　24,303 . . . . B3　49
Faulkton, S. Dak., 1,051 . . . E6　77
Fauquier, co., Va.,
　24,066 . . . . B5　85
Faust, Alta., Can., 763 . . . . B3　38
Favara, It., 27,900 . . . . F4　9
Fawnie Nose, mtn., B.C.,
　Can. . . . . C5　37
Faxon, Pa., 1,841 . . . . *D7　81
Fayette, Ala., 4,227 . . . . . . B2　46
Fayette, Iowa, 1,597 . . . . . . B6　60
Fayette, Miss., 1,626 . . . . . D2　68
Fayette, Mo., 3,294 . . . . . . B5　69
Fayette, Ohio, 1,090 . . . . . A1　78
Fayette, co., Ala., 16,148 . . B2　46
Fayette, co., Ga., 8,199 . . . C2　55
Fayette, co., Ill., 21,946 . . . D4　58
Fayette, co., Ind., 24,454 . . E7　59
Fayette, co., Iowa, 28,581 . . B6　60
Fayette, co., Ky., 131,906 . . B5　62
Fayette, co., Ohio, 24,775 . . C2　78
Fayette, co., Pa., 169,340 . . G2　81
Fayette, co., Tenn.,
　24,557 . . . . B2　83
Fayette, co., Tex., 20,384 . . E4　84
Fayette, co., W. Va.,
　61,731 . . . . C3　87
Fayette City, Pa., 1,159 . . *G2　81
Fayetteville, Ark., 20,274 . . A1　49
Fayetteville, Ga., 1,389 . . . C2　55
Fayetteville, N.Y., 4,702 . . B5　75
Fayetteville, N.C., 55,000
　(*195,000) . . . . B4　76

Fayetteville, Pa., 950.....G6 81
Fayetteville, Tenn., 6,804..B5 83
Fayetteville, W. Va., 1,848.........C3, D7 87
Fayetteville North, N.C., 3,071.............*B4 76
Fayville, Mass., 900......g9 65
Feasterville, Pa., 6,000...o21 81
Feather Falls, Calif., 650..C3 50
Fécamp, Fr., 19,491.....C4 5
Fedala, Mor., 35,010.....B3 22
Federalsburg, Md., 2,060..C6 53
Federal Way, Wash., 7,000..............*B3 86
Fedscreek, Ky., 500......C7 62
Feeding Hills, Mass., 4,500................B2 65
Feilding, N.Z., 8,172.....N15 26
Feira de Santana, Braz., 61,612...............*E7 27
Fejer, co., Hung., 300,119............*B4 10
Felanitx, Sp., 11,759....C7 8
Feldkirch, Aus., 17,343...E4 6
Felicity, Ohio, 878......D1 78
Felipe Carrillo Puerto, Mex., 1,249..........D7 34
Fellsmere, Fla., 732......E6 54
Felton, Calif., 1,600.....D2 50
Feltre, It., 8,500........A3 9
Fenelon Falls, Ont., Can., 1,359..................C6 41
Fengshan, Taiwan, 5,000...............*G9 17
Fennimore, Wis., 1,747....F3 88
Fennville, Mich., 705.....F4 66
Fenton, Mich., 8,067.....F7 66
Fenton, Mo., 1,059.....f13 69
Fentress, co., Tenn., 13,288..............C9 83
Fenwick, Ont., Can., 685..D5 41
Fenyang, China, 30,000...D7 17
Feodosiya, Sov. Un., 51,000...............I10 12
Ferdinand, Ind., 1,427...H4 59
Ferentino, It., 16,836....D4 9
Fergana, Sov. Un., 87,000............*E10 13
Fergus, Ont., Can., 3,831..D4 41
Fergus, co., Mont., 14,018..............C7 70
Fergus Falls, Minn., 13,733................D2 67
Ferguson, Mo., 22,149............C7, f13 69
Fermanagh, co., N. Ire., 51,300............*C3 4
Ferme-Neuve, Que., Can., 1,971..................C2 42
Fermo, It., 11,400......C4 9
Fernandina Beach, Fla., 7,276...............B5, k9 54
Fernando Póo, reg., Equat. Gui., 71,000.........H6 22
Fern Creek, Ky., 1,500...A5 62
Ferndale, Calif., 1,371...B1 50
Ferndale, Md., 3,000.....B4 53
Ferndale, Mich., 31,347...*F7 66
Ferndale, Pa., 2,717.....F4 81
Ferndale, Wash., 1,442...A3 86
Fernie, B.C., Can., 2,661..E10 37
Fern Park, Fla., 3,000...D5 54
Fernwood, N.Y., 170......B4 75
Ferozepore, India, 47,060 (*97,932)............B5 20
Ferrara, It., 102,000....B3 9
Ferreñafe, Peru, 12,200...C2 31
Ferriday, La., 4,563......C4 63
Ferris, Ont., Can., 3,004..............*A5 41
Ferris, Tex., 1,807....C4, n10 84
Ferris, mts., Wyo......D5 89
Ferry, co., Wash., 3,889..A7 86
Ferryland, Newf., Can., 713.................E5 44
Ferrysburg, Mich., 2,590.*E4 66
Ferryville, Tun., 29,353...F2 9
Fertile, Minn., 968.......C2 67
Fès (Fez), Mor., 216,133..B3 22
Fessenden, N. Dak., 920...C6 77
Festus, Mo., 7,021...C7, g13 69
Feteşti, Rom., 15,383.....C8 10
Fetters Hot Springs, Calif., 750................*C2 50
Ffestiniog, Wales, 6,700..D5 4
Fianarantsoa, Malag., 36,189..............E9 24
Fidenza, It., 9,800......B3 9
Fieldale, Va., 1,499.....D3 85
Fier, Alb., 11,000......*B2 14
Fierro Urco, vol., Peru...B2 31
Fife, co., Sask., Can., 323,200............*B5 4
Fife, Wash., 1,463.....*B3 86
Figeac, Fr., 6,933.......E4 5
Figueira da Foz, Port., 10,855..............B1 8
Figueras, Sp., 17,548....A7 8

Fiji Island, br. dep., Oceania, 455,000......H8 2
Filbert, W. Va., 950......D3 87
Filer, Idaho, 1,249......G4 57
Filiatra, Grc., 6,753....*D3 14
Fillmore, Calif., 4,808...E4 50
Fillmore, Utah, 1,602.....B5 72
Fillmore, co., Minn., 23,768...............G6 67
Fillmore, co., Nebr., 9,425.................D8 71
Finchley, Eng., 69,311...k12 4
Finderne, N.J., 2,000....*B3 74
Findlay, Ohio, 30,344....A2 78
Findlay, Ill., 759.......D5 58
Findlay, mtn., B.C., Can...D9 37
Finistère, dept., Fr., 727,847..............*C2 5
Finland, country, Eur., 4,523,200...........E12 11
Finney, co., Kans., 16,093.D3 61
Finneytown, Ohio, 5,000..*C1 78
Finnmark, co., Nor., 74,600............*B13 11
Finspång, Swe., 15,200...u33 11
Finsterwalde, Ger., 20,700................C6 6
Firat (Euphrates), riv., Asia.................D12 14
Fircrest, Wash., 3,565....f10 86
Firebaugh, Calif., 2,627..D3 50
Firenze (Florence), It., 455,000..............C3 9
Firenzuola, It., 743.....B3 9
Firminy, Fr., 26,065.....E6 5
Fisher, Ill., 1,330......C5 58
Fisher, co., Tex., 7,865...C2 84
Fisher, peak, Va........D2 85
Fishersville, Va., 700....B4 85
Fishguard, Wales, 4,900...E4 4
Fishing Creek, Md., 700...D5 53
Fishkill, N.Y., 997......D7 75
Fiskdale, Mass., 850.....B3 65
Fitchburg, Mass., 43,021..A4 65
Fitzgerald, Ga., 8,781...E3 55
Fitz Roy, mtn., Arg......D2 28
Fiume, see Rijeka, Yugo.
Five Points, Calif., 15,000...............*F3 50
Five Points, N. Mex., 3,000................*B3 48
Flagler, co., Fla., 4,566..C5 54
Flagler Beach, Fla., 970..C5 54
Flagstaff, Ariz., 24,592..B3 48
Flagtown, N.J., 650......B3 74
Flanagan, Ill., 841......C5 58
Flanders, N.Y., 2,000...*n16 75
Flandreau, S. Dak., 2,129..F9 77
Flat Creek, Ala., 800..B2, E4 46
Flathead, co., Mont., 32,965...............B2 70
Flathead, mts., Mont.....B2 70
Flatonia, Tex., 1,009....E4 84
Flat River, Mo., 4,515...D7 69
Flat Rock, Newf., Can., 632.................*E5 44
Flat Rock, Mich., 4,696...F7 66
Flat Rock, N.C., 1,808...f10 76
Flatwoods, Ky., 3,741....B7 62
Fleetwing Estates, Pa., 1,100...............*F11 81
Fleetwood, Pa., 2,647...F10 81
Fleming, co., Ky., 10,890.B6 62
Flemingsburg, Ky., 2,067..B6 62
Flemington, N.J., 3,232...B3 74
Flemington, Pa., 1,608...D7 81
Flensburg, Ger., 96,900...A4 6
Flers, Fr., 14,634.......C3 5
Fletcher, N.C., 800.....f10 76
Fletcher, Okla., 884.....C4 79
Flin Flon, Man., Can., 11,104.............B1, g7 40
Flint, Mich., 200,000 (*445,000)............F7 66
Flint, co., Wales, 152,300.............*D5 4
Flintridge, Calif., 5,000.*F4 50
Flomaton, Ala., 1,454...D2 46
Floodwood, Minn., 677...D6 67
Flora, Ill., 5,331.......E5 58
Flora, Ind., 1,742.......C4 59
Florala, Ala., 3,011.....D3 46
Floral City, Fla., 900...D4 54
Floral Park, Mont., 4,079...............*D4 70
Floral Park, N.Y., 17,762.k13 75
Flordell Hills, Mo., 1,119................*C7 69
Florence, Ala., 31,649...A2 46
Florence, Ariz., 2,143.C3, D2 48
Florence, Calif., 38,164..*E4 50
Florence, Colo., 2,821...C5 51
Florence, Kans., 853.....D7 61
Florence, Ky., 5,837...A5, A7 62
Florence, N.J., 4,000....C3 74
Florence, Oreg., 1,642...D2 80
Florence, S.C., 24,722..C8 82
Florence, Wis., 800......C5 88

Florence, co., S.C., 84,438..............C8 82
Florence, co., Wis., 3,437..C5 88
Florence, see Firenze, It.
Florencia, Col., 17,709...C2 32
Flores, Guat., 1,596.....H12 33
Flores, isl., Indon......G6 19
Flores, dept., Ur., 23,400..*E1 30
Floresville, Tex., 2,126...............E3, k7 84
Florham Park, N.J., 7,222.B4 74
Floriano, Braz., 16,063...D6 27
Florianópolis, Braz., 74,323................D3 30
Florida, Cuba, 30,200....D4 35
Florida, N.Y., 1,656..D6, m14 75
Florida, Ur., 20,934.....E1 30
Florida, dept., Ur., 64,200..............*E1 30
Florida, state, U.S., 4,951,560...........E10 45
Florida, bay, Fla.......E10 54
Florida City, Fla., 4,114..............G6, t13 54
Florida Keys, is., Fla....H6 54
Florin, Pa., 1,518.....*G9 81
Florina, Grc., 11,933....E5 10
Flórina, prov., Grc., 67,356.............*B3 14
Florissant, Mo., 38,166...f13 69
Flossmoor, Ill., 5,921....k9 58
Flour Bluff, Tex., 3,500.*F4 84
Flourtown, Pa., 4,000...o21 81
Flower Hill, N.Y., 4,594.*E7 75
Flower Village, Calif., 5,000................*E4 50
Floyd, co., Ga., 69,130...B1 55
Floyd, co., Ind., 53,008...H6 59
Floyd, co., Iowa, 21,102..A5 60
Floyd, co., Ky., 41,642...C7 62
Floyd, co., Tex., 12,369..B2 84
Floyd, co., Va., 10,462...D2 85
Floydada, Tex., 3,769....C2 84
Flushing, Mich., 6,023...E7 66
Flushing, Ohio, 1,189....B4 78
Fluvanna, co., Va., 7,227..C4 85
Foam Lake, Sask., Can., 933.................F4 39
Foard, co., Tex., 3,125...B3 84
Focşani, Rom., 28,244....C8 10
Foggia, It., 124,500.....D5 9
Fogo, Newf., Can., 1,152..D4 44
Fohnsdorf, Aus., 11,517...E7 6
Foix, Fr., 7,164........F4 5
Folcroft, Pa., 7,013....*G11 81
Foley, Ala., 2,889......E2 46
Foley, Minn., 1,112.....E5 67
Foligno, It., 32,400....C4 9
Folkestone, Eng., 43,600..E7 4
Folkston, Ga., 1,810....F4 55
Follansbee, W. Va., 4,052...............A4, B2 87
Follonica, It., 7,147....C3 9
Folly Beach, S.C., 1,137...............F8, k12 82
Folsom, Calif., 3,925....C3 50
Folsom, Pa., 5,000.....*G11 81
Fomento, Cuba, 8,800....C4 35
Fonda, Iowa, 1,026.....B3 60
Fonda, N.Y., 1,004......C6 75
Fond du Lac, Wis., 32,719.............E5, k9 88
Fond du Lac, co., Wis., 75,085................E5 88
Fondi, It., 13,700......D4 9
Fonsagrada, Sp., 950.....A2 8
Fontainebleau, Fr., 20,583...............C5 5
Fontana, Calif., 14,659..m14 50
Fontana, Wis., 1,326.....F5 88
Fontanelle, Iowa, 729....C3 60
Fontenay-le-Comte, Fr., 10,109...............D3 5
Fontenay [-sous-Bois], Fr., 37,484...............g10 5
Fonthill, Ont., Can., 2,324................D5 41
Foochow (Minhow), China, 616,000..............F8 17
Footville, Wis., 675.....F4 88
Forbach, Fr., 21,704.....C7 5
Forbes, Austl., 7,370....F8 25
Forbes, mtn., Alta., Can..D2 38
Forchheim, Ger., 20,900..D5 6
Ford, co., Ill., 16,606...C5 58
Ford, co., Kans., 20,938..E4 61
Ford City, Calif., 3,926..E4 50
Ford City, Pa., 5,440....E2 81
Fords, N.J., 12,500.....*B4 74
Fords Prairie, Wash., 1,404................*C3 86
Fordyce, Ark., 3,890....D3 49
Foreman, Ark., 1,001....D1 49
Forest, Bel., 51,503.....B6 5
Forest, Ont., Can., 2,188..D2 41
Forest, Miss., 3,917.....C4 68
Forest, Ohio, 1,314.....B2 78
Forest, co., Pa., 4,485...C3 81

Forest, co., Wis., 7,542...C5 88
Forest Acres, S.C., 3,842..C6 82
Forestburg, Alta., Can., 677.................C4 38
Forest City, Iowa, 3,329..A4 60
Forest City, N.C., 6,556..............B1, f11 76
Forest City, Pa., 2,651...C11 81
Forest Grove, Oreg., 5,628..............B3, g11 80
Forest Heights, Md., 3,524................*C4 53
Forest Hills, N.B., Can., 715.................*D4 43
Forest Hill, Ont., Can., 20,489...............m15 41
Forest Hill, Tex., 3,221..*C4 84
Forest Hills, Pa., 8,796..k14 81
Forest Hills, Tenn., 2,101................*A5 83
Forest Homes, Ill., 2,025.*E3 58
Forest Knolls, Calif., 600..g7 50
Forest Lake, Minn., 2,809.E6 67
Forest Lawn, Alta., Can., 12,263................D4 38
Forest Park, Ga., 14,201..............B5, C2 55
Forest Park, Ill., 14,452..k9 58
Forestview, Ill., 1,042..*B6 58
Forest View, S.C., 1,000.*B3 82
Forestville, Md., 1,500..*C4 53
Forestville, N.Y., 905....C1 75
Forfar, Scot., 10,300....B5 4
Forges-les-Eaux, Fr., 2,914................C4 5
Forge Village, Mass., 1,400............A5, f10 65
Forked River, N.J., 900...D4 74
Forks, Wash., 1,156.....B1 86
Forli, It., 62,700......B4 9
Formiga, Braz., 18,763...C3 30
Formosa, Arg., 16,506....E4 29
Formosa, prov., Arg., 178,458..............E4 29
Formosa, see Taiwan, Asia
Forney, Tex., 1,544...C4, n10 84
Forres, Scot., 4,700.....B5 4
Forrest, Ill., 1,220.....C5 58
Forrest, co., Miss., 52,722.D4 68
Forrest City, Ark., 10,544.B5 49
Forreston, Ill., 1,153....A4 58
Forst, Ger., 28,700.....C7 6
Forsyth, Ga., 3,697.....C3 55
Forsyth, Mont., 2,032...D10 70
Forsyth, co., Ga., 12,170..B2 55
Forsyth, co., N.C., 189,428..............A2 76
Fortaleza, Braz., 354,942..D7 27
Fort Atkinson, Wis., 7,908.F5 88
Fort Bend, co., Tex., 40,527...............E5 84
Fort Benton, Mont., 1,887..C6 70
Fort Bragg, Calif., 4,433..C2 50
Fort Branch, Ind., 1,983...H2 59
Fort Chipewyan, Alta., Can., 717.............f8 38
Fort Cobb, Okla., 687....B3 79
Fort Collins, Colo., 25,027...............A5 51
Fort Collins West, Colo., 1,569..............*A5 51
Fort Coulonge, Que., Can., 1,823................B8 41
Fort Covington, N.Y., 976.................f10 75
Fort-Dauphin, Malag., 11,200...............E9 24
Fort Davis, Tex., 850....o13 84
Fort-de-France, Mart., 84,811..............I14 35
Fort Deposit, Ala., 1,466..D3 46
Fort Dodge, Iowa, 29,654..B3 60
Fort Edward, N.Y., 3,737..B7 75
Fort Erie, Ont., Can., 9,027................E6 41
Fort Fairfield, Maine, 3,300, (5,876▲)......B7 64
Fort Frances, Ont., Can., 9,481...............o16 41
Fort Gaines, Ga., 1,320...E1 55
Fort-George, Que., Can., 1,074................h11 42
Fort Gibson, Okla., 1,407.B6 79
Fort Hall, Idaho, 700....F6 57
Fort Hancock, Tex., 600..o12 84
Fort Howard, Md., 500....B5 53
Fort Huachuca, Ariz......D3 48
Fort Johnson, N.Y., 876..*C6 75
Fort Kent, Maine, 2,787, (4,761▲).............A4 64
Fort Knox, Ky..........C4 62
Fort-Lamy, Chad, 88,162..F8 22
Fort Langley, B.C., Can., 962.................f13 37
Fort Laperrine, see Tamanrasset, Alg.
Fort Lauderdale, Fla., 83,648...........F6, r13 54

Fort Levenworth, Kans., 8,000......C8, k15　61
Fort Lee, N.J., 21,815.....h9　74
Fort-Liberté, Hai., 1,506...E8　35
Fort Loramie, Ohio, 687...B1　78
Fort Lupton, Colo., 2,194..A6　51
Fort Macleod, Alta., Can., 2,490.............E4　38
Fort Madison, Iowa, 15,247............D6　60
Fort McKinley, Ohio, 8,000...........*C1　78
Fort Meade, Fla., 4,014...E5　54
Fort Mill, S.C., 3,315.....A6　82
Fort Morgan, Colo., 7,379.............A7　51
Fort Myers, Fla., 22,523.............F5　54
Fort Myers Beach, Fla., 2,463.............F5　54
Fort Nelson, B.C., Can., 1,607............m18　37
Fort Oglethorpe, Ga., 2,251.............B1　55
Fort Payne, Ala., 7,029...A4　46
Fort Peck, Mont., 650....B10　70
Fort Pierce, Fla., 25,256..E6　54
Fort Pierre, S. Dak., 2,649.............F5　77
Fort Plain, N.Y., 2,809...C6　75
Fort Qu'Appelle, Sask., Can., 1,521........G4　39
Fort Recovery, Ohio, 1,336.............B1　78
Fort Riley, Kans., 1,500...C7　61
Fort St. James, B.C., Can., 1,081.......B5　37
Fort St. John, B.C., Can., 3,619......A7, m18　37
Fort Saskatchewan, Alta., Can., 2,972........C4　38
Fort Scott, Kans., 9,410...E9　61
Fort Shawnee, Ohio, 4,000.............B1　78
Fort Smith, Ark., 52,991..B1　49
Fort St. John, B.C., Can., 3,619......A7, m18　37
Fort Stockton, Tex., 6,373.............D1　84
Fort Sumner, N. Mex., 1,809.............B6　48
Fort Thomas, Ky., 14,896..A7　62
Fortuna, Calif., 3,523.....B1　50
Fortune, Newf., Can., 1,360.............E4　44
Fort Valley, Ga., 8,310....D3　55
Fort Vermilion, Alta., Can., 768...........f7　38
Fort Victoria, Rh., 9,400..E6　24
Fortville, Ind., 2,209.....E6　59
Fort Walton Beach, Fla., 12,147...........u15　54
Fort Washington, Pa., 3,400............o21　81
Fort Washington Forest, Md., 1,350........C4　53
Fort Wayne, Ind., 174,000 (*242,000)............B7　59
Fort William, Ont., Can., 45,214, (*93,251)......o17　41
Fort William, Scot., 2,900.B4　4
Fort Worth, Tex., 360,000 (*555,000)......C4, n9　84
Fort Wright, Ky., 2,184...A7　62
Forty Fort, Pa., 6,431............D10, n17　81
Foshan, China, 5,000....B11　17
Fossano, It., 11,000......B1　9
Fossil, Oreg., 672........B6　80
Fossombrone, It., 4,659...C4　9
Fosston, Minn., 1,704....C3　67
Foster, co., N. Dak., 5,361.............C7　77
Foster Brook, Pa., 950...C4　81
Foster Village, Haw., 2,500............g10　56
Fostoria, Ohio, 15,732...A2　78
Fostoria, Tex., 666......*D8　84
Fougères, Fr., 24,279....C3　5
Fouliang, China, 92,000..*E8　17
Fouling, China, 32,000...F6　17
Foumban, Cam., 18,000...G7　22
Founing, China, 85,000...E8　17
Fountain, Colo., 1,602....C6　51
Fountain, co., Ind., 18,706.............D3　59
Fountain, peak, Calif.....E6　50
Fountain City, Ind., 833..E8　59
Fountain City, Wis., 934...D2　88
Fountain Green, Utah, 544...............B6　72
Fountain Hill, Pa., 5,428..E11　81
Fountain Inn, S.C., 2,385.B3　82
Fountain Place, La., 5,000...........*D4　63
Fountain Valley, Calif., 2,068............*F5　50

Four Corners, Oreg., 4,743.............*C4　80
Fourmies, Fr., 14,508.....B6　5
Four Oaks, N.C., 1,040...B4　76
Fouyang, China, 65,000...E8　17
Fowler, Calif., 1,892.....D4　50
Fowler, Colo., 1,240......C6　51
Fowler, Ind., 2,491.......C3　59
Fowler, Kans., 717........E3　61
Fowler, Mich., 854........E6　66
Fowlerville, Mich., 1,674.F6　66
Foxboro, Mass., 6,000....B5　65
Fox Chapel, Pa., 3,302...*E1　81
Fox Farm, Wyo., 1,371...*E8　89
Fox Harbour, Newf., Can., 746.............E5　44
Fox Lake, Ill., 3,886...A5, h8　58
Fox Lake, Wis., 1,181....E5　88
Fox Point, Wis., 7,315...........E5, m12　88
Fox River Grove, Ill., 1,866..............h8　58
Foxworth, Miss., 950.....D4　68
Frackville, Pa., 5,654....E9　81
Fraga, Sp., 8,691.........B6　8
Framingham, Mass., 44,526..........B5, g10　65
Franca, Braz., 646........C3　30
Francavilla Fontana, It., 27,000.............D6　9
France, country, Eur., 49,440,000...............　5
Francesville, Ind., 1,002..C4　59
Franche-Comté, fr. prov., Fr., 757,000...........D6　5
Francistown, Bots., 10,000.E5　24
Franconia, Va., 3,000....*B5　85
Franconville, Fr., 11,185..g9　5
Frankenberg, Ger., 8,100.C4　6
Frankenmuth, Mich., 1,728.............E7　66
Frankenthal, Ger., 33,900.D4　6
Frankford, Ont., Can., 1,642.............C7　41
Frankfort, Ill., 1,523.....m9　58
Frankfort, Ind., 15,302...D4　59
Frankfort, Kans., 1,106...C7　61
Frankfort, Ky., 18,365....B5　62
Frankfort, Mich., 1,690...D4　66
Frankfort, N.Y., 3,872....B5　75
Frankfurt [am Main], Ger., 683,100 (*1,495,000)....C4　6
Frankfurt [an der Oder], Ger., 57,700...........B7　6
Franklin, Idaho, 7,222....*F2　57
Franklin, Ind., 11,292....F5　59
Franklin, Kans., 600......E9　61
Franklin, Ky., 5,319......D3　62
Franklin, La., 8,673......E4　63
Franklin, Mass., 8,000....B5　65
Franklin, Mich., 2,262...*F7　66
Franklin, Nebr., 1,194....D7　71
Franklin, N.H., 6,742.....E4　73
Franklin, N.J., 3,624.....A3　74
Franklin, N.C., 2,173.....f9　76
Franklin, Ohio, 7,917.....C1　78
Franklin, Pa., 1,352......*E4　81
Franklin, Pa., 9,586......D2　81
Franklin, Tenn., 6,977....B5　83
Franklin, Tex., 1,065.....D4　84
Franklin (Independent City) Va., 7,264.........D6　85
Franklin, Wis., 10,006...n11　88
Franklin, co., Ala., 21,988..A2　46
Franklin, co., Ark., 10,213.............B2　49
Franklin, co., Fla., 6,576..C2　54
Franklin, co., Ga., 13,274.B3　55
Franklin, co., Idaho, 8,457.............G7　57
Franklin, co., Ill., 39,281..E5　58
Franklin, co., Ind., 17,015..F7　59
Franklin, co., Iowa, 15,472.............B4　60
Franklin, co., Kans., 19,548.............D8　61
Franklin, co., Ky., 29,421..B5　62
Franklin, co., Maine, 20,069.............C2　64
Franklin, co., Mass., 54,864.............A2　65
Franklin, co., Miss., 9,286..D3　68
Franklin, co., Mo., 44,566.............C6　69
Franklin, co., Nebr., 5,449.............D7　71
Franklin, co., N.Y., 44,742.............A6　75
Franklin, co., N.C., 28,755.............A4　76
Franklin, co., Ohio, 682,962............B2　78
Franklin, co., Pa., 88,172..G6　81
Franklin, co., Tenn., 25,528.............B5　83
Franklin, co., Tex., 5,101..C5　84
Franklin, co., Vt., 29,474..B2　73
Franklin, co., Va., 25,925..D3　85

Franklin, co., Wash., 23,342.............C6　86
Franklin, dist., N. W. Ter., Can., 3,424........B13　36
Franklin, par., La., 26,088.............B4　63
Franklin Furnace, Ohio, 950.............D3　78
Franklin Grove, Ill., 773..B4　58
Franklin Lakes, N.J., 3,316............*B4　74
Franklin Park, Ill., 18,322..k9　58
Franklin Park, N.J., 900..C3　74
Franklin Park, Va., 1,300............*B5　85
Franklin Square, N.Y., 33,000.............G2　52
Franklinton, La., 3,141...D5　63
Franklinton, N.C., 1,513..A4　76
Franklinville, N.J., 1,000.D2　74
Franklinville, N.Y., 2,124.C2　75
Franklinville, N.C., 686..B3　76
Frankston, Tex., 953.....C5　84
Frankton, Ind., 1,445....D6　59
Frascati, It., 13,500...D4, h9　9
Fraser, Mich., 7,027....*F8　66
Fraser, riv., B.C., Can....C6　37
Fraser, mtn., B.C., Can...............C8　37
Fraserburgh, Scot., 10,500.B6　4
Frauenfeld, Switz., 14,702.E4　6
Fray Bentos, Ur., 12,900..E1　30
Frazee, Minn., 1,083.....D3　67
Frazeyburg, Ohio, 842....B3　78
Frazier Park, Calif., 900..E4　50
Frederic, Wis., 857......C1　88
Fredericia, Den., 29,870..J3　11
Frederick, Md., 21,744...B3　53
Frederick, Okla., 5,879...C2　79
Frederick, co., Md., 71,930.............B3　53
Frederick, co., Va., 21,941.............A4　85
Fredericksburg, Iowa, 797.B5　60
Fredericksburg, Pa., 700..*F9　81
Fredericksburg, Tex., 4,629.............D3　84
Fredericksburg (Independent City), Va., 13,639......B5　85
Fredericktown, see Georgetown, Md.
Fredericktown, Mo., 3,484.............D7　69
Fredericktown, Ohio, 1,531.............B3　78
Fredericktown, Pa., 1,200.F1　81
Fredericton, N.B., Can., 19,683............D3　43
Frederiksborg, co., Den., 181,663............*J5　11
Frederikshavn, Den., 22,522............I4　11
Frederiksted, Vir. Is., (U.S.), 277.........H12　35
Fredonia, Kans., 3,233...E8　61
Fredonia, N.Y., 9,388....C1　75
Fredonia, Pa., 657.......D1　81
Fredonia, Wis., 710......E6　88
Fredrikstad, Nor., 13,700...........H4, p28　11
Freeborn, co., Minn., 37,891.............G5　67
Freeburg, Ill., 2,191.....E4　58
Freedom, Calif., 4,206...*D3　50
Freedom, Pa., 2,895......E1　81
Freehold, N.J., 9,140....C4　74
Freel, peak, Calif........C4　50
Freeland, Mich., 900.....E6　66
Freeland, Pa., 5,068.....D10　81
Freelandville, Ind., 650...G3　59
Freeman, S. Dak., 1,140...G8　77
Freemansburg, Pa., 1,652.............E11　81
Freeport, Fla., 900......u15　54
Freeport, Ill., 26,628....A4　58
Freeport, Maine, 2,000, (4,055▲).........E2, g7　64
Freeport, Minn., 615.....E4　67
Freeport, N.Y., 38,429...G2　52
Freeport, Pa., 2,439......E2　81
Freeport, Tex., 11,619.........E5, s14　84
Freer, Tex., 3,300.......F3　84
Freestone, co., Tex., 12,525.............D4　84
Freetown, N.Y., 1,450............*m16　75
Freetown, S.L., 127,917...G2　22
Fregenal de la Sierra, Sp., 10,498.............C2　8
Freiberg, Ger., 47,700....C6　6
Freiburg [im Breisgau], Ger., 150,400........D3　6
Freising, Ger., 27,600....D5　6
Freistadt, Aus., 5,375....D7　6
Fréjus, Fr., 16,953.......F3　5
Fremantle, Austl., 25,233..F2　25

Fremont, Calif., 43,790..........D2, h9　50
Fremont, Ind., 937.......A8　59
Fremont, Mich., 3,384....E5　66
Fremont, Nebr., 19,689...........C9, g11　71
Fremont, N.C., 1,609.....B5　76
Fremont, Ohio, 17,573....A2　78
Fremont, co., Colo., 20,196.............C5　51
Fremont, co., Idaho, 8,679.............E7　57
Fremont, co., Iowa, 10,282.............D2　60
Fremont, co., Wyo., 26,186.............C4　89
French Camp, Calif., 1,000...........*D3　50
French Guiana, dep., S.A., 33,505............C5　27
French Lick, Ind., 1,954..G4　59
French Polynesia, Fr. dep., Oceania, 89,000..........*H11　2
French Somaliland, see Afars & Issas, Afr.
French Southern & Antarctic Ter., Fr. dep., Oceania, 150........H11　2
Frenchtown, N.J., 1,340..B2　74
Frenchville, Maine, 700 (1,421▲).........A4　64
Frendale, Pa., 1,900....*D8　81
Freshfield, mtn., Alta., Can..............D9　37
Freshwater, Newf., Can., 1,396..........*f9　44
Fresnillo [de González Echeverría], Mex., 35,582.............C4　34
Fresno, Calif., 163,000 (*272,000).........D4　50
Fresno, co., Calif., 365,945.............D4　50
Freudenstadt, Ger., 14,200.............D4　6
Frewsburg, N.Y., 1,623...C1　75
Friant, Calif., 300.......D4　50
Friars Point, Miss., 1,029.A3　68
Frias, Arg., 7,941.......E2　29
Fribourg, Switz., 37,700..E3　6
Fribourg, canton, Switz., 162,000...........*E3　6
Friday Harbor, Wash., 706...............A2　86
Fridley, Minn., 24,789...m12　67
Friedberg, Ger., 17,300...C4　6
Friedens, Pa., 900.......F4　81
Friedland, Ger., 8,500...B6　6
Friedrichshafen, Ger., 39,000.............E4　6
Friend, Nebr., 1,069.....D8　71
Friendship, N.Y., 1,231..C2　75
Friern Barnet, Eng., 28,807............k12　4
Fries, Va., 1,039........D2　85
Friesland, prov., Neth., 479,900...........*A6　5
Frio, co., Tex., 10,112...E3　84
Friona, Tex., 2,048......B1　84
Frisco, Pa., 900........*E1　81
Frisco, Tex., 1,184.....*C4　84
Frisco City, Ala., 1,177..D2　46
Fritch, Tex., 1,617......B2　84
Fritzlar, Ger., 8,500.....C4　6
Friuli-Venezia Giulia, dist., It., 1,204,298......*B4　9
Frontenac, Kans., 1,713..E9　61
Frontenac, Mo., 3,089...*C7　69
Frontenac, co., Ont., Can., 87,534.............C8　41
Frontenac, co., Que., Can., 30,600............D7　42
Frontera, Mex., 8,375...D6　34
Frontier, co., Nebr., 4,311.............D5　71
Frontignan, Fr., 5,341...F5　5
Frontino, peak, Col.....B2　32
Front Royal, Va., 7,949..B4　85
Frosinone, It., 26,400...D4　9
Frostburg, Md., 6,722...k13　53
Frostproof, Fla., 2,664..E5　54
Frouard, Fr., 6,916......C7　5
Fruita, Colo., 1,830.....B2　51
Fruitdale, Oreg., 2,158..*E3　80
Fruitdale, Tex., 1,418...*C4　84
Fruitland, Idaho, 804....F2　57
Fruitland, Ill., 1,000....*B3　58
Fruitland, Md., 1,147....D6　53
Fruitland Park, Fla., 774..D5　54
Fruitport, Mich., 1,037...E4　66
Fruitridge, Calif., 17,000..*C3　50
Fruitvale, Wash., 3,345..*C5　86
Fruitville, Fla., 2,131..E4, q11　54
Frunze, Sov. Un., 355,000...........E10　13
Frydek-Mistek, Czech., 28,500.............D5　7

Fryeburg, Maine, 950,
(1,874 ▲) D2   64
Fthiotis (Phthiotis), prov.,
Grc., 160,035 . . . . *C4   14
Fuchin, China, 40,000 . . . . B11   17
Fuchow, China, 10,000 . . . F8   17
Fuchū, Jap., 126,519 . . . . *I9   18
Fuente Alamo, Sp., 9,270 . . D5   8
Fuente de Cantos, Sp.,
8,941 . . . . C2   8
Fuenteovejuna, Sp., 5,914 . . C3   8
Fuji, vol., Jap. I9, n17   18
Fujieda, Jap., 42,000,
(70,789 ▲) o17   18
Fujimi, Jap., 4,800 . . . . . . n17   18
Fujinomiya, Jap., 54,000
(80,000 ▲) n17   18
Fujisawa, Jap., 175,183 . . . *I9   18
Fuji-Yoshida, Jap.,
45,384 . . . . n17   18
Fukagawa, Jap.,
15,200 . . . . E10   18

Fukien, prov., China,
14,650,000 . . . . F8   17
Fukuchiyama, Jap.,
58,223 . . . . I7, n14   18
Fukue, Jap., 8,700 . . . . . . o16   18
Fukui, Jap., 169,636 . . . . . H8   18
Fukui, pref., Jap.,
750,557 . . . . *H8   18
Fukuoka, Jap., 8,000 . . . . F10   18
Fukuoka, Jap., 749,808 . . . J5   18
Fukuoka, pref., Jap.,
3,964,611 . . . . *J5   18
Fukushima, Jap.,
5,800 . . . . I8, n16   18
Fukushima, Jap.,
126,000 . . . . H10   18
Fukushima, pref., Jap.,
1,983,754 . . . . *H10   18
Fukuyama, Jap., 170,158 . . I6   18
Fulda, Ger., 44,800 . . . . . . C4   6
Fulda, Minn., 1,202 . . . . . . G3   67
Fullerton, Calif., 56,180 . . n13   50
Fullerton, Ky., 1,082 . . . . . B7   62

Fullerton, Md., 3,000 . . . . . *B5   53
Fullerton, Nebr., 1,475 . . . . C8   71
Fullerton, Pa., 5,500 . . . . *E10   81
Fulton, Ill., 3,387 . . . . B3   58
Fulton, Ky., 3,265 . . . . B2   62
Fulton, Miss., 1,706 . . . . . . A5   68
Fulton, Mo., 11,131 . . . . . . C6   69
Fulton, N.Y., 14,261 . . . . . . B4   75
Fulton, co., Ark., 6,657 . . . A4   49
Fulton, co., Ga., 556,326 . . C2   55
Fulton, co., Ill., 41,954 . . . C3   58
Fulton, co., Ind., 16,957 . . B5   59
Fulton, co., Ky., 11,256 . . . B2   62
Fulton, co., N.Y., 51,304 . . B6   75
Fulton, co., Ohio, 29,301 . . A1   78
Fulton, co., Pa., 10,597 . . . G5   81
Fultondale, Ala., 2,001 . . . E4   46
Fulton Heights, Colo.,
1,250 . . . . *C6   51
Fumay, Fr., 6,185 . . . . C6   5
Funabashi, Jap., 223,989 . . n19   18
Funchal, Port., 43,301 . . . h12   8
Fundación, Col., 14,128 . . . A3   32

Funkstown, Md., 968 . . . . . A2   53
Fuquay Springs, N.C.,
3,389 . . . . *B4   76
Furano, Jap., 13,000 . . . . . E11   18
Furman University, S.C.,
1,500 . . . . *B3   82
Furnas, co., Nebr., 7,711 . . D6   71
Fürstenfeld, Aus., 6,415 . . . E8   6
Fürstenwalde, Ger.,
31,600 . . . . B7   6
Fürth, Ger., 97,600 . . . . . . D5   6
Furukawa, Jap.,
6,500 . . . . H8, m16   18
Fusagasugá, Col., 18,755 . . C3   32
Fuse, Jap., 271,704 . . I7, o14   18
Fushun, China, 985,000 . . . C9   17
Fusin, China, 188,600 . . . . C9   17
Füssen, Ger., 10,700 . . . . . E5   6
Fusung, China, 5,000 . . . . E3   18
Futamata, Jap., 11,442 . . . o16   18
Fuyu, China, 45,000 . . . . . C2   18
Fuyu, China, 45,000 . . . . . B9   17
Fuyuan, China, 5,000 . . . . B7   18

G

Gaberones, Bots., 10,000 . . . E5   24
Gabès, Tun., 24,420 . . . . . . B7   22
Gabin, Pol., 3,108 . . . . B5   7
Gabon (Gabun), country,
Afr., 468,000 . . . . I7   22
Gabrovo, Bul., 37,919 . . . . D7   10
Gadag, India, 76,614 . . . . . E6   20
Gadsden, Ala., 58,088 . . . . A3   46
Gadsden, co., Fla., 41,989 . . B2   54
Gadyach, Sov. Un.,
10,000 . . . . F9   12
Găești, Rom., 7,179 . . . . . . C7   10
Gaeta, It., 21,500 . . . . D4   9
Gaffney, S.C., 10,435 . . . . A4   82
Gafsa, Tun., 24,345 . . . . . . B6   22
Gage, co., Nebr., 26,818 . . D9   71
Gages Lake, Ill., 3,395 . . . *A5   58
Gagnon, Que., Can.,
1,900 . . . . h13   42
Gagny, Fr., 29,004 . . . . . . g11   5
Gahanna, Ohio, 2,717 . . . k11   78
Gaillac, Fr., 6,205 . . . . F4   5
Gaines, co., Tex., 12,267 . . C1   84
Gainesboro, Tenn., 1,021 . . C8   83
Gainesville, Fla., 29,701 . . C4   54
Gainesville, Ga., 16,523 . . B3   55
Gainesville, Tex., 13,083 . . C4   84
Gainesville East, Fla.,
2,393 . . . . *C4   54
Gainesville North, Fla.,
4,290 . . . . *C4   54
Gainesville West, Fla.,
2,725 . . . . *C4   54
Gainsborough, Eng.,
17,200 . . . . D6   4
Gairdner, lake, Austl F6   25
Gairloch, Scot., 1,991 . . . . B4   4
Gaithersburg, Md., 3,847 . . B3   53
Galacz, see Galati, Rom.
Galápagos, Is., see Colón,
Archipiélago de, Ec.
Galashiels, Scot., 12,200 . . C5   4
Galati, Rom., 107,200 . . . C8   10
Galatia, Ill., 830 . . . . F5   58
Galatina, It., 18,200 . . . . D7   9
Galax (Independent City),
Va., 5,254 . . . . D2   85
Galdar, Sp., 6,165 . . . . . . m14   8
Galeana, Mex., 876 . . . . . . A3   34
Galena, Ill., 4,410 . . . . A3   58
Galena, Kans., 3,827 . . . . E9   61
Galena Park, Tex.,
10,852 . . . . r14   84
Gales, peak, Oreg. g11   80
Galesburg, Ill., 37,243 . . . C3   85
Galesburg, Mich., 1,410 . . F5   66
Galesville, Md., 625 . . . . . C4   53
Galesville, Wis., 1,199 . . . D2   88
Galeton, Pa., 1,646 . . . . . C6   81
Galeville, N.Y., 1,000 . . . *B4   75
Galicia, reg., Pol.,
Sov. Un. D6   7
Galicia, reg., Sp.,
2,602,962 . . . . A1   8
Galien, Mich., 750 . . . . . . G4   66
Galion, Ohio, 12,650 . . . . B3   78
Gallarate, It., 37,700 . . . . B1   9
Gallatin, Mo., 1,658 . . . . . B4   69

Gallatin, Tenn., 7,901 . . . . A5   83
Gallatin, co., Ill., 7,638 . . . F5   58
Gallatin, co., Ky., 3,867 . . B5   62
Gallatin, co., Mont.,
26,045 . . . . E5   70
Galle, Cey., 55,848 . . . . . . G7   20
Gallia, co., Ohio, 26,120 . . D3   78
Gallipoli, It., 16,196 . . . . . D6   9
Gallipoli,
see Gelibolu, Tur.
Gallipolis, Ohio, 8,775 . . . D3   78
Gallitzin, Pa., 2,783 . . . . . F4   81
Gällivare, Swe., 25,363 . . D9   11
Galloway, W. Va., 300 . . . . B4   87
Gallup, N. Mex., 14,089 . . B4   48
Galt, Calif., 2,613 . . . . C3   50
Galt, Ont., Can., 27,830 . . D4   41
Galty, mts., Ire. D2   4
Galva, Ill., 3,060 . . . . B3   58
Galveston, Ind., 1,111 . . . . C5   59
Galveston, Tex., 65,000
(*163,000) E5, r15   84
Galveston, co., Tex.,
140,364 . . . . E5   84
Galway, Ire., 24,500 . . . . . D2   4
Galway, co., Ire.,
148,200 . . . . *D2   4
Gamagori, Jap., 81,112 . . . o16   18
Gamarra, Col., 4,664 . . . . B3   32
Gambia, country, Afr.,
315,500 . . . . F1   22
Gambia, riv., Afr. F2   22
Gambier, Ohio, 1,148 . . . . B3   78
Gamboa, C.Z., 3,489 . . . . *B2   32
Gambrills, Md., 600 . . . . . B4   53
Ganado, Tex., 1,626 . . . . . E4   84
Gananoque, Ont., Can.,
5,096 . . . . C8   41
Gand, see Gent, Bel.
Gander, Newf., Can.,
5,725 . . . . D4   44
Gandía, Sp., 15,812 . . . . . C5   8
Gangaw, Bur., 3,800 . . . . . D9   20
Ganges, riv., Asia D8   20
Gangtok, Sikkim, 6,848 . . C8   20
Gannat, Fr., 5,376 . . . . . . D5   5
Gannett, peak, Wyo C3   89
Gantt, S.C., 900 . . . . B3   82
Gao, Mali, 6,500 . . . . E5   22
Gap, Fr., 20,478 . . . . E7   5
Gap, Pa., 800 . . . . G9   81
Garanhuns, Braz.,
34,050 . . . . *D7   27
Garber, Okla., 905 . . . . . . A4   27
Garberville, Calif., 1,000 . . B2   50
Garça, Braz., 18,155 . . . . . C3   30
Garciasville, Tex., 350 . . . F3   84
Gard, dept., Fr., 435,482 . . *F6   5
Gardelegen, Ger., 12,400 . . B5   6
Garden, co., Nebr.,
3,472 . . . . C3   71
Gardena, Calif., 35,943 . . n12   50
Graden City, Fla., 1,500 . . m8   54
Garden City, Ga., 5,451 . . D5   55
Garden City, Idaho,
1,681 . . . . *F2   57
Garden City, Kans.,
11,811 . . . . E3   61

Garden City, Mich.,
38,017 . . . . p15   66
Graden City, Mo., 600 . . . C3   69
Garden City, N.Y.,
24,661 . . . . G2   52
Garden City, Pa.,
2,000 . . . . *G11   81
Garden City Park, N.Y.,
6,600 . . . . *G2   52
Gardendale, Ala.,
4,712 . . . . B3, E4   46
Garden Grove, Calif.,
84,238 . . . . n13   50
Garden Home, Oreg.,
2,000 . . . . *B4   80
Garden Lakes, Ga.,
1,300 . . . . *B1   55
Garden View, Pa., 2,418 . . *D7   81
Gardez, Afg., 17,540 . . . . B4   20
Gardiner, Maine, 6,897 . . . D3   64
Gardiner, Mont., 650 . . . . E6   70
Gardner, Ill., 1,041 . . . . . . B5   58
Gardner, Kans., 1,619 . . . D9   61
Gardner, Mass., 19,038 . . A4   65
Garfield, N.J., 29,253 . . . h8   74
Garfield, Wash., 607 . . . . B8   86
Garfield, co., Colo.,
12,017 . . . . B2   51
Garfield, co., Mont.,
1,981 . . . . C9   70
Garfield, co., Nebr.,
2,699 . . . . C6   71
Garfield, co., Okla.,
52,975 . . . . A4   79
Garfield, co., Utah, 3,577 . . C6   72
Garfield, co., Wash.,
2,976 . . . . C8   86
Garfield Heights, Ohio,
38,455 . . . . h9   78
Garfield peak, Wyo D5   89
Gargalianoi, Grc., 6,637 . . *D3   14
Garibaldi, Oreg., 1,163 . . . B3   80
Garibaldi, mtn., B.C.,
Can. E6   37
Garland, Md., 1,200 . . . . *B4   53
Garland, N.C., 642 . . . . . . C4   76
Garland, Tex., 38,501 . . . n10   84
Garland, Utah, 1,119 . . . . A5   72
Garland, co., Ark., 46,697 . . C2   49
Garmisch-Partenkirchen,
Ger., 26,800 . . . . E5   6
Garnavillo, Iowa, 662 . . . . B6   60
Garner, Iowa, 1,800 . . . . . A4   60
Garner, N.C., 4,282 . . . . . B4   76
Garnett, Kans., 3,034 . . . . D8   61
Garoua, Cam. G7   22
Garrard, co., Ky., 9,747 . . C5   62
Garrett, Ind., 4,725 . . . . . B7   59
Garrett, Ky., 100 . . . . C7   62
Garrett, co., Md., 20,420 . . k12   53
Garrett Park, Md., 965 . . . B3   53
Garrett Park Estates, Md.,
2,000 . . . . *B3   53
Garrettsville, Ohio, 1,662 . . A4   78
Garrison, Md., 600 . . . . . . B4   53
Garrison, N. Dak., 2,367 . . C4   77
Garrison, Tex., 951 . . . . . . D5   84
Garrovillas, Sp., 5,764 . . . C2   8

Garson, Ont., Can.,
3,786 . . . . *p19   41
Gartok, China, 5,000 . . . . B7   20
Garvin, co., Okla., 28,290 . . C4   79
Garwolin, Pol., 5,315 . . . . C6   7
Garwood, N.J., 5,426 . . . . *B4   74
Gary, Ind., 178,320 . . . . . A3   59
Gary, W. Va., 1,393 . . . . . D3   87
Garyville, La., 2,389 . . D5, h10   63
Garza, co., Tex., 6,611 . . . C2   84
Garzón, Col., 11,999 . . . . C2   32
Gas City, Ind., 5,249 . . . . D6   59
Gasconade, co., Mo.,
12,195 . . . . C6   69
Gascony (Gascogne),
former prov., Fr.,
996,000 . . . . E3   5
Gaspé, Que., Can., 2,603 . . k14   42
Gaspe East, co., Que.,
Can., 41,333 . . . . *k14   42
Gaspe West, co., Que.,
Can., 20,529 . . . . *k13   42
Gasport, N.Y., 900 . . . . . . B2   75
Gassaway, W. Va., 1,223 . . C4   87
Gaston, Ind., 801 . . . . D7   59
Gaston, N.C., 1,214 . . . . . A5   76
Gaston, co., N.C., 135,775 . . B1   76
Gastonia, N.C., 45,429 . . . B1   76
Gatchina, Sov. Un.,
47,900 . . . . H14, s31   11
Gate City, Va., 2,142 . . . . f9   85
Gates, N.Y., 16,405 . . . . . *B3   75
Gates, co., N.C., 9,254 . . . A6   76
Gateshead, Eng., 102,600 . . C6   4
Gates Mills, Ohio, 1,588 . . *A4   78
Gatesville, Tex., 4,626 . . . D4   84
Gatineau, Que., Can.,
13,022 . . . . D2   42
Gatineau, co., Que., Can.,
13,022 . . . . C2   42
Gatlinburg, Tenn.,
1,764 . . . . D10   83
Gatun, C.Z., 692 . . . . *B2   32
Gauley Bridge, W. Va.,
950 . . . . C3, D7   87
Gävle, Swe., 57,000 . . . . . G7   11
Gävleborg, co., Swe.,
294,300 . . . . *G7   11
Gavrilovka, Sov. Un.,
10,000 . . . . G11   12
Gawler, Austl., 5,639 . . . . G2   26
Gaya, India, 151,105 . . . . D7   20
Gaylord, Mich., 2,568 . . . C6   66
Gaylord, Minn., 1,631 . . . F4   67
Gaysin, Sov. Un., 10,000 . . G7   12
Gays Mills, Wis., 634 . . . . E3   88
Gaza Strip, Israeli occ.,
Asia, 325,000 . . . . C2   15
Gaziantep, Tur.,
124,097 . . . . D11   14
Gdańsk (Danzig), Pol.,
309,700 . . . . A5   7
Gdynia, Pol., 159,300 . . . . A5   7
Gearhart, mtn., Oreg. E6   80
Geary, N.B., Can., 938 . . . D3   43
Geary, Okla., 1,416 . . . . . B3   79
Geary, co., Kans., 28,779 . . D7   61

Geauga, co., Ohio, 47,573..........A4 78
Gedaref, Sud., 17,537.....F5 23
Gediz, Tur., 7,306.........C7 14
Geelong, Austl., 18,138 (*111,278).........G7, n14 25
Geislingen, Ger., 25,800..D4 6
Geistown, Pa., 3,186.....F4 81
Gelderland, prov., Neth., 1,287,800.............*A6 5
Gelibolu (Gallipoli), Tur., 12,945..............B6 14
Gelsenkirchen, Ger., 379,300.............C3 6
Gem, co., Idaho, 9,127....E2 57
Gemlik, Tur., 12,640......B7 14
Geneina, Sud., 11,817....F2 23
General Belgrano, Arg., 3,789...............B5 28
General Madariaga, Arg., 7,073...............B5 28
General Pico, Arg., 15,000..B4 28
General Roca, Arg., 21,969..............B3 28
Genesee, Idaho, 535.......C2 57
Genesee, Mich., 800......E7 66
Genesee, co., Mich., 374,313.............E7 66
Genesee, co., N.Y., 53,994..B2 75
Geneseo, Ill., 5,761.......B3 58
Geneseo, N.Y., 4,415.....C3 75
Geneva, Ala., 3,840......D4 46
Geneva, Ill., 8,573.......F1 58
Geneva, Ind., 1,053......C8 59
Geneva, Nebr., 1,352.....D8 71
Geneva, N.Y., 17,286.....C4 75
Geneva, Ohio, 5,677......A5 78
Geneva-on-the-Lake, Ohio, 631............A5 78
Geneva, co., Ala., 22,310..D4 46
Genéve (Geneva), Switz., 175,500 (*315,000).....E3 6
Genéve, canton, Switz., 259,234.............*E3 6
Genevia, Ark., 6,000..C3, D6 49
Genichesk, Sov. Un., 25,000.............H10 12
Genk, Bel., 47,416........B6 5
Gennevilliers, Fr., 42,595..g10 5
Genoa, Ill., 2,862........A5 58
Genoa, Nebr., 1,009......C8 71
Genoa, Ohio, 1,957.........A2, e7 78
Genoa City, Wis., 1,005............F5, n11 88
Genova (Genoa), It., 825,500.............B2 9
Gent (Ghent), Bel., 157,811 (*330,000).....B5 5
Genthin, Ger., 15,200.....B6 6
Gentilly, Que., Can., 677..C5 42
Gentilly, Fr., 19,211......g10 5
Gentry, co., Mo., 8,793....A3 69
Genzano di Roma, It., 12,727..............h9 9
George, Iowa, 1,200......A2 60
George, S. Afr., 14,759....G4 24
George, co., Miss., 11,098.............E5 68
Geroge, hill, Md........k12 53
Georgetown, Ont., Can., 10,298.............D5 41
Georgetown, P.E.I., Can., 744................C7 43
Georgetown, Conn., 1,200..D3 52
Georgetown, Del., 1,765..C7 53
Georgetown, Guy., 72,965.............C5 27
Gerogetown, Idaho, 551...G7 57
Georgetown, Ill., 3,544...D6 58
Georgetown, Ind., 713...H6 59
Georgetown, Ky., 6,986...B5 62
Georgetown, Mass., 2,300..A6 65
Georgetown, Ohio, 2,674..D2 78
Georgetown, S.C., 12,621..E9 82
Georgetown, Tex., 5,218..D4 84
Geroge Town, see Penang, Mala.
Georgetown, co., S.C., 34,798.............E9 82
George West, Tex., 1,878..E3 84
Georgia (Georgian S.S.R.), rep., Sov. Un., 4,460,000.............*A3 15
Georgia, state, U.S., 3,943,116..............
Georgiana, Ala., 2,093...D3 46
Georgia Southern, Ga., 1,700..............D5 55
Gera, Ger., 103,000......C6 6
Geraldine, Austl., 12,118..E1 25
Geraldton, Ont., Can., 3,375............o18 41
Gerber, Calif., 775.......B2 50
Gering, Nebr., 4,585.....C2 71
Gerlachovka, mtn., Czech..D6 7
Germantown, Conn., 2,893.............*D3 52

Germantown, Ill., 983.....E4 58
Germantown, Ohio, 3,999..C1 78
Germantown, Tenn., 1,104..............B2 83
Germantown, Wis., 622................E5, m11 88
Germany, East, country, Eur., 17,011,900.......... 6
Germany, West, country, Eur., 59,296,600.......... 6
Germiston, S. Afr., 148,102.............F5 24
Gero, Jap., 9,500........n16 18
Gerona, Sp., 32,784......B7 8
Gerona, prov., Sp., 351,369.............*B7 8
Gers, dept., Fr., 182,264..*F4 5
Gertrudis Sánchez, Mex., 28,808..............h9 34
Getafe, Sp., 21,895...B4, p17 8
Gettysburg, Pa., 7,960....G7 81
Gettysburg, S. Dak., 1,950..............E6 77
Geyserville, Calif., 750...C2 50
Ghana, country, Afr., 7,740,000...........G4 22
Gharyān, Libya, 2,796.....B7 22
Ghazni, Afg., 27,084.....B4 20
Ghazzah (Gaza), see Gaza Strip, Asia
Ghent, see Gent, Bel.
Gheorgheni, Rom., 11,969.............B7 10
Gherla, Rom., 7,617......B6 10
Giant, mtn., N.Y..........A7 75
Gibara, Cuba, 8,400......D5 35
Gibbon, Minn., 896.......F4 67
Gibbon, Nebr., 1,083.....D7 71
Gibbsboro, N.J., 2,141...*D3 74
Gibbstown, La., 25........F2 63
Gibbstown, N.J., 4,065...D2 74
Gibraleón, Sp., 8,865....D2 8
Gibraltar, Gib., 24,502...D3 8
Gibraltar, Mich., 2,196...*F7 66
Gibraltar, Br. dep., Eur., 25,000............*D3 8
Gibsland, La., 1,150......B2 63
Gibson, co., Ind., 29,949..H2 59
Gibson, co., Tenn., 44,699.............A3 83
Gibsonburg, Ohio, 2,540............A2, e7 78
Gibson City, Ill., 3,453...C5 58
Gibsonia, Pa., 1,150.....h14 81
Gibsons, B.C., Can., 1,091..............E6 37
Gibsonton, Fla., 2,000...p11 54
Gibsonville, N.C., 1,784..A3 76
Giddings, Tex., 2,821....D4 84
Gideon, Mo., 1,411......E8 69
Gien, Fr., 8,812.........D5 5
Giessen, Ger., 70,000....C4 6
Giffard, Que., Can., 10,129.............N17 42
Gifford, Fla., 3,509......E6 54
Gifu, Jap., 358,190...I8, n15 18
Gifu, pref., Jap., 1,700,365............*I8 18
Gigante, Col., 4,594......C2 32
Gig Harbor, Wash., 1,094............B3, f10 86
Gijon, Sp., 124,714......A3 8
Gila, co., Ariz., 25,745...C3 48
Gila, riv., Ariz., N. Mex..D4 45
Gila Bend, Ariz., 1,938...C2 48
Gilbert, Ariz., 1,831...C3, D2 48
Gilbert, Minn., 2,591.....C6 67
Gilbert, peak, Wash......C4 86
Gilbert & Ellice Is., Br. dep., Oceania, 51,000...F8 2
Gilberton, Pa., 1,712....*E9 81
Gilbertville, Iowa, 653...B5 60
Gilbert Plains, Man., Can., 849................D1 40
Gilbertville, Mass., 1,250..B3 65
Gilbertsville, Pa., 750....F10 81
Gilchrist, co., Fla., 2,868..C4 54
Giles, co., Tenn., 22,410..B4 83
Giles, co., Va., 17,219....C2 85
Gilford Park, N.J., 1,400.............*D4 74
Gillespie, Ill., 3,569......D4 58
Gillespie, co., Tex., 10,048.D3 84
Gillett, Wis., 1,374......D5 88
Gillette, Wyo., 3,580.....B7 89
Gilliam, co., Oreg., 3,069..B6 80
Gillingham, Eng., 75,800..E7 4
Gilly, Bel., 23,858.......B6 5
Gilman, Ill., 1,704.......C5 58
Gilmer, Tex., 4,312......C5 84
Gilmer, co., Ga., 8,922...B2 55
Gilmer, co., W. Va., 8,050..............C4 87
Gilmore City, Iowa, 688..B3 60
Gilpin, co., Colo., 685...B5 51
Gilroy, Calif., 7,348.....D3 50
Gimli, Man., Can., 1,841..D3 40
Ginosa, It., 17,800......D6 9

Ginzo, Sp., 9,130........A2 8
Gioia del Colle, It., 24,000.............D6 9
Gioiosa Ionica, It., 5,002..E6 9
Girard, Ill., 1,734.......D4 58
Girard, Kans., 2,350.....E9 61
Girard, Ohio, 12,997....A5 78
Girard, Pa., 2,451.......B1 81
Girardot, Col., 66,584, (76,990 ▲).........C3 32
Girardville, Pa., 2,958...E9 81
Giresun (Kerasund) Tur., 19,902.............B12 14
Giridih, Inida, 36,881....D8 20
Girishk, Afg., 5,000......B3 20
Gironde, dept., Fr., 935,448.............*E3 5
Girvan, Scot., 6,100......C4 4
Gisborne, N.Z., 24,939 (*27,804).........M17 26
Gisors, Fr., 6,398........C4 5
Giulianova, It., 9,100....C4 9
Giurgiu, Rom., 34,400...D7 10
Givet, Fr., 7,444........B6 5
Givors, Fr., 17,066......E6 5
Gjinokaster, Alb., 13,100..B3 14
Gjinokaster, pref., Alb., 168,000.............*B3 14
Gjövik, Nor., 23,700.....G4 11
Glace Bay, N.S., Can., 24,186.............C10 43
Glacier, co., Mont., 11,565.............B3 70
Glacier, peak, Wash......A4 86
Gladbrook, Iowa, 949....B5 60
Glades, co., Fla., 2,950...F5 54
Glade Spring, Va., 1,407..f10 85
Gladewater, Tex., 5,742..C5 84
Gladstone, Austl., 12,372..D9 25
Gladstone, Austl., 1,036...F6 25
Gladstone, Man., Can., 944................D2 40
Gladstone, Mich., 5,267..C4 66
Gladstone, Mo., 14,502...h10 69
Gladstone (Peapack-Gladstone), N.J., 1,804.............B3 74
Gladstone, Oreg., 3,854...........B4, h12 80
Gladstone (Peapack-Gladstone), N.J., 1,804..B3 74
Gladwin, Mich., 2,226...E6 66
Gladwin, co., Mich., 10,769.............D6 66
Gladwyne, Pa., 2,500...*F11 81
Glamoč, Yugo., 986......C3 10
Glamorgan, co., Wales, 1,242,000............*E5 4
Glandorf, Ohio, 747.....A1 78
Glarus, Switz., 5,852....E4 6
Glarus, canton, Switz., 40,148..............*E4 6
Glasco, Kans., 812.......C6 61
Glasco, N.Y., 800........C7 75
Glascock, co., Ga., 2,672..C4 55
Glasford, Ill., 1,012.....C4 58
Glasgow, Mo., 1,200.....B5 69
Glasgow, Ky., 10,069....C4 62
Glasgow, Mo., 1,200.....B5 69
Glasgow, Mont., 6,398...B10 70
Glasgow, Scot., 1,036,300..C4 4
Glasgow, Va., 1,091......C3 85
Glasgow, W. Va., 914....C6 87
Glassboro, N.J., 10,253...D2 74
Glasscock, co., Tex., 1,118..............D2 84
Glassport, Pa., 8,418.....F2 81
Glastonbury, Conn., 6,000..............C6 52
Glauchau, Ger., 33,700...C6 6
Gleason, Tenn., 900......A3 83
Gleasondale, Mass., 650...g9 65
Glenarden, Md., 1,336...*C4 53
Glen Allen, Va., 900.....C5 85
Glen Alpine, N.C., 734................B1, f11 76
Glen Avon Heights, Calif., 3,416.............*F5 50
Glenboro, Man., Can., 797................E2 40
Glen Burnie, Md., 22,500..B4 53
Glen Carbon, Ill., 1,241...E4 58
Glencliff, Tenn., 3,000...*A5 83
Glencoe, Ala., 2,592.....B4 46
Glencoe, Ont., Can., 1,156..............E3 41
Glencoe, Ill., 10,472...A6, h9 58
Glencoe, Minn., 3,216....F4 67
Glen Cove, N.Y., 25,048..h13 75
Glencullen, Oreg., 1,000..*B4 80
Glendale, Ariz., 30,760.............C2, D1 48
Glendale, Calif., 119,442............m12 50
Glendale, Mo., 7,048....*C7 69
Glendale, Ohio, 2,823............C1, m13 78

Glendale, S.C., 750......B4 82
Glen Dale, W. Va., 1,905..B4 87
Glendale, Wis., 10,432...*E6 88
Glendive, Mont., 7,058...C12 70
Glendora, Calif., 29,513..m13 50
Glendora, N.J., 5,000...*D2 74
Glen Ellyn, Ill., 18,620...k8 58
Glen Gardner, N.J., 787..B3 74
Glengarry, co., Ont., Can., 19,217.............B10 41
Glen Haven, Ga., 4,000..*C2 55
Glen Head, N.Y., 4,400..*F2 52
Glen Innes, Austl., 5,754..E9 25
Glen Jean, W. Va., 900.........D3, D7 87
Glen Lake, B.C., Can., 663................E5 37
Glen Lyon, Pa., 4,173....D9 81
Glen Moore, Pa., 1,700..*G9 81
Glenmora, La., 1,447.....D3 63
Glenn, co., Calif., 17,245..C2 50
Glenn Dale, Md., 600....C4 53
Glenns Ferry, Idaho, 1,374..............G3 57
Glennville, Ga., 2,791....E5 55
Glen Oak Acres, Ill., 1,500.............*A6 58
Glenolden, Pa., 7,249....p20 81
Glenorchy, Austl., 39,034..o15 25
Glen Raven, N.C., 2,418..A3 76
Glen Riddle, Pa., 800....p20 81
Glen Rock, N.J., 12,896............h8, D5 74
Glen Rock, Pa., 1,546....G8 81
Glenrock, Wyo., 1,584...D7 89
Glen Rogers, W. Va., 950................*D3 87
Glen Rose, Tex., 1,422...C4 84
Glens Falls, N.Y., 18,580..B7 75
Glenshaw, Pa., 24,939...*E1 81
Glenside, Pa., 25,000....o21 81
Glen Ullin, N. Dak., 1,210..............D4 77
Glenview, Ill., 23,521....h9 58
Glenview Countryside, Ill., 2,000.............*E2 58
Glenville, Minn., 643....G5 67
Glenville, W. Va., 1,828..C4 87
Glenwillard, Pa., 1,100...*E1 81
Glenwood, Newf., Can., 1,130..............D4 44
Glenwood, Iowa, 4,783...C2 60
Glenwood, Minn., 2,631..E3 67
Glenwood, Va., 1,857...*D3 85
Glenwood Landing, N.Y., 4,000.............*F2 52
Glenwood Park, N.Y., 1,317.............*D6 75
Glenwood Springs, Colo., 3,637.............B3 51
Glidden, Iowa, 993......B3 60
Glidden, Wis., 700.......B3 88
Gliwice, Pol., 145,900..C5, g9 7
Globe, Airz., 6,299...C3, D3 48
Globino, Sov. Un., 10,000..G9 12
Gloucester, Eng., 70,800..E5 4
Gloucester, Mass., 25,789............A6, f13 65
Gloucester, co., N.B., Can., 66,343.............B4 43
Gloucester, co., Eng., 1,024,100............*E5 4
Gloucester, co., N.J., 134,840.............D2 74
Gloucester, co., Va., 11,919.............C6 85
Gloucester City, N.J., 15,511.............D2 74
Glouster, Ohio, 2,255....C3 78
Gloversville, N.Y., 21,741..B6 75
Glovertown, Newf., Can., 1,197..............D4 44
Glovertown South, Newf., Can., 663.............*D5 44
Gloverville, S.C., 1,551...E4 82
Glubczyce, Pol., 5,020...C4 7
Glubokoye, Sov. Un., 25,000.............D6 12
Glucholazy, Pol., 12,500..C4 7
Gluck, S.C., 900........C2 82
Glukhov, Sov. Un., 10,000.............F9 12
Glussk, Sov. Un., 10,000..E7 12
Glyndon, Md., 900......B4 53
Glynn, co., Ga., 41,954..E5 55
Gmunden, Aus., 12,518..E6 6
Gnadenhutten, Ohio, 1,257..............B4 78
Gniezno, Pol., 46,400....B4 7
Goa, Damão and Diu, ter., India, 684,941...D5, E5 20
Goat, mtn., Mont........C3 70
Gobles, Mich., 816......F5 66
Gobo, Jap., 22,200......J7 18
Goch, Ger., 15,200......C3 6
Godavari, riv., India.....E6 20
Goderich, Ont., Can., 6,411.............D3 41

Godfrey, Ill., 4,000.......E3 58
Godwin Austen, peak, Pak..A6 20
Goffstown, N.H., 1,300....E4 73
Gogebic, co., Mich.,
  24,370.................n12 66
Goiana, Braz., 19,026....*D7 27
Goiás, Braz., 7,121.......B2 30
Goiás, state, Braz.,
  1,954,862...............B2 30
Gojo, Jap., 20,600......o14 18
Golchika, Sov. Un.,
  1,300.................B11 13
Golconda, Ill., 864......F5 58
Gold Beach, Oreg.,
  1,756.................E2 80
Gold Coast, see Ghana,
  country, Afr.
Gold Coast, see
  Southport, Austl.
Golden, B.C., Can.,
  1,776.................D9 37
Golden, Colo., 7,118.....B5 51
Golden City, Mo., 714....D3 69
Golden Acres, Tex.,
  2,500................*F5 84
Goldendale, Wash., 2,536..D5 86
Golden Glades, Fla.,
  3,000................*G6 54
Golden Hill, Minn.,
  2,190................*F6 67
Golden Hinde, mtn., B.C.,
  Can...................E5 37
Golden Meadow, La.,
  3,097.................E5 63
Golden Valley, Minn.,
  21,248................n12 67
Golden Valley, co., Mont.,
  1,203.................D7 70
Golden Valley, co., N. Dak.,
  3,100.................D2 77
Gold Hill, Ore., 608.....E3 80
Gold Mine, Ala., 50.....*A2 46
Goldsboro, N.C., 28,873..B5 76
Goldsmith, Tex., 670.....D1 84
Goldthwaite, Tex., 1,383..D3 84
Goleta, Calif., 5,000....E4 50
Golf Manor, Ohio, 4,648..o13 78
Goliad, Tex., 1,782......E4 84
Goliad, co., Tex., 5,429..E4 84
Golspie, Scot., 1,323....A5 4
Gomel, Sov. Un., 199,000..E8 12
Gómez Palacio, Mex.,
  61,174................B4 34
Gonaïves, Hai., 13,634....E7 35
Gonda, India, 43,496.....C7 20
Gondar, Eth., 25,000.....F5 23
Gönen, Tur., 10,890......B6 14
Gonesse, Fr., 8,517......g10 5
Gonzales, Calif., 2,165...D3 50
Gonzales, La., 3,252..D5, h10 63
Gonzales, Tex., 5,829....E4 84
Gonzales, co., Tex.,
  17,845................E4 84
Goochland, co., Va.,
  9,206.................C5 85
Goodhue, co., Minn.,
  33,035................F6 67
Gooding, Idaho, 2,750....G4 57
Gooding, co., Idaho,
  9,544.................F4 57
Goodland, Ind., 1,202....C3 59
Goodland, Kans., 4,459...C2 61
Goodlettsville, Tenn.,
  3,163...............A5, E9 83
Goodman, Miss., 932.....C4 68
Good Pine, La., 600......C3 63
Goodsprings, Ala., 900...B2 46
Goodview, Minn., 1,348...F7 67
Goodwater, Ala., 2,023...B3 46
Goodwell, Okla., 771.....e9 79
Goodyear, Ariz.,
  1,821..............C3, D2 48
Goose Bay, Newf., Can.,
  3,040...............B1, h9 44
Goose Creek, S.C.,
  830..................F7, k11 82
Goosport, La., 18,500....*D2 63
Göppingen, Ger., 48,100..D4 6
Gorakhpur, India,
  180,255...............C7 20
Gordo, Ala., 1,714.......B2 46
Gordon, Ga., 1,793.......D3 55
Gordon, Nebr., 2,223.....B3 71
Gordon, Pa., 888........*E9 81
Gordon, co., Ga., 19,228..B2 55
Gordonsville, Va., 1,109..B4 85
Gore, Eth., 10,000.......G5 23
Gore, N.Z., 7,270.......Q10 26
Gore Bay, Ont., Can., 716..B2 41
Gorgas, Ala., 500.......B2 46
Gorham, Maine, 2,500
  (5,767▲).............E2, g7 64
Gorham, N.H., 2,000.....C5 73
Gorham, N.Y., 800.......C3 75
Gorizia, It., 43,400.....B4 9
Gorki (Gorkiy), Sov. Un.,
  1,085,000.............D7 13
Gorlice, Pol., 12,800....D6 7

Görlitz, Ger., 89,300....C7 6
Gorlovka, Sov. Un.,
  309,000............G12, q21 12
Gorman, Tex., 1,142.....C3 84
Gorna-Dzhumaya, see
  Blagoevgrad, Bul.
Gorna Oryakhovitsa, Bul.,
  10,303................D7 10
Gorno-Altaysk, Sov. Un.,
  30,000...............D11 12
Gorodenka, Sov. Un.,
  10,000................G5 12
Gorodishche, Sov. Un.,
  10,000................q22 12
Gorodnya, Sov. Un.,
  10,000................F8 12
Gorodok, Sov. Un.,
  10,000................D7 12
Gorodok, Sov. Un.,
  10,000................G4 12
Gorontalo, Indon.,
  71,232................E6 19
Gorzow [Wielkopolski], Pol.,
  64,500................B3 7
Gosainthan, peak, China..C8 20
Gosford, Austl., 7,317...F8 26
Goshen, Calif., 1,061...*D4 50
Goshen, Ind., 13,718.....A6 59
Goshen, N.Y.,
  4,133.............D6, m14 75
Goshen, Ohio, 900.......C1 78
Goshen, co., Wyo.,
  11,941................D8 89
Goshogawara, Jap.,
  17,100 (47,433▲).....F10 18
Goslar, Ger., 40,900.....C5 6
Gosper, co., Nebr., 2,489..D6 71
Gospic, Yugo., 6,857.....C2 10
Gosport, Ind., 646......F4 59
Gostivar, Yugo., 12,776..E5 10
Gostyn, Pol., 11,100.....C4 7
Gostynin, Pol., 10,300...B5 7
Göteborg, Swe., 404,700..I4 11
Göteborg, och Bohus, co.,
  Swe., 633,000........*I4 11
Gotemba, Jap., 33,900....n17 18
Gotha, Ger., 56,300......C5 6
Gothenburg, Nebr.,
  3,050.................D5 71
Gotland, co., Swe.,
  54,200...............*I8 11
Göttingen, Ger., 82,600..C4 6
Gottwaldov Zlin, Czech.,
  55,600................D4 7
Gouda, Neth., 44,000.....A6 5
Goulburn, Austl., 20,849..F8 25
Gould, Ark., 1,210......D4 49
Goulding, Fla., 900.....*u14 54
Goulds, Fla., 5,121......s13 54
Gournay-en-Bray, Fr.,
  3,195.................C4 5
Gouverneur, N.Y., 4,946...f9 75
Gove, co., Kans., 4,107...D3 61
Governador Valadares, Braz.,
  70,494................B4 30
Gowanda, N.Y., 3,352....C2 75
Gowrie, Iowa, 1,127......B3 60
Goya, Arg., 20,804......E4 29
Graaff-Reinet, S. Afr.,
  16,936................G4 24
Gračanica, Yugo., 7,668..C4 10
Grace, Idaho, 725.......G7 57
Grace, mtn., Mass........A3 65
Grace Park, Pa., 2,000..*G11 81
Graceville, Fla., 2,307...u16 54
Graceville, Minn., 823...E2 67
Gradacac, Yugo., 5,897...C4 10
Gradizhsk, Sov. Un.,
  10,000................G9 12
Grado, Sp., 3,671.......A2 8
Grady, co., Ga., 18,015...F2 55
Grady, co., Okla., 29,590..C4 79
Graehl, Alsk., 560......*C10 47
Graettinger, Iowa, 879...A3 60
Grafton, Austl., 15,944..E9 25
Grafton, Ill.,1,084......E3 58
Grafton, Mass., 2,000....B4 65
Grafton, N. Dak., 7,064..B8 77
Grafton, Ohio, 1,683.....A3 78
Grafton, Va., 900.......h15 85
Grafton, W. Va.,
  5,791..............B4, B7 87
Grafton, Wis., 3,748..E5, m12 88
Grafton, co., N.H.,
  48,857................D4 73
Graham, N.C., 7,723......A3 76
Graham, Tex., 8,505......C3 84
Graham, co., Ariz., 14045..C3 48
Graham, co., Kans.,
  5,586.................C4 61
Graham, co., N.C., 6,432...f9 76
Grahamstown, S. Afr.,
  32,611................G5 24
Grainger, co., Tenn.,
  12,506...............C10 83
Grajewo, Pol., 6,171.....B7 7
Gramalote, Col., 3,098...B3 32
Grambling, La., 3,144....B3 63

Gramercy, La., 2,094.....h10 63
Grammichele, It., 14,486..F5 9
Granada, Nic., 28,507....E7 34
Granada, Sp., 157,178....D4 8
Granada, prov., Sp.,
  769,408..............*D4 8
Granbury, Tex., 2,227....C4 84
Granby, Que., Can.,
  31,463................D5 42
Granby, Mo., 1,808......E3 69
Grand, co., Colo., 3,537..A4 51
Grand, co., Utah, 6,345...B7 72
Grand, isl., La..........E6 63
Grand Bank, Newf., Can.,
  2,703.................E4 44
Grand Bay, N.B., Can.,
  725...................D3 43
Grand Bend, Ont., Can.,
  928...................D3 41
Grand Blanc, Mich.,
  1,565.................F7 66
Grand-Bourg, Guad.,
  2,489................I14 35
Grand Centre, Alta.,
  Can., 1,493...........B5 38
Grand Coteau, La., 1,165..D3 63
Grand Coulee, Wash.,
  1,058.................B6 86
Grande-Entrée, Que.,
  Can., 715.............B8 43
Grande Prairie, Alta., Can.,
  8,352..............B1, f7 38
Grande Rivière, Que., Can.,
  1,176...............*k14 42
Grandes-Bergeronnes,
  Que., Can., 779.......A8 42
Grand Falls, N.B., Can.,
  3,983.................B2 43
Grand Falls, Newf., Can.,
  6,606.................D4 44
Grandfalls, Tex., 1,012...D1 84
Grandfather, mtn., N.C...A1 76
Grandfield, Okla., 1,606..C3 79
Grand Forks, B.C., Can.,
  2,347.................E8 37
Grand Forks, N. Dak.,
  38,230................C8 77
Grand Forks, co., N. Dak.,
  48,677................C8 77
Grand Gorge, N.Y., 600...C6 75
Grand Haven, Mich.,
  11,066................E4 66
Grand Island, Nebr.,
  25,742................D7 71
Grand Island, N.Y.,
  1,700................*B2 75
Grand Isle, La., 2,074....E6 63
Grand Isle, co., Vt.,
  2,927.................B1 73
Grand Junction, Colo.,
  18,694................B2 51
Grand Junction, Iowa,
  949...................B3 60
Grand Ledge, Mich.,
  5,165.................F6 66
Grand Marais, Minn.,
  1,301.................k9 67
Grand Meadow, Minn.,
  837...................G6 67
Grand' Mère, Que., Can.,
  15,806................C5 42
Grand Prairie, Tex.,
  30,386................n10 84
Grand Rapids, Man.,
  Can., 986.............C2 40
Grand Rapids, Mich., 198,000
  (*405,000)............F5 66
Grand Rapids, Minn.,
  7,265.................C5 67
Grand Rapids, Ohio,
  670.................A2, f6 78
Grand Saline, Tex.,
  2,006.................C5 84
Grand Terrace, Calif.,
  1,450................*F5 50
Grand Teton, mtn., Wyo...C2 89
Grand Tower, Ill., 847...F4 58
Grand Traverse, co., Mich.,
  33,490................D5 66
Grand Valley, Ont., Can.,
  634...................D4 41
Grandview, Man., Can.,
  1,057.................D1 40
Grandview, Ill., 100.....D6 58
Grand View, Ind., 599....I4 59
Grandview, Mo.,
  6,027.............C3, k10 69
Grandview, Tex., 961....*C4 84
Grandview, Wash.,
  3,366.................C6 86
Grandview Heights, Ohio,
  8,270................m10 78
Grandview Heights, Pa.,
  3,800................*G9 81
Grandville, Mich., 7,975..F5 66
Granger, Tex., 1,339.....D4 84
Granger, Utah., 10,000..*A5 72
Granger, Wash., 1,424....C5 86

Grangeville, Idaho, 3,642..D2 57
Grangeville, Pa., 1,100..*G8 81
Granite, Md., 700.......B4 53
Granite, Okla., 952......C2 79
Granite, peak, Mont......E7 70
Granite, co., Mont.,
  3,014.................D3 70
Granite, peak, Mont......E7 70
Granite, peak, Wyo......D4 89
Granite City, Ill., 40,073..E3 58
Granite Falls, Minn.,
  3,171.................F3 67
Granite Falls, N.C., 2,644..B1 76
Granite Falls, Wash., 599..A4 86
Granite Quarry, N.C.,
  1,059.................B2 76
Graniteville, Mass., 900...f10 65
Graniteville, S.C., 3,000..D4 82
Granja de Torrehermosa, Sp.,
  6,314.................C3 8
Granollers, Sp., 20,194...B7 8
Grant, Mich., 732.......E5 66
Grant, Nebr., 1,166......D4 71
Grant, co., Ark., 8,294...C3 49
Grant, co., Ind., 75,741...C6 59
Grant, co., Kans., 5,269...E2 61
Grant, co., Ky., 9,489....B5 62
Grant, co., Minn., 8,840..E2 67
Grant, co., Nebr., 1,009...C4 71
Grant, co., N. Mex.,
  18,700................C4 48
Grant, co., N. Dak.,
  6,248.................D4 77
Grant, co., Okla., 8,140..A4 79
Grant, co., Oreg., 7,726..C7 80
Grant, co., S. Dak., 9,913..E9 77
Grant, co., Wash., 46,477..B6 86
Grant, co., W. Va., 8,304..B4 87
Grant, co., Wis., 44,419...F3 88
Grant, par., La., 13,300...C3 63
Grant City, Mo., 1,061...A3 69
Grantham, Eng., 25,400...D6 4
Grant Park, Ill., 757....B6 58
Grants, N. Mex., 10,274..B5 48
Grantsboro, N.C., 150....B6 76
Grantsburg, Wis., 900....C1 88
Grants Pass, Oreg.,
  10,118................E3 80
Grantsville, Utah,
  2,166..............A5, D1 72
Grantsville, W. Va., 866...C3 87
Grant Town, W. Va.,
  1,105..............A7, B4 87
Grantville, Ga., 1,158...C2 55
Granville, Fr., 9,827....C3 5
Granville, Ill., 1,048....B4 58
Granville, N.Y., 2,715...B7 75
Granville, Ohio, 2,868...B3 78
Granville, W. Va., 806...*B5 87
Granville, co., N.C.,
  33,110................A4 76
Grapeland, Tex., 1,113...D5 84
Grapeville, Pa., 1,600...*F2 81
Grapevine, Ky., 500.....C2 62
Grapevine, Tex.,
  2,821..............C4, n9 84
Grasonville, Md., 925....C5 53
Grasse, Fr., 26,258......F7 5
Grassflat, Pa., 850......D5 81
Grass Lake, Mich., 1,037..F6 66
Grass Valley, Calif., 4,876..C3 50
Gratiot, co., Mich.,
  37,012................E6 66
Graton, Calif., 1,055...*C2 50
Graubünden, canton, Switz.,
  147,458..............*E4 6
Graulhet, Fr., 7,996.....F5 5
Gravatá, Braz., 15,550...*D7 27
Grave, peak, Idaho......C4 57
Gravelbourg, Sask., Can.,
  1,499................H2 39
Gravenhurst, Ont., Can.,
  3,077.................C5 41
Graves, co., Ky., 30,021...B2 62
Gravesend, Eng.,
  53,300.............E7, m13 4
Gravina [in Puglia], It.,
  31,977................D6 9
Gray, Ga., 1,320.........C3 55
Gray, Ky., 650..........D5 62
Gray, Maine, 600........g7 64
Gray, co., Kans., 4,380...E3 61
Gray, co., Tex., 31,535...B2 84
Grayling, Mich., 2,015...D6 66
Grays, peak, Colo........B5 51
Grays Harbor, co., Wash.,
  54,465................B2 86
Grayslake, Ill., 4,347..A5, h8 58
Grayson, Ky., 1,692......B7 62
Grayson, co., Ky., 15,834..C3 62
Grayson, co., Tex.,
  73,043................C4 84
Grayson, co., Va., 17,390..D1 85
Graysville, Ala., 2,870..*B3 46
Grayville, Ill., 2,280....E5 58
Graz, Aus., 243,400......E7 6
Great Barrington, Mass.,
  3,500.................B4 65

Great Bear, lake, Can......C9 36
Great Bend, Kans.,
  16,670...............D5 61
Great Bend, Pa., 777.....C10 81
Great Blue, hill, Mass.....B5 65
Great Divide, basin, Wyo..E4 89
Greater Antilles, is., W.I..B3 27
Great Falls, Mont.,
  55,244...............G5 70
Great Falls, S.C., 3,030...B6 82
Greathouse, peak, Mont...D7 70
Great Neck, N.Y., 4,948..h13 75
Great Neck Estates, N.Y.,
  3,262................n15 75
Great Salt, lake, Utah.....A5 72
Great Slave, lake, Can....D11 36
Great Whale River, Que.,
  Can., 718............g11 42
Great Yarmouth, Eng.,
  52,700...............D7 4
Greece, N.Y., 33,500....*B3 75
Greece, country, Eur.,
  8,510,000.............C4 14
Greeley, Colo., 26,314....A6 51
Greeley, Nebr., 656......C7 71
Greeley, co., Kans., 2,087.D2 61
Greeley, co., Nebr., 4,595.C7 71
Green, co., Ky., 11,249....C4 62
Green, co., Wis., 25,851...F4 88
Green, riv., U.S..........B6 72
Greenacres, Calif., 1,000.*E4 50
Green Acres, Md., 1,000.*C3 53
Green Acres, N.Y., 2,500.*E2 75
Greenacres, Wash.,
  2,074...............B8, g14 86
Greenacres City, Fla.,
  1,026................F6 54
Greenback, Tenn., 285....D9 83
Green Bay, Wis., 85,000
  (*119,000).........D6, g10 88
Greenbelt, Md., 7,479....B4 53
Greenbrae, Calif., 2,000.*D2 50
Greenbrier, co., W. Va.,
  34,446...............D4 87
Green Brook, N.J., 3,622.*B4 74
Greenbush, Mass., 600...h12 65
Greenbush, Minn., 706...B2 67
Greencastle, Ind., 8,506..E4 59
Greencastle, Pa., 2,988...G6 81
Green City, Mo., 628....A5 69
Green Cove Springs, Fla.,
  4,233..............C5, n8 54
Greendale, Ind., 2,861...F8 59
Greendale, Wis.,
  6,843..............F6, n12 88
Greene, Iowa, 1,427.....B5 60
Greene, N.Y., 1,927.....C5 75
Greene, co., Ala., 13,600..C1 46
Greene, co., Ark., 25,198..A5 49
Greene, co., Ga., 11,193..C3 55
Greene, co., Ill., 17,460..D3 58
Greene, co., Ind., 26,327..F4 59
Greene, co., Iowa, 14,379.B3 60
Greene, co., Miss., 8,366..D5 68
Greene, co., Mo., 126,276.D4 69
Greene, co., N.Y., 31,372.C6 75
Greene, co., N.C., 16,741.B5 76
Greene, co., Ohio, 94,642..C2 78
Greene, co., Pa., 39,424...G1 81
Greene, co., Tenn.,
  42,163..............C11 83
Greeneville, Tenn.,
  11,759..............C11 83
Greenfield, Calif., 6,927..D3 50
Greenfield, Ill., 1,064....D3 58
Greenfield, Ind., 9,049....E6 59
Greenfield, Iowa, 2,243...C3 60
Greenfield, Mass., 17,690.A2 65
Greenfield, Mo., 1,172...D4 69
Greenfield, Ohio, 5,422...C2 78
Greenfield, Tenn., 1,779..A3 83
Greenfield, Wis., 17,636..n12 88
Greenfield Park, Que., Can.,
  7,807...............q20 42
Greenfield Village, Utah,
  1,000...............*D2 82
Green Forest, Ark., 1,083..A2 49
Green Harbor, Mass., 700.B6 65
Green Haven, Md.,
  1,302...............*B2 53
Greenhills, Ohio, 5,407...n12 78
Green Hills, Tenn.,
  14,000..............*A5 83
Green Island, N.Y.,
  3,533...............*C7 75
Green Lake, Sask., Can.,
  756.................C2 39
Green Lake, Wis., 1,033...E5 88
Green Lake, co., Wis.,
  15,418..............E4 88
Greenland, Dan. dep., N.A.,
  40,000..............B16 33
Greenlawn, N.Y., 6,500...F3 52
Greenlee, co., Ariz.,
  11,509..............C4 48
Green Lookout, mtn.,
  Wash...............D3 86

Green Manorville, Conn.,
  1,300...............*B6 52
Green Meadows, Md.,
  1,500...............*C4 53
Greenock, Pa., 1,500.....*E1 81
Greenock, Scot., 74,700
  (*108,000)..........C4 4
Greenport, N.Y., 2,608...m16 75
Green Ridge, Pa.,
  3,500...............*G11 81
Green River, Utah,
  1,075...............B6 72
Green River, Wyo., 3,497.E3 89
Greensboro, Ala., 3,081...C2 46
Greensboro, Fla., 709....B2 54
Greensboro, Ga., 2,773...C3 55
Greensboro, Md., 1,160..C6 53
Greensboro, N.C., 136,000
  (*185,000)..........A3 76
Greensburg, Ind., 7,492...F7 59
Greensburg, Kans., 1,988.E4 61
Greensburg, Ky., 2,334...C4 62
Greensburg, Pa., 17,383..F2 81
Green's Harbour, Newf.,
  Can., 713...........*E5 44
Greenspond, Newf., Can.,
  728.................D5 44
Green Springs, Ohio,
  1,262...............A2 78
Greensville, co., Va.,
  16,155..............D5 85
Greentown, Ind., 1,763...D6 59
Green Tree, Pa., 5,226....*E1 81
Greenup, Ill., 1,477.....D5 58
Greenup, Ky., 1,240.....B7 62
Greenup, co., Ky., 29,238.B7 62
Greenvale, N.Y., 1,220...*F2 52
Greenview, Ill., 796.....C4 58
Greenville, Ala., 6,894...D3 46
Greenville, Calif., 1,140..B3 50
Greenville, Fla., 1,318....B3 54
Greenville, Ill., 4,569....E4 58
Greenville, Ky., 3,198....C2 62
Greenville, Maine, 1,400..C3 64
Greenville, Mich., 7,440..E5 66
Greenville, Miss., 41,502..B2 68
Greenville, N.H., 1,251...F4 73
Greenville, N.Y., 2,800...h13 75
Greenville, N.C., 22,860..B5 76
Greenville, Ohio, 10,585..B1 78
Greenville, Pa., 8,765....D1 81
Greenville, R.I., 3,000....B10 52
Greenville, S.C., 67,000
  (*180,000)..........B3 82
Greenville, Tex., 19,087..C4 84
Greenville, co., S.C.,
  209,776.............A3 82
Greenville Junction,
  Maine, 600..........C3 64
Greenwich, Conn., 53,793.E2 52
Greenwich, Eng., 83,800.m13 4
Greenwich, N.Y., 2,263...B7 75
Greenwich, Ohio, 1,371..A3 78
Greenwood, Ark., 1,558..B1 49
Greenwood, B.C., Can.,
  932.................E8 37
Greenwood, Ind.,
  7,169..............E5, m10 59
Greenwood, Miss., 20,436.B3 68
Greenwood, Pa., 1,500....E5 81
Greenwood, S.C., 16,644..C3 82
Greenwood, Wis., 1,041..D3 88
Greenwood, co., Kans.,
  11,253..............E7 61
Greenwood, co., S.C.,
  44,346..............C3 82
Greenwood Lake, N.Y.,
  1,236...............*D6 75
Greer, S.C., 8,967.......B3 82
Greer, co., Okla., 8,877...C2 79
Gregg, co., Tex., 69,436..C5 84
Gregory, S. Dak., 1,478..G6 77
Gregory, Tex., 1,970.....*F4 84
Gregory, co., S. Dak.,
  7,399...............G6 77
Greifswald, Ger., 47,200..A6 6
Greilickville, Mich.,
  900.................D5 66
Greinwich Terrace, La.,
  2,000...............*D2 63
Greiz, Ger., 39,100......C6 6
Grenada, Miss., 7,914....B5 68
Grenada, co., Miss.,
  18,409..............B4 68
Grenada, Br. dep., N.A.,
  88,677..............J14 35
Grenfell, Sask., Can.,
  1,256...............G4 39
Grenloch, N.J., 550......D2 74
Grenoble, Fr., 156,707...E6 5
Grenville, Que., Can.,
  1,330...............D3 42
Grenville, co., Ont., Can.,
  22,864..............C9 41
Gresham, Oreg., 3,944...B4 80
Gretna, Fla., 647.......B2 54
Gretna, La., 21,967....E5, k11 63
Gretna, Nebr., 745.....C9, g12 71

Gretna, Va., 900........D3 85
Grey, co., Ont., Can.,
  62,005..............C4 41
Greybull, Wyo., 2,286....B4 89
Greylock, mtn., Mass.....A1 65
Greymouth, N.Z., 8,881..O13 26
Gridley, Calif., 3,343....C3 50
Gridley, Ill., 889.......C5 58
Griffin, Ga., 21,735.....C2 55
Griffing Park, Tex.,
  2,267...............*E5 84
Griffith, Austl., 9,510....F8 25
Griffith, Ind., 12,810....A3 59
Grifton, N.C., 1,816.....B5 76
Griggs, co., N. Dak.,
  5,023...............C7 77
Griggsville, Ill., 1,240....D3 58
Grimes, co., Tex., 12,709..D4 84
Grimma, Ger., 16,100....C6 6
Grimsby, Ont., Can.,
  5,148...............D5 41
Grimsby, Eng., 96,700...D6 4
Grimshaw, Alta., Can.,
  1,095...............A2 38
Grindstone, Pa., 1,094...*G2 81
Grinnell, Iowa, 7,367....C5 60
Griswold, Iowa, 1,207...C2 60
Grodno, Sov. Un., 88,000.E4 12
Grodzisk, Pol., 6,015....B4 7
Grodzisk Mazowiecki,
  Pol., 19,500........m13 7
Groesbeck, Ohio, 9,000..*C1 78
Groesbeck, Tex., 2,498...D4 84
Grojec, Pol., 6,841......C6 7
Grombalia, Tun., 5,043..F3 9
Gronau, Ger., 25,600....B3 6
Groningen, Neth.,
  151,100.............A7 5
Groningen, prov., Neth.,
  477,700.............*A7 5
Grosse Ile, Mich., 6,318..*B7 66
Grossenhain, Ger., 19,500.C6 6
Grosse Pointe, Mich.,
  6,631...............p16 66
Grosse Pointe Farms,
  Mich., 12,172.......*p16 66
Grosse Pointe Park, Mich.,
  15,457..............p16 66
Grosse Pointe Shores,
  Mich., 2,301........*F8 66
Grosse Pointe Woods,
  Mich., 18,580.......p16 66
Grosseto, It., 38,200....C3 9
Grossglockner, mtn., Aus..E6 6
Grossmont, Calif., 3,000..o16 50
Gros Ventre, range, Wyo..C2 89
Groton, Conn., 29,937...D8 52
Groton, Mass., 1,250...A4, f9 65
Groton, N.Y., 2,123.....C4 75
Groton, S. Dak., 1,063...E7 77
Grottaferrata, It., 5,377..h9 9
Grottaglie, It., 23,223...D6 9
Grottoes, Va., 969......B4 85
Grove, Okla., 975.......A7 79
Grove City, Ohio,
  8,107..............C2, m10 78
Grove City, Pa., 8,368...D1 81
Grove Hill, Ala., 1,834...D2 46
Groveland, Fla., 1,747...D5 54
Groveland, Mass., 1,800..A5 65
Groveport, Ohio,
  2,043..............C2, m11 78
Grover City, Calif., 5,210.E3 50
Groves, Tex., 17,304....E6 84
Groveton, N.H., 2,004...B4 73
Groveton, Pa., 1,300....*E1 81
Groveton, Tex., 1,148...D5 84
Groveton, Va., 1,200....g12 85
Grovetown, Ga., 1,396...C4 55
Groveville, N.J., 2,500...C3 74
Groznyy, Sov. Un.,
  314,000.............E7 13
Grudziadz, Pol., 68,000..B5 7
Grulla, Tex., 1,500......F3 84
Grundy, Va., 2,287......e9 85
Grundy, co., Ill., 22,350..B5 58
Grundy, co., Iowa, 14,132.B5 60
Grundy, co., Mo., 12,220.A4 69
Grundy, co., Tenn.,
  11,512..............D8 83
Grundy Center, Iowa,
  2,403...............B5 60
Gruver, Tex., 1,030.....A2 84
Gruz, Yugo., 10,000.....D4 10
Gryazi, Sov. Un.,
  10,000..............E12 12
Guadalajara, Mex.,
  736,800............C4, m12 34
Guadalajara, Sp., 21,230.B4 8
Guadalajara, prov., Sp.,
  183,545.............*B4 8
Guadalcanal, Sp., 6,931..C3 8
Guadalupe, Ariz., 2,000..D2 48
Guadalupe, Calif., 2,614.E3 50
Cuadalupe, co., N. Mex.,
  5,610...............B6 48
Guadalupe, co., Tex.,
  29,017..............E4 84

Guadalupe, peak, Tex.,...E2 84
Guadeloupe, Fr. dep., N.A.,
  283,223.............H14 35
Guaira, dept., Par.,
  100,446.............E4 29
Gualeguay, Arg., 16,542..A5 28
Gualeguaychú, Arg.,
  29,863..............A5 28
Guam, U.S., dep.,
  Oceania, 70,000.....F6 2
Guanabacoa, Cuba,
  41,000..............C2 35
Guanabara, state, Braz.,
  3,307,163...........*C4 30
Guanacaste, prov., C.R.,
  146,600.............*E8 34
Guanajay, Cuba, 13,700..C2 35
Guanajuato, Mex.,
  28,212............C4, m13 34
Guanajuato, state, Mex.,
  1,735,490...........C4 34
Guanare, Ven., 18,452...B4 32
Guane, Cuba, 4,400......C1 35
Guánica, P.R., 4,100....*G11 35
Guantánamo, Cuba,
  100,500.............D6 35
Guarabira, Braz., 15,848.*D7 27
Guaranda, Ec., 9,900....B2 31
Guarapuava, Braz.,
  13,546..............D2 30
Guaratinguetá, Braz.,
  38,293..............C3 30
Guarda, Port., 9,094....B2 8
Guareña, Sp., 9,742.....C2 8
Guárico, state, Ven.,
  244,966.............B4 32
Guarujá, Braz., 6,506....n8 30
Guatemala, Guat.,
  572,900.............E6 34
Guatemala, country, N.A.,
  4,278,500...........D6 34
Guaxupé, Braz.,
  14,168.............C3, k8 30
Guayabal, Cuba, 9,000..D5 35
Guayama, P.R., 19,183..n13 36
Guayaquil, Ec., 510,804..B2 31
Guayas, prov., Ec.,
  979,225.............B1 31
Guaymas, Mex., 34,865..B2 34
Gubakha, Sov. Un.,
  53,800..............*D8 13
Gubat, Phil., 8,392.....*C6 19
Gubbio, It., 8,600......C4 9
Gudur, India, 25,618....F6 20
Guebwiller, Fr., 10,568..D7 5
Guecho, Sp., 22,951....A4 8
Guelma, Alg., 34,829....A6 22
Guelph, Ont., Can.,
  39,838..............D4 41
Güemes, Arg., 5,688....D2 29
Guéret, Fr., 11,384.....D4 5
Guerneville, Calif., 900..*C2 50
Guernsey, Wyo., 800....D8 89
Guernsey, Br. dep., Eur.,
  49,000..............F5 4
Guernsey, co., Ohio,
  38,579..............B4 78
Guerrero, state, Mex.,
  1,186,716...........D5 34
Gueydan, La., 2,156.....D3 63
Guiana, French, see French
  Guiana, dep., S.A.
Guiana, Netherlands,
  see Surinam,
  Neth. dep., S.A.
Guidonia, It., 22,205..D4, h9 9
Guildford, Eng.,
  54,300............E6, m11 4
Guilford, Conn., 2,600...D6 52
Guilford, Maine, 1,400...C3 64
Guilford, N.C., 1,000...*A3 76
Guilford, co., N.C.,
  269,513.............A3 76
Guilford, College, N.C.,
  1,700...............*A3 76
Guimarães, Port.,
  23,229..............B1 8
Guin, Ala., 1,462.......B2 46
Guinea, country, Afr.,
  3,500,000...........F2 22
Guinea, Portugese see
  Portuguese Guinea,
  dep., Afr.
Güines, Cuba, 39,500....C2 35
Guingamp, Fr., 8,912....C2 5
Guipúzcoa, prov., Sp.,
  478,337.............*A4 8
Güira de Melena, Cuba,
  18,900..............C2 35
Güiria, Ven., 10,061....A5 32
Guise, Fr., 6,284.......C5 5
Gujarat, state, India,
  20,633,350..........D5 20
Gujranwala, Pak.,
  196,154.............B5 21
Gulbarga, India, 97,069..E6 20
Gulf, co., Fla., 9,937....C1 54
Gulf Hammock, Fla., 350..C4 54

Gulfport, Fla.,
9,730............E4, p10 54
Gulfport, Miss., 33,000
(*137,000).........E2, E4 68
Gull Lake, Sask., Can.,
1,038................G1 39
Gulyay-Pole, Sov. Un.,
10,000..............H11 12
Gumma, pref., Jap.,
1,605,584...........*H9 18
Gummersbach, Ger.,
32,000...............C3 6
Gunnedah, Austl., 6,546...E8 26
Gunnison, Colo., 3,477...C4 51
Gunnison, Utah, 1,059.....B6 72
Gunnison, co., Colo.,
5,477...............C3 51

Guntersville, Ala., 6,592...A3 46
Guntur, India, 187,122...E7 20
Gurabo, P.R., 3,957....*G11 35
Gurdon, Ark., 2,166.....D2 49
Gurnee, Ill., 2,167.......E2 58
Guryev, Sov. Un.,
91,000................E8 13
Gusev (Gumbinnen) Sov. Un.,
25,000................A7 7
Gusinje, Yugo., 2,757....D4 10
Gus-Khrustalnyy,
Sov. Un., 59,000.....D13 12
Gustine, Calif., 2,300....D3 50
Güstrow, Ger.,
38,000................B6 6
Gütersloh, Ger., 53,400....C4 6
Guthrie, Ky., 1,211......D12 62

Guthrie, Okla., 9,502......B4 79
Guthrie, co., Iowa,
13,607................C3 60
Guthrie Center, Iowa,
2,071................C3 60
Guttenberg, Iowa, 2,087..B6 60
Guttenberg, N.J., 5,118...h8 74
Guyana, country, S.A.,
631,000..............C5 27
Guyenne, former prov., Fr.,
2,061,000............E4 5
Guymon, Okla.,
5,768................e9 79
Guysborough, co., N.S.,
Can., 490.............D8 43
Gvardeysk, Sov. Un.,
5,000................A6 7

Gwadar Gwadur, Pak.,
8,146................C3 20
Gwalior, India, 300,587....C6 20
Gwelo, Rh., 32,200......D5 24
Gwinn, Mich., 1,200.....B3 66
Gwinnett, co., Ga.,
43,541..............C2 55
Gyangtse, China,
10,000...............C8 20
Gympie, Austl.,
11,277..........E9, n14 25
Gyongyos, Hung.,
28,668...............B4 10
Györ, Hung., 75,300....B3 10
Gyor-Sopron, co., Hung.,
391,734.............*B3 10
Gyula, Hung., 19,990.....B5 10

H

Haakon, co., S. Dak.,
3,303................F4 77
Haapsalu, Sov. Un.,
10,000................B4 12
Haarlem, Neth., 172,000...A6 5
Habersham, Ga., 400.....B3 55
Habersham., co., Ga.,
18,116...............B3 55
Haboro, Jap., 21,800....D10 18
Hachiman, Jap., 13,000...n15 18
Hachinohe, Jap.,
189,387..............F10 18
Hachioji, Jap.,
207,753..........I9, n18 18
Hackberry, La., 800......E2 63
Hackensack, N.J.,
30,521............B4, h8 74
Hackettstown, N.J., 5,276..B3 74
Haddonfield, N.J., 13,201..D2 74
Haddon Heights, N.J.,
9,260................D2 74
Hadera, Isr., 27,200....B2, g5 15
Haderslev, co., Den.,
72,153..............*J3 11
Haditha, Iraq, 5,434......C3 15
Hadley, Mass., 800
(3,099▲)............B2 65
Haeju, Kor., 82,135......G2 18
Hagaman, N.Y., 1,292....*C6 75
Hagar Shores (Lake
Michigan Beach),
Mich., 1,092.........*F4 66
Hagen, Ger., 198,900....C3 6
Hagerman, N. Mex.,
1,144................C6 48
Hagerstown, Ind., 1,730...E7 59
Hagerstown, Md., 36,660..A2 53
Hagersville, Ont., Can.,
2,075................E4 41
Hagginwood, Calif.,
11,469..............*C3 50
Hagi, Jap., 42,000.......I5 18
Ha Giang, Viet., 25,000..G6 17
Haguenau, Fr., 20,457....C7 5
Hague, The ('s Gravenhage),
see The Hague, Neth.
Hahira, Ga., 1,297.......F3 55
Hahnville, La.,
1,297............E5, k11 63
Hai Duong, Viet.,
24,752..............*A3 19
Haifa, Isr., 191,200
(*300,000)........B3, g5 15
Hā'il, Sau. Ar., 30,000....D3 15
Hailar (Hulun), China,
43,200................B8 17
Hailey, Idaho, 1,185.....F4 57
Haileybury, Ont., Can.,
2,638................p20 41
Haileyville, Okla., 922...C6 79
Hailun, China, 48,000....C3 18
Hailung, China, 20,000....E2 18
Hainan, isl., China......B4 19
Hainaut, prov., Bel.,
1,248,854............*B5 5
Haines City, Fla., 9,135...D5 54
Haines Falls, N.Y., 700...C6 75
Hainesport, N.J., 1,500...D3 74
Haiphong, Viet.,
182,496..............A3 19
Haiti, country, N.A.,
4,485,000............E7 35
Hajdu-Bihar, co., Hung.,
393,332.............*B5 10

Hajduhadhaz, Hung.,
11,221...............B5 10
Hajdunanas, Hung.,
14,003...............B5 10
Hajduszoboszlo, Hung.,
16,709...............B5 10
Hakalau, Haw., 650.....D6 56
Hakodate, Jap., 243,418..F10 18
Halawa Heights, Haw.,
2,000................g10 56
Halberstadt, Ger., 45,700..C5 6
Halden, Nor., 10,000....H4 11
Haldimand, co., Ont.,
Can., 28,197.........E5 41
Hale, co., Ala., 19,537....C2 46
Hale, co., Tex., 36,798...B2 84
Haleakala, crater, Haw....C5 56
Hale Center, Tex., 2,196..B2 84
Haledon, N.J., 6,161....*B4 74
Haleiwa, Haw., 2,504...B3, f9 56
Hales Corners, Wis.,
5,549................n11 88
Halesite, N.Y., 3,200....*n15 75
Halethorpe, Md.,
23,000............B4, h10 53
Haleyville, Ala., 3,740....A2 46
Half Moon Bay, Calif.,
1,957................k8 50
Halfway, Md., 5,000.....A2 53
Haliburton, Ont., Can.,
853..................B6 41
Haliburton, co., Ont., Can.,
8,928................B6 41
Halifax, N.S., Can., 92,511
(*183,946)...........E6 43
Halifax, Eng., 95,900.....D6 4
Halifax, N.C., 58,956.....A5 76
Halifax, Mass., 600
(1,599▲)............C6 65
Halifax, Pa., 824........F8 81
Halifax, Va., 792........D4 85
Halifax, co., N.S., Can.,
225,723..............E7 43
Halifax, co., Va., 33,637..D4 85
Hall, Aus., 10,016.......E5 6
Hall, co., Ga., 49,739....B3 55
Hall, co., Nebr., 35,757...D7 71
Hall, co., Tex., 7,322....B2 84
Halland, co., Swe.,
171,200..............I15 11
Hallandale, Fla.,
10,483...........G6, s13 54
Halle, Ger., 278,000.....C5 6
Hallein, Aus., 13,329.....E6 6
Hallettsville, Tex., 2,808..E4 84
Hallock, Minn., 1,527....B2 67
Hallowell, Maine, 3,169..D3 64
Halls, Tenn., 1,890......B2 83
Hallstead, Pa., 1,580....C10 81
Hallsville, Tex., 684.....C5 84
Halmstad, Swe., 40,100...I5 11
Hälsingborg, Swe.,
77,600...............I5 11
Halstad, Minn., 639.....C2 67
Halstead, Kans.,
1,598............E6, g11 61
Haltia, mtn., Fin........C9 11
Haltom City, Tex.,
23,133.............*C4 84
Halton, co., Ont., Can.,
106,967..............D4 41
Hamada, Jap., 44,439....I6 18
Hamadān, Iran, 99,909...F7 16
Hamāh, Syr., 97,390.....E11 14

Hamamatsu, Jap.,
392,632..........I8, o16 18
Hamar, Nor., 13,500....G4 11
Hama-tombetsu, Jap.,
3,200...............D11 18
Hambantota, Cey.,
4,345................G7 20
Hamblen, co., Tenn.,
33,092..............C10 83
Hamburg, Ark., 2,904....D4 49
Hamburg, Ger., 1,854,600..B5 6
Hamburg, Iowa, 1,647...D2 60
Hamburg, N.J., 1,532....A3 74
Hamburg, N.Y., 9,493....C2 75
Hamburg, Pa., 3,747....E10 81
Hamburg, state, Ger.,
1,860,000...........*B5 6
Hamburg, mts., N.J......A3 74
Hamden, Conn., 41,056...D6 52
Hamden, Maine, 800....*D4 64
Hamden, Ohio, 1,035....C3 78
Hamden Highlands,
Maine, 900...........D4 64
Häme, prov., Fin.,
592,400............*G11 11
Hämeenlinna, Fin.,
28,300..............G11 11
Hamel, Minn., 1,472....*E5 67
Hameln, Ger., 49,200....B4 6
Hamhung, Kor., 112,184..G3 18
Hami (Kumul) (Qomul),
China, 30,000........C3 17
Hamilton, Ala., 1,934....A2 46
Hamilton, Austl., 10,052..G7 25
Hamilton, Bermuda,
2,878................p20 35
Hamilton, Ont., Can.,
273,991 (*395,189).....D5 41
Hamilton, Ill., 2,516.....C2 58
Hamilton, Mass., 900
(5,488▲).........A6, f12 65
Hamilton, Mich., 700....F4 66
Hamilton, Mo., 1,701....B3 69
Hamilton, Mont., 2,475...D2 70
Hamilton, N.Y., 3,499....C5 75
Hamilton, N.Z., 63,000
(*63,303)............L15 26
Hamilton, Ohio, 71,000
(*110,000)...........C1 78
Hamilton, Scot., 43,100...C4 4
Hamilton, Tex., 3,106....D3 84
Hamilton, co., Fla., 7,705..B3 54
Hamilton, co., Ill., 10,010..E5 58
Hamilton, co., Ind.,
40,132..............D5 59
Hamilton, co., Iowa,
20,032..............B4 60
Hamilton, co., Kans.,
3,144................E2 61
Hamilton, co., Nebr.,
8,714................D7 71
Hamilton, co., N.Y.,
3,499................C5 75
Hamilton, co., Ohio,
864,121.............C1 78
Hamilton, co., Tenn.,
237,905.............D8 83
Hamilton, co., Tex.,
8,488................D3 84
Hamilton, mtn., N.Y.....B6 75
Hamilton Acres, Alsk.,
1,600...............*C10 47
Hamilton Park, Pa.,
3,500...............*G9 81

Hamilton Square, N.J.,
8,500................C3 74
Hamina, Fin., 9,800.....G12 11
Hamiota, Man., Can.,
779..................D1 40
Hamirpur, India, 10,000...C7 20
Hamlet, N.C., 4,810.....C3 76
Hamlin, Tex., 3,791.....C2 84
Hamlin, co., S. Dak.,
6,303................F8 77
Hamm [in Westfalen], Ger.,
71,200...............C3 6
Hammon, Okla., 656....B2 79
Hammond, Ind., 111,698..A2 59
Hammond, La.,
10,563...........D5, h11 63
Hammond, Wis., 645....D1 88
Hammond East, La.,
1,462..............*D5 63
Hammondsport, N.Y.,
1,176................C3 75
Hammonton, N.J., 9,854..D3 74
Hampden, Newf., Can.,
682..................D3 44
Hampden, Maine, 800
(4,583▲)............*D4 64
Hampden, co., Mass.,
429,353..............B2 65
Hampden Highlands,
Maine, 900...........D4 64
Hampshire, Ill., 1,309....A5 58
Hampshire, co., Mass.,
103,229..............B2 65
Hampshire, co., W. Va.,
11,705................B6 87
Hampshire (Southampton),
co., Eng., 1,336,084....E6 4
Hampstead, Que., Can.,
4,557...............*D4 42
Hampton, Ark., 1,011....D3 49
Hampton, Ga., 1,253....C2 55
Hampton, Iowa, 4,501...B4 60
Hampton, N.H., 4,200...F6 73
Hampton, N.J., 1,135....B3 74
Hampton, S.C., 2,486....F5 82
Hampton, Tenn., 1,048...C11 83
Hampton
(Independent City)
Va., 89,258.......C6, h15 85
Hampton, co., S.C.,
17,425..............F5 82
Hampton Bays, N.Y.,
2,550...............n16 75
Hamtramck, Mich.,
34,137..............p15 66
Hana, Haw., 435........C6 56
Hanahan, S.C.,
7,000............F7, k11 82
Hanamaki, Jap., 29,700
(62,710▲)...........G10 18
Hanamaulu, Haw., 977...B2 56
Hanapepe, Haw., 1,383...B2 56
Hanau, Ger., 48,900.....C4 6
Hanceville, Ala., 1,174...A3 46
Hancock, Md., 2,004....A1 53
Hancock, Mich., 5,022...A2 66
Hancock, Minn., 942....E3 67
Hancock, N.Y., 1,830....D5 75
Hancock, co., Ga., 9,979..C3 55
Hancock, co., Ill., 24,574..C2 58
Hancock, co., Ind.,
26,665...............E6 59
Hancock, co., Iowa,
14,604...............A4 60

Hancock, co., Ky., 5,330...C3 62
Hancock, co., Maine, 32,293............D4 64
Hancock, Mich., 5,022....A2 66
Hancock, co., Miss., 14,039............E4 68
Hancock, co., Ohio, 53,686............A2 78
Hancock, co., Tenn., 7,757............C10 83
Hancock, co., W. Va., 39,615............A4 87
Hand, co., S. Dak., 6,712..F6 77
Handa, Jap., 76,027......o15 18
Handley, W. Va., 900....C6 87
Handsboro, Miss., 1,577............E2, E4 68
Haney, B.C., Can., 2,117............E6, f13 37
Hanford, Calif., 10,133...D4 50
Hanford Northwest, Calif., 1,364............*D4 50
Hangchow, China, 784,000............E9 17
Hangö, Fin., 8,200......H10 11
Hankinson, N. Dak., 1,285............D9 77
Hanley Hills, Mo., 3,308............*C7 69
Hanna, Alta., Can., 2,645............D5 38
Hanna, Wyo., 625........E6 89
Hanna City, Ill., 1,056....C4 58
Hannibal, Mo., 20,028.....B6 69
Hannibal, N.Y., 611......B4 75
Hannover (Hanover), Ger., 567,400............B4 6
Hanoi, Viet., 414,620.....G6 17
Hanover, Ont., Can., 4,401............C3 41
Hanover, Ill., 1,396......A3 58
Hanover, Ind., 1,170......G7 59
Hanover, Kan., 773........C7 61
Hanover, Mass., 700 (5,923▲)............B6, h12 65
Hanover, N.H., 5,649.....D3 73
Hanover, N.J., 4,379......*B4 74
Hanover, Pa., 15,538......G8 81
Hanover, co., Va., 27,550..C5 85
Hanover, reg., Ger........B4 6
Hanover Green, Pa., 1,000............*D9 81
Hansford, co., Tex., 6,208..A2 84
Hanson, Mass., 700 (4,370▲)............B6 65
Hanson, co., S. Dak., 4,584............G8 77
Hants, co., N.S., Can., 26,444............D6 43
Hantsport, N.S., Can., 1,381............D5 43
Hapeville, Ga., 10,082............B5, C2 55
Happy Valley, Newf., Can., 2,861............B1, h9 44
Harahan, La., 9,275......k11 63
Haralson, co., Ga., 14,543............C1 55
Härar, Eth., 25,000......G6 23
Harbin, China, 1,814,000............D3 18
Harbor Beach, Mich., 2,282............E8 66
Harborcreek, Pa., 800...B2 81
Harbor Isle, N.Y., 1,300..*E7 75
Harbor Springs, Mich., 1,433............C6 66
Harbour Breton, Newf., Can., 1,076............E4 44
Harbour Grace, Newf., Can., 2,650............E5 44
Harbour Main, Newf., Can., 469............E5 44
Hardee, co., Fla., 12,370...E5 54
Hardeeville, S.C., 700....G5 82
Hardeman, co., Tenn., 21,517............B2 83
Hardeman, co., Tex., 8,275............B3 84
Hardin, Ill., 1,040........D3 58
Hardin, Mo., 727.........B4 69
Hardin, co., Ill., 5,879....F5 58
Hardin, co., Iowa, 22,533..B4 60
Hardin, co., Ky., 67,789...C4 62
Hardin, co., Mont., 2,789..E9 70
Hardin, co., Ohio, 29,633..B2 78
Hardin, co., Tenn., 17,397............B3 83
Hardin, co., Tex., 24,629..D5 84
Harding, co., N. Mex., 1,874............B7 48
Harding, co., S. Dak., 2,371............E2 77
Hardinsburg, Ky., 1,377...C3 62
Hardshell, Ky., 350......C6 62
Hardwar, India, 58,513....C6 20
Hardwick, Ga., 3,500.....C3 55
Hardwick, Vt., 1,521.....B3 73

Hardy, co., W. Va., 9,308..B6 87
Hare Bay, Newf., Can., 1,467............D4 44
Harfleur, Fr., 10,514.....C4 5
Harford, co., Md., 76,722..A5 53
Hargeisa, Som., 53,000....G6 23
Harihar, India, 22,829.....F6 20
Harkers Island, N.C., 1,362............C6 76
Harlan, Iowa, 4,775......C2 60
Harlan, Ky., 4,177.......D6 62
Harlan, co., Ky., 51,107...D6 62
Harlan, co., Nebr., 5,081..D6 71
Harlem, Fla., 1,256......F6 54
Harlem, Ga., 1,423.......C4 55
Harlem, Mont., 1,267.....B8 70
Harlem, Neth., 12,000....A6 5
Harlingen, Tex., 41,207...F4 84
Harlow, Eng., 61,100.....k13 4
Harlowton, Mont., 1,734............D7 70
Harmarville, Pa., 1,500...h14 81
Harmon, co., Okla., 5,852............C2 79
Harmony, Ind., 750......E3 59
Harmony, Minn., 1,214...G6 67
Harmony, Pa., 1,142......E1 81
Harnett, co., N.C., 49,189..B4 76
Harney, co., Oreg., 6,744..D7 80
Harney, peak, S. Dak.....F2 77
Harnösand, Swe., 17,200..F8 11
Haro, Sp., 8,554........A4 8
Harper, Kans., 1,899.....E5 61
Harper, Lib., 8,000......H3 22
Harper, co., Kans., 9,541............E5 61
Harper, co., Okla., 5,956..A2 79
Harper Woods, Mich., 19,995............*F7 66
Harrah, Okla., 934.......B4 79
Harriman, Tenn., 5,931...D1 83
Harrington, Del., 2,495...C6 53
Harrington Park, N.J., 3,581............h9 74
Harris, co., Ga., 11,167...D2 55
Harris, co., Tex., 1,243,158............E5 84
Harris, hill, Mass........A3 65
Harrisburg, Ark., 1,481...B5 49
Harrisburg, Ill., 9,171....F5 58
Harrisburg, Oreg., 939....C3 80
Harrisburg, Pa., 73,500 (*265,000)............F8 81
Harris Hill, N.Y., 5,000...*C2 75
Harrison, Ark., 6,580.....A2 49
Harrison, Mich., 1,072....D6 66
Harrison, N.J., 11,743....k8 74
Harrison, N.Y., 13,200............D2, h13 75
Harrison, Ohio, 3,878....C3 78
Harrison, co., Ind., 19,207............H5 59
Harrison, co., Iowa, 17,600............C2 60
Harrison, co., Ky., 13,704............B5 62
Harrison, co., Miss., 119,489............E4 68
Harrison, co., Mo., 11,603............A3 69
Harrison, co., Ohio, 17,995............B4 78
Harrison, co., Tex., 45,594............C5 84
Harrison, co., W. Va., 77,856............B4 87
Harrisonburg, La., 594....C4 63
Harrisonburg (Independent City), Va., 11,916......B4 85
Harrisonville, Mo., 3,510..C3 69
Harriston, Ont., Can., 1,631............D4 41
Harrisville, Pa., 896......D2 81
Harrisville, R.I., 1,400....B10 52
Harrisville, W. Va., 1,428..B3 87
Harrisville, N.Y., 842.....A5 75
Harrodsburg, Ky., 6,061..C5 62
Harrogate, Eng., 57,500..C6 4
Harrow, Ont., Can., 1,787............E2 41
Harrow, Eng., 209,500...*E6 4
Hart, Mich., 1,990.......E4 66
Hart, co., Ga., 15,229....B4 55
Hart, co., Ky., 14,119....C4 62
Hart, mtn., Man., Can....C1 40
Hartford, Ala., 1,956.....D4 46
Hartford, Conn., 162,178............B6 52
Hartford, Ill., 2,355......E3 58
Hartford, Ky., 1,618......C3 62
Hartford, Mich., 2,305....F4 66
Hartford, Wis., 5,627............E5, m11 88
Hartford, co., Conn., 689,555............B5 52
Hartford City, Ind., 8,053............D7 59
Hartington, Nebr., 1,648..B8 71

Hartland, N.B., Can., 1,025............C2 43
Hartland, Maine, 1,050 (1,447▲)............D3 64
Hartland, Wis., 2,088............E5, m11 88
Hartlepool, Eng., 18,200...C6 4
Hartley, Iowa, 1,738......A2 60
Hartley, co., Tex., 2,171...B1 84
Hartsdale, N.Y., 11,500...*D7 75
Hartselle, Ala., 5,000.....A3 46
Hartshorne, Okla., 1,903..C6 79
Hartsville, S.C., 6,392....C7 82
Hartsville, Tenn., 1,712...A5 83
Hartville, Ohio, 1,353....B4 78
Hartwell, Ga., 4,599......B4 55
Hartwick, N.Y., 600......C5 75
Harvard, Ill., 5,019......A5 58
Harvard, Nebr., 1,261....D7 71
Harvard, mtn., Colo......C4 51
Harvey, Ill., 33,230......B6, k9 58
Harvey, La., 11,000......E5, k11 63
Harvey, Mich., 900......B3 66
Harvey, N. Dak., 2,365...C6 77
Harvey, co., Kans., 25,865............D6 61
Harvey, mtn., Mass......B1 65
Harwich, Eng., 13,800...E7 4
Harwich, Mass., 850 (3,747▲)............C7 65
Harwich Port, Mass., 1,000............C7 65
Harwick, Pa., 1,500......*E1 81
Harwood Heights, Ill., 5,688............*B6 58
Hasbrouck Heights, N.J., 13,046............h8 74
Hashimoto, Jap., 20,300..o14 18
Haskell, Okla., 3,121.....B6 79
Haskell, Tex., 4,016......C3 84
Haskell, co., Kans., 2,990............E3 61
Haskell, co., Okla., 1,887..B6 79
Haskell, co., Tex., 11,174..C3 84
Haslett, Mich., 1,500....*F6 66
Hassan, India, 32,172.....F6 20
Hasselt, Bel., 36,618.....B6 5
Hässleholm, Swe., 13,500..I5 11
Hastings, Ont., Can., 897..C7 41
Hastings, Eng., 66,600...E7 4
Hastings, Fla., 617.......C5 54
Hastings, Mich., 6,375...F5 66
Hastings, Minn., 10,588............F6 67
Hastings, Nebr., 21,412...D7 71
Hastings, N.Z., 26,867 (*37,466)............M16 26
Hastings, Pa., 1,751......E4 81
Hastings, co., Ont., Can., 93,377............C7 41
Hastings-on-Hudson, N.Y., 9,777............h13 75
Hatboro, Pa., 7,315......F11 81
Hatch, N. Mex., 888.....C5 48
Hatfield, Mass., 1,400 (2,350▲)............B2 65
Hatfield, Pa., 1,941......F11 81
Hatfield, Rh., 11,990....D6 24
Ha Tien, Viet., 4,700.....C2 19
Hatteras, N.C., 700......B7 76
Hattiesburg, Miss., 34,989..D4 68
Hatton, N. Dak., 856.....C8 77
Hatton Fields, Calif., 2,362............*D3 50
Hatvan, Hung., 19,952...B4 10
Hatzic, B.C., Can., 724...fl3 37
Haubstadt, Ind., 1,029...H2 59
Haugesund, Nor., 27,100............H1 11
Hauppauge, N.Y., 5,500............*D3 75
Haute-Garonne, dept., Fr., 594,633............*F4 5
Haute-Loire, dept., Fr., 211,036............*E5 5
Haute-Marne, dept., Fr., 208,446............*C6 5
Hauterive, Que., Can., 5,980............k13 42
Hautes-Alpes, dept., Fr., 85,436............*E7 5
Haute-Saône, dept., Fr., 208,440............*D6 5
Haute-Savoie, dept., Fr., 329,230............*D7 5
Hautes-Pyrénées, dept., Fr., 211,433............*F4 5
Haute-Vienne, dept., Fr., 332,514............*E4 5
Hautmont, Fr., 18,594...B6 5
Haut-Rhin, dept., Fr., 547,920............*C7 5
Hauula, Haw., 806....B4, f10 56
Havana (La Habana), Cuba, 946,300 (*1,700,000)............C2 35
Havana, Fla., 2,090......B2 54
Havana, Ill., 4,363.......C3 58

Havelock, Ont., Can., 1,260............C7 41
Havelock, N.C., 2,433....C6 76
Haven, Kans., 982...E6, g11 61
Haverford, Pa., 5,500....*F10 81
Haverhill, Mass., 46,346..A5 65
Haverstraw, N.Y., 7,293............D7, m15 75
Havertown, Pa., 36,000..*G10 81
Haviland, Kans., 725.....E4 61
Havlickuv Brod, Czech., 14,900............D3 7
Havre, Mont., 10,740....B7 70
Havre-Aubert, Que., Can., 494............B8 43
Havre de Grace, Md., 8,510............A5 53
Havza, Tur., 9,443......B10 14
Hawaii, co., Haw., 61,332............D5 56
Hawaii, state, U.S., 632,772............D5 56
Hawaii, isl., Haw........D6 56
Hawaiian Gardens, Calif., 15,000............*F4 50
Hawarden, Iowa, 2,544....A1 60
Hawera, N.Z., 7,542....M15 26
Hawesville, Ky., 882.....C3 62
Hawi, Haw., 985........C6 56
Hawick, Scot., 15,900....C5 4
Hawkesbury, Ont., Can., 8,661............B10 41
Hawkins, co., Tenn., 30,468............C10 83
Hawkinsville, Ga., 3,967..D3 55
Hawk Run, Pa., 850.....E5 81
Hawks Bill, mtn., Va.....B4 85
Hawley, Minn., 1,270....D2 67
Hawley, Pa., 1,433......D11 81
Haworth, N.J., 3,215....h9 74
Haw River, N.C., 1,500..A3 76
Hawthorne, Calif., 33,035............n12 50
Hawthorne, Fla., 1,167...C4 54
Hawthorne, Nev., 2,838..B2 72
Hawthorne, N.J., 17,735..B4 74
Hawthorne, N.Y., 5,000..g13 75
Haxtun, Colo., 990......A8 51
Hayange, Fr., 11,009....C7 5
Hayden, Ariz., 1,760..C3, D3 48
Hayden, Idaho, 901......B2 57
Haydenville, Mass., 750..B2 65
Haydenville, Ohio, 800....C3 78
Hayes, La., 800.........D3 63
Hayes, co., Nebr., 1,919..D4 71
Hayesville, Oreg., 4,568..*C4 80
Hayfield, Minn., 889.....G6 67
Haynau, see Chojnow, Pol.
Haynesville, La., 3,031...B2 63
Hay River, N. W. Ter., Can., 1,338............D10 36
Hays, Kans., 11,947.....D4 61
Hays, Mont., 600.......C8 70
Hays, co., Tex., 19,934...D3 84
Hay Springs, Nebr., 823..B3 71
Haysville, Kans., 5,836...B5 61
Hayti, Mo., 3,737.......E8 69
Hayward, Calif., 72,700...h8 50
Hayward, Wis., 1,540....B2 88
Haywood, N.C., 713.....B3 76
Haywood, co., N.C., 39,711............f9 76
Haywood, co., Tenn., 23,393............B2 83
Hazard, Ky., 5,958......C6 62
Hazardville, Conn., 4,000..B6 52
Hazebrouck, Fr., 17,446..B5 5
Hazel Crest, Ill., 8,907...k9 58
Hazel Dell, Wash., 2,500..*D3 86
Hazel Green, Wis., 807...F3 88
Hazel Park, Mich., 25,631............p15 66
Hazelwood, Mo., 6,045...*C7 69
Hazelwood, N.C., 1,925..f10 76
Hazen, Ark., 1,456......C4 49
Hazen, N. Dak., 1,222...C4 77
Hazlehurst, Ga., 3,699...E4 55
Hazlehurst, Miss., 3,400..D3 68
Hazlet, N.J., 12,400.....C4 74
Hazleton, Iowa, 665.....B6 60
Hazleton, Pa., 32,056....E10 81
Hazleton, peak, Wyo.....C3 89
Headland, Ala., 2,650....D4 46
Healdsburg, Calif., 5,132..C2 50
Healdton, Okla., 2,898...C4 79
Heard, co., Ga., 5,333...C1 55
Hearne, Tex., 5,072......D4 84
Hearst, Ont., Can., 2,373..o19 41
Heart's Content, Newf., Can., 607............E5 44
Heart's Delight, Newf., Can., 631............*E5 44
Heath, Ohio, 6,066......B3 78
Heavener, Okla., 1,891...C7 79
Hebbronville, Tex., 4,000............F3 84
Heber, Utah, 2,936...A6, D2 72

Heber Springs, Ark., 2,265.........B3 49
Hébertville, Que., Can., 1,604............A6 42
Hébertville Station, Que., Can., 1,257.........*A6 42
Hebrides, sea, Scot.......B3 4
Hebron, Ill., 701.......A5 58
Hebron, Ind., 1,401.....B3 59
Hebron, Nebr., 1,920....D8 71
Hebron, N. Dak., 1,340..D3 77
Hebron, Ohio, 1,260.....C3 78
Hecelchakán, Mex., 3,879.C6 34
Hechingen, Ger., 9,600...D4 6
Hector, Minn., 1,177.....F4 67
Hedemora, Swe., 6,000...G6 11
Hedmark, co., Nor., 177,200............*G4 11
Hedrick, Iowa, 762......C5 60
Hedwig Village, Tex., 1,182............*E5 84
Heerlen, Neth., 75,300...B6 5
Heflin, Ala., 2,400......B4 46
Hegeler, Ill., 1,640.....*C6 58
Hegins, Pa., 800........E8 81
Heide, Ger., 20,000......A4 6
Heidelberg, Ger., 125,600...........D4 6
Heidelberg, Miss., 1,049..D5 68
Heidelberg, Pa., 2,118..*E1 81
Heidenheim, Ger., 50,000.D5 6
Heidrick, Ky., 500.......D6 62
Heilbronn, Ger., 92,800..D4 6
Heiligenstadt, Ger., 12,500............C5 6
Heilungkiang, prov., China, 14,860,000.........B10 17
Heislerville, N.J., 600...E3 74
Hejaz, pol. div., Sau. Ar., 2,000,000..........D2 15
Hekla, peak, Ice.......n23 11
Helena, Ark., 11,500.....C5 49
Helena, Ga., 1,290......D4 55
Helena, Mont., 20,227...D5 70
Helensburgh, Scot., 9,800.B4 4
Hellam, Pa., 1,234......G8 81
Hellertown, Pa., 6,716..E11 81
Hellville, Malag., 7,497..C9 23
Helmetta, N.J., 779......C4 74
Helmond, Neth., 44,600..B6 5
Helmstedt, Ger., 29,600..B5 6
Helper, Utah, 2,459.....B6 72
Helsingfors, see Helsinki, Fin.
Helsingør, Den., 26,658....I5 11
Helsinki, Fin., 476,400...G11 11
Hemel Hempstead, Eng., 60,500...........k12 4
Hemet, Calif., 7,943.....F5 50
Hemingford, Nebr., 904...B2 71
Hemingway, S.C., 951....D9 82
Hemlock, Mich., 900.....E6 66
Hemlock (Eureka), S.C., 1,423............B5 82
Hemmingford, Que., Can., 778............D4 42
Hemphill, Tex., 913......D6 84
Hemphill, co., Tex., 3,185............B2 84
Hempstead, N.Y., 37,192...........k13 75
Hempstead, Tex., 1,505...D4 84
Hempstead, co., Ark., 19,661............D2 49
Henday, Fr., 7,204.......F3 5
Hendek, Tur., 9,880......B8 14
Henderson, Ky., 16,892....C2 62
Henderson, Minn., 728....F5 67
Henderson, Nebr., 730....D8 71
Henderson, Nev., 12,525..C4 72
Henderson, N.C., 12,740..A4 76
Henderson, Tenn., 2,691..B3 83
Henderson, Tex., 9,666...C5 84
Henderson, co., Ill., 8,237............C3 58
Henderson, co., Ky., 33,519............C2 62
Henderson, co., N.C., 36,163............f10 76
Henderson, co., Tenn., 16,115............B3 83
Henderson, co., Tex., 21,786............C5 84
Hendersonville, N.C., 5,911............f10 76
Hendersonville, Tenn., 950............A5 83
Hendon, Eng., 151,500...k12 4
Hendricks, Minn., 797....F2 67
Hendricks, co., Ind., 40,896............E4 59
Hendry, co., Fla., 8,119...F5 54
Hengelo, Neth., 64,800...A7 5
Hengyang, China, 235,000...........F7 17
Henlawson, W. Va., 1,670............D5 87
Hennebont, Fr., 7,623....D2 5

Hennepin, co., Minn., 842,854...........E5 67
Hennessey, Okla., 1,228..A4 79
Henning, Minn., 980.....D3 67
Henrico, co., Va., 117,339...........C5 85
Henrietta, N.Y., 7,500...B3 75
Henrietta, N.C., 950..B2, f11 76
Henrietta, Tex., 3,062...C3 84
Henry, Ill., 2,480.......B4 58
Henry, co., Ala., 75,286..D4 46
Henry, co., Ga., 17,619..C2 55
Henry, co., Ill., 49,317..B3 58
Henry, co., Ind., 48,899..E7 59
Henry, co., Iowa, 18,187..C6 60
Henry, co., Ky., 10,987..B4 62
Henry, co., Mo., 19,226..C4 69
Henry, co., Ohio, 25,392..A1 78
Henry, co., Tenn., 22,275..A3 83
Henry, co., Va., 40,335..D3 85
Henryetta, Okla., 6,551..B6 79
Hensall, Ont., Can., 926..D3 41
Henryville, Que., Can., 711............D4 42
Henzada, Bur., 61,972...E10 20
Heppner, Oreg., 1,661....B7 80
Herat, Afg., 100,000.....B3 20
Hérault, dept., Fr., 516,658...........*F5 5
Herbert, Sask., Can., 1,008............G2 39
Herblay, Fr., 10,220.....g9 5
Hercegovina, reg., Yugo..D3 10
Herculaneum, Mo., 1,767.........C7, g13 69
Heredia, C.R., 19,249....E8 34
Heredia, prov., C.R., 77,300...........*E8 34
Hereford, Eng., 42,400...D5 4
Hereford, Tex., 7,652....B1 84
Hereford, co., Eng., 134,100...........*D5 4
Herencia, Sp., 8,606.....C4 8
Herford, Ger., 55,600....B4 6
Herington, Kans., 3,702..D7 61
Herisau, Switz., 14,361..E4 6
Herkimer, N.Y., 9,396...B6 75
Herkimer, co., N.Y., 66,370............B5 75
Herman, Minn., 764.....E2 67
Hermann, Mo., 2,536.....C6 69
Hermansville, Mich., 700..C3 66
Hermantown, Minn., 1,000............D6 67
Herminie, Pa., 1,571.....F2 81
Hermiston, Oreg., 4,402..B7 80
Hermon, N.Y., 612.......f9 75
Hermosa Beach, Calif., 16,115...........*F4 50
Hermosillo, Mex., 95,978..B2 34
Hernando, Miss., 1,898...A4 68
Hernando, co., Fla., 11,205............D4 54
Herndon, Va., 1,960..B5, g12 85
Herning, Den., 24,790....I3 11
Heron Lake, Minn., 852...G3 67
Herrin, Ill., 9,474.......F4 58
Hershey, Pa., 7,000.....F8 81
Herstal, Bel., 29,606....B6 5
Hertford, Eng., 17,300.........E6, k12 4
Hertford, N.C., 2,012....A6 76
Hertford, co., Eng., 829,200...........*E6 4
Hertford, co., N.C., 22,718............A5 76
Herzliya, Isr., 30,000..B2, g5 15
Hespeler, Ont., Can., 4,519.D4 41
Hesperia, Mich., 822....E4 66
Hesse, reg., Ger.........C4 6
Hessen, state, Ger., 5,082,000..........*C4 6
Hesston, Kans., 1,103...D6 61
Hettinger, N. Dak., 1,769..D3 77
Hettinger, co., N. Dak., 6,317............D3 77
Heuvelton, N.Y., 810....f9 75
Heves, Hung., 9,923.....B5 10
Heves, co., Hung., 348,756...........*B5 10
Hewitt, N.J., 1,571......A4 74
Hewlett, N.Y., 7,500....*G2 52
Hewlett Harbor, N.Y., 1,610............*G2 52
Heyworth, Ill., 1,196.....C5 58
Hialeah, Fla., 66,972.........G6, s13 54
Hiawatha, Iowa, 1,336...*C6 60
Hiawatha, Kans., 3,391...C8 61
Hiawatha, Utah, 439.....B6 72
Hibbing, Minn., 17,731..C6 67
Hibernia, N.J., 250......B4 74
Hickman, Ky., 1,537.....B2 62
Hickman, co., Ky., 6,747..B2 62
Hickman, co., Tenn., 11,862............B4 83
Hickory, N.C., 19,328....B1 76
Hickory, co., Mo., 4,516..D4 69

Hickory East, N.C., 3,274............*B1 76
Hickory Hills, Ill., 2,707..*B6 58
Hicksville, N.Y., 53,000...........E7, n15 75
Hicksville, Ohio, 3,116....A1 78
Hico, Tex., 1,020.......D3 84
Hidalgo, Tex., 1,078.....F3 84
Hidalgo, co., N. Mex., 4,961............D4 48
Hidalgo, co., Tex., 180,904...........F3 84
Hidalgo, state, Mex., 994,598.........C5, m14 34
Hidalgo del Parral, Mex., 41,474............B3 34
Higashiizu, Jap., 11,600..o18 18
Higbee, Mo., 646.......B5 69
Higgins, Tex., 711.......A2 84
Higginsville, Mo., 4,003..B4 69
High Bridge, N.J., 2,148..B3 74
Highgrove, Calif., 2,000..*F5 50
High Knob, mtn., Va.....A4 85
Highland, Calif., 7,000..*E5 50
Highland, Ill., 5,637.....E4 58
Highland, Ind., 20,354...A3 59
Highland, Kans., 755.....C8 61
Highland, Mich., 700....o14 66
Highland, N.Y., 2,931....D7 75
Highland, Wis., 741......E3 88
Highland, co., Ohio, 29,716............C2 78
Highland, co., Va., 3,221..B3 85
Highland City, Fla., 1,020............*E5 54
Highland Creek, Ont., Can.............D5 41
Highland Crest, Kans., 4,000............*B8 61
Highland Falls, N.Y., 4,469............*D7 75
Highland Heights, Ky., 3,491............A7 62
Highland Heights, Ohio, 2,929............*A4 78
Highland Park, Ill., 30,054.........A6, h9 58
Highland Park, Mich., 38,063...........p15 66
Highland Park, N.J., 11,049............*C4 74
Highland Park, Pa., 1,534............*F6 81
Highland Park, Tex., 10,411............B5 84
Highlands, Fla., 4,000....*B5 54
Highlands, N.J., 3,536....C5 74
Highlands, Tex., 5,500...r14 84
Highlands, co., Fla., 21,338............E5 54
Highland Springs, Va., 6,800.........C5, m18 85
Highmore, S. Dak., 1,078.F6 77
High Point, N.C., 62,500 (*112,000)........B3 76
High Point, mtn., N.J.....A3 74
High Prairie, Alta., Can., 1,756............B2 38
High River, Alta., Can., 2,276............D4 38
Highshoals, N.C., 900....B1 76
High Spire, Pa., 2,999....F8 81
High Springs, Fla., 2,329............C4 54
Hightstown, N.J., 4,317..C3 74
Highway City, Calif., 1,381............*D4 50
Highway Village, Tex., 1,927............*F4 84
Highwood, Ill., 4,499..A6, h9 58
High Wycombe, Eng., 53,400...........E6 4
Higüey, Dom. Rep., 10,560............E9 35
Hikone, Jap., 46,000 (62,740▴)..........n15 18
Hilbert, Wis., 736......E3 88
Hildburghausen, Ger., 7,870............C5 6
Hildesheim, Ger., 99,200..B4 6
Hill, co., Mont., 18,653..B6 70
Hill, co., Tex., 23,650...D4 84
Hilla (Hillah), Iraq., 46,441...........B6 23
Hillburn, N.Y., 1,068....*D6 75
Hill City, Kans., 2,421...C4 61
Hillcrest, N.J., 1,922...*B2 74
Hillcrest, N.Y., 3,000....*D6 75
Hillcrest Center, Calif., 15,000...........*E4 50
Hillcrest Heights, Md., 20,000...........*C3 53
Hillcrest Mines, Alta., Can., 618..........E3 38
Hiller, Pa., 1,746......*G2 81
Hilliard, Fla., 1,075.....B5 54
Hilliard, Ohio, 5,633....k10 78
Hillsboro, Ill., 4,232.....D4 58

Hillsboro, Kans., 2,441....D6 61
Hillsboro, N.H., 1,700....E4 73
Hillsboro, N. Dak., 1,278............C8 77
Hillsboro, Ohio, 5,474...C2 78
Hillsboro, Oreg., 8,232.........B3, g12 80
Hillsboro, Tenn., 200....B6 83
Hillsboro, Tex., 7,402...C4 84
Hillsboro, Wis., 1,366...E3 88
Hillsboro, co., N.H., 178,161...........F4 73
Hillsborough, Calif., 7,554............*D2 50
Hillsborough, N.B., Can., 679............D5 43
Hillsborough, N.C., 1,349..A3 76
Hillsborough, co., Fla., 397,788...........E4 54
Hillsdale, Mich., 7,629...G6 66
Hillsdale, Mo., 2,788....*C7 69
Hillsdale, N.J., 8,734....g8 74
Hillsdale, co., Mich., 34,742............G6 66
Hillside, Ill., 7,794.....*B6 58
Hillside, N.J., 22,304....k8 74
Hillside Manor, N.Y., 14,000...........*G2 52
Hillsville, Pa., 950......D1 81
Hillsville, Va., 905......D2 85
Hilltop, N.J., 1,500....*D2 74
Hillwood, Va., 1,400....*B5 85
Hilo, Haw., 25,966....D6, n16 56
Hilton, N.Y., 1,800.....B3 75
Hilversum, Neth., 103,400...........A6 5
Himeji, Jap., 367,807....I7 18
Himi, Jap., 29,900 (62,452▴)..........H8 18
Hinche, Hai., 5,234.....E7 35
Hinckley, Ill., 940......B5 58
Hinckley, Minn., 851....D6 67
Hindenburg, see Zabrze, Pol.
Hinds, co., Miss., 187,045..C3 68
Hines, Oreg., 1,207.....D7 80
Hinesville, Ga., 3,174...E5 55
Hingham, Mass., 12,500.........B6, h12 65
Hinojosa [del Duque], Sp., 14,767............C3 8
Hinsdale, Ill., 14,738....k9 58
Hinsdale, Mass., 900 (1,414▴)..........B1 65
Hinsdale, N.H., 1,235....F3 73
Hinsdale, co., Colo., 208..D3 51
Hinton, Alta., Can., 3,529............C2 38
Hinton, Okla., 907......B3 79
Hinton, W. Va., 5,197...D4 87
Hiram, Ohio, 1,011......A4 78
Hiratsuka, Jap., 134,931...........n17 18
Hiroo, Jap., 9,800......E11 18
Hirosaki, Jap., 80,000...F10 18
Hiroshima, Jap., 504,245..I6 18
Hiroshima, pref., Jap., 2,281,146..........*I6 18
Hirson, Fr., 11,715......C5 5
Hispaniola, isl., N.A.....D8 35
Hissar, India, 60,222....C4 20
Hita, Jap., ,43,000 (66,787▴)..........*J5 18
Hitachi, Jap., 179,703...H10 18
Hitchcock, Tex., 5,216...r14 84
Hitchcock, co., Nebr., 4,829............D4 71
Hitchins, Ky., 800......B7 62
Hitoyoshi, Jap., 29,600 (44,831▴)..........J5 18
Hixon, Tenn., 2,000..D8, E10 83
Hjørring, Den., 15,038...I3 11
Hjørring, co., Den., 177,778...........*I3 11
Hlohovec, Czech., 12,700............D4 7
Hlomsak, Thai., 7,906...*E11 20
Hoa Binh, Viet., 25,000..*A3 19
Hobart, Austl., 53,226 (*141,238).........o15 25
Hobart, Ind., 20,875....A3 59
Hobart, Okla., 5,132....B2 79
Hobbs, N. Mex., 26,275..C7 48
Hobgood, N.C., 630.....A5 76
Hoboken, Bel., 30,557...B6 5
Hoboken, N.J., 48,441...k8 74
Hocking, co., Ohio, 20,168............C3 78
Hockley, Tex., 200......q14 84
Hockley, co., Tex., 22,340..C1 84
Hoddesdon, Eng., 18,600..k13 4
Hodge, La., 878........B3 63
Hodgeman, Kans., 3,115..D4 61
Hodgenville, Ky., 1,985..C4 62
Hodgkins, Ill., 1,126....*B6 58
Hódmezővásárhely, Hung., 40,000...........B5 10
Hodonín, Czech., 18,000..D4 7
Hoeryong, Kor., 24,330..E4 18

Hof, Ger., 55,900........C5   6
Hofei, China, 304,000....E8   17
Hoffman, Minn., 605.....E3   67
Hoffman Estates, Ill.,
   8,296................h8   58
Hofu, Jap., 68,000
   (94,342▲)............I5   18
Hogansville, Ga., 3,658...C2   55
Hogback, mtn., S.C........A3   82
Hohenwald, Tenn., 2,194..B4   83
Ho-Ho-Kus (Hohokus),
   N.J., 3,988...........h8   74
Hoisington, Kans., 4,248..D5   61
Hokah, Minn., 685.......G7   67
Hoke, co., N.C., 16,356...B3   76
Hokendauqua, Pa.,
   1,400..............*E10   81
Hokes Bluff, Ala., 1,619...B4   46
Hokkaido, pref., Jap.,
   5,171,800..........*E10   18
Hokkaido, isl., Jap......E10   18
Holbaek, co., Den.,
   127,747.............*J4   11
Holbrook, Ariz., 4,481....B3   48
Holbrook, Mass., 7,900
   (10,104▲)........B5, h11   65
Holbrook, N.Y., 4,300....*n15   75
Holden, Mass., 2,200
   (10,117▲)...........B4   65
Holden, Mo., 1,951......C4   69
Holden, W. Va., 1,900....D2   87
Holdenville, Okla., 5,712..B5   79
Holdrege, Nebr., 5,226....D6   71
Holgate, Ohio, 1,374.....A1   78
Holguín, Cuba, 102,100..D5   35
Hollabrunn, Aus., 5,832..D8   6
Holladay, Utah, 33,000...*C3   72
Holland, Mich., 24,777...F4   66
Holland, N.Y., 950......C2   75
Holland, Ohio,
   924............A2, E6   78
Hollandale, Miss., 2,646..B3   68
Holley, N.Y., 1,788......B2   75
Holliday, Tex., 1,139.....C3   84
Hollidaysburg, Pa.,
   6,475...............F5   81
Hollins, Va., 3,000......C3   85
Hollis, Alsk., 292.......n23   47
Hollis, Okla., 3,006......C2   79
Hollister, Calif., 6,071...D3   50
Hollister, Mo., 600......E4   69
Holliston, Mass., 2,700
   (6,222▲).............h10   65
Holloway Terrace, Del.,
   1,100..............*A6   53
Hollsopple, Pa., 900.....F4   81
Holly, Colo., 1,108......C8   51
Holly, Mich., 3,269......F7   66
Holly Hill, Fla., 4,182....C5   54
Holly Hill, S.C., 1,235...E7   82
Holly Oak, Del., 1,000...A7   53
Holly Ridge, N.C., 731...C5   76
Holly Springs, Miss.,
   5,621...............A4   68
Hollywood, Fla.,
   35,237.........F6, r13   54
Hollywood, La., 1,750...*D2   63
Hollywood, Pa., 2,000...*F11   81
Hollywood Heights, Ill,
   1,000..............*E3   58
Holmdel Gardens, Kans.,
   1,436.............*D6   61
Holmen, Wis., 635......E2   88
Holmes, Pa., 3,000.....*G11   81
Holmes, co., Fla.,
   10,844..............u16   54
Holmes, co., Miss.,
   27,096..............B3   68
Holmes, co., Ohio, 21,591..B4   78
Holmes, mtn., Wyo.......B2   89
Holmes Beach, Fla.,
   1,143..............*E4   54
Holmes Run Acres, Va.,
   1,000..............*B5   85
Holmes Run Park, Va.,
   4,000..............*B5   85
Holon, Isr., 55,200......B2   15
Holopaw, Fla., 250......D5   54
Holstebro, Den., 18,563...I3   11
Holstein, Iowa, 1,413....B2   60
Holt, Ala., 3,000.......B2   46
Holt, Mich., 5,000......F6   66
Holt, co., Mo., 7,885....A2   69
Holt, co., Nebr., 13,722..B7   71
Holton, Kans., 3,028.....C8   61
Holtville, Calif., 3,538...F6   50
Holyhead, Wales,
   10,300.............D4   4
Holyoke, Colo., 1,555....A8   51
Holyoke, Mass., 52,689..B2   65
Holyoke, range, Mass.....B2   65
Holyrood, Kans., 737.....D5   61
Holzminden, Ger.,
   22,500.............C4   6
Homalin, Bur., 10,000...D9   20
Homeacre, Pa., 3,508...*E2   81
Home Corner, Ind.,
   2,636..............C6   59

Homécourt, Fr., 10,141...C6   5
Homedale, Idaho, 1,381...F2   57
Homedale, Ohio, 670....*B2   78
Home Gardens, Calif.,
   1,541..............*F5   50
Homer, Alsk., 900....D6, h16   47
Homer, Ill., 1,276......C6   58
Homer, La., 4,665......B2   63
Homer, Mich., 1,629....F6   66
Homer, N.Y., 3,622.....C4   75
Homer City, Pa., 2,471...E3   81
Homerville, Ga., 2,634...E4   55
Homestead, Fla.,
   9,152...........G6, t13   54
Homestead, Pa., 7,502...k14   81
Homestead Valley, Calif.,
   1,000..............*C2   50
Hometown, Ill., 7,479...*B6   58
Homewood, Ala., 20,289...E4   46
Homewood, Calif., 100...C3   50
Homewood, Ill.,
   17,399..........B6, k9   58
Homeworth, Ohio, 600...B4   78
Hominy, Okla., 2,866....A5   79
Homs, Syr., 137,217.....B5   23
Honaker, Va., 851......e10   85
Honan, prov., China,
   48,670,000..........E7   17
Honda, Col., 19,945.....B3   32
Hondo, Tex., 4,992.....E3   84
Honduras, country, N.A.,
   2,163,000...........D7   34
Honea Path, S.C., 3,453...C3   82
Honeoye Falls, N.Y.,
   2,229..............C3   75
Honesdale, Pa., 5,569....C11   81
Honey Brook, Pa., 1,023..F10   81
Honey Grove, Tex.,
   2,071..............C5   84
Honfleur, Fr., 8,970.....C4   5
Hon Gai, Viet., 35,412...*A3   19
Hongwon, Kor., 25,663...G3   18
Hong Kong, Br. dep., Asia,
   3,133,131...........G7   17
Honokaa, Haw., 1,300....C6   56
Honolulu, Haw.,
   294,194........B4, g10   56
Honolulu, co., Haw.,
   500,409............B3   56
Honshū, isl., Jap........H8   18
Honto, see Nevelsk,
   Sov. Un.
Hood, co., Tex., 5,443....C4   84
Hood, mtn., Oreg.......B5   80
Hoodoo, peak, Wash.....A5   86
Hood River, Oreg., 3,657..B5   80
Hood River, co., Oreg.,
   13,395.............B5   80
Hoodsport, Wash., 580...B2   86
Hooker, Okla., 1,684.....e9   79
Hooker, co., Nebr., 1,130..C4   71
Hooker, mtn., B.C., Can...C8   37
Hooks, Tex., 2,048.....*C5   84
Hooksett, N.H., 1,000...E5   73
Hoolehua, Haw., 1,000...B4   56
Hooper, Nebr., 832......C9   71
Hooper, Utah, 300....A5, C2   72
Hooper Bay, Alsk., 460...C6   47
Hoopeston, Ill., 6,606....C6   58
Hoorn, Neth., 16,100....A6   5
Hoosac, range, Mass.....A1   65
Hoosick Falls, N.Y.,
   4,023..............C7   75
Hooverson Heights, W. Va.,
   1,800..............*B2   87
Hooversville, Pa., 1,120...F4   81
Hopatcong, N.J., 3,391...B3   74
Hope, Ark., 8,399......D2   49
Hope, B.C., Can., 2,751...E7   37
Hope, Ind., 1,489.......F6   59
Hopedale, Ill., 737......C4   58
Hopedale, La., 720......E6   63
Hopedale, Mass.,
   3,987...........B4, h9   65
Hopedale, Ohio, 932.....B5   78
Hopeh (Hopei), prov.,
   China, 42,500,000....D8   17
Hopelawn, N.J., 1,500...*B4   74
Hope Mills, N.C., 1,109...C4   76
Hope Ranch, Calif., 1,000.*E4   50
Hope Valley, R.I., 1,000..C10   52
Hopewell, N.J., 1,928....C3   74
Hopewell
   (Independent
   City), Va., 17,895..C5, n18   85
Hopewell, W. Va., 1,230..*B4   87
Hopewell Junction, N.Y.,
   900...............D7   75
Hopkins, Minn., 12,187...n12   67
Hopkins, Mo., 710......A3   69
Hopkins, co., Ky., 38,458..C2   62
Hopkins, co., Tex.,
   18,594.............C5   84
Hopkinsville, Ky., 19,465..D2   62
Hopkinton, Iowa, 768....B6   60
Hopkinton, Mass.,
   3,000 (4,932▲).....B4, h9   65
Hopland, Calif., 800.....C2   50

Hoppo, China, 67,000....G6   17
Hopwood, Pa., 1,615.....G2   81
Hoquiam, Wash., 10,762...C2   86
Hordaland, co., Nor.,
   236,100............*G1   11
Horicon, Wis., 2,996.....E5   88
Hornell, N.Y., 13,907....C3   75
Hornersville, Mo., 752....E7   69
Horni Pocernice, Czech.,
   7,579..............n18   7
Hornsea, Eng., 6,000.....D6   4
Hornsey, Eng., 2,634....k12   4
Horqueta, Par., 17,389...D4   29
Horry, co., S.C., 68,247...D9   82
Horseback Knob, hill,
   Ohio...............C2   78
Horse Cave, Ky., 1,780...C4   62
Horseheads, N.Y., 7,854...C4   75
Horsens, Den., 37,261....J3   11
Horsham, Austl., 10,557...G7   25
Horsham, Pa., 4,000....*F11   81
Horta, Port. (Azores),
   8,564..............k9   22
Horten, Nor., 13,500..H4, p28   11
Horton, Kans., 2,361....C8   61
Hortonville, Wis., 1,366...D5   88
Hoshiarpur, India, 50,739..B6   20
Hospers, Iowa, 600......A2   60
Hospitalet, Sp., 122,813...B7   8
Hot Springs, N.C.,
   723...............f10   76
Hot Springs, S. Dak.,
   4,943.............G2   77
Hot Springs, co., Ark.,
   21,893.............C2   49
Hot Springs, co., Wyo.,
   6,365..............C4   89
Hot Springs, see Truth or
   Consequences, N. Mex.
Hot Springs
   [National Park],
   Ark., 28,337......C2, C6   49
Houghton, Mich., 3,393...A2   66
Houghton, N.Y., 1,600...C2   75
Houghton, Wash., 2,426..e11   86
Houghton, co., Mich.,
   35,654.............B2   66
Houghton Lake, Mich.,
   800...............D6   66
Houghton Lake Heights,
   Mich., 1,000........D6   66
Houilles, Fr., 26,370.....g9   5
Houlton, Maine, 6,500
   (8,289▲)............B5   64
Houma, La., 22,561...E5, k10   63
Housatonic, Mass., 1,400..B1   65
Houston, B.C., Can.,
   699...............B4   37
Houston, Minn., 1,082....G7   67
Houston, Miss., 2,577....B5   68
Houston, Mo., 1,660....D6   69
Houston, Pa., 1,865.....F1   81
Houston, Tex., 1,150,000
   (*1,595,000)......E5, r14   84
Houston, co., Ala.,
   50,718.............D4   46
Houston, co., Ga.,
   39,154.............D3   55
Houston, co., Minn.,
   16,588.............G7   67
Houston, co., Tenn.,
   4,794..............A4   83
Houston, co., Tex.,
   19,376.............D5   84
Houtzdale, Pa., 1,239....E5   81
Hove, Eng., 72,000.....E6   4
Howard, Kans., 1,017....E7   61
Howard, S. Dak., 1,208...F8   77
Howard, Wis., 3,485...D5, g9   88
Howard, co., Ark., 10,878..C2   49
Howard, co., Ind., 69,509..C5   59
Howard, co., Iowa,
   12,734.............A5   60
Howard, co., Md., 36,152..B4   53
Howard, co., Mo., 10,859..B5   69
Howard, co., Nebr.,
   6,541..............C7   71
Howard, co., Tex., 40,139..C2   84
Howard City, Mich.,
   1,004..............E5   66
Howard Lake, Minn.,
   1,007..............E4   67
Howe, Ind., 500.......A7   59
Howell, Mich., 4,861....F7   66
Howell, co., Mo., 22,027..E6   69
Howells, Nebr., 694.....C8   71
Howick, Que., Can., 647..D4   42
Howland, Maine, 1,362...C4   64
Howley, mtn., Newf., Can..D2   44
Howrah, India, 512,598...D8   20
Howson, peak, B.C.,
   Can............B4, n17   37
Hoxie, Ark., 1,886......A5   49
Hoxie, Kans., 1,289.....C3   61
Hoya, Ger., 4,300......B4   6
Hoyerswerda, Ger.,
   24,500.............C7   6
Hoyt Lakes, Minn., 3,186..C6   67

Hradec Králové, Czech.,
   57,100.............C3   7
Hranice, Czech., 10,800...D4   7
Hrinova, Czech., 6,831....D5   7
Hrubieszow, Pol., 13,100..C7   7
Hsichang (Sichang), China,
   50,000.............F5   17
Hsifeng, China, 33,886...C9   17
Hsinchu, Taiwan,
   114,000............G9   17
Hsinkao, mtn., Taiwan....G9   17
Hsinmin, China, 35,000...C9   17
Hsipaw, Bur., 5,000.....*D10   20
Huacho, Peru, 22,200....D2   31
Huaillay, Peru, 593......D2   31
Huaiyin, China, 77,000...E8   17
Hualgayoc, Peru, 1,173...C2   31
Hualien, Taiwan,
   32,230.............G9   17
Huamachuco, Peru, 2,324..C2   31
Huamantla, Mex.,
   10,154.............n15   34
Huancabamba, Peru,
   2,443..............C2   31
Huancané, Peru, 2,236....E4   31
Huancavelica, Peru,
   11,000.............D2   31
Huancavelica, dept., Peru,
   315,730............D2   31
Huancayo, Peru, 46,000..D2   31
Huanjen, China, 5,000...F2   18
Huanta, Peru, 5,600.....D3   31
Huánuco, Peru, 24,600...C2   31
Huánuco, dept., Peru,
   355,003............C2   31
Huaral, Peru, 5,012.....D2   31
Huarás, Peru, 20,500....C2   31
Huariaca, Peru, 1,593....D2   31
Huarmey, Peru, 1,333....D2   31
Huascaran, mtn., Peru....C2   31
Huatabampo, Mex.,
   10,228.............B3   34
Huatien, China, 35,000...C10   17
Huatusco [de Chicuellar],
   Mex., 8,680........n15   34
Huauchinango, Mex.,
   12,317.............m14   34
Huaytará, Peru, 718.....D2   31
Hubbard, Iowa, 806.....B4   60
Hubbard, Ohio, 7,137....A5   78
Hubbard, Tex., 1,628....D4   84
Hubbard, co., Minn.,
   9,962..............C3   67
Hubbell, Mich., 1,429....A2   66
Huberdeau, Que., Can.,
   605...............D3   42
Huber Heights, Ohio,
   15,000.............*C1   78
Hubli, India, 171,326.....E6   20
Huddersfield, Eng.,
   131,800............D6   4
Huddy, Ky., 600.......C7   62
Hudiksvall, Swe., 12,000..G7   11
Hudson, Que., Can.,
   1,671...........D3, q18   42
Hudson, Iowa, 1,423.....B5   60
Hudson, Mass., 9,666..B4, g9   65
Hudson, Mich., 2,546....G6   66
Hudson, N.H., 3,800....F5   73
Hudson, N.Y., 11,075....C7   75
Hudson, N.C., 1,536.....B1   76
Hudson, Ohio, 2,438.....A4   78
Hudson, Pa., 900......*D9   81
Hudson, Wis., 4,325.....D1   88
Hudson, co., N.J.,
   610,734............B4   74
Hudson, bay, Can.......D16   36
Hudson, mtn., Maine.....B3   64
Hudson Bay, Sask., Can.,
   1,601..............E4   39
Hudson Falls, N.Y., 7,752..B7   75
Hudson Heights, Que.,
   Can., 1,540......D8, q18   42
Hudsonville, Mich., 2,649..F5   66
Hudspeth, co., Tex.,
   3,343..............o12   84
Hue, Viet., 105,800.....B3   19
Hueco, mts., Tex........o11   84
Huedin, Rom., 5,134....B6   10
Huehuetenango, Guat.,
   6,187.............*D6   34
Huelma, Sp., 7,739......D4   8
Huelva, Sp., 74,384.....D2   8
Huelva, prov., Sp.,
   399,934...........*D2   8
Huércal-Overa, Sp.,
   13,016.............D5   8
Huerfano, Colo., 7,867...D5   51
Huesca, Sp., 24,377.....A5   8
Huesca, prov., Sp.,
   233,543...........*A5   8
Huéscar, Sp., 5,499.....D4   8
Hueytown, Ala., 5,997...E4   46
Hughes, Ark., 1,960.....C5   49
Hughes, co., Okla.,
   15,144.............B5   79
Hughes, co., S. Dak.,
   12,725.............F6   77

Hughes Springs, Tex.,
1,813.............*C5 84
Hughestown, Pa., 1,615..*D9 81
Hughesville, Pa., 2,218....D8 81
Hughson, Calif., 1,898....*D3 50
Hugo, Colo., 811.........B7 51
Hugo, Okla., 6,287.......C6 79
Hugoton, Kans., 2,912....E2 61
Huguley, Ala., 2,189.....*C4 46
Huhehot (Kweisui), China,
314,000...............C7 17
Huichon, Kor., 14,619.....F3 18
Huila, dept., Col.,
416,289...............C2 32
Huixtla, Mex., 12,327....D6 34
Hukou, China, 5,000.....F8 17
Hulan, China, 60,000.....B10 17
Hulen, Ky., 500.........D6 62
Hull, Que., Can.,
56,929...............D2 42
Hull, Eng., 301,000.....D6 4
Hull, Iowa, 1,484.......A1 60
Hull, Mass., 7,055....B6, g12 65
Hull, co., Que., Can.,
84,803...............D2 42
Hulmeville, Pa., 968.....*F11 81
Humacao, P.R., 8,005...*G12 35
Humansville, Mo., 745....D4 69
Humble, Tex., 1,711.E5, q14 84
Humboldt, Sask., Can.,
3,245................E3 39
Humboldt, Iowa, 4,497....B3 60
Humboldt, Kans., 2,285....E8 61
Humboldt, Nebr., 1,322...D10 71
Humboldt, Tenn., 8,482...B3 83
Humboldt, co., Calif.,
104,892..............B2 50
Humboldt, co., Iowa,
13,156...............B3 60
Humboldt, co., Nev.,
5,708................A2 72
Humenné, Czech., 11,100..D6 7
Humeston, Iowa, 638.....D4 60
Hummelstown, Pa.,
4,474................*F8 81

Humphrey, Nebr., 801....C8 71
Humphreys, co., Miss.,
19,093...............B3 68
Humphreys, co., Tenn.,
11,511...............A4 83
Humphreys, peak, Ariz...B2 48
Humpolec, Czech., 5,083..D3 7
Hunan, prov., China,
36,220,000...........F7 17
Hunchun, China, 25,000..C11 17
Hunedoara, Rom.,
51,200...............C6 10
Hungary, country, Eur.,
10,135,000...........B4 10
Hungnam, Kor., 143,600..G3 18
Hunt, mtn., Wyo.........B5 89
Hunt, co., Tex., 39,399...C4 84
Hunterdon, N.J., 54,107..B3 74
Huntersville, N.C., 1,004..B2 76
Huntingburg, Ind., 4,146..H4 59
Huntingdon, Que., Can.,
3,134................D3 42
Huntingdon, Pa., 7,234...F6 81
Huntingdon, Tenn.,
2,119................A3 83
Huntingdon, co., Que., Can.,
14,752...............D3 42
Huntingdon, co., Pa.,
39,457...............F5 81
Huntingdon
[& Peterborough],
co., Eng., 166,000...*D7 4
Huntington, Ind., 16,185..C7 59
Huntington, Mass., 950
(1,392 ▲)............B2 65
Huntington, N.J., 700....B2 74
Huntington, N.Y.,
12,500.............E7, n15 75
Huntington, Oreg., 689...C9 80
Huntington, Tex., 1,009..D5 84
Huntington, Utah, 787....B6 72
Huntington, W. Va.,
80,000 (*238,000).......C2 87
Huntington, co., Ind.,
33,814...............C6 59

Huntington Bay, N.Y.,
1,267................*G3 52
Huntington Beach, Calif.,
86,646...............n13 50
Huntington Beach, N.Y.,
3,789................*D3 75
Huntington Park, Calif.,
29,920...............F4 50
Huntington Station, N.Y.,
26,000...............F3 52
Huntington Woods, Mich.,
8,746................p15 66
Huntingtown, Md., 200...C4 53
Huntley, Ill., 1,143.....A5 58
Huntly, Scot., 3,800.....B5 4
Huntsville, Ala., 72,365...A3 46
Huntsville, Ark., 1,050...A2 49
Huntsville, Ont., Can.,
3,189................B5 41
Huntsville, Mo., 1,526...B5 69
Huntsville, Tex., 11,999..D5 84
Hupeh (Hupei),
prov., China,
30,790,000...........E7 17
Hurley, N. Mex., 1,851...C4 48
Hurley, N.Y., 900.......D6 75
Hurley, Wis., 2,763.....B3 88
Hurleyville, N.Y., 900...D6 75
Hurlock, Md., 1,035.....C3 53
Huron, Calif., 1,269.....*D4 50
Huron, Ont., Can.,
53,805...............D3 41
Huron, Ohio, 5,197......A3 78
Huron, S. Dak., 14,180...F7 77
Huron, co., Mich., 34,006..E7 66
Huron, co., Ohio, 47,326..A3 78
Huron, lake, Can., U.S...B10 45
Hurricane, Utah, 1,251...C5 72
Hurricane, W. Va.,
1,970................C2 87
Hurst, Ill., 863........F4 58
Hurst, Tex., 10,165.....*C4 84
Hurtsboro, Ala., 1,056...C4 46
Huşi, Rom., 18,055......B9 10
Huskerville, Nebr., 1,000..D9 71

Huskvarna, Swe., 13,800...I6 11
Hustisford, Wis., 708.....E5 88
Husum, Ger., 23,800.....A4 6
Hutchins, Tex., 1,100.....n10 84
Hutchinson, Kans.,
37,574............D6, f11 61
Hutchinson, Minn., 6,207..F4 67
Hutchinson, S. Dak.,
11,085...............G8 77
Hutchinson, Tex., 34,419..B2 84
Huttig, Ark., 936.......D3 49
Huxley, Iowa, 629....C4, e8 60
Huy, Bel., 13,447.......B6 5
Hvannadalshnvkúr, mtn.,
Ice..................n24 11
Hvittingfoss, Nor., 576...p28 11
Hwaining see Anking, China
Hwang Ho (Yellow),
riv., China........D8, f14 16
Hyannis, Mass., 5,700....C7 65
Hyannis Port, Mass., 500..C7 65
Hyattsville, Md.,
15,168.............C4, f9 53
Hybla Valley, Va., 1,500..*B5 85
Hyde, N.C., 5,456......B6 76
Hyde, Pa., 850.........D5 81
Hyde, S. Dak., 2,602....F6 77
Hyde Park, N.Y., 2,800...D7 75
Hyde Park, Pa., 2,500...*F9 81
Hyderabad, India,
931,082..............E6 20
Hyderabad, Pak., 416,441
(*460,000)...........C4 20
Hyde Villa, Pa., 1,300...*F9 81
Hydro, Okla., 697.......B3 79
Hyères, Fr., 18,671.....F7 5
Hymera, Ind., 1,015.....F3 59
Hyndman, Pa., 1,124.....G4 81
Hyogo, pref., Jap.,
4,309,944............*I7 18
Hyopchon, Kor., 7,000....I4 18
Hyrum, Utah, 1,728.....A6 72
Hyrynsalmi, Fin., 1,300..E13 11
Hythe, Alta., Can., 449...B1 38
Hythe, Eng., 10,200.....E7 4

I

Iaeger, W. Va., 930......D3 87
Iasi (Jassy), Rom.,
124,700..............B8 10
Iba, Phil., 4,241........*B5 19
Ibadan, Nig., 627,379.....G5 22
Ibagué, Col., 125,233....C2 32
Ibaraki, pref., Jap.,
2,056,154............*H10 18
Ibarra, Ec., 25,835......A2 31
Ibb, Yemen, 25,000......G3 15
Iberia, Mo., 694........C5 69
Iberia, par., La., 51,657..E4 63
Iberville, Que., Can.,
7,588................D4 42
Iberville, co., Que., Can.,
18,080...............D4 42
Iberville, par., La....D4, h9 63
Ibitinga, Braz., 8,881.....C3 30
Ibiza, Sp., 11,259......C6 8
Ica, Peru, 38,300.......D2 31
Ica, dept., Peru, 261,126..D2 31
Ice, mtn., B.C., Can......B7 37
Iceland, country, Eur.,
189,000..............n23 11
Ichang, China, 81,000....E7 17
Ichikawa, Jap., 207,988..N18 18
Ichinomiya, Jap.,
203,743..............n15 18
Ichinoseki, Jap., 28,700..G10 18
Ichnya, Sov. Un., 10,000..F9 12
Ida, Mich., 800.........G7 66
Ida, co., Iowa, 10,269....B2 60
Idabel, Okla., 4,967.....D7 79
Ida Grove, Iowa, 2,265...B2 60
Idaho, co., Idaho, 13,542..D3 57
Idaho, state, U.S., 667,191...57
Idaho Falls, Idaho,
35,711...............F6 57
Idaho Springs, Colo.,
1,480................B5 51
Idalou, Tex., 1,274.....C2 84
Idamay, W. Va., 800.....A7 87
Idanha-a-Nova, Port.,
4,459................C2 8
Idaville, Ind., 600......C4 59
Idrija, Yugo., 6,024.....B2 10

Ieper (Ypres), Bel.,
18,121...............B5 5
Ierapetra, Grc., 6,488....E5 14
Iesi, It., 21,900........C4 9
Ifni, Sp. dep., Afr.,
49,889...............C2 22
Igarapava, Braz., 9,083...C3 30
Igarka, Sov. Un.,
14,300...............C11 13
Igdir, Tur., 12,730......C15 14
Ighil Izane, Alg., 35,380..A5 22
Iglesias, It., 28,004.....E2 9
Igloo, S. Dak., 1,000....G2 77
Igualada, Sp., 19,866....B6 8
Iguatu, Braz., 16,540....*D7 27
Ihsing, China, 93,000....*E8 17
Iida, Jap., 48,000
(79,145▲)..........I8, n16 18
Iide-san, mtn., Jap......H9 18
Iijima, Jap., 3,400......n16 18
Iisalmi, Fin., 6,000.....F12 11
Iizuka, Jap., 82,033
(*110,000)...........J5 18
Ijebu Ode, Nig., 27,558..G5 22
Ijuí, Braz., 19,671......D2 30
Ikeda, Jap., 82,478.....D14 18
Ikhtiman, Bul., 9,063....D6 10
Ilagan, Phil., 6,375.....B6 19
Ilan (Sanhsing), China,
40,000...............B10 17
Ilan, Taiwan, 38,910....*G9 17
Ile-a-la-Cross, Sask.,
Can., 570............m7 39
Ile-de-France, former
prov., Fr., 7,733,000....C5 5
Île-Perrot, Que., Can.,
3,106................q19 42
Ilford, Eng., 178,210.....k13 4
Ilfracombe, Eng., 8,400...E4 4
Ilgin, Tur., 8,116.......C8 14
Ilhavo, Port., 6,969.....B1 8
Ilhéus, Braz., 45,712....E7 27
Ilia (Elis), prov., Grc.,
188,861..............*D3 14
Ilinskaya, Sov. Un.,
10,000...............I13 12

Ilion, N.Y., 10,199......B5 75
Illampu, mtn., Bol.......C2 29
Illapel, Chile, 10,400....A2 28
Ille-et-Vilaine, dept., Fr.,
614,268..............*C3 5
Illinois, state, U.S.,
10,081,158...........58
Illinois, peak, Idaho.....B3 57
Illinois, peak, Mont......C1 70
Illiopolis, Ill., 995.....D4 58
Illmo, Mo., 1,174.......D8 69
Illora, Sp., 13,458......D4 8
Ilmenau, Ger., 17,700...C5 6
Ilo, Peru, 1,043........E3 31
Ilocos Norte, prov., Phil.,
287,333..............*B6 19
Ilocos Sur, prov., Phil.,
338,058..............C6 19
Iloilo, Phil., 151,266....C6 19
Iloilo, prov., Phil.,
966,266..............*C6 19
Ilorin, Nig., 208,546.....G5 22
Ilovaysk, Sov. Un.,
10,000...............r21 12
Imabari, Jap., 104,470...I6 18
Imabetsu, Jap., 2,300....F10 18
Iman, Sov. Un., 18,000..E16 13
Imari, Jap., 41,000
(67,316▲)............*J4 18
Imazu, Jap., 3,800......n15 18
Imbabura, prov., Ec.,
174,039..............A2 31
Imlay City, Mich., 1,968..E7 66
Immenstadt, Ger.,
10,000...............E5 6
Immokalee, Fla., 3,224...F5 54
Imola, It., 29,000.......B3 9
Imperia, It., 36,500.....C2 9
Imperial, Calif., 3,271...F6 50
Imperial, Sask., Can.,
557..................F3 39
Imperial, Mo., 500...C7, g13 69
Imperial, Nebr., 1,423...D4 71
Imperial, Pa., 2,000.....k13 81
Imperial, co., Calif.,
78,019...............F6 50

Imperial Beach, Calif.,
17,773...............o15 50
Imperoyal, N.S., Can.,
490..................E6 43
Imphal, India, 67,717....D9 20
Ina, Jap., 25,500
(51,944▲)............n16 18
Inatori, Jap., 9,100......o18 18
Inca, Sp., 13,816.......C7 8
Inchŏn, Kor., 485,500....H3 18
Indaw, Bur., 2,138......D10 20
Independence, Calif., 950..D4 50
Independence, Iowa,
5,498................B6 60
Independence, Kans.,
11,222...............E8 61
Independence, La., 1,941..D5 63
Independence, Minn.,
1,446................*F5 67
Independence, Mo.,
62,328.............B3, h11 69
Independence, Ohio,
6,868................h9 78
Independence, Oreg.,
1,930.............C3, k11 80
Independence, Wis., 954..D2 88
Independence, co., Ark.,
20,048...............B4 49
Independence Hill, Ind.,
1,824................*B3 59
India, country, Asia,
475,353,000..........D6 20
Indialantic, Fla., 1,653...*D6 54
Indian, ocean...........G2 2
Indiana, Pa., 13,005.....E3 81
Indiana, co., Pa., 75,366..E3 81
Indiana, state, U.S.,
4,662,498............59
Indianapolis, Ind., 515,000
(*900,000).........E5, k10 59
Indian Head, Sask., Can.,
1,802................G4 39
Indian Head, Md., 780...C3 53
Indian Hill, Ohio,
4,526................o13 78
Indian Lake, N.Y., 500...B6 75

Indian Mound Beach, Mass., 600............*C6 65
Indianola, Iowa, 8,281....C4 60
Indianola, Miss., 6,714....B3 68
Indianola, Nebr., 754....D5 71
Indianola, Pa., 1,000......*E1 81
Indian, peak, Wyo.......B3 89
Indian River, co., Fla., 25,309...............E6 54
Indian Rocks Beach, Fla., 1,940..............p10 54
Indiantown, Fla., 1,411...E6 54
Indio, Calif., 9,745.......F5 50
Indochina, reg., Asia.....B3 19
Indonesia, country, Asia, 575,893...............F6 19
Indore, India, 394,941...D6 20
Indramaju, Indon., 21,190..............G3 19
Indre, dept., Fr., 251,432..............*D4 5
Indre-et-Loire, dept., Fr., 395,210..............*D4 5
Indus, riv., Asia..........C4 20
Industrial, S.C., 1,000....B6 82
Industrial City, Ala., 1,500................*E4 46
Industry, Pa., 2,338......*E1 81
Ine, Jap., 2,000..........n14 18
Infantes, Sp., 9,909......C4 8
Infiesto, Sp., 1,650.......A3 8
Ingalls, Ind., 873.........E6 59
Ingalls Park, Ill., 6,840...B5 58
Ingersoll, Ont., Can., 6,874................D4 41
Ingham, Austl., 5,358.....C8 25
Ingham, co., Mich., 211,296..............F6 66
Ingleside, Nebr., 400.....D7 71
Ingleside, Tex., 3,022.....F4 84
Inglewood, Calif., 63,390..n12 50
Inglewood, Nebr., 480...............C9, g11 71
Inglewood, Tenn., 13,500.............*A5 83
Ingolstadt, Ger., 65,400...D5 6
Ingomar, Pa., 1,500.....h13 81
Ingonish Beach, N.S., Can., 658..............C9 43
Ingram, Pa., 4,730.......k13 81
Inhambane, Moz..........E7 24
Inharrime, Moz..........E7 24
Inishbofin, isl., U.K......D1 4
Inishtrahull, isl., U.K.....C3 4
Inishturk, isl., U.K.......D1 4
Inkerman, Pa., 1,000....*D9 81
Inkom, Idaho, 528.......G6 57
Inkster, Mich., 39,097....p15 66
Inman, Kans., 729........D6 61
Inman, S.C., 1,714.......A3 82
Inman Mills, S.C., 1,769................*A3 82
Inner Mongolia, prov., China, 9,200,000......C8 17
Innisfail, Alta., Can., 2,270................C4 38
Innisfail, Austl., 7,419.....C8 25
Innsbruck, Aus., 104,900...E5 6
Ino, Jap., 14,000.........J6 18
Inowroclaw, Pol., 49,900.............B5 7
Insein, Bur., 27,030......E10 20
Institute, W. Va., 2,600...C3 87
Intercession City, Fla., 500................D5 54
Intercity, Wash., 1,475...*B3 86
Interlaken, N.J., 1,168....*C4 74
International Falls, Minn., 6,778...............B5 67
Intersection, mtn., B.C., Can.................C7 37
Invercargill, N.Z., 43,572 (*46,016)............Q12 26
Inverell, Austl., 8,411.....E9 25
Invermere, B.C., Can., 744................D9 37
Inverness, Calif., 550....C2 50
Inverness, N.S., Can., 2,109...............C8 43
Inverness, Fla., 1,878.....D4 54
Inverness, Ill., 1,110......*B6 58
Inverness, Miss., 1,039....C4 68
Inverness, Scot., 30,000...B4 4
Inverness, co., N.S., Can., 18,718..............C8 43

Inverness, co., Scot., 81,900...............*B4 4
Invisible, mtn., Idaho.....F5 57
Inwood, Iowa, 638.......A1 60
Inwood, N.Y., 9,500.....k13 75
Inyan Kara, mtn., Wyo...B8 89
Inyo, co., Calif., 11,684...D5 50
Inyokern, Calif., 550.....E5 50
Ioannina, Grc., 34,997...C3 14
Ioannina, prov., Grc., 155,326.............*C3 14
Iola, Kans., 6,885........E8 61
Iola, Wis., 831...........D4 88
Iona, Idaho, 702.........F7 57
Ione, Calif., 1,118.......C3 50
Ionia, Mich., 6,754.......F5 66
Ionia, co., Mich., 43,132...F5 66
Iosco, co., Mich., 16,505...D7 66
Iota, La., 1,245..........D3 63
Iowa, La., 1,857.........D2 63
Iowa, co., Iowa, 16,396...C5 60
Iowa, co., Wis., 19,631...E3 88
Iowa, state, U.S., 2,757,537................ 60
Iowa City, Iowa, 40,467...C6 60
Iowa Falls, Iowa, 6,322...B4 60
Iowa Park, Tex., 3,295...C3 84
Ipameri, Braz., 8,987.....B3 30
Ipava, Ill., 623..........C3 58
Ipiales, Col., 23,320......C2 32
Ipin, China, 177,500.....F5 17
Ipoh, Mala., 125,770.....E2 19
Ipswich, Austl., 54,534...E9 25
Ipswich, Eng., 119,400...D7 4
Ipswich, Mass., 5,400....A6 65
Ipswich, S. Dak., 1,131...E6 77
Iquique, Chile, 50,700....D2 29
Iquitos, Peru, 55,700.....B3 31
Iraan, Tex., 1,255........D2 84
Iraklion, Grc., 63,458....E5 14
Iraklion, prov., Grc., 208,374.............*E5 14
Iran (Persia), country, Asia, 23,100,000.......F8 16
Irapuato, Mex., 83,768...........C4, m13 34
Iraq, country, Asia, 8,855,000............C3 15
Irbid, Jordan, 44,685...B3, g5 15
Irbil, Iraq, 34,313......D15 15
Iredell, co., N.C., 62,526...B2 76
Ireland (Eire), country, Eur., 2,880,800......D3 4
Ireton, Iowa, 510........B1 60
Iri, Kor., 64,400.........I3 18
Iringa, Tan., 9,587.......B7 24
Irion, co., Tex., 1,183....D2 84
Irkutsk, Sov. Un., 401,000............D13 13
Iron, co., Mich., 17,184...B2 66
Iron, co., Mo., 8,041.....D7 69
Iron, co., Utah, 10,795...C5 72
Iron, co., Wis., 7,830....B3 88
Iron, mts., Va...........D1 85
Irondale, Ala., 3,501.....E5 46
Irondale, Ohio, 705......B5 78
Irondequoit, N.Y., 60,704..............B3 75
Ironia, N.J., 900.........B3 74
Iron Mountain, Mich., 9,299................C2 66
Iron River, Mich., 3,754...B2 66
Iron River, Wis., 650.....B2 88
Ironton, Minn., 724......D5 67
Ironton, Mo., 1,310......D7 69
Ironton, Ohio, 15,745....D3 78
Ironwood, Mich., 10,265.............n11 66
Iroquois, N.B., Can., 818................*B1 43
Iroquois, Ont., Can., 1,136................C9 41
Iroquois, co., Ill., 33,562...C6 58
Iroquois Falls, Ont., Can., 1,681...............*o19 41
Irosin, Phil., 8,031.......*C6 19
Irrawaddy, riv., Bur.....D10 20
Irtysh, riv., Sov. Un............D9, D10 13
Irún, Sp., 29,814........A5 8
Irvine, Ky., 2,955........C6 62
Irvine, Scot., 18,400.....C4 4
Irving, Tex., 45,985.....n10 84
Irvington, Ky., 1,190.....D3 62
Irvington, N.J., 59,379...k8 74

Irvington, N.Y., 5,686....g13 75
Irvona, Pa., 781.........E4 81
Irwin, Pa., 4,270........F2 81
Irwin, S.C., 1,113.......*B6 82
Irwin, co., Ga., 9,211.....E3 55
Irwindale, Calif., 1,518...*E4 50
Isabel, mtn., Wyo........D2 89
Isabela, P.R., 7,302.....*G11 35
Isabela, prov., Phil., 442,062.............*D6 19
Isabella, Pa., 900........G2 81
Isabella, Tenn., 415......D9 83
Isabella, co., Mich., 35,348..............E6 66
Isahaya, Jap., 36,100 (63,886*).............J5 18
Isanti, Minn., 521.......E5 67
Isanti, co., Minn., 13,530...E5 67
Ise (Uji-yamada), Jap., 102,395..........I8, o15 18
Iselin, N.J., 17,000......B4 74
Iselin, Pa., 500..........E3 81
Isère, dept., Fr., 729,789.............*E6 5
Isernia, It., 8,600........D5 9
Iseyin, Nig., 49,680.....G5 22
Isezaki, Jap., 62,000 (86,861*).........H9, m18 18
Ishikawa, pref., Jap., 980,499.............*H8 18
Ishim, Sov. Un., 39,000...D9 13
Ishimbay, Sov. Un., 53,500.............*D8 13
Ishinomaki, Jap., 62,000..............G10 18
Ishioka, Jap., 21,100....m19 18
Ishpeming, Mich., 8,857...B3 66
Isigny-sur-Mer, Fr., 2,391...C3 5
Isiro (Paulis), Con. K., 9,700...............H3 23
İskenderun (Alexandretta), Tur., 62,061........D11 14
Iskilip, Tur., 12,210.....B10 14
Isla Cristina, Sp., 8,276....D2 8
Islamorado, Fla., 700....H6 54
Island, co., Wash., 19,638...A3 86
Island Falls, Maine, 800 (1,018*)............B4 64
Island Heights, N.J., 1,150................D4 74
Island Lake, Ill., 1,639...*E2 58
Island Park, N.Y., 3,846...*E7 75
Island Pond, Vt., 1,319...B4 73
Islav, isl., U.K...........C3 4
Isle, Minn., 529.........D5 67
Isle-aux-Morts, Newf., Can., 884............E2 44
Isle of Ely, co., Eng., 89,112..............*D7 4
Isle of Hope, Ga., 1,900................*D6 55
Isle of Man, Br. dep.; Eur., 48,000..............C4 4
Isle of Man, isl., U.K.....C4 4
Isle of Palms, S.C., 1,186................k12 82
Isle of Wight, co., Eng., 95,479.............*E6 4
Isle of Wight, isl., U.K....E6 4
Isle Royale, isl., Mich.....h9 66
Isleton, Calif., 1,039.....C3 50
Isle-Verte, Que., Can., 1,517................A8 42
Islington, Mass., 3,800...h11 65
Islip, N.Y., 12,000......n15 75
Islip Terrace, N.Y., 3,600..............*n15 75
Isola Capo Rizzuto, It., 9,218................E6 9
Isparta, Tur., 35,981.....D8 14
Israel, country, Asia, 2,376,000............C2 15
Issaquah, Wash., 1,870....e11 86
Issaquena, co., Miss., 3,576................C2 68
Issoire, Fr., 10,454.......E5 5
Issoudun, Fr., 13,900....D4 5
Issyk-kul, lake, Sov. Un...E10 13
Issy [les-Moulineaux], Fr., 51,776..............g10 5
İstanbul (Constantinople), Tur., 1,466,535........B7 14
Istmina, Col., 3,996......B2 32

Itá, Par., 18,777.........E4 29
Itabaiana, Braz., 11,847...*E7 27
Itabaiana, Braz., 11,050..............*D7 27
Itaberaba, Braz., 8,555...*E6 27
Itabira, Braz., 15,539....B4 30
Itabuna, Braz., 54,268...E7 27
Itajaí, Braz., 38,889.....D3 30
Itajubá, Braz., 31,262....C3 30
Italy, Tex., 1,183........C4 84
Italy, country, Eur., 50,900,000............. 9
Itami, Jap., 121,380....o14 18
Itaperuna, Braz., 18,095...C4 30
Itapetininga, Braz., 29,468.........C3, m7 30
Itapeva, Braz., 13,510...C3 30
Itápolis, Braz., 7,430.....k7 30
Itapúa, dept., Par., 111,424.............E4 29
Itaqui, Braz., 13,223.....D1 30
Itararé, Braz., 12,812....C3 30
Itasca, Ill., 3,930........k8 58
Itasca, Tex., 1,383.......C4 84
Itasca, co., Minn., 38,006...C5 67
Itatiba, Braz., 12,336....m8 30
Itaúna, Braz., 22,319....C4 30
Itawamba, co., Miss., 15,080..............A5 68
Ithaca, Mich., 2,611.....E6 66
Ithaca, N.Y., 28,799.....C4 75
Itō, Jap., 59,404.......o18 18
Itoigawa, Jap., 21,700...H8 18
Itta Bena, Miss., 1,914...B3 68
Itu, Braz., 23,435.....C3, m8 30
Ituango, Col., 3,466.....B2 32
Ituiutaba, Braz., 29,724...B3 30
Ituna, Sask., Can., 837...F4 39
Itung, China..........C10 17
Itzehoe, Ger., 36,100....B4 6
Iuka, Miss., 2,010.......A5 68
Iva, S.C., 1,357.........C2 82
Ivanhoe, Calif., 1,616...*D4 50
Ivanhoe, Minn., 719......F2 67
Ivanhoe, Va., 800.......D2 85
Ivano-Frankovsk, Sov. Un., 78,000..............G5 12
Ivanovka, Sov. Un., 5,000...............q21 12
Ivanovo, Sov. Un., 368,000.............C13 12
Ivanteyevka, Sov. Un., 10,000..............n17 12
Ivory Coast, country, Afr., 3,750,000............G3 22
Ivoryton, Conn., 1,000...D7 52
Ivrea, It., 23,723........B1 9
Ivry-sur-Seine, Fr., 53,406..............g10 5
Ivywild, Colo., 8,000.....C6 51
Iwaki-yama, mtn., Jap...F10 18
Iwakuni, Jap., 105,931...I6 18
Iwamisawa, Jap., 46,000 (65,508*)............E10 18
Iwamurada, Jap., 7,600..m17 18
Iwanai, Jap., 21,500.....E10 18
Iwate, pref., Jap., 1,411,118...........*G10 18
Iwate-yama, mtn., Jap...G10 18
Iwaya, Jap., 13,700....o14 18
Iwo, Nig., 158,583......G5 22
Ixmiquilpan, Mex., 2,480..............m14 34
Ixtacalco, Mex., 25,546...h9 34
Ixtacihuatl, mtn., Mex....n14 34
Ixtapalapa, Mex., 25,717...h9 34
Ixtlán de Juárez, Mex., 1,165...............o15 34
Ixtlán del Río, Mex., 8,330............C4, m11 34
Izamal, Mex., 8,633......C7 34
Izard, co., Ark., 6,766....A4 49
Izhevsk, Sov. Un., 351,000.............D8 13
Izmail, Sov. Un., 55,000...I7 12
Izmir (Smyrna), Tur., 360,829.............C6 14
Izmit (Kocaeli), Tur., 73,488..............B7 14
Izúcar de Matamoros, Mex., 16,556.........n14 34
Izuhara, Jap., 17,400....I4 18
Izumo, Jap., 38,100 (68,765*)..............I6 18
Izyum, Sov. Un., 34,000..G11 12

J

Jabalpur (Jubbulpore),
India, 295,375
(*367,014)............D6   20
Jaboatão, Braz., 33,963...*D7   27
Jaboticabal, Braz.,
20,231............C3, k7   30
Jaca, Sp., 9,856............A5   8
Jacala de Ledesma,
Mex., 1,968............m14   34
Jacareí, Braz., 28,131.....m9   30
Jacarèzinho, Braz.,
14,813............C3   30
Jachymov, Czech., 6,806...C2   7
Jacinto City, Tex., 9,547..r14   84
Jack, co., Tex., 7,418....C3   84
Jack, mtn., Mont........D4   70
Jack, mtn., Va........B3   85
Jackfork, mtn., Okla......C6   79
Jacks, mtn., Pa........E6   81
Jacksboro, Tex., 3,816....C3   84
Jackson, Ala., 4,959......D2   46
Jackson, Calif., 1,852....C3   50
Jackson, Ga., 2,545....C3   55
Jackson, Ky., 1,852....C6   62
Jackson, La., 1,824....D4   63
Jackson, Mich., 49,000
(*125,000)............F6   66
Jackson, Minn., 3,370....G3   67
Jackson, Miss., 165,000
(*230,000)............C3   68
Jackson, Mo., 4,875......D8   69
Jackson, N.C., 765......A5   76
Jackson, Ohio, 6,980.....C3   78
Jackson, S.C., 1,746.....E4   82
Jackson, Tenn., 34,376....B3   83
Jackson, Wyo., 1,437.....C2   89
Jackson, co., Ala.,
36,681............A3   46
Jackson, co., Ark., 22,843..B4   49
Jackson, co., Colo., 1,758..A4   51
Jackson, co., Fla., 36,208..B1   54
Jackson, co., Ga., 18,499..B3   55
Jackson, co., Ill., 42,151...F4   58
Jackson, co., Ind., 30,556..G5   59
Jackson, co., Iowa,
20,754............B7   60
Jackson, co., Kans.,
10,309............C8   61
Jackson, co., Ky., 10,677...C5   62
Jackson, co., Mich.,
131,994............F6   66
Jackson, co., Minn.,
15,501............G3   67
Jackson, co., Miss.,
55,522............E5   68
Jackson, co., Mo.,
622,732............C3   69
Jackson, co., N.C., 17,780..f9   76
Jackson, co., Ohio,
29,372............C3   78
Jackson, co., Okla.,
29,736............C2   79
Jackson, co., Oreg.,
73,962............E3   80
Jackson, co., S. Dak.,
1,985............G4   77
Jackson, co., Tenn., 9,233..C8   83
Jackson, co., Tex., 14,040..E4   84
Jackson, co., W. Va.,
18,541............C3   87
Jackson, co., Wis., 15,151..D3   88
Jackson, par., La., 15,828..B3   63
Jackson, mtn., Maine.....D2   64
Jackson Center, Ohio,
980............B1   78
Jacksonville, Ala., 5,678..B4   46
Jacksonville, Ark.,
14,488............C3, D6   49
Jacksonville, Fla., 190,000
(*525,000)............B5, m8   54
Jacksonville, Ill., 21,690..D3   58
Jacksonville, N.C., 13,491..C5   76
Jacksonville, Oreg., 1,172..E4   80
Jacksonville, Tex., 9,590..D5   84
Jacksonville Beach, Fla.,
12,049............B5, m9   54
Jacmel, Hai., 8,643......E7   35
Jacobabad, Pak., 22,835...C4   20
Jacobina, Braz., 12,373...*E6   27
Jacomino, Cuba, 6,121...*C2   35
Jacques-Cartier, Que., Can.,
40,807............D4, p20   42
Jacques-Cartier, co., Que.,
Can., 1,747,696.......q19   42
Jacques Cartier, mtn.,
Que............k13   42
Jadotville, Con. K.,
74,500............C5   24
Jaén, Sp., 64,917........D4   8
Jaén, prov., Sp., 736,391..*D4   8
Jaffna, Cey., 77,181......G7   20

Jaffrey, N.H., 1,700
(3,154▲)............F3   73
Jaguarão, Braz., 12,336....E2   30
Jaqüey Grande, Cuba,
6,600............C3   35
Jaipur, India, 403,444.....C6   20
Jaisalmer, India, 8,362....C5   20
Jajce, Yugo., 6,839.......C3   10
Jajpur, India, 13,802......D8   20
Jakarta, see Djakarta, Indon.
Jakobstad (Pietersaari),
Fin., 7,378............F10   11
Jal, N. Mex., 3,051......C7   48
Jalalabad, Afg., 14,756...B5   20
Jalapa, Guat., 6,610......*F6   34
Jalapa Enríquez
(Jalapa), Mex.,
66,269............D5, n15   34
Jalca Grande, Peru,
1,189............C2   31
Jalgaon, India, 80,351.....D6   20
Jalisco, state, Mex.,
4,189............C4, m12   34
Jalna, India, 67,158......E6   20
Jalpa, Mex., 6,213...C4, m12   34
Jalpan, Mex., 1,258..C5, m14   34
Jamaica, country, N.A.,
1,773,000............E5   35
James, riv., S. Dak......F7   77
Jamesburg, N.J., 2,853....C4   74
James City, N.C., 1,500...B5   76
James City, co., Va.,
11,539............C6   85
Jamesport, Mo., 622......B4   69
Jamestown, Calif., 900....D3   50
Jamestown, Ind., 827......E4   59
Jamestown, Ky., 792......D4   62
Jamestown, N.Y., 41,818...C1   75
Jamestown, N.C., 1,338....B3   76
Jamestown, N. Dak.,
15,163............D7   77
Jamestown, Ohio, 1,730...C2   78
Jamestown, Pa., 897......D1   81
Jamestown, R.I., 2,267...D11   52
Jamestown, Tenn.,
1,727............C9   83
Jamesville, N.Y., 1,000...*C4   75
Jamiltepec, Mex., 3,737...D5   34
Jammu, India, 102,738....B5   20
Jammu and Kashmir,
Disputed reg., Pak.,
4,700,000............B6   20
Jamnagar, India, 139,692..D5   20
Jamshedpur, India,
291,791............D8   20
Jämtland, co., Swe.,
137,600............*F6   11
Janesville, Iowa, 648.....B5   60
Janesville, Minn., 1,426...F5   67
Janesville, Wis., 35,164...F4   88
Janin, Jordan, 14,402.....B3   15
Janos, Mex., 987.........A3   34
Janoshalma, Hung.,
10,767............B4   10
Janow Lubelski, Pol.,
3,793............C7   7
Januária, Braz., 9,741.....B4   30
Jaoho (Tuanshantzu), China,
30,000............B11   17
Japan, country, Asia.,
98,274,961............I6   18
Japan, sea, Asia........F6   18
Jaral [del Progreso], Mex.,
7,055............m13   34
Jarales, N. Mex., 300.....B5   48
Jarocin, Pol., 19,100.....C4   7
Jaroslaw, Pol., 26,500....C7   7
Jarvis, Ont., Can., 783....E4   41
Jarvisburg, N.C., 500.....A7   76
Jasonville, Ind., 2,436....F3   59
Jasper, Ala., 10,799......B2   46
Jasper, Alta., Can.,
2,360............C1   38
Jasper, Fla., 2,103........B4   54
Jasper, Ga., 1,036.......B2   55
Jasper, Ind., 7,910.......H4   59
Jasper, Minn., 850.......G2   67
Jasper, Mo., 746........D3   69
Jasper, Tenn., 1,450......D8   83
Jasper, Tex., 4,889.......D6   84
Jasper, co., Ga., 6,135....C3   55
Jasper, co., Ill., 11,346....D5   58
Jasper, co., Ind., 18,842...B3   59
Jasper, co., Iowa, 35,282...C4   60
Jasper, co., Miss., 16,909..C4   68
Jasper, co., Mo., 78,863...D3   69
Jasper, co., S.C., 12,237...G5   82
Jasper, co., Tex., 22,100...D5   84
Jasper Place, Alta., Can.,
30,530............C4   38
Jaszapati, Hung., 9,423...B5   10

Jaszbereny, Hung.,
22,284............B4   10
Jatibonico, Cuba, 5,700..D4   35
Játiva, Sp., 19,896........C5   8
Jaú, Braz., 31,229.....C3, m7   30
Jauja, Peru, 12,700......D2   31
Jaumave, Mex., 2,266....C5   34
Jaunpur, India, 61,851....C7   20
Java, isl., Indon........G3   19
Javellanos, Cuba, 12,400..C3   35
Jawor, Pol., 14,500......C4   7
Jaworzno, Pol., 57,800....g10   7
Jay, Fla., 672............u14   54
Jay, N.Y., 500.........f11   75
Jay, Okla., 1,120........A7   79
Jay, co., Ind., 22,572....D7   59
Jayanca, Peru, 3,413......C2   31
Jeanerette, La., 5,568....E4   63
Jeannette, Pa., 16,565....F2   81
Jeberos, Peru, 981.......C2   31
Jedburgh, Scot., 3,600....C5   4
Jedrzejow, Pol., 13,400...C6   7
Jeff, Ky., 500..........C6   62
Jeff Davis, co., Ga., 8,914..E4   55
Jeff Davis, co., Tex.,
1,582............o12   84
Jefferson, Ga., 1,746.....B3   55
Jefferson, Iowa, 4,570....B3   60
Jefferson, La., 24,000....*E5   63
Jefferson, Mass., 700....B4   65
Jefferson, N.C., 814......A1   76
Jefferson, Ohio, 2,116....A5   78
Jefferson, Oreg.,
716............C3, k11   80
Jefferson, Pa., 8,280.....*E1   81
Jefferson, Tex., 3,082....C5   84
Jefferson, Wis., 4,548....E5   88
Jefferson, co., Ala.,
634,864............B3   46
Jefferson, co., Ark.,
81,373............C3   49
Jefferson, co., Colo.,
127,520............B5   51
Jefferson, co., Fla., 9,543..B3   54
Jefferson, co., Ga., 17,468..C4   55
Jefferson, co., Idaho,
11,672............F6   57
Jefferson, co., Ill., 32,315..E5   58
Jefferson, co., Ind.,
24,061............G7   59
Jefferson, co., Iowa,
15,818............C6   60
Jefferson, co., Kans.,
11,252............C8   61
Jefferson, co., Ky.,
610,947............B4   62
Jefferson, co., Miss.,
10,142............D2   68
Jefferson, co., Mo.,
66,377............C7   69
Jefferson, co., Mont.,
4,297............D4   70
Jefferson, co., Nebr.,
11,620............D8   71
Jefferson, co., N.Y.,
87,835............A5   75
Jefferson, co., Ohio,
99,201............B5   78
Jefferson, co., Okla.,
8,192............C4   79
Jefferson, co., Oreg.,
7,130............C5   80
Jefferson, co., Pa., 46,792..D3   81
Jefferson, co., Tenn.,
21,493............C10   83
Jefferson, co., Tex.,
245,659............E5   84
Jefferson, co., Wash.,
9,639............B2   86
Jefferson, co., W. Va.,
18,665............B7   87
Jefferson, co., Wis.,
50,094............E5   88
Jefferson, par., La.,
208,769............E5   63
Jefferson City, Mo.,
28,228............C5   69
Jefferson City, Tenn.,
4,550............C10   83
Jefferson Davis, co., Miss.,
13,540............D4   68
Jefferson Davis, par., La.,
29,825............D3   63
Jeffersontown, Ky.,
3,341............A4, B4   62
Jefferson Village, Va.,
2,000............*B5   85
Jeffersonville, Ga., 1,013...D3   55
Jeffersonville, Ind.,
20,060............H6   59
Jeffersonville, Ky., 500....C6   62

Jeffersonville, Ohio, 897...C2   78
Jeffery City, Wyo., 800...*D4   89
Jehossee Island, S.C.....K11   82
Jekabpils, Sov. Un.,
10,000............C5   12
Jelenia Gora, Pol., 53,000..C3   7
Jelgava, Sov. Un., 36,300..C4   12
Jellico, Tenn., 2,210......C9   83
Jelm, mtn., Wyo........E7   89
Jemison, Ala., 977.......C3   46
Jena, Ger., 82,100.......C5   6
Jena, La., 2,098.........C3   63
Jenison, Mich., 2,000....*F4   66
Jenkinjones, W. Va.,
300............*D3   87
Jenkins, Ky., 3,202......C7   62
Jenkins, co., Ga., 9,148....D5   55
Jenkinsville, S.C., 500....C5   82
Jenkintown, Pa.,
5,017............F11, o21   81
Jenks, Okla., 1,734......A6   79
Jenners, Pa., 900.......F3   81
Jennings, Fla., 516.......B3   54
Jennings, La., 11,887.....D3   63
Jennings, Mo., 19,935....f13   69
Jennings, co., Ind., 17,267..G6   59
Jennings Lodge, Oreg.,
1,000............*B4   80
Jensen Beach, Florida,
1,500............E6   54
Jenny Jump, mtn., N.J...B3   74
Jequié, Braz., 40,158.....*E6   27
Jerauld, co., S. Dak.,
4,048............F7   77
Jérémie, Hai., 11,048.....E6   35
Jerez de García Salinas,
Mex., 15,016..........C4   34
Jerez, de la Frontera, Sp.,
96,209............D2   8
Jericho, N.Y., 10,795.....*E7   75
Jericho, Va., 2,300......*D6   85
Jermyn, Pa., 2,568......C10   81
Jerome, Idaho, 4,761.....G4   57
Jerome, Ill., 1,666......*D4   58
Jerome, Pa., 1,241.......F4   81
Jerome, co., Idaho,
11,712............G4   57
Jersey, Br. dep., Eur.,
63,000............F5   4
Jersey, co., Ill., 17,023....D3   58
Jersey City, N.J.,
276,101............B4, k8   74
Jersey Shore, Pa., 5,613...D7   81
Jerseyside, Newf., Can.,
923............*E5   44
Jerseyville, Ill., 7,420....D3   58
Jerusalem, Isr., 175,500
(*260,000)............C3, h5   15
Jerusalem, Jordan,
60,488............C3, h5   15
Jesenik, Czech., 5,873....C4   7
Jessamine, co., Ky.,
13,625............C5   62
Jesselton, Mala., 21,719...D5   19
Jessup, Md., 900........B4   53
Jessup, Pa., 5,456.......m18   81
Jesup, Ga., 7,304.......E5   55
Jesup, Iowa, 1,594......B5   60
Jesús Carranza, Mex.,
2,336............D6   34
Jesús María, Arg., 6,284...A4   28
Jesús María, Mex., 300....B5   34
Jetmore, Kans., 1,028....D4   61
Jever, Ger., 9,400.......B3   6
Jewell, Iowa, 1,113.......B4   60
Jewell, Kans., 582.......C5   61
Jewell, co., Kans., 7,217...C5   61
Jewell Ridge, Va., 500....e10   85
Jewett, Ohio, 925........B4   78
Jewett City, Conn.,
3,608............C9   52
Jeypore, India, 25,291....E7   20
Jhalrapatan, India, 9,128..D6   20
Jhansi, India, 140,217
(*169,712)............C4   20
Jhelum, Pak., 41,160
(*52,585)............B5   20
Jibhalanta (Uliassutai),
Mong., 5,000..........B4   17
Jicin, Czech., 12,200......C3   7
Jihlava, Czech., 35,600...D3   7
Jimã, Eth., 10,000.......G5   23
Jimbolia, Rom., 11,281....C5   10
Jimena, Sp., 10,123......D3   8
Jim Hogg, co., Tex., 5,022..F3   84
Jim Thorpe (Mauch
Chunk), Pa.,
5,945............E10   81
Jim Wells, co., Tex.,
34,548............F3   84
Jindrichuv Hradec, Czech.,
10,300............D3   7

Jinja, Ug., 29,741.......H4 23
Jinotepe, Nic., 9,311......E7 34
Jipijapa, Ec., 13,367......B1 31
Jiquilpan de Juárez, Mex.,
  11,862................n12 34
Jirgalanta Kobdo, Mong.,
  5,800.................B3 17
Joanna, S.C., 1,831.......C4 82
João Pessoa, Braz.,
  135,820................D7 27
Jocobus, Pa., 968........*G8 81
Jocotepec, Mex., 8,017...m12 34
Jódar, Sp., 14,424.......D4 8
Jo Daviess, co., Ill.,
  21,821.................A3 58
Jodhpur, India, 224,760...C5 20
Joe Batt's Arm, Newf.,
  Can., 1,058............D4 44
Joensuu, Fin., 28,300.....F13 11
Joeuf, Fr., 12,588.......C6 5
Joffre, mtn., Alta., Can...D3 38
Joffre, mtn., B.C., Can...D10 37
Joggins, N.S., Can.,
  909....................D5 43
Jogjakarta (Jokjakarta),
  Indon., 308,530........G4 19
Johannesburg, S. Afr.,
  594,290 (*2,075,000)....F5 24
John Day, Oreg., 1,520....C8 80
Johns Island, S.C.,
  500.................F7, k11 82
Johnson, Kans.,
  860...................E2 61
Johnson, Vt., 941 (1,478*)..B2 73
Johnson, co., Ark., 12,421..B2 49
Johnson, co., Ga., 8,048...D4 55
Johnson, co., Ill., 6,928...F5 58
Johnson, co., Ind., 43,704..F5 59
Johnson, co., Iowa,
  53,663.................C6 60
Johnson, co., Kans.,
  143,792................D9 61
Johnson, co., Ky., 19,748..C7 62
Johnson, co., Mo., 28,981..C4 69
Johnson, co., Nebr.,
  6,281..................D9 71
Johnson, co., Tenn.,
  10,765.................C12 83
Johnson, co., Tex., 34,720..C4 84
Johnson, co., Wyo., 5,475..D9 89
Johnsonburg, Pa., 4,966...D4 81
Johnson City, N.Y.,
  20,442.................C5 75

Johnson City, Tenn.,
  31,187................C11 83
Johnson City, Tex., 611...D3 84
Johnson Creek, Wis., 986...E5 88
Johnsonville, S.C., 882...D9 82
Johnston, Iowa, 800.......e8 60
Johnston, R.I., 19,547...B10 52
Johnston, S.C., 2,119.....D4 82
Johnston, co., N.C.,
  60,939.................B4 76
Johnston, co., Okla.,
  8,517..................C5 79
Johnston City, Ill., 3,891..F5 58
Johnstown, Colo., 976.....A6 51
Johnstown, N.Y., 10,390...B6 75
Johnstown, Ohio, 2,881....B3 78
Johnstown, Pa., 44,000
  (*120,000)..............F4 81
Johore, state, Mala.,
  1,179,200..............E2 19
Johore Bahru, Mala.,
  74,909.................E2 19
Joigny, Fr., 7,144........D5 5
Joinville, Braz., 44,255...D3 30
Jojutla, Mex., 11,555.....n14 34
Joliet, Ill., 76,000..... B5, k8 58
Joliette, Que., Can.,
  18,088.................C4 42
Joliette, co., Que., Can.,
  18,088.................C3 42
Jolo Phil., 33,259........D6 19
Jonava, Sov. Un., 10,000..A8 7
Jones, Okla., 794.........B4 79
Jones, co., Ga., 8,468....C3 55
Jones, co., Iowa, 20,693..B6 60
Jones, co., Miss., 59,542..D4 68
Jones, co., N.C. 10,221...B5 76
Jones, co., S. Dak., 2,066..G5 77
Jones, co., Tex., 19,299...C3 84
Jonesboro, Ark., 21,418...B5 49
Jonesboro, Ga., 3,014....C2 55
Jonesboro, Ill., 1,636....F4 58
Jonesboro, Ind., 2,260....D6 59
Jonesboro, La., 3,848.....B3 63
Jonesboro, Tenn., 1,148..C11 83
Jones Mill, Ark.,
  950...............C3, D6 49
Jonesport, Maine, 800....D5 64
Jonesville, La., 2,347....C4 63
Jonesville, Mich., 1,896...G6 66
Jonesville, N.C., 1,895...A2 76
Jonesville, S.C., 1,439...B4 82
Jonesville, Va., 711........f8 85

Jönköping, Swe., 51,100...I6 11
Jönköping, co., Swe.,
  286,300...............*I5 11
Jonquière, Que., Can.,
  28,588.................A6 42
Jonuta, Mex., 2,274......D6 34
Joplin, Mo., 38,958......D3 69
Joppa, Ill., 578.........F5 58
Jordan, Minn., 1,479.....F5 67
Jordan, N.Y., 1,381......B4 75
Jordan, country, Asia,
  1,976,000..............C3 15
Jorhat, India, 24,953....C9 20
Jos, Nig., 31,582
  (*38,527)..............G6 22
José Batlle y Ordóñez, Ur.,
  1,781..................E1 30
Joseph, Oreg., 788.......B9 80
Josephine, co., Oreg., 29,917..E3 80
Joshua Tree, Calif.,
  1,300..................E5 50
Jourdanton, Tex., 1,504...E3 84
Jovellanos, Cuba, 12,400..C3 35
Juab, co., Utah, 4,597....B5 72
Juana Díaz, P.R.,
  4,618................*G11 35
Juan Aldama, Mex.,
  7,742..................C4 34
Juanita, Wash., 1,500....*B3 86
Juanjui, Peru, 5,200.....C2 31
Juárez, Arg., 7,602......B5 28
Juarez, Mex.,
  844....................B4 34
Juàzeiro, Braz., 21,196...D6 27
Juazeiro do Norte, Braz.,
  53,421................*D7 27
Juba, Sud., 40,299.......H4 23
Júcaro, Cuba, 1,411......D4 35
Juchipila, Mex., 3,459...m12 34
Juchitán [de Zaragoza],
  Mex., 19,797...........D5 34
Juddah (Jidda) Sau, Ar.,
  147,900................E2 15
Jude, isl., Newf., Can.....E4 44
Judenburg, Aus., 9,869....E7 6
Judith Basin, co., Mont.,
  3,085..................C6 70
Judith, mtn., Mont.......C7 70
Judith, peak, Mont.......C7 70
Judson, S.C., 2,000......*B3 82
Judsonia, Ark., 977......B4 49
Juiz de Fora, Braz.,
  124,979............C4, g6 30

Jujuy, Arg., 31,091......D2 29
Jujuy, prov., Arg.,
  239,783................D2 29
Jukao, China, 80,000....*E9 17
Julesburg, Colo., 1,840...A8 51
Juliaca, Peru, 20,800....E3 31
Julian, Calif., 500......F5 50
Julianehaab, Grnld.,
  1,741.................C16 33
Jullundur, India, 222,569
  (*265,030).............B6 20
Julimes, Mex., 1,900.....B3 34
Jumet, Bel., 28,713......B6 5
Jumilla, Sp., 16,199.....C5 8
Junagadh, India,
  74,298.................D5 20
Juncos, P.R., 6,247.....*G12 35
Junction, Tex., 2,441....D3 84
Junction City, Ark., 749...D3 49
Junction City, Kans.,
  18,700.................C7 61
Junction City, Ky., 1,047..C5 62
Junction City, Ohio, 763..C3 78
Junction City, Oreg.,
  1,614..................C3 80
Jundiaí, Braz.,
  79,536.............C3, m8 30
Juneau, Alsk.,
  6,797............D13, k22 47
Juneau, Wis., 1,718......E5 88
Juneau, co., Wis., 17,490..E3 88
Jungfrau, mtn., Switz.,...E3 6
Juniata, co., Pa., 15,874..F6 81
Juniata Terrace, Pa.,
  1,130..................E6 81
Junín, Arg., 52,054......A4 28
Junín, Peru, 5,100.......D2 31
Junín, dept., Peru,
  546,662................D2 31
Juniper, N.B., Can., 691..C2 43
Junipero Serra, peak,
  Calif..................D3 50
Jupiter, Fla., 1,058.....F6 54
Jura, dept., Fr., 225,682..*D6 5
Jura, isl., Scot.........C4 4
Jurbarkas, Sov. Un.,
  5,000..................A7 7
Juruá, riv.,.............C4 31
Justice, Ill., 2,803.....*B6 58
Jüterbog, Ger., 13,500...C6 6
Jutiapa, Guat., 5,162....E7 34
Juwain, Afg., 5,000......B3 20
Jyvaskylä, Fin., 43,600...F11 11

K

Kaala, peak, Haw.,.......f9 56
Kaalaea, Haw., 300.....g10 56
Kabaena, isl., Mala......G6 19
Kabong, Mala., 1,957....E4 19
Kabul, Afg., 236,000....B4 20
Kachuga, Sov. Un.,
  53,500................D13 13
Kadinhan, Tur., 6,848...C9 14
Kadiri, India, 24,307...F6 20
Kadiyevka, Sov. Un.,
  192,000........G12, o21 12
Kaduna, Nig., 149,910...F6 22
Kaédi, Maur., 9,197.....E2 22
Kaeryong, Kor., 6,200...H4 18
Kaesong, Kor.,
  100,000...............G3 18
Kāf, Sau. Ar.,..........C2 15
Kafr az Zayyāt, Eg.,
  U.A.R., 25,100........D2 14
Kagawa, pref., Jap.,
  900,845..............*I7 18
Kagizman, Tur., 7,176...B14 14
Kagoshima, Jap.,
  328,446...............K5 18
Kagoshima, pref., Jap.,
  1,853,541............*K5 18
Kagul, Sov. Un.,
  20,000................C9 10
Kahoka, Mo., 2,160.....*A6 69
Kahoolawe, isl., Haw.....C5 56
Kahuka, Haw., 1,238..B4, f10 56
Kahului, Haw., 4,223....C5 56
Kaifeng, China, 299,100..E7 17
Kailua, Haw., 33,000...g11 56
Kaimana, Irian, 800.....F8 19
Kainan, Jap., 52,519....I7 18
Kaiping, China, 40,000..C9 17
Kairouan, Tun., 33,968..A7 22

Kaiserslautern, Ger.,
  86,800................D3 6
Kaiyuan, China, 25,000..E2 18
Kaizuka, Jap., 69,635...o14 18
Kajaani, Fin., 14,700...E12 11
Kajikazawa, Jap., 3,700..n17 18
Kakegawa, Jap., 29,600..o17 18
Kakinada, India.,
  122,865...............E7 20
Kakogawa, Jap.,
  101,841..............*I7 18
Kalabagh, Pak., 10,523...B5 20
Kalach, Sov. Un., 16,900..F13 12
Kalaheo, Haw., 1,735....B2 56
Kalama, Wash., 1,088...C3 86
Kalamai (Kalamata), Grc.,
  38,211................D4 14
Kalamazoo, Mich., 86,000
  (*190,000).............F5 66
Kalamazoo, co., Mich.,
  169,712...............F5 66
Kalaotoa, isl., Indon.....G6 19
Kalapana, Haw., 60.....D7 56
Kalgan (Changkiakow),
  China, 229,300........C7 17
Kalgoorlie, Austl., 9,163
  (*19,892)..............F3 25
Kalimnos, Grc., 10,211..D6 14
Kalinin, Sov. Un.,
  292,000...............C10 12
Kaliningrad, Sov. Un.,
  76,000................n17 12
Kaliningrad (Königsberg),
  Sov. Un., 238,000......D3 12
Kalinkovichi, Sov. Un.,
  10,000................E7 12
Kalispell, Mont., 10,151..B2 70
Kalisz, Pol., 74,600.....C5 7

Kalkaska, Mich., 1,321...D5 66
Kalkaska, co., Mich.,
  4,382.................D5 66
Kallithea, Grc., 54,720..*D4 14
Kalmar, Swe., 31,600....I7 11
Kalmar, co., Swe.,
  235,600..............*I7 11
Kalocsa, Hung., 13,663...B4 10
Kalona, Iowa, 1,429.....C6 60
Kalone, peak, B.C., Can..C4 37
Kaluga, Sov. Un.,
  157,000...............D11 12
Kalush, Sov. Un., 10,000..G5 12
Kama, riv., Sov.
  Un.................C8, D8 13
Kamaishi, Jap., 82,104...G10 18
Kamakura, Jap.,
  118,329...............n18 18
Kamenets-Podolskiy,
  Sov. Un., 40,299......G6 12
Kamen-na-Obi, Sov. Un.,
  37,000................D11 13
Kamensk-Shakhtinskiy,
  Sov. Un., 62,000......G13 12
Kamensk-Uralskiy,
  Sov. Un., 152,000.....D9 13
Kamenz, Ger., 14,900...C7 6
Kameoka, Jap., 22,100...o14 18
Kamiah, Idaho, 1,245...C2 57
Kamioka, Jap., 21,000...m16 18
Kammuri-Yama, mtn.,
  Jap...................I6 18
Kamouraska, co., Que.,
  Can., 27,138..........B8 42
Kampala, Ug., 46,735...H4 23
Kampen, Neth., 27,200...A6 5

Kampot, Camb., 12,600...C2 19
Kamsack, Sask., Can.,
  2,968.................F5 39
Kamuela, Haw., 800.....C6 56
Kamyshin, Sov. Un.,
  65,000................F15 12
Kanab, Utah, 1,645.....C5 72
Kanabec, co., Minn.,
  9,007.................E5 67
Kanagawa, pref., Jap.,
  4,430,743.............*I9 18
Kanash, Sov. Un.,
  29,000................D16 12
Kanawha, Iowa, 735.....B4 60
Kanawha, co., W. Va.,
  252,925...............C3 87
Kanayama, Jap., 4,100...n16 18
Kanazawa, Jap.,
  335,828...............H8 18
Kanchanaburi, Thai.,
  12,957................C1 19
Kancheepuram
  (Conjeeveram), India,
  92,714................F6 20
Kanchenjunga, peak,
  Nep...................C8 20
Kandahar, Afg., 100,000..B4 20
Kandalaksha, Sov. Un.,
  37,045................C6 13
Kandangan, Indon.,
  9,774.................F5 19
Kandira, Tur., 4,876....B8 14
Kandiyohi, co., Minn.,
  29,987................E3 67
Kandy, Cey., 57,200.....G7 20
Kane, Pa., 5,380........C4 81
Kane, co., Ill., 208,246..B5 58
Kane, co., Utah, 2,667...C5 72

Kaneohe, Haw., 16,000.............B4, g10 56
Kanggye, Kor., 30,013....F3 18
Kangnung, Kor., 41,700...H4 18
Kangting, China, 30,000...E5 17
Kanhsien, China, 98,600...F7 17
Kanjiža, Yugo., 10,709....B5 10
Kankakee, Ill., 27,666....B6 58
Kankakee, co., Ill., 92,063............B6 58
Kankan, Guinea, 29,000...F3 22
Kanker, India, 6,437....D7 20
Kannan, China, 5,000....Cl 18
Kannapolis, N.C., 36,500..B2 76
Kano, Nig., 295,432......F6 22
Kanopolis, Kan., 732....D5 61
Kanoya, Jap., 33,600....K5 18
Kanpur, India, 881,177 (*1,000,000)...........C7 20
Kansas, Ill., 815.........D6 58
Kansas, state, U.S., 2,178,611... 61
Kansas, riv., Kans........C7 61
Kansas City, Kans., 121,901............C9, k16 61
Kansas City, Mo., 545,000 (*1,165,000)......B3, h10 69
Kansk, Sov. Un., 90,000..D12 13
Kansong, Kor., 5,000....G4 18
Kansu, prov., China, 12,800,000..........D5 17
Kantunilkín, Mex., 1,038..C7 34
Kanye, Bots., 34,100....E5 24
Kaohsiung (Takao), Taiwan, 410,000............G9 17
Kaolack, Sen., 69,600.....F1 22
Kaoyao, China, 49,000...G7 17
Kapaa, Haw., 3,500......A2 56
Kapanga, Con. K.......B4 24
Kapfenberg, Aus., 23,859..E7 6
Kapit, Indon., 1,834.....E4 19
Kaplan, La., 5,267......D3 63
Kaposvar, Hung., 47,300..B3 10
Kapuskasing, Ont., Can., 8,888............o19 41
Kapuvár, Hung., 10,902..B3 10
Karachev, Sov., Un., 10,000............E10 12
Karachi, Pak., 1,447,419...C4 20
Karaga, Sov. Un., 10,000............D19 13
Karaganda, Sov. Un., 482,000............E10 13
Karakose, Tur., 19,776...C14 14
Karaman, Tur., 21,688...D9 14
Karapinar, Tur., 10,767...D9 14
Kara Shahr (Yenki), China, 10,000.........C2 17
Karatsu, Jap., 59,000.....J4 18
Karbalā, Iraq, 44,600....C3 15
Karcag, Hung., 20,803...B5 10
Kardhitsa, Grc., 23,708...C3 14
Karelia (Kerelo-Finnish S.S.R), former rep., Sov. Un............*C6 16
Kargil, India, 5,000......B6 20
Kargopol, Sov. Un., 5,000............A12 12
Kariba, Rh., 5,950......D5 24
Karikal, India, 22,252....F6 20
Karima, Sud., 5,989.....E4 23
Karkaralinsk, Sov. Un., 12,200............E10 13
Karl-Marx-Stadt (Chemnitz), Ger., 287,400............C6 6
Karlovac, Yugo., 38,803...C2 10
Karlovasi, Grc., 5,308....*D6 14
Karlovy Vary, Czech., 43,100............C2 7
Karlshamn, Swe., 11,700..I6 11
Karlskoga, Swe., 36,100..H6 11
Karlskrona, Swe., 33,300..I6 11
Karlsruhe, Ger., 249,900..D4 6
Karlstad, Minn., 720....B2 67
Karlstad, Swe., 44,700...H5 11
Karmutzen, mtn., B.C., Can............D4 37
Karnak, Ill., 667.........F5 58
Karnes, co., Tex., 14,995............E4 84
Karnes City, Tex., 2,693..E4 84
Kars, Tur., 32,141......B14 14
Karsakpay, Sov. Un., 12,000............E9 13
Karshi, Sov. Un., 19,000..F9 13
Kartal, Tur., 10,800.....*B7 14
Kartaly, Sov. Un., 33,400..D9 13
Kartuzy, Pol., 5,991......A5 7
Karviná, Czech., 54,600...D5 7
Karwar, India, 12,134....F5 20
Kasaragod, India, 27,635..F6 20
Kasba Tadla, Mor., 11,733............B3 22
Kāshān, Iran, 45,955.....B8 23
Kashgar (Sufu), China, 91,000............F10 16
Kashima, Jap., 2,600....n19 18

Kashira, Sov. Un., 10,000............D12 12
Kashiwazaki, Jap., 44,000............H9 18
Kasimov, Sov. Un., 33,500............D13 12
Kaslo, B.C., Can., 646....E9 37
Kasota, Minn., 649......F5 67
Kassala, Sud., 35,621....E5 23
Kassel, Ger., 212,200....C4 6
Kasson, Minn., 1,732....F6 67
Kastamonu (Kastamuni), Tur., 20,307........B9 14
Kastoria, Grc., 10,162....B3 14
Kasukabe, Jap., 26,800...n18 18
Kasumi, Jap., 11,700....I7 18
Kasur, Pak., 74,546.....B5 20
Katahdin, mtn., Maine...C4 64
Katanga, prov., Con. K., 1,664,200............C5 24
Katanning, Austl., 3,505..F2 25
Katata, Jap., 8,700.....n14 18
Katerini, Grc., 28,046....B4 14
Katharina, mtn., Eg., U.A.R............C4 23
Katherine, Austl., 1,268..B5 25
Kathleen, Fla., 900......D4 54
Kathwood, S.C., 2,000...*D4 82
Katiola, I.C., 7,900......G3 22
Katmandu, Nep., 122,500............C8 20
Katni (Murwara), India, 46,169............D7 20
Katonah, N.Y., 2,500....A5 75
Katoomba (Blue Mountains), Austl., 28,119............F8 26
Katowice (Stalinogród), Pol., 282,500......C5, g10 7
Katrineholm, Swe., 19,000............H7, u34 11
Katsuyama, Jap., 21,900............m15 18
Katy, Tex., 1,569........F4 84
Kauai, isl., Haw.........A2 56
Kauai, co., Haw., 28,176..B2 56
Kaufbeuren, Ger., 34,700..E5 6
Kaufman, Tex., 3,087....C4 84
Kaufman, co., Tex., 29,931............C4 84
Kaukauna, Wis., 10,096............D5, h9 88
Kaumakani, Haw., 921...B2 56
Kaunakakai, Haw., 800...B4 56
Kaunas, Sov. Un., 247,000............D4 12
Kavaje, Alb., 13,700.....*B2 14
Kaválla, Grc., 44,517....B5 14
Kaválla, prov., Grc., 140,751............*B5 14
Kavarna, Bul., 5,625.....D9 10
Kawagoe, Jap., 127,155...n18 18
Kawaguchi, Jap., 249,112............n18 18
Kawaikini, peak, Haw....A2 56
Kawasaki, Jap., 854,866............I9, n18 18
Kawkareik, Bur., 10,000..*B1 19
Kawkawlin, Mich., 650...E7 66
Kay, co., Okla., 51,042...A4 79
Kayes, Mali, 28,500.....F2 22
Kayford, W. Va., 400............C3, D6 87
Kayseri, Tur., 102,596...C10 14
Kaysville, Utah, 3,608............A6, C2 72
Kazachye, Sov. Un., 900..B16 13
Kazakh S.S.R., rep., Sov. Un., 11,800,000...*E9 16
Kazan, Sov. Un., 762,000..D7 13
Kazanluk, Bul., 19,386...D7 10
Keansburg, N.J., 6,854...C4 74
Kearney, Nebr., 14,210...D6 71
Kearney, Mo., 678....B3, h11 69
Kearney, co., Nebr., 6,580............D7 71
Kearns, Utah, 21,000....*A5 72
Kearny, N.J., 37,472....h8 74
Kearny, co., Kans., 3,108..D2 61
Kearsarge, Mich., 500...A2 66
Keasbey, N.J., 1,500.....*B4 74
Kebnekaise, mtn., Swe....D8 11
Kecskemét, Hung., 48,600............B4 10
Kedah, state, Mala., 849,900............*D2 19
Kedainiai, Sov. Un., 8,602............A7 7
Kedgwick, N.B., Can., 1,095............B2 43
Keegan, Maine, 700.....A5 64
Keego Harbor, Mich., 2,761............o15 66
Keene, N.H., 17,562....F3 73
Keene, Tex., 1,532......n9 84
Keeseville, N.Y., 2,213...f11 75
Keewatin, Ont., Can., 2,197............E4 40

Keewatin, Minn., 1,651....C5 67
Keewatin, dist., N.W. Ter., Can., 2,345....D15 36
Kefallinia, prov., Grc., 47,314............*C3 14
Keighley, Eng., 56,700...D6 4
Keiser, Pa., 1,132........*D8 81
Keith, Scot., 4,200......B5 4
Keith, co., Nebr., 7,958...C4 71
Keithsburg, Ill., 963.....B3 58
Keizer, Oreg., 5,288....*C4 80
Kekaha, Haw., 2,082....B2 56
Kelantan, state, Mala., 618,900............D2 19
Keller, Tex., 827........n9 84
Kellerman, Ala., 500....B2 46
Kellogg, Idaho, 5,061....B2 57
Kellogg, Iowa, 623......C5 60
Kelly Brook, mtn., Maine..A3 64
Kelly Lake, Minn., 900...C5 67
Kelowna, B.C., Can., 13,188............E8 37
Kelseyville, Calif., 800...C2 50
Kelso, Mo., 258.........D8 69
Kelso, Wash., 8,379....C3 86
Kelso, Scot., 3,800......C5 4
Keltys, Tex., 1,056......*D5 84
Kelvington, Sask., Can., 885............E4 39
Kem, Sov. Un., 10,000..E16 11
Kemah, Tex., 950.......*E5 84
Kemerovo, Sov. Un., 298,000............D11 13
Kemi, Fin., 28,800......E11 11
Kemmerer, Wyo., 2,028..E2 89
Kemp, Tex., 816.........C4 84
Kemper, co., Miss., 12,277............C5 68
Kempsey, Austl., 8,173...F9 25
Kempshall, mtn., N.Y.....A6 75
Kempten, Ger., 43,800...E5 6
Kemptville, Ont., Can., 1,959............B9 41
Kenansville, N.C., 703...C4 76
Kenbridge, Va., 1,188...D4 85
Kendal, Eng., 18,700....C5 4
Kendall, Fla., 6,000.....s13 54
Kendall, co., Ill., 17,540..B5 58
Kendall, co., Tex., 5,889..E3 84
Kendall Park, N.J., 4,000..C3 74
Kendallville, Ind., 6,765..B7 59
Kendari, Indon.........F6 19
Kendrapara, India, 15,830............D8 20
Kendrick, Fla., 500.....C4 54
Kenedy, Tex., 4,301....E4 84
Kenedy, co., Tex., 884...F4 84
Kenhorst, Pa., 2,815....*F9 81
Kenilworth, Ill., 2,959...H9 58
Kenilworth, N.J., 8,379..*B4 74
Kenitra, Mor., 86,775...B3 22
Kenly, N.C., 1,174......B4 76
Kenmare, N. Dak., 2,463..B3 77
Kenmawr, Pa., 3,000....*E1 81
Kenmore, N.Y., 21,146..C2 75
Kenmore, Wash., 1,000..*B3 86
Kennaday, peak, Wyo....E6 89
Kennebec, co., Maine, 89,150............D3 64
Kennebunk, Maine, 3,000 (4,551▲)..........E2 64
Kennebunkport, Maine, 800 (1,851▲).........E2 64
Kennedale, Tex., 1,521...n9 84
Kennedy, N.Y., 600.....C1 75
Kenner, La., 17,037.....E5 63
Kennesaw, Ga., 1,507..A4, B2 55
Kenneth City, Fla., 2,114............*E4 54
Kennett, Mo., 9,098....E7 69
Kennett Square, Pa., 4,355............G10 81
Kennewick, Wash., 14,244.C6 86
Kennydale, Wash., 850...e11 86
Kénogami, Que., Can., 11,816............A6 42
Kenora, Ont., Can., 10,904............o16 41
Kenora, dist., Ont., Can., 51,474............o16 41
Kenosha, Wis., 67,899...........F6, n12 88
Kenosha, co., Wis., 100,615............F5 88
Kenova, W. Va., 4,577...C2 87
Kensington, Calif., 6,161............*D3 50
Kensington, Conn., 5,600............C5 52
Kensington, Kans., 619...C4 61
Kensington, Md., 2,175..B3 53
Kensington, N.Y., 1,166..*G2 52
Kensington Estates, Md., 1,600............*B3 53
Kensington Park, Fla., 2,969............*E4 54

Kent, Wash., 9,017....B3, f11 86
Kent, co., N.B., Can., 26,667............C4 43
Kent, co., Ont., Can., 89,427............E2 41
Kent, co., Del., 65,651...B6 53
Kent, co., Eng., 1,237,800..........*E7 4
Kent, co., Md., 15,481...B5 53
Kent, co., Mich., 363,187..E5 66
Kent, co., R.I., 112,619...C10 52
Kent, co., Tex., 1,727....C2 84
Kent City, Mich., 617....E5 66
Kentfield, Calif., 5,000...*C2 50
Kentland, Ind., 1,783....C3 59
Kentland, Md., 1,800....*C4 53
Kenton, Ohio, 8,747....B2 78
Kenton, Tenn., 1,095....A2 83
Kenton, co., Ky., 120,700..B5 62
Kentucky, state, U.S., 3,038,156............ 62
Kent Village, Md., 2,500............*C4 53
Kentville, N.S., Can., 4,612............D5 43
Kentwood, La., 2,607....D5 63
Kenvil, N.J., 2,000......B3 74
Kenvir, Ky., 950........D6 62
Kenwood, Ohio, 2,000...*C1 78
Kenya, country, Afr., 9,643,000............H5 23
Kenya, mtn., Ken........I5 23
Kenyon, Minn., 1,624...F6 67
Keokuk, Iowa, 16,316...D6 60
Keokuk, co., Iowa, 15,492............C5 60
Keosauqua, Iowa, 1,023..D6 60
Keota, Iowa, 1,096......C6 60
Keota, Okla., 579.......B7 79
Kepno, Pol., 7,810......C5 7
Kerala, state, India, 16,903,715..........F6 20
Kerang, Austl., 4,165....G7 25
Kerby, Oreg., 600......E3 80
Kerch, Sov. Un., 107,000............I11 12
Keremeos, B.C., Can., 563............E8 37
Kerens, Tex., 1,123.....C4 84
Kerhonkson, N.Y., 750...D6 75
Kerintji, mtn., Indon.....F2 19
Kérkhoven, Minn., 645...E3 67
Kérkira, Grc., 26,991....C2 14
Kerkira, prov., Grc., 101,770............*C2 14
Kerkrade, Neth., 50,800..B7 5
Kerman, Calif., 1,970....*D4 50
Kermān, Iran, 62,157....C6 15
Kermānshāh, Iran, 125,439............B7 23
Kermit, Tex., 10,465....D1 84
Kermit, W. Va., 743.....D2 87
Kermode, mtn., B.C., Can............C2 37
Kern, co., Calif., 291,984..E4 50
Kernersville, N.C., 2,942..A2 76
Kernville, Calif., 500....E4 50
Kerr, co., Tex., 16,800...D3 84
Kerrobert, Sask., Can., 1,220............F1 39
Kerrville, Tex., 8,901....D3 84
Kerry, co., Ire., 112,600..*D2 4
Kershaw, S.C., 1,567....B6 82
Kershaw, co., S.C., 33,585............C6 82
Kesan, Tur., 15,061.....B6 14
Kesennuma, Jap., 44,000............G10 18
Keski-Suomi, prov., Fin., 247,900............*K5 11
Keswick, Ont., Can., 695..C5 41
Keszthely, Hung., 14,854..B3 10
Keta, Ghana, 16,700....G5 22
Ketapang, Indon., 4,385..F3 19
Ketchikan, Alsk., 6,483............D13, n24 47
Ketchum, Idaho, 1,400...F4 57
Ketona, Ala., 900.......E5 46
Ketrzyn Mazowiecki, Pol., 17,000............A6 7
Kettering, Eng., 38,800...D6 4
Kettering, Ohio, 54,462...C1 78
Kettle Falls, Wash., 905..A7 86
Kety, Pol., 10,400.....D5, a10 7
Kewanee, Ill., 16,324....B4 58
Kewaskum, Wis., 1,572..E5 88
Kewaunee, Wis., 2,772..D6 88
Kewanna, Ind., 683.....B5 59
Kewaunee, co., Wis., 18,282............D6 88
Keweenaw, co., Mich., 2,417............A2 66
Keya Paha, co., Nebr., 1,672............B6 71
Key Biscayne, Fla., 2,500............*G6 54
Keyes, Calif., 1,546.....*D4 50
Keyes, Okla., 627.......e8 79

Keyport, N.J., 6,440......C4   74
Keyser, W. Va., 6,192......B6   87
Keystone, Iowa, 522......C5   60
Keystone, W. Va., 75...D3   87
Keysville, Fla., 500......E2   54
Keysville, Va., 733......C4   85
Keytesville, Mo., 644......B5   69
Key West, Fla., 33,956...H5   54
Kezar Falls, Maine, 500...E2   64
Kezhma, Sov. Un.,
    3,000......D13   13
Kezmarok, Czech., 7,372...D6   7
Kfar Ata, Isr., 16,300......B3 15
Kfar Sava, Isr., 19,000....B2   15
Khabarovsk, Sov. Un.,
    408,000......E16   13
Khairpur, Pak., 18,186....C4   20
Khalkidhiki (Chalcidice),
    prov., Grc., 79,849.....*B4 14
Khalkis, Grc., 24,745......C4   14
Khambhaliya, India,
    20,064......D5   20
Khanabad, Afg., 30,000....A4   20
Khanaqin, Iraq, 10,090....C4   15
Khandwa, India, 63,505...D6   20
Khania, Grc., 131,061......*E4 14
Khaniá (Canea), Grc.,
    38,467......E5   14
Khanpur, Pak., 13,484....C5   20
Khan Yunis, Palestine,
    10,000......C2, h5   15
Kharagpur, India,
    147,253......D8   20
Kharkov, Sov. Un.,
    1,006,000......G11   12
Kharmanli, Bul., 9,240....E7   10
Kharovsk, Sov. Un.,
    5,000......B13   12
Khartoum, Sud., 138,000
    (*390,000)......E4   23
Khartoum North, Sud.,
    56,000......E4   23
Khartsyzsk, Sov. Un.,
    10,000......q21   12
Khash, Afg., 5,000......B3   20
Khaskovo, Bul., 27,394....E7   10
Khatanga, Sov. Un.,
    10,000......B13   16
Khénifra, Mor., 18,503....B5   22
Kherson, Sov. Un.,
    192,000......H9   12
Khilok, Sov. Un., 18,600..D14   13
Khimki, Sov. Un.,
    51,000......n17   12
Khios, Grc., 24,053......C6   14
Khios, (Chios), prov., Grc.,
    62,223......*C6   14
Khmelnik, Sov. Un.,
    10,000......G6   12
Khmelnitskiy, Sov. Un.,
    72,000......G6   12
Kholm, Sov. Un., 10,000...C8   12
Kholmsk (Maoka),
    Sov. Un., 33,000......E17   16
Khong, Laos, 10,000......C3   19
Khong Sedone, Laos,
    10,000......*B3   19
Khorog, Sov. Un., 9,000...F10   13
Khorol, Sov. Un., 10,000..G9   12
Khotan (Hotien), China,
    50,000......A6   20
Khotin, Sov. Un., 10,000..G6   12
Khulna, Pak., 80,917....D8   20
Khust, Sov. Un., 10,000...G4   12
Kiamichi, mtn., Okla......C6   79
Kiamusze (Chiamussu),
    China, 146,000......C5   18
Kiangsi, prov., China,
    18,610,000......F9   17
Kiangsu, prov., China,
    42,630,000......E8   17
Kiaohsien, China, 75,000..D9   17
Kičevo, Yugo., 10,273....E5   10
Kidder, co., N. Dak.,
    5,386......C6   77
Kidderminster, Eng.,
    43,100......D5   4
Kiel, Ger., 270,900......A5   6
Kiel, Wis., 2,524......E5, k9   88
Kielce, Pol., 97,900......C6   7
Kiester, Minn., 741......G5   67
Kiev (Kiyev), Sov. Un.,
    1,248,000......F8   12
Kifisia, Grc., 14,193......*C24 14
Kigali, Rwanda, 4,000......I4   23
Kikinda, Yugo., 33,906....C5   10
Kikladhes (Cyclades), prov.,
    Grc., 99,959......*D5   14
Kikwit, Con. K., 11,000...B3   24
Kilauea, crater, Haw......D6   56
Kilbride, Newf., Can.,
    607......*E5   44
Kilchu, Kor., 30,026......F4   18
Kildare, co., Ire., 66,500..*D3 4
Kilgore, Tex., 10,092......C5   84
Kilimanjaro, mtn., Tan.....I5   23
Kilis (Killis), Tur.,
    33,005......D11   14

Kiliya, Sov. Un., 10,000...I7   12
Kilkenny, Ire., 10,100....D3   4
Kilkenny, co., Ire.,
    60,500......*D3   4
Kilkís, Grc., 10,963......E6   10
Kilkís, prov., Grc.,
    102,812......*B4   14
Killaloe Station, Ont.,
    Can., 932......B7   41
Killarney, Man., Can.,
    1,729......E2   40
Killarney, Ire., 6,900....D2   4
Killbuck, Ohio, 865......B4   78
Killeen, Tex., 23,377......D4   84
Killian, S.C., 800......C6   82
Killona, La., 650......h11   63
Kilmallie, Scot., 5,049....B4   4
Kilmarnock, Scot.,
    48,000......C4   4
Kilmarnock, Va., 927......C6   85
Kimchaek, (Songjin), Kor.,
    67,778......F4   18
Kimball, Minn., 535......E4   67
Kimball, Nebr., 4,384......C2   71
Kimball, S. Dak., 912......G7   77
Kimball, W. Va., 1,175....*D3   87
Kimball, co., Nebr.,
    7,975......C2   71
Kimberly, B.C., Can.,
    6,013......E9   37
Kimberly, S. Afr., 75,376
    (*79,031)......F4   24
Kimberly, Ala., 763......B3   46
Kimberly, Idaho, 1,298....G4   57
Kimberly, W. Va., 900....D6   87
Kimberly, Wis., 5,322....h9   88
Kimble, co., Tex., 3,943...D3   84
Kimry, Sov. Un., 40,000..C11   12
Kinabalu, mtn., Mala......D5   19
Kincaid, Ill., 1,544......D4   58
Kincardine, Ont., Can.,
    2,841......C3   41
Kincardine, co., Scot.,
    25,600......*B5   4
Kinde, Mich., 624......E8   66
Kinder, La., 2,299......D3   63
Kinderhook, N.Y., 1,078...C7   75
Kindersley, Sask., Can.,
    2,990......F1   39
Kindia, Guinea, 25,000...F2   22
Kindu [-Port Empain],
    Con. K., 14,200......I3   23
Kineo, mtn., Maine......C3   64
Kineshma, Sov. Un.,
    91,000......C14   12
King, N.C., 950......A2   76
King, Wis., 700......D4   88
King, co., Tex., 640......C2   84
King, co., Wash., 935,014..B4   86
King, mtn., Oreg......D8   80
King, mtn., Oreg......E3   80
King and Queen, co., Va.,
    5,889......C6   85
Kingaroy, Austl., 5,070...E9   25
King City, Calif., 3,060...D3   50
King City, Ont., Can.,
    1,864......k14   41
King City, Mo., 1,009....A3   69
Kingfield, Maine, 700
    (864▲)......D2   64
Kingfisher, Okla., 3,249...B4   79
Kingfisher, co., Okla.,
    10,635......B3   79
King George, co., Va.,
    7,243......B5   85
King George, mtn., B.C.,
    Can......D10   37
Kingman, Ariz., 6,021....B1   48
Kingman, Kans.,
    3,582......E5, g10   61
Kingman, co., Kans.,
    9,958......E5   61
King of Prussia, Pa.,
    6,000......*F11   81
Kings, co., N.B., Can.,
    25,908......D4   43
Kings, co., N.S., Can.,
    41,747......E5   43
Kings, co., P.E.I., Can.,
    17,893......C7   43
Kings (Brooklyn Borough), co.,
    N.Y., 2,627,319......E7   75
Kings, peak, Calif......B1   50
Kings, peak, Utah......A6   72
Kingsburg, Calif., 3,093...D4   50
Kingscote, Austl., 1,074...G6   25
Kingsford, Mich., 5,084...C2   66
Kingsford Heights, Ind.,
    1,276......*A4   59
Kings Gardens, Kans., 400.A4   61
Kingsley, Iowa, 1,044.....B2   60
Kingsley, Mich., 586......D5   66
King's Lynn, Eng.,
    27,500......D7   4
Kings Mills, Ohio,
    700......C1, n13   78
Kings Mountain, N.C.,
    8,256......B1   76

Kings Park, N.Y., 7,000...n15   75
King's Point, Newf.,
    Can., 542......D3   44
Kings Point, N.Y., 5,410...F1   52
Kingsport, Tenn., 26,314..C11   83
Kingston, Ont., Can.,
    53,526......C8   41
Kingston, Idaho, 500......B2   57
Kingston, Jam., 421,718...F5   35
Kingston, Mass., 1,500
    (4,302▲)......C6   65
Kingston, N.H., 600
    (1,672▲)......F6   73
Kingston, N.J., 900......C3   74
Kingston, N.Y., 29,260...D6   75
Kingston, Ohio, 1,006.....C3   78
Kingston, Okla., 639......D5   79
Kingston, Pa.,
    20,261......D10, n17   81
Kingston, R.I., 3,500......D10 52
Kingston, Tenn., 2,010...D9   83
Kingston, W. Va.,
    400......D3, D6   87
Kingston-on-Thames,
    Eng., (part of
    London), 36,100......m11   4
Kingstree, S.C., 3,847......D8 82
Kingsville, Ont., Can.,
    3,041......E2   41
Kingsville, Ohio, 950......A5   78
Kingsville, Tex., 25,297...F4   84
King William, co., Va.,
    7,563......C5   85
King William's Town,
    S. Afr., 14,678......G5   24
Kingwood, W. Va., 2,530..B5   87
Kinistino, Sask., Can.,
    764......E3   39
Kinloch, Mo., 6,501......f13   69
Kinmundy, Ill., 813......E5   58
Kinnaird, B.C., Can.,
    2,123......E9   37
Kinnelon, N.J., 4,431......B4   74
Kinney, co., Tex., 2,452...E2   84
Kinomoto, Jap., 5,000....n15   18
Kinross, co., Scot., 6,600...*B5 4
Kinshasa (Leopoldville),
    Con. K., 402,500......A3   24
Kinsley, Kans., 2,263......E4   61
Kinsman, Ohio, 900......A5   78
Kinston, N.C., 24,819....B5   76
Kinwood, Tex., 2,500......*E5   84
Kiowa, Kans., 1,674......E5   61
Kiowa, Okla., 607......C6   79
Kiowa, co., Colo., 2,425...C8   51
Kiowa, co., Kans., 4,626..E4   61
Kiowa, co., Okla.,
    14,825......C2   79
Kiparissia, Grc., 4,602....*D3 14
Kipling, Sask., Can., 773..G4   39
Kippens, Newf., Can.,
    1,079......*D2   44
Kipushi, Con. K., 15,100..C5   24
Kirbyville, Tex., 1,660....D6   84
Kirensk, Sov. Un.,
    12,500......D13   13
Kirghiz, S.S.R., rep.,
    Sov. Un., 2,490,000...E10   16
Kirin (Chilin), China,
    568,000......E3   18
Kirin, prov., China,
    12,550,000......C10   17
Kirkagac, Tur., 11,345....C6   14
Kirkcaldy, Scot., 52,600...B5   4
Kirkcudbright, co., Scot.,
    28,300......*C4   4
Kirkland, Ill., 928......A5   58
Kirkland, Wash.,
    6,025......B3, e11   86
Kirkland Lake, Ont., Can.,
    15,366......o20   41
Kirklareli, Tur., 20,196...B6   14
Kirklin, Ind., 767......D5   59
Kirksville, Mo., 13,123...A5   69
Kirkuk, Iraq, 120,593....B3   15
Kirkwood, Md., 2,500....*C3   53
Kirkwood, Mo., 29,421...f13   69
Kirn, Ger., 9,600......D3   6
Kirov, Sov. Un., 296,000..D7   13
Kirovabad, Sov. Un.,
    123,000......E7   13
Kirovograd, Sov. Un.,
    142,000......G9   12
Kirovsk, Sov. Un., 52,800..C6   13
Kirsanov, Sov. Un.,
    10,000......E14   12
Kirsehir (Kir-Shehr), Tur.,
    20,248......C10   14
Kiruna, Swe., 20,100.....D9   11
Kiryū, Jap.,
    127,800......H9, m18   18
Kisangani (Stanleyville),
    Con. K., 126,500......H3   23
Kisarazu, Jap., 36,200....n18   18
Kiselevsk, Sov. Un.,
    142,000......*D11   13

Kishangarh, India,
    25,244......C5   20
Kishinev, Sov. Un.,
    254,000......H7   12
Kishiwada, Jap.,
    143,710......o14   18
Kishorganj, Pak., 19,067..D9   20
Kiskoros, Hung., 9,972....B4   10
Kiskundorozsma, Hung.,
    8,705......B5   10
Kiskunfelegyhaza, Hung.,
    22,925......B4   10
Kiskunhalas, Hung.,
    18,314......B4   10
Kiskunmajsa, Hung.,
    7,611......B4   10
Kislovodsk, Sov. Un.,
    83,000......*E7   13
Kiso-sammyaku, mts.,
    Jap......n16   18
Kissimmee, Fla., 6,845....D5   54
Kistler, W. Va.,
    1,084......D3, D5   87
Kisujszallas, Hung.,
    11,304......B5   10
Kisumu, Ken., 23,526.....I4   23
Kisvarda, Hung., 13,284...A6   10
Kita-dake, mtn., Jap......I9   18
Kitakyūshū, Jap.,
    1,042,388......J5   18
Kitale, Ken., 9,342......H4   23
Kitami, Jap., 51,000......E11   18
Kit Carson, co., Colo.,
    6,957......B8   51
Kitchener, Ont., Can.,
    74,485......D4   41
Kitega, Burundi, 2,800...I4   23
Kitimat, B.C., Can.,
    8,217......B3   37
Kitsap, co., Wash.,
    84,176......B3   86
Kittanning, Pa., 6,793....E2   81
Kittery, Maine, 9,000
    (10,689▲)......E2   64
Kittery Point, Maine,
    1,350......E2   64
Kittitas, co., Wash.,
    20,467......B5   86
Kitts, Ky., 950......D6   62
Kittson, co., Minn., 8,343..B2 67
Kityang, China, 54,000....G8   17
Kitzbühel, Aus., 7,744.....E6   6
Kitzingen, Ger., 17,800...D5   6
Kitzmiller, Md., 535......m12   53
Kiukiang, China, 64,600...F8   17
Kizel, Sov. Un., 60,000...*D8   13
Kizyl-Arvat, Sov. Un.,
    26,000......F8   13
Kladno, Czech.,
    50,800......C3, n17   7
Klagenfurt, Aus., 69,218..E7   6
Klaipeda (Memel),
    Sov. Un., 105,000......D3   12
Klamath, co., Oreg.,
    47,475......E4   80
Klamath, mts., Calif......B2   50
Klamath Falls, Oreg.,
    16,949......E5   80
Klamath Glen, Calif., 500..B2   50
Klang, Mala., 75,649......E2   19
Klatovy, Czech., 14,000...D2   7
Kleberg, Tex., 3,572......*C4   84
Kleberg, co., Tex., 30,052..F4 84
Klemme, Iowa, 615......A4   60
Kletnya, Sov. Un.,
    10,000......E9   12
Kletsk, Sov. Un., 10,000...E6   12
Kleve, Ger., 21,100......C3   6
Klickitat, Wash., 850....D4   86
Klickitat, co., Wash.,
    13,455......D5   86
Klintsy, Sov. Un., 42,033..E9   12
Ključ, Yugo., 2,322......C3   10
Klobuck, Pol., 10,100.....C5   7
Klodzko, Pol., 24,800.....C4   7
Klosterneuburg, Aus.,
    22,787......D8   6
Kluang, Mala., 31,181.....E2   19
Kluczbork, Pol., 14,800....C5   7
Klyuchevskaya, vol.,
    Sov. Un......D19   13
Knezha, Bul., 13,133......D7   10
Knightdale, N.C., 690......B4   76
Knights Landing, Calif.,
    800......C3   50
Knightstown, Ind.,
    2,496......E6   59
Knightsville, Ind., 722....I3   59
Knittlefeld, Aus., 14,259...E7 6
Knob Noster, Mo., 2,292..C4   69
Knockmealdown, mts.,
    Ire......D2   4
Knollwood, Ohio, 2,500...*C2   78
Knoolwood Park, Mich.,
    2,100......*F6   66
Knott, co., Ky., 17,362....C6   62
Knowlton, Que., Can.,
    1,396......D5   42

Knox, Ind., 3,458........B4 59
Knox, Pa., 250.........*E1 81
Knox, co., Ill., 61,280....B3 58
Knox, co., Ind., 41,561....G3 59
Knox, co., Ky., 25,258....D6 62
Knox, co., Maine, 28,575..D4 64
Knox, co., Mo., 6,558.....A5 69
Knox, co., Nebr., 13,300..B8 71
Knox, co., Ohio, 38,808..B3 78
Knox, co., Tenn.,
  250, 523.............C10 83
Knox, co., Tex., 7,857....C3 84
Knox City, Tex., 1,805....C3 84
Knoxville, Ill., 2,560....C3 58
Knoxville, Iowa, 8,521....C4 60
Knoxville, Tenn., 186,000
  (*315,000)......D10, E11 83
Knysna, S. Afr., 11,045....G4 24
Kobe, Jap., 1,216,666....o14 18
Kobelyaki, Sov. Un.,
  10,000..............G10 12
Kóbenhavn (Copenhagen),
  co., Den., 1,321,805...*J5 11
Koblenz, Ger., 101,400....C3 6
Kobrin, Sov. Un., 25,000..E5 12
Kočani, Yugo., 10,986.....E6 10
Koch, mtn., Mont........E5 70
Kochi, Jap., 217,889......J6 18
Kochi, pref., Jap.,
  812,714.............*j6 18
Kodak, Ky., 500.........C6 62
Kodiak, Alsk., 2,628.....D9 47
Kodiak, isl., Alsk........D9 47
Koforidua, Ghana,
  34,900..............G4 22
Kofu, Jap., 172,457...I9, n17 18
Koga, Jap., 50,202......m18 18
Kohala, Haw., 550.......C6 56
Kohat, Pak., 30,016......B5 20
Kohler, Wis., 1,524..E5, k10 88
Kokand, Sov. Un.,
  117,000.............E10 13
Kokchetav, Sov. Un.,
  67,000..............D9 13
Kokkola, Fin., 16,200....F10 11
Kokomo, Ind., 47,197....D5 59
Kokonor, lake, China.....D4 17
Kokstad, S. Afr., 7,926...G5 24
Kolar Gold Fields, India
  146,811.............F6 20
Kolarovo, Bul., 31,169....D8 10
Kolarovo, Czech., 10,800..E4 7
Kolhapur, India, 187,442..E5 20
Kolin, Czech., 23,300.....C3 7
Köln (Cologne), Ger.,
  857,400.............C3 6
Kolo, Pol., 11,600.......B5 7
Koloa, Haw., 1,426......B2 56
Kolomna, Sov. Un.,
  125,000.......D12, n18 12
Kolomyya, Sov. Un.,
  45,000..............G5 12
Kolonodale, Indon.......F6 19
Kolpino, Sov. Un.,
  50,000..............s31 11
Kolwezi, Con. K., 48,000..C5 24
Kolyberovo, Sov. Un.,
  10,000..............n18 12
Kolyma, riv., Sov. Un....C18 16
Komádi, Hung., 7,362....B5 10
Komandorski Village,
  Calif., 1,006.......*D2 50
Komarno, Czech., 24,900..E5 7
Komarno, Sov. Un.,
  5,000...............D7 7
Komárom, Hung., 9,862...B4 10
Komárom, co., Hung.,
  286,200............*B4 10
Komatsu, Jap., 69,000....H8 18
Komatsushima, Jap.,
  27,100..............I7 18
Kommunarsk, Sov. Un.,
  110,000........G12, q21 12
Komotini (Komotine),
  Grc., 28,355........B5 14
Kompong Cham, Camb.,
  28,000.............*C2 19
Kompong Chhnang,
  Camb., 12,900......*C2 19
Kompong Kleang, Camb.,
  10,000.............*C2 19
Kompong Speu, Camb.,
  7,500..............*C2 19
Kompong Thom, Camb.,
  9,600...............C2 19
Komrat, Sov. Un.,
  10,000..............H7 12
Komsomolsk [-na Amure],
  Sov. Un., 192,000...D16 13
Konawa, Okla., 1,555....C5 79
Kondoa, Tan., 2,816......A7 24
Kondopoga, Sov. Un.,
  5,000...............F16 11
Kong, reg., I.C.........G4 22
Kongju, Kor.,
  23,400..............H3 18
Kongsberg, Nor., 9,700...H3 11
Konin, Pol., 20,800......B5 7

Konosha, Sov. Un.,
  10,000..............A13 12
Konotop, Sov. Un.,
  56,000..............F9 12
Konskie, Pol., 10,500....C6 7
Konstantinovka, Sov. Un.,
  94,000..............q20 12
Konstanz, Ger., 55,400...E4 6
Kontum, Viet., 8,760.....C3 19
Konya, Tur., 119,841....D9 14
Konyang, Kor., 2,000.....I3 18
Koochiching, co., Minn.,
  18,190..............B4 67
Koontz Lake, Ind., 1,000..B5 59
Kooskia, Idaho, 801......C3 57
Kootenai, co., Idaho.,
  29,556..............B2 57
Kopeysk, Sov. Un.,
  168,000............*D9 13
Köping, Swe., 17,700..H6, t33 11
Kopparberg, co., Swe.,
  286,600............*G6 11
Koppel, Pa., 1,389.......E1 81
Kopperston, W. Va.,
  950.................*D3 87
Koprivnica, Yugo., 1,329..B3 10
Kopychintsy, Sov. Un.,
  10,000..............G5 12
Korçë, Alb., 39,386.....B3 14
Korçë, pref., Alb.,
  175,000............*B3 14
Korea, North, country,
  Asia, 10,029,000....F4 18
Korea, South, country,
  Asia, 29,207,856....H4 18
Korets, Sov. Un., 10,000..F6 12
Korhogo, I.C., 14,000....G3 22
Kórinthos (Corinth), Grc.,
  15,892..............D4 14
Kóriyama, Jap., 127,000
  (223,183*)..........H10 18
Korkino, Sov. Un.,
  87,000.............*D9 13
Korla, see Kuerhlo, China
Kormend, Hung., 7,581....B3 10
Korneuburg, Aus., 8,276..D8 6
Koropi, Grc., 7,862.....*D4 14
Korosten, Sov. Un.,
  33,800..............F7 12
Korsakov (Otomari), Sov.
  Un., 43,800.........E17 13
Kortrijk, Bel., 43,606....B5 5
Kos, Grc., 8,138........D6 14
Koscian, Pol., 16,600....B4 7
Koscierzyna, Pol., 12,200..A4 7
Kosciusko, Miss., 6,800...B4 68
Kosciusko, co., Ind.,
  40,373..............B6 59
Kosciusko, mtn., Austl....G8 25
Koshan, China, 25,000...B10 17
Kosice, Czech., 88,300....D6 7
Kosong, Kor., 14,842.....G4 18
Kosove (Kosovo), pref.,
  Alb., 53,000........*A3 14
Kosovska Mitrovica, Yugo.,
  26,620..............D5 10
Kossuth, co., Iowa,
  25,314..............A3 60
Kosti, Sud., 22,688......F4 23
Kostroma, Sov. Un.,
  193,000............C13 12
Kostrzyn, Pol., 23,000....B3 7
Koszalin, Pol., 50,000....A4 7
Koszeg, Hung., 9,818....B3 10
Kotabaru, Indon., 3,756...F5 19
Kota Bharu, Mala.,
  38,103..............D2 19
Kotah, India, 120,345....C6 20
Kotelnikovskiy, Sov. Un.,
  17,605..............H14 12
Köthen, Ger., 37,600....C5 6
Kotka, Fin., 31,100.....G12 11
Kotlas, Sov. Un., 56,000..C7 13
Kotor, Yugo., 4,833......D4 10
Kotovsk, Sov. Un.,
  10,000..............H7 12
Kotung, China, 5,000....B7 18
Kotzebue, Alsk., 1,290...*B7 47
Koudougou, Upper Volta,
  8,000...............F4 22
Kountze, Tex., 1,768.....D5 84
Kouts, Ind., 1,007.......B3 59
Kouvola, Fin., 18,200...G12 11
Kovel, Sov. Un., 42,600...F5 12
Kovrov, Sov. Un.,
  105,000............C13 12
Kowa, Jap., 10,300......o15 18
Kowloon, Hong Kong,
  726,976............G7 17
Kowon, Kor., 5,000.....G3 18
Kozan, Tur., 15,159.....D10 14
Kozani, Grc., 21,537....*B3 14
Kozani, prov., Grc.,
  190,835............*B3 14
Kozhikode, India, 192,521..F6 20
Kozienice, Pol., 4,099....C6 7
Kozle, Pol., 12,000......C5 7
Kozloduy, Bul., 7,422....D6 10

Kozuchow, Pol., 8,782....C3 7
Kragujevac, Yugo.,
  52,491..............D5 10
Kraków (Cracow), Pol.,
  505,400.............C5 7
Kraljevo, Yugo., 20,409...D5 10
Kralupy [nad Vltavou],
  Czech., 11,100.......n17 7
Kramatorsk, Sov. Un.,
  126,000........G11, q20 12
Kranj, Yugo., 21,354.....B2 10
Kraslice, Czech., 6,294...C2 7
Krasnik Lubelski, Pol.,
  21,000..............C7 7
Krasnoarmeysk, Sov. Un.,
  54,000..............F15 12
Krasnodar, Sov. Un.,
  368,000.............I12 12
Krasnograd, Sov. Un.,
  10,000..............G10 12
Krasnoselye, Sov. Un.,
  10,000..............G9 12
Krasnoslobodsk, Sov. Un.,
  5,000...............D14 12
Krasnovodsk, Sov. Un.,
  39,272..............E8 13
Krasnoyarsk, Sov. Un.,
  541,000.............D12 13
Krasnystaw, Pol., 11,500..C7 7
Krasnyy Liman, Sov. Un.,
  10,000..............q20 12
Krasnyy Luch, Sov. Un.,
  98,000..............q21 12
Krasnyy Sulin, Sov. Un.,
  66,600..............H13 12
Krasnyy Yar, Sov. Un.,
  10,000..............F15 12
Kratie, Camb., 11,900....C3 19
Krebs, Okla., 1,342......C6 79
Krefeld, Ger., 217,200....C3 6
Kremenchug, Sov. Un.,
  100,000.............G9 12
Kremenets, Sov. Un.,
  10,000..............F5 12
Kremennaya, Sov. Un.,
  5,000...............p21 12
Krems, Aus., 21,046.....D7 6
Kreole, Miss., 1,870..E5, E3 68
Krichev, Sov. Un., 5,000..E8 12
Krishnagiri, India, 19,774..F6 20
Kristiansand, Nor.,
  27,900..............H2 11
Kristianstad, Swe., 26,100..I6 11
Kristianstad, co., Swe.,
  256,600............*I5 11
Kristiansund, Nor.,
  17,200..............F2 11
Krivoy Rog, Sov. Un.,
  448,000.............H9 12
Križevci, Yugo., 6,498....B3 10
Krnov, Czech., 21,800....C4 7
Kromeriz, Czech.,
  20,900..............D4 7
Kromy, Sov. Un.,
  10,000..............E10 12
Kronoberg, co., Swe.,
  159,100............*I6 11
Kronshtadt, Sov. Un.,
  40,000..............B7 12
Kroonstad, S. Afr., 42,438..F5 24
Kropotkin, Sov. Un.,
  59,000..............I13 12
Krosno, Pol., 23,400.....D6 7
Krosno Odrzanskie, Pol.,
  5,841...............B3 7
Krotoszyn, Pol., 19,800...C4 7
Krotz Springs, La., 1,057..D4 63
Krsko, Yugo., 629.......C2 10
Krugersdorp, S. Afr.,
  89,947..............F5 24
Krumroy, Ohio, 1,400...*A4 78
Krusevac, Yugo., 22,140..D5 10
Krusevo, Yugo., 4,099....E6 10
Krymskaya, Sov. Un.,
  10,000..............I11 12
Krynki, Pol., 5,290......B7 7
Ksar el Kebir, Mor.,
  34,035..............B3 22
Ksar es Souk, Mor., 6,554..B4 22
Kuala Lipis, Mala., 8,753..E2 19
Kuala Lumpur, Mala.,
  316,230.............E2 19
Kuala Trengganu, Mala.,
  29,446..............D2 19
Kuantan, Mala., 23,034...E2 19
Kubokawa, Jap., 6,800....J6 19
Kuching, Mala., 50,579...E4 19
Kudat, Mala., 3,660......D5 19
Kuerhlo (Korla), China,
  10,000..............C2 17
Kufstein, Aus., 11,215....E6 6
Kuji, Jap., 18,600......F10 19
Kuju-San, mtn., Jap.......J5 18
Kuki, Jap., 15,400......m18 18
Kükong, China, 81,700...G7 17
Kula, Bul., 5,566.......D6 10
Kula, Tur., 9,180.......*C7 14
Kula, Yugo., 13,612......C4 10

Kulebaki, Sov. Un.,
  34,000..............D14 12
Kulhakangri, peak, Bhutan,
  China...............C9 20
Kuling, China, 5,000.....F8 17
Kulmbach, Ger., 23,500...C5 6
Kulpmont, Pa., 4,288.....E9 81
Kumagava, Jap.,
  109,575............m18 18
Kumamoto, Jap., 407,052..J5 18
Kumamoto, pref., Jap.,
  1,770,736..........*J5 18
Kumanovo, Yugo.,
  30,734..............D5 10
Kumasi, Ghana, 220,922..G4 22
Kumbakonam, India,
  92,581..............F6 20
Kumchon, Kor., 42,100
  (57,200*)...........H4 18
Kumha, Kor., 1,400......G3 18
Kumihama, Jap., 4,100...n14 19
Kumla, Swe.,
  10,000..........H6, t33 11
Kuna, Idaho, 516.......F2 57
Kungchuling, China,
  25,000..............E2 18
Kunming (Yunnanfu),
  China, 880,000......F5 17
Kunsan, Kor., 100,400....I3 18
Kunszentmarton, Hung.,
  8,783...............B5 10
Kuolayarvi, Sov. Un.,
  10,000..............D13 11
Kuopio, Fin., 47,700....F12 11
Kuopio, prov., Fin.,
  453,881............*F12 11
Kupang, Indon., 7,171....H6 19
Kupyansk, Sov. Un.,
  32,400.............G11 12
Kurashiki, Jap., 144,461..I6 18
Kurdzhali, Bul., 10,480...E7 10
Kure, Jap., 225,013......I6 18
Kuressaare, Sov. Un.,
  10,000..............B4 12
Kurgan, Sov. Un.,
  182,000.............D9 13
Kuri, India, 10,000......C5 20
Kurnool, India, 100,815...E6 20
Kursk, Sov. Un., 233,000..F11 12
Kurthwood, La., 70......C2 63
Kurtistown, Haw., 1,025..D6 56
Kurume, Jap., 158,974....J5 18
Kurunegala, Cey.,
  13,510..............G7 20
Kusatsu, Jap., 24,800...n14 18
Kushchevskaya, Sov. Un.,
  10,000..............H12 12
Kushevat, Sov. Un.,
  1,000...............C9 13
Kushimoto, Jap., 15,800..J7 18
Kushiro, Jap., 174,105...E12 18
Kushka, Sov. Un., 4,600..F9 13
Kustanay, Sov. Un.,
  105,000.............D9 13
Küstrin, see Kostrzyn, Pol.
Kutahya (Kutaiah), Tur.,
  39,663..............C7 14
Kutaradja, Indon.,
  34,207..............k11 19
Kutna Hora, Czech.,
  16,900..............D3 7
Kutno, Pol., 26,900......B5 7
Kutztown, Pa., 3,312....E10 81
Kuwait, Kuw., 96,860....D4 15
Kuwait, country, Asia,
  321,621.............D4 15
Kuwana, Jap.,
  75,712..........I8, n18 18
Kuybyshev, Sov. Un.,
  948,000.............D8 13
Kuybyshev, Sov. Un.,
  265,000............*D10 13
Kuznetsk, Sov. Un.,
  64,000..............E16 12
Kwangju, Kor., 300,100
  (365,600*)..........I3 18
Kwangsi Chuang, auton.
  reg., China, 19,390,000..G6 17
Kwangtung, prov., China,
  37,960,000..........G7 17
Kweichow, prov., China,
  16,890,000..........F6 17
Kweilin, China, 145,100...F7 17
Kweisui, see Huhehot,
  China
Kweiyang, China,
  504,000.............G7 17
Kwidzyn, Pol., 21,700....B5 7
Kyaiklat, Bur., 15,781...E10 20
Kyaikto, Bur., 10,000...*B1 19
Kyakhta, Sov. Un.,
  21,700..............D13 13
Kyaukse, Bur., 8,659....D10 20
Kybartai, Sov. Un., 7,274..A7 7
Kyje, Czech., 5,836.....n18 7
Kyle, Sask., Can., 535....G1 39
Kyle, Tex., 1,023........E4 84
Kylestrome, Scot.......*A4 4

Kyllburg, Ger., 1,250 . . . . *C3 6
Kymi, prov., Fin., 343,100 . . . . *G12 11
Kynlyn, Del., 1,600 . . . . . . *A6 53
Kyomipo, see Songnim, Kor.

Kyongju, Kor., 47,800 (85,900▲) I4 18
Kyongsong, Kor., 25,925 . . . F4 18
Kyoto, Jap., 1,365,007 (*1,625,000) I7, n14 18

Kyoto, pref., Jap., 2,102,808 . . . . *I7 18
Kyritz, Ger., 8,679 . . . . B6 6
Kyshtym, Sov. Un., 31,100 . . . . *D9 13

Kyūshū, isl., Jap J5 18
Kyustendil, Bul., 38,199 . . . D6 10
Kyzyl, Sov. Un., 40,000 . . . D12 13
Kzyl-Orda, Sov. Un., 78,000 . . . . E9 13

L

Labadieville, La., 650 . . . . E5, k10 63
La Baie Shawinigan, Que., Can., 1,085 . . . . C5 42
La Barca, Mex., 16,273 . . . . C4, m12 34
La Barge, Wyo., 700 . . . . . . D2 89
Labe, Guinea, 12,500 . . . . . . F2 22
Labelle, Que., Can., 1,224 . . . . C3 42
La Belle, Fla., 1,262 . . . . . . F5 54
La Belle, Mo., 866 . . . . A6 69
Labelle, co., Que., Can., 1,224 . . . . C2 42
Labette, co., Kans., 26,805 . . . . E8 61
Labin, Yugo., 6,152 . . . . C2 10
La Boca, C.Z., 48 . . . . *B2 32
Laboulaye, Arg., 11,334 . . . . A4 28
Labrador, reg., Newf., Can. g9 44
Laburnum Manor, Va., 2,500 . . . . *C5 85
La Canada, Calif., 17,800 . . . . m12 50
La Carlota, Phil., 15,286 . . *C6 19
La Carolina, Sp., 12,138 . . . C4 8
Lac au Saumon, Que., Can., 1,548 . . . . *k13 42
Lac-aux-Sables, Que., Can., 857 . . . . C5 42
Lac-Beauport, Que., Can., 9,192 . . . . C9 42
Lac-Bouchette, Que., Can., 911 . . . . A5 42
Laccadive, is., India F5 20
Lac-Carre, Que., Can., 687 . . . . C3 42
Lac-du-Bonnet, Man., Can., 569 . . . . D3 40
Lac du Flambeau, Wis., 700 . . . . B4 88
La Ceiba, Hond., 24,863 . . . D7 34
La Ceja, Col., 9,424 . . . . B2 32
Lac-Etchemin, Que., Can., 2,297 . . . . C7 42
Lacey, Wash., 6,630 . . . . . . B3 86
Lacey Park, Pa., 4,000 . . . *F11 81
La Chaux-de-Fonds, Switz., 41,300 . . . . E3 6
Lachine, Que., Can., 38,630 . . . . D4, q19 42
La Chorrera, Pan., 13,696 . . . . B2 32
Lachute, Que., Can., 7,560 . . . . D3 42
La Ciotat, Fr., 18,827 . . . . . F6 5
Lackawanna, N.Y., 28,717 . . . . C2 75
Lackawanna, co., Pa., 234,531 . . . . D10 81
Lac la Biche, Alta., Can., 1,314 . . . . B5 38
Lac la Hache, B.C., Can., 775 . . . . D7 37
Laclede, co., Mo., 18,991 . . D5 69
Lac-Mégantic, Que., Can., 7,015 . . . . D7 42
Lacolle, Que., Can., 1,187 . . . . D4 42
Lacombe, Alta., Can., 3,029 . . . . C4 38
Lacombe, La., 650 . . . D6, h12 63
Lacon, Ill., 2,175 . . . . B5 58
Laconia, N.H., 15,288 . . . . . D5 73
La Conner, Wash., 638 . . . . A3 86
Lacoochee, Fla., 1,523 . . . . . D4 54
La Coruña, Sp., 177,502 . . . A1 8
La Coruña, prov., Sp., 971,641 . . . . *A1 8
La Courneuve, Fr., 25,792 . . . . g10 5
Lac Qui Parle, co., Minn., 13,330 . . . . F2 67
La Crescent, Minn., 2,624 . . . . G7 67

La Crescenta, Calif., 12,000 . . . . *F4 50
La Cresta Village, Calif., 1,000 . . . . *E4 50
La Crosse, Ind., 632 . . . . . . B4 59
La Crosse, Kans., 1,767 . . . D4 61
La Crosse, Va., 726 . . . . D4 85
La Crosse, Wis., 47,575 . . . . E2 88
La Crosse, co., Wis., 72,465 . . . . E2 88
La Cruz, Col., 4,014 . . . . . . C2 32
La Cruz, Mex., 2,740 . . . . . C3 34
La Cygne, Kans., 810 . . . . . D9 61
Lacy-Lakeview, Tex., 2,272 . . . . *D4 84
Ladd, Ill., 1,255 . . . . B4 58
Ladera Heights, Calif., 1,500 . . . . *F4 50
Ladner, B.C., Can., 5,000 . . . . E6, f12 37
Ladoga, Ind., 974 . . . . E4 59
Ladoga, lake, Sov. Un. A8 12
Ladonia, Tex., 890 . . . . C5 84
La Dorado, Col., 26,168 . . B3 32
Ladue, Mo., 9,466 . . . . *C7 69
Lady Laurier, mtn., B.C., Can. A6 37
Ladysmith, B.C., Can., 2,173 . . . . E6, g12 37
Ladysmith, S. Afr., 22,955 . . . . F5 24
Ladysmith, Wis., 3,584 . . . . C2 88
La Esperanza, Cuba, 1,867 . . . . C2 35
La Estrada, Sp., 2,540 . . . . A1 8
La Farge, Wis., 833 . . . . E3 88
Lafayette, Ala., 2,605 . . . . . C4 46
Lafayette, Calif., 22,000 . . . *D2 50
Lafayette, Colo., 2,612 . . . . B5 51
La Fayette, Ga., 5,588 . . . . B1 55
Lafayette, Ind., 45,214 . . . . D4 59
Lafayette, La., 50,312 . . . . . D3 63
Lafayette, N.J., 200 . . . . A3 74
Lafayette, Oreg., 553 . . B3, h11 80
Lafayette, Tenn., 1,590 . . . C7 83
Lafayette, co., Ark., 11,030 . . . . D2 49
Lafayette, co., Fla., 2,889 . . C3 54
Lafayette, co., Miss., 21,355 . . . . A4 68
Lafayette, co., Mo., 25,274 . . . . C4 69
Lafayette, co., Wis., 18,142 . . . . F3 88
Lafayette, par., La., 84,656 . . . . D3 63
Lafayette Hill, Pa., 3,500 . . . . *F11 81
La Feria, Tex., 3,047 . . . . . . F4 84
La Ferté-Bernard, Fr., 5,979 . . . . C4 5
Lafferty, Ohio, 950 . . . . B4 78
Lafitte, La., 1,000 . . . . k11 63
Laflèche, Sask., Can., 749 . . . . H2 39
La Flèche, Fr., 9,439 . . . . . D3 5
Laflèche (Mackayville), Que., Can., 10,984 . . . . . *D4 42
La Follette, Tenn., 6,204 . . C9 83
La Fontaine, Ind., 779 . . . . C6 59
Lafourche, par., La., 55,381 . . . . E5 63
La France, S.C., 800 . . . . . B2 82
Laghouat, Alg., 20,777 . . . . B5 22
La Gloria, Col., 2,915 . . . . . B3 52
Lagny, Fr., 11,945 . . . . C5 5
Lagos, Nig., 665,246 . . . . . G5 22
Lagos, Port., 7,143 . . . . D1 8
Lagos de Moreno, Mex., 23,636 . . . . C4, m13 34
La Grand' Combe, Fr., 14,440 . . . . E5 5
La Grande, Oreg., 9,014 . . . B8 80
La Grange, Ga., 23,632 . . . . C1 55
La Grange, Ill., 16,326 . . . . B6, k9 58

Lagrange, Ind., 1,990 . . . . . A7 59
La Grange, Ky., 2,168 . . . . B4 62
La Grange, Mo., 1,347 . . . . A6 69
La Grange, N.C., 2,133 . . . . B5 76
Lagrange, Ohio, 1,007 . . . . A3 78
La Grange, Tex., 3,623 . . . . E4 84
Lagrange, co., Ind., 17,380 . . . . A7 59
La Grange Highlands, Ill., 5,000 . . . . *B6 58
La Grange Park, Ill., 15,430 . . . . k9 58
Lagro, Ind., 763 . . . . C6 59
La Guadeloupe, Que., Can., 1,728 . . . . D7 42
La Guaira, Ven., 20,497 . . . A4 32
La Guajira, intendencia, Col., 147,140 . . . . A3 32
La Guardia, Sp., 9,311 . . . . B1 8
Laguna, Braz., 17,451 . . . . . D3 27
Laguna, prov., Phil., 472,064 . . . . *C6 19
Laguna Beach, Calif., 9,288 . . . . F5, n13 50
Lagunas, Peru, 1,548 . . . . . C2 31
Laguna Shores, Tex., 1,500 . . . . *F4 84
La Habra, Calif., 35,253 . . n13 50
La Habra Heights, Calif., 1,500 . . . . *F4 50
Lahad Datu, Mala., 1,544 . . . . D5 19
Lahaina, Haw., 3,600 . . . . . C5 56
La Harpe, Ill., 1,322 . . . . . . C3 58
Lahij, S. Yem., 10,000 . . . . G3 15
Lahore, Pak., 1,227,996 . . . B5 20
Lahr, Ger., 22,600 . . . . D3 6
Lahti, Fin., 72,000 . . . . G11 11
La Huaca, Peru, 2,012 . . . . B1 31
Laie, Haw., 1,800 . . . . . B4, f10 56
Laigle, Fr., 5,520 . . . . C4 5
Laingsburg, Mich., 1,057 . . F6 66
Lairg, Scot., 962 . . . . A4 4
La Jara, Colo., 724 . . . . D5 51
Lajes, Braz., 35,112 . . . . . . D2 30
Lajosmizse, Hung., 4,735 . . B4 10
La Joya, Mex., 17,197 . . . . h9 34
La Junta, Colo., 8,026 . . . . D7 51
Lake, co., Calif., 13,786 . . . C2 50
Lake, co., Colo., 7,101 . . . . B4 51
Lake, co., Fla., 57,383 . . . . D5 54
Lake, co., Ill., 293,656 . . . . A6 58
Lake, co., Ind., 513,269 . . . B3 59
Lake, co., Mich., 5,338 . . . E5 66
Lake, co., Minn., 13,702 . . C7 67
Lake, co., Mont., 13,104 . . C2 70
Lake, co., Ohio, 148,700 . . A4 78
Lake, co., Oreg., 7,158 . . . E6 80
Lake, co., S. Dak., 11,764 . . F8 77
Lake, co., Tenn., 9,572 . . . A2 83
Lake, mtn., Wyo. E6 89
Lake Alfred, Fla., 2,191 . . . D5 54
Lake Andes, S. Dak., 1,097 . . . . G7 77
Lake Arrowhead, Calif., 500 . . . . E5 50
Lake Arthur, La., 3,541 . . . D3 63
Lake Barcroft, Va., 1,800 . . . . *B5 85
Lake Benton, Minn., 905 . . F2 67
Lake Bluff, Ill., 4,345 . . A6, h9 58
Lake Butler, Fla., 1,311 . . . B4 54
Lake Charles, La., 60,000 (*122,000) D2 63
Lake City, Fla., 9,465 . . . . B4 54
Lake City, Iowa, 2,114 . . . B3 60
Lake City, Mich., 718 . . . . D5 66
Lake City, Minn., 3,494 . . . F6 67
Lake City, Pa., 1,722 . . . . . B1 81
Lake City, S.C., 6,059 . . . . D8 82
Lake City, Tenn., 1,914 . . . C9 83
Lake Cowichan, B.C., Can., 2,149 . . . . g11 37
Lake Crystal, Minn., 1,652 . . . . F4 67
Lake Delton, Wis., 714 . . . . E4 88

Lake Erie Beach, N.Y., 950 . . . . *C1 75
Lake Fenton, Mich., 1,500 . . . . *F7 66
Lakefield, Ont., Can., 2,167 . . . . C6 41
Lakefield, Minn., 1,789 . . . G3 67
Lake Forest, Fla., 8,000 . . . m8 54
Lake Forest, Ill., 13,345 . . . . A6, h9 58
Lake Forest, S.C., 1,500 . . *B3 82
Lake Forest Park, Wash., 1,500 . . . . *B3 86
Lake Geneva, Wis., 4,929 . . F5 88
Lake George, N.Y., 1,026 . . . . B7 75
Lake Hamilton, Fla., 930 . . . . *D5 54
Lake Harbor, Fla., 500 . . . *F6 54
Lake Helen, Fla., 1,096 . . . D5 54
Lake Hiawatha, N.J., 6,000 . . . . B4 74
Lake Hills, Wash., 4,500 . . *B3 86
Lake Hopatcong, N.J., 1,500 . . . . *B3 74
Lakehurst, N.J., 2,780 . . . . C4 74
Lake in the Hills, Ill., 2,046 . . . . *A5 58
Lake Jackson, Tex., 9,651 . . . . E5, r14 84
Lake James, Ind., 600 . . . . A7 59
Lakeland, Fla., 41,350 . . . . D5 54
Lakeland, Ga., 2,236 . . . . . E3 55
Lakeland, Miss., 900 . . . . . C3 68
Lakeland Village, Calif., 3,593 . . . . *F5 50
Lake Linden, Mich., 1,314 . . . . A2 66
Lake Lotawana, Mo., 1,499 . . . . *C3 69
Lake Luzerne, N.Y., 900 . . B7 75
Lake Manawa, Iowa, 1,000 . . . . C2 60
Lake Mary, Fla., 900 . . . . . D5 54
Lake Mills, Iowa, 1,758 . . . A4 60
Lake Mills, Wis., 2,951 . . . E5 88
Lake Mohawk, N.J., 4,300 . . . . A3 74
Lakemont, Pa., 2,000 . . . . . F5 81
Lakemore, Ohio, 2,765 . . . . A4 78
Lake Odessa, Mich., 1,806 . . . . F5 66
Lake of the Woods, lake, Can., U.S. A4 67
Lake of the Woods, co., Minn., 4,304 . . . . B3 67
Lake Orion, Mich., 2,698 . . F7 66
Lake Orion Heights, Mich., 1,918 . . . . *F7 66
Lake Oswego, Oreg., 8,906 . . . . B4, h12 80
Lake Ozark, Mo., 500 . . . . C5 69
Lake Park, Fla., 3,589 . . . . F6 54
Lake Park, Iowa, 952 . . . . . A2 60
Lake Park, Minn., 730 . . . . D2 67
Lake Placid, Fla., 1,007 . . . E5 54
Lake Placid, N.Y., 2,998 . . . . A7, f10 75
Lakeport, Calif., 2,747 . . . . C2 50
Lake Preston, S. Dak., 955 . . . . F8 77
Lake Providence, La., 5,781 . . . . B4 63
Lake Ronkonkoma, N.Y., 6,100 . . . . F4 52
Lake Shore, Fla., 11,000 . . m8 54
Lakeside, Calif., 7,000 . . . . F5, o16 50
Lakeside, N.S., Can., 988 . . E6 43
Lakeside, La., 1,233 . . . . . *C3 63
Lakeside, Ohio, 800 . . . . . . A3 78
Lakeside, Oreg., 500 . . . . . . D2 80
Lakeside, Va., 19,000 . . . . *C5 85
Lakeside Park, Ky., 2,214 . . A7 62
Lake Stevens, Wash., 1,100 . . . . A3 86

Lake Success, N.Y., 2,954..h13 75
Lake Telemark, N.J.,
800.................*B3 74
Lake Toxaway, N.C., 700..f10 76
Lakeview, Ont., Can.,
17,000.................m14 41
Lakeview, Ga., 3,000....*B1 55
Lake View, Iowa, 1,165...B2 60
Lakeview, Mich., 10,384..*F5 66
Lakeview, Mich., 1,126...E5 66
Lake View, N.Y., 4,000...*C2 75
Lakeview, N.Y., 9,000...*E7 75
Lakeview, Ohio, 1,008...B2 78
Lakeview, Oreg., 3,260...E6 80
Lake View, S.C., 865....C9 82
Lakeview, Tex., 3,849...*E6 84
Lake Villa, Ill., 903.....h8 58
Lake Village, Ark., 2,998..D4 49
Lakeville, Conn., 900....B3 52
Lakeville, Ind., 757......A5 59
Lakeville, Minn., 924....F5 67
Lakeville, N.Y., 800.....C3 75
Lakeville, Ohio, 4,181...A5 78
Lake Waccamaw, N.C.,
780.................C4 76
Lake Wales, Fla., 8,346...E5 54
Lakewood, Calif., 67,126..n12 50
Lakewood, N.B., Can.,
836.................*C2 43
Lakewood, Colo., 51,000..*B5 51
Lakewood, N.J., 16,020...C4 74
Lakewood, N.Y., 3,933...C1 75
Lakewood, Ohio,
66,154.............A4, h9 78
Lakewood, Tenn., 1,896..*A5 83
Lakewood, Tex., 1,882...*E5 84
Lakewood Center, Wash.,
20,000.............*B3 86
Lake Worth, Fla., 20,758..F6 54
Lake Zurich, Ill., 3,851...h8 58
Lakhimpur, India, 25,055..C7 20
Lakin, Kans., 1,432......E2 61
Lakonia (Laconia), prov.,
Grc., 118,661........*D4 14
Lakota, N. Dak., 1,658...B7 77
La Laguna, Sp., 15,899..m13 8
La Libertad, dept., Peru,
609,105.............C2 31
Lalín, Sp., 1,353........A1 8
La Línea, Sp., 59,456....D3 8
Lalitpur, India, 20,792...D6 20
La Loche, Sask., Can.,
717.................m7 39
La Maddalena, It.,
11,169..............D2 9
La Malbaie, Que., Can.,
2,580...............B7 42
Lamar, Colo., 7,369......C8 51
Lamar, Mo., 3,608.......D3 69
Lamar, S.C., 1,121.......C7 82
Lamar, co., Ala., 14,271..B1 46
Lamar, co., Ga., 10,240...C2 55
Lamar, co., Tex., 34,234..C5 84
La Marque, Tex., 13,969..r15 84
Lamartine, Que., Can.,
40..................B7 42
Lamas, Peru, 7,300......C2 31
Lamb, co., Tex., 21,896...B1 84
Lamballe, Fr., 5,069.....C2 5
Lambayeque, Peru,
10,600..............C2 31
Lambayeque, dept., Peru,
353,657.............C2 31
Lambert, Miss., 1,181....A3 68
Lamberton, Minn., 1,141..F3 67
Lambertville, Mich.,
1,168...............*G7 66
Lambertville, N.J., 4,269..C3 74
Lambeth, Ont., Can.,
2,293...............E3 41
Lambton, Que., Can.,
699.................D6 42
Lambton, co., Ont., Can.,
102,131.............E2 41
Lamego, Port.............B2 8
Lamèque, N.B., Can.,
1,082...............B5 43
La Mesa, Calif., 30,441..o15 50
Lamesa, Tex., 12,438.....C2 84
Lamia, Grc., 21,509......C4 14
La Mirada, Calif.,
22,444..............*F4 50
La Moille, Ill., 655.......B4 58
Lamoille, co., Vt., 11,027..B2 73
Lamoni, Iowa, 2,463.....D4 60
Lamont, Calif., 6,177.....E4 50
Lamont, Alta., Can., 705..C6 38
Lamont, Okla., 543......A4 79
La Monte, Mo., 801......C4 69
La Moure, N. Dak.,
1,068...............D7 77
La Moure, co., N. Dak.,
8,705...............D7 77
Lampa, Peru, 2,619......E3 31
Lampang, Thai., 36,486..*B1 19
Lampasas, Tex., 5,016....D3 84
Lampasas, co., Tex.,
9,418...............D3 84

Lamphun, Thai., 10,600...*B1 19
Lampman, Sask., Can.,
637.................H4 39
Lanai City, Haw., 2,200...C5 56
Lanao del Norte, prov.,
Phil., 270,603........*D6 19
Lanark, Ont., Can., 918...C8 41
Lanark, Ill., 1,473.......A4 58
Lanark, Scot., 8,400.....C5 4
Lanark, co., Ont., Can.,
918.................C8 41
Lanark, co., Scot.,
1,618,000...........*C5 4
Lanark Village, Fla., 600..C2 54
Lancashire, co., Eng.,
5,176,000...........*C5 4
Lancaster, Calif., 28,000..E4 50
Lancaster, N.B., Can.,
13,848..............D3 43
Lancaster, Ont., Can.,
584.................B10 41
Lancaster, Eng., 48,500
(*95,000)...........C5 4
Lancaster, Ky., 3,021....C5 62
Lancaster, Mass., 750
(3,958▲)............B4 65
Lancaster, Mo., 740......A5 69
Lancaster, N.H., 2,392
(3,138▲)............C4 73
Lancaster, N.Y., 12,254...C2 75
Lancaster, Ohio, 29,916...G3 78
Lancaster, Pa., 59,000
(*128,500)..........F9 81
Lancaster, S.C., 7,999....B6 82
Lancaster, Tex., 7,501...n10 84
Lancaster, Wis., 3,703....F3 88
Lancaster, co., Nebr.,
155,272.............D9 71
Lancaster, co., Pa.,
278,359.............G9 81
Lancaster, co., S.C.,
39,352..............B6 82
Lancaster, co., Va., 9,174..C6 85
Lancaster Mills, S.C.,
6,255...............*B6 82
Lancer, Ky., 500.........C7 62
Lanchow, China, 699,000..D5 17
Lanciano, It., 13,300.....C5 9
Lancut, Pol., 10,900......C7 7
Landau [an der Isar], Ger.,
6,000...............D6 6
Landau [in der Pfalz], Ger.,
28,700..............D4 6
Landeck, Aus., 6,514.....E5 6
Lander, Wyo., 4,182.....B4 89
Lander, co., Nev., 1,566...A3 72
Landerneau, Fr., 11,834...C1 5
Landes, dept., Fr.,
260,495.............*F3 5
Landing, N.J., 1,500.....*B3 74
Landis, N.C., 1,763......B2 76
Landisville, Pa., 1,690..*F11 81
Landivisiau, Fr., 4,121...C1 5
Lando, S.C., 700........B5 82
Landover Hills, Md.,
1,850...............*C4 53
Landrum, S.C., 1,930....A3 82
Landsberg, Ger., 13,400..D5 6
Landshut, Ger., 50,700...D6 6
Landskrona, Swe., 28,900..J5 11
Lane, co., Kans., 3,060...D3 61
Lane, co., Oreg., 162,890..D4 80
Lanesboro, Mass., 900
(2,933▲)............A1 65
Lanesboro, Minn., 1,063..G7 67
Lanett, Ala., 7,674......C4 46
Langadhás, Grc., 6,739...*B4 14
Langdale, Ala., 2,528.....C4 46
Langdon, N. Dak., 2,151..B7 77
L'Ange-Gardien, Que.,
Can., 1,543.........n17 42
Langeloth, Pa., 1,112.....F1 81
Langenburg, Sask., Can.,
757.................G5 39
Langensalza, Ger., 16,200..C2 6
Langenthal, Switz.,
10,974..............E3 6
Langesund, Nor.,
2,200.............H3, p27 11
Langford, B.C., Can.,
1,024...............h12 37
Langhorne, Pa., 1,101...F12 81
Langlade, co., Wis.,
19,916..............C4 88
Langley, B.C., Can.,
2,365...............f13 37
Langley, Ky., 700........C7 62
Langley, S.C., 1,300.....D4 82
Langley Park, Md.,
11,800..............*C3 53
Langnau in Emmental,
Switz., 9,201........E3 6
Langon, Fr., 4,197.......D3 5
Langres, Fr., 9,577......D6 5
Langsa, Indon.,
4,749............E1, m11 19
Lang Son, Viet.,
25,000.............*G13 16

Langstaff, Ont., Can.,
1,153...............k15 41
Languedoc, former prov.,
Fr., 2,413,000.......F5 5
Lanham, Md., 4,500.....C4 53
Lanhsi, China, 5,000.....C3 18
Lanier, co., Ga., 5,097...E3 55
Lannion, Fr., 6,497......C2 5
Lannon, Wis., 1,084....m11 88
L'Annonciation, Que.,
Can., 1,042.........C3 42
Lanoraie, Que., Can.,
1,060...............D4 42
Lansdale, Pa., 12,612....F11 81
Lansdowne, Md., 9,000...B4 53
Lansdowne, Pa.,
12,601..........G11, p20 81
Lansdowne House, Ont.,
Can., 612...........n18 41
L'Anse, Mich., 2,397.....B2 66
Lansford, Pa., 5,958....E10 81
Lansing, Ont., Can......m15 41
Lansing, Ill., 20,926...B6, k9 58
Lansing, Iowa, 1,325.....A6 60
Lansing, Kans., 1,264....B8 61
Lansing, Mich., 132,000
(*250,000)..........F6 66
Lansing, Ohio, 1,200....*C4 78
Lantana, Fla., 5,021.....F6 54
Laoag, Phil., 25,105......B6 19
Laoighis, co., Ire.,
44,700..............*D3 4
Lao Kay, Viet., 25,000...*G13 16
Laon, Fr., 25,078.......C5 5
Laona, Wis., 700........C5 88
La Oroya, Peru, 24,800...D2 31
Laos, country, Asia,
91,428..............*B2 19
Lapa, Braz., 7,167.......D3 30
La Palma, Sp., 8,669.....D2 8
La Pampa, prov., Arg.,
158,489.............B3 28
La Paz, Arg., 11,028......A5 28
La Paz, Bol., 450,000....C2 29
La Paz, Col., 4,278......A3 32
La Paz, Mex., 24,253.....C2 34
La Paz, Mex., 3,526......C4 34
La Paz, dept., Bol.,
948,446.............C2 29
Lapeer, Mich., 6,160.....E7 66
Lapeer, co., Mich.,
41,926..............E7 66
Lapel, Ind., 1,772.......D6 59
La Piedad [Cavadas],
Mex., 24,377.......m12 34
Laplace, La., 3,541......h11 63
Lapland, reg., Eur......C12 11
La Plata, Arg.,
258,000...........A5, g8 28
La Plata, Col., 5,863.....C2 32
La Plata, Md., 1,214......C4 53
La Plata, Mo., 1,365.....A5 69
La Plata, co., Colo.,
19,225..............D3 51
La Pocatière, Que., Can.,
3,086...............B7 42
La Pola, Sp., 5,430......A3 8
La Porte, Ind., 21,157....A4 59
La Porte, Tex., 4,512....r14 84
La Porte, co., Ind.,
95,111..............A4 59
La Porte City, Iowa,
2,117...............B5 60
Lappeenranta, Fin.,
21,600.............G13 11
Lappi, prov., Fin.,
152,607.............*D11 11
Laprairie, Que., Can.,
7,328...............D4 42
Laprairie, co., Que., Can.,
31,157..........D4, q20 42
La Presa, Calif., 1,300...*F5 50
La Providence, Que.,
Can., 4,251.........*D5 42
La Pryor, Tex., 900......E3 84
La Puebla, Sp., 9,931....C7 8
La Puebla de Montalbán,
Sp., 7,700..........C3 8
La Puente, Calif., 24,723..*F4 50
La Purisima, Mex., 748...B2 34
La Quiaca, Arg., 6,768....D2 29
L'Aquila, It., 36,200.....C4 9
Lara, state, Ven., 489,140..A3 32
Larache, Mor., 30,763....A3 22
Laramie, Wyo., 17,520...E7 89
Laramie, co., Wyo.,
60,149..............E8 89
Laramie, peak, Wyo......D7 89
Larchmont, N.Y., 6,860..h13 75
Laredo, Sp., 6,206......A4 8
Laredo, Tex., 74,000
(*79,000)...........F3 84
Largo, Fla., 5,302...E4, p10 54
Lariat, Colo., 900.......D4 51
La Ricamarie, Fr., 11,902..E6 5
Larimer, Pa., 1,500.....*F2 81
Larimer, co., Colo.,
53,343..............A5 51

Larimore, N. Dak.,
2,046...............C8 77
Larino, It., 8,678.......D5 9
La Rioja, Arg., 23,809....E2 29
La Rioja, prov., Arg.,
128,270.............E2 29
La Rioja, Cuba, 1,818....D5 35
Lárisa (Larissa), Grc.,
55,391..............C4 14
Larisa (Larissa), prov.,
Grc., 237,776.......*C4 14
Larkana, Pak., 48,008....C4 20
Larkspur, Calif., 5,710...h7 50
Larksville, Pa., 4,390....n17 81
Larne, N. Ire., 16,600....C4 4
Larned, Kans., 5,001.....D4 61
La Rochelle, Fr., 66,590..D3 5
La Roche-sur-Yon, Fr.,
24,019..............D3 5
La Roda, Sp., 12,190....C4 8
La Romana, Dom. Rep.,
22,310..............E9 35
La Ronge, Sask., Can.,
707.................B3 39
Larose, La., 2,796.......E5 63
La Rue, Ohio, 842.......B2 78
Larue, co., Ky., 10,346...C4 62
Larvik, Nor., 10,600..H4, p28 11
Larwill, Ind., 994.......B6 59
La Salle, Que., Can.,
30,904..............q19 42
La Salle, Colo., 1,070....A6 51
La Salle, Ill., 11,897.....B4 58
La Salle, co., Ill., 110,800..B5 58
La Salle, co., Tex., 5,972..E3 84
La Salle, par., La.,
13,011..............C3 63
Las Animas, Colo., 3,402..C7 51
Las Animas, co., Colo.,
19,983..............D6 51
La Sarre, Que., Can.,
3,944...............o20 41
Lascahobas, Hai., 2,167..E8 35
L'Ascension, Que., Can.,
1,197...............A6 42
La Scie, Newf., Can.,
939.................D4 44
Las conchas, Arg.,
24,809..............g7 28
Las Cruces, N. Mex.,
29,367..............C5 48
La Selle, peak, Hai......E8 37
La Serena, Chile, 40,900..E1 29
La Seyne [-sur-Mer], Fr.,
33,570..............F6 5
Las Flores, Arg., 9,287...B5 28
La Sierra, Calif., 7,000..n14 50
Lasithi (Lasithion), prov.,
Grc., 73,880........*E5 14
Las Matas de Farfan,
Dom. Rep., 3,585...*E8 35
La Solana, Sp., 14,948...C4 8
Las Palmas, prov., Sp.,
453,793............m14 8
Las Palmas
[de Gran Canaria],
Sp., 193,862.......m14 8
La Spezia, It., 121,923...B2 9
Las Piedras, Ur., 40,658..E1 30
Lassen, co., Calif.,
17,053..............B3 50
Lassen, peak, Calif......B3 50
L'Assomption, Que., Can.,
4,448...............D4 42
L'Assomption, co., Que.,
Can., 39,400........D4 42
Las Varillas, Arg., 5,950..A4 28
Las Vegas, Nev., 120,000
(*245,000)..........C4 72
Las Vegas, N. Mex.,
6,028............B6, D7 48
Las Vigas, Mex., 4,762..n15 34
Las Villas, prov., Cuba,
1,030,162...........C3 35
Latacunga, Ec., 14,856...B2 31
Latah, co., Idaho, 21,170..C2 57
Laterrière, Que., Can.,
651.................A6 42
La Teste-de-Buch, Fr.,
8,907...............E3 5
Latham, N.Y., 7,100....*C7 75
Lathrop, Calif., 1,123...*D3 50
Lathrop, Mo., 1,006.....B3 69
Lathrup Village, Mich.,
3,556...............*F7 66
Latimer, co., Okla., 7,738..C6 79
Latina, It., 39,500...D4, k9 9
Latium, reg., It.........C4 9
Laton, Calif., 1,052.....D4 50
Latour, peak, Idaho......B2 57
La Trinité, Mart., 3,631..I14 35
Latrobe, Pa., 11,932.....F3 81
Latta, S.C., 1,901.......C9 82
Lattimer Mines, Pa., 600..E10 81
Lattingtown, N.Y.,
1,461...............*E7 75
La Tuque, Que., Can.,
13,023..............B5 42

Latvia (S.S.R.), rep., Sov. Un., 2,200,000........C4 12
Lauderdale, Minn., 2,386................n12 67
Lauderdale, co., Ala., 61,622.............A2 46
Lauderdale, co., Miss., 67,119.............C5 68
Lauderdale, co., Tenn., 21,844.............B2 83
Lauderdale-by-the-Sea, Fla., 1,327...........*F6 54
Launceston, Austl., 37,210 (*60,453)...........o15 25
Launceston, Eng., 4,500...E4 4
La Unión, Chile, 11,600....C5 28
La Unión, Col., 3,875.....C2 32
La Unión, Mex., 1,435.............D4, o13 34
La Unión, Peru, 1,672.....C2 31
La Unión, Sal., 11,432...E7 34
La Unión, Sp., 11,687....D5 8
La Union, prov., Phil., 293,300............*B6 19
Laupheim, Ger., 8,700....D4 6
Laurel, Del., 2,709.......C6 53
Laurel, Fla., 1,000......E4 54
Laurel, Ind., 848........F7 59
Laurel, Md., 8,503.......B4 53
Laurel, Miss., 27,889....D4 68
Laurel, Mont., 4,601.....E8 70
Laurel, Nebr., 922.......B8 71
Laurel, co., Ky., 24,901...C5 62
Laurel Bay, S.C., 4,000....G6 82
Laureldale, Pa., 4,051....F10 81
Laurel Gardens, Pa., 1,500..............*E1 81
Laurel Heights, Wash., 900.................*B3 86
Laurel Hill, N.C., 900....C3 76
Laurel Run, Pa., 855....n17 81
Laurel Springs, N.J., 2,028...............*D3 74
Laurence Harbor, N.J., 3,000...............C4 74
Laurens, Iowa, 1,799...B3 60
Laurens, S.C., 9,598.....B3 82
Laurens, co., Ga., 32,313..D4 55
Laurens, co., S.C., 47,609..C3 82
Laurentides, Que., Can., 1,698...............D4 42
Lauria Inferiore, It., 4,530.................D5 9
Laurier, Que., Can., 653..C6 42
Laurierville, Que., Can., 872.................C6 42
Laurinburg, N.C., 8,242...C3 76
Laurium, Mich., 3,058....A2 66
Lausanne, Switz., 132,300, (*202,100).........E3 6
Lautaro, Chile, 10,400....B2 28
Lauzon, Que., Can., 11,533............C6, n17 42
Lavaca, co., Tex., 20,174...E4 84
Lava Hot Springs, Idaho, 593................G6 57
Laval, Fr., 39,283........C3 5
Laval, Que., Can., 194,446.............D4 42
Laval-des-Rapides, Que., Can., 19,227.........*D4 42
La Vale, Md., 5,000.....k13 53
Lavalleja, dept., Ur., 65,600.............*E1 30
Lavallette, N.J., 832....D4 74
Laval-Ouest, Que., Can., 5,440.............*p19 42
Lavaltrie, Que., Can., 1,034..............D4 42
Lavaur, Fr., 4,137.......F4 5
La Vega, Dom. Rep., 19,830..............E8 35
Lavello, It., 13,745......D5 9
La Verne, Calif., 6,516...m13 50
Laverne, Okla., 1,937....A2 79
Laviana, Sp., 12,455.....A3 8
La Victoria, Ven., 22,293..............A4 32
La Villa, Tex., 1,261....*F4 84
La Vista, Ga., 4,000.....C2 55
La Vista, Nebr., 800.....g13 71
La Viuda, mtn., Peru....C2 31
Lavonia, Ga., 2,088......B3 55
Lavras da Mangabeira, Braz., 2,835.........*D7 27
Lawn, Newf., Can., 716...E4 44
Lawndale, Calif., 21,740..*F4 50
Lawndale, N.C., 723......B1 76
Lawnside, N.J., 2,155....*D2 74
Lawnton, Pa., 3,500.....*F8 81
Lawrence, Ind., 10,103...........E5, k10 59
Lawrence, Kans., 32,858.........D9, m15 61
Lawrence, Mass., 70,933...A5 65
Lawrence, Mich., 773....F4 66
Lawrence, N.Y., 5,813....G2 52
Lawrence, Pa., 1,048....F1 81

Lawrence, co., Ala., 24,501..............A2 46
Lawrence, co., Ark., 17,267..............A4 49
Lawrence, co., Ill., 18,540..............E6 58
Lawrence, co., Ind., 36,564..............G4 59
Lawrence, co., Ky., 12,134..............B7 62
Lawrence, co., Miss., 10,215..............D3 68
Lawrence, co., Mo., 23,260..............D4 69
Lawrence, co., Ohio, 55,438..............D3 78
Lawrence, co., Pa., 112,965.............E1 81
Lawrence, co., S. Dak., 17,075..............F2 77
Lawrence, co., Tenn., 28,049..............B4 83
Lawrenceburg, Ind., 5,004................F8 59
Lawrenceburg, Ky., 3,523................B5 62
Lawrenceburg, Tenn., 8,042................B4 83
Lawrence Park, Pa., 4,403................B1 81
Lawrenceville, Ga., 3,804............A6, C3 55
Lawrenceville, Ill., 5,492................E6 58
Lawrenceville, N.J., 3,000................C3 74
Lawrenceville, Va., 1,941..D5 85
Lawson, Mo., 778.......B3 69
Lawtey, Fla., 623........B4 54
Lawton, Mich., 1,402....F5 66
Lawton, Okla., 61,697....C3 79
Layland, W. Va., 400....D7 87
Layton, Utah, 9,027.....C2 72
Laytonville, Calif., 900...C2 50
Lazio, pol. dist., It., 3,958,957..........*D4 9
Lea, co., N. Mex., 53,429..C7 48
Leachville, Ark., 1,507....B5 49
Lead, S. Dak., 6,211.....F2 77
Lead, mtn., Maine.......D4 64
Leader, Sask., Can., 1,211..G1 39
Leadville, Colo., 4,008...B4 51
Leadwood, Mo., 1,500....D7 69
League City, Tex., 2,622..*E5 84
Leake, co., Miss., 18,660..C4 68
Leakesville, Miss., 1,014..D5 68
Leakey, Tex., 587........E3 84
Leaksville, N.C., 6,684...A3 76
Lealman, Fla., 20,000....p10 54
Leamington, Ont., Can., 9,030................E2 41
Leamington, Eng., 43,500..D6 4
Leaside, Ont., Can., 18,579.............m15 41
Leatherhead, Eng., 36,900.............m12 4
Leatherwood, Ky., 1,000..C6 62
Leavenworth, Kans., 22,052...........C9, k16 61
Leavenworth, Wash., 1,480................B5 86
Leavenworth, co., Kans., 48,524.............C8 61
Leavittsburg, Ohio, 3,000..A5 78
Leawood, Kans., 7,466...D9 61
Lebanon, Ill., 2,863.....E4 58
Lebanon, Ind., 9,523.....D5 59
Lebanon, Ky., 4,813.....C4 62
Lebanon, Mo., 8,220.....D5 69
Lebanon, N.H., 9,299....D3 73
Lebanon, N.J., 800......B3 74
Lebanon, Ohio, 5,993....G1 78
Lebanon, Oreg., 5,858...........C4, k12 80
Lebanon, Pa., 30,045....F9 81
Lebanon, Tenn., 10,512..A5 83
Lebanon, Va., 2,085.....f9 85
Lebanon, co., Pa., 90,853..F9 81
Lebanon, country, Asia, 2,265,000..........F10 14
Lebanon Junction, Ky., 1,527................C4 62
Lebedyan, Sov. Un., 10,000.............E12 12
Le Blanc, Fr., 5,279.....D4 5
Le Blanc-Mesnil, Fr., 35,708.............g10 5
Lebork, Pol., 22,700.....A4 7
Le Bourget, Fr., 10,077...g10 5
Le Bouscat, Fr., 21,404...E3 5
Lebrija, Sp., 12,297.....D2 8
Le Cateau, Fr., 9,055....B5 5
Lecce, It., 76,400.......D7 9
Lecco, It., 49,800.......B2 9
Le Center, Minn., 1,597...F5 67
Le Chambon-Feugerolles, Fr., 20,320.........E6 5
Le Chesnay, Fr., 13,249...g9 5

Le Claire, Iowa, 1,546..............C7, g11 60
Lecompte, La., 1,485.....C3 63
Le Coteau, Fr., 6,571....D6 5
Le Creusot, Fr., 33,737...D6 5
Leczyca, Pol., 12,600....B5 7
Ledgewood, N.J., 1,000...B3 74
Ledo, India, 5,000......C10 20
Leduc, Alta., Can., 2,356..C4 38
Lee, Mass., 3,200 (5,271▲)..........B1 65
Lee, co., Ala., 49,754....C4 46
Lee, co., Ark., 21,001....C5 49
Lee, co., Fla., 54,539....F5 54
Lee, co., Ga., 6,204.....E2 55
Lee, co., Ill., 38,749....B4 58
Lee, co., Iowa, 44,207....D6 60
Lee, co., Ky., 7,420.....C6 62
Lee, co., Miss., 40,589...A5 68
Lee, co., N.C., 29,197....B3 76
Lee, co., S.C., 21,832....C7 82
Lee, co., Tex., 8,949....D4 84
Lee, co., Va., 25,824....f8 85
Leechburg, Pa., 3,545....E2 81
Leedon, Estates, Pa., 1,800..............*G11 81
Leeds, Ala., 6,162....C3, E5 46
Leeds, Eng., 513,800....D6 4
Leeds, co., Ont., Can., 46,889..............C8 41
Leelanau, co., Mich., 9,321................D5 66
Lee Park, Pa., 3,500....n17 81
Leer, Ger., 20,500......B3 6
Leesburg, Fla., 11,172...D5 54
Leesburg, N.J., 700.....E3 74
Leesburg, Ohio, 932.....C2 78
Leesburg, Va., 2,869....A5 85
Lee's Summit, Mo., 8,267...........C3, k11 69
Leesville, La., 4,689....C2 63
Leesville, S.C., 1,619....D4 82
Leetes Island, Conn., 400..D6 52
Leetonia, Ohio, 2,543....B5 78
Leetsdale, Pa., 2,153....h13 81
Leeuwarden, Neth., 85,700..............A6 5
Leeward, is., see Antigua, Montserrat, St. Kitts-Nevis-Anguilla, and Virgin Islands, (Br.), Br. dep., N.A.
Leflore, co., Miss., 47,142..B3 68
Le Flore, co., Okla., 29,106..............C7 79
Lefors, Tex., 864........B2 84
Le François, Mart., 2,849..I14 37
Leganés, Sp., 8,539.....p17 8
Legaspi, Phil., 36,374...C6 19
Legion, Tex., 1,691.....*E3 84
Legnano, It., 43,800....B2 9
Legnica, Pol., 69,800....C4 7
Lago, mtn., Wash........A5 86
Le Grand, Calif., 900....D3 50
Le Havre, Fr., 183,776...C3 5
Lehi, Utah, 4,377....A6, D2 72
Lehigh, Iowa, 846......B3 60
Lehigh, co., Pa., 227,536..E10 81
Lehigh Acres, Fla., 4,200..F5 54
Lehighton, Pa., 6,318...E10 81
Lehrte, Ger., 21,300....B4 6
Leiah, Pak., 14,914.....B5 20
Leicester, Eng., 270,400 (*430,000).........D6 4
Leicester, Mass., 1,850 (8,177▲)..........B4 65
Leicester, co., Eng., 696,600...........*D6 4
Leiden, Neth., 98,800....A6 5
Leigh Creek, Austl., 1,020..E2 26
Leighton, Ala., 1,158....A2 46
Leinster, prov., Ire., 1,412,600.........*D3 4
Leipsic, Ohio, 1,802....A2 78
Leipzig, Ger., 587,200...C6 6
Leiria, Port., 7,477.....C1 8
Leisure City, Fla., 3,001..s13 54
Leitchfield, Ky., 2,982...C3 62
Leith, Pa., 1,622......*G2 81
Leitrim, co., Ire., 30,500..............*D3 4
Leiva, mtn., Col........C3 32
Lejunior, Ky., 900......D6 62
Le Kef, Tun., 14,743....A6 22
Leksands, Swe., 1,800...G6 11
Leland, Miss., 6,295....B3 68
Leland Grove, Ill., 1,731..*D4 58
Le Locle, Switz., 13,762..E3 6
Le Mans, Fr., 132,181...D4 5
Le Marin, Mart., 2,004..............I14 35
Le Mars, Iowa, 7,847....B1 60
Lemay (Luxemburg), Mo., 23,000............*C7 69
Leme, Braz., 11,785.....m8 30
Lemeta, Alsk., 1,015...*C10 47
Lemgo, Ger., 21,400....B4 6
Lemhi, co., Idaho, 5,816..E4 57
Lemmon, S. Dak., 2,412..E3 77

Lemon Grove, Calif., 21,000..........F5, o15 50
Lemont, Ill., 4,034....B6, k9 58
Lemont, Pa., 1,153.....E6 81
Lemoore, Calif., 2,561...D4 50
Le Moule, Guad., 8,189..H14 35
Le Moyen, La., 200.....D3 63
Lemoyne, Pa., 4,662....*F8 81
Le Moyne, Que., Can., 8,057..............*D4 42
Lena, Ill., 1,552.......A4 58
Lena, Sp., 2,252.......A3 8
Lena, riv., Sov. Un.,..........C15 13
Lenawee, co., Mich., 77,789.............G6 66
Lenexa, Kans., 2,487....D9 61
Leninabad, Sov. Un., 86,000..............E9 13
Leningrad, Sov. Un., 3,180,000 (*3,950,000)......H14, s31 11
Leninogorsk, Sov. Un., 69,000.............D11 13
Leninsk, Sov. Un., 5,000..G15 12
Leninsk-Kuznetskiy, Sov. Un., 140,000.....D11 13
Lenkoran, Sov. Un., 30,000.............F7 13
Lennox, Calif., 31,224...*E4 50
Lennox, S. Dak., 1,353...G9 77
Lennox & Addington, co., Ont., Can., 23,717...C7 41
Lennoxville, Que., Can., 3,699.............D6 42
Lenoir, N.C., 10,257....B1 76
Lenoir, co., N.C., 55,276..B5 76
Lenoir City, Tenn., 4,979..D9 83
Lenox, Iowa, 1,178.....D3 60
Lenox, Mass., 1,750....B1 65
Lenox Avenue, N.Y., 1,400.............*C4 75
Lennox & Addington co., Ont., Can., 23,717...C7 41
Lennoxville, Que., Can., 3,699.............D6 42
Lens, Fr., 42,590......B5 5
Lenwood, Calif., 2,407...*E5 50
Leo, Ind., 600.........B7 59
Leoben, Aus., 36,257....E7 6
Léogâne, Hai., 3,607....E7 35
Leominster, Mass., 27,929..A4 65
Leon, Iowa, 2,004......D4 60
León (de Los Aldamas), Mex., 209,870....C4, m13 34
León, Nic., 44,053.....E7 34
León, Sp., 73,483......A3 8
Leon, co., Fla., 74,225...B2 54
Leon, co., Tex., 9,951...D5 84
León, prov., Sp., 584,594..*A3 8
León, reg., Sp., 1,291,452..B3 8
Leonard, Tex., 1,117....C4 84
Leonardo, N.J., 3,000....C4 74
Leonardtown, Md., 1,281..D4 53
Leonforte, It., 17,927...F5 9
Leonia, N.J., 8,394.....h9 74
Leonora, Austl., 970....E3 25
Leopoldina, Braz., 17,726............C4, g6 30
Leoti, Kans., 1,401.....D2 61
Leovo, Sov. Un., 10,000...H7 12
Lepanto, Ark., 1,585....B5 49
Lepe, Sp., 10,038......D2 8
Lepel, Sov. Un., 10,000..D7 12
Le Petit-Quevilly, Fr., 21,098.............C4 5
L'Épiphanie, Que., Can., 2,663..............D4 42
Le Puy [-en-Velay], Fr., 25,125.............E5 5
Le Raincy, Fr., 14,908...g11 5
Lercara Friddi, It., 11,872.............F4 9
Lérida, Sp., 50,047.....B6 8
Lérida, prov., Sp., 333,765...........*B6 8
Le Roy, Ill., 2,436.....C5 58
Le Roy, Kans., 601.....D8 61
Le Roy, Minn., 971.....G6 67
Le Roy, N.Y., 4,662.....C3 75
Lerwick, Scot., 5,900...g10 4
Les Cayes, Hai., 11,608..E7 35
Les Éboulements, Que., Can., 619.............B7 42
Lesh, Alb., 1,609......B2 14
Leskovac, Yugo., 33,941..D5 10
Leslie, Mich., 1,807....F6 66
Leslie, co., Ky., 10,941...C6 62
Les Lilas, Fr., 17,721...g10 5
Les Saules, Que., Can., 4,098..............n17 42
Lesotho, (Basutoland), country, Afr., 733,000..F5 24
Les Sables-d'Olonne, Fr., 18,401.............D3 5
Lesser Antilles, is., W.I.....B4 27

Lester, Pa., 2,000......*G11 81
Lester, W. Va., 626......D6 87
Lester Prairie, Minn., 966..F4 67
Le Sueur, Minn., 3,310....F5 67
Le Sueur, co., Minn.,
  19,906..............F5 67
Lesvos (Lesbos), prov.,
  Grc., 140,251......*C6 14
Leszno, Pol., 30,900......C4 7
Letcher, co., Ky., 30,102..C7 62
Le Teil, Fr., 8,236......E6 5
Lethbridge, Alta., Can.,
  35,454........E4, h8 38
Leticia, Col., 4,013......D4 32
Letpadan, Bur., 15,896..*H12 16
Le Tréport, Fr., 6,136....B4 5
Leucadia, Calif., 5,665...*F5 50
Leuser mtn.,
  Indon.............m11 19
Leuven, Bel., 32,524.....B6 5
Levack, Ont., Can.,
  3,178.............*A3 41
Levadhia, Grc., 12,609....C4 14
Levallois-Perret, Fr.,
  61,804........C4, g10 5
Level Green, Pa., 1,500...*F2 81
Levelland, Tex., 10,153...C1 84
Level Park, Mich., 3,017..*F5 66
Leven, Scot., 8,900......B5 4
Levice, Czech., 13,800.....D5 7
Levin, N.Z., 7,934......N15 26
Lévis, Que., Can.,
  15,112.........C6, n17 42
Lévis, co., Que., Can.,
  51,842............C6 42
Levittown, N.Y., 11,861..*C3 74
Levittown, N.Y., 65,700..*G2 52
Levittown, Pa., 70,000..*F12 81
Levkas, Grc., 6,552......C3 14
Levoca, Czech., 7,584....D6 7
Levy, co., Fla., 10,364....C4 54
Lewes, Del., 3,025......C7 53
Lewes, Eng., 13,900......E7 4
Lewis, co., Idaho, 4,423..C2 57
Lewis, co., Ky., 13,115...B6 62
Lewis, co., Mo., 10,984..A6 69
Lewis, co., N.Y., 23,249..B5 75
Lewis, co., Tenn., 6,269...B4 83
Lewis, co., Wash.,
  41,858............C3 86
Lewis, co., W. Va.,
  19,711............C4 87
Lewis and Clark, co.,
  Mont., 28,006.......C4 70
Lewisburg, Ala., 2,500...E4 46
Lewisburg, Ohio, 1,415....C1 78
Lewisburg, Pa., 5,523....E8 81
Lewisburg, Tenn., 6,338...B5 83
Lewisburg, W. Va.,
  2,259.............D4 87
Lewisdale, Md., 5,000...*C3 53
Lewis Gardens, Va.,
  1,380.............*C5 85
Lewisporte, Newf., Can.,
  2,702.............D4 44
Lewis Run, Pa., 714......C4 81
Lewiston, Idaho, 12,691..C1 57
Lewiston, Maine,
  40,804.........D2, f7 64
Lewiston, Mich., 600.....D6 66
Lewiston, Minn., 890.....G7 67
Lewiston, N.Y., 3,320....B1 75
Lewiston, Utah, 1,336....A6 72
Lewiston Orchards, Idaho,
  11,500............C1 57
Lewistown, Ill., 2,603....C3 58
Lewistown, Mont., 7,408..C7 70
Lewistown, Pa., 12,640...E6 81
Lewisville, Ark., 1,373....D2 49
Lewisville, Ind., 592.....F7 59
Lewisville, N.B., Can.,
  3,094.............C5 43
Lewisville, Tex.,
  3,956.........C4, m9 84
Lexington, Ill., 1,244....C5 58
Lexington, Ky., 88,000,
  (*160,000)........B5 62
Lexington, Mass.,
  27,691.........B5, g11 65
Lexington, Mich., 722....E8 66
Lexington, Minn., 1,457..*E5 67
Lexington, Miss., 2,839...B3 68
Lexington, Mo., 4,845....B4 69
Lexington, Nebr., 5,572..D6 71
Lexington, N.C., 16,093...B2 76
Lexington, Ohio, 1,311...B3 78
Lexington, Okla., 1,216...B4 79
Lexington, S.C., 1,127....D5 82
Lexington, Tenn., 3,943..B3 83
Lexington, Va., 7,537....C3 85
Lexington, co., S.C.,
  60,726............D5 82
Lexington Park, Md.,
  8,000.............*D5 53
Leyte, prov., Phil.,
  963,364...........*C6 19
Leyte, isl., Phil........C6 19
Leyton, Eng., 93,857.....k12 4

Lézignan, Fr., 6,939......F5 5
Lezirias, reg., Port......f10 8
Lgov, Sov. Un., 10,000....f10 12
Lhasa, China, 50,000.....F3 17
L' Hay-les-Roses, Fr.,
  17,968............g10 5
Liaoning, prov., China,
  24,090,000.........C9 17
Liaoyang, China,
  135,000............C9 17
Líbano, Col., 18,640.....C3 32
Libby, Mont., 2,828......B1 70
Liberal, Kans., 13,813....E3 61
Liberal, Mo., 612.......D3 69
Liberec, Czech., 66,400....C3 7
Liberia, country, Afr.,
  1,066,000..........G3 22
Liberty, Ind., 1,745......E8 59
Liberty, Ky., 1,578......C5 62
Liberty, Mo., 8,909..B3, h11 69
Liberty, N.Y., 4,704......D6 75
Liberty, N.C., 1,438......B3 76
Liberty, Pa., 3,624......*E1 81
Liberty, S.C., 2,657......B2 82
Liberty, Tex., 6,127..D6, q15 84
Liberty, co., Fla., 3,138...B2 54
Liberty, co., Ga., 14,487..E5 55
Liberty, co., Mont., 2,624..B5 70
Liberty, co., Tex., 31,595..D5 84
Liberty Acres, Calif.,
  5,200.............*E4 50
Liberty Center, Ohio
  867...............A1 78
Liberty Corner, N.J., 800..B3 74
Liberty Lake, Wash.,
  800..............g14 86
Liberty Plain, Mass.,
  900..............h12 65
Libertyville, Ill.,
  9,241.........A6, h9 58
Libourne, Fr., 15,170.....E3 5
Library, Pa., 3,000......*E1 81
Libreville, Gabon, 46,000..H6 22
Libya, country, Afr.,
  1,559,400..........C2 23
Licata, It., 38,500......F4 9
Lice, Tur., 6,725........C13 14
Licking, Mo., 954.......D6 69
Licking, co., Ohio, 90,242..B3 78
Lida, Sov. Un., 28,000....E5 12
Lidgerwood, N. Dak.,
  1,081.............D8 77
Lidice, Czech........C3, n17 7
Lidingö, Swe.,
  30,800........H8, t36 11
Lidköping, Swe., 16,900...H5 11
Liechtenstein, country,
  Eur., 19,085........E4 6
Liège, Bel., 153,240
  (*550,000).........B6 5
Liège, prov., Bel.,
  1,003,526..........B6 5
Lienyün, China, 85,000...E8 17
Lienz, Aus., 11,132......E6 6
Liepāja, Sov. Un., 77,000..C3 12
Lier, Bel., 28,755......B6 5
Liestal, Switz., 10,262...E3 6
Lighthouse Point, Fla.,
  2,453.............*F6 54
Lighthouse, point, Fla....C2 80
Lighthouse, point, Mich...C5 66
Ligonier, Ind., 2,595.....B6 59
Ligonier, Pa., 2,276......F3 81
Liguria, pol. dist., It.,
  1,735,349.........*B2 9
Liguria, reg., It........B2 9
Lihue, Haw., 3,908......B2 56
Likhoslavl, Sov. Un.,
  5,000.............C10 12
Likino-Dulevo, Sov. Un.,
  10,000............n18 12
Lilbourn, Mo., 1,216......E8 69
Lilesville, N.C., 635......C2 76
Lille, Fr., 193,096
  (*865,000).........B5 5
Lillehammer, Nor., 6,000..G4 11
Lillestrom, Nor.,
  10,600.........H4, p29 11
Lillington, N.C., 1,186....B4 76
Lillooet, B.C., Can.,
  1,304.............D7 37
Lillooet, range, B.C.,
  Can...............E7 37
Lilly, Pa., 1,642........F4 81
Lilly Grove, W. Va.,
  1,255.............*D3 87
Lima, N.Y., 1,630.......C3 75
Lima, Ohio, 51,037......B1 78
Lima, Peru, 1,716,000,
  (*2,000,000).......D2 31
Lima, dept., Peru,
  2,093,435..........D2 31
Limbé, Hai., 3,208......E7 35
Limburg, Ger., 15,600....C4 6
Limburg, prov., Bel.,
  574,606...........*B6 5
Limburg, prov., Neth.,
  894,300...........*B6 5

Limeil-Brévannes, Fr.,
  8,377.............h10 5
Limeira, Braz., 45,256.....m8 30
Limerick, Ire., 55,900....D2 4
Limerick, co., Ire.,
  137,300...........*D2 4
Limestone, Maine, 1,900...B5 64
Limestone, co., Ala.,
  36,513............A2 46
Limestone, co., Tex.,
  20,413............D4 84
Limoeiro do Norte, Braz.,
  5,705.............*D7 27
Limoges, Fr., 117,827....E4 5
Limon, Colo., 1,811......B7 51
Limón, C.R., 19,432......F8 34
Limón, prov., C.R.,
  62,800...........*I12 33
Limousin, former prov., Fr.,
  487,000...........E4 5
Limoux, Fr., 9,603......F5 5
Linares, Chile, 27,600....B2 28
Linares, Col., 1,344......C2 32
Linares, Mex., 13,592.....C5 34
Linares, Sp., 50,527.....C4 8
Linares, prov., Chile,
  171,302............B2 28
Linch, Wyo., 600.......*C6 89
Lincoln, Arg., 12,695.....A4 28
Lincoln, Calif., 3,197.....C3 50
Lincoln, Eng., 77,400.....D6 4
Lincoln, Ill., 17,364.....C4 58
Lincoln, Kans., 1,717.....C5 61
Lincoln, Maine, 3,700.....C4 64
Lincoln, Mass., 2,000....g10 65
Lincoln, Nebr.,
  146,000
  (*162,000)......D9, h11 71
Lincoln, N.H., 1,000
  (1,228▲)..........*C4 73
Lincoln, Pa., 1,686......*E1 81
Lincoln, R.I., 7,600
  (13,551▲).........B11 52
Lincoln, co., Ark., 14,447..D4 49
Lincoln, co., Colo., 5,310..C7 51
Lincoln, co., Ont., Can.,
  126,674............D5 41
Lincoln, co., Eng.,
  764,200...........*D6 4
Lincoln, co., Ga., 5,906...C4 55
Lincoln, co., Idaho, 3,686..G4 57
Lincoln, co., Kans., 5,556..C5 61
Lincoln, co., Ky., 16,503...C5 62
Lincoln, co., Maine,
  18,497............D3 64
Lincoln, co., Minn., 9,651..F2 67
Lincoln, co., Miss., 26,759..D3 68
Lincoln, co., Mo., 14,783..B6 69
Lincoln, co., Mont.,
  12,537............B1 70
Lincoln, co., Nebr.,
  28,491............D5 71
Lincoln, co., Nev., 2,431...C4 72
Lincoln, co., N. Mex.,
  7,744.............C6 48
Lincoln, co., N.C., 28,814..B1 76
Lincoln, co., Okla.,
  18,783............B5 79
Lincoln, co., Oreg.,
  24,635............C3 80
Lincoln, co., S. Dak.,
  12,371............G9 77
Lincoln, co., Tenn.,
  23,829............B5 83
Lincoln, co., Wash.,
  10,919............B7 86
Lincoln, co., W. Va.,
  20,267............C2 87
Lincoln, co., Wis., 22,338..C4 88
Lincoln, co., Wyo., 9,023..D2 89
Lincoln, par., La., 28,535..B3 63
Lincoln Acres, Calif.,
  3,500.............o15 50
Lincoln City, Oreg.,
  1,342.............C3 80
Lincoln Heights, Ohio,
  7,798.............o13 78
Lincoln Highway, Nebr.,
  950...............*C5 71
Lincoln Park, Colo.,
  2,085.............*C5 51
Lincoln Park, Ga., 1,840..*D2 55
Lincoln Park, Mich.,
  53,933............p15 66
Lincoln Park, N.J., 6,048..B4 74
Lincoln Park, N.Y.,
  1,100.............*D6 75
Lincoln Park, Pa., 1,500..*F9 81
Lincolnton, Ga., 1,450....C4 55
Lincolnton, N.C., 5,699...B1 76
Lincoln Village, Calif.,
  6,000.............*D3 50
Lincoln Village, Ohio,
  3,000.............*C3 78
Lincolnwood, Ill., 13,546..h9 58
Lincroft, N.J., 3,000.....C4 74
Lind, Wash., 697.......C7 86
Linda, Calif., 6,129......*C3 50

Lindale, Ga., 2,600......*B1 55
Lindale, Tex., 1,285......C5 84
Lindau, Ger., 24,200.....E4 6
Linden, Ala., 2,516......C2 46
Linden, Ind., 619.......D4 59
Linden, Mich., 1,146.....F7 66
Linden, N.J., 39,931.....k8 74
Linden, Tenn., 1,086.....B4 83
Linden, Tex., 1,832......C5 84
Lindenhurst, Ill., 1,259...h8 58
Lindenhurst, N.Y.,
  24,599............G3 52
Lindenwold, N.J., 7,335...D3 74
Lindesberg, Swe., 6,000...H6 11
Lindi, Tan, 10,315......D7 24
Lindon, Utah, 1,150.....*A6 72
Lindsay, Calif., 5,397....D4 50
Lindsay, Ont., Can.,
  11,399............C6 41
Lindsay, Okla., 4,258.....C4 79
Lindsborg, Kans., 2,609...D6 61
Lindstrom, Minn., 835....E6 67
Linesville, Pa., 1,255.....C1 81
Lineville, Ala., 1,612.....B4 46
Lingayen, Phil., 8,221....B6 19
Lingen, Ger., 25,200.....B3 6
Linglestown, Pa., 800....F8 81
Lingyuan, China, 20,000..C8 17
Linhai, China, 26,000....F9 17
Lini, China, 80,000......D8 17
Linière, Que., Can., 1,269..C7 42
Linköping, Swe., 69,000...H6 11
Linn, Mo., 1,050.......C6 69
Linn, co., Iowa, 136,899..B6 60
Linn, co., Kans., 8,274....D9 61
Linn, co., Mo., 16,815....B4 69
Linn, co., Oreg., 58,867...C4 80
Linntown, Pa., 1,628....*E7 81
Lino Lakes, Minn., 2,329..*E5 67
Lins, Braz., 32,204......C3 30
Linthicum Heights,
  Md., 10,500......B4, h11 53
Linton, Ind., 5,736......F3 59
Linton, N. Dak., 1,826....D5 77
Linwood, Mass., 1,000....B4 65
Linwood, Mich., 650.....E7 66
Linwood, N.J., 3,847.....E3 74
Linwood, Pa., 4,460....*G11 81
Linworth, Ohio, 600.....k10 78
Linyü, China, 60,000.....C8 17
Linz, Aus., 198,800......D7 6
Lipa, Phil., 17,470..C6, p13 19
Lipari, It., 3,731.......E5 9
Lipetsk, Sov. Un.,
  205,000...........E12 12
Lipkany, Sov. Un.,
  10,000............A8 10
Lipno, Pol., 10,800......B5 7
Lipova, Rom., 10,064....B5 10
Lippstadt, Ger., 37,500...C4 6
Lipscomb, Ala., 2,811..B3, E4 46
Lipscomb, co., Tex.,
  3,406.............A2 84
Liria, Sp., 9,723........C5 8
Lisboa, see Lisbon, Port.
Lisbon, Iowa, 1,227.....C6 60
Lisbon, Maine, 1,300..D2, f7 64
Lisbon, N.H., 1,220
  (1,788▲)..........C4 73
Lisbon, N. Dak., 2,093...D8 77
Lisbon, Ohio, 3,579......B5 78
Lisbon Falls, Maine,
  2,700..........D5, f7 64
Lisbon (Lisboa), Port.,
  802,230
  (*1,300,000).......C1, f9 8
Lisburn, N. Ire., 18,100...C3 4
Lishu, China, 5,000......E2 18
Lisichansk, Sov. Un.,
  10,000............q21 12
Lisieux, Fr., 21,156......C4 5
Lisle, Ill., 5,037.......k8 58
L'Islet, Que., Can., 816...B7 42
L'Islet, co., Que., Can.,
  24,798............B7 42
L'isletville, Que., Can.,
  1,184.............B7 42
Lisman, Ala., 909.......C1 46
Lismore, Austl., 19,740...E9 25
Listowel, Ont., Can.,
  4,002.............D4 41
Litchfield, Conn., 1,363
  (6,264▲)..........B4 52
Litchfield, Ill., 7,330....D4 58
Litchfield, Mich., 993....F6 66
Litchfield, Minn., 5,078...E4 67
Litchfield, co., Conn.,
  119,856...........B3 52
Litchfield Park, Ariz.,
  1,500.............D1 48
Lithgow, Austl., 12,813...F9 25
Lithonia, Ga., 1,667..B5, C2 55
Lithuania (S.S.R.), rep.,
  Sov. Un., 2,900,000....D4 12
Lititz, Pa., 5,987.......F9 81
Litokhoron, Grc., 5,032..*B4 14
Litomerice, Czech.,
  16,900............C3 7

Litomysl, Czech., 6,384....D7　7
Little, mtn., Wyo............E5　89
Little Belt, mtn., Mont.,...D6　70
Little Canada, Minn.,
　3,512.................*E5　67
Little Catalina, Newf.,
　Can., 752.............D5　44
Little Chute, Wis.,
　5,099.............D5, h9　88
Little Current, Ont., Can.,
　1,527.................B3　41
Little Falls, Minn., 7,551..E4　67
Little Falls, N.J., 9,730....B4　74
Little Falls, N.Y., 8,935...B6　75
Little Ferry, N.J., 6,175...h8　74
Littlefield, Tex., 7,236...C1　84
Littlefork, Minn., 805.....B5　67
Little River, co., Ark.,
　9,211.................D1　49
Little Rock, Ark.,
　136,000
　(*286,000).........C3, D6　49
Little Rock, river, Iowa....A1　70
Little Silver, N.J., 5,202...C4　74
Littlestown, Pa., 2,756....G7　81
Littleton, Colo., 13,670...B6　51
Littleton, Mass., 750
　(5,109▲)...............f9　65
Littleton, N.H., 3,500
　(5,003▲)..............C4　73
Littleton, N.C., 1,024....A5　76
Littleton Common, Mass.,
　2,300................f10　65
Little Valley, N.Y., 1,244..C2　75
Liuho, China., 5,000......E2　18
Lively, Ont., Can., 3,211..A3　41
Live Oak, Calif., 2,276....C3　50
Live Oak, Fla., 6,544......B4　54
Live Oak, co., Tex., 7,846..E3　84
Livermore, Calif., 16,058..h9　50
Livermore, Ky., 1,506.....C2　62
Livermore, peak, Tex.....o12　84
Livermore Falls, Maine,
　2,882................D2　64
Liverpool, N.S., Can.,
　3,712................E5　43
Liverpool, Eng., 739,700
　(*1,680,000)..........D5　4
Liverpool, N.Y., 3,308....B4　75
Liverpool, Pa., 894.......E7　81
Livingston, Ala., 1,544....C1　46
Livingston, Calif., 2,188...D3　50
Livingston, Guat., 2,606...D7　34
Livingston, Ill., 964......E4　58
Livingston, La.,
　1,183.............D5, g10　63
Livingston, Mont., 8,229..E6　70
Livingston, N.J., 23,124...B4　74
Livingston, Tenn., 2,817...C8　83
Livingston, Tex., 3,398....D5　84
Livingstone, Zambia,
　33,600................D5　24
Livingston, co., Ill.,
　40,341................C5　58
Livingston, co., Ky.,
　7,029.................A3　62
Livingston, co., Mich.,
　38,233................F6　66
Livingston, co., Mo.,
　15,771................B4　69
Livingston, co., N.Y.,
　44,053................C3　75
Livingston, par., La.,
　26,974................D5　63
Livingston Manor, N.Y.,
　2,080................D6　75
Livno, Yugo., 5,170.......D3　10
Livny, Sov. Un., 10,000..E11　12
Livonia, Mich., 66,702....F7　66
Livonia, N.Y., 946........C3　75
Livorno (Leghorn), It.,
　165,800................C3　9
Livramento, Braz., 37,666..E1　30
Livry-Gargan, Fr.,
　29,679................g11　5
Lizard Head, peak,
　Wyo..................D3　89
Ljubljana, Yugo.,
　134,169................B2　10
Ljungby, Swe., 9,300......I5　11
Llandrindod Wells, Wales,
　3,300.................D5　4
Llandudno, Wales,
　17,200................D5　4
Llanelly, Wales, 29,500....E4　4
Llanes, Sp., 20,421.......A3　8
Llano, Tex., 2,656........D3　84
Llano, co., Tex., 5,240....D3　84
Llanquihue, prov., Chile,
　167,491................C2　28
Lloyd, Ky., 600..........B7　62
Lloyd Harbor, N.Y.,
　2,879................*G3　52
Lloydminster, Alta., Can.,
　5,667.................D1　39
Lloydminster, Sask., Can.,
　5,667.................D1　39
Lloyd Place, Va., 2,282...*D6　85

Lluchmayor, Sp.,
　10,664................C7　8
Llullaillaco, vol., Chile....D2　29
Löbau, Ger., 16,800.....C7　6
Loberia, Arg., 7,916......B5　28
Lobito, Ang., 31,630.....C2　24
Lobos, Arg., 8,372....B5, g7　28
Locarno, Switz., 10,500...E4　6
Lochdale, B.C., Can......f12　37
Lochearn, Md., 2,000....*B4　53
Loches, Fr., 5,902........D4　5
Loch Raven, Md.,
　23,278...............*B4　53
Lockeport, N.S., Can.,
　1,231................F4　43
Lockhart, Tex.,
　6,084.............E4, h8　84
Lock Haven, Pa., 11,748...D7　81
Lockland, Ohio, 5,292....o13　78
Lockney, Tex., 2,141.....B2　84
Lockport, Ill., 8,785....B5, k8　58
Lockport, La.,
　2,221..............E5, k10　63
Lockport, N.Y., 26,443...B2　75
Lockwood, Mo., 835......D4　69
Locumba, Peru, 634......E3　31
Locust, N.J., 800........C4　74
Locust Grove, Okla.,
　828.................A6　79
Locust Valley, N.Y.,
　3,400................F2　52
Lod (Lydda), Isr.,
　21,000............C2, h5　15
Lodève, Fr., 6,869.......F5　5
Lodeynoye Pole, Sov. Un.,-
　10,000...............A9　12
Lodge Grass, Mont., 687...E9　70
Lodhran, Pak., 4,890......C5　20
Lodi, Calif., 27,018.......C3　50
Lodi, N.J., 23,502........h8　74
Lodi, Ohio, 2,213........A3　78
Lodi, Wis., 1,620........E4　88
Łódź, Pol., 734,300......C5　7
Loei, Thai., 7,268.......*B2　19
Logan, Iowa, 1,605......C2　60
Logan, Kans., 846.......C4　61
Logan, Ohio, 6,417......C3　78
Logan, Utah, 18,731.....A6　72
Logan, W. Va., 4,185..D3, D5　87
Logan, co., Ark., 15,957...B2　49
Logan, co., Colo., 20,302..A7　51
Logan, co., Ill., 33,656....C4　58
Logan, co., Kans., 4,036...D2　61
Logan, co., Ky., 20,896....D3　62
Logan, co., Nebr., 1,108...C5　71
Logan, co., N. Dak.,
　5,369................D6　77
Logan, co., Ohio, 34,803..B2　78
Logan, co., Okla., 18,662..B4　79
Logan, co., W. Va.,
　61,570................D3　87
Logan, mtn., Yukon, Can..D6　36
Logansport, Ind., 21,106...C5　59
Logansport, La., 1,371....C2　63
Loganville, Ga., 926......C3　55
Logroño, Sp., 61,292.....A4　8
Loggieville, N.B., Can.,
　691..................B4　43
Logroño, prov., Sp.,
　229,852..............*A4　8
Logrosán, Sp., 6,595.....C3　8
Lohardaga, India,
　13,203................D4　20
Lohrville, Iowa, 615......B3　60
Loire, dept., Fr.,
　696,348..............*E6　5
Loire, riv., Fr...........D3　5
Loire-Atlantique, dept.,
　Fr., 803,372...........*D3　5
Loiret, dept., Fr.,
　389,854..............*D4　5
Loir-et-Cher, dept., Fr.,
　250,741..............*D4　5
Loja, Ec., 26,785........B2　31
Loja, Sp., 12,439........D3　8
Loja, prov., Ec., 285,448..B2　31
Lokhvitsa, Sov. Un.,
　10,000................F9　12
Lom, Bul., 15,182.......D6　10
Loma Linda, Calif.,
　6,000................*E5　50
Lomas de Zamora, Arg.,
　275,219............A5, g7　28
Lombard, Ill., 28,151.....k8　58
Lombardia, pol. dist., It.,
　7,406,152.............*B2　9
Lombardy, reg., It........B2　9
Lomé, Togo, 80,000......G5　22
Lometa, Tex., 817........D3　84
Lomira, Wis., 807........E5　88
Lomita, Calif., 14,983....*E4　50
Lomonosov, Sov. Un.,
　30,000...............s30　11
Lompoc, Calif., 23,998....E3　50
Lomza, Pol., 21,700......B7　7
Lonaconing, Md., 2,077...k13　53
London, Ont., Can.,
　169,569 (*181,283).....E3　41

London, Eng.,
　7,972,900
　(*10,975,000).......E6, k12　4
London, Ky., 4,035......C5　62
London, Ohio, 6,379......C2　78
London, W. Va., 500....*C6　87
London, co., Eng.,
　3,195,114............*E6　4
Londonderry, N. Ire.,
　55,000................C3　4
Londonderry, co., N. Ire.,
　114,700...............*C3　4
London Mills, Ill., 617....C3　58
Londrina, Braz., 74,110...C2　30
Lone Oak, Ky., 2,104....A2　62
Lone Pine, Calif., 1,400...D4　50
Lone Star, Tex., 1,513....*C5　84
Lone Wolf, Okla., 617....C2　79
Lone Tree, Iowa, 717.....C6　60
Long, co., Ga., 3,874.....E5　55
Long Beach, Calif.,
　344,168...........F4, n12　50
Long Beach, Ind., 2,007..A4　59
Long Beach, Miss.,
　4,770.............E2, E4　68
Long Beach, N.Y.,
　28,490...........E7, n15　75
Long Beach, Wash., 665...C1　86
Longboat Key, Fla.,
　1,000................q10　54
Long Branch, Ont., Can.,
　11,039...............m14　41
Long Branch, N.J.,
　26,228...............C5　74
Long Creek, mtn., Wyo...D4　89
Longford, co., Ire.,
　28,900..............*D3　4
Longhurst, N.C., 1,546...A4　76
Long Island, isl., N.Y.....n15　75
Long Island, Tenn.,
　1,925...............*C11　83
Long Lake, Ill., 3,502....h8　58
Long Lake, Minn., 996...*F5　67
Long Lake, N.Y., 700....B6　75
Longleaf, La., 600.......C3　63
Long Leaf Park, N.C.,
　2,238...............*C5　76
Longmeadow, Mass.,
　10,565...............B2　65
Longmont, Colo.,
　11,489...............A5　51
Long Pond, Newf., Can.,
　1,244................E5　44
Longport, N.J., 1,077....E13　74
Long Prairie, Minn.,
　2,414................E4　67
Longreach, Austl., 3,864..D7　25
Longs, peak, Colo........A5　51
Long Range, mtn., Newf.,
　Can............D3, h10　44
Longueuil, Que., Can.,
　24,131............D4, p19　42
Long Valley, N.J., 1,220...B3　74
Longview, Alta., Can.,
　246.................D3　38
Long View, Ky., 500.....C4　62
Long View, N.C., 2,997...B1　76
Longview, Tex., 40,050...C5　84
Longview, Wash., 23,349..C3　86
Longwood, Fla., 1,689...*D5　54
Longwood Park, N.C.,
　1,144...............*B3　76
Longwy, Fr., 21,939.....C6　5
Long Xuyen, Viet.,
　23,300..............*C3　19
Lonoke, Ark., 2,359...C4, D6　49
Lonoke, co., Ark., 24,551..C4　49
Lons-le-Saunier, Fr.,
　15,924...............D6　5
Loogootee, Ind., 2,858....G4　59
Lookout, Ky., 900.......C7　62
Lookout Mountain, Tenn.,
　1,817...............E10　83
Loon Lake, mtn., N.Y.....f10　75
Lopei, China, 5,000......C5　18
Lora, Sp., 11,864........D3　8
Lorado, W. Va., 700..D3, D6　87
Lorain, Ohio, 68,932.....A3　78
Lorain, Pa., 1,324......*E4　81
Lorain, co., Ohio,
　217,500...............A3　78
Loraine, Tex., 837.......C2　84
Lorca, Sp., 21,000.......D5　8
Lordsburg, N. Mex.,
　3,436................C4　48
Loreauville, La., 655.....D4　63
Lorena, Braz., 26,068....G3　30
Lorenzo, Tex., 1,188.....C2　84
Loreto, Mex., 1,706......B2　34
Loreto, Par., 11,321......D4　29
Loreto, dept., Peru,
　411,340...............C3　31
Loretteville,
　Que., Can.,
　6,522............C6, n17　42
Loretto, Pa., 1,338......F4　81
Loretto, Tenn., 929......B4　83
Lorica, Col., 12,880......B2　32

Lorient, Fr., 60,566......F2　5
L'Orignal, Ont., Can.,
　1,189................B10　41
Loris, S.C., 1,702........C10　82
Lorne, N.B., Can., 890...B3　43
Lorneville, N.B., Can.,
　666..................D3　43
Lörrach, Ger., 30,500....E3　6
Lorraine, former prov., Fr.,
　1,956,000.............C6　5
Los Alamitos, Calif.,
　4,312...............*F5　50
Los Alamos, N. Mex.,
　13,037...............B5　48
Los Alamos, co., N. Mex.,
　13,037...............B5　48
Los Altos, Calif., 19,696...k8　50
Los Altos Hills, Calif.,
　3,412...............*D2　50
Los Andes, Chile, 20,400..A2　28
Los Angeles, Calif., 2,810,000
　(*8,455,000).......E4, m12　50
Los Angeles, co., Calif.,
　6,038,771.............E4　50
Los Angeles, Chile,
　33,000...............B2　28
Los Banos, Calif., 9,943...D3　50
Los Barrios, Sp., 3,583....D3　8
Los Fresnos, Tex., 1,289...F4　84
Los Gatos, Calif.,
　15,676................D2　50
Loshan, China, 5,000.....F5　17
Los Mochis, Mex., 38,307..B3　34
Los Nietos, Calif., 9,000..*E4　50
Los Palacios, Cuba, 7,000..C2　35
Los Reyes [de Salgado],
　Mex., 9,796......D4, n12　34
Los Ríos, prov., Ec.,
　250,062..............B2　31
Los Tequés, Ven., 36,073..A4　32
Lost Nation, Iowa, 567....C7　60
Lot, dept., Fr., 149,929...*E4　5
Lota, Chile, 27,700......B2　28
Lotbinière, co., Que., Can.,
　30,234...............C6　42
Lot-et-Garonne, dept., Fr.,
　275,028..............*E4　5
Lothair, Ky., 1,082.......C6　62
Lott, Tex., 924..........D4　84
Loudon, Tenn., 3,812....D9　83
Loudon, co., Tenn.,
　23,757...............D9　83
Loudonville, N.Y., 7,000..*C6　75
Loudonville, Ohio, 2,611..B3　78
Loudoun, co., Va., 24,549..B5　85
Loudun, Fr., 5,587.......D4　5
Loughborough, Eng.,
　39,000................D6　4
Louisa, Ky., 2,071.......B7　62
Louisa, co., Iowa, 10,290..C6　60
Louisa, co., Va., 12,959...C5　85
Louisbourg, N.S., Can.,
　1,417...............D10　43
Louisburg, Kans., 862.....D9　61
Louisburg, N.C., 2,862....A4　76
Louisdale, N.S., 793......D8　43
Louisiana, Mo., 4,286....B6　69
Louisiana, state, U.S.,
　3,257,022.............　63
Louis Trichardt, S. Afr.,
　9,890................E5　24
Louisville, Que., Can.,
　4,138................C5　42
Louisville, Colo., 2,073...B5　51
Louisville, Ga., 2,413.....C4　55
Louisville, Ill., 906......E5　58
Louisville, Ky., 392,000
　(*820,000).........A4, B4　62
Louisville, Miss., 5,066...B4　68
Louisville, Nebr.,
　1,194.............D9, h12　71
Louisville, Ohio, 5,116....B4　78
Loulé, Port., 6,479......D1　8
Louny, Czech., 12,300....C2　7
Loup, co., Nebr., 1,097...C6　71
Loup, riv., Nebr..........C8　71
Loup City, Nebr., 1,415...C7　71
Lourdes, Newf., Can.,
　975.................D2　44
Lourdes, Fr., 16,023......F4　5
Lourenço Marques, Moz.,
　65,716...............F6　24
Loures, Port., 6,089......f9　8
Louth, Eng., 11,400......D7　4
Louth, co., Ire., 69,200...*C3　4
Loutrá Aidhipsoú, Grc.,
　1,859...............*C4　14
Louvain, see Leuven, Bel.
Louviers, Fr., 13,160.....C4　5
Love, co., Okla., 5,862....D4　79
Lovech, Bul., 11,730......D7　10
Lovejoy, Ill., 1,922......*E3　58
Loveland, Colo., 9,734...A5　51
Loveland, Ohio,
　5,008.............C1, n12　78
Loveland Park, Ohio,
　1,000.............C1, n13　78
Lovell, Wyo., 2,451......B4　89

Lovelock, Nev., 1,948....A2 72
Lovely, Ky., 600.......C7 62
Loves Park, Ill., 10,880...A4 58
Lovilia, Iowa, 630......C5 60
Loving, N. Mex., 1,646...C6 48
Loving, co., Tex., 226...D1 84
Lovington, Ill., 1,200...D5 58
Lovington, Iowa, 800....e8 60
Lovington, N. Mex.,
9,660.............C7 48
Lowden, Iowa, 641......C7 60
Lowell, Ind., 3,063......B3 59
Lowell, Mass., 92,107..A5, f10 65
Lowell, Mich., 2,545.....F5 66
Lowell, N.C., 3,048......B1 76
Lowell, Ohio, 783.......C4 78
Lowell, Wash., 1,086....*B3 86
Lowellville, Ohio, 2,055...A5 78
Lower Burrell, Pa.,
11,952...........*F2 81
Lower Caraquet, N.B.,
Can., 807.........*B5 43
Lower Hutt, N.Z.,
57,403..........*N15 26
Lower Paia, Haw., 925...C5 56
Lower West Pubnico, N.S.,
Can., 618.........F4 43
Lowestoft, Eng., 47,100...D7 4
Lowicz, Pol., 18,300.....B5 7
Lowmoor, Va., 900......C3 85
Lowndes, co., Ala.,
15,417............C3 46
Lowndes, co., Ga., 49,270.F3 55
Lowndes, co., Miss.,
46,639............B5 68
Lowville, N.Y., 3,616....B5 75
Loxton, Austl., 2,321....G3 26
Loyal, Wis., 1,146......D3 88
Loyalhanna, Pa., 1,000...*F2 81
Loyall, Ky., 1,260......D6 62
Loyalton, Calif., 936....C3 50
Loyalty, is., Pac. O.....H8 2
Loyang, China, 171,200...E7 17
Lozere, dept., Fr.,
81,868...........*E5 5
Loznica, Yugo., 10,611...C4 10
Lozovatka, Sov. Un.,
10,000...........G9 12
Lualualei, Haw., 2,100...g9 56
Luanda, Ang., 224,540...B2 24
Luang Prabang, Laos,
25,000...........B2 19
Luanshya, Zambia,
72,100...........C5 24
Luban, Pol., 16,200.....C3 7
Lubartow, Pol., 5,542....C7 7
Lübben, Ger., 9,433.....C6 6
Lubbock, Tex., 157,000
(*176,000)........C2 84
Lubbock, co., Tex.,
156,271...........C2 84
Lubec, Maine, 1,200.....D6 64
Lübeck, Ger., 240,200...B5 6
Lublin, Pol., 197,100....C7 7
Lubliniec, Pol., 17,000...C5 7
Lubny, Sov. Un., 29,442..F9 12
Lubrin, Sp., 5,417......D4 8
Lubumbashi
(Elisabethville),
Con. K., 183,700....C5 24

Lubutu, Con. K.........I3 23
Lucan, Ont., Can., 986...D3 41
Lucas, Ohio, 719.......B3 78
Lucas, co., Iowa, 10,923...C4 60
Lucas, co., Ohio, 456,931..A2 78
Lucasville, Ohio, 1,277...D3 78
Lucca, It., 89,500......C3 9
Luce, co., Mich., 7,827...B5 66
Lucedale, Miss., 1,977...E5 68
Lucena, Phil., 40,652..C6, p13 19
Lucenec, Czech., 16,100..D5 7
Lucera, It., 24,500.....D5 9
Lucerne, see Luzern, Switz.
Lucernemines, Pa., 1,524..E3 81
Luceville, Que., Can.,
1,419............A9 42
Luck, Wis., 853........C1 88
Luckau, Ger., 6,145....C6 6
Luckenwalde, Ger.,
28,600...........B6 6
Luckey, Ohio, 946....A2, f7 78
Lucknow, Ont., Can.,
1,031............D3 41
Lucknow, India, 595,440
(*675,000)........C7 20
Lucknow, Pa., 900.....*F8 81
Lucy, La., 725........h10 63
Lüdenscheid, Ger., 58,700.C3 6
Ludhiana, India, 244,032..B6 20
Ludington, Mich., 9,421...E4 66
Ludlam, Fla., 35,000....*G6 54
Ludlow, Eng., 6,800....D5 4
Ludlow, Ky., 6,233.....A7 62
Ludlow, Mass., 11,500...B3 65
Ludlow, Pa., 800.......C4 81
Ludlow, Vt., 1,658
(2,386▲).........E2 73
Ludowici, Ga., 1,578....E5 55
Ludvika, Swe., 12,300...G6 11
Ludwigsburg, Ger.,
75,000...........D4 6
Ludwigshafen, Ger.,
172,100...........D4 6
Ludwigslust, Ger., 12,000.B5 6
Lueders, Tex., 654.....C3 84
Lufkin, Tex., 17,641....D5 84
Luga, Sov. Un., 43,000...B7 12
Lugano, Switz., 20,900
(*48,400).........E4 6
Lugansk, Sov. Un.,
314,000........G12, q22 12
Lugo, It., 12,800......B3 9
Lugo, Sp., 45,497......A2 8
Lugo, prov., Sp., 479,530..*A2 8
Lugoff, S.C., 800......C6 82
Lugoj, Rom., 30,258....C5 10
Luhsien, China, 289,000..F6 17
Luichow, China, 158,800..C6 17
Luján, Arg., 29,383.....g7 28
Lukovit, Bul., 7,755....D7 10
Lukow, Pol., 12,100....C7 7
Lukoyanov, Sov. Un.,
5,000............D15 12
Luleå, Swe., 32,300....E10 11
Luling, La., 2,122......k11 63
Luling, Tex., 4,412....E4, h8 84
Luluabourg, Con. K.,
115,000...........B4 24
Lumber City, Ga., 1,360..E4 55

Lumberport, W. Va.,
1,031...........A6, B4 87
Lumberton, Miss., 2,108..D4 68
Lumberton, N.J., 700....D3 74
Lumberton, N.C., 15,305..C3 76
Lumby, B.C., Can., 1,842..D8 37
Lumpkin, Ga., 1,348....D2 55
Lumpkin, co., Ga., 7,241..B2 55
Lumsden, Sask., Can.,
685.............G3 39
Luna, co., N. Mex., 9,839..C5 48
Luna Pier (Lakewood),
Mich., 1,344.......G7 66
Lund, Swe., 41,700......J5 11
Lundale, W. Va., 950....D3 87
Lundar, Man., Can., 713..D2 40
Lüneburg, Ger., 60,800...B5 6
Lunel, Fr., 7,758.......F6 5
Lunenburg, N.S., Can.,
3,056............E5 43
Lunenburg, Mass., 1,000..A4 65
Lunenburg, co., N.S.,
Can., 34,998.......E5 43
Lunenburg, co., Va.,
12,523............D4 85
Lunéville, Fr., 21,618...C7 5
Lungchi, China, 81,200...G8 17
Lunino, Sov. Un., 10,000..E15 12
Lupeni, Rom., 21,188....C6 10
Lupin, see Manchouli,
China
Luque, Par., 22,469.....E4 29
Luray, Va., 3,014......B4 85
Lure, Fr., 6,408.......D7 5
Lurgan, N. Ire., 18,400...C3 4
Lusaka, Zambia, 122,300..D5 24
Lusambo, Con. K., 9,800..I2 23
Luseland, Sask.,
Can., 665.........E1 39
Lusk, Wyo., 1,890......D8 89
Lutcher, La., 3,274...D5, h10 63
Lutesville, Mo., 658....D8 69
Lutherville-Timonium,
Md., 14,200.......B4 53
Luton, Eng., 136,400....E6 4
Lutsk, Sov. Un., 69,000..F5 12
Lutugino, Sov. Un.,
5,000............q22 12
Lutz, Fla., 950........D4 54
Luverne, Ala., 2,238....D3 46
Luverne, Minn., 4,249...G2 67
Luwuk, Indon.........F6 19
Luxembourg, Lux.,
73,900...........C7 5
Luxembourg, country,
Eur., 314,889......C7 5
Luxembourg, prov., Bel.,
216,848..........*C6 5
Luxemburg, Wis., 730...D6 88
Luxeuil-les-Bains, Fr.,
8,161............D7 5
Luxor, see Al Uqsur,
Eg., U.A.R.
Luxora, Ark., 1,236.....B6 49
Luzern, Switz., 73,000...E4 6
Luzern, canton, Switz.,
273,000..........*E4 6
Luzerne, Pa., 5,118.....n17 81
Luzerne, co., Pa., 346,972.D9 81
Luzon, isl., Phil........B6 19

Lvov, Sov. Un., 469,000...G5 12
Lyallpur, Pak., 425,248...B5 20
Lyaskovets, Bul., 5,560...D7 10
Lycoming, co., Pa.,
109,367...........D7 81
Lydia Mills, S.C., 1,177..*C4 82
Lydick, Ind., 1,217.....*A5 59
Lyell, mtn., B.C., Can....D9 37
Lyford, Tex., 1,554.....F4 84
Lykens, Pa., 2,527......E8 81
Lyle, Minn., 607.......G6 67
Lyman, Nebr., 626......C1 71
Lyman, S.C., 1,261.....B3 82
Lyman, co., S. Dak.,
4,428............G6 77
Lynbrook, N.Y., 20,784...G2 52
Lyndhurst, N.J., 21,867...h8 74
Lyndhurst, Ohio, 16,805...g9 78
Lyndon, Kans., 953......D8 61
Lyndon, Ky., 6,000......A4 62
Lyndonville, N.Y., 755...B2 75
Lyndonville, Vt., 1,477...B3 73
Lyndora, Pa., 5,700.....E2 81
Lynn, Ind., 1,260......D8 59
Lynn, Mass., 94,478...B6, g12 65
Lynn, co., Tex., 10,914...C2 84
Lynnfield, Mass., 8,398...f11 65
Lynn Garden, Tenn.,
5,261...........*C11 83
Lynn Haven, Fal., 3,078..u16 54
Lynn Lake, Man.,
Can., 1,881......A1, f7 40
Lynnville, Ky., 1,711...*B4 62
Lynnwood, Pa., 1,200...*D9 81
Lynnwood, Wash., 7,207..*B3 86
Lynwood, Calif., 31,614..n12 50
Lyon, Fr., 528,535....E6, F2 6
Lyon, co., Iowa, 14,468...A1 60
Lyon, co., Kans., 26,928..D7 61
Lyon, co., Ky., 5,924....C1 62
Lyon, co., Minn., 22,655..F3 67
Lyon, co., Nev., 6,143...B2 72
Lyon Mountain, N.Y.,
900.............f11 75
Lyonnais, former prov.,
Fr., 1,621,000......E6 5
Lyons, Ga., 3,219......D4 55
Lyons, Ill., 10,891......k9 58
Lyons, Ind., 651.......G3 59
Lyons, Kans., 4,592....D5 61
Lyons, Mich., 687......F6 66
Lyons, Nebr., 974......C9 71
Lyons, N.Y., 4,397.....B4 75
Lyons Falls, N.Y., 887...B5 75
Lysa, Czech., 6,500.....n18 7
Lysaya Gora, Sov. Un.,
10,000...........G8 12
Lysekil, Swe., 7,800....H4 11
Lyster Station, Que.,
Can.............C6 42
Lysva, Sov. Un., 76,000..D8 13
Lytle, Tex., 798.......E3 84
Lyubar, Sov. Un., 10,000..G6 12
Lyubertsy, Sov. Un.,
100,000..........N17 12

M

Maastricht, Neth.,
94,200...........B6 5
Mabank, Tex., 944......C4 84
Mabel, Minn., 815......G7 67
Mableton, Ga., 5,500....A4 55
Mabscott, W. Va.,
1,591.........D3, D7 87
Mabton, Wash., 958....C5 86
McAdam, N.B., Can.,
2,472............D2 43
McAdenville, N.C., 748..*B1 76
McAdoo, Pa., 3,560.....E9 81
Macaé, Braz., 19,830....C4 30
McAlester, Okla., 17,419..C6 79
McAllen, Tex., 35,411...F3 84
Macamic, Que., Can.,
1,614...........*o20 41
Macao, Port. dep., Asia,
169,299..........G7 17
Macapá, Braz., 27,585...C5 27
McArthur, Ohio, 1,529...C3 78

MacArthur, W. Va.,
1,418...........*D3 87
Macas Ec., 1,355.......D3 27
Macau, Braz., 11,876....D7 27
McBee, S.C., 512.......C7 82
McBride, B.C., Can., 590..C7 37
McCall, Idaho, 1,423....E2 57
McCamey, Tex., 3,375...D1 84
McCarthy, mtn., Mont....E4 70
McCaysville, Ga., 1,871..B2 55
McChesneytown, Pa.,
1,140...........*F2 81
McClain, co., Okla.,
12,740............C4 79
McCleary, Wash., 1,115..B2 86
MacClenny, Fla., 2,671..B4 54
MacClesfield, Eng.,
38,000...........D5 4
McCloud, Calif., 2,140...B2 50
McClure, Ohio, 651.....A2 78
McClure, Pa., 1,001....E7 81

McColl, S.C., 2,474.....B8 82
McComas, W. Va., 950...D3 87
McComb, Miss., 12,020..D3 68
McComb, Ohio, 1,176...A2 78
McCone, co., Mont.,
33,21............C11 70
McConnellsburg, Pa.,
1,245............G6 81
McConnelsville, Ohio,
2,257............C4 78
McCook, Nebr., 8,301...D5 71
McCook, Co., S. Dak.,
8,268............G8 77
McCormick, S.C.,
1,998............D3 82
McCormick, co., S.C.,
8,629............D3 82
McCracken, co., Ky.,
57,306............A2 62
McCreary, Man., Can.,
597.............D2 40

McCreary, co., Ky.,
12,463............D5 62
McCrory, Ark., 1,053...B4 49
McCulloch, co., Tex.,
8,815............D3 84
McCurtain, Okla., 528...B7 79
McCurtain, co., Okla.,
25,851............C7 79
McDermott, Ohio, 900...D2 78
McDonald, Ohio, 2,727..A5 78
McDonald, Pa., 3,141...k13 81
MacDonald, W. Va.,
300..........D3, D7 87
McDonald, co., Mo.,
11,798............E3 69
McDonough, Ga.,
2,224............C2 55
McDonough, co., Ill.,
28,928............C3 58
McDowell, co., N.C.,
26,742............f10 76

McDowell, co., W. Va., 71,359.............D3 87
McDuffie, co., Ga., 12,627...............C4 55
Macedon, N.Y., 963......B3 75
Macedonia, reg., Eur.....*B4 14
Macedonia, rep., Yugo., 1,406,003..........*D5 10
Maceío, Braz., 153,305...D7 27
Macerata, It., 24,800.....C4 9
McEwen, Tenn., 979.....A4 83
McFarland, Calif., 3,686..E4 50
McFarland, Wis., 1,272...E4 88
McGehee, Ark., 4,448....D4 49
McGill, Nev., 2,195......B4 72
MacGillicuddy's Reeks, mts., Ire................E2 4
McGrann, Pa., 800......*E2 81
McGraw, N.Y., 1,276.....C4 75
MacGregor, Man., Can., 642...................E2 40
McGregor, Iowa, 1,040...A6 60
McGregor, Tex., 4,642....D4 84
McGuffey, Ohio, 647.....B2 78
McGuire, mtn., Idaho....D4 57
Machado, Braz., 8,373..C3, k9 30
Machala, Ec., 29,036....B2 31
McHenry, Ill., 3,336...A5, h8 58
McHenry, co., Ill., 84,210................A5 58
McHenry, co., N. Dak., 11,099..............B5 77
Machias, Maine, 1,600, (2,614▲)............D5 64
Măcin, Rom., 6,533......C9 10
McIntoch, Minn., 785.....C3 67
McIntosh, co., Ga., 6,364..E5 55
McIntosh, co., N. Dak., 6,702................D6 77
McIntosh, co., Okla., 12,371...............B6 79
Mack, Ohio, 5,000......*D2 78
Mackay, Austl., 18,637...D8 25
Mackay, Idaho, 652.....F5 57
Mackayville, see Laflèche, Que., Can.
McKean, co., Pa., 54,517..C4 81
McKeesport, Pa., 45,489...........F4, r14 81
McKees Rocks, Pa., 13,185...........F1, k13 81
McKenney, Va., 519.....D5 85
McKenzie, Tenn., 3,780..A3 83
McKenzie, co., N. Dak., 7,296................C2 77
McKenzie, dist., N. W. Ter., Can., 14,895...............D11 36
Mackenzie, mts., Can.....C7 33
McKenzie, riv., N. W. Ter., Can........C8 36
Mackinac, co., Mich., 10,853...............B5 66
Mackinac Island, Mich., 942....................C6 66
Mackinaw, Ill., 1,163.....C4 58
Mackinaw City, Mich., 934....................C6 66
McKinley, Minn., 408.....C6 67
McKinley, co., N. Mex., 37,209...............B4 48
McKinley, mtn., Alsk....C9 47
McKinley Heights, Ohio, 1,500................*A5 78
McKinleyville, Calif., 5,000.................B1 50
McKinney, Tex., 13,763..C4 84
McKittrick Summit, mtn., Calif.................E4 50
Macklin, Sask., Can., 690...................E1 39
McKnight, Pa., 15,000...*E1 81
McKownville, N.Y., 2,000................*C7 75
McLaughlin, S. Dak., 983....................E5 77
McLean, Tex., 1,330.....B2 84
McLean, Va., 12,500....g12 85
McLean, co., Ill., 83,877...C5 58
McLean, co., Ky., 9,355..C2 62
McLean, co., N. Dak., 14,030...............C4 77
McLean, mtn., Maine.....A4 64
McLeansboro, Ill., 2,951..E5 58
McLennan, Alta., Can., 1,078................B2 38
McLennan, co., Tex., 150,091..............D4 84
McLeod, co., Minn., 24,401...............F4 67
McLeod Lake, B.C., Can., 123..............B6, n18 37
McLoud, Okla., 837.....B4 79
McLoughlin, mtn., Oreg...E4 80
McLouth, Kans., 494.............C8, k15 61
McMasterville, Que., Can., 2,075..........*D4 42

McMechen, W. Va., 2,999..........B2, B4 87
McMillan Manor, Calif., 1,193................*E4 50
McMinn, co., Tenn., 33,662..............D9 83
McMinnville, Oreg., 7,656............B3, h11 80
McMinnville, Tenn., 9,013................D8 83
McMullen, co., Tex., 1,116................E3 84
McMurray, Alta., Can., 1,186............A5, f8 38
McNair, Tex., 1,880.....E5 84
McNairy, co., Tenn., 18,085..............B3 83
McNary, Ariz., 1,608....A5 48
McNeill, mtn., B.C., Can..B2 37
Macomb, Ill., 16,094.....C3 58
Macomb, co., Mich., 405,804.............F8 66
Macon, Fr., 25,714......D6 5
Macon, Ga., 128,000 (*200,000)..........D3 55
Macon, Ill., 1,229.......D5 58
Macon, Miss., 2,432.....B5 68
Macon, Mo., 4,547......B5 69
Macon, co., Ga., 13,170..D2 55
Macon, co., Ill., 118,257..D5 58
Macon, co., Mo., 16,473..B5 69
Macon, co., N.C., 14,935...f9 76
Macon, co., Tenn., 12,197..C7 83
Macoupin, co., Ill., 43,524...............D4 58
McPherson, Kans., 9,996..D6 61
McPherson, co., Kans., 24,285...............D6 61
McPherson, co., Nebr., 735...................C4 71
McPherson, co., S. Dak., 5,821................E6 77
McRae, Ga., 2,738.....D4 55
McRoberts, Ky., 1,363...C7 62
McSherrystown, Pa., 2,839................G7 81
Macksville, Kans., 546....E5 61
MacTier, Ont., Can., 851..B5 41
Macungie, Pa., 1,266....E10 81
McVeigh, Ky., 800.......C7 62
Ma'dabā, Jordan, 11,224..C3 15
Madagascar, isl., Afr.....D8 24
Madawaska, Maine, 4,400 (5,507▲)..........A4 64
Madawaska, co., N.B., Can., 38,983..........B1 43
Madeira, Ohio, 6,744....o13 78
Madeira, riv., Braz......D4 27
Madeira Beach, Fla., 3,943................*E4 54
Madeira Is., reg., Port. 268,937.............B1 22
Madelia, Minn., 2,190....F4 67
Madera, Calif., 14,430....D3 50
Madera, Mex., 7,314.....B3 34
Madera, Pa., 900........E5 81
Madera, co., Calif., 40,468...............D4 50
Madhya Pradesh, state, India, 32,372,408.......D6 20
Madill, Okla., 3,084.....C5 79
Madīnat ash Sha'b, S. Yem................G4 15
Madison, Ala., 1,435.....A3 46
Madison, Ala., 900......C3 46
Madison, Conn., 1,500...D6 52
Madison, Fla., 3,239.....B3 54
Madison, Ga., 2,680.....C3 55
Madison, Ill., 6,861......C3 58
Madison, Ind., 10,488....G7 59
Madison, Kans., 1,105...D7 61
Madison, Maine, 2,800 (3,935▲)............D3 64
Madison, Minn., 2,380...E2 67
Madison, Mo., 528......B5 69
Madison, Nebr., 1,513...C8 71
Madison, N.J., 15,122....B4 74
Madison, N.C., 1,905....A3 76
Madison, Ohio, 1,347....A4 78
Madison, S. Dak., 5,420..G9 77
Madison, Tenn., 16,000............A5, E9 83
Madison, W. Va., 2,215.............C3, D5 87
Madison, Wis., 168,000 (*228,000)..........E4 88
Madison, co., Ala., 117,348.............A3 46
Madison, co., Ark., 9,068..B2 49
Madison, co., Fla., 14,154..B3 54
Madison, co., Ga., 11,246..B3 55
Madison, co., Idaho, 9,417..F7 57
Madison, co., Ill., 224,689..E4 58
Madison, co., Ind., 125,819.............D6 59
Madison, co., Iowa, 12,295...............C3 60
Madison, co., Ky., 33,482..C5 62

Madison, co., Miss., 32,904..............C4 68
Madison, co., Mo., 9,366..D7 69
Madison, co., Mont., 5211................E4 70
Madison, co., Nebr., 25,145..............C8 71
Madison, co., N.Y., 54,635..............C5 75
Madison, co., N.C., 17,217..............f10 76
Madison, co., Ohio, 26,454..............C2 78
Madison, co., Tenn., 60,655..............B3 83
Madison, co., Tex., 6,749..D5 84
Madison, co., Va., 8,187..B4 85
Madison, par., La., 16,444..B4 63
Madison Heights, Mich., 33,343.............*F7 66
Madison Heights, Va., 700...................C3 85
Madison Township, Pa., 1,491........F10, o19 81
Madisonville, Ky., 13,110..C2 62
Madisonville, La., 860.............D5, h11 63
Madisonville, Tenn., 1,812................D9 83
Madisonville, Tex., 2,324..D5 84
Madoc, Ont., Can., 1,347..C7 41
Madras, India, 1,729,141 (*2,000,000)........F7 20
Madras, Oreg., 1,515....C5 80
Madras, state, India, 33,686,953..........F6 20
Madre de Dios, dept, Peru, 25,269.............D3 31
Madrid, Iowa, 2,286..C4, e8 60
Madrid, N.Y., 700.......f9 75
Madrid, Sp., 2,259,931........B4, p17 8
Madrid, prov., Sp., 2,606,254..........*B4 8
Madridejos, Phil., 3,041...*C6 19
Madridejos, Sp., 9,795....C4 8
Madura, India, 424,810...G6 20
Maebashi, Jap., 198,745........H9, M18 18
Maeser, Utah, 929......A7 72
Mafeking, S. Afr., 8,362...F5 24
Mafra, Braz., 12,981....D3 30
Magadan, Sov. Un., 72,000..............D18 13
Magallanes, prov., Chile, 73,426......E2, h11 28
Magangué, Col., 27,354 (64,651▲)...........B3 32
Magdalena, Mex., 9,445...A2 34
Magdalena, N. Mex., 1,211................B5 48
Magdalena, dept., Col., 789,410.............A3 32
Magdalena, riv., Col.....C3 27
Magdalena Contreras, Mex., 12,516.........h9 34
Magdalen Islands, co., Que., Can., 12,479....B8 43
Magdeburg, Ger., 265,500..B5 6
Magé, Braz., 10,712.....h6 30
Magee, Miss., 2,039.....D4 68
Magelang, Indon., 91,636..G4 19
Magenta, It., 18,417.....B2 9
Maglie, It., 13,028......D7 9
Magna, Utah, 7,300...A5, C2 72
Magnitogorsk, Sov. Un., 348,000.............D8 13
Magnolia, Ark., 10,651...D2 49
Magnolia, Miss., 2,083...D3 68
Magnolia, N.J., 4,199....D2 74
Magnolia, N.C., 621.....C4 76
Magnolia, Ohio, 1,596...B4 78
Magoffin, co., Ky., 11,156..C6 62
Magog, Que., Can., 13,139..............D5 42
Magrath, Alta., Can., 1,338................E4 38
Magwe, Bur., 13,270....D9 20
Mahameru, mtn., Indon...G4 19
Mahanoy City, Pa., 8,536..E9 81
Maharashtra, state, India, 39,553,718..........D5 20
Mahaska, co., Iowa, 23,602..............C5 60
Mahbubnagar, India, 35,588..............E6 20
Mahdia, Tun., 10,880....A7 22
Mahe, India, 7,951......F6 20
Mahnomen, Minn., 1,462..C3 67
Mahnomen, co., Minn., 6,341................C2 67
Mahogany, mtn., Oreg...D9 80
Mahomet, Ill., 1,367....C5 58
Mahón, Sp., 16,619.....C8 8
Mahone Bay, N.S., Can., 1,103................E5 43
Mahoning, co., Ohio, 300,480.............B5 78

Mahopac, N.Y., 1,500............D7, m15 75
Mahtomedi, Minn., 2,127..E7 67
Mahwah, N.J., 4,500....A4 74
Maiden, N.C., 2,039....B1 76
Maidstone, Sask., Can., 577...................D1 39
Maidstone, Eng., 61,300..E7 4
Maiduguri, Nig., 139,965..F7 22
Maimana, Afg., 30,000...A3 20
Maine, former prov., Fr., 682,000.............C3 5
Maine, state, U.S., 969,265..............64
Maine-et-Loire, dept., Fr., 556,272............*D3 5
Maintirano, Malag., 3,100................D8 24
Main Topsail, mtn., Newf., Can..........D3 44
Mainz, Ger., 139,700....C4 6
Maipú, Arg., 5,469.....B5 28
Maiquetía, Ven., 75,687..A4 32
Maisonette, N.B., Can., 627...................B4 43
Maisons-Alfort, Fr., 51,186..............g10 5
Maisons-Laffitte, Fr., 19,132..............g9 5
Maitland, Austl., 28,424...F9 25
Maitland (Lake Maitland), Fla., 3,570..*D5 54
Maize, Kans., 623......g12 61
Maizuru, Jap., 78,000 (96,641▲)........I7, n14 18
Majagual, Col., 2,197....B3 32
Majestic, Ky., 503......C7 62
Major, co., Okla., 7,808..A3 79
Majunga, Malag., 34,119..D9 24
Makaha, Haw., 2,720....g9 56
Makarov Shirutoru, Sov. Un., 5,000....B11 18
Makarska, Yugo., 3,637..D3 10
Makasar (Macassar), Indon., 367,882......G5 19
Makawao, Haw., 977.....C5 56
Makaweli, Haw., 400....B2 56
Makeyevka, Sov. Un., 381,000........G11, q20 12
Makhachkala, Sov. Un., 140,000.............E7 13
Makhlata, Bul., 6,537....D7 10
Makri, India, 5,000......E7 20
Makurazaki, Jap., 18,200..K5 18
Makurdi, Nig., 16,713....G6 22
Malabar, Fla., 800......D6 54
Malacca, Mala., 69,848...E2 19
Malacca, state, Mala., 372,100.............E2 19
Malad City, Idaho, 2,274..G6 57
Málaga, Col., 9,674.....B3 32
Málaga, N.J., 800.......D2 74
Málaga, Sp., 301,048....D3 8
Málaga, prov., Sp., 775,167............*D3 8
Malagasy Republic, country, Afr., 618,000...E9 24
Malakal, Sud., 9,680....G4 23
Malakoff, Fr., 33,603....g10 5
Malakoff, Tex., 1,657....C4 84
Malang, Indon., 332,023..G4 19
Malange, Ang., 12,815...B3 24
Malartic, Que., Can., 6,998...............k11 42
Malatya, Tur., 83,692...C12 14
Malawi (Nyasaland), country, Afr., 3,753,000..C6 24
Malaya, reg., Mala., 7,810,100...........E2 19
Malaya Vishera, Sov. Un., 25,000.........B9 12
Malaybalay, Phil., 7,624..D7 19
Malaysia, country, Asia, 9,136,500..........E4 19
Malbork, Pol., 27,200....A5 7
Malchin, Ger., 6,825....B6 6
Malden, Mass., 57,676...........B5, g11 65
Malden, Mo., 5,007....E8 69
Malden, W. Va., 1,000...C6 87
Maldive Islands, country, Asia, 95,000.........G5 20
Maldonado, Ur., 12,100..E2 30
Maldonado, dept., Ur., 61,500............*E2 30
Maler-Kotla, India, 32,575..............B6 20
Malheur, co., Oreg., 22,764..............D9 80
Mali, country, Afr., 4,576,000...........F3 22
Malibu, Calif., 4,500....m11 50
Malin, Oreg., 568......E5 80
Malinec, Czech., 6,551...D5 7
Malita, Phil., 5,947.....*D7 19
Malkara, Tur., 9,364....B6 14
Mallawī, Eg., U.A.R., 43,200..............C4 23

Malleco, prov., Chile 174,205............B2 28
Mallory, W. Va., 800.....*D3 87
Mallow, Ire., 5,500.....D2 4
Malmédy, Bel., 6,355.....B7 5
Malmesbury, S. Afr., 8,267...............G3 24
Malmö, Swe., 237,500....J5 11
Malmöhus, co., Swe., 632,200...........*J5 11
Maloarkhangelsk, Sov. Un., 10,000...........E11 12
Malolos, Phil., 13,339....o13 19
Malone, Fla., 661.......B1 54
Malone, N.Y., 8,737.....f10 75
Maloyaroslavets, Sov. Un., 25,000...........D11 12
Malta, Mont., 2,239.......B9 70
Malta, Ohio, 983........C4 78
Malta, country, Eur., 326,000...............A7 22
Malton, Ont., Can., 2,148.............D5, m14 41
Malton, Eng., 4,200......C6 4
Malvern, Ark., 9,566.....C3 49
Malvern, Iowa, 1,193....D2 60
Malvern, Ohio, 1,320....B4 78
Malvern, Pa., 2,268..F10, o19 81
Malverne, N.Y., 9,899...*G2 52
Mamanguape, Braz., 8,512...............*D7 27
Mamaroneck, N.Y., 19,074...............h13 75
Mamba, Jap., 1,600......m17 18
Mamers, Fr., 4,869......C4 5
Mammoth, Ariz., 1,913...C3 48
Mammoth, W. Va., 800..............C3, C6 87
Mamou, Guinea, 9,000...F2 22
Mamou, La., 2,928......D3 63
Man, W. Va., 1,486...D3, D5 87
Man, Isle of, see Isle of Man, Br. dep., Eur.
Manabi, prov., Ec., 612,542...............B1 31
Manacor, Sp., 19,224....C7 8
Manado, Indon., 127,614..E6 19
Managua, Nic., 234,580...E7 34
Manahawkin, N.J., 800...D4 74
Manakara, Malag., 12,000...............E9 24
Manama, Bahrain, 55,541..D5 15
Mananjary, Malag., 15,600...............E9 24
Manasquan, N.J., 4,022...C4 74
Manassas, Va., 3,555..B5, g12 85
Manassas Park, Va., 5,342...............*B5 85
Manatee, co., Fla., 69,168..E4 54
Manatí, P.R., 9,682.....*G11 35
Manaus, Braz., 154,040..D4 27
Manawa, Wis., 1,037....D5 88
Mancelona, Mich., 1,141..D5 66
Mancha, reg., Sp........C4 8
Mancha Real, Sp., 7,855..D4 8
Manchaug, Mass., 900....B4 65
Manche, dept., Fr., 446,878...............*C3 5
Manchester, Conn., 42,102...............B6 52
Manchester, Eng., 654,700 (*2,850,000)....D5 4
Manchester, Ga., 4,115...D2 55
Manchester, Iowa, 4,611...B6 60
Manchester, Ky., 1,868...C6 62
Manchester, Md., 1,108...A4 53
Manchester, Mass., 3,932...........A6, f12 65
Manchester, Mich., 1,568..F6 66
Manchester, Mo., 2,021...f12 69
Manchester, N.H., 92,500, (*139,000)...........F5 73
Manchester, N.Y., 1,344...C3 75
Manchester, Ohio, 2,172...D2 78
Manchester, Pa., 1,454....F8 81
Manchester, Tenn., 3,930..B5 83
Manchester Depot, Vt., 620................E1 73
Manchouli Lupin, China, 25,000...............B8 17
Manchuria, reg., China..B10 17
Mandalay, Bur., 195,000..D10 20
Mandan, N. Dak., 10,525..D5 77
Mandarin, Fla., 900...B5, m8 54
Manderson, Wyo., 167....B5 89
Mandeville, Jam., 9,175...............E5 35
Mandeville, La., 1,740.............D5, h11 63
Mandsaur, India, 41,876..D6 20
Manduria, It., 22,500...D6 9
Mandvi, India, 29,305...D4 20
Manfalut, Eg., U.A.R., 23,900...............C4 23
Mangalore, India, 142,669...............F5 20
Mangham, La., 521......B4 63

Mangum, Okla., 3,950....C2 79
Manhasset, N.Y., 9,000...F2 52
Manhattan, Ill., 1,117....*B6 58
Manhattan, Kans., 22,993..C7 61
Manhattan, N.Y., 1,698,281...........*B5 75
Manhattan Beach, Calif., 34,513...............n12 50
Manheim, Pa., 4,790.....F9 81
Manhuaçu, Braz., 10,546..C4 30
Manila, Ark., 1,753......B5 49
Manila, Phil., 1,138,611..o13 19
Manilla, Iowa, 939......C2 60
Manisa, Tur., 59,675.....C6 14
Manistee, Mich., 8,324...D4 66
Manistee, co., Mich., 19,042...............D4 66
Manistique, Mich., 4,875..C4 66
Manito, Ill., 1,093......C4 58
Manitoba, prov., Can., 921,686..............40
Manitoba, lake, Man., Can..............D2 40
Manitou, Man., Can., 863................E2 40
Manitou Beach, Mich., 1,800...............*G6 66
Manitoulin, dist., Ont., Can., 11,176........B2 41
Manitou Springs, Colo., 3,626...............C6 51
Manitowoc, Wis., 33,215...........D6, h10 88
Manitowoc, co., Wis., 75,215...............D6 88
Maniwaki, Que., Can., 6,349................C2 42
Manizales, Col., 221,916..B2 32
Mankato, Kans., 1,231...C5 61
Mankato, Minn., 28,454..F5 67
Manlius, N.Y., 2,781....C5 75
Manlléu, Sp., 9,410.....A7 8
Manly, Iowa, 1,425......A4 60
Mannar, Cey., 5,190.....G6 20
Mannheim, Ger., 321,100..D4 6
Manning, Alta., Can., 896................A2 38
Manning, Iowa, 1,676....C2 60
Manning, S.C., 3,917....D7 82
Mannington, W. Va., 2,996............A6, B4 87
Mannville, Alta., Can., 632................C5 38
Manomet, Mass., 500....C6 65
Manomet, hill, Mass....C6 65
Manono, Con., K., 19,500..B5 24
Manor, Pa., 1,136......*F2 81
Manorhaven, N.Y., 3,566...............*E7 75
Manosque, Fr., 7,454....F6 5
Manresa, Sp., 52,216....B6 8
Manseau, Que., Can., 837................C5 42
Mansfield, Eng., 54,100 (*190,000)..........D6 4
Mansfield, Ill., 843......C5 58
Mansfield, La., 5,839....B2 63
Mansfield, Mass., 5,000 (7,773▲).............B5 65
Mansfield, Mo., 949.....D5 69
Mansfield, Ohio, 47,325..B3 78
Mansfield, Pa., 2,678....C7 81
Mansfield, Tex., 1,375...n9 84
Mansfield, mtn., Vt......B2 73
Mansfield Southeast, Ohio, 2,961.........*B3 78
Manson, Iowa, 2,052.....B3 60
Mansura, La., 1,579.....C3 63
Manta, Ec., 33,622......B1 31
Manteca, Calif., 11,208..D3 50
Manteno, Ill., 2,225.....B6 58
Mantes [la-Jolie], Fr., 18,902...............C4 5
Manti, Utah, 1,739......B6 72
Manton, Mich., 1,050....D5 66
Mantova, It., 63,700.....B9 9
Mantua, N.J., 2,000.....D2 74
Mantua, Ohio, 1,194.....A4 78
Manuel Benavides, Mex., 902................B4 34
Manuels, Newf., Can., 724................*E5 44
Manville, N.J., 10,995...B3 74
Manville, R.I., 3,500....B11 52
Many, La., 3,164.......C2 63
Manzanares, Sp., 17,847..C4 8
Manzanillo, Cuba, 51,900..D5 35
Manzanillo, Mex., 19,950.............D4, n11 34
Mapastepec, Mex., 4,664................D6 34
Maple, Ont., Can., 1,552................k14 41
Maple Bluff, Wis., 1,565..E4 88
Maple Creek, Sask., Can., 2,291................H1 39
Maple Heights, Ohio, 31,667................h9 78

Maple Lake, Minn., 1,018..E4 67
Maple Lane, Ind., 1,350..*A5 59
Maple Mount, Ky., 500...C2 62
Maple Plain, Minn., 754................m11 67
Maple Rapids, Mich., 683................E6 66
Maple Shade, N.J., 12,947...............D2 74
Mapleton, Iowa, 1,686...B2 60
Mapleton, Maine, 500 (1,514▲)............B4 64
Mapleton, Minn., 1,107...G5 67
Mapleton, Oreg., 700....C3 80
Mapleton, Utah, 1,516...D2 72
Maplewood, La., 2,432...D2 63
Maplewood, Minn., 21,438...............m12 67
Maplewood, Mo., 12,552..f13 69
Maplewood, N.J., 23,977..B4 74
Maplewood, N.Y., 650...*C7 75
Maplewood Park, Pa., 1,800...............*G11 81
Maquoketa, Iowa, 5,909..B7 60
Marabá, Braz., 8,533....D6 27
Maracaibo, Ven., 502,700..A3 32
Maracju, Braz., 1,848....F5 27
Maracay, Ven., 153,700..A4 32
Maradi, Niger, 10,100...F6 22
Maragogipe, Braz., 12,575...............*E7 27
Marana, Ariz., 500......C3 48
Maranguape, Braz., 8,715...............*D7 27
Maranhão, state, Braz., 2,492,139...........*D6 27
Marañón, riv., Peru......B2 31
Maraş (Marash), Tur., 54,447...............D11 14
Marathon, Ont., Can., 2,568................o18 41
Marathon, Fla., 3,097....H5 54
Marathon, Iowa, 516....B3 60
Marathon, N.Y., 1,079...C4 75
Marathon, Tex., 800..D1, o13 84
Marathon, Wis., 1,022...D4 88
Marathon, co., Wis., 88,874...............D4 88
Maravatío de Ocampo, Mex., 5,388.........n13 34
Mara Vista, Mass., 800...C6 65
Marbella, Sp., 8,982....D3 8
Marble, Minn., 879......C5 67
Marble Cliff, Ohio, 622..m10 78
Marble Falls, Tex., 2,161..D3 84
Marblehead, Mass., 18,521............B6, f12 65
Marblehead, Ohio, 858...A3 78
Marbleton, Que., Can., 661................D6 42
Marburg, Ger., 47,600...C4 6
Marbury, Md., 500......C3 53
Marceline, Mo., 2,872...B5 69
Marcellus, Mich., 1,073..F5 66
Marcellus, N.Y., 1,697...C4 75
Marche, former prov., Fr., 222,000...........D4 5
Marche, pol. dist., It., 1,347,489...........*C4 9
Marchena, Sp., 17,030...D3 8
Marches, reg., It........C4 9
Marcola, Oreg., 500....C4 80
Marcos Juarez, Arg., 12,955...............A4 28
Marcus, Iowa, 1,307....B2 60
Marcus Hook, Pa., 3,299.G11 81
Marcy, mtn., N.Y........A7 75
Mardan, Pak., 73,246...B5 20
Mar Del Plata, Arg., 203,093...............B5 28
Mardin, Tur., 28,382....D3 14
Marechal Deodoro, Braz., 5,269...............*D7 27
Marengo, Ill., 3,568....A5 58
Marengo, Ind., 803......H5 59
Marengo, Iowa, 2,264....C5 60
Marengo, co., Ala., 27,098...............C2 46
Marenisco, Mich., 700...n12 66
Marfa, Tex., 2,799.....o12 84
Margão, India, 17,175...E5 20
Margaret, Ala., 715.....B3 46
Margaretville, N.Y., 833..C6 75
Margate, Eng., 45,400...E7 4
Margate, Fla., 2,646....*F6 54
Margate City, N.J., 9,474..E3 74
Margelan, Sov. Un., 80,000...............E10 13
Margherita, mtn., Con. K., Ug................H3 23
Maria la Baja, Col., 5,739................A2 32
Mariana, is., Pac. O.....E6 2
Marianao, Cuba, 454,700...............D2 35
Marianna, Ark., 5,134...C5 49
Marianna, Fla., 7,152....B1 54
Marianna, Pa., 1,088...*F1 81

Marianske Lazne, Czech. 12,600...............D2 7
Maribo, co., Den., 131,699...............*J4 11
Maribor, Yugo., 82,387...B2 10
Maricopa, Calif., 754....E4 50
Maricopa, co., Ariz., 663,510...............C2 48
Mariemont, Ohio, 4,120..o13 78
Marienville, Pa., 800....D3 81
Maries, co., Mo., 7,282..C6 69
Mariestad, Swe., 11,900..H5 11
Marietta, Fla., 2,000....m8 54
Marietta, Ga., 25,565..A5, c2 55
Marietta, Ohio, 16,847...C4 78
Marietta, Okla., 1,933...D4 79
Marietta, Pa., 2,385.....F8 81
Marietta, S.C., 900.....A2 82
Marietta East, Ga., 4,535...............*A5 55
Marieville, Que., Can., 3,809...............D4 42
Marília, Braz., 51,789....C3 30
Marín, Sp., 7,261......A1 8
Marin, co., Calif., 146,820..C2 50
Marin City, Calif., 2,500..*C2 50
Marinduque, prov., Phil., 114,586...........*C6 19
Marine, Ill., 813.......E4 58
Marine City, Mich., 4,404.F8 66
Marinette, Wis., 13,329..C6 88
Marinette, co., Wis., 34,660...............C5 88
Maringouin, La., 1,168...D4 63
Marinha Grande, Port., 4,698................C1 8
Marino, It., 9,700.......H9 9
Marion, Ala., 3,807.....C2 46
Marion, Ill., 11,274.....F5 58
Marion, Ind., 37,854....C6 59
Marion, Iowa, 15,267...B6 60
Marion, Kans., 2,169....D6 61
Marion, Ky., 2,468......A3 62
Marion, La., 685.......B3 63
Marion, Mass., 1,300 (2,881▲)............C6 65
Marion, Mich., 898.....D5 66
Marion, N.Y., 850......B3 75
Marion, N.C., 3,345..B1, f10 76
Marion, Ohio, 37,079...B2 78
Marion, S.C., 7,174....C9 82
Marion, Va., 8,385.....f10 85
Marion, Wis., 1,200....D5 88
Marion, co., Ala., 21,837..A2 46
Marion, co., Ark., 6,041..A3 49
Marion, co., Fla., 51,616..C4 54
Marion, co., Ga., 5,477..D2 55
Marion, co., Ill., 39,349..E5 58
Marion, co., Ind., 697,567..E5 59
Marion, co., Iowa, 25,886..C4 60
Marion, co., Kans., 15,143...............D6 61
Marion, co., Ky., 16,887..C4 62
Marion, co., Miss., 23,293..D4 68
Marion, co., Mo., 29,522..B6 69
Marion, co., Ohio, 60,221..B2 78
Marion, co., Oreg., 120,888...............C4 80
Marion, co., S.C., 32,014..C9 82
Marion, co., Tenn., 21,036...............D8 83
Marion, co., Tex., 8,049..C5 84
Marion, co., W. Va., 63,717...............B4 87
Marionville, Mo., 1,251..D4 69
Mariposa, Calif., 700....D4 50
Mariposa, co., Calif., 5,064................D3 50
Marissa, Ill., 1,722.....E4 58
Maris Town, Miss., 500...C3 68
Mariupol see Zandanov, Sov. Un.
Markdale, Ont., Can., 1,090................C4 41
Marked Tree, Ark., 3,216..B5 49
Markesan, Wis., 1,060...E5 88
Markham, Ont., Can., 4,294.............D5, k15 41
Markham, Ill., 14,595...k9 58
Markham, mtn., Ant.....L7 2
Markle, Ind., 789.......C7 59
Markovka, Sov. Un., 5,000................G12 12
Marks, Miss., 2,572.....A3 68
Marksville, La., 4,257...C3 63
Marktredwitz, Ger., 15,500...............C6 6
Marlbank, Ont., Can., 237................C7 41
Marlboro, Mass., 18,819............B4, g9 65
Marlboro, N.H., 1,097...F3 73
Marlboro, N.J., 600....C4 74
Marlboro, N.Y., 1,733...D6 75
Marlboro, co., S.C., 28,529...............B8 82
Marlene Village, Oreg., 1,100...............*B3 80

Marlette, Mich., 1,640.....E7 66
Marley, Md., 2,000......B4 53
Marlin, Tex., 6,918......D4 84
Marlinton, W. Va., 1,586..C4 87
Marlow, Okla., 4,027.....C4 79
Marlowe, W. Va., 700....B7 87
Marlton, N.J., 3,000.....D3 74
Marmande, Fr., 10,199...E4 5
Marmet, W. Va.,
  2,500............C3, C6 87
Marmora, Ont., Can.,
  1,381..............C7 41
Marmora, N.J., 500......E3 74
Marmora, peak, It.......D2 9
Marne, Mich., 500......E5 66
Marne, dept., Fr.,
  442,195.........*C6 5
Maroa, Ill., 1,235......C5 58
Maroantsetra, Malag.,
  5,300............D9 24
Maromokotro, mtn.,
  Malag.............C9 24
Maroua, Cam.........F7 22
Marovoay, Malag.,
  14,000............D9 24
Marquesas, Is.,
  Fr. Polynesia........G11 2
Marquês de Valença,
  Braz., 18,935.......C4, h6 30
Marquette, Kans., 607....D6 61
Marquette, Mich., 19,824..B3 66
Marquette, co., Mich.,
  56,154............B3 66
Marquette, co., Wis.,
  8,516............E4 88
Marquette Heights, Ill.,
  2,517............C4 58
Marrakech, Mor., 243,134..B3 22
Marrero, La., 21,500....k11 63
Marromeu, Moz.........D7 24
Mars, Pa., 1,522......E1 81
Mars, hill, Maine......g7 64
Marsala, It., 39,600....F4 9
Marseille, Fr.,
  778,071............F6 5
Marseilles, Ill., 4,340....B5 58
Marshall, Ark., 1,095....B3 49
Marshall, Ill., 3,270......D6 58
Marshall, Mich., 6,736....F6 66
Marshall, Minn., 7,363....F3 67
Marshall, Mo., 9,572....B4 69
Marshall, N.C., 926.....F10 76
Marshall, Tex., 23,846....C5 84
Marshall, Va., 500......B5 85
Marshall, Wis., 736......E4 88
Marshall, co., Ala., 48,018..A3 46
Marshall, co., Ill., 13,334..B4 58
Marshall, co., Ind., 32,443..B5 59
Marshall, co., Iowa,
  37,984............C4 60
Marshall, co., Kans.,
  15,598............C7 61
Marshall, co., Ky., 16,736..A3 62
Marshall, co., Minn.,
  14,262............B2 67
Marshall, co., Miss.,
  24,503............A4 68
Marshall, co., Okla.,
  7,263............C5 79
Marshall co., S. Dak.,
  6,663............E8 77
Marshall, co., Tenn.,
  16,859............B5 83
Marshall, co., W. Va.,
  38,041............B4 87
Marshallberg, N.C., 600...C6 76
Marshall Northeast, Tex.,
  1,192............*C5 84
Marshallton, Del., 3,000...A6 35
Marshallton, Pa., 2,316...*D8 81
Marshalltown, Iowa,
  22,521............B5 60
Marshallville, Ga., 1,308...D3 55
Marshallville, Ohio, 611..B4 78
Marshfield, Mass.,
  1,500 (6,748▲).....B6, h13 65
Marshfield, Mo., 2,221...D5 69
Marshfield, Wis., 14,153..D3 88
Marshfield Hills, Mass.,
  900............B6, h13 65
Mars Hill, Ind.,
  5,600............E5, m10 59
Mars Hill, Maine, 1,458
  (2,062▲)............B5 64
Mars Hill, N.C., 1,574...f10 76
Marshville, N.C., 1,322...C2 76
Marsing, Idaho, 555......F2 57
Marston, Mo., 631......E8 69
Mart, Tex., 2,197......D4 84
Martel, Que., Can.,
  1,009............A6 42
Martí, Cuba, 652........D5 35
Martigues, Fr., 9,852....F6 5
Martin, Ky., 992........C7 62
Martin, Mich., 483......F5 66
Martin, S. Dak., 1,184...G4 77
Martin, Tenn., 4,750....A3 83
Martin, co., Fla., 16,932..E6 54

Martin, co., Ind., 10,608...G4 59
Martin, co., Ky., 10,201...C7 62
Martin, co., Minn.,
  26,986............G4 67
Martin, co., N.C., 25,611..B5 76
Martin, co., Tex., 5,068..C2 84
Martina [Franca], It.,
  25,500............D6 9
Martinez, Calif.,
  9,604............C2, h8 50
Martinez, Ga., 950......*C4 55
Martinique, Fr. dep.,
  N.A., 292,062.......I14 35
Martinsburg, Pa., 1,772...F5 81
Martinsburg, W. Va.,
  15,179............B6 87
Martins Creek, Pa., 900...B2 81
Martins Ferry, Ohio,
  11,919............B5 78
Martinsville, Ill., 1,351...D6 58
Martinsville, Ind., 7,525...F5 59
Martinsville, N.J., 800...B3 74
Martinsville
  (Independent City), Va.,
  18,798............D3 85
Martos, Sp., 16,900.....D4 8
Marudi, Mala., 2,663....E5 19
Maruf, Afg., 5,000......B4 20
Marugame, Jap., 44,000
  (58,826▲)..........I6 18
Marvell, Ark., 1,690.....C5 49
Mary, Sov. Un., 54,000...F9 13
Maryborough, Austl.,
  19,647............E9 25
Maryborough, Austl.,
  7,694............G7 25
Maryfield, Sask., Can.,
  476............H5 39
Maryland, state, U.S.,
  3,100,689..........53
Maryland Heights, Mo.,
  6,000............f13 69
Maryport, Eng., 12,300...C5 4
Marys, peak, Oreg......C3 80
Mary's Harbour, Newf.,
  Can., 264..........B4 44
Marystown, Newf., Can.,
  1,691............E4 44
Marysville, Calif., 9,553...C3 50
Marysville, B.C., Can.,
  1,057............E10 37
Marysville, N. B., Can.,
  3,233............D3 43
Marysville, Kans., 4,143...C7 61
Marysville, Mich., 4,065...F8 66
Marysville, Ohio, 4,952...B2 78
Marysville, Pa., 2,580....F8 81
Marysville, Wash., 3,117..A3 86
Maryvale, Ariz., 2,000....*C2 48
Maryville, Mo., 7,807....A3 69
Maryville, Tenn.,
  10,348..........D10, E11 83
Masan, Kor., 158,600.....I4 18
Masaya, Nic., 24,302.....E7 34
Masbate, Phil., 17,574....C6 19
Masbate, prov., Phil.,
  335,971............*H7 19
Mascara, Alg., 46,209....A5 22
Mascot, Tenn., 950..C10, E12 83
Mascota, Mex., 5,267....m11 34
Mascouche, Que., Can.,
  1,152............D4 42
Mascoutah, Ill., 4,664....E4 58
Mashhad Meshed, Iran,
  241,989............B6 15
Masindi, Ug., 5,000.....H4 23
Masisea, Peru, 1,742....C3 31
Maskinongé, Que., Can.,
  893............C4 42
Maskinonge, co., Que.,
  Can., 21,274........C4 42
Mason, Mich., 4,522.....F6 66
Mason, Ohio 4,727...C1, n13 78
Mason, Tex., 1,910......D3 84
Mason, W. Va., 1,005....B2 87
Mason, co., Ill., 15,193...C4 58
Mason, co., Ky., 18,454..B6 62
Mason, co., Mich., 21,929..D4 66
Mason, co., Tex., 3,780...D3 84
Mason, co., Wash., 16,251..B2 86
Mason, co., W. Va.,
  24,459............C3 87
Mason City, Ill., 2,160...C4 58
Mason City, Iowa, 30,711..A4 60
Masontown, Pa., 4,730...G2 81
Masontown, W. Va., 841..B5 87
Mass, Mich., 500....B1, m12 66
Massa, It., 59,200......B3 9
Massac, co., Ill., 14,341..F5 58
Massachusetts, state, U.S.,
  5,148,578..........65
Massaemett, mtn., Mass...A2 65
Massafra, It., 20,005....D6 9
Massa Marittima, It.,
  5,700............C3 9
Massanutten, mtn., Va....B4 85
Massapequa, N.Y.,
  36,000............G3 52

Massapequa Park, N.Y.,
  19,904............*E7 75
Massaua, Eth., 25,000....E5 23
Massena, N.Y., 15,478....f10 75
Masset, B.C., Can., 547...C1 37
Massey, Ont., Can., 1,324..A2 41
Massillon, Ohio, 31,326...B4 78
Massive, mtn., Colo......B4 51
Masson, Que., Can.,
  1,933............D2 42
Masterton, N.Z., 15,128..N15 26
Mastic, N.Y., 3,000......*n15 75
Mastic Beach, N.Y.,
  4,000............*F4 52
Mastung, Pak., 2,792.....C4 20
Masuda, Jap., 30,500
  (52,729▲)..........I5 18
Masulipatnam, India,
  101,417............E7 20
Masuria, reg., Pol.......B6 7
Masury, Ohio, 6,200.....A5 78
Matachewan, Ont., Can.,
  923............p19 41
Matadi, Con. K., 59,000...B2 24
Matagalpa, Nic., 15,030...E7 34
Matagorda, co., Tex.,
  25,744............E5 84
Matamoras, Pa., 2,087...D12 81
Matamoros, Mex., 92,327..B5 34
Matamoros [de la Laguna],
  Mex., 13,770........B4 34
Matane, Que., Can.,
  9,190............G20 36
Matane, co., Que., Can.,
  35,078............*G20 36
Matanzas, Cuba, 80,300...C3 35
Matanzas, prov., Cuba,
  395,780............C3 35
Matapedia, co., Que.,
  Can., 35,586.......*G20 36
Matara, Cey., 27,735.....G7 20
Mataram, Indon........G5 19
Mataró, Sp., 41,128.....B7 8
Matawan, N.J., 5,097....C4 74
Matehuala, Mex.,
  19,927............C4 34
Matera, It., 39,900......D6 9
Mateszalka, Hung.,
  11,249............B6 10
Mateur, Tun., 12,714.....F2 9
Matewan, W. Va., 896...D2 87
Matfield, Mass., 900.....B6 65
Mather, Pa., 1,033......G1 81
Mather, peak, Wyo......B5 89
Mathews, co., Va., 7,121..C6 85
Mathis, Tex., 6,075.....E4 84
Mathura, India, 116,959..C6 20
Matoaca, Va., 1,200.....n18 85
Matoaka, W. Va., 613....D3 87
Mato Grosso, state, Braz.,
  910,262............B1 30
Matozinhos, Port., 37,694..B1 8
Matrah, Mus. & Om.,
  14,000............E6 15
Matruh, Eg., U.A.R.,
  3,047............B3 23
Matsudo, Jap., 160,001..*I9 18
Matsue, Jap., 110,534....I6 18
Matsuida, Jap., 7,700....m17 18
Matsumae, Jap., 19,111..F10 18
Matsumoto, Jap.,
  154,131............H9, m16 18
Matsuyama, Jap., 282,651..J6 18
Matsuzaka, Jap.,
  63,000 (99,814▲)...I8, o15 18
Matsuzaki, Jap., 4,700....o17 18
Mattancheri, India,
  83,896............G6 20
Mattapoisett, Mass.,
  1,800 (3,117▲).......C6 65
Mattawa, Ont., Can.,
  3,314............A6, p20 41
Mattawamkeag, Maine,
  700 (945▲)........C4 64
Matterhorn, mtn., Switz...E3 6
Matteson, Ill., 3,898.....k9 58
Matthews, Ind., 627.....D7 59
Matthews, N.C., 609.....B2 76
Matthews, mtn., Mo......D7 69
Matthew Town, Ba. Is.,
  995............D7 35
Mattituck, N.Y., 1,500...n16 75
Mattoon, Ill., 19,088.....D5 58
Mattydale, N.Y., 10,500..*B4 75
Matucana, Peru, 1,746...D2 31
Matun, Afg., 5,000......B4 20
Maturín, Ven., 54,362....B5 32
Maubeuge, Fr., 27,214...B5 5
Maubin, Bur., 22,130....*E10 20
Mauch Chunk, see
  Jim Thorpe, Pa.
Maud, Ohio, 600....C1, n13 78
Maud, Okla., 1,137......B5 79
Maud, Tex., 951........C5 84
Maugansville, Md., 900...A2 53
Maugerville, N.B., Can.,
  631............D3 43

Maui (incl. Kalawao), co.,
  Haw., 42,855........B4 56
Maui, isl., Haw.........C6 56
Mauldin, S.C., 1,462....*B3 82
Maule, prov., Chile,
  79,763............B2 28
Maumee, Ohio,
  12,063............A2, e6 78
Mauna Kea, vol., Haw....D6 56
Maunaloa, Haw., 789....B4 56
Mauna Loa, vol., Haw....D6 56
Mauritania, country, Afr.,
  1,070,000..........E2 22
Mauritius, country, Afr.,
  752,000............*H24 2
Maury, co., Tenn.,
  41,699............B4 83
Mauston, Wis., 3,531....E3 88
Maverick, co., Tex.,
  14,508............E2 84
Maxcanú, Mex., 5,139...C7 34
Max Meadows, Va., 900..D2 85
Maxton, N.C., 1,755....C3 76
Maxville, Ont., Can.,
  804............B10 41
Maxwell, Iowa, 773...C4, e9 60
May, mtn., Alta., Can....B1 38
Mayagüez, Dom. Rep.,
  50,147............G11 35
Mayari, Cuba, 7,400.....D6 35
Maybee, Mich., 459.....F7 66
Maybeury, W. Va., 900...D3 87
Maybole, Scot., 4,600....C4 4
Maybrook, N.Y., 1,442...D6 75
Mayen, Ger., 17,300.....C3 6
Mayenne, Fr., 10,270....C3 5
Mayenne, dept., Fr.,
  250,030............*C3 5
Mayer, Ariz., 300......B2 48
Mayerthorpe, Alta., Can.,
  663............C3 38
Mayes, co., Okla., 20,073..A6 79
Mayesville, S.C., 750....D7 82
Mayfield, Ky., 10,762....B2 62
Mayfield, N.Y., 818.....B6 75
Mayfield, Ohio, 1,977....*A4 78
Mayfield, Pa., 1,996.....C11 81
Mayfield Heights, Ohio,
  13,478............A4 78
Mayking, Ky., 750......C7 62
Maykop, Sov. Un.,
  95,000............*E7 13
Maymyo, Bur., 22,287...D10 20
Maynard, Iowa, 515.....B6 60
Maynard, Mass.,
  7,695............B5, g10 65
Mayo, Yukon, Can., 342..D6 36
Mayo, Fla., 687........B3 54
Mayo, Md., 500........C4 53
Mayo, S.C., 500........A4 82
Mayo, co., Ire., 115,600..*D2 4
Mayodan, N.C., 2,259...A3 76
Mayon, vol., Phil.......C6 19
May Pen, Jam., 14,214...F5 35
Mayport, Fla., 450.....B5, m9 54
Mays Landing, N.J.,
  1,500............E3 74
Maysville, Ky., 8,484....B6 62
Maysville, Mo., 942.....B3 69
Maysville, N.C., 851....C5 76
Maysville, Okla., 1,530...C4 79
Mayville, Mich., 896....E7 66
Mayville, N.J., 550.....E3 74
Mayville, N.Y., 1,619....C1 75
Mayville, N. Dak., 2,168..C8 77
Mayville, Wis., 3,607....E5 88
Maywood, Calif., 14,588..*F4 50
Maywood, Ill., 28,805...k9 58
Maywood, N.J., 11,460...h8 74
Maywood, N.Y., 3,000...*C7 75
Mazamet, Fr., 14,863....F5 5
Mazapil, Mex., 2,437....C4 34
Mazara Del Vallo, It.,
  36,827............F4 9
Mazar-I-Sharif, Afg.,
  70,000............A4 20
Mazarrón, Sp., 11,569...D5 8
Mazatenango, Guat.,
  11,067............E6 34
Mazatlán, Mex., 75,751...C3 34
Mazomanie, Wis., 1,069..E4 88
Mazon, Ill., 683........B5 58
Mazzarino, It., 17,789...F5 9
Mbalmayo, Cam........H7 22
Mbandaka
  (Coquilhatville), Con.
  K., 37,500.........H1 23
Mbeya, Tan., 6,932.....B6 24
Mead, Wash., 800...B8, g14 86
Meade, Kans., 2,019....E3 61
Meade, co., Kans., 5,505..E3 61
Meade, co., Ky., 18,938...C3 62
Meade, co., S. Dak.,
  12,044............F3 77
Meade, peak, Idaho.....G7 57
Meaderville, Mont., 600..*D4 70
Meadowbrook, Ind.,
  2,300............*B7 59

Meadowbrook, W. Va., 200.....A7 87
Meadow Lake, Sask., Can., 2,803.....n7 39
Meadow Lands, Pa., 1,967.....F1 81
Meadow Park, Fla., 3,500..F6 54
Meadowview, Va., 750....f10 85
Meadville, Pa., 16,671....C1 81
Meaford, Ont., Can., 3,834.....C4 41
Meagher, co., Mont., 2,616.....D6 70
Meath, co., Ire., 67,300...*D3 4
Meaux, Fr., 22,251.....C5 5
Mebane, N.C., 2,364.....A3 76
Mecca, Ind., 500.....E3 59
Mecca Makkah, Sau. Ar., 158,900.....E2 15
Mechanic Falls, Maine, 2,195.....D2 64
Mechanicsburg, Ohio, 1,810.....B2 78
Mechanicsburg, Pa., 8,123..F7 81
Mechanicsville, Iowa, 1,010.....C6 60
Mechanicsville, Va., 1,500..C5 85
Mechanicville, N.Y., 6,831.....C7 75
Mechelen, Bel., 64,772...B6 5
Mecklenburg, co., N.C., 272,111.....B2 76
Mecklenburg, co., Va., 31,428.....D4 85
Mecklenburg, state, Ger., 2,139,640.....*B6 6
Mecosta, co., Mich., 21,051.....E5 66
Medan, Indon., 466,370.....E1, m11 19
Medaryville, Ind., 758....B4 59
Medéa, Alg., 14,194.....A5 22
Medellín, Col., 772,887 (*1,025,000).....B2 32
Medfield, Mass., 2,900 (6,021▲).....h10 65
Medford, Mass., 64,971.....B5, g11 65
Medford, N.J., 1,600.....D3 74
Medford, Okla., 1,223.....A4 79
Medford, Oreg., 24,425...E4 80
Medford, Wis., 3,260.....C3 88
Medford Lakes, N.J., 2,876.....D3 74
Medgidia, Rom., 17,943...C9 10
Media, Pa., 5,803...G11, p20 81
Mediapolis, Iowa, 1,040..C6 60
Mediaş, Rom., 32,503.....B7 10
Medical Lake, Wash., 4,765.....B8, g13 86
Medicine Bow, peak, Wyo..E6 89
Medicine Hat, Alta., Can., 24,484.....D5, g8 38
Medicine Lodge, Kans., 3,072.....E5 61
Medicine Park, Okla., 600..C3 79
Medina, N.Y., 6,681.....B2 75
Medina, Ohio, 8,235.....A4 78
Medina, Wash., 2,285....e11 86
Medina, co., Ohio, 65,315..A4 78
Medina, co., Tex., 18,904..E3 84
Medina del Campo, Sp., 14,327.....B3 8
Medina Sidonia, Sp., 8,704.....D3 8
Mediterranean, sea.....D21 2
Medora, Ind., 716.....G5 59
Medvezhegorsk, Sov. Un., 19,200.....F16 11
Medway, Mass., 1,800 (5,168▲)..B5, h10 65
Medzhibozh, Sov. Un., 10,000.....G6 12
Meekatharra, Austl., 640...E2 25
Meeker, Colo., 1,655.....A3 51
Meeker, Okla., 664.....B5 79
Meeker, co., Minn., 18,887.....E4 67
Meerane, Ger., 24,500....C6 6
Meerut, India, 200,470, (*283,997).....C6 20
Mégantic, co., Que., Can., 57,400.....C6 42
Megantic, mtn., Que., Can.....D6 42
Megara, Grc., 15,450....C4 14
Meggett, S.C., 188...F7, k11 82
Megunticook, mtn., Maine.....D3 64
Mehun-sur-Yèvre, Fr., 4,735.....D5 5
Meigs, Ga., 1,236.....E2 55
Meigs, co., Ohio, 22,159...C3 78
Meigs, co., Tenn., 5,160...D9 83
Meihsien, China, 85,000...G8 17
Meiktila, Bur., 25,180...D10 20
Meiners Oaks, Calif., 3,513.....*E4 50

Meiningen, Ger., 23,700...C5 6
Meissen, Ger., 47,800.....C6 6
Mejillones, Chile, 3,363...F3 27
Meknès, Mor., 175,943...B3 22
Mekong, riv., Asia.....B2 19
Melbourne, Austl., 75,709 (*2,228,511).....G8, n15 25
Melbourne, Fla., 11,982...D6 54
Melbourne, Iowa, 517.....C4 60
Melbourne Beach, Fla., 1,004.....D6 54
Melcher, Iowa, 867.....C4 60
Melfi, It., 18,208.....D5 9
Melfort, Sask., Can., 4,039.....E3 39
Melilla, Sp. dep., Afr., 79,056.....A4 22
Melipilla, Chile, 15,600...A2 28
Melita, Man., Can., 1,038.....E1 40
Melito di Porto Salvo, It., 8,880.....F5 9
Melitopol, Sov. Un., 104,000.....H10 12
Mellen, Wis., 1,182.....B3 88
Mellette, co., S. Dak., 2,664.....G5 77
Melnik, Czech., 13,100...n18 7
Melo, Ur., 33,741.....E2 30
Melocheville, Que., Can., 1,666.....q19 42
Melouprey, Camb., 10,000.....*C3 19
Melrose, Fla., 800.....C4 54
Melrose, Mass., 29,619.....B5, g11 65
Melrose, Minn., 2,135....E4 67
Melrose, N. Mex., 698....B7 48
Melrose, Wis., 516.....D3 88
Melrose Park, Fla., 4,000..*F6 54
Melrose Park, Ill., 22,291..F2 58
Melrose Park, N.Y., 2,058.....*C4 75
Melrose Park, Pa., 6,000.....*F11 81
Melun, Fr., 26,873.....C5 5
Melville, Sask., Can., 5,191.....G4 39
Melville, La., 1,939.....D4 63
Melville, isl., N.W. Ter., Can.....A11 36
Melvin, Ky., 750.....C7 62
Melvindale, Mich., 13,089.....*F7 66
Memel, see Klaipeda, Sov. Un.
Memmingen, Ger., 29,800..E5 6
Memphis, Fla., 2,647.....p10 54
Memphis, Mich., 996.....F8 66
Memphis, Mo., 2,106.....A5 69
Memphis, Tenn., 542,000, (*725,000).....B1, E8 83
Memphis, Tex., 3,332.....B2 84
Memramcook, N.B., Can., 402.....C5 43
Memramcook East, N.B., Can., 720.....*C5 43
Mena, Ark., 4,388.....C1 49
Menahga, Minn., 799.....D3 67
Menands, N.Y., 2,702....C7 75
Menard, Tex., 1,914.....D3 84
Menard, co., Ill., 9,248....C4 58
Menard, co., Tex., 2,964..D3 84
Menasha, Wis., 14,647.....D5, h9 88
Mende, Fr., 8,337.....E5 5
Mendenhall, Miss., 1,946..D4 68
Mendham, N.J., 2,371.....B3 74
Mendocino, Calif., 900...C2 50
Mendocino, co., Calif., 51,059.....C2 50
Mendon, Ill., 784.....C2 58
Mendon, Mass., 900 (2,068▲).....h9 65
Mendon, Mich., 867.....F5 66
Mendon, Ohio, 663.....B1 78
Mendota, Calif., 3,086...D3 50
Mendota, Ill., 6,714.....B4 58
Mendota Heights, Minn., 5,028.....*F5 67
Mendoza, Arg., 109,122...A3 28
Mendoza, prov., Arg., 825,535.....A3 28
Menemen, Tur., 15,155.....*C6 14
Menfi, It., 12,492.....F4 9
Mengtzu, China, 9,000....G5 17
Menifee, co., Ky., 4,276...C6 62
Menindee, Austl., 629....F7 25
Meningie, Austl., 569....G6 25
Menlo Park, Calif., 26,958..k8 50
Menlo Park, N.J., 1,630...B4 74
Menlo Park Terrace, N. J., 2,800.....*B4 74
Menominee, Mich., 11,289.....C3 66
Menominee, co., Mich., 24,685.....C3 66

Menominee, co., Wis., 2,600.....C5 88
Menominee, riv., Mich....C3 66
Menomonee Falls, Wis., 18,276.....E5, m11 88
Menomonie, Wis., 8,624...D2 88
Mentana, It., 5,489.....g9 9
Menton, Fr., 19,904.....F7 5
Mentone, Calif., 2,000...*E5 50
Mentone, Ind., 813.....B5 59
Mentor, Ohio, 4,354.....A4 78
Mentor Headlands, Ohio, 1,500.....*A4 78
Mentor-on-the-Lake, Ohio, 3,290.....A4 78
Meppel, Neth., 17,700....A7 5
Meppen, Ger., 14,900.....B3 6
Meoqui, Mex., 10,287....B3 34
Mequon, Wis., 8,543..E5, m12 88
Merano, It., 31,400.....A3 9
Merauke, W. Irian, 3,600.....G10 19
Merca, Som., 15,000.....H6 23
Mercara, India, 14,453...F6 20
Merced, Calif., 20,068...D3 50
Merced, co., Calif., 90,446.....D3 50
Mercedes, Arg., 14,813...E4 29
Mercedes, Arg., 32,628.....A5, g7 28
Mercedes, Arg., 35,449...A3 28
Mercedes, Tex., 10,943....F4 84
Mercedes, Ur., 31,225....E1 30
Mercer, Pa., 2,800.....D1 81
Mercer, Wis., 750.....*B3 88
Mercer, co., Ill., 17,149...B3 58
Mercer, co., Ky., 14,596...C5 62
Mercer, co., Mo., 5,750...A4 69
Mercer, co., N.J., 266,392..C3 74
Mercer, co., N. Dak., 6,805.....C4 77
Mercer, co., Ohio, 32,559..B1 78
Mercer, co., Pa., 127,519..D1 81
Mercer, co., W. Va., 68,206.....D3 87
Mercer Island, Wash., 14,200.....B3, e11 86
Mercersburg, Pa., 1,759...G6 81
Mercerville, N.J., 15,500..C3 74
Merchantville, N.J., 4,075.....*D2 74
Meredith, N.H., 1,000 (2,434▲).....D4 73
Meredosia, Ill., 1,034.....D3 58
Merefa, Sov. Un., 10,000..G11 12
Mergui, Bur., 33,697.....F10 20
Mérida, Mex., 170,834....C7 34
Mérida, Sp., 34,297.....C2 8
Mérida, Ven., 46,339.....B3 32
Mérida, state, Ven., 270,668.....B3 32
Meriden, Conn., 51,850...C5 52
Meridian, Idaho, 2,081...F2 57
Meridian, Miss., 49,374...C5 68
Meridian, Pa., 1,649.....*E2 81
Meridian, Tex., 993.....D4 84
Merioneth, co., Wales, 38,400.....*D5 4
Merion Park, Pa., 1,000..*F11 81
Merion Station, Pa., 5,500.....*F11 81
Meriwether, co., Ga., 19,756.....C2 55
Merkel, Tex., 2,312.....C3 84
Merksem, Bel., 36,098....B6 5
Merlin, Ont., Can., 595...E2 41
Merlo, Arg., 8,385.....g7 28
Mermentau, La., 716.....D3 63
Mermentau, riv., La.....E2 63
Merowe, Sud., 1,620.....E4 23
Merredin, Austl., 3,619...F2 25
Merriam, Kans., 5,084....B8 61
Merrick, N.Y., 22,500....G2 52
Merrick, co., Nebr., 8,363..C7 71
Merrickville, Ont., Can., 947.....C9 41
Merrifield, Va., 1,000.....g12 85
Merrill, Iowa, 645.....B1 60
Merrill, Mich., 963.....E6 66
Merrill, Oreg., 804.....E5 80
Merrill, Wis., 9,451.....C4 88
Merrillan, Wis., 591.....D3 88
Merrillville, Ind., 3,200...B3 59
Merrimac, Mass., 2,000 (3,261▲).....A5 65
Merrimack, N.H., 400.....F5 73
Merrimack, co., N.H., 67,785.....E4 73
Merrionette Park, Ill., 2,354.....*B6 58
Merritt, B.C., Can., 3,039..D7 37
Merritt Island, Fla., 10,000.....D6 54
Mer Rouge, La., 853.....B4 63
Merryville, La., 1,232....D2 63
Merseburg, Ger., 50,800..C4 6
Mersey, riv., Eng.....D5 4
Mersin, Tur., 68,485.....D10 14

Mersing, Mala., 7,228.....E2 19
Merthyr Tydfil, Wales, 58,700.....E5 4
Meru, mtn., Tan......I5 23
Merzifon, Tur., 22,096...B10 14
Mesa, Ariz., 50,529...C3, D2 48
Mesa, co., Colo., 50,715...C2 51
Mesagne, It., 23,000.....D6 9
Meshkovskaya, Sov. Un...G13 12
Mesilla, N. Mex., 1,264...E3 48
Mesilla Park, N. Mex., 1,500.....E3 48
Mesologion, Grc., 11,266..C3 14
Mesquite, Tex., 27,526...n10 84
Messina, It., 259,700.....E5 9
Messina, S. Afr., 10,295...E6 24
Messini, Grc., 8,249.....*D3 14
Messinia (Messenia), prov., Grc., 211,970...*D4 14
Mestre, It., 73,435.....B4 9
Meta, dept., Col., 165,530..C3 32
Meta, riv., Col.....B4 32
Métabetchouan, Que., Can., 1,962.....A6 42
Metairie, La., 95,000.....k11 63
Metamora, Ill., 1,808.....C4 58
Metamora, Ohio, 598.....A2 78
Metán, Arg., 6,915.....E3 29
Metcalfe, co., Ky., 8,367...D4 62
Meteghan, N.S., Can., 925.....E3 43
Methuen, Mass., 28,114...A5 65
Metkovic, Yugo., 4,488...D3 10
Metropolis, Ill., 7,339.....F5 58
Metter, Ga., 2,362.....D4 55
Metuchen, N.J., 14,041...B4 74
Metz, Fr., 102,771 (*150,000).....C7 5
Metzger, Oreg., 2,500....h12 80
Meudon, Fr., 34,878.....g9 5
Meulaboh, Indon., 2,575.....m11 19
Meurthe-et-Moselle, dept., 678,078.....*C7 5
Meuse, dept., Fr., 215,985.....*C6 5
Mexia, Tex., 6,121.....D4 84
Mexicali, Mex., 174,540...A1 34
Mexico, Ind., 750.....C5 59
Mexico, Maine, 4,000.....D2 64
Mexico, Mo., 12,889.....B6 69
Mexico, N.Y., 1,465.....B4 75
Mexico, country, N.A., 40,913,000.....G10 33, 34
México, state, Mex., 1,897,851.....D5, n14 34
Mexico, gulf, N.A.....G11 33
Mexico City, Mex., 2,832,133 (*5,215,000).....n14 34
Meyersdale, Pa., 2,901....G3 81
Mezen, Sov. Un., 7,300...C7 13
Mézières, Fr., 11,799....C6 5
Mezokovesd, Hung., 18,640.....B5 10
Mezotur, Hung., 16,000...B5 10
Mglin, Sov. Un., 10,000...E9 12
Miajadas, Sp., 8,632.....C3 8
Miami, Ariz., 3,350..C3, D3 48
Miami, Fla., 320,000 (*1,530,000).....G6, s13 54
Miami, Okla., 12,869.....A7 79
Miami, W. Va., 500.....D6 87
Miami, co., Ind., 38,000...C5 59
Miami, co., Kans., 19,884..D9 61
Miami, co., Ohio, 72,901..B1 78
Miami Beach, Fla., 63,145.....G6, s13 54
Miamisburg, Ohio, 9,893..C1 78
Miami Shores, Fla., 8,865.....G6, s13 54
Miami Shores, Ohio, 1,200.....*C1 78
Miami Springs, Fla., 11,229.....G6, s13 54
Miamitown, Ohio, 500....o12 78
Mianwali, Pak., 23,341...B5 20
Miaoli, Taiwan, 5,000....*G9 17
Miass, Sov. Un., 109,000.....*D9 13
Micanopy, Fla., 658.....C4 54
Michalovce, Czech., 16,300.....D6 7
Michigan, lake, U.S.....E12 33
Michigan, state, U.S., 7,823,194.....66
Michigan Center, Mich., 5,000.....F6 66
Michigan City, Ind., 36,653.....A4 59
Michoacán, state, Mex., 1,851,876.....D4, n13 34
Michurinsk, Sov. Un., 85,000.....E13 12
Mickleyville, Ind., 4,700..m10 59
Micoud, St. Lucia, 2,040.....J14 35
Middelburg, Neth., 23,400..B5 5

Middelburg, S. Afr.,
8,681................G5 24
Middleboro, Mass., 6,300
(11,065▲)............C6 65
Middlebranch, Ohio, 600..B4 78
Middle Brook, Newf.,
Can., 744............D4 44
Middleburg, Fla., 750.....B5 54
Middleburg, N.Y., 1,317..C6 75
Middleburg, Pa., 1,366....E7 81
Middleburg, Va., 761.....B5 85
Middleburgh Heights,
Ohio, 7,282...........h9 78
Middlebury, Conn., 500...C4 52
Middlebury, Ind., 917.....A6 59
Middlebury, Vt., 3,688....C1 73
Middle Caraquet, N.B.,
Can., 895............*B5 43
Middlefield, Conn., 600
(3,255▲)............C5 52
Middlefield, Ohio, 1,467...A4 78
Middle Granville, N.Y.,
600................B7 75
Middle Haddam, Conn.,
500................C5 52
Middle Musquodoboit,
N.S., Can., 741.......D6 43
Middleport, N.Y., 1,882...B2 75
Middleport, Ohio, 3,373...C3 78
Middleport, Pa., 775.....*E9 81
Middle River, Md.,
14,500..............*B5 53
Middlesboro, Ky., 12,607..D6 62
Middlesbrough, Eng.,
158,100.............C6 4
Middlesex, N.J., 10,520...B4 74
Middlesex, N.C., 588.....B4 76
Middlesex, co., Ont., Can.,
221,422.............D3 41
Middlesex, co., Conn.,
88,865..............D6 52
Middlesex, co., Eng.,
2,230,093...........*E6 4
Middlesex, co., Mass.,
1,238,742...........A5 65
Middlesex, co., N.J.,
433,856.............C4 74
Middlesex, co., Va., 6,319..C6 85
Middleton, N.S., Can.,
1,921...............E4 43
Middleton, Idaho, 541....F2 57
Middleton, Mass.,
3,718..............A5, f11 65
Middleton, Wis., 4,410....E4 88
Middletown, Calif.,
750................C2 50
Middletown, Conn.,
33,250..............C6 52
Middletown, Del., 2,191..B6 53
Middletown, Ind., 2,033...D6 59
Middletown, Ky., 90.....A4 62
Middletown, Md., 1,036...B2 53
Middletown, N.J., 8,000
(39,675▲)...........C4 74
Middletown, N.Y., 23,475..D6 75
Middletown, Ohio, 42,115..C1 78
Middletown, Pa., 11,182...F8 81
Middletown, R.I.,
19,562..............C11 52
Middletown Heights, Pa.,
1,000..............*G11 81
Middleville, Mich., 1,196..F5 66
Middleville, N.Y., 648....B6 75
Midfield, Ala., 3,556....*E4 46
Midland, Calif., 600.....F6 50
Midland, Ont., Can.,
8,656...............C5 41
Midland, La., 500.......D3 63
Midland, Md., 737......K13 53
Midland, Mich., 27,779...E6 66
Midland, N.C., 750......B2 76
Midland, Pa., 6,425......E1 81
Midland, Tex., 62,625....D1 84
Midland, Wash., 900....*D3 86
Midland, co., Mich.,
51,450..............E6 66
Midland, co., Tex.,
67,717..............D1 84
Midland Park, Kans.,
3,000...............B5 61
Midland Park, N.J.,
7,543...............B4 74
Midland Park, S.C., 600..K11 82
Midleton, Ire., 2,772.....E2 4
Midlothian, Ill., 11,789....k9 58
Midlothian, Tex.,
1,521.............C4, n10 84
Midlothian, co., Scot.,
593,000............*C5 4
Midnapore, India,
59,532..............D8 20
Midstate Mill, N.C.,
1,090...............*C3 76
Midvale, Ohio, 683......B4 78
Midvale, Utah, 5,802.....D2 72
Midway, Ky., 1,044......B5 62
Midway, Oreg., 19,000..*B4 80
Midway, Pa., 1,568.......G7 81

Midway City, Calif.,
2,500...............*F5 50
Midway Park, N.C., 4,164..C5 76
Midway Is., U.S. dep.,
Oceania, 2,500........E9 2
Midwest, Wyo., 900.....C6 89
Midwest City, Okla.,
36,058..............B4 79
Mid-Western, reg., Nig.,
2,535,839...........G6 22
Midyat, Tur., 9,621.....D13 14
Mie, pref., Jap.,
1,514,467...........*I8 18
Miechow, Pol., 6,878.....C6 7
Miechowice, Pol., 13,831...g9 7
Miedzyrzec, Pol., 11,900...C7 7
Mielec, Pol., 24,100......C6 7
Mieres, Sp., 19,308.......A3 8
Mifflin, co., Pa., 44,348...F6 81
Mifflinburg, Pa., 2,476....E7 81
Mifflintown, Pa., 887.....E7 81
Mifflinville, Pa., 1,027....D9 81
Migdal Ashqelon, Isr.,
28,400..............C2 15
Migennes, Fr., 6,352......D5 5
Mignon, Ala., 2,271......B3 46
Mihama, Jap., 12,500....o15 18
Mihara, Jap., 82,175.....*i6 18
Mikhaylovgrad, Bul.,
8,067...............D6 10
Mikhaylovka, Sov. Un.,
10,000.............H10 12
Mikhaylovka, Sov. Un.,
31,000.............F14 12
Mikindani, Tan., 4,807....C8 24
Mikkeli, Fin., 19,800.....G12 11
Mikkeli, prov., Fin.,
235,403............*G12 11
Mikolow, Pol., 19,500.....g9 7
Mikulczyce, Pol.........g9 7
Mikulov, Czech., 5,220...D4 7
Milaca, Minn., 1,821.....E5 67
Milam, co., Tex., 22,263...D4 84
Milan, Ill., 3,941.......B3 58
Milan, Ind., 1,174.......F7 59
Milan, Mich., 3,616......F7 66
Milan, Mo., 1,670.......A4 69
Milan, N. Mex., 2,658...*B2 48
Milan, Ohio, 1,309.......A3 78
Milan, Tenn., 5,208......B3 83
Milano (Milan), It.,
1,666,300 (*2,860,000)...B2 9
Milan, see Milano, It.
Milas, Tur., 11,700.....*D6 14
Milazzo, It., 12,900......E5 9
Milbank, S. Dak., 3,500...E9 77
Milbridge, Maine, 500
(1,101▲)............D5 64
Mildmay, Ont., Can., 847...C3 41
Mildred, Pa., 800........D9 81
Mildura, Austl., 12,931...F7 25
Miles, Austl., 1,479.....*E9 25
Miles, Tex., 626........D2 84
Miles City, Mont., 9,665..D11 70
Milford, Conn., 41,662...E4 52
Milford, Del., 5,795.....C7 53
Milford, Ill., 1,699......C6 58
Milford, Ind., 1,167......B6 59
Milford, Iowa, 1,476.....A2 60
Milford, Maine, 1,000
(1,572▲)............D4 64
Milford, Mass., 15,749..B4, h9 65
Milford, Mich., 4,323..F7, o14 66
Milford, Nebr., 1,462....D8 71
Milford, N.H., 4,000.....F4 73
Milford, N.J., 1,114......B2 74
Milford, N.Y., 548.......C6 75
Milford, Ohio, 4,131......C1 78
Milford, Pa., 1,198.....D12 81
Milford, Utah, 1,471.....B5 72
Milford Center, Ohio, 794..B2 78
Milford Haven, Wales,
12,900..............E4 4
Milford Mills, Md.,
5,000...............*B4 53
Milford Station, N.S.,
Can., 528...........D6 43
Miliana, Alg., 8,642......A5 22
Milk, riv., Alta., Can.....E5 38
Milk River, Alta., Can.,
801................E4 38
Mill, riv., Mass.........h9 65
Millard, Nebr., 1,014....g12 71
Millard, co., Utah, 7,866..B5 72
Millau, Fr., 21,229......E5 5
Millbourne, Pa., 793....*G11 81
Millbrae, Calif., 15,873....h8 50
Millbrook, Ala., 900......C3 46
Millbrook, Ont., Can.,
891................C6 41
Millbrook, N.J., 1,500...*B3 74
Millbrook, N.Y., 1,717....D7 75
Millburn, N.J., 18,799....B4 74
Millbury, Mass., 5,500....B4 65
Millbury, Ohio, 730......e7 78
Mill City, Oreg., 1,289....C4 80
Milldale, Conn., 1,000...C4 52
Milledgeville, Ga., 11,117..C3 55

Milledgeville, Ill., 1,208...B4 58
Mille Lacs, co., Minn.,
14,560..............E5 67
Mille Lacs, lake, Minn....D5 67
Millen, Ga., 3,633.......D5 55
Miller, S. Dak., 2,081.....F7 77
Miller, co., Ark., 31,686...D2 49
Miller, co., Ga., 6,908....E2 55
Miller, co., Mo., 13,800...C5 69
Millerovo, Sov. Un.,
32,400.............G13 12
Millersburg, Ky., 913.....B5 62
Millersburg, Ohio, 3,101..B4 78
Millersburg, Pa., 2,984...E8 81
Millers Falls, Mass., 1,199..A3 65
Millersport, Ohio, 752....C3 78
Millersville, Pa., 3,883....F9 81
Millerton, N.Y., 1,027....D7 75
Mill Hall, Pa., 1,891......D7 81
Millicent, Austl., 4,528....G7 25
Milligan, Fla., 800......u15 54
Millington, Mich., 1,159...E7 66
Millington, N.J., 1,300...*B3 74
Millington, Tenn., 6,059..*B1 83
Millinocket, Maine, 7,453..C4 64
Millis, Mass., 2,900
(4,374▲).........B5, h10 65
Millport, Ala., 943.......B1 46
Mills, Wyo., 1,477.......D6 89
Mills, co., Iowa, 13,050...C2 60
Mills, co., Tex., 4,467....D3 84
Millsboro, Del., 536......C2 53
Millsboro, Pa., 950.......G1 81
Millside, Del., 1,000....*A6 53
Millstadt, Ill., 1,830......E3 58
Milltown, N.B., Can.,
1,892...............D2 43
Milltown, Ind., 793......H5 59
Milltown, Mont., 750....D3 70
Milltown, N.J., 5,435....C4 74
Milltown, Wis., 608......C1 88
Millvale, Pa., 6,624.....k14 81
Mill Valley, Calif.,
10,411............D2, h7 50
Millville, Mass., 1,567....B4 65
Millville, N.J., 19,096....E2 74
Millville, Ohio, 676.....n12 78
Millville, Pa., 950.......D9 81
Millwood, Wash., 1,776..g14 86
Milmont Park, Pa.,
2,000..............*G11 81
Milo, Maine, 1,900......C4 64
Milpitas, Calif., 6,572...*D3 50
Milroy, Ind., 900........F7 59
Milroy, Pa., 1,666.......E6 81
Milstead, Ga., 1,047...B6, C3 55
Milton, N.S., Can., 1,121..E5 43
Milton, Del., 1,617......C7 53
Milton, Fla., 4,108......u14 54
Milton, Ind., 700........E7 59
Milton, Iowa, 800.......D5 60
Milton, Mass., 26,375..B5, g11 65
Milton, N.H., 800
(1,418▲)............D5 73
Milton, N.J., 400........A3 74
Milton, N.Y., 800........D7 75
Milton, Pa., 7,972.......D8 81
Milton, Wash., 2,218....f11 86
Milton, W. Va., 1,714....C2 87
Milton, Wis., 1,671......F5 88
Milton-Freewater, Oreg.,
4,110...............B8 80
Milton Junction, Wis.,
1,433...............F5 88
Miltonvale, Kans., 814....C6 61
Milton West, Ont., Can.,
5,629...............D5 41
Milverton, Ont., Can.,
1,111...............D4 41
Milwaukee, Wis., 745,000
(*1,350,000)......E5, m12 88
Milwaukee, co., Wis.,
1,036,041...........E6 88
Milwaukie, Oreg.,
9,099............B4, h12 80
Mimico, Ont., Can.,
18,212............D5, m15 41
Mims, Fla., 1,307.......D6 54
Minamata, Jap., 33,700
(45,577▲)...........J5 18
Minas, Ur., 24,400.......E1 30
Minas de Riotinto, Sp.,
9,060...............D2 8
Minas Gerais, state, Braz.,
9,798,880...........B4 30
Minatare, Nebr., 894....C2 71
Minatitlán, Mex., 35,350..D6 34
Minato, Jap., 7,100.....m19 18
Minbu, Bur., 9,096......D9 20
Minco, Okla., 1,021......B4 79
Mindanao, isl., Phil......D6 19
Minden, Ont., Can., 658..C6 41
Minden, Ger., 49,200....B4 6
Minden, La., 12,785.....B2 63
Minden, Nebr., 2,383....D7 71
Minden, W. Va.,
1,114...........D3, D7 87
Mindoro, isl., Phil.......C6 19

Minechoag, mtn., Mass....B3 65
Minehead, Eng., 7,500....E5 4
Mine Hill, N.J., 3,362....*B3 74
Mineola, N.Y.,
22,052...........E7, n15 75
Mineola, Tex., 3,810.....C5 84
Miner, Mo., 548.........E8 69
Miner, co., S. Dak., 5,398..G8 77
Mineral, co., Colo., 424...D4 51
Mineral, co., Mont., 3,037..C1 70
Mineral, co., Nev., 6,329..B2 72
Mineral, co., W. Va.,
22,354..............B6 87
Mineral City, Ohio, 917...B4 78
Mineral del Oro, Mex.,
3,507..............n13 34
Mineral Point, Wis., 2,385..F3 88
Mineral Ridge, Ohio
2,000..............*A5 78
Mineral Wells, Tex.,
11,053..............C3 84
Minersville, Pa., 6,606....E9 81
Minerva, Ohio, 3,833.....B4 78
Minerva Park, Ohio,
1,169..............*C3 78
Minervino Murge, It.,
18,427..............D6 9
Minetto, N.Y., 800.......B4 75
Mineville, N.Y., 1,181....A7 75
Mingenew, Austl., 668....E2 25
Mingo, co., W. Va.,
39,742..............D2 87
Mingo Junction, Ohio,
4,987...............B5 78
Mingshui, China, 5,000...C2 18
Minho, prov., Port.,
825,788............*B1 8
Minhow, see Foochow, China
Minidoka, co., Idaho,
14,394.............G5 57
Minier, Ill., 847........C4 58
Minitonas, Man., Can.,
606................C1 40
Minna, Nig., 12,810.....G6 22
Minneapolis, Kans., 2,024..C6 61
Minneapolis, Minn.,
450,000
(*1,615,000)......F5, n12 67
Minnedosa, Man., Can.,
2,211...............D2 40
Minnehaha, Wash.,
2,000..............*D3 86
Minnehaha, co., S. Dak.,
86,575.............G9 77
Minneola, Kans., 679.....E3 61
Minneota, Minn., 1,297...F3 67
Minnesota, state, U.S.,
3,413,864........... 67
Minnesota, riv., Minn....F3 67
Minnesota Lake, Minn.,
697................G5 67
Minnetonka, Minn.,
25,037.............*F5 67
Minnetrista, Minn.,
2,076..............*E5 67
Mino, Jap., 20,700......n15 18
Minoa, N.Y., 1,984.....*B4 75
Minocqua, Wis., 800.....C4 88
Minokamo, Jap., 16,900..n15 18
Minonk, Ill., 2,001......C4 58
Minot, N. Dak., 33,477...B4 77
Minquadale, Del., 1,330.*A6 53
Minsk, Sov. Un., 644,000..E6 12
Minster, Ohio, 2,193.....B1 78
Minturno, It., 3,125......D4 9
Minūf, Eg., U.A.R.,
36,900.............*G8 14
Minusinsk, Sov. Un.,
44,600.............D12 13
Minya Konka, peak,
China..............F5 17
Miraflores, Col., 3,257....C3 32
Miraflores, Peru, 16,146...A3 31
Miraj, India, 53,345......E5 20
Mira Loma, Calif., 3,982..*E5 50
Miramar, Fla., 5,485....s13 54
Miranda, state, Ven.,
492,349.............A4 32
Miranda de Ebro, Sp.,
27,881..............A4 8
Mirassol, Braz., 13,674...C3 30
Mirebalais, Hai., 1,835...E7 35
Mirecourt, Fr., 8,572.....C7 5
Mirgorod, Sov. Un.,
10,000.............G9 12
Miri, Mala., 13,350......E4 19
Mirror, Alta., Can., 577...C4 38
Mirzapur, India, 100,097..C7 20
Misakubo, Jap., 3,200...n16 18
Misamis Occidental, prov.,
Phil., 248,371.......*D6 19
Misamis Oriental, prov.,
Phil., 388,615.......*D7 19
Misantla, Mex.,
9,201............D5, h15 34
Misenheimer, N.C., 950...B2 76
Mishan, China, 5,000.....D6 18
Mishawaka, Ind., 33,361..A5 59

Mishicot, Wis., 762...D6, h10 88
Mishima, Jap., 71,239..I9, n17 18
Misiones, dept., Par.,
43,449............E4 29
Misiones, prov., Arg.,
331,000............E4 29
Miskolc, Hung., 159,800...A5 10
Misrātah, Libya, 59,902..B8 22
Missaukee, co., Mich.,
6,784............D5 66
Mission, Kans., 4,626....*B9 61
Mission, Tex., 14,081......F3 84
Mission City, B.C.,
Can., 3,251......E6, f13 37
Mission Hills, Kans., 3,621..B9 61
Missisquoi, co., Que.,
Can., 29,526......D4 42
Mississippi, co., Ark.,
70,174............B5 49
Mississippi, co., Mo.,
20,695............E8 69
Mississippi, state, U.S.,
2,178,141............68
Mississippi, riv., U.S..B8, D8 45
Mississippi City, Miss.,
4,169............E2, E4 45
Missoula, Mont., 27,090..D2 70
Missoula, co., Mont.,
44,663............D2 70
Missoula Southwest,
Mont., 3,900......*D2 70
Missouri, state, U.S.,
4,319,813............69
Missouri, riv., U.S........B7 45
Missouri Valley, Iowa,
3,567............C2 60
Mistassini, Que., Can.,
3,461............h12 42
Mistelbach [an der Zaya],
Aus., 5,434........D8 6
Misti, vol., Peru.........E3 31
Mistretta, It., 9,979......F5 9
Mitaka, Jap., 135,873....*I9 18
Mitake, Jap., 9,600...I8, n16 18
Mitcham, Eng., 63,653...m12 4
Mitchell, Austl., 1,705....E8 25
Mitchell, Ont., Can.,
2,247............D3 41
Mitchell, Ind., 3,552.....G5 59
Mitchell, Nebr., 1,920....C2 71
Mitchell, S. Dak., 12,555..G7 77
Mitchell, co., Ga., 19,652..E2 55
Mitchell, co., Iowa,
14,043............A5 60
Mitchell, co., Kans.,
8,866............C5 61
Mitchell, co., N.C.,
13,906............e10 76
Mitchell, co., Tex., 11,255..C2 84
Mitchell, mtn., N.C.......f10 76
Mitchellsburg, Ky., 500...C5 62
Mitchellville, Iowa, 1,107..C4 60
Mitilíni (Mytilene), Grc.,
25,758............C6 14
Mito, Jap., 154,983..H10, m19 18
Mitterteich, Ger., 6,500...D6 6
Mittweida, Ger., 20,900...C6 6
Mitú, Col., 1,623.........C3 32
Miura, Jap., 42,601......n18 18
Mixquiahuala, Mex.,
7,173............m13 34
Miyagi, pref., Jap.,
1,753,126..........*G10 18
Miyako, Jap., 45,000
(56,575▲)............G10 18
Miyakonojo, Jap., 64,000
(108,220▲)............K5 18
Miyazaki, Jap., 131,000
(182,870▲)............K5 18
Miyazaki, pref., Jap.,
1,080,692..........*K5 18
Miyazu, Jap., 23,300....n14 18
Mizil, Rom., 7,460.......C8 10
Mjölby, Swe., 10,700.....H6 11
Mladá Boleslav, Czech.,
26,200............C3, n18 7
Mlawa, Pol., 16,900......B6 7
Moab, Utah, 4,682.......B7 72
Mobara, Jap., 42,486....n19 18
Moberly, Mo., 13,170....B5 69
Mobile, Ala., 220,000
(*345,000)............E1 46
Mobile, co., Ala., 314,301..E1 46
Mobridge, S. Dak., 4,391..E5 77
Moca, mun., P.R., 21,990..E8 35
Moçambique, Moz.,
12,166............D8 24
Moçâmedes, Ang., 7,185..D2 24
Mocanaqua, Pa., 1,104...D9 81
Mochudi, Bots., 17,700...C5 24
Mocksville, N.C., 2,379...B2 76
Moclips, Wash., 500......B1 86
Mocoa, Col., 2,571.......C2 32
Mococa, Braz., 14,306..C3, k8 30
Mocorito, Mex., 4,223....B3 34
Moctezuma, Mex.,
2,298............B3 34
Modena, It., 149,800.....B3 9

Modesto, Calif., 36,585....D3 50
Modica, It., 30,200.......F5 9
Modlin, Pol...........B6, k13 7
Mödling, Aus., 17,274....D8 6
Modoc, co., Calif., 8,308..B3 50
Modřany, Czech., 10,100..n17 7
Moe, Austl., 16,544..G8, n15 25
Moffat, co., Colo., 7,061..A2 51
Mogadiscio, Som.,
120,600............H7 23
Mogadore, Ohio, 3,851...A4 78
Mogaung, Bur., 2,940...C10 20
Mogi das Cruzes, Braz.,
63,748..........C3, m8 30
Mogilev, Sov. Un.,
145,000............E8 12
Mogilev-Podolskiy,
Sov. Un., 46,300......G6 12
Mogilno, Pol., 5,193......B4 7
Mogí Mirim, Braz.,
18,345..........C3, m8 30
Mogocha, Sov. Un.,
18,000............D14 13
Mogok, Bur., 8,369.....D10 20
Moguer, Sp., 7,222......D2 8
Mohács, Hung., 15,860...C4 10
Hohall, N. Dak., 1,204...B4 77
Mohave, co., Ariz., 7,736..B1 48
Mohawk, Mich., 750.....A2 66
Mohawk, N.Y., 3,533....C5 75
Mohnton, Pa., 2,223....F10 81
Mohon, Fr., 9,043.......C6 5
Moineşti, Rom., 12,934...B8 10
Moissac, Fr., 4,770......E4 5
Mojave, Calif., 3,000....E4 50
Mokelumne Hill, Calif.,
560............C3 50
Mokena, Ill., 1,376......k9 58
Mokpo, Kor., 157,400....I3 18
Mol, Yugo., 8,079.......C5 10
Mola di Bari, It., 22,852...D6 9
Molalla, Oreg., 1,501....B4 80
Mold, Wales, 6,857......*D5 4
Moldavia, reg., Rom.....B8 10
Moldavia (S.S.R.), rep.,
Sov. Un., 3,040,000...H7 12
Molepolole, Bots., 29,600..E5 24
Molfetta, It., 63,100......D6 9
Molina, Chile, 7,600.....B2 28
Molina de Segura, Sp.,
8,578............C5 8
Moline, Ill., 42,705......B3 58
Moline, Kans., 698......E7 61
Moline, Mich., 550......F5 66
Moline Acres, Mo.,
3,132............*C7 69
Molino, Fla., 800......u14 54
Molino de Rosas, Mex.,
10,235............h9 34
Moliterno, It., 5,657.....D5 9
Mollendo, Peru, 14,893...E3 31
Mölndal, Swe., 26,500.....I5 11
Molodechno, Sov. Un.,
26,000............D6 12
Molotovsk, Sov. Un.,
97,000............E18 11
Molotovskoye, Sov. Un.,
10,000............I13 12
Molus, Ky., 500........D6 62
Mombasa, Ken., 179,575...I5 23
Mombetsu, Jap., 31,000
(40,389▲)............D11 18
Momence, Ill., 2,949.....B6 58
Momostenango, Guat.,
5,002............*D6 34
Mompós, Col., 10,965....B3 32
Monaca, Pa., 8,394......E1 81
Monaco, country, Eur.,
22,297............F7 5
Monagas, state, Ven.,
246,217............B5 32
Monaghan, S.C., 750....B3 82
Monaghan, co., Ire.,
45,700............*C3 4
Monahans, Tex., 8,567...D1 84
Monarch, S.C., 1,990....B4 82
Monarch, mtn., B.C.,
Can............D5, n17 37
Monashee, mts., B.C.,
Can............D8 37
Monastir, Tur., 12,596....A7 22
Monaville, W. Va., 825...*D5 87
Monchegorsk, Sov. Un.,
30,000............D15 11
Mönchengladbach, Ger.,
154,300 (*340,000)....C3 6
Moncks Corner, S.C.,
2,030............E7 82
Monclova, Mex., 43,077..B4 34
Moncton, N.B., Can.,
43,840 (*55,768)......C5 43
Mondoñedo, Sp., 9,153...A2 8
Mondoví, It., 8,800......B1 9
Mondovi, Wis., 2,320....D2 88
Monessen, Pa., 18,424...F2 81
Monett, Mo., 5,359......E4 69
Monette, Ark, 981......B5 49
Monfalcone, It., 26,818...B4 9

Monforte de Lemos, Sp.,
13,502............A2 8
Monfort Heights, Ohio,
6,000............*C1 78
Monghyr, India, 89,768...C8 20
Mong Mit, Bur., 5,000...D10 20
Mongolia, country, Asia,
1,019,000............B4 17
Moniquirá, Col., 4,882...B3 32
Moniteau, co., Mo.,
10,500............C5 69
Monmouth, Ill., 10,372...C3 58
Monmouth, Oreg.,
2,229............C3, k11 80
Monmouth, co., N.J.,
334,401............C4 74
Monmouth, co., Wales,
451,400............*E5 4
Monmouth, mtn., B.C.,
Can............D6 37
Monmouth, peak, Oreg...C3 80
Monmouth Beach, N.J.,
1,363............C5 74
Monmouth Junction,
N.J., 900............C3 74
Mono, Calif., 2,213......D4 50
Monon, Ind., 1,417......C4 59
Monona, Iowa, 1,346.....A6 60
Monona, Wis., 8,178.....E4 88
Monona, co., Iowa, 13,916..B1 60
Monongah, W. Va.,
1,321............A7, B4 87
Monongahela, Pa., 8,388..F2 81
Monongalia, co., W. Va.,
55,617............B4 87
Monopoli, It., 24,000.....D6 9
Monor, Hung., 14,830....B4 10
Monóvar, Sp., 9,933.....C5 8
Monponsett, Mass., 600..B9 65
Monreale, It., 18,500.....E4 9
Monroe, Conn., 950......D3 52
Monroe, Ga., 6,826......C3 55
Monroe, Iowa, 1,366.....C4 60
Monroe, La., 52,219......B3 63
Monroe, Mich., 22,968...G7 66
Monroe, N.Y.,
3,885............D6, m14 75
Monroe, N.C., 10,913....C2 76
Monroe, Ohio, 1,475.....*C1 78
Monroe, Utah, 955.......B5 72
Monroe, Va., 800........C3 85
Monroe, Wash., 1,901....B4 86
Monroe, Wis., 8,050......F4 88
Monroe, co., Ala., 22,372..D2 46
Monroe, co., Ark., 17,327..C4 49
Monroe, co., Fla., 47,921..G5 54
Monroe, co., Ga., 10,495..D3 55
Monroe, co., Ill., 15,507..E3 58
Monroe, co., Ind., 59,225..F4 59
Monroe, co., Iowa, 10,463..D5 60
Monroe, co., Ky., 11,799..D4 62
Monroe, co., Mich.,
101,120............G7 66
Monroe, co., Miss., 33,953..B5 68
Monroe, co., Mo., 10,688..B5 69
Monroe, co., N.Y.,
625,128............B3 75
Monroe, co., Ohio, 15,268..C4 78
Monroe, co., Pa., 39,567..D11 81
Monroe, co., Tenn.,
23,316............D9 83
Monroe, co., W. Va.,
11,584............D4 87
Monroe, co., Wis., 31,241..E3 88
Monroe City, Mo., 2,377..B6 69
Monroeville, Ala., 3,632..D2 46
Monroeville, Ind., 1,294..C8 59
Monroeville, Ohio, 1,371..A3 78
Monroeville, Pa., 22,446..*E1 81
Monrovia, Calif., 27,079..m13 50
Monrovia, Lib., 81,000...G2 22
Mons, Bel., 26,973......B5 5
Monson, Maine, 700
(852▲)............C3 64
Monson, Mass., 2,500
(6,712▲)............B3 65
Montague, Calif., 896....B2 50
Montague, P.E.I., Can.,
1,126............C7 43
Montague, Mass., 600
(7,836▲)............A2 65
Montague, Mich., 2,366..E4 66
Montague, co., Tex.,
14,893............C4 84
Montague City, Mass.,
600............A2 65
Mont Alto, Pa., 1,039....G6 81
Montalvo, Calif., 2,028...*E4 50
Montana, state, U.S.,
674,767............70
Montánchez, Sp., 4,190...C2 8
Montargis, Fr., 15,996....D5 5
Montauban, Que., Can.,
623............C5 42
Montauban, Fr., 30,242...E4 5
Montauk, N.Y., 600....m17 75
Monta Vista, Calif.,
2,000............*D3 50

Monta Vista, Wash.,
1,500............*B3 86
Montbéliard, Fr., 21,699..D7 5
Mont Belvieu, Tex.,
1,200............E5, r15 84
Montbrison, Fr., 9,051....E6 5
Montcalm, co., Que.,
Can., 18,766........C3 42
Montcalm, co., Mich.,
35,795............E5 66
Mont-Carmel, Que.,
Can., 895............B8 42
Montceau-les-Mines, Fr.,
29,364............D6 5
Montchanin [-les-Mines],
Fr., 6,405............D6 5
Montclair (Monte Vista),
Calif., 13,546........m13 50
Montclair, N.J., 43,129...B4 74
Mont Clare, Pa., 1,124...o19 81
Montcoal, W. Va.,
275............D3, D6 87
Mont-De-Marsan, Fr.,
20,203............F3 5
Montebello, Calif.,
40,613............m12 50
Montebello, Que., Can.,
1,486............D3 42
Monte Caseros, Arg.,
12,930............A5 28
Montecelio, It., 5,000....g9 9
Montecristi, Dom. Rep.,
6,140............E8 35
Montefrio, Sp., 5,137....D3 8
Montego Bay, Jam.,
23,471............E5 35
Montegut, La., 700......E5 63
Monteith, mtn., B.C.,
Can............B6 38
Montélimar, Fr., 15,914...E6 5
Montellano, Sp., 9,334...D3 8
Montello, Wis., 1,021....E4 88
Montemorelos, Mex.,
11,641............B5 34
Montemor-o-Novo, Port.,
5,047............C1 8
Montenegro, Braz.,
14,491............D2 30
Montenegro (Crna Gora),
rep., Yugo., 471,894..*D4 10
Monte Plata, Dom. Rep.,
2,110............E9 35
Montepulciano, It.,
17,552............C3 9
Montereau, Fr., 14,121...C5 5
Monterey, Calif., 25,436..D3 50
Monterey, Ohio, 1,500...*C1 78
Monterey, Tenn., 2,069...C8 83
Monterey, co., Calif.,
224,316............D3 50
Monterey Park, Calif.,
37,821............m12 50
Montería, Col., 70,531
(126,329▲)............B2 32
Monteros, Arg., 7,745....E2 29
Monterotondo, It., 9,340...g9 9
Monterrey, Mex., 596,939..B4 34
Montesano, Wash., 2,486..C2 86
Monte Sant' Angelo, It.,
21,601............D5 9
Montes Claros, Braz.,
40,545............B4 30
Monte Sereno, Calif.,
1,506............*D3 50
Montevallo, Ala., 2,755...B3 46
Montevarchi, It., 9,100...C3 9
Montevideo, Minn., 5,693..F3 67
Montevideo, Ur.,
1,173,100............E1 30
Montevideo, dept., Ur.,
1,173,100............*E1 30
Monte Vista, Colo., 3,385..D4 51
Montezuma, Ga., 3,744...D2 55
Montezuma, Ind., 1,231...E3 59
Montezuma, Iowa, 1,416..C5 60
Montezuma, co., Colo.,
14,024............D2 51
Montfort, Wis., 538......F3 88
Montgomery, Ala., 146,000
(*167,000)............C3 46
Montgomery, Alta., Can.,
5,077............D3 38
Montgomery, Ill.,
2,744............B5, k8 58
Montgomery, La., 866....C3 63
Montgomery, Minn.,
2,118............F5 67
Montgomery, N.Y., 1,312..D6 75
Montgomery, Ohio,
3,075............*C1 78
Montgomery, Pak., 75,180..B5 20
Montgomery, Pa., 2,150..D8 81
Montgomery, W. Va.,
3,000............C3, C6 87
Montgomery, co., Ala.,
169,210............C3 46
Montgomery, co., Ark.,
5,370............C2 49

Montgomery, co., Ga., 6,284..............D4   55
Montgomery, co., Ill., 31,244.............D4   58
Montgomery, co., Ind., 32,089.............D4   59
Montgomery, co., Iowa, 14,467.............C2   60
Montgomery, co., Kans., 45,007............E8   61
Montgomery, co., Ky., 13,461.............B6   62
Montgomery, co., Md., 340,928............B3   53
Montgomery, co., Miss., 13,320............B4   68
Montgomery, co., Mo., 11,097.............C6   69
Montgomery, co., N.Y., 57,240............C6   75
Montgomery, co., N.C., 18,408............B3   76
Montgomery, co., Ohio, 527,080...........C1   78
Montgomery, co., Pa., 516,682............F11   81
Montgomery, co., Tenn., 55,645...........A4   83
Montgomery, co., Tex., 26,839............D5   84
Montgomery, co., Va., 32,923.............C2   85
Montgomery, co., Wales, 43,700...........*D5   4
Montgomery City, Mo., 936...............C6   69
Monticello, Ark., 4,412....D4   49
Monticello, Fla., 2,490....B3   54
Monticello, Ga., 1,931....C3   55
Monticello, Ill., 3,511....C5   58
Monticello, Ind., 4,035....C4   59
Monticello, Iowa, 3,190....B6   60
Monticello, Ky., 2,940....D5   62
Monticello, Maine, 600 (1,109▲)...........B5   64
Monticello, Minn., 1,477..E5   67
Monticello, Miss., 1,432..D3   68
Monticello, N.Y., 5,222..D6   75
Monticello, Utah, 1,845..C7   72
Monticello, Wis., 789....F4   88
Montigny-lès-Metz., Fr., 22,388...............C7   5
Montijo, Port., 17,751..C1, f10   8
Montijo, Sp., 14,961......C2   8
Montilla, Sp., 19,755....D3   8
Montivilliers, Fr., 8,427..C4   5
Mont-Joli, Que., Can., 6,178...............G20   36
Mont-Laurier, Que., Can., 5,859................C2   42
Montluçon, Fr., 55,184...D5   5
Montmagny, Que., Can., 6,850..............C7   42
Montmagny, co., Que., Can., 26,450..........C7   42
Montmartre, Sask., Can., 482................G4   39
Montmorenci, S.C., 900................D4   82
Montmorency, Que., Can., 5,985........C6, n17   42
Montmorency, Fr., 16,369..............g10   5
Montmorency, co., Mich., 4,424..............C6   66
Montmorency No. 1, co., Que., Can., 20,734.....B6   42
Montmorency No. 2, co., Que., Can., 4,974....C7   42
Montmorillon, Fr., 4,766..D4   5
Montoro, Sp., 14,950....C3   8
Montour, co., Pa., 16,730.D8   81
Montour Falls, N.Y., 1,533...............C4   75
Montoursville, Pa., 5,211..D8   81
Montpelier, Idaho, 3,146..G7   57
Montpelier, Ind., 1,954...C7   59
Montpelier, Ohio, 4,131..A1   78
Montpelier, Vt., 8,782....C2   73
Montpellier, Fr., 118,864..F5   5
Montréal, Que., Can., 1,201,116 (*2,109,509).......D4, q19   42
Montreal, Wis., 1,361....B3   88
Montréal West, Que., Can., 6,446..........*D4   42
Montreuil-sur-Mer, Fr., 3,253...............B4   5
Montreux, Switz., 19,000..E3   6
Mont-Rolland, Que., Can., 1,457...............D3   42
Montrose, Ala., 500......E2   46
Montrose, Calif., 6,000...*E4   50
Montrose, B.C., Can., 862..E9   37
Montrose, Colo., 5,044....C3   51
Montrose, Iowa, 632.....D6   60
Montrose, Mich., 1,466...E7   66
Montrose, Pa., 1,100....*F10   81

Montrose, Pa., 2,363.....C10   81
Montrose, Scot., 10,900....B5   4
Montrose, co., Colo., 18,286..............C2   51
Montrose Hill, Pa., 2,000..*E1   81
Montrouge, Fr., 45,260...g10   5
Montserrat, Br. dep., N.A., 12,108.........H13   35
Montvale, N.J., 3,699.....g8   74
Montville, Conn., 1,060...D8   52
Montville, N.J., 800......B4   74
Monument, peak, Idaho...G4   57
Monument Beach, Mass., 900................C6   65
Monywa, Bur., 26,172....D10   20
Monza, It., 89,000.......B2   9
Monzón, Peru, 514.......C2   31
Moodus, Conn., 1,300....D7   52
Moody, Tex., 1,074......D4   84
Moody, co., S. Dak., 8,810..F9   77
Mooers, N.Y., 543.......f11   75
Moonachie, N.J., 3,052...*B4   74
Moon Crest, Pa., 1,500...*E1   81
Moon Run, Pa., 800.....k13   81
Moonta, Austl., 1,122....F6   25
Moora, Austl., 1,175......F2   25
Moorcraft, Wyo., 826....B8   89
Moore, Okla., 1,783......B4   79
Moore, co., N.C., 36,733..B3   76
Moore, co., Tenn., 3,454..B5   83
Moore, co., Tex., 14,773..B2   84
Moorefield, W. Va., 1,434..B6   87
Moore Haven, Fla., 790...F5   54
Mooreland, Okla., 871....A2   79
Moorestown, N.J., 12,497..D3   74
Mooresville, Ind., 3,856..E5   59
Mooresville, N.C., 6,918..B2   76
Moorhead, Minn., 22,934..D2   67
Moorhead, Miss., 1,754...B3   68
Mooringsport, La., 864...B2   63
Moorpark, Calif., 3,500...E4   50
Moose, mtn., Sask., Can...H4   39
Mooseheart, Ill., 1,200..B5, k8   58
Moose Jaw, Sask., Can., 33,206..........G3, n7   39
Moose Lake, Minn., 1,514...............D6   67
Moosic, Pa., 4,243.......m18   81
Moosic, mts., Pa........m18   81
Moosomin, Sask., Can., 1,781...............G5   39
Moosonee, Ont., Can., 975................o19   41
Moosup, Conn., 3,000....C9   52
Mopti, Mali, 12,700......F4   22
Moquegua, Peru, 7,700...E3   31
Moquegua, dept., Peru, 41,072..............E3   31
Mor, Hung., 11,482......B4   10
Mora, Minn., 2,329.......E5   67
Mora, N. Mex., 400......B6   48
Mora, Sp., 10,657.......C4   8
Mora, Swe., 6,032.......G6   11
Mora, co., N. Mex., 6,028..A6   48
Morada, Calif., 2,156....*D3   50
Moradabad, India, 180,100, (*191,828)..........C6   20
Moraine, Ohio, 2,262....*C1   78
Morales, Mex., 4,380....k13   34
Moramanga, Malag., 5,700...............D9   24
Moran, Kans., 549........E8   61
Morant Bay, Jam., 5,053..F5   35
Moratalla, Sp., 5,879.....C5   8
Moravia, Iowa, 621......D5   60
Moravia, N.Y., 1,575....C4   75
Moravia (Morava), reg., Czech., 3,532,444.....D4   7
Moray, co., Scot., 50,900..*B5   4
Morbihan, dept., Fr., 530,833.............*D2   5
Morden, Man., Can., 2,793...............E2   40
Moreauville, La., 815.....C4   63
Moree, Austl., 7,774......E8   25
Morehead, Ky., 4,170....B6   62
Morehead City, N.C., 5,583...............C6   76
Morehouse, par., La., 33,709..............B4   63
Morehouse, Mo., 1,417...E8   69
Moreland Hills, Ohio, 2,188...............*A4   78
Morelia, Mex., 100,828.........D4, n13   34
Morelos, state, Mex., 386,264.........D5, n14   34
Morenci, Ariz., 2,431.....C4   48
Morenci, Mich., 2,053.....G6   66
Möre og Romsdal, co., Nor., 216,500.......*F2   11
Morez, Fr., 5,777.......D7   5
Morgan, Minn., 975......F4   67
Morgan, Utah, 1,299.....A6   72
Morgan, co., Ala., 60,454..A3   46
Morgan, co., Colo., 21,192.............A7   51
Morgan, co., Ga., 10,280..C3   55

Morgan, co., Ill., 36,571...D3   58
Morgan, co., Ind., 33,875..F5   59
Morgan, co., Ky., 11,056..C6   62
Morgan, co., Mo., 9,476...C5   69
Morgan, co., Ohio, 12,747..C4   78
Morgan, co., Tenn., 14,304.............C9   83
Morgan, co., Utah, 2,837..A6   72
Morgan, co., W. Va., 8,376...............B6   87
Morgan City, La., 13,540.............E4, k9   63
Morganfield, Ky., 3,741...C2   62
Morgan Hill, Calif., 4,068..D3   50
Morganton, N.C., 9,186...B1   76
Morgantown, Ind., 971...F5   59
Morgantown, Ky., 1,318..C3   62
Morgantown, W. Va., 22,487..........A7, B5   87
Morganza, La., 937.......D4   63
Mori, Jap., 13,400.......E10   18
Moriguchi, Jap., 138,865..............*I7   18
Morinville, Alta., Can., 935................C4   38
Morioka, Jap., 176,967...G10   18
Morlaix, Fr., 18,866......C2   5
Morningdale, Mass., 900..B4   65
Morningside, Md., 1,708..*C4   53
Morningside, Minn., 1,981................*F5   67
Morning Sun, Iowa, 875...C6   60
Morocco, Ind., 1,341.....C3   59
Morocco, country, Afr., 13,451,000..........B4   22
Morococha, Peru, 1,522..D2   31
Morogoro, Tan., 14,507...B7   24
Moroléon, Mex., 17,954..m13   34
Morón, Cuba, 24,100....C4   35
Morona-Santiago, prov., Ec., 25,503..........B2   31
Morondava, Malag., 10,700..............E8   24
Moroni, Utah, 879.......B6   72
Morozovsk, Sov. Un., 28,000..............G13   12
Morrill, Nebr., 884.......C2   71
Morrill, co., Nebr., 7,057..C2   71
Morrilton, Ark., 5,997....B3   49
Morris, Ala., 638.........B3   46
Morris, Man., Can., 1,370..E3   40
Morris, Ill., 7,935.......B5   58
Morris, Minn., 4,199.....E3   67
Morris, N.Y., 677.......C5   75
Morris, Okla., 982.......B6   79
Morris, co., Kans., 7,392..D7   61
Morris, co., N.J., 261,620..B3   74
Morris, co., Tex., 12,576..C5   84
Morris, mtn., N.Y........A6   75
Morrisburg, Ont., Can., 1,820...............C9   41
Morrisdale, Pa., 800......E5   81
Morrison, Ill., 4,159.....A4   58
Morrison, Tenn., 294....*C5   83
Morrison, co., Minn., 26,641..............D4   67
Morrisonville, Ill., 1,129..D4   58
Morris Plains, N.J., 4,703..B4   74
Morristown, Ind., 704....E6   59
Morristown, Minn., 616...F5   67
Morristown, N.J., 17,712..B4   74
Morristown, N.Y., 541....f9   75
Morristown, Tenn., 21,267.............C10   83
Morrisville, N.Y., 1,686..C5   75
Morrisville, Vt., 2,047....B2   73
Morro Bay, Calif., 3,692..E3   50
Morro do Chapéu, Braz., 2,039...............E6   27
Morropón, Peru, 3,909...C2   31
Morrow, Ohio, 1,477.....C1   78
Morrow, co., Ohio, 19,405..B3   78
Morrow, co., Oreg., 4,871..B7   80
Morse, La., 682.........D3   63
Morshansk, Sov. Un., 48,000..............E13   12
Mortara, It., 10,500......B2   9
Morteros, Arg., 5,993....A4   28
Morton, Ill., 8,248......C4   58
Morton, Minn., 464......F4   67
Morton, Pa., 2,207.....*G11   81
Morton, Tex., 2,731.....C1   84
Morton, Wash., 1,183....C3   86
Morton, co., Kans., 3,354..E2   61
Morton, co., N. Dak., 20,992.............D4   77
Morton Grove, Ill., 25,154..h9   58
Mortons Gap, Ky., 1,308..C2   62
Moruya, Austl., 1,181....G8   26
Morven, N.C., 518.......C2   76
Morwell, Austl., 16,578.............G8, n15   25
Moscow, Idaho, 13,783..C2   57
Moscow, Pa., 1,212.....m18   81
Moscow (Moskva), Sov. Un., 6,423,000 (*8,500,000)......D11, n17   12

Moselle, dept., Fr., 919,412..............*C7   5
Moses Lake, Wash., 11,299..............B6   86
Moshi, Tan., 13,726......I5   23
Mosinee, Wis., 2,067.....D4   88
Mosjøen, Nor., 4,600.....E5   11
Moskva, see Moscow, Sov. Un.
Mosonmagyaróvar, Hung., 21,199........B3   10
Mosquera, Col., 766.....C2   32
Moss, Nor., 22,000...H4, p28   11
Mossbank, Sask., Can., 568................H3   39
Mossel Bay, S. Afr., 12,225.............G4   24
Mossman, Austl., 1,617...C8   25
Mossoro, Braz., 38,833...*D7   27
Moss Point, Miss., 6,631.............E3, E5   68
Most, Czech., 51,400.....C2   7
Mostaganem, Alg., 68,921..A5   22
Mostar, Yugo., 35,242...D3   10
Mosul, Iraq, 179,646....B3   15
Motala, Swe., 27,100.....H6   11
Motherwell [& Wishaw], Scot., 73,800.........C5   4
Motley, co., Tex., 2,870...B2   84
Motomachi, Jap., 5,900..o18   18
Motril, Sp., 19,185......D4   8
Mott, N. Dak., 1,463.....D3   77
Motul [de Felipe Carrillo Puerto], Mex., 10,351..C7   34
Motupe, Peru, 4,396.....C2   31
Moulins, Fr., 23,909.....D5   5
Moulmein, Bur., 108,000..E10   20
Moulton, Ala., 1,716.....A2   46
Moulton, Iowa, 773......D5   60
Moultrie, Ga., 15,764....E3   55
Moultrie, co., Ill., 13,635..D5   58
Mound, Minn., 5,990.....n11   67
Mound Bayou, Miss., 1,354..............B3   68
Mound City, Ill., 1,669...F4   58
Mound City, Kans., 661...D9   61
Mound City, Mo., 1,249..A2   69
Moundridge, Kans., 1,214..D6   61
Mounds, Ill., 1,835......F4   58
Mounds, Okla., 674......B5   79
Mounds View, Minn., 6,416..............*F5   67
Moundsville, W. Va., 15,163..........B2, B4   87
Moundville, Ala., 922.....C2   46
Mountain, prov., Phil., 435,839...........*B6   19
Mountainair, N. Mex., 1,605...............B5   48
Mountain Brook, Ala., 12,680.............E5   46
Mountain City, Tenn., 1,379.............C12   83
Mountain Dale, N.Y., 900................D6   75
Mountain Grove, Mo., 3,176...............D5   69
Mountain Home, Ark., 2,105...............A3   49
Mountain Home, Idaho., 10,075.............F3   57
Mountain Iron, Minn., 1,808...............C6   67
Mountain Lake, Minn., 1,943...............G4   67
Mountain Lake Park, Mo., 975...........m12   53
Mountain Lakes, N.J., 4,037...............B4   74
Mountain Pine, Ark., 1,300...........C2, C5   49
Mountainside, N.J., 6,325...............B4   74
Mountain View, Ark., 983................B3   49
Mountain View, Calif., 30,889..............k8   50
Mountainview, Haw., 566..D6   56
Mountain View, Idaho, 4,898..............*F2   57
Mountain View, Mo., 936..D6   69
Mountain View, Okla., 864................B3   79
Mountain View, Wyo., 400................*D2   89
Mount Airy, Md., 1,352...B3   53
Mount Airy, N.C., 7,055...A2   76
Mount Angel, Oreg., 1,428...........B4, h12   80
Mount Arlington, N.J., 1,246...............B3   74
Mount Athos, see Ayion Oros, Grc.
Mount Ayr, Iowa, 1,738..D3   60
Mount Berry, Ga., 1,000..B1   55
Mount Bethel, N.J., 600...B3   74
Mount Brydges, Ont., Can., 1,016..........E3   41

Mount Carmel, Newf.,
  Can., 673.............E5 44
Mount Carmel, Ill., 8,594..E6 58
Mount Carmel, Ohio,
  700.................o13 78
Mount Carmel, Pa.,
  10,760...............E9 81
Mount Carroll, Ill., 2,056..A4 58
Mount Clare, W. Va.,
  900..................B4 87
Mount Clemens, Mich.,
  21,016............F8, o16 66
Mount Dora, Fla., 3,756...D5 54
Mount Edgecumbe, Alsk.,
  1,884................m22 47
Mount Ephraim, N.J.,
  5,447................*D2 74
Mount Forest, Ont., Can.,
  2,623................D4 41
Mount Gambier, Austl.,
  17,146...............G7 25
Mount Gay, W. Va.,
  2,500................*D3 87
Mount Gilead, N.C.,
  1,229................B3 76
Mount Gilead, Ohio,
  2,788................B3 78
Mount Healthy, Ohio,
  6,553................o12 78
Mount Hermon, Mass.,
  600..................A3 65
Mount Holly, N.J.,
  13,271...............C3 74
Mount Holly, N.C., 5,120..B1 76
Mount Holly Springs, Pa.,
  1,840................F7 81
Mount Hope, Ont., Can.,
  807..................D5 42
Mount Hope, Kans.,
  539...............E6, g11 61
Mount Hope, N.J., 600....B3 74
Mount Hope, W. Va.,
  2,000.............D3, D7 87
Mount Horeb, Wis., 1,991..E4 88
Mount Houston, Tex.,
  2,500................*E5 84
Mount Isa, Austl., 16,713..D6 25
Mount Jackson, Va., 722..B4 85
Mount Jewett, Pa., 1,226..C4 81
Mount Joy, Pa., 3,292.....F9 81
Mount Kisco, N.Y.,
  6,941.............D7, m15 75
Mountlake Terrace,
  Wash., 9,122.........*B3 86
Mount Lebanon, Pa.,
  35,361...............F1 81
Mount Magnet, Austl.,
  900..................E2 25
Mount Morgan, Austl.,
  4,051................D9 25
Mount Moriah, Newf.,
  Can., 716............*D2 44
Mount Morris, Ill., 3,075..A4 58
Mount Morris, Mich.,
  3,484................E7 66
Mount Morris, N.Y.,
  3,250................C3 75
Mount Olive, Ala., 40..B3, E4 46
Mount Olive, Ill., 2,295...D4 58
Mount Olive, N.C., 4,673..B4 76
Mount Oliver, Pa., 5,980..k14 81
Mount Orab, Ohio, 1,058..C2 78
Mount Pearl Park, Newf.,
  Can., 2,785..........f9 44
Mount Penn, Pa., 3,574..*F10 81
Mount Pleasant, Iowa,
  7,339................D6 60
Mount Pleasant, Mich.,
  14,875...............E6 66
Mount Pleasant, N.C.,
  1,041................B2 76
Mount Pleasant, Pa.,
  6,107................F2 81
Mount Pleasant, S.C.,
  5,116.............F8, k12 82
Mount Pleasant, Tenn.,
  2,921................B4 83
Mount Pleasant, Tex.,
  8,027................C5 84
Mount Pleasant, Utah,
  1,572................B6 72
Mount Pocono, Pa., 935..D11 81
Mount Prospect, Ill.,
  30,202.............A6, h9 58
Mount Pulaski, Ill., 1,689..C4 58
Mountrail, co., N. Dak.,
  10,077...............B3 77

Mount Rainier, Md.,
  9,855................f9 53
Mount Royal, Que., Can.,
  21,182...............*D4 42
Mount Royal, N.J., 700...D2 74
Mount Savage, Md.,
  1,750................k13 53
Mount Shasta, Calif.,
  2,272................B2 50
Mount Sterling, Ill.,
  2,262................D3 58
Mount Sterling, Ky.,
  5,370................B6 62
Mount Sterling, Ohio,
  1,388................C2 78
Mount Union, Pa., 4,091..F6 81
Mount Vernon, Ala., 553..D1 46
Mount Vernon, Ga., 200..D4 55
Mount Vernon, Ill.,
  15,566...............E5 58
Mount Vernon, Ind.,
  5,970................I2 59
Mount Vernon, Iowa
  2,593................C6 60
Mount Vernon, Ky.,
  1,177................C5 62
Mount Vernon, Md., 500..D6 53
Mount Vernon, Mo.,
  2,381................D4 69
Mount Vernon, N.Y.,
  3,200................*C2 75
Mount Vernon, N.Y.,
  72,918...............h13 75
Mount Vernon, Ohio,
  13,284...............B3 78
Mount Vernon, Tex.,
  1,338................C5 84
Mount Vernon, Wash.,
  7,921................A3 86
Mount Victory, Ohio, 598..B2 78
Mountville, Pa., 1,411....*G9 81
Mount Washington, Ky.,
  1,173.............A4, B4 62
Mount Wolf, Pa., 1,514...F8 81
Mount Zion, Ill., 925.....D5 58
Moura, Port., 9,509......C2 8
Mourne, mts., N. Ire.....C3 4
Mouscron, Bel., 36,554...B5 5
Mousie, Ky., 500.........C7 62
Moville, Iowa, 1,156.....B1 60
Moweaqua, Ill., 1,614....D4 58
Mower, co., Minn.,
  48,498...............G6 67
Moyeuvre-Grande, Fr.,
  15,146...............C7 5
Moyobamba, Peru, 8,850..C2 31
Mozambique, Port. dep.,
  Afr., 6,592,994.......D7 24
Mozhaysk, Sov. Un.,
  10,000...............D11 12
Mozyr, Sov. Un., 25,000..E7 12
Mtsensk, Sov. Un.,
  10,000...............E11 12
Mung Hot, Thai.,.......*B1 19
Muang Nan, Thai.,
  13,802...............*B2 19
Muchkap, Sov. Un.,
  10,000...............F14 12
Mucuri, Braz., 603......E7 27
Mudanya, Tur., 5,900....*B7 14
Mudgee, Austl., 5,313....F7 26
Muenster, Tex., 1,190....C4 84
Mufulira, Zambia,
  75,900...............C5 24
Mugía, Sp., 7,061.......A1 8
Mugla, Tur., 14,053.....D7 14
Mühldorf, Ger., 10,800..D6 6
Muhlenberg, co., Ky.,
  27,791...............C2 62
Muhlenburg Park, Pa.,
  1,000................*F9 81
Mühlhausen, Ger.,
  45,300...............C5 6
Muir, Mich., 610........E6 66
Mukachevo, Sov. Un.,
  51,000...............G4 12
Mukden (Shenyang),
  China, 2,411,000......C9 17
Mukilteo, Wash., 1,128...B3 86
Mukwonago, Wis.,
  1,877.............F5, n11 88
Mula, Sp., 14,312.......C5 8
Mulberry, Ark., 934......B1 49
Mulberry, Fla., 2,922....E5 54
Mulberry, Ind., 1,062....D4 59
Mulberry, Kans., 642....E9 61
Mulchén, Chile, 10,700...B2 28

Muldraugh, Ky., 1,743....C4 62
Muldrow, Okla., 1,137....B7 79
Mulege, Mex., 883.......B2 34
Muleng, China, 5,000....D5 18
Muleshoe, Tex., 3,871....B1 84
Mulga Mine, Ala.,
  482...............B3, E4 46
Mulgrave, N.S., Can.,
  1,145................D8 43
Mulhacén, mtn., Sp.,.....D4 8
Mülheim [an der Ruhr],
  Ger., 190,800.........C3 6
Mulhouse, Fr., 108,995...D7 5
Mullan, Idaho, 1,477.....B3 57
Mullens, W. Va., 3,544...D3 87
Mullewa, Austl., 799.....E2 25
Mullica Hill, N.J., 500...D2 74
Mullingar, Ire., 6,500....D3 4
Mullins, S.C., 6,229.....C9 82
Multan, Pak., 340,399....B5 20
Multnomah, co., Oreg.,
  522,813..............B4 80
Mulvane, Kans., 2,981....E6 61
Muna, Mex., 4,443.......C7 34
München (Munich),
  Ger., 1,214,600.......D5 6
Munchŏn, Kor., 12,005...G3 18
Muncie, Ind., 69,500
  (*107,000)...........D7 59
Muncy, Pa., 2,830.......D8 81
Mundare, Alta., Can.,
  603..................C4 38
Munday, Tex., 1,978.....C3 84
Mundelein, Ill.,
  14,368.............A5, h9 58
Münden, Ger., 20,200....C4 6
Munford, Tenn., 1,014...B2 83
Munfordville, Ky., 1,157..C4 62
Munhall, Pa., 17,312.....k14 81
Munich, see München,
  Ger.
Munising, Mich., 4,228...B4 66
Munroe Falls, Ohio,
  1,828................*A4 78
Munsan, Kor., 5,000.....H3 18
Munsey Park, N.Y.,
  2,847................*E7 75
Munster, Fr., 4,965......C7 5
Munster, Ind., 12,581....A2 59
Münster [In Westfalen],
  Ger., 190,800.........C3 6
Munster, prov., Ire.,
  858,700..............*D2 4
Muntenia, prov., Rom.,
  4,991,289............*C8 10
Muntenia, reg., Rom......C7 10
Muntok, Indon., 6,929....F3 19
Muong Hou Nua, Laos,
  10,000...............*D11 20
Muong Sing, Laos,
  10,000...............D11 20
Murakami, Jap., 24,600..G9 18
Murcia, Sp., 126,000.....C5 8
Murcia, reg., Sp.,
  1,171,439............C5 8
Murfreesboro, Ark., 1,096..C2 49
Murfreesboro, N.C.,
  2,643................A5 76
Murfreesboro, Tenn.,
  18,991...............B5 83
Muriae, Braz., 22,571....C4 30
Murmansk, Sov. Un.,
  254,000..............C15 11
Murom, Sov. Un.,
  83,000...............D13 12
Muroran, Jap., 161,252...E10 18
Muroto, Jap., 20,500.....J7 18
Murphy, Mo.,...........g13 69
Murphy, N.C., 2,235.....F8 76
Murphysboro, Ill., 9,393..F4 58
Murray, Iowa, 613.......C4 60
Murray, Ky., 9,303......B3 62
Murray, Utah,
  16,806............A6, C2 72
Murray, co., Ga., 10,447..B2 55
Murray, co., Minn.,
  14,743...............F3 67
Murray, co., Okla.,
  10,622...............C4 79
Murray, riv., Austl.......G7 25
Murray City, Ohio, 717..C3 78
Murrells Inlet, S.C., 500..D9 82
Murrysville, Pa., 1,000...k15 81
Murud, India, 9,744......E5 20
Murwillumbah, Austl.,
  7,153................D9 26

Mürzzuschlag, Aus.,
  11,586...............E7 6
Mus, Tur., 11,965.......C13 14
Musala, peak, Bul.......D6 10
Musan, Kor., 20,717.....E4 18
Musashino, Jap.,
  133,516..............*I9 18
Muscat, Mus. & Om.,
  6,000................D2 20
Muscat & Oman,
  country, Asia, 565,000..F6 15
Muscatine, Iowa, 22,194..C6 60
Muscatine, co., Iowa,
  33,840...............C6 60
Muscle Shoals, Ala.,
  4,084................A2 46
Musclow, mtn., B.C.,
  Can.................C4 37
Muscoda, Wis., 927.....E3 88
Muscogee, co., Ga.,
  158,623..............D2 55
Musconetcong, mtn.,
  N.J..................B2 74
Muse, Pa., 1,386........F1 81
Musgravetown, Newf.,
  Can., 597............D5 44
Mushketovo, Sov. Un.,
  10,000...............r20 12
Muskego, Wis.,
  10,497............F5, n11 88
Muskegon, Mich., 43,000
  (*172,000)...........E4 66
Muskegon, co., Mich.,
  149,943..............E4 66
Muskegon Heights, Mich.,
  19,552...............E4 66
Muskingum, co., Ohio,
  79,159...............B3 78
Muskö, Swe.............u36 11
Muskogee, Okla., 38,059..B6 79
Muskogee, co., Okla.,
  61,866...............B6 79
Muskoka, dist., Ont.,
  Can., 26,705.........B5 41
Musquash, mtn., Maine...C5 64
Musquodoboit Harbour,
  N.S., Can., 654.......E6 43
Musselburgh, Scot.,
  17,700...............C5 4
Musselshell, co., Mont.,
  4,888................D8 70
Mustafa, Kemalpasa, Tur.,
  20,886...............B7 14
Muswellbrook, Austl.,
  6,288................F9 25
Mutankiang, China,
  151,400..............D4 18
Mutsu, Jap., 24,700.....F10 18
Mutton, mts.,
  Oreg.................C5 80
Muttontown, N.Y.,
  1,265................*E7 75
Muzaffarpur, India,
  109,048..............C8 20
Muzambinho, Braz.,
  6,731................k8 30
Muztagh Ata, mtn.,
  China................A7 20
Mwanza, Tan., 19,877...I4 23
Myaungmya, Bur.,
  20,770...............*E9 20
Myers, S.C., 1,000......k12 82
Myerstown, Pa., 3,268...F9 81
Myingyan, Bur., 36,536..D10 20
Myitkyina, Bur., 12,833..C10 20
Myjava, Czech., 9,935....D4 7
Mymensingh, Pak.,
  53,256...............D9 20
Myrtle Beach, S.C.,
  7,834................D10 82
Myrtle Creek, Oreg.,
  2,231................D3 80
Myrtle Grove, Fla.,
  13,000...............u14 54
Myrtle Point, Oreg.,
  2,886................D2 80
Mysen, Nor., 2,525......p29 11
Myslenice, Pol., 6,520....D5 7
Myslowice, Pol., 42,700..g10 7
Mysore, India, 253,865...F6 20
Mysore, state, India,
  23,586,772...........F6 20
Mystic, Conn., 6,500.....D9 52
Mystic, Iowa, 761.......D5 60
My Tho, Viet, 40,070....C3 19
Mytischi, Sov. Un.,
  107,000..............n17 12

N

Naalehu, Haw., 1,000.....D6　56
Nabeul, Tun., 14,047......A7　22
Nabnasset, Mass., 1,500...A5　65
Nābulus, Jordan,
　45,768..............B3, g5　15
Naches, Wash., 680......C5　86
Nachod, Czech., 17,800....C4　7
Nacogdoches, Tex.,
　12,674..............D5　84
Nacogdoches, co., Tex.,
　28,046..............D5　84
Nacozari [de García],
　Mex., 2,745............A3　34
Nădlac, Rom., 12,284....B5　10
Nadvornaya, Sov. Un.,
　10,000...............G5　12
Naesong, Kor., 5,000.....H4　18
Naestved, Den., 19,617....J4　11
Naga, Phil., 55,506......C6　19
Nagano, Jap., 172,836....H9　18
Nagano, pref., Jap.,
　1,958,007............*H9　18
Nagaoka, Jap., 106,000...H9　18
Nagasaki, Jap., 405,479....J4　18
Nagasaki, pref., Jap.,
　1,641,245............*J4　18
Nagercoil, India,
　106,207.............G6　20
Nagoya, Jap.,
　1,935,430..........J8, n15　18
Nagpur, India, 643,659....D6　20
Nags Head, N.C., 700....B7　76
Nagua, Dom. Rep., 6,180..E9　35
Nagykanizsa, Hung.,
　34,222..............B3　10
Nagykoros, Hung., 19,908..B4　10
Naha, Ryukyu Is.,
　246,900.............F10　17
Nahant, Mass., 3,960.....g10　65
Nahariya, Isr., 15,900....A3　15
Nahunta, Ga., 952.......E5　55
Naicam, Sask., Can., 672.E3　39
Nairn, Scot., 4,900......B5　4
Nairn, co., Scot., 8,300...*B5　4
Nairobi, Ken., 266,795....I5　23
Najin, Kor., 34,338......E5　18
Nakaminato, Jap.,
　26,900..............m19　18
Nakamura, Jap.,
　17,900..............J6　18
Nakatsu, Jap., 43,000.....J5　18
Nakhichevan [na Arakse],
　Sov. Un., 27,000......F7　16
Nakhon Ratchasima,
　Thai., 42,218........C2　19
Nakina, Ont., Can., 747..o18　41
Nakiri, Jap., 7,000......o15　18
Naklo, Pol., 15,000......B4　7
Nakskov, Den., 16,639....J4　11
Nakuru, Ken., 38,181.....I5　23
Nakusp, B.C., Can., 992...D9　37
Nalchik, Sov. Un.,
　106,000.............*E7　13
Namcha Barwa, mtn.,
　China...............F4　17
Namangan, Sov. Un.,
　138,000.............E10　12
Nambour, Austl., 6,211....E9　25
Nam Dinh, Viet, 86,132...A3　19
Namiquipa, Mex., 908....B3　34
Nampa, Idaho, 18,897.....F2　57
Nampo (Chinnampo),
　Kor., 82,162.........G2　18
Nampula, Moz..........D7　24
Namur, Bel., 32,511......B6　5
Namur, prov., Bel.,
　369,432.............*B6　5
Namwŏn, Kor., 25,900.....I3　18
Nanaimo, B.C., Can.,
　14,135............E5, f12　37
Nanakuli, Haw.,
　2,745.............B3, g9　56
Nanam, Kor., 21,258......F4　18
Nanao, Jap., 32,300......H8　18
Nance, co., Nebr., 5,635...C7　71
Nanchang, China,
　508,000.............F8　17
Nancheng, China, 18,000..E6　17
Nanchung, China,
　164,700.............E6　17
Nancy, Fr., 128,677......C7　5
Nanda Devi, peak, India..B7　20
Nanga Parbat, peak,
　Pak................A5　20
Nanhai (Fatshan), China,
　122,500............*G7　17
Nanju, Kor., 15,000......I3　18
Nanking, China,
　1,419,000...........E8　17
Nanning, China, 264,000..G6　17
Nanping, China, 29,000....F8　17

Nansemond, co., Va.,
　31,366..............D6　85
Nanterre, Fr., 83,416......g9　5
Nantes, Fr., 240,028......D3　5
Nanticoke, Md., 600.....D6　53
Nanticoke, Pa.,
　15,601............D10, n16　81
Nanton, Alta., Can.,
　1,054..............D4　38
Nantucket, Mass., 2,900...D7　65
Nantucket, co., Mass.,
　3,559..............D7　65
Nantung, China, 260,400..*E9　17
Nanty Glo, Pa., 4,608....F4　81
Nanuet, N.Y., 8,700......g12　75
Nanyang, China, 50,000...E7　17
Naoma, W. Va., 600......D6　87
Naousa, Grc., 15,492.....*B4　14
Napa, Calif., 22,170......C2　50
Napa, co., Calif., 65,890...C2　50
Napanee, Ont., Can.,
　4,500..............C8　41
Napanoch, N.Y., 950.....D6　75
Naperville, Ill.,
　18,734............B5, k8　58
Napier, N.Z., 28,645
　(*38,309)...........M16　26
Napierville, Que., Can.,
　1,812..............D4　42
Napierville, co., Que.,
　Can., 11,216.........D4　42
Naples, Fla., 4,655.......F5　54
Naples (Napoli), It.,
　1,204,900...........D5　9
Naples, N.Y., 1,237......C3　75
Naples, Tex., 1,692......C5　84
Napo, riv., Ec., Peru.....B2　31
Napoleon, N. Dak.,
　1,078..............D6　77
Napoleon, Ohio, 6,739....A1　78
Napoleonville, La.,
　1,148.............E4, k9　63
Napoli, see Naples, It.
Nappanee, Ind., 3,895....B5　59
Nara, Jap., 160,641......o14　18
Naracoorte, Austl., 4,377..G7　25
Naranja, Fla., 2,700...G6, s13　54
Narbada, riv., India......D6　20
Narberth, Pa., 5,109..F11, o20　81
Narbonne, Fr., 33,891....F5　5
Nardó, It., 24,000.......D7　9
Nariño, dept., Col.,
　705,611.............C2　32
Narita, Jap., 20,800......n19　18
Narodnaya, mtn.,
　Sov. Un.............C9　13
Naro-Fominsk, Sov. Un.,
　35,419.............D11　12
Narol, Man., Can., 592...D3　40
Narrabri, Austl., 5,953....F8　25
Narragansett, R.I.,
　2,000..............D11　52
Narrandera, Austl., 4,897..F8　25
Narrogin, Austl., 4,864....F2　25
Narrows, Va., 2,508......C2　85
Narrowsburg, N.Y., 500...D5　75
Narva, Sov. Un., 27,600...B7　12
Narvik, Nor., 13,600......C7　11
Naryan-Mar, Sov. Un.,
　11,400.............C8　13
Nassawadox, Va., 650.....C7　85
Nash, Tex., 1,124.......C5　84
Nash, co., N.C., 61,002...A4　76
Nashua, Iowa, 1,737.....B5　60
Nashua, Mont., 796......B10　70
Nashua, N.H., 39,096.....F5　73
Nashville, Ark., 3,579....D2　49
Nashville, Ga., 4,070.....E3　55
Nashville, Ill., 2,606.....E4　58
Nashville, Mich., 1,525...F5　66
Nashville, N.C., 1,423....B5　76
Nashville, Tenn., 275,000
　(*470,000).........A5, E9　83
Nashwauk, Minn., 1,712...C5　67
Našice, Yugo., 4,157.....C4　10
Nasik, India, 131,103.....E5　20
Nassau, Ba. Is.,
　6,000............B5, m17　35
Nassau, N.Y., 1,248......C7　75
Nassau, co., Fla., 17,189..B5　54
Nassau, co., N.Y.,
　1,300,171...........E7　75
Nässjö, Swe., 18,400......I6　11
Nasukoin, mtn., Mont.....B2　70
Natagaima, Col., 8,372....C2　32
Natal, Braz., 154,276.....D7　27
Natal, B.C., Can., 829....E10　37
Natal, prov., S. Afr.,
　2,979,920...........F6　24
Natalia, Tex., 1,200......E3　84
Natchez, Miss., 23,791...D2　68

Natchitoches, La., 13,924..C2　63
Natchitoches, par., La.,
　35,653.............C2　63
Natick, Mass.,
　28,831...........B5, g10　65
National City, Calif.,
　32,771..........F5, o15　50
National Park, N.J.,
　3,380.............*D2　74
Natívitas, Mex., 2,613....h9　34
Natoma, Kans., 775......C4　61
Natrona, co., Wyo.,
　49,623.............D6　89
Natrona, Heights, Pa.,
　15,710...........E2, h15　81
Natural Bridge, N.Y., 750..A5　75
Naturita, Colo., 979......C2　51
Nauen, Ger., 12,300......B6　6
Naugatuck, Conn.,
　19,511.............D4　52
Naughton, Ont., Can.,
　954...............A3　41
Naumburg [an der Saale],
　Ger., 37,700.........C5　6
Nauru, country, Oceania,
　5,000..............G8　2
Nauta, Peru, 689........B3　31
Nautla, Mex., 1,409..C5, m15　34
Nauvoo, Ill., 1,039.......C2　58
Navalmoral de la Mata,
　Sp., 9,073...........C3　8
Navarra (Navarre), prov.,
　Sp., 402,042........*A5　8
Navarre, Ohio, 1,698.....B4　78
Navarre, reg., Sp.,
　402,042.............A5　8
Navarro, co., Tex.,
　34,423.............C4　84
Navasota, Tex., 4,937.....D4　84
Navassa, N.C., 500......C4　76
Navesink, N.J., 1,500.....C4　74
Navojoa, Mex., 30,560....B3　34
Navolato, Mex., 9,118....C3　34
Navplion, Grc., 7,080....*D4　14
Navy Yard City, Wash.,
　3,341.............*B3　86
Nayarit, state, Mex.,
　389,929..........C4, m11　34
Nayoro, Jap., 25,600.....D11　18
Nazaré, Braz., 14,644....*E7　27
Nazaré, Port., 9,241......C1　8
Nazareth, Isr., 26,400..B3, g5　15
Nazareth, Ky., 500......C4　62
Nazareth, Pa., 6,209.....E11　81
Nazas, Mex., 2,738.......B4　34
Nazca, Peru, 13,600......D3　31
Nazilli, Tur., 36,660.....D7　14
Ndola, Zambia, 88,900....C5　24
Neah Bay, Wash., 600....A1　86
Neath, Wales, 30,600.....E5　4
Neba, Jap., 800........n16　18
Nebraska, state, U.S.,
　1,411,330...........　71
Nebraska City, Nebr.,
　7,252...........D10, h13　71
Necedah, Wis., 691......D3　88
Nechako, mts., B.C., Can..C5　37
Necochea, Arg., 17,808....B5　28
Nederland, Tex., 12,036...E6　84
Nedrow, N.Y., 2,500.....*C4　75
Needham, Mass., 25,793..g11　65
Needle, mtn., Wyo.......B3　89
Needles, Calif., 4,590.....E6　50
Needville, Tex., 861.....r14　84
Ñeembucú, dept., Par.,
　50,861.............E4　29
Neenah, Wis., 18,057..D5, h9　88
Neepawa, Man., Can.,
　3,197.............D2　40
Neffs, Ohio, 800........B5　78
Neffsville, Pa., 900......F9　81
Negapattinam, India,
　59,063.............F6　20
Negaunee, Mich., 6,126...B3　66
Negley, Ohio, 500.......B5　78
Negotin, Yugo., 8,639....C6　10
Negra, mts., Peru........C2　31
Negreira, Sp., 5,725......A1　8
Negro, riv., S.A.........D4　27
Negros, isl., Phil........D6　19
Negros Occidental, prov.,
　Phil., 1,332,323......*C6　19
Negros Oriental, prov.,
　Phil., 597,761.......*D6　19
Neguac, N.B., Can., 559..B4　43
Neiba, Dom. Rep., 4,620..E8　35
Neillsville, Wis., 2,728....D3　88
Neiva, Col., 75,886......C2　32
Nejd, pol. div., Sau. Ar.,
　5,000,000...........D3　15
Nekoosa, Wis., 2,515.....D4　88

Neligh, Nebr., 1,776......B7　71
Nellore, India, 106,776...F6　20
Nelson, B.C., Can.,
　7,074..............E9　37
Nelson, Nebr., 695......D7　71
Nelson, N.Z., 26,218
　(*27,615)...........N14　26
Nelson, co., Ky., 22,168..C4　62
Nelson, co., N. Dak.,
　7,034..............C7　77
Nelson, co., Va., 12,752..C4　85
Nelsonville, Ohio, 4,834..C3　78
Nemacolin, Pa., 1,404....G2　81
Nemaha, co., Kans.,
　12,897.............C7　61
Nemaha, co., Nebr.,
　9,099.............D10　71
Nemunas (Niemen), riv.,
　Sov. Un.............D3　12
Nemuro, Jap., 45,149....E12　18
Neodesha, Kans., 3,594...E8　61
Neoga, Ill., 1,145.......D5　58
Neola, Iowa, 870.......C2　60
Neon, Ky., 766.........C7　62
Neopit, Wis., 1,359......D5　88
Neosho, Mo., 7,452.....E3　69
Neosho, co., Kans.,
　19,455.............E8　61
Nepal, country, Asia,
　9,900,000...........C7　20
Nephi, Utah, 2,566......B6　72
Neptune, N.J., 13,000....C4　74
Neptune Beach, Fla.,
　2,868...........B5, m9　54
Neptune City, N.J.,
　4,013.............*C4　74
Nerchinsk, Sov. Un.,
　28,700.............D14　13
Nerekhta, Sov. Un.,
　19,900.............C13　12
Nerja, Sp., 7,224.......D4　8
Nerva, Sp., 12,686......D2　8
Nesconset, N.Y., 2,500...F4　52
Nescopeck, Pa., 1,934....D9　81
Neshoba, co., Miss.,
　20,927.............C4　68
Nesquehoning, Pa.,
　3,000..............E10　81
Ness, co., Kans., 5,470...D3　61
Ness City, Kans., 1,653...D4　61
Nes Ziona, Isr., 10,917..*C2　15
Netarts, Oreg., 600......B3　80
Netcong, N.J., 2,765.....B3　74
Netherlands, country,
　Eur., 12,535,500.......A6　5
Netherlands Antilles,
　dep., N.A., 188,914...*A4　32
Nettleton, Miss., 1,389...A5　68
Nettuno, It., 14,100......k9　9
Neubrandenburg, Ger.,
　33,400.............B6　6
Neuburg, Ger., 16,500....D5　6
Neuchâtel, Switz., 35,600,
　(*51,900)...........E3　6
Neuchâtel, canton, Switz.,
　147,633.............E3　6
Neufchâtel-en-Bray, Fr.,
　5,590..............C4　5
Neuhaldensleben, Ger.,
　22,000.............B5　6
Neuilly [sur-Marne], Fr.,
　15,082.............g11　5
Neuilly-sur-Seine, Fr.,
　72,773.............g10　5
Neumarkt, Ger., 15,800...D5　6
Neumünster, Ger.,
　74,800.............A4　6
Neunkirchen, Aus.,
　10,027.............E8　6
Neuquén, Arg., 16,738....B3　28
Neuquén, Prov., Arg.,
　111,008.............B3　28
Neuruppin, Ger., 22,000..B6　6
Neustadt, Ont., Can., 493..C4　41
Neustadt [an der Aisch],
　Ger., 8,900.........C5　6
Neustadt [an der
　Weinstrasse], Ger.,
　31,600.............D4　6
Neustadt [bei Coburg],
　Ger., 12,600.........D4　6
Neustadt [im
　Schwarzwald], Ger.,
　6,900..............A5　6
Neustadt [in Holstein],
　Ger., 14,500.........C5　6
Neustrelitz, Ger., 28,000..B6　6
Neu-Ulm, Ger., 24,300...D5　6
Neuville, Que., Can.,
　802...............C6, o16　42
Neuwied, Ger., 26,400....C3　6

Nevada, Iowa, 4,840....B4 60
Nevada, Mo., 8,416......D3 69
Nevada, Ohio, 919......B2 78
Nevada, co., Ark., 10,700..D2 49
Nevada, co., Calif., 20,911............C3 50
Nevada, state, U.S., 285,278............ 72
Nevada City, Calif., 2,353..C3 50
Nevada de Colima, mtn., Mex............n12 34
Nevada de Toluca, mtn., Mex............n14 34
Nevado del Huilo, peak, Col............C2 32
Nevelsk, Sov. Un., 10,980............C10 18
Nevers, Fr., 39,085.......D5 5
Nevesinje, Yugo., 2,272..D4 10
Neville Island, Pa., 2,400............*E1 81
Nevsehir, Tur., 18,662...C10 14
New Albany, Ind., 38,218............H6 59
New Albany, Miss., 5,151..A4 68
New Albin, Iowa, 643.....A6 60
New Alexandria, Va., 1,500............*B5 85
New Amsterdam, Guy., 14,059............C5 27
Newark, Ark., 728.......B4 49
Newark, Calif., 9,884.....h8 50
Newark, Del., 11,404.....A6 53
Newark, Eng., 24,700.....D6 4
Newark, N.J., 405,220..B4, k8 74
Newark, N.Y., 12,868.....B3 75
Newark, Ohio, 41,790.....B3 78
Newark Valley, N.Y., 1,234............C4 75
New Athens, Ill., 1,923...E4 58
Newaygo, Mich., 1,447...E5 66
Newaygo, co., Mich., 24,160............E5 66
New Baden, Ill., 1,464....E4 58
New Baltimore, Mich., 3,159............F8 66
New Baltimore, N.Y., 500..C7 75
New Beaver, Pa., 1,383...*E1 81
New Bedford, Mass., 99,000 (*156,000)............C6 65
Newberg, Oreg., 4,204............B4, h12 80
New Berlin, Ill., 744.....D4 58
New Berlin, N.Y., 1,262...C5 75
New Berlin, Wis., 15,788..n11 88
New Berlinville, Pa., 1,151............*F9 81
New Bern, N.C., 15,717...B5 76
Newbern, Tenn., 1,695...A2 83
Newberry, Fla., 1,105....C4 54
Newberry, Mich., 2,612...B5 66
Newberry, S.C., 8,208....C4 82
Newberry, co., S.C., 29,416............C4 82
New Bethlehem, Pa., 1,599............D3 81
New Bloomfield (Bloomfield), Pa., 987...F7 81
New Boston, Ill., 726.....B3 58
New Boston, Mich., 900..p15 66
New Boston, Ohio, 3,984..D3 87
New Boston, Tex., 2,773...C5 84
New Braunfels, Tex., 15,631............E3, h7 84
New Bremen, Ohio, 1,972..B1 78
New Brighton, Minn., 6,448............*E5 67
New Brighton, Pa., 8,397...E1 81
New Britain, Conn., 82,201............C5 52
New Britain, Isl., N. Gui............G7 2
New Brockton, Ala., 1,093............D4 46
New Brunswick, N.J., 40,139............C4 74
New Brunswick, prov., Can., 616,788............C3 43
New Brunswick Heights, N.J., 200............*C4 74
New Buffalo, Mich., 2,128............G4 66
Newburg, Mo., 884.......D6 69
Newburgh, Ont., Can., 569............C8 41
Newburgh, Ind., 1,450....I3 59
Newburgh, N.Y., 27,000 (*138,000)............D6 75
Newburgh Heights, Ohio, 3,512............h12 78
Newbury, Eng., 21,000...E6 4
Newbury, Mass., 800.....A6 65
Newburyport, Mass., 14,004............A6 65
New Caledonia, Fr., dep., Oceania, 85,000....H7 2
New Canaan, Conn., 13,466............E3 52

New Carlisle, Que., Can., 1,333............A4 43
New Carlisle, Ind., 1,376..A4 59
New Carlisle, Ohio, 4,107..C1 78
New Cassel, N.Y., 8,400...*E7 75
New Castile, reg., Sp., 4,210,817............C4 8
New Castle, Ala., 950..B3, E5 46
Newcastle, Austl., 144,100..F9 25
Newcastle, Calif., 900.....C3 50
Newcastle, N.B., Can., 5,236............B4 43
Newcastle, Ont., Can., 1,272............D6 41
New Castle, Del., 4,469...A6 53
New Castle, Ind., 20,349..E7 59
New Castle, Pa., 44,790...D1 81
Newcastle, Tex., 617......C3 84
Newcastle, Wyo., 4,345...C8 89
New Castle, co., Del., 307,446............A6 53
Newcastle Bridge, N.B., Can., 483............C3 43
Newcastle Mine, Alta., Can., 949............D4 38
New Castle Northwest, Pa., 2,007............*E1 81
Newcastle-on-Tyne, Eng., 263,400............C6 4
New Chicago, Ind., 2,312..A3 59
New City, N.Y., 9,500............D7, m15 75
Newcomb, N.Y., 500......B6 75
Newcomerstown, Ohio, 4,273............B4 78
New Concord, Ohio, 2,127............C4 78
New Cumberland, Pa., 9,257............F8 81
New Cumberland, W. Va., 2,076......A2, A4 87
New Cumnock, Scot., 3,871............C4 4
New Delhi, India, 261,545............C6 20
New Denver, B.C., Can., 564............D9 37
New Eagle, Pa., 2,670....*F1 81
New Egypt, N.J., 1,737...C3 74
Newell, Iowa, 893........B2 60
Newell, W. Va., 1,842............A2, A4 87
New Ellenton, S.C., 2,309..E4 82
Newellton, La., 1,453....B4 63
New England, N. Dak., 1,095............D3 77
Newfane, N.Y., 1,600....B2 75
Newfield, N.J., 1,299....D2 74
New Florence, Mo., 616...C6 69
New Florence, Pa., 958...F3 81
Newfoundland, prov., Can., 493,396............ 44
Newfoundland, N.J., 800..A4 74
New Franklin, Mo., 1,096..B5 69
New Freedom, Pa., 1,395..G8 81
New Germany, N.S., Can., 623............E5 43
New Glarus, Wis., 1,468...F4 88
New Glasgow, N.S., Can., 9,782............D7 43
New Gretna, N.J., 500....D4 74
New Guinea, isl., Oceania..G6 2
New Guinea, Territory of, Austl. trust., Oceania 1,449,000............h12 25
Newgulf, Tex., 1,419.....*E5 84
Newhall, Calif., 7,000....E4 50
Newhall, Iowa, 601......C6 60
New Hamburg, Ont., Can., 2,181............D4 41
New Hampshire, state, U.S., 606,921............ 73
New Hampton, Iowa, 3,593............A5 60
New Hanover, co., N.C., 71,742............C5 76
New Harbour, Newf., Can., 756............E5 44
New Harmony, Ind., 1,121............H2 59
New Hartford, Conn. 1,200............B5 52
New Hartford, Iowa, 649..B5 60
New Hartford, N.Y., 2,468............*B5 75
New Haven, Conn., 146,000 (*472,000)......D5 52
New Haven, Ill., 642.....F5 58
New Haven, Ind., 3,396...B7 59
New Haven, Ky., 1,009...C4 62
New Haven, Mich., 1,198..F8 66
New Haven, Mo., 1,223...C6 69
New Haven, W. Va., 1,314............C3 87
New Haven, co., Conn., 660,315............D4 52
New Hebrides, Br. and Fr. dep., Oceania, 65,000...H8 2

New Holland, Ga., 800....B3 55
New Holland, Ohio, 798...C2 78
New Holland, Pa., 3,425...F9 81
New Holstein, Wis., 2,401............E5, k9 88
New Hope, Ala., 953......A3 46
New Hope, Minn., 3,552...*E5 67
New Hope, Pa., 958......F12 81
New Hudson, Mich., 600..o14 66
New Hyde Park, N.Y., 10,808............G2 52
New Iberia, La., 29,062...D4 63
Newington, Conn., 17,664..C6 52
New Jersey, state, U.S., 6,066,782............ 74
New Kensington, Pa., 23,485............E2, h14 81
New Kent, co., Va., 4,504..C6 85
Newkirk, Okla., 2,092....A4 79
New Knoxville, Ohio, 792..B1 78
Newland, N.C., 564...A1, e11 76
New Lebanon, Ohio, 1,459............*C1 78
New Lenox, Ill., 2,367............B6, k9 58
New Lexington, Ohio 4,514............C3 78
New Lisbon, Wis., 1,337...E3 88
New Liskeard, Ont., Can., 4,896............p20 41
New London, Conn., 33,000 (*198,000)...D8 52
New London, Iowa, 1,694..D6 60
New London, Minn., 721..E4 67
New London, Mo., 875....B6 69
New London, N.H., 1,100..E4 73
New London, Ohio, 2,392..A3 78
New London, Wis., 5,288..D5 88
New London, co., Conn., 185,745............C8 52
New Madison, Ohio, 910..C1 78
New Madrid, Mo., 2,867...E8 69
New Madrid, co., Mo., 31,350............E8 69
New Malden, Eng., 46,587............m11 4
Newman, Calif., 2,558....D3 50
Newman, Ill., 1,052......D6 58
Newman Grove, Nebr., 880............C8 71
Newmanstown, Pa., 1,200..F9 81
Newmarket, Ont., Can., 8,932............C5 41
New Market, Ind., 578...E4 59
Newmarket, N.H., 2,745...E6 73
New Market, N.J., 6,500..*B4 74
New Market, Va., 783....B4 85
New Martinsville, W. Va., 5,607............B4 87
New Matamoras, Ohio, 925............C4 78
New Meadows, Idaho, 647............E2 57
New Mexico, state, U.S., 121,666............ 48
New Miami, Ohio, 2,360............C1, n12 78
New Milford, Conn., 3,700............C3 52
New Milford, N.J., 18,810..h8 74
New Milford, Ohio, 500...A4 78
New Milford, Pa., 1,129..C10 81
New Monmouth, N.J., 3,000............C4 74
Newnan, Ga., 12,169.....C2 55
New Norfolk, Austl., 5,775............o15 25
New Orleans, La., 665,000 (*1,060,000)......E5, h11 63
New Oxford, Pa., 1,407...G7 81
New Palestine, Ind., 725..E6 59
New Paltz, N.Y., 4,161...D6 75
New Paris, Ind., 800.....B6 59
New Paris, Ohio, 1,679...C1 78
New Philadelphia, Ohio, 14,241............B4 78
New Philadelphia, Pa., 1,702............E9 81
New Plymouth, Idaho, 940............F2 57
New Plymouth, N.Z., 31,843 (*35,280)......M15 26
Newport, Ark., 7,007.....B4 49
Newport, Del., 1,239.....A6 53
Newport, Eng., 19,000....E6 4
New Port, Ind., 627......E3 59
Newport, Ky., 30,070............A7, B5 62
Newport, Maine, 1,700...D3 64
Newport, Mich., 650......G7 66
Newport, Minn., 2,349...n13 67
Newport, N.H., 3,700....E3 73
Newport, N.J., 600......E2 74
Newport, N.C., 861......C6 76
Newport, Ohio, 480......C4 78
Newport, Oreg., 5,344...C2 80
Newport, Pa., 1,861.....F7 81

Newport, R.I., 35,901....D11 52
Newport, Tenn., 6,448...D10 83
Newport, Vt., 5,019......B3 73
Newport, Wales, 108,000...E5 4
Newport, Wash., 1,513....A8 86
Newport, co., R.I., 81,891............C11 52
Newport Beach, Calif., 26,564............F5, n13 50
Newport News (Independent City), Va., 135,000 (*280,000)........D6, k15 85
New Port Richey, Fla., 3,520............D4 54
Newportville, Pa., 700...*F11 81
New Prague, Minn., 2,533..F5 67
New Providence, N.J., 10,243............*B4 74
New Providence, Tenn., 4,451............A4 83
New Providence, isl., Ba. Is............B5, m17 35
Newquay, Eng., 11,600....E4 4
New Richland, Minn., 1,046............G5 67
New Richmond, Que., Can., 411............A4 43
New Richmond, Ohio, 2,834............D1 78
New Richmond, Wis., 3,316............C1 88
New Road, N.S., Can., 1,109............E6 43
New Roads, La., 3,965...D4 63
New Rochelle, N.Y., 76,812............h13, n15 75
New Rockford, N. Dak., 2,177............C6 77
Newry, N. Ire., 12,200...C3 4
Newry, S.C., 700........B2 82
New Salem, N. Dak., 986..D4 77
New Salem, Pa., 860......*G2 81
New Sarpy, La., 1,259...k11 63
New Sharon, Iowa, 1,063..C5 60
New Shrewsbury, N.J., 7,313............C4 74
New Smyrna Beach, Fla., 8,781............C6 54
New South Wales, state, Austl., 4,231,103......F8 25
New Straitsville, Ohio, 1,019............C3 78
New Tazewell, Tenn., 768............C10 83
Newton, Ala., 958......D4 46
Newton, Ill., 2,901......E5 58
Newton, Iowa, 15,381....C4 60
Newton, Kans., 14,877............D6, f12 61
Newton, Mass., 92,384............B5, g11 65
Newton, Miss., 3,178.....C4 68
Newton, N.J., 6,563.....A3 74
Newton, N.C., 6,658.....B1 76
Newton, Tex., 1,233.....D6 84
Newton, co., Ark., 5,963..B2 49
Newton, co., Ga., 20,999..C3 55
Newton, co., Ind., 11,502..B3 59
Newton, co., Miss., 19,517............C4 68
Newton, co., Mo., 30,093..E3 69
Newton, co., Tex., 10,372..D6 84
Newton Brook, Ont., Can............k15 41
Newton Falls, N.Y., 750............A6, f9 75
Newton Falls, Ohio, 5,038..A5 78
Newtonville, N.Y., 1,500..*C7 75
New Toronto, Ont., Can., 13,384............D5, m14 41
Newtown, Newf., Can., 585............D5 44
Newtown, Conn., 1,261...D3 52
New Town, N. Dak., 1,586............C3 77
Newtown, Ohio, 1,750............C1, o13 78
Newtown, Pa., 2,323.....F12 81
Newtown [& Llanllwchaiarn], Wales, 5,500............D5 4
Newtownards, N. Ire., 13,200............C4 4
Newtown Square, Pa., 9,270............p20 81
New Ulm, Minn., 12,587..F4 67
New Vienna, Ohio, 858....C2 78
Newville, Pa., 1,656......F7 81
New Washington, Ohio, 1,162............B3 78
New Waterford, N.S., Can., 10,592............C9 43
New Waterford, Ohio, 711..B5 78
New Westminster, B.C., Can., 33,654............E6, f13 37
New Whiteland, Ind., 3,488............E5 59

New Wilmington, Pa.,
2,203.................D1 81
New Windsor, Ill., 658....B3 58
New Windsor, Md., 738..A3 53
New Windsor, N.Y.,
4,500.................*D6 75
New York, N.Y., 8,020,000
(*17,030,000)......E7, h13 75
New York, co., N.Y.,
1,698,281.............k13 75
New York, state, U.S.,
16,782,304.................... 75
New York Mills, Minn.,
828...................D3 67
New York Mills, N.Y.,
3,788.................*B5 75
New Zealand, country,
Oceania, 2,676,919....N15 26
Nezhin, Sov. Un., 59,000..F8 12
Nez Perce, Idaho, 667.....C2 57
Nez Perce, co., Idaho,
27,066................C2 57
N'gaoundéré, Cam.......G7 22
Nha Trang, Viet., 49,150..C3 19
Niagara, Wis., 2,098.....C6 88
Niagara, co., N.Y.,
242,269...............B2 75
Niagara Falls, Ont., Can.,
53,365, (*56,621).......D5 41
Niagara Falls, N.Y.,
102,394...............B1 75
Niagara-on-the-Lake, Ont.,
Can., 2,712...........D5 41
Niagara University, N.Y.,
2,100.................*B1 75
Niamey, Niger, 40,000....F5 22
Niantic, Conn., 3,400....D8 52
Niantic, Ill., 629........D4 58
Nicaragua, country, N.A.,
1,655,000.............E7 34
Nicaragua, lake, Nic......E7 34
Nicastro, It., 21,500......E6 9
Nice, Fr., 292,958........F7 5
Niceville, Fla., 4,517....u15 54
Nichinan, Jap., 38,100
(57,612▲)..............K5 18
Nicholas, co., Ky., 6,677..B6 62
Nicholas, co., W. Va.,
25,414................C4 87
Nicholasville, Ky., 4,275...C5 62
Nicholls, Ga., 930.......E4 55
Nichols, N.Y., 685.......C4 75
Nichols, S.C., 617.......C9 82
Nichols Hills, Okla., 4,897..B4 79
Nicholson, Pa., 942......C10 81
Nickerson, Kans., 1,091..D5 61
Nicolet, Que., Can.,
4,441.................C5 42
Nicolet, co., Que., Can.,
30,827................C5 42
Nicollet, Minn., 493......F4 67
Nicollet, co., Minn.,
23,196................F4 67
Nicoma Park, Okla.,
1,263.................B4 79
Nicosia, Cyp., 47,000....A4 23
Nicosia, It., 17,600......F5 9
Nicotera, It., 9,143......E5 9
Nicoya, C.R., 3,196......E7 34
Niedersachsen (Lower
Saxony), state, Ger.,
6,641,400.............*B4 6
Nienburg, Ger., 22,100...B4 6
Nievre, dept., Fr.,
245,921...............*D5 5
Nigde, Tur., 18,042.....D10 14
Niger, country, Afr.,
2,850,000.............F6 22
Niger, riv., Afr..........F5 22
Nigeria, country, Afr.,
56,400,000............G6 22
Nigrita, Grc., 9,979.....*B4 14
Niigata, Jap., 356,302....H9 18
Niigata, pref., Jap.,
2,398,931.............*H9 18
Niihama, Jap., 125,155...J6 18
Niihau, isl., Haw.........B1 56
Niimi, Jap., 17,000.......I6 18
Níjar, Sp., 2,052........D4 8
Nijmegen, Neth., 137,800.B6 5
Nikitovka, Sov. Un.,
10,000...............q21 12
Nikko, Jap., 32,031......H9 18
Niland, Calif., 800.......F6 50
Nile, riv., Afr...........D4 23
Ninette, Man., Can., 673..E2 40
Ninety Six, S.C., 1,435...C3 82
Ningan, China, 40,000...D4 18
Ninghsien, China, 5,000..D6 17
Ningpo (Ninghsien),
China, 237,500........F9 17
Ningsia Hui, auton. reg.,
China, 1,810,000......D6 17
Ningsia, see Yinchwan,
China
Ningte, China, 30,000....F8 17
Ninh Binh, Viet., 25,000..A3 19
Niobrara, Nebr., 736.....B7 71

Niort, Fr., 37,512........D3 5
Niota, Tenn., 679........D9 83
Nipawin, Sask., Can.,
3,836.................D3 39
Nipigon, lake, Ont.,
Can..................o17 41
Nipissing, dist., Ont.,
Can., 70,568..........A5 41
Nipomo, Calif., 750......E3 50
Niquero, Cuba, 8,600....D5 35
Nirasaki, Jap., 14,500...n17 18
Niš, Yugo., 81,073.......D5 10
Nisa, Port., 5,617.......C2 8
Nishio, Jap., 46,000
(70,432▲)............o16 18
Nisihomiya, Jap.,
336,873..............*I7 18
Nisko, Pol., 6,590.......C7 7
Nisswa, Minn., 742......D4 67
Niterói, Braz.,
228,826...........C4, h6 30
Nitra, Czech., 35,800....D5 7
Nitro, W. Va., 6,894.....C3 87
Niue, N.Z., dep., Oceania,
5,194.................*H9 2
Nivelles, Bel., 14,345....B6 5
Nivernais, former prov.,
Fr., 236,00...........D5 5
Niverville, Man., Can.,
474...................E3 40
Nixa, Mo., 944..........D4 69
Nixon, N.J., 10,000......B4 74
Nixon, Tex., 1,751....E4, k8 84
Nizhneudinsk, Sov. Un.,
35,900...............D12 13
Nizhneye, Sov. Un.,
10,000...............q21 12
Nizhniy Tagil, Sov. Un.,
370,000...............D9 13
Nkangsamba, Cam........H6 22
Noank, Conn., 1,200.....D9 52
Nobel, Ont., Can., 693...B4 41
Nobeoka, Jap., 124,000..J5 18
Noble, Ill., 761.........E5 58
Noble, Okla., 995........B4 79
Noble, co., Ind., 28,162...B7 59
Noble, co., Ohio, 10,982..C4 78
Noble, co., Okla., 10,376..A4 79
Nobles, co., Minn., 23,365..G3 67
Noblesville, Ind., 7,664...D6 59
Noboribetsu, Jap.,
39,000...............E10 18
Nocatee, Fla., 750.......E5 54
Nochixtán, Mex., 3,172..o15 34
Nocona, Tex., 3,127......C4 84
Nodaway, co., Mo.,
22,215................A3 69
Noel, Mo., 736..........E3 69
Nogales, Ariz., 7,286.....D3 48
Nogales, Mex., 37,657....A2 34
Nogales, Mex., 11,219...n15 34
Nogata, Jap., 57,839.....J5 18
Nogent-le-Rotrou, Fr.,
9,428.................C4 5
Nogent [sur-Marne], Fr.,
24,501...............g10 5
Noginsk, Sov. Un.,
98,000...........D12, n18 12
Nogoyá, Arg., 10,911.....A5 28
Nógrád, co., Hung.,
236,393..............*A4 10
Nohar, India, 13,728.....C5 20
Noheji, Jap., 12,000.....F10 18
Noisy-le-Sec, Fr.,
31,187...............g10 5
Nokomis, Sask., Can., 560..F3 39
Nokomis, Fla., 2,253.....E4 54
Nokomis, Ill., 2,476.....D4 58
Nola, It., 16,400........D5 9
Nolan, co., Tex., 18,963..C2 84
Nome, Alsk., 2,316.......C6 47
Nominingue, Que., Can.,
744...................C2 42
Nomme, Sov. Un.,
18,026...............*B5 12
Nonoava, Mex., 1,993....B3 34
Noranda, Que., Can.,
11,477...............*o20 41
Nora Springs, Iowa,
1,275.................A5 60
Norborne, Mo., 965......B4 69
Norco, Calif., 4,964.....*F5 50
Norco, La., 4,682.....D5, h11 63
Norcross, Ga., 1,605...A5, C2 55
Nord, dept., Fr.,
2,293,112............*B5 5
Nordegg, Alta., Can....C2, g7 38
Norden, Ger., 16,200....B3 6
Nordenham, Ger., 26,900..B4 6
Nordhausen, Ger., 40,800..C5 6
Nordhorn, Ger., 40,400...B3 6
Nordland, co., Nor.,
225,982..............*D6 11
Nördlingen, Ger., 14,400..D5 6
Nordrhein-Westfalen, state,
Ger., 15,901,700......*C3 6
Nord-Tröndelag, co.,
Nor., 116,800........*E4 11

Nordvik, Sov. Un., 2,500..B14 13
Norfolk, Nebr., 13,640...B8 71
Norfolk, N.Y., 1,353......f9 75
Norfolk (Independent
City), Va., 323,000
(*675,500)........D6, k15 85
Norfolk, co., Ont., Can.,
50,475................E4 41
Norfolk, co., Eng.,
569,000..............*D7 4
Norfolk, co., Mass.,
510,256...............B5 65
Norilsk, Sov. Un.,
117,000..............C11 13
Norlina, N.C., 911.......A4 76
Norma, N.J., 700........E2 74
Normal, Ala., 1,500.....*A3 46
Normal, Ill., 20,676......C5 58
Norman, co., Minn.,
11,253................C2 67
Norman, Okla., 33,412...B4 79
Normandin, Que., Can.,
1,838................*G19 36
Normandy, Fla., 1,900...*B5 54
Normandy, Mo., 4,452...f13 69
Normandy, former prov.,
Fr., 2,407,000........C4 5
Normandy Heights, Ohio,
630..................n12 78
Normandy Park, Wash.,
3,224................*B4 86
Norman's Cove, Newf.,
Can., 571............*D5 44
Norquay, Sask., Can.,
498...................F4 39
Norrbotten, co., Swe.,
262,600.............*E10 11
Norridge, Ill., 17,126....k9 58
Norridgewock, Maine,
800 (1,634▲).........D3 64
Norris, S.C., 594........B2 82
Norris, Tenn., 1,389.....C9 83
Norris Arm, Newf., Can.,
1,226.................D4 44
Norris City, Ill., 1,243...F5 58
Norris Point, Newf.,
Can..................D3 44
Norristown, Pa.,
38,925...........F11, o20 81
Norrköping, Swe.,
92,300...........H7, u34 11
Norrtälje, Swe.,
8,900...........H8, t36 11
Norseman, Austl., 1,849...F3 25
Norte de Santander, dept.,
Col., 534,486.........B3 32
North, S.C., 1,047.......D5 82
North, isl., N.Z..........L14 26
North, sea, Eur..........D8 3
North Abington,
Mass., 3,600.....B6, h12 65
North Adams, Mass.,
19,905................A1 65
North Adams, Mich., 494..G6 66
North Albany, Oreg.,
900..................k11 80
North America, cont.,
291,800,000.............. 33
North Amherst, Mass.,
1,100.................B2 65
North Amityville, N.Y.,
11,000...............*E7 75
Northampton, Austl., 714..E1 25
Northampton, Eng.,
105,400..............D6 4
Northampton, Mass.,
30,058................B2 65
Northampton, Pa.,
8,866................E11 81
Northampton, co., Eng.,
411,200..............*D6 4
Northampton, co., N.C.,
26,811................A5 76
Northampton, co., Pa.,
201,412..............E11 81
Northampton, co., Va.,
16,966................C7 85
North Andover, Mass.,
10,908................A5 65
North Anson, Maine, 700..D3 64
North Apollo, Pa., 1,741..E2 81
North Arlington, N.J.,
17,477................h8 74
North Asheboro, N.C.,
3,805................*B3 76
North Atlanta, Ga.,
12,661................A5 55
North Attleboro, Mass.,
14,777................C5 65
North Augusta, S.C.,
10,348................E3 82
North Aurora, Ill., 4,734..k8 58
North Babylon, N.Y.,
25,000..............*n15 75
North Baltimore, Ohio,
3,011.................A2 78
North Bangor, N.Y., 500..f10 75

North Battleford, Sask.,
Can., 11,230......E1, n7 39
North Bay, Ont., Can.,
23,781...........A5, p20 41
North Bay, Fla., 2,006...*G6 54
North Beach, Md., 606...C4 53
North Belle Vernon, Pa.,
3,148................*F2 81
North Bellmore, N.Y.,
23,000...............*E7 75
North Bellport, N.Y.,
4,200................n15 75
North Belmont, N.C.,
4,000.................B1 76
North Bend, Nebr., 1,174..C9 71
North Bend, Ohio, 622...o12 78
North Bend, Oreg.,
7,512.................D2 80
North Bend, Pa., 800....D6 81
North Bend, Wash., 945..B4 86
North Bennington, Vt.,
1,437.................F1 73
North Bergen, N.J.,
42,387................h8 74
North Berwick, Maine,
1,295 (1,844▲).......E2 64
North Billerica, Mass.,
4,000.............A5, f10 65
North Bonneville, Wash.,
494...................D4 86
Northboro, Mass., 2,900
(6,687▲)..............B4 65
North Brabant, prov.,
Neth., 1,512,800.....*B6 5
North Braddock, Pa.,
13,204...............k14 81
North Branch, Mich., 901..E7 66
North Branch, Minn.,
949...................E6 67
North Branch, N.J., 700..B3 74
Northbridge, Mass., 2,180
(10,800▲).............B4 65
Northbrook, Ill., 15,204...h9 58
North Brookfield, Mass.,
2,615 (3,616▲)........B3 65
North Brother, mtn.,
Maine.................C4 64
North Brunswick, N.J.,
10,099...............*C4 74
North Caldwell, N.J.,
4,163.................B4 74
North Canton, Ga., 1,000..B2 55
North Canton, Ohio,
7,727.................B4 78
North Carolina, state,
U.S., 4,556,155........... 76
North Catasauqua, Pa.,
2,805...............*E11 81
North Cedar, Iowa,
1,500................*B5 60
North Charleroi, Pa.,
2,259................*F1 81
North Charleston, S.C.,
23,500...........F8, k12 82
North Chelmsford, Mass.,
4,500.................A5 65
North Chicago, Ill.,
22,938...........A6, h9 58
North Chili, N.Y., 1,350..*B3 75
North Chillicothe, Ill.,
2,259.................C4 58
North City, Wash., 2,000..*B3 86
Northcliffe, Austl., 578....F2 25
North Cohasset, Mass.,
500..................h12 65
North College Hill, Ohio,
12,035...............o12 78
North Collins, N.Y.,
1,574.................C2 75
North Conway, N.H.,
1,104.................B4 73
North Corbin, Ky., 950...D5 62
North Creek, N.Y., 900...B7 75
Northcrest, Calif.,
1,945................*B1 50
North Dakota, state, U.S.
632,446.................. 77
North Dartmouth, Mass.,
4,000.................C6 65
North Decatur, Ga.,
9,000................*C2 55
North Dighton, Mass.,
1,200.................C5 65
North Druid Hills, Ga.,
4,000................*C2 55
North East, Md., 1,628...A6 53
North East, Nor..........E5 13
North East, Pa., 4,217....B2 81
Northeastern Polder,
prov., Neth., 28,800...*A6 5
Northeast Harbor, Maine,
600...................D4 64
Northeast New Guinea,
reg., N. Gui.,
1,320,000............k12 25
North Easton, Mass.,
3,300.................B5 65
Northeim, Ger., 19,300...C4 6

North English, Iowa,
1,004............C5 60
Northern Arm, Newf.,
Can., 606.......D4 44
Northern, reg., Nig.,
29,758,875.......F6 22
Northern Ireland, reg.,
U.K., 1,425,462.......C3 4
Northern Territory, ter.,
Austl., 37,166.......C5 25
North Fairfield, Ohio,
547............A3 78
North Falmouth, Mass.,
600............C6 65
Northfield, B.C., Can.,
610............f2 37
Northfield, Ill., 4,005.....*B6 58
Northfield, Mass., 1,179...A3 65
Northfield, Minn., 8,707...F5 67
Northfield, N.H., 1,243....E4 73
Northfield, N.J., 5,849....E3 74
Northfield, Ohio, 1,055...h9 78
Northfield, Vt., 2,159......C2 73
North Fond du Lac, Wis.,
2,549............E5, k9 88
North Fork, Calif., 500....D4 50
Northfork, W. Va., 798...*D3 87
North Freedom, Wis., 579..E4 88
North Glen Ellyn, Ill.,
1,500............*B5 58
North Grafton, Mass.,
3,000............B4 65
North Great River, N.Y.,
8,000............n15 75
North Greenville, Miss.,
2,516............*B2 68
North Grosvenor Dale,
Conn., 2,000.......B9 52
North Gulfport, Miss.,
3,323............*E4 68
North Haledon, N.J.,
6,026............*B4 74
North Hampton, Ohio,
495............C2 78
North Hartsville, S.C.,
1,899............*C7 82
North Hatley, Que., Can.,
719............D6 42
North Haven, Conn.,
15,935............D5 52
North Head, N.S., Can.,
609............E3 43
North Henderson, N.C.,
1,995............*A4 76
North Highlands, Calif.,
21,271............*C3 50
North Holland
(Noordholland), prov.,
Neth., 2,073,100......*A6 5
North Hornell, N.Y.,
917............*C3 75
North Hudson, Wis.,
1,019............*D1 88
North Industry, Ohio,
1,800............B4 78
North Irwin, Pa., 1,143...*F2 81
North Judson, Ind., 1,942.B4 59
North Kamloops, B.C.,
Can., 6,456.......D7 37
North Kansas City, Mo.,
5,657............h10 69
North Kingstown, R.I.,
3,500............C11 52
North Kingsville, Ohio,
1,854............A5 78
North La Junta, Colo.,
1,000............C7 51
Northlake, Ill., 14,115.....K9 58
North Larchmont, N.Y.,
9,000............*D2 75
North Las Vegas, Nev.,
18,442............C4 72
North Lewisburg, Ohio,
879............B2 78
North Liberty, Ind.,
1,241............A5 59
North Lima, Ohio, 600...B5 78
North Lindenhurst, N.Y.,
11,200............n15 75
North Little Rock,
Ark., 58,032.....C3, D6 49
North Manchester, Ind.,
4,377............C6 59
North Mankato, Minn.,
6,618............F4 67
North Massapequa, N.Y.,
24,500............*E7 75
North Merrick, N.Y.,
15,000............*E7 75
North Miami, Fla.,
28,708............G6, s13 54
North Miami Beach, Fla.,
21,405............s13 54
Northmoor, Mo., 696...h10 69
North Muskegon, Mich.,
3,855............E4 66
North New Hyde Park,
N.Y., 15,500.........*E7 75

North Norwich, N.Y.,
500............C5 75
North Ogden, Utah,
2,621............A6, C2 72
North Olmsted, Ohio,
16,290............h9 78
North Oxford, Mass.,
1,500............B4 65
North Palisade, mtn.,
Calif.............D4 50
North Palm Beach, Fla.,
2,684............*F6 54
North Park, Ill., 14,500....A4 58
North Patchogue, N.Y.,
6,000............n14 75
North Pembroke, Mass.,
500............B6 65
North Perkin, Ill., 2,025..*C4 58
North Pelham, N.Y.,
5,326............h13 75
North Plainfield, N.J.,
16,993............B4 74
North Plains, Oreg.,
500............B4, g12 80
North Platte, Nebr.,
17,184............C5 71
North Platte, riv., U.S.....B6 45
North Pleasanton, Tex.,
1,018............*E3 84
Northport, Ala., 5,245.....B2 46
Northport, Mich., 530....C5 66
Northport, N.Y., 6,424....n15 75
Northport, Wash., 482....A8 86
North Prairie, Wis., 489...F5 88
North Princeton, N.J.,
4,506............*C3 74
North Providence, R.I.,
21,206............B11 52
North Quincy, Ill., 2,256..D2 58
North Reading, Mass.,
8,331............f11 65
North Richland Hills,
Tex., 8,662.......C4 84
Northridge, Ohio, 7,000..*C1 78
North Riverside, Ill.,
8,401............*B6 58
North Rockville Centre,
N.Y., 800.........*E7 75
North Rose, N.Y., 850....B4 75
North Royalton, Ohio,
9,290............h9 78
North Sacramento, Calif.,
12,922............*C3 50
North Salem, Ind., 626...E4 59
North Salt Lake, Utah,
1,655............*A6 72
North Scituate, Mass.,
2,700............h12 65
North Seaford, N.Y.,
3,000............*E7 75
North Shreveport, La.,
7,701............*B2 63
North Springfield, Va.,
5,000............*B5 85
North St. Paul, Minn.,
10,531............m13 67
North Sudbury, Mass.,
700............g10 65
North Swansea, Mass.,
700............C5 65
North Sydney, N.S., Can.,
8,657............C9 43
North Syracuse, N.Y.,
8,076............B4 75
North Tarrytown,
N.Y., 8,600......g13, m15 75
North Terre Haute, Ind.,
3,500............E3 59
North Tewksbury, Mass.,
900............A5 65
North Tonawanda, N.Y.,
35,968............B2 75
North Troy, Vt., 961......B3 73
North Tunica, Miss.,
1,025............*A3 68
North Turlock, Calif.,
2,535............*D3 50
North Turner, mtn.,
Mass.............C4 65
Northumberland, Pa.,
4,165............E8 81
Northumberland, co.,
N.B., Can., 50,035.....B3 43
Northumberland, co.,
Ont., Can., 41,892......C6 41
Northumberland, co.,
Eng., 826,500.........*C6 4
Northumberland, co., Pa.,
104,138..............D8 81
Northumberland, co., Va.,
10,185..............C6 85
North Uxbridge, Mass.,
1,680............B4 65
Northvale, N.J., 2,892.....g9 74
North Valley Stream,
N.Y., 11,700.........*E7 75
North Vancouver, B.C.,
Can., 23,656.....E6, f12 37

North Vandergrift, Pa.,
1,827............*E2 81
North Vassalboro, Maine,
800............D3 64
North Vernon, Ind., 4,307..F6 59
Northville, Mich., 3,967...p15 66
Northville, N.Y., 1,156....B6 75
North Wales, Pa., 3,673...F11 81
North Walsham, Eng.,
5,100............D7 4
North Warren, Pa., 1,458..C3 81
Northwest Park
Apartments, Md.,
3,000............*B3 53
North Westport, Mass.,
1,500............C5 65
North West River, Newf.,
Can., 753..........B1, h9 44
Northwest Territories,
ter., Can., 22,998.....C10 36
North Wilbraham, Mass.,
700............B3 65
North Wildwood, N.J.,
3,598............E3 74
North Wilkesboro, N.C.,
4,197............A1 76
Northwood, Iowa, 1,768..A4 60
Northwood, Mich.,
4,000............*E5 66
Northwood, N.H., 350....E5 73
Northwood, N. Dak.,
1,195............C8 77
Northwoods, Mo., 4,701..*C7 69
North York, Pa., 2,290....G8 81
Norton, N.S., Can., 846...D4 43
Norton, Kans., 3,345.....C4 61
Norton, Mass., 1,550.....C5 65
Norton, Ohio, 11,800....A4 78
Norton (Independent
City), Va., 5,013.......f9 85
Norton, co., Kans., 8,035..C4 61
Nortonville, Kans.,
595............C8, k15 61
Nortonville, Ky., 755.....C2 62
Norvelt, Pa., 1,211.......*F2 81
Norwalk, Calif., 88,739...n12 50
Norwalk, Conn., 67,775...E3 52
Norwalk, Iowa, 1,630..C4, f8 60
Norwalk, Ohio, 12,900....A3 78
Norwalk, Wis., 484.......E3 88
Norway, Iowa, 516.......C6 60
Norway, Maine, 2,700
(3,733▲)............D2 64
Norway, Mich., 3,171.....C3 66
Norway, S.C., 525........E5 82
Norway, country, Eur.,
3,708,000............E5 11
Norway House, Man.,
Can., 543..........C3 40
Norwayne, Mich., 6,000..*F7 66
Norwell, Mass., 600
(5,207▲)............h12 65
Norwich, Ont., Can.,
1,703............E4 41
Norwich, Conn., 38,506...C8 52
Norwich, Eng., 119,500...D7 4
Norwich, N.Y., 9,175.....C5 75
Norwood, Ont., Can.,
1,060............C7 41
Norwood, Mass.,
24,898............B5, h11 65
Norwood, Minn., 945.....F5 67
Norwood, N.J., 2,852.....h9 74
Norwood, N.Y., 2,200....f10 75
Norwood, N.C., 1,844....B2 76
Norwood, Ohio, 34,580...o13 78
Norwood, Pa., 6,729.....p20 81
Norwood, Tenn., 350....*D10 83
Norwottock, mtn., Mass...B2 65
Noshiro, Jap., 41,000
(61,921▲)............F10 18
Nossa Senhora das Dores,
Braz., 4,740.......*E7 27
Notch, mtn., Mass.......A3 65
Noto, It., 21,000........F5 9
Notodden, Nor., 7,600....H3 11
Notre Dame, Ind.,
6,500............*A5 59
Notre-Dame-de-Lourdes,
Man., Can., 511......E2 40
Notre Dame du Lac,
Que., Can., 1,695......B9 42
Notre-Dame-du-Laus,
Que., Can., 565.......C2 42
Nottingham, Eng.,
315,100............D6 4
Nottingham, co., Eng.,
926,000............*D6 4
Nottingham, Pa., 2,500..*F11 81
Nottoway, co., Va.,
15,141............C4 85
Nova Cruz, Braz., 6,780..*D7 27
Nova Friburgo, Braz.,
49,901............C4, h6 30
Nova Iguaçu, Braz.,
134,708............h6 30
Nova Lima, Braz.,
21,135............C4 30

Nova Lisboa, Ang.,
38,745............C3 24
Novara, It., 92,000........B2 9
Nova Scotia, prov., Can.,
737,007............D6 43
Novato, Calif., 17,881....C2 50
Nova Varos, Yugo.,
3,186............D4 10
Novaya Ladoga, Sov. Un.,
25,000............A9 12
Novaya Zemlya, is.,
Sov. Un.............B8 16
Nova Zagora, Bul.,
11,031............D8 10
Nové Zámky, Czech.,
22,600............E5 7
Novgorod, Sov. Un.,
76,000............B8 12
Novgorod-Severskiy,
Sov. Un., 10,000.....E9 12
Novi, Mich., 6,390.......p15 66
Novigrad, Yugo., 531.....C2 10
Novi Ligure, It., 26,972...B2 9
Novi Pazar, Bul., 5,461...D8 10
Novi Pazar, Yugo.,
20,712............D5 10
Novi Sad, Yugo., 102,469..C4 10
Novoaydar, Sov. Un.,
10,000............G12, q21 12
Novocherkassk, Sov. Un.,
69,000............H13 12
Novoekonomicheskoye,
Sov. Un., 10,000.....q20 12
Novogrudok, Sov. Un.,
25,000............E5 12
Novo-Kazalinsk,
Sov. Un., 19,499.....E9 16
Novokuznetsk, Sov. Un.,
475,000............D11 13
Novomoskovsk, Sov. Un.,
37,500............G10 12
Novomoskovsk, Sov. Un.,
114,000............D12 12
Novorossiysk, Sov. Un.,
104,000............I11 12
Novoshakhtinsk,
Sov. Un., 108,000....H12 12
Novosibirsk, Sov. Un.,
1,029,000............D11 13
Novosil, Sov. Un.,
10,000............E11 12
Novoukrainka, Sov. Un.,
10,000............G8 12
Nový Bohumín, Czech.,
11,000............D5 7
Nový Bydžov, Czech.,
6,120............C3 7
Nový Jičín, Czech.,
16,600............D5 7
Novyye Senzhary,
Sov. Un.............G10 12
Novyy Oskol, Sov. Un.,
10,000............F11 12
Nowa Sól, Pol., 28,500....C3 7
Nowata, Okla., 4,163.....A6 79
Nowata, co., Okla.,
10,848............A6 79
Nowra, Austl., 6,221......G8 26
Nowshera, Pak., 21,516...B5 20
Nowy Dwór, Pol., 5,046...k13 7
Nowy Sacz, Pol., 36,400...D6 7
Nowy Targ, Pol., 18,200...D6 7
Noxen, Pa., 800....D9, m16 81
Noxubee, co., Miss.,
16,826............B5 68
Noya, Sp., 4,236........A1 8
Noyon, Fr., 9,317........C5 5
Nsawam, Ghana, 20,200...G4 22
Ñuble, prov., Chile,
285,730............B2 28
Nuckolls, co., Nebr.,
8,217............D7 71
Nucla, Colo., 906.......C2 51
Nueces, co., Tex.,
221,573............F4 84
Nueva Casas Grandes,
Mex., 11,687..........A3 34
Nueva Ecija, prov., Phil.,
608,362............*C6 19
Nueva Esparta, state
Ven., 89,492........A5 32
Nueva Gerona, Cuba,
9,000............D2 35
Nueva Imperial, Chile,
6,400............B2 28
Nueva Rosita, Mex.,
34,302............B4 34
Neuva San Salvador, Sal.,
27,039............*E7 34
Nueva Vizcaya, prov.,
Phil., 138,090........*B6 19
Nueve de Julio, Arg.,
13,678............B4 28
Nuevitas, Cuba, 16,300...D5 35
Nuevo Laredo, Mex.,
92,627............B5 34
Nuevo León, state, Mex.,
1,078,848............B5 34

Nules, Sp., 8,460........C5 8
Numazu, Jap.,
  159,880..........I9, n17 18
Nu Mine, Pa., 500.......E3 81
Nunda, N.Y., 1,224......C3 75
Nungan, China, 35,000...C10 17
Nunkiang, China, 5,000..B10 17
Nuoro, It., 24,500......D2 9
Nuquí, Col., 1,500......C3 27
Nuremberg, Pa., 900.....E9 81
Nuri, Mex., 1,125.......B3 34

Nürnberg, Ger., 466,200...D5 6
Nushki, Pak., 2,142......C4 20
Nutley, N.J., 29,513....B4, h8 74
Nutter Fort, W. Va.,
  2,440................B4 87
Nutting Lake, Mass.,
  2,500................f10 65
Nuwara Eliya, Cey.,
  11,983...............G7 20
Nyack, N.Y., 5,400...D7, m15 75
Nyamandhlovu, Rh., 350..D5 24

Nyandoma, Sov. Un.,
  17,800...............A13 12
Nyasa, lake, Afr..........C6 24
Nybro, Swe., 8,700.......I6 11
Nye, co., Nev., 4,374.....B3 72
Nyiregyhaza, Hung.,
  41,800...............B5 10
Nykøbing [På] Falster,
  Den., 17,850..........A1 7
Nykøbing [På Mors], Den.,
  9,326................I3 11

Nyköping, Swe.,
  24,300............H7, u34 11
Nyland Acres, Calif.,
  1,619...............*E4 50
Nymburk, Czech.,
  12,600.............C3, n19 7
Nynäshamn, Swe.,
  9,400.............H7, u35 11
Nyngan, Austl., 2,584......F8 25
Nysa, Pol., 26,400........C4 7
Nyssa, Oreg., 2,611....D10 80

O

Oahu, isl., Haw.......B4, g9 56
Oak Bay, B.C., Can.,
  16,935...............h12 37
Oak Bluffs, Mass., 1,419..D6 65
Oakbrook Terrace, Ill.,
  1,121...............*F2 58
Oak Creek, Colo., 666....A4 51
Oak Creek, Wis., 9,372..n12 88
Oakdale, Calif., 4,980....D3 50
Oakdale, La., 6,618.......D3 63
Oakdale, Mass., 500.......B4 65
Oakdale, N.Y., 4,300....*n16 75
Oakdale, Pa., 1,695.....k13 81
Oakes, N. Dak., 1,650....D7 77
Oakfield, Maine, 500
  (848▲).............B4 64
Oakfield, N.Y., 2,070....B2 75
Oakford, Pa., 1,300..F12, o22 81
Oak Forest, Ill., 11,107...k9 58
Oak Grove, Ga., 3,500...*C2 55
Oak Grove, La., 1,797....B4 63
Oak Grove, Oreg.,
  5,500.............B4, h12 80
Oakharbor, Ohio, 2,903...A2 78
Oak Harbor, Wash.,
  3,942...............A3 86
Oak Hill, Fla., 758.......D6 54
Oak Hill, Mich., 800.....D4 66
Oak Hill, Ohio, 1,748....D3 78
Oak Hill, Tenn., 4,490...*A5 83
Oak Hill, W. Va.,
  4,711.............D3, D7 87
Oakhurst, N.J., 4,500....C4 74
Oakhurst, Okla., 2,000...A5 79
Oakland, Calif.,
  367,548...........D2, h8 50
Oakland, Ill., 939.......D5 58
Oakland, Iowa, 1,340....C2 60
Oakland, Maine, 2,000...D3 64
Oakland, Md., 1,977....m12 53
Oakland, Mo., 1,552....*C7 69
Oakland, Nebr., 1,429...C9 71
Oakland, N.J., 9,446....A4 74
Oakland, Oreg., 856.....D3 80
Oakland, Pa., 2,303....*D1 81
Oakland, co., Mich.,
  690,259............F7 66
Oakland City, Ind.,
  3,016...............H3 59
Oaklandon, Ind., 1,000...k11 59
Oakland Park, Fla.,
  5,331.............F6, r13 54
Oak Lawn, Ill.,
  49,084...........B6, k9 58
Oaklawn, Kans., 5,000...B5 61
Oakley, Idaho, 613......G5 57
Oakley, Kans., 2,190.....C3 61
Oakley Park, Mich.,
  1,100..............*F7 66
Oaklyn, N.J., 4,778....*D2 74
Oakman, Ala., 849......B2 46
Oakmont, Pa., 7,504..E2, h14 81
Oak Park, Ill.,
  61,093...........B6, k9 58
Oak Park, Mich.,
  36,632.............p15 66
Oak Ridge, N.C., 500....A3 76
Oakridge, Oreg., 1,973...D4 80
Oak Ridge, Tenn., 27,169..C9 83
Oak Ridges, Ont., Can.,
  1,864...............k15 41
Oaks, Pa., 950.........o20 81
Oaktown, Ind., 798......G3 59
Oak View, Calif., 2,448..*E4 50
Oak View, Md., 1,000...*C3 53
Oakville, Ont., Can.,
  42,109.............D5 41
Oakville, Conn., 7,000...C4 52
Oakville, Mo., 1,000.....g13 69
Oakville, Tenn., 9,000..B2, E8 83

Oakwood, Ill., 861.......C6 58
Oakwood, Ohio, 686.....A1 78
Oakwood (Oakwood
  Village), Ohio, 3,283...*A4 78
Oakwood (Far Hills),
  Ohio, 10,493.........C1 78
Oakwood, Pa., 2,267....*E1 81
Oakwood, Tex., 716.....D5 84
Oakwood Beach, N.J.,
  600.................D1 74
Oakwood Villa, Fla.,
  4,500...............*B5 54
Oamaru, N.Z., 13,186....P13 26
Oamishirasato, Jap.,
  7,700...............n19 18
Oaxaca (de Juarez),
  Mex., 72,370.........D5 34
Oaxaca, state, Mex.,
  1,727,266...........D5 34
Ob, river, Sov. Un....C9 D11 13
Obama, Jap., 21,800...n14 18
Oban, Scot., 6,800.......B4 4
Oberhausen, Ger.,
  260,000.............C3 6
Oberlin, Kans., 2,337....C3 61
Oberlin, La., 1,794......D3 63
Oberlin, Ohio, 8,198.....A3 78
Oberlin, Pa., 2,500.....*F8 81
Oberstdorf, Ger., 8,300...E5 6
Obetz, Ohio, 1,984...C3, m11 78
Obihiro, Jap., 117,253...E11 18
Obion, Tenn., 1,097......A2 83
Obion, co., Tenn.,
  26,957..............A2 83
Oblong, Ill., 1,817......D6 58
Obluchye, Sov. Un.,
  15,000..............E16 13
O'Brien, co., Iowa,
  18,840..............A2 60
Observation, peak, Calif...B3 50
Obuasi, Ghana, 22,800...G4 22
Ocala, Fla., 13,598......C4 54
Ocaña, Col., 28,028......B3 32
Ocaña, Sp., 6,686........C4 8
Occidental, mts., Peru...D2 31
Ocean, co., N.J., 108,241..D4 74
Oceana, W. Va., 1,303...D3 87
Oceana, co., Mich.,
  16,547..............E4 66
Ocean Bluff, Mass.,
  900...............B6, h13 65
Ocean City, Md., 983.....D7 53
Ocean City, N.J., 7,618....E3 74
Ocean Falls, B.C., Can.,
  3,056...............C4 37
Ocean Gate, N.J., 706....D4 74
Ocean Grove, Mass.,
  2,000...............C5 65
Ocean Grove, N.J., 6,000..C4 74
Oceanlake, Oreg.,
  1,342..............*C3 80
Oceano, Calif., 1,317....*E3 50
Ocean Park, Wash., 750...C1 86
Oceanport, N.J., 4,937....C4 74
Oceanside, Calif., 31,824...F5 50
Oceanside, N.Y., 34,000..*G2 52
Ocean Springs, Miss.,
  5,025.............E3, E5 68
Oceanville, N.J., 600.....E4 74
Oceanway, Fla., 2,000....m8 54
Ocheyedan, Iowa, 662....A2 60
Ochiltree, co., Tex.,
  9,380...............A2 84
Ocilla, Ga., 3,217.......E3 55
Ockelbo, Swe., 2,490....G7 11
Ocenle Mari, Rom.,
  4,420...............C7 10
Ocho Rios, Jam.,
  4,758...............E5 35
Ocoee, Fla., 2,628......D5 54

Ocoña, Peru, 932........E3 31
Oconee, co., Ga., 6,304....C3 55
Oconee, co., S.C., 40,204...B1 82
Oconomowoc, Wis., 6,682..E5 88
Oconto, Wis., 4,805......D6 88
Oconto Falls, Wis., 2,331..D5 88
Ocotlán, Mex.,
  25,416...........C4, m12 34
Ocracoke, N.C., 600......B7 76
Ocros, Peru, 1,321.......D2 31
Oda, Ghana, 19,700......G4 22
Odate, Jap., 34,800
  (59,662▲).........F10 18
Odawara, Jap.,
  143,377..........I9, n18 18
Odda, Nor., 5,197........G2 11
Odebolt, Iowa, 1,331.....B2 60
Odell, Ill., 936.........B5 58
Odem, Tex., 2,088........F4 84
Odemis, Tur., 28,482.....C6 14
Odendaalsrus, S. Afr.,
  15,126..............F5 24
Odense, Den., 111,145....J4 11
Odense, co., Den.,
  207,273............*J4 11
Odenton, Md., 3,000......B4 53
Oder (Odra), riv., Eur...B7 6
Odessa, Ont., Can.,
  852.................C8 41
Odessa, Mo., 2,034.......B4 69
Odessa, N.Y., 573........C4 75
Odessa, Sov. Un.,
  709,000.............H8 12
Odessa, Tex., 80,338......D1 84
Odessa, Wash., 1,231.....B7 86
Odin, Ill., 1,242........E4 58
Odin, mtn., B.C., Can....D8 37
Odon, Ind., 1,192.......G4 59
O'Donnell, Tex., 1,356...C2 84
Odorhei, Rom., 14,162...B7 10
Oella, Md., 500.........B4 53
Oelsnitz, Ger., 18,500...C6 6
Oelwein, Iowa, 8,282.....B6 60
O'Fallon, Ill., 5,796.....E4 58
O'Fallon, Mo., 3,770.....f12 69
Offaly, co., Ire., 51,700..*D3 4
Offenbach, Ger., 117,500..C4 6
Offenburg, Ger., 27,600...D3 6
Ofunato, Jap., 28,400....G10 18
Oga, Jap., 23,600
  (43,333▲).........G9 18
Ōgaki, Jap., 113,671..I8, n15 18
Ogallala, Nebr., 4,250.....C4 71
Ogbomosho, Nig.,
  319,881.............G5 22
Ogden, Iowa, 1,525.......B3 60
Ogden, Kans., 1,780......C7 61
Ogden, Pa., 1,600......*G11 81
Ogden, Utah, 72,000
  (*170,000).........A6, C2 72
Ogden Dunes, Ind., 947..*A3 59
Ogdensburg, N.J., 1,212...A3 74
Ogdensburg, N.Y., 16,122..f9 75
Ogemaw, co., Mich.,
  9,680...............D6 66
Ogle, co., Ill., 38,106.....A4 58
Ogles, Ill., 1,000......*E4 58
Oglesby, Ill., 4,215......B4 58
Oglethorpe, Ga., 1,169...D2 55
Oglethorpe, co., Ga.,
  7,926...............C3 55
Ogletown, Del., 3,500...*A6 53
Ogoamas, mtn., Indon...E6 19
Ogulin, Yugo., 3,519.....C2 10
Ogunquit, Maine, 800....E2 64
Ohara, Jap., 12,300......n19 18
O'Higgins, prov., Chile,
  259,772.............A2 28
Ohio, co., Ind., 4,165...G7 59
Ohio, co., Ky., 17,725.....C3 62

Ohio, co., W. Va., 68,437..A4 87
Ohio, state, U.S.,
  9,706,397........... 78
Ohio, river, U.S........C10 45
Ohio City, Ohio, 851.....B1 78
Ohioville, Pa., 3,050....*E1 81
Ohrid, Yugo., 16,626....E5 10
Oil City, La., 1,430......B2 63
Oil City, Pa., 17,692.....D2 81
Oildale, Calif., 21,000....E4 50
Oilton, Okla., 1,100......A5 79
Oise, dept., Fr., 481,289..*C5 5
Ōita, Jap., 226,417......J5 18
Oita, pref., Jap.,
  1,187,480..........*J5 18
Ojai, Calif., 4,495.......E4 50
Ojinaga, Mex., 8,252.....B4 34
Ojocaliente, Mex., 6,779...C4 34
Ojos del Salado, mtn.,
  Arg., Chile..........F4 27
Ojus, Fla., 5,000.....G6, s13 54
Oka, Que., Can.,
  1,375............D3, q18 42
Oka, river,
  Sov. Un...........D11, o18 12
Okaloosa, co., Fla.,
  61,175.............u15 54
Okanagan Landing, B.C.,
  Can., 535...........D8 37
Okanogan, Wash., 2,001...A6 86
Okanogan, co., Wash.,
  25,520..............A6 86
Okarche, Okla., 584......B4 79
Okauchee, Wis., 1,879...*E5 88
Okawville, Ill., 931.......E4 58
Okaya, Jap., 56,986..H9, m17 18
Okayama, Jap., 291,825...I6 18
Okayama, pref., Jap.,
  1,645,135..........*I6 18
Okazaki, Jap., 194,409...o16 18
Okecie, Pol.........B6, m13 7
Okeechobee, Fla., 2,947....E6 54
Okeechobee, co., Fla.,
  6,424...............E5 54
Okeene, Okla., 1,164......A3 79
Okehampton, Eng., 3,800..E4 4
Okemah, Okla., 2,836.....B5 79
Okfuskee, co., Okla.,
  11,706..............B5 79
Okha, Sov. Un., 35,000...D17 13
Okhotsk, Sov. Un.,
  2,000...............D17 13
Okhotsk, sea, Sov. Un....D17 13
Oklahoma, Pa., 983......*F2 81
Oklahoma, co., Okla.,
  439,506.............B4 79
Oklahoma, state, U.S.,
  2,328,284........... 79
Oklahoma City, Okla.,
  375,000 (*585,000).....B4 79
Oklawaha, Fla., 600....C5 54
Oklee, Minn., 529........C3 67
Okmulgee, Okla., 15,951...B6 79
Okmulgee, co., Okla.,
  36,945..............B5 79
Okolona, Ky., 9,000.....A4 62
Okolona, Miss., 2,622....B5 68
Okotoks, Alta., Can.,
  1,043...............D4 38
Oktibbeha, co., Miss.,
  26,175..............B5 68
Okushiri, Jap., 5,000....E9 18
Olaa (Keaau), Haw.,
  1,334...............D6 56
Olancha, peak, Calif....D4 50
Olanta, S.C., 568........D8 82
Olathe, Kans., 10,987....D9 61
Olavarriá, Arg., 34,175...B4 28
Oława, Pol., 12,800......C4 7
Olbia, It., 11,000........D2 9

Olcott, N.Y., 1,300.......B2 75
Old Bethpage, N.Y.,
5,000..............*E7 75
Old Bridge, N.J., 8,000...C4 74
Old Brookville, N.Y.,
1,126..............*E7 75
Old Castile, reg., Sp.,
2,218,884..........B4 8
Oldenburg, Ind., 694.....F7 59
Oldenburg [in Holstein],
Ger., 9,350.........A5 6
Oldenburg [in Oldenburg],
Ger., 126,500.......B4 6
Old Forge, N.Y., 850....B6 75
Old Forge, Pa.,
8,928..........D10, m17 81
Old Fort, N.C., 787.....F10 76
Oldham, Eng., 114,200...D5 4
Oldham, Ky., 13,388....B4 62
Oldham, co., Tex., 1,928.B1 84
Oldham Village, Mass.,
800...............*B6 65
Old Hickory, Tenn.,
4,300...........A5, E9 83
Old Hometown, Tenn.,
2,500..............*B1 83
Old Man, mtn., Newf.,
Can...............D3 44
Old Orchard Beach,
Maine, 4,580......E2, g7 64
Old Perlican, Newf., Can.,
599...............D5 44
Olds, Alta., Can., 2,433..D3 38
Old Saybrook, Conn.,
2,300.............*D7 52
Oldsmar, Fla., 878......o10 54
Old Speck, mtn., Maine..D2 64
Old Tappan, N.J., 2,330..*B4 74
Old Town, Maine,
8,626.............D4 64
Oldtown, N.C., 1,000...*A2 76
Old Westbury, N.Y.,
2,064.............*E7 75
Olean, N.Y., 21,868.....C2 75
O'Leary Station, P.E.I.,
Can., 755..........C5 43
Oleiros, Sp., 76........A1 8
Olekminsk, Sov. Un.,
5,500.............C15 13
Olesno, Pol., 6,058.....C5 7
Olhão, Port., 16,017....D2 8
Olímpia, Braz., 14,629...C3 30
Olimpo, dept., Par.,
2,705.............D4 29
Olin, Iowa, 703........B6 60
Olinda, Braz., 100,545...*D7 27
Oliva, Sp., 14,579......C5 8
Oliva de la Frontera, Sp.,
12,899............C2 8
Olive Hill, Ky., 1,398...B6 62
Olivehurst, Calif., 6,000..C3 50
Oliveira, Braz., 12,919...C4 30
Olivenza, Sp., 11,469...C2 8
Oliver, B.C., Can., 1,774..E8 37
Oliver, Pa., 1,250......G2 81
Oliver, co., N. Dak.,
2,610.............C4 77
Oliver Springs, Tenn.,
1,163.............C9 83
Olivet, Mich., 1,185....F6 66
Olivette, Mo., 8,257....*C7 69
Olivia, Minn., 2,355....F4 67
Olkusz, Pol., 13,300....g11 7
Olla, La., 1,246.......C3 63
Olmos, Peru, 2,163.....C2 31
Olmos Park, Tex., 2,457..k7 84
Olmsted, Ohio, 4,773...*A4 78
Olmsted, co., Minn.,
65,532............G6 67
Olmsted Falls, Ohio,
2,144.............h9 78
Olney, Ill., 8,780......E5 58
Olney, Md., 800.......B3 53
Olney, Tex., 3,872......C3 84
Olomouc, Czech.,
72,200............D4 7
Oloron-Ste. Marie, Fr.,
12,778............F3 5
Olot, Sp., 17,185......A7 8
Olpe, Kans., 722.......D7 61
Olshany, Sov. Un.,
10,000............F10 12
Olsztyn, Pol., 72,300....B6 7
Olten, Switz., 21,400....E3 6
Oltenia, prov., Rom.,
1,717,982..........*C6 10
Oltenia, reg., Rom.,
1,562,000..........C6 10
Olteniţa, Rom., 14,111...C8 10
Olton, Tex., 1,917......B1 84
Olvera, Sp., 8,341......D3 8
Olympia, Wash., 18,273..B3 86
Olympia Fields, Ill.,
1,503.............*B6 58
Olympus, mtn., Grc.....B4 14
Olympus, mtn., Wash....B2 86
Olyphant, Pa.,
5,864...........D10, m18 81

Omagh, N. Ire., 8,109.....C3 4
Omaha, Nebr.,
352,000
(*500,000).......C10, g13 71
Omak, Wash., 4,068.....A6 86
Omar, W. Va., 900...D3, D5 87
Omdurman, Sud.,
171,000...........E4 23
Omega, Ga., 940.......E3 55
Omemee, Ont., Can., 809..C6 41
Omerville, Que., Can.,
1,094.............D5 42
Ometepec, Mex., 4,990...D5 34
Omigawa, Jap., 5,400....n19 18
Ominato, Jap., 21,600...F10 18
Ōmiya, Jap., 215,646..I9, n18 18
Omro, Wis., 1,991......D5 88
Omsk, Sov. Un.,
721,000...........D10 13
Ōmuta, Jap., 193,875.....J5 18
Onalaska, Wis., 3,161....E2 88
Onamia, Minn., 645.....D5 67
Onancock, Va., 1,759....C7 85
Onarga, Ill., 1,397......C5 58
Onawa, Iowa, 3,176.....B1 60
Onaway, Mich., 1,388....C6 66
Ondor Haan, Mong.,
4,500.............B7 17
Oneco, Fla., 2,500...E4, q10 54
Onega, Sov. Un., 17,000...C6 13
Onega, lake, Sov. Un.....G16 11
Oneida, Ill., 672.......B3 58
Oneida, N.Y., 11,677....B5 75
Oneida, Ohio, 1,500....C1 78
Oneida, Tenn., 2,480....C9 83
Oneida, co., Idaho, 3,603..G6 57
Oneida, co., N.Y.,
264,401...........B5 75
Oneida, co., Wis., 22,112..C4 88
O'Neill, Nebr., 3,181....B7 71
Oneonta, Ala., 4,136....B3 46
Oneonta, N.Y., 14,531...C5 75
Ongjin, Kor., 32,965....H2 18
Ōno, Jap., 22,700
(43,747▲)..........n15 18
Onoda, Jap., 43,584....*J15 18
Onomichi, Jap., 90,740...I6 18
Onondaga, N.Y., 1,500..*C4 75
Onondaga, co., N.Y.,
423,028...........C4 75
Onset, Mass., 2,000....C6 65
Onslow, co., N.C.,
82,706............C5 76
Onsŏng, Kor., 10,116....E4 18
Onsted, Mich., 526......F6 66
Ontake-san, mtn., Jap....n16 18
Ontario, Calif.,
46,617.........E5, m13 50
Ontario, N.Y., 750......B3 75
Ontario, Ohio, 3,049....B3 78
Ontario, Oreg., 5,101....C10 80
Ontario, co., Ont., Can.,
135,895...........C5 41
Ontario, co., N.Y., 68,070..C3 75
Ontario, prov., Can.,
6,960,870..........41
Onteniente, Sp., 18,787...C5 8
Ontonagon, Mich.,
2,358..........B1, m12 66
Ontonagon, co., Mich.,
10,584............m12 66
Oolitic, Ind., 1,140.....G4 59
Oostburg, Wis., 1,065...E6 88
Oostende, Bel., 56,494...B5 5
Ootacamund, India,
50,140............F6 20
Oot Park, N.Y., 2,000..*B4 75
Opal Cliffs, Calif., 3,825..*D2 50
Opa-Locka, Fla., 9,810...sl3 54
Opatow, Pol., 5,459....C6 7
Opava, Czech., 43,600...D4 7
Opelika, Ala., 15,678....C4 46
Opelousas, La., 17,417...D3 63
Opochka, Sov. Un.,
10,000............C7 12
Opoczno, Pol., 10,700....C6 7
Opole, Pol., 68,800....C4 7
Opole Lubelskie, Pol.,
5,574.............C6 7
Oppeln see Opole, Pol.
Oppdal, Nor..........F3 11
Oppland, co., Nor.,
167,500...........*G4 11
Opportunity, Wash.,
13,200.........B8, g14 86
Oquawka, Ill., 1,090....C3 58
Oradea (Oradea Mare),
Rom., 117,300.......B5 10
Oradell, N.J., 7,487.....h8 74
Oran (Ouahran), Alg.,
392,637...........A4 22
Oran, Mo., 1,090.......D8 69
Oran, dept., Alg.,
1,990,729..........*B5 22
Orange, river, Afr......F3 24
Orange, Austl., 21,000...F8 25
Orange, Calif., 67,206...n13 50

Orange, Conn., 8,547....D4 52
Orange, Fr., 17,520.....E6 5
Orange, Mass., 4,000
(6,154▲)..........A3 65
Orange, N.J., 35,789....B4 74
Orange, Ohio, 2,006....*A4 78
Orange, Tex., 25,605....D6 84
Orange, Va., 2,955......B4 85
Orange, co., Calif.,
703,925...........F5 50
Orange, co., Fla.,
263,540...........D5 54
Orange, co., Ind., 16,877.G4 59
Orange, co., N.Y.,
209,141...........D6 75
Orange, co., N.C., 42,970.A3 76
Orange, co., Tex., 60,357.D6 84
Orange, co., Vt., 16,014..D3 73
Orange, co., Va., 12,900..B4 85
Orangeburg, N.Y.,
3,500.............*D6 75
Orangeburg, S.C., 13,852.E6 82
Orangeburg, co., S.C.,
68,559............E6 82
Orange City, Fla., 1,598..D5 54
Orange City, Iowa,
2,707.............A1 60
Orange Cove, Calif.,
2,885.............*D4 50
Orange Free State, prov.,
S. Afr., 1,386,547....F5 24
Orange Grove, Tex.,
1,109.............F4 84
Orange Park, Fla.,
2,624..........B5, m8 54
Orangevale, Calif.,
8,000.............*C3 50
Orangeville, Ont., Can.,
4,593.............D4 41
Oranienburg, Ger.,
21,100............B6 6
Oras, Phil., 4,863......*C7 19
Orăştie, Rom., 10,488....C6 10
Oraviţa, Rom., 8,175....C5 10
Orchard Avenue, Wash.,
5,000.............*B8 86
Orchard Beach, Md.,
1,691.............*B4 53
Orchard Homes, Mont.,
2,019.............D2 70
Orchard Lake, Mich.,
1,127.............*F7 66
Orchard Park, N.Y.,
3,506.............C2 75
Orchard Valley, Wyo.,
1,449.............E8 89
Orchards, Wash., 1,500...D3 86
Orcotuna, Peru, 3,400...D2 31
Orcutt, Calif., 1,500....E3 50
Ord, Nebr., 2,413......C7 71
Órdenes, Sp., 1,311.....A1 8
Ordu, Tur., 20,029.....B11 14
Orduña, Sp., 5,950.....A4 8
Ordville, Nebr., 950....*C2 71
Ordway, Colo., 1,254....C7 51
Ordzhonikidze, Sov. Un.,
194,000...........*E7 13
Ordzhonnikidze
(Dzaudzhikau),
Sov. Un., 208,000.....E7 13
Örebro, Swe.,
76,800..........H6, t33 11
Örebro, co., Swe.,
263,300...........*H6 11
Oregon, Ill., 3,732.....A4 58
Oregon, Mo., 887......B2 69
Oregon, Ohio,
13,319...........A2, e7 78
Oregon, Wis., 1,701....F4 88
Oregon, co., Mo., 9,845..E6 69
Oregon, state, U.S.,
1,768,687..........80
Oregon City, Oreg.,
7,996..........B4, h12 80
Orekhov, Sov. Un.,
10,000............H10 12
Orekhovo-Zuyevo, Sov.
Un., 113,000.....D12, n18 12
Orel, Sov. Un.,
183,000...........E11 12
Oreland, Pa., 6,700....*F11 81
Orenburg (Chkalov),
Sov. Un., 306,000.....D8 13
Orense, prov., Sp.,
451,474...........*A2 8
Orestes, Ind., 507......D6 59
Orestias, Grc., 10,281....B6 14
Orford, mtn., Que., Can..D5 42
Orfordville, Wis., 665....F4 88
Orgeyev, Sov. Un.,
10,000............H7 12
Orick, Calif., 1,000.....B1 50
Orient, Ill., 588.......F5 58
Orient, N.Y., 600......m16 75
Oriental, N.C., 522.....B6 76
Oriente, prov., Cuba,
1,797,606..........D6 35
Orihuela, Sp., 15,873....C5 8

Orillia, Ont., Can.,
15,345............C5 41
Orinda, Calif., 10,280...*D2 50
Orinoco, river, Ven.....B5 32
Orion, Ill., 1,269......B3 58
Oriskany, N.Y., 1,687...B5 75
Oriskany Falls, N.Y., 972.C5 75
Orissa, state, India,
17,548,846.........E7 20
Oristano, It., 14,300....E2 9
Orizaba, Mex.,
69,706.........D5, n15 34
Orkney, co., Scot.,
18,500............*A5 4
Orkney, isl., Scot......*A5 4
Orland, Calif., 2,534....C2 50
Orland, Fla., 450 (1,195▲).D4 64
Orlando, Fla., 88,135....D5 54
Orland Park, Ill., 4,509...k9 58
Orleanais, former prov.,
Fr., 782,000.......D4 5
Orleans, Calif., 500.....B2 50
Orléans, Ont., Can.,
1,381.............h12 41
Orléans, Fr., 84,289
(*126,000).........D4 5
Orleans, Ind., 1,659....G5 59
Orleans, Mass., 950
(2,342▲)..........C7 65
Orleans, Nebr., 608.....D6 71
Orleans, Vt., 1,240.....B3 73
Orleans, co., N.Y., 34,159.B2 75
Orleans, co., Vt., 20,143..B3 73
Orleans, par., La.,
627,525...........E6 63
Orléansville, see
El Asnam, Alg.
Orlovista, Fla., 4,000...*D5 54
Ormoc, prov., Phil.,
13,640............*C6 19
Ormond Beach, Fla.,
8,658.............C5 54
Ormsby, co., Nev., 8,063..B2 72
Ormstown, dept., Que.,
Can., 1,527........D3 42
Orne, dept., Fr.,
280,549...........*C3 5
Örnsköldsvik, Swe., 8,400.F8 11
Orocué, Col., 1,600....C3 32
Orofino, Idaho, 2,471...C2 57
Oro Grande, Calif., 700...E5 50
Oromocto, N.B., Can.,
12,170............D3 43
Orono, Ont., Can., 964..D6 41
Orono, Maine, 8,341....D4 64
Orono, Minn., 5,643....*E5 67
Oronogo, Mo., 513.....D3 69
Oroquieta, Phil., 5,331..*D6 19
Oroshaza, Hung., 26,550..B5 10
Oroville, Calif., 6,115....C3 50
Oroville, Wash., 1,437...A6 86
Orpington, Eng., 80,271..m13 4
Orrick, Mo., 800.......B3 69
Orrville, Ohio, 6,511....B4 78
Orsainville, Que., Can.,
4,236.............n17 42
Orsha, Sov. Un., 74,000...D8 12
Orsk, Sov. Un., 199,000...D8 13
Orşova, Rom., 6,527....C6 10
Orthez, Fr., 5,125......F3 5
Ortigueira, Sp., 1,590...A2 8
Orting, Wash., 1,520....B3 86
Ortiz, Mex., 1,401......B2 34
Ortona a Mare, It.,
10,700............C5 9
Ortonville, Mich., 771...F7 66
Ortonville, Minn., 2,674..E2 67
Oruro, Bol., 82,000....C2 29
Oruro, dept., Bol.,
210,260...........C2 29
Orvieto, It., 9,600.....C4 9
Orwell, Ohio, 819......A5 78
Orwigsburg, Pa., 2,131..E9 81
Oryakhovo, Bul., 6,972..D6 10
Osage, Iowa, 3,753.....A5 60
Osage, co., Kans., 12,886.D8 61
Osage, co., Mo., 10,867..C6 69
Osage, co., Okla.,
32,441............A4 79
Osage Beach, Mo., 741...C5 69
Osage City, Kans., 2,213..D8 61
Ōsaka, Jap., 3,156,222
(*9,400,000).....I7, o14 18
Ōsaka, Jap., 2,500.....n16 18
Ōsaka, pref., Jap.,
6,657,189.........*I7 18
Osakis, Minn., 1,396....E3 67
Osawatomie, Kans.,
4,622.............D9 61
Osborne, Kans., 2,049...C5 61
Osborne, co., Kans.,
7,506.............C5 61
Osbornsville, N.J., 150..*C4 74
Osburn, Idaho, 1,788...B3 57
Osceola, Ark., 6,189....B6 49
Osceola, Ind., 1,350....A5 59
Osceola, Iowa, 3,350....C4 60
Osceola, Mo., 1,066....C4 69

Osceola, Nebr., 1,013.....C8 71
Osceola, Wis., 942.......C1 88
Osceola, co., Fla., 19,029..E5 54
Osceola, co., Iowa, 10,064..A2 60
Osceola, co., Mich.,
  13,595................E5 66
Osceola Mills, Pa., 1,777..E5 81
Oschatz, Ger., 15,500.....C6 6
Oschersleben, Ger.,
  19,100................B5 6
Oscoda, Mich., 2,000.....D7 66
Oscoda, co., Mich., 3,447..D6 66
Osgood, Ind., 1,434......F7 59
Osgoode Station, Ont.,
  Can., 673..............B9 41
Osh, Sov. Un., 90,000....E10 13
Oshamambe, Jap.,
  11,000................E10 18
Oshawa, Ont., Can.,
  62,415................D6 41
Oshkosh, Nebr., 1,025.....C3 71
Oshkosh, Wis.,
  45,110............D5, h8 88
Oshogbo, Nig., 210,384....G5 22
Osijek, Yugo., 71,843.....C4 10
Osinniki, Sov. Un.,
  71,000...............*D11 13
Osipenko, Sov. Un.,
  73,000................H11 12
Oskaloosa, Iowa, 11,536...C5 60
Oskaloosa, Kans.,
  807................C8, k15 61
Oskarshamn, Swe., 12,900..I7 11
Oslo, Nor., 477,100
  (*670,000)........G4, p28 11
Oslo, co., Nor.,
  483,200...............*H4 11
Osmaniye, Tur.,
  27,451................D11 14
Osmond, Nebr., 719......B8 71
Osnabruck, Ger.,
  142,600...............B4 6
Osorno, Chile, 55,100.....C2 28
Osorno, prov., Chile,
  144,088...............C2 28
Osoyoos, B.C., Can.,
  1,022.................E8 37
Osprey, Fla., 800........E4 54
Oss, Neth., 30,700.......B6 5
Ossa, mtn., Austl........o15 25
Osseo, Minn., 2,726.....m12 67
Osseo, Wis., 1,114.......D2 88
Ossian, Ind., 1,108......C7 59
Ossian, Iowa, 827........A6 60
Ossining, N.Y.,
  21,241...........D7, m15 75
Ostashkov, Sov. Un.,
  10,000................C9 12
Osteen, Fla., 550........D5 54
Östergötland, co., Swe.,
  358,000...............*H6 11
Östersund, Swe., 24,900...F6 11
Osterville, Mass., 1,200...C7 65
Östfold, co., Nor.,
  209,100...............*H4 11
Ostrava, Czech.,
  244,900...............D5 7
Ostróda, Pol., 19,000.....B5 7

Ostrogozhsk, Sov. Un.,
  1,000.................F12 12
Ostroleka, Pol., 17,100....B6 7
Ostrov, Czech., 16,600....C2 7
Ostrov, Sov. Un., 10,000..C7 12
Ostrow, Pol., 13,400......B6 7
Ostrowiec, Pol., 41,700....C6 7
Ostrów Wielkopolski,
  Pol., 44,800..........C4 7
Ostrzeszów, Pol., 5,403....C4 7
Ostuni, It., 23,500.......D6 9
Ōsuka, Jap., 4,500......o16 18
Osuna, Sp., 19,569.......D3 8
Oswego, Ill., 1,510.....B5, k8 58
Oswego, Kans., 2,027......E8 61
Oswego, N.Y., 22,155.....B4 75
Oswego, co., N.Y., 86,118..B4 75
Oswestry, Eng., 11,700....D5 4
Oświęcim, Pol.,
  34,100.............C5, g10 7
Ōtaki, Jap., 4,300.......n19 18
Ōtaré, mtn., Col.........C3 32
Ōtaru, Jap., 196,771.....E10 18
Otavalo, Ec., 8,630.......A2 31
Otay, Calif., 1,500......*F5 50
Oteen, N.C., 1,000......f10 76
Otego, N.Y., 875.........C5 75
Otero, co., Colo., 24,128...D7 51
Otero, co., N. Mex.,
  36,976................C6 48
Othello, Wash., 2,669.....C6 86
Otho, Iowa, 593.........B3 60
Otis Orchards, Wash.,
  750..................g14 86
Otisville, Mich., 701......E7 66
Otisville, N.Y., 896......*D6 75
Ote, co., Nebr., 16,503...D9 71
Otsego, Mich., 4,142.....F5 66
Otsego, co., Mich.,
  7,545.................C6 66
Otsego, co., N.Y., 51,942...C5 75
Ōtsu, Jap., 38,402.......I7 18
Ōtsu, Jap., 121,041.....o14 18
Ōtsuki, Jap., 28,500.....n17 18
Ottawa, Ont., Can.,
  268,206 (*429,750)..B9, h12 41
Ottawa, Ill., 19,408......B5 58
Ottawa, Kans., 10,673....D8 61
Ottawa, Ohio, 3,245......A1 78
Ottawa, co., Kans.,
  6,779.................C6 61
Ottawa, co., Mich.,
  98,719................F4 66
Ottawa, co., Ohio, 35,323..A2 78
Ottawa, co., Okla.,
  28,301................A7 79
Ottawa, river, Ont.,
  Que., Can.............E18 36
Ottawa Hills, Ohio,
  3,870.............A2, e6 78
Otterbien, Ind., 788......D3 59
Otter Lake, Mich., 562....E7 66
Otter River, Mass., 600....A3 65
Otterville, Ont., Can.,
  725..................E4 41
Ottoville, Ohio, 793......B1 78
Ottumwa, Iowa, 33,871....C5 60
Otuzco, Peru, 3,534......C2 31
Otwell, Ind., 600........H3 59

Otwock, Pol., 38,000.....m14 7
Ouachita, co., Ark.,
  31,641................D3 49
Ouachita, par., La.,
  101,663...............B3 63
Ouachita, river, U.S......D8 45
Ouagadougou, Upper
  Volta, 59,126..........F4 22
Ouahigouya, Upper
  Volta, 10,000.........F4 22
Ouargla, Alg., 11,279.....B6 22
Oudtshoorn, S. Afr.,
  22,229................G4 24
Ouezzane, Mor., 26,203...B3 22
Ouidah, Dah., 14,000.....G5 22
Oullins, Fr., 24,356......E6 5
Oulu, Fin., 63,800.......E11 11
Oulu, prov., Fin.,
  413,800...............*E11 11
Ouray, Colo., 785........C3 51
Ouray, co., Colo., 1,601...C3 51
Ourinhos, Braz., 25,717...C3 30
Ouro Fino, Braz.,
  8,044..............C3, m8 30
Ouro Prêto, Braz., 14,722..C4 30
Outagamie, co., Wis.,
  101,794...............D5 88
Outes, Sp., 869..........A1 8
Outlook, Sask., Can.,
  1,340.................F2 39
Outreau, Fr., 13,548......B4 5
Outremont, Que., Can.,
  30,753................p19 42
Ouyen, Austl., 1,644......F7 25
Ovada, It., 9,594........B2 9
Ovalle, Chile, 25,300.....A2 28
Ovar, Port., 7,298.......B1 8
Overbrook, Kans., 509.....D8 61
Overijssel, prov., Neth.,
  835,500...............*A7 5
Overland, Mo., 22,763....f13 69
Overland Park, Kans.,
  56,395................B9 61
Overlea, Md.,
  11,500............B4, g11 53
Overton, Nebr., 523......D6 71
Overton, Nev., 700.......C4 72
Overton, Tex., 1,950......C5 84
Overton, co., Tenn.,
  14,661................C8 83
Ovid, Mich., 1,505.......E6 66
Ovid, N.Y., 789.........C4 75
Oviedo, Fla., 1,926.......D5 54
Oviedo, Sp., 127,058.....A3 8
Oviedo, prov., Sp.,
  989,344...............*A3 8
Ovruch, Sov. Un., 10,000..F7 12
Owasso, Okla., 2,032.....A6 79
Owatonna, Minn., 14,776..F5 67
Owego, N.Y., 5,439......C4 75
Owen, Wis., 1,098.......D3 88
Owen, co., Ind., 11,400...F4 59
Owen, co., Ky., 8,237.....B5 62
Owens, N.C., 5,207......*C4 76
Owensboro, Ky., 42,471...C3 62
Owensboro East, Ky.,
  2,244.................*C3 62
Owensboro West, Ky.,
  1,366.................*C3 62

Owen Sound, Ont., Can.,
  17,421................C4 41
Owensville, Ind.,
  1,121.................H2 59
Owensville, Mo.,
  2,379.................C6 69
Owensville, Ohio, 609.....C1 78
Owenton, Ky., 1,376......B5 62
Owings Mills, Md., 100...*B4 53
Owingsville, Ky., 1,040....B6 62
Owl Creek, mts., Wyo.....C4 89
Owosso, Mich., 17,006....E6 66
Owsley, co., Ky., 5,369....C6 62
Owyhee, co., Idaho,
  6,375.................G2 57
Oxbow, Sask., Can.,
  1,359.................H4 39
Oxbow, Mich., 1,700.....*F7 66
Oxelösund, Swe.,
  10,000................o35 11
Oxford, Ala., 3,603.......B4 46
Oxford, N.S., Can.,
  1,471.................D6 43
Oxford, Eng., 107,100....E6 4
Oxford, Ga., 1,047.......C3 55
Oxford, Ind., 1,108.......C3 59
Oxford, Iowa, 633........C6 60
Oxford, Kans., 989.......E6 61
Oxford, Maine, 500......D2 64
Oxford, Md., 852.........C5 53
Oxford, Mass., 7,100.....B4 65
Oxford, Mich., 2,357.....F7 66
Oxford, Miss., 5,283......A4 68
Oxford, Nebr., 1,090......D6 71
Oxford, N.J., 1,000.......B3 74
Oxford, N.Y., 1,871......C5 75
Oxford, N.C., 6,978......A4 76
Oxford, Ohio, 7,828......C1 78
Oxford, Pa., 3,376.......G10 81
Oxford, co., Ont., Can.,
  70,499................D4 41
Oxford, co., Eng.,
  324,100...............*E6 4
Oxford, co., Maine
  44,345................D2 64
Oxnard, Calif., 58,269....E4 50
Oxnard Beach, Calif.,
  2,000................*E4 50
Oyo, Nig., 112,349.......G5 22
Oyonnax, Fr., 14,830.....D6 5
Oyrot Tura, see Gorno
  Altaysk, Sov. Un.
Oyster Bay, N.Y.,
  6,500.............E7, n15 75
Oyster Bay Cove, N.Y.,
  988..................*E7 75
Ozamiz, Phil., 17,940....D6 19
Ozark, Ala., 9,534.......D4 46
Ozark, Ark., 1,965.......B2 49
Ozark, Mo., 1,536.......D4 69
Ozrak, co., Mo., 6,744....E5 69
Ozaukee, co., Wis.,
  38,441................E6 88
Ozd, Hung., 34,155......A5 10
Ozieri, It., 11,884.......D2 9
Ozona, Fla., 700........o10 54
Ozona, Tex., 3,361......D2 84
Ozorkow, Pol., 168,00.....C5 7
Ozu, Jap., 20,000........J6 18

P

Paarl, S. Afr., 41,540.....G3 24
Paauilo, Haw., 1,059......C6 56
Pabianice, Pol., 58,200....C5 7
Pabna, Pak., 32,340......D8 20
Pacasmayo, Peru, 6,615...C2 31
Pace, Fla., 900.........ul4 54
Pacheco, Calif., 1,518....*C2 50
Pachuca [de Soto],
  Mex., 64,571......C5, m14 34
Pacific, Mo., 2,795....C7, g12 69
Pacific, Wash., 1,577.....f11 86
Pacific, co., Wash.,
  14,674................C2 86
Pacific, ocean..........F6 2
Pacifica, Calif., 20,995....h8 50
Pacific Grove, Calif.,
  12,208................D3 50
Packard, mtn., Mass......B3 65
Pacolet, S.C., 1,252......B4 82
Pacolet Mills, S.C.,
  1,476.................B4 82
Paczków, Pol., 6,955.....C4 7

Padang, Indon.,
  143,615...............F2 19
Padangpandjang, Indon.,
  25,509................F2 19
Padangsidimpuan,
  Indon., 5,709......E1, m11 19
Paddock Lake, Wis., 912..n11 88
Paden City, W. Va.,
  3,137.................B4 87
Paderborn, Ger., 57,000...C4 6
Padova (Padua), It.,
  207,600...............B3 9
Paducah, Ky., 34,479.....A2 62
Paducah, Tex., 2,392......B2 84
Paektu-san, mtn., Kor.....F4 18
Pagadian, Phil., 17,865....*D6 19
Page, Ariz., 2,500.......A4 48
Page, W. Va., 800....C3, D6 87
Page, co., Iowa, 21,023....D2 60
Page, co., Va., 15,572....B4 85
Pagedale, Mo., 5,106.....*C7 69
Pageland, S.C., 2,020......B7 82

Page Manor, Ohio,
  5,000................*C1 78
Pago Pago, Am. Sam.,
  1,251................*G9 2
Pagosa Springs, Colo.,
  1,374.................D3 51
Pahala, Haw., 1,392......D6 56
Pahang, state, Mala.,
  387,400...............E2 19
Pahlavi, Iran, 31,349......A7 23
Pahoa, Haw., 1,046.......D7 56
Pahokee, Fla., 4,709......F6 54
Paia, Haw., 2,149........C5 56
Painesdale, Mich., 950....A2 66
Painesville, Ohio, 16,116...A4 78
Paint, Pa., 1,275.......*F4 81
Painted Post, N.Y., 2,570..C3 75
Paintsville, Ky., 4,025.....C7 62
Paisley, Ont., Can., 759....C3 41
Paisley, Scot., 96,700.....C4 4
Paita, Peru, 7,177........C1 31
Pajaro, Calif., 1,273.....*D3 50

Pakanbaru, Indon.,
  69,147................E2 19
Pakistan, country, Asia,
  10,070,900.........C4, D9 20
Pakokku, Bur., 30,943....D10 20
Paks, Hung., 10,452......B4 10
Pakse, Laos, 25,000......B3 19
Palacios, Tex., 3,676......E4 84
Palafrugell, Sp., 7,905....B7 8
Palaiseau, Fr., 16,326.....h9 5
Palamós, Sp., 7,639......B7 8
Palana, Sov. Un.,
  1,000.................D18 13
Palanpur, India, 29,139...D5 20
Palas de Rey, Sp., 769....A2 8
Palatine, Ill., 19,146....A5, h8 58
Palatka, Fla., 11,028......C5 54
Palawan, prov., Phil.,
  162,669...............C5 19
Palawan, isl., Phil........C5 19
Palazzolo Acreide, It.,
  11,024................F5 9

Palembang, Indon.,
458,661.............F2 19
Palencia, Sp., 48,216.....A3 8
Palencia, prov., Sp.,
231,977...........*A3 8
Palermo, It., 614,000......E4 9
Palestine, Ill., 1,564.....D6 58
Palestine, Tex., 13,974...D5 84
Palestine, reg., Asia......C2 15
Palestrina, It., 9,154....h9 9
Palghat, India, 77,620....F6 20
Palisades, Idaho, 75....*F7 57
Palisades Park, N.J.,
11,943...........h8 74
Palma [de Mallorca], Sp.,
159,084...........C7 8
Palmares, Braz., 17,327..*D7 27
Palma Soriano, Cuba,
47,900...........D5 35
Palm Bay, Fla., 2,808.....D6 54
Palm Beach, Fla., 6,055...F6 54
Palm Beach, co., Fla.,
228,106...........F6 54
Palmdale, Calif., 7,400....E4 50
Palm Desert, Calif.,
1,295...........*F5 50
Palmeira dos Indios, Braz.,
15,642...........*D7 27
Palmer, Alsk., 1,181..C10, g17 47
Palmer, Mass., 4,000
(10,358▲).........B3 65
Palmer, Mich., 850.......B3 66
Palmer, Tenn., 1,069.....D8 83
Palmer Heights, Pa.,
2,597...........*E11 81
Palmer Park, Md., 4,000..*C4 53
Palmerston, Ont., Can.,
1,554...........D4 41
Palmerston North, N.Z.,
46,832 (*49,140)....N15 26
Palmerton, Pa., 5,942.....E10 81
Palmetto, Fla., 5,556..E4, p10 54
Palmetto, Ga., 1,466......C2 55
Palm Harbor, Fla., 1,000..o10 54
Palmi, It., 15,400........E5 9
Palmira, Col., 106,502....C2 32
Palmira, Cuba, 8,700.....C3 35
Palm Springs, Calif.,
13,468...........F5 50
Palm Springs, Fla., 2,503..*F6 54
Palmyra, Ill., 811.......D4 58
Palmyra, Mo., 2,933......B6 69
Palmyra, N.J., 7,036.....C2 74
Palmyra, N.Y., 3,486.....B3 75
Palmyra, Pa., 6,999......F8 81
Palmyra, Wis., 1,000.....F5 88
Palo Alto, Calif.,
52,287...........D2, k8 50
Palo Alto, Pa., 1,445....*E9 81
Palo Alto, co., Iowa,
14,736...........A3 60
Palomar, mtn., Calif......F5 50
Palombara Sabina, It.,
6,215...........g9 9
Palo Pinto, co., Tex.,
20,516...........C3 84
Palopo, Indon., 4,208.....F6 19
Palos Heights, Ill., 3,775..*B6 58
Palos Hills, Ill., 3,766...*B6 58
Palos Park, Ill., 2,169....k9 58
Palos Verdes Estates,
Calif., 9,564.......n12 50
Palouse, Wash., 926......C8 86
Palpa, Peru, 2,171.......D3 31
Pamekasan, Indon.,
24,912...........G4 19
Pamiers, Fr., 13,297.....F4 5
Pamlico, co., N.C., 9,850..B6 76
Pampa, Tex., 24,664......B2 84
Pampanga, prov., Phil.,
617,259...........*B6 19
Pampas, Peru, 1,622......D3 31
Pampas, reg., Arg.......*G4 27
Pamplico, S.C., 988......C8 82
Pamplona, Col., 25,502...B3 32
Pamplona, Sp., 97,880....A5 8
Pana, Ill., 6,432........D4 58
Panagyurishte, Bul.,
12,015...........D7 10
Panama, Okla., 937......B7 79
Panamá, Pan., 318,500...B2 32
Panama, country, N.A.,
1,246,000.........B2 32
Panama City, Fla.,
33,275...........u16 54
Panao, Peru, 954........C2 31
Panay, isl., Phil.......C6 19
Pancevo, Yugo., 40,740...C5 10
Pandharpur, India,
45,421...........E6 20
Pando, Ur., 6,248.......E1 30
Pando, dept., Bol.,
19,804...........B2 29
Pandora, Ohio, 782......B2 78
Panevėžys, Sov. Un.,
41,100...........D5 12
Panfilov, Sov. Un.,
27,300...........E10 13

Pangasinan, prov., Phil.,
1,124,144.........*B6 19
Pangkalpinang, Indon.,
58,540...........F3 19
Panguitch, Utah, 1,435....C5 72
Panhandle, Tex., 1,958...B2 84
Panjim, India, 31,950....E5 20
Panna, India, 16,737.....D7 20
Panola, co., Miss., 28,791..A3 68
Panola, co., Tex., 16,870...C5 84
Panora, Iowa, 1,019......C3 60
Pantelleria, It., 2,294....F3 9
Pantin, Fr., 46,292......g10 5
Pánuco, Mex., 8,810..C5, k14 34
Paola, It., 9,197........E6 9
Poala, Kans., 4,784......D9 61
Paoli, Ind., 2,754.......G5 59
Paoli, Pa., 9,000........o20 81
Paonia, Colo., 1,083.....C3 51
Paoting (Tsingyuan),
China, 265,000......D8 17
Paotow, China, 400,000...C7 17
Paoying, China, 85,000...C7 17
Papa, Hung., 25,629.....B3 10
Papaikou, Haw., 1,591....D6 56
Papantla [de Olarte],
Mex., 18,865......C5, m15 34
Papeete, Oceania,
18,089...........H11 2
Papenburg, Ger., 150,000..B3 6
Papillion, Nebr.,
4,079...........C9, g12 71
Papineau, co., Que., Can.,
32,697...........D2 42
Papineauville, Que., Can.,
1,300...........D2 42
Papua, Austl. dep.,
Oceania, 523,000....k12 25
Paracatu, Braz., 5,909....B3 30
Paraćin, Yugo., 15,627...D5 10
Paradis, La., 800........k11 63
Paradise, Calif., 11,000...C3 50
Paradise, Pa., 750.......F9 81
Paradise Valley, Ariz.,
4,650...........D2 48
Paragould, Ark., 9,947...A5 49
Paraguaçu Paulista, Braz.,
11,391...........C2 30
Paraguarí, Par., 12,405...E4 29
Paraguarí, dept., Par.,
159,161...........E4 29
Paraguay, country, S.A.,
1,920,000.........D4 29
Paraguay, riv., Braz.,
Par.............F5 27
Paraíba do Sul, Braz.,
7,675...........h6 30
Paraíba [do Sul], riv.,
Braz.............F6 27
Paraíso, C.Z., 3,113.....*B2 32
Paraíso, Mex., 4,049.....D6 34
Paraisópolis, Braz., 6,582..C3 30
Parakhino-Paddubye,
Sov. Un., 20,000....B9 12
Paramaribo, Sur.,
122,600...........C5 27
Paramé, Fr., 8,811......C2 5
Paramount, Calif.,
27,249...........*F4 50
Paramus, N.J., 23,238...h8 74
Paraná, Arg., 107,551....A4 28
Paraná, state, Braz.,
4,227,763.........C2 30
Paraná, riv., S.A.......E4 29
Paranaguá, Braz., 27,728..D3 30
Paray-Le-Monial, Fr.,
9,557...........D6 5
Parchim, Ger., 18,900....B5 6
Parchment, Mich., 1,565...F5 66
Pardeeville, Wis., 1,331...E4 88
Pardess Hanna, Isr.,
8,200...........B2 15
Pardubice, Czech., 55,300..C3 7
Parecis, mts., Braz.......E5 27
Parent, Que., Can., 1,298..k12 42
Parepare, Indon.,
62,683...........F5 19
Paricutín, vol., Mex......m12 34
Parintins, Braz., 9,068...*D5 27
Paris, Ark., 3,007.......B2 49
Paris, Ont., Can., 5,820..D4 41
Paris, Fr., 2,790,091
(*7,750,000)......C5, g10 5
Paris, Idaho, 746.......G7 57
Paris, Ill., 9,823.......D6 58
Paris, Ky., 7,791.......B5 62
Paris, Mo., 1,393.......B6 69
Paris, S.C., 1,000......*B3 82
Paris, Tenn., 9,325.....A3 83
Paris, Tex., 20,977.....C5 84
Paris, peak, Idaho......G7 57
Park, co., Colo., 1,822...B5 51
Park, co., Mont., 13,168...E6 70
Park, co., Wyo., 16,874...B3 89
Park City, Ill., 2,131....*A6 58
Park City, Kans., 3,000...B5 61
Park City, Utah,
1,366...........A6, D2 72

Parkdale, P.E.I., Can.,
1,735...........C6 43
Parke, co., Ind., 14,804...E3 59
Parker, Ariz., 1,937.....B1 48
Parker, Fla., 2,669......u16 54
Parker, Pa., 945........D2 81
Parker, S. Dak., 1,142...G8 77
Parker, co., Tex., 22,880..C4 84
Parker City, Ind., 1,181..D7 59
Parkersburg, Iowa, 1,468..B5 60
Parkersburg, W. Va.,
44,797...........B3 87
Parkers Prairie, Minn.,
884.............D3 67
Parkes, Austl., 8,223.....F7 26
Parkesburg, Pa., 2,759...G10 81
Park Falls, Wis., 2,919...C3 88
Park Forest, Ill.,
31,324...........B6, m9 58
Parkhill, Ont., Can.,
1,169...........D3 41
Park Hills, Ky., 4,076....A7 62
Parkin, Ark., 1,489......B5 49
Parkland, Pa., 1,200....*F11 81
Parkland, Wash., 18,000..f11 86
Parklawn, Va., 1,000....*B5 85
Park Place, Pa., 230....*B3 81
Park Rapids, Minn.,
3,047...........D3 67
Park Ridge, Ill.,
39,065...........B6, h9 58
Park Ridge, N.J., 6,389...g8 74
Park Ridge Manor, Ill.,
900.............*B6 58
Park River, N. Dak.,
1,813...........B8 77
Parkrose, Oreg., 24,000..*B4 80
Parkside, Pa., 2,426....*G11 81
Parksley, Va., 850.......C7 85
Parkston, S. Dak., 1,514..G8 77
Parksville, B.C., Can.,
1,183...........E5 37
Parksville, N.Y., 900....D6 75
Parkton, N.C., 906......C3 76
Parkview, Ohio, 2,018...*A4 78
Parkview, Pa., 1,000....*E2 81
Parkville, Md., 47,800...C3 53
Parkville, Mo., 1,229..B3, h10 69
Parkville, Pa., 1,300....*G8 81
Parkway Village, Ky.,
949.............*B4 62
Parkwood, Md., 1,400...*B3 53
Parlier, Calif., 1,946....D4 50
Parma, Idaho, 1,295.....F2 57
Parma, It., 157,300......B3 9
Parma, Mich., 770.......F6 66
Parma, Mo., 1,060......E8 69
Parma, Ohio, 82,845...A4, h9 78
Parma Heights, Ohio,
18,100...........h9 78
Parmar, co., Tex., 9,583..B1 84
Parnaíba, Braz., 39,951...D6 27
Parnaíba, riv., Braz......D6 27
Pärnu, Sov. Un., 36,100..B5 12
Parowan, Utah, 1,486....C5 72
Parral, Chile, 14,600.....B2 28
Parras de la Fuente, Mex.,
19,768...........B4 34
Parrish, Ala., 1,608.....B2 46
Parrish, Fla., 800......E4, p11 54
Parrsboro, N.S., Can.,
1,834...........D5 43
Parry, is., N.W. Ter.,
Can.............m28 36
Parry, mtn., B.C., Can...C3 37
Parry Sound, Ont.,
Can., 6,004......B4, p20 41
Parry Sound, dist.,
Ont., Can., 29,632....B4 41
Parshall, N. Dak., 1,915...C3 77
Parsippany, N.J., 5,000..*B4 74
Parsons, Kans., 13,929...E8 61
Parsons, Tenn., 1,859....B3 83
Parsons, W. Va., 1,798...B5 87
Parthenay, Fr., 8,350....D3 5
Partinico, It., 26,119.....E4 9
Pasadena, Calif.,
116,407.........E4, m12 50
Pasadena, Md., 1,500....B4 53
Pasadena, Tex., 58,737...r14 84
Pasadena Hills, Mo.,
1,315...........*C7 69
Pasadena Park, Wash.,
2,000...........*B8 86
Pasay (Rizal), Phil.,
132,673..........C6, o13 19
Pascagoula, Miss.,
17,155.........E3, E5 68
Pascani [-Gară], Rom.,
15,008...........B8 10
Pasco, Wash., 14,522....C6 86
Pasco, co., Fla., 36,785...D4 54
Pasco, dept., Peru,
130,507...........D2 31
Pascoag, R.I., 3,400.....B2 52

Pasig, Phil., 62,130......o13 19
Paso de los Libres, Arg.,
11,665...........E4 29
Paso Robles, Calif., 6,677..E3 50
Pasquotank, co., N.C.,
25,630...........A6 76
Pasrur, Pak., 9,403......B5 20
Passadumkeag, mtn.,
Maine............C4 64
Passaic, N.J., 53,963...B4, h8 74
Passaic, co., N.J., 406,618..A4 74
Passau, Ger., 31,400.....D6 6
Pass Christian, Miss.,
3,881...........E2, E4 68
Passo Fundo, Braz.,
47,299...........D2 30
Passos, Braz., 28,555....C3 30
Pastaza, prov., Ec., 13,693..B2 31
Pasto, Col., 82,546......C2 32
Pasuruan, Indon., 62,872..G4 19
Pataskala, Ohio, 1,046....C3 78
Patchogue, N.Y., 9,768...n15 75
Paternó, It., 44,400......F5 9
Paterson, N.J.,
143,663.........B4, h8 74
Pathankot, India, 46,330..B6 20
Pathfork, Ky., 500......D6 62
Patiala, India, 125,234...B6 20
Patna, India, 363,700....C8 20
Patos, Braz., 27,275.....*D7 27
Patos de Minas, Braz.,
31,471...........B3 30
Patrai, Grc., 95,364.....C3 14
Patrick, co., Va., 15,282...D2 85
Patrocínio, Braz., 13,933...B3 30
Pattani, Thai., 16,804....D2 19
Patten, Maine, 1,200
(1,312▲).........C4 64
Patterson, Calif., 2,429..*D3 50
Patterson, La., 2,923.....E4 63
Patterson, N.Y., 900.....D7 75
Patterson Gardens, Mich.,
1,747...........*G7 66
Patton, Pa., 2,880......E4 81
Pattonsburg, Mo., 753....A3 69
Pattullo, mtn., B.C., Can..A3 37
Pátzcuaro, Mex.,
14,324.........D4, n13 34
Patzicía, Guat., 5,021...*E6 34
Patzún, Guat., 5,103....*E6 34
Pau, Fr., 59,937.......F3 5
Paucarbamba, Peru,
1,173...........D3 31
Paudalho, Braz., 6,889..*D7 27
Pauk, Bur., 5,000.......D9 20
Paulding, Ohio, 2,936....A1 78
Paulding, co., Ga., 13,101..C2 55
Paulding, co., Ohio,
16,792...........A1 78
Paulina (Remy), La.,
1,150.........D5, h10 63
Paulina, mts., Oreg......D5 80
Paulina, peak, Oreg......D5 80
Pauline, mtn., B.C., Can...C8 37
Paullina, Iowa, 1,329....B2 60
Paulsboro, N.J., 8,121...D2 74
Pauls Valley, Okla.,
6,856...........C4 79
Paungde, Bur., 17,286...E10 20
Pavia, It., 79,400.......B2 9
Pavlodar, Sov. Un.,
120,000...........D10 13
Pavlograd, Sov. Un.,
43,000...........G10 12
Pavlovo, Sov. Un.,
55,000...........D14 12
Pavlovsk, Sov. Un.,
30,000...........F13 12
Pavlovskiy Posad,
Sov. Un., 58,000....n18 12
Pawcatuck, Conn., 6,500..D9 52
Paw Creek, N.C., 1,000...B2 76
Pawhuska, Okla., 5,414...A5 79
Pawling, N.Y., 1,734.....D7 75
Pawnee, Ill., 1,517......D4 58
Pawnee, Okla., 2,303....A5 79
Pawnee, co., Kans.,
10,254...........D4 61
Pawnee, co., Nebr., 5,356..D9 71
Pawnee, co., Okla.,
10,884...........A5 79
Pawnee City, Nebr.,
1,343...........D9 71
Paw Paw, Mich., 2,970...F5 66
Paw Paw, W. Va., 789....B6 87
Paw Paw Lake, Mich.,
3,518...........*F4 66
Pawtucket, R.I., 77,538..B11 52
Paxtang, Pa., 1,916....*F8 81
Paxton, Ill., 4,370......C5 58
Payen, China, 5,000.....D3 17
Payette, Idaho, 4,451....E2 57
Payette, co., Idaho,
12,363...........E2 57
Payne, Ohio, 1,287.....A1 78
Payne, co., Okla., 44,231..A4 79
Paynesville, Minn., 1,754..E4 67
Paysandú, Ur., 51,645...E1 30

Paysandú, dept., Ur.,
87,000..............*E1 30
Payson, Utah, 4,237...A6, D2 72
Pazardzhik, Bul., 55,410...D7 10
Pazin, Yugo., 3,004.......C1 10
Peabody, Kans., 1,309.....D6 61
Peabody, Mass.,
32,202.............A6, f12 65
Peace, riv., Alta., B.C.,
Can..................E10 36
Peace Dale, R.I., 2,000...D11 52
Peace River, Alta., Can.,
2,543.............A2, f7 38
Peach, co., Ga., 13,846....D3 55
Peach Creek, W. Va.,
700..................D5 87
Peak Hill, Austl., 1,380....E2 25
Peaked, mtn., Maine.......B4 64
Peapack-Gladstone, see
Gladstone, N.J.
Pearisburg, Va., 2,268.....C2 85
Pearl, Miss., 5,081.......*C3 68
Pearland, Tex., 1,497.....r14 84
Pearl Beach, Mich.,
1,224................*F8 66
Pearl City, Haw.,
9,000.............B4, g10 56
Pearl River, La., 964......D6 63
Pearl River, N.Y.,
14,500................g12 75
Pear Ridge, Tex., 3,470....E2 63
Pearsall, Tex., 4,957......E3 84
Pearsall, peak, Oreg......E3 80
Pearson, Ga., 1,615.......E4 55
Pebane, Moz............D7 24
Peć, Yugo., 28,297........D5 10
Peçanha, Braz., 3,602.....B4 30
Pecatonica, Ill., 1,659....A4 58
Pechenga, Sov. Un.,
13,200................C6 13
Pechora, riv., Sov. Un.....C8 13
Peckville (Blakely), Pa.,
6,374.................A9 81
Pecos, N. Mex., 584.....*B6 48
Pecos, Tex., 12,728...D1, o13 84
Pecos, co., Tex., 11,957....D1 84
Pecos, riv., N. Mex.,
Tex..................D6 45
Pécs, Hung., 127,000......B4 10
Pedley, Calif., 1,600.....*F5 50
Pedreiras, Braz., 10,189...*D6 27
Pedricktown, N.J., 750....D2 74
Pedro Juan Caballero,
Par., 12,521..........D4 29
Pedro Velho, Braz.,
2,041................*D7 27
Peebles, Ohio, 1,601......D2 78
Peebles, Scot., 5,300......C4 4
Peebles, co., Scot.,
13,300...............*C5 4
Peekaboo, mtn., Maine....C5 64
Peekskill, N.Y.,
18,504............D7, m15 75
Peel, co., Ont., Can.,
111,575...............D5 41
Pego, Sp., 8,291..........C5 8
Pegu, Bur., 47,378.......E10 20
Pehan, China, 18,000....B10 17
Pehuajo, Arg., 13,537.....B4 28
Peine, Ger., 29,800.......B5 6
Peiping, see Peking, China
Pekalongan, Indon.,
100,261...............G3 19
Pekan, Mala., 7,129.......E2 19
Pekin, Ill., 29,624........C4 58
Peking (Peiping), China,
3,500,000.............D8 17
Pelahatchie, Miss., 1,066...C4 68
Pelaihari, Indon..........F4 19
Pelée, mtn., Mart........I14 35
Pelham, Ga., 4,609.......E2 55
Pelham, N.Y., 1,964.....*D7 75
Pelham Manor, N.Y.,
6,114................h13 75
Pelhrimov, Czech.,
7,200.................D3 7
Pelican Rapids, Minn.,
1,693................D2 67
Pelican, mtn., Alta., Can...B4 38
Pell Lake, Wis., 900......n11 88
Pella, Iowa, 6,087.......C5 60
Pella, prov., Grc.,
133,224..............*B4 14
Pell City, Ala., 4,165.....B3 46
Peloponnesos
(Peloponnesus), reg.,
Grc..................D4 14
Pelotas, Braz., 121,280....E2 30
Pelzer North, S.C.,
1,400................*B2 82
Pematangsiantar, Indon.,
112,687..............m11 19
Pemberton, N.J., 1,250....D3 74
Pemberville, Ohio, 1,237...A4 78
Pembina, co., N. Dak.,
12,946................B8 77
Pembroke, Ont., Can.,
16,791............B7, p20 41

Pembroke, Ga., 1,450.....D5 55
Pembroke, Mass., 700....B6 65
Pembroke, N.C., 1,372....C3 76
Pembroke, Va., 1,038.....C2 85
Pembroke, Wales, 13,500..E4 4
Pembroke, co., Wales,
94,700...............*E4 4
Pembroke Pines, Fla.,
1,429................*F6 54
Pemiscot, co., Mo.,
38,095................E8 69
Penang (George Town),
Mala., 234,903
(*325,000)............D2 19
Penang, state, Mala.,
697,000...............D2 19
Penápolis, Braz., 14,400...C2 30
Pen Argyl, Pa., 3,693....E11 81
Peñarroya-Pueblonuevo,
Sp., 24,152...........C3 8
Penbrook, Pa., 3,671......F8 81
Pender, Nebr., 1,165......B9 71
Pender, co., N.C.,
17,372................C4 76
Pendleton, Ind., 2,472....E6 59
Pendleton, Oreg., 14,434..B8 80
Pendleton, S.C., 2,358....B2 82
Pendleton, co., Ky.,
9,968.................B5 62
Pendleton, co., W. Va.,
8,093.................C5 87
Pend Oreille, co., Wash.,
6,914.................A8 86
Penedo, Braz., 17,084.....E7 27
Penetanguishene, Ont.,
Can..................C5 41
Penfield, N.Y., 4,000.....*B3 75
Penfield Junction, Ohio,
2,300................*A3 78
Pengpu, China, 253,000...E8 17
Peniche, Port., 11,357.....C1 8
Peninsula, Ohio, 644......A4 78
Penki, China, 449,000.....C9 17
Penn, Pa., 858..........*F3 81
Pennask, mtn., B.C., Can...E7 37
Penndel, Pa., 2,158......*F12 81
Penne, It., 5,054.........C4 9
Pennines, mts., Eng.......C5 4
Pennington, Ala., 400.....C1 46
Pennington, N.J., 2,063....C3 74
Pennington, co., Minn.,
12,468................B2 67
Pennington, co., S. Dak.,
58,195................G3 77
Pennington Gap, Va.,
1,799.................f8 85
Pennsauken, N.J., 33,771..D2 74
Pennsboro, W. Va., 1,660..B4 87
Pennsburg, Pa., 1,698....F11 81
Penns Grove, N.J., 6,176...D2 74
Pennside, Pa., 3,000.....*F10 81
Pennsville, N.J., 5,000.....D1 74
Pennsylvania, state, U.S.,
11,319,366............. 81
Penn Valley, Pa., 3,500..*F11 81
Penn Wynne, Pa., 4,500..*C11 81
Penn Yan, N.Y., 5,770....C3 75
Penny Hill, Del., 1,000...*A6 53
Penobscot, co., Maine,
126,346...............C4 64
Pensacola, Fla., 60,000
(*188,000)...........u14 54
Pentecost, Miss., 100.....B3 68
Penticton, B.C., Can.,
13,859................E8 37
Penton, Miss., 100.......A3 68
Pentwater, Mich., 1,030...E4 66
Penza, Sov. Un., 315,000..D7 13
Penzance, Eng., 18,800....E4 4
Penzberg, Ger., 10,300....E5 6
Penzhino, Sov. Un.,......D17 13
Peoria, Ariz., 3,802....C2, D1 48
Peoria, Ill., 136,000
(*300,000)............C4 58
Peoria, co., Ill., 189,044..C4 58
Peoria Heights, Ill., 7,064..C4 58
Peotone, Ill., 1,788......B6 58
Pepin, Wis., 825.........D1 88
Pepin, co., Wis., 7,332....D2 88
Pepper Pike, Ohio,
3,217................*A4 78
Pequannock, N.J., 3,500..B4 74
Perak, state, Mala.,
1,508,000............*E2 19
Percy, Ill., 810..........E4 58
Perdido, mtn., Sp........A6 8
Pereira, Braz., 7,173......C2 30
Pereira, Col., 147,487.....C2 32
Perekop, Sov. Un.,
10,000................H9 12
Pereslavl-Zalesskiy,
Sov. Un., 22,200.....C12 12
Pereyaslav-Khmelnitskiy,
Sov. Un., 10,000......F8 12
Pergamino, Arg., 45,366...A4 28
Perham, Minn., 2,019.....D3 67
Périgueux, Fr., 38,529.....E4 5
Perija, mts., Col..........B3 32

Perkasie, Pa., 4,650......F11 81
Perkins, co., Nebr., 4,189..D4 71
Perkins, co., S. Dak.,
5,977.................E3 77
Perleberg, Ger., 13,500....B5 6
Perlis, state, Mala.,
109,100..............*D2 19
Perl-Mack, Colo., 4,000..*B6 51
Perm, Sov. Un., 764,000..D8 13
Përmet, Alb., 2,302......B3 14
Pernambuco, state, Braz.,
788,569..............*D7 27
Pernik, Bul., 75,844......D6 10
Perpignan, Fr., 83,025.....F5 5
Perquimans, co., N.C.,
8,675.................A6 76
Perrine, Fla., 6,424....G6, s13 54
Perris, Calif., 2,950......F5 50
Perry, Fla., 8,030........B3 54
Perry, Iowa, 6,442.......C3 60
Perry, Mich., 1,370......F6 66
Perry, Mo., 802.........B6 69
Perry, N.Y., 4,629.......C3 75
Perry, Ohio, 885.........A4 78
Perry, Okla., 5,210.......A4 79
Perry, co., Ala., 17,358....C2 46
Perry, co., Ark., 4,927....C3 49
Perry, co., Ill., 19,184....E4 58
Perry, co., Ind., 17,232...H4 59
Perry, co., Ky., 34,961....C6 62
Perry, co., Miss., 8,745....D4 68
Perry, co., Mo., 14,642...D8 69
Perry, co., Ohio, 27,864...C3 78
Perry, co., Pa., 26,582....F7 81
Perry, co., Tenn., 5,273...B4 83
Perry, peak, Mass........B1 65
Perry Hall (Fullerton),
Md., 3,800...........B5 53
Perry Heights, Ohio,
2,000................*B4 78
Perryman, Md., 900.....B5 53
Perryopolis, Pa., 1,799...*F2 81
Perrysburg, Ohio,
5,519.............A2, e6 78
Perryton, Tex., 7,903.....A2 84
Perryville, Mo., 5,117.....D8 69
Pershing, co., Nev., 3,199..A2 72
Persia, see Iran, country,
Asia
Persimmon Grove, Ky.,
100..................A7 62
Person, co., N.C., 26,394..A3 76
Perth, Austl., 96,217
(*558,297)............F2 25
Perth, N.S., Can., 909....C2 43
Perth, Ont., Can., 5,360...C8 41
Perth, Scot., 41,100......B5 4
Perth, co., Ont., Can.,
57,452................D3 41
Perth, co., Scot., 124,700..*B5 4
Perth Amboy, N.J.,
38,007............B4, k7 74
Pertuis, Fr., 6,774.......F6 5
Peru, Ill., 11,443........B4 58
Peru, Ind., 14,453.......C5 59
Peru, Nebr., 1,151......D10 71
Peru, country, S.A.,
11,650,000............D3 31
Perugia, It., 75,000......C4 9
Pervomaysk, Sov. Un.,
30,000................G8 12
Pervomaysk, Sov. Un.,
10,000................q21 12
Pervouralsk, Sov. Un.,
108,000...............D8 13
Pesaro, It., 49,000.......C4 9
Pescara, It., 95,800......C5 9
Peshtera, Bul., 13,777.....D7 10
Peshtigo, Wis., 2,504.....C6 88
Peski, Sov. Un., 25,500..F14 12
Peso da Régua, Port.,
5,623.................B2 8
Pesqueira, Braz., 19,778..*D7 27
Pest, co., Hung., 818,600..*B4 10
Petacas, mtn., Col........C2 32
Petah Tiqva, Isr., 58,700..B2 15
Petal, Miss., 4,007.......D4 68
Petaluma, Calif., 18,058...C2 50
Petatlán, Mex., 4,875.....D4 34
Peterborough, Ont., Can.,
47,185................C6 41
Peterborough, Eng.,
63,800................D6 4
Peterborough (Peterboro),
N.H., 1,700..........F4 73
Peterborough, co., Ont.,
Can., 76,375.........C6 41
Peterhead, Scot., 12,800...B6 4
Petermann, ranges,
Austl.................D4 25
Peters, mtn., Va.........C2 85
Petersburg, Alsk.,
1,502.............D13, m23 47
Petersburg, Ill., 2,359....C4 58
Petersburg, Ind., 2,939...H3 59
Petersburg, Mich., 1,018...G7 66
Petersburg, Tex., 1,400...C2 84

Petersburg, W. Va., 2,079..B5 87
Petersburg (Independent
City), Va., 38,000
(*121,000)........C5, n18 85
Petilia Policastro, It.,
8,662.................E6 9
Pétionville, Hai., 9,417....E7 35
Petite-de-Grat, N.S.,
Can., 865............D9 43
Petite-Rivière-de-l'
Artibonite, Hai., 4,383...E7 35
Petit-Goâve, Hai., 5,378...E7 35
Peto, Mex., 7,243........C7 34
Petoskey, Mich., 6,138....C6 66
Petrich, Bul., 13,456......E6 10
Petrikov, Sov. Un.,
10,000................E7 12
Petrinja, Yugo., 7,345.....C3 10
Petrodvorets, Sov. Un.,
30,000................s30 11
Petrokrepost, Sov. Un.,
30,000................s32 11
Petroleum, co., Mont.,
894..................C8 70
Petrolia, Ont., Can.,
3,708.................E2 41
Petrolina, Braz., 14,652...*D6 27
Petropavlovsk, Sov. Un.,
153,000...............D9 13
Petropavlovsk
[-Kamchatskiy], Sov.
Un., 106,000.........D18 13
Petrópolis, Braz.,
93,849.............C4, h6 30
Petros, Tenn., 850.......C9 83
Petroseni, Rom., 28,400...C6 10
Petrovgrad, see
Zrenjanin, Yugo.
Petrovsk, Sov. Un.,
10,000...............E15 12
Petrovskoye, Sov. Un.,
29,000...............I14 12
Petrovsk-Zabaykalskiy,
Sov. Un., 59,000......D13 13
Petrozavodsk, Sov. Un.,
145,000..............A10 12
Pettis, co., Mo., 35,120....C4 69
Petty Harbour, Newf.,
Can., 908............E5 44
Pewaukee, Wis.,
2,484.............E5, m11 88
Pézenas, Fr., 7,198.......F5 5
Pforzheim, Ger., 85,800...D4 6
Phalodi, India, 15,722.....C5 20
Phan Rang, Viet., 21,940..C3 19
Phan Thiet, Viet., 55,180..C3 19
Pharr, Tex., 15,279......F3 84
Phelps, Ky., 725.........C7 62
Phelps, N.Y., 1,887.......C3 75
Phelps, co., Mo., 25,396..D6 69
Phelps, co., Nebr., 9,800..D6 71
Phenix City, Ala., 27,630..C4 46
Phet Buri, Thai., 14,288...C1 19
Phetchabun, Thai., 5,887..B2 19
Phichit, Thai., 9,257.....*B2 19
Philadelphia, Miss.,
5,017.................C4 68
Philadelphia, N.Y., 868...A5 75
Philadelphia, Pa., 2,040,000
(*5,025,000)......G11, p21 81
Philadelphia, co., Pa.,
2,002,512............G11 81
Phil Campbell, Ala., 898...A2 46
Philip, S. Dak., 1,114....C4 77
Philippeville, Bel., 1,559..*B6 5
Philippi, W. Va., 2,228....B4 87
Philippines, country,
Asia, 32,345,000.......B6 19
Philippolis, S. Afr., 2,077..G5 24
Philipsburg, Mont., 1,107..D3 70
Philipsburg, Pa., 3,872....E5 81
Phillips, Tex., 3,605......B2 84
Phillips, Wis., 1,524......C3 88
Phillips, co., Ark.,
43,997................C5 49
Phillips, co., Colo., 4,440..A8 51
Phillips, co., Kans., 8,709..C4 61
Phillips, co., Mont., 6,027..B8 70
Phillipsburg, Ga., 2,037..*E3 55
Phillipsburg, Kans.,
3,233.................C4 61
Phillipsburg, N.J., 18,502..B2 74
Phillipsville, N.C., 1,311..*f9 76
Philmont, N.Y., 1,750....C7 75
Philo, Ohio, 913.........C4 78
Philomath, Ga., 200.....C4 55
Philomath, Oreg., 1,359...C3 80
Phitsanulok, Thai.,
30,364................B2 19
Phnom Penh, Camb.,
403,500...............C2 19
Phoenix, Ariz., 520,000
(*840,000).......C2, D2 48
Phoenix, Ill., 4,203......k9 58
Phoenix, N.Y., 2,408.....B4 75
Phoenixville, Pa.,
13,797..........F10, o19 81
Phong Saly, Laos, 10,000..G5 17

Phrae, Thai., 16,006......*B2 19
Phuket, Thai., 28,033.....D1 19
Piacenza, It., 96,700.....B2 9
Pialba, Austl., 3,544......B9 26
Piaseczno, Pol., 17,400...m14 7
Piatra-Neamt, Rom.,
  37,000................B8 10
Piatt, co., Ill., 14,960.....D5 58
Piauí, state, Braz.,
  1,263,368.............*D6 27
Piazza Armerina, It.,
  24,887................F5 9
Picadome, Ky., 900......B5 62
Picardy (Picardie),
  former prov., Fr.,
  1,051,000.............C5 5
Picayune, Miss., 7,834....E4 68
Picher, Okla., 2,553......A7 79
Pichincha, prov., Ec.,
  587,835...............B2 31
Pickaway, co., Ohio,
  35,855................C2 78
Pickens, S.C., 2,198......B2 82
Pickens, co., Ala., 21,882..B1 46
Pickens, co., Ga., 8,903...B2 55
Pickens, co., S.C., 46,030..B2 82
Pickering, Ont., Can.,
  1,755.................D5 41
Pickett, co., Tenn., 4,431..C8 83
Pickstown, S. Dak., 400...H7 77
Pico Duarte, peak,
  Dom. Rep.............E8 35
Pico Rivera, Calif.,
  49,150................N12 50
Picton, Ont., Can., 4,862..D7 41
Pictou, N.S., Can., 4,534..D7 43
Pictou, co., N.S., Can.,
  43,908................D7 43
Pidurutalagala, peak,
  Cey...................G7 20
Piedmont, Ala., 4,794.....B4 46
Piedmont, Calif., 11,117...h8 50
Piedmont, Mo., 1,555.....D7 69
Piedmont, S.C., 2,108.....B3 82
Piedmont, W. Va., 2,307...B5 87
Piedmont, reg., It.........B1 9
Piedrabuena, Sp., 6,210...C3 8
Piedras Negras, Mex.,
  42,992................B4 34
Pieksämäki, Fin., 10,600..F12 11
Piélagos, Sp., 8,040.......A4 8
Piemonte, pol. dist., It.,
  3,914,250.............*B1 9
Piendamó, Col., 3,499....C2 32
Pierce, Fla., 800..........E5 54
Pierce, Nebr., 1,216......B8 71
Pierce, co., Ga., 9,678....E4 55
Pierce, co., Nebr., 8,722..B8 71
Pierce, co., N. Dak., 7,394..B5 77
Pierce, co., Wash.,
  321,590...............C3 86
Pierce, co., Wis., 22,503..D1 88
Pierce City, Mo., 1,006...E3 69
Pierceton, Ind., 1,186.....B6 59
Piermont, N.Y., 1,839....D7 75
Pierre, S. Dak., 10,088....F5 77
Pierrefitte [sur-Seine], Fr.,
  14,770................g10 5
Pierrefonds, Que., Can.,
  12,171................q19 42
Pierreville, Que., Can.,
  1,559.................C5 42
Pierz, Minn., 816.........E4 67
Pieš'any, Czech.,
  18,700................D4 7
Pietermaritzburg, S. Afr.,
  91,988................F6 24
Pietersburg, S. Afr.,
  28,071................E5 24
Pigeon, Mich., 1,191......E7 66
Pigeon Cove, Mass.,
  1,600.................A6 65
Piggott, Ark., 2,776......A5 49
Pigüé, Arg., 5,869........B4 28
Pike, co., Ala., 25,987....D4 46
Pike, co., Ark., 7,864.....C2 49
Pike, co., Ga., 7,138......C2 55
Pike, co., Ill., 20,552.....D3 58
Pike, co., Ind., 12,797....H3 59
Pike, co., Ky., 68,264.....C7 62
Pike, co., Miss., 35,063...D3 68
Pike, co., Mo., 16,706....B6 69
Pike, co., Ohio, 19,380....C2 78
Pike, co., Pa., 9,158......D11 81
Pikes, peak, Colo.........C5 51
Pikesville, Md.,
  21,500................B4, g10 53
Piketon, Ohio, 1,244.....C2 78
Pikeville, Ky., 4,754......C7 62
Pikeville, Tenn., 951......D8 83
Piła, Pol., 36,600.........B4 7
Pilar, Braz., 7,201........*D7 27
Pilar, Par., 10,062........E4 29
Pilcomayo, riv., S.A.......D3 29
Pilgrim Gardens, Pa.,
  5,000.................*B11 81
Pilot Mound, Man., Can.,
  802...................E2 40

Pilot Mountain, N.C.,
  1,310.................A2 76
Pilot, peak, Wyo.........B3 89
Pilot Point, Tex., 1,254...C4 84
Pilot Rock, Oreg., 1,695...B8 80
Pima, co., Ariz., 265,660..C2 48
Pimmit Hills, Va., 1,000..*B5 85
Pinal, co., Ariz., 62,673...C3 48
Pinar del Río, Cuba,
  58,100................C2 35
Pinar del Río, prov., Cuba,
  448,442...............C2 35
Pinardville, N.H., 2,700...*E4 73
Pincher Creek, Alta., Can.,
  2,961.................E4 38
Pinckneyville, Ill., 3,085...E4 58
Pinconning, Mich., 1,329..E7 66
Pindamonhangaba, Braz.,
  19,144................C3 30
Pine, co., Minn., 17,004..D6 67
Pine, riv., Mich..........D5 66
Pine Beach, N.J., 985.....*D4 74
Pine Bluff, Ark., 44,037...C3 49
Pine Bluffs, Wyo., 1,121..E8 89
Pine Bluff Southeast, Ark.,
  2,679.................*C4 49
Pine Bush, N.Y., 1,100...D6 75
Pine Castle, Fla., 8,500...D5 54
Pine City, Minn., 1,972...E6 67
Pineda, Fla., 150.........D6 54
Pinedale, Ariz., 80........B3 48
Pinedale, Wyo., 965......D3 89
Pine Falls, Man., Can.,
  1,244.................D3 40
Pine Grove, Pa., 2,267....E9 81
Pine Hill, N.J., 3,939.....D3 74
Pine Hills, Fla., 7,000....*D5 54
Pinehurst, Idaho, 1,800...B2 57
Pinehurst, Mass., 3,500...f11 65
Pinehurst, N.C., 1,124....B3 76
Pinehurst, Wash., 3,000..*B3 86
Pine Island, Minn., 1,308..F6 67
Pine Island, N.Y., 800....D6 75
Pine Knot, Ky., 800.......D5 62
Pinelake, Ind., 1,400.....*A4 59
Pine Lake, Mass., 800....g10 65
Pineland, Tex., 1,236.....D6 84
Pine Lawn, Mo., 5,943...f13 69
Pinellas, co., Fla.,
  374,665...............D4 54
Pinellas Park, Fla.,
  10,848................E4, p10 54
Pine Ridge, S. Dak.,
  1,300.................G3 77
Pinerolo, It., 24,500......B1 9
Pinetops, N.C., 1,372.....B5 76
Pineville, Ky., 3,181......D6 62
Pineville, La., 8,636......C3 63
Pineville, N.C., 1,514.....B2 76
Pineville, W. Va., 1,137...D3 87
Piney Point, Tex., 1,790..*E5 84
Piney View, W. Va., 800..D7 87
Pinghsiang, China, 22,000..F7 17
Pingliang, China, 55,000..D6 17
Pingtung, Taiwan,
  93,500................*G9 17
Pinhal, Braz., 14,260..C3, m8 30
Pinhsien, China, 6,000....D3 18
Pinkney (South Gastonia),
  N.C., 3,762............*B1 76
Pinole, Calif., 6,064......h8 50
Pinon, Ariz., 100.........A3 48
Pinos, Mex., 3,125........C4 34
Pinoso, Sp., 5,114........C5 8
Pinos-Puente, Sp., 8,653..D4 8
Pinsk, Sov. Un., 41,548...E6 12
Pinson, Ala., 1,121.......E5 46
Pinsonfork, Ky., 800......*C7 62
Pioche, Nev., 900.........C4 72
Piombino, It., 38,200.....C3 9
Piotrków [Trybunalski],
  Pol., 55,400...........C5 7
Piper City, Ill., 807......C5 58
Pipestone, Minn., 5,324...G2 67
Pipestone, co., Minn.,
  13,605................F2 67
Piqua, Ohio, 19,219......B1 78
Piracicaba, Braz.,
  80,670...............C3, m8 30
Piraçununga, Braz.,
  12,546................C3, k8 30
Piraeus, see Piraievs, Grc.
Piraievs (Piraeus), Grc.,
  183,877...............D4 14
Pirajú, Braz., 10,658......C3 30
Pirajuí, Braz., 6,465......C3 30
Piran, Yugo., 5,464.......B4 9
Pirapóra, Braz., 13,772...B4 30
Pirgos, Grc., 20,558......D3 14
Piriápolis, Ur., 4,400.....E1 30
Pirmasens, Ger., 52,900...D3 6
Pirna, Ger., 41,000.......C6 6
Pirot, Yugo., 18,585......D6 10
Piryatin, Sov. Un., 10,000..F9 12
Pisa, It., 96,400..........C3 9
Piscataquis, co., Maine,
  17,379................C3 64
Pisco, Peru, 17,222.......D2 31

Písek, Czech., 19,500.....D3 7
Pisinimo, Ariz., 200.......C2 48
Pismo Beach, Calif., 1,762..E3 50
Pissis, mtn., Arg.........E2 29
Pisticci, It., 13,300.......D6 9
Pistoia, It., 60,500.......C3 9
Pitalito, Col., 10,818......C2 32
Pitangui, Braz., 7,421.....B4 30
Pitcairn, Pa., 5,383......k14 81
Piteå, Swe., 7,400........E9 11
Pitești, Rom., 45,600.....C7 10
Pithiviers, Fr., 7,318......C5 5
Pitkin, co., Colo., 2,381...B4 51
Pitlochry, Scot., 2,400....B5 4
Pitman, N.J., 8,644.......D2 74
Pitrufquén, Chile, 6,500...B2 28
Pitt, co., N.C., 69,942.....B5 76
Pittsboro, N.C., 1,215.....B3 76
Pittsboro, Ind., 826.......E5 59
Pittsburg, Calif., 19,062...g9 50
Pittsburg, Kans., 18,678...E9 61
Pittsburg, Tex., 3,796.....C5 84
Pittsburg, co., Okla.,
  34,360................C6 79
Pittsburgh, Pa.,
  604,332.............F1, k13 81
Pittsfield, Ill., 4,089......D3 58
Pittsfield, Maine, 3,350...D3 64
Pittsfield, Mass., 57,897..B1 65
Pittsfield, Mich., 1,500...*F7 66
Pittsfield, N.H., 1,500....E5 73
Pittsford, N.Y., 1,843....B3 75
Pittston, Pa.,
  12,407..............D10, n17 81
Pittsylvania, co., Va.,
  58,296................D3 85
Piuka, Jap., 5,200........D11 18
Piura, Peru, 39,800.......C1 31
Piura, dept., Peru,
  431,487...............C1 31
Piute, co., Utah, 1,436....B5 72
Pixley, Calif., 1,327......E4 50
Pizzo, It., 9,560.........E6 9
Placentia, Calif., 5,861...*F5 50
Placentia, Newf., Can.,
  1,610.................E5 44
Placer, co., Calif., 56,998..C3 50
Placerville, Calif., 4,997..C3 50
Placetas, Cuba, 32,500...C4 35
Placida, Fla., 150.........F4 54
Plain City, Ohio, 2,146...B2 78
Plain Dealing, La.,
  1,357.................B2 63
Plainfield, Conn., 2,100...C9 52
Plainfield, Ill., 9,600..B5, k8 58
Plainfield, Ind., 5,460....E5 59
Plainfield, N.J., 45,330...B4 74
Plainfield, Tenn.,
  2,127.................*D10 83
Plainfield Heights, Mich.,
  1,000.................*F5 66
Plainsboro, N.J., 600.....C3 74
Plainsville, Pa., 500......*D10 81
Plainview, Minn., 1,833...F6 67
Plainview, Nebr., 1,467...B8 71
Plainview, N.Y.,
  30,500................*G3 52
Plainview, Tex., 18,735...B2 84
Plainville, Conn., 13,149..C5 52
Plainville, Kans., 3,104...C4 61
Plainwell, Mich., 3,125...F5 66
Plaisance, Hai., 1,692....E7 35
Plaistow, N.H., 1,200....F5 73
Planada, Calif., 1,704....*D3 50
Plandome, N.Y., 1,379...*E7 75
Plandome Heights, N.Y.,
  1,025.................*E7 75
Plano, Calif., 1,500......*D4 50
Plano, Ill., 4,059.........B5 58
Plano, Tex., 3,695....C4, m10 84
Plantagenet, Ont., Can.,
  854...................B9 41
Plant City, Fla., 15,711...D4 54
Plantsite, Ariz., 1,552....*D6 48
Plantsville, Conn., 2,500..C5 52
Plaquemine, La.,
  7,689...............D4, h9 63
Plaquemines, par., La.,
  22,545...............*D4 63
Plasencia, Sp., 21,297....B2 8
Plaster Rock, N.B., Can.,
  1,267.................C2 43
Plato, Col., 13,364.......B3 32
Platón, Sánchez, Mex.,
  4,127................m14 34
Platte, S. Dak., 1,167....G7 77
Platte, co., Mo., 23,350...B3 69
Platte, co., Nebr., 23,992..C8 71
Platte, co., Wyo., 7,195...D7 89
Platte City, Mo.,
  1,188...............B3, h10 69
Platteville, Wis., 6,957...F3 88
Plattsburg, Mo., 1,663....B3 69
Plattsburgh, N.Y., 21,090..f11 75
Plattsmouth, Nebr.,
  6,244...............D10, h13 71
Plauen, Ger., 79,000.....C6 6
Pleasant Dale, Nebr., 190..D9 71

Pleasant Gap, Pa., 1,500...E6 81
Pleasant Grove, Ala.,
  3,977.................E4 46
Pleasant Grove, Utah,
  4,772...............A6, D2 72
Pleasant Hill, Calif.,
  21,500................h8 50
Pleasant Hill, Ill., 950....D3 58
Pleasant Hill, Iowa, 1,006..e8 60
Pleasant Hill, La., 907....C2 63
Pleasant Hill, Mo., 2,689..C3 69
Pleasant Hill, Ohio, 1,060..B1 78
Pleasant Hill, Pa., 1,200..*F9 81
Pleasant Hill, Va., 2,636..*D6 85
Pleasant Hills, Pa.,
  8,573.................*F2 81
Pleasanton, Calif., 4,203...h9 50
Pleasanton, Kans., 1,098..D9 61
Pleasanton, Tex., 3,467...E3 84
Pleasant Ridge, Mich.,
  3,807.................*F7 66
Pleasants, co., W. Va.,
  7,124.................B3 87
Pleasant Valley, Mo.,
  1,109................h11 69
Pleasant Valley, N.Y.,
  1,000.................D7 75
Pleasant View, Colo.,
  100...................*B5 51
Pleasant View, Utah, 927..A5 72
Pleasantville, Iowa, 1,202..C4 60
Pleasantville, N.J., 15,172..E3 74
Pleasantville, N.Y.,
  6,361................m15 75
Pleasantville, Ohio, 940...C2 81
Pleasure Beach, Conn.,
  1,264.................*E4 52
Pleasure Ridge Park, Ky.,
  13,000................A4 62
Pleasureville, Pa.,
  1,000.................*G8 81
Pleiku, Viet., 7,240......*C3 19
Plenita, Rom., 6,735.....C6 10
Plentywood, Mont.,
  2,121................B12 70
Plesetsk, Sov. Un., 18,000..C7 13
Plessisville, Que., Can.,
  6,570.................C6 42
Pleszew, Pol., 11,700.....C4 7
Pleven, Bul., 79,234......D7 10
Pleven, co., Bul.,
  1,056,436.............*D7 10
Pljevlja, Yugo., 10,240...D4 10
Płock, Pol., 50,000.......B5 7
Ploërmel, Fr., 3,840......D2 5
Ploiești, Rom., 127,800...C8 10
Plomarion, Grc., 5,172...*C6 14
Płonsk, Pol., 10,600......B6 7
Plovdiv, Bul., 222,737....D7 10
Plovdiv, co., Bul.,
  876,993...............*D7 10
Plum, Pa., 10,241........*E1 81
Plumas, co., Calif., 11,620..B3 50
Plymouth, Conn., 950....C4 52
Plymouth, Eng., 210,100..E4 4
Plymouth, Ind., 7,558....B5 59
Plymouth, Mass., 11,100..C6 65
Plymouth, Mich.,
  8,766...............F7, p15 66
Plymouth, Minn., 9,576..*F5 67
Plymouth, N.H., 2,400...D4 73
Plymouth, N.C., 4,753....B6 76
Plymouth, Ohio, 1,822...B3 78
Plymouth, Pa.,
  10,401..............D10, n17 81
Plymouth, Wis.,
  5,128...............E5, k10 88
Plymouth, co., Iowa,
  23,906................B1 60
Plymouth, co., Mass.,
  248,449...............C6 65
Plymouth Meeting, Pa.,
  4,000................*F11 81
Plymouth Valley, Pa.,
  1,700................*F11 81
Plymptonville, Pa.,
  1,220................*D5 81
Plzeň, Czech., 139,600...D2 7
Pocahontas, Ark., 3,665...A5 49
Pocahontas, Iowa, 2,011..B3 60
Pocahontas, Va., 1,313...e10 85
Pocahontas, co., Iowa,
  14,234................B3 60
Pocahontas, co., W. Va.,
  10,136................C4 87
Pocatello, Idaho, 39,194...G6 57
Pochep, Sov. Un., 10,000..E9 12
Pochutla, Mex., 3,066....D5 34
Pocomoke City, Md.,
  3,329.................D6 53
Poços de Caldas, Braz.,
  32,291...............C3, k8 30
Podgorica, see Titograd,
  Yugo.
Podolsk, Sov. Un.,
  144,000.............D11, n17 12
Podor, Sen., 3,400........E2 22
Poe, S.C., 1,000.........*B3 82

Poggibonsi, It., 7,236......C3　9
Pohang, Kor., 52,700.......H4　18
Pohjois-Karjala, prov.,
　Fin., 203,000.........*F13　11
Poinsett, co., Ark., 30,834..B5　49
Point Comfort, Tex.,
　1,453................*E4　84
Pointe-à-Pitre, Guad.,
　27,966...............H14　35
Pointe-au-Pic, Que., Can.,
　1,333.................B7　42
Pointe-aux-Trembles,
　Que., Can., 21,926.....p20　42
Pointe-Claire, Que.,
　Can., 22,709........D4, q19　42
Pointe Coupee, par., La.,
　22,488................D4　63
Pointe-du-Lac, Que.,
　Can., 934.............C5　42
Point Edward, Ont., Can.,
　2,744.................D2　41
Pointe-Gatineau, Que.,
　Can., 8,854...........D2　42
Pointe-Noire, Con. B.,
　79,500................I7　22
Point Leamington, Newf.,
　Can., 901.............D4　44
Point Lookout, Mo., 200...E4　69
Point Marion, Pa., 1,853...F2　81
Point Pleasant, N.J.,
　10,182................C4　74
Point Pleasant Beach, N.J.,
　3,873.................C4　74
Poissy, Fr., 28,499.......C4　5
Poitiers, Fr., 62,178.....D4　5
Poitou, former prov., Fr.,
　1,037,000.............D3　5
Pokaran, India, 5,284.....C5　20
Pokotu, China..........B9　17
Pokrovskoye, Sov. Un.,
　10,000...............H12　12
Poland, Ohio, 2,766.....*A5　78
Poland, country, Eur.,
　31,350,000............C5　7
Polgar, Hung., 7,697......B5　10
Poli, China, 35,000......B11　17
Polikhnitos, Grc., 5,131..*C6　14
Polk, Pa., 3,574.........D2　81
Polk, co., Ark., 11,981...C1　49
Polk, co., Fla., 195,139..E5　54
Polk, co., Ga., 28,015....C1　55
Polk, co., Iowa, 266,315..C4　60
Polk, co., Minn., 36,182..C2　67
Polk, co., Mo., 13,753....D4　69
Polk, co., Nebr., 7,210...C8　71
Polk, co., N.C., 11,395...f10　76
Polk, co., Oreg., 26,523..C3　80
Polk, co., Tenn., 12,160..D9　83
Polk, co., Tex., 13,861...D5　84
Polk, co., Wis., 24,968...C1　88
Pollensa, Sp., 8,984......C7　8
Pollocksville, N.C., 414..C5　76
Polo, Ill., 2,551.........B4　58
Polotsk, Sov. Un., 30,000..D7　12
Polson, Mont., 2,314.....C2　70
Poltava, Sov. Un.,
　158,000..............G10　12
Pomabamba, Peru, 2,346..C2　31
Pombal, Braz., 8,120....*D7　27
Pombetsu, Jap., 6,600...E11　18
Pomerania, reg., Pol....B4　7
Pomeroy, Iowa, 816......B3　60
Pomeroy, Ohio, 3,345....C3　78
Pomeroy, Pa., 1,085....*G10　81
Pomeroy, Wash., 1,677...C8　86
Pomoho Camp, Haw., 350..f9　56
Pomona, Calif.,
　67,157............E5, m13　50
Pompano Beach, Fla.,
　15,992............F6, r13　54
Pompton Lakes, N.J.,
　9,445................A4　74
Pompton Plains, N.J.,
　7,500................B4　74
Ponca, Nebr., 924........B9　71
Ponca City, Okla., 24,411..A4　79
Ponce, P.R., 114,286....G11　35
Ponchatoula, La.,
　4,727............D5, h11　63
Pondera, co., Mont.,
　7,653................B4　70
Pondicherry, India,
　40,421...............F6　20
Ponoka, Alta., Can.,
　3,938................C4　38
Ponta Delgada, Azores Is.,
　Port., 22,316........m10　22
Ponta Grossa, Braz.,
　77,803...............D2　30
Pont-A-Mousson, Fr.,
　12,802...............C7　5
Ponta Porã, Braz., 9,160..C1　30
Pontarlier, Fr., 15,382...D7　5
Pontedera, It., 12,400....C3　9
Ponteix, Sask., Can., 887..H2　39
Ponte Nova, Braz.,
　22,536...............C4　30

Pontevedra, Sp., 19,739....A1　8
Pontevedra, prov., Sp.,
　680,229..............*A1　8
Pontiac, Ill., 8,435.......C5　58
Pontiac, Mich.,
　82,233...........F7, o15　66
Pontiac, co., Que., Can.,
　19,947...............A7　41
Pontianak, Indon.,
　146,547..............F3　19
Pontivy, Fr., 8,775.......C2　5
Pont-l'-Abbé, Fr., 5,541...D1　5
Pontoise, Fr., 15,853.....C4　5
Pontotoc, Miss., 2,108....A4　68
Pontotoc, co., Miss.,
　17,232...............A4　68
Pontotoc, co., Okla.,
　28,089...............C5　79
Pontremoli, It., 4,839....B2　9
Pont-Rouge, Que.,
　Can., 2,988.......C6, n16　42
Pont-Viau, Que., Can.,
　16,077.............*D4　42
Poole, Eng., 93,800......E5　4
Pooler, Ga., 1,073.......D5　55
Poona, India, 597,562
　(*800,000)...........E5　20
Popasnaya, Sov. Un.,
　10,000..............q21　12
Popayán, Col., 58,500....C2　32
Pope, co., Ark., 21,177...B2　49
Pope, co., Ill., 4,061....F5　58
Pope, co., Minn., 11,914..E3　67
Poplar, Calif., 1,478....*D4　50
Poplar, Mont., 1,565....B11　70
Poplar Bluff, Mo., 15,926..E7　69
Poplar Heights, Va.,
　1,000...............*B5　85
Poplarville, Miss., 2,136..E4　68
Popocatepetl, vol., Mex...n14　34
Popovka, Sov. Un.,
　10,000..............H11　12
Popovo, Bul., 6,469.......D8　10
Poquonock, Conn., 850....B6　52
Poquonock Bridge, Conn.,
　2,500................D8　52
Poquoson, Va., 4,278..C6, h15　85
Porbandar, India,
　74,476...............D4　20
Porcuna, Sp., 10,516.....D3　8
Pordenone, It., 34,055....B4　9
Poreč, Yugo., 2,992......C1　10
Pori, Fin., 57,200.......G9　11
Porlamar, Ven., 21,787...A5　32
Poronaysk, Shikuka,
　Sov. Un., 33,000......E17　13
Porrentruy, Switz., 7,095..E3　6
Porsgrunn, Nor., 10,700..p27　11
Port Adelaide, Austl.,
　39,749...............F6　25
Portadown, N. Ire.,
　19,300...............C3　4
Portage, Ind., 16,490....A3　59
Portage, Mich., 27,642...F5　66
Portage, Pa., 3,933......F4　81
Portage, Wis., 7,822.....E4　88
Portage, co., Ohio, 91,798..A4　78
Portage, co., Wis., 36,964..D4　88
Portage Lakes, Ohio,
　10,000.............*A4　78
Portage-la-Prairie,
　Man., Can., 12,388..E2, h8　40
Portageville, Mo., 2,505..E8　69
Port Alberni, B.C., Can.,
　11,560...............E5　37
Portalegre, Port., 11,017..C2　8
Portales, N. Mex., 9,695..B7　48
Port Alfred, Que., Can.,
　9,066................A7　42
Port Alfred, S. Afr.,
　6,184................G5　24
Port Alice, B.C., Can.,
　1,065................D4　37
Port Allegany, Pa., 2,742..C5　81
Port Allen, La., 5,026..D4, h9　63
Port Angles, Wash.,
　12,653...............A2　86
Port Angeles East, Wash.,
　1,283...............*A2　86
Port Antonio, Jam.,
　7,827................E5　35
Port Arthur, Ont., Can.,
　45,276..............o17　41
Port Arthur, Tex., 66,676..E6　84
Port Arthur (Lüshun),
　China, 126,000........D9　17
Port Augusta, Austl.,
　10,128...............F6　25
Port-au-Prince, Hai.,
　240,000..............E7　35
Port Barre, La., 1,876....D4　63
Port Byron, Ill., 1,153...B3　58
Port Byron, N.Y., 1,201...B4　75
Port Carbon, Pa., 2,775..E9　81
Port-Cartier, Que., Can.,
　3,458...............k13　42
Port Charlotte, Fla.,
　11,000...............F4　54

Port Chester, N.Y.,
　24,755.........E7, n15　75
Port Chicago, Calif.,
　1,900................G8　50
Port Clinton, Ohio, 6,870..A3　78
Port Colborne, Ont., Can.,
　14,886...............E5　41
Port Coquitlam, B.C.,
　Can., 8,111.....E6, f13　37
Port Crane, N.Y., 1,200...C5　75
Port Credit, Ont.,
　Can., 7,203......D5, m14　41
Port Dickinson, N.Y.,
　2,295................C5　75
Port Dickson, Mala.,
　4,415................E2　19
Port Dover, Ont., Can.,
　3,064................E4　41
Port Edward, B.C., Can.,
　887..................B2　37
Port Edwards, Wis., 1,849..D4　88
Port Elgin, N.B., Can.,
　661..................C5　43
Port Elgin, Ont., Can.,
　1,632................C3　41
Port Elizabeth, S. Afr.,
　249,211, (*290,693)...G5　24
Porter, Ind., 3,193......A3　59
Porter, co., Ind., 60,279..B3　59
Porterdale, Ga., 2,365....C3　55
Porterville, Calif., 7,991..D4　50
Port Étienne, Maur.,
　5,283................D1　22
Port Ewen, N.Y., 2,300...D7　75
Port-Francqui, Con. K.,
　3,553................I2　23
Port-Gentil, Gabon,
　20,732...............I6　22
Port Gibson, Miss., 2,861..D3　68
Port Hammond, B.C.,
　Can., 1,267.........f13　37
Port Harcourt, Nig.,
　179,563..............H6　22
Port Hawkesbury, N.S.,
　Can., 1,346..........D8　43
Port Hedland, Austl.,
　1,785................D2　25
Port Henry, N.Y., 1,767...A7　75
Port Hope, Ont., Can.,
　8,091................D6　41
Port Hueneme, Calif.,
　11,067...............E4　50
Port Huron, Mich., 36,500
　(*65,000)............F8　66
Portimão, Port., 12,129...D1　8
Port Isabel, Tex., 3,575..F4　84
Port Jefferson, N.Y.,
　4,440................F4　52
Port Jefferson Station,
　N.Y., 1,370.........n15　75
Port Jervis, N.Y., 8,601..D6　75
Portland, Austl., 6,674...G7　25
Portland, Conn., 7,496...C6　52
Portland, Ind., 6,999....D8　59
Portland, Maine, 70,000
　(*167,000).......E2, g7　64
Portland, Mich., 3,330...F6　66
Portland, Oreg.,
　365,000 (*825,000)..B4, g12　80
Portland, Tenn., 2,424...A5　83
Port Lavaca, Tex., 8,864..E4　84
Port Leyden, N.Y., 898...B5　75
Port Lincoln, Austl.,
　8,867................F6　25
Port McNicoll, Ont.,
　Can., 1,053..........C5　41
Port Macquarie, Austl.,
　7,090................F9　25
Port Monmouth, N.J.,
　5,500................C4　74
Port Moody, B.C.,
　Can., 4,789.....E6, f13　37
Port Neches, Tex., 8,696...E6　84
Portneuf, Que., Can.,
　1,380................C6　42
Portneuf, co., Que., Can.,
　1,380................C5　42
Port Norris, N.J., 1,800..E2　74
Pôrto, Port., 303,424
　(*750,000)...........B1　8
Pôrto Alegre, Braz.,
　617,629..............E2　30
Porto Alexandre, Ang.,
　2,874................D2　24
Pôrto Amélia, Moz.,
　10,000...............C8　24
Pôrto de Moz, Braz., 879..D5　27
Pôrto Feliz, Braz.,
　11,786............C3, m8　30
Portoferraio, It., 6,000..C3　9
Port-of-Spain, Trin.,
　93,954..............K14　35
Portogruaro, It., 7,100...B4　9
Portola, Calif., 1,874....C3　50
Portomaggiore, It., 4,300..B3　9

Pôrto Nacional, Braz.,
　4,926................E6　27
Porto-Novo, Dah., 69,500..G5　22
Port Orange, Fla., 1,801..C6　54
Port Orchard, Wash.,
　2,778............B3, e10　86
Port Orford, Oreg., 1,171..E2　80
Portolo, Calif., 1,874....C3　50
Porto Torres, It., 9,166..D2　9
Pôrto União, Braz., 9,954..D2　30
Pôrto Velho, Braz.,
　19,387...............D4　27
Portoviejo, Ec., 32,228...B1　31
Portpatrick, Scot., 1,063..C4　4
Port Perry, Ont., Can.,
　2,262................C6　41
Port Pirie, Austl., 13,947..F6　25
Port Reading, N.J., 4,000..k8　74
Port Richey, Fla., 1,931..D4　54
Port Said (Būr Sa'īd),
　Eg., U.A.R., 256,100...G9　14
Port Saint Joe, Fla.,
　4,217............C1, v16　54
Port St. Lucie, Fla.,
　2,000................E6　54
Port Sewall, Fla., 300...E6　54
Portsmouth, Eng., 224,900
　(*445,000)...........E6　4
Portsmouth, N.H., 26,900..E6　73
Portsmouth, Ohio,
　33,637...............D3　78
Portsmouth, R.I., 3,000..C12　52
Portsmouth,
　(Independent City),
　Va., 114,773.....D6, k15　85
Port Stanley, Ont., Can.,
　1,460................E3　41
Port Sudan, Sud., 56,000..E5　23
Port Sulphur, La., 2,868..E6　63
Port Townsend, Wash.,
　5,074................A3　86
Portugal, country, Eur.,
　9,140,000............C1　8
Portugal Cove, Newf.,
　Can., 1,141........*E5　44
Portugalete, Sp., 22,584..A4　8
Portuguesa, state, Ven.,
　203,707..............B4　32
Portuguese Guinea, dep.,
　Afr., 544,184........F1　22
Portuguese Timor, dep.,
　Asia, 517,079........G7　19
Port Vue., Pa., 6,635...*F2　81
Port Wakefield, Austl.,
　1,083..............*F6　25
Port Washington, N.Y.,
　15,800.............h13　75
Port Washington, Wis.,
　5,984................E6　88
Port Wentworth, Ga.,
　3,705................D5　55
Posadas, Arg., 37,588.....E4　29
Posadas, Sp., 8,999......D3　8
Posen, Ill., 4,517.......k9　58
Posen, see Poznan, Pol.
Posey, co., Ind., 19,214..H2　59
Poseyville, Ind., 997....H2　59
Poso, Indon., 2,875......F6　19
Post, Tex., 4,663........C2　84
Post Falls, Idaho, 1,983..B2　57
Postojna, Yugo., 4,848...C2　10
Poston, S.C., 250........D9　82
Postville, Iowa, 1,554...A6　60
Potchefstroom, S. Afr.,
　41,927...............F5　24
Poteau, Okla., 4,428.....B7　79
Poteet, Tex., 2,811......E3　84
Potenza, It., 30,800.....D5　9
Potgietersrus, S. Afr.,
　11,491...............E5　24
Poth, Tex., 1,119........E3　84
Potlatch, Idaho, 880.....C2　57
Potomac, Md., 1,000......B3　53
Potomac Heights, Md.,
　2,000................C3　53
Potomac Park, Md.,
　1,300..............k13　53
Potosí, Bol., 54,000.....C2　29
Potosi, Mo., 2,805......D7　69
Potosí, dept., Bol.,
　534,399..............C2　29
Pototan, Phil., 5,475...*C6　19
Potsdam, Ger., 109,900...B6　6
Potsdam, N.Y., 8,673....f10　75
Pottawatomie, co., Kans.,
　11,957...............C7　61
Pottawatomie, co., Okla.,
　41,486...............B5　79
Pottawattamie, co., Iowa,
　83,102...............C2　60
Potter, co., Pa., 16,483..C6　81
Potter co., Tex.,
　115,580..............B2　84
Potterville, Mich., 1,028.*F6　66
Pottstown, Pa., 26,144...F10　81
Pottsville, Pa., 21,659...E9　81
Pouch Cove, Newf., Can.,
　1,324................E5　44

Poughkeepsie, N.Y., 36,000
(*139,000)..............D7 75
Poulsbo, Wash., 1,505.....B3 86
Poultney, Vt., 1,810.........D1 73
Pound, Va., 1,135.........e9 85
Pouso Alegre, Braz.,
18,852................C3 30
Póvoa, de Varzim, Port.,
17,696................B1 8
Powassan, Ont., Can.,
1,064.................A5 41
Poway, Calif., 4,500......F5 50
Powder River, co., Mont.,
2,485................E11 70
Powell, Mo., 100.........E3 69
Powell, Wyo., 4,740......B4 89
Powell, co., Ky., 6,674....C6 62
Powell, co., Mont., 7,002..D4 70
Powell River, B.C., Can.,
10,748................E5 37
Powellton, W. Va., 1,256..C3 87
Power, co., Idaho, 4,111...G6 57
Powers, Oreg., 1,366.....E2 80
Poweshiek, co., Iowa,
19,300................C5 60
Powhatan, co., Va.,
6,747.................C5 85
Powhatan Point, Ohio,
2,147.................C5 78
Poynette, Wis., 1,090.....E4 88
Požarevac, Yugo., 24,293..C5 10
Poza Rica de Hidalgo,
Mex., 19,564..........m15 34
Poznań, Pol., 429,300....B4 7
Pozoblanco, Sp., 16,020....C3 8
Pozzallo, It., 12,253........F5 9
Pozzuoli, It., 55,000......D5 9
Prachin Buri, Thai.,
13,420................C2 19
Prachuap Khiri Khan,
Thai., 6,228..........*C1 19
Praco, Ala., 900.........E4 46
Prades, Fr., 5,676........F5 5
Praestø, co., Den.,
121,976..............*J5 11
Prague, Czech.,
1,008,900.........C3, n17 7
Prague, Okla., 1,545......B5 79
Praha, see Prague, Czech.
Prairie, co., Ark., 10,515..C4 49
Prairie, co., Mont.,
2,318................D11 70
Prairie City, Iowa, 943...C4 60
Prairie du Chien, Wis.,
5,649.................E2 88
Prairie du Sac, Wis.,
1,676.................E4 88
Prairie Grove, Ark., 1,056..B1 49
Prairie Village, Kans.,
25,356...............*B9 61
Pran Buri, Thai...........C1 19
Prato, It., 120,400........C3 9
Pratt, Kans., 8,156.......E5 61
Pratt, Minn.............*C6 87
Pratt, co., Kans., 12,122...E5 61
Prattville, Ala., 6,616.....C3 46
Prattville, Okla., 2,530...*A5 79
Pravdinsk (Friedland),
Sov. Un., 10,000......A6 7
Pravia, Sp., 1,804........A2 8
Preble, co., Ohio, 32,498...C1 78
Premont, Tex., 3,049......F3 84
Prentiss, Miss., 1,321.....D4 68
Prentiss, co., Miss.,
17,949................A5 68
Prenzlau, Ger., 19,700....F6 6
Prerov, Czech., 31,400....D4 7
Prescott, Ariz., 13,823....B2 48
Prescott, Ark., 3,533......D2 49
Prescott, Ont., Can.,
5,366.................C9 41
Prescott, Wis., 1,536.....D1 88
Prescott, co., Ont., Can.,
5,366................B10 41
Presidencia Roque Sáenz
Peña, Arg., 23,100......E3 29
Presidente Hayes, dept.,
Par., 31,600..........D4 29
Presidente Prudente, Braz.,
54,055................C2 30
Presidio, Tex., 1,200.....p12 84
Presidio, co., Tex., 5,460..o12 84
Presov, Czech., 36,300....D6 7
Presque Isle, Maine,
12,886................B4 64
Presque Isle, co., Mich.,
13,117................C6 66
Preston, Ont., Can.,
11,577................D4 41
Preston, Eng., 111,700....D5 4
Preston, Idaho, 3,640....G7 57
Preston, Ky., 200.........B6 62
Preston, Minn., 1,491....G6 67
Preston, co., W. Va.,
27,233................B5 87

Preston, peak, Calif.......B2 50
Prestonburg, Ky., 3,133....C7 62
Prestonville, Ky., 211......B4 62
Prestwick, Scot., 12,600...*C4 4
Pretoria, S. Afr., 303,684,
(*422,590)............F5 24
Preveza, Grc., 11,172.....C3 14
Preveza, prov., Grc.,
62,523...............*C3 14
Prey Veng, Camb., 8,800..*C3 19
Pribram, Czech., 25,700...D3 7
Price, Que., Can.,
3,094...............*G20 36
Price, Utah, 6,802.........B6 72
Price, co., Wis., 14,370....C3 88
Pricedale, Pa., 1,300......*F2 81
Prichard, Ala., 47,371.....E1 46
Priestly, mtn., B.C., Can...B3 37
Priest River, Idaho,
1,749.................A2 57
Prilep, Yugo., 37,486......E5 10
Priluki, Sov. Un., 40,000...F9 12
Primera, Tex., 1,066......*F4 84
Primghar, Iowa,
1,131.................A2 60
Primorsk, Sov. Un.,
8,000.................A6 7
Primorsko-Akhtarsk,
Sov. Un., 10,000......H12 12
Primos, Pa., 1,000.......*G11 81
Primrose, Pa., 950.......*E9 81
Prince, co., P.E.I., Can.,
40,894................C5 43
Prince Albert, Sask.,
Can., 24,168.......D3, n7 39
Prince Edward, co., Ont.,
Can., 21,108..........C7 41
Prince Edward, co., Va.,
14,121................C4 85
Prince Edward Island,
prov., Can., 104,629...C6 43
Prince George, B.C.,
Can., 13,877.......C6, n18 37
Prince George, co., Va.,
20,270................C5 85
Prince Georges, co., Md.,
357,395...............C4 53
Prince of Wales, isl., N.
W. Ter., Can..........B14 36
Prince Rupert, B.C.,
Can., 11,987......B2, n16 37
Princess Anne, Md.,
1,351.................D6 53
Princeton, Ala., 150......A3 46
Princeton, B.C., Can.,
2,163.................E7 37
Princeton, Fla.,
1,719.............G6, s13 54
Princeton, Ill., 6,250.....B4 58
Princeton, Ind., 7,906.....H2 59
Princeton, Ky., 5,618......C2 62
Princeton, Minn., 2,353....E5 67
Princeton, Mo., 1,443.....A4 69
Princeton, N.J., 11,890....C3 74
Princeton, N.C., 981.......B4 76
Princeton, W. Va.,
8,393.................D3 87
Princeton, Wis., 1,509.....E4 88
Princeville, Que., Can.,
3,174.................C6 42
Princeville, Ill., 1,281.....C4 58
Princeville, N.C., 797......B5 76
Prince William, co., Va.,
50,164................B5 85
Prineville, Oreg., 3,263....C6 80
Prineville Southeast,
Oreg., 1,299.........*C6 80
Pringle, Pa., 1,418......*D10 81
Prinsburg, Minn., 462....F3 67
Priozersk, Sov. Un.,
32,800...............G14 11
Pristina, Yugo.,
38,891................D5 10
Pritzwalk, Ger., 9,416.....B6 6
Privas, Fr., 8,663.........E6 5
Privolnoye, Sov. Un.,
9,000.................H9 12
Prizren, Yugo., 28,050....D5 10
Prizzi, It., 9,752.........F4 9
Probolinggo, Indon.,
68,378................G4 19
Proctor, Minn., 2,963.....D6 67
Proctor, Vt., 1,978.......D1 73
Proctorville, Ohio, 831....D3 78
Progreso, Hond., 6,921...*D7 34
Progreso, Mex., 13,694....C7 34
Progress, Pa., 1,700......*F8 81
Project City, Calif.,
900...................B2 50
Prokopyevsk, Sov. Un.,
291,000..............D11 13
Prokuplje, Yugo.,
13,690................D5 10
Proletarskaya, Sov. Un.,
10,000................H13 12

Prome, Bur., 36,997......E10 20
Prophetstown, Ill., 1,802..B4 58
Propriá, Braz., 15,947....*D7 27
Prosotsani, Grc., 5,320...*B4 14
Prospect, Conn., 4,367....C5 52
Prospect, Ohio, 1,067.....B2 78
Prospect, Pa., 903........E1 81
Prospect Heights, Ill.,
7,000................*B6 58
Prospect Park, N.J., 5,201..B4 74
Prospect Park, Pa., 6,596..p20 81
Prosser, Wash., 2,763.....C6 86
Prostejov, Czech., 33,600..D4 7
Provadiya, Bul., 12,463....D8 10
Provence, former prov., Fr.,
1,750,000.............F7 5
Providence, Ky., 3,771....C2 62
Providence, R.I., 180,000
(*865,000)...........B11 52
Providence, Tenn., 3,830..*A5 83
Providence, Utah, 1,189...*A6 72
Providence, co., R.I.,
568,778..............B10 52
Provincetown, Mass.,
3,389.................B7 65
Provins, Fr., 10,310......C5 5
Provo, Utah, 42,000
(*116,000).........A6, D2 72
Provost, Alta., Can., 1,022..C5 38
Prowers, co., Colo.,
13,296................D8 51
Prozor, Yugo., 5,506......D3 10
Pruden, Ky., 100.........*D6 62
Prudnik, Pol., 18,400.....C4 7
Pruszkow, Pol.,
37,700.............B6, m13 7
Pruzhany, Sov. Un.,
10,000................E5 12
Pryor, Okla., 6,476.......A6 79
Pryor, mts., Mont........E8 70
Przasnysz, Pol., 7,015.....B6 7
Przemysl, Pol., 49,300.....D7 7
Przeworsk, Pol., 8,569....C7 7
Pskov, Sov. Un., 101,000...C7 12
Pszczyna, Pol., 16,100...D5, h9 7
Ptolemais, Grc., 12,747...*B3 14
Ptuj, Yugo., 7,365........B2 10
Puebla, state, Mex.,
1,973,837..........D5, n14 34
Puebla de Don Fadrique,
Sp., 7,142............D4 8
Puebla del Caramiñal,
Sp., 8,337.............A1 8
Puebla [de Zaragoza],
Mex., 289,049.....D5, n14 34
Pueblo, Colo., 102,000
(*123,000)...........C6 51
Pueblo, co., Colo.,
118,707...............C6 51
Puenteareas, Sp., 14,634...A1 8
Puente Ceso, Sp., 9,780...A1 8
Puentedeume, Sp., 7,755..A2 8
Puente-Genil, Sp., 25,000..D3 8
Puerto Alvaro Obregón,
Mex., 8,320.........*D6 34
Puerto Armuelles, Pan.,
10,712...............*B1 32
Puerto Barrios, Guat.,
15,155................D7 34
Puerto Berrío, Col.,
15,812................B3 32
Puerto Cabello, Ven.,
52,493................A4 32
Puerto Casado, Par.,
6,708.................D4 29
Puerto Cortés, Hond.,
17,048................D7 34
Puerto de la Cruz, Sp.,
5,855................m13 8
Puerto Eten, Peru, 2,576...C2 31
Puerto La Cruz, Ven.,
59,033................A5 32
Puertollano, Sp., 53,136...C3 8
Puerto Maldonado, Peru,
3,500.................D4 31
Puerto Montt, Chile,
41,700................C2 28
Puerto Padre, Cuba,
15,900................D5 35
Puerto Peñasco, Mex.,
3,370.................A2 34
Puerto Pinasco, Par.,
7,576.................D4 29
Puerto Plata, Dom. Rep.,
18,530................E8 35
Puerto Rico, U.S., dep.,
N.A., 2,349,544......G11 35
Puerto Sastre, Par., 5,058..D4 29
Puerto Supe, Peru, 2,180..D2 31
Puerto Tejada, Col.,
14,863................C2 32
Puerto Vallarto, Mex.,
7,484............C3, m11 34
Puerto Wilches, Col.,
4,635.................B3 32

Puglia, pol. dist., It.,
3,421,217............*D6 9
Pugwash, N.S., Can., 815..D6 43
Puhi, Haw., 704..........B2 56
Puhsi, China, 5,000.......B2 18
Pukchong, Kor., 30,709...F4 18
Puksubaek-san, mtn., Kor..F3 18
Pula, Yugo., 36,838.......C1 10
Pulaski, Miss., 200.......C4 68
Pulaski, N.Y., 2,256......B4 75
Pulaski, Tenn., 6,616.....B4 83
Pulaski, Va., 10,469......C2 85
Pulaski, Wis., 1,540......D5 88
Pulaski, co., Ark., 242,980..C3 49
Pulaski, co., Ga., 8,204....D3 55
Pulaski, co., Ill., 10,490....F4 58
Pulaski, co., Ind., 12,837..B4 59
Pulaski, co., Ky., 34,403...C5 62
Pulaski, co., Mo., 46,567..D5 69
Pulaski, co., Va., 27,258...C2 85
Pulawy, Pol., 15,800......C6 7
Pul-I-Khumri, Afg.,
12,246................A4 20
Pullman, Wash.,
12,957................C8 86
Pulog, mtn., Phil.........n13 19
Pultusk, Pol., 11,400.....B6 7
Puluntohai, see Bulun
Tukhoi, China
Pungsan, Kor., 17,453....F4 18
Punjab, state, India
20,306,812............B6 20
Puno, Peru, 25,100.......E3 31
Puno, dept., Peru,
646,385...............E3 31
Punta Alta, Arg., 31,186..B4 28
Punta Arenas, Chile,
49,500...............h11 28
Punta Gorda, Fla.,
3,157.............A2 35, F4 54
Puntarenas, C.R.,
19,582...............*F8 34
Puntarenas, prov., C.R.,
148,100..............*F8 34
Punxsutawney, Pa., 8,805..E4 81
Puquio, Peru, 6,183.......D3 31
Purcell, Mo., 265........D3 69
Purcell, Okla., 3,729......B4 79
Purcellville, Va., 1,419....A5 85
Purèpero, Mex., 10,093...n12 34
Puri, India, 60,815.......E8 20
Purnea, India, 40,602.....C8 20
Pursat, Camb., 14,500....C2 19
Pursglove, W. Va., 600....B4 87
Purulia, India, 48,134....D8 20
Purús, riv., Peru.........D3 31
Purvis, Miss., 1,614......D4 68
Pusan, Kor., 1,419,800....I4 18
Pushkin, Sov. Un., 55,000..B8 12
Pushkino, Sov. Un.,
10,000............C11, m17 12
Pushmataha, Ala., 200....C1 46
Pushmataha, co., Okla.....C6 79
Puspokladany, Hung.,
15,735................B5 10
Pustelnik, Pol., 5,000.....k14 7
Putao, Bur., 10,000......C10 20
Puteaux, Fr., 39,640......g9 5
Putivl, Sov. Un., 10,000...F9 12
Putnam, Conn., 6,952.....B9 52
Putnam, co., Fla., 32,212..C5 54
Putnam, co., Ga.,
7,798.................C3 55
Putnam, co., Ill., 4,570....B4 58
Putnam, co., Ind., 24,927..E4 59
Putnam, co., Mo., 6,999...A4 69
Putnam, co., N.Y., 41,811..D7 75
Putnam, co., Ohio, 28,331..B1 78
Putnam, co., Tenn.,
29,236................C8 83
Putnam, co., W. Va.,
23,561................C3 87
Puttalam, Cey., 10,162....G6 20
Putumayo, comisaría,
Col., 56,284..........C2 32
Puukolii, Haw., 418......C5 56
Puunene, Haw., 2,500....C5 56
Puxico, Mo., 743.........E7 69
Puyallup, Wash.,
12,063.............B3, f11 86
Puy-de-Dôme, dept., Fr.,
508,928.............*E5 5
Puyo, Ec., 2,290.........B2 31
Pwllheli, Wales, 3,600.....D4 4
Pyapon, Bur., 19,174.....E10 20
Pyatigorsk, Sov. Un.,
74,000...............*E7 13
Pyinmana, Bur., 22,066...E10 20
Pyŏngchang, Kor., 4,300..H4 18
Pyŏngtaek, Kor., 15,200...H3 18
Pyŏngyang, Kor., 653,100..G2 18
Pyrénées-Orientales, dept.,
Fr., 251,231.........*F5 5
Pyskowice, Pol., 22,900....g9 7
Pyu, Bur., 10,443........E10 20

Q

Qana, Leb., 3,000.......A3 15
Qatar, country, Asia, 55,000..............D5 15
Quakenbruck, Ger., 7,857..B3 6
Quaker Hill, Conn., 2,000..D8 52
Quakertown, Pa., 6,305...F11 81
Quanah, Tex., 4,564......B3 84
Quang Ngai, Viet., 8,640..B3 19
Quang Tri, Viet., 10,740..B3 19
Quantico, Va., 1,015......B5 85
Quapaw, Okla., 850......A7 79
Quaraí, Braz., 10,575......E1 30
Quarryville, Pa., 1,427...G9 81
Quartu Sant' Elena, It., 22,916..............E2 9
Quartz Hill, Calif., 3,325................*E4 50
Quay, co., N. Mex., 12,279..............B7 48
Québec, Que., Can., 171,979 (*357,568........C6, n17 42
Québec, co., Que., Can., 331,307............B5 42
Québec, prov., Can., 5,780,845.............42

Québec-Quest, Que., Can., 8,733........*C6 42
Quedlinburg, Ger., 31,100..............C5 6
Queen Annes, co., Md., 16,569.............B5 53
Queen Bess, mtn., B.C., Can..................D5 37
Queen City, Tex., 1,081..*C5 84
Queen Elizabeth, is., N.W. Ter., Can.......m31 36
Queens, borough and co., N.Y., 1,809,578......E7 75
Queens, co., N.B., Can., 11,640.............D4 43
Queens, co., N.S., Can., 13,155.............E4 43
Queens, co., P.E.I., Can., 45,842.............C6 43
Queensland, state, Austl., 1,661,240..........D7 25
Queenstown, S. Afr., 33,182.............G5 24
Quelimane, Moz..........D7 24
Querétaro, Mex., 67,674............C4, m13 34

Querétaro, state, Mex., 355,045.....C4, m13 34
Quesada, Sp., 7,609.......D4 8
Quesnel, B.C., Can., 4,673................C6 37
Questa, N. Mex., 650......A6 48
Quetta, Pak., 79,493.....B4 20
Quezaltenango, Guat., 27,672.............E6 34
Quezaltepeque, Sal., 9,395...............*E7 34
Quezon, prov., Phil., 653,426............*C6 19
Quezon City, Phil., 397,990............C6 19
Quibdó, Col., 19,989.....B2 32
Quidnessett, R.I., 1,000................C11 52
Quidnick, R.I., 2,000....C10 52
Quiindy, Par., 2,150......E4 29
Quilá, Mex., 1,451......C3 34
Quillota, Chile, 29,400...A2 28
Quilmes, Arg., 310,000....g7 28
Quilon, India, 91,018.....G6 20
Quilpie, Austl., 859......E7 25
Quilpué, Chile, 26,600.....A2 28

Quimper, Fr., 45,989.....C2 5
Quimperlé, Fr., 10,272....D2 5
Quincy, Calif., 1,700....C3 50
Quincy, Fla., 8,874......B2 54
Quincy, Ill., 43,793......D2 58
Quincy, Mass., 87,409..........B5, h11 65
Quincy, Mich., 1,602.....G6 66
Quincy, Wash., 3,269.....B6 86
Quinnville, R.I., 400.....B11 52
Quintana de la Serena, Sp., 7,861...........C3 8
Quintanar, Sp., 9,483....C4 8
Quintana Roo, Ter., Mex., 50,169.........D7 34
Quinter, Kans., 776......C3 61
Quinton, Okla., 898......B6 79
Quiroga, Sp., 8,380......A2 8
Quitman, Ga., 5,071......F3 55
Quitman, Miss., 2,030....C5 68
Quitman, Tex., 1,237.....C5 84
Quitman, co., Ga., 2,432..E1 55
Quitman, co., Miss., 21,019...............A3 68
Quito, Ec., 354,746......B2 31
Quixadá, Braz., 8,747....*D7 27

R

Raba, Indon., 6,781......G5 19
Rabat, Mor., 227,445.....B3 22
Rabun, Ala., 300........D2 46
Rabun, co., Ga., 7,456....B3 55
Raceland, Ky., 1,115......B7 62
Raceland, La., 3,666...E5, k10 63
Rach Gia, Viet., 36,930...............*C2 19
Raciborz, Pol., 35,500....C5 7
Racine, Wis., 97,000 (*129,000)........F6, n12 88
Racine, co., Wis., 141,781..F5 88
Radauti, Rom., 15,949....B7 10
Radcliff, Ky., 3,384......C4 62
Radeberg, Ger., 16,300...C6 6
Radford (Independent City), Va., 9,371......C2 85
Radiant Valley, Md., 1,500................C4 53
Radnor, Pa., 1,000......*G11 81
Radnor, co., Wales, 18,400...............*D5 4
Radom, Pol., 139,700....C6 7
Radomir, Bul., 5,778......D6 10
Radomsko, Pol., 28,300...C5 7
Radville, Sask., Can., 1,067................H3 39
Radzionkow, Pol., 26,200..g9 7
Rae Bareli, India, 29,940..C7 20
Raeford, N.C., 3,058.....C3 76
Rafaela, Arg., 34,046....A4 28
Ragland, Ala., 1,166.....B3 46
Ragunda, Swe., 202......F7 11
Ragusa, It., 48,000.......F5 9
Rahimyar-Khan, Pak., 14,919.............C5 20
Rahway, N.J., 27,699..B4, k7 74
Raichur, India, 63,329....E6 20
Raigarh, India, 36,933....D7 20
Rainbow City, Ala., 1,625................*A3 46
Rainbow City, C.Z., 3,688................*B2 32
Rainier, Oreg., 1,152.....A4 80
Rainier, mtn., Wash.......C4 86
Rains, co., Tex., 2,993....C5 84
Rainsville, Ala., 398.....A4 46
Rainy River, Ont., Can., 1,168...............*o16 41
Rainy River, dist., Ont., Can., 26,531.......o16 41
Raipur, India, 139,792....D7 20
Rajahmundry, India, 130,002.............E7 20
Rajasthan, state, India, 20,155,602...........C5 20
Rajkot, India, 193,498.....D5 20
Rakovnik, Czech., 12,000..C2 7

Rakvere, Sov. Un., 25,000..............B6 12
Raleigh, N.C., 111,000, (*166,000)...........B4 76
Raleigh, Tenn., 3,000..B2, E8 83
Raleigh, W. Va., 750.....D7 87
Raleigh, co., W. Va., 77,826.............D3 87
Ralls, Tex., 2,229.......C2 84
Ralls, co., Mo., 8,078....B6 69
Ralston, Nebr., 2,977.....g12 71
Rām Allāh, Jordan, 14,759.............C3 15
Ramat Gan, Isr., 95,800...B2 15
Rambervillers, Fr., 7,042...C7 5
Ramea, Newf., Can., 970..E3 44
Ramenskoye, Sov. Un., 10,000..........D12, n18 12
Ramle, Isr., 23,900......C2 15
Ramleh, Eg., U.A.R., 52,000..............*G8 14
Ramona, Calif., 3,000....F5 50
Rampur, India, 135,407...C6 20
Rampur-Baolia, Pak., 56,885.............D8 20
Ramsay, Mich., 1,158....n12 66
Ramseur, N.C., 1,258.....B3 76
Ramsey, N.J., 9,527......A4 74
Ramsey, co., Minn., 422,525............E5 67
Ramsey, co., N. Dak., 13,443.............B7 77
Ramsgate, Eng., 37,700...E7 4
Rancagua, Chile, 53,300..A2 28
Ranches of Taos, N. Mex., 1,600..............A6 48
Ranchi, India, 122,416....D8 20
Rancho Cordova, Calif., 20,000.............*C3 50
Rand, W. Va., 3,000.....C6 87
Randall, co., Tex., 33,913..B2 84
Randallstown, Md., 3,000..B4 53
Randers, Den., 42,238.....I4 11
Randers, co., Den., 170,231.............*I4 11
Randleman, N.C., 2,232...B3 76
Randolph, Maine, 1,724...D3 64
Randolph, Mass., 18,900.........B5, h11 65
Randolph, Nebr., 1,063...B8 71
Randolph, Vt., 2,122.....D2 73
Randolph, Wis., 1,507....E4 88
Randolph, co., Ala., 19,477.............B4 46
Randolph, co., Ark., 12,520.............A4 49
Randolph, co., Ga., 11,078.............E2 55

Randolph, co., Ill., 29,988.............E4 58
Randolph, co., Ind., 28,434.............D7 59
Randolph, co., Mo., 22,014.............B5 69
Randolph, co., N.C., 61,497.............B3 76
Randolph, co., W. Va., 26,349.............C5 87
Randolph Hills, Md., 2,000...............*B3 53
Rangely, Colo., 1,464....A2 51
Ranger, Tex., 3,313.......C3 84
Rangoon, Bur., 821,800...E10 20
Rangpur, Pak., 31,759....C8 20
Raniganj, India, 30,113...D8 20
Rankin, Pa., 5,164......k14 81
Rankin, Tex., 1,214.....D2 84
Rankin, co., Miss., 34,322..C4 68
Ranlo, N.C., 2,000......*B1 76
Ranshaw, Pa., 1,078.....*E9 81
Ransom, co., N. Dak., 8,078..............D8 77
Ranson, W. Va., 1,974....B7 87
Rantoul, Ill., 27,553.....C5 58
Rapallo, It., 22,700......B2 9
Rapid City, S. Dak., 42,399.............F2 77
Rapides, par., La., 111,351............C3 63
Rappahannock, co., Va., 5,368................B4 85
Raritan, N.J., 6,137......B3 74
Raseiniai, Sov. Un., 6,181..A7 7
Rashīd (Rosetta), Eg., U.A.R., 32,800........G8 14
Rasht, Iran, 109,491.....A7 23
Rasskazovo, Sov. Un., 43,500.............E13 12
Rastatt, Ger., 24,100.....D4 6
Rat Buri, Thai., 20,380....C1 19
Rathenow, Ger., 28,600...B6 6
Ratibor, see Raciborz, Pol.
Ratnagiri, India, 31,091...E5 20
Raton, N. Mex., 8,146....A6 48
Rauch, Arg., 5,274.......B5 28
Rauma, Fin., 21,700......G9 11
Ravalli, co., Mont., 12,341.............D2 70
Rava-Russkaya, Sov. Un., 10,000..............F4 12
Raven, Va., 900.........e10 85
Ravena, N.Y., 2,718......C7 75
Ravenna, It., 57,300.....B4 9
Ravenna, Ky., 921.......C6 62
Ravenna, Nebr., 1,417....C7 71
Ravenna, Ohio, 10,918....A4 78

Ravensburg, Ger., 31,300..E4 6
Ravenswood, W. Va., 3,410...............C3 87
Rawalpindi, Pak., 197,370 (*340,175)..........B5 20
Rawa Mazowiecka, Pol., 6,908..............C6 7
Rawdon, Que., Can., 2,388..............C4 42
Rawicz, Pol., 13,300.....C4 7
Rawlins, Wyo., 8,968.....E5 89
Rawlins, co., Kans., 5,279..C2 61
Ray, Ariz., 1,000.....C3, D3 48
Ray, N. Dak., 1,049......B2 77
Ray, co., Mo., 16,075.....B3 69
Raybon, Ga., 400........E5 55
Raychikhinsk, Sov. Un., 30,000.............B4 18
Raymond, Alta., Can., 2,362..............E4 38
Raymond, Miss., 1,381....C3 68
Raymond, Wash., 3,301...C2 86
Raymondville, Tex., 6,385................F4 84
Rayne, La., 8,634........D3 63
Raynham Center, Mass., 200................C5 65
Rayong, Thai., 9,701....*C2 19
Raytown, Mo., 16,075....C4 55
Raytown, Mo., 17,083....h11 69
Rayville, La., 4,052......B4 63
Razgrad, Bul., 15,023....D8 10
Razlog, Bul., 6,857.......E6 10
Reading, Eng., 121,500...E6 4
Reading, Mass., 19,259.........A5, f11 65
Reading, Mich., 1,128....G6 66
Reading, Ohio, 12,832..........C1, o13 78
Reading, Pa., 93,000 (*200,000)..........F10 81
Reagan, co., Tex., 3,782..D2 84
Real, co., Tex., 2,079....E3 84
Ream, Camb., 5,000.....*C2 19
Ream, W. Va., 800......*D3 87
Reamstown, Pa., 950.....F9 81
Recanati, It., 6,288......C4 9
Rechitsa, Sov. Un., 33,800.............E8 12
Recife, Braz., 788,569....D7 27
Recklinghausen, Ger., 129,700.............C3 6
Reconquista, Arg., 12,729..E4 29
Rector, Ark., 1,757......A5 49
Red, riv., U.S..........D8 20
Red, sea, Afr...........D9 21
Red, sea, Asia..........D9 21
Red Bank, N.J., 12,482....C4 74

Red Bank, Tenn., 10,777............*D8 83
Red Bay, Ala., 1,954....A1 46
Red Bluff, Calif., 7,202....B2 50
Red Boiling Springs, Tenn., 597............C8 83
Red Bud, Ill., 2,280......E4 58
Redcliff, Alta., Can., 2,221............D5 38
Red Cloud, Nebr., 1,525...D7 71
Red Deer, Alta., Can., 19,612............C4, g8 38
Reddell, La., 500......D3 63
Redding, Calif., 12,773....B2 50
Redfield, Iowa, 966......C3 60
Redfield, S. Dak., 2,952...F7 77
Redford Heights, Mich., 71,276.............*F7 66
Red Hill, Pa., 1,086....*F11 81
Red Hook, N.Y., 1,731...D7 75
Redington Beach, Fla., 1,368............*E4 54
Redington Shores, Fla., 917.............*E4 54
Red Jacket, W. Va., 950...D2 87
Red Key, Ind., 1,746......D7 59
Red Lake, Ont., Can., 2,051............o16 41
Red Lake, co., Minn., 5,830............C2 67
Red Lake Falls, Minn., 1,520............C2 67
Redlands, Calif., 26,829...E5 50
Red Lion, Pa., 5,594......G8 81
Red Lodge, Mont., 2,278...E7 70
Redmond, Oreg., 3,340...C5 80
Redmond, Wash., 1,426...e11 86
Red Oak, Ga., 900......B5 55
Redon, Fr., 6,444.......D3 5
Redondela, Sp., 3,261...A1 8
Redondo Beach, Calif., 46,986............n12 50
Redore, Minn., 170......C6 67
Red River, co., Tex., 15,682............C5 84
Red River, par., La., 9,978............B2 63
Red Springs, N.C., 2,767...C3 76
Redstone, Ala., 1,000...*A3 46
Redstone, Colo., 100......B3 51
Red Tank, C.Z., 1,949....*B2 32
Redtop, Mo., 128........D4 69
Redwater, Alta., Can., 1,135............C4 38
Red Willow, co., Nebr., 12,940............D5 71
Red Wing, Minn., 10,528..F6 67
Redwood, co., Minn., 21,718............F3 67
Redwood City, Calif., 46,290............D2, k8 50
Redwood Estates, Calif., 930.............*D3 50
Redwood Falls, Minn., 4,285............F3 67
Reed City, Mich., 2,184...E5 66
Reedley, Calif., 5,880....D4 50
Reedsburg, Wis., 4,371....E3 88
Reeds Lake, Mich., 10,924.............*F5 66
Reedsport, Oreg., 2,998..D2 80
Reedsville, Pa., 950......E6 81
Reese Village, Tex., 1,433.............*C2 84
Reeves, co., Tex., 17,644..o13 84
Reform, Ala., 1,241......B1 46
Refuge, Tex., 75.........D5 84
Refugio, co., Tex., 10,975..E4 84
Regensburg, Ger., 125,300............D6 6
Reggio di Calabria, It., 126,000............E5 9
Reggio nell 'Emilia, It., 90,000.............B3 9
Reghin, Rom., 18,091.....B7 10
Regina, Sask., Can., 112,141............G3, n8 39
Region Occidental (Chaco), dept., Par., 54,277.............*D3 29
Regla, Cuba, 32,400......C2 35
Rehoboth Beach, Del., 1,507............C7 53
Rehovot, Isr., 30,400......C2 15
Reichenbach, Ger., 29,600............C6 6
Reidsville, Ga., 1,229.....D4 55
Reidsville, N.C., 14,036...A3 76
Reigate, Eng., 54,900............E6, m12 4
Reims, Fr., 133,914......C6 5
Reinbeck, Iowa, 1,621....B5 60
Reindeer, lake, Can....E13 36
Reinosa, Sp., 10,044.....A3 8
Reistertown, Md., 5,000...B4 53
Rembertow, Pol., 24,300............B6, k14 7
Remedios, Cuba, 12,400...C4 35

Remerton, Ga., 571......F3 55
Remington, Ind., 1,207...C3 59
Remiremont, Fr., 9,350...C7 5
Remscheid, Ger., 128,700..C3 6
Remsen, Iowa, 1,338......B2 60
Rendsburg, Ger., 35,700...A4 6
Renfrew, Ont., Can., 8,935............B8 41
Renfrew, co., Ont., Can., 8,935............B7 41
Renfrew, co., Scot., 346,100............*C4 4
Rengo, Chile, 11,000......A2 28
Rennes, Fr., 151,948......C3 5
Reno, Nev., 51,470.......B2 72
Reno, co., Kans., 59,055...E5 61
Renovo, Pa., 3,316.......D6 81
Rensselaer, Ind., 4,740...C3 59
Rensselaer, N.Y., 10,506...C6 75
Rensselaer, co., N.Y., 142,585............C7 75
Renton, Wash., 18,453............B3, f11 86
Renville, Minn., 1,373....F3 67
Renville, co., Minn., 23,249............F3 67
Renville, co., N. Dak., 4,698............B4 77
Republic, Mich., 950......B3 66
Republic, Mo., 1,519......D4 69
Republic, Pa., 1,921......G2 81
Republic, Wash., 1,064...A7 86
Republic, co., Kans., 9,768............C7 61
Requena, Sp., 8,228.......C5 8
Reserve, La., 5,500......h10 63
Resistencia, Arg., 80,000..E4 29
Resita, Rom., 46,100......C5 10
Restigouche, co., N.B., Can., 40,973............B2 43
Reszel, Pol., 5,693.......A6 7
Retalhuleu, Guat., 9,304...E6 34
Rethimni (Rhethymnon), prov., Grc., 69,943....*E5 14
Rethimnon, Grc., 14,999...E5 14
Reus, Sp., 41,014........B6 8
Reutlingen, Ger., 70,800..D4 6
Revel, Fr., 4,288........F5 5
Revelo, Ky., 500........D5 62
Revelstoke, B.C., Can., 3,624............D8 37
Revere, Mass., 40,080....g11 65
Revere, Minn., 201......F3 67
Revin, Fr., 11,244.......C6 5
Revloc, Pa., 900........F4 81
Rewa, India, 43,065......D7 20
Rewari, India, 36,994....C6 20
Rexburg, Idaho, 7,025....F7 57
Reykjavík, Ice., 73,388 (*90,000)............n22 11
Reynolds, Ga., 1,087.....D2 55
Reynolds, co., Mo., 5,161..D6 69
Reynoldsburg, Ohio, 7,793............C3, m11 78
Reynoldsville, Pa., 3,158..D4 81
Reynosa, Reinosa, Mex., 74,140............B5 34
Rezé, Fr., 28,276........D3 5
Rezekne, Sov. Un., 13,139............C6 12
Rhea, co., Tenn., 15,863...D9 83
Rheden, Neth., 9,200....A7 6
Rhein (Rhine), riv., Eur...C3 6
Rheine, Ger., 47,000.....B3 6
Rheinland-Pfalz, state, Ger., 3,582,000......C3 6
Rhinebeck, N.Y., 2,093...D7 75
Rhineland, reg., Ger......C3 6
Rhinelander, Wis., 8,790..C4 88
Rhode Island, state, U.S., 859,488............52
Rhodesia, Br. dep., Afr., 4,013,000............D5 24
Rhodhiss, N.C., 837......B1 76
Rhondda, Wales, 100,100..E5 4
Rhône, dept., Fr., 1,116,664............*E6 5
Rhyl, Wales, 21,400......D5 4
Rialto, Calif., 18,567....m14 50
Rianjo, Sp., 9,971.......A1 8
Ribadavia, Sp., 7,031....A1 8
Ribadeo, Sp., 9,567......A2 8
Ribadesella, Sp., 8,228...A3 8
Ribatejo, prov., Port., 464,874.............*C1 8
Ribe, co., Den., 185,048...*J3 11
Ribeirão Prêto, Braz., 116,153............C3, k8 30
Ribera, It., 18,547.......F4 9
Ricany, Czech., 6,376....o18 7
Rice, co., Kans., 13,909...D5 61
Rice, co., Minn., 38,988...F5 67
Rice Lake, Wis., 7,303....C2 88
Riceville, Iowa, 898......A5 60
Rich, Miss., 100.........A3 68
Rich, co., Utah, 1,685....A6 72
Richardson, Tex., 16,810............n10 84

Richardson, co., Nebr., 13,903............D10 71
Richelieu, co., Que., Can., 38,565............D4 42
Richfield, Calif., 100......C2 50
Richfield, Minn., 46,444..n12 67
Richfield, Utah, 4,412....B5 72
Richfield Springs, N.Y., 1,630............C6 75
Richford, Vt., 1,663......B3 73
Rich Hill, Mo., 1,699......C3 69
Richibucto, N.B., Can., 1,375............C5 43
Richland, Ga., 1,472......D2 55
Richland, Mo., 1,662......D5 69
Richland, Pa., 1,276......*F9 81
Richland, Wash., 23,548...C6 86
Richland, co., Ill., 16,299..E5 58
Richland, co., Mont., 10,504............C12 70
Richland, co., N.Dak., 18,824............D9 77
Richland, co., Ohio, 117,761............B3 78
Richland, co., S.C., 200,102............D6 82
Richland, co., Wis., 17,684............E3 88
Richland, par., La., 23,824............B4 63
Richland Center, Wis., 4,746............E3 88
Richland Hills, Tex., 7,804.............*C4 84
Richlands, N.C., 1,079....C5 76
Richlands, Va., 4,963.....e10 85
Richmond, Calif., 71,854............D2, h8 50
Richmond, Que., Can., 4,072............D5 42
Richmond, Eng., 40,600..m11 4
Richmond, Ind., 44,194...E8 59
Richmond, Ky., 12,168...C5 62
Richmond, Maine, 1,400............D3, f8 64
Richmond, Mich., 2,667...F8 66
Richmond, Mo., 4,604....B4 69
Richmond, Tex., 3,668............E5, r14 84
Richmond, Utah, 977.....A6 72
Richmond (Independent City), Va., 216,000 (*485,000)........C5, m18 85
Richmond (Staten Island), borough and co., N.Y., 221,991............E6 75
Richmond, co., N.S., Can., 11,374............D9 43
Richmond, co., Que., Can., 4,072............D5 42
Richmond, co., Ga., 135,601............C4 55
Richmond, co., N.C., 39,299............B3 76
Richmond, co., Va., 6,375............C6 85
Richmond Beach, Wash., 7,000............B3 86
Richmond Heights, Fla., 4,311............s13 54
Richmond Heights, Mo., 15,622............f13 69
Richmond Highlands, Wash., 6,000.........*B3 86
Richmond Hill, Ont., Can., 16,446............D5, k15 41
Richmond Hill., N.C., 2,943.............*B3 76
Rich Square, N.C., 1,134...A5 76
Richton, Miss., 1,089....D5 68
Richwood, Ohio, 2,137...B2 78
Richwood, W. Va., 4,110...C4 87
Riddle, Oreg., 992.......E3 80
Ridge, Va., 2,000.......*C5 85
Ridgecrest, Calif., 5,099..*E5 50
Ridgecrest, Wash., 4,000..*B3 86
Ridgedale, Mo., 135......E4 69
Ridgedale, Tenn., 1,000..C10 83
Ridge Farm, Ill., 894.....D6 58
Ridgefield, Conn., 3,000...D3 52
Ridgefield, N.J., 10,788...h8 74
Ridgefield, Park, N.J., 12,701............B4, h8 74
Ridgeland, S.C., 1,192....G6 82
Ridgeley, W. Va., 1,229...B6 87
Ridgely, Tenn., 1,464.....A2 83
Ridgetown, Ont., Can....E3 41
Ridgeville, Ga., 200......E5 55
Ridgeville, Ind., 950......D7 59
Ridgewood, Ill., 5,586....*B5 58
Ridgewood, N.J., 25,391..B4 74
Ridgewood Heights, Ohio, 1,500.............*C1 78
Ridgway, Ill., 1,055......F5 58
Ridgway, Pa., 6,387......D4 81
Ridley Farms, Pa., 1,500..............*G11 81

Ridley Park, Pa., 7,387....p20 81
Ried, Aus., 9,471........D6 6
Riegelsville, Pa., 953.....B2 81
Riesa, Ger., 36,800......C6 6
Rieti, It., 24,200........C4 9
Rifle, Colo., 2,135.......B3 51
Riga, Sov. Un., 632,000...C5 12
Rigaud, Que., Can., 1,990............D3 42
Rigby, Idaho, 2,281......F7 57
Riihimäki, Fin., 20,200...G11 11
Rijeka, Yugo., 100,989...C2 10
Riley, co., Kans., 41,914...C7 61
Rimbey, Alta., Can., 1,266............C3 38
Rimersburg, Pa., 1,323...D2 81
Rimini, It., 69,000.......B4 9
Rîmnicu-Sărat, Rom., 19,095............C8 10
Rîmnicu-Vîlcea, Rom., 18,984............C7 10
Rimouski, Que., Can., 17,739............A9 42
Rimouski, co., Que., Can., 65,295............A9 42
Rincon, Ga., 1,057.......D5 55
Rindjani, peak, Indon....G5 19
Ringgold, Ga., 1,311.....B1 55
Ringgold, La., 953.......B2 63
Ringgold, co., Iowa, 7,910............D3 60
Ringkøbing, co., Den., 205,772............*I3 11
Ringling, Okla., 1,170....C4 79
Ringsaker, Nor.,.........G4 11
Ringsted, Den., 9,694....A1 7
Ringwood, N.J., 4,182....A4 74
Rio Arriba, co., N. Mex., 24,193............A5 48
Riobamba, Ec., 41,625...B2 31
Rio Blanco, co., Colo., 5,150............B2 51
Rio Branco, Braz., 17,245..C4 31
Río Caribe, Ven., 7,774...A5 32
Rio Claro, Braz., 48,548............C3, m8 30
Río Cuarto, Arg., 70,505..A4 28
Rio de Janeiro, Braz., 3,307,163 (*4,700,000)......C4, h6 30
Rio de Janeiro, state, Braz., 3,402,728....C4, h6 30
Rio Dell, Calif., 3,000....B1 50
Río Gallegos, Arg., 14,439............E3, h12 28
Rio Grande, Braz., 83,189............E2 30
Río Grande, Mex., 8,357...C4 34
Rio Grande, N.J., 950....E3 74
Rio Grande, co., Colo., 11,160............D4 51
Rio Grande (Rio Bravo del Norte), river, Mex., U.S.............E6 45
Rio Grande do Norte, state, Braz., 1,157,258..*D7 27
Rio Grande do Sul, state, Braz., 5,448,823....E2 30
Ríohacha, Col., 11,708...A3 32
Rio Hondo, Tex., 1,344...F4 84
Rio Linda, Calif., 6,000.............*C3 50
Riom, Fr., 14,418.......E5 5
Rio Muni, reg., Equat. Gui., 195,000......H7 22
Río Negro, prov., Arg., 412,652............C3 28
Rio Negro, Braz., 10,225............D3 30
Río Negro, dept. Ur., 192,595............*E1 30
Rionero in Vulture, It., 14,378............D5 9
Rio Pardo, Braz., 14,412..D2 30
Río Piedras, P.R., 65,406.............*G11 35
Río Tercero, Arg., 18,540..A4 28
Rio Verde, Braz., 11,268..B2 30
Río Verde (Ríoverde), Mex., 14,825.......m13 34
Rio Vista, Calif., 2,855....C3 50
Ripley, Miss., 2,668......A5 68
Ripley, N.Y., 1,247......C1 75
Ripley, Ohio, 2,174......D2 78
Ripley, Tenn., 3,782......B2 83
Ripley, W. Va., 2,756....C3 87
Ripley, co., Ind., 20,641...F7 59
Ripley, co., Mo., 9,096...E7 69
Ripoll. Sp., 9,034.......A7 8
Ripon, Calif., 1,894......*D3 50
Ripon, Eng., 10,700.....C6 4
Ripon, Wis., 6,163......E5 88
Rishon le-Zion, Isr., 30,000............C2 15
Rising Star, Tex., 997....C3 84
Rising Sun, Ind., 2,230...G8 59
Rison, Ark., 889........D3 49
Ritchey, Mo., 128.......E3 69

Ritchie, co., W. Va., 10,877....B3 87
Rittman, Ohio, 5,410....B4 78
Ritzville, Wash., 2,173....B7 86
Riva, It., 6,839....B3 9
Rivadavia, Arg., 5,643....A3 28
Rive-de-Gier, Fr., 16,565....E6 5
Rivera, Ur., 41,266....E1 30
Rivera, dept., Ur., 75,800....*E1 30
Riverbank, Calif., 2,786....D3 50
Riverdale, Calif., 1,012....D4 50
Riverdale, Ga., 1,045....*C2 55
Riverdale, Ill., 13,761....k9 58
Riverdale, Md., 4,389..C4, f9 53
Riverdale, N.J., 2,596....B4 74
Riverdale, N. Dak., 700...C4 77
Riverdale, Oreg., 1,500...*B4 80
Riverdale, Utah, 1,848..*A6 72
Riverdale Heights, Md., 4,389....*C4 53
River Edge, N.J., 13,264...h8 74
River Falls, Wis., 4,857...D1 88
River Forest, Ill., 12,695...k9 58
River Grove, Ill., 11,111...k9 58
Riverhead, N.Y., 6,700...n15 75
River Hebert, N.S., Can., 1,382....D5 43
River Hills, Wis., 1,257...m12 88
Riverina, reg., Austl.....F7 25
Riverland Terrace, S.C., 3,000....k12 82
River Pines, Mass., 1,500....*A5 65
River Plaza, N.J., 4,500..*C4 74
River Rouge, Mich., 18,147....F7, p15 66
Rivers, Man., Can., 1,574....D1 40
Riverside, Calif., 84,332....F5, n14 50
Riverside, Ont., Can., 18,089....E2 41
Riverside, Colo., 180....B5 51
Riverside, Ill., 9,750....k9 58
Riverside, Mich., 800....*F6 66
Riverside, Mo., 1,315....*B3 69
Riverside, N.J., 8,474....C3 74
Riverside, N.Y., 1,030....*C3 75
Riverside, Pa., 1,580....E8 81
Riverside, S.C., 1,200....*B3 82
Riverside, co., Calif., 306,191....F5 50
Riverton, Ill., 1,591....D4 58
Riverton, N.J., 3,324....C3 74
Riverton, Utah, 1,993....D2 72
Riverton, Wyo., 6,845....C4 89
Riverton Heights, Wash., 19,000....*B3 86
River Vale, N.J., 5,616..*A5 74
River View, Ala., 1,171....C4 46
Riverview, Fla., 4,000....m8 54
Riverview, Fla., 1,000....p11 54
Riverview, Mich., 7,237...p15 66
Riverview, Mo., 3,706....*C7 69
Riverview (Pasco West), Wash., 2,894....*C6 86
Rives, Mo., 134....E7 69
Rivesville, W. Va., 1,191....A7, B4 87
Riviera Beach, Fla., 13,046....F6 54
Riviera Beach, Md., 4,902....*B4 53
Rivière-Bleue, Que., Can., 1,540....B8 42
Rivière-du-Loup, Que., Can., 10,835....B8 42
Rivière-du-Loup, co., Que., Can., 40,239....B9 42
Rivière-du-Moulin, Que., Can., 4,386....A6 42
Riyadh (Ar Riyād), Sau. Ar., 169,185....E4 15
Rizal, Prov., Phil., 1,456,362....*B6 19
Rize, Tur., 22,181....B13 14
Rjukan, Nor., 5,677....H3 11
Roachdale, Ind., 927....E4 59
Roane, co., Tenn., 39,133....D9 83
Roane, co., W. Va., 15,720....C3 87
Roan Mountain, Tenn., 800....C11 83
Roanne, Fr., 51,723....D5 5
Roanoke, Ala., 5,288....B4 46
Roanoke, Ill., 1,821....C4 58
Roanoke, Ind., 935....C7 59
Roanoke (Independent City), Va., 103,000 (*186,000)....C3 85
Roanoke, co., Va., 61,693....C2 85
Roanoke Rapids, N.C., 13,320....A5 76
Roaring Springs, Pa., 2,937....F5 81

Robbins, Ill., 7,511....k9 58
Robbins, N.C., 1,294....B3 76
Robbinsdale, Minn., 16,381....E5, m12 67
Robersonville, N.C., 1,810....B5 76
Robert Lee, Tex., 990....D2 84
Roberts, co., S. Dak., 13,190....E9 77
Roberts, co., Tex., 1,075....B2 84
Robertsdale, Pa., 800....F5 81
Robertsdale, Ala., 1,474....E2 46
Robertson, co., Ky., 2,443..B5 62
Robertson, co., Tenn., 27,335....A5 83
Robertson, co., Tex., 16,157....D4 84
Robertsonville, Que., Can., 1,156....C6 42
Roberval, Que., Can., 7,739....A5 42
Robeson, N.C., 89,102....C3 76
Robesonia, Pa., 1,579....*F9 81
Robinson, Ill., 7,226....D6 58
Robinson, Pa., 900....F3 81
Robinson, Tex., 2,111....*D4 84
Robinsonville, Miss., 115....A3 68
Robinwood, Ala., 1,500....*B3 46
Roblin, Man., Can., 1,368....D1 40
Robson, mtn., Can.....C1 38
Robstown, Tex., 10,266....F4 84
Roby, Mo., 100....D5 69
Roby, Tex., 913....C2 84
Roccastrada, It., 3,109....C3 9
Rocha, Ur., 19,484....E2 30
Rocha, dept., Ur., 55,000....*E2 30
Rochdale, Eng., 86,300....D5 4
Rochdale, Mass., 1,300....B4 65
Rochefort, Fr., 28,648....E3 5
Rochelle, Ga., 1,235....E3 55
Rochelle, Ill., 7,554....B4 58
Rochelle Park, N.J., 6,119....h8 74
Rochester, Ind., 4,883....B5 59
Rochester, Mich., 5,431....F7 66
Rochester, Minn., 47,797....F6 67
Rochester, N.H., 15,927....E6 73
Rochester, N.Y., 298,000 (*680,000)....B3 75
Rochester, Pa., 5,952....E1 81
Rock, co., Minn., 11,864....G2 67
Rock, co., Nebr., 2,554....B6 71
Rock, co., Wis., 113,913....F4 88
Rockaway, N.J., 5,413....B3 74
Rockaway, Oreg., 771....B3 80
Rockbridge, co., Va., 24,039....C3 85
Rockcastle, co., Ky., 12,334....C5 62
Rockcliffe Park, Ont., Can., 2,084....*B9 41
Rock Creek Hills, Md., 1,500....*B3 53
Rockdale, Ill., 1,272..B5, m8 58
Rockdale, Md., 1,500....*B4 53
Rockdale, Tex., 4,481....D4 84
Rockdale, co., Ga., 10,572....C3 55
Rock Falls, Ill., 10,261....B4 58
Rockford, Ill., 143,000 (*226,000)....A4 58
Rockford, Iowa, 941....A5 60
Rockford, Mich., 2,074....E5 66
Rockford, Ohio, 1,155....B1 78
Rockford, Tenn., 900....D10, E11 83
Rock Hall, Md., 1,073....B5 53
Rockhampton, Austl., 46,052....D9 25
Rock Hill, Mo., 6,523....*C7 69
Rock Hill, S.C., 29,404....B5 82
Rockingham, N.C., 5,748....C3 76
Rockingham, co., N.H., 99,029....E5 73
Rockingham, co., N.C., 71,404....A3 76
Rockingham, co., Va., 40,485....B4 85
Rock Island, Que., Can., 1,608....D5 42
Rock Island, Ill., 51,863...B3 58
Rock Island, co., Ill., 150,991....B3 58
Rockland, Ont., Can., 3,037....B9 41
Rockland, Maine, 8,769....B3 64
Rockland, Mass., 13,119....B6, h12 65
Rockland, co., N.Y., 192,724....D6 75
Rockledge, Fla., 3,481....D6 54
Rockledge, Pa., 2,587....o21 81
Rocklin, Calif., 1,495....*C3 50
Rockmart, Ga., 3,938....C1 55

Rockport, Ind., 2,474....I3 59
Rockport, Maine, 900....D3 64
Rockport, Mass., 3,100....A6 65
Rock Port, Mo., 1,310....A2 69
Rockport, Tex., 2,989....F4 84
Rock Rapids, Iowa, 2,780....A1 60
Rocksprings, Tex., 1,182...D2 84
Rock Springs, Wyo., 10,371....E3 89
Rockton, Ill., 1,833....A4 58
Rock Valley, Iowa, 2,072...A1 60
Rockville, Conn., 9,478....B7 52
Rockville, Ind., 2,756....E3 59
Rockville, Md., 26,090....B3 53
Rockville Centre, N.Y., 26,413....n15 75
Rockwall, Tex., 2,166....C4, n10 84
Rockwall, co., Tex., 5,878....C4 84
Rockwell City, Iowa, 2,313....B3 60
Rockwood, Mich., 2,026...F7 66
Rockwood, Pa., 1,101....F3 81
Rockwood, Tenn., 5,345...D9 83
Rocky Ford, Colo., 4,929...C7 51
Rocky Grove, Pa., 3,168...D2 81
Rocky Hill, Conn., 7,404....C6 52
Rocky Mount, N.C., 32,147....B5 76
Rocky Mount, Va., 1,412..C3 85
Rocky Mountain House, Alta., Can., 2,360....C3 38
Rocky Point, N.Y., 2,300....*n15 75
Rocky Point, Wash., 1,000....*B3 86
Rocky Ripple, Ind., 967...k10 59
Rocky River, Ohio, 18,097....A4, h9 78
Roddickton, Newf., Can., 1,185....C3, h10 44
Roderfield, W. Va., 1,020....D3 87
Rodessa, La., 700....B1 63
Rodez, Fr., 20,924....E5 5
Rodgers Forge, Md., 7,645....*B4 53
Rodhopi (Rhodope), prov., Grc., 109,201....*B5 14
Ródhos, Grc., 27,393....D7 14
Rodney, Ont., Can., 1,041....E3 41
Rodney Village, Del., 1,200....B6 53
Roebling, N.J., 3,600....C3 74
Roebuck Plaza, Ala., 900....*B3 46
Roeland Park, Kans., 10,403....B9 61
Roermond, Neth., 34,500....B6 5
Roeselare, Bel., 35,645....B5 5
Roessleville, N.Y., 14,000....*C7 75
Rogachev, Sov. Un., 25,000....E8 12
Rogaland, cc., Nor., 239,000....*H1 11
Rogatica, Yugo., 3,044....D4 10
Roger Mills, co., Okla., 5,090....B2 79
Rogers, Ark., 5,700....A1 49
Rogers, Tex., 936....D4 84
Rogers, Va., 50....f10 85
Rogers, co., Okla., 20,614..A6 79
Rogers City, Mich., 4,722..C7 66
Rogers Heights, Md., 2,000....*C4 53
Rogersville, Tenn., 3,121..C10 83
Rogozno, Pol., 5,536....B4 7
Rohnerville, Calif., 1,000..*B1 50
Roi Et, Thai., 13,055....B2 19
Rojas, Arg., 6,608....A4 28
Rokitno, Sov. Un., 9,000..F6 12
Rokycany, Czech., 12,000..D2 7
Roland Terrace, Md., 2,000....*B4 53
Rolette, co., N. Dak., 10,641....B6 77
Rolfe, Iowa, 819....B3 60
Rolla, Mo., 11,132....D6 69
Rolla, N. Dak., 1,398....A6 77
Rolling Fork, Miss., 1,619..C3 68
Rolling Hills, Kans., 1,600..B5 61
Rolling Hills Estates, Calif., 3,941....*F4 50
Rolling Meadows, Ill., 13,177....h8 58
Rollingwood, Calif., 2,200....*D2 50
Roma, Austl., 6,000....E8 25
Roma, Tex., 1,496....F3 84
Roma, see Rome, It.
Roman, Rom., 32,900....B8 10

Romania, country, Eur., 19,025,000....B7 10
Romans [-sur-Isère], Fr., 26,377....E6 5
Romblon, Phil., 3,342....*C6 19
Romblon, prov., Phil., 131,658....*C6 19
Rome, Ga., 32,226....B1 55
Rome, Ill., 1,500....C4 58
Rome, It., 2,455,300...D4, h8 9
Rome, N.Y., 51,646....B5 75
Rome, Ohio, 50....*A5 78
Romeo, Ill., 3,574....*B5 58
Romeo, Mich., 3,327....F7 66
Romilly [-sur-Seine], Fr., 15,753....C5 5
Romita, Mex., 11,912....m11 34
Romney, W. Va., 2,203....B6 87
Romny, Sov. Un., 35,792..F9 12
Romorantin, Fr., 11,777...D4 5
Romulus, Mich., 2,500....p15 66
Ronan, Mont., 1,334....C2 70
Ronceverte, W. Va., 1,882....D4 87
Ronciglione, It., 7,079....C4 9
Ronda, Sp., 17,703....D3 8
Rondônia, prov., Braz., 70,783....B3 29
Ronkonkoma, N.Y., 7,700..F4 52
Rønne, Den., 13,195....A3 7
Ronse, Bel., 25,106....B5 5
Roodhouse, Ill., 2,352....D3 58
Rooks, co., Kans., 9,734..C4 61
Roosendaal, Neth., 41,400..B6 5
Roosevelt, N.Y., 13,700..G2 52
Roosevelt, Utah, 1,812...A6 72
Roosevelt, co., Mont., 11,731....B11 70
Roosevelt, co., N. Mex., 16,198....B7 48
Roosevelt, riv., Braz.....B3 29
Roosevelt Park, Mich., 2,578....E4 66
Roquetas, Sp., 5,514....B6 8
Rorschach, Switz., 13,400 (*24,400)....E4 6
Rosa, mtn., It., Switz.....B2 9
Rosario, Arg., 671,852....A4 28
Rosário, Braz., 6,999....*D6 27
Rosario, Mex., 11,703....C3 34
Rosario, Par., 6,058....D4 29
Rosario, Ur., 7,600....E1 30
Rosário do Sul, Braz., 15,786....E2 30
Rosario Tala, Arg., 10,584....A5 28
Rosburg, Wash., 50....B5 89
Roscoe, N.Y., 800....D6 75
Roscoe, Pa., 1,315....F2 81
Roscoe, Tex., 1,490....C2 84
Roscommon, co., Ire., 56,100....*D2 4
Roscommon, co., Mich., 867....D6 66
Roseau, Dominica, 10,417....I14 35
Roseau, Minn., 2,146....B3 67
Roseau, co., Minn., 12,154....B3 67
Roseboro, N.C., 1,354....C4 76
Rosebud, Tex., 1,644....D4 84
Rosebud, co., Mont., 6,187....D10 70
Roseburg, Oreg., 11,467...D3 80
Rosedale, Fla., 4,085....*E4 54
Rosedale, Miss., 2,339....B2 68
Rosedale Station, Alta., Can.....D4 38
Rose Hill, Kans., 273....E6 61
Rosehill, N.C., 1,255....C4 76
Roseland, Fla., 145....E6 54
Roseland, Ind., 971....A5 59
Roseland, La., 1,254....D5 63
Roseland, N.J., 2,804....*B4 74
Roseland, Ohio, 8,204....*B3 78
Roselle, Ill., 4,827....k8 58
Roselle, N.J., 21,032....k7 74
Roselle Park, N.J., 12,546..k7 74
Rosemead, Calif., 15,476..*F4 50
Rosemère, Que., Can., 6,158....p19 42
Rosemont, Ill., 2,600....*E3 58
Rosemont, Pa., 4,000....*F11 81
Rosemount, Minn., 1,068..F5 67
Rosenberg, Tex., 9,698....E5, r14 84
Rosendael, Fr., 19,960....B5 5
Rosendale, N.Y., 1,033....*C6 75
Rosenheim, Ger., 31,600...E6 6
Roseto, Pa., 1,630....E11 81
Rosetown, Sask., Can., 2,450....F1, n7 39
Roseville, Calif., 13,421...C3 50
Roseville, Ill., 1,065....C3 58
Roseville, Mich., 50,195...o16 66
Roseville, Minn., 29,581..m12 67
Roseville, Ohio, 1,749....C3 78
Rosewood, Calif., 1,100..*B1 50

Rosewood Heights, Ill., 4,800................*E3 58
Rosiclare, Ill., 1,700........F5 58
Roşiorii-de-Vede, Rom., 17,320................C7 10
Roskilde, co., Den., 90,337.................*J5 11
Roslavl, Sov. Un., 36,000..E9 12
Roslyn, N.Y., 2,681......*E7 75
Roslyn, Pa., 8,500.......*F11 81
Roslyn, Wash., 1,283......B4 86
Roslyn Estates, N.Y., 1,289................*G2 52
Roslyn Harbor, N.Y., 925.................*E7 75
Roslyn Heights, N.Y., 7,600.............D2, h13 75
Rosny-sous-Bois, Fr., 21,001................g10 5
Ross, Calif., 2,551.......*C2 50
Ross, co., Ohio, 61,215....C2 78
Ross and Cromarty, co., Scot., 57,400........*B4 4
Rossano, It., 12,400.......E6 9
Rossford, Ohio, 4,406..A2, e6 78
Rossiter, Pa., 950........E4 81
Rossland, B.C., Can., 4,354.................E9 37
Rossmoor, Calif., 9,000..*F5 50
Rossmoyne, Ohio, 2,000..*C1 78
Rossosh, Sov. Un., 10,000...............F12 12
Rossville, Ga., 4,665.......B1 55
Rossville, Ill., 1,470......C6 58
Rosthern, Sask., Can., 1,264................E2 39
Rostock, Ger., 166,500.....A6 6
Rostov, Sov. Un., 29,230..C12 12
Rostov [-na-Donu], Sov. Un., 689,000.....H12 12
Roswell, Ga., 2,983........B2 55
Roswell, N. Mex., 39,593..C6 48
Rotan, Tex., 2,788........C2 84
Rotenburg [an der Fulda], Ger., 7,700...........B4 6
Rothenburg ob der Tauber, Ger., 11,100...........D5 6
Rothesay, Scot., 7,300.....C4 4
Rothschild, Wis., 2,550...D4 88
Rothsville, Pa., 900.......F9 81
Rotondella, It., 5,643.....D6 9
Rotorua, N.Z., 25,978....M16 26
Rotterdam, Neth., 731,100 (*1,005,000)..........B6 5
Rotterdam, N.Y., 22,000..*C6 75
Rottweil, Ger., 17,900....D4 6
Roubaix, Fr., 112,856.....B5 5
Roudnice nad Labem, Czech., 10,000........n17 7
Rouen, Fr., 120,857.......C4 5
Roulette, Pa., 700........C5 81

Round Lake, Ill., 997......h8 58
Roundlake, Miss., 175.....A3 68
Round Lake Beach, Ill., 5,011.................h8 58
Round Lake Heights, Ill., 1,099.............*h8 58
Round Lake Park, Ill., 2,565.................*h8 58
Round Pond, Ark., 50.....B5 49
Round Rock, Tex., 1,878..D4 84
Roundup, Mont., 2,842...D8 70
Rouses Point, N.Y., 2,160................f11 75
Rouseville, Pa., 923......D2 81
Routt, co., Colo., 5,900....A3 51
Rouville, co., Que., Can., 25,979...............D4 42
Rouzerville, Pa., 900......G7 81
Rovana, Calif., 400.......*D4 50
Rovaniemi, Fin., 21,500..D11 11
Rovato, It., 6,288.........B2 9
Rovenki, Sov. Un., 55,000...........G12, q22 12
Rovereto, It., 25,638......B3 9
Rovigo, It., 34,400........B3 9
Rovinj, Yugo., 7,156......C1 10
Rovno, Sov. Un., 77,000...F6 12
Rovnoye, Sov. Un., 10,000...............F16 12
Rowan, co., Ky., 12,808..B6 62
Rowan, co., N.C., 82,817..B2 76
Rowan Mill, N.C., 1,089..*B2 76
Rowena, N.C., 1,408......C3 76
Rowland, N.C., 1,408......C3 76
Rowland, Pa., 100.........D11 81
Rowlesburg, W. Va., 970.................B5 87
Rowlett, Tex., 1,015......*C4 84
Rowley, Mass., 1,500......A6 65
Roxana, Ill., 2,090.......f13 69
Roxas (Capiz), Phil., 30,033...............C6 19
Roxboro, N.C., 5,147......A4 76
Roxburgh, co., Scot., 42,400..............*C5 4
Roxton Falls, Que., Can., 972.................D5 42
Roy, N. Mex., 633........B6 48
Roy, Utah, 9,239......A5, C2 72
Royal, Fla., 200..........D4 54
Royal Center, Ind., 966...C4 59
Royal Mills, N.C., 600....A4 76
Royal Oak, Mich., 80,612...........F7, o15 66
Royal Oak Township, Mich., 8,147.........*F7 66
Royalton, Ill., 1,225......F4 58
Royalton, Pa., 1,128......*F8 81
Royan, Fr., 16,521........E3 5
Royersford, Pa., 3,969....F10 81
Royse City, Tex., 1,274....C4 84

Royston, Ga., 2,333.......B3 55
Roznava, Czech., 10,200..D6 7
Rtishchevo, Sov. Un., 32,000...............E14 12
Ruapehu, mtn., N.Z.....M15 26
Rubezhnoye, Sov. Un., 50,000...............p21 12
Rubidoux, Calif., 10,400..............n14 50
Rudbar, Afg., 5,000.......B3 20
Rudolf, lake, Afr..........F9 21
Rudolstadt, Ger., 27,700...C5 6
Rueil-Malmaison, Fr., 54,786...............g9 5
Rufino, Arg., 12,045......A4 28
Rufisque, Sen., 49,700....F1 22
Rugby, N. Dak., 2,972....B6 77
Ruidoso, N. Mex., 1,557..C6 48
Rule, Tex., 1,347.........C3 84
Ruleville, Miss., 1,902....B3 68
Ruma, Yugo., 19,570.....C4 10
Rumford, Maine, 7,300...D2 64
Rumoi, Jap., 40,231......E10 18
Rumson, N.J., 6,405.....C4 74
Runge, Tex., 1,036.......E4 84
Runnels, co., Tex., 15,016..D3 84
Runnelstown, Miss., 125..D4 68
Runnemede, N.J., 8,396..D2 74
Rupert, Idaho, 4,153......G5 57
Rupert, W. Va., 921......D4 87
Rural Hall, N.C., 1,503..A2 76
Ruse (Ruschuk), Bul., 109,900.............*D7 10
Ruse (Ruschuk), co., Bul., 527,708.........*D8 10
Rush, co., Ind., 20,393....E7 59
Rush City, Minn., 1,108..E6 67
Rushford, Minn., 1,335...G7 67
Rush Springs, Okla., 1,303................C4 79
Rushville, Ill., 2,819......C3 58
Rushville, Ind., 7,264.....E7 59
Rushville, Nebr., 1,228....B3 71
Rusk, Tex., 4,900........D5 84
Rusk, co., Tex., 36,421....C5 84
Rusk, co., Wis., 14,794....C2 88
Ruskin, Fla., 1,894....E4, p11 54
Russas, Braz., 7,102......*D7 27
Russell (Russell City), Calif., 1,100.........*D3 50
Russell, Man., Can., 1,263................D1 40
Russell, Kans., 6,113.....D5 61
Russell, Ky., 1,458.......B7 62
Russell, co., Ala., 46,351..C4 46
Russell, co., Ont., Can., 20,892..............B9 41
Russell, co., Kans., 11,348...............D5 61
Russell, co., Ky., 11,076..D4 62
Russell, co., Va., 26,290...f9 85

Russell Gardens, N.Y., 1,156................*E7 75
Russells Point, Ohio, 1,111................*B2 78
Russell Springs, Ky., 1,125................D4 62
Russellton, Pa., 1,613.....E2 81
Russellville, Ala., 6,628...A2 46
Russellville, Ark., 8,921...B2 49
Russellville, Ky., 5,861....D3 62
Russian Soviet Federated Socialist Republic, rep., Sov. Un.............C8 12
Russiaville, Ind., 1,200....D5 59
Ruston, La., 13,991.......B3 63
Rutchenkovo, Sov. Un., 25,000...............r20 12
Rute, Sp., 10,077.........D3 8
Ruteng, Indon...........G6 19
Ruth, Miss., 150.........D3 68
Ruth, Nev., 800..........B4 72
Ruthenia, reg., Sov. Un...D7 7
Rutherford, N.J., 20,473...........B4, h8 74
Rutherford, Tenn., 983...A3 83
Rutherford, co., N.C., 45,091..............B1 76
Rutherford, co., Tenn., 52,368...............B5 83
Rutherford Heights, Pa., 1,700................*F8 81
Rutherfordton, N.C., 3,392.............B1, f11 76
Rutland, Mass., 1,800....B4 65
Rutland, Vt., 18,325......D2 73
Rutland, co., Eng., 26,400..............*D6 4
Rutland, co., Vt., 46,719..D1 73
Rutledge, Pa., 947.......*G11 81
Ruvo [di Puglia], It., 23,746................D6 9
Ruxton, Md., 2,100......*B4 53
Ruzayevka, Sov. Un., 34,500...............D15 12
Ruzomberok, Czech., 18,600................D5 7
Rwanda, country, Afr., 2,800,000............I3 23
Ryazan, Sov. Un., 262,000..............D12 12
Rybinsk (Shcherbakov), Sov. Un., 195,000.....B12 12
Rybnik, Pol., 36,800...C5, g9 7
Rydal, Pa., 1,500........*F11 81
Ryde, Eng., 19,800.......E6 4
Rye, N.Y., 15,232....h13, n15 75
Rylsk, Sov. Un., 10,000...F10 12
Ryotsu, Jap., 13,200......G9 18
Rypin, Pol., 7,350........B5 7
Rzeszow, Pol., 67,200....C6 7
Rzhev, Sov. Un., 55,000..C10 12

S

Saalfeld, Ger., 26,900.....C5 6
Saar, state, Ger., 1,116,000...............D3 6
Saarbrücken, Ger., 134,300 (*365,000).....D3 6
Saarlouis, Ger., 36,400....D3 6
Sabac, Yugo., 30,231......C4 10
Sabadell, Sp., 105,152.....B7 8
Sabae, Jap., 35,100.......n15 18
Sabah (North Borneo), reg., Mala., 506,600....D5 19
Sabana de la Mar, Dom. Rep., 2,840...........E9 35
Sabana Grande, P.R., 3,318...............*G11 35
Sabanalarga, Col., 20,254..A3 32
Sabang, Indon., 6,855....K11 19
Sabará, Braz., 10,004....B4 30
Sabaudia, It., 6,262......D4 9
Sabetha, Kans., 2,318....C8 61
Sabina, Ohio, 2,313......C2 78
Sabinal, Tex., 1,747......E3 84
Sabinas, Mex., 16,076....B4 34
Sabinas Hidalgo, Mex., 11,598...............B4 34
Sabine, co., Tex., 7,302...D6 84
Sabine, par., La., 18,564..C2 63
Sablé [-sur-Sarthe], Fr., 6,885................D3 5
Sabzawar, Afg., 10,000....B3 20

Sac, co., Iowa, 17,007....B2 60
Sac City, Iowa, 3,354.....B2 60
Sachsen, former state, Ger., 5,558,566......*C6 6
Sachsen-Anhalt (Saxony-Anhalt), former state, Ger., 4,160,539......*C5 6
Sackets Harbor, N.Y., 1,279................B4 75
Sackville, N.B., Can., 3,038.................D5 43
Saco, Maine, 10,515...E2, g7 64
Sacramento, Calif., 270,000 (*695,000).....A6 50
Sacramento, co., Calif., 502,778..............C3 50
Sacré-Coeur Saguenay, Que., Can., 1,108......A8 42
Sá da Bandeira, Ang., 13,867...............C2 24
Sa'dah, Yemen, 25,000...F3 15
Saddle Brook, N.J., 13,834..............*A4 74
Saddle River, N.J., 1,776................*A4 74
Saddle Rock, N.Y., 1,109................*G2 52
Saegertown, Pa., 1,131....C1 81
Saeki, Jap., 32,000.......J5 18
Safad, Isr., 11,500....B3, g5 15

Safety Harbor, Fla., 1,787.............D4, p10 54
Safford, Ariz., 5,165.....C4 48
Safi, Mor., 81,072........B3 22
Safranbolu, Tur., 7,383...B9 14
Saga, Jap., 134,575.......J5 18
Saga, pref., Jap., 871,885.*J5 18
Sagadahoc, co., Maine, 22,793...............E3 64
Sagaing, Bur., 15,439....D10 20
Sagamihara, Jap., 163,383..............*i9 18
Sagamore, Pa., 800.......E3 81
Sagamore Hills, Ohio, 4,500................h9 78
Sagara, Jap., 9,800......o17 18
Sag Harbor, N.Y., 2,346..n16 75
Saginaw, Mich., 96,000 (*182,000)...........E7 66
Saginaw, Tex., 1,001.....n9 84
Saginaw, co., Mich., 190,752.............E6 66
Sagle, Idaho, 100........A2 57
Saguache, Colo., 722.....C4 51
Saguache, co., Colo., 4,473................C4 51
Sagua de Tanamo, Cuba, 1,700................D6 35
Sagua la Grande, Cuba, 33,900...............C3 35

Saguenay, co., Que., Can., 81,900..........A8 42
Sagunto, Sp., 40,293.....C5 8
Sahagún, Col., 11,560....B2 32
Saharanpur, India, 185,213..............C6 20
Sahuaripa, Mex., 4,114...B3 34
Sahuayo (de Díaz), Mex., 25,661..............m12 34
Saidpur, Pak., 60,628....C8 20
Saijo, Jap., 10,600.......H6 18
Saigon, Viet., 1,250,800..C3 19
Saijo, Jap., 37,200.......*I6 18
Saiki, Jap., 32,200.......J5 18
St. Adelphe, Que., Can., 787.................C5 42
St. Affrique, Fr., 5,670....F5 5
St. Agapit, Que., Can., 1,117................C6 42
St. Agathe-de-Monts, Que., Can., 5,725.......C3 42
St. Alban, Que., Can., 786.................C5 42
St. Alban's, Newf., Can., 1,547................E4 44
St. Albans, Eng., 50,500.............E6, k12 4
St. Albans, W. Va., 15,103...............C3 87
St. Albans Bay, Vt., 200...B1 73

St. Albert, Alta., Can.,
4,059..................C4 38
St. Alexandre
[-de-Kamouraska],
Que., Can., 872........B8 42
St. Alexis-des-Monts,
Que., Can., 1,964......C3 42
St. Amand-Mont-Rond,
Fr., 10,890...........D5 5
St. Ambroise, Que., Can.,
1,576.................A6 42
St. André-Avellin, Que.,
Can., 1,066...........D2 42
St. Andrews, N.B., Can.,
1,531.................D2 43
St. Andrews, Scot., 10,100..B5 4
St. Andrews, S.C.,
5,500...............F7, k11 82
St. Andrews East, Que.,
Can., 1,183...........D3 42
St. Ann, Mo., 12,155...*C7 69
Ste. Anne, Que., Can.,
900...................D4 42
Ste. Anne, Guad., 3,190..H14 35
St. Anne, Ill., 1,378.....B6 58
Ste. Anne-de-Beaupré,
Que., Can., 1,878......B7 42
Ste. Anne (-de-Bellevue),
Que., Can., 4,044.....q19 42
Ste. Anne-de-la-Pérade,
Que., Can., 1,184.....C5 42
St. Anselme, Que., Can.,
1,131.................C7 42
St. Ansgar, Iowa, 1,014...A5 60
St. Anthony, Newf., Can.,
1,820.................C4 44
St. Anthony, Minn.,
5,084................*F5 67
St. Antoine des Laurentides,
Que., Can., 3,005.....*D3 42
St. Apollinaire, Que.,
Can., 968.........C6, o16 42
St. Aubert, Que., Can.,
735...................B7 42
St. Augustine, Fla.,
14,734.............C5, n9 54
St. Avold, Fr., 15,247.....C7 5
St. Barthélemy, Que.,
Can., 620.............C4 42
St. Basile [-de-Portneuf],
Que., Can., 1,709......C6 42
St. Bernard, Ohio, 6,778..o12 78
St. Bernard, par., La.,
32,186................E6 63
St. Bernice, Ind., 900....E2 59
St. Bonaventure, N.Y.,
2,000................*C2 75
St. Boniface, Man., Can.,
37,600................E3 40
St. Bride, mtn., Alta.,
Can...................D3 38
St. Brieuc, Fr., 43,142....C2 5
St. Bruno-Lac-St. Jean,
Que., Can., 1,158......A6
St. Camille [-de-Belle-
chasse], Que., Can.,
689...................C7 42
St. Casimir, Que., Can.,
1,386.................C5 42
Ste. Catharines, Ont.,
Can., 84,472 (*95,577)..D5 41
Ste. Catherine, Que.,
Can., 893.........C6, n16 42
St. Césaire, Que., Can.,
2,097.................D4 42
St. Chamond, Fr., 17,107..E6 5
St. Charles, Ill., 11,158...B5 58
St. Charles, Mich., 1,959..E6 66
St. Charles, Minn., 1,882..G6 67
St. Charles, Mo.,
21,189............C7, f12 69
St. Charles, co., Mo.,
52,970................C7 69
St. Charles, par., La.,
21,219................E5 63
St. Charles
[-de-Bellechasse],
Que., Can., 981.......C7 42
St. Chrysostome, Que.,
Can., 972.............D4 42
St. Clair, Mich., 4,538....F8 66
St. Clair, Mo., 2,711.....C6 69
St. Clair, Pa., 5,159......E9 81
St. Clair, co., Ala., 25,388..B3 46
St. Clair, co., Ill., 262,509..E3 58
St. Clair, co., Mich.,
107,201...............F8 66
St. Clair, co., Mo., 8,421..C4 69
Ste. Claire, Que., Can.,
1,838.................C7 42
St. Clair Shores, Mich.,
76,657...............*o16 66
St. Clairsville, Ohio, 3,865..B5 78
St. Claude, Man., Can.,
609...................E2 40
St. Claude [-sur-Bienne],
Fr., 12,114...........D6 5
St. Cloud, Fla., 4,353....D5 54

St. Cloud, Fr., 26,476.....g9 5
St. Cloud, Minn.,
37,746................E4 67
St. Constant, Que., Can.,
2,739................q19 42
St. Croix, Que., Can.,
1,363.............C6, o16 42
St. Croix, co., Wis.,
29,164................C1 88
St. Croix Falls, Wis.,
1,249.................C1 88
St. Cyrille [-de-L'Islet],
Que., Can., 655.......B7 42
St. Cyrille [-de-Wendover],
Que., Can., 1,138......D5 42
St. Damase, Que., Can.,
879...................D4 42
St. Davids, Pa., 1,200...*G11 81
St. Denis, Fr., 94,264..C5, g10 5
St. Denis
[-de-la-Bouteillerie],
Que., Can., 269.......B8 42
St. Denis [River
Richelieu], Que.,
1,063.................D4 42
St. Dié, Fr., 23,108......C7 5
St. Dizier, Fr., 34,407....C6 5
St. Donat-de-Mont-calm,
Que., Can., 1,414......C3 42
St. Edward, Nebr., 777...C8 71
St. Éleuthère, Que., Can.,
1,014.................B8 42
St. Elias, mts., N.A......C11 47
St. Elmo, Ill., 1,503......D5 58
Ste. Émélie [-de-l'Energie],
Que., Can., 721.......C4 42
St. Ephrem, Que., Can.,
898...................C7 42
St. Esprit, Que., Can.,
778...................D4 42
St. Étienne, Fr., 201,242
(*290,000)...........E6 5
St. Eustache, Que., Can.,
5,463.............D4, p19 42
St. Fabien, Que., Can.,
1,466.................A9 42
St. Felicien, Que., Can.,
5,133.................A5 42
St. Félix-de-Valois,
Que., Can., 1,399......C4 42
St. Ferdinand, Que.,
Can., 2,706...........C6 42
St. Flavien, Que., Can.,
610...................C6 42
Ste. Flore, Que., Can.,
622...................C5 42
St. Flour, Fr., 5,846.....E5 5
Ste. Foy, Que., Can.,
29,716................C6 42
St. Francis, Kans., 1,800..C2 61
St. Francis, Wis., 10,065..E2 88
St. François [-du-Lac],
Que., Can., 977.......C5 42
St. Francisville, Ill., 1,040..E6 58
St. Francisville, La., 1,661..D4 63
St. Francois, co., Mo.,
36,516................D7 69
St. Fulgence, Que., Can.,
1,094.................A7 42
St. Gabriel [-de-Brandon],
Que., Can., 3,425......C4 42
St. Gallen, see Sankt
Gallen, Switz.
St. Gaudens, Fr., 7,949....F4 5
Ste. Genevieve, Mo.,
4,443.................D7 69
Ste. Genevieve, co., Mo.,
12,116................D7 69
Ste. Geneviève-de-
Pierrefonds, Que.,
Can., 2,397..........*D4 42
St. George, Austl., 2,231..E8 25
St. George, N.B., Can.,
1,133.................D3 43
St. George, Ont., Can.,
791...................D4 41
St. George, Mo., 1,323...*C7 69
St. George, S.C., 1,833...E6 82
St. Georges, Que., Can.,
1,775.................C5 42
St. George's, Grenada,
7,303................J14 35
St. Georges [-de-Windsor],
Que., Can., 345.......D6 42
St. Georges-Ouest,
Que., Can., 4,755.....*C7 42
St. Gérard, Que., Can.,
662...................D6 42
St. Germain,
[-de-Grantham],
Que., Can., 1,015.....D5 42
St. Germain-en-Laye, Fr.,
34,621................g9 5
St. Gervais, Que., Can.,
576...................C7 42
St. Gilles, Que., Can.,
822...................C6 42

St. Gilles-du-Gard, Fr.,
4,791.................F6 5
St. Girons, Fr., 7,368....F4 5
St. Helena, Calif., 2,722..A5 50
St. Helena, dep., Afr.,
5,200................H20 2
St. Helena, par., La.,
9,162.................D5 63
St. Helens, Eng., 107,500..*D5 4
St. Helens, Oreg., 5,022..B4 80
St. Helier, Jersey, 26,500..F5 4
St. Henry, Ohio, 978.....B1 78
St. Hilaire Est, Que.,
Can., 2,911...........D4 42
St. Hyacinthe, Que., Can.,
22,354................D5 42
St. Hyacinthe, co.,
Que., Can., 22,354....D4 42
St. Ignace, Mich., 3,334..C6 66
St. Jacobs, Ont., Can.,
669...................D4 41
St. Jacques, Que., Can.,
2,038.................D4 42
St. James, Man., Can.,
33,977................E3 40
St. James, Minn.,
4,174.................G4 67
St. James, Mo., 2,384....D6 69
St. James, N.Y., 5,500....F4 52
St. James, par., La.,
18,369................D5 63
St. Jean, Que., Can.,
26,988................D4 42
St. Jean, co., Que., Can.,
38,470................D4 42
St. Jean-Baptiste, Man.,
Can., 521.............E3 40
St. Jean-D'Angély, Fr.,
8,660.................E3 5
St. Jean-de-Dieu, Que.,
Can., 1,177...........A9 42
St. Jean-de-Luz, Fr.,
10,241................F3 5
St. Jean-de-Matha, Que.,
Can., 846.............C4 42
St. Jean-Eudes, Que.,
Can., 2,873..........*A7 42
St. Jérôme, Que., Can.,
24,546................D3 42
Saint John, N.B., Can.,
55,153 (*95,563).......D3 43
St. John, Ind., 1,128.....B3 59
St. John, Kans., 1,753....E5 61
St. John, co., N.B., Can.,
89,251................D4 43
St. John's, Antigua,
21,396...............H14 35
St. Johns, Ariz., 1,310...B4 48
St. John's, Newf., Can.,
63,633 (*90,838).......E5 44
St. Johns, Mich., 5,629...F6 66
St. Johns, Mo., 7,342....*C7 69
St. Johns, co., Fla.,
30,034................B5 54
St. Johnsbury, Vt., 6,809..C3 73
St. Johnsville, N.Y.,
2,193................*B6 75
St. John the Baptist, par.,
La., 18,439...........D5 63
St. Joseph, Ill., 1,210....C5 58
St. Joseph, La., 1,653....C4 63
St. Joseph, Mich.,
11,755................F4 66
St. Joseph, Minn., 1,487..E4 67
St. Joseph, Mo., 79,673...B3 69
St. Joseph, co., Ind.,
238,614...............A5 59
St. Joseph, co., Mich.,
42,332................G5 66
St. Joseph-de-Beauce,
Que., Can., 2,484......C7 42
St. Joseph-de-Sorel,
Que., Can., 3,588.....*D4 42
St. Joseph-de-St.
Hyacinthe, Que., Can.,
3,799................*D5 42
St. Jovite, Que., Can.,
2,692.................C3 42
St. Junien, Fr., 8,449.....E4 5
St. Kitts-Nevis-Anguilla,
Br., dep., N.A.,
56,591...........G13, H13 35
St. Lambert, Que., Can.,
14,531...............p19 42
St. Landry, par., La.,
81,493................D3 63
St. Laurent, Man., Can.,
869...................D3 40
St. Laurent, Que., Can.,
49,805...............p19 42
St. Lawrence, Newf.,
Can., 2,095...........E4 44
St. Lawrence, Pa., 929...*F10 81
St. Lawrence, co., N.Y.,
111,239...............A6 75
St. Lawrence, co., N.A...G20 36
St. Léonard, N.B., Can.,
1,666.................B2 43

St. Léonard [-de-Noblat],
Fr., 3,671............E4 5
St. Lô, Fr., 17,137......C3 5
St. Louis, Mich., 3,808...E6 66
St. Louis, Sen., 48,800....E1 22
St. Louis (Independent
City), Mo., 675,000
(*2,255,000).........C37 69
St. Louis, co., Minn.,
231,588...............C6 67
St. Louis, co., Mo.,
703,532...............C7 69
St. Louis Park, Minn.,
48,021...............n12 67
St. Lucie, co., Fla.,
39,294................E6 54
St. Maixent-l' École, Fr.,
7,068.................D3 5
St. Malo, Fr., 17,137.....C2 5
St. Mandé, Fr., 24,325....g10 5
St. Marc, Hai., 9,401.....E7 35
St. Marc [-des-Carrières],
Que., Can., 2,622......C5 42
Ste. Marie, Que., Can.,
181...................C6 42
St. Maries, Idaho, 2,435..B2 57
St. Martin, par., La.,
29,063................D4 63
St. Martinville, La.,
6,468.................D4 63
St. Mary, par., La.,
48,833................E4 63
St. Mary, peak, Austl.....*F6 25
St. Mary-of-the-Woods,
Ind., 800.............E3 59
St. Marys, Ont., Can.,
4,482.................D3 41
St. Marys, Ga., 3,272....F5 55
St. Marys, Ind., 1,100....A5 59
St. Marys, Kans., 1,509...C7 61
St. Marys, Ohio, 7,737...B3 78
St. Marys, Pa., 8,065....D4 81
St. Marys, W. Va.,
2,443.................B3 87
St. Marys, co., Md.,
38,915................D4 53
St. Matthews, Ky.,
8,738.............A4, B4 62
St. Matthews, S.C., 2,433..D6 82
St. Maur-des-Fossés, Fr.,
70,397...............g10 5
St. Maurice, co., Que.,
Can., 109,873.........C4 42
St. Michael, Minn., 707...E5 67
St. Michael, Pa., 1,292...*E4 81
St. Michaels, Md., 1,484..C5 53
St. Michel, Que., Can.,
55,978...............p19 42
St. Nazaire, Fr., 58,286...D2 5
St. Noël, Que., Can.,
1,124...............*G20 36
St. Norbert, Man., Can.,
695...................E3 40
St. Omer, Fr., 19,283.....B5 5
St. Ouen, Fr., 51,956.....g10 5
St. Pacôme, Que., Can.,
1,242.................B8 42
St. Pamphile, Que., Can.,
1,839.................C8 42
St. Paris, Ohio, 1,460....B2 78
St. Pascal, Que., Can.,
2,144.................B8 42
St. Paul, Alta., Can.,
2,823.................B5 38
St. Paul, Minn.,
313,411...........E5, n12 67
St. Paul, Nebr., 1,714....C7 71
St. Paul, Va., 1,156......f9 85
St. Paulin, Que., Can.,
920...................C4 42
St. Paul Park, Minn.,
5,111.............F5, n12 67
St. Pauls, N.C., 2,249....C4 76
St. Peter, Minn., 8,484...F5 67
St. Peter Port, Guernsey,
15,700................F5 4
St. Petersburg, Fla.,
200,000 (*420,000)..E4, p10 54
St. Petersburg Beach,
Fla., 6,268..........p10 54
St. Pie, Que., Can., 1,434..D5 42
St. Pierre, Mart., 5,436..I14 35
St. Pierre-Jolys, Man.,
Can., 856.............E3 40
St. Pierre & Miquelon,
Fr. dep., N.A., 4,990...E3 44
St. Pol-de-Léon, Fr.,
6,037.................C2 5
St. Pourçain [-sur-Sioule],
Fr., 3,182............D5 5
St. Prosper, Que., Can.,
158...................C7 42
St. Quentin, N.B., Can.,
2,089.................B2 43
St. Quentin, Fr., 61,071...C5 5
St. Raphaël, Que., Can.,
1,134.................C7 42
St. Raphaël, Fr., 9,470....F7 5

St. Raymond, Que., Can., 3,931 . . . . .C6 42
St. Regis Park, Ky., 1,179 . .B4 62
St. Rémi, Que., Can., 2,276 . . . . .D4, q19 42
St. Romuald, Que., Can., 5,681 . . . . .C6, n17 42
Ste. Rosalie, Que., Can., 1,255 . . . .*D5 42
Ste. Rose, Que., Can., 7,571 . . . .*D4 42
Ste. Rose, Guad., 2,237 . . .H14 35
St. Rose, La., 1,099 . . . . . . .k11 63
Ste. Rose-de-Lima, Que., Can., 2,965 . . . . .D2 42
Ste. Rose-du-Dégelé, Que., Can., 1,943 . . . . . .B9 42
Ste. Rose-du-Lac, Man., Can., 790 . . . . .D2 40
Saintes, Fr., 25,717 . . . . . . .E3 5
St. Sauveur [-des-Monts], Que., Can., 1,702 . . . . . .D3 42
Ste. Savine, Fr., 11,864 . . . .C5 5
St. Servan [-sur-Mer], Fr., 14,963 . . . . .C3 5
St. Siméon, Que., Can., 1,197 . . . . .B8 42
St. Simons Island, Ga., 3,199 . . . . .E5 55
St. Stephen, N.B., Can., 3,380 . . . . .D2 43
St. Stephen, S.C., 1,462 . . . .E8 82
St. Tammany, par., La., 38,643 . . . . .D5 63
Ste. Thérèse-de-Blainville, Que., Can., 11,771 . . . . .D4, p19 42
St. Thomas, Ont., Can., 22,469 . . . . .E3 41
St. Tite, Que., Can., 3,250 . . . . .C5 42
St. Ulric, Que., Can., 1,021 . . . .*k13 42
St. Vincent-de-Paul, Que., Can., 11,214 . . . . .*D4 42
St. Walburg, Sask., Can., 689 . . . . .D1 39
St. Yrieix-la-Perche, Fr., 4,368 . . . . .E4 5
Saintonge, former prov., Fr., 286,000 . . . . .E3 5
Saitama, pref., Jap., 3,014,983 . . . .*I9 18
Sajama, mtn., Bol. C2 29
Sakai, Jap., 466,412 . . . . . .o14 18
Sakāka, Sau. Ar. D3 15
Sakania, Con. K., 12,100 . .C5 24
Sakashita, Jap., 3,100 . . . . .n16 18
Sakata, Jap., 63,000 . . . . . .G9 18
Sakchu, Kor., 13,568 . . . . . .F2 18
Sakhalin, isl., Sov. Un. D17 16
Sakon Nakhon, Thai., 15,997 . . . . .B2 19
Sakti, India, 8,125 . . . . .D7 20
Sala, Swe., 11,000 . . .H7, t34 11
Sala Consilina, It., 6,897 . . .D5 9
Saladillo, Arg., 7,586 . . . . . .B5 28
Salado, riv., Arg. A3 28
Salamà, Guat., 2,760 . . . . .*D7 34
Salamanca, Mex., 32,663 . . . . .m13 34
Salamanca, N.Y., 8,480 . . . .C2 75
Salamanca, Sp., 90,498 . . . .B3 8
Salamanca, prov., Sp., 405,729 . . . .*B3 8
Salamina, Col., 14,263 . . . . .B2 32
Salamis, Grc., 11,161 . . . . .*D4 14
Salas, Sp., 2,522 . . . . .A2 8
Salaverry, Peru, 3,403 . . . . .C2 31
Salcedo, Ec., 3,442 . . . . .B2 31
Saldanha, S. Afr., 2,243 . . .G3 24
Saldus, Sov. Un., 10,000 . . .C4 12
Sale, Austl., 7,899 . . . . .I6 26
Salé, Mor., 75,799 . . . . .B3 22
Salekhard, Sov. Un., 16,567 . . . . .C9 13
Salem, Ill., 6,165 . . . . .E5 58
Salem, India, 249,145 . . . . . .F6 20
Salem, Ind., 4,546 . . . . .G5 59
Salem, Mass., 39,211 . .A6, f12 65
Salem, Mo., 3,870 . . . . .D6 69
Salem, N.H., 6,500 . . . . .F5 73
Salem, N.J., 8,941 . . . . .D2 74
Salem, N.Y., 1,076 . . . . .B7 75
Salem, Ohio, 13,854 . . . . . . .B5 78
Salem, Oreg., 49,142 . .C4, k12 80
Salem, S. Dak., 1,188 . . . . . .G8 77
Salem, Utah, 920 . . . . .D2 72
Salem, Va., 16,058 . . . . .C2 85
Salem, W. Va., 2,366 . . . . .B4, B6 87
Salem, co., N.J., 58,711 . . . .D2 74
Salem Depot, N.H., 2,523 . .F5 73
Salem Heights, Oreg., 10,770 . . . .*C4 80
Salemi, It., 13,300 . . . . .F4 9
Salerno, It., 125,700 . . . . . .D5 9
Salford, Eng., 152,600 . . . . .D5 4

Salgotarjan, Hung., 31,626 . . . . .A4 10
Salida, Calif., 1,109 . . . . . .*D3 50
Salida, Colo., 4,560 . . . . . . .C5 51
Salies-de-Béarn, Fr., 2,859 . . . . .F3 5
Salihli, Tur., 24,100 . . . . . .*C7 14
Salin, Bur., 5,000 . . . .*D9 20
Salina, Kans., 43,202 . . . . . .D6 61
Salina, Okla., 972 . . . . .A6 79
Salina, Utah, 1,618 . . . . .B6 72
Salinas, Calif., 52,207 . . . . .D3 50
Salinas, P.R., 3,666 . . . . . .*G11 35
Salina Springs, Ariz., 200 . .A4 48
Saline, Mich., 2,334 . . . . . . .F7 66
Saline, co., Ark., 28,956 . . . .C3 49
Saline, co., Ill., 26,227 . . . . .F5 58
Saline, co., Kans., 54,715 . . .D6 61
Saline, co., Mo., 25,148 . . . .B4 69
Saline, co., Nebr., 12,542 . . .D8 71
Salineville, Ohio, 1,898 . . . .B5 78
Salisbury, Eng., 35,600 . . . . .E6 4
Salisbury, Md., 16,302 . . . . .D6 53
Salisbury, Mass., 1,000 . . . . .A6 65
Salisbury, Mo., 1,787 . . . . . . .B5 69
Salisbury, N.C., 21,297 . . . .B2 76
Salisbury, Rh., 220,000 . . . .D6 24
Salisbury West, N.C., 1,323 . . . .*B2 76
Sallisaw, Okla., 3,351 . . . . . .B7 79
Salmon, Idaho, 2,944 . . . . . .D5 57
Salmon Arm, B.C., Can., 1,506 . . . . .D8 37
Salmon Falls, N.H., 1,210 . .E6 73
Salo, Fin., 11,000 . . . . . . .G10 11
Salon-de-Provence, Fr., 17,267 . . . . .F6 5
Salonta, Rom., 16,276 . . . . .B5 10
Salsk, Sov. Un., 18,500 . . .H13 12
Salsomaggiore, It., 8,600 . . .B2 9
Salta, Arg., 108,000 . . . . . . .D2 29
Salta, prov., Arg., 412,652 . . . . .D2 29
Saltillo, Mex., 98,839 . . . . . .B4 34
Salt Lake, co., Utah, 383,035 . . . . .A5 72
Salt Lake City, Utah, 190,000 (*498,000) . .A6, C2 72
Salto, Braz., 12,643 . . . . . .m8 30
Salto, Ur., 57,714 . . . . .E1 30
Salto, dept., Ur., 92,600 . . .*E1 30
Saltpond, Ghana, 9,900 . . . .G4 22
Salt River, Ky., 400 . . . . .C4 62
Saltsburg, Pa., 1,054 . . . . . . .F3 81
Salt Springs, Fla., 755 . . . . .C5 54
Saltville, Va., 2,844 . . . . . . .f10 85
Saluda, S.C., 2,000 . . . . .D4 82
Saluda, co., S.C., 14,554 . . .C4 82
Saluda Gardens, S.C., 2,000 . . . .*D5 82
Salur, India, 26,111 . . . . . . .E7 20
Saluzzo, It., 11,100 . . . . .B1 9
Salvador, Braz., 630,878 . . .E7 27
Salvatierra, Mex., 14,451 . . . . .m13 34
Salween, Asia D10 20
Salween, riv., Bur. D10 20
Salyersville, Ky., 1,173 . . . . .C6 62
Salzburg, Aus., 110,500 . . . .E6 6
Salzburg, state, Aus., 347,292 . . . . .E6 6
Salzgitter, Ger., 113,300 . . .B5 6
Salzwedel, Ger., 20,700 . . . .B5 6
Samani, Jap., 3,200 . . . . . .E11 18
Samaniego, Col., 3,181 . . . .C2 32
Samar, prov., Phil., 867,994 . . . . .C7 19
Samar, isl., Phil. C7 19
Samarinda, Indon., 68,095 . . . . .F5 19
Samarkand, Sov. Un., 233,000 . . . . .F9 13
Samarra, Iraq, 8,867 . . . . . .C3 15
Sambalpur, India, 38,915 . . .D7 20
Sambas, Indon., 12,000 . . . .E3 19
Sambor, Sov. Un., 41,200 . . . . .G4 12
Samchŏk, Kor., 21,500 . . . .H4 18
Samchonpo, Kor., 31,400 . . .I4 18
Samokov, Bul., 12,784 . . . . .D6 10
Samos, prov., Grc., 52,022 . . . .*D6 14
Samoset, Fla., 4,824 . . . . . .q10 54
Sampson, co., N.C., 48,013 . . . . .B4 76
Samson, Ala., 1,932 . . . . . . .D3 46
Samsun, Tur., 87,688 . . . . .B11 14
Samtown, La., 4,008 . . . . . .*C3 63
San'ā', Yemen, 89,000 . . . . .F3 15
San Agustín, 3,250 . . . . .C2 32
San Andreas, Calif., 1,800 . .C3 50
San Andrés de Giles, Arg., 5,392 . . . . .g7 28
San Andrés Tuxtla, Mex., 20,256 . . . . .D5 34
San Angelo, Tex., 58,815 . .D2 84
San Anselmo, Calif., 11,584 . . . . .h7 50

San Antonio, Chile, 26,900 . . . . .A2 28
San Antonio, Tex., 670,000 (*820,000) . . .E3, k7 84
San Antonio de Areco, Arg., 7,436 . . . . .g7 28
San Antonio de los Baños, Cuba, 25,500 . . . . .C2 35
San Antonio Heights, Calif., 1,100 . . . .*E5 50
San Augustine, Tex., 2,584 . . . . .D5 84
San Augustine, co., Tex., 7,722 . . . . .D5 84
San Bartolomeo [in Galdo], It., 8,767 . . . .D5 9
San Benedetto del Tronto, It., 22,500 . . . . .C4 9
San Benito, Tex., 16,422 . . .F4 84
San Benito, co., Calif., 15,396 . . . . .D3 50
San Bernardino, Calif., 91,922 (460,000) . . .E5, m14 50
San Bernardino, co., Calif., 503,591 . . . . .E5 50
San Bernardo, Chile, 45,200 . . . . .A2 28
Sanborn, Iowa, 1,323 . . . . . .A2 60
Sanborn, co., S. Dak., 4,641 . . . . .G7 77
San Bruno, Calif., 29,063 . . . . .D2, h8 50
San Carlos, Arg., 809 . . . . . .C2 28
San Carlos, Calif., 21,370 . .k8 50
San Carlos, Chile, 13,600 . . .B2 28
San Carlos, Phil., 9,779 . . .o13 19
San Carlos, Ur., 13,695 . . . .E2 30
San Carlos [de Bariloche], Arg., 15,995 . . . . .C2 28
San Cataldo, It., 22,544 . . .F4 9
San Clemente, Calif., 13,167 . . . . .F5 50
San Clemente, Sp., 6,948 . . .C4 8
San Cristóbal, Dom. Rep., 16,580 . . . . .E8 35
San Cristóbal, Ven., 116,200 . . . . .B3 32
San Cristóbal de las Casas, Mex., 23,343 . . . . .D6 34
Sancti-Spíritus, Cuba, 49,000 . . . . .D4 35
Sanda, Jap., 18,800 . . . . . . .o14 18
Sandakan, Mala., 28,806 . . .D5 19
Sandefjord, Nor., 7,000 . . .p28 11
Sanders, co., Mont., 6,880 . .C1 70
Sandersville, Ga., 5,425 . . . .D4 55
Sandia, Peru, 1,482 . . . . .D4 31
San Diego, Calif., 680,000 (*1,085,000) F5, o15 50
San Diego, Tex., 4,351 . . . .F3 84
San Diego, co., Calif., 1,033,011 . . . . .F5 50
Sandikli, Tur., 9,357 . . . . . . .C8 14
Sandila, India, 18,407 . . . . .C7 20
San Dimas, Calif., 7,200 . .*F4 50
Sandoa, Con. K. B4 24
Sandomierz, Pol., 14,200 . . .C6 7
Sandoná, Col., 6,776 . . . . . .C2 32
San Donà di Piave, It., 11,100 . . . . .B4 9
Sandoval, Ill., 1,356 . . . . . . .E4 58
Sandoval, co., N. Mex., 14,201 . . . . .B5 48
Sandpoint, Idaho, 4,355 . . . .A2 57
Sandspit, B.C., Can., 466 . . . . .C2 37
Sands Point, N.Y., 2,283 . .*G2 52
Sand Springs, Okla., 7,754 . . . . .A5 79
Sandstone, Minn., 1,552 . . . .D6 67
Sandusky, Mich., 2,066 . . . .E8 66
Sandusky, Ohio, 31,989 . . . .A3 78
Sandusky, co., Ohio, 56,486 . . . . .A2 78
Sandusky South, Ohio, 4,724 . . . .*A3 78
Sandviken, Swe., 22,000 . . .G7 11
Sandwich, Ill., 4,500 . . . . . . .B5 58
Sandwich, Mass., 1,200 . . . .C7 65
Sandy, Oreg., 1,147 . . . . .B4 80
Sandy, Pa., 2,070 . . . .*D4 81
Sandy, Utah, 3,322 . . . . .D2 72
Sandy Beach, N.Y., 950 . . .*C2 75
Sandy Hook, Conn., 800 . .D3 52
Sandy Springs, Ga., 12,500 . . . . .A5 55
San Elizario, Tex., 1,064 . .o11 84
San Estanislao, Par., 10,948 . . . . .D4 29
San Felipe, Chile, 19,000 . .A2 28
San Felipe, N. Mex., 1,100 . . . . .B5, D6 48
San Felipe, Ven., 28,744 . . .A4 32
San Felíu de Guixols, Sp., 10,307 . . . . .B7 8
San Fernando, Arg., 84,000 . . . . .A5, g7 28

San Fernando, Calif., 16,093 . . . . .m12 50
San Fernando, Chile, 21,800 . . . . .A2 28
San Fernando, Phil., 4,427 . . . . .B6, n13 19
San Fernando, Phil., 33,335 . . . . .o13 19
San Fernando, Sp., 52,389 . . . . .D2 8
San Fernando, Trin., 39,830 . . . . .A5 32
San Fernando de Apure, Ven., 24,470 . . . . .B4 32
San Fernando de Atabapo, Ven., 898 . . . . .C4 32
Sanford, Fla., 19,175 . . . . . .D5 54
Sanford, Maine, 10,800 . . . .E4 64
Sanford, N.C., 12,573 . . . . .B3 76
San Francisco, Arg., 38,353 . . . . .A4 28
San Francisco, Calif., 748,000 (*4,195,000) D2, h8 50
San Francisco, Col., 1,248 . . . . .C2 32
San Francisco del Oro, Mex., 11,333 . . . . .B3 34
San Francisco del Rincón, Mex., 20,878 . . . . .m13 34
San Francisco de Macorís, Dom. Rep., 27,050 . . . . .E8 35
San Gabriel, Calif., 22,561 . . . . .m12 50
San Gabriel, Ec., 6,803 . . . .A2 31
San Gabriel Chilac, Mex., 6,211 . . . . .D5, n15 34
Sangamon, co., Ill., 146,539 . . . . .D4 58
Sanger, Calif., 9,627 . . . . . . .D4 50
Sanger, Tex., 1,190 . . . . .C4 84
Sangerhausen, Ger., 23,800 . . . . .C5 6
San Germán, P.R., 7,790 . . . .*G11 35
San Gil, Col., 18,518 . . . . . .B3 32
San Giovanni in Fiore, It., 17,400 . . . . .E6 9
Sangju, Kor., 21,600 . . . . . .H4 18
San Gorgonio, mtn., Calif. E5 50
Sanhsing, see Illan, China
San Ignacio, Par., 10,766 . .E4 29
Sanilac, co., Mich., 32,314 . . . . .E8 66
San Isidro, Arg., 196,188 . .g7 28
San Jacinto, Calif., 2,553 . .F5 50
San Jacinto, co., Tex., 6,153 . . . . .D5 84
San Javier, Chile, 8,500 . . . .B2 28
Sanjo, Jap., 55,000 . . . . .H9 18
San Joaquin, co., Calif., 249,989 . . . . .C3 50
San Jose, Ariz., 100 . . . . .C4 48
San Jose, Calif., 204,196 . . . . .D3, k9 50
San José, C.R., 101,162 . . . .F8 34
San Jose, Fla., 8,000 . . . . . . .M8 54
San Jose, Ill., 1,093 . . . . .C4 58
San José, Ur., 21,200 . . . . . .E1 30
San José, dept., Ur., 77,300 . . . .*E1 30
San José, prov., C.R., 430,300 . . . .*F8 34
San José de Feliciano, Arg., 3,721 . . . . .A5 28
San José de los Molinos, Peru, 1,221 . . . . .D2 31
San Juan, Arg., 106,564 . . .A3 28
San Juan, Colo., 100 . . . . . . .D6 51
San Juan, Dom. Rep., 21,630 . . . . .E8 35
San Juan, P.R., 432,377 (*588,805) *G11 35
San Juan, Tex., 4,371 . . . . .G2 84
San Juan, co., Colo., 849 . . . . .D3 51
San Juan, co., N. Mex., 53,306 . . . . .A4 48
San Juan, co., Utah, 9,040 . . . . .C6 72
San Juan, co., Wash., 2,872 . . . . .A2 86
San Juan, prov., Arg., 352,461 . . . . .A3 28
San Juan Bautista, Calif., 1,046 . . . .*D3 50
San Juan Bautista, Par., 9,054 . . . . .E4 29
San Juan Capistrano, Calif., 2,551 . . . . .F5 50
San Juan de los Lagos, Mex., 14,319 . . . . .m12 34
San Juan de los Morros, Ven., 28,556 . . . . .B4 32
San Juan del Río, Mex., 11,177 . . . . .m13 34
San Julián, Arg., 3,649 . . . .D3 28

Sankt Gallen, Switz., 77,400............E4 6
Sankt Gallen, canton, Switz., 327,600.......*E4 6
Sankt Pölten, Aus., 40,112...............D7 6
Sankt Veit [an der Glan], Aus., 10,950..........E7 6
San Leandro, Calif., 65,962...............h8 50
San Lorenzo, Arg., 20,920...............A4 28
San Lorenzo, Calif., 23,773...............*D2 50
San Lorenzo, P.R., 5,551................*G12 35
San Lorenzo del Escorial, Sp., 7,965..B3, o16 8
Sanlúcar, Sp., 32,580......D2 8
San Luis, Arg., 40,420.....A3 28
San Luis, Colo., 800.....D5 51
San Luis, Cuba, 15,700....D6 35
San Luis, prov., Arg., 174,251.............A3 28
San Luis de la Paz, Mex., 8,361.........m13 34
San Luis Obispo, Calif., 20,437...............E3 50
San Luis Obispo, co., Calif., 81,044...........E3 50
San Luis Potosí, Mex., 159,980............C4, k13 34
San Luis Potosí, state, Mex., 1,048,297....C4, k13 34
San Manuel, Ariz., 4,600...............*C3 48
San Marco [in Lamis], It., 19,014.............D5 9
San Marcos, Tex., 12,713............E4, h8 84
San Marino, Calif., 13,658.............m12 50
San Marino, country, Eur., 17,000.............C4 9
San Martín, Arg., 20,466..A3 28
San Martín (General San Martín), Arg., 279,213.............g7 28
San Martin, Calif., 1,162................*D3 50
San Martín, dept., Peru, 120,913.............C2 31
San Mateo, Calif., 69,870..h8 50
San Mateo, Ven., 1,849....B5 32
San Mateo, co., Calif., 444,387............D2 50
San Miguel, Sal., 40,432...E7 34
San Miguel, co., Colo., 2,944...............D2 51
San Miguel, co., N. Mex., 23,468.............B6 48
San Miguel de Allende, Mex., 14,891........m13 34
San Miguel de Tucumán, Arg., 271,546........F4 27
San Nicolás, Arg., 47,728..A4 28
San Nicolás Totolapan, Mex., 3,924..........h9 34
Sannois, Fr., 16,490.....g10 5
Sano, Jap., 49,000 (68,931▲).........m18 18
Sanok, Pol., 18,300.......D7 7
San Onofre, Col., 10,737...B2 32
San Pablo, Calif., 19,687..*D2 50
San Patricio, co., Tex., 45,021.............E4 84
San Pedro, Arg., 6,105....D3 29
San Pedro, Arg., 15,354............A5, f7 28
San Pedro, Par., 16,691....D4 29
San Pedro, Tex., 7,634....*F4 84
San Pedro, dept., Par., 91,000.............D4 29
San Pedro de las Colonias, Mex., 26,018........B4 34
San Pedro de Lloc, Peru, 5,286...............C2 31
San Pedro de Macorís, Dom. Rep., 21,820....E9 35
San Pedro Mártir, mts., Mex..................A1 34
San Pedro Sula, Hond., 58,632.............D7 34
Sanpete, co., Utah, 11,053.............B6 72
San Rafael, Arg., 46,599...A3 28
San Rafael, Calif., 20,460...........D2, h7 50
San Rafael, mts., Calif....E4 50
San Ramon, Peru, 1,275...D2 31
San Ramon, Ur., 5,672....g9 28
San Remo, It., 47,200.....C1 9
San Roque, Sp., 13,676....D3 8
San Saba, Tex., 2,728....D3 84
San Saba, co., Tex., 6,381...............D3 84
San Salvador, Sal., 255,744............E7 34

San Salvador de Jujuy, Arg., 44,188..........F4 27
San Sebastián, P.R., 4,019................*G11 35
San Sebastián, Sp., 135,149.............A4 8
San Sepolcro, It., 7,242....C4 9
San Severo, It., 49,800....D5 9
Sansom Park Village, Tex., 4,175..........*C4 84
Sans Souci, S.C., 7,000...*B3 82
Santa, Peru, 1,089.......C2 31
Santa Ana, Calif., 100,350...........F5, n13 50
Santa Ana, Mex., 5,934...A2 34
Santa Ana, Sal., 72,839...E7 34
Santa Ana, mts., Calif....n13 50
Santa Anita, Mex., 15,263..h9 34
Santa Anna,Tex., 1,320....D3 84
Santa Barbara, Braz., 13,571.............m8 30
Santa Barbara, Calif., 58,768.............E4 50
Santa Bárbara, Mex., 15,846.............B3 34
Santa Barbara, co., Calif., 168,962............E3 50
Santa Catalina, isl., Calif................F4 50
Santa Catarina, state, Braz., 2,146,909.......D2 30
Santa Clara, Calif., 58,880............D2, k9 50
Santa Clara, Cuba, 115,300.............C4 35
Santa Clara, Ur., 2,499....E2 30
Santa Clara, co., Calif., 642,315.............D3 50
Santa Cruz, Bol., 67,000...C3 29
Santa Cruz, Calif., 25,596.............D2 50
Santa Cruz, C.R., 3,849....E7 34
Santa Cruz, co., Ariz., 10,808.............D3 48
Santa Cruz, co., Calif., 84,219.............D2 50
Santa Cruz, prov., Arg., 52,853.............D3 28
Santa Cruz de la Palma, Sp., 8,835..........m13 8
Santa Cruz de la Zarza, Sp., 5,588..........C4 8
Santa Cruz del Sur, Cuba, 4,200..........D5 35
Santa Cruz de Tenerife, Sp., 133,100........m13 8
Santa Cruz de Tenerife, prov., Sp., 490,655....*m13 8
Santa Cruz do Rio Pardo, Braz., 13,789........C3 30
Santa Cruz do Sul., Braz., 18,898.............D2 30
Santa Elena, Tex., 250...F3 84
Santa Eugenia [de Ribeira], Sp., 4,543....A1 8
Santa Eulalia del Río, Sp., 7,564...........C6 8
Santa Fe, Arg., 208,350.............A4 28
Santa Fé, Cuba, 11,900...D2 35
Santa Fe, Mex., 9,032.....h9 34
Santa Fe, N. Mex., 33,394............B6, D6 48
Santafé, Sp., 8,387.......D4 8
Santa Fe, co., N. Mex., 44,970.............B5 48
Santa Fe, prov., Arg., 1,865,537............A4 28
Santa Fe Springs, Calif., 16,342.............F4 50
Santai, China, 24,000....E6 17
Santa Inés Ahuatempan, Mex., 3,649..........n14 34
Santa Isabel, Equat. Gui., 11,098.............H6 22
Santa Isabel, P.R., 4,712................*G11 35
Santa Lucía, Cuba, 1,969..D6 35
Santa Lucia, Ur., 12,647...E1 30
Santa Margarita, Calif., 1,000...............E3 50
Santa Maria, Braz., 78,682.............D2 30
Santa Maria, Calif., 20,027.............E3 50
Santa Maria [Capua Vetere], It., 30,024.....D5 9
Santa Maria Colotepec, Mex., 2,054..........D5 34
Santa María del Oro, Mex., 4,227..........B3 34
Santa Marta, Col., 104,471.............A3 32
Santa Marta, Sp., 5,142...C2 8
Santa Monica, Calif., 83,249.............m12 50
Santana, Port., 4,953.....h12 8
Santander, Col., 11,426....C2 32

Santander, Sp., 118,435....A4 8
Santander, dept., Col., 1,001,213...........B3 32
Santander, prov., Sp., 432,132............*A4 8
Santanoni, peak, N.Y.....A6 75
Santañy, Sp., 6,295......C7 8
Santa Paula, Calif., 13,279.............E4 50
Santaquin, Utah, 1,183....B6 72
Santarém, Braz., 24,924...D5 27
Santarém, Port., 16,449...C1 8
Santa Rita, Braz., 20,623...............*D7 27
Santa Rita, Guam, 1,630...*F6 2
Santa Rita, N. Mex., 1,700...............C4 48
Santa Rosa, Arg., 23,458...B4 28
Santa Rosa, Calif., 41,615..C2 50
Santa Rosa, N. Mex., 2,220...............B6 48
Santa Rosa, co., Fla., 29,547.............G2 54
Santa Rosa de Copán, Hond., 7,946.........*E7 34
Santa Rosa, de Osos, Col., 6,860..........B2 32
Santa Rosalia, Mex., 5,361...............B2 34
Santa Susana, Calif., 2,310...............*E4 50
Santa Tomé de Guayana, Ven., 75,000........B5 32
Santa Úrsula Coapa, Mex., 4,830..........h9 34
Santa Venetia, Calif., 3,000...............*D2 50
Santa Vitória do Palma, Braz., 8,224.........E2 30
Santee, Calif., 9,000......o16 50
Santiago, Braz., 15,140...D2 30
Santiago, Chile, 646,500...A2 28
Santiago, Dom. Rep., 85,640.............E8 35
Santiago, Mex., 702......C3 34
Santiago, Pan., 8,746.....B1 32
Santiago, Par., 7,834.....E4 29
Santiago, sp., 37,916.....A1 8
Santiago, prov., Chile, 2,436,398............A2 28
Santiago, mts., Tex.......D1 84
Santiago, peak, Calif.....n14 50
Santiago, peak, Tex.......E1 84
Santiago de Cao, Peru, 957................C2 31
Santiago de Cuba, Cuba, 248,100............D6 35
Santiago del Estero, Arg., 80,000.............E3 29
Santiago del Estero, prov., Arg., 477,156........E3 29
Santiago Ixcuintla, Mex., 11,017........C3, m11 34
Santiago Tepalcatlalpan, Mex., 4,174..........h9 34
Santisteban, del Puerto, Sp., 8,678..........C4 8
Santo Amaro, Braz., 17,226.............*E7 27
Santo Angelo, Braz., 25,415.............D2 30
Santo Antônio, Braz., 2,978...............*E7 27
Santo Domingo, Dom. Rep., 369,980........E9 35
Santo Domingo Pueblo, N. Mex., 900........B5 48
San Tomas, Calif., 1,500...............*D3 50
Santoña, Sp., 9,082......A4 8
Santos, Braz., 262,048...........C3, m8 30
Santos Dumont, Braz., 20,414...........C4, g6 30
Santo Tomás, Peru, 877...D3 31
Santo Tomas, Ven., 100...B5 32
San Valentín, mtn., Chile................H3 27
San Vicente, Sal., 15,433..E7 34
San Vicente de Alcántara, Sp., 8,212..........C2 8
San Vincente del Caguán, Col., 1,764..........C3 32
San Vito al Tagliamento, It., 5,065...........B4 9
San Ygnacio, Tex., 800....F3 84
São Bernardo [do Campo], Braz., 61,645...........C3, m8 30
São Borja, Braz., 20,339...D1 30
São Carlos, Braz., 50,010...........C3, m8 30
São Cristovão, Braz., 7,624..............*E7 27
São Francisco, riv., Braz.................A4 30
São Francisco do Sul, Braz., 11,593..........D3 30

São Gabriel, Braz., 22,967...............E2 30
São João da Boa Vista, Braz., 25,226........C3, k8 30
São João del Rei, Braz., 34,654...........C4, g5 30
São João Nepomuceno, Braz., 9,436.......C4, g6 30
São José do Rio Pardo, Braz., 14,186.........k8 30
São José do Rio Prêto, Braz., 66,476........C3 30
São José dos Campos, Braz., 55,349......C3, m9 30
São Leopoldo, Braz. 41,023.............D2 30
São Lourenço, Braz., 14,680.............C3 30
São Luís, Braz., 124,606...D6 27
São Luís Gonzaga, Braz., 12,926............D2 30
São Manuel, Braz., 10,009...........C3, m7 30
Saône-et-Loire, dept., Fr., 535,772.........*D6 5
São Paulo, Braz., 3,825,351.......C3, m8 30
São Paulo, state, Braz., 12,974,699......C3, m8 30
São Roque, Braz., 12,409..m8 30
São Sebastião do Paraíso, Braz., 14,451.......C3 30
São Tomé & Principe, Port. dep., Afr., 63,676..H6 22
São Vicente, Braz., 73,578.............C3 30
São Vicente, Port., 6,663..h11 8
Sapai, Grc., 2,589.......*B5 14
Saposoa, Peru, 3,243......C2 31
Sapozhok, Sov. Un., 10,000.............E13 12
Sapphire, mts., Mont......D3 70
Sappington, Mo., 15,000...f13 69
Sapporo, Jap., 794,908...E10 18
Sapri, It., 6,188.........D5 9
Sapulpa, Okla. 14,282....B5 79
Sara Buri, Thai., 18,861..*C2 19
Sarah, Miss., 125........A3 68
Sarajevo, Yugo., 143,117............D4 10
Sara Kaeo, Thai........*C2 19
Saraland, Ala., 4,595.....E1 46
Saranac, Mich., 1,081....F5 66
Saranac, N.Y., 600.......f11 75
Saranac Lake, N.Y., 6,421..............B3 75
Saranap, Calif., 6,450....*D2 50
Sarandí del Yí, Ur., 4,437..............E1 30
Sarandi Grande, Ur., 4,539..............E1 30
Saransk, Sov. Un., 124,000............D15 12
Sarapul, Sov. Un., 78,000.............D8 12
Sarasota, Fla., 34,083..........E4, q10 54
Sarasota, co., Fla., 76,895.............E4 54
Saratoga, Calif., 14,861..*D3 50
Saratoga, Tex., 900......D5 84
Saratoga, Wyo., 1,133....E6 89
Saratoga, co., N.Y., 101,345............B7 75
Saratoga Place, Va., 1,478..............*D6 85
Saratoga Springs, N.Y., 17,288............B7 75
Saratov, Sov. Un., 644,000............F15 12
Saravane, Laos, 25,000...*B3 19
Sarawak, reg., Mala., 819,800............E4 19
Saraykoy, Tur., 6,984....D7 14
Sarcelles, Fr., 35,885.....g10 5
Sarcoxie, Mo., 1,056.....D3 69
Sardegna, pol. dist., It., 1,419,362.........*E2 9
Sardinia, Ohio, 799......C2 78
Sardinia, isl., It.........D2 9
Sardis, Ala., 300.........C3 46
Sardis, B.C., Can., 898...f14 37
Sardis, Miss., 2,098......A4 68
Sardis, Ohio, 500........C5 78
Sarepta, La., 737........B2 63
Sargent, Nebr., 876......C6 71
Sargent, co., N. Dak., 6,856..............D8 77
Sarikamis, Tur., 17,529..B14 14
Sariwon, Kor., 42,957....G2 18
Sarlat, Fr., 5,251........E4 5
Sarmiento, mtn., Chile....I3 27
Sarnia, Ont., Can., 50,976............E2 41
Sarny, Sov. Un., 10,000...F6 12
Saronno, It., 25,190......B2 9
Sarospatak, Hung., 9,610..A5 10
Sarpsborg, Nor., 13,300...p29 11

Sarpy, co., Nebr., 31,281..C9 71
Sarreguemines, Fr.,
  17,866...............C7   5
Sartell, Minn., 791......E4 67
Sartène, Fr., 4,067......D2   9
Sarthe, dept., Fr.,
  443,019.............*D4   5
Sartrouville, Fr., 31,267....g9   5
Sarufusu, Jap., 4,100....D11 4
Sarvar, Hung., 11,021....B3 10
Sarzana, It., 8,600......B2   9
Sasaram, India, 37,782....D7 20
Sasebo, Jap., 247,069....J4 18
Saskatchewan, prov., Can.,
  925,181.................39
Saskatchewan, riv., Can...F13 36
Saskatoon, Sask., Can.,
  95,526...........E2, n7 39
Sasovo, Sov. Un.,
  26,000.............D13 12
Sassafras, mtn., S.C......A2 82
Sassari, It., 94,200......D2   9
Satah, mtn., B.C., Can....C5   9
Satanta, Kans., 686......E3 61
Saticoy, Calif., 2,500.....E4 50
Satka, Sov. Un., 45,500....D8 13
Satoraljaujhely, Hung.,
  16,197..............A5 10
Satsuma, Ala., 1,491.....E1 46
Sattahip, Thai., 4,478...*C2 19
Satu-Mare, Rom., 60,800..B6 10
Saucillo, Mex., 6,842.....B3 34
Sauda, Nor., 5,723......H2 11
Saudi Arabia, country,
  Asia, 6,750,000.......D3 15
Saugatuck, Mich., 927....F4 66
Saugerties, N.Y., 4,353...C7 75
Saugor, India, 85,491.....D6 20
Saugus, Mass.,
  23,000...........B5, g11 65
Sauk, co., Wis., 36,179....E4 88
Sauk Centre, Minn.,
  3,573...............E4 67
Sauk City, Wis., 2,095....E4 88
Sauk Rapids, Minn.,
  4,570...............E4 67
Sauk Village, Ill., 5,774...*B6 58
Saukville, Wis., 1,038....E6 88
Sault-au-Mouton, Que.,
  Can., 876............A8 42
Sault Ste. Marie, Mich.,
  18,722..............B6 66
Sault Ste. Marie, Ont.,
  Can., 43,088.........p18 41
Saumur, Fr., 20,773......D4   5
Saunders, co., Nebr.,
  17,270..............C9 71
Sauquoit, N.Y., 1,715...*B5 75
Sausalito, Calif.,
  5,331............D2, h8 50
Sava, Yugo............C4 10
Savage, Md., 1,400......B4 53
Savage, Minn.,
  1,603............F5, n11 67
Savanna, Ill., 4,950......A3 58
Savanna, Okla., 620......C6 79
Savanna-la-Mar, Jam.,
  9,783...............E4 35
Savannah, Ga., 134,000
  (*196,000)...........D5 55
Savannah, Mo., 2,455.....B3 69
Savannah, N.Y., 655......B4 75
Savannah, Tenn., 4,315....B3 83
Savannah Beach, Ga.,
  1,385...............D6 55
Saveni, Rom., 6,470......B8 10
Saverne, Fr., 9,056......C7   5
Savigliano, It., 14,800....B1   9
Savoie, dept., Fr.,
  266,678.............*F3   5
Savona, B.C., Can., 532...D7 37
Savona, It., 75,100......B2   9
Savona, N.Y., 904......C3 75
Savonlinna, Fin., 14,700..G13 11
Savoy (Savoie), former
  prov., Fr., 546,000.....E7   5
Savran, Sov. Un., 10,000..G8 12
Sawahlunto, Indon.,
  12,295..............F2 19
Sawan Khalok, Thai.,
  7,873...............B1 19
Sawbill Landing, Minn.,
  100................C7 67
Sawhāj, Eg., U.A.R.,
  48,300..............C4 23
Sawtooth, mts., Idaho.....E3 57
Sawyer, Mich., 300......G4 66
Sawyer, co., Wis., 9,475...C2 88
Sawyerville, Que., Can.,
  789................D6 42
Sawyerwood, Ohio,
  5,400..............*A4 78
Saxapahaw, N.C., 600....B3 78
Saxis, Va., 577........C7 85
Saxon, S.C., 1,700......B4 82
Saxony, reg., Ger.......C6   6
Saxonburg, Pa., 876.....E2 81
Saxton, Pa., 977.......F5 81

Sayabec, Que., Can.,
  2,314..............*G20 36
Sayán, Peru, 1,229......D2 31
Saybrook, Ill., 859......C5 58
Sayhūt, S. Arabia.......F5 15
Sayre, Ala., 950.......B3 46
Sayre, Okla., 2,913.....B2 79
Sayre, Pa., 7,917......C9 81
Sayreton, Ala., 900....C3, E4 46
Sayreville, N.J., 22,553....C4 74
Sayula, Mex.,
  11,616..........D4, n12 34
Sayville, N.Y., 12,000....G4 52
Scafell Pikes, mtn., Eng....C4   4
Scalp Level, Pa., 1,455....F4 81
Scandia, Kans., 643.....C6 61
Scanlon, Minn., 1,126....D6 67
Scansano, It., 8,560......C3   9
Scapegoat, mtn., Mont....C4 70
Scappoose, Oreg., 923....B4 80
Scarboro, Maine, 800
  (6,418▲)..........E2, g7 64
Scarborough, Ont., Can...m15 41
Scarborough, Eng.,
  41,900..............C6   4
Scarbro, W. Va., 900......D7 87
Scarsdale, N.Y., 18,345...h13 75
Sceaux, Fr., 19,024......g10   5
Schaefferstown, Pa., 800...F9 81
Schaffhausen, Switz.,
  36,300 (*56,200).......E4   6
Schaffhausen, canton,
  Switz., 33,200.......*E4   6
Schaghticoke, N.Y., 720...C7 75
Schaller, Iowa, 896......B2 60
Schaumburg, Ill., 3,296...h8 58
Schefferville, Que., Can.,
  3,178...............h13 42
Schenectady, N.Y.,
  81,682..............C7 75
Schenectady, co., N.Y.,
  152,896.............C6 75
Schererville, Ind., 3,347...B3 59
Schertz, Tex., 2,281.....h7 84
Schiedam, Neth., 81,400..B6   5
Schiller Park, Ill., 8,610...k9 58
Schiltigheim, Fr., 25,081...C7   5
Schio, It., 28,298......B3   9
Schivelbein, see Świdwin,
  Pol.
Schleicher, co., Tex.,
  2,791...............D2 84
Schleswig, Ger., 33,800...A4   6
Schleswig, Iowa, 863.....B2 60
Schleswig-Holstein, reg.,
  Ger................A4   6
Schleswig-Holstein, state,
  Ger., 2,438,800.......A4   6
Schley, co., Ga., 3,256....D2 55
Schlüchtern, Ger., 5,800...C4   6
Schmalkalden, Ger.,
  14,000..............C5   6
Schneidemuhl, see Pila,
  Pol.
Schofield, Wis., 3,038....D4 88
Schoharie, N.Y., 1,168....C6 75
Schoharie, co., N.Y.,
  22,616..............C6 75
Schönebeck, Ger.,
  44,900..............B5   6
Schongau, Ger., 8,800....E5   6
Schoolcraft, Mich., 1,205..F5 66
Schoolcraft, co., Mich.,
  8,953...............B4 66
Schooley, mtn., N.J......B3 74
Schramberg, Ger., 18,100..D4   6
Schram City, Ill., 698....D4 58
Schriever, La., 650....E5, k10 63
Schrobenhausen, Ger.,
  8,700...............D5   6
Schroon Lake, N.Y., 800...B7 75
Schulenburg, Tex., 2,207...E4 84
Schuyler, Nebr., 3,096....C8 71
Schuyler, co., Ill., 8,746...C3 58
Schuyler, co., Mo., 5,052...A5 69
Schuyler, co., N.Y.,
  15,044..............C4 75
Schuylerville, N.Y., 1,233..B7 75
Schuylkill, co., 173,027...E9 81
Schuylkill Haven, Pa.,
  6,470...............E9 81
Searsport, Maine, 900
  (1,838▲)............D4 64
Schwabach, Ger., 23,700..D5   6
Schwäbisch Gmünd, Ger.,
  40,100..............D4   6
Schwäbisch Hall, Ger.,
  21,900..............D4   6
Schwandorf, Ger., 16,100..D6   6
Schwaner, mts., Indon....F4 19
Schwaz, Aus., 9,455.....E5   6
Schwedt, Ger., 5,961....B7   6
Schweinfurt, Ger., 57,700..C5   6
Schwenningen, Ger.,
  31,700..............D4   6
Schwerin, Ger., 93,800...B5   6
Schwyz, Switz., 11,007...E4   6
Schwyz, canton, Switz.,
  78,048.............*E4   6
Sciacca, It., 25,000.....F4   9

Scio, Ohio, 1,135.......B4 78
Scioto, co., Ohio, 84,216...D2 78
Sciotodale, Ohio, 800....*D2 78
Scituate, Maine, 4,000
  (11,214▲).......B6, h13 65
Scobey, Mont., 1,726.....B11 70
Scotch Plains, N.J.,
  18,491..............B4 74
Scotia, Calif., 1,122.....B1 50
Scotia, N.Y., 7,625......C7 75
Scotland, Ont., Can., 612..D4 41
Scotland, S. Dak., 1,077...G8 77
Scotland, co., Mo.,
  6,484...............A5 69
Scotland, co., N.C.,
  25,183..............C3 76
Scotland, reg., U.K.,
  5,178,490............B4   4
Scotland Neck, N.C.,
  2,974...............A5 76
Scotlandville, La.,
  21,000............D4, g9 63
Scotstown, Que., Can.,
  1,038...............D6 42
Scott, La., 902.........D3 63
Scott, co., Ark., 7,297....C1 49
Scott, co., Ill., 6,377....D3 58
Scott, co., Ind., 14,643...G6 59
Scott, co., Iowa, 119,067..C7 60
Scott, co., Kans., 5,228...D3 61
Scott, co., Ky., 15,376...B5 62
Scott, co., Minn., 21,909..F5 67
Scott, co., Miss., 21,187..C4 68
Scott, co., Mo., 32,748...D8 69
Scott, co., Tenn., 15,413..C9 83
Scott, co., Va., 25,813....f9 85
Scott, mtn., Idaho......E3 57
Scott, mtn., Okla.......C3 79
Scott, mtn., Oreg.......E4 80
Scott, peak, Idaho......E6 57
Scott City, Kans., 3,555...D3 61
Scott City, Mo., 1,963....D8 69
Scottdale, Ga., 9,175...*B5 55
Scottdale, Pa., 6,244....F2 81
Scotts, mtn., N.J.......B2 74
Scottsbluff, Nebr., 13,377..C2 71
Scotts Bluff, co., Nebr.,
  33,809..............C2 71
Scottsboro, Ala., 6,449...A3 46
Scottsburg, Ind., 4,806...G6 59
Scottsdale, Ariz.,
  54,504............C3, D2 48
Scottsville, Ky., 3,324....D3 62
Scottsville, N.Y., 2,045...B3 75
Scottville, Mich., 1,245...E4 66
Scranton, Iowa, 865.....B3 60
Scranton, Kans., 576....D8 61
Scranton, Pa.,
  103,500
  (*208,000)......D10, m18 81
Scranton, S.C., 613......D8 82
Screven, Ga., 1,010.....E4 55
Screven, co., Ga., 14,919..D5 55
Scribner, Nebr., 1,021....C9 71
Scunthorpe, Eng., 68,900..D6   4
Scurry, co., Tex., 20,369...C2 84
Seaboard, N.C., 624.....A5 76
Sea Bright, N.J., 1,138...C5 74
Seabrook, Md., 3,000...*C4 53
Seabrook, N.J., 1,900....E2 74
Seabrook, Tex., 950.....r14 84
Sea Cliff, N.Y., 5,669....F2 52
Seadrift, Tex., 1,082....E4 84
Seaford, Del., 4,430.....C6 53
Seaford, N.Y., 20,000....G3 52
Seaford, Va., 1,100.....h15 85
Seaforth, Ont., Can.,
  2,255...............D3 41
Sea Girt, N.J., 1,798.....C4 74
Seagoville, Tex., 3,745...n10 84
Seagraves, Tex., 2,307...C1 84
Sea Isle City, N.J., 1,393..E3 74
Seal Beach, Calif., 6,994..*F5 50
Seal Cove, N.B., Can.,
  549................E3 43
Sealevel, N.C., 500.....C6 76
Sealy, Tex., 2,328......E4 84
Seaman, Ohio, 714......D2 78
Searcy, Ark., 7,272.....B4 49
Searcy, co., Ark., 8,124...I3 49
Seaside, Calif., 19,353...*D3 50
Seaside, Oreg., 3,877....B3 80
Seaside Heights, N.J.,
  954................D4 74
Seaside Park, N.J., 1,054..D4 74
Seat Pleasant, Md.,
  5,365............C4, f9 53
Seattle, Wash., 560,000
  (*1,050,000)....B3, e11 86
Seaview, Wash., 600....C1 86
Sebastian, Fla., 698.....E6 54
Sebastian, co., Ark.,
  66,685..............B1 49
Sebastopol, Calif., 2,694...C2 50
Sebeka, Minn., 823......D3 67
Sebeș, Rom., 11,628.....C6 10

Sebewaing, Mich., 2,026...E7 66
Sebinkarahisar, Tur.,
  8,747..............B12 14
Sebnitz, Ger., 14,800....C7   6
Sebree, Ky., 1,139......C2 62
Sebring, Fla., 6,939.....E5 54
Sebring, Ohio, 4,439.....B4 78
Sebringville, Ont., Can.,
  520................D3 41
Secane, Pa., 2,000.....*B11 81
Secaucus, N.J., 12,154....h8 74
Sechura, Peru, 3,826.....C1 31
Sector Popular, Mex.,
  18,089..............h9 34
Secunderabad, India,
  187,471.............E6 20
Security, Colo., 13,500....C6 51
Sedalia, Mo., 23,874....C4 69
Sedan, Fr., 20,336......C6   5
Sedan, Kans., 1,677.....E7 61
Sedgefield, N.C., 1,000..*A3 76
Sedgewick, Alta., Can.,
  655................C5 38
Sedgwick, Kans.,
  1,095...........E6, g12 61
Sedgwick, co.,
  Colo., 4,242.........A8 51
Sedgwick, co.,
  Kans., 343,231.......E6 61
Sedro Woolley, Wash.,
  3,705...............A3 86
Seekonk, Mass., 8,399...C5 65
Seeley, Calif., 700......F6 50
Seeley Lake, Mont., 500..C3 70
Seelyville, Ind., 1,114....F3 59
Segorbe, Sp., 7,538.....C5   8
Ségou, Mali., 28,000....F3 22
Segovia, Sp., 33,360....B3   8
Segovia, prov., Sp.,
  195,602.............*B3   8
Segré, Fr., 5,203.......D3   5
Seguin, Tex., 14,299...E4, h8 84
Sehwan, Pak., 3,827.....C4 20
Seiling, Okla., 910......A3 79
Seinäjoki, Fin., 15,800...F10 11
Seine, dept., Fr.,
  5,646,446..........C5, g1   5
Seine-et-Marne, dept.,
  Fr., 524,486........*C5   5
Seine-et-Oise, dept., Fr.,
  2,298,931..........*C5   5
Seine-Maritime, dept., Fr.,
  1,035,844...........C4   5
Seis de Septiembre, Arg.,
  344,041.............g7 28
Seixal, Port., 4,125.....f9   8
Seki, Jap., 4,000......o15 18
Sekondi-Takoradi, Ghana,
  123,300.............H4 22
Selah, Wash., 2,824.....C5 86
Selangor, state, Mala.,
  1,276,200...........E2 19
Selanovtsi, Bul., 7,259...D7 10
Selb, Ger., 19,200......C6   6
Selby, S. Dak., 979.....E5 77
Selbyville, Del., 1,080...D7 53
Selden, N.Y., 1,604...*E3 75
Sélestat, Fr., 13,818....C7   5
Selidovka, Sov. Un.,
  10,000..............q20 12
Selinsgrove, Pa., 3,948...E8 81
Selkirk, Man., Can.,
  8,576...............D3 40
Selkirk, Scot., 5,600...*C5   4
Selkirk, co., Scot., 5,634..*C5   4
Selle, Pic la, peak, Hai...E8 35
Sellersburg, Ind., 3,007...H6 59
Sellersville, Pa., 2,497...F11 81
Selma, Ala., 28,385.....C2 46
Selma, Calif., 7,173.....D4 50
Selma, Ind., 562.......D7 59
Selma, N.C., 3,197......B4 76
Selmer, Tenn., 1,897....B3 83
Selvas, reg., Braz.....*D4 27
Selwyn, mtn., B.C., Can..B6 37
Semarang, Indon.,
  487,006.............G4 19
Sembilan, state, Mala.,
  466,300............*E2 19
Semenovka, Sov. Un.,
  9,000...............E9 12
Semeru, mtn., Indon......G4 19
Seminole, Ala., 200......E2 46
Seminole, Fla., 1,500...*E4 54
Seminole, Okla., 11,464...B5 79
Seminole, Tex., 5,737....C1 84
Seminole, co., Fla.,
  54,947..............D5 54
Seminole, co., Ga., 6,802..F2 55
Seminole, co., Okla.,
  28,066..............B5 79
Semipalatinsk, Sov. Un.,
  188,000............D11 13
Semnān, Iran, 29,036...A8 23
Senador Pompeu, Braz.,
  8,210..............*D7 27
Senath, Mo., 1,369......E7 69

Senatobia, Miss., 3,259....A4 68
Sendai, Jap., 480,925....G10 18
Sendai (Kagoshima, Perf.)
 Jap., 32,000............K5 18
Seneca, Ill., 1,719........B5 58
Seneca, Kans., 2,072.....C7 61
Seneca, Mo., 1,478........E3 69
Seneca, Pa., 950..........D2 81
Seneca, S.C., 5,547.......B2 82
Seneca, co., N.Y., 31,984...C4 75
Seneca, co., Ohio, 59,326..A2 78
Seneca, mtn., N.Y..........C2 75
Seneca Falls, N.Y., 7,439...C4 75
Seneca Gardens, Ky.,
 928................*H6 62
Sengel, country, Afr.,
 3,400,000............F2 22
Senftenberg, Ger., 21,000..C7 6
Senhor do Bonfim, Braz.,
 13,958..............*E7 27
Senigallia, It., 16,700.....C4 9
Senlis, Fr., 9,371.........C5 5
Senneterre, Que., Can.,
 3,246................B2 42
Sens, Fr., 20,015.........C5 42
Senta, Yugo., 24,987......C5 10
Sentinel, Okla., 1,154.....B2 79
Sentinel, peak, B.C., Can..B6 37
Seoul (Sŏul), Kor.,
 3,470,900............H3 18
Sept Îles (Seven Islands),
 Que., Can., 14,196....h13 42
Sequatchie, co., Tenn.,
 5,915................D8 83
Sequim, Wash., 1,164....A2 86
Sequoia, Calif., 3,300.....D4 50
Sequoyah, co., Okla.,
 18,001...............B7 79
Serafimovich, Sov. Un.,
 8,800................G14 12
Seraing, Bel., 41,239......B6 5
Serang, Indon., 11,163.....G3 19
Serbia, reg., Yugo........D5 10
Serbia, rep., Yugo.,
 7,642,227............*D5 10
Serdobsk, Sov. Un.,
 10,000...............E15 12
Sered, Czech., 6,208......D4 7
Seremban, Mala.,
 52,091...............E2 19
Sergeant Bluff, Iowa, 813..B1 60
Sergipe, state, Braz.,
 760,273.............*E7 27
Seria, Bru., 17,595........E4 19
Seringapatam, India,
 11,423...............F6 20
Serón, Sp., 7,091.........D4 8
Serov, Sov. Un.,
 104,000..............D9 13
Serowe, Bots., 34,100.....E5 24
Serpa, Port., 7,273........D2 8
Serpukhov, Sov. Un.,
 113,000..............D11 12
Serrai, Grc., 40,063.......B4 14
Serrai, prov., Grc.,
 248,041.............*B4 14
Serra Talhada, Braz.,
 12,164..............*D7 27
Serrinha, Braz., 10,284...*E7 27
Sesser, Ill., 1,764.........E4 58
Sesto [Fiorentino], It.,
 22,453...............C3 9
Sestri Levante, It., 9,100..B2 9
Sestroretsk, Sov. Un.,
 34,000...............A8 12
Setana, Jap., 3,500.......E9 18
Setauket, N.Y., 1,500......F4 52
Sète (Cette), Fr., 36,301...F5 5
Sete Lagoas, Braz., 36,302..B4 30
Seth, W. Va., 800.....C3, D6 87
Seth Ward, Tex., 1,328....*B2 84
Sétif, Alg., 93,561........A6 22
Seto, Jap., 86,424.....I8, n16 18
Settat, Mor., 29,617.......B3 22
Setúbal, Port., 44,435.....C1 8
Sevastopol, Sov. Un.,
 169,000..............I9 12
Seven Devils, mts., Idaho..D2 57
Seven Harbors, Mich.,
 2,000...............*F7 66
Seven Hills, Ohio, 5,708..*A4 78
Seven Mile, Ohio, 690.....C1 78
Sevenoaks, Eng., 17,700..m13 4
Severn, Md., 900..........B4 53
Severna Park, Md.,
 3,500................B4 53
Sevier, co., Ark., 10,156..D1 49
Sevier, co., Utah, 10,565..B6 72
Sevierville, Tenn., 2,890..D10 83
Sevilla, Col., 26,757......C2 32
Sevilla (Seville), Sp.,
 442,300..............D3 8
Sevilla (Seville), prov.,
 Sp., 1,234,435.......*D3 8
Seville, Fla., 623.........C5 54
Seville, Ohio, 1,190......A4 78

Sevlievo, Bul., 9,856.......D7 10
Sevran, Fr., 17,969........g11 5
Sèvres, Fr., 20,129........g9 5
Sewanee, Tenn., 1,464....B6 83
Seward, Alsk., 1,891..C10, g17 47
Seward, Nebr., 4,208.....D8 71
Seward, co., Kans.,
 15,930...............E3 61
Seward, co., Nebr.,
 13,581...............D8 71
Sewaren, N.J., 1,500......k7 74
Sewell, Ky., 265..........C6 62
Sewell, N.J., 1,700........D2 74
Sewickley, Pa., 6,157..E1, h13 81
Sewickley Heights, Pa.,
 931.................*E1 81
Sexsmith, Alta., Can., 531..B1 38
Seychelles, Br. dep., Afr.,
 47,000..............G24 2
Seymour, Conn., 10,100...D4 52
Seymour, Ind., 11,629.....G6 59
Seymour, Iowa, 1,117.....D4 60
Seymour, Mo., 1,046......D5 69
Seymour, Tex., 3,789......C3 84
Seymour, Wis., 2,045...D5, g9 88
Seymourville, La., 1,000...h9 63
Sezimbra, Port., 6,957.....C1 8
Sezze, It., 7,544..........D4 9
Sfax, Tun., 65,645........B7 22
Sfîntul-Gheorghe, Rom.,
 17,638...............C7 10
's Gravenhage,
 see The Hague, Neth.
Shabbona, Ill., 690.......B5 58
Shackelford, co., Tex.,
 3,990................C3 84
Shady Cove, Oreg., 875...E4 80
Shady Side, Md., 900.....C4 53
Shadyside, Ohio, 5,028...C5 78
Shaft (William Penn),
 Pa., 850............*E9 81
Shafter, Calif., 5,312......E4 50
Shahjahanpur, India,
 110,432 (*117,702).....C6 20
Shāhrūd, Iran, 17,058.....B6 15
Shaker Heights, Ohio,
 36,460............A4, n9 78
Shakhty, Sov. Un.,
 201,000.............H13 12
Shakopee, Minn.,
 6,294.............F5, n11 67
Shalimar, Fla., 754.......u15 54
Shallowater, Tex., 1,001..C2 84
Shām, Jabal ash, mtn.,
 Mus. & Om...........D2 20
Shamokin, Pa., 13,674....E8 81
Shamokin Dam, Pa.,
 1,093...............E8 81
Shamrock, Fla., 600......C3 54
Shamrock, Tex., 3,113....B2 84
Shandaken, N.Y., 500....C6 75
Shangchiu, China,
 134,400.............E8 17
Shanghai, China,
 6,900,000...........E9 17
Shannon, Ga., 1,629.....B1 55
Shannon, Ill., 766.......A4 58
Shannon, co., Mo., 7,087..D6 69
Shannon, co., S. Dak.,
 6,000...............G3 77
Shannontown, S.C.,
 7,064..............*D7 82
Shansi, prov., China,
 15,960,000..........D7 17
Shantung, prov., China,
 54,030,000..........D8 17
Shaohsing, China, 130,600..E9 17
Shaoyang, China, 117,700..F7 17
Sharasume (Chenghwa),
 China, 25,000........B2 17
Shari, Jap., 9,500........E12 18
Sharkey, co., Miss.,
 10,738..............C3 68
Sharon, Mass.,
 10,070...........B5, h11 65
Sharon, Pa., 25,267......D1 81
Sharon, Tenn., 966.......A3 83
Sharon, Wis., 1,167......F5 88
Sharon Hill, Pa., 7,123...p20 81
Sharon Park, Ohio, 800...n12 78
Sharon Springs, Kans.,
 966.................D2 61
Sharonville, Ohio, 6,457..n13 78
Sharpes, Fla., 700........D6 54
Sharpsburg, Md., 861.....B2 53
Sharpsburg, Pa., 6,096...k14 81
Sharpsville, Ind., 663.....D5 59
Sharpsville, Pa., 6,061....D1 81
Sharptown, Md., 620......C6 53
Shasi, China, 85,800......E7 17
Shasta, co., Calif., 59,468..B3 50
Shasta, mtn., Calif........B2 50
Shastsk, Sov. Un., 10,000..D13 12
Shattuck, Okla., 1,625....A2 79
Shaunavon, Sask., Can.,
 2,154...............H1 39
Shavertown, Pa., 2,000...*B8 81

Shaw, Miss., 2,062........B3 68
Shawano, Wis., 6,103.....D5 88
Shawbridge, Que., Can.,
 1,034...............D3 43
Shawinigan, Que., Can.,
 32,169 (*63,518).....C5 42
Shawinigan-Sud, Que.,
 Can., 12,683........C5 43
Shawmut, Ala., 1,898.....C4 46
Shawnee, Kans., 9,072....B8 61
Shawnee, Ohio, 1,000.....C3 78
Shawnee, Okla., 24,326...B5 79
Shawnee, co., Kans.,
 141,286.............D8 61
Shawneetown, Ill., 1,399...F5 58
Shawville, Que., Can.,
 1,534...............B8 41
Shchelkovo, Sov. Un.,
 66,000..............n18 12
Shchetovo, Sov. Un.,
 10,000..............q22 12
Shchigry, Sov. Un.,
 10,000..............F11 12
Shchors, Sov. Un., 10,000..F8 12
Sheartown, Newf., Can.,
 680................*E5 44
Sheboygan, Wis.,
 45,747...........E5, k10 88
Sheboygan, co., Wis.,
 86,484..............E6 88
Sheboygan Falls, Wis.,
 4,061............E5, k10 88
Shediac, N.B., Can.,
 2,159...............C5 43
Sheep, mtn., Wyo.........B5 89
Sheep, mtn., Wyo.........C2 89
Sheeps Heaven, mtn.,
 Mass...............A1 65
Sheerness, Eng., 13,700...E7 4
Sheet Harbour, N.S.,
 Can., 883...........E7 43
Sheffield, Ala., 13,491....A2 46
Sheffield, Eng., 495,300
 (*735,000)..........D6 4
Sheffield, Ill., 1,078......B4 58
Sheffield, Iowa, 1,156.....B4 60
Sheffield, Ohio, 1,664.....A3 78
Sheffield, Pa., 1,971......C3 81
Sheffield Lake, Ohio,
 6,884..............*A3 78
Shefford, co., Que., Can.,
 54,963..............D5 42
Sheila, N.B., Can., 553....B5 43
Shelagyote, peak, B.C.,
 Can................B4 37
Shelbiana, Ky., 500.......C7 62
Shelbina, Mo., 2,067.....B5 69
Shelburn, Ind., 1,299.....F3 59
Shelburne, N.S., Can.,
 2,408...............F4 43
Shelburne, Ont., Can.,
 1,239...............C4 41
Shelburne, co., N.S., Can.,
 15,208..............F4 43
Shelburne Falls, Mass.,
 2,097...............A2 65
Shelby, Ind., 500.........B3 59
Shelby, Iowa, 533........C2 60
Shelby, Mich., 1,603......E4 66
Shelby, Miss., 2,384......B3 68
Shelby, Mont., 4,017......B5 70
Shelby, Nebr., 613........C8 71
Shelby, N.C., 16,941......B1 76
Shelby, Ohio, 9,106.......B3 78
Shelby, co., Ala., 32,132..B3 46
Shelby, co., Ill., 23,404...D5 58
Shelby, co., Ind., 34,093...E6 59
Shelby, co., Iowa, 15,825..C2 60
Shelby, co., Ky., 18,493...B4 62
Shelby, co., Mo., 9,063....B5 69
Shelby, co., Ohio, 33,586..B1 78
Shelby, co., Tenn.,
 627,019.............B2 83
Shelby, co., Tex., 20,479..D5 84
Shelby City, Ky., 350......C5 62
Shelby Village, Mich.,
 1,900..............*F7 66
Shelbyville, Ill., 4,821.....D5 58
Shelbyville, Ind., 14,744..F6 59
Shelbyville, Ky., 4,525....B4 62
Shelbyville, Mo., 657.....B5 69
Shelbyville, Tenn., 10,466..B5 83
Sheldon, Ill., 1,137.......C6 58
Sheldon, Iowa, 4,251.....A2 60
Shell Beach, Calif., 1,820..*E3 50
Shellbrook, Sask., Can.,
 1,042...............D2 39
Shell Camp, Tex., 500....*C5 84
Shelley, Idaho, 2,612.....F6 57
Shell Lake, Wis., 1,016....C2 88
Shellman, Ga., 1,050......E2 55
Shellman Bluff, Ga.,
 150.................E5 55
Shell Rock, Iowa, 1,112...B5 60
Shellsburg, Iowa, 625.....B6 60
Shelter Island, N.Y., 550..m16 75
Shelton, Conn., 18,190...D4 52
Shelton, Nebr., 904.......D7 71

Shelton, Wash., 5,651....B2 86
Shenandoah, Iowa, 6,567..D2 60
Shenandoah, Pa., 11,073...E9 81
Shenandoah, Va., 1,839...B4 85
Shenandoah, co., Va.,
 21,825..............B4 85
Shenandoah, mtn., Va....B3 85
Shenandoah Heights, Pa.,
 1,721..............*E9 81
Shendi, Sud., 11,031......E4 23
Shenorock, N.Y., 1,600...*D7 75
Shensi, prov., China,
 18,130,000..........E6 17
Shenyang, see Mukden,
 China
Shepetovka, Sov. Un.,
 10,000..............F6 12
Shepherd, Mich., 1,293...E6 66
Shepherd Brook, mtn.,
 Maine...............B3 64
Shepherdstown, W. Va.,
 1,328...............B7 87
Shepherdsville, Ky.,
 1,525...............D4 62
Shepparton, Austl.,
 13,579..............H5 26
Sheppton, Pa., 800.......E9 81
Sherborn, Mass., 500
 (1,806▲)............h10 65
Sherbrooke, Que., Can.,
 66,554.............D6, k12 42
Sherbrooke, co., Que.,
 Can., 80,490........D5 42
Sherburn, Minn., 1,227...G4 67
Sherburne, N.Y., 1,717...C5 75
Sherburne, co., Minn.,
 12,861..............E5 67
Shereshevo, Sov. Un.,
 10,000..............B8 7
Sheridan, Ark., 1,938.....C3 49
Sheridan, Colo., 3,559....B6 51
Sheridan, Ind., 2,165.....D5 59
Sheridan, Mich., 606.....E5 66
Sheridan, Mont., 539.....E4 70
Sheridan, Oreg., 1,763....B3 80
Sheridan, Wyo., 11,651...B8 89
Sheridan, co., Kans.,
 4,267...............C3 61
Sheridan, co., Mont.,
 6,458..............B12 70
Sheridan, co., Nebr.,
 9,049...............B3 71
Sheridan, co., N. Dak.,
 4,350...............C5 77
Sheridan, co., Wyo.,
 18,989..............B5 89
Sheridan, mtn., Wyo......B2 89
Sheridan Beach, Wash.,
 1,500..............*B3 86
Sheringham, Eng., 4,600..D7 4
Sherman, N.Y., 873.......C1 75
Sherman, Tex., 24,988...C4 84
Sherman, co., Kans.,
 6,682...............C2 61
Sherman, co., Nebr.,
 5,382...............C6 71
Sherman, co., Oreg.,
 2,446...............B6 80
Sherman, co., Tex., 2,605..A2 84
Sherridon, Man., Can.,
 40..................B1 40
Sherrill, N.Y., 2,922......B5 75
's Hertogenbosch, Neth.,
 75,700..............B6 5
Sherwood, Ark., 1,846..C3, D6 49
Sherwood, Ohio, 587.....A1 78
Sherwood, Oreg., 680....h12 80
Sherwood, Tenn., 650....B6 83
Sherwood Park, Alta.,
 Can., 2,923..........C4 38
Sheshebee, Minn., 100...D5 67
Shetland, co., Scot.,
 17,500.............*g10 4
Shetland, is., Scot........g1 4
Shiawassee, co., Mich.,
 53,446..............F6 66
Shibam, S. Yem., 8,000...F4 15
Shibarghan (Shibargan),
 Afg., 22,464.........A4 20
Shibata, Jap., 39,200
 (73,992▲)...........H9 18
Shibecha, Jap., 5,100.....E12 18
Shibetsu, Jap., 15,400....D11 18
Shibetsu, Jap., 3,300.....E12 18
Shibīn al Kawm, Eg.,
 U.A.R., 47,100.......G8 14
Shickshinny, Pa., 1,843...D9 81
Shidler, Okla., 870.......A5 79
Shiga, pref., Jap., 853,385..*I8 18
Shigatse (Zhikatse)
 China, 10,000........C8 20
Shihchiachuang, China,
 126,000............*D7 17
Shikarpur, Pak., 53,910...C4 20
Shikoku, isl., Jap........J6 18
Shilka, Sov. Un., 23,000..D14 13
Shillington, Pa., 5,639....F10 81
Shillong, India, 72,438....C9 20

Shiloh, Ohio, 724........B3 78
Shiloh, Ohio, 9,500......C1 78
Shimabara, Jap., 30,800
  (44,175▲)..............J5 18
Shimada, Jap., 45,000
  (63,493▲)............o17 18
Shimane, pref., Jap.,
  821,620..............*I16 18
Shimanovsk, Sov. Un.,
  17,000................D15 13
Shimizu, Jap.,
  218,559............I9, n17 18
Shimoda, Jap., 19,800....o17 18
Shimodate, Jap., 26,300
  (51,717▲)............m18 18
Shimoga, India, 63,764...F6 20
Shimonoseki, Jap.,
  254,376................I5 18
Shimotsuma, Jap.,
  11,400...............m18 18
Shiner, Tex., 1,945......E4 84
Shinglehouse, Pa., 1,298..C5 81
Shingu, Jap., 40,051.....J7 18
Shinjo, Jap., 24,800
  (43,037▲).............G10 18
Shinkolobwe, Con. K.,
  10,900................C5 24
Shinnston, W. Va.,
  2,724.............A7, B4 87
Shinshiro, Jap., 16,600..o16 18
Shiocton, Wis., 685....D5, h8 88
Shiogama, Jap., 58,363..G10 18
Shiojiri, Jap., 18,600..m16 18
Ship Bottom, N.J., 717...D4 74
Shipman, Va., 500.......C4 85
Shippegan, N.B., Can.,
  1,631.................B5 43
Shippegan Gully, N.B.,
  Can., 761............*B5 43
Shippensburg, Pa., 6,138..F7 81
Shirane-san, mtn., Jap...H9 18
Shīrāz, Iran, 170,659....G8 16
Shīrbin, Eg., U.A.R.,
  13,293................G8 14
Shiremanstown, Pa.,
  1,212................*F8 81
Shiribeshi-yama, mtn.,
  Jap..................E10 18
Shirley, Ind., 1,038.....E6 59
Shirley, Mass., 1,850
  (5,202▲)..............A4 65
Shirley, Mont...........D11 70
Shirley, N.Y., 4,500....*n15 75
Shirley, mtn., Wyo......D6 89
Shirntoru, see Makarov,
  Sov. Un.
Shiroishi, Jap., 22,600
  (41,928▲).............G10 18
Shirotori, Jap., 4,100..n15 18
Shishido, Jap., 11,018..m19 18
Shitara, Jap., 3,400....n16 18
Shively, Ky., 15,155..A4, B4 62
Shizuoka, Jap.,
  367,705............I9, o17 18
Shizuoka, pref., Jap.,
  2,912,521............*I9 18
Shkodër (Scutari), Alb.,
  43,234................A2 14
Shkodër (Scutari), pref.,
  Alb., 150,000.........*A2 14
Shoal Lake, Man., Can.,
  774...................D1 40
Shoals, Ind., 1,022.....G4 59
Shoemakersville, Pa.,
  1,464................E10 81
Sholapur, India, 337,583...E6 20
Shore Acres, Calif.,
  3,093................*D2 50
Shore Acres, Mass., 900..h13 65
Shoreview, Minn., 7,157..*F5 67
Shorewood, Minn., 3,197..*F5 67
Shorewood, Wis.,
  15,900............E5, m12 88
Shorewood Hills, Wis.,
  2,320................*E4 88
Short Beach, Conn., 1,500..D5 52
Shortsville, N.Y., 1,382..C3 75
Shoshone, Idaho, 1,416..G4 57
Shoshone, co., Idaho,
  20,876................B3 57
Shoshoni, Wyo., 766.....C4 89
Show Low, Ariz., 1,994..B3 48
Shpola, Sov. Un., 10,000..G8 12
Shreve, Ohio, 1,617.....B3 78
Shreveport, La., 160,000
  (*260,000)............B2 63
Shrewsbury, Eng., 50,700..D5 4
Shrewsbury, Mass., 16,622..B4 65
Shrewsbury, Mo., 4,730..*C7 69
Shrewsbury, N.J., 3,222..C4 74
Shrewsbury, Pa., 943....G8 81
Shropshire, co., Eng.,
  307,100..............*D5 4
Shrub Oak, N.Y., 2,200..*D7 75
Shuangcheng, China,
  81,000................D3 18
Shuangshan, China,
  5,000.................E1 18

Shuangyang, China,
  5,000.................E2 18
Shubenacadie, N.S., Can.,
  579...................D6 43
Shuksan, mtn., Wash.....A4 86
Shulan, China, 5,000....D3 18
Shulaps, peak, B.C., Can..D6 37
Shullsburg, Wis., 1,324...F3 88
Shumen, co., Bul.,
  1,408,188............*D8 10
Shumerlya, Sov. Un.,
  26,800................D16 12
Shuya, Sov. Un., 67,000..C13 12
Shuzenji, Jap., 4,300....o17 18
Shwangliao
  (Chengchiatun), China,
  120,100...............C9 18
Shwebo, Bur., 17,842....D10 20
Shwegyin, Bur., 10,000..*B1 20
Si, riv., China.........G7 17
Sialkot, Pak., 143,889....B5 20
Siam, see Thailand, Asia
Siangtan, China, 183,600...F7 17
Sian (Hsian), China,
  1,310,000.............E6 17
Šiauliai, Sov. Un.,
  68,000................D4 12
Sibenik, Yugo., 26,253...D2 10
Sibert, Ky., 700........C6 62
Sibi, Pak., 11,842......C4 20
Sibiu, Rom., 98,400....C7 10
Sibley, Iowa, 2,852.....A2 60
Sibley, La., 595........B2 63
Sibley, co., Minn., 16,228..F4 67
Sibolga, Indon., 37,171..E1 19
Sibsagar, India, 15,106...C9 20
Sibu, Mala., 29,630.....E4 19
Sicard, La., 2,000......B3 63
Sicilia, pol. dist., It.,
  4,810,000............*F4 9
Sicily, isl., It.........F4 9
Sicily Island, La., 761...C4 63
Sicklerville, N.J., 750...D3 74
Sicuaní, Peru, 7,036....D3 31
Siderno Marina, It., 6,915..E6 9
Sidhirokastron, Grc.,
  8,177................*B4 14
Sidi-bel-Abbès, Alg.,
  105,357...............A4 22
Sidi Ifni, Ifni, 12,751..C2 22
Sidmouth, Eng., 10,000..E5 4
Sidney, B.C., Can.,
  1,558..............E6, g12 37
Sidney, Iowa, 1,057.....D2 60
Sidney, Mont., 4,564....C12 70
Sidney, Nebr., 8,004....C3 71
Sidney, N.Y., 5,157.....C5 75
Sidney, Ohio, 14,663....B1 78
Sidney Center, N.Y., 500..C5 75
Siedlce, Pol., 34,900....B7 7
Siegburg, Ger., 34,000...C3 6
Siegen, Ger., 49,500....C4 6
Siemianowice Śląskie,
  Pol., 65,200..........g10 7
Siem Reap, Camb.,
  10,200................C2 19
Siena, It., 48,200......C3 9
Sieradz, Pol., 14,400....C5 7
Siero, Sp., 30,931......A3 8
Sierpc, Pol., 11,700....B5 7
Sierra, co., Calif., 2,247..C3 50
Sierra, co., N. Mex., 6,409..C5 48
Sierra Blanca, Tex., 800..o12 84
Sierra Leone, country,
  Afr., 2,180,354.......G2 22
Sierra Madre, Calif.,
  9,732................m12 50
Sierra Nevada, mts., Calif..C3 50
Sierraville, Calif., 150..C3 50
Sierra Vieja, mts., Tex...o12 84
Sierra Vista, Ariz., 4,635..*D3 48
Sifton, Man., Can., 245..D1 40
Sighet, Rom., 22,361....B6 10
Sighişoara, Rom., 20,363..B7 10
Sigli, Indon., 3,327....k11 19
Signal, mtn., Va........g11 85
Signal Hill, Calif., 4,627..*F4 50
Signal Hill, Ill., 1,000..*E3 58
Signal Mountain, Tenn.,
  3,413.............D8, E10 83
Sigourney, Iowa, 2,387...C5 60
Siguiri, Guinea, 12,700...F3 22
Sihaus, Peru, 1,432.....C2 31
Siirt, Tur., 22,944.....D13 14
Sikar, India, 50,636....C6 20
Sikasso, Mali, 13,600...F3 22
Sikeston, Mo., 13,765...E8 69
Sikionía, Grc., 6,069...*C4 14
Sikkim, country, Asia,
  170,000...............C8 20
Silao, Mex., 24,229....m13 34
Silchar, India, 41,062...D9 20
Siler City, N.C., 4,455...B3 76
Silesia, reg., Pol......C4 7
Siletz, Oreg., 583......C3 80
Silifke, Tur., 9,843....D9 14
Siliguri, India, 65,471..C8 20
Silistra, Bul., 16,180...C8 10

Sillery, Que., Can.,
  14,109...............n17 42
Siloam Springs, Ark.,
  3,953.................A1 49
Silsbee, Tex., 6,277....D5 84
Siluria, Ala., 736......B2 46
Silva, Mo., 100........D7 69
Silva Jardim, Braz., 1,774..h6 30
Silver Bay, Minn., 3,723..C7 67
Silver Bow, co., Mont.,
  46,454................E4 70
Silver Bow Park, Mont.,
  4,798.................D4 70
Silver City, N. Mex.,
  6,972.................C4 48
Silver Creek, N.Y., 3,310..C1 75
Silverdale, Wash.,
  1,000.............B3, e10 86
Silver Grove, Ky., 1,207..A7 62
Silver Hill, Md., 1,700...f9 53
Silver Lake, Ind., 514...B6 59
Silver Lake, Mass., 150..f11 65
Silver Lake, Minn., 646..F4 67
Silver Lake, Ohio, 2,655..*A4 78
Silver Lake, Wis.,
  250...............F5, n11 88
Silver Spring, Md.,
  80,000............C3, f8 53
Silver Springs, N.Y., 792..C2 75
Silverthrone, mtn., B.C.,
  Can..................D4 37
Silvertip, mtn., Mont....C3 70
Silverton, Colo., 822....D3 51
Silverton, Idaho, 700....B3 57
Silverton, Ohio, 6,682...o13 78
Silverton, Oreg.,
  3,081.............B4, h12 80
Silverton, Tex., 1,098...B2 84
Silvia, Col., 3,180.....C2 32
Silvis, Ill., 3,973.....B3 58
Silvis Heights, Ill., 2,000..*B3 58
Silwān, Jordan, 5,000...*C3 15
Simcoe, Ont., Can., 8,754..E4 41
Simcoe, co., Ont., Can.,
  141,271...............C4 41
Simav, Tur., 6,528......C7 14
Simferopol, Sov. Un.,
  203,000...............I10 12
Simi, Calif., 2,107....*E4 50
Simití, Col., 2,825.....B3 32
Simla, India, 42,597....B6 20
Simleul-Silvaniei, Rom.,
  8,560.................B6 10
Simmesport, La., 2,125...D4 63
Simpson, N.C., 302......B5 76
Simpson, Pa., 1,500.....C11 81
Simpson, co., Ky., 11,548..D3 62
Simpson, co., Miss.,
  20,454................D4 68
Simpsonville, S.C., 2,282..B3 82
Simsbury, Conn., 3,200...B5 52
Sinaia, Rom., 9,006.....C7 10
Sinajana, Guam, 2,861...*F6 2
Sinaloa [de Leyva], Mex.,
  1,692.................B3 34
Sinaloa de Leyva, state,
  Mex., 838,404........C3 34
Sinanju, Kor., 16,493....G2 18
Sincé, Col., 10,631.....B2 32
Sincelejo, Col., 44,001..B2 32
Sinclair, Wyo., 621.....E5 89
Sinclairville, N.Y., 726..C1 75
Sind, reg., Pak.........C4 20
Sinelnikovo, Sov. Un.,
  10,000................G10 12
Sines, Port., 4,893.....D1 8
Singa, Sud., 9,436......F4 23
Singapore, Singapore,
  925,241...............E2 19
Singapore, country, Asia,
  1,820,000.............E2 19
Singaradja, Indon.,
  12,345................G5 19
Singkawang, Indon.,
  7,127.................E3 19
Sinhung, Kor., 7,583....F3 18
Sining (Hsining)
  China, 300,000........D5 17
Siniscola, It., 6,559...D2 9
Sinj, Yugo., 4,133.....D3 10
Sinkiang Uighur, prov.,
  China, 5,640,000......C2 17
Sinking Spring, Pa.,
  2,244................*F9 81
Sînnicolau-Mare, Rom.,
  9,956.................B5 10
Sinnuris, Eg., U.A.R.,
  23,537................H8 14
Sinop, Tur., 10,214.....A10 14
Sinpo, Kor., 26,086.....F4 18
Sintang, Indon., 4,474...E4 19
Sint-Niklaas, Bel., 47,819..B6 5
Sinton, Tex., 6,008.....E4 84
Sintra, Port., 7,150....f9 8
Sinŭiju, Kor., 118,414...F2 18
Sion, Switz., 16,051....E3 6
Sioux, co., Iowa, 26,375..A1 60
Sioux, co., Nebr., 2,575..B2 71

Sioux, co., N. Dak., 3,662..D5 77
Sioux Center, Iowa, 3,034..A1 60
Sioux City, Iowa, 87,000
  (*100,500)............B1 60
Sioux Falls, S. Dak.,
  65,466................G9 77
Sioux Lookout, Ont.,
  Can., 2,453..........o17 41
Sioux Rapids, Iowa, 962..B2 60
Sipes (Midway), Fla.,
  1,500................*D5 54
Sipsey, Ala., 900.......B2 46
Siracusa, It., 89,409...F5 9
Sirājganj, Pak., 47,152..D8 20
Sir Douglas, mtn., Alta.,
  Can..................D3 38
Siren, Wis., 679........C1 88
Siret, Rom., 5,664......B8 10
Siros, Grc., 14,402.....D5 14
Sirpur, India, 4,466....E6 20
Sirsa, India, 33,363....C6 20
Sir Wilfrid, mtn., Que.,
  Can..................C2 42
Sisak, Yugo., 19,238....C3 10
Siskiyou, co., Calif.,
  32,885................B2 50
Sisseton, S. Dak., 3,218..E9 77
Sister Bay, Wis., 520...C6 88
Sisters, Oreg., 602.....C5 80
Sistersville, W. Va., 2,331..B4 87
Sitapur, India, 53,884...C7 20
Sitionuevo, Col., 5,969..A3 32
Sitka, Alsk., 3,237....D12 47
Sivas, Tur., 93,368.....C11 14
Siverek, Tur., 26,134...D21 14
Sivrihisar, Tur., 7,186..C8 14
Skagit, co., Wash., 51,350..A4 86
Skamania, co., Wash.,
  5,207.................D3 86
Skanderborg, co., Den.,
  137,865..............*I3 11
Skaneateles, N.Y., 2,921..C4 75
Skara, Swe., 9,100.....H5 11
Skegness, Eng., 12,400...D7 4
Skellefteå, Swe., 22,700..E9 11
Skidmore, Tex., 700.....E4 84
Skien, Nor., 45,400
  (*72,600)..........H3, p27 11
Skierniewice, Pol.,
  23,400................C6 7
Skihist, mtn., B.C., Can..D7 37
Skikda (Philippeville),
  Alg., 87,922.........A6 22
Skokie, Ill., 67,865...A6, h9 58
Skole, Sov. Un., 5,000..D7 7
Skopin, Sov. Un., 10,000..E13 12
Skopje (Skoplje), Yugo.,
  165,529...............D5 10
Skövde, Swe., 23,900....H5 11
Skovorodino, Sov. Un.,
  26,000................D15 13
Skowhegan, Maine, 6,900
  (7,661▲)..............D3 64
Skradin, Yugo., 928.....D2 10
Skvira, Sov. Un., 10,000..G7 12
Skyland, N.C., 1,500....f10 76
Sky Manor, N.J., 900....C4 74
Slagelse, Den., 20,562...A1 7
Slamet, mtn., Indon.....G3 19
Slănic, Rom., 6,842.....C7 10
Slany, Czech., 12,000...n17 7
Slater, Iowa, 979....C4, e8 60
Slater, Mo., 2,767......B4 69
Slater, S.C., 900.......A3 82
Slatersville, R.I., 1,200..B10 52
Slatina, Rom., 13,381...C7 10
Slatington, Pa., 4,316...E10 81
Slaton, Tex., 6,568.....C2 84
Slavgorod, Sov. Un.,
  38,413................D10 13
Slavonia, reg., Yugo....C3 10
Slavonska Pozega, Yugo.,
  13,112................C3 10
Slavyanoserbsk, Sov.
  Un., 5,000...........q21 12
Slavyansk, Sov. Un.,
  86,000...........G11, q20 12
Slavyanskaya, Sov. Un.,
  83,000................I12 12
Slayton, Minn., 2,487...G3 67
Sleepy Eye, Minn., 3,492..F4 67
Sleepy Hollow, Calif.,
  1,200................*D2 50
Sleepy Hollow, Va.,
  1,200................*B5 85
Slickville, Pa., 950....*F2 81
Slidell, La., 6,356....D6, h12 63
Slide, mtn., N.Y........C6 75
Sliderock, mtn., Mont...D3 70
Slieve Donard, mtn.,
  N. Ire...............C3 4
Sligo, Ire., 13,300....C2 4
Sligo, Pa., 814.........D3 81
Sligo, co., Ire., 51,100..*C2 4
Slinger, Wis., 1,141....E5 88
Slingerlands, N.Y., 1,500..*C7 75
Slippery Rock, Pa., 2,563..D1 81
Sliven, Bul., 46,175....D8 10

Sloan, Iowa, 704.........B1 60
Sloan, N.Y., 5,493.......C2 75
Sloatsburg, N.Y., 2,820..A4 75
Slobozia, Rom., 9,632.....C8 10
Slocomb, Ala., 1,368......D4 46
Slonim, Sov. Un., 10,000..E5 12
Slope, co., N. Dak., 1,893.D2 77
Slough, Eng., 84,200..E6, k11 4
Slovakia (Slovensko), reg., Czech., 4,174,046..D5 7
Slovan, Pa., 1,018........F1 81
Slovenia, reg., Yugo......C2 10
Slovenia, rep., Yugo., 1,584,368..........*C2 10
Slupca, Pol., 5,133.......B4 7
Slupsk, Pol., 53,000......A4 7
Slutsk, Sov. Un., 5,000...s31 11
Slyudyanka, Sov. Un., 17,500..........D13 13
Smackover, Ark., 2,434....D3 49
Smederevo, Yugo., 27,104..C5 10
Smela, Sov. Un., 44,534...G8 12
Smelterville, Idaho, 1,127..B2 57
Smethport, Pa., 1,725.....C5 81
Smethwick, Eng., 68,500...D5 4
Smidovich, Sov. Un., 5,000..........B6 18
Smith, co., Kans., 7,776...C5 61
Smith, co., Miss., 14,303..C4 68
Smith, co., Tenn., 12,059..C8 83
Smith, co., Tex., 86,350...C5 84
Smith, peak, Idaho........A2 57
Smith Center, Kans., 2,339..........C5 61
Smithers, B.C., Can., 2,487..........B4 37
Smithers, W. Va., 1,696..........C3, C6 87
Smithfield, N.C., 6,315....B4 76
Smithfield, Ohio, 1,312....B5 78
Smithfield, Pa., 2,547....*E5 81
Smithfield, Pa., 939......G2 81
Smithfield, Utah, 2,512...A6 72
Smithfield, Va., 917..D6, k14 85
Smithmill, Pa., 600.......E5 81
Smith River, Calif., 500...B1 50
Smithsburg, Md., 586.....A2 53
Smiths Falls, Ont., Can., 9,603..........C8 41
Smithton, Austl., 2,693...o15 25
Smithtown, N.Y., 9,600...F4 52
Smithville, Mo., 1,254..........B3, h10 69
Smithville, Ohio, 1,024....B4 78
Smithville, Tenn., 2,348...D8 83
Smithville, Tex., 2,933....D4 84
Smock, Pa., 1,012......*G2 81
Smokey Dome, mtn., Idaho..........F4 57
Smoky, mts., Idaho........F4 57
Smoky Lake, Alta., Can., 626..........B4 38
Smolensk, Sov. Un., 170,000..........D8 12
Smooth Rock Falls, Ont., Can., 1,131..........o19 41
Smyre, N.C., 1,197......*B1 76
Smyrna, Del., 3,241......B6 53
Smyrna, Ga., 10,157...A5, C2 55
Smyrna, Tenn., 3,612.....B5 83
Smyrna, see Izmir, Tur.
Smyth, co., Va., 31,066...f10 85
Snake, riv., U.S..........B3 45
Sneads, Fla., 1,399.......B2 54
Sneads Ferry, N.C., 500...C5 76
Sneek, Neth., 21,100......A6 5
Snezhnoye, Sov. Un., 55,000..........q21 12
Snohomish, Wash., 3,894..B3 86
Snohomish, co., Wash., 172,199..........A4 86
Snoqualmie, Wash., 1,216..B4 86
Snow, mtn., Calif.........C2 50
Snow, mtn., Maine........C2 64
Snow, peak, Wash.........A7 86
Snowdon, mtn., Wales.....D4 4
Snowflake, Ariz., 1,728...B3 48
Snow Hill, Md., 2,311.....D7 53
Snow Hill, N.C., 1,043....B5 76
Snow Lake, Man., Can., 881..........B1 40
Snowshoe, peak, Mont.....B1 70
Snowyside, peak, Idaho....F4 57
Snyatyn, Sov. Un., 10,000..A7 10
Snyder, Okla., 1,663......C3 79
Snyder, Tex., 13,850......C2 84
Snyder, co., Pa., 25,922...E7 81
Soap Lake, Wash., 1,591...B6 86
Soatá, Col., 4,361........B3 32
Sobinka, Sov. Un., 10,000..........D13 12
Sobota Rimavska, Czech., 10,700........D6 7
Sobral, Braz., 32,281.....*D6 27
Socaste, S.C., 900........D9 82
Sochaczew, Pol., 17,300...B6 7
Sochi, Sov. Un., 174,000..*E6 13
Society, is., Fr. Polynesia..H10 2

Society Hill, S.C., 677.....B8 82
Socorro, Col., 13,716......B3 32
Socorro, N. Mex., 5,271....B5 48
Socorro, co., N. Mex., 10,168..........C5 48
Soc Trang, Viet., 16,890...D3 19
Socuéllamos, Sp., 14,828...C4 8
Soda Springs, Idaho, 3,456..........G7 57
Soddy, Tenn., 2,206..D8, E10 83
Söderhamn, Swe., 13,000...G7 11
Södertälje, Swe., 35,300...t35 11
Sodus, N.Y., 1,722........B3 75
Soest, Ger., 33,300.......C4 6
Sofia (Sofiya), Bul., 800,953..........D6 10
Sofiya, see Sofia, Bul.
Sofiya, co., Bul., 1,457,742.........*D6 10
Sofiyevka, Sov. Un., 10,000..........G9 12
Sogamoso, Col., 32,274....B3 32
Sogn og Fjordane, co., Nor., 100,900........*G1 11
Sointula, B.C., Can., 682..D4 37
Soissons, Fr., 23,150......C5 5
Sokal, Sov. Un., 10,000....F5 12
Sokcho, Kor., 53,600 (60,300▲)..........G4 18
Soke, Tur., 23,593........D6 14
Soke of Peterborough, co., Eng., 74,442......*D6 4
Sokol, Sov. Un., 36,000...B13 12
Sokolow, Pol., 7,515......B7 7
Sokoto, Nig., 47,643......F6 22
Solana, Fla., 1,309.......F5 54
Solana Beach, Calif., 3,000..........*F5 50
Solano, Phil., 12,095.....*B6 19
Solano, co., Calif., 134,597..........C2 50
Soldiers Grove, Wis., 663..E3 88
Soledad, Calif., 3,715.....D3 50
Soledad, Col., 37,617......A3 32
Solikamsk, Sov. Un., 82,000..........D8 13
Soliman, Tun., 6,980......F3 9
Solingen, Ger., 172,300...C3 6
Sollefteå, Swe., 9,900.....F7 11
Sóller, Sp., 6,817........C7 8
Solna, Swe., 53,700......H7 11
Solomon, Kans., 1,008....D6 61
Solomon Is., Br. dep., Oceania, 102,000......G7 2
Solon, Iowa, 604.........C6 60
Solon, Maine, 500 (669▲)..D3 64
Solon, Ohio, 6,333.......A4 78
Solonika, see Thessaloniki, Grc.
Solon Springs, Wis., 530..B2 88
Solothurn, Switz., 18,600 (*36,100)..........E3 6
Solothurn, canton, Switz., 200,816..........E3 6
Solovyevsk, Sov. Un., 10,000..........D15 13
Soltau, Ger., 14,400......B4 6
Solvang, Calif., 1,325....*E3 50
Solvay, N.Y., 8,551.......B4 75
Soma, Tur., 13,100......*C6 14
Somali Republic, country, Afr., 2,300,000........H6 23
Sombor, Yugo., 37,802....C4 10
Sombra, Ont., Can., 520..E2 41
Sombrerete, Mex., 9,289..C4 34
Somerdale, N.J., 4,839....D2 74
Somers, Conn., 850.......B7 52
Somers, Mont., 800.......B2 70
Somerset, Man., Can., 587..E2 40
Somerset, Ky., 7,112......C5 62
Somerset, Md., 1,444....*C3 53
Somerset, Mass., 12,196...C5 65
Somerset, Ohio, 1,361.....C3 78
Somerset, Pa., 6,347......F3 81
Somerset, Wis., 729.......C1 88
Somerset, co., Eng., 616,100..........*E5 4
Somerset, co., Maine, 39,749..........C2 64
Somerset, co., Md., 19,623..........D6 53
Somerset, co., N.J., 143,913..........C3 74
Somerset, co., Pa., 77,450..........G3 81
Somerset, isl., N. W. Ter., Can..........B15 36
Somerset East, S. Afr., 9,801..........G5 24
Somers Point, N.J., 4,504..E3 74
Somersworth, N.H., 8,529..E6 73
Somerton, Ariz., 2,119....C1 48
Somervell, co., Tex., 2,577..C4 84
Somerville, Mass., 94,697..........B5, g11 65
Somerville, N.J., 12,458...B3 74
Somerville, Tenn., 1,820..B2 83
Somerville, Tex., 1,177....D4 84

Somme, dept., Fr., 488,225..........C5 5
Somogy, co., Hung., 371,783..........*B3 10
Somonauk, Ill., 1,010.....B5 58
Sonchon, Kor., 22,725.....G2 18
Sønderborg, Den., 20,653..A4 6
Sønderborg, co., Den., 49,604..........*A4 6
Sonderhausen, Ger., 19,000..........C5 6
Sondrio, It., 20,200......A2 9
Songjin, see Kimchaek, Kor.
Songkhla, Thai., 31,014...D2 19
Songnim (Kyŏmipo), Kor., 53,035........G2 18
Son La, Viet., 10,000.....G5 17
Sonneberg, Ger., 28,900...C5 6
Sonobe, Jap., 8,500......n14 18
Sonoma, Calif., 3,351.....C2 50
Sonoma, co., Calif., 181,901..........C2 50
Sonora, Ariz., 1,244..C3, D3 48
Sonora, Calif., 2,725.....D3 50
Sonora, Tex., 2,619.......D2 84
Sonora, state, Mex., 783,378..........B2 34
Sonpur, India, 7,108......D7 20
Sonsón, Col., 16,955......B2 32
Sonsonate, Sal., 23,666...E7 34
Son Tay, Viet., 16,640....G6 17
Soochow (Suchou), China, 633,000........E9 17
Soperton, Ga., 2,317......D4 55
Sophia, W. Va., 1,284.....D3 87
Sopot, Pol., 45,100.......A5 7
Sopron, Hung., 43,400....B3 10
Sora, It., 9,000..........D4 9
Sorbas, Sp., 5,961........D4 8
Sorel, Que., Can., 17,147..C4 42
Sorento, Ill., 681........E4 58
Soresina, It., 9,100......B2 9
Soria, Sp., 19,301........B4 8
Soria, prov., Sp., 147,052..*B4 8
Soriano, dept., Ur., 74,000..........*E1 30
Sorø, co., Den., 129,580..*J4 11
Sorocaba, Braz., 109,999..........C3, m8 30
Soroki, Sov. Un., 15,000..G7 12
Sorong, W. Irian, 8,000...F8 19
Soroti, Ug., 6,645........H4 23
Sorrento, It..............D5 9
Sorrento, La., 1,151..D5, h10 63
Sorrento, Maine, 185....*D5 64
Sorsogon, Phil., 13,983...C6 19
Sorsogon, prov., Phil., 347,771..........*C6 19
Sortavala, Sov. Un., 16,400..........G14 11
Sor Trondelag, co., Nor., 219,200..........*F4 11
Sosnovka, Sov. Un., 10,000..........E13 12
Sosnowiec, Pol., 137,300..........C5, g10 7
Sotteville-lès-Rouen, Fr., 25,625..........C4 5
Soudan, Minn., 850.......C6 67
Souderton, Pa., 5,381....F11 81
Souflion, Grc., 6,693....*B6 14
Soufriere, St. Lucia, 2,692..........J14 35
Souk-el Arba, Tun., 6,469..........F2 9
Sŏul, see Seoul, Kor.
Soulanges, co., Que., Can., 10,075........D3 42
Sound Beach, N.Y., 1,800..........*n15 75
Soure, Braz., 6,666......*D6 27
Souris, Man., Can., 1,841..........E1 40
Souris East, P.E.I., Can., 1,537..........C7 43
Sourlake, Tex., 1,602.....D5 84
South, div., Ice., 13,416..*n21 11
South, isl., N.Z..........O12 26
South Acton, Mass., 1,100..........g10 65
South Africa, country, Afr., 17,057,000......F5 24
South Amboy, N.J., 8,422..........C4, m7 74
South America, cont., 166,127,000..........27
South Amherst, Mass., 600..........B2 65
South Amherst, Ohio, 1,657..........A3 78
Southampton, Ont., Can., 1,818..........C3 42
Southampton, Eng., 207,200..........E6 4
Southampton, N.Y., 4,833..........n16 75

Southampton, Pa., 4,500..........*F11 81
Southampton, co., Va., 19,931..........D5 85
Southampton, isl., Can...D16 36
South Apopka, Fla., 2,484..........*D5 54
South Arabia, see Southern Yemen, Asia, 758,000........G4 15
South Ashburnham, Mass., 800..........A4 65
South Australia, state, Austl., 1,090,723.....E5 25
South Barre, Mass., 800...B3 65
South Bathurst, N.S., Can., 1,390........*B4 43
South Bay, Fla., 1,631....F6 54
South Bellingham, Mass., 3,000..........B5 65
South Belmar, N.J., 1,537..........C4 74
South Belmont, N.C., 2,286..........*B1 76
South Beloit, Ill., 3,781...A4 58
South Bend, Ind., 133,000 (*272,000)..........A5 59
South Bend, Wash., 1,671..C2 86
South Bennettsville, S.C., 1,025..........*B8 82
South Berwick, Maine, 1,850..........E2 64
South Boise, Idaho, 1,530..........*F2 57
Southboro, Mass., 1,114..........B4, g9 65
South Boston (Independent City), Va., 5,974..........D4 85
South Bound Brook, N.J., 3,626..........B3 74
Southbridge, Mass., 16,523..........B3 65
South Broadway, Wash., 3,661..........*C5 86
South Brook, Newf., Can., 621........*D3 44
South Burlington, Vt., 6,903..........*C1 73
South Carolina, state, U.S., 2,382,594........82
South Charleston, Ohio, 1,505..........C2 78
South Charleston, W. Va., 19,180..........C6 87
South Chelmsford, Mass., 500..........C1 65
South Chicago Heights, Ill., 4,043..........m9 58
South China, sea, Asia...H14 16
South Cleveland, Tenn., 1,512..........*D9 83
South Clinton, Tenn., 1,356..........*C9 83
South Coatesville, Pa., 2,032..........*G10 81
South Coffeyville, Okla., 622..........A6 79
South Congaree, S.C., 650..........D5 82
South Connellsville, Pa., 2,434..........G2 81
South Corning, N.Y., 1,448..........*C3 75
South Dakota, state, U.S., 680,514..........77
South Dartmouth, Mass., 5,500..........C6 65
South Dayton, N.Y., 696...C1 75
South Daytona, Fla., 1,954..........C5 54
South Decatur, Ga., 26,000..........*C2 55
South Deerfield, Mass., 1,253..........B2 65
Sough Dennis, Mass., 600..C7 65
South Duxbury, Mass., 1,000..........B6 65
South Easton, Mass., 900..B5 65
South Elgin, Ill., 3,589..........B5, h8 58
South El Monte, Calif., 4,850..........*E5 50
Southend-on-Sea, Eng., 165,900..........E7 4
Southern Cross, Austl., 779..........F2 25
Southern Pines, N.C., 5,198..........B3 76
Southern Rhodesia, see Rhodesia
Southern Shops, S.C., 1,435..........*B4 82
Southern View, Ill., 1,485..........*D4 58
Southern Yemen, Asia, 1,146,000........G4 15
South Essex, Mass., 600...A6 65

South Euclid, Ohio,
  27,569............g9   78
South Fallsburg, N.Y.,
  1,290...............D6   75
South Farmingdale, N.Y.,
  18,000...............*E7   75
South Fayetteville, N.C.,
  3,411................*B3   76
Southfield, Mass., 150...B1   65
South Floral Park, N.Y.,
  1,090................*E7   75
South Fork, Pa., 2,053...F4   81
South Fort George, B.C.,
  Can., 1,964..........C6   37
South Fort Mitchell, Ky.,
  4,086................A7   62
South Fulton, Tenn.,
  2,512................A3   83
South Gate, Calif.,
  53,831...............n12   50
Southgate, Ky., 2,070...A7   62
Southgate, Mich.,
  29,404...............*F7   66
South Glastonbury, Conn.,
  1,000................C6   52
South Glens Falls, N.Y.,
  4,129................*B7   75
South Grafton, Mass.,
  3,000................B4   65
South Greensburg, Pa.,
  3,058................*F2   81
South Greenwood, S.C.,
  2,520................C3   82
South Hackensack, N.J.,
  1,841................*B4   74
South Hadley, Mass.,
  4,000................B2   65
South Hadley Falls, Mass.,
  8,000................B3   65
South Hamilton,
  Mass., 3,000.......A6, f12   65
South Hanover, Mass.,
  600..................h12   65
South Harriman, Tenn.,
  2,884................D9   83
South Harwich, Mass.,
  650..................C7   65
South Haven, Mich.,
  6,149................F4   66
South Hempstead, N.Y.,
  3,000................*E7   75
South Henderson, N.C.,
  2,017................*A4   76
South Hill, Va., 2,569...D4   85
South Holland, Ill.,
  14,587...............k9   58
South Holland
  (Zuidholland), prov.,
  Neth., 2,787,200....*A6   5
South Hooksett, N.H.,
  1,000................D4   73
South Houston, Tex.,
  7,523................r14   84
South Huntington, N.Y.,
  7,500................*D3   75
South Hutchinson, Kans.,
  1,672................A4   61
Southington, Conn.,
  14,000...............C5   52
South International Falls,
  Minn., 2,479.........B5   67
South Jacksonville, Ill.,
  2,654................D3   58
South Jordan, Utah,
  1,354................*A6   72
Southkent, Mich.,
  15,000...............*F5   66
South Laguna, Calif.,
  2,000................*F5   50
Southlake, Tex., 1,023...*C4   84
South Lancaster, Mass.,
  2,100................B4   65
Southland, Mich.,
  2,000................*F6   66
Southlawn, Ill., 3,000...*D4   58
South Lebanon, Ohio,
  2,720................C1   78
South Lyon, Mich.,
  1,735.............F7, p14   66
South Mansfield, La., 616..B2   63
South Miami, Fla.,
  9,846.............G6, s13   54
South Milwaukee,
  Wis., 20,307......F6, n12   88
South Modesto, Calif.,
  9,000................*D3   50
South Monroe, Mich.,
  2,919................*G7   66
Southmont, N.C., 600....B2   76
Southmont, Pa., 2,857...*F4   81
South Montrose, Pa.,
  250..................C10   81
South Mt. Vernon, Ohio,
  1,420................*B3   78
South Nelson, N.S., Can.,
  792..................*C4   43
South Nelson Village,
  B.C., Can., 939......*E9   37

South New Castle, Pa.,
  955..................*D1   81
South Nyack, N.Y.,
  3,113................g9   75
South Ogden, Utah,
  7,405.............A6, C2   72
Southold, N.Y., 1,000...m16   75
South Orange, N.J.,
  16,175...............B4   74
South Oroville, Calif.,
  3,704................*C3   50
South Paris, Maine,
  2,000................D2   64
South Park, Ill., 2,500...*B5   58
South Pasadena, Calif.,
  19,706...............*E4   50
South Patrick Shores,
  Fla., 3,000..........*D6   54
South Pekin, Ill., 1,007...C4   58
South Pittsburg, Tenn.,
  4,130................D8   83
South Plainfield, N.J.,
  17,879...............B4   74
South Point, Ohio,
  1,663................D3   78
South Porcupine, Ont.,
  Can., 5,144..........o19   41
Southport, Fla., 900....u16   54
Southport (Gold Coast),
  Austl., 33,716.......F9   25
Southport, Eng., 80,200..D5   4
Southport, Ind., 892..E5, m10   59
Southport, N.Y., 6,900...*C4   75
Southport, N.C., 2,034...D4   76
South Portland, Maine,
  22,788............E2, g7   64
South Pottstown, Pa.,
  1,850................*F10   81
South Range, Mich., 760..A2   66
South Renovo, Pa., 777....D6   81
South Revelstoke, B.C.,
  Can., 737............D8   37
South River, Ont., Can.,
  1,044................B5   42
South River, N.J.,
  13,397...............C4   74
South Rockwood, Mich.,
  1,337................*F7   66
South Roxana, Ill.,
  2,200................*E4   58
South Russell, Ohio,
  1,276................*A4   78
South St. Paul, Minn.,
  24,429............F5, n12   67
South Salisbury, N.C.,
  3,065................*B2   76
South Salt Lake, Utah,
  9,520................C2   72
South San Francisco,
  Calif., 39,418.......h8   50
South San Gabriel,
  Calif., 26,213.......*F4   50
South Shields, Eng.,
  109,100..............C6   4
South Shore, Mo., 200....f12   69
Southside Estates, Fla.,
  4,000................*B5   54
South Side Place, Tex.,
  1,282................r14   84
South Sioux City, Nebr.,
  7,200................B9   71
South Stickney, Ill.,
  25,000...............k9   58
South Streator, Ill.,
  1,923................*B5   58
South Swansea, Mass.,
  1,000................C5   65
South Taft, Calif.,
  1,910................*E4   50
South Temple, Pa.,
  1,500................*F10   81
South Toms River, N.J.,
  1,603................D4   74
South Torrington, Wyo.,
  500..................D8   89
South Trail, Fla., 5,471...q10   54
South Tucson, Ariz.,
  7,004................C3   48
South Uniontown, Pa.,
  3,603................*G2   81
South Walpole, Mass.,
  600..................h10   65
South Waverly, Pa.,
  1,382................C8   81
South Webster, Ohio,
  803..................D3   78
Southwest, Pa., 800.....F2   81
South West, div., Ice.,
  77,976...............n22   11
South West Africa, country,
  Afr., 564,000........E3   24
South Westbury, N.Y.,
  12,300...............*E7   75
Southwestern, mts., Va...B4   85
South West Fargo,
  N. Dak., 3,920.......D9   77

Southwest Greensburg,
  Pa., 3,264...........*F2   81
Southwest Harbor, Maine,
  950..................D4   64
South Whitley, Ind.,
  1,325................B6   59
Southwick, Mass., 1,400...B2   65
South Williamson, Ky.,
  1,097................C7   62
South Williamsport, Pa.,
  6,972................D7   81
South Wilmington, Ill.,
  730..................B5   58
South Windermere, S.C.,
  1,500................*F8   82
South Windham, Maine,
  1,400.............E2, g7   64
South Windsor, Conn.,
  800..................B6   52
Southwood Acres, Conn.,
  5,000................*B6   52
South Yarmouth, Mass.,
  2,100................C7   65
South Zanesville, Ohio,
  1,557................C3   78
Sovetskaya Gavan, Sov.
  Un., 49,000..........E17   13
Sovetsk, (Tilsit), Sov. Un.,
  85,900...............A6   7
Soviet Union (U.S.S.R.),
  country, Europe, Asia,
  233,000,000.........   13
Spa, Bel., 9,055.........B6   5
Spain, country, Eur.,
  31,500,000..........   8
Spalding, Eng., 15,100...D6   4
Spalding, Nebr., 683.....C7   71
Spalding, co., Ga., 35,404..C2   55
Spanaway, Wash., 3,500...B3   86
Spangler, Pa., 2,658.....E4   81
Spaniard's Bay, Newf.,
  Can., 1,289..........E5   44
Spanish, Ont., Can.,
  1,536................A2   41
Spanish Fork, Utah,
  6,472.............A6, D2   72
Spanish Sahara, dep.,
  Afr., 25,000.........D2   22
Spanish Town, Jam.,
  14,439...............F5   35
Sparkill, N.Y., 1,200....*D6   75
Sparkman, Ark., 787.....D3   49
Sparks, Ga., 1,158......E3   55
Sparks, Nev., 16,618....B2   72
Sparlingville, Mich.,
  1,877................*F8   66
Sparrows Point, Md.,
  2,800................B5   53
Sparta, Ga., 1,921......C4   55
Sparta, Ill., 3,452......E4   58
Sparta, Mich., 2,749....E5   66
Sparta, N.J., 700.......A3   74
Sparta, N.C., 1,047.....A1   76
Sparta, Tenn., 4,510....D8   83
Sparta, Wis., 6,080.....E3   88
Sparta, mtn., N.J.......B3   74
Spartanburg, S.C.,
  44,352...............B4   82
Spartanburg, co., S.C.,
  156,830..............B3   82
Sparti (Sparta), Grc.,
  10,412...............D4   14
Spassk-Dalniy, Sov. Un.,
  29,400...............E16   13
Spearfish, S. Dak., 3,682..F2   77
Spearman, Tex., 3,555....A2   84
Spearville, Kans., 602...E4   61
Speed, Ind., 800........H6   59
Speedway, Ind.,
  11,319............E5, k10   59
Speers, Pa., 1,479......*F2   81
Speight, Ky., 500.......C7   62
Spenard, Alsk., 10,000...*C10   47
Spencer, Ind., 2,557....F4   59
Spencer, Iowa, 8,864....A2   60
Spencer, Mass., 5,593...B4   65
Spencer, Nebr., 671.....B7   71
Spencer, N.Y., 879.....C4   75
Spencer, N.C., 2,904....B2   76
Spencer, Ohio, 742.....A3   78
Spencer, Okla., 1,189...*B4   79
Spencer, W. Va., 2,660...C3   87
Spencer, Wis., 897.....D3   88
Spencer, co., Ind., 16,074..H4   59
Spencer, co., Ky., 5,680...B4   62
Spencerport, N.Y., 2,676..B3   75
Spencerville, Ohio, 2,061...B1   78
Sperry, Okla., 883.....A6   79
Speyer, Ger., 40,100....D4   6
Spiceland, Ind., 863....E7   59
Spinazzola, It., 10,850...D6   9
Spindale, N.C., 4,082....B1   76
Spink, co., S. Dak., 11,706..F7   77
Spirit Lake, Idaho 693....B3   57
Spirit Lake, Iowa, 2,685...A2   60
Spirit River, Alta., Can.,
  890..................B1   38
Spiro, Okla., 1,450.....B7   79

Spišská Nová Ves, Czech.,
  16,900...............D6   7
Spittal, Aus., 10,045....E6   6
Split, Yugo., 99,462.....D3   10
Spokane, Wash., 170,000
  (*245,000)........B8, g14   86
Spokane, co., Wash.,
  278,333..............B8   86
Spoleto, It., 24,500.....C4   9
Spooner, Wis., 2,398....C2   88
Spotswood, N.J., 5,788...C4   74
Spotsylvania, co., Va.,
  13,819...............B5   85
Sprague, W. Va., 3,073...D7   87
Spray, N.C., 4,318.....A3   76
Spreckels, Calif., 800...*D3   50
Spreckelsville, Haw.,
  1,200................C5   56
Spremberg, Ger., 22,900...C7   6
Spring, Tex., 1,000.....q14   84
Spring Arbor, Mich.,
  900..................F6   66
Springboro, Ohio, 917...C1   78
Spring City, Pa., 3,162...F10   81
Spring City, Tenn., 1,800..D9   83
Springdale, Ark., 10,076..A1   49
Springdale, Newf., Can.,
  2,100................D3   44
Springdale, Ohio, 3,556...n13   78
Springdale, Pa.,
  5,602.............E2, h14   81
Springdale, S.C., 1,000...*D5   82
Springer, N. Mex., 1,564..A6   48
Springfield, Colo., 1,791..D8   51
Springfield, Fla., 4,628...v16   54
Springfield, Ill., 88,000
  (*134,000)..........D4   58
Springfield, Ky., 2,382...C4   62
Springfield, Mass.,162,000
  (*500,000)..........B2   65
Springfield, Minn., 2,701..F4   67
Springfield, Mo., 110,000
  (*122,000)..........D4   69
Springfield, Nebr.,
  506..............C9, g12   71
Springfield, N.J.,
  14,467...............B4   74
Springfield, Ohio, 81,000
  (*118,000)..........C2   78
Springfield, Oreg., 19,616..C4   80
Springfield, Pa., 26,733...*B11   81
Springfield, S.C., 787...E5   82
Springfield, S. Dak.,
  1,194................H8   77
Springfield, Tenn., 9,221..A5   83
Springfield, Vt., 6,700...E3   73
Springfield, Va., 15,000...g12   85
Springfield Place, Mich.,
  5,136................*F5   66
Spring Glen, Fla., 5,000...*B5   54
Spring Green, Wis., 1,146..E3   88
Spring Grove, Minn.,
  1,342................G7   67
Spring Grove, Pa., 1,675...G8   81
Springhill, N.S., Can.,
  5,836................D6   43
Spring Hill, Kans., 909...D9   61
Springhill, La., 6,437....A2   63
Spring Hill, Pa., 1,127...*F4   81
Spring Hope, N.C., 1,336..B4   76
Spring Lake, Mich., 2,063..E4   66
Spring Lake, N.J., 2,922..C4   74
Spring Lake, N.C., 4,110...B3   76
Spring Lake Heights, N.J.,
  3,309................C4   74
Spring Lake Park, Minn.,
  3,260................*E5   67
Springlee, Ky., 987.....*H6   62
Spring Mills, S.C., 1,069...*B6   82
Springmont, Pa., 1,000...*F10   81
Springport, Mich., 693...F6   66
Springsure, Aust., 814....B8   25
Springvale, Maine, 2,500..E2   64
Spring Valley, Calif.,
  13,200...............o16   50
Spring Valley, Ill., 5,371...B4   58
Spring Valley, Minn.,
  2,628................G6   67
Spring Valley, N.Y.,
  8,397................g12   75
Spring Valley, Ohio, 678..C1   78
Spring Valley, Tex.,
  3,004................*E5   84
Springville, Iowa, 785...B6   60
Springville, N.Y., 4,137...C2   75
Springville, Utah,
  7,913.............A6, D2   72
Spruce Knob, mtn.,
  W. Va................C5   87
Spruce Pine, N.C., 2,504..f10   76
Spur, Tex., 2,170......C2   84
Squamish, B.C., Can.,
  1,557................E6   37
Squatteck, Que., Can.,
  1,088................B9   42
Squaw Lake, Minn., 129...C4   67
Squaw Rapids, Sask.,
  Can., 1,024.........D4   39

Srbobran, Yugo., 14,392...C4 10
Sredne-Kolymsk, Sov.
  Un., 3,000............C18 13
Sremska, Mitrovica, Yugo.,
  20,790................C4 10
Sretensk, Sov. Un.,
  24,600................D14 13
Srinagar, India, 285,257...B6 20
Staatsburg, N.Y., 800.....D7 75
Stade, Ger., 30,500.......B4 6
Stafford, Eng., 49,200.....D5 4
Stafford, Kans., 1,862.....E5 61
Stafford, Tex., 1,485......*E5 84
Stafford, co., Eng.,
  1,787,300.............*D5 4
Stafford, co., Kans.,
  7,451.................D5 61
Stafford, co., Va., 16,876..B5 85
Stafford Springs, Conn.,
  3,322.................B7 52
Staffordsville, Ky., 700....C7 62
Staines, Eng., 52,400.....m11 4
Stains, Fr., 27,503........g10 5
Stambaugh, Mich., 1,876..B2 66
Stamford, Conn., 92,713...E2 52
Stamford, N.Y., 1,166.....C6 75
Stamford, Tex., 5,259.....C3 84
Stamps, Ark., 2,591.......D2 49
Stanaford, W. Va.,
  950................D3, D7 87
Stanberry, Mo., 1,409.....A3 69
Standale, Mich., 1,000....*F5 66
Standerton, S. Afr.,
  16,897................F5 24
Standish, Mich., 1,214....E7 66
Stanfield, Oreg., 745......B7 80
Stanford, Calif., 9,000....*D2 50
Stanford, Ky., 2,019.......C5 62
Stanford, Mont., 615......C6 70
Stanhope, N.J., 1,814......B3 74
Stanislaus, co., Calif.,
  157,294...............D3 50
Stanke Dimitrov, Bul.,
  19,239................D6 10
Stanley, N.C., 2,132......B1 76
Stanley, N. Dak., 1,795....B3 77
Stanley, Va., 1,039.......B4 85
Stanley, Wis., 2,014......D3 88
Stanley, co., S. Dak.,
  4,085.................F5 77
Stanleytown, Va., 500.....D3 85
Stanleyville, N.C., 1,138..*A2 76
Stanly, co., N.C., 40,873..B2 76
Stanstead, Que., Can.,
  1,116.................D5 42
Stanstead, co., Que., Can.,
  36,095................D5 42
Stanton, Calif., 11,163...*F5 50
Stanton, Del., 2,000.....*A6 53
Stanton, Mich., 1,139.....E5 66
Stanton, Nebr., 1,317.....C8 71
Stanton, Tex., 2,228.......C2 84
Stanton, co., Kans., 2,108..E2 61
Stanton, co., Nebr., 5,783..C8 71
Stantonsburg, N.C., 897...B5 76
Stanwood, Wash., 1,123....A3 86
Staples, Minn., 2,706.....D4 67
Star, N.C., 745...........B3 76
Starachowice, Pol.,
  38,100................C6 7
Staraya Russa, Sov. Un.,
  25,409................C8 12
Stara Zagora, Bul.,
  88,522................D7 10
Stara-Zagora, co., Bul.,
  821,764..............*D7 10
Starbuck, Minn., 1,099....E3 67
Star City, Ark., 1,573.....D4 49
Star City, W. Va., 1,236...B5 87
Stargard, Pol., 36,800....B3 7
Stargo, Ariz., 1,075.......C4 48
Stark, co., Ill., 8,152.....B4 58
Stark, co., N. Dak.,
  18,451................D3 77
Stark, co., Ohio, 340,345..B4 78
Starke, Fla., 4,806.......C4 54
Starke, co., Ind., 17,911...B4 59
Starkey, Va., 800.........C3 85
Starkville, Miss., 9,041...B5 68
Starobelsk, Sov. Un.,
  10,000................G12 12
Starodub, Sov. Un.,
  10,000................E9 12
Starogard, Pol., 28,600...B5 7
Starr, co., Tex., 17,137...F3 84
Startex, S.C., 950........B3 82
Staryy Oskol, Sov. Un.,
  10,000................F11 12
Stassfurt, Ger., 26,300...C5 6
State Center, Iowa, 1,142..B4 60
State College, Miss.,
  6,300.................B5 68
State College, Pa., 27,584..E6 81
State Road, N.C., 600.....A2 76
Statesboro, Ga., 8,356....D5 55
Statesville, N.C., 19,844..B2 76
Staunton, Ill., 4,228......D4 58

Staunton (Independent
  City), Va., 22,232......B3 85
Stavanger, Nor., 78,400
  (*106,000)............H1 11
Stavropol, Sov. Un.,
  158,000...............I13 12
Stawell, Austl., 5,504.....H4 25
Stayner, Ont., Can.,
  1,671.................C4 41
Stayton, Oreg.,
  2,108..............C4, k12 80
Steamboat Springs, Colo.,
  1,843.................A4 51
Stearns, Ky., 950.........D5 62
Stearns, co., Minn.,
  80,345................E4 67
Steblev, Sov. Un., 10,000..G8 12
Steele, Mo., 2,301........E8 69
Steele, co., Minn., 25,029..F5 67
Steele, co., N. Dak.,
  4,719.................C8 77
Steeleville, Ill., 1,569.....E4 58
Steelton, Pa., 11,266......F8 81
Steelville, Mo., 1,127.....D6 69
Steep Rock Lake, Ont.,
  Can., 40.............o17 41
Stefanesti, Rom., 7,770...B8 10
Steger, Ill., 6,432.....B6, m9 58
Steiermark (Styria),
  state, Aus., 1,137,865...*E7 6
Steilacoom, Wash.,
  1,569...............B3, f10 86
Steinbach, Man., Can.,
  3,739.................E3 40
Stellarton, N.S., Can.,
  5,327.................D7 43
Stendal, Ger., 37,000.....B5 6
Stephen, Minn., 858......B2 67
Stephens, Ark., 1,275.....D2 49
Stephens, co., Ga., 18,391..B3 55
Stephens, co., Okla.,
  37,990................C4 79
Stephens, co., Tex., 8,885..C3 84
Stephens City, Va., 876....A4 85
Stephenson, Mich., 820....C3 66
Stephenson, co., Ill.,
  46,207................A4 58
Stephenville, Newf., Can.,
  6,043.................D2 44
Stephenville, Tex., 7,359..C3 84
Stephenville Crossing,
  Newf., Can., 2,209......D2 44
Stepnoy, Sov. Un.,
  34,000...............H15 12
Sterling, Colo., 10,751.....A7 51
Sterling, Ill., 15,688......B4 58
Sterling, Kans., 2,303.....D5 61
Sterling, Mass., 950
  (3,193▲).............B4 65
Sterling, co., Tex., 1,177...D2 84
Sterling City, Tex., 854....D2 84
Sterlington, La., 1,300....B3 63
Sterlitamak, Sov. Un.,
  131,000...............D8 13
Sternberk, Czech.,
  11,200................D4 7
Stettin, see Szczecin, Pol.
Stettler, Alta., Can.,
  3,638.................C4 38
Stetson, mtn., Maine.....C4 .64
Steuben, co., Ind.,
  17,184................A7 59
Steuben, co., N.Y.,
  97,691................C3 75
Steubenville, Ohio,
  32,000 (*124,000)......B5 78
Stevens, co., Kans., 4,400..E3 61
Stevens, co., Minn.,
  11,262................E2 67
Stevens, co., Wash.,
  17,884................A7 86
Stevenson, Ala., 1,456....A4 46
Stevenson, Wash., 927....D4 86
Stevens Point, Wis.,
  17,837................D4 88
Stevensville, Mich., 697...F4 66
Stevensville, Mont., 784...D2 70
Steveston, B.C., Can.,
  4,000................F12 37
Stewardson, Ill., 656.....D5 58
Stewart, Minn., 676......F4 67
Stewart, co., Ga., 7,371...D2 55
Stewart, co., Tenn., 7,851..A4 83
Stewart Manor, N.Y.,
  2,422................*E7 75
Stewartstown, Pa., 1,164...G8 81
Stewartsville, N.J., 950...B2 74
Stewartville, Minn.,
  2,186.................G6 67
Stewiacke, N.S., Can.,
  1,042.................D6 43
Steyr, Aus., 38,306.......D7 6
Stickney, Ill., 6,239......*B6 58
Stigler, Okla., 1,923......B6 79
Stillwater, Minn.,
  8,310.................E6 67
Stillwater, N.Y., 1,356....C7 75
Stillwater, Okla., 23,965..A4 79

Stillwater, co., Mont.,
  5,526.................E7 70
Stilwell, Okla., 1,916.....B7 79
Stinnett, Tex., 2,695......B2 84
Štip, Yugo., 18,650........E6 10
Stirling, Ont., Can.,
  1,315.................C7 41
Stirling, N.J., 1,500......B4 74
Stirling, Scot., 27,600....B4 4
Stirling, co., Scot.,
  196,000..............*C5 4
Stittsville, Ont., Can.,
  1,508.................B9 41
Stockbridge, Ga., 1,201....C2 55
Stockbridge, Mass., 900...B1 65
Stockbridge, Mich., 1,097..F6 66
Stockdale, Tex., 1,111..E4, k8 84
Stockerau, Aus., 11,853...D8 6
Stockholm, Swe.,
  806,900
  (*1,125,000).......H8, t36 11
Stockholm, co., Swe.,
  463,000..............*H8 11
Stockport, Eng., 142,700..D5 4
Stockton, Ala., 950.......E2 46
Stockton, Calif.,
  97,500 (*188,000)..D3, h10 50
Stockton, Ill., 1,800......A3 58
Stockton, Kans., 2,073....C4 61
Stockton, Mo., 838.......D4 69
Stockton-on-Tees, Eng.,
  83,700................C6 4
Stoddard, co., Mo.,
  29,490................E8 69
Stoke-on-Trent, Eng.,
  266,100...............D5 4
Stokes, co., N.C., 22,314...A2 76
Stokesdale, N.C., 900.....A3 76
Stokke, Nor., 801........p28 11
Stolberg, Ger., 37,500....C3 6
Stone, Ky., 700..........C7 62
Stone, co., Ark., 6,294....B3 49
Stone, co., Miss., 7,013...E4 68
Stone, co., Mo., 8,176....E4 69
Stoneboro, Pa., 1,267.....D1 81
Stonega, Va., 800........f9 85
Stoneham, Mass., 17,821..g11 65
Stone Harbor, N.J., 834...E3 74
Stonehaven, Scot., 4,500..B5 4
Stoneleigh, Md., 8,000....*B4 53
Stone Mountain, Ga.,
  1,976..............B5, C2 55
Stone Park, Ill., 4,242....*B6 58
Stones River Homes,
  Tenn., 1,800.........*B5 83
Stoneville, N.C., 968......A3 76
Stonewall, Man., Can.,
  1,420.................D3 40
Stonewall, Miss., 1,126...C5 68
Stonewall, co., Tex.,
  3,017.................C2 84
Stonewood, W. Va.,
  2,202................*B4 87
Stoney Creek, Ont., Can.,
  6,043.................D5 41
Stonington, Conn.,
  1,622.................D9 52
Stonington, Ill., 1,076....D4 58
Stonington, Maine, 800
  (1,408▲).............D4 64
Stony Brook, N.Y.,
  4,000...............*n15 75
Stony Creek Mills, Pa.,
  1,500...............*F10 81
Stony Mountain, Can.,
  1,130.................D3 40
Stony Plain, Alta., Can.,
  1,311.................C3 38
Stony Point, N.Y., 3,000...A5 75
Stony Point, N.C., 1,300...B1 76
Stony Prairie, Ohio,
  1,720................*A2 78
Storey, co., Nev., 568.....B2 72
Storm Lake, Iowa, 7,728..B2 60
Stormont, co., Ont., Can.,
  57,867................B9 41
Stornoway, Scot., 5,300...A3 4
Storozhinets, Sov. Un.,
  10,000................G5 12
Storrs, Conn., 8,000......B7 52
Story, co., Iowa, 49,327...B4 60
Story City, Iowa, 1,943...B4 60
Stottville, N.Y., 1,040....C7 75
Stouffville, Ont., Can.,
  3,188.............D5, k15 41
Stoughton, Sask., Can.,
  606..................H4 39
Stoughton, Mass.,
  16,328.............B5, h11 65
Stoughton, Wis., 5,555...F4 88
Stovall, Miss., 125.......A3 68
Stover, Mo., 757.........C4 69
Stow, Ohio, 12,194......A4 78
Stowe, Pa., 3,501........F10 81
Stowe Township, Pa.,
  11,730...............*E2 81
Stoyoma, mtn., B.C., Can..E7 37
Strabane, N. Ire., 7,786....C3 4

Strabane, Pa., 1,940......F1 81
Strafford, Mo., 400.......D4 69
Strafford, Pa., 2,500.....*G10 81
Strafford, co., N.H.,
  59,799................E5 73
Strakonice, Czech.,
  14,100................D2 7
Straldzha, Bul., 5,348....D8 10
Stralsund, Ger., 67,000...A6 6
Strängnäs, Swe., 8,300...t35 11
Stranraer, Scot., 9,400...C4 4
Strasbourg, Sask., Can.,
  636..................F3 39
Strasbourg, Fr.,
  228,971 (*320,000)..C7, D3 6
Strasburg, N. Dak., 612...D5 77
Strasburg, Ohio, 1,687....B4 78
Strasburg, Pa., 1,416.....G9 81
Strasburg, Va., 2,428.....B4 85
Stratford, Calif., 900.....D4 50
Stratford, Ont., Can.,
  20,467................D3 41
Stratford, Conn., 45,012..E4 52
Stratford, Iowa, 703......B4 60
Stratford, N.J., 4,308.....D2 74
Stratford, Okla., 1,058....C5 79
Stratford, Tex., 1,380.....A1 84
Stratford, Wis., 1,106....D3 88
Stratford Hills, Va.,
  2,500................*C5 85
Stratford-on-Avon, Eng.,
  17,000................D6 4
Strathmore, Calif., 1,095..D4 50
Strathmore, Alta., Can.,
  924...................D4 38
Strathroy, Ont., Can.,
  5,150.................E3 41
Straubing, Ger., 36,300...D6 6
Strawberry, mts., Oreg...C8 80
Strawberry Point, Calif.,
  1,500................*C2 50
Strawberry Point, Iowa,
  1,303.................B6 60
Strawn, Tex., 817........C3 84
Straznice, Czech., 4,989..D4 7
Streamwood, Ill., 6,751..*A5 58
Streator, Ill., 16,868.....B5 58
Streetsboro, Ohio, 3,000..*A4 78
Streetsville, Ont., Can.,
  5,056...............m14 41
Strehaia, Rom., 8,545....C6 10
Stringtown, Ky., 100.....B5 62
Stromsburg, Nebr., 1,244..C8 71
Strong City, Kans., 659...D7 61
Stronghurst, Ill., 815....C3 58
Strongsville, Ohio, 8,504..A4 78
Stroud, Okla., 2,456......B5 79
Stroudsburg, Pa., 6,070...E11 81
Stroudsburg West, Pa.,
  1,569...............*E11 81
Struer, Den., 8,335.......I3 11
Strum, Wis., 663.........D2 88
Strumica, Yugo., 15,978..E6 10
Struthers, Ohio, 15,631..A5 78
Stryker, Ohio, 1,205......A1 78
Stryy, Sov. Un., 36,180...G4 12
Strzegom, Pol., 13,100....C4 7
Strzelce, Pol., 10,300....C5 7
Strzelin, Pol., 7,334......C4 7
Strzelno, Pol., 5,264......B5 7
Strzemieszyce, Pol.,
  11,900................g10 7
Stuart, Fla., 4,791.......E6 54
Stuart, Iowa, 1,486......C3 60
Stuart, Nebr., 794.......B6 71
Stuart, Va., 974.........D2 85
Stuarts Draft, Va., 600...B3 85
Stung Treng, Camb.,
  3,400.................C3 19
Sturbridge, Mass., 800...B3 65
Sturgeon, Mo., 620.......B5 69
Sturgeon, Pa., 1,000.....*F1 81
Sturgeon Bay, Wis.,
  7,353.................D6 88
Sturgeon Falls, Ont.,
  Can., 6,288...........A5 41
Sturgis, Sask., Can., 611..F4 39
Sturgis, Ky., 2,209.......C2 62
Sturgis, Mich., 8,915.....G5 66
Sturgis, S. Dak., 4,639...F2 77
Sturtevant, Wis.,
  1,488.............F6, n12 88
Stutsman, co., N. Dak.,
  25,137................C7 77
Stuttgart, Ark., 9,661....C4 49
Stuttgart, Ger., 629,400
  (*1,455,000).........D4 6
Styria, reg., Aus.........E7 6
Suakin, Sud., 4,228......E5 23
Suao, Taiwan, 5,000....*G9 21
Sublette, Kans., 1,077....E3 61
Sublette, co., Wyo.,
  3,778.................D2 89
Subotica, Yugo.,
  74,832................B4 10
Succasunna, N.J., 3,300..B3 74
Suceava, Rom., 23,200....B8 10
Sucha, Pol., 5,866........D5 7

Suchan, Sov. Un., 48,505..............E16 13
Suchitoto, Sal., 4,447......*E7 34
Süchow, China, 676,000..E8 17
Sucre, Bol., 55,000........C2 29
Sucre, state, Ven., 401,992................A5 32
Sucy-en-Brie, Fr., 13,258..g11 5
Sudan, Tex., 1,235........B1 84
Sudan, reg., Afr..........E7 21
Sudbury, Ont., Can., 80,120 (*110,694)..A4, p19 41
Sudbury, Mass., 1,200..........B5, g10 65
Sudbury, dist., Ont., Can., 165,862..............A3 41
Sudbury Center, Mass., 800................*B5 65
Sudirman, mts., W. Irian..F9 19
Sudzha, Sov. Un., 10,000................F10 12
Sueca, Sp., 20,612........C5 8
Suez, Eg., U.A.R., 219,000................H9 14
Suffern, N.Y., 6,121..D6, m14 75
Suffield, Conn., 1,110....B6 52
Suffolk (Independent City), Va., 12,609..D6, k14 85
Suffolk, co., Eng., 495,000................*D7 4
Suffolk, co., Mass., 791,329................B5 65
Suffolk, co., N.Y., 666,784................n15 75
Sugar, mtn., Mich..........k9 66
Sugar Creek, Mo., 2,663..h11 69
Sugarcreek, Ohio, 982...*B4 78
Sugar Grove, Va., 800................D1, f10 85
Sugar Hill, Ga., 1,175....B2 55
Sugar Land, Tex., 2,802..........E5, r14 84
Sugarloaf, mtn., Maine....C2 64
Sugar Notch, Pa., 2,524..n17 81
Suḩār, Mus. & Om., 4,000................E6 15
Suhl, Ger., 25,500........C5 6
Suihua (Peilintzu), China, 40,000..........B10 17
Suileng, China, 5,000....C3 18
Suipin, China, 5,000....C5 18
Suita, Jap., 196,779....*I7 18
Suitland, Md., 14,000....f9 53
Sukabumi, Indon., 78,806..G3 19
Sukaradja, Indon., 16,632..F4 19
Sukarnapura (Hollandia), W. Irian, 14,500......F10 19
Sukumo, Jap., 14,700....J6 18
Sukkur, Pak., 103,216....C4 20
Sullana, Peru, 26,330....B1 31
Sulligent, Ala., 1,346....B1 46
Sullivan, Ill., 3,946.....D5 58
Sullivan, Ind., 4,979....F3 59
Sullivan, Mo., 4,098.....C6 69
Sullivan, co., Ind., 21,721..F3 59
Sullivan, co., Mo., 8,783...A4 69
Sullivan, co., N.H., 28,067................E3 73
Sullivan, co., N.Y., 45,272................D6 75
Sullivan, co., Pa., 6,251....D8 81
Sullivan, co., Tenn., 114,139................C11 83
Sullivans Island, S.C., 1,358................k12 82
Sully, Iowa, 631..........C5 60
Sully, co., S. Dak., 2,607..F5 77
Sulmona, It., 18,400....C4 9
Sulphur, La., 11,429....D2 63
Sulphur, Okla., 4,737....C5 79
Sulphur South, La., 1,351................*D2 63
Sulphur Springs, Tex., 9,160................C5 84
Sultan, Wash., 821........B4 86
Sulu, prov., Phil., 326,898................*D6 19
Sumach, Wash., 1,345...*C5 86
Sumas, Wash., 629......A3 86
Sumatra, is., Indon......F2 19
Sumenep, Indon., 17,824..G7 19
Sumiton, Ala., 1,287....*B2 46
Summerdale, Pa., 1,200..*F8 81
Summerfield, N.C., 700...A3 76
Summerland, B.C., Can., 4,307................E8 37
Summers, co., W. Va., 15,640................D4 87
Summerside, P.E.I., Can., 8,611................C6 43
Summersville, W. Va., 2,008..........C4, C7 87
Summerton, S.C., 1,504...D7 82
Summerville, Ga., 4,706...B1 55
Summerville, Pa., 895....D3 81
Summerville, S.C., 3,633................E7, h11 82
Summit, Ill., 10,374.......k9 58

Summit, Miss., 1,663......D3 68
Summit, N.J., 23,677......B4 74
Summit, co., Colo., 2,073..B4 51
Summit, co., Ohio, 513,569................A4 78
Summit, co., Utah, 5,673..A6 72
Summit Hill, Pa., 4,386................E10 81
Summitville, Ind., 1,048..D6 59
Sumner, Ill., 1,035.....E6 58
Sumner, Iowa, 2,170....B5 60
Sumner, Wash., 3,156....B3 86
Sumner, co., Kans., 25,316................E6 61
Sumner, co., Tenn., 32,217................A5 83
Sumoto, Jap., 35,400.....I7 18
Sumperk, Czech., 19,400................D4 7
Sumter, Ala., 20,041.....C1 46
Sumter, S.C., 23,062.....D7 82
Sumter, co., Fla., 11,869..D4 54
Sumter, co., Ga., 24,652..D2 55
Sumter, co., S.C., 74,941..D7 82
Sumy, Sov. Un., 117,000..F10 12
Sun, La., 224............D6 63
Sunagawa, Jap., 24,200..E10 18
Sunburst, Mont., 882.....B5 70
Sunbury, Ohio, 1,360....B3 78
Sunbury, Pa., 13,687....E8 81
Sunbury, co., N.B., Can., 22,796................D3 43
Sunchŏn, Kor., 20,682....I3 18
Sunchŏn, Kor., 49,800...G2 18
Sun City, Ariz., 2,000....*C2 48
Suncook, N.H., 3,900....E5 73
Sun Crest, Calif., 1,166..*F5 50
Sundance, Wyo., 908....B8 89
Sundance, mtn., Wyo.....B8 89
Sundbyberg, Swe., 27,100................t35 11
Sunderland, Ont., Can., 634................C5 41
Sunderland, Eng., 190,500................C6 4
Sundown, Tex., 1,186....C1 84
Sundre, Alta., Can., 853..D3 38
Sundsvall, Swe., 30,300..F7 11
Sunfield, Mich., 625....F5 66
Sunflower, co., Miss., 45,750................B3 68
Sungari, riv., China......C5 18
Sungchiang, China, 70,000................E7 17
Sungurlu, Tur., 10,619..B10 14
Suniland, Fla., 1,500....*G6 54
Sunman, Ind., 618......F7 59
Sunny Acres, Ky., 844....A7 62
Sunnyland, Fla., 4,761...q11 54
Sunnyland, Ill., 4,000....*C4 58
Sunnymead, Calif., 3,404................*F5 50
Sunnyside, Utah, 1,740..B6 72
Sunnyside, Wash., 6,208..C5 86
Sunnyvale, Calif., 52,898..k8 50
Sunol, Calif., 750......h9 50
Sun Prairie, Wis., 4,008..E4 88
Sunray, Tex., 1,967.....B2 84
Sunridge, Ont., Can., 756..B5 41
Sunrise Heights, Mich., 1,569................*F5 66
Sunset, La., 1,307......D3 63
Sunset, Utah, 4,235......*A5 72
Sunset Beach, Calif., 1,300................*F5 50
Sunset Hills, Mo., 3,525................*C7 69
Sunset Park, Kans., 1,000................*B5 61
Sunwui, China, 85,000...G7 17
Superior, Ariz., 5,000..C3, D3 48
Superior, Mont., 1,242...C2 70
Superior, Nebr., 2,935...E7 71
Superior, W. Va., 900...*D3 87
Superior, Wis., 33,563...B1 88
Superior, Wyo., 241.....E4 89
Superior, lake, Can., U.S................A9 45
Suquamish, Wash., 1,000..B3 86
Şūr, Mus. & Om..........E6 15
Surabaja (Soerabaja), Indon., 989,734......G4 19
Surakarta (Soerakarta), Indon., 363,167......G4 19
Surany, Czech., 5,381...D5 7
Surat, India, 288,026....D5 20
Surbiton, Eng., 62,940..m11 4
Suresnes, Fr., 39,100....g9 5
Surfside, Fla., 3,157....s13 54
Surgoinsville, Tenn., 1,132................C11 83
Surgut, Sov. Un., 3,500..C10 13
Suri, India, 22,841......D8 20
Surigao, Phil., 15,661....D7 19
Surigao del Norte, prov., Phil., 194,981......*D7 19
Surigao del Sur, prov., Phil., 165,016........*D7 19

Surinam, dep., Sur., 345,000................C5 27
Suriname, riv., Sur........C5 27
Surrey, co., Eng., 935,700................*E6 4
Surry, N.H., 200.........E3 73
Surry, co., N.C., 48,205..A2 76
Surry, co., Va., 6,220....C6 85
Susa, It., 5,891..........B1 9
Susana Knolls, Calif., 900................*E4 50
Susanville, Calif., 6,912..B3 50
Susice, Czech., 6,793....D2 7
Susquehanna, Pa., 2,591..C10 81
Susquehanna, co., Pa., 33,137................C10 81
Sussex, N.B., Can., 3,457................D4 43
Sussex, N.J., 1,656......A3 74
Sussex, Wis., 1,087.....m11 88
Sussex, co., Del., 73,195..C6 53
Sussex, co., Eng., 1,105,700................*E7 4
Sussex, co., N.J., 49,255..A3 74
Sussex, co., Va., 12,411..D5 85
Susurluk, Tur., 11,450...C7 14
Sutersville, Pa., 964....*F2 81
Sutherland, Iowa, 883....B2 60
Sutherland, Nebr., 867...C4 71
Sutherland, co., Scot., 13,200................*B4 4
Sutherlin, Oreg., 2,452..D3 80
Sutter, Calif., 1,219....*C3 50
Sutter, co., Calif., 33,380..C3 50
Sutter Creek, Calif., 1,444..C3 50
Sutton, Que., Can., 1,755................D5 42
Sutton, Eng., 78,969.....m12 4
Sutton, Nebr., 1,252.....D8 71
Sutton, W. Va., 967.....C4 87
Sutton, co., Tex., 3,738..D2 84
Sutton-in-Ashfield, Eng., 40,700................D6 4
Sutton West, Ont., Can., 1,470................C5 41
Suttsu, Jap., 5,100......E10 18
Suva, Fiji, 47,850.......H8 2
Suwa, Jap., 46,276.....m17 18
Suwalki, Pol., 21,300....A7 7
Suwannee, Fla., 200....C3 54
Suwannee, co., Fla., 14,961................B3 54
Suwŏn, S. Kor., 101,000 (123,100*)......H3 18
Suyo, Peru, 744........B1 31
Suzuka, Jap., 60,000....o15 18
Svalbard (Spitzbergen), Nor., 1,200......B5 13
Svedala, Swe., 3,114....A2 7
Svendborg, co., Den., 150,365................*J4 11
Sverdlovsk, Sov. Un., 919,000................D9 13
Sverdrup, is., Can......m30 36
Svetlaya, Sov. Un., 10,000................C9 18
Svilajnac, Yugo., 5,905..C5 10
Svilengrad, Bul., 9,918..E8 10
Svirstroy, Sov. Un., 10,000................A9 12
Svishtov, Bul., 12,949...D7 10
Svitavy, Czech., 13,900..D4 7
Svobodnyy, Sov. Un., 58,000................D15 13
Swain, co., N.C., 8,387..f9 76
Swainsboro, Ga., 5,943..D4 55
Swampscott, Mass., 13,294..........B6, g12 65
Swan Hill, Austl., 7,376..G7 25
Swan Hills, Alta., Can., 643................B3 38
Swanlake, Idaho, 150....G6 57
Swan Lake, Miss., 300....B3 68
Swannanoa, N.C., 2,189..f10 76
Swan River, Man., Can., 3,163................C1 40
Swansboro, N.C., 1,104..C5 76
Swansea, Ont., Can., 9,628................m15 41
Swansea, Ill., 3,018....f14 69
Swansea, Mass., 200....C5 65
Swansea, S.C., 776.....D5 82
Swansea, Wales, 170,400..E5 4
Swansea Center, Mass., 700................*C5 65
Swanton, Ohio, 2,306....A2 78
Swanton, Vt., 2,390.....B1 73
Swarthmore, Pa., 5,753..p20 81
Swartz Creek, Mich., 3,006................F7 66
Swatow Shantou, China, 280,400................G8 17
Swayzee, Ind., 1,007....C6 59
Swaziland, Br. dep., Afr., 285,000................F6 24
Swea City, Iowa, 805....A3 60
Swedeborg, Mo., 175....D5 69
Swedeland, Pa., 950.....o20 81

Sweden, country, Eur., 7,604,000................F7 11
Swedesboro, N.J., 2,449..D2 74
Sweeny, Tex., 3,087.....r14 84
Sweet, Idaho, 100......F2 57
Sweet Briar, Va., 950....C3 85
Sweet Grass, co., Mont., 3,290................E7 70
Sweet Home, Oreg., 3,353..C4 80
Sweetsburg, Que., Can., 958................D5 42
Sweetsers, Ind., 896....C6 59
Sweet Springs, Mo., 1,452..C4 69
Sweetwater, Tenn., 4,145..D8 83
Sweetwater, Tex., 13,914..C2 84
Sweetwater, co., Wyo., 17,920................E3 89
Swepsonville, N.C., 800...A3 76
Swidnica, Pol., 43,100...C4 7
Swidwin, Pol., 10,900...B3 7
Swiebodzice, Pol., 17,100..C4 7
Swiebodzin, Pol., 13,000..B3 7
Swiecie, Pol., 14,500....B5 7
Swietochlowice, Pol., 58,200................g9 7
Swift, co., Minn., 14,936..E3 67
Swift Current, Sask., Can., 12,186..........G2, n7 39
Swindon, Eng., 96,200...E6 4
Swinemünde, see Swinoujscie, Pol.
Swinoujscie, Pol., 20,100..B3 7
Swisher, co., Tex., 10,607..B2 84
Swissvale, Pa., 15,089...k14 81
Switzer, W. Va., 1,131...D5 87
Switzerland, co., Ind., 7,092................G7 59
Switzerland, country, Eur., 5,825,000......E4 6
Swoyerville, Pa., 6,751................D10, n17 81
Sycamore, Ill., 6,961....B5 58
Sycamore, Ohio, 998....B2 78
Sycemore Hills, Mo., 942................*C7 69
Sydenham, Ont., Can., 803................C8 41
Sydney, Austl., 158,801 (*2,539,627)......F9 25
Sydney, N.S., Can., 33,617................C9 43
Sydney Mines, N.S., Can., 9,122................C9 43
Sykesville, Md., 1,196...B4 53
Sykesville, Pa., 1,479...D4 81
Syktyvkar, Sov. Un., 84,000................C8 13
Sylacauga, Ala., 12,857..B3 46
Sylhet, Pak., 37,740....D9 20
Sylva, N.C., 1,564......f9 76
Sylvan, Oreg., 1,000....g12 80
Sylvan Beach, N.Y., 600..B5 75
Sylvania, Ala., 4,000....A4 46
Sylvania, Ga., 3,469....D5 55
Sylvania, Ky., 1,500....A3 62
Sylvania, Ohio, 5,187..A2, e6 78
Sylvan Lake, Alta., Can., 1,381................C3 38
Sylvester, Ga., 3,610....E3 55
Syosset, N.Y., 21,500...F2 52
Syracuse, Ind., 1,595....B6 59
Syracuse, Kans., 1,888...E2 61
Syracuse, Nebr., 1,261................D9, h12 71
Syracuse, N.Y., 210,000 (*495,000)......B4 75
Syracuse, Ohio, 731.....D4 78
Syracuse, Utah, 1,061...C2 72
Syr Darya, riv., Sov. Un..E9 13
Syria, country, Asia, 5,399,000................F6 16
Syriam, Bur., 15,070....*B1 19
Syzran, Sov. Un., 159,000................D7 13
Szabadszallas, Hung., 4,878................B4 10
Szabolcs-Szatmar, co., Hung., 587,257......*B5 10
Szamotuly, Pol., 12,200..B4 7
Szarvas, Hung., 12,277..B5 10
Szczebrzeszyn, Pol., 5,122..C7 7
Szczecinek, Pol., 25,100..B4 7
Szczecin Stettin, Pol., 299,200................B3 7
Szechwan, prov., China, 72,160,000................E5 17
Szeged, Hung., 107,300..B5 10
Szekesfehervar, Hung., 61,400................B4 10
Szekszard, Hung., 16,409..B4 10
Szentendre, Hung., 10,307..B4 10
Szentes, Hung., 24,807...B5 10
Szeping, China, 125,900..C9 17
Szolnok, Hung., 51,300...B5 10
Szolnok, co., Hung., 462,516................*B5 10
Szombathely, Hung., 57,600................B3 10

T

Tabaco, Phil., 8,308......*C6   19
Tabasco, state, Mex.,
   496,340.............D6   34
Taber, Alta., Can., 3,951..E4   38
Taboada, Sp., 8,162......A2   8
Tabor, Czech., 19,600....D3   7
Tabor, Iowa, 909.........D2   60
Tabor, N.J., 1,500.......*B4   74
Tabora, Tan., 15,361......B6   24
Tabor City, N.C., 2,338...C4   76
Tabrīz, Iran, 289,996.....B4   15
Tabūk, Sau. Ar.............D2   15
Tachikawa, Jap.,100,719..n18   18
Táchira, state, Ven.,
   399,163.............B3   32
Tacloban, Phil., 35,974...C6   19
Tacna, Peru, 13,514......E5   31
Tacna, dept., Peru, 42,874..E3   31
Tacoma, Wash.,
   150,000
   (*330,000).........B3, f11   86
Tacuarembó, Ur., 29,011..E1   30
Tacuarembó, dept., Ur.,
   76,300.............*E1   30
Tadoussac, Que., Can.,
   1,083..............A8   42
Tadzhik, rep., Sov. Un.,
   2,432,000...........F9   16
Taegu, Kor., 811,400.....I4   18
Taejon, Kor., 307,400....H3   18
Tafalla, Sp., 7,320......A5   8
Tafí Viejo, Arg., 15,374..E2   29
Tafí Viejo, Arg., 15,374..E2   29
Taft, Calif., 3,822.......E4   50
Taft, Fla., 1,214........D5   54
Taft, Tex., 3,463........F4   84
Taft Heights, Calif.,
   2,661..............*E4   50
Taft Southwest, Tex.,
   1,927..............*F4   84
Taganrog, Sov. Un.,
   220,000............H12   12
Taguchi, Jap., 4,400.....n16   18
Tahat, mtn., Alg.........D6   22
Tahlequah, Okla., 5,840..B7   79
Tahoka, Tex., 3,012......C2   84
Tahoua, Niger, 12,400....F6   22
Taian, China, 80,000....*D8   17
T'aichung, Taiwan,
   232,000............G9   17
Taihsien, China, 2,600...E6   17
Taikang, China, 5,000....C2   18
Tailai, China, 5,000.....C1   18
T'ainan, Taiwan, 288,000..G9   17
Taipei (Taihoku),
   Taiwan, 1,027,600.....G9   17
Taiping, Mala., 48,206...E2   19
Taira, Jap., 70,921......H10   18
T'aitung, Taiwan, 29,010..G9   17
Taiwan (Formosa),
   country (Nationalist
   China), Asia,
   12,070,000..........G9   17
Taiyüan (Yangkü),
   China, 1,020,000......D7   17
Taizz, Yemen, 25,000....G3   15
Tajimi, Jap., 60,175...I8, n16   18
Tājūrā', Libya, 2,670.....B7   22
Tak, Thai., 13,398.......*B1   19
Takada, Jap., 49,000.....H9   18
Takamatsu, Jap., 243,444..I7   18
Takaoka, Jap., 139,502...H8   18
Takasaki, Jap.,
   130,735............H9, m18   18
Takatsuki, Jap., 130,735..o14   18
Takayama, Jap.,
   59,600.............H8, m16   18
Takefu, Jap., 41,000.....n15   18
Takeo, Camb., 7,400.....*C2   19
Takingeun, Indon.,
   1,411..............*m11   19
Takoma Park, Md., 16,799..f8   53
Takut, Bur., 5,000......*D10   20
Talā, Eg., U.A.R.,
   18,570.............*G8   14
Tala, Mex., 12,547......m12   34
Tala, Ur., 3,213.........E1   30
Talagante, Chile, 11,560...A2   28

Talai, China, 24,921......D2   18
Talara, Peru, 12,985......B1   31
Talavera de la Reina,
   Sp., 31,900..........C3   8
Talbert, Ky., 150........C6   62
Talbot, co., Ga., 7,127...D2   55
Talbot, co., Md., 21,578...C5   53
Talbotton, Ga., 1,163....D2   55
Talca, Chile, 68,100......B2   28
Talca, prov., Chile,
   206,255............B2   28
Talcahuano, Chile,
   83,600.............B2   28
Talcher, India, 8,147.....D8   20
Talco, Tex., 1,024.......C5   84
Tali, China, 15,000......E6   17
Taliaferro, co., Ga., 3,370..C4   55
Talien, see Dairen, China
Talihina, Okla., 1,048....C6   79
Talisayan, Phil., 10,646..*D6   19
Talladega, Ala., 17,742....B3   46
Talladega, co., Ala.,
   65,495.............B3   46
Tallahassee, Fla., 48,174..B2   54
Tallahatchie, co., Miss.,
   24,081.............B3   68
Tallapoosa, Ga., 2,744....C1   55
Tallapoosa, co., Ala.,
   35,007.............C4   46
Tallassee, Ala., 4,934....C4   46
Talleyville, Del., 2,000..*A6   53
Tallinn, Sov. Un., 311,000..B5   12
Tallmadge, Ohio, 10,246..A4   78
Tallulah, La., 9,413......B4   63
Talnoye, Sov. Un., 10,000..G8   12
Talsi, Sov. Un., 10,000...C4   12
Taltal, Chile, 4,901......E1   29
Tama, Iowa, 2,925.......C5   60
Tama, co., Iowa, 21,413...B5   60
Tamale, Ghana, 40,400...G4   22
Taman, Sov. Un., 10,000..I11   12
Tamano, Jap., 66,232.....I6   18
Tamanrasset, Alg., 1,714..D6   22
Tamaqua, Pa., 10,173...E10   81
Tamatave, Malag.,
   39,627.............D9   24
Tamaulipas, state, Mex.,
   1,024,182...........C5   34
Tamazula de Gordiano,
   Mex., 10,672........n12   34
Tambov, Sov. Un.,
   203,000............E13   12
Tampa, Fla., 308,000
   (*420,000)..........E4, p11   54
Tampico, Mex.,
   122,535............C5, k15   34
Tampere, Fin., 133,300...G10   11
Tams, W. Va., 500.......D3   87
Tamworth, Austl., 21,682..F9   25
Tanabe, Jap., 44,000.....J7   18
Tananarive, Malag.,
   270,300............D6   24
Tanchon, Kor., 32,761....F4   18
Tandag, Phil., 6,735.....*D7   19
Tăndărei, Rom., 2,353....C8   10
Tandjungpandan, Indon.,
   15,708.............F3   19
Taney, co., Mo., 10,238...E4   69
Taneytown, Md., 1,519...A3   53
Tanga, Tan., 38,053......B7   24
Tanganyika, lake, Afr....C6   24
Tangermünde, Ger.,
   13,800.............B5   6
Tanger (Tangier), Mor.,
   141,714............A3   22
Tangier, Va., 876........C7   85
Tangipahoa, par., La.,
   59,434.............D5   63
Tangshan, China, 65,000..*D8   17
Tangyüan, China, 5,000...C4   18
Tanjay, Phil., 12,355....*D6   19
Tanjore, India, 111,099...F6   20
Tank, Pak., 6,899........B5   20
Tanque Verde, Ariz.,
   1,053..............*C4   48
Tanshui, Taiwan, 10,000..*F9   17
Tantā, Eg., U.A.R.,
   209,500............G8   14

Tanzania, country, Afr.,
   10,123,000..........B6   24
Taonan, China, 65,000...B9   17
Taormina, It., 5,800.....F5   9
Taos, N. Mex., 2,163.....A6   48
Taos, co., N. Mex.,
   15,934.............A6   48
Taourirt, Mor., 7,343.....B4   22
Tapachula, Mex.,
   41,578.............E6   34
Tappahannock, Va.,
   1,086..............C6   85
Tappan, N.Y., 3,300......g13   75
Taquara, Braz., 11,282...D2   30
Taquaritinga, Braz.,
   11,624.............k7   30
Tara, Mo., 2,000........*C7   69
Tara, Sov. Un., 20,400...D10   13
Tarabulus (Tripoli),
   Leb., 115,000........E10   14
Tarakan, Laos, 10,000...*B2   19
Tarancón, Sp., 7,714.....B4   8
Taranto, It., 199,800....D6   9
Tarapacá, prov., Chile,
   122,665............D1   29
Tarapoto, Peru, 9,249....C2   31
Tarare, Fr., 12,131......E6   5
Tarascon-sur-Ariège, Fr.,
   3,680..............F6   5
Tarazona, Sp., 12,059....B5   8
Tarbes, Fr., 46,600......F4   5
Tarboro, N.C., 8,411.....B5   76
Taree, Austl., 10,050....E9   26
Tarentum, Pa., 8,232..E2, h14   81
Tarfaya, Mor., 1,521.....C2   22
Tarifa, Sp., 7,737.......D3   8
Tarija, Bol., 16,869......D3   29
Tarija, dept., Bol.,
   126,752............D3   29
Tarkio, Mo., 2,160.......A2   69
Tarkwa, Ghana, 13,500
   (*25,232)...........G4   22
Tarlac, Phil., 42,019..B6, o13   19
Tarlac, prov., Phil.,
   426,647............*B6   19
Tarma, Peru, 7,876......D2   31
Tarn, dept., Fr., 319,560..*F5   5
Tarn-et-Garonne, dept., Fr.,
   175,847............*E4   5
Tarnobrzeg, Pol., 4,140...C6   7
Tarnów, Pol., 75,100.....C6   7
Tarnowskie Góry, Pol.,
   28,000.............g9   7
Taroudant, Mor., 17,141..B3   22
Tarpon Springs, Fla.,
   6,768..............D4   54
Tarquinia, It., 9,776.....C3   9
Tarragona, Sp., 43,519...B6   8
Tarragona, prov., Sp.,
   362,679............*B6   8
Tarrant, Ala., 7,810...C3, E3   46
Tarrant, co., Tex.,
   538,495............C4   84
Tarrasa, Sp., 92,234.....B7   8
Tarrytown, N.Y.,
   11,280.............D7, m15   75
Tarshiha, Isr., 1,609.....A3   15
Tarsney, Mo., 400.......k11   69
Tarsus, Tur., 51,184.....D10   14
Tartu, Sov. Un., 77,000...B6   12
Tashkent, Sov. Un.,
   1,092,000...........E9   13
Tashkurghan, Afg.,
   20,000.............A4   20
Tasmania, state, Austl.,
   371,217............o14   25
Tatamagouche, N.S.,
   Can., 581...........D6   43
Tatarbunary, Sov. Un.,
   10,000.............C9   10
Tate, Ga., 900..........B2   55
Tate, co., Miss., 18,138...A4   68
Tateville, Ky., 725......D5   62
Tateyama, Jap.,
   39,700.............I9, o18   18
Tatta, Pak., 9,716.......D4   20
Tattnall, co., Ga., 15,837..D4   55
Tatuí, Braz., 22,550...C3, m8   30

Tatum, N. Mex., 1,168...C7   48
Tatung, China, 228,500...C7   17
Taubaté, Braz., 64,863...C3   30
Taung, S. Afr., 860......F4   24
Taungdwingyi, Bur.,
   16,233.............D10   20
Taunggyi, Bur., 8,652....D10   20
Taunton, Eng., 36,400...E5   4
Taunton, Mass., 41,132...C5   65
Taurage, Sov. Un., 10,465..D4   12
Tauranga, N.Z., 23,390...L16   26
Taurianova, It., 14,300...E6   9
Tauste, Sp., 6,634.......B5   8
Tavares, Fla., 2,724.....D5   54
Tavas, Tur., 7,110......*D7   14
Tavda, Sov. Un., 47,954..D9   13
Tavira, Port., 7,496.....D2   8
Tavistock, Ont., Can.,
   1,232..............D4   41
Tavoy, Bur., 40,312.....F10   20
Tavsanli, Tur., 11,500...*C7   14
Tawas City, Mich., 1,810..D7   66
Taylor, Mich., 49,658...*F7   66
Taylor, Pa., 6,148..D10, m18   81
Taylor, Tex., 9,434......D4   84
Taylor, co., Fla., 13,168...B3   54
Taylor, co., Ga., 8,311...D2   55
Taylor, co., Iowa, 10,288..D3   60
Taylor, co., Ky., 16,285...C4   62
Taylor, co., Tex., 101,078..C3   84
Taylor, co., W. Va.,
   15,010.............B4   87
Taylor, co., Wis., 17,843...C3   88
Taylor Mill, Ky., 710....A7   62
Taylors, S.C., 1,500.....B3   82
Taylorsport, Ky., 200....A7   62
Taylorsville, Ky., 937....B4   62
Taylorsville, Miss., 1,132..D4   68
Taylorsville, N.C., 1,470..B1   76
Taylorville, Ill., 8,801....D4   58
Tayshet, Sov. Un.,
   28,900.............D12   13
Taza, Mor., 31,667......B4   22
Tazewell, Tenn., 1,264...C10   83
Tazewell, Va., 3,000.....e10   85
Tazewell, co., Ill., 99,789..C4   58
Tazewell, co., Va.,
   44,791.............e10   85
Tbilisi, Sov. Un.,
   805,000............E7   13
Tchula, Miss., 882.......B3   68
Tczew, Pol., 36,000......A5   7
Teague, Tex., 2,728......D4   84
Teaneck, N.J., 42,085....h8   74
Tecuala, Mex., 10,868...C3   34
Tecuci, Rom., 23,400....C8   10
Tecumseh, Ont., Can.,
   4,476..............E2   41
Tecumseh, Mich., 7,045..F7   66
Tecumseh, Nebr., 1,887...D9   71
Tecumseh, Okla., 2,630...B5   79
Tegucigalpa, Hond.,
   134,075............E7   34
Teguise, Sp., 5,547......m15   8
Tehachapi, Calif., 3,838...E4   50
Tehama, co., Calif.,
   25,305............B2   50
Tehrán, Iran, 1,512,082
   (*1,590,000).........B5   15
Tehuacan, Mex.,
   31,897.............D5, n15   34
Tehuantepec, Mex.,
   13,458.............D5   34
Teide, Pico de, peak,
   Sp., (Can. Is.).......m13   8
Tejo (Tagus), riv., Eur....C1   8
Tekamah, Nebr., 1,788...C9   71
Tekax de Alvaro
   Obregón, Mex., 7,849..C7   34
Tekirdag, Tur., 23,987...B6   14
Tekoa, Wash., 911......B8   86
Tela, Hond., 13,619.....*D7   34
Tel Aviv-Yafo (Tel
   Aviv-Jaffa), Isr.,
   392,900 (*715,000)..B2, g5   15
Telde, Sp., 14,100.......m14   8
Telemark, Nor.,
   149,900............*H3   11

Telfair, co., Ga., 11,715....E4   55
Telford, Pa., 2,763......F11   81
Tell, Wis................I4   59
Tell City, Ind., 7,715......I4   59
Teller, co., Colo., 2,495....C5   51
Telluride, Colo., 677......D3   51
Telok Anson, Mala.,
37,042...............E2   19
Teloloapan, Mex.,
8,065..........D5, n14   34
Telukbetung, Indon.,
132,312..............G3   19
Tempe, Ariz., 45,919..C3, D2   48
Temperance, Mich.,
2,215...............G7   66
Tempio Pausania, It.,
8,300...............D2   9
Temple, Okla., 1,282......C3   79
Temple, Pa., 1,633........F10   81
Temple, Tex., 30,419......D4   84
Temple City, Calif.,
26,500..............*F5   50
Temple Hill, Ky., 100....D4   62
Temple Terrace, Fla.,
3,812...............o11   54
Templeton, Mass., 750....A3   65
Templin, Ger., 11,600......B6   6
Temryuk, Sov. Un.,
10,000..............I11   12
Temuco, Chile, 72,100....B2   28
Tenafly, N.J., 14,264...B5, h9   74
Tenaha, Tex., 1,097......D5   84
Tenancingo [de Degollado,
Mex.,], 9,320......D5, n14   34
Tenango del Valle, Mex.,
7,685................n14   34
Tenasserim, Bur., 1,194...F10   20
Tengchung, China.......F4   17
Tengri Khan, mtn.,
China...............E11   13
Tenino, Wash., 836......C3   86
Tennessee, state, U.S.,
3,567,089............   83
Tennessee, riv., U.S...B3, D8   83
Tensas, par., La., 11,796..B4   63
Teocaltiche, Mex.,
10,959...........C4, m12   34
Teófilo Otoni, Braz.,
41,013..............B4   30
Tepatitlán [de Morelos],
Mex., 19,835......C4, m12   34
Tepic, Mex., 54,069..C4, m11   34
Teplice, Czech., 44,000...C2   7
Teramo, It., 25,600......C4   9
Teresina, Braz., 100,006..D6   27
Teresópolis, Braz.,
29,540...........C4, h6   30
Termez, Sov. Un., 24,000..F9   13
Termini Imerese, It.,
24,000..............F4   9
Termoli, It., 9,686......C5   9
Ternate, Indon., 21,200...E7   19
Terneuzen, Neth., 12,100..B5   5
Terney, Sov. Un., 10,000..D8   18
Terni, It., 99,600......C4   9
Ternopol, Sov. Un.,
61,000..............G5   12
Terra Alta, W. Va., 1,504..B5   87
Terrace, B.C., Can., 4,682..B3   37
Terrace Park, Ohio,
2,023..............*C1   78
Terracina, It., 17,300....D4   9
Terra Linda, Calif.,
3,000..............*D2   50
Terrebonne, Que.,
Can., 6,207......D4, p19   42
Terrebonne, co., Que.,
Can., 102,275........D3   42
Terrebonne, par., La.,
60,771..............E5   63
Terre Haute, Ind., 72,500..F3   59
Terre Hill, Pa., 1,129....F9   81
Terrell, Tex., 13,803.....C4   84
Terrell, co., Ga., 12,742..E2   55
Terrell, co., Tex., 2,600..D1   84
Terrell Hills, Tex., 5,572..k7   84
Terry, Mont., 1,140......D11   70
Terry, co., Tex., 16,286...C1   84
Terrytown, La., 5,000....*k11   63
Terrytown, Nebr., 164....C2   71
Terryville, Conn., 5,000..C4   52
Teruel, Sp., 19,726......B5   8
Teruel, prov., Sp.,
215,183............*B5   8
Tešanj, Yugo., 3,150....C3   10
Teterow, Ger., 11,100....B6   6
Teton, co., Idaho, 2,639..F7   57
Teton, co., Mont., 7,295..C4   70
Teton, co., Wyo., 3,062...C2   89
Tétouan, Mor., 101,352..A3   22
Tetovo, Yugo., 25,203...D5   10
Tetu, China, 22,024.....B3   18
Teutopolis, Ill., 1,140....D5   58
Tewksbury, Mass.,
1,151...........A5, f11   65
Texarkana, Ark., 19,788..D1   49
Texarkana, Tex., 30,218...C5   84

Texas, Md., 120.........B4   53
Texas, co., Mo., 17,758....D5   69
Texas, co., Okla., 14,162...e9   79
Texas, state, U.S.,
9,579,677............   84
Texas City, Tex.,
32,065..........E5, r15   84
Texhoma, Okla., 911......e9   79
Teziutlán, Mex.,
17,400..........D5, n15   34
Thailand (Siam),
country, Asia,
30,591,000..........B2   19
Thames, N.Z., 5,315....L15   26
Thamesville, Ont., Can.,
1,054...............E3   41
Thanh Hoa, Viet., 31,211..B3   19
Thann, Fr., 7,736........D7   5
Thaon [-les-Vosges], Fr.,
8,166...............C7   5
Tharptown, Pa., 1,085....*E8   81
Tharrawaddy, Bur.,
8,977..............E10   20
Thatcher, Ariz., 1,581...C4   48
Thatcher, Idaho, 100....G7   57
Thaton, Bur., 38,047....E10   20
Thayer, Mo., 1,713......E6   69
Thayer, co., Nebr., 9,118..D8   71
Thayetmyo, Bur.,
11,164.............*E10   20
The Dalles, Oreg.,
10,493..............B5   80
The Father, mtn.,
N. Gui..............k13   25
The Hague
('s Gravenhage), Neth.,
604,100 (*830,000)......A6   5
The Pas, Man., Can.,
4,671............C1, g7   40
The Plains, Ohio, 1,400...C3   78
Theresa, N.Y., 956.....A5, f9   75
Thermalito, Calif., 1,200..*C3   50
Thermopolis, Wyo., 3,995..C4   89
Thesprotía, prov., Grc.,
52,125.............*C3   14
Thessalon, Ont., Can.,
1,725...............p19   41
Thessaloníki (Salonika),
Grc., 250,920
(*378,444)..........B4   14
Thessaloníki(Salonika),
prov., Grc., 544,394....*B4   14
Thessaly, reg., Grc......C4   14
Thetford Mines, Que.,
Can., 21,618.........C6   42
The Village, Okla.,
12,118.............*B4   79
Thibodaux, La.,
13,403..........E5, k10   63
Thief River Falls, Minn.,
7,151...............B2   67
Thiensville, Wis......E5, m12   88
Thiers, Fr., 12,418......E5   5
Thiès, Sen., 69,000......F1   22
Thimbu, Bhu...........C8   20
Thionville, Fr., 31,811...C7   5
Thisted, co., Den.,
86,703.............*I3   11
Thivai (Thebes), Grc.,
15,779.............*C4   14
Thomas, Okla., 1,211...B3   79
Thomas, W. Va., 830....B5   87
Thomas, co., Ga., 34,319...F3   55
Thomas, co., Kans., 7,358..C2   61
Thomas, co., Nebr., 1,078..C5   71
Thomaston, Ala., 857....C2   46
Thomaston, Conn., 4,700..C4   52
Thomaston, Ga., 9,336...D2   55
Thomaston, Maine, 2,300..D3   64
Thomaston, N.Y., 2,767..*E7   75
Thomasville, Ala., 3,182...D2   46
Thomasville, Ga., 18,246...F3   55
Thomasville, N.C., 15,190..B2   76
Thompson, Conn., 500...B9   52
Thompson Falls, Mont.,
1,274...............C1   70
Thompsonville, Conn.,
21,000..............A6   52
Thomson, Ga., 4,522.....C4   55
Thorburn, N.S., Can.,
1,000...............D7   43
Thornaby-on-Tees, Eng.,
22,900..............C6   4
Thornbury, Ont., Can.,
1,097...............C4   41
Thorndale, Tex., 995.....D4   84
Thornton, Colo., 11,353..*B6   51
Thornton, Idaho, 200....F7   57
Thornton, Ill., 3,667....*B6   58
Thornton, Miss., 250....B3   68
Thorntown, Ind., 1,486...D4   59
Thornwood, N.Y., 3,500..*D7   75
Thorofare, N.J., 900.....D2   74
Thorold, Ont., Can.,
8,633...............D5   41
Thorp, Wis., 1,496......D3   88
Thorpe, W. Va., 1,102...D3   87
Thorsby, Ala., 968.......C3   46

Thouars, Fr., 11,257......D3   5
Thousand Oaks, Calif.,
2,934..............*E4   50
Three Forks, Mont.,
1,161...............E5   70
Three Hills, Alta., Can.,
1,491...............D4   38
Three Oaks, Mich., 1,763..G4   66
Three Rivers, Mass., 2,400..B3   65
Three Rivers, Mich.,
7,092...............G5   66
Three Rivers, Miss., 150..E5   68
Three Rivers, Tex.,
1,932...............E3   84
Throckmorton, Tex.,
1,299...............C3   84
Throckmorton, co., Tex.,
2,767...............C3   84
Throop, Pa., 4,732......m18   81
Thule, Grnld., 206......*B14   33
Thun, Switz., 32,000.....E3   6
Thunder Bay, dist., Ont.,
Can., 138,518........o17   41
Thunderbolt, Ga., 1,925...D5   55
Thurgau, canton, Switz.,
166,420............*E4   6
Thüringia, former state,
Ger., 2,927,497......*C5   6
Thuringia, reg., Ger......C5   6
Thurles, Ire., 6,700......D3   4
Thurmont, Md., 1,998....A3   53
Thurso, Que., Can.,
3,310...............D2   42
Thurso, Scot., 9,100......A5   4
Thurston, co., Nebr.,
7,237...............B9   71
Thurston, co., Wash.,
55,049..............C3   86
Thysville, Con. K., 11,600..B2   24
Tiberias, Isr., 22,300...B3, g5   15
Tibet, prov., China,
1,300,000...........B8   20
Tiburon, Calif., 1,500....*C2   50
Tice, Fla., 4,377........F5   54
Ticino, canton, Switz.,
195,566............*E4   6
Tickfaw, La., 317.......D5   63
Ticonderoga, N.Y., 3,568..B7   75
Ticul, Mex., 10,893......C7   34
Tidioute, Pa., 860......C3   81
Tiehling, China, 45,000...C9   17
Tienen, Bel., 22,736.....B6   5
Tienshui, China, 63,000...E6   17
Tientsin, China,
2,850,000...........D8   17
Tie Plant, Miss., 350....B4   68
Tierra Blanca, Mex.,
16,556..........D5, n15   34
Tierra del Fuego, isl.,
Chile...............h12   28
Tietê, Braz., 8,729....C3, m8   30
Tiff City, Mo., 100......E3   69
Tiffin, Ohio, 21,478.....A2   78
Tiflis, see Tbilisi, Sov. Un.
Tift, co., Ga., 23,487.....E3   55
Tifton, Ga., 9,903......E3   55
Tiftona, Tenn., 1,500....*D8   83
Tigard, Oreg., 1,844.....h12   80
Tigil, Sov. Un., 1,200....D18   13
Tignish, P.E.I., Can., 994..C6   43
Tigris, riv., Asia.......F7   13
Tijuana, Mex., 152,374...A1   34
Tikhvin, Sov. Un., 34,300..B9   12
Tiksi, Sov. Un., 1,000....B15   13
Tilburg, Neth., 141,600...B6   5
Tilbury, Ont., Can., 3,030..E2   41
Tilden, Ill., 808........E4   58
Tilden, Nebr., 917......B8   71
Tilghman, Md., 900.....C5   53
Tiline, Ky., 150........A3   62
Tillamook, Oreg., 4,244...B3   80
Tillamook, co., Oreg.,
18,955..............B3   80
Tillicum, Wash., 1,900..*B3   86
Tillman, co., Okla.,
14,654..............C2   79
Tillsonburg, Ont., Can.,
6,600...............E4   41
Tilton, Ill., 2,598......C6   58
Tilton, N.H., 1,129......E4   73
Tiltonsville, Ohio, 2,454..B5   78
Timaru, N.Z., 27,314....P13   26
Timbauba, Braz.,
21,019.............*D7   27
Timberlake, Va., 2,700..*C3   85
Times Beach, Mo., 986..*C7   69
Timiskaming, dist., Ont.,
Can., 50,971........o19   41
Timişoara, Rom., 147,800..C5   10
Timmins, Ont., Can.,
29,270.............o19   41
Timmonsville, S.C.,
2,178...............C8   82
Timoneng, Guam, 5,380..*F6   2
Timor, isl., Indon........G6   19
Timor Portuguese, see
Portuguese Timor,
dep., Asia

Timpson, Tex., 1,120.....D5   84
Tineo, Sp., 21,338.......A2   8
Tinley Park, Ill., 8,750....k9   58
Tinsley, Miss., 250.......C3   68
Tioga, N. Dak., 2,087....B2   77
Tioga, co., N.Y., 43,597...C4   75
Tioga, co., Pa., 36,614....C7   81
Tippah, co., Miss., 15,093..A5   68
Tipp City, Ohio, 4,267....C1   78
Tippecanoe, co., Ind.,
89,122..............D4   59
Tipperary, Ire., 4,500....D2   4
Tipperary, co., Ire.,
122,800............*D3   4
Tipton, Calif., 900......D4   50
Tipton, Ind., 5,604......D5   59
Tipton, Iowa, 2,862......C6   60
Tipton, Mo., 1,639......C5   69
Tipton, Okla., 1,117.....C2   79
Tipton, co., Ind., 15,856..D5   59
Tipton, co., Tenn., 28,564..B2   83
Tiptonville, Tenn., 2,068..A2   83
Tiranë (Tirana), Alb.,
152,000.............B2   14
Tiranë (Tirana), pref.,
Alb................*B2   14
Tirano, It., 7,517.......A3   9
Tiraspol, Sov. Un.,
75,000..............H7   12
Tire, Tur., 26,643......C6   14
Tîrgoviște, Rom., 27,200..C7   10
Tîrgu-jiu, Rom., 19,618...C6   10
Tîrgul-Neamt, Rom.,
10,373..............B8   10
Tîrgul-Ocna, Rom.,
11,227..............B8   10
Tîrgu-Mureș, Rom.,
71,200..............B7   10
Tîrgu-Sacuesc, Rom.,
7,500...............B8   10
Tîrnăveni, Rom., 14,883..B7   10
Tírnavos, Grc., 10,805...*C4   14
Tirol, state, Aus.,
462,899.............E5   6
Tirol, reg., Aus.........E5   6
Tiruchirappalli, India,
249,862.............F6   20
Tirunelveli, India,
87,988..............G6   20
Tisdale, Sask., Can.,
2,402...............E3   39
Tishomingo, Okla., 2,381..C5   79
Tishomingo, co., Miss.,
13,899..............A5   68
Tiskilwa, Ill., 951.......B4   58
Tisza, riv., Hung., Yugo..B5   10
Tiszafured, Hung., 10,318..B5   10
Tiszakecske, Hung., 6,626..B5   10
Titicaca, lake, Bol., Peru..C2   29
Titograd, Yugo., 29,043...D4   10
Titovo Užice, Yugo.,
20,069..............D4   10
Titov Veles, Yugo.,
26,618..............E5   10
Titus, co., Tex., 16,785...C5   84
Titusville, Fla., 6,410....D6   54
Titusville, N.J., 1,000...C3   74
Titusville, Pa., 8,356....C2   81
Tiverton, Eng., 13,100...E5   4
Tiverton, R.I., 6,500....C12   52
Tivoli, It., 37,700....D4, h9   9
Tivoli, Tex., 500.......E4   84
Tixtla, Mex., 8,500.....o14   34
Tizapán, Mex., 5,620....h9   34
Tizimín, Mex., 15,723...C7   34
Tizi-Ouzou, Alg., 26,363..A5   22
Tiznit, Mor., 7,694......C3   22
Tjilatjap, Indon., 28,309..G3   19
Tjirebon, Indon., 153,405..G3   19
Tlalpan, Mex., 22,957...h9   34
Tlaxcala, state, Mex.,
346,699.............D5   34
Tlaxiaco, Mex., 6,082...D5   34
Tlemcen, Alg., 82,527...B4   22
Toast, N.C., 2,023......A2   76
Toba, Jap., 30,098.....o15   18
Tobarra, Sp., 8,243.....C5   8
Tobol, riv., Sov. Un.....D9   13
Tobolsk, Sov. Un., 36,484..D9   13
Tobyhanna, Pa., 900....D11   81
Tocantins, riv., Braz.....D6   27
Toccoa, Ga., 7,303......B3   55
Toccoa Falls, Ga., 300...B3   55
Tochigi, Jap., 55,000..H9, m8   18
Tochigi, pref., Jap.,
1,521,656..........*H9   18
Tocopilla, Chile, 21,000..D1   29
Todd, co., Ky., 11,364...D2   62
Todd, co., Minn., 23,119..D4   67
Todd, co., S. Dak., 4,661..G5   77
Togo, country, Afr.,
1,680,000...........G5   22
Tokat, Tur., 32,654.....B11   14
Tokenon, Kor., 15,711...G2   18
Tokushima, Jap., 193,233..I7   18
Tokushima, pref., Jap.,
815,115............*I7   18
Tokuyama, Jap., 84,687..I6   18

Tokyo, Jap., 8,893,094
　(*16,900,000)......I9, n18　18
Tokyo, pref., Jap.,
　10,869,244............*I9　18
Tolbukhin (Dobrich), Bul.,
　55,111.................D8　10
Toledo, Ill., 998.........D5　58
Toledo, Iowa, 2,417......B5　60
Toledo, Ohio, 318,003..A2, e6　78
Toledo, Oreg., 3,053......C3　80
Toledo, Sp., 40,651.......C3　8
Toledo, prov., Sp.,
　521,637...............*C3　8
Toler, Ky., 700..........C7　62
Tolima, dept., Col.,
　841,424...............C2　32
Tolland, co., Conn.,
　68,737................B7　52
Tolleson, Ariz., 3,886.....D1　48
Tolmin, Yugo., 1,638.....B1　10
Tolna, Hung., 8,748......B4　10
Tolna, co., Hung.,
　267,415...............*B4　10
Tolono, Ill., 1,802........D5　58
Tolosa, Sp., 16,281.......A4　8
Toluca, Ill., 1,352........B4　58
Toluca [de Lerdo], Mex.,
　77,124.............D5, n14　34
Tomah, Wis., 5,321.......E3　88
Tomahawk, Wis., 3,348...C4　88
Tomakomai, Jap.,
　81,812...............E10　18
Tomakovka, Sov. Un.,
　10,000...............H10　12
Tomar, Port., 8,034.......C1　8
Tomari, Sov. Un.,
　16,100...............E17　13
Tomaszow, Pol., 7,338.....C7　7
Tomaszow Mazowiecki,
　Pol., 57,200...........C6　7
Tomball, Tex., 1,713......D5　84
Tombouctou (Timbuktu),
　Mali, 7,500............E4　22
Tombstone, Ariz., 1,283....D4　48
Tomé, Chile, 26,900......B2　28
Tomelloso, Sp., 27,815....C4　8
Tom Green, co., Tex.,
　64,630................D2　84
Tomkins Cove, N.Y.,
　800................D7, m14　75
Tommot, Sov. Un.,
　4,800................D15　13
Tompkins, co., N.Y.,
　66,164................C4　75
Tomsk, Sov. Un.,
　302,000...............D11　13
Toms River, N.J., 8,000...D4　74
Tonalá, Mex., 13,208.....D6　34
Tonasket, Wash., 958.....A6　86
Tonawanda, N.Y., 21,946.B2　75
Tondano, Indon., 15,007...E6　19
Tønder, Den., 7,192.......A4　6
Tønder, co., Den., 42,842..*J3　11
Tonga, Br. dep., Oceania,
　72,000................H9　2
Tonganoxie, Kans.,
　1,354.............C8, k15　61
Tonka Bay, Minn., 1,204..*F5　67
Tonkawa, Okla., 3,415....A4　79
Tonkin, reg., Viet.,
　11,000,000.............A3　19
Tonk Raj (Tonk),
　India, 42,833..........C6　20
Tonopah, Nev., 1,679.....B3　72
Tönsberg, Nor.,
　12,400.............H4, p28　11
Tooele, Utah, 9,133...A5, D2　72
Tooele, co., Utah, 17,868..A5　72
Toole, co., Mont., 7,904...B5　70
Toombs, co., Ga., 16,837..D4　55
Toowoomba, Austl.,
　55,774................E9　25
Topanga, Calif., 3,500....*F4　50
Topeka, Kans., 124,000
　(*146,000)........C8, k13　61
Topol'čany, Czech.,
　10,400................D5　7
Topolovgrad, Bul., 6,591..D8　10
Toppenish, Wash., 5,667..C5　86
Topsfield, Mass., 2,200....A6　65
Topsham, Maine,
　2,300...............E3, g8　64
Topton, Pa., 1,684......F10　81
Torbay, Newf., Can.,
　1,445................E5　44
Torhout, Bel., 13,465.....B5　5
Toride, Jap., 17,100.....n19　18
Torino Turin, It.,
　1,116,600.............B1　9
Toro, Sp., 10,218........B3　8
Torokszentmiklós, Hung.,
　17,952...............B5　10
Toronto, Ont., Can.,
　672,407..........D5, m15　41
Toronto, Ohio, 7,780.....B5　78
Toropets, Sov. Un.,
　25,000...............C8　12

Torquay, Eng., 52,000.....E5　4
Torrance, Calif., 100,991..n12　50
Torrance, co., N. Mex.,
　6,497.................B5　48
Torre Annunziata, It.,
　59,000................D5　9
Torre del Greco, It.,
　81,700................D5　9
Torredonjimeno, Sp.,
　14,204................D4　8
Torrelavega, Sp., 14,800...A3　8
Torremaggiore, It.,
　17,318................D5　9
Torrens, lake, Austl.......F6　25
Torrente, Sp., 24,042.....C5　8
Torreón, Mex., 179,901
　(*310,000)............B4　34
Torre Pacheco, Sp.,
　9,541.................D5　8
Torres Novas, Port.,
　7,291.................C1　8
Torrevieja, Sp., 9,234.....D5　8
Torrington, Conn.,
　30,045................B4　52
Torrington, Wyo., 4,188...D8　89
Torrox, Sp., 7,384........D4　8
Tortilla Flat, Ariz., 100...C3　48
Tortona, It., 20,400......B2　9
Tortosa, Sp., 18,900......B6　8
Torun, Pol., 111,300......B5　7
Torzhok, Sov. Un.,
　32,000...............C10　12
Toscana, pol. dist., It.,
　3,286,160.............*C3　9
Tosno, Sov. Un., 10,000..C10　12
Tosya, Tur., 13,699.....B10　14
Totana, Sp., 9,949........D5　8
Totkomlos, Hung., 8,122..B5　10
Totonicapán, Guat.,
　6,405.................D6　34
Totowa, N.J., 10,897.....B4　74
Tottenham, Eng.,
　113,126..............k12　4
Tottori, Jap., 75,000.....I7　18
Tottori, pref., Jap.,
　579,853..............*I7　18
Totz, Ky., 700...........D6　62
Toubkal, mtn., Mor.......C3　22
Tougaloo, Miss., 1,000...C3　68
Toul, Fr., 14,155.........C6　5
Toulon, Fr., 161,786......F6　5
Toulon, Ill., 1,213........B4　58
Toulouse, Fr., 323,724....F4　5
Toungoo, Bur., 31,589...E10　20
Touraine, former prov.,
　Fr., 392,000...........D4　5
Tourcoing, Fr., 89,258....B5　5
Tourlaville, Fr., 11,569...C3　5
Tours, Fr., 92,944........D4　5
Towaco, N.J., 1,000......B4　74
Towanda, Kans.,
　1,031..............E7, k12　61
Towanda, Pa., 4,293......C9　81
Tower City, Pa., 1,968....E8　81
Town and Country, Mo.,
　1,440................*C7　69
Towner, N. Dak., 948.....B5　77
Towner, co., N. Dak.,
　5,624.................B6　77
Townley, Ala., 450.......B2　46
Town of Pines, Ind., N.Y.,
　939.................*A4　59
Town of Tonawanda, N.Y.,
　88,556...............*B2　75
Towns, co., Ga., 4,538....B3　55
Townsend, Mass., 1,200...A4　65
Townsend, Mont., 1,528...D5　70
Townsville, Austl., 58,760.C8　25
Towson, Md., 48,500.B4, g11　53
Toyama, Jap., 239,810....H8　18
Toyama, pref., Jap.,
　1,025,465.............*H8　18
Toyohashi, Jap.,
　238,672..........I8, o16　18
Tozeur, Tun., 11,820......B6　22
Trabzon (Trebizond),
　Tur., 53,039.........B12　14
Tracadie, N.B., Can.,
　1,651.................B5　43
Tracy, Calif., 14,443..D3, h10　50
Tracy, Minn., 2,862.......F3　67
Tracy City, Tenn., 1,577..D7　83
Traer, Iowa, 1,623........B5　60
Trafford, Pa., 4,330.....k14　81
Traiguén, Chile, 10,000...B2　28
Trail, B.C., Can.,
　11,580.............E9, o19　37
Trail Creek, Ind., 2,346...A4　59
Trailer Estates, Fla.,
　1,562................*E4　54
Traill, co., N. Dak.,
　10,583...............C8　77
Trainer, Pa., 2,358......*G11　81
Tralee, Ire., 11,200......D2　4
Tranås, Swe., 15,400.....H6　11
Trani, It., 38,129........D6　9
Transcona, Man., Can.,
　14,248...............E3　40

Transilvania, prov.,
　Rom., 3,420,859......*B6　10
Transvaal, prov., S. Afr.,
　6,273,477.............E5　24
Transylvania, co., N.C.,
　16,372................f10　76
Transylvania, reg., Rom...B6　10
Trapani, It., 78,800......E4　9
Trappe, Pa., 1,264......*F11　81
Traralgon, Austl., 12,300..I6　26
Trás-os-Montes, reg.,
　Port., 558,700.........B2　8
Trás-os-Montes e Alto
　Douro, prov., Port.,
　639,846..............*B2　8
Traunstein, Ger., 14,400...E6　6
Travelers Rest, S.C.,
　1,973.................B3　82
Traverse, co., Minn.,
　7,503.................E2　67
Traverse City, Mich.,
　18,432................D5　66
Travis, co., Tex., 212,136.D4　84
Travnik, Yugo., 9,984....C3　10
Treasure, co., Mont.,
　1,345.................D9　70
Treasure Island, Fla.,
　3,506................*E4　54
Trebic, Czech., 19,200....D3　7
Trebinje, Yugo., 4,072....D4　10
Trebisov, Czech., 9,300...D6　7
Trego, co., Kans., 5,473..D4　61
Treinta y Tres, Ur.,
　21,035................E2　30
Treinta y Tres, dept., Ur.,
　43,200...............*E2　30
Trélazé, Fr., 9,400.......D3　5
Trelew, Arg., 11,852.....C3　28
Trelleborg, Swe., 19,200..J5　11
Tremont, Ill., 1,558......C4　58
Tremont, Pa., 1,893......E9　81
Tremonton, Utah, 2,115..A5　72
Trempealeau, co., Wis.,
　23,377................D2　88
Trencin, Czech., 22,300...D5　7
Trenggauu, state, Mala.,
　346,000...............*D2　19
Trenque Lauquén, Arg.,
　10,887................B4　28
Trentino-Alto-Adige,
　pol. dist., It., 785,967..*A3　9
Trento, It., 80,300.......A3　9
Trenton, N.S., Can.,
　3,140.................D7　43
Trenton, Ont., Can.,
　13,183................C7　41
Trenton, Fla., 941........C4　54
Trenton, Ga., 1,301......B1　55
Trenton, Ill., 2,095.......E4　58
Trenton, Mich.,
　18,439.........F7, p15　66
Trenton, Mo., 6,262.....A4　69
Trenton, Nebr., 914......D4　71
Trenton, N.J., 114,167....C3　74
Trenton, Ohio, 3,064.....C1　78
Trenton, Tenn., 4,225....B3　83
Trentwood, Wash., 1,387.*B8　86
Tres Arroyos, Arg.,
　33,318................B4　28
Trescow, Pa., 1,145......E10　81
Trés Corações, Braz.,
　17,498................C3　30
Três Lagoas, Braz., 14,520.C2　30
Treutlen, co., Ga., 5,874..D4　55
Treviglio, It., 23,413.....B2　9
Treviso, It., 79,200......B4　9
Trevorton, Pa., 2,597.....E8　81
Trevose, Pa., 6,000.....*F12　81
Trevose Heights, Pa.,
　1,500................*F12　81
Treynor, Iowa, 476.......C2　60
Trezevant, Tenn., 944.....A3　83
Triangle, Va., 2,948......B5　85
Tribbett, Miss., 200......B3　68
Tribune, Kans., 1,036.....D2　61
Trichinopoly, see
　Tiruchirappal, India
Trichur, India, 73,038....F6　20
Trier, Ger., 86,800.......D3　6
Trieste, It., 277,600......B4　9
Trigg, co., Ky., 8,870....D2　62
Triglav, mtn., Yugo.......B1　10
Trigueros, Sp., 6,454.....D2　8
Trikkala, Grc., 27,876....C3　14
Trikkala, prov., Grc.,
　142,781..............*C3　14
Tri Lakes, Ind., 1,089....*B7　59
Trimble, co., Ky., 5,102..B4　62
Trimont, Minn., 942.....G4　67
Trincomalee, Cey.,
　26,356................G7　20
Tring-Jonction, Que.,
　Can., 1,214...........C6　42
Trinidad, Bol., 8,695.....B3　29
Trinidad, Colo., 10,691...D6　51
Trinidad, Cuba, 19,700...D4　35
Trinidad, Tex., 786.......C4　84
Trinidad, Ur., 15,455.....E1　30

Trinidad and Tobago,
　country, N.A., 922,000..A5　32
Trinité, Mart., 3,631.....I14　35
Trinity, Tex., 1,787......D5　84
Trinity, co., Calif., 9,706...B2　50
Trinity, co., Tex., 7,539..D5　84
Trinity, mts., Calif.......B2　50
Trino, It., 8,100.........B2　9
Trion, Ga., 2,227........B1　55
Tripoli, Iowa, 1,179......B5　60
Tripolis, Grc., 18,500....D4　14
Tripoli, see Tarabulus,
　Leb.
Tripoli (Ţarābulus), Libya,
　212,600..............B7　22
Tripp, S. Dak., 837......G8　77
Tripp, co., S. Dak., 8,761.G6　77
Tristate Village, Ill.,
　1,700................*B5　58
Triumph, La., 900.......E6　63
Trivandrum, India,
　239,815..............G6　20
Trnava, Czech., 33,000...D4　7
Trois-Pistoles, Que.,
　Can., 4,349...........A8　42
Trois-Rivières, Que., Can.,
　56,413 (*87,432).......C5　42
Troitsk, Sov. Un., 80,000.D9　13
Trollhättan, Swe., 33,100.H5　11
Troms, co., Nor.,
　130,900..............*C8　11
Tromsö, Nor., 33,400.....C8　11
Trona, Calif., 1,500......E5　50
Trondheim, Nor.,
　113,600..............F4　11
Troodos, mtn., Cyp......E9　14
Tropea, It., 6,702........E5　9
Trotwood, Ohio, 4,992...C1　78
Troup, Tex., 1,667.......C5　84
Troup, co., Ga., 47,189...C1　55
Trousdale, co., Tenn.,
　4,914.................A5　83
Trouville, Fr., 6,622......C3　5
Trowbridge, Eng., 16,200.E5　4
Troy, Ala., 10,234.......D4　46
Troy, Ill., 1,778.........E4　58
Troy, Kans., 1,051.......C8　61
Troy, Mich., 19,382.....*F7　66
Troy, Mo., 1,779........C7　69
Troy, N.Y., 67,492......C7　75
Troy, N.C., 2,346.......B3　76
Troy, Ohio, 13,685......B1　78
Troy, Pa., 1,478........C8　81
Troyes, Fr., 67,406......C6　5
Trubchevsk, Sov. Un.,
　10,000...............E9　12
Trucial Coast, country,
　Asia, 86,000..........E5　15
Trucksville, Pa., 2,300..*D10　81
Trujillo, Peru, 99,800....C2　31
Trujillo, Sp., 13,326.....C3　8
Trujillo, Ven., 18,957....B3　32
Trujillo, state, Ven.,
　326,634..............B3　32
Truman, Minn., 1,256....G4　67
Trumann, Ark., 4,511....B5　49
Trumansburg, N.Y.,
　1,768.................C4　75
Trumbull, Conn., 20,379..E4　52
Trumbull, co., Ohio,
　208,526..............A5　78
Truro, N.S., Can.,
　12,421...............D6　43
Truro, Eng., 13,900......E4　4
Trussville, Ala., 2,510.B3, E5　46
Truth or Consequences,
　N. Mex., 4,269........C5　48
Trutnov, Czech., 23,000..C3　7
Tryon, N.C., 2,223......f10　76
Trysil, Nor., 787........G5　11
Tsangwu, see Wuchow,
　China
Tselinograd (Akmolinsk),
　Sov. Un., 139,000.....D10　13
Tsinan (Chinan), China
　862,000..............D8　17
Tsinghai (Chinghai),
　prov., China, 2,050,000..D8　17
Tsingtao (Chingtao),
　China, 1,121,000......D9　17
Tsingyuan, see Paoting,
　China
Tsitsihar, China, 668,000..B9　17
Tskhinvali, Sov. Un.,
　24,000...............A14　14
Tsu, Jap., 117,214...I8, o15　18
Tsuchiura, Jap.,
　56,000..........H10, m19　18
Tsuni, China, 97,500.....F6　17
Tsuruga, Jap.,
　39,200...........I8, n15　18
Tsuruoka, Jap., 67,000...G9　18
Tsushima, Jap., 46,559...n15　18
Tsuyama, Jap., 50,000...I7　18
Tubarão, Braz., 29,615...D3　30
Tübingen, Ger., 52,000...D4　6
Tuchola, Pol., 5,750......B4　7
Tuckahoe, N.Y., 750....h13　75

Tucker, Ga., 4,000.......A5   55
Tucker, co., W. Va.,
  7,750.................B5   87
Tuckerman, Ark., 1,539...B4   49
Tuckerton, N.J., 1,536...D4   74
Tucson, Ariz., 240,000
  (*310,000)............C3   48
Tucumán, Arg., 280,000...E2   29
Tucumán, prov., Arg.,
  780,348..............E2   29
Tucumcari, N. Mex.,
  8,143................B7   48
Tudela, Sp., 16,456......A5   8
Tuguegarao, Phil., 23,584..B6   19
Tuktoyaktuk, N.W. Ter.,
  Can., 409............C7   36
Tukwila, Wash., 1,804....fl1   86
Tula, Sov. Un., 351,000..D11   12
Tulancingo, Mex.,
  26,839...........C5, m14   34
Tulare, Calif., 13,824.....D4   50
Tulare, co., Calif.,
  168,403.............D4   50
Tularosa, N. Mex., 3,200..C5   48
Tulcán, Ec., 16,448......A2   31
Tulcea, Rom., 24,639.....C9   10
Tuléar, Malag., 33,850...E8   24
Tulelake, Calif., 950.....B3   50
Tulia, Tex., 4,410.......B2   84
Tūl Karm, Jordan,
  20,690...............B3   15
Tullahoma, Tenn.,
  12,242...............B5   83
Tullamore, Ire., 6,700...D3   4
Tulle, Fr., 19,084.......E4   5
Tullytown, Pa., 2,452....*F12   81
Tulsa, Okla., 315,000
  (*420,000)...........A6   79
Tulsa, co., Okla.,
  346,038.............B6   79
Tuluá, Col., 56,539......C2   32
Tulufan, see Turfan,
  China.
Tulun, Sov. Un., 34,000..D13   13
Tumaco, Col., 25,145....C2   32
Tumbarumba, Austl.,
  1,511................G7   26
Tumbes, Peru, 7,416.....B1   31
Tumbes, Peru, 30,035....B1   31
Tumen, China, 28,000....C10   17
Tumkur, India, 47,277...F6   20
Tumwater, Wash., 3,885...B3   86

Tunbridge Wells, Eng.,
  40,400...............E7   4
Tunghwa, China, 129,100..F2   18
Tungliao (Payintala),
  China, 40,000.........C9   17
Tunguragua (Tungurahua),
  prov., Ec., 178,709....B2   31
Tunhua, China, 35,000...C10   17
Tunica, Miss., 1,445.....A3   68
Tunica, co., Miss., 16,826..A3 68
Tunis, Tun., 410,000.....A7   22
Tunisia, country, Afr.,
  4,458,000............A6   22
Tunja, Col., 40,451......B3   32
Tunkhannock, Pa.,
  2,297...............C10   81
Tuntutuliak, Alsk., 144...C7   47
Tuolumne, Calif., 1,403...D3   50
Tuolumne, co., Calif.,
  14,404..............C4   50
Tupelo, Miss., 17,221.....A5   68
Tupper Lake, N.Y.,
  5,200..............A6, f10   75
Tupungato, mtn., Arg.....A3   28
Tura, Sov. Un., 2,000....C13   13
Turbaco, Col., 14,255....A2   32
Turčiansky Svatý Martin,
  Czech., 22,400........D5   7
Turda, Rom., 37,800.....B6   10
Turek, Pol., 13,500......B5   7
Turfan (Tulufan) China
  25,000..............C2   17
Turgay, Sov. Un., 5,800..E9   13
Turgovishte, Bul., 10,505..D8   10
Turgtlu, Tur., 31,459.....C6   14
Turka, Sov. Un., 10,000..G4   12
Turkestan, Sov. Un.,
  38,152..............E9   13
Turkeve, Hung., 10,339...B5   10
Turkey, Tex., 813........B2   84
Turkey, country, Asia,
  30,677,000..........C9   14
Turkmen, S.S.R., rep.,
  Sov. Un., 1,850,000...*F8   16
Turks and Caicos Islands,
  br. dep., N.A., 5,668...D8   35
Turku, Fin., 130,800.....G10   11
Turku-Pori, prov., Fin.,
  607,073.............*G10   11
Turley, Okla., 4,000......A6   79
Turlock, Calif., 9,116....D3   50
Turner, Kans., 1,800.....B8   61

Turner, co., Ga., 8,439....E3   55
Turner, co., S. Dak.,
  11,159...............G8   77
Turners Falls, Mass.,
  4,400................A2   65
Turner Valley, Alta., Can.,
  702..................D3   38
Turnhout, Bel., 36,444....B6   5
Turnov, Czech., 11,500...C3   7
Tŭrnovo, Bul., 37,269....D7   10
Turnu Măgurele, Rom.,
  18,055...............D7   10
Turnu Severin, Rom.,
  32,486...............C6   10
Turquino, peak, Cuba....D5   35
Turtkul, Sov. Un., 23,700..E9   13
Turtle Creek, Pa., 10,607..k14 81
Turukhansk, Sov. Un.,
  5,000................C11   13
Tuscaloosa, Ala., 63,370..B2   46
Tuscaloosa, co., Ala.,
  109,047.............B2   46
Tuscany, reg., It.........C3   9
Tuscarawas, co., Ohio,
  76,789..............B4   78
Tuscola, Ill., 3,894......D5   58
Tuscola, co., Mich.,
  43,305..............E7   66
Tusculum College, Tenn.,
  1,433...............*C5   83
Tuscumbia, Ala., 8,994...A2   46
Tuskegee, Ala., 7,240.....C4   46
Tuskegee Institute, Ala.,
  3,400...............C4   46
Tustin, Calif., 2,006.....*F5   50
Tuticorin, India, 124,230..G6   20
Tutrakan, Bul., 7,203.....C8   10
Tuttlingen, Ger., 24,900...E4   6
Tutwiler, Miss., 912......A3   68
Tuxedo, Man., Can.,
  1,627...............E3   40
Tuxedo, Md., 1,000......C4   53
Tuxedo Park, N.Y.,
  880.............D6, m14   75
Tuxpan, Mex.,
  14,971...........C3, m11   34
Tuxpan, Mex., 10,833....n12   34
Tuxpan de Rodriguez
  Cano, Mex.,
  23,262...........C5, m15   34
Tuxtla Guiterrez, Mex.,
  24,648..............D6   34

Tuy, Sp., 2,779..........A1   8
Tuzla, Yugo., 37,673.....C4   10
Tweed, Ont., Can.,
  1,791...............C7   41
Twenty-Nine Palms, Calif.,
  2,000...............E5   50
Twickenham, Eng.,
  100,822............m11   4
Twig, Minn., 175........D6   67
Twiggs, co., Ga., 7,935...D3   55
Twillingate, Newf., Can.,
  947.................D4   44
Twin City, Ga., 1,095....D4   55
Twin Falls, Idaho,
  20,893..............G4   57
Twin Falls, co., Idaho,
  41,842..............G4   57
Twin Lakes, Calif.,
  1,849..............*D2   50
Twin Lakes, Ohio, 900...*A4   78
Twin Lakes, Wis.,
  1,497.............F5, n11   88
Twin Oaks, Pa., 1,500...*G11   81
Twin Orchards, N.Y.,
  1,000..............*C5   75
Twin Rocks, Pa., 950....F4   81
Twinsburg, Ohio, 4,098...A4   78
Two Harbors, Minn.,
  4,695...............C7   67
Two Rivers, Wis.,
  12,393...........D6, h10   88
Tyler, Minn., 1,138......F2   67
Tyler, Tex., 51,230......C5   84
Tyler, co., Tex., 10,666...D5   84
Tyler, co., W. Va.,
  10,026..............B4   87
Tyler Heights, W. Va.,
  3,000..............*C3   87
Tyler Park, Va., 1,000...*B5   85
Tylertown, Miss., 1,532...D3   68
Tyndall, S. Dak., 1,262...H8   77
Tynemouth, Eng., 71,900..C6   4
Tyre (Sur), Leb.,
  10,400............A3, g5   15
Tyrell, co., N.C., 4,520...B6   76
Tyrone, Pa., 7,792......E5   81
Tyrone, co., N. Ire.,
  134,700............*C3   4
Tyumen, Sov. Un.,
  178,000............D9   13
Tzekung, China,
  291,300............F5   17

U

Ubá, Braz., 21,768.....C4, g6   30
Ube, Jap., 158,986.......J5   18
Ubeda, Sp., 28,956......C4   8
Uberaba, Braz., 72,053...B3   30
Uberlândia, Braz., 70,719..B3   30
Ubon, Thai., 27,222......B2   19
Ucayali, riv., Peru......C3   31
Uccle, Bel., 71,725......B6   5
Udaipur, India, 111,139...D5   20
Uddevalla, Swe., 34,700..H4   11
Udine, It., 89,900........A4   9
Udon Thani, Thai.,
  30,884..............B2   19
Ueda, Jap., 73,940...H9, m17   18
Uelen, Sov. Un., 800.....C21   13
Uelkal, Sov. Un., 800....C21   13
Uelzen, Ger., 25,000.....B5   6
Ueno, Jap., 36,100......o15   18
Ufa, Sov. Un., 665,000...D8   13
Uganda, country, Afr.,
  7,740,000............H4   23
Uglegorsk (Esutoru),
  Sov. Un., 20,000.....B11   18
Uglich, Sov. Un.,
  28,890..............C12   12

Uherské Hradiště, Czech.,
  12,800..............D4   7
Uhrichsville, Ohio, 6,201..B4   78
Uinta, co., Wyo., 7,484...E2   89
Uintah, co., Utah,
  11,852..............B7   72
Uitenhage, S. Afr.,
  48,755..............G5   24
Uji-yamada, see Ise, Jap.
Ujjain, India, 144,161.....D6   20
Ukhta, Sov. Un.,
  15,000..............C8   13
Ukiah, Calif., 9,900......C2   50
Ukraine (S.S.R.), rep.,
  Sov. Un., 45,500,000...*E6   16
Ulan Bator (Urga), Mong.,
  195,300.............B6   17
Ulan-Ude, Sov. Un.,
  213,000.............D13   13
Ulla, Sov. Un., 10,000...D7   12
Ulm, Ger., 93,800.......D4   6
Ulman, Mo., 100........C5   69
Ulsan, Kor., 53,100......I4   18
Ulster, co., N.Y.,
  118,804.............D6   75

Ulster, prov., Ire.,
  208,000............*C3   4
Ulugh Muztagh, mtn.,
  China...............A8   20
Ulverston, Eng., 10,500...C5   4
Ulyanovsk, Sov. Un.,
  265,000.............D7   13
Ulysses, Kans., 3,157.....E2   61
Uman, Sov. Un., 44,546..G8   12
Umatilla, Fla., 1,717.....D5   54
Umatillia, co., Oreg.,
  44,352..............B7   80
Umbria, pol. dist., It.,
  794,745............*C4   9
Umbria, reg., It.........C4   9
Umeå, Swe., 24,100......F9   11
Umm Ruwāba, Sud.,
  7,805...............F4   23
Umtali, Rh., 39,600......D6   24
Umvuma, Rh., 1,750.....D6   24
Una, S.C., 1,500........*B4   82
Unadilla, Ga., 1,304......D3   55
Unadilla, N.Y., 1,586.....C5   75
Unayzah, Sua., Ar.,
  50,000..............D3   15

Uncasville, Conn., 1,500...D8   52
Uncompahgre, mts.,
  Colo................C3   51
Underwood, N. Dak., 819..C4   77
Unecha, Sov. Un., 10,000..E9   12
Unggi, Kor., 20,882......E5   18
Unicoi, co., Tenn.,
  15,082..............C11   83
Union, Miss., 1,726......C4   68
Union, Mo., 3,937.......C6   69
Union, N.J., 51,499......B4   74
Union, Ohio, 1,072......C1   78
Union, Oreg., 1,490......B9   80
Union, S.C., 10,191......B4   82
Union, co., Ark., 49,518...D3   49
Union, co., Fla., 6,043...B4   54
Union, co., Ga., 6,510...B2   55
Union, co., Ill., 17,645...F4   58
Union, co., Ind., 6,457...E8   59
Union, co., Iowa, 13,712..C3   60
Union, co., Ky., 14,537...C2   62
Union, co., Miss., 18,904..A4   68
Union, co., N.J., 504,255..B4   74
Union, co., N. Mex.,
  6,068...............A7   48

Union, co., N.C.,
  48,389..............B2   76
Union, co., Ohio,
  22,853..............B2   78
Union, co., Oreg.,
  18,180..............B8   80
Union, co., Pa., 25,646...E7   81
Union, co., S.C., 30,015...B4   82
Union, co., S. Dak.,
  10,197..............H9   77
Union, co., Tenn.,
  8,498..............C10   83
Union, par., La.,
  17,624..............B3   63
Union Beach, N.J., 5,862..C4   74
Union City, Calif., 6,618..h8   50
Union City, Ga., 2,118....C2   55
Union City, Ind., 4,047...D8   59
Union City, Mich., 1,669..F5   66
Union City, N.J., 52,180..h8   74
Union City, Ohio, 1,657..B1   78
Union City, Pa., 3,819...C2   81
Union City, Tenn., 8,837..A2   83
Uniondale, N.Y., 20,500..*G2   52
Unión de Reyes, Cuba,
  5,500..............C3   35
Union Gap, Wash., 2,100..C5   86
Union Grove, Wis.,
  1,970..............F5, n11   88
Union Lake, Mich.,
  2,000..............*F7   66
Union of Soviet Socialist
  Republics, country,
  Europe, Asia, 233,000,000..   13
Union Park, Fla., 1,000...*D5   54
Union Point, Ga., 1,615...C3   55
Union Springs, Ala.,
  3,704..............C4   46
Union Springs, N.Y.,
  1,066..............C4   75
Uniontown, Ala., 1,993...C2   46
Uniontown, Ky., 1,255...C2   62
Uniontown, Ohio, 1,668..B4   78
Uniontown, Pa., 17,942..G2   81
Union Village, R.I.,
  1,500..............B10   52
Unionville, Conn., 2,300..B5   52
Unionville, Ga., 1,607..*E3   55
Unionville, Mo., 1,896...A4   69
United, Pa., 2,044......F3   81
United Arab Republic
  (Egypt), country, Afr.,
  27,285,000..............C3   23

United Kingdom of
  Great Britain and
  Northern Ireland
  country, Eur.,
  54,213,000..............   4
United States, country,
  N.A., 200,300,000..........   45
United States Air Force
  Acad., Colo., 5,500.....C6   51
Unity, Sask., Can., 1,902...E1   39
University, Miss.,
  4,200..............A4   68
University City, Mo.,
  51,249..............C7, f13   69
University Gardens, Md.,
  1,000..............*C4   53
University Heights, Ohio,
  16,641..............h9   78
University Hills, Md.,
  1,700..............*C4   53
University Park, Md.,
  3,098..............*C4   53
University Park, N.Mex.,
  3,800..............*C5   48
University Park, Tex.,
  23,202..............n10   84
University View, Ohio,
  1,300..............*C3   78
Unterwalden, canton,
  Switz., 45,323........*E4   6
Unye, Tur., 11,350......B11   14
Upington, S. Afr., 20,366..F4   24
Upland, Calif.,
  15,918..............E5, m13   50
Upland, Ind., 1,999......D7   59
Upland, Pa., 4,343......*G10   81
Upper Arlington, Ohio,
  28,486..............B3, k10   78
Upper Brookville, N.Y.,
  1,045..............*E7   75
Upper Darby, Pa.,
  93,158..............G11, p20   81
Upper Nyack, N.Y.,
  1,833..............*D7   75
Upper Saddle River, N.J.,
  3,570..............A4   74
Upper Sandusky, Ohio,
  4,941..............B2   78
Upper Silesia, reg., Pol.....g9   7
Upper Volta, country,
  Afr., 4,750,000..........F4   22
Uppsala, Swe.,
  80,500............H7, t35   11

Uppsala, co., Swe.,
  170,000..............*H7   11
Upshur, co., Tex., 19,793..C5   84
Upshur, co., W. Va.,
  18,292..............C4   87
Upson, co., Ga., 23,800....D2   55
Upton, Mass., 1,150....B4, h9   65
Upton, Wyo., 1,244......B8   89
Upton, co., Tex., 6,239....D2   84
Urakawa, Jap., 12,300....E11   18
Ural, riv., Sov. Un......E8   13
Uralsk, Sov. Un.,
  111,000..............D8   13
Urania, La., 1,063.......C3   63
Uranium City, Sask.,
  Can., 1,665..........E12   36
Uravan, Colo., 750......C2   51
Urawa, Jap., 221,337..I9, n18   18
Urbana, Ill., 27,294......C5   58
Urbana, Ohio, 10,461....B2   78
Urbancrest, Ohio, 1,029..m10   78
Urbandale, Iowa,
  10,310..............C4, e8   60
Urbino, It., 6,500......C4   9
Urfa, Tur., 59,863......D12   14
Uri, canton, Switz.,
  32,021..............E4   6
Urla, Tur., 10,800......*C6   14
Urmia, salt lake, Iran....D15   14
Uruapan del Progreso,
  Mex., 45,727......D4, n13   34
Uruguaiana, Braz.,
  48,358..............D1   30
Uruguay, country, S.A.,
  2,592,563............E1   30
Uruguay, riv., Arg.,
  Ur................E1   30
Urumchi (Tihwa), China,
  275,000..............C2   17
Urusha, Sov. Un.,
  10,000..............D15   13
Uryupinsk, Sov. Un.,
  29,900..............F14   12
Usak, Tur., 29,021......C7   14
Üsküdar, Tur., 111,821..B7   14
Usman, Sov. Un.,
  50,000..............E12   12
Usolye-Sibirskoye, Sov.
  Un., 60,000..........D13   13
Ussuriysk, Sov. Un.,
  113,000..............E16   13
Ústí nad Labem, Czech.,
  66,700..............C3   7

Ust-Kamenogorsk, Sov.
  Un., 195,000.........E11   13
Ust-Kut, Sov. Un.,
  21,900..............D13   13
Ust-Maya, Sov. Un.,
  2,300..............C16   13
Ust-Srednikan, Sov. Un.,
  800................C18   13
Ust-Tsilma, Sov. Un.,
  7,900..............C8   13
Ust-Usa, Sov. Un., 2,500..C8   13
Ustyuzhna, Sov. Un.,
  10,000..............B11   12
Usumbura, see
  Bujumbura, Burundi
Utah, co., Utah, 106,991..A6   72
Utah, state, U.S.,
  890,627..............   72
Utica, Ill., 1,014......B4   58
Utica, Mich., 1,454...F7, o15   66
Utica, N.Y., 97,000
  (*302,000)............B5   75
Utica, Ohio, 1,854......B3   78
Utica, S.C., 1,294......*B1   82
Utica Heights, Mich.,
  2,700..............*F8   66
Utiel, Sp., 10,076......C5   8
Utrecht, Neth., 261,000
  (*405,000)............A6   5
Utrecht, prov., Neth.,
  686,600..............*A6   5
Utrera, Sp., 35,200.....D3   8
Utsunomiya, Jap.,
  265,696..............H9   18
Uttaradit, Thai., 9,109...*B2   19
Uttar Pradesh, state,
  India,73,746,401........C6   20
Utuado, P.R., 9,870.....*G11   35
Uusimaa, prov., Fin.,
  668,211..............*G11   11
Uvalde, Tex., 10,293.....E3   84
Uvalde, co., Tex., 16,814...E3   84
Uvaly, Czech., 4,706.....n18   7
Uwajima, Jap., 53,000.....J6   18
Uxbridge, Ont., Can.,
  2,316..............C5   41
Uxbridge, Mass., 3,400...B4   65
Uzbek S.S.R., rep.,
  Sov. Un., 10,050,000...*E9   16
Uzhgrood, Sov. Un.,
  55,000..............G4   12
Uzunkopru, Tur.,
  18,300..............B6   14

V

Vaasa, Fin., 44,400.......F9   11
Vaasa, prov., Fin.,
  603,964..............*F9   11
Vac, Hung., 24,748......B4   10
Vacaville, Calif., 10,898...C3   50
Vacherie, La., 950......h11   63
Vadnais Heights, Minn.,
  2,459..............*F5   67
Vail Homes, N.J., 1,204..*C4   74
Valais, canton, Switz.,
  177,783..............E3   6
Valatie, N.Y., 1,237......C7   75
Val-Barrette, Que., Can.,
  557................*G20   36
Val-David, Que., Can.,
  1,118..............C3   42
Valdepeñas, Sp., 25,706...C4   8
Valdese, N.C., 2,941......B1   76
Valdivia, Chile, 61,300...B2   28
Valdivia, prov., Chile
  259,798..............B2   28
Val-d' Or, Que., Can.,
  10,983..............o20   41
Valdosta, Ga., 30,652....F3   55

Vale, Oreg., 1,491.......D9   80
Valença, Braz., 17,137.....E7   27
Valence, Fr., 52,532......E6   5
Valencia, Sp., 13,159.....C2   8
Valencia, Sp., 505,066.....C5   8
Valencia, Ven., 183,500..A4   32
Valencia, co., N. Mex.,
  39,085..............B4   48
Valencia, prov., Sp.,
  1,429,708............*C2   8
Valenciennes, Fr., 45,379
  (*172,000)............B5   5
Valentine, Nebr., 2,875....B5   71
Valera, Ven., 46,643......B3   32
Valhalla, N.Y.,
  4,500..............D7, m15   75
Valjevo, Yugo., 22,070....C4   10
Valka, Sov. Un., 25,000...C6   12
Valki, Sov. Un., 10,000...G10   12
Valladolid, Sp., 151,807..B3   8
Valladolid, prov., Sp.,
  363,106..............*B3   8
Valle d' Aosta, pol. dist.,
  It., 100,959..........*B1   9

Valle de la Pascua, Ven.,
  24,308..............*B4   32
Valle del Cauca, dept.,
  Col., 1,733,053.....   C2   32
Valle de Santiago, Mex.,
  21,795..............m13   34
Vallée-Jonction, Que.,
  Can., 1,405..........C7   42
Vallejo, Calif.,
  60,877..............C2   50
Valletta, Malta, 17,700
  (*203,000)............A7   22
Valley, Nebr., 1,452..C9, g12   71
Valley, co., Idaho,
  3,663..............E3   57
Valley, co., Mont.,
  17,080..............B10   70
Valley, co., Nebr., 6,590...C6   71
Valley Brook, Okla.,
  1,378..............*B4   79
Valley Center, Kans.,
  2,570..............E6, g12   61
Valley City, N. Dak.,
  7,809..............D7   77

Valley Cottage, N.Y.,
  3,000..............g13   75
Valleydale, Calif., 1,000..*F4   50
Valley Falls, Kans.,
  1,193..............C8, k15   61
Valleyfield, Que.,
  Can., 27,297.......D3, q18   42
Valley Mills, Tex., 1,061..D4   84
Valley Park, Miss., 100...C3   68
Valley Park, Mo., 3,452...fl2   69
Valley Station, Ky.,
  14,000..............A4   62
Valley Stream, N.Y.,
  38,591..............k13   75
Valley View, Ill., 1,741...*B5   58
Valley View, Ohio,
  1,221..............*A4   78
Valley View, Pa., 1,540....E9   81
Valmiera, Sov. Un.,
  10,000..............C5   12
Valparaíso, Chile, 252,900
  (*440,000)............A2   28
Valparaiso, Fla., 5,975....u15   54
Valparaiso, Ind., 16,938...B3   59

Valparaíso, prov., Chile,
618,112................A2   28
Valverde, Dom. Rep.,
17,885................D2   8
Val Verde, co., Tex.,
24,461................E2   84
Van, Tex., 1,103........C5   84
Van, Tur., 22,043......C14   14
Van, prov., Tur.,
211,034..............*C14   14
Van Alstyne, Tex., 1,608..C4   84
Van Buren, Ark., 6,787...B1   49
Van Buren, Ind., 929.....C6   59
Van Buren, Maine,
3,500................A5   64
Van Buren, co., Ark.,
7,228................B3   49
Van Buren, co., Iowa,
9,778................D5   60
Van Buren, co., Mich.,
48,395...............F4   66
Van Buren, co., Tenn.,
3,671................D6   83
Vance, co., N.C.,
32,002...............A4   76
Vanceburg, Ky., 1,881...B6   62
Vancouver, B.C., Can.,
384,552 (*790,165)..E6, f12   37
Vancouver, Wash.,
32,464...............D3   86
Vancouver, isl., B.C., Can..G8   36
Vandalia, Ill., 5,537......E4   58
Vandalia, Mo., 3,055.....B6   69
Vandalia, Ohio, 6,342...*C1   78
Vanderbilt, Pa., 826......F2   81
Vanderburgh, co., Ind.,
165,794..............H2   59
Vandercook Lake, Mich.,
5,000................*F6   66
Vandergrift, Pa., 8,742....E2   81
Vanderhoof, B.C., Can.,
1,460................C5   37
Vandling, Pa., 578.......C11   81
Vänern (Väner), lake,
Swe.................H5   11
Vänersborg, Swe., 18,500..H5   11
Van Horn, Tex., 1,953...o12   84
Vankleek Hill, Ont.,
Can., 1,735..........B10   41
Van Lear, Ky., 921.......C7   62
Vannes, Fr., 30,411......D2   5
Vanves, Fr., 25,585......g10   5
Van Wert, Ohio, 11,323...B1   78
Van Wert, co., Ohio,
28,840...............B1   78
Van Winkle, Miss., 2,000..C3   68
Van Yen, Viet., 10,000...*G5   17
Van Zandt, co., Tex.,
19,091...............C5   84
Var, dept., Fr., 469,557..*F7   5
Varaždin, Yugo., 26,239...B3   10
Varazze, It., 9,200.......B2   9
Varberg, Swe., 14,500....I5   11
Varel, Ger., 12,400......B4   6
Varennes, Que., Can.,
2,240.............D4, p20   42
Varese, It., 70,800.......B2   9
Varginha, Braz., 24,944...C3   30
Varkaus, Fin., 22,200....F12   11
Varmland, co., Swe.,
291,000..............*H5   11
Varnamo, Swe., 13,200...I6   11
Varna (Stalin), Bul.,
180,062..............D8   10
Varnsdorf, Czech.,
13,400...............C3   7
Varnville, S.C., 1,461.....F5   82
Vas, co., Hung., 283,096..*B3   10
Vasilkov, Sov. Un.,
10,000...............F8   12
Vaslui, Rom., 14,850.....B8   10
Vassar, Mich., 2,680......E7   66
Västerås, Swe.,
80,500............H7, t34   11
Västerbotten, co., Swe.,
238,600..............*F9   11
Västernörrland, co., Swe.,
283,300..............*F8   11
Västervik, Swe., 18,200...I7   11
Västmanland, co., Swe.,
235,881..............*H7   11
Vasto, It., 12,600........C5   9
Vatican City, country,
Eur., 1,000........D4, h8   9
Vaucluse, dept., Fr.,
303,536..............*F6   5
Vaud, canton, Switz.,
425,912..............*E2   6
Vaudreuil, Que.,
Can., 200........D3, q18   42
Vaudreuil co., Que.,
Can., 28,681.........D3   42
Vaughn, N. Mex., 1,170..B6   48
Vaupés, comisaría, Col.,
13,403...............C3   32
Växjö, Swe., 24,000......I6   11
Veachland, Ky., 700......B4   62
Veazie, Maine, 1,354....*D4   64

Vecses, Hung., 15,537.....B4   10
Veedersburg, Ind., 1,762..D3   59
Vegas, Heights, Nev.,
1,200................*G6   72
Vegreville, Alta., Can.,
2,908................C4   38
Vejle, Den., 31,362.......J3   11
Vejle, co., Den., 213,705..*J3   11
Velda Village Hills, Mo.,
1,365................*C7   69
Vélez-Rubio, Sp., 4,484...D4   8
Velikiye Luki, Sov. Un.,
68,000...............C8   12
Velikiy Ustyug, Sov. Un.,
37,026...............C7   13
Velizh, Sov. Un., 10,000...D8   12
Velletri, It., 18,200...D4, h9   9
Vellore, India, 113,742...F6   20
Velma, Okla., 700........C4   79
Velsk, Sov. Un., 14,300...C7   13
Velva, N. Dak., 1,330....B5   77
Venado Tuerto, Arg.,
23,433...............A4   28
Venango, co., Pa., 65,295..D2   81
Vendée, hills, Fr........*D3   5
Venetian Village, Ill.,
2,200................*A6   58
Veneto, pol. dist., It.,
3,846,562............*B4   9
Veneto, reg., It.........A3   9
Venezia, see Venice, It.
Venezuela, country, S.A.,
7,555,799............C4   27
Venice, Fla., 3,444.......E4   54
Venice, Ill., 5,380.......E3   58
Venice (Venezia), It.,
335,700..............B4   9
Vénissieux, Fr., 29,040...E6   5
Venlo, Neth., 80,000.....B7   5
Ventimiglia, It., 12,200...C1   9
Ventnor City, N.J., 8,688..E4   74
Ventspils, Sov. Un.,
27,400...............C3   12
Ventura, Calif., 29,114...E4   50
Ventura, co., Calif.,
199,138..............E4   50
Ventura North
(Chrisman), Calif.,
3,923................*E4   50
Veracruz, state, Mex.,
2,727,899..........D5, n15   34
Veracruz [Llave], Mex.,
144,681............D5, n15   34
Veradale, Wash., 2,000...*B8   86
Veraval, India, 60,857....D5   20
Vercelli, It., 53,800......B2   9
Verchères, Que., Can.,
1,768................D4   42
Verchères, Que., Can.,
25,697...............D9   42
Verden, Ger., 17,500.....B4   6
Verdun, Que., Can.,
78,317...............q19   42
Verdun [-Sur-Meuse], Fr.,
21,982...............C6   5
Verdunville, W. Va.,
2,260................D2   87
Vereeniging, S. Afr.,
78,835...............F5   24
Verga, N.J., 800........*D2   74
Vergennes, Vt., 1,921.....C1   73
Verkhneye, Sov. Un.,
10,000...........G12, q21   12
Verkhoyansk, Sov. Un.,
1,200................C16   13
Vermilion, Alta., Can.,
2,449................C5   38
Vermilion, Ohio, 5,220...A3   78
Vermilion, co., Ill.,
96,176...............C6   58
Vermilion, par., La.,
38,855...............E3   63
Vermilion Heights, Ill.,
1,568................*C6   58
Vermillion, S. Dak.,
6,102................H9   77
Vermillion, co., Ind.,
17,683...............E3   59
Vermont, Ill., 903........C3   58
Vermont, state, U.S.,
389,881.............   73
Vernal, Utah, 3,655......A7   72
Vernon, Ala., 1,492......B1   46
Vernon, B.C., Can.,
10,250............D8, n19   37
Vernon, Fr., 17,247......C4   5
Vernon, N.Y., 913.......*B5   75
Vernon, Tex., 12,141.....B3   84
Vernon, co., Mo., 20,540..D3   69
Vernon, co., Wis., 25,663..E3   88
Vernon, par., La., 18,301..C2   63
Vernonia, Oreg., 1,089....B3   80
Vernon Valley, N.Y.,
5,998...............n15   75
Vero Beach, Fla., 8,849...E6   54
Veroia, Grc., 25,765.....B4   14
Vernona, It., 233,600.....B3   9
Vernona, N.J., 13,782....B4   74

Vernona, Pa., 4,032.....k14   81
Vernona, Wis., 1,471.....E4   88
Verona Park, Mich.,
1,884................*F5   66
Verplanck, N.Y., 2,400..*D7   75
Versailles, Fr., 86,759..C4, g9   5
Versailles, Ind., 1,158....F7   59
Versailles, Ky., 4,060....B5   62
Versailles, Mo., 2,047....C5   69
Versailles, Ohio, 2,159...B1   78
Versailles, Pa., 2,297....*F2   81
Verviers, Bel., 35,453....B6   5
Veseloye, Sov. Un.,
25,000..............H10   12
Vesoul, Fr., 13,678......D7   5
Vest-Agder, co., Nor.,
114,000.............*H2   11
Vestal, N.Y., 6,000......C4   75
Vestavia Hills, Ala.,
4,029................*B3   46
Vestfold, co., Nor.,
164,600.............*H4   11
Vestry, Miss., 150.......E5   68
Vesuvius, vol., It........D5   9
Veszprem, Hung.,
25,495...............B3   10
Veszprem, co., Hung.,
393,331.............*B3   10
Veszto, Hung., 9,645....B5   10
Vevay, Ind., 1,503.......G7   59
Vevey, Switz., 18,200....E3   6
Vezirkopru, Tur., 8,224..B10   14
Viadana, It., 5,587.......B3   9
Vian, Okla., 930........B7   79
Viareggio, It., 50,300....C3   9
Viborg, co., Den.,
161,232.............*I3   11
Vibo Valentia, It.,
12,800...............E6   9
Vicco, Ky., 900.........C6   62
Vicenza, It., 102,700....B3   9
Vichada, comisaría, Col.,
10,130...............C3   32
Vichy, Fr., 30,614.......D5   5
Vicksburg, Mich., 2,224..F5   66
Vicksburg, Miss., 29,143..C3   68
Victor, N.Y., 1,943......C3   75
Victoria, Arg., 15,108....A4   28
Victoria, B.C., Can.,
54,941 (*154,152)..E6, f12   37
Victoria, Newf., Can.,
1,506................E5   44
Victoria, Chile, 14,200...B2   28
Victoria, Hong Kong,
674,962..............G7   17
Victoria, Kans., 1,170...D4   61
Victoria, Tex., 33,047...E4   84
Victoria, Va., 1,737.....D4   85
Victoria, co., N.B., Can.,
19,712...............B2   43
Victoria, co., N.S., Can.,
8,226................C9   43
Victoria, co., Ont., Can.,
29,750...............C6   43
Victoria, co., Tex.,
46,475...............E4   84
Victoria, state, Austl.,
3,217,832............G7   25
Victoria, isl., Can.......B11   36
Victoria, lake, Afr.......I4   23
Victoria, mtn., Pap......k12   25
Victoria de las Tunas,
Cuba, 31,100.........D5   35
Victoria Harbour, Ont.,
Can., 1,066..........C5   41
Victoriaville, Que., Can.,
18,720...............C6   42
Victor Mills, S.C., 2,018..*B3   82
Victorville, Calif., 9,655...E5   50
Victory Gardens, N.J.,
1,085................*B3   74
Victory Heights, N.Y.,
600.................*C4   75
Vidal, Calif., 100........E6   50
Vidalia, Ga., 7,569......D4   55
Vidalia, La., 4,313......C4   63
Vidin, Bul., 18,580......D6   10
Vidor, Tex., 4,938.......D6   84
Vienna (Wien), Aus.,
1,634,300 (*2,010,000)..D8   6
Vienna, Ga., 2,090......D3   55
Vienna, Ill., 1,094......F5   58
Vienna, Va., 11,440..B5, g12   85
Vienna, W. Va., 9,381...B3   87
Vienne, Fr., 26,977......E6   5
Vienne, dept., Fr.,
26,977..............*D4   5
Vientiane, Laos, 162,300..B2   19
Vierzon, Fr., 31,549.....D5   5
Vieste, It., 12,679.......D6   9
Vietnam, North, country,
Asia, 17,800,000......B3   19
Vietnam, South, country,
Asia, 15,317,000......C3   19
Vietnam, reg., Asia B3   19
View Park, Calif., 2,500..*E4   50
Vigan, Phil., 10,498......B6   19
Vigevano, It., 61,500.....B2   9

Vigo, Sp., 144,914......A1   8
Vigo, co., Ind., 108,458...F3   59
Vijayavada, India,
230,397..............E7   20
Vila Nova de Gaia, Port.,
45,739...............B1   8
Vilas, co., Wis., 9,332....B4   88
Vila Teixeira da Silva,
Ang., 4,897..........C3   24
Vileyka, Sov. Un., 10,000..D6   12
Viljandi, Sov. Un., 12,941..B5   12
Vilkovo, Sov. Un., 20,000..I7   12
Villacarrillo, Sp., 13,090..C4   8
Villach, Aus., 32,971....E6   6
Villa Dolores, Arg.,
16,741...............A3   28
Villafranca de los Barros,
Sp., 16,671..........C2   8
Villafranca del Panadés,
Sp., 11,985..........B6   8
Villafranca di Verona, It.,
6,015................B3   9
Villagarcía, de Arosa, Sp.,
4,986................A1   8
Village-Richelieu, Que.,
Can., 1,612.........*D4   42
Villa Grove, Ill., 2,421....D5   58
Villaguay, Arg., 12,463...A5   28
Villa Heights, Md.,
1,000................*C4   53
Villahermosa, Mex.,
52,262...............D6   34
Villa María, Arg., 42,629..A4   28
Villanova, Pa., 5,000....*G11   81
Villanueva de Córdoba,
Sp., 15,719..........C3   8
Villanueva del Arzobispo,
Sp., 9,712...........C4   8
Villanueva de La Serena,
Sp., 20,812..........C3   8
Villanueva y Geltrú, Sp.,
25,669...............B6   8
Villa Obregón, Mex.,
31,416...............h9   34
Villa Park, Ill., 25,697....k8   58
Villa Rica, Ga., 3,450....C1   55
Villarreal, Sp., 19,700....C5   8
Villarrica, Par., 15,600...E4   29
Villarrobledo, Sp.,
21,356...............C4   8
Villas, N.J., 2,500.......E3   74
Villavicencio, Col.,
45,277...............C3   32
Villefranche-sur-Saône,
Fr., 24,516..........E6   5
Villejuif, Fr., 46,116.....g10   5
Ville Marie, Que., Can.,
1,710................p20   41
Villemomble, Fr., 24,540..g10   5
Villeneuve-le-Roi, Fr.,
22,300...............h10   5
Villeneuve St Georges,
Fr., 28,231..........h10   5
Villeneuve-sur-Lot, Fr.,
17,295...............E4   5
Ville Platte, La., 7,512...D3   63
Ville St Georges, Que.,
Can., 4,082..........C7   42
Villeta, Par., 14,729.....E4   29
Villeurbanne, Fr.,
105,416..............E6   5
Villingen, Ger., 31,900...D4   6
Villisca, Iowa, 1,690.....D3   60
Vilnius, Sov. Un.,
271,000..............D5   12
Vilvoorde, Bel., 31,441...B6   5
Vilyuy, riv., Sov. Un.....C15   13
Vilyuysk, Sov. Un.,
3,600................C15   13
Vimianzo, Sp., 654......A1   8
Viña del Mar, Chile,
115,500..............A2   28
Vinalhaven, Maine, 900...D4   64
Vincennes, Fr., 50,436...g10   5
Vincennes, Ind., 20,061...G3   59
Vincent, Ala., 1,402......B3   46
Vincent, Ohio, 2,100....*A3   78
Vine Grove, Ky., 2,435...C4   62
Vine Hill (Martinez
East), Calif., 3,958....*C2   50
Vineland, N.J., 37,685...E2   74
Vineyard Haven (Tisbury),
Mass., 2,169.........D6   65
Vinh Yen, Viet., 3,820...G6   17
Vinita, Okla., 6,027......A6   79
Vinita Park, Mo., 2,204..*C7   69
Vinkovci, Yugo., 23,113...C4   10
Vinnitsa, Sov. Un.,
139,000..............G7   12
Vinson Massif, mtn., Ant..L15   2
Vinton, Iowa, 4,899......B5   60
Vinton, La., 2,987.......D2   63
Vinton, Va., 3,432......C3   85
Vinton, co., Ohio, 10,274..C3   78
Vintondale, Pa., 938.....F4   81
Virden, Man., Can.,
2,708................E1   40

Virden, Ill., 3,309.......D4 58
Virginia, Ill., 1,669.......D3 58
Virginia, Minn., 14,034...C6 67
Virginia, state, U.S.,
  3,966,949.............. 85
Virginia Beach
  (Independent City),
  Va., 85,218.........D7, k16 85
Virginia City, Nev., 500...B2 72
Virginia Gardens, Fla.,
  2,159................*G6 54
Virgin Islands, Br. dep.,
  N.A., 7,340............G12 35
Virgin Islands of the U.S.,
  dep., N.A., 32,099.....G12 35
Viroflay, Fr., 16,004......g9 5
Viroqua, Wis., 3,926.....E3 88
Virovitica, Yugo.,
  14,027................C3 10
Visakhapatnam, India,
  182,004...............E7 20
Visalia, Calif., 21,054.....D4 50
Visalia North (Crowley),
  Calif., 3,950..........D4 50
Visby, Swe., 16,000.......I8 11
Vista, Calif., 19,625.....F5 50
Vista Park, Calif., 3,500..*E4 50
Vitanovak, Yugo., 1,127..D5 10
Vitebsk, Sov. Un.,
  174,000..............D8 12
Viterbo, It., 29,000......C4 9

Vitim, Sov. Un., 2,300...D14 13
Vitória, Braz., 82,748.....C4 30
Vitoria, Sp., 73,701......A4 8
Vitória da Conquista,
  Braz., 46,778.........A4 30
Vitry [-sur-Seine], Fr.,
  65,734...............g10 5
Vittoria, It., 45,000......F5 9
Vittorio Veneto, It.,
  21,500...............B4 9
Vivian, La., 2,624.......B2 63
Vizcaya, prov., Sp.,
  754,383.............*A4 8
Vizianagram, India,
  76,808...............E7 20
Vizzini, It., 10,806.......F5 9
Vlaardingen, Neth.,
  71,900...............B6 5
Vladimir, Sov. Un.,
  181,000.............C13 12
Vladimiro
  Aleksandrovskoye,
  Sov. Un., 10,000.......E6 18
Vladimir Volynskiy,
  Sov. Un., 10,000......F5 12
Vladivostok, Sov. Un.,
  338,000.............E5 18
Vlasotince, Yugo., 5,924...D6 10
Vlissingen, Neth.,
  28,900...............B5 5
Vlonë, Alb., 58,000......B2 14

Vlonë, pref., Alb.,
  58,000..............*B2 14
Vodnany, Czech., 4,576..*D3 7
Voeune Sai, Camb.,
  10,000...............F7 22
Voghera, It., 35,747......B2 9
Voiron, Fr., 11,150.......E6 5
Volga, riv., Sov. Un......E7 13
Volgograd, Sov. Un.,
  663,000.............G14 12
Volkhov, Sov. Un., 16,500..B9 12
Volkovysk, Sov. Un.,
  10,000...............E5 12
Vologda, Sov. Un.,
  152,000.............B12 12
Volokolamsk, Sov. Un.,
  10,000...............C10 12
Volos, Grc., 49,221.......C4 14
Volsk, Sov. Un., 67,000..*D7 13
Volta Redonda, Braz.,
  83,973............C4, h5 30
Volterra, It., 9,300.......C3 9
Volusia, co., Fla., 125,319..C5 54
Voorheesville, N.Y.,
  1,288...............*C7 75
Vorarlberg, state, Aus.,
  226,323.............E4 6
Vordingborg, Den.,
  11,780..............A1 7
Vorkuta, Sov. Un.,
  60,000...............C9 13

Voronezh, Sov. Un.,
  535,000.............F12 12
Vosges, dept., Fr.,
  380,676.............*C7 5
Votkinsk, Sov. Un.,
  68,000.............*D8 13
Voznesensk, Sov. Un.,
  10,000...............H8 12
Vranje, Yugo., 16,457.....D5 10
Vratsa, Bul., 19,448.......D6 10
Vratsa, co., Bul., 771,486..D6 10
Vrsac, Yugo., 31,551.....C5 10
Vsetin, Czech., 18,200.....D5 7
Vukovar, Yugo., 25,826...C4 10
Vulcan, Alta., Can.,
  1,310...............D4 38
Vulcan, Mo., 100........D7 69
Vyazma, Sov. Un.,
  26,700..............D10 12
Vyazniki, Sov. Un.,
  39,392..............C14 12
Vyborg, Sov. Un.,
  57,000...............A7 12
Vyksa, Sov. Un.,
  28,600..............D14 12
Vyshniy Volochek,
  Sov. Un., 71,000.....C10 12
Vysoké Tatry, Czech.,
  9,000................D6 7
Vytegra, Sov. Un.,
  11,800..............A11 12

W

Wabana (Bell Island),
  Newf., Can., 8,026......E5 44
Wabash, Ind., 13,448.....C6 59
Wabash, co., Ill., 14,047...C6 58
Wabash, co., Ind., 32,605..C6 59
Wabasha, Minn., 2,500....F6 67
Wabasha, co., Minn.,
  17,007...............F6 67
Wabasso, Fla., 500.......E6 54
Wabaunsee, co., Kans.,
  6,648................D7 61
Wacissa, Fla., 300.......B3 54
Waco, Tex., 105,000
  (*136,000)............D4 84
Waconia, Minn., 2,048....F5 67
Waddington, B.C., Can....F8 36
Waddington, N.Y., 921.....f9 75
Wadena, Sask., Can.,
  1,311................F4 39
Wadena, Minn., 4,381....D3 67
Wadena, co., Minn.,
  12,199...............D4 67
Wadesboro, N.C., 3,744...C2 76
Wadley, Ga., 1,898.......D4 55
Wad Medani, Sud.,
  56,000...............F4 23
Wadsworth, Ohio, 10,635..A4 78
Waelder, Tex., 1,270......E4 84
Wagga Wagga, Austl.,
  25,939...............G8 25
Wagner, S. Dak., 1,586....G7 77
Wagoner, Okla., 4,469....B6 79
Wagoner, co., Okla.,
  15,673..............B6 79
Wagon Mound, N. Mex.,
  760.................B6 48
Wagrowiec, Pol., 13,400..B4 7
Wahiawa, Haw.,
  15,512...........B3, f9 56

Wahkiakum, co., Wash.,
  3,426...............C2 86
Wahneta, Fla., 1,796.....*E5 54
Wahoo, Nebr., 3,610..C9, g11 71
Wahpeton, N. Dak., 6,453..D9 77
Waialua, Haw., 2,689...B3, f9 56
Waianae, Haw., 4,120..B3, g9 56
Waikabubak, Indon......G5 19
Wailua, Haw., 1,129......A2 56
Wailuku, Haw., 150.......C5 56
Waimanalo, Haw.,
  3,400............B4, g11 56
Waimea, Haw., 1,312.....B2 56
Waimea, Haw., 400........f9 56
Wainwright, Alta., Can.,
  3,351................C5 38
Waipahu, Haw., 8,000..B3, g9 56
Waipio Acres, Haw.,
  1,158................g9 56
Waite Park, Minn., 2,016..E4 67
Waitsburg, Wash., 1,010...C7 86
Wajima, Jap., 20,300.....H8 18
Wakamatsu, Jap., 70,200..H9 18
Wakarusa, Ind., 1,145.....A5 59
Wakaw, Sask., Can., 974...E3 39
Wakayama, Jap.,
  328,657...........I7, o14 18
Wakayama, pref., Jap.,
  1,026,975............*I7 18
Wake, co., N.C., 197,617..B4 76
WaKeeney, Kans., 2,808...C4 61
Wakefield, Mass.,
  24,295............B5, f11 65
Wakefield, Mich., 3,231..n12 66
Wakefield, Nebr., 1,068....B9 71
Wakefield, R.I., 4,000....D11 52
Wakefield, Va., 1,015.....D6 85
Wake Forest, N.C., 2,681..B4 76
Wakulla, co., Fla.........B2 54

Walbridge, Ohio, 2,142....e6 78
Walbrzych, Pol., 117,000...C4 7
Walden, N.Y., 5,079.......D6 75
Waldo, Ark., 1,722.......D2 49
Waldo, co., Maine,
  22,632...............D3 64
Waldorf, Md., 1,200......C4 53
Waldron, Ark., 1,619......C1 49
Waldwick, N.J., 10,495....A4 74
Wales, reg., U.K.,
  2,620,632............D5 4
Walhalla, N. Dak., 1,432..A8 77
Walhalla, S.C., 3,431.....B1 82
Walker, La., 912........g10 63
Walker, Minn., 1,180......C4 67
Walker, co., Ala., 54,211..B2 46
Walker, co., Ga., 45,264...B1 55
Walker, co., Tex., 21,475..D5 84
Walkersville, Md., 1,020...B3 53
Walkerton, Ont., Can.,
  3,851................C3 41
Walkerton, Ind., 2,044....B5 59
Walkertown, N.C., 1,240..A2 76
Walkerville, Mont., 1,453..D4 70
Wall, Pa., 1,493.........*F2 81
Wallace, Idaho, 2,412.....B3 57
Wallace, N.C., 2,968......C4 76
Wallace, co., Kans., 2,069..D2 61
Wallaceburg, Ont., Can.,
  7,881................E2 41
Wallasey, Eng., 103,400...D5 4
Walla Walla, Wash.,
  24,536...............C7 86
Walla Walla, co., Wash.,
  42,195...............C7 86
Walled Lake, Mich.,
  3,550...............o15 66
Waller, Tex., 900........D5 84
Waller, co., Tex., 12,071..E4 84

Wallingford, Conn.,
  29,920...............D5 52
Wallingford, Vt., 800......E2 73
Wallington, Eng.,
  32,500..............m12 4
Wallington, N.J., 9,261....h8 74
Wallis, Tex., 1,000.......E4 84
Wallkill, N.Y., 1,215......D6 75
Wallowa, Oreg., 989.....B9 80
Wallowa, co., Oreg., 7,102..B9 80
Wallsend, Eng., 49,600....C6 4
Walnut, Calif., 934......*F4 50
Walnut, Ill., 1,192.......B4 58
Walnut Cove, N.C., 1,288..A2 76
Walnut Creek, Calif.,
  23,368...............h8 50
Walnut Heights, Calif.,
  5,080..............*D2 50
Walnut Park, Calif.,
  7,500..............*F4 50
Walnutport, Pa., 1,609...E10 81
Walnut Ridge, Ark., 3,547..A5 49
Walpole, Mass.,
  7,700............B5, h10 65
Walsall, Eng., 120,600.....D6 4
Walsenburg, Colo., 5,071..D6 51
Walsh, co., N. Dak.,
  17,997..............B8 77
Walterboro, S.C., 5,417....F6 82
Walters, Okla., 2,825.....C3 79
Walthall, co., Miss.,
  13,512..............D6 68
Waltham, Mass.,
  55,413..........B5, g11 65
Walthamstow, Eng.,
  108,788.............k12 4
Walthill, Nebr., 844......B9 71
Walton, Ind., 1,079.......C5 59
Walton, Ky., 1,530....A7, B5 62

Walton, N.Y., 3,855......C5 75
Walton, co., Fla., 15,576..u15 54
Walton, co., Ga., 20,481...C3 55
Walton Hills, Ohio,
1,776................*A4 78
Walvis Bay, S. Afr.,
12,235................E2 24
Walworth, Wis., 1,494....F5 88
Walworth, co., S. Dak.,
8,097.................E5 77
Walworth, co., Wis.,
52,368................F5 88
Wamac, Ill., 1,394......E4 58
Wamego, Kans., 2,363....C7 61
Wampum, Pa., 1,085......E1 81
Wanamassa, N.J., 2,100...C4 74
Wanaque, N.J., 7,126.....A4 74
Wanganui, N.Z., 35,629
(*38,174)............M15 26
Wangaratta, Austl.,
13,783...............H6 26
Wangching, China......C10 17
Wanhsien, China, 90,000..E6 17
Wankie, Rh., 20,200.....D5 24
Wantagh, N.Y., 34,000...G2 52
Wapakoneta, Ohio, 6,756..B1 78
Wapato, Wash., 3,137....C5 86
Wapello, Iowa, 1,745....C6 60
Wapello, co., Iowa,
46,126...............C5 60
Wappingers Falls, N.Y.,
4,816................D7 75
War, W. Va., 3,006.....D3 87
Warangal, India, 156,106..E6 20
Ward, W. Va., 700......C6 87
Ward, co., N. Dak., 47,072..B4 77
Ward, co., Tex., 14,917..D1 84
Warden, Wash., 949.....C6 86
Ward Ridge, Fla., 1,886...*C1 54
Wardville, La., 1,086....*C3 63
Ware, Mass., 6,700.....B3 65
Ware, co., Ga., 34,219...E4 55
Wareham, Mass., 2,100...C6 65
Warehouse Point, Conn.,
1,400................B6 52
Waren, Ger., 19,700....B6 6
Ware Shoals, S.C., 2,671..C3 82
Warfield, B.C., Can.,
2,212................E9 37
Warner Robins, Ga.,
18,633...............D3 55
Warr Acres, Okla., 7,135..B4 79
Warren, Ark., 6,752.....D3 49
Warren, Ill., 1,470......A4 58
Warren, Ind., 1,241.....C7 59
Warren, Mass., 1,616....B3 65
Warren, Mich.,
89,246..........F7, p16 66
Warren, Minn., 2,007....B2 67
Warren, Ohio, 59,648....A5 78
Warren, Pa., 14,505.....C3 81
Warren, R.I., 9,749.....C11 52
Warren, co., Ga., 7,360..C4 55
Warren, co., Ill., 21,587..C3 58
Warren, co., Ind., 8,545..D3 59
Warren, co., Iowa, 20,829..C4 60
Warren, co., Ky., 45,491..C3 62
Warren, co., Miss., 42,206..C3 68
Warren, co., Mo., 8,750..C6 69
Warren, co., N.J., 63,220..B3 74
Warren, co., N.Y., 44,002..B7 75
Warren, co., N.C., 17,591..A4 76
Warren, co., Ohio, 65,711..C1 78
Warren, co., Pa., 45,582...C3 81
Warren, co., Tenn.,
23,102...............D8 83
Warren, co., Va., 14,655..B4 85
Warrensburg, Mo., 9,689..C4 69
Warrensburg, N.Y., 2,240..B7 75
Warrensville Heights,
Ohio, 10,609.........h9 78
Warrenton, Ga., 1,770...C4 55
Warrenton, Mo., 1,869...C6 69
Warrenton, N.C., 1,063..A4 76
Warrenton, Oreg., 1,717..A3 80
Warrenton, Va., 3,522...B5 85
Warrenville, Ill., 3,500...k8 58
Warrenville, S.C., 1,128..D4 82
Warrick, co., Ind., 23,577..H3 59
Warrington, Eng.,
76,000...............D5 4
Warrington, Fla.,
18,000...............u14 54
Warrior, Ala., 2,448.....B3 46
Warrnambool, Austl.,
17,497...........G7, n14 25
Warroad, Minn., 1,309...B3 67
Warsaw, Ill., 1,938.....C2 58
Warsaw, Ind., 7,234.....B6 59
Warsaw, Mo., 1,054.....C4 69
Warsaw, N.Y., 3,653....C2 75
Warsaw, N.C., 1,964....B4 76
Warsaw (Warszawa),
Pol., 1,221,900....B6, m14 7
Warson Woods, Mo.,
1,746................*C7 69
Warwick, Que., Can.,
2,487................D6 42

Warwick, Eng., 16,600...D6 4
Warwick, N.Y.,
3,261.............D6, m14 75
Warwick, R.I., 77,637...C10 52
Warwick, co., Eng.,
2,076,700...........*D6 4
Wasatch, co., Utah, 5,308..A6 72
Wasco, Calif., 6,841....E4 50
Wasco, co., Oreg., 20,205..B5 80
Waseca, Minn., 6,102....F5 67
Waseca, co., Minn.,
16,041...............F5 67
Washabaugh, co., S. Dak.,
1,042................G4 77
Washakie, co., Wyo.,
8,883................C5 89
Washburn, Ill., 1,064....C4 58
Washburn, Maine, 1,100..B4 64
Washburn, Wis., 1,896...B3 88
Washburn, co., Wis.,
10,301...............C2 88
Washington, D.C.,
815,000
(*2,695,000)......C3, f8 53
Washington, Ga., 4,440..C4 55
Washington, Ill., 5,919..C4 58
Washington, Ind., 11,230..G3 59
Washington, Iowa, 6,037..C6 60
Washington, Kans., 1,506..C6 61
Washington, La., 1,291..D3 63
Washington, Mo., 7,961..C6 69
Washington, N.J., 5,723..B3 74
Washington, N.C.,
10,150...............B5 76
Washington, Pa., 23,545..F1 81
Washington, co., Ala.,
15,372...............D1 46
Washington, co., Ark.,
55,797...............A1 49
Washington, co., Colo.,
6,625................B7 51
Washington, co., Fla.,
11,249...............u16 54
Washington, co., Ga.,
18,903...............C4 55
Washington, co., Idaho,
8,378................E2 57
Washington, co., Ill.,
13,569...............E4 58
Washington, co., Ind.,
17,819...............G5 59
Washington, co., Iowa,
19,406...............C6 60
Washington, co., Ky.,
11,168...............C4 62
Washington, co., Maine,
32,908...............D5 64
Washington, co., Md.,
91,219...............A2 53
Washington, co., Minn.,
52,432...............E6 67
Washington, co., Miss.,
78,638...............B3 66
Washington, co., Mo.,
14,346...............D7 69
Washington, co., Nebr.,
12,103...............C9 71
Washington, co., N.Y.,
48,476...............B7 75
Washington, co., N.C.,
13,937...............B6 76
Washington, co., Ohio,
51,689...............C4 78
Washington, co., Okla.,
42,347...............A6 79
Washington, co., Oreg.,
92,237...............B3 80
Washington, co., Pa.,
217,271..............F1 81
Washington, co., R.I.,
59,054...............D10 52
Washington, co., Tex.,
19,145...............D4 84
Washington, co., Utah,
10,271...............C5 72
Washington, co., Vt.,
42,860...............C2 73
Washington, co., Va.,
38,076................f9 85
Washington, co., Wis.,
46,119...............E5 88
Washington, par., La.,
44,015...............D5 63
Washington, state, U.S.,
2,853,214............86
Washington, mtn., N.H....C5 73
Washington Court House,
Ohio, 12,388........C2 78
Washington Heights,
N.Y., 1,231.........*D6 75
Washington North, Pa.,
2,077...............*F1 81
Washington Park, Ill.,
6,601................E3 58
Washington Terrace,
Utah, 6,441.........*A5 72
Washingtonville, N.Y.,
1,178...............*D6 75

Washington West, Pa.,
3,951................*F1 81
Washita, co., Okla.,
18,121...............B2 79
Washoe, co., Nev., 84,743..A2 72
Washougal, Wash., 2,672..D3 86
Washtenaw, co., Mich.,
172,440..............F7 66
Waskom, Tex., 1,336....C5 84
Watauga, co., N.C.,
17,529...............A1 76
Watchung, N.J., 3,312...*B4 74
Waterbury, Conn.,
106,000 (*195,000)...C4 52
Waterbury, Vt., 2,984....C2 73
Waterford, Calif., 1,780..*D3 50
Waterford, Ont., Can.,
2,221................E4 41
Waterford, Conn., 6,000..D8 52
Waterford, N.Y., 2,749...C7 75
Waterford, Pa., 1,390....C1 81
Waterford, Wis.,
1,500.............F5, n11 88
Waterford, co., Ire.,
73,000..............*D3 4
Waterloo, Ont., Can.,
21,366...............D4 41
Waterloo, Que., Can.,
4,543................D5 42
Waterloo, Ill., 3,739....E3 58
Waterloo, Ind., 1,432....B7 59
Waterloo, Iowa, 78,000
(*124,000).........B5 60
Waterloo, N.Y., 5,098...C4 75
Waterloo, Wis., 1,947...E5 88
Waterloo, co., Ont., Can.,
176,754..............D4 41
Waterman, Ill., 916.....B5 58
Waterproof, La., 1,412..C4 63
Watertown, Conn., 6,000..C4 52
Watertown, Fla., 2,109..B4 54
Watertown, Mass.,
39,092...............g11 65
Watertown, Minn., 1,046..*F5 67
Watertown, N.Y., 33,306..B5 75
Watertown, S. Dak.,
14,077...............F8 77
Watertown, Tenn., 919...A5 83
Watertown, Wis., 13,943..E5 88
Water Valley, Miss., 3,206..A4 68
Waterville, Que., Can.,
1,330................D6 42
Waterville, Maine, 18,695..D3 64
Waterville, Minn., 1,623..F5 67
Waterville, N.Y., 1,901..C5 75
Waterville, Ohio,
1,856.............A2, f6 78
Waterville, Wash., 1,013..B5 86
Watervliet, Mich., 1,818..F4 66
Watervliet, N.Y., 13,917..C7 75
Watford, Ont., Can.,
1,293................E3 41
Watford City, N. Dak.,
1,865................C2 77
Watkins Glen, N.Y., 2,813..C4 75
Watonga, Okla., 3,252...B3 79
Watonwan, co., Minn.,
14,460...............F4 67
Watrous, Sask., Can.,
1,461................F3 39
Watseka, Ill., 5,219....C6 58
Watsontown, Pa., 2,431..D8 81
Watsonville, Calif.,
13,293...............D3 50
Wattrelos, Fr., 41,319..B5 5
Wattsville, S.C., 1,438..B4 82
Wauchula, Fla., 3,411...E5 54
Wauconda, Ill., 5,343...h8 58
Waukegan, Ill., 55,719..A6, h9 58
Waukesha, Wis., 30,004..E5 88
Waukesha, co., Wis.,
158,249..............E5 88
Waukon, Iowa, 3,639....A6 60
Waunakee, Wis., 1,611..E4 88
Waupaca, Wis., 3,984...D4 88
Waupaca, co., Wis.,
35,340...............D5 88
Waupun, Wis., 7,935....E5 88
Waurika, Okla., 1,933...C4 79
Wausau, Wis., 31,943...D4 88
Wauseon, Ohio, 4,311...A1 78
Waushara, co., Wis.,
13,497...............D4 88
Wautoma, Wis., 1,466..D4 88
Wauwatosa, Wis.,
56,923...............m12 88
Waverly, Ill., 1,375....D4 58
Waverly, Iowa, 6,822...B5 60
Waverly, N.Y., 5,629...C4 75
Waverly, Ohio, 3,830...C3 78
Waverly, Tenn., 2,891..A4 83
Waverly, Va., 1,601....C5 85
Waxahachie, Tex.,
12,749...........C4, n10 84
Waycross, Ga., 20,944...E4 55
Wayland, Ky., 1,340....C7 62
Wayland, Mass., 950...g10 65

Wayland, Mich., 2,019....F5 66
Wayland, N.Y., 2,003....C3 75
Waymart, Pa., 1,106....C11 81
Wayne, Mich., 16,034...p15 66
Wayne, Nebr., 4,217....B8 71
Wayne, N.J., 29,353....B4 74
Wayne, Pa., 10,500..F11, o20 81
Wayne, W. Va., 1,274....C2 87
Wayne, co., Ga., 17,921..E5 55
Wayne, co., Ill., 19,008..E5 58
Wayne, co., Ind., 74,039..E7 59
Wayne, co., Iowa, 9,800..D4 60
Wayne, co., Ky., 14,700..D5 62
Wayne, co., Mich.,
2,666,297............F7 66
Wayne, co., Miss., 16,258..D5 68
Wayne, co., Mo., 8,638..D7 69
Wayne, co., Nebr., 9,959..B8 71
Wayne, co., N.Y., 73,837..B3 75
Wayne, co., N.C., 82,059..B4 76
Wayne, co., Ohio, 75,497..B4 78
Wayne, co., Pa., 28,237..C11 81
Wayne, co., Tenn., 11,908..B4 83
Wayne, co., Utah, 1,728..B6 72
Wayne, co., W. Va.,
38,977...............C2 87
Waynesboro, Ga., 5,359..C4 55
Waynesboro, Miss., 3,892..D5 68
Waynesboro, Pa., 10,427..G6 81
Waynesboro, Tenn., 1,343..B4 83
Waynesboro (Independent
City), Va., 15,694....B4 85
Waynesburg, Ohio, 1,442..B4 78
Waynesburg, Pa., 5,188..G1 81
Waynesville, Mo., 2,377..D5 69
Waynesville, N.C., 6,159..f10 76
Waynesville, Ohio, 1,298..C1 78
Waynoka, Okla., 1,794...A3 79
Wayzata, Minn., 3,219...*F5 67
Weakley, co., Tenn.,
24,227...............A3 83
Weatherford, Okla., 4,499..B3 79
Weatherford, Tex., 9,759..C4 84
Weatherly, Pa., 2,591...E10 81
Weaver, Ala., 1,401.....B4 46
Weaverville, Calif., 2,000..B2 50
Weaverville, N.C., 1,411..f10 76
Webb, co., Tex., 64,791..F3 84
Webb City, Mo., 6,740...D3 69
Weber, co., Utah, 110,744..A6 72
Weber City, Va., 1,274..*f9 85
Webster, Mass., 13,680..B4 65
Webster, N.Y., 3,617....B3 75
Webster, S. Dak., 2,409..E8 77
Webster, co., Ga., 3,247..D2 55
Webster, co., Iowa, 47,810..B3 60
Webster, co., Ky., 14,244..C2 62
Webster, co., Miss., 10,580..B4 68
Webster, co., Mo., 13,753..D5 69
Webster, co., Nebr., 6,224..D7 71
Webster, co., W. Va.,
13,719...............C4 87
Webster, par., La.,
39,701...............B2 63
Webster City, Iowa, 8,671..B4 60
Webster Groves, Mo.,
28,990...............f13 69
Webster Springs
(Addison), W. Va.,
1,132................C4 87
Wedgeport, N.S., Can.,
665..................F4 43
Wedowee, Ala., 917.....B4 46
Weed, Calif., 4,200.....B2 50
Weed Heights, Nev.,
1,092...............*B2 72
Weedon, Que., Can.,
1,426................D6 42
Weedsport, N.Y., 1,731..B4 75
Weehawken, N.J., 13,504..h8 74
Weeks, La., 1,138......E4 63
Weeping Water,
Nebr., 1,048......D9, h12 71
Weert, Neth., 12,900....B6 5
Weiden, Ger., 42,200...D6 6
Weifang, China, 148,900..D8 17
Weihai, China, 45,000...D9 17
Weilheim, Ger., 12,400..E5 6
Weimar, Ger., 64,200...C5 6
Weimar, Tex., 2,006....E4 84
Weinan, China.........E6 17
Weinheim, Ger., 27,900..D4 6
Weippe, Idaho, 700.....C3 57
Weirton, W. Va.,
28,201...........A2, A4 87
Weiser, Idaho, 4,208....E2 57
Weissenburg [in Bayern],
Ger., 13,900.........D5 6
Weissenfels, Ger., 46,500..C5 6
Wejherowo, Pol., 27,400..A5 7
Welborn, Kans., 6,500..B8 61
Welch, W. Va., 5,313...D3 87
Welcome, S.C., 1,500...*B3 82
Weld, co., Colo., 72,344..A6 51
Weldon, N.C., 2,165....A5 76
Weleetka, Okla., 1,231..B5 79
Welland, Ont., Can.,
36,079...............E5 41

Welland, co., Ont., Can.,
164,741 . . . .*E5 41
Wellesley, Mass.,
26,071 . . . . .B5, g10 65
Wellford, S.C., 1,040 . . . . .B3 82
Wellington, Austl., 5,597 . .F7 26
Wellington, Ont., Can.,
1,064 . . . . .D7 41
Wellington, Kans., 8,809 . .E6 61
Wellington, N.Z., 131,655
(*282,487) N15 26
Wellington, Ohio, 3,599 . . .A3 78
Wellington, Tex., 3,137 . . .B4 84
Wellington, Utah, 1,066 . .B6 72
Wellington, co., Ont.,
Can., 84,702 . . . . .D4 41
Wellman, Iowa, 1,085 . . . . .C6 60
Wells, B.C., Can., 740 . . . .C7 37
Wells, Minn., 2,897 . . . . . .G5 67
Wells, Nev., 1,071 . . . . . . .A4 72
Wells, co., Ind., 21,220 . . . .C7 59
Wells, co., N. Dak., 9,237 . .C6 77
Wellsboro, Pa., 4,369 . . . . .C7 81
Wellsburg, W. Va.,
5,514 . . . . .A4, B2 87
Wellston, Mo., 7,979 . . . . .f13 69
Wellston, Ohio, 5,728 . . . .C3 78
Wellsville, Kans., 984 . . . . .D8 61
Wellsville, Mo., 1,523 . . . . .B6 69
Wellsville, N.Y., 5,967 . . . .C3 75
Wellsville, Ohio, 7,117 . . . .B5 78
Wellsville, Utah, 1,106 . . . .A6 72
Wels, Aus., 41,060 . . . . . . .D7 6
Welsh, La., 3,332 . . . . .D3 63
Wembley, Eng., 124,843 . .k11 4
Wenatchee, Wash., 16,726 . .B5 86
Wenchow (Yungkia),
China, 201,600 . . . . .F9 17
Wendell, Idaho, 1,232 . . . . .G4 57
Wendell, N.C., 1,620 . . . . .B4 76
Wenham, Mass.,
2,798 . . . . .A6, f12 65
Wenona, Ill., 1,005 . . . . . .*B4 58
Wenonah, N.J., 2,100 . . . .D2 74
Wentworth, co., Ont.,
Can., 358,837 . . . . .D4 41
Wentzville, Mo., 2,742 . . . .C7 69
Werdau, Ger., 24,500 . . . . .C6 6
Wernersville, Pa., 1,462 . .*F9 81
Wernigerode, Ger.,
33,100 . . . . .C5 6
Wesconnett, Fla., 6,000 . . .m8 54
Wesel, Ger., 32,000 . . . . . .C3 6
Weslaco, Tex., 15,649 . . . . .F3 84
Weslaco North, Tex.,
1,049 . . . .*F3 84
Wesleyville, Newf., Can.,
1,285 . . . . .D5 44
Wesleyville, Pa., 3,534 . . . .B2 81
Wessington Springs,
S. Dak., 1,488 . . . . .F7 77
Wesson, Miss., 1,157 . . . . .D3 68
West, Tex., 2,352 . . . . .D4 84
West Alexandria, Ohio,
1,524 . . . . .C1 78
West Allis, Wis., 68,157 . .m12 88
West Amityville, N.Y.,
5,000 . . . .*E7 75
West Babylon, N.Y.,
23,500 . . . .*n15 75
West Baden Springs, Ind.,
879 . . . . .G4 59
West Barrington, R.I.,
4,200 . . . . .B11 52
West Baton Rouge, par.,
La., 14,796 . . . . .D4 63
West Belmar, N.J., 2,000 . .*C4 74
West Bend, Iowa, 910 . . . . .B3 60
West Bend, Wis., 9,969 . . . .E5 88
West Bengal, state, India,
34,926,279 . . . .*D8 20
West Berlin, N.J., 3,363 . . .D3 74
West Blocton, Ala., 156 . . . .B2 46
West Bountiful, Utah,
945 . . . .*A6 72
West Boylston, Mass.,
3,400 . . . . .B4 65
West Branch, Iowa, 1,298 . .C6 60
West Branch, Mich.,
2,025 . . . . .D6 66
West Bridgewater, Mass.,
1,200 . . . . .B5 65
West Bridgewater, Pa.,
1,292 . . . .*E1 81
West Bromwich, Eng.,
97,700 . . . . .D6 4
Westbrook, Maine,
13,820 . . . . .E2, g7 64
Westbrook, Minn.,
1,012 . . . . .F3 67
West Brookfield, Mass.,
1,350 . . . . .B3 65
Westbrook Park, Pa.,
5,000 . . . .*B11 81
West Brownsville, Pa.,
1,907 . . . .*F2 81
West Brunswick, N.J.,
2,000 . . . .*C4 74

West Burlington, Iowa,
3,015 . . . . .D6 60
Westbury, N.Y., 14,618 . . . .E7 75
Westby, Wis., 1,544 . . . . . .E3 88
West Caldwell, N.J.,
8,314 . . . .*B4 74
West Cape May, N.J.,
1,030 . . . . .F3 74
West Carroll, par., La.,
14,177 . . . . .B4 63
West Carrollton, Ohio,
4,749 . . . . .C1 78
West Carthage, N.Y.,
2,167 . . . . .B5 75
Westchester, Ill., 18,092 . . .k9 58
West Chester, Pa.,
15,705 . . . . .G10 81
Westchester, co., N.Y.,
853,198 . . . . .D7 75
West Chicago, Ill., 8,174 . . .k8 58
West City, Ill., 814 . . . . . . .F5 58
West Clarkston, Wash.,
2,851 . . . .*C8 86
West Collingswood, N.J.,
2,000 . . . .*D2 74
West Collingswood
Heights, N.J., 1,300 . . . .*D2 74
West Columbia, S.C.,
6,410 . . . . .D5 82
West Columbia, Tex.,
2,947 . . . . .E5, r14 84
West Concord, Mass.,
2,500 . . . . .B5, g10 65
West Concord, N.C.,
5,510 . . . .*B2 76
West Conshohocken, Pa.,
2,254 . . . . .o20 81
West Corners, N.Y.,
3,000 . . . .*C5 75
West Covina, Calif.,
60,329 . . . . .m13 50
Westdale, Ill., 2,000 . . . . .*B6 58
West Decatur, Pa., 750 . . . .E5 81
West Derry, Pa., 1,000 . . .*F3 81
West Des Moines, Iowa,
13,720 . . . . .C4, e8 60
West Easton, Pa., 1,228 . .*E11 81
West Elizabeth, Pa., 921 . .*F2 81
West Elkton, Ohio, 345 . .*C1 75
West Elmira, N.Y.,
6,000 . . . .*C4 75
West End, Ark., 2,208 . . .*C3 49
West End, Fla., 3,124 . . . .*C4 54
West End, N.Y., 1,500 . . .*C5 75
West End Anniston, Ala.,
2,500 . . . .*B4 46
West Endicott, N.Y.,
3,000 . . . .*C5 75
Westerly, R.I., 10,300 . . . . .D9 52
Western, reg., Nig.,
10,265,846 . . . . .G5 22
Western Australia, state,
Austl., 835,570 . . . . .D3 25
Western Hills, Colo.,
3,500 . . . .*B6 51
Western Peninsula, div.,
Ice., 11,394 . . . .*m21 11
Westernport, Md., 3,559 . .m12 53
Western Samoa, country,
Oceania, 124,000 . . . . . .G9 2
Western Springs, Ill.,
13,233 . . . . .k9 58
Westerville, Ohio,
7,011 . . . . .B3, k11 78
West Fairview, Pa., 1,718 . .F8 81
West Farmington, Maine,
500 . . . . .D2 64
West Feliciana, par., La.,
12,395 . . . . .D4 63
Westfield, Ala., 2,000 . . . . .E4 46
Westfield, Ind., 1,217 . . . . .D5 59
Westfield, Mass., 26,302 . . .B2 65
Westfield, N.J., 31,447 . . . .B4 74
Westfield, N.Y., 3,878 . . . .C1 75
Westfield, Pa., 1,333 . . . . . .C6 81
Westfield, Wis., 919 . . . . . .E4 88
West Flanders, prov.,
Bel., 1,068,976 . . . .*B5 5
West Frankfort, Ill.,
9,027 . . . . .F5 58
Westgate, Fla., 2,500 . . . . .F6 54
West Glens Falls, N.Y.,
2,725 . . . .*B7 75
West Grove, Pa., 1,607 . . .G10 81
Westhampton Beach,
N.Y., 1,460 . . . . .n16 75
West Hartford, Conn.,
62,382 . . . . .B6 52
West Hartlepool, Eng.,
78,600 . . . . .C6 4
West Hartsville, S.C.,
2,427 . . . .*C7 82
West Haven, Conn.,
43,002 . . . . .D5 52
West Haverstraw, N.Y.,
5,020 . . . .*D7 75
West Hazleton, Pa., 6,278 . .E9 81
West Helena, Ark., 8,385 . .C5 49

West Hempstead, N.Y.,
26,500 . . . .*G2 52
West Hill, Ont.,
Can. D5, k15 41
West Hillsboro, N.C.,
1,065 . . . .*A3 76
West Hollywood, Calif.,
28,870 . . . .*E4 50
West Hollywood, Fla.,
52,000 . . . . .r13 54
West Homestead, Pa.,
4,155 . . . .*F2 81
West Indies, Atl. O. 35
West Irian, Indon. dep.,
Asia, 750,000 . . . . .F9 19
West Islip, N.Y., 23,000 . .*n15 75
West Jefferson, N.C.,
1,000 . . . . .A1 76
West Jefferson, Ohio,
2,774 . . . . .C2, m10 78
West Jordan, Utah,
3,009 . . . . .A5, D2 78
West Junction, Tenn.,
11,000 . . . . .B1, E8 83
West Kankakee, Ill., 3,300 .B6 58
West Kingston, R.I., 900 .D10 52
West Kittanning, Pa.,
1,101 . . . .*E3 81
West Lafayette, Ind.,
17,731 . . . . .D4 59
West Lafayette, Ohio,
1,476 . . . . .B4 78
Westlake, La., 3,311 . . . . . .D2 63
Westlake, Ohio, 12,906 . . . .h9 78
Westlands, Mass., 2,000 . . .f10 65
West Lanham Hills, Md.,
1,000 . . . .*C4 53
West Lawn, Pa., 2,059 . . . .F10 81
West Lebanon, Pa., 1,054 . .*F9 81
West Leechburg, Pa.,
1,323 . . . .*E2 81
West Leisenring, Pa., 800 . .G2 81
West Liberty, Iowa, 2,042 . .C6 60
West Liberty, Ky., 1,165 . . .C6 62
West Liberty, Ohio, 1,522 . .B2 78
West Liberty, W. Va.,
2,200 . . . . .B2 87
West Linn, Oreg.,
3,933 . . . . .B4, h12 80
Westlock, Alta., Can.,
1,838 . . . . .B4 38
West Logan, W. Va., 855 . .*D3 87
West Long Branch, N.J.,
5,337 . . . . .C4 74
West Lorne, Ont., Can.,
1,070 . . . . .E3 41
West Manayunk, Pa.,
1,900 . . . .*F11 81
West Marion, N.C.,
1,600 . . . .*f10 76
West Mayfield, Pa.,
2,201 . . . .*E1 81
Westmeath, co., Ire.,
52,800 . . . .*D3 4
West Medway, Mass.,
2,000 . . . . .B5, h10 65
West Melbourne, Fla.,
2,266 . . . .*D6 54
West Memphis, Ark.,
19,374 . . . . .B5 49
West Miami, Fla., 5,296 . . .s13 54
West Middlesex, Pa.,
1,301 . . . . .D1 81
West Mifflin, Pa., 27,289 . .F2 81
West Milton, Ohio, 2,972 . .C1 78
West Milwaukee, Wis.,
5,043 . . . . .m12 88
Westminster, Calif.,
44,851 . . . . .n12 50
Westminster, Colo., 1,700 . .A6 51
Westminster, Md., 6,123 . . .A4 53
Westminster, Mass., 1,400 . .A4 65
Westminster, S.C., 2,413 . . .B1 82
West Monroe, La.,
15,215 . . . . .B3 63
Westmont, Ill., 5,997 . . . . .k9 58
Westmont, N.J., 8,000 . . . .D2 74
Westmont, Pa., 6,573 . . . . .F4 81
Westmoreland, co., Va.,
11,042 . . . . .B6 85
Westmoreland City, Pa.,
1,300 . . . .*F2 81
Westmorland, Calif.,
1,414 . . . . .F6 50
Westmorland, co., N.B.,
Can., 93,679 . . . . .C5 43
Westmorland, co., Eng.,
67,000 . . . .*C5 4
Westmount, Que., Can.,
25 012 . . . .*D4 42
West Mystic, Conn., 650 . . .D9 52
West Newton, Pa., 3,982 . . .F2 81
West New York, N.J.,
35,547 . . . . .h8 74
West Nyack, N.Y., 4,000 . .*D7 75
Weston, Ont., Can.,
9,715 . . . . .m14 41
Weston, Conn., 700 . . . . . .E3 52

Weston, Mass., 8,261 . . . . .g10 65
Weston, Mo., 1,057 . . .B3, h10 69
Weston, Ohio, 1,075 . . . . . .A2 78
Weston, W. Va., 8,754 . . . .B4 87
Weston, co., Wyo., 7,929 . .C8 89
Weston-Super-Mare, Eng.
43,200 . . . . .E5 4
West Orange, N.J.,
39,895 . . . . .B4 74
West Orange, Tex.,
4,848 . . . .*D6 84
Westover, W. Va.,
4,749 . . . . .A7, B5 87
West Palm Beach, Fla.,
61,000 (*210,000) F6 54
West Paterson, N.J.,
7,602 . . . .*B4 74
West Pensacola, Fla.,
33,500 . . . . .v14 54
West Pittston, Pa., 6,998 . .m17 81
West Plains, Mo., 5,836 . . . .E6 69
West Point, Ga., 4,610 . . . .D1 55
West Point, Ky., 2,005 . . . .C4 62
West Point, Miss., 8,550 . . .B5 68
West Point, Nebr., 2,921 . . .C9 71
West Point, N.Y.,
4,500 . . . . .D7, m15 75
West Point, Va., 1,678 . . . .C6 85
Westport, Conn., 20,955 . . .E3 52
West Portland, Oreg.,
2,000 . . . .*B4 80
West Portland Park,
Oreg., 2,500 . . . .*B4 80
West Portsmouth, Ohio,
3,100 . . . . .D2 78
West Pueblo, Colo.,
1,700 . . . .*C6 51
West Roanoke Rapids,
N.C., 2,000 . . . .*A5 76
West Rockingham, N.C.,
1,128 . . . .*B3 76
West Rutland, Vt., 2,302 . .D1 73
West Sacramento, Calif.,
16,500 . . . .*C3 50
West Salem, Ill., 956 . . . . . .E5 58
West Salem, Ohio, 1,017 . . .B3 78
West Salem, Wis., 1,070 . . .E2 88
West Sayville, N.Y.,
3,500 . . . . .G4 52
West Seneca, N.Y.,
39,653 . . . .*C2 75
West Slope, Oreg., 5,000 . .g12 80
West Spitsbergen, isl.,
Nor. A21 2
West Springfield, Mass.,
24,924 . . . . .B2 65
West St. Paul, Minn.,
15,144 . . . . .n12 67
West Terre Haute, Ind.,
3,006 . . . . .F3 59
West Union, Iowa, 2,551 . . .B6 60
West Union, Ohio, 1,762 . .D2 78
West Union, W. Va.,
1,186 . . . . .B4, B6 87
West Unity, Ohio, 1,192 . . .A1 78
West University Place,
Tex., 14,628 . . . . .r14 84
West Van Lear, Ky., 900 . . .C7 62
West View, Ohio, 1,303 . . . .h9 78
West View, Pa., 8,079 . . . .h13 81
West View Park, Tenn.,
1,000 . . . . .C11 83
Westville, Ill., 3,497 . . . . . .C6 58
Westville, N.J., 4,951 . . . . .D2 74
Westville Grove, N.J.,
3,000 . . . .*D2 74
West Virginia, state, U.S.,
1,860,421 87
West Warren, Mass.,
1,124 . . . . .B3 65
West Warwick, R.I.,
21,915 . . . . .C10 52
Westwego, La., 9,815 . . . .k11 63
West Wenatchee, Wash.,
2,518 . . . .*B5 86
West Winfield, N.Y., 960 . .C5 75
West Winter Haven, Fla.,
5,050 . . . .*D5 54
Westwood, Calif., 1,600 . . .B3 50
Westwood, Kans., 2,040 . . .B9 61
Westwood, Ky., 5,000 . . . . .B7 62
Westwood, Mass.,
7,200 . . . . .B5, h11 65
Westwood, Mich., 6,500 . .*F5 66
Westwood, N.J.,
9,046 . . . . .D5, h8 74
Westwood Lakes, Fla.,
28,000 . . . . .s13 54
Westworth Village, Tex.,
3,321 . . . .*C4 84
West Wyalong, Austl.,
2,399 . . . . .F6 26
West Wyoming, Pa.,
3,166 . . . . .n17 81
West Wyomissing, Pa.,
2,500 . . . .*F9 81
West Yarmouth, Mass.,
2,100 . . . . .C7 65

West York, Pa., 5,526.....G8 81
West Yuma, Ariz., 2,781..*C1 48
Wetaskiwin, Alta., Can., 5,300...........C4 38
Wethersfield, Conn., 20,561............C6 52
Wetumka, Okla., 1,798..B5 79
Wetumpka, Ala., 3,672...C3 46
Wetzel, co., W. Va., 19,347............B4 87
Wetzlar, Ger. 37,900....C4 6
Wewahitchka, Fla., 1,436..B1 54
Wewoka, Okla., 5,954...B5 79
Wexford, Ire., 11,500.....D3 4
Wexford, co., Ire., 83,400.............*D3 4
Wexford, co., Mich., 18,466.............D5 66
Weyauwega, Wis., 1,239...D5 88
Weyburn, Sask., Can., 9,101............H4, o8 39
Weymouth, N.S., Can., 671..............E4 43
Weymouth, Mass., 48,177...........B6, h12 65
Weymouth and Melcombe Regis, Eng., 41,800.............E5 4
Whangarei, N.Z., 27,560...........K15 26
Wharton, N.J., 5,006...B3 74
Wharton, Tex., 5,734...E4 84
Wharton, W. Va., 1,055..D6 87
Wharton, co., Tex., 38,152.............E4 84
Wharton West, Tex., 1,609.............*E4 84
What Cheer, Iowa, 956....C5 60
Whatcom, co., Wash., 70,317............A4 86
Wheatland, Wyo., 2,350...D8 89
Wheatland, co., Mont., 3,026.............D7 70
Wheatley, Ont., Can., 1,362.............E2 41
Wheaton, Ill., 28,233..B5, k8 58
Wheaton, Md., 63,000...*B3 53
Wheaton, Minn., 2,102..E2 67
Wheat Ridge, Colo., 29,000............*B5 51
Wheeler, Tex., 1,174.....B2 84
Wheeler, co., Ga., 5,342...D4 55
Wheeler, co., Nebr., 1,297.............C7 71
Wheeler, co., Oreg., 2,722.............C6 80
Wheeler, co., Tex., 7,947.............B2 84
Wheeler, peak, N. Mex.....A6 48
Wheelersburg, Ohio, 2,682.............D3 78
Wheeling, Ill., 11,756.....h9 58
Wheeling, W. Va., 48,000 (*117,000)...A4, B2 87
Wheelwright, Ky., 1,518...C7 62
Whippany, N.J., 6,300....B4 74
Whitaker, Pa., 2,130....*F2 81
Whitakers, N.C., 1,004....A5 76
Whitby, Ont., Can., 14,685............D6 41
Whitby, Eng., 12,100....C6 4
White, co., Ark., 32,745..B4 49
White, co., Ga., 6,935....B3 55
White, co., Ill., 19,373...E5 58
White, co., Ind., 19,709...C4 59
White, co., Tenn., 15,577.............D8 83
White Bear Lake, Minn., 19,410.....E5, m12 67
White Castle, La., 2,253.............D4, h9 63
White City, Fla., 600......C1 54
White Cloud, Mich., 1,001.............E5 66
White Deer, Tex., 1,057..B2 84
Whitefield, N.H., 1,200....C4 73
Whitefish, Mont., 2,965..B2 70
Whitefish Bay, Wis., 18,390............*E6 88
White Hall, Ill., 3,012.....D3 58
Whitehall, Mich., 2,590...E4 66
Whitehall, Mont., 898....E4 70
Whitehall, N.Y., 4,016....B7 75
Whitehall, Ohio, 20,818..m11 78
Whitehall, Pa., 16,075....*F1 81
Whitehall, Wis., 1,446....D2 88
Whitehaven, Eng., 27,600..C5 4
White Haven, Pa., 1,778.............D10 81
Whitehaven, Tenn., 16,000............E8 83
Whitehorse, Yukon, Can., 5,031.............D6 36
Whitehouse, Ohio, 1,135.............A2, e6 78
White Lake, Mich. 300...*F7 66
Whiteland, Ind., 1,368....*E5 59
White Oak, N.C., 150.....C4 76

White Oak, Ohio, 7,000...o12 78
White Oak, Pa., 9,047....*F2 81
White Oak, Tex., 1,250..*C5 84
White Pigeon, Mich., 1,399.............G5 66
White Pine, co., Nev., 9,808.............B4 72
White Pine, Tenn., 1,035.............C10 83
White Plains, N.Y., 50,040..........D7, m15 75
White River Junction, Vt., 2,600...........D3 73
White Rock, B.C., Can., 6,453........E6, f13 37
White Salmon, Wash., 1,590.............D4 86
Whitesboro, N.Y., 4,784.............*B5 75
Whitesboro, Tex., 2,485...C4 84
Whitesburg, Ky., 1,774...C7 62
Whites Creek, Tenn., 100..E9 83
White Settlement, Tex., 11,513............*B5 84
Whiteside, co., Ill., 59,887............B3 58
White Stone, Va., 395....C6 85
White Sulphur Springs, Mont., 1,519........D6 70
White Sulphur Springs, W. Va., 2,676......D4 87
Whitesville, W. Va., 774...D6 87
Whiteville, N.C., 4,683...C4 76
Whitewright, Tex., 1,315..C4 84
Whitefield, co., Ga., 42,109............B2 55
Whiting, Ind., 8,137......A3 59
Whiting, Wis., 1,193......D4 88
Whitinsville, Mass., 5,102.............B4 65
Whitley, co., Ind., 20,954............B6 59
Whitley, co., Ky., 25,815............D5 62
Whitley City, Ky., 1,034...D5 62
Whitman, Mass., 10,485..........B6, h12 65
Whitman, co., Wash., 31,263............B8 86
Whitmire, S.C., 2,663.....N4 82
Whitmore City, Haw., 1,820.............f9 56
Whitnel, N.C., 1,232......B1 76
Whitney, Idaho, 11,500...F2 57
Whitney, S.C., 2,100......B4 82
Whitney, Tex., 1,050......D4 84
Whitney, mtn., Calif........D4 50
Whitney Point, N.Y., 1,108.............C5 75
Whittier, Calif., 33,663............F4, n12 50
Whitwell, Tenn., 1,857...D8 83
Wiarton, Ont., Can., 2,138.............C3 41
Wibaux, co., Mont., 766..D12 70
Wichita, Kans., 288,000 (*365,000)........E6, g12 61
Wichita, Oreg., 6,000....*B4 80
Wichita, co., Kans., 2,765..D2 61
Wichita, co., Tex., 123,528.............B3 84
Wichita Falls, Tex., 98,000 (*115,000)......C3 84
Wickenburg, Ariz., 2,445.............C2 48
Wickett, Tex., 900.......D1 84
Wickliffe, Ohio, 15,760...........A4, g9 78
Wickliffe, Ky., 917.......A2 62
Wickliffe, Ohio, 6,000...*A5 78
Wicklow, co., Ire., 60,300.............*D3 4
Wicomico, co., Md., 49,050............D6 53
Wiconisco, Pa., 1,402.....E8 81
Wielun, Pol., 12,400.....C6 7
Wiener Neustadt, Aus., 33,845............E8 6
Wiesbaden, Ger., 258,200.............C4 6
Wiggins, Miss., 1,591.....E4 68
Wigtown, co., Scot., 28,800.............*C4 4
Wilbarger, co., Tex., 17,748............B3 84
Wilber, Nebr., 1,358......D9 71
Wilberforce, Ohio, 2,800..C2 78
Wilbur, Wash., 1,138.....B7 86
Wilburton, Okla., 1,772...C6 79
Wilcox, co., Ala., 18,739.............D2 46
Wilcox, co., Ga., 7,905....E3 55
Wilden, Pa., 1,787.......*E11 81
Wilder, Vt., 1,400.......D3 73
Wildwood, Fla., 2,170.....D4 54
Wildwood, N.J., 4,690.....F3 74
Wildwood, Tex., 2,500...*E2 81

Wildwood Crest, N.J., 3,011.............F3 74
Wilhelm, mtn., N. Gui....k12 25
Wilhelmina, mtn., W. Irian.............F9 19
Wilhelm-Pieck-Stadt Guben, Ger., 22,500...C7 6
Wilhelmshaven, Ger., 100,500.............B4 6
Wilkes, co., Ga., 10,961...C4 55
Wilkes, co., N.C., 45,269...A1 76
Wilkes-Barre, Pa., 56,000 (*250,000).......D10, n17 81
Wilkesboro, N.C., 1,568...A1 76
Wilkie, Sask., Can., 1,612.............E1 39
Wilkin, co., Minn., 10,650............D2 67
Wilkinsburg, Pa., 30,066............F2, k14 81
Wilkinson, co., Ga., 9,250.............D3 55
Wilkinson, co., Miss., 13,235............D2 68
Will, co., Ill., 191,617.....B6 58
Willacoochee, Ga., 1,061..E3 55
Willacy, co., Tex., 20,084............F4 84
Willamina, Oreg., 960....B3 80
Willard, Ohio, 5,457.....A3 78
Willcox, Ariz., 3,018.....C4 48
Willemstad, Neth., 43,547............A4 32
Willesden, Eng., 170,835..........E6, k11 4
Williams, Ariz., 3,559....B2 48
Williams, Calif., 1,370....C2 50
Williams, co., N. Dak., 22,051............B2 77
Williams, co., Ohio, 29,968............A1 78
Williams Bay, Wis., 1,347..F5 88
Williamsburg, Iowa, 1,342.............C5 60
Williamsburg, Ky., 3,478..D5 62
Williamsburg, Ohio, 1,956.............C1 78
Williamsburg, Pa., 1,792..F5 81
Williamsburg (Independent City), Va., 6,832.........C6 85
Williamsburg, co., S.C., 40,932............D8 82
Williams Lake, B.C., Can., 2,120........C6, n18 37
Williamson, N.Y., 1,690...B3 75
Williamson, W. Va., 6,746.............D2 87
Williamson, co., Ill., 46,117............F4 58
Williamson, co., Tenn., 25,267............A5 83
Williamson, co., Tex., 35,044............D4 84
Williamsport, Ind., 1,353..D3 59
Williamsport, Md., 1,853..A2 53
Williamsport, Pa., 41,967..D7 81
Williamston, Mich., 2,214..F6 66
Williamston, N.C., 6,886...B5 76
Williamston, S.C., 3,721...B3 82
Williamstown, Ky., 1,611..B5 62
Williamstown, Mass., 5,500 A1 65
Williamstown, N.J., 2,800.............D3 74
Williamstown, Pa., 2,097..E8 81
Williamstown, W. Va., 2,632.............B3 87
Williamsville, N.Y., 6,512..C2 75
Willimantic, Conn., 13,881............C8 52
Willis Beach, Nebr., 100..B9 71
Williston, Fla., 1,582.....C4 54
Williston, N. Dak., 11,866..B2 77
Williston, S.C., 2,722.....E5 82
Williston Park, 8,255.....G2 52
Willits, Calif., 3,410......C2 50
Willmar, Minn., 10,417...E3 67
Willoughby, Ohio, 15,058.............A4 78
Willow Brook, Calif., 22,000.............*F4 50
Willowdale, Ont., Can.,...........D5, k15 41
Willow Grove, Pa., 11,500..........F11, o21 81
Willowwick, Ohio, 18,749.............A4, h9 78
Willow Run, Mich., 4,100.............*F7 66
Willows, Calif., 4,139......C2 50
Willow Springs, Ill., 3,158..k9 58
Willow Springs, Mo., 1,913.............E6 69
Wills Point, Tex., 2,281.............*C5 84
Wilmer, Tex., 1,785.......n10 84
Wilmerding, Pa., 4,349....B6 81

Wilmette, Ill., 31,685..A6, h9 58
Wilmington, Del., 95,827..A6 53
Wilmington, Ill., 4,210....B5 58
Wilmington, Mass., 3,000.............A5, f11 65
Wilmington, N.C., 44,013..C5 76
Wilmington, Ohio, 8,915..C2 78
Wilmington Manor, Del., 2,200.............*A6 53
Wilmore, Ky., 2,773.....C5 62
Wilson, Ark., 1,191......B5 49
Wilson, Conn., 3,000.....B6 52
Wilson, Kans., 1,084.....D5 61
Wilson, N.Y., 1,320......B2 75
Wilson, N.C., 28,753.....B5 76
Wilson, Okla., 1,647.....C4 79
Wilson, Pa., 8,465.......E11 81
Wilson, co., Kans., 13,077............E8 61
Wilson, co., N.C., 57,716..B5 76
Wilson, co., Tenn., 27,668............A5 83
Wilson, co., Tex., 13,267..E3 84
Wilton, Conn., 5,500.....E3 52
Wilton, Maine, 1,800....D2 64
Wilton, N.H., 1,425......F4 73
Wilton Junction (Wilton), Iowa, 1,750...........C6 60
Wilton Manors, Fla., 8,257.............*F6 54
Wiltshire, co., Eng., 447,300.............*F6 4
Wimbledon, Eng., 56,994............m12 4
Winamac, Ind., 2,375....B4 59
Winchendon, Mass., 3,800.............A3 65
Winchester, Ont., Can., 1,429.............B9 41
Winchester, Eng., 29,500..E6 4
Winchester, Ill., 1,657....D3 58
Winchester, Ind., 5,742...D8 59
Winchester, Ky., 10,187...C5 62
Winchester, Mass., 19,376.............g11 65
Winchester, Mo., 1,299...*C7 69
Winchester, Nev., 600....C4 72
Winchester, Tenn., 4,760..B5 83
Winchester (Independent City), Va., 15,110....A4 85
Windber, Pa., 6,994......F4 81
Winder, Ga., 5,555.......C3 55
Windfall, Ind., 1,135.....D6 59
Windgap, Pa., 1,930.....E11 81
Windham, Ohio, 3,777....A4 78
Windham, co., Conn., 68,572............B8 52
Windham, co., Vt., 29,776............F3 73
Windhoek, S.W. Afr., 36,051............E3 24
Wind Lake, Wis., 1,800...F5 88
Windom, Minn., 3,691....G3 67
Windsor, Newf., Can......D4 44
Windsor, N.S., Can., 3,823.............E5 43
Windsor, Ont., Can., 114,367 (*193,365)......E1 41
Windsor, Que., Can., 6,589.............D5 42
Windsor, Colo., 1,509...*A6 51
Windsor, Conn., 13,500...B6 52
Windsor, Ill., 1,021......D5 58
Windsor, Mo., 2,714.....C4 69
Windsor, N.C., 1,813.....A6 76
Windsor, Pa., 1,029......G8 81
Windsor, Vt., 3,256......E3 73
Windsor, co., Vt., 42,483............D2 73
Windsor Heights, Iowa, 4,715.............e8 60
Windsor Hills, Calif., 3,500.............*F4 50
Windsor Locks, Conn., 11,411............B6 52
Windward Islands, see Dominica, Grenada, St. Lucia and St. Vincent, br. dep., N.A.
Windy Hill, S.C., 2,201..*C8 82
Windy Hills, Ky., 1,371..*H6 62
Winfield, Ala., 2,907.....B2 46
Winfield, Ill., 2,452......*B5 58
Winfield, Kans., 11,117...E7 61
Winfield, N.J., 2,458......k7 74
Wingate, N.C., 1,966.....C2 76
Wingham, Ont., Can., 2,922.............D3 41
Wink, Tex., 1,863.......D1 84
Winkelman, Ariz., 1,123...C3 48
Winkler, Man., Can., 2,529.............E3 40
Winkler, co., Tex., 13,652............D1 84
Winn, par., La., 16,034....C3 63
Winneab, Ghana, 25,400...G4 22
Winnebago, Ill., 1,059....A4 58
Winnebago, Minn., 2,088..G4 67

Winnebago, co., Ill., 209,765..............A4 58
Winnebago, co., Iowa, 13,099..............A4 60
Winnebago, co., Wis., 107,928..............H9 88
Winneconne, Wis., 1,273...D5 88
Winnemucca, Nev., 3,453..A3 72
Winner, S. Dak., 3,705....G6 77
Winneshiek, co., Iowa, 21,651..............A6 60
Winnetka, Ill., 13,368..A6, h9 58
Winnfield, La., 7,022....C3 63
Winnie, Tex., 1,114......*E5 84
Winnipeg, Man., Can., 265,429 (*475,989)..E3, h8 40
Winnipeg, lake, Man., Can...................C2 40
Winnipegosis, Man., Can., 980..............D2 40
Winnipegosis, lake, Man. Can., 980.............C2 40
Winnsboro, La., 4,437....B4 63
Winnsboro, S.C., 3,479....C5 82
Winnsboro, Tex., 2,675....C5 84
Winnsboro Mills, S.C., 2,411..............*C5 82
Winona, Minn., 26,771....F7 67
Winona, Miss., 4,282.....B4 68
Winona, co., Minn., 40,937..............F7 67
Winona Lake, Ind., 1,928..B6 59
Winooski, Vt., 7,420......C1 73
Winschoten, Neth., 16,600..............A7 5
Winslow, Ariz., 8,862.....B3 48
Winslow, Ind., 1,089......H3 59
Winslow, Maine, 4,000....D3 64
Winslow, Wash., 919.....e10 86
Winsted, Conn., 8,136.....B4 52
Winsted, Minn., 1,163.....F4 67
Winston, Fla., 3,323.......D4 54
Winston, Miss., 19,246....B4 68
Winston, Oreg., 2,395.....*D3 80
Winston, co., Ala., 14,858..A2 46
Winston-Salem, N.C., 143,000 (*216,000).....A2 76
Winter Garden, Fla., 5,513..............D5 54
Winter Haven, Fla., 16,277..............D5 54
Winter Park, Fla., 17,162..............D5 54
Winters, Calif., 1,700.....C2 50
Winters, Tex., 3,266.......D3 84
Winterset, Iowa, 3,639....C4 60
Wintersville, Ohio, 3,597..B5 78
Winterthur, Switz., 86,900..............E4 6
Winterton, Newf., Can., 808..............E5 44
Winterville, N.C., 1,418...B5 76
Winthrop, Maine, 2,300..D3 64
Winthrop, Mass., 20,303..........B6, g12 65
Winthrop, Minn., 1,381...F4 67
Winthrop Harbor, Ill., 4,427............A6, h9 58
Wirt, co., W. Va., 4,391...B3 87
Wisbech, Eng., 17,500....D7 4
Wiscasset, Maine, 950.....D3 64
Wisconsin, state, U.S., 3,951,777...........B8 45
Wisconsin Dells, Wis., 2,105..............E4 88
Wisconsin Rapids, Wis., 15,042..............D4 88
Wise, Va., 2,614..........f9 85
Wise, co., Tex., 17,012....C4 84
Wise, co., Va., 43,579.....e9 85
Wishek, N. Dak., 1,290...D6 77
Wisła, riv., Pol...........B5 7
Wismar, Ger., 56,600.....B5 6

Wisner, La., 1,254........C4 63
Wisner, Nebr., 1,192......C9 71
Withamsville, Ohio, 2,811..............C1 78
Witt, Ill., 1,101..........D4 58
Wittenberg, Ger., 45,700...C6 6
Wittenberge, Ger., 46,100..............B5 6
Wixom, Mich., 1,531....o14 66
Włocławek, Pol., 66,900...B5 7
Woburn, Mass., 31,214..........B5, g11 65
Wolcott, Conn., 1,500....C5 52
Wolcott, N.Y., 1,630.....B4 75
Wolfe, co., Que., Can., 18,335..............D6 42
Wolfe, co., Ky., 6,534....C6 62
Wolfeboro, N.H., 1,300...D5 73
Wolfe City, Tex., 1,317....C4 84
Wolfenbüttel, Ger., 40,000..............B5 6
Wolf Lake, Mich., 1,900...E4 66
Wolf Point, Mont., 3,585..B11 70
Wolfsburg, Ger., 76,100...B5 6
Wolfville, N.S., Can., 2,413..............D5 43
Wollongong, Austl., 150,208.............F9 25
Wolseley, Sask., Can., 1,031..............G4 39
Wolverhampton, Eng., 150,300.............D5 4
Wolverine Lake, Mich., 2,404..............*F7 66
Wolverton, Eng., 13,000...D6 4
Womelsdrof, Pa., 1,471....F9 81
Wonder Lake, Ill., 4,000............A5, h8 58
Wonsan, Kor., 112,952...G3 18
Wood, co., Ohio, 72,596..A2 78
Wood, co., Tex., 17,653...C5 84
Wood, co., W. Va., 78,331.............B3 87
Wood, co., Wis., 59,105..D3 88
Woodbine, Iowa, 1,304...C2 60
Woodbine, N.J., 2,823....E4 74
Woodbourne, N.Y., 900...D6 75
Woodbridge, Ont., Can., 2,315........D5, k14 41
Woodbridge, Conn., 5,182..............D4 52
Woodbridge, N.J., 19,000............B4, k7 74
Woodbridge, Va., 1,500...B5 85
Woodburn, Oreg., 3,120..........B4, h12 80
Woodbury, Conn., 1,700...C4 52
Woodbury, Ga., 1,230....D2 55
Woodbury, N.J., 12,453..D2 74
Woodbury, N.Y., 2,200...*E7 75
Woodbury, Tenn., 1,562..B5 83
Woodbury, co., Iowa, 107,849.............B1 60
Woodbury Heights, N.J., 1,723..............*D2 74
Woodcliff Lake, N.J., 2,742...............g8 74
Woodcroft, Ind., 2,000...*E5 59
Wood Dale, Ill., 4,424.....k9 58
Woodford, Eng., 61,259..k13 4
Woodford, co., Ill., 24,579..............C4 58
Woodford, co., Ky., 11,913.............B5 62
Wood Green, Eng., 47,897.............k12 4
Woodlake, Calif., 2,623....D4 50
Woodland, Calif., 13,524..C3 50
Woodland, Maine, 1,450..C5 64
Woodland, Pa., 900......E5 81
Woodland, Wash., 1,336..D3 86
Woodland Beach, Mich., 1,944..............*G7 66

Woodlawn, Ky., 50......A2 62
Woodlawn, Md., 6,000...*B4 53
Woodlawn, Md., 3,000...*C4 53
Woodlawn, Ohio, 3,007..n13 78
Woodlawn Beach, N.Y., 2,000............C2 75
Woodlawn Orchards, Mich., 2,000.........*F6 66
Woodlawn Park, Ky., 1,137..............*H6 62
Woodley Hills, Va., 2,000..............*B5 85
Woodlyn, Pa., 6,000.....*B10 81
Wood Lynne, N.J., 3,128..............*D2 74
Woodmere, N.Y., 18,200.............G2 52
Wood-Ridge, N.J., 7,964..h8 74
Woodridge, N.Y., 1,034..D6 75
Wood River, Ill., 11,694...E3 58
Woodroffe, mtn., Austl....E5 25
Woodruff, S.C., 3,679.....B3 82
Woodruff, co., Ark., 13,954.............B4 49
Woodruff Place, Ind., 1,501..............*E5 59
Woods, co., Okla., 11,932.............A3 79
Woodsboro, Tex., 2,081....E4 84
Woods Cross, Utah, 1,098..C2 72
Woodsfield, Ohio, 2,956...C4 78
Woodside, Calif., 3,592....*D2 50
Woodson, co., Kans., 5,423.............E8 61
Woodson Terrace, Mo., 6,048.............*C7 69
Woodstock, N.B., Can., 4,305.............C2 43
Woodstock, Ont., Can., 20,486.............D4 41
Woodstock, Ill., 9,910....A5 58
Woodstock, Vt., 1,415....D2 73
Woodstock, Va., 2,083....B4 85
Woodstown, N.J., 2,942..D2 74
Woodsville, N.H., 1,600...C3 73
Woodville, Calif., 1,045...*D4 50
Woodville, Miss., 1,856...D2 68
Woodville, Ohio, 1,700.............A2, f7 78
Woodville, Tex., 1,920...D5 84
Woodward, Ala., 1,000...........B3, E4 46
Woodward, Iowa, 967.....C4 60
Woodward, Okla., 7,747..A2 79
Woodward, co., Okla., 13,902.............A2 79
Woodway, Tex., 1,244...*D4 84
Woolwich, Eng., 148,700............m13 4
Woonsocket, R.I., 46,678.............A10 52
Woonsocket, S. Dak., 1,035.............F7 77
Wooster, Ohio, 17,406....B4 78
Worcester, Eng., 67,300..D5 4
Worcester, Mass., 177,000 (*335,000).........B4 65
Worcester, N.Y., 799....C6 75
Worcester, S. Afr., 32,274.............G3 24
Worcester, co., Eng., 588,200............*D5 4
Worcester, co., Md., 23,733.............D7 53
Worcester, co., Mass., 583,228............A3 65
Worden, Ill., 1,060.......E4 58
Workington, Eng., 29,800.............C5 4
Worland, Wyo., 5,806...B5 89
World, 3,287,000,000........ 2
Wormleysburg, Pa., 1,794..............*F8 81

Worms, Ger., 63,400.....D4 6
Worth, Ill., 11,702.......k9 58
Worth, co., Ga., 16,682...E3 55
Worth, co., Iowa, 10,259..A4 60
Worth, co., Mo., 3,936....A3 69
Wortham, Tex., 1,087....D4 84
Worthing, Eng., 79,700...E6 4
Worthington, Ind., 1,635..F4 59
Worthington, Ky., 1,235...B7 62
Worthington, Minn., 9,015.............G3 67
Worthington, Ohio, 9,239..........B2, k10 78
Wrangel, isl., Sov. Un.....B21 13
Wrangell, Alsk., 1,315..........D13, m23 47
Wrangell, mtn., Alsk......f19 47
Wray, Colo., 2,082.......A8 51
Wrens, Ga., 1,628........C4 55
Wrentham, Mass., 1,909..............B5 65
Wrexham, Wales, 36,100..D5 4
Wright, co., Iowa, 19,447.............B4 60
Wright, co., Minn., 29,935.............E4 67
Wright, co., Mo., 14,183..D5 69
Wright City, Okla., 1,161..C6 79
Wrightstown, N.J., 4,846.............C3 74
Wrightsville, Ga., 2,056...D4 55
Wrightsville, Pa., 2,345...F8 81
Wrocław (Breslau), Pol., 461,900...........C4 7
Wuchow (Tsangwu), China, 110,800.......G7 17
Wuhan, China, 2,146,000..E7 17
Wuhu, China, 242,100.............E8 17
Wuppertal, Ger., 421,800.............C3 6
Württemberg, reg., Ger....D4 6
Würzburg, Ger., 120,000...D4 6
Wurzen, Ger., 23,500.....C6 6
Wusih, China, 613,000....E9 17
Wusu, China, 10,000.....C1 17
Wyandanch, N.Y., 9,000..............*n15 75
Wyandot, co., Ohio, 21,648.............B2 78
Wyandotte, Mich., 43,519.........F7, p15 66
Wyandotte, co., Kans., 185,495.............C9 61
Wyckoff, N.J., 11,205....*A4 74
Wymore, Nebr., 1,975...D9 71
Wyncote, Pa., 6,000.....*F11 81
Wyndmoor, Pa., 5,800...*F11 81
Wynne, Ark., 4,922......B5 49
Wynnewood, Okla., 2,509.............C4 79
Wynnewood, Pa., 7,200..*F11 81
Wynyard, Sask., Can., 1,686..........F3, n8 39
Wyoming, Del., 1,172....B6 53
Wyoming, Ill., 1,559.....B4 58
Wyoming, Mich., 45,829..*F5 66
Wyoming, Minn., 435.....E6 67
Wyoming, Ohio, 7,736...c13 78
Wyoming, Pa., 4,127....n17 81
Wyoming, co., N.Y., 34,793.............C2 75
Wyoming, co., Pa., 16,813.............D9 81
Wyoming, co., W. Va., 34,836.............D3 87
Wyoming, state, U.S., 330,066............. 89
Wyomissing, Pa., 5,044...F10 81
Wythe, co., Va., 21,975.............D1 85
Wytheville, Va., 5,634..............D1 85

X

Xanthi, Grc., 26,377.....B5 14
Xauen, Mor., 13,712.....A3 22

Xavier, Kans., 600.......B8 61
Xenia, Ohio, 20,445.....C2 78

Xilitla, Mex., 3,098......m14 34
Xingú, riv., Braz.........D5 27

Xochimilco, Mex., 30,031..........h9, n14 34

Y

Yadkin, co., N.C.,
22,804 . . . . A2 76
Yadkinville, N.C., 1,644 . . A2 76
Yaizu, Jap., 77,008 . . . . . . o17 18
Yakima, Wash., 43,284 . . . . C5 86
Yakima, co., Wash.,
145,112 . . . . C5 86
Yakutsk, Sov. Un.,
82,000 . . . . C15 13
Yalobusha, co., Miss.,
12,502 . . . . A4 68
Yalta, Sov. Un., 43,994 . . . I10 12
Yalu, China, 10,000 . . . . . . B9 17
Yalvac, Tur., 10,378 . . . . . . C8 14
Yamachiche, Que., Can.,
1,186 . . . . C5 42
Yamagata, Jap., 133,000 . . G10 18
Yamagata, pref., Jap.,
1,263,103 . . . . *G10 18
Yamaguchi, Jap.,
66,000 . . . . I5 18
Yamaguchi, pref, Jap.,
1,543,573 . . . . *I5 18
Yamanashi, pref., Jap.,
763,194 . . . . *I9 18
Yamaska, co., Que., Can.,
16,058 . . . . C5 42
Yambol, Bul., 58,405 . . . . . D8 10
Yamethin, Bur., 12,030 . . D10 20
Yamhill, co., Oreg.,
32,478 . . . . B3 80
Yanam, India, 7,032 . . . . . E7 20
Yanbu', Sau. Ar., 20,000 . . E2 15
Yancey, co., N.C.,
14,008 . . . . f10 76
Yanceyville, N.C., 1,113 . . A3 76
Yangchow, China,
180,200 . . . . E8 17
Yangtze, riv., China E8 17
Yankton, S. Dak., 9,279 . . H8 77
Yankton, co., S. Dak.,
17,551 . . . . G8 77
Yaoundé, Cam.,
93,269 . . . . H7 22
Yaracuy, state, Ven.,
175,291 . . . . A4 32
Yardley, Pa., 2,271 . . . . . . F12 81
Yarım, Yemen, 20,000 . . . . G3 15
Yarkand (Soche), China,
80,000 . . . . F10 16
Yarmouth, N.S., Can.,
8,636 . . . . F3 43
Yarmouth, Maine,
3,000 . . . . E2, g7 64
Yarmouth, co., N.S.,
Can., 23,386 . . . . F4 43
Yaroslavl, Sov. Un.,
454,000 . . . . C12 12

Yartsevo, Sov. Un.,
25,800 . . . . D9 12
Yarumal, Col., 16,823 . . . . B2 32
Yasinovataya, Sov. Un.,
10,000 . . . . q20 12
Yates, co., N.Y., 18,614 . . . C3 75
Yates Center, Kans.,
2,080 . . . . E8 61
Yatsushiro, Jap., 69,000 . . . J5 18
Yauco, P.R., 8,996 . . . . . . *G11 35
Yavapai, co., Ariz.,
28,912 . . . . B2 48
Yavorov, Sov. Un.,
10,000 . . . . G4 12
Yawatahama, Jap.,
36,900 . . . . J6 18
Yazd (Yezd), Iran,
63,502 . . . . B8 23
Yazoo, co., Miss.,
31,653 . . . . C3 68
Yazoo City, Miss.,
11,236 . . . . C3 68
Yeadon, Pa., 11,610 . . . . . p20 81
Yeagertown, Pa.,
1,349 . . . . E6 81
Yecla, Sp., 18,400 . . . . C5 8
Yefremov, Sov. Un.,
42,900 . . . . E12 12
Yegoryevsk, Sov.
Un., 61,000 . . . . . . D12, n19 12
Yelan, Sov. Un.,
10,000 . . . . F14 12
Yelets, Sov. Un., 85,000 . . E12 12
Yell, co., Ark., 11,940 . . . . B2 49
Yellow, sea, China D9 17
Yellowknife, N.W. Ter.,
Can., 3,141 . . . . D11 36
Yellow Medicine, co.,
Minn., 15,523 . . . . F2 67
Yellow Springs, Ohio,
4,167 . . . . C2 78
Yellowstone, co., Mont.,
79,016 . . . . D8 70
Yellowstone, riv., U.S. B2 89
Yellowstone National
Park (part), co., Wyo.,
420 . . . . B2 89
Yemen, country, Asia
5,000,000 . . . . F3 15
Yenakiyevo
(Ordzhonikidze), Sov.
Un., 92,000 . . . . q20 12
Yenangyaung, Bur.,
11,098 . . . . *G4 17
Yencheng, China,
105,000 . . . . *E9 17
Yenchi (Chutzuchieh),
China, 70,000 . . . . C10 17

Yenisey, riv., Sov. Un. C11 16
Yeniseysk, Sov. Un.,
18,300 . . . . D12 13
Yeovil, Eng., 24,700 . . . . . . E5 4
Yerevan, Sov. Un.,
623,000 . . . . E7 13
Yerupaja, mtn., Peru D2 31
Yessey, Sov. Un., 10,000 . . C13 13
Yevpatoriya, Sov. Un.,
61,000 . . . . I9 12
Yeysk, Sov. Un., 61,000 . . H12 12
Yiannitsa, Grc., 19,693 . . . *B4 14
Yinchwan (Ningsia),
China, 84,000 . . . . D6 17
Yingkow, China,
131,400 . . . . C9 17
Yoakum, Tex., 5,761 . . . . . E4 84
Yoakum, co., Tex., 8,032 . . C1 84
Yoichi, Jap., 20,300 . . . . . E10 18
Yokkaichi, Jap.,
218,981 . . . . I8, o15 18
Yokohama, Jap.,
1,788,915 . . . . I9, n18 18
Yokosuka, Jap.,
317,411 . . . . I9, n18 18
Yokote, Jap., 26,900 . . . . G10 18
Yolo, co., Calif., 65,727 . . . C2 50
Yolyn, W. Va., 800 . . . . D5 87
Yonago, Jap., 99,484 . . . . . I6 18
Yonezawa, Jap., 68,000 . . H10 18
Yonghung, Kor., 18,445 . . . G3 18
Yonkers, N.Y.,
190,634 . . . . E7, n15 75
Yonne, dept., Fr.,
269,826 . . . . *D5 5
Yorba Linda, Calif.,
1,198 . . . . *F5 50
York, Ala., 2,932 . . . . C1 46
York, Eng., 104,300 . . . . . . D6 4
York, Maine, 1,000 . . . . E1 64
York, Nebr., 6,173 . . . . D8 71
York, Pa., 51,500
(*153,000) G8 81
York, S.C., 4,758 . . . . B5 82
York, co., N.B., Can.,
52,672 . . . . C3 43
York, co., Ont., Can.,
1,733,108 . . . . D5 43
York, co., Eng.,
4,801,000 . . . . *D6 4
York, co., Maine, 99,402 . . E2 64
York, co., Nebr., 13,724 . . . D8 71
York, co., Pa., 238,336 . . . . G8 81
York, co., S.C., 78,760 . . . . A5 82
York, co., Va., 21,583 . . . . . C6 85
Yorkshire, N.Y., 450 . . . . . C2 75
Yorkton, Sask., Can.,
9,995 . . . . F4, n8 39

Yorktown, Ind., 1,137 . . . . . D6 59
Yorktown, N.Y., 3,576 . . . *D7 75
Yorktown, Tex., 2,527 . . . . E4 84
Yorktown Heights, N.Y.,
7,500 . . . . A5 75
Yorktown Manor, R.I.,
1,300 . . . . C11 52
Yorkville, Ill., 1,568 . . . . . . B5 58
Yorkville, N.Y., 3,749 . . . . B5 75
Yorkville, Ohio, 1,801 . . . . B5 78
Yoshiwara, Jap., 90,224 . . n17 18
Young, co., Tex., 17,254 . . . C3 84
Youngstown, N.Y., 1,848 . . B2 75
Youngstown, Ohio,
155,000 (*485,000) A5 78
Youngsville, La., 946 . . . . . D3 63
Youngsville, Pa., 2,211 . . . C3 81
Youngtown, Ariz., 1,709 . . . D1 48
Youngwood, Pa., 2,813 . . . . F2 81
Yozgat, Tur., 18,305 . . . . C10 14
Ypacaraí, Par., 8,118 . . . . . E4 29
Ypsilanti, Mich.,
20,957 . . . . F7, p4 66
Yreka, Calif., 4,759 . . . . . . B2 50
Ystad, Swe., 13,700 . . . . . . J5 11
Yuanling, China, 28,000 . . . F7 17
Yuba, co., Calif., 33,859 . . . C3 50
Yuba City, Calif., 11,507 . . C3 50
Yuba City South, Calif.,
3,200 . . . . *C3 50
Yūbari, Jap., 85,141 . . . . . E10 18
Yucatán, state, Mex.,
614,049 . . . . C7 34
Yugoslavia, country, Eur.,
19,400,000 . . . . C3 10
Yukon, Fla., 2,000 . . . B5, m8 54
Yukon, Okla., 3,076 . . . . . . B4 79
Yukon, ter., Can.,
14,628 . . . . D6 36
Yukon, riv., N.A. C9 47
Yuma, Ariz., 28,005 . . . . . . C1 48
Yuma, Colo., 1,919 . . . . . . A8 51
Yuma, co., Ariz., 55,833 . . . C1 48
Yuma, co., Colo., 8,912 . . . A8 51
Yunnan, prov., China,
19,100,000 . . . . G5 17
Yurécuaro, Mex.,
12,084 . . . . m12 34
Yuryevets, Sov. Un.,
10,000 . . . . C14 12
Yuryev-Polskiy, Sov. Un.,
10,000 . . . . C12 12
Yuty, Par., 16,262 . . . . E4 29
Yuzha, Sov. Un., 25,000 . . C13 12
Yuzhno-Sakhalinsk
(Toyohara), Sov. Un.,
87,000 . . . . E17 13
Yverdon, Switz., 16,338 . . . E3 6

Z

Zabkowice, Pol., 12,600 . . . C4 7
Zabrze, Pol., 199,400 . . C5, g9 7
Zacatecas, Mex., 31,701 . . C4 34

Zacatecas, state, Mex.,
817,831 . . . . C4, m12 34
Zachary, La., 3,268 . . . . . . D4 63

Zadar, Yugo., 25,132 . . . . . C2 10
Zagorsk, Sov. Un.,
78,000 . . . . C12 12

Zagreb, Yugo., 430,802 . . . C2 10
Zāhedān, Iran, 17,495 . . . . G9 16
Zahle, Leb., 30,400 . . . . . . G5 15

Zaječar, Yugo., 18,545....D6 10
Zákinthos, Grc., 9,506.....D3 14
Zákinthos (Zante),
   prov., Grc., 35,509.....*D3 14
Zakopane, Pol., 25,800....D5 7
Zala, co., Hung.,
   274,161................*B3 10
Zalaegerszeg, Hung.,
   23,738.................B3 10
Zalău, Rom., 13,378.....B6 10
Zambales, prov., Phil.,
   213,442...............*B5 19
Zambezi, riv., Afr........H8 21
Zambia (Northern
   Rhodesia), country,
   Afr., 3,500,000........C5 24
Zamboanga, Phil.,
   25,000................D6 19
Zamboanga del Norte,
   prov., Phil., 281,429....*D6 19
Zamboanga del Sur.,
   prov., Phil., 742,404....*D6 19
Zamora, Sp., 42,060......B3 8
Zamora, prov., Sp.,
   301,129...............*B3 8
Zamora de Hidalgo,
   Mex., 34,372......C4, m12 34
Zamość, Pol., 29,600......C7 7
Zanesville, Ohio, 39,077...C4 78
Zanjān, Iran, 47,159......A7 23
Zanzibar, Tan.,
   57,923................B7 24
Zapata, Tex., 2,300.......F3 84
Zapata, co., Tex.,
   4,393.................F3 84

Zaporozhye, Sov. Un.,
   507,000..............H10 12
Zaragoza, prov., Sp.,
   656,772..............*B5 8
Zárate, Arg., 45,735...A5, g7 28
Zaraysk, Sov. Un.,
   10,000...............D12 12
Zaria, Nig., 166,170......F6 22
Zashiversk, Sov. Un.,
   800..................C17 13
Zatec, Czech., 14,800.....C2 7
Zavala, co., Tex.,
   12,696................E3 84
Zavitaya, Sov. Un.,
   14,500...............D15 13
Zawiercie, Pol.,
   34,700.............C5, g10 7
Zaysan, Sov. Un., 15,600..E11 13
Zdolbunov, Sov. Un.,
   10,000................F6 12
Zduńska Wola, Pol.,
   26,900................C5 7
Zebulon, N.C., 1,534......B4 76
Zeeland, Mich., 3,702.....F5 66
Zeeland, prov., Neth.,
   283,900...............B5 5
Zehdenick, Ger., 12,800....B6 6
Zeigler, Ill., 2,133........F4 58
Zeist, Neth., 54,700......A6 5
Zeitz, Ger., 46,100.......C6 6
Zelienople, Pa., 3,284......E1 81
Zella-Mehlis, Ger.,
   16,400................C5 6
Zemetchino, Sov. Un.,
   10,000...............E14 12

Zenica, Yugo., 32,552.....C3 10
Zephyrhills, Fla., 2,887....D4 54
Zerbst, Ger., 17,900......C6 6
Zeya, Sov. Un., 15,100...D15 13
Zgierz, Pol., 38,700......C5 7
Zhdanov (Mariupol),
   Sov. Un., 321,000....H11 12
Zhitomir, Sov. Un.,
   120,000...............F7 12
Zhizdra, Sov. Un.,
   10,000...............E10 12
Zhmerinka, Sov. Un.,
   25,000................G7 12
Ziebach, co., S. Dak.,
   2,495.................F4 77
Zielona Gora, Pol.,
   57,900................C3 7
Ziguinchor, Sen.,
   29,800................F1 22
Zile, Tur., 21,339.......B10 14
Zilina, Czech., 34,300....D5 7
Zilwaukee, Mich., 1,793...E7 66
Zima, Sov. Un.,
   38,549..............D13 13
Zimnicea, Rom., 12,445...D7 10
Zinder, Niger, 13,300......F6 22
Zion, Ill., 14,106......A6, h9 58
Zionsville, Ind.,
   1,822.............E5, k9 59
Zipaquirá, Col., 22,648....B3 32
Zitácuaro, Mex., 23,883...n13 34
Zittau, Ger., 43,100......C7 6
Zlatoust, Sov. Un.,
   175,000..............D8 13
Zlynka, Sov. Un., 10,000...E8 12

Znamenka, Sov. Un.,
   37,300................G9 12
Znojmo, Czech., 24,500....D4 7
Zolochev, Sov. Un.,
   28,600................G5 12
Zolotonosha, Sov. Un.,
   10,000................G9 12
Zonguldak, Tur., 54,010...B8 14
Zrenjanin (Petrovgrad),
   Yugo., 48,954.........C5 10
Zug, Switz., 19,792.......E4 6
Zug, canton, Switz.,
   52,489...............*E4 6
Zulia, state, Ven.,
   919,863...............B3 32
Zumbrota, Minn.,
   1,830.................F6 67
Zuni, N. Mex., 3,700.....B4 48
Zürich, Switz., 438,800
   (*725,000)............*E4 6
Zürich, canton, Switz.,
   1,032,000............*E4 6
Zutphen, Neth., 25,200...A7 5
Zuwārah, Libya, 2,380....B7 22
Zvenigorodka, Sov. Un.,
   10,000................G8 12
Zvolen, Czech.,
   19,600................D5 7
Zweibrucken, Ger.,
   32,900................D3 6
Zwickau, Ger., 129,000....C6 6
Zwolle, La., 1,326........C2 63
Zwolle, Neth., 57,400.....A7 5
Zyrardów, Pol.,
   30,900..........B6, m12 7

GLOSSARY OF FOREIGN GEOGRAPHICAL TERMS

Arab	Arabic	*Kor*	Korean
Bantu	Bantu	*Lao*	Laotian
Bur	Burmese	*Lapp*	Lappish
Camb	Cambodian	*Mal*	Malayan
Celt	Celtic	*Mong*	Mongolian
Chn	Chinese	*Nor*	Norwegian
Czech	Czech	*Per*	Persian
Dan	Danish	*Pol*	Polish
Du	Dutch	*Port*	Portuguese
Fin	Finnish	*Rom*	Romanian
Fr	French	*Rus*	Russian
Ger	German	*Siam*	Siamese
Grc	Greek	*So. Slav*	Southern Slavonic
Hung	Hungarian	*Sp*	Spanish
Ice	Icelandic	*Swe*	Swedish
India	India	*Tib*	Tibetan
Indian	American Indian	*Tur*	Turkic
It	Italian	*Viet*	Vietnamese
Jap	Japanese		

A

å, *Dan., Nor* ... river
aan, *Du* ... at, on
abad, *India, Per* ... dwelling, town
abu, abou, *Arab* ... father
ålen, *Nor* ... spit
alf, elf, *Swe* ... river
alp, *Ger* ... mountain
alt, *Ger* ... old
alta, -o, *It., Port., Sp* ... high
altipiano, *It* ... plateau
älv, älven, *Swe* ... river
amarillo, *Sp* ... yellow
arquipélago, *Port* ... archipelago
arroyo, *Sp* ... brook, dry bed of stream
as, *Dan., Nor., Swe* ... hill, ridge
austral, *Sp* ... southern

B

baai, *Du* ... bay
bab, *Arab* ... gate, strait
bach, *Ger* ... brook, stream
backe, *Swe* ... hill
bad, *Ger* ... bath
bahía, *Port., Sp* ... bay, gulf
bahr, *Arab* ... bay, river
baia, *It* ... bay, gulf
baie, *Fr* ... bay, gulf
bajo, *Sp* ... low, lower
bakke, *Dan., Nor* ... hill
balkan, *Tur* ... mountain range
ban, *Lao, Mal* ... village
ban, *Siam* ... house
bana, *Jap* ... cape
bandar, *Per* ... harbor
batang, *Mal* ... river
belyy, belaya, *Rus* ... white
ben, *Celt* ... mountain, summit
bender, bandar, *Arab., India* ... market town, port
beni, bani, *Arab* ... sons of, tribe of
berg, *Du., Ger., Nor., Swe* ... mountain, hill
bir, bi'r, *Arab* ... well
birkat, *Arab* ... pool, well
bjeli, -a, -o, *So. Slav* ... white
bjerg, bjaerg, *Dan., Nor* ... mountain
blanc, *Fr* ... white
blanco, *Sp* ... white
blau, *Ger* ... blue
bleu, *Fr* ... blue
bodden, *Ger* ... ground
bogaz, bogazi, *Tur* ... strait
bois, *Fr* ... forest, wood
boloto, *Rus* ... marsh
bolshoy, bolshoye, *Rus* ... great
boreal, *Sp* ... northern
borg, *Dan., Nor., Swe* ... castle
borgo, *It* ... town
bosch, *Du* ... forest, wood
bouche, *Fr* ... river, mouth
bourg, *Fr* ... town, borough
bro, *Dan., Nor., Swe* ... bridge
brücke, brücken, *Ger* ... bridge, bridges
brun, *Fr* ... brown
bucht, *Ger* ... bay, bight
bugt, *Dan., Nor* ... bay, gulf
bukt, bukten, *Swe* ... bay, gulf
bulak, *Tur* ... spring
būr, *Arab* ... port
burg, *Du., Ger* ... castle, town
buri, *Siam* ... city
burun, burnu, *Tur* ... cape
büyük, *Tur* ... great
by, *Dan., Nor., Swe* ... town, village

C

cabeza, *Sp* ... summit
cabo, *Port., Sp* ... cape
cairn, carn, *Celt* ... rocky headland
campo, *It., Port., Sp* ... field
campos, *Port. (Brazil)* ... plains
cañon, *Sp* ... canyon
cap, *Fr* ... cape
capo, *It* ... cape
casa, *It., Port., Sp* ... house
castello, *It., Port* ... castle, fort
castillo, *Sp* ... castle, fort
catingas, *Port. (Brazil)* ... open brushlands
cayo, *Sp* ... rock, shoal, islet
central, *Fr* ... middle
cerro, *Sp* ... hill
chai, ciai, *Tur* ... river
champ, *Fr* ... field
chapada, *Port. (Brazil)* ... hills, ridge
chateau, *Fr* ... castle
cherniy, chernyaya, *Rus* ... black
chin, *Chn* ... market town
chott, shat, *Arab* ... salt river or lake
chou, *Chn* ... island
cidade, *Port* ... city
città, *It* ... town, city
ciudad, *Sp* ... town, city
col, *Fr* ... pass
colina, *Sp* ... hill
colorado, *Sp* ... red
cordillera, *Sp* ... mountain chain
costa, *It., Port., Sp* ... coast
côte, côtes, *Fr* ... coast, hills, peak, ridge
crkva, *So. Slav* ... church
crni, *So. Slav* ... black
cuchilla, *Sp* ... mountain range
cumbre, *Sp* ... peak, ridge

D

daal, dal, *Du* ... valley
dag, *Tur* ... mountain
daglari, *Tur* ... mountains, range
dake, take, *Jap* ... peak, ridge
dal, *Dan., Du., Nor., Swe* ... valley
dalay, *Mong* ... lake
dar, *Arab* ... land, country
darya, daria, *Per* ... river, sea
dasht, *Per* ... plain, desert
dawhat, *Arab* ... bay, inlet
deccan, *India* ... south
deir, *Arab* ... convent
denis, -z, *Tur* ... sea, lake
désert, *Fr* ... desert
deserto, *It* ... desert
desierto, *Sp* ... desert
détroit, *Fr* ... strait
djebel, jebel, *Arab* ... mountain
dolok, *Mal* ... mountain
dorf, *Ger* ... village
dorp, *Du* ... village
drift, *Du., Ger* ... current
duinen, *Du* ... dunes
dun, *Celt* ... fortified hill
dyk, *Du* ... dam, dyke
dzong, *Tib* ... fort, administrative capital

E

eau, *Fr* ... water
ecuador, *Sp* ... equator
eiland, *Du* ... island
elf, älf, *Swe* ... river
elv, *Dan., Nor* ... river
erg, *Arab* ... dune, region of dunes
eski, *Tur* ... old
est, *Fr* ... east
estado, *Sp* ... state
este, *It., Port., Sp* ... east
estrecho, *Sp* ... strait
étang, *Fr* ... pond, lake
état, *Fr* ... state
étroit, *Fr* ... narrow

F

feld, *Ger* ... field, plain
fels, *Ger* ... rock
festung, *Ger* ... fort
firth, *Scotch* ... estuary
fiume, *It* ... river
fjäll, fjället, *Swe* ... mountain
fjärd, *Swe* ... bay, inlet
fjeld, *Nor* ... mountain, hill
fjell, *Nor* ... mountain
fjord, fjorden, *Dan., Nor* ... fiord, inlet
fjördhur, *Ice* ... fiord, inlet
fleuve, *Fr* ... river
flod, *Dan, Swe* ... river
flói, *Ice* ... bay
fluss, *Ger* ... river
foce, *It* ... river mouth
fontein, *Du* ... a spring
fors, *Swe* ... waterfall, torrent
forst, *Ger* ... forest
fos, *Dan., Nor* ... waterfall
fuente, *Sp* ... spring, fountain
fuerte, *Sp* ... fort
furt, *Ger* ... ford

G

gamla, *Swe* ... old
gamle, *Dan., Nor* ... old
gat, *Dan., Nor* ... passage, channel
gavan', *Rus* ... harbor
gebel, *Arab* ... mountain
gebergte, *Du* ... mountain range
gebiet, *Ger* ... district, territory
gebirge, *Ger* ... range, mountains
ghat, *India* .. mountain pass, river passage
gobi, *Mong* ... desert
göl, gölu, *Tur* ... lake
golf, *Du., Ger* ... gulf, bay
golfe, *Fr* ... gulf, bay
golfo, *It., Port., Sp* ... gulf, bay
gong, *India* ... village
gora, *Pol., Rus., So. Slav* ... mountain
gornji, -a, -o, *So. Slav* ... upper
gorny, *Pol* ... upper
gorod, grad, *Rus., So. Slav* ... town
grand, grande, *Fr* ... large, great
grande, *It., Port., Sp* ... large, great
grod, gorod, *Pol., Rus* ... town
grön, *Dan* ... green
groot, *Du* ... great
gross, *Ger* ... great
guba, *Rus* ... bay, gulf
gunto, *Jap* ... archipelago

H

haf, *Swe* ... sea
hafen, *Ger* ... port, harbor
haff, *Ger* ... gulf, inland sea
hai, *Chn* ... sea, lake
hamn, *Swe* ... harbor
hamun, *Per* ... swampy lake, plain
haus, hausen, *Ger* ... house, houses
haut, *Fr* ... high, summit, upper
havet, *Nor* ... bay
havn, *Dan., Nor* ... harbor, port
havre, *Fr* ... harbor, port
hawr, *Arab* ... lake, marsh
haz, -a, *Hung* ... house, dwelling of
heim, *Ger* ... hamlet
hem, *Swe* ... hamlet
higashi, *Jap* ... east
hinterland, *Ger* ... back country
hissar, hisar, *Tur* ... castle, fort
ho, *Chn* ... river
hoch, *Ger* ... high
hoek, *Du* ... cape
hof, *Ger* ... court, farm house
höfn, *Ice* ... harbor
hoku, *Jap* ... north
holm, *Dan., Nor., Swe* ... island
hora, *Czech* ... mountain
horn, *Ger* ... peak
hoved, *Dan., Nor* ... cape, headland
hsien, *Chn* ... district, district capital
hügel, *Ger* ... hill
huk, *Dan., Nor., Swe* ... point
hus, *Dan., Nor., Swe* ... house
hwang, *Chn* ... yellow

I

ile, *Fr* ... island
ilha, *Port* ... island
indre, *Dan., Nor* ... inner
indsö, *Dan., Nor* ... lake
inférieur, *Fr* ... lower
insel, *Ger* ... island
insjö, *Swe* ... lake
irmak, *Tur* ... river
isla, *Sp* ... island
isola, *It* ... island
istmo, *It., Sp* ... isthmus

J

jabal, *Arab* ... mountain, plateau, ridge
järvi, *Fin* ... lake
jebel, djebel, *Arab* ... mountain
jima, shima, *Jap* ... island
jökel, jökelen, *Nor* ... glacier
joki, *Fin* ... river
jökull, *Ice* ... ice-covered mountain
juzna, *So. Slav* ... south, southern

K

kaap, *Du* ... cape
kafr, kefr, *Arab* ... village
kaikyo, *Jap* ... strait
kaise, *Lapp* ... mountain
kala, kalat, *Arab., Per* ... castle, fortress, village
kale, *Tur* ... castle, fort
kamen', *Rus* ... rock
kang, *Chn* ... village
kap, *Ger* ... cape
kapp, *Nor* ... cape
kara, *Tur* ... black
kaupunki, *Fin* ... town, city
kavīr, *Per* ... salt desert
kebir, *Arab* ... great
kefr, kafr, *Arab* ... village
ken, *Jap* ... prefecture
kend, kand, *Per* ... village
khalīj, *Arab* ... bay, gulf
khrebet, *Rus* ... mountain range
ki, *Jap* ... tree, forest
kil, cill, *Celt* ... church, cell
kirche, *Ger* ... church
kirchen, *Ger* ... parish
kio, kyo, *Jap* ... town, capital
kis, *Hung* ... little, small
klein, *Du., Ger* ... small
köbstad, *Dan* ... city
köl, *Mong., Tur* ... lake, marsh
kompong, *Camb* ... village
kong, *Chn* ... river
kopf, *Ger* ... head, summit, peak
köping, *Swe* ... market, borough
kraal, *Du* ... native village
krasniy, krasnaya, *Rus.* ... beautiful, fair, red
kuala, *Mal* ... junction, river mouth
kuchuk, *Tur* ... small
kuh, koh, *Per* ... mountain
kul, *Mong., Tur* ... lake
kum, qum, *Tur* ... desert
kuppe, *Ger* ... summit
küste, *Ger* ... coast
kyzyl, kizil, *Tur* ... red

L

laag, *Du* ... low
lac, *Fr* ... lake
lago, *It., Sp* ... lake
lâgoa, *Port* ... lagoon
laguna, *It., Port., Sp* ... lagoon, lake
lahti, *Fin* ... bay, gulf
län, *Swe* ... county
landsby, *Dan., Nor* ... village
lao, *Viet* ... island
lilla, *Swe* ... small

GLOSSARY OF FOREIGN GEOGRAPHICAL TERMS *(Continued)*

lille, *Dan., Nor*....................small
liman, *Tur*.....................bay, port
ling, *Chn*................mountain, range
llanos, *Sp*...............prairies, plains
loch, *Celt*........lake, bay (Scotland)
lough, *Celt*........lake, bay (Ireland)

M

maha, *India*...................great
malyy, malaya, *Rus*.............small
mar, *Port., Sp*...................sea
mare, *It., Rom*..................sea
mare, *Rom*....................great
mark, *Ger*............boundary, limit
massif, *Fr*.............mountain range
mato, *Port*...........jungle, copse
medio, *Sp*...................middle
meer, *Du., Ger*...........lake, sea
mer, *Fr*.......................sea
mesa, *Sp*.........flat-topped mountain
meseta, *Sp*....................hill
midden, *Du*...................middle
mina, *Port., Sp*.................mine
mittel, *Ger*...................middle
mont, *Fr*............mount, mountain
montagna, *It*................mountain
montagne, *Fr*...............mountain
montaña, *Sp*.................mountain
monte, *It., Port., Sp*...mount, mountain
more, *Rus., So. Slav*.............sea
morro, *Port., Sp*................hill
moyen, *Fr*....................middle
mühle, *Ger*...................mill
mund, munde, *Ger*........river mouth
mündung, *Ger*.........river mouth
muong, *Lao*.........town, village
mura, *Jap*...................village
muz, *Tur*.....................ice
mys, *Rus*...............cape, point

N

nada, *Jap*....................sea
nadi, *India*..........river, creek
naes, näs, *Dan., Nor., Swe*.......cape
nagar, nagon, *India*.........town, city
nagy, *Hung*...........large, great
naka, *Jap*...................middle
neder, *Du*....................low
nedre, *Nor*....................lower
negro, *It., Port., Sp*............black
nejd, *Arab*................highland
neu, *Ger*.....................new
nevado, *Sp*...............mountain
nez, *Fr*...............point, cape
nieder, *Ger*...........low, lower
nieuw, *Du*...................new
nizhne, nizhniy, nizhnyaya, *Rus*....lower
noir, *Fr*....................black
nong, *Siam*....marsh, pond, lake
noord, *Du*...................north
nor, *Tib*....................lake
nord, *Dan., Fr., Ger., It., Nor*.....north
norr, norra, *Swe*..............north
norte, *Port., Sp*..............north
nos, *Rus*....................cape
nouvelle, *Fr*..................new
novi, -a, -o, *So. Slav*..........new
novo, *Port*...................new
novy, -e, -a, *Czech*...........new
novyy, novyye, novaya, novo, *Rus*..new
nowa, nowy, *Pol*..............new
nuevo, *Sp*...................new
nuovo, *It*...................new
nuur, *Mong*..................lake
ny, *Dan., Swe*................new
nyasa, *Bantu*................lake

O

o; *Jap*.................great, large
ö, *Dan., Nor., Swe*...........island
ober, *Ger*...................upper
occidental, *Sp*.............western

odde, *Dan., Nor*............point, cape
oedjoeng, *Mal*..................cape
oeste, *Port., Sp*..............west
ojo, *Sp*...................spring
oost, *Du*.....................east
op, *Du*.......................on
oriental, *Sp*...............eastern
oro, *Sp*.....................gold
óros, *Grc*................mountain
ost, *Ger., Swe*................east
öst, öster, östre, *Dan., Nor., Swe.*
..................east, eastern
ostrog, *Rus*...................fort
ostrov, *Rus*...................island
ouadi, *Arab*......intermittent stream
ouest, *Fr*....................west
öy, *Nor*....................island
ozero, *Rus*...................lake

P

paa, *Fin*...................mountain
padang, *Mal*.........plain, field
pampas, *Sp. (Argentina)*.....grassy plains
para, *Indian (Brazil)*...........river
pas, *Fr*.......channel, strait, pass
paso, *Sp*.............mountain pass
passo, *It., Port*........mountain pass
patam *India*............city, town
pequeño *Sp*.................small
peresheyek, *Rus*............isthmus
pertuis, *Fr*...................strait
peski, *Rus*.........desert, sands
petit, petite, *Fr*........small, little
pic, *Fr*............mountain peak
piccolo, *It*...................small
pico, *Port., Sp*.......mountain peak
piedra, *Sp*...........stone, rock
pik, *Rus*............mountain peak
planalto, *Port*...............plateau
plata, *Sp*...................silver
plato, *Rus*..................plateau
playa, *Sp*...........shore, beach
po, *Chn*....................lake
pointe, *Fr*...................point
polder, *Du., Ger*......reclaimed marsh
polje, *So. Slav*................field
poluostrov, *Rus*...........peninsula
pont, *Fr*...................bridge
ponta, *Port*.......point, headland
ponte, *It., Port*.............bridge
pore, pur, *India*.........city, town
porto, *It*..........port, harbor
pôrto, *Port*........port, harbor
prado, *Sp*........field, meadow
presqu'ile, *Fr*............peninsula
proliv, *Rus*...................strait
pu, *Chn*........commercial village
pueblo, *Sp*..........town, village
puerto, *Sp*........port, harbor
pulau, *Mal*..................island
punkt, *Ger*...................point
punt, *Du*....................point
punta, *It., Sp*...............point
pur, pura, *India*.........city, town
puy, *Fr*......................peak

R

rann, *India*...............wasteland
ra's, *Arab*..........cape, summit
reg, *Arab*........coarse gravel desert
reka, *Rus., So. Slav*.............river
represa, *Port*..............reservoir
retto, *Jap*................archipelago
ria, *Sp*...............river mouth
ribeira, -ão, *Port*.........stream, river
rio, *It., Port*..................river
río, *Sp*......................river
rivière, *Fr*...................river
roca, *Sp*.....................rock
rochedos, *Port. (Brazil)*...rocks in water
rouge, *Fr*....................red
rud, *Per*.....................river

S

saari, *Fin*...................island
sable, *Fr*....................sand
sahra, *Arab*.................desert
sal, *Sp*......................salt
samar, *Mong*..........path, route
san, *Chn., Jap., Kor*......mountain, hill
san, santa, santo, *It., Port., Sp*.....saint
são, *Port*....................saint
sat, satu, *Rom*...............village
schloss, *Ger*............castle, fort
sebkha, *Arab*.............salt marsh
see, *Ger*.............lake, sea
sehir, shehr, *Tur*..............town
selat, *Mal*...........channel, strait
selatan, *Mal*........south, southern
selvas, *Port. (Brazil)*
.............tropical rain forests
seno, *Sp*....................bay
serra, *It., Port*.....pass, mountain ridge
serranía, *Sp*.........mountain ridge
seto, *Jap*..........strait, channel
severnaya, *Rus*..............north
shahr, shehr, *Per*..............town
sha'īb, *Arab*
......depression, intermittent stream
shan, *Chn*......range, mountain, hill
shaṭṭ, chott, *Arab*......salt river or lake
shima, sima, *Jap*...............island
shimo, *Jap*...................lower
shiu, *Chn., Jap*..............province
shoto, *Jap*...............archipelago
si, *Chn*............west, western
sierra, *Sp*...........mountain range
sint, *Sp*......................saint
sjö, *Nor., Swe*............lake, sea
sö, *Dan., Nor*............lake, sea
söder, *Swe*...................south
soengai, sungei, *Mal*............river
sopka, *Rus*........extinct volcano
source, *Fr*.................spring
spitze, *Ger*........summit, point
sredniy, sredne, srednyaya, *Rus*...middle
staat, *Ger*...................state
stad, *Dan., Du., Nor., Swe*.....city, town
stadt, *Ger*............city, town
stari, -a, -o, *So. Slav*............old
stary, *Czech., Pol*.............old
staryy, staraya, *Rus*...........old
stato, *It*...................state
sten, *Dan., Nor., Swe*........stone
step, *Rus*.........treeless plain, steppe
stor, *Dan., Nor., Swe*.......great, large
straat, *Du*..................strait
strand, *Dán., Du., Ger., Nor., Swe*
.................shore, beach
stretto, *It*...................strait
strom, *Ger*.................stream
ström, *Dan., Nor., Swe*.......river
stroom, *Du*........stream, river
su, suyu, *Tur*........water, river
sud, *Fr., Sp*.................south
süd, *Ger*...................south
sul, *Port*........south, southern
sund, *Dan., Nor., Swe*........sound
supérieure, *Fr*...............upper
sur, *Fr*......................on
sur, *Sp*.....................south
syd, *Dan., Nor., Swe*.........south

T

tafelland, *Du., Ger*....plateau, tableland
tagh, *Mong., Tur*...........mountain
tai, *Jap*...........large, great
taiga, *Rus*....northern coniferous forest
take, dake, *Jap*..........peak, ridge
tandjung, tanjong, *Mal*............cape
tao, -u, *Chn*................island
targ, targu, *Rom*.........market, town
tash, *Per., Tur*.........rock, stone
tau, *Tur*..........mountain range
tell, tel, *Arab*................hill
terra, *It*....................land
terre, *Fr*...........earth, land

U

thal, *Ger*....................valley
tierra, *Sp*...........earth, land
torp, *Swe*..........village, cottage
torre, *It., Port., Sp*...........tower
tsi, *Chn*........village, borough
tsu, *Jap*....................port
tundra, *Rus*.......marshy arctic plains
tung, *Chn*..........east, eastern
turn, turnu, *Rom*...........tower
tuz, *Tur*.....................salt

U

udd, udde, *Swe*..............cape
ufer, *Ger*.......beach, shore, river bank
uj, *Hung*....................new
ulan, *Mong*..................red
umi, *Jap*...............sea, gulf
unter, *Ger*..................lower
ura, *Jap*.......bay, shore, creek
ust, *Rus*...........river mouth
uula, *Mong*.......mountain, range
utara, *Mal*........north, northern

V

vall, *Swe*...................coast
valle, *Port., Sp*.............valley
vallée, *Fr*..................valley
valli, *It*.........lake, lagoon
var, *Hung*..................fortress
varos, *Hung., So. Slav*..........town
varre, *Lapp*...............mountain
vecchio, *It*...................old
veld, *Du*........open plain, field
velho, *Port*....................old
velikiy, *Rus., So. Slav*..........great
verde, *It., Port., Sp*...........green
verkhniy, verkhnyaya, *Rus*
.............upper, higher
vert, *Fr*....................green
ves, *Czech*...............village
vest, *Dan., Nor., Swe*..........west
viejo, *Sp*...................old
vieux, *Fr*...................old
vik, viken, *Swe*................bay
villa, *Port., Sp*........small town
villar, *Sp*........village, hamlet
ville, *Fr*...........town, city
vinh, *Viet*...................bay
vishni, visni, *Rus*.............high
vostok, *Rus*.................east
volcán, *Sp*.................volcano

W

wadi, wādī, wad, *Arab*
...............intermittent stream
wald, *Ger*........forest, woodland
wan, *Chn., Jap*.........bay, gulf
weiler, *Ger*........hamlet, village
weiss, *Ger*..................white
westersch, *Du*..............western
wiek, *Ger*....................bay
wüste, *Ger*.................desert

Y

yama, *Jap*................mountain
yang, *Chn*................channel
yeni, *Tur*....................new
yokara, *Tur*.................upper
yoma, *Bur*........mountain range
yug, *Rus*...................south
yuzhno, *Rus*........south, southern

Z

zaki, saki, *Jap*..............cape
zaliv, *Rus*............bay, gulf
zapad, zapadnyy, *Rus*..........west
zapadni, -a, -o, *So. Slav*....west, western
zee, *Du*.....................sea
zemlya, *Rus*................land
zuid, *Du*...................south

WORLD POLITICAL INFORMATION TABLE

This table lists all countries and dependencies in the world, U.S. States, Canadian provinces, and other important regions and political subdivisions. Besides specifying the form of government for all political areas, the table classifies them into six groups according to their political status. Units labeled **A** are independent sovereign nations. (Several of these are designated as members of the British Commonwealth of Nations.) Units labeled **B** are independent as regards internal affairs, but for purposes of foreign affairs they are under the protection of another country. Areas under military government are also labeled **B.** Units labeled **C** are colonies, overseas territories, dependencies, etc., of other countries. Together the **A, B,** and **C** areas comprise practically the entire inhabited area of the world. The areas labeled **D** are physically separate units, such as groups of islands, which are *not* separate countries, but form part of a nation or dependency. Units labeled **E** are States, provinces, Soviet Republics, or similar major administrative subdivisions of important countries. Units in the table with no letter designation are regions or other areas that do not constitute separate political units by themselves.

Region or Political Division	Area in sq. miles	Estimated Population 1/1/1965	Pop. per sq. mi.	Form of Government and Ruling Power	Capital; Largest City (unless same)	Predominant Languages
Aden, see Southern Yemen	....	....	......	....	....	....
Afars & Issas (French Somaliland)	8,378	80,000	9.5	Overseas Territory (France) C	Djibouti	Somali, French
Afghanistan†	250,000	15,200,000	61	Monarchy A	Kabul	Pushtu (Afghan), Persian
Africa	11,685,000	290,200,000	25	....	........; Cairo	....
Alabama	51,609	3,462,000	67	State (U.S.) E	Montgomery; Birmingham	....
Alaska	586,400	247,000	0.4	State (U.S.) E	Juneau; Anchorage	English, Indian, Eskimo
Albania†	11,100	1,846,000	166	People's Republic A	Tiranë	Albanian
Alberta	255,285	1,449,000	5.7	Province (Canada) E	Edmonton	English
Algeria†	919,595	10,700,000	12	Republic A	Algiers (Alger)	Arabic, French
American Samoa	76	21,000	276	Unincorporated Territory (U.S.) C	Pago Pago	Polynesian, English
Andaman & Nicobar Is.	3,215	74,000	23	Territory (India) D	Port Blair	Andaman, Nicobar Malay
Anguilla	35	6,000	171	Part of St. Kitts-Nevis-Anguilla‡ D	........; South Hill	English
Andorra	175	12,000	69	Principality A	Andorra	Catalan
Angola	481,353	5,125,000	11	Overseas Province (Portugal) C	Luanda	Bantu languages
Antarctica	5,100,000	....	....	....	....	....
Antigua (incl. Barbuda)	171	59,000	345	Associated State (U.K.) B	St. John's	English
Arabian Peninsula	1,145,606	14,636,000	13	....	........; Mecca	Arabic
Argentina†	1,072,072	22,200,000	21	Federal Republic A	Buenos Aires	Spanish
Arizona	113,909	1,635,000	14	State (U.S.) E	Phoenix	....
Arkansas	53,104	1,889,000	36	State (U.S.) E	Little Rock	....
Armenia (S.S.R.)	11,500	2,100,000	183	Soviet Socialist Republic (Sov. Un.) E	Yerevan	Armenian
Aruba	69	63,000	913	Division of Netherlands Antilles (Neth.) D	Oranjestad	Dutch, Spanish, English, Papiamento
Ascension I.	34	400	12	Dependency of St. Helena (U.K.) D	Georgetown	English
Asia	17,085,000	1,877,000,000	110	....	........; Tōkyō	....
Australia†	2,967,909	11,335,000	3.8	Monarchy (Federal) (Br. Commonwealth of Nations) A	Canberra; Sydney	English
Australian Capital Territory	939	86,000	92	Federal Territory (Australia) E	Canberra	English
Austria†	32,374	7,235,000	223	Federal Republic A	Vienna (Wien)	German
Azerbaidzhan (S.S.R.)	33,450	4,440,000	133	Soviet Socialist Republic (Sov. Un.) E	Baku	Turkic languages, Russian, Armenian
Azores Is.	893	332,000	372	Part of Portugal (3 Districts) D	........; Ponta Delgada	Portuguese
Baden-Wurttemberg	13,803	8,245,000	597	State (Germany, West) E	Stuttgart	German
Bahama Is.	4,403	136,000	31	Colony (U.K.) C	Nassau	English
Bahrain	231	166,000	719	Sheikdom (U.K. protection) B	Manama	Arabic
Balearic Is.	1,936	453,000	234	Part of Spain (Baleares Province) D	Palma de Mallorca	Catalan
Baltic Republics	67,150	6,350,000	95	Soviet Union	........; Riga	Lithuanian, Latvian, Estonian, Russian
Barbados†	166	242,000	1,458	Self-Governing Member (Br. Comm. of Nations) A	Bridgetown	English
Basutoland, see Lesotho	....	....	....	....	....	....
Bavaria (Bayern)	27,239	9,970,000	366	State (Germany, West) E	München (Munich)	German
Bechuanaland, see Botswana	....	....	....	....	....	....
Belgium†	11,781	9,400,000	798	Monarchy A	Brussels (Bruxelles)	Flemish, French
Benelux	25,363	21,932,000	864	....	Brussels (Bruxelles)	Dutch, Flemish, French, Luxembourgeois
Berlin, West	186	2,200,000	11,828	State (Germany, West) E	Berlin (West)	German
Bermuda	21	60,000	2,857	Colony (U.K.) C	Hamilton	English
Bhutan	18,200	750,000	41	Monarchy (Indian protection) B	Thimbu and Paro	Tibetan dialects
Bismarck Archipelago	20,415	193,000	9.5	Part of Australian Trust Ter. of New Guinea (3 Districts) D	........; Rabaul	Malay-Polynesian and Papuan languages
Bolivia†	424,164	3,675,000	8.7	Republic A	Sucre and La Paz; La Paz	Spanish, Quechua, Aymará, Guaraní
Bonin Islands	40	200	5.0	U.S. Military Administration B	....	English
Borneo, Indonesian (Kalimantan)	208,286	4,470,000	21	Part of Indonesia (4 Provinces) D	........; Bandjermasin	Bahasa Indonesia (Indonesian)
Botswana (Bechuanaland)†	222,000	555,000	2.5	Republic (Br. Commonwealth of Nations) A	Gaberones; Kanye	Bechuana, other Bantu languages
Brazil†	3,286,487	80,250,000	24	Federal Republic A	Brasília; Rio de Janeiro	Portuguese
Bremen	156	732,000	4,692	State (Germany, West) E	Bremen	German
British Antarctic Territory (excl. Antarctic mainland)	2,040	No perm. pop.	....	Colony (U.K.) C	Stanley, Falkland Islands	....
British Columbia	366,255	1,770,000	4.8	Province (Canada) E	Victoria; Vancouver	English
British Commonwealth of Nations	10,861,111	796,398,000	73	....	London	....
British Guiana, see Guyana	....	....	....	....	....	....
British Honduras	8,867	105,000	12	Colony (U.K.) C	Belize	English, Spanish, Indian languages
British Indian Ocean Territory	29	1,400	48	Colony (U.K.) C	Victoria, Seychelles	Creole, English, French
Brunei	2,226	105,000	47	Protectorate (U.K.) C	Brunei	Malay-Polynesian languages
Bulgaria†	42,829	8,175,000	191	People's Republic A	Sofia (Sofiya)	Bulgarian
Burma†	261,790	24,500,000	94	Federal Republic A	Rangoon	Burmese, English
Burundi (Urundi)†	10,747	2,775,000	258	Republic A	Bujumbura	Bantu and Hamitic languages
Byelorussia (S.S.R.)†	80,150	8,500,000	106	Soviet Socialist Republic (Sov. Un.) E	Minsk	Byelorussian, Polish
California	158,693	18,338,000	116	State (U.S.) E	Sacramento; Los Angeles	....
Cambodia†	69,898	6,100,000	87	Monarchy A	Phnom Penh	Cambodian (Khmer), French
Cameroon†	183,569	4,750,000	26	Federal Republic A	Yaoundé; Douala	Native languages, French
Canada†	3,851,809	19,445,000	5.0	Monarchy (Federal) (Br. Commonwealth of Nations) A	Ottawa; Montreal	English, French
Canal Zone	558	50,000	90	Under U.S. Jurisdiction C	Balboa Heights; Rainbow City	Spanish, English
Canary Is.	2,808	1,005,000	358	Part of Spain (2 Provinces) D	........; Las Palmas	Spanish
Canton & Enderbury	27	300	11	U.K.-U.S. Administration C	Canton Island	Malay-Polynesian languages, English
Cape of Good Hope	278,380	5,830,000	21	Province (South Africa) E	Cape Town	English, Afrikaans, Bantu languages
Cape Verde Is.	1,557	229,000	147	Overseas Province (Portugal) C	Praia; Mindelo	Portuguese
Caroline Is.	457	62,000	136	Part of U.S. Pacific Is. Trust Ter. (4 Districts) D	....	Malay-Polynesian languages
Cayman Is.	100	9,000	90	Colony (U.K.) C	Georgetown	English
Celebes (Sulawesi)	72,987	7,700,000	105	Part of Indonesia (2 Provinces) D	........; Makassar	Malay-Polynesian languages
Central African Republic†	240,535	1,350,000	5.6	Republic A	Bangui	Bantu languages, French
Central America	205,801	13,800,000	67	....	........; Guatemala	Spanish, Indian languages
Central Asia, Soviet	478,150	16,800,000	35	Soviet Union	........; Tashkent	Uzbek, Russian, Kirghiz, Turkoman, Tadzhik
Ceylon†	25,332	11,000,000	434	Commonwealth (Br. Commonwealth of Nations) A	Colombo	Sinhalese, Tamil, English
Chad†	495,800	2,900,000	5.8	Republic A	Fort Lamy	Hamitic languages, Arabic, French
Channel Is. (Guernsey, Jersey, etc.)	75	112,000	1,493	....	........; St. Helier	English, French
Chile†	292,258	8,450,000	29	Republic A	Santiago	Spanish

† *Member of the United Nations (1967).* ‡ *Anguilla unilaterally declared its independence from St. Kitts-Nevis-Anguilla in July 1967.*

Region or Political Division	Area in sq. miles	Estimated Population 1/1/1965	Pop. per sq. mi.	Form of Government and Ruling Power	Capital; Largest City (unless same)	Predominant Languages
China (excl. Taiwan)	3,691,500	700,000,000	190	People's Republic...A	Peking (Peiching); Shanghai	Chinese, Mongolian, Turkish, Tungus
China (Nationalist), see Taiwan						
Christmas I. (Indian Ocean)	52	3,500	67	External Territory (Australia)...C		Chinese, Malay, English
Christmas I. (Pacific Ocean)	222	400	1.8	Part of Gilbert & Ellice Is. (U.K.); also claimed by U.S.		Malay-Polynesian languages, English
Cocos (Keeling) Is.	5	700	140	External Territory (Australia)...C		Malay, English
Colombia†	439,515	15,600,000	35	Republic...A	Bogotá	Spanish
Colorado	104,247	2,003,000	19	State (U.S.)...E	Denver	
Commonwealth of Nations, see Br. Commonwealth of Nations						
Comoro Is.	838	192,000	229	Overseas Territory (France)...C	Moroni; Dzaoudzi	Malagasy, French
Congo (Rep. of Congo; Capital: Brazzaville)†	132,000	1,050,000	8.0	Republic...A	Brazzaville	Bantu languages, French
Congo, The (Rep. of The Congo; Capital: Kinshasa)†	905,567	15,500,000	17	Republic...A	Kinshasa	Bantu languages, French
Connecticut	5,009	2,752,000	549	State (U.S.)...E	Hartford	
Cook Is.	93	19,000	204	Island Territory (New Zealand)...C	Avarua	Malay-Polynesian languages
Corsica	3,352	280,000	84	Part of France (Corse Department)...D	Ajaccio; Bastia	French, Italian
Costa Rica†	19,650	1,425,000	73	Republic...A	San José	Spanish
Crete	3,217	480,000	149	Part of Greece (4 Prefectures)...D	......; Iráklion	Greek
Cuba†	44,218	7,100,000	161	Republic...A	Havana (La Habana)	Spanish
Curaçao	173	133,000	769	Division of Netherlands Antilles (Neth.)...D	Willemstad	Dutch, Spanish, English, Papiamento
Cyprus†	3,572	590,000	165	Republic (Br. Commonwealth of Nations)...A	Nicosia	Greek, Turkish, English
Czechoslovakia†	49,371	14,100,000	286	People's Republic...A	Prague (Praha)	Czech, Slovak
Dahomey†	43,484	2,300,000	53	Republic...A	Porto Novo; Cotonou	Native languages, French
Delaware	2,057	494,000	240	State (U.S.)...E	Dover; Wilmington	
Denmark†	16,619	4,740,000	285	Monarchy...A	Copenhagen (København)	Danish
Denmark and Possessions	857,159	4,817,000	5.6		Copenhagen (København)	Danish, Faeroese, Greenlandic
District of Columbia	69	810,000	11,739	District (U.S.)...E	Washington	
Dominica	290	65,000	224	Associated State (U.K.)...B	Roseau	English, French
Dominican Republic†	18,816	3,500,000	186	Republic...A	Santo Domingo	Spanish
Ecuador†	104,506	4,950,000	47	Republic...A	Quito; Guayaquil	Spanish, Quechua
Egypt, see United Arab Republic						
El Salvador†	8,260	2,875,000	348	Republic...A	San Salvador	Spanish
England (excl. Monmouthshire)	50,332	45,150,000	897	United Kingdom	......; London	English
England & Wales	58,348	47,825,000	820	Administrative division of United Kingdom...E	London	English, Welsh
Equatorial Guinea	10,830	266,000	25	African Province (Spain)...C	Bata and Santa Isabel; Santa Isabel	Bantu languages, Spanish
Estonia (S.S.R.)	17,400	1,250,000	72	Soviet Socialist Republic (Sov. Un.)...E	Tallinn	Estonian, Russian
Ethiopia†	471,778	21,500,000	46	Monarchy...A	Addis Ababa	Amharic and other Semitic languages, English, various Hamitic languages
Eurasia	20,910,000	2,478,900,000	119		......; Tōkyō	
Europe	3,825,000	601,900,000	157		......; London	
Faeroe Is.	540	37,000	69	Self-Governing Territory (Denmark)...C	Thórshavn	Danish, Faeroese
Falkland Is. (excl. Deps.)	4,618	2,200	0.5	Colony (U.K.)...C	Stanley	English
Fernando Poo	785	71,000	90	Part of Equatorial Guinea...D	......; Santa Isabel	Bantu languages, Spanish
Fiji	7,055	455,000	64	Colony (U.K.)...C	Suva	Malaya-Polynesian languages, English, Hindi
Finland†	130,120	4,600,000	35	Republic...A	Helsinki	Finnish, Swedish
Florida	58,560	5,913,000	101	State (U.S.)...E	Tallahassee; Miami	
France†	210,039	48,800,000	232	Republic...A	Paris	French
France and Possessions	238,869	50,366,000	211		Paris	
Franklin	549,253	6,300	0.01	District of Northwest Territories, Canada...E	......; Cambridge Bay	English, Eskimo, Indian
French Guiana	35,100	36,000	1.0	Overseas Department (France)...C	Cayenne	French
French Polynesia	1,543	89,000	58	Overseas Territory (France)...C	Papeete	Malay-Polynesian languages, French
French Somaliland see Afars & Issas						
French Southern & Antarctic Ter. (excl. Adélie Coast)	2,918	150	0.05	Overseas Territory (France)...C		French
French West Indies	1,112	620,000	558		......; Fort-de-France	French
Gabon†	103,347	465,000	4.5	Republic...A	Libreville	Bantu languages, French
Galápagos Is.	3,075	2,500	0.8	Province (Ecuador)...D	Puerto Baquerizo	Spanish
Gambia†	4,003	320,000	80	Self-Governing Member (Br. Comm. of Nations)...A	Bathurst	Mandingo, Fula, English
Georgia (S.S.R.)	26,900	4,460,000	166	Soviet Socialist Republic (Sov. Un.)...E	Tbilisi	Georgic, Armenian, Russian
Georgia	58,876	4,312,000	73	State (U.S.)...E	Atlanta	
Germany (Entire)	137,746	75,800,000	550		......; Berlin	German
Germany, East	41,816	17,250,000	413	People's Republic...A	Berlin (East)	German
Germany, West (incl. West Berlin)	95,930	58,550,000	610	Federal Republic...A	Bonn; Berlin (West)	German
Ghana†	92,100	7,600,000	83	Republic (Br. Commonwealth of Nations)...A	Accra	Twi, Fanti, Ewe-Fon, English
Gibraltar	2	25,000	12,500	Colony (U.K.)...C	Gibraltar	Spanish, English
Gilbert & Ellice Is.	342	51,000	149	Colony (U.K.)...C	Tarawa	Malay-Polynesian languages
Great Britain & Northern Ireland, see United Kingdom						
Greece†	50,944	8,500,000	167	Monarchy...A	Athens (Athínai)	Greek
Greenland	840,000	40,000	0.05	Overseas Territory (Denmark)...C	Godthaab	Greenlandic, Danish, Eskimo
Grenada	133	93,000	699	Associated State (U.K.)...B	St. George's	English
Guadeloupe (incl. Dependencies)	687	308,000	448	Overseas Department (France)...C	Basse-Terre; Pointe-à-Pitre	French
Guam	212	70,000	330	Unincorporated Territory (U.S.)...C	Agana	English, Chamorro
Guatemala†	42,042	4,375,000	104	Republic...A	Guatemala	Spanish, Indian languages
Guernsey (incl. Dependencies)	30	49,000	1,633	Bailiwick (U.K.)...C	St. Peter Port	English, French
Guinea†	94,926	3,500,000	37	Republic...A	Conakry	Native languages, French
Guyana†	83,000	631,000	7.6	Self-Governing Member (Br. Comm. of Nations)...A	Georgetown	English
Haiti†	10,714	4,600,000	429	Republic...A	Port-au-Prince	Creole, French
Hamburg	288	1,860,000	6,458	State (Germany, West)...E	Hamburg	German
Hawaii	6,424	710,000	111	State (U.S.)...E	Honolulu	English, Japanese, Hawaiian
Hesse (Hessen)	8,150	5,082,000	624	State (German, West)...E	Wiesbaden; Frankfurt am Main	German
Hispaniola	29,530	8,100,000	274		......; Santo Domingo	French, Spanish
Holland, see Netherlands						
Honduras†	43,277	2,125,000	49	Republic...A	Tegucigalpa	Spanish
Hong Kong	398	3,750,000	9,422	Colony (U.K.)...C	Victoria	Chinese, English
Hungary†	35,919	10,135,000	282	People's Republic...A	Budapest	Hungarian
Iceland†	39,800	190,000	4.8	Republic...A	Reykjavík	Icelandic
Idaho	83,557	702,000	8.4	State (U.S.)...E	Boise (Boise City)	
Ifni	580	51,000	88	African Province (Spain)...C	Sidi Ifni	Spanish, Arabic
Illinois	56,400	10,584,000	188	State (U.S.)...E	Springfield; Chicago	
India (incl. part of Kashmir)†	1,227,180	479,000,000	390	Republic (Br. Commonwealth of Nations)...A	New Delhi; Calcutta	Hindi and other Indo-Aryan languages, Dravidian languages, English
Indiana	36,291	4,914,000	135	State (U.S.)...E	Indianapolis	
Indonesia (excl. West Irian)†	574,670	103,350,000	180	Republic...A	Djakarta	Bahasa Indonesia (Indonesian), Chinese, English
Iowa	56,290	2,783,000	49	State (U.S.)...E	Des Moines	
Iran (Persia)†	636,300	23,100,000	36	Monarchy...A	Tehrān	Persian, Turkish dialects, Kurdish
Iraq†	173,260	7,050,000	41	Republic...A	Baghdad	Arabic, Kurdish

†Member of the United Nations (1967).

Region or Political Division	Area in sq. miles	Estimated Population 1/1/1965	Pop. per sq. mi.	Form of Government and Ruling Power	Capital; Largest City (unless same)	Predominant Languages
Ireland†	27,136	2,855,000	105	Republic.....A	Dublin	English, Irish
Isle of Man	227	48,000	211	Possession (U.K.).....C	Douglas	English
Israel†	7,992	2,520,000	315	Republic‡‡.....A	Jerusalem; Tel Aviv-Yafo	Hebrew, Arabic
Italy†	116,304	50,900,000	438	Republic.....A	Rome (Roma)	Italian
Ivory Coast†	124,504	3,775,000	30	Republic.....A	Abidjan	French, native languages
Jamaica†	4,232	1,750,000	414	Self-Governing Member (Br. Commonwealth of Nations).....A	Kingston	English
Japan†	142,727	97,400,000	682	Monarchy.....A	Tōkyō	Japanese
Java (Djawa) (incl. Madura)	51,040	67,000,000	1,313	Part of Indonesia (5 Provinces).....D	........; Djakarta	Bahasa Indonesia (Indonesian), Chinese, English
Jersey†	45	63,000	1,400	Bailiwick (U.K.).....C	St. Helier	English, French
Jordan†	37,738	1,900,000	50	Monarchy‡‡.....A	Amman	Arabic
Kansas	82,264	2,251,000	27	State (U.S.).....E	Topeka; Wichita	
Kashmir, Jammu &	86,024	4,700,000	55	In dispute (India & Pakistan).....	Srinagar	Kashmiri, Punjabi
Kazakh S.S.R.	1,050,000	11,800,000	11	Soviet Socialist Republic (Sov. Un.).....E	Alma-Ata	Turkic languages, Russian
Keewatin	228,160	2,400	0.01	District of Northwest Territories, Canada.....E	........; Baker Lake	English, Eskimo, Indian
Kentucky	40,395	3,138,000	78	State (U.S.).....E	Frankfort; Louisville	
Kenya†	224,960	9,200,000	41	Republic (Br. Comm. of Nations).....A	Nairobi	Swahili and other Bantu languages, English
Kerguelen	2,700	150	0.06	Part of French Southern & Antarctic Ter. (Fr.).....D		French
Kirghiz S.S.R.	76,650	2,490,000	32	Soviet Socialist Republic (Sov. Un.).....E	Frunze	Turkic languages, Persian
Korea (Entire)	84,544	39,500,000	467		........; Seoul (Sŏul)	Korean
Korea, North	46,540	11,500,000	247	People's Republic.....A	Pyongyang	Korean
Korea South	38,004	28,000,000	737	Republic.....A	Seoul (Sŏul)	Korean
Kuwait†	6,200	405,000	65	Sheikdom.....A	Kuwait	Arabic
Labrador	112,826	16,000	0.1	Part of Newfoundland Province, Canada.....D	........; Goose Bay	English, Eskimo
Laos†	91,429	2,000,000	22	Monarchy.....A	Vientiane	Lao, French
Latin America	7,928,469	237,100,000	30		........; Buenos Aires	
Latvia (S.S.R.)	24,600	2,200,000	89	Soviet Socialist Republic (Sov. Un.).....E	Riga	Latvian, Russian
Lebanon†	4,015	2,265,000	564	Republic.....A	Beirut	Arabic, French, English
Lesotho (Basutoland)†	11,716	740,000	63	Monarchy (Br. Comm. of Nations).....A	Maseru	Kaffir, other Bantu languages
Liberia†	43,000	1,050,000	24	Republic.....A	Monrovia	Native languages, English
Libya†	679,362	1,580,000	2.3	Monarchy.....A	Tripoli and Bengasi; Tripoli	Arabic
Liechtenstein	62	18,000	290	Principality.....A	Vaduz	German
Lithuania (S.S.R.)	25,150	2,900,000	115	Soviet Socialist Republic (Sov. Un.).....E	Vilnius	Lithuanian, Polish, Russian
Louisiana	48,523	3,480,000	72	State (U.S.).....E	Baton Rouge; New Orleans	
Lower Saxony (Niedersachsen)	18,296	6,855,000	375	State (Germany, West).....E	Hannover (Hanover)	German
Luxembourg†	998	332,000	333	Grand Duchy.....A	Luxembourg	Luxembourgeois, French
Macao	6	175,000	29,167	Overseas Province (Portugal).....C	Macao	Chinese, Portuguese
Mackenzie	527,490	16,300	0.03	District of Northwest Territories, Canada.....E	........; Yellowknife	English, Eskimo, Indian
Madeira Is.	308	270,000	877	Part of Portugal (Funchal District).....D	Funchal	Portuguese
Maine	33,215	989,000	30	State (U.S.).....E	Augusta; Portland	
Malagasy Republic (Madagascar)†	226,658	6,200,000	27	Republic.....A	Tananarive	French, Malagasy
Malawi (Nyasaland)†	46,066	3,900,000	85	Republic (Br. Comm. of Nations).....A	Zomba; Blantyre-Limbe	Bantu languages
Malaya	50,700	7,950,000	157	Part of Malaysia.....A	Kuala Lumpur	Malay, Chinese, English
Malaysia†	128,430	9,310,000	72	Self-Governing Member (Br. Comm. of Nations).....A	Kuala Lumpur	Malay, Chinese, English
Maldive Is.†	115	95,000	826	Sultanate (Br. Comm. of Nations).....A	Male	Arabic
Mali†	463,950	4,550,000	9.8	Republic.....A	Bamako	Native languages, French, Arabic
Malta†	122	325,000	2,664	Self-Governing Member (Br. Comm. of Nations).....A	Valletta	English, Maltese
Manitoba	251,000	963,000	3.8	Province (Canada).....E	Winnipeg	English
Mariana Is. (excl. Guam)	154	11,000	71	District of U.S. Pacific Is. Trust Ter..D	Saipan	Malay-Polynesian languages
Maritime Provinces (excl. Newfoundland)	51,963	1,489,000	29	Canada.....	........; Halifax	English
Marshall Is.	61	17,000	279	District of U.S. Pacific Is. Trust Ter..D	Majuro	Malay-Polynesian languages
Martinique	425	312,000	734	Overseas Department (France).....C	Fort-de-France	French
Maryland	10,577	3,480,000	329	State (U.S.).....E	Annapolis; Baltimore	
Massachusetts	8,257	5,387,000	652	State (U.S.).....E	Boston	
Mauritania†	397,685	1,000,000	2.5	Republic.....A	Nouakchott	Arabic, French
Mauritius (incl. Dependencies)	809	752,000	930	Monarchy (Br. Comm. of Nations).....A	Port Louis	Indo-Aryan languages, French, Creole, English
Mexico†	761,604	40,250,000	53	Federal Republic.....A	Mexico City	Spanish
Michigan	58,216	8,269,000	142	State (U.S.).....E	Lansing; Detroit	
Middle America	1,058,469	76,300,000	72		........; Mexico City	
Midway Is.	2	2,500	1,250	Possession (U.S.).....C		English
Minnesota	84,068	3,613,000	43	State (U.S.).....E	St. Paul; Minneapolis	
Mississippi	47,716	2,320,000	49	State (U.S.).....E	Jackson	
Missouri	69,686	4,446,000	64	State (U.S.).....E	Jefferson City; St. Louis	
Moldavia (S.S.R.)	13,000	3,250,000	250	Soviet Socialist Republic (Sov. Un.).....E	Kishinev	Moldavian, Russian, Ukrainian
Monaco	0.6	22,000	36,666	Principality.....A	Monaco	French, Italian
Mongolia†	592,700	1,079,000	1.8	People's Republic.....A	Ulan Bator	Mongolian
Montana	147,138	717,000	4.9	State (U.S.).....E	Helena; Great Falls	
Montserrat	39	13,000	333	Colony (U.K.).....C	Plymouth	English
Morocco†	171,835	13,150,000	77	Monarchy.....A	Rabat; Casablanca	Arabic, Berber, French
Mozambique	302,329	6,900,000	23	Overseas Province (Portugal).....C	Lourenço Marques	Bantu Languages, Portuguese
Muscat & Oman	82,000	580,000	7.1	Sultanate.....A	Muscat; Matrah	Arabic
Natal	33,578	3,270,000	97	Province (South Africa).....E	Pietermaritzburg; Durban	English, Afrikaans, Bantu languages
Nauru	8	5,000	625	Republic (Br. Comm. of Nations).....A		Malay-Polynesian languages, Chinese, English
Nebraska	77,227	1,507,000	20	State (U.S.).....E	Lincoln; Omaha	
Nepal†	54,362	9,900,000	182	Monarchy.....A	Katmandu	Nepali, Tibeto-Burman languages
Netherlands†	12,584	12,200,000	969	Monarchy.....A	The Hague ('s Gravenhage) and Amsterdam; Amsterdam	Dutch
Netherlands and Possessions	68,099	12,793,000	188		The Hague and Amsterdam; Amsterdam	
Netherlands Antilles	371	208,000	561	Self-Governing Territory (Netherlands).....C	Willemstad	Dutch, Spanish, English, Papiamento
Netherlands Guiana, see Surinam	....	....	....			
Netherlands New Guinea, see West Irian						
Nevada	110,540	426,000	3.9	State (U.S.).....E	Carson City; Las Vegas	
New Brunswick	28,354	620,000	22	Province (Canada).....E	Fredericton; Saint John	English, French
New Caledonia (incl. Deps.)	7,202	85,000	12	Overseas Territory (France).....C	Nouméa	Malay-Polynesian languages, French
New England	66,608	11,060,000	166	United States.....E	........; Boston	English
Newfoundland	156,185	495,000	3.2	Province (Canada).....E	St. John's	English
Newfoundland (excl. Labrador)	43,359	479,000	11		........; St. John's	English
New Guinea, North-East	69,695	1,320,000	19	Part of Australian Trust Ter. of New Guinea (3 Districts).....D	........; Lae	Papuan and Negrito languages
New Guinea, Ter. of	94,430	1,575,000	17	Trust Territory (Austl.; administered from Papua).....C	Port Moresby, Papua; Rabaul	Papuan and Negrito languages, English
New Hampshire	9,304	639,000	69	State (U.S.).....E	Concord; Manchester	
New Hebrides	5,700	65,000	11	Condominium (France-U.K.).....C	Vila	Malay-Polynesian languages, French
New Jersey	7,836	6,587,000	841	State (U.S.).....E	Trenton; Newark	
New Mexico	121,666	1,048,000	8.6	State (U.S.).....E	Santa Fe; Albuquerque	

† *Member of the United Nations (1967).*   ‡‡ *As of late 1967, the Gaza Strip was under Israeli military occupation. Data for Israel, Jordan, Syria and the United Arab Republic do not reflect de facto changes which took place during 1967.*

Region or Political Division	Area in sq. miles	Estimated Population 1/1/1965	Pop. per sq. mi.	Form of Government and Ruling Power	Capital; Largest City (unless same)	Predominant Languages
New South Wales	309,433	4,160,000	13	State (Australia)...E	Sydney	English
New York	49,576	17,834,000	360	State (U.S.)...E	Albany; New York	
New Zealand†	103,736	2,625,000	25	Monarchy (Br. Commonwealth of Nations)...A	Wellington; Auckland	English
Nicaragua†	53,938	1,620,000	30	Republic...A	Managua	Spanish
Niedersachsen, see Lower Saxony						
Niger†	489,200	3,275,000	6.7	Republic...A	Niamey	Hausa, Arabic, French
Nigeria†	356,669	43,200,000	121	Republic (Br. Commonwealth of Nations)††...A	Lagos	Hausa, Ibo, Yoruba, English
Niue	100	5,000	50	Island Territory (New Zealand)...C	Alofi	Malay-Polynesian languages, English
Norfolk Island	14	1,000	71	External Territory (Australia)...C	Kingston	English
North America	9,420,000	289,700,000	31		........; New York	
North Borneo, see Sabah						
North Carolina	52,712	4,877,000	93	State (U.S.)...E	Raleigh; Charlotte	
North Dakota	70,665	642,000	9.1	State (U.S.)...E	Bismarck; Fargo	
Northern Ireland	5,452	1,460,000	267	Administrative division of United Kingdom...E	Belfast	English
Northern Rhodesia, see Zambia						
Northern Territory	520,280	51,000	0.1	Territory (Australia)...E	Darwin	English, Aboriginal languages
North Polar Regions						
North Rhine-Westphalia (Nordrhein-Westfalen)	13,119	16,540,000	1,261	State (Germany, West)...E	Düsseldorf; Köln	German
Northwest Territories	1,304,903	25,000	0.02	Territory (Canada)...E	Yellowknife	English, Eskimo, Indian
Norway†	125,182	3,710,000	30	Monarchy...A	Oslo	Norwegian (Riksmål and Landsmål)
Nova Scotia	21,425	761,000	36	Province (Canada)...E	Halifax	English
Nyasaland, see Malawi						
Oceania (incl. Australia)	3,295,000	17,400,000	5.3		........; Sydney	
Ohio	41,222	10,372,000	252	State (U.S.)...E	Columbus; Cleveland	
Oklahoma	69,919	2,512,000	36	State (U.S.)...E	Oklahoma City	
Ontario	412,582	6,670,000	16	Province (Canada)...E	Toronto	English
Orange Free State	49,866	1,580,000	32	Province (South Africa)...E	Bloemfontein	English, Afrikaans, Bantu languages
Oregon	96,981	1,896,000	20	State (U.S.)...E	Salem; Portland	
Orkney Is.	376	18,400	49	Part of Scotland, U.K. (Orkney County)...D	Kirkwall	English
Pacific Islands Trust Territory	672	90,000	134	Trust Territory (U.S.)...E	Saipan	Malay-Polynesian languages, English
Pakistan (incl. part of Kashmir)†	399,737	102,700,000	257	Federal Republic (Br. Comm. of Nations)...A	Islamabad and Dacca; Karachi	Urdu, Bengali, English
Pakistan, East	54,501	54,600,000	1,002	Province (Pakistan)...D	Dacca	Bengali, English
Pakistan, West (incl. Karachi and part of Kashmir)	345,236	48,100,000	139	Pakistan...........; Karachi		Urdu, English
Palestine (Gaza Strip)	146	400,000	2,740	Military Government (U.A.R.)‡‡...B	Gaza	Arabic
Panama†	29,209	1,225,000	42	Republic...A	Panamá	Spanish
Papua (excl. New Guinea, Ter. of)	86,100	560,000	6.5	External Territory (Australia)...C	Port Moresby	Papuan and Negrito languages, English
Paraguay†	157,048	1,920,000	12	Republic...A	Asuncion	Spanish, Guaraní
Pennsylvania	45,333	11,511,000	254	State (U.S.)...E	Harrisburg; Philadelphia	
Persia, see Iran						
Peru†	496,224	11,500,000	23	Republic...A	Lima	Spanish, Quechua
Philippines†	115,831	31,800,000	275	Republic...A	Quezon City; Manila	Tagalog and other Malay-Polynesian languages, English
Pitcairn (excl. Dependencies)	2	100	50	Colony (U.K.)...C	Adamstown	English
Poland†	120,665	31,350,000	260	People's Republic...A	Warsaw (Warszawa)	Polish
Portugal†	35,510	9,140,000	257	Republic...A	Lisbon (Lisboa)	Portuguese
Portugal and Possessions	840,838	22,697,000	27		Lisbon (Lisboa)	
Portuguese Guinea	13,948	525,000	38	Overseas Province (Portugal)...C	Bissau	Native languages, Portuguese
Portuguese India (former) (Goa, Damão & Diu; Dadra & Nagar Haveli)						
Portuguese Timor	5,763	548,000	95	Overseas Province (Portugal)...C	Dili	Malay, Papuan languages, Portuguese
Prairie Provinces	757,985	3,359,000	4.4	Canada...........; Winnipeg		English
Prince Edward Island	2,184	108,000	49	Province (Canada)...E	Charlottetown	English
Puerto Rico	3,435	2,600,000	757	Commonwealth (U.S.)...C	San Juan	Spanish, English
Qatar	8,500	65,000	7.6	Sheikdom (U.K. protection)...B	Doha	Arabic
Quebec	594,860	5,620,000	9.4	Province (Canada)...E	Quebec; Montreal	French, English
Queensland	667,000	1,606,000	2.4	State (Australia)...E	Brisbane	English
Reunion	969	385,000	397	Overseas Department (France)...C	St. Denis	French
Rhineland-Palatinate (Rheinland-Pfalz)	7,657	3,545,000	463	State (Germany, West)...E	Mainz; Ludwigshafen am Rhein	German
Rhode Island	1,214	897,000	739	State (U.S.)...E	Providence	
Rhodesia	150,333	4,200,000	28	Self-Governing Colony (U.K.)*...C	Salisbury	Bantu langues, English
Rhodesia & Nyasaland, Federation of, see Malawi, Rhodesia, and Zambia						
Rio Muni, see Equatorial Guinea						
Rodrigues	42	19,000	452	Dependency of Mauritius (U.K.)...D	Port Mathurin	English, French
Romania†	91,699	19,025,000	207	People's Republic...A	Bucharest (Bucureşti)	Romanian, Hungarian
Ruanda-Urundi, see Rwanda and Burundi						
Russian Soviet Federated Socialist Republic	6,592,850	126,300,000	19	Soviet Federated Socialist Republic (Sov. Un.)...E	Moscow (Moskva)	Russian, Finno-Ugric languages, various Turkic, Iranian, and Mongol languages
Russian S.F.S.R. in Europe	1,527,400	92,900,000	61	Soviet Union...........; Moscow		Russian, Finno-Ugric languages
Rwanda†	10,169	2,800,000	275	Republic...A	Kigali	Bantu and Hamitic languages
Ryukyu Is. (Southern)	848	940,000	1,108	U.S. Military Administration...B	Naha	Japanese
Saar (Saarland)	991	1,116,000	1,126	State (Germany, West)...E	Saarbrücken	German
Sabah (North Borneo)	29,388	515,000	18	Administrative division of Malaysia...E	Jesselton; Sandakan	Malay, Chinese
St. Helena (incl. Dependencies)	162	4,600	28	Colony (U.K.)...C	Jamestown	English
St. Kitts-Nevis-Anguilla	138	64,000	464	Associated State (U.K.)...B	Basseterre	English
St. Lucia	238	94,000	395	Associated State (U.K.)...B	Castries	English
St. Pierre & Miquelon	93	5,000	54	Overseas Territory (France)...C	St. Pierre	French
St. Vincent	150	85,000	567	Internally Self-Governing (U.K.)...B	Kingstown	English
Samoa (Entire)	1,173	145,000	124		........; Apia	Malay-Polynesian languages, English
San Marino	24	17,000	708	Republic...A	San Marino	Italian
Sao Tome & Principe	372	55,000	148	Overseas Province (Portugal)...C	São Tomé	Bantu languages, Portuguese
Sarawak	48,342	845,000	17	Administrative division of Malaysia...E	........; Kuching	Malay, Chinese, English
Sardinia	9,301	1,440,000	155	Part of Italy (3 Provinces)...D	........; Caglairi	Italian
Saskatchewan	251,700	947,000	3.8	Province (Canada)...E	Regina	English
Saudi Arabia†	830,000	7,000,000	8.4	Monarchy...A	Riyadh; Mecca	Arabic
Scandinavia (incl. Finland and Iceland)	510,029	20,952,000	41		........; Copenhagen (København)	Swedish, Danish, Norwegian, Finnish, Icelandic
Schleswig-Holstein	6,045	2,405,000	398	State (Germany, West)...E	Kiel	German
Scotland	30,411	5,215,000	171	Administrative division of United Kingdom...E	Edinburgh; Glasgow	English
Senegal†	75,955	3,480,000	46	Republic...A	Dakar	Wolof, Poular, French
Seychelles	156	47,000	301	Colony (U.K.)...C	Victoria	French, Creole, English

† Member of the United Nations (1967). †† The Eastern Region of Nigeria unilaterally declared itself the independent Republic of Biafra in May 1967. * Rhodesia unilaterally declared its independence from the United Kingdom on November 11, 1965. ‡‡ As of late 1967, the Gaza Strip was under Israeli military occupation. Data for Israel, Jordan, Syria, and the United Arab Republic do not reflect de facto changes which took place during 1967.

Region or Political Division	Area in sq. miles	Estimated Population 1/1/1965	Pop. per sq. mi.	Form of Government and Ruling Power	Capital; Largest City (unless same)	Predominant Languages
Shetland Is.	550	17,500	32	Part of Scotland, U.K. (Zetland County) ... D	Lerwick	English
Siam, see Thailand	...	...	...	...	...	...
Sicily	9,926	4,810,000	485	Part of Italy (Sicilia Autonomous Region) ... D	Palermo	Italian
Sierra Leone†	27,699	2,250,000	81	Monarchy (Br. Commonwealth of Nations) ... A	Freetown	Temne, Mende, English
Sikkim	2,744	170,000	62	Monarchy (Indian protection) ... B	Gangtok	Tibeto-Burman languages
Singapore†	224	1,840,000	8,214	Republic (Br. Comm. of Nations) ... A	Singapore	Chinese, Malay, English
Solomon Is. (Austl. Trust)	4,320	62,000	14	Part of Australian Trust Ter. of New Guinea (Bougainville District) ... D	Sohano; Kieta	Malay-Polynesian languages
Solomon Is., British	11,500	133,000	12	Protectorate (U.K.) ... C	Honiara	Malay-Polynesian languages
Somali Republic†	246,201	2,350,000	9.5	Republic ... A	Mogadiscio	Somali
South Africa†	471,445	17,700,000	38	Federal Republic ... A	Pretoria and Cape Town; Johannesburg	English, Afrikaans, Bantu languages
South America	6,870,000	160,800,000	23	...	...; Buenos Aires	...
South Arabia, see Southern Yemen	...	...	...	...	...	...
South Australia	380,070	1,042,000	2.7	State (Australia) ... E	Adelaide	English
South Carolina	31,055	2,524,000	81	State (U.S.) ... E	Columbia	...
South Dakota	77,047	711,000	9.2	State (U.S.) ... E	Pierre; Sioux Falls	...
Southern Rhodesia, see Rhodesia	...	...	...	...	...	...
Southern Yemen	111,100	1,300,000	11.7	People's Republic ...	Madīnat ash Sha'b; Aden	Arabic; English
South Georgia	1,450	500	0.3	Dependency of Falkland Is. (U.K.) ... D	Grytviken	English, Norwegian
South Polar Regions	...	...	...	...	...	...
South West Africa	318,261	555,000	1.7	Mandate (South Africa)** ... C	Windhoek	Bantu languages, Hottentot, Bushman, Afrikaans, English
Soviet Union (Union of Soviet Socialist Republics)†	8,599,300	229,500,000	27	Federal Soviet Republic ... A	Moscow (Moskva)	Russian and other Slavic languages, various Finno-Ugric, Turkic, and Mongol languages, Caucasian languages, Persian
Soviet Union in Europe	1,919,750	156,500,000	82	Soviet Union ...	...; Moscow (Moskva)	Russian, Ruthenian, various Finno-Ugric and Caucasian languages
Spain†	194,885	31,500,000	162	Monarchy (Regency) ... A	Madrid	Spanish, Catalan, Galician, Basque
Spain and Possessions	309,007	32,020,000	104	...	Madrid	...
Spanish Possessions in North Africa	12	158,000	13,167	Five Possessions (no central government) (Spain) ... C	...; Melilla	Spanish, Arabic, Berber
Spanish Sahara	102,700	45,000	0.4	African Province (Spain) ... C	Aiún	Arabic, Spanish
Spitsbergen, see Svalbard	...	...	...	...	...	...
Sudan†	967,499	13,350,000	14	Republic ... A	Khartoum	Arabic, native languages, English
Sumatra (Sumatera)	182,860	17,150,000	94	Part of Indonesia (6 Provinces) ... D	...; Medan	Bahasa Indonesia, English, Chinese
Surinam (Neth. Guiana)	55,144	385,000	7.0	Self-Governing Territory (Netherlands) ... C	Paramaribo	Dutch, Indo-Aryan languages
Svalbard (Spitsbergen)	24,102	No perm. pop.	...	Dependency (Norway) ... C	Longyearbyen	Norwegian, Russian
Swaziland	6,705	295,000	44	Territory (Protectorate)(U.K.) ... C	Mbabane	Swazi and other Bantu languages, English
Sweden†	173,666	7,675,000	44	Monarchy ... A	Stockholm	Swedish
Switzerland	15,941	6,075,000	381	Federal Republic ... A	Bern (Berne); Zürich	German, French, Italian
Syria†	71,498	5,100,000	71	Republic‡‡ ... A	Damascus (Esh Sham)	Arabic
Tadzhik S.S.R.	55,250	2,410,000	44	Soviet Socialist Republic (Sov. Un.) ... E	Dushanbe	Tadzhik, Turkic languages, Russian
Taiwan (Formosa) (Nationalist China)†	13,885	12,250,000	882	Republic ... A	Taipei	Chinese
Tanganyika, see Tanzania	...	...	...	...	...	...
Tanzania (Tanganyika & Zanzibar)†	362,820	10,425,000	29	Republic (Br. Comm. of Nations) ... A	Dar es Salaam	Swahili and other Bantu languages, English Arabic
Tasmania	26,383	371,000	14	State (Australia) ... E	Hobart	English
Tennessee	42,244	3,737,000	88	State (U.S.) ... E	Nashville; Memphis	...
Texas	267,339	10,669,000	40	State (U.S.) ... E	Austin; Houston	...
Thailand (Siam)†	198,500	30,100,000	152	Monarchy ... A	Bangkok (Krung Thep)	Thai, Chinese
Tibet	471,660	1,300,000	2.8	Autonomous Region (China) ... E	Lhasa	Tibetan
Togo†	21,850	1,620,000	74	Republic ... A	Lomé	Native languages, French
Tokelau (Union) Is.	4	2,000	500	Island Territory (New Zealand) ... C	...; Fakaofo	Malay-Polynesian languages
Tonga	270	72,000	267	Protected Monarchy (U.K.) ... C	Nukualofa	Malay-Polynesian languages, English
Transcaucasia	71,850	11,000,000	153	Soviet Union ...	...; Baku	...
Transvaal	109,621	7,020,000	64	Province (South Africa) ... E	Pretoria; Johannesburg	English, Afrikaans, Bantu languages
Trinidad & Tobago†	1,980	960,000	485	Self-Governing Member (Br. Comm. of Nations) ... A	Port-of-Spain	English, Spanish
Tristan da Cunha	40	300	7.5	Dependency of St. Helena (UK.) ... D	Edinburgh	English
Trucial Coast	32,300	120,000	3.7	Seven Sheikdoms (no central government) (U.K. protection) ... B	...; Dubayy	Arabic
Tunisia†	48,332	4,600,000	95	Republic ... A	Tunis	Arabic, French
Turkey†	301,381	31,300,000	104	Republic ... A	Ankara; İstanbul	Turkish
Turkey in Europe	9,120	2,600,000	285	Turkey ...	...; İstanbul	Turkish
Turkmen S.S.R.	188,450	1,850,000	9.8	Soviet Socialist Republic (Sov. Un.) ... E	Ashkhabad	Turkic languages, Russian
Turks & Caicos Is.	166	6,000	36	Colony (U.K.) ... C	Grand Turk	English
Uganda†	91,076	7,450,000	82	Self-Governing Member (Br. Commonwealth of Nations) ... A	Kampala	Bantu languages
Ukraine (S.S.R.)†	232,050	45,500,000	196	Soviet Socialist Republic (Sov. Un.) ... E	Kiev	Ukrainian, Russian
Union of Soviet Socialist Republics, see Soviet Union	...	...	...	...	...	...
United Arab Republic (Egypt)†	386,000	29,000,000	75	Republic‡‡ ... A	Cairo (Al Qāhirah)	Arabic
United Kingdom of Great Britain & Northern Ireland†	94,211	54,500,000	578	Monarchy (Br. Commonwealth of Nations) ... A	London	English, Welsh, Gaelic
United Kingdom & Possessions	299,733	64,224,000	214	...	London	...
United States†	*3,675,633	193,850,000‡	53	Federal Republic ... A	Washington; New York	English
United States and Possessions	3,680,757	196,723,000	53	...	Washington; New York	English, Spanish
Upper Volta†	105,869	4,775,000	45	Republic ... A	Ouagadougou	Voltaic and Mande languages, French
Uruguay†	72,173	2,600,000	36	Republic ... A	Montevideo	Spanish
Utah	84,916	1,008,000	12	State (U.S.) ... E	Salt Lake City	...
Uzbek S.S.R.	171,900	10,050,000	58	Soviet Socialist Republic (Sov. Un.) ... E	Tashkent	Turkic languages, Sart, Russian
Vatican City (Holy See)	0.2	1,000	5,000	Ecclesiastical State ... A	Vatican City	Italian, Latin
Venezuela†	352,144	8,600,000	24	Federal Republic ... A	Caracas	Spanish
Vermont	9,609	396,000	41	State (U.S.) ... E	Montpelier; Burlington	...
Victoria	87,884	3,155,000	36	State (Australia) ... E	Melbourne	English
Vietnam (Entire)	127,243	33,400,000	262	...	...; Saigon	Annamese, Chinese
Vietnam, North	61,294	17,500,000	286	People's Republic ... A	Hanoi	Annamese, Chinese
Vietnam, South	65,949	15,900,000	241	Republic ... A	Saigon	Annamese, Chinese
Virgin Is., British	59	8,000	136	Colony (U.K.) ... C	Road Town	English
Virgin Is. of the U.S.	133	38,000	286	Unincorporated Territory (U.S.) ... C	Charlotte Amalie	English
Virginia	40,815	4,400,000	108	State (U.S.) ... E	Richmond; Norfolk	...
Wake I.	3	1,200	400	Possession (U.S.) ... C	...	English
Wales (incl. Monmouthshire)	8,016	2,675,000	334	United Kingdom ...	Cardiff	English, Welsh
Wallis & Futuna	77	9,000	117	Overseas Territory (France) ... C	Mata-Utu	Malay-Polynesian languages
Washington	68,192	3,051,000	45	State (U.S.) ... E	Olympia; Seattle	...
Western Australia	975,920	814,000	0.8	State (Australia) ... E	Perth	English
Western Samoa	1,097	124,000	104	Self-Governing Member (Br. Commonwealth of Nations) ... A	Apia	Malay-Polynesian languages, English
West Indies	91,064	22,250,000	244	...	...; Havana	...
West Irian	159,376	775,000	4.8	Under Indonesian Administration ... C	Sukarnapura (Hollandia)	Various Papuan languages
West Virginia	24,181	1,797,000	74	State (U.S.) ... E	Charleston; Huntington	...
White Russia, see Byelorussia	...	...	...	...	...	...
Wisconsin	56,154	4,166,000	74	State (U.S.) ... E	Madison; Milwaukee	...
World	57,280,000	3,237,000,000	57	...	...; New York	...
Wyoming	97,914	355,000	3.6	State (U.S.) ... E	Cheyenne	...
Yemen†	75,300	5,000,000	66	Republic ... A	Şan'ā'	Arabic
Yugoslavia†	98,766	19,400,000	196	Socialist Federal Republic ... A	Belgrade (Beograd)	Serbo-Croatian-Slovenian, Macedonian
Yukon	207,076	17,000	0.08	Territory (Canada) ... E	Whitehorse	English, Eskimo, Indian
Zambia (Northern Rhodesia)†	290,586	3,650,000	13	Republic (Br. Comm. of Nations) ... A	Lusaka; Kitwe	Bantu languages, English
Zanzibar	1,020	335,000	328	Part of Tanzania ... D	...; Zanzibar	Arabic, English

*† Member of the United Nations (1967). * Total area of the United States includes 3,548,974 square miles of land; 66,237 square miles of inland water; and 60,422 square miles of Great Lakes area, not included in any State. ** The United Nations declared an end to the mandate of South Africa over South West Africa in October 1966. Administration of the territory by South Africa is not recognized by the United Nations.*
‡ Total 1965 estimated population of the United States includes 193,200,000 residents of the 50 States and D.C., and 650,000 armed forces overseas, not included in any State. ‡‡ As of late 1967, the Gaza Strip was under Israeli military occupation. Data for Israel, Jordan, Syria and the United Arab Republic do not reflect de facto changes which took place during 1967.

WORLD FACTS AND COMPARISONS

MOVEMENTS OF THE EARTH

The earth makes one complete revolution around the sun every 365 days, 5 hours, 48 minutes, and 46 seconds.

The earth makes one complete rotation on its axis in 23 hours and 56 minutes.

The earth revolves in its orbit around the sun at a speed of 66,700 miles per hour.

The earth rotates on its axis at an equatorial speed of more than 1,000 miles per hour.

MEASUREMENTS OF THE EARTH

Estimated age of the earth, at least 3 billion years.
Equatorial diameter of the earth, 7,926.68 miles.
Polar diameter of the earth, 7,899.99 miles.
Mean diameter of the earth, 7,918.78 miles.
Equatorial circumference of the earth, 24,902.45 miles.
Polar circumference of the earth, 24,818.60 miles.
Difference between equatorial and polar circumference of the earth, 83.85 miles.

Weight of the earth, 6,600,000,000,000,000,000,000 tons, or 6,600 billion billion tons.
Total area of the earth, 196,940,400 square miles.
Total land area of the earth (including inland water and Antarctica), 57,280,000 square miles.

THE EARTH'S INHABITANTS

Total population of the earth is estimated to be 3,237,000,000 (January 1, 1965).
Estimated population density of the earth, 57 per square mile.

THE EARTH'S SURFACE

Highest point on the earth's surface, Mount Everest, China (Tibet)–Nepal, 29,028 feet.
Lowest point on the earth's land surface, shores of the Dead Sea, Israel-Jordan, 1,286 feet below sea level.
Greatest ocean depth, the Marianas Trench, south of Guam, Pacific Ocean, 36,201 feet.

EXTREMES OF TEMPERATURE AND RAINFALL OF THE EARTH

Highest temperature ever recorded, 136.4°F. at Azizia, Libya, Africa, on September 13, 1922.

Lowest temperature ever recorded, −126.9°F. at Vostok, Antarctica, on August 24, 1960.

Highest mean annual temperature, 88°F. at Lugh Ferrandi, Somali Republic.

Lowest mean annual temperature, −67°F at Vostok, Antarctica.

At Baguio, Luzon, in the Philippines, 46 inches of rainfall was reported in a 24-hour period, July 14–15, 1911. This is believed to be the world's record for a 24-hour rainfall.

An authenticated rainfall of 366 inches in 1 month—July, 1861—was reported at Cherrapunji, India. More than 131 inches fell in a period of 7 consecutive days in June, 1931. Average annual rainfall at Cherrapunji is 450 inches.

THE CONTINENTS

CONTINENT	Area (sq. mi.)	Population Estimated Jan. 1, 1965	Population per sq. mi.	Mean Elevation (feet)	Highest Elevation (Feet)	Lowest Elevation (Feet)	Highest Recorded Temperature	Lowest Recorded Temperature
North America	9,420,000	289,700,000	31	2,000	Mt. McKinley, United States (Alaska), 20,320	Death Valley, California, 282 below sea level	Death Valley, California, 134°F.	Snag, Yukon, Canada, −81°F.
South America	6,870,000	160,800,000	23	1,800	Mt. Aconcagua, Argentina, 22,834	Salinas Grandes, Península Valdés, Argentina, 131 below sea level	Rivadavia, Argentina, 120°F.	Sarmiento, Argentina, −27.4°F.
Europe	3,825,000	601,900,000	157	980	Mt. Elbrus, Soviet Union, 18,481	Caspian Sea, Soviet Union—Iran, 92 below sea level	Sevilla (Seville), Spain, 122°F.	Ust-Shchugor, Soviet Union, −67°F.
Asia	17,085,000	1,877,000,000	110	3,000	Mt. Everest, China (Tibet)-Nepal, 29,028	Dead Sea, Israel-Jordan, 1,286 below sea level	Tirat Zvi, Israel, 129.2°F.	Oymyakon, Soviet Union, −89.9°F.
Africa	11,685,000	290,200,000	25	1,900	Mt. Kilimanjaro, Tanzania, 19,340	Qattara Depression, U.A.R. (Egypt), 436 below sea level	Azizia, Libya, 136.4°F.	Ifrane, Morocco, −11.2°F.
Oceania, incl. Australia	3,295,000	17,400,000	5	.....	Mt. Wilhelm, New Guinea, Ter. of, 15,400	Lake Eyre, South Australia, 39 below sea level	Cloncurry, Queensland, Australia, 127.5°F.	Charlotte Pass, New South Wales, Australia, −8°F.
Australia	2,967,909	11,335,000	4	1,000	Mt. Kosciusko, New South Wales, 7,316	Lake Eyre, South Australia, 39 below sea level	Cloncurry, Queensland, 127.5°F.	Charlotte Pass, New South Wales, −8°F.
Antarctica	5,100,000	Uninhabited	...	6,000	Vinson Massif, 16,864	Sea level	Esperanza (Antarctic Peninsula), 58.3°F.	Vostok, −126.9°F.
World	57,280,000	3,237,000,000	57	.....	Mt. Everest, China (Tibet)-Nepal, 29,028	Dead Sea, Israel-Jordan, 1,286 below sea level	Azizia, Libya, 136.4°F.	Vostok, −126.9°F.

APPROXIMATE POPULATION OF THE WORLD, 1650–1965*

AREA	1650	1750	1800	1850	1900	1914	1920	1939	1950	1965
North America	5,000,000	5,000,000	13,000,000	39,000,000	106,000,000	141,000,000	147,000,000	186,000,000	219,000,000	289,700,000
South America	8,000,000	7,000,000	12,000,000	20,000,000	38,000,000	55,000,000	61,000,000	90,000,000	111,000,000	160,800,000
Europe	100,000,000	140,000,000	190,000,000	265,000,000	400,000,000	470,000,000	453,000,000	526,000,000	530,000,000	601,900,000
Asia	335,000,000	476,000,000	593,000,000	754,000,000	932,000,000	1,006,000,000	1,000,000,000	1,247,000,000	1,418,000,000	1,877,000,000
Africa	100,000,000	95,000,000	90,000,000	95,000,000	118,000,000	130,000,000	140,000,000	170,000,000	199,000,000	290,200,000
Oceania, incl. Australia	2,000,000	2,000,000	2,000,000	2,000,000	6,000,000	8,000,000	9,000,000	11,000,000	13,000,000	17,400,000
Australia					4,000,000	5,000,000	6,000,000	7,000,000	8,000,000	11,335,000
World	550,000,000	725,000,000	900,000,000	1,175,000,000	1,600,000,000	1,810,000,000	1,810,000,000	2,230,000,000	2,490,000,000	3,237,000,000

*Figures prior to 1965 are rounded to the nearest million. Figures in italics represent very rough estimates.

LARGEST COUNTRIES OF THE WORLD IN POPULATION

	Population 1/1/1965
1 China (excl. Taiwan)	700,000,000
2 India (incl. part of Kashmir)	479,000,000
3 Soviet Union	229,500,000
4 United States	193,850,000
5 Indonesia	103,350,000
6 Pakistan (incl. part of Kashmir)	102,700,000
7 Japan	97,400,000
8 Brazil	80,250,000
9 Germany, West (incl. West Berlin)	58,550,000
10 United Kingdom of Great Britain & Northern Ireland	54,500,000
11 Italy	50,900,000
12 France	48,800,000
13 Nigeria	43,200,000
14 Mexico	40,250,000
15 Philippines	31,800,000
16 Spain	31,500,000
17 Poland	31,350,000
18 Turkey	31,300,000
19 Thailand	30,100,000
20 United Arab Republic (Egypt)	29,000,000
21 Korea, South	28,000,000
22 Burma	24,500,000
23 Iran	23,100,000
24 Argentina	22,200,000
25 Ethiopia	21,500,000

LARGEST COUNTRIES OF THE WORLD IN AREA

	Area (sq. mi.)
1 Soviet Union	8,599,300
2 Canada	3,851,809
3 China (excl. Taiwan)	3,691,500
4 United States	3,675,633
5 Brazil	3,286,487
6 Australia	2,967,909
7 India (incl. part of Kashmir)	1,227,180
8 Argentina	1,072,072
9 Sudan	967,499
10 Algeria	919,595
11 Congo, The (Kinshasa)	905,567
12 Greenland (Den.)	840,000
13 Saudi Arabia	830,000
14 Mexico	761,604
15 Libya	679,362
16 Iran	636,300
17 Mongolia	592,700
18 Indonesia	574,670
19 Peru	496,224
20 Chad	495,800
21 Niger	489,200
22 Angola (Port.)	481,353
23 Ethiopia	471,778
24 South Africa	471,445
25 Mali	463,950

PRINCIPAL MOUNTAINS OF THE WORLD

NORTH AMERICA

	Height (feet)
McKinley, △Alaska (△United States; △North America)	20,320
Logan, △Canada (△St. Elias Mts.)	19,850
Citlaltépetl (Orizaba), △Mexico	18,701
St. Elias, Alaska–Canada	18,008
Popocatépetl, Mexico	17,887
Foraker, Alaska	17,395
Ixtacihuatl, Mexico	17,343
Lucania, Yukon, Canada	17,147
Whitney, △California	14,494
Elbert, △Colorado (△Rocky Mts.)	14,431
Massive, Colorado	14,418
Harvard, Colorado	14,414
Rainier, △Washington (△Cascade Range)	14,410
Williamson, California	14,384
Blanca Pk., Colorado (△Sangre de Cristo Range)	14,317
Uncompahgre Pk., Colorado (△San Juan Mts.)	14,306
Grays Pk., Colorado (△Front Range)	14,274
Evans, Colorado	14,264
Longs Pk., Colorado	14,256
Shasta, California	14,162
Pikes Peak, Colorado	14,110
Wrangell, Alaska	14,005
Colima, Nevado de, Mexico	13,993
Tajumulco, △Guatemala (△Central America)	13,846
Mauna Kea, △Hawaii (△Hawaii I.)	13,796
Gannett Pk., △Wyoming	13,785
Grand Teton, Wyoming	13,766
Mauna Loa, Hawaii	13,680
Kings Pk., △Utah	13,528
Waddington, Canada (△Coast Mts.)	13,260
Cloud Pk., Wyoming (△Big Horn Mts.)	13,175
Wheeler Pk., △New Mexico	13,160
Boundary Pk., △Nevada	13,140
Robson, Canada (△Canadian Rockies)	12,972
Granite Pk., △Montana	12,799
Humphreys Pk., △Arizona	12,670
Borah Pk., △Idaho	12,662
Chirripó Grande, △Costa Rica	12,533
Adams, Washington	12,307
Gunnbjörn, △Greenland	12,139
San Gorgonio, California (△Southern California)	11,502
Chiriquí, △Panama	11,411
Hood, △Oregon	11,235
Lassen Pk., California	10,457
Duarte, Pico, △Dominican Rep. (△West Indies)	10,417
Haleakala, Hawaii (△Maui)	10,025
Parícutin, Mexico	9,213
Selle, Massif de la, △Haiti	8,793
Guadalupe Pk., △Texas	8,751
Olympus, Washington (△Olympic Mts.)	7,965
Santa Ana, △El Salvador	7,812
Blue Mountain Pk., △Jamaica	7,402
Harney Pk., △South Dakota (△Black Hills)	7,242
Mitchell, △North Carolina (△Appalachian Mts.)	6,684
Clingmans Dome, North Carolina–Tennessee (△Great Smoky Mts.)	6,642
Turquino, Pico de, △Cuba	6,542
Washington, △New Hampshire (△White Mts.)	6,288
Rogers, △Virginia	5,729
Marcy, △New York (△Adirondack Mts.)	5,344
Katahdin, △Maine	5,268
Kawaikini, △Hawaii (△Kauai)	5,170
Spruce Knob, △West Virginia	4,860
Pelée, △Martinique	4,583
Mansfield, △Vermont (△Green Mts.)	4,393
Punta, Cerro de, △Puerto Rico	4,389
Black Mtn., △Kentucky	4,145
Kilauea, Hawaii (Hawaii I.)	4,090
Kaala Pk., Hawaii (△Oahu)	4,025

SOUTH AMERICA

	Height (feet)
Aconcagua, △Argentina (△Andes Mts.; △South America)	22,834
Ojos del Salado, Nudos, Argentina–△Chile	22,590
Pissis, Argentina	22,546
Tupungato, Argentina–Chile	22,310
Huascarán, △Peru	22,205
Llullaillaco, Argentina–Chile	22,146
Mercedario, Argentina	21,885
Yerupaja, Peru	21,758
Incahuasi, Argentina–Chile	21,719
Illampu, △Bolivia	21,490
Ancohuma, Bolivia	21,489
Sajama, Nevado, Bolivia	21,391
Illimani, Bolivia	21,151
Chimborazo, △Ecuador	20,577
Cotopaxi, Ecuador	19,344
Misti, El, Peru	19,144
Cristóbal Colón, △Colombia	18,947

	Height (feet)
Huila, Colombia (△Cordillera Central)	18,865
Bolívar (La Columna), △Venezuela	16,411
Fitz Roy, Argentina	11,600
Bandeira, Pico da, △Brazil	9,462

EUROPE

	Height (feet)
Elbrus, Soviet Union (△Caucasus Mts., △Europe)	18,481
Shkhara, Soviet Union	17,059
Dykh-Tau, Soviet Union	17,054
Kazbek, Soviet Union	16,554
Blanc, Mont, △France (△Alps)	15,781
Rosa, Monte (Dufourspitze) △Switzerland	15,200
Rosa, Monte (Grenzgipfel) △Italy–Switzerland	15,194
Weisshorn, Switzerland	14,803
Matterhorn, Switzerland	14,685
Finsteraarhorn, Switzerland	14,026
Jungfrau, Switzerland	13,668
Grossglockner, △Austria	12,461
Teide, Pico de, △Spain (△Canary Is.)	12,162
Mulhacén, △Spain (continental)	11,424
Aneto, Pico de, Spain (△Pyrenees)	11,168
Etna, Italy (△Sicily)	11,122
Perdido (Perdu), Spain	11,007
Clapier, France-Italy (△Maritime Alps)	10,817
Zugspitze, △Germany	9,721
Coma Pedrosa, Andorra	9,665
Musala, △Bulgaria	9,592
Corno, Italy (△Apennines)	9,560
Olympus, △Greece	9,550
Triglav, △Yugoslavia	9,393
Korab, △Albania	9,068
Cinto, France (△Corsica)	8,891
Gerlachovka, △Czechoslovakia (△Carpathian Mts.)	8,737
Negoi, △Romania	8,346
Rysy Pk., Czechoslovakia	8,212
Glittertinden, △Norway (△Scandinavia)	8,104
Parnassós, Greece	8,061
Idhi (Ida), Greece (△Crete)	8,058
Pico, △Portugal (△Azores Is.)	7,713
Kebnekaise, △Sweden	6,965
Hvannadalshnúkur, △Iceland	6,952
Malhão, △Portugal (continental)	6,532
Narodnaya, Soviet Union (△Ural Mts.)	6,184
Marmora, Punta La, Italy (△Sardinia)	6,017
Hekla, Iceland	4,747
Nevis, Ben, △United Kingdom (△Scotland)	4,406
Haltia, △Finland	4,344
Vesuvius, Italy	3,842
Snowdon, △Wales	3,560
Carrantuohill, △Ireland	3,414
Kekes, △Hungary	3,330
Scafell Pikes, △England	3,210
Stromboli, Italy	3,038

ASIA

	Height (feet)
Everest, △China (△Tibet)–△Nepal (△Himalaya Mts.; △Asia; △World)	29,028
Godwin Austen (K²), △Pakistan (△Kashmir) (△Karakoram Range)	28,250
Kanchenjunga, Nepal–△Sikkim	28,168
Makalu, China (Tibet)–Nepal	27,790
Dhaulagiri, Nepal	26,810
Nanga Parbat, Pakistan (Kashmir)	26,660
Annapurna, Nepal	26,504
Gasherbrum, Pakistan (Kashmir)	26,470
Gosainthan, China (Tibet)	26,291
Nanda Devi, △India	25,645
Rakaposhi, Pakistan (Kashmir)	25,551
Kamet, India	25,447
Namcha Barwa, China (Tibet)	25,445
Gurla Mandhata, China (Tibet)	25,355
Ulugh Muztagh, China (△Kunlun Mts.)	25,340
Tirich Mir, Pakistan (△Hindu Kush)	25,230
Minya Konka, China	24,900
Kulhakangri, △Bhutan	24,784
Communism Pk., Soviet Union (△Pamir-Alay Mts.)	24,590
Pobeda Pk., China–Soviet Union (△Tien Shan)	24,409
Muztagh Ata, China	24,388
Api, Nepal	23,398
Lenin Pk., Soviet Union	23,382
Tengri Khan, Soviet Union	22,940
Kailas, China (Tibet)	22,028
Hkakabo Razi, △Burma	19,296
Demavend, △Iran	18,934
Ararat, △Turkey	16,946
Sukarno Peaks, △West Irian (△New Guinea)	16,503
Klyuchevskaya, Soviet Union (△Kamchatka)	15,912
Wilhelmina, West Irian	15,518

	Height (feet)
Tabun Bogdo (Khuitun), △Mongolia (△Altai Mts.)	15,266
Belukha, Soviet Union	15,157
Turgun Uula, Mongolia	14,052
Kinabalu, △Malaysia (△Borneo)	13,455
Hsinkao, △Taiwan (Formosa)	13,113
Erciyas, Turkey	12,848
Munku-Sardyk, Mongolia–Soviet Union (△Sayan Mts.)	12,821
Kerintji, △Indonesia (△Sumatra)	12,467
Fuji, △Japan (△Honshu)	12,388
Hadūr Shu'ayb, △Yemen (△Arabian Peninsula)	12,336
Rindjani, Indonesia (△Lombok)	12,224
Mahameru, Indonesia (△Java)	12,060
Qalate Qarrāde, △Iraq	12,000
Razih, Jabal, △Saudi Arabia	11,999
Rantemario, Indonesia (△Celebes)	11,286
Qurnet es Sa'uda, △Lebanon	10,131
Shām, Jabal ash, △Muscat and Oman	9,902
Apo, △Philippines (△Mindanao)	9,692
Pulog, Philippines (△Luzon)	9,626
Phu Bia, △Laos	9,242
Hermon, Lebanon–△Syria	9,232
Paektu-san, △Korea	9,003
Anai Mudi, △India (peninsular)	8,841
Doi Nthanon, △Thailand	8,514
Pidurutalagala, △Ceylon	8,281
Mayon, Philippines (Luzon)	8,077
Asahi, Japan (△Hokkaido)	7,513
Tahan, Gunong, Malaysia (△Malaya)	7,174
Troodos, △Cyprus	6,403
Kuju-San, Japan (△Kyushu)	5,866
Atzmon, △Israel	3,962
Krakatoa (Rakata), Indonesia	2,667
Carmel, Israel	1,791

AFRICA

	Height (feet)
Kilimanjaro (Kibo), △Tanzania (△Africa)	19,340
Kenya, △Kenya	17,040
Margherita, Mt., △Congo K.–△Uganda	16,795
Ras Dashan, △Ethiopia	15,158
Meru, Tanzania	14,980
Elgon, Kenya–Uganda	14,178
Toubkal, Djebal, △Morocco (△Atlas Mts.)	13,661
Cameroon, △Cameroon	13,354
Thabana Ntlenyana, △Lesotho (△Southern Africa)	11,425
Emi Koussi, △Chad (△Tibesti Mts.)	11,204
Injasuti, South Africa	11,182
Neiges, Piton des, △Reunion	10,069
Tahat, △Algeria (△Ahaggar Mts.)	9,852
Maromokotro, △Malagasy Republic	9,462
Santa Isabel, △Equatorial Guinea (△Fernando Poo)	9,350
Cano, △Cape Verde Is	9,281
Katrīnah, Jabal, △United Arab Republic (Egypt)	8,652
São Tomé, Pico de, △Sao Tome	6,640

OCEANIA

	Height (feet)
Wilhelm, △New Guinea, Ter. of	15,400
Giluwe, △Papua	13,660
Bangeta, New Guinea, Ter. of	13,473
Victoria, Papua (△Owen Stanley Range)	13,363
Cook, △New Zealand (△South Island)	12,349
Balbi, △Solomon Is. (△Bougainville)	10,170
Ruapehu, New Zealand (△North Island)	9,175
Egmont, New Zealand	8,260
Orohena, △Fr. Polynesia (△Tahiti)	7,618
The Father, New Guinea, Ter. of (△Bismarck Archipelago)	7,532
Kosciusko, △Australia (△New South Wales)	7,316
Mauga Silisili, △Western Samoa	6,095
Hombolt, △New Caledonia	5,380
Panié, New Caledonia	5,348
Ossa, Australia (△Tasmania)	5,305
Bartle Frere, Australia (△Queensland)	5,287
Woodroffe, Australia (△South Australia)	4,970
Victoria, △Fiji (△Viti Levu)	4,341
Bruce, Australia (△Western Australia)	4,024

ANTARCTICA

	Height (feet)
Vinson Massif (△Antarctica)	16,864
Kirkpatrick	14,856
Markham	14,272
Jackson	13,747
Sidley	13,717
Wade	12,280

△ *Highest mountain in state, country, range, or region named.*

GREAT OCEANS AND SEAS OF THE WORLD

OCEANS AND SEAS	Area (sq. mi.)	Average Depth (feet)	Greatest Depth (feet)	OCEANS AND SEAS	Area (sq. mi.)	Average Depth (feet)	Greatest Depth (feet)	OCEANS AND SEAS	Area (sq. mi.)	Average Depth (feet)	Greatest Depth (feet)
Pacific Ocean	63,855,000	14,050	36,201	Bering Sea	876,000	4,710	16,800	Hudson Bay	476,000	420	850
Atlantic Ocean	31,744,000	12,690	27,498	Caribbean Sea	750,000	7,310	24,580	Japan, Sea of	389,000	4,490	12,280
Indian Ocean	28,371,000	13,000	26,400	Gulf of Mexico	596,000	4,960	14,360	North Sea	222,000	310	2,170
Arctic Ocean	5,427,000	5,010	17,880	Okhotsk, Sea of	590,000	2,760	11,400	Black Sea	178,000	3,610	7,360
Mediterranean Sea	967,000	4,780	15,900	East China Sea	482,000	620	9,840	Red Sea	169,000	1,610	7,370
South China Sea	895,000	5,420	18,090	Yellow Sea	480,000	150	300	Baltic Sea	163,000	180	1,440

PRINCIPAL LAKES OF THE WORLD

LAKES	Area (sq. mi.)	LAKES	Area (sq. mi.)	LAKES	Area (sq. mi.)
Caspian, Soviet Union–Iran (salt)	152,084	Ontario, United States–Canada	7,540	Torrens, Australia (salt)	△2,200
Superior, United States–Canada	31,820	Ladoga, Soviet Union	7,092	Albert, Uganda–Congo K	2,162
Victoria, Kenya–Uganda–Tanzania	26,828	Balkhash, Soviet Union	6,678	Vänern, Sweden	2,156
Aral, Soviet Union (salt)	26,518	Chad, Chad–Nigeria–Cameroon	△6,300	Winnipegosis, Canada	2,103
Huron, United States–Canada	23,010	Onega, Soviet Union	3,821	Bangweulu, Zambia	△1,900
Michigan, United States	22,400	Eyre, Australia (salt)	△3,700	Nipigon, Canada	1,870
Great Bear, Canada	12,275	Titicaca, Peru–Bolivia	3,500	Manitoba, Canada	1,817
Baykal, Soviet Union	12,159	Athabasca, Canada	3,120	Great Salt, United States (salt)	1,700
Great Slave, Canada	10,980	Nicaragua, Nicaragua	2,972	Koko Nor, China	1,650
Tanganyika, Congo K.–Tanzania–Burundi–Zambia	10,965	Rudolf, Kenya–Ethiopia (salt)	2,473	Dubawnt, Canada	1,600
Nyasa, Malawi–Tanzania–Mozambique	10,900	Reindeer, Canada	2,467	Gairdner, Australia (salt)	△1,500
Erie, United States–Canada	9,940	Issyk-Kul, Soviet Union	2,393	Lake of the Woods, United States–Canada	1,485
Winnipeg, Canada	9,465	Urmia, Iran (salt)	△2,229	Van, Turkey (salt)	1,470

△ Due to seasonal fluctuations in water level, areas of these lakes vary considerably.

PRINCIPAL RIVERS OF THE WORLD

River	Length (miles)	River	Length (miles)	River	Length (miles)
Nile, Africa	4,132	Amu Darya, Asia	1,628	Si, Asia	930
Amazon, South America	3,900	Kolyma, Asia	1,615	Oka, Europe	920
Mississippi–Missouri–Red Rock, North America	3,860	Murray, Australia	1,600	Canadian, North America	906
Ob-Irtysh, Asia	3,461	Ganges, Asia	1,550	Dnestr, Europe	876
Yangtze, Asia	3,430	Pilcomayo, South America	1,550	Brazos, North America	870
Hwang Ho, Asia	2,903	Angara, Asia	1,549	Salado, South America	870
Congo, Africa	2,900	Ural, Asia	1,522	Fraser, North America	850
Amur, Asia	2,802	Vilyuy, Asia	1,513	Parnaíba, South America	850
Irtysh, Asia	2,747	Arkansas, North America	1,450	Colorado, North America (Texas)	840
Lena, Asia	2,653	Colorado, North America (U.S.–Mexico)	1,450	Rhine, Europe	820
Mackenzie, North America	2,635	Irrawaddy, Asia	1,425	Narbada, Asia	800
Mekong, Asia	2,600	Dnepr, Europe	1,420	Athabasca, North America	765
Niger, Africa	2,590	Aldan, Asia	1,392	Donets, Europe	735
Yenisey, Asia	2,566	Negro, South America	1,305	Pecos, North America	735
Missouri, North America	2,466	Paraguay, South America	1,290	Green, North America	730
Paraná, South America	2,450	Kama, Europe	1,261	Elbe, Europe	720
Mississippi, North America	2,348	Juruá, South America	1,250	James, North America	710
Plata-Paraguay, South America	2,300	Xingú, South America	1,230	Ottawa, North America	696
Volga, Europe	2,293	Don, Europe	1,224	White, North America	690
Madeira, South America	2,060	Ucayali, South America	1,220	Cumberland, North America	687
Indus, Asia	1,980	Columbia, North America	1,214	Gambia, Africa	680
Purús, South America	1,900	Saskatchewan, North America	1,205	Yellowstone, North America	671
St. Lawrence, North America	1,900	Peace, North America	1,195	Tennessee, North America	652
Rio Grande, North America	1,885	Orange, Africa	1,155	Gila, North America	630
Brahmaputra, Asia	1,800	Tigris, Asia	1,150	Vistula, Europe	630
Orinoco, South America	1,800	Sungari, Asia	1,140	Loire, Europe	625
São Francisco, South America	1,800	Pechora, Europe	1,118	Tagus, Europe	625
Yukon, North America	1,800	Tobol, Asia	1,093	North Platte, North America	618
Danube, Europe	1,770	Snake, North America	1,038	Albany, North America	610
Darling, Australia	1,750	Uruguay, South America	1,025	Tisza, Europe	607
Salween, Asia	1,730	Red, North America	1,018	Back, North America	605
Euphrates, Asia	1,675	Churchill, North America	1,000	Ouachita, North America	605
Syr Darya, Asia	1,653	Marañón, South America	1,000	Cimarron, North America	600
Zambezi, Africa	1,650	Ohio, North America	981	Sava, Europe	585
Tocantins, South America	1,640	Magdalena, South America	950	Nemunas (Niemen), Europe	582
Araguaia, South America	1,630	Roosevelt (River of Doubt), South America	950	Branco, South America	580
		Godavari, Asia	930	Oder, Europe	565

PRINCIPAL ISLANDS OF THE WORLD

Island	Area (sq. mi.)	Island	Area (sq. mi.)	Island	Area (sq. mi.)
Greenland, Arctic Region	840,000	Hispaniola, West Indies	29,530	Ceram, Indonesia	6,046
New Guinea, Oceania	316,856	Sakhalin, Soviet Union	29,344	New Caledonia, Oceania	5,671
Borneo, Indonesia	286,967	Tasmania, Australia	26,383	Flores, Indonesia	5,513
Madagascar, Indian Ocean	227,800	Ceylon, Indian Ocean	25,332	Samar, Philippines	5,124
Baffin, Canadian Arctic	183,810	Banks, Canadian Arctic	23,230	Negros, Philippines	4,903
Sumatra, Indonesia	182,860	Devon, Canadian Arctic	20,861	Palawan, Philippines	4,500
Honshū, Japan	88,930	Tierra del Fuego, Argentina-Chile	18,600	Panay, Philippines	4,448
Great Britain, North Atlantic Ocean	88,756	Kyūshū, Japan	16,215	Jamaica, West Indies	4,232
Ellesmere, Canadian Arctic	82,119	Melville, Canadian Arctic	16,141	Hawaii, Oceania	4,030
Victoria, Canadian Arctic	81,930	Southampton, Hudson Bay, Canada	15,700	Cape Breton, Canada	3,970
Celebes, Indonesia	72,986	West Spitsbergen, Arctic Region	15,260	Bougainville, Oceania	3,880
South Island, New Zealand	58,093	New Britain, Oceania	14,592	Mindoro, Philippines	3,794
Java, Indonesia	50,745	Formosa, China Sea	13,885	Cyprus, Mediterranean Sea	3,572
North Island, New Zealand	44,281	Hainan, South China Sea	13,127	Kodiak, Gulf of Alaska	3,569
Cuba, West Indies	44,218	Timor, Timor Sea	13,094	Puerto Rico, West Indies	3,435
Newfoundland, North Atlantic Ocean	43,359	Prince of Wales, Canadian Arctic	12,830	Corsica, Mediterranean Sea	3,352
Luzon, Philippines	40,814	Vancouver, Canada	12,408	Crete, Mediterranean Sea	3,217
Iceland, North Atlantic Ocean	39,800	Sicily, Mediterranean Sea	9,926	New Ireland, Oceania	3,205
Mindanao, Philippines	36,906	Somerset, Canadian Arctic	9,370	Leyte, Philippines	3,090
Ireland, North Atlantic Ocean	32,596	Sardinia, Mediterranean Sea	9,301	Wrangel, Soviet Arctic	2,819
Novaya Zemlya, Soviet Arctic	31,390	Shikoku, Japan	7,245	Guadalcanal, Oceania	2,500
Hokkaidō, Japan	29,950	North East Land, Svalbard Group	6,350	Long Island, United States	1,620

LARGEST METROPOLITAN AREAS AND CITIES OF THE WORLD, 1964

This table lists every metropolitan area in the world with 1,000,000 or more population. For ease of comparison, each metropolitan area has been defined by Rand McNally & Company according to consistent rules. A metropolitan area includes a central city, neighboring communities linked to it by continuous built-up areas, and more distant communities if the bulk of their population is supported by commuters to the central city. All populations are estimates for January 1, 1964. The "city proper" figures refer to the area locally considered to be the city, provided it is under a single municipal government. Some metropolitan areas, such as Tōkyō–Yokohama, have more than one central city; in such cases the "city proper" figure is for the first-named city only.

Rank 1964		Estimated Population, 1/1/1964 Metropolitan Area	City Proper
1	New York, New York	16,325,000	8,085,000
2	Tōkyō–Yokohama, Japan	15,400,000	8,850,000
3	London, England	11,025,000	3,175,000
4	Ōsaka–Kōbe, Japan	8,700,000	3,250,000
5	Moscow (Moskva), Soviet Union	8,450,000	6,475,000
6	Paris, France	8,000,000	2,800,000
7	Buenos Aires, Argentina	7,700,000	2,950,000
8	Shanghai, China	7,600,000	10,400,000▲
9	Los Angeles, California	7,475,000	2,660,000
10	Chicago, Illinois	7,090,000	3,575,000
11	Calcutta, India	6,700,000	3,000,000
12	Mexico City, Mexico	6,100,000	3,050,000
13	São Paulo, Brazil	5,450,000	4,425,000
14	Rio de Janeiro, Brazil	5,250,000	3,600,000
15	Essen–Dortmund–Duisburg, Germany (West)	5,200,000	729,000
16	Bombay, India	4,700,000	4,500,000
17	Cairo (Al Qāhirah), United Arab Republic	4,600,000	3,800,000
18	Peking (Peiping), China	4,200,000	7,000,000▲
19	Detroit–Windsor, Michigan–Canada	4,170,000	1,610,000
20	Philadelphia, Pennsylvania	4,150,000	2,040,000
21	Berlin, Germany	4,025,000	2,180,000
22	Leningrad, Soviet Union	4,000,000	3,100,000
23	San Francisco–Oakland–San Jose, California	3,730,000	750,000
24	Boston, Massachusetts	3,480,000	665,000
25	Tientsin (Tienching), China	3,400,000	3,800,000▲
26	Victoria, Hong Kong	3,275,000	725,000
27	Seoul, Korea (South)	3,200,000	3,125,000
28	Djakarta, Indonesia	3,150,000	3,150,000
29	Manila, Philippines	2,900,000	1,190,000
30	Delhi–New Delhi, India	2,900,000	2,575,000
31	Manchester, England	2,850,000	652,000
32	Milano (Milan), Italy	2,775,000	1,675,000
33	Mukden (Shenyang), China	2,650,000	2,650,000
34	Birmingham, England	2,640,000	1,115,000
35	Wuhan, China	2,600,000	2,600,000
36	Madrid, Spain	2,575,000	2,450,000
37	Rome (Roma), Italy	2,500,000	2,340,000
38	Santiago, Chile	2,400,000	640,000
39	Sydney, Australia	2,340,000	168,000
40	Lima, Peru	2,300,000	1,975,000
41	Hamburg, Germany (West)	2,300,000	1,855,000
42	Washington, D.C.	2,265,000	785,000
43	Budapest, Hungary	2,265,000	1,920,000
44	Cleveland, Ohio	2,260,000	865,000
45	Montreal, Canada	2,250,000	1,225,000
46	Johannesburg–Germiston, South Africa	2,200,000	575,000
47	Barcelona, Spain	2,175,000	1,650,000
48	St. Louis, Missouri	2,155,000	720,000
49	Nagoya, Japan	2,150,000	1,750,000
50	Madras, India	2,150,000	1,825,000
51	Bangkok (Krung Thep), Thailand	2,100,000	1,500,000
52	Karachi, Pakistan	2,100,000	1,550,000
53	Melbourne, Australia	2,055,000	75,000
54	Chungking (Chungching), China	2,050,000	2,400,000▲
55	Canton (Kuangchou), China	2,050,000	2,050,000
56	Vienna (Wien), Austria	2,025,000	1,660,000
57	Tehrān, Iran	2,000,000	1,900,000
58	Athens (Athínai), Greece	1,975,000	650,000
59	Brussels (Bruxelles), Belgium	1,975,000	169,000
60	Pittsburgh, Pennsylvania	1,975,000	575,000
61	Toronto, Canada	1,960,000	665,000
62	Katowice–Zabrze–Bytom, Poland	1,960,000	285,000
63	Harbin (Haerhpin), China	1,950,000	1,950,000
64	İstanbul, Turkey	1,950,000	1,625,000
65	Glasgow, Scotland	1,885,000	1,030,000
66	Singapore, Singapore	1,825,000	1,100,000
67	Napoli (Naples), Italy	1,765,000	1,225,000
68	Caracas, Venezuela	1,750,000	890,000
69	Amsterdam, Netherlands	1,730,000	866,000
70	Alexandria (Al Iskandarīyah), United Arab Republic	1,700,000	1,650,000
71	Saigon, Vietnam (South)	1,700,000	1,350,000
72	Donetsk–Makeyevka, Soviet Union	1,700,000	785,000
73	Baltimore, Maryland	1,700,000	930,000
74	Liverpool, England	1,685,000	738,000
75	Nanking (Nanching), China	1,650,000	1,650,000
76	Sian (Hsian), China	1,600,000	1,600,000
77	Warsaw (Warszawa), Poland	1,575,000	1,210,000
78	Köln (Cologne), Germany (West)	1,550,000	835,000
79	Kyōto, Japan	1,550,000	1,330,000
80	Havana (La Habana), Cuba	1,550,000	875,000
81	Minneapolis–St. Paul, Minnesota	1,540,000	470,000
82	Miami–Fort Lauderdale, Florida	1,500,000	335,000
83	München (Munich), Germany (West)	1,500,000	1,175,000
84	Lahore, Pakistan	1,450,000	1,350,000
85	Frankfurt am Main, Germany (West)	1,450,000	695,000
86	Taipei, Taiwan	1,425,000	1,025,000
87	Gorki (Gorkiy), Soviet Union	1,425,000	1,060,000
88	Kitakyūshū–Shimonoseki, Japan	1,425,000	1,065,000
89	Houston, Texas	1,420,000	1,045,000
90	Stuttgart, Germany (West)	1,415,000	642,000
91	Bucharest (Bucureşti), Romania	1,400,000	1,265,000
92	Kiev (Kiyev), Soviet Union	1,390,000	1,280,000
93	Copenhagen (København), Denmark	1,380,000	705,000
94	Ahmadabad, India	1,375,000	1,250,000
95	Lisbon (Lisboa), Portugal	1,375,000	825,000
96	Buffalo–Niagara Falls, New York–Canada	1,370,000	515,000
97	Leeds–Bradford, England	1,360,000	514,000
98	Bogotá, Colombia	1,350,000	1,150,000
99	Torino (Turin), Italy	1,350,000	1,110,000
100	Chengtu, China	1,350,000	1,350,000
101	Hyderabad, India	1,350,000	950,000
102	Montevideo, Uruguay	1,335,000	1,180,000
103	Bangalore, India	1,325,000	950,000
104	Cincinnati, Ohio	1,315,000	495,000
105	Milwaukee, Wisconsin	1,315,000	760,000
106	Pusan, Korea (South)	1,300,000	1,300,000
107	Dairen (Talien), China	1,300,000	1,250,000
108	Tsingtao (Chingtao), China	1,300,000	1,300,000
109	Recife (Pernambuco), Brazil	1,250,000	900,000
110	Taiyüan (Yangkü), China	1,250,000	1,250,000
111	Kharkov, Soviet Union	1,250,000	1,020,000
112	Baku, Soviet Union	1,235,000	710,000
113	Tashkent, Soviet Union	1,205,000	1,055,000
114	San Diego–Tijuana, California–Mexico	1,200,000	640,000
115	Fushun, China	1,200,000	1,200,000
116	Dallas, Texas	1,180,000	750,000
117	Stockholm, Sweden	1,180,000	800,000
118	Casablanca, Morocco	1,175,000	1,100,000
119	Mannheim–Ludwigshafen–Heidelberg, Germany (West)	1,170 000	323,000
120	Newcastle-on-Tyne, England	1,155,000	262,000
121	Changchun (Hsinking), China	1,150,000	1,150,000
122	Surabaja, Indonesia	1,125,000	1,050,000
123	Atlanta, Georgia	1,115,000	515,000
124	Kansas City, Missouri	1,110,000	525,000
125	Prague (Praha), Czechoslovakia	1,110,000	1,011,000
126	Dnepropetrovsk, Soviet Union	1,090,000	755,000
127	Kanpur (Cawnpore), India	1,075,000	950,000
128	Kuybyshev, Soviet Union	1,075,000	920,000
129	Bandung, Indonesia	1,075,000	1,025,000
130	Novosibirsk, Soviet Union	1,065,000	1,000,000
131	Kunming, China	1,050,000	1,050,000
132	Düsseldorf, Germany (West)	1,050,000	704,000
133	Sverdlovsk, Soviet Union	1,040,000	885,000
134	Seattle, Washington	1,035,000	565,000
135	Tsinan (Chinan), China	1,025,000	1,025,000
136	Denver, Colorado	1,020,000	520,000
137	Antwerpen (Antwerp), Belgium	1,015,000	248,000
138	Rotterdam, Netherlands	1,010,000	732,000
139	Lyon, France	1,000,000	545,000

▲ Municipal boundaries of Shanghai, Peking, Tientsin, and Chungking now include extensive rural zones, which have been excluded in estimating their metropolitan populations.

PRINCIPAL WORLD CITIES AND POPULATIONS

This table includes all cities with 500,000 or more population, as well as many smaller cities of importance. The populations for all United States cities are estimates for January 1, 1965. The populations for foreign cities listed in the table of World Metropolitan Areas on the preceding page are estimates for January 1, 1964. For other cities, the populations are recent census figures or official estimates. Metropolitan populations are given for as many cities as possible, and identified by a star symbol (*). Some metropolitan areas, such as Minneapolis-St. Paul, include more than one large city. In such cases, the entry for the first named city carries the entire metropolitan population, and other cities in the metropolitan area carry a reference to the first-named city with a star symbol.

Aachen, Germany (West) (*450,000)....174,700
Abidjan, Ivory Coast....180,000
Accra, Ghana....337,800
Addis Ababa, Ethiopia....448,512
Adelaide, Australia (*660,000)....21,300
Aden, Southern Yemen (*138,441)....99,285
Agra, India (*508,680)....462,020
Ahmadabad, India (*1,375,000)....1,250,000
Akron, Ohio (*615,000)....298,000
Albany, New York (*605,000)....127,000
Aleppo (Halab), Syria....425,467
Alexandria (Al Iskandarīyah), U.A.R. (*1,700,000)....1,650,000
Algiers (Alger), Algeria (*995,000)....883,879
Allahabad, India (*430,730)....411,955
Alma-Ata, Soviet Union....580,000
'Ammān, Jordan (*246,475)....224,974
Amritsar, India (*398,047)....376,295
Amsterdam, Netherlands (*1,730,000)....866,000
Ankara (Angora), Turkey....650,067
Anshan, China....805,000
Antwerpen (Antwerp), Belgium (*1,015,000)....248,000
Apia, Western Samoa....21,699
Asunción, Paraguay....305,200
Athens (Athínai), Greece (*1,975,000)....650,000
Atlanta, Georgia (*1,230,000)....535,000
Auckland, New Zealand (*499,700)....147,900

Baghdad, Iraq (*650,000)....355,958
Baku, Soviet Union (*1,235,000)....710,000
Baltimore, Maryland (*1,730,000)....925,000
Bamako, Mali....135,000
Banaras (Benares), India (*489,864)....471,258
Bandung, Indonesia (*1,075,000)....1,025,000
Bangalore, India (*1,325,000)....950,000
Bangkok (Krung Thep), Thailand (*2,100,000)....1,500,000
Bangui, Central African Republic....79,600
Barcelona, Spain (*2,175,000)....1,650,000
Barranquilla, Colombia....431,000
Basel (Bâle), Switzerland (*505,000)....211,500
Beirut (Beyrouth), Lebanon....400,000
Belém (Pará), Brazil (*405,000)....359,988
Belfast, Northern Ireland (*580,000)....412,500
Belgrade (Beograd), Yugoslavia....585,234
Belo Horizonte, Brazil (*775,000)....642,912
Bengasi (Banghāzī), Libya....136,600
Berlin, East, Germany (*Berlin)....1,061,200
Berlin, West, Germany (*4,025,000)....2,180,000
Bern (Berne), Switzerland (*225,000)....167,400
Bilbao, Spain (*565,000)....297,942
Birmingham, Alabama (*655,000)....345,000
Birmingham, England (*2,640,000)....1,115,000
Bogotá, Colombia (*1,350,000)....1,150,000
Bologna, Italy....475,700
Bombay, India (*4,700,000)....4,500,000
Bonn, Germany (West) (*285,000)....143,000
Bordeaux, France (*480,000)....249,688
Boston, Massachusetts (*3,540,000)....670,000
Bradford, England (*Leeds)....297,000
Brasília, Brazil....150,000
Brazzaville, Congo....133,700
Bremen, Germany (West)....581,000
Brighton, England (*405,000)....162,900
Brisbane, Australia (*649,500)....619,000
Bristol, England (*605,000)....433,900
Brussels (Bruxelles), Belgium (*1,975,000)....169,000
Bucharest (București), Romania (*1,400,000)....1,265,000
Budapest, Hungary (*2,265,000)....1,920,000
Buenos Aires, Argentina (*7,700,000)....2,950,000
Buffalo, New York (*1,370,000)....505,000
Bujumbura, Burundi....50,000

Cairo (Al Qāhirah), U.A.R. (*4,600,000)....3,800,000
Calcutta, India (*6,700,000)....3,000,000
Cali, Colombia....591,000
Canberra, Australia....77,644
Canton (Kuangchou), China (*2,050,000)....2,050,000
Cape Town, South Africa (*807,211)....508,341
Caracas, Venezuela (*1,750,000)....890,000
Cardiff, Wales (*605,000)....260,600
Casablanca, Morocco (*1,175,000)....1,100,000
Changchun (Hsinking), China (*1,150,000)....1,150,000
Changsha, China....703,000
Chelyabinsk, Soviet Union (*950,000)....767,000
Chengchow, China....766,000
Chengtu, China (*1,350,000)....1,350,000
Chicago, Illinois (*7,225,000)....3,520,000
Chittagong, Pakistan (364,205)....180,000
Chungking (Chungching), China (2,400,000▲)....*2,050,000
Cincinnati, Ohio (*1,310,000)....495,000
Cleveland, Ohio (*2,250,000)....855,000
Colombo, Ceylon (*800,000)....510,947
Columbus, Ohio (*825,000)....540,000
Conakry, Guinea (*109,500)....43,000
Copenhagen (København), Denmark (*1,380,000)....705,000
Córdoba, Argentina....580,000
Coventry, England (*580,000)....313,900

Dacca, Pakistan (*750,000)....362,006
Dairen (Talien), China (*1,300,000)....1,250,000
Dakar, Senegal (*435,000)....374,700
Dallas, Texas (*1,280,000)....790,000
Damascus (Dimashq), Syria....529,963
Dar es Salaam, Tanzania....128,742
Dayton, Ohio (*720,000)....260,000
Delhi, India (*2,900,000)....2,575,000
Denver, Colorado (*1,035,000)....520,000
Detroit, Michigan (*4,370,000)....1,600,000
Djakarta (Batavia), Indonesia (*3,150,000)....3,150,000
Dnepropetrovsk, Soviet Union (*1,090,000)....755,000
Donetsk (Stalino), Soviet Union (*1,700,000)....785,000
Dortmund, Germany (West) (*Essen)....652,000
Dresden, Germany (East) (*625,000)....494,600
Dublin (Baile Átha Cliath), Ireland (*690,000)....537,448
Duisburg, Germany (West) (*Essen)....497,500
Durban, South Africa (*659,934)....560,010
Düsseldorf, Germany (West) (*1,050,000)....704,000

Edinburgh, Scotland (*615,000)....476,200
Edmonton, Canada (*337,568)....281,027
El Paso, Texas (*650,000)....309,000
Essen, Germany (West) (*5,200,000)....729,000

Firenze (Florence), Italy (*560,000)....455,000
Foochow, China....616,000
Fortaleza, Brazil (*525,000)....354,942
Fort-Lamy, Chad....91,700
Fort Worth, Texas (*540,000)....360,000
Frankfurt [am Main], Germany, (West) (*1,450,000)....695,000
Freetown, Sierra Leone....128,000
Fukuoka, Japan (*790,000)....647,122
Fushun, China (*1,200,000)....1,200,000

Gdańsk (Danzig), Poland (*550,000)....301,700
Genève (Geneva), Switzerland (*305,000)....174,700
Genova (Genoa), Italy (*865,000)....825,500
Gent (Ghent), Belgium (*330,000)....157,811
Georgetown, Guyana (*148,402)....79,965
Glasgow, Scotland (*1,885,000)....1,030,000
Gorki (Gorkiy), Soviet Union (*1,425,000)....1,060,000
Göteborg, Sweden (*515,000)....410,700
Guadalajara, Mexico (*830,000)....736,800
Guatemala, Guatemala....417,200
Guayaquil, Ecuador....510,800

Halle [an der Saale], Germany (East) (*425,000)....278,000
Hamburg, Germany (West) (*2,300,000)....1,855,000
Hamilton, Canada (*395,189)....273,991
Hangchow, China....784,000
Hannover (Hanover), Germany (West) (*740,000)....567,400
Hanoi, Vietnam (North) (*643,576)....414,620
Harbin (Haerhpin), China (*1,950,000)....1,950,000
Hartford, Connecticut (*885,000)....158,000
Havana (La Habana), Cuba (*1,550,000)....875,000
Helsinki, Finland (*635,000)....476,400
Hiroshima, Japan (*560,000)....431,336
Honolulu, Hawaii (*560,000)....315,000
Houston, Texas (*1,490,000)....1,100,000
Howrah, India (*Calcutta)....512,598
Huhehot (Kweisui), China....314,000
Hull (Kingston-upon-Hull), England (*360,000)....301,000
Hyderabad, India (*1,350,000)....950,000
Hyderabad, Pakistan (*460,000)....416,441

Ibadan, Nigeria....459,196
Inchŏn, Korea (South)....430,100
Indianapolis, Indiana (*900,000)....530,000
Indore, India....394,941
Irkutsk, Soviet Union....390,000
İstanbul, Turkey (*1,950,000)....1,625,000
Ivanovo, Soviet Union....368,000
İzmir (Smyrna), Turkey (*500,000)....360,829

Jabalpur (Jubbulpore), India (*367,014)....295,375
Jacksonville, Florida (*525,000)....198,000
Jaipur, India....403,444
Jamshedpur, India (*328,044)....291,791
Jerusalem, Israel (*260,000)....175,500
Jerusalem, Jordan (*Jerusalem)....60,488
Johannesburg, South Africa (*2,200,000)....575,000
Juddah, Saudi Arabia....147,900

Kabul, Afghanistan....236,000
Kalgan, China....299,300
Kampala, Uganda (*123,332)....46,735
Kanpur (Cawnpore), India (*1,075,000)....950,000
Kansas City, Missouri (*1,140,000)....530,000
Karachi, Pakistan (*2,100,000)....1,900,000
Karaganda, Soviet Union....462,000
Karl-Marx-Stadt (Chemnitz), Germany (East) (*400,000)....287,400
Katmandu, Nepal....122,500
Katowice, Poland (*1,960,000)....285,000
Kaunas, Soviet Union....247,000
Kawasaki, Japan (*Tōkyō)....632,975
Kazan, Soviet Union....725,000
Khabarovsk, Soviet Union....377,000
Kharkov, Soviet Union (*1,250,000)....1,020,000
Khartoum, Sudan (*370,000)....132,000
Kiev (Kiyev), Soviet Union (*1,390,000)....1,280,000
Kigali, Rwanda....4,000
Kingston, Jamaica....421,718
Kinshasa, The Congo....402,500
Kirin, China....568,000
Kitakyūshū, Japan (*1,425,000)....1,065,000
Kōbe, Japan (*Ōsaka)....1,113,977
Köln (Cologne), Germany (West) (*1,550,000)....835,000
Kowloon, Hong Kong (*Victoria)....726,976
Kraków (Cracow), Poland....495,600
Krasnoyarsk, Soviet Union....483,000
Krivoy Rog, Soviet Union....448,000
Kuala Lumpur, Malaysia (*400,000)....316,230
Kunming, China (*1,050,000)....1,050,000
Kuwait, Kuwait (*151,247)....96,860
Kuybyshev, Soviet Union (*1,075,000)....920,000
Kweiyang, China....504,000
Kyōto, Japan (*1,550,000)....1,330,000

Lagos, Nigeria....665,246
Lahore, Pakistan (*1,450,000)....1,350,000
Lanchow, China....699,000
La Paz, Bolivia....450,000
La Plata, Argentina (*410,000)....295,000
Leeds, England (*1,360,000)....514,000
Le Havre, France (*223,000)....183,776
Leicester, England (*430,000)....270,400
Leipzig, Germany (East) (*735,000)....587,200
Leningrad, Soviet Union (*4,000,000)....3,100,000
Libreville, Gabon....31,027
Liège, Belgium (*550,000)....153,240
Lille, France (*865,000)....193,096
Lima, Peru (*2,300,000)....1,975,000
Lisbon (Lisboa), Portugal (*1,375,000)....825,000
Liverpool, England (*1,685,000)....738,000
Łódź, Poland (*875,000)....726,800
Lomé, Togo....80,000
London, England (*11,025,000)....3,175,000
Los Angeles, California (*7,635,000)....2,695,000
Louisville, Kentucky (*795,000)....392,000
Lourenço Marques, Mozambique (*183,800)....78,500
Loyang, China....171,200
Luanda, Angola....225,000
Lubumbashi, The Congo....183,700
Lucknow, India (*675,000)....595,440
Lusaka, Zambia....114,400
Luxembourg, Luxembourg....73,900
Lvov, Soviet Union....469,000
Lyon (Lyons), France (*1,000,000)....545,000

Macao, Macao (*169,299)....153,630
Madras, India (*2,150,000)....1,825,000
Madrid, Spain (*2,575,000)....2,450,000
Madura, India (*500,000)....424,810
Magdeburg, Germany (East) (*370,000)....265,500
Managua, Nicaragua....234,800
Manchester, England (*2,850,000)....652,000
Manila, Philippines (*2,900,000)....1,190,000
Mannheim, Germany (West) (*1,170,000)....323,000
Maracaibo, Venezuela....432,902
Marseille (Marseilles), France (*870,000)....778,071
Mecca (Makkah), Saudi Arabia....158,900
Medan, Indonesia....466,370
Medellín, Colombia (*750,000)....614,000
Melbourne, Australia (*2,055,000)....75,000
Memphis, Tennessee (*700,000)....525,000
Mexico City, Mexico (*6,100,000)....3,050,000
Miami, Florida (*1,500,000)....325,000
Middlesbrough, England (*545,000)....158,100
Milano (Milan), Italy (*2,775,000)....1,675,000
Milwaukee, Wisconsin (*1,330,000)....765,000
Minneapolis, Minnesota (*1,590,000)....465,000
Minsk, Soviet Union....644,000
Mogadiscio, Somali Rep....90,600
Monrovia, Liberia....81,000
Monterrey, Mexico (*695,000)....596,939
Montevideo, Uruguay (*1,335,000)....1,180,000
Montreal, Canada (*2,250,000)....1,225,000
Moscow (Moskva), Soviet Union (*8,450,000)....6,475,000
Mukden (Shenyang), China (*2,650,000)....2,650,000
München (Munich), Germany (West) (*1,500,000)....1,175,000

Nagasaki, Japan....344,153
Nagoya, Japan (*2,150,000)....1,750,000
Nagpur, India (*700,000)....643,659
Nairobi, Kenya....266,795
Nanchang, China....508,000
Nanking (Nanching), China (*1,650,000)....1,650,000
Napoli (Naples), Italy (*1,765,000)....1,225,000
Nashville, Tennessee (*450,000)....261,000
Newark, New Jersey (*New York)....395,000
Newcastle-on-Tyne, England (*1,155,000)....262,000
New Delhi, India (*Delhi)....261,545
New Orleans, Louisiana (*985,000)....655,000
New York, New York (*16,550,000)....8,080,000
Niamey, Niger....30,030
Nice, France....292,958
Norfolk, Virginia (*655,500)....322,000
Nottingham, England (*630,000)....315,100
Novokuznetsk (Stalinsk), Soviet Union....410,000
Novosibirsk, Soviet Union (*1,065,000)....1,000,000
Nürnberg (Nuremberg), Germany (West) (*675,000)....466,200

Oakland, California (*San Francisco)....378,000
Odessa, Soviet Union....709,000
Oklahoma City, Oklahoma (*585,000)....380,000
Omaha, Nebraska (*495,000)....340,000
Omsk, Soviet Union....674,000
Ōsaka, Japan (*8,700,000)....3,250,000
Oslo, Norway (*635,000)....477,100
Ottawa, Canada (*429,750)....268,206
Ouagadougou, Upper Volta....59,126

Palembang, Indonesia....458,661
Palermo, Italy....614,000
Panamá, Panama (*330,000)....306,000
Paotow, China....400,000
Paris, France (*8,000,000)....2,800,000
Patna, India (*450,000)....363,700
Peking (Peiping), China (7,000,000▲)....*4,200,000
Penang (George Town), Malaysia (*325,000)....234,903
Perm, Soviet Union....722,000
Perth, Australia (*485,000)....95,000
Philadelphia, Pennsylvania (*4,200,000)....2,030,000
Phnom Penh, Cambodia....403,500
Phoenix, Arizona (*810,000)....520,000
Pittsburgh, Pennsylvania (*1,955,000)....560,000
Poona, India (*800,000)....597,562
Port-au-Prince, Haiti....240,000
Portland, Oregon (*795,000)....380,000
Pôrto (Oporto), Portugal (*750,000)....303,424
Pôrto Alegre, Brazil (*850,000)....617,629
Port-of-Spain, Trinidad & Tobago (*170,000)....93,954
Porto Novo, Dahomey....65,000
Port Said (Būr Sa'īd), U.A.R....245,318
Portsmouth, England (*445,000)....224,900
Poznań, Poland....422,700
Prague (Praha), Czechoslovakia (*1,110,000)....1,011,000
Pretoria, South Africa (*422,590)....303,684
Providence, Rhode Island (*850,000)....195,000
Pusan, Korea (South) (*1,300,000)....1,300,000
Pyŏngyang, Korea (North)....653,100

Quebec, Canada (*357,568)....171,979
Quezon City, Philippines (*Manila)....397,990
Quito, Ecuador....355,200

Rabat, Morocco (*310,000)....227,445
Rangoon, Burma....821,800
Rawalpindi, Pakistan (*340,175)....197,370
Recife (Pernambuco), Brazil (*1,250,000)....900,000
Reykjavík, Iceland (*92,000)....75,000
Richmond, Virginia (*455,000)....223,000
Riga, Soviet Union....632,000
Rio de Janeiro, Brazil (*5,250,000)....3,600,000
Riyadh (Ar Riyāḍ), Saudi Arabia....169,185
Rochester, New York (*645,000)....305,000
Rome (Roma), Italy (*2,500,000)....2,340,000
Rosario, Argentina....595,000
Rostov [-na-Donu], Soviet Union (*780,000)....689,000
Rotterdam, Netherlands (*1,010,000)....732,000

Sacramento, California (*655,000)....265,000
Saigon, Vietnam (South) (*1,700,000)....1,350,000
St. Louis, Missouri (*2,195,000)....710,000
St. Paul, Minnesota (*Minneapolis)....308,000
St. Petersburg, Florida (*415,000)....200,000
Salisbury, Rhodesia (*315,300)....220,000
Salt Lake City, Utah (*488,000)....195,000
Salvador, Brazil....630,878
Ṣan'ā', Yemen....89,000
San Antonio, Texas (*790,000)....645,000
San Bernardino, California (*575,000)....102,000
San Diego, California (*1,210,000)....636,000
San Francisco, California (*3,805,000)....745,000
San Jose, California (*San Francisco)....308,000
San José, Costa Rica (*320,000)....101,162
San Juan, Puerto Rico (*660,000)....432,377
San Salvador, Salvador (*360,000)....255 744
Santiago, Chile (*2,400,000)....640,000
Santo Domingo, Dominican Republic....367,053
Santos, Brazil (*400,000)....262,048
São Paulo, Brazil (*5,450,000)....4,425,000
Sapporo, Japan (*615,000)....523,839
Saratov, Soviet Union (*770,000)....644,000
Seattle, Washington (*1,045,000)....565,000
Semarang, Indonesia....487,006
Sendai, Japan (*515,000)....425,272
Seoul, Korea (South) (*3,200,000)....3,125,000
Sevilla (Seville), Spain....442,300
Shanghai, China (10,400,000▲)....*7,600,000
Sheffield, England (*735,000)....495,300
Shihchiachuang, China....598,000
Shizuoka, Japan (*485,000)....323,819
Sian (Hsian), China (*1,600,000)....1,600,000
Singapore, Singapore (*1,825,000)....1,100,000
Sofia (Sofiya), Bulgaria (*769,700)....695,400
Soochow (Suchou), China....663,000
Southampton, England (*355,000)....207,200
Springfield, Massachusetts (*495,000)....174,000
Srinagar, India (*295,084)....285,257
Stockholm, Sweden (*1,180,000)....800,000
Stoke-on-Trent, England (*440,000)....266,100
Strasbourg, France (*320,000)....228,971
Stuttgart, Germany (West) (*1,415,000)....642,000
Suchow, China....676,000
Sucre, Bolivia....55,000
Suez, U.A.R....203,610
Surabaja, Indonesia (*1,125,000)....1,050,000
Sverdlovsk, Soviet Union (*1,040,000)....885,000
Sydney, Australia (*2,340,000)....168,000
Syracuse, New York (*485,000)....216,000
Szczecin (Stettin), Poland....286,300

Taegu, Korea (South)....716,600
Taipei, Taiwan (*1,425,000)....1,025,000
Taiyüan (Yangkü), China (*1,250,000)....1,250,000
Tallinn, Soviet Union....311,000
Tampa, Florida (*395,000)....305,000
Tananarive, Malagasy Republic....254,271
Tangier, Morocco....141,714
Tangshan, China....800,000
Tashkent, Soviet Union (*1,205,000)....1,055,000
Tbilisi, Soviet Union (*860,000)....768,000
Tegucigalpa, Honduras....133,887
Tehrān, Iran (*2,000,000)....1,900,000
Tel Aviv -Yafo, Israel (*715,000)....392,900
The Hague ('s Gravenhage), Netherlands (*830,000)....602,400
Thessaloníki (Salonika), Greece (*373,635)....250,920
Tientsin (Tienching), China (3,800,000▲)....*3,400,000
Tiranë, Albania....140,300
Tōkyō, Japan (*15,400,000)....8,850,000
Toledo, Ohio (*540,000)....354,000
Torino (Turin), Italy (*1,350,000)....1,110,000
Toronto, Canada (*1,960,000)....665,000
Tripoli (Tarābulus), Libya....212,600
Tsinan (Chinan), China (*1,025,000)....1,025,000
Tsingtao (Chingtao), China (*1,300,000)....1,300,000
Tsitsihar, China....668,000
Tula, Soviet Union....351,000
Tunis, Tunisia....410,000

Ufa, Soviet Union....630,000
Ulan Bator, Mongolia....195,300
Utrecht, Netherlands (*410,000)....264,200

Valencia, Spain (*660,000)....505,066
Valletta, Malta (*208,000)....18,300
Valparaíso, Chile (*440,000)....252,900
Vancouver, Canada (*790,165)....384,522
Venezia (Venice), Italy....355,700
Victoria, Hong Kong (*3,275,000)....725,000
Vienna (Wien), Austria (*2,025,000)....1,660,000
Vientiane, Laos....162,300
Vilnius, Soviet Union....271,000
Vladivostok, Soviet Union....338,000
Volgograd (Stalingrad), Soviet Union (*775,000)....665,000
Voronezh, Soviet Union....535,000

Warsaw (Warszawa), Poland (*1,575,000)....1,210,000
Washington, D.C. (*2,485,000)....810,000
Wellington, New Zealand (*267,400)....125,900
Wiesbaden, Germany (West) (*520,000)....258,200
Winnipeg, Canada (*475,989)....265,429
Wrocław (Breslau), Poland....451,600
Wuhan, China (*2,600,000)....2,600,000
Wuppertal, Germany (West) (*900,000)....421,800
Wusih, China....613,000

Yaoundé, Cameroon....92,600
Yaroslavl, Soviet Union....454,000
Yerevan, Soviet Union....578,000
Yokohama, Japan (*Tōkyō)....1,375,710
Youngstown, Ohio (*490,000)....162,000

Zagreb, Yugoslavia....430,802
Zaporozhye, Soviet Union....507,000
Zürich, Switzerland (*715,000)....440,000

* *Population of metropolitan area, including suburbs. See headnote.*
▲ *Population of entire municipality or district, including rural area. Starred population in these entries refers to urban portion of municipality only.*

America (1492–1850) continued

DATE	EXPLORER	COUNTRY REPRESENTED	DESCRIPTION
1577–80	Francis Drake	England	Explored west coast of North America to 46° or 48° N. and named it New Albion; circumnavigated the earth.
1583	Humphrey Gilbert	England	Made first effort to establish an English colony in North America; ship lost returning to England.
1585–87	John Davis	England	Made several voyages in search of Northwest Passage; discovered Davis Strait and Baffin Bay.
1602–03	Sebastian Vizcaino and Martin Aguilar	Spain	Sailed along coast of California to about 42° or 43° N.; discovered Monterey Bay but missed that of San Francisco; Aguilar reported large river near 43° N.
1603–15	Samuel de Champlain	France	Explored and mapped St. Lawrence R., New England coast, Ottawa R., Lake Huron, Lake Ontario; discovered Lake Champlain (1609).
1607–14	John Smith	England	Explored and mapped vicinity of Jamestown, Virginia (1608) and coast of New England (1614).
1609–11	Henry Hudson	Holland and England	Explored Hudson R. to Albany for Holland (1609); discovered and explored Hudson Bay for England (1610–1611).
1612–13	Thomas Button	England	Explored Hudson Bay in search of strait to the Western Ocean.
1615–16	William Baffin	England	Made two voyages in search of Northwest Passage; explored Baffin Bay to 78° N.
1631–32	Luke Foxe and William James	England	Explored northern and southern extensions of Hudson Bay without finding passage westwards.
1634	Jean Nicollet	France	Crossed Lake Huron to Mackinac Strait and Green Bay; reported "Western Sea" three days distant.
1658–59	Pierre Radisson and Sieur des Groseillers	France	Explored upper Mississippi R. and western shores of Lake Superior.
1669–70	John Lederer	England	Crossed the Blue Ridge and explored the Shenandoah Valley.
1669–87	Robert Cavalier, Sieur de la Salle	France	Explored Lake Ontario and upper Ohio R. (1669) and the Great Lakes to head of Lake Michigan (1679); descended Illinois and Mississippi rivers to Gulf of Mexico (1681–82); killed in Texas after failing to locate Mississippi R. by sea (1684–87).
1673	Jacques Marquette and Louis Joliet	France	Descended Mississippi R. from the Wisconsin R. to the Arkansas and returned to the Great Lakes via the Illinois-Chicago portage.
1680	Louis Hennepin	France	Explored upper Mississippi R. from the Illinois R. to the Minnesota.
1688	Louis de la Hontan	France	Explored upper Mississippi region; spread reports of fictitious "Long River" leading to Western Sea.
1699	Pierre le Moyne, Sieur d'Iberville	France	Entered mouth of Mississippi from Gulf of Mexico and explored delta.
1701–02	Eusebio Francisco Kino	Spain	Explored the Gila and lower Colorado rivers; proved that California was not an island.
1718–19	Bernard de la Harpe	France	Explored the Red and Arkansas rivers.
1721	Pierre François Xavier de Charlevoix	France	Visited French settlements in North America from Quebec to New Orleans.
1728–41	Vitus Bering	Russia	Confirmed existence of strait between Asia and America (1728); discovered northwest coast and named Mt. St. Elias (1741).
1730–43	Sieur de La Vérendrye and sons	France	Explored territory northwest of Lake Superior; discovered Lake Winnipeg; sons may have seen Rocky Mountains.
1742	Christopher Middleton	England	Discovered 'Repulse Bay in search of passage to Western Sea.
1749	Celoron de Bienville	France	Buried plates along the Ohio R., claiming formal possession for France.
1750	Thomas Walker	England	Discovered Cumberland Gap route into Kentucky.
1750	Christopher Gist	England	Explored Ohio R. and Kentucky areas

Ancient and Medieval (to the Discovery of America)

DATE	EXPLORER	COUNTRY REPRESENTED	DESCRIPTION
600 B.C.	Phoenician Sailors	Egypt	Reported by Herodotus to have sailed around Africa from east to west in three years, under orders of King Necho.
500–450 B.C.	Himilco	Carthage	Said to have explored the west coast of Europe, possibly reaching Britain.
500 B.C.	Hanno	Carthage	Explored west coast of Africa to Sierra Leone or about 5°N.
450 B.C.	Herodotus	Greece	Visited Black Sea, eastern Mediterranean, and Egypt, and described the world of his time.
334–323 B.C.	Alexander the Great	Macedonia	Explored and conquered all of southwestern Asia from Egypt to the Jaxartes and Indus rivers.
320 B.C.	Pytheas	Marseilles	Visited Britain and northwestern Europe and, possibly, either Iceland or Norway, which he called Thule.
59–44 B.C.	Julius Caesar	Rome	Added information about Gaul, Britain, and Germany to current geographical knowledge.
20 B.C.	Strabo	Rome	Traveled widely throughout Mediterranean lands; compiled most complete geography of ancient times.
570 A.D.	St. Brendan	Ireland	Alleged to have sailed the western seas for seven years in search of tropical islands; may have reached Madeira or West Indies.
690 A.D.	Bishop Arculf	France	Visited Jerusalem and other holy places; described Egypt.
721–31 A.D.	Willibard	England	Visited and described the Holy Land, Constantinople, and Rome.
890 A.D.	Othere	Norway	Sailed around North Cape, along the Lapland coast, and discovered the White Sea.
925–950 A.D.	Al Masudi	Baghdad	Traveled in India, Ceylon, China, Russia, Persia, and Egypt.
982 A.D.	Eric the Red	Norway	Discovered and colonized southern Greenland.
1000 A.D.	Leif Ericson	Norway	Discovered Labrador, Newfoundland, and nearby coasts.
1003–06 A.D.	Thorfinn Karlsefni	Iceland	Explored and attempted to colonize northeast coast of North America.
1099–1154 A.D.	Idrisi	Spain and Sicily	Traveled in north Africa and Asia Minor; compiled a description and map of the world.
1106 A.D.	Daniel of Kiev	Russia	Visited Jaffa, Jerusalem, the Jordan, and Damascus on pilgrimage to the Holy Land.
1160–73 A.D.	Benjamin of Tudela	Spain	Traveled through Egypt, Assyria, Persia, and central Asia, visiting Jewish centers.
1245–47 A.D.	John de Plano Carpini	Italy	Traveled through Poland, Russia, and central Asia to Karakoram, in Mongolia, as legate of the pope.
1253–55 A.D.	William of Rubruck	France	Visited Karakoram, in Mongolia, by way of southern Russia and Turkestan.
1270 A.D.	Lancelot Malocello	Italy	Rediscovered the Fortunate or Canary Islands.
1271–95 A.D.	Marco Polo	Italy	Journeyed to China by way of central Asia; returned by sea by way of Sumatra, Ceylon, India, and Persia; reported existence of Japan and Madagascar.
1281–91 A.D.	Vivaldi Brothers	Italy	Attempted voyage to India by sea along west coast of Africa, but never returned.
1323–28 A.D.	Friar Odoric	Italy	Traveled to China by way of India and Malaya; returned through central Asia.
1325–54 A.D.	Ibn Battuta		Visited every Islamic country from Spain to India; traveled widely in Far East, Arabia, and western Africa.
1346 A.D.	Jayme Ferrer	Catalonia	Credited by 14th-century maps with having rounded Cape Bojador on west coast of Africa.
1427–31 A.D.	Diogo de Seville	Portugal	Discovered some of the Azores Islands.
1433–35 A.D.	Gil Eannes	Portugal	Rounded Cape Bojador in exploration of west coast of Africa.
1435–36 A.D.	Affonso Baldaya	Portugal	Landed on coast of Africa in vicinity of Rio de Oro.

Date	Explorer	Country	Description
1441–46 A.D.	Nuno Tristam	Portugal	Reached the Sénégal R. along west coast of Africa.
1445 A.D.	Dinis Diaz	Portugal	Rounded Cape Verde on west coast of Africa.
1455–57 A.D.	Alvise da Cadamosto	Portugal	Explored the Sénégal and Gambia rivers; discovered Cape Verde Islands.
1472 A.D.	Fernando Póo	Portugal	Discovered island bearing his name in Gulf of Guinea.
1482–86 A.D.	Diogo Cão	Portugal	Discovered mouth of Congo R. (1482), reached Cape Negro at 16° S. (1486).
1487 A.D.	Pedro de Covilhã	Portugal	Traveled to India via Egypt and Arabia; visited east coast of Africa, south to Zambezi R.
1487–88 A.D.	Bartolomeu Dias	Portugal	Discovered Cape of Good Hope; explored coast east to Mossel Bay.

America (1492–1850)

Date	Explorer	Country	Description
1492–1502	Christopher Columbus	Spain	Discovered the West Indies (1492); in three later voyages explored coasts of northern South America and Central America.
1497–98	John and Sebastian Cabot	England	Discovered shores of Nova Scotia and Newfoundland, and visited southern Greenland.
1499–1500	Amerigo Vespucci, Juan de la Cosa and Alonso de Ojeda	Spain	Discovered and explored northeastern coast of South America.
1499–1500	Vicente Yáñez Pinzón	Spain	Discovered mouth of Amazon R.
1500	Pedro Álvares Cabral	Portugal	Discovered or visited coast of Brazil on voyage to India.
1500–01	Gaspar Corte Real	Portugal	Made two voyages to northeastern North America, but never returned.
1501–02	Amerigo Vespucci	Portugal	Explored coast of Brazil to 30° S. or farther.
1513	Juan Ponce de León	Spain	Discovered and explored coasts of Florida.
1513	Vasco Núñez de Balboa	Spain	Crossed Isthmus of Panama and discovered the South Sea (Pacific Ocean).
1515	Juan Díaz de Solis	Spain	Discovered mouth of Río de la Plata.
1517	Francisco Fernández de Córdoba	Spain	Discovered Yucatán and evidence of Mayan culture.
1518	Juan de Grijalva	Spain	Explored east coast of Mexico north of Yucatán.
1519	Alvárez Pineda	Spain	Explored Gulf of Mexico and may have discovered mouth of Mississippi R.
1519–22	Ferdinand Magellan	Spain	Discovered Strait of Magellan (1520) during first circumnavigation of the earth.
1519–27	Hernando Cortes	Spain	Explored and conquered Mexico.
1523–41	Francisco Pizarro	Spain	Explored northwestern South America and conquered Peru.
1524	Giovanni da Verrazano	France	Discovered New York Bay and explored coast northward.
1524–25	Estéban Gomez	Spain	Sailed along east coast of North America from Nova Scotia to Florida.
1527–37	Cabeza de Vaca	Spain	Wandered for nine years along and near coast of Gulf of Mexico from Florida to Mexico.
1534–41	Jacques Cartier	France	Explored Gulf of St. Lawrence (1534) and river as far as sites of Quebec and Montreal (1536).
1535–36	Diego de Almagro	Spain	Explored and conquered Chile.
1536–38	Gonzalo Jiménez de Quesada	Spain	Explored and conquered New Granada, and founded Bogotá.
1539	Francisco de Ulloa	Spain	Explored Gulf of California to its head.
1539–43	Hernando de Soto	Spain	Explored southeastern United States from Florida to Tennessee; discovered Mississippi R. (1541).
1540	Hernando de Alarcón	Spain	Sailed up Gulf of California and entered Colorado R.
1540–42	Francisco Vasquez de Coronado	Spain	Led expedition into southwestern United States; explored Great Plains northward to Kansas; Grand Canyon of Colorado R. discovered by one of his party.
1541	Francisco de Orellana	Spain	Crossed the Andes and descended Amazon R. to its mouth.
1542–43	Bartolomé Ferrelo and Juan Rodriguez Cabrillo	Spain	Discovered San Diego Bay and explored California coast to about 42° N. or Cape Mendocino.
1562–65	René de Laudonnière and Jean de Ribaut	France	Failed in effort to establish a permanent colony on coast of South Carolina.
1766–68	Jonathan Carver	England	Explored the upper Mississippi region and reported existence of the Oregon or River of the West.
1769–75	Daniel Boone	England	Explored eastern Kentucky (1769–71) and blazed the famous Wilderness Road (1775).
1769	José Ortega	Spain	Discovered San Francisco Bay during overland expedition into upper California.
1770–72	Samuel Hearne	England	Traced the Coppermine R. to the Northern Ocean and discovered Great Slave Lake.
1774–75	Juan Pérez and Bruno Heceta	Spain	Sent to explore northwest coast, reaching 55° N.; Heceta observed entrance to Columbia R.; Pérez discovered Nootka Sound.
1778–79	James Cook	England	Rediscovered Hawaiian Islands; explored and charted northwest coast from 45° N. to Arctic Ocean.
1788–92	Robert Gray	United States	Explored northwest coast; discovered Grays Harbor; entered and named the Columbia R. (1792).
1789–93	Alexander Mackenzie	England	Traced Mackenzie R. to its mouth (1789); crossed Rocky Mountains via Peace R. and reached Pacific Ocean.
1792–94	George Vancouver	England	Explored and mapped Puget Sound; charted inside passage and inlets along northwest coast.
1804–06	Meriwether Lewis and William Clark	United States	Ascended Missouri R. to its source, crossed Rocky Mountains and descended Columbia R. to Pacific Ocean.
1805–07	Zebulon M. Pike	United States	Explored and mapped upper Mississippi R. (1805); and southwestern section of Louisiana Territory (1806–07).
1807–08	Manuel Lisa and John Colter	United States	Explored Northern Rockies (Yellowstone-Big Horn region) as trappers and fur traders.
1811–12	Wilson Price Hunt (Astorians)	United States	Discovered overland route to Pacific via the Snake and Columbia rivers.
1819–20	Stephen H. Long	United States	Explored the high plains between Platte and Arkansas rivers; called the Great Plains the "Great American Desert."
1821	William Becknell	United States	Opened trade route between Missouri R. and Santa Fe.
1823–29	Jedediah Smith	United States	Located famous South Pass across Rocky Mts.; crossed desert between Colorado R. and California.
1824–28	Peter Skene Ogden	England	Explored upper Snake R. and northern Great Basin; discovered Humboldt R. and Great Salt Lake.
1829–30	Ewing Young and party	United States	Opened up Spanish Trail between Santa Fe and Los Angeles.
1832–33	Nathaniel J. Wyeth	United States	Led first expedition along Oregon Trail to Columbia R.
1833	Joseph E. Walker	United States	Crossed Great Basin between Great Salt Lake and California.
1841	Charles Wilkes	United States	Visited Oregon country and California during official Pacific exploring expedition by sea.
1842–45	John C. Frémont	United States	First official government explorer to re-trace explorations of fur trappers in the Far West.

Africa

Date	Explorer	Country	Description
1520–27	Francisco Alvarez	Portugal	Visited Ethiopia and described it in detail.
1541	Christopher da Gama	Portugal	Led expedition into Ethiopia.
1578–89	Duarte López	Portugal	Visited the Kingdom of Congo; his reports a chief source of information until 19th century.
1604–22	Pedro Páez	Portugal	First European to visit Ethiopian sources of the Nile R.
1616	Gaspar Boccaro	Portugal	Explored interior from upper Zambezi R. to west coast.
1618–19	George Thompson	England	Explored the Gambia R.
1625–35	Jerome Lobo	Portugal	Lived in Ethiopia as a missionary.
1698–1700	C. J. Poncet	France	Traveled as a physician into Ethiopia to treat the Emperor.
1768–73	James Bruce	England	Explored Ethiopia, especially source of the Blue Nile R.
1777–79	William Patterson	England	Made several trips into the Kaffir country as a naturalist.
1795–1805	Mungo Park	England	Explored the Gambia R. and was first modern European to reach the Niger R.
1797–98	John Barrow	England	Journeyed from Cape of Good Hope to upper Orange R.

PRINCIPAL DISCOVERIES AND EXPLORATIONS (Continued)

Arctic Regions continued

DATE	EXPLORER	COUNTRY REPRESENTED	DESCRIPTION
1871–74	Julius Payer and Carl Weyprecht	Austria	Discovered Franz Josef Land Archipelago.
1876	Albert H. Markham	England	Reached 83° 20′ on northwest coast of Greenland.
1878–79	Nils A. E. Nordenskjöld	Sweden	Completed the Northeast Passage in two seasons in ship *Vega*.
1879–81	George W. DeLong	United States	Explored Arctic Ocean northwest of Bering Strait; ship *Jeannette* and most of party lost.
1881–83	Adolphus W. Greely	United States	Explored northern Greenland and Ellesmere Island; party established new record of 83° 24′ N.
1888–96	Fridtjof Nansen	Norway	Made first crossing of Greenland (1888); reached record of 86° 14′ during drift of ship *Fram* (1895).
1897	Salomon A. Andrée	Sweden	Attempted balloon flight to North Pole from Spitsbergen (Svalbard); remains of party found in 1930 on White Island.
1898–1902	Otto Sverdrup	Norway	Explored northern Ellesmere Island and discovered Axel Heiberg Island.
1899–1900	Umberto Cagni	Italy	Reached new record at 86° 34′ N. by sledge from Franz Josef Land; member of Abruzzi expedition.
1900–09	Robert E. Peary	United States	Made repeated efforts to reach North Pole, succeeding (April 6, 1909) by sledge from Grant Land.
1903–6	Roald Amundsen	Norway	Completed first trip through Northwest Passage from east to west.
1907–9	Frederick A. Cook	United States	Claimed to have reached North Pole on April 20, 1908.
1925–26	Lincoln Ellsworth	United States	Made flight with Amundsen from Spitsbergen (Svalbard) to 87° 43′ N. and return; co-leader of dirigible flight over North Pole (1926).
1926	Richard Byrd and Floyd Bennett	United States	Made successful flight from Spitsbergen (Svalbard) to North Pole and return.
1926–28	Umberto Nobile	Italy	Made numerous dirigible flights across arctic region; rescued after *Italia* crashed on ice in 1928.
1937–38	Otto Schmidt	Russia	Spent nine months with scientific expedition near North Pole.

Antarctic Regions

DATE	EXPLORER	COUNTRY REPRESENTED	DESCRIPTION
1738–39	J.B.C. Bouvet de Lozier	France	Discovered Bouvet Island south of Africa in latitude 54° S.
1768–75	James Cook	England	Established non-existence of southern continent in habitable latitudes; reached record of 71° 10′ S.
1771–73	Yves Joseph de Kerguélen-Trémarec	France	Discovered and explored Kerguélen Island in latitude 49° 50′ S., longitude 69° 30′ E.
1819	William Smith	England	Discovered South Shetland Islands.
1819–21	Fabian von Bellingshausen	Russia	Circumnavigated Antarctica; discovered Alexander I Land.
1821	Nathaniel Palmer	United States	Discovered Palmer Peninsula on sealing expedition.
1823	James Weddell	England	Discovered Weddell Sea; reached 74° 15′ S.
1837–40	Jules Dumont d'Urville	France	Discovered Adélie Land south of Tasmania.
1839–40	Charles Wilkes	United States	Sighted Antarctic coast between 108° and 148° E.
1840–43	James Ross	England	Charted coast in neighborhood of Ross Sea; reached record of 78° 9′ S.
1902–04	Robert F. Scott	England	Explored coast of Edward VII Land; reached 82° 17′ S.
1903–05	Jean B. Charcot	France	Explored Palmer Peninsula; discovered Loubet Coast.
1908–09	Ernest Shackleton	England	Explored head of Ross Sea; reached 88° 23′ S.
1910–12	Roald Amundsen	Norway	Discovered Queen Maud Range; reached South Pole Dec. 16, 1911.
1910–12	Robert Scott	England	Reached South Pole January 18, 1912; entire party perished during return.
1911–13 1929–31	Douglas Mawson	England and Australia	Explored coast from King George V Land to Enderby Land in two expeditions.
1914–17	Ernest Shackleton	England	Discovered Caird Coast; ship lost in Weddell Sea, but party rescued after many hardships.

Africa continued

DATE	EXPLORER	COUNTRY REPRESENTED	DESCRIPTION
1797–1800	Frederick Hornemann	England	Traveled from Egypt to Marzūq and the Niger R., disguised as an Arab.
1798–99	Francisco de Lacerda	Portugal	Explored southeastern interior north of Zambezi R.
1801	John Trutter and William Somerville	England	Explored Bechuanaland, north of Orange R.
1802–06	Pedro Baptista and A. Jose	Portugal	Made first recorded crossing of continent eastward from Angola.
1812–14	Johann L. Burckhardt	Switzerland	Traveled up the Nile R. and across to the Red Sea.
1822–25	Dixon Denham and Hugh Clapperton	England	Crossed desert from Tripoli to Lake Chad and westward to the Niger R.
1825–26	Alexander G. Laing	England	Reached Timbuktu from Tripoli, but was murdered on return trip.
1827–28	René Caillé	France	Traveled from Guinea Coast to Fez and Tangier by way of Timbuktu.
1830–34	Richard Lander	England	Explored the lower Niger R. and located its mouth.
1849–73	David Livingstone	England	Discovered Zambezi R. (1851), Victoria Falls (1855), and Lake Nyasa (1859); explored upper Congo tributaries; found by Stanley on Lake Tanganyika in 1871.
1856–59	Richard Burton	England	Discovered Lake Tanganyika and explored surrounding area.
1858–63	John Speke	England	Discovered Victoria Nyanza as source of the Nile R.
1861–69	Samuel Baker	England	Explored upper Nile R.; discovered Lake Albert.
1863–71	Georg A. Schweinfurth	Germany	Explored extensively in the Sudan and equatorial Africa.
1871–90	Henry Stanley	United States	Continued Livingstone's explorations in the lakes region; descended Congo R. to Atlantic Ocean (1877); discovered Stanley Pool and Lake Edward.
1877–86	Serpa Pinto	Portugal	Crossed the continent from Angola to Mozambique.
1879–90	Joseph Thomson	England	Explored new areas in Tanganyika, Kenya, and Uganda.
1888	Samuel Teleki	Hungary	Discovered lakes Rudolph and Stephanie.

Asia

DATE	EXPLORER	COUNTRY REPRESENTED	DESCRIPTION
1497–99	Vasco da Gama	Portugal	Discovered sea route to India by way of South Africa and Indian Ocean.
1502–07	Ludovici di Varthema	Portugal	Traveled as convert to Islam in Arabia, Persia, India, and East Indies.
1511	Mathias Albuquerque	Portugal	Conquered Malacca, East Indian spice center.
1520–21	Thomé Pires	Portugal	Sent to Peking as commercial envoy.
1537–58	Fernão Mendes Pinto	Portugal	Described travels in India, China, and Japan.
1549–51	Francis Xavier	Portugal	Introduced Christianity into Japan.
1561–63	Anthony Jenkinson	England	Visited Persia by overland route from Russia.
1578–1610	Matteo Ricci	Portugal	Established first Christian missions in China.
1603–05	Benedict de Goez	Portugal	Made first overland trip to China after Marco Polo.
1632–68	Jean B. Tavernier	France	Traveled as commercial trader in Persia, India, and East Indies.
1656	Pieter van Goyer and Jacob von Keyser	Holland	Visited Peking by overland route from Canton.
1665–77	John Chardin	France	Described extensive travels in Persia and India.
1683–93	Engelbert Kaempfer	Holland	As physician with Dutch embassy, visited and described Thailand (Siam) and Japan.
1715–47	John Bell	Russia	Traveled as physician with Russian embassies to Persia and through Siberia to China.
1716–21	Ipolito Desideri	Italy	Reached Tibetan city of Lhasa from Kashmir.
1761–64	Carsten Niebuhr	Denmark	Explored Yemen, reaching cities of San'ā and Mocha (Al Mukäh); also visited Oman, Syria, and Palestine.
1795–97	W. R. Broughton	England	Explored coasts of Hokkaido and Korea.

Date	Name	Country	Description
1928–30	Hubert Wilkins	England	Made first Antarctic explorations by air.
1928–47	Richard Byrd	United States	Established base at Little America and made first flight over South Pole (1929); second expedition remained through winter of 1934; third expedition (1939–40) made extensive aerial explorations; fourth expedition concentrated on scientific work.
1935–36	Lincoln Ellsworth	United States	Explored by air between Palmer Peninsula and Little America.
1947–48	Finn Ronne	United States	Explored Palmer Peninsula and Weddell Sea by land and air.
1955–58	Vivian Fuchs and Edmund Hillary	United Kingdom and New Zealand	Commonwealth Trans-Antarctic Expedition crossed the Continent through the South Pole from Weddell Sea to McMurdo Sound.
1957–58	I. G. Y. (International Geophysical Year)	Arg.; Austl.; Bel.; Chile; Fr.; Jap.; N.Z.; Nor.; S. Afr.; Sov. Un.; U.K.; U.S.	Established research stations; field expeditions led to new discoveries of physical features, as well as new information on ice conditions; extensive oceanographic surveys and mapping conducted.
1959–61	Australian National Antarctic Expedition	Australia	Gathered data on weather, cosmic rays, geomagnetism, seismology; field explorations and mapping; extensive aerial surveys.

Pacific Ocean and Australia

Date	Name	Country	Description
1520–21	Ferdinand Magellan	Spain	Crossed the Pacific from South America to the Philippines during first circumnavigation of the earth.
1542	Lopez de Villalobos	Spain	Sailed from Mexico to the Philippines; discovered Caroline and Palau Islands.
1565	Andrés de Urdaneta	Spain	Discovered northern sailing route from Philippines to Mexico in latitude of the Forties.
1567–95	Alvaro de Mendana	Spain	Discovered Solomon, Marshall, and Ellice Islands (1567); also Marquesas and Santa Cruz (1595).
1578	Francis Drake	England	Crossed the Pacific from California to the East Indies on first English circumnavigation.
1606	Pedro de Quiros	Spain	Discovered Tahiti and New Hebrides Islands.
1606	Luis de Torres	Spain	Sailed through Torres Strait between Australia and New Guinea.
1616	Dirk Hartog	Holland	Explored section of west coast of Australia.
1616	William Van Schouten and Jacob Lemaire	Holland	Rounded Cape Horn and crossed Pacific; discovered Bismarck Archipelago.
1642–44	Abel Tasman	Holland	Discovered Tasmania and part of New Zealand; explored the north coast of Australia.
1699	William Dampier	England	Explored west and northwest coasts of Australia.
1721	Jacob Roggeveen	Holland	Discovered Easter Island and Samoa.
1767–69	Louis de Bougainville	France	Explored South Pacific islands, including Tahiti, Samoa, and the New Hebrides.
1768–79	James Cook	England	Made three voyages into the Pacific; explored coasts of New Zealand and eastern Australia (1769–70); proved non-existence of continental land north of Antarctic Circle (1772–75); discovered Hawaiian Islands and explored northwest coast of North America (1776–79).
1785–88	Jean de La Pérouse	France	Explored North Pacific Ocean, especially coasts of Siberia and Japan; lost at sea.
1798	George Bass	England	Discovered strait separating Tasmania from Australia.
1802–03	Matthew Flinders	England	Explored south coast of Australia and sailed completely around the continent.
1816–22	John Oxley	England	Explored the interior of New South Wales, Australia.
1828–45	Charles Sturt	England	Discovered the Darling R.; descended Murray R. to its mouth; reached center of continent (1845).
1833–35	Charles Darwin	England	Explored South Pacific islands as a naturalist.
1839–41	Edward Eyre	England	Crossed southern Australia from Spencer Gulf to King George Sound.
1844–48	Ludwig Leichhardt	Germany	Explored interior of northern Queensland and Arnhem Land.
1858–62	John Stuart	England	Explored interior of South Australia and made unsuccessful attempt to cross the continent (1860); succeeded (1862).
1860–61	Robert Burke and W. J. Wills	England	Succeeded in crossing Australia from Melbourne to Gulf of Carpentaria.
1873	Peter E. Warburton	England	Crossed western Australia from Alice Springs to the coast, using camels.
1874	John Forrest	England	Crossed desert region of Australia from Perth to Adelaide.
1875–76	Ernest Giles	England	Made trip across desert from Port Augusta to Perth and return.

Date	Name	Country	Description
1839–46	Evariste Regis Huc	France	Traveled through interior of China, Mongolia and Tibet.
1851–54	Matthew C. Perry	United States	Opened Japan to foreign trade.
1862–67	Peter Kropotkin	Russia	Made geographical surveys of North Manchuria.
1867–88	Nikolai Przhevalsky	Russia	Led expeditions into Central Asia, Mongolia, and Tibet; rediscovered Lop Nor.
1868–72	Ferdinand Richthofen	Germany	Explored and described most of Chinese Empire.
1869–70	Joseph Halévy	France	Explored interior of southwestern Arabia.
1873	Jean Dupuis	France	Explored Tonkin route into China.
1885–1908	Sven Hedin	Sweden	Traveled extensively in Persia, Turkestan, China, and Tibet.
1886–1904	Francis Younghusband	England	Explored and surveyed in Kashmir, Central Asia, and Tibet.
1889–92	William W. Rockhill	United States	Explored eastern Tibet.
1899–1914	Gertrude Bell	England	Traveled widely in Palestine, Mesopotamia, and inner Arabia.
1899–1926	Aurel Stein	England	Made archaeological explorations in India, Persia, and central Asia.
1901–06	Ellsworth Huntington	United States	Explored upper Euphrates R. and Chinese Turkestan.
1914–29	Roy Chapman Andrews	United States	Explored western China and Mongolia as a naturalist, discovering many animal fossils.
1917–32	St. John Philby	England	Crossed Arabia from sea to sea; explored oases of Nejd.

Arctic Regions

Date	Name	Country	Description
1553–54	Hugh Willoughby and Richard Chancellor	England	Attempted exploration of Northeast Passage; Willoughby lost, but Chancellor reached Archangel and opened trade with Russia.
1576–78	Martin Frobisher	England	Made three voyages in search of Northwest Passage; discovered Frobisher Bay.
1580	Arthur Pet and Charles Jackman	England	Reached the Kara Sea, exploring Northeast Passage.
1585–87	John Davis	England	Reached latitude 73° N. in Baffin Bay, exploring Northwest Passage.
1594–97	Willem Barents	Holland	Discovered Spitsbergen (Svalbard) and reached Novaya Zemlya along Northeast Passage.
1607–11	Henry Hudson	England and Holland	Made several voyages in search of both Northeast and Northwest Passages to India; reached 73° N. on east Greenland coast.
1615–16	William Baffin and Robert Bylot	England	Explored Baffin Bay; reached 78° N.
1648	Simon Dezhnev	Russia	Explored northeastern Siberian coast from the Kolyma to Anadyr rivers.
1728	Vitus Bering	Russia	Discovered Bering Strait and the St. Lawrence and Diomede Islands.
1737–42	Dimitri Laptev	Russia	Explored north Siberian coast from Lena R. to Cape Baranov.
1742	T. Chelyuskin	Russia	Discovered northernmost point of Asia by land.
1773	C. J. Phipps	England	Reached 80° 48' north of Spitsbergen (Svalbard).
1818–27	William E. Parry	England	Explored Canadian arctic and Spitsbergen (Svalbard) areas; reached 82° 45' (1827).
1820–22	William Scoresby	England	Discovered Scoresby Sound in eastern Greenland; published standard description of Arctic regions.
1825–28	Frederick W. Beechey	England	Explored arctic coast of North America from Bering Strait to Point Barrow.
1829–49	John and James Ross	England	Discovered Boothia Peninsula and Gulf; James located North Magnetic Pole (1831); both participated in search for Franklin (1848–49).
1845–48	John Franklin	England	Lost two ships and 129 men in attempt to sail through Northwest Passage; reached King William Island.
1850–54	Richard Collinson and Robert McClure	England	Reached Melville Sound from Bering Strait and proved existence of northwest waterway passage.
1853–55	Elisha K. Kane	United States	Explored Smith Sound and Kane Basin; reached 80° 10' N.
1857–58	Francis L. McClintock	England	Discovered McClintock Channel and relics of Franklin expedition on King William Island.
1860–71	Charles F. Hall	United States	On third expedition, explored northern shores of Ellesmere Island and Greenland, reaching 82° 26' N.

WORLD AIR DISTANCE TABLE

	Apia	Azores Islands	Berlin	Bombay	Buenos Aires	Calcutta	Cape Town	Cape Verde Islands	Chicago	Darwin	Denver	Gibraltar	Hong Kong	Honolulu	Istanbul	Juneau	London	Los Angeles	Manila	Melbourne	Mexico City	Moscow
Apia, Western Samoa		9644	9743	8154	6931	7183	9064	10246	6557	3843	5653	10676	5591	2604	10175	5415	9789	4828	4993	3113	5449	9116
Azores Islands	9644		2185	5967	5417	6549	5854	1499	3093	10209	3991	1249	7572	7180	2975	4526	1527	4794	8250	12101	4385	3165
Berlin, Germany	9743	2185		3910	7376	4376	5977	3194	4402	8036	5077	1453	5500	7305	1078	4560	574	5782	6128	9919	6037	996
Bombay, India	8154	5967	3910		9273	1041	5134	6297	8054	4503	8383	4814	2673	8020	2991	6866	4462	8701	3148	6097	9722	3131
Buenos Aires, Argentina	6931	5417	7376	9273		10242	4270	4208	5596	9127	5928	5963	11463	7558	7568	7759	6918	6118	11042	7234	4633	8375
Calcutta, India	7183	6549	4376	1041	10242		6026	7148	7981	3744	8050	5521	1534	7037	3646	6326	4954	8148	2189	5547	9495	3447
Cape Town, South Africa	9064	5854	5977	5134	4270	6026		4509	8449	6947	9327	5076	7372	11532	5219	10330	6005	9969	7525	6412	8511	6294
Cape Verde Islands	10246	1499	3194	6297	4208	7148	4509		4066	10664	4975	1762	8539	8311	3507	5911	2731	5772	9221	10856	4857	3982
Chicago, U.S.A.	6557	3093	4402	8054	5596	7981	8449	4066		9346	920	4258	7790	4244	5476	2305	3950	1745	8128	9668	1673	4984
Darwin, Australia	3843	10209	8036	4503	9127	3744	6947	10664	9346		8557	9265	2642	5355	7390	7105	8598	7835	1979	1964	9081	7046
Denver, U.S.A.	5653	3991	5077	8383	5928	8050	9327	4975	920	8557		5122	7465	3338	6154	1831	4688	831	7661	8759	1434	5485
Gibraltar, Gibraltar	10676	1249	1453	4814	5963	5521	5076	1762	4258	9265	5122		6828	8075	1874	5273	1094	5936	7483	10798	5629	2413
Hong Kong, Asia	5591	7572	5500	2673	11463	1534	7372	8539	7790	2642	7465	6828		5537	4980	5634	5981	7240	693	4607	8776	4439
Honolulu, Hawaii, U.S.A.	2604	7180	7305	8020	7558	7037	11532	8311	4244	5355	3338	8075	5537		8104	2815	7226	2557	5296	5513	3781	7033
Istanbul (Constantinople), Turkey	10175	2975	1078	2991	7568	3646	5219	3507	5476	7390	6154	1874	4980	8104		5498	1551	6843	5659	9088	7102	1088
Juneau, Alaska, U.S.A.	5415	4526	4560	6866	7759	6326	10330	5911	2305	7105	1831	5273	5634	2815	5498		4418	1842	5869	8035	3219	4534
London, United Kingdom	9789	1527	574	4462	6918	4954	6005	2731	3950	8598	4688	1094	5981	7226	1551	4418		5439	6667	10501	5541	1549
Los Angeles, U.S.A.	4828	4794	5782	8701	6118	8148	9969	5772	1745	7835	831	5936	7240	2557	6843	1842	5439		7269	7931	1542	6068
Manila, Philippines	4993	8250	6128	3148	11042	2189	7525	9221	8128	1979	7661	7483	693	5296	5659	5869	6667	7269		3941	8829	5130
Melbourne, Australia	3113	12101	9919	6097	7234	5547	6412	10856	9668	1964	8759	10798	4607	5513	9088	8035	10501	7931	3941		8422	8963
Mexico City, Mexico	5449	4385	6037	9722	4633	9495	8511	4857	1673	9081	1434	5629	8776	3781	7102	3219	5541	1542	8829	8422		6688
Moscow, Soviet Union	9116	3165	996	3131	8375	3447	6294	3982	4984	7046	5485	2413	4439	7033	1088	4534	1549	6068	5130	8963	6688	
New Orleans, U.S.A.	6085	3524	5116	8865	4916	8803	8316	4194	833	9545	1082	4757	8480	4207	6171	2905	4627	1673	8724	9275	934	5756
New York, U.S.A.	7242	2422	3961	7794	5297	7921	7801	5271	713	9959	1631	3627	8051	4959	5009	2854	3459	2451	8493	10355	2085	4662
Nome, Alaska, U.S.A.	5438	4954	4342	5901	8848	4036	10107	6438	3314	6235	2925	5398	4547	3004	5101	1094	4381	2876	4817	7558	4309	4036
Oslo, Norway	9247	2234	515	4130	7613	4459	6494	3444	4040	8022	4653	1791	5337	6784	1518	4045	714	5325	6016	9926	5706	1016
Panamá, Panama	6514	3778	5849	9742	3381	10114	7014	3734	2325	10352	2636	4926	10084	5245	6750	4460	5278	3001	10283	9022	1495	6711
Paris, France	9990	1659	542	4359	6877	4889	5841	2666	4133	8575	4885	964	5956	7434	1401	4628	213	5601	6673	10396	5706	1541
Peking (Peiping), China	5903	6565	4567	2964	11974	2024	7763		6592	3728	6348	6009	1226	5067	4379	4522	5054	6250	1770	5667	7733	3597
Port Said, U.A.R.	10485	3391	1747	2659	7362	3506	4590	3672	6103	7159	6819	2179	4975	8738	693	6215	2154	7528	5619	8658	7671	1710
Quebec, Canada	7406	2240	3583	7371	5680	7481	7857	3355	878	9724	1752	3383	7650	5000	4644	2660	3101	2579	8124	10497	2454	4242
Reykjavik, Iceland	8678	1777	1479	5191	7099	5409	7111	3248	2954	8631	3596	2047	6031	6084	2558	3268	1171	4306	6651	10544	4622	2056
Rio de Janeiro, Brazil	8120	4428	6144	8257	1218	9376	3769	3040	5296	9960	5871	4775	10995	8190	6395	7598	5772	6296	11254	8186	4770	7179
Rome, Italy	10475	2125	734	3843	6929	4496	5249	2772	4808	8190	5561	1034	5768	8022	854	5247	887	6326	6457	9934	6353	1474
San Francisco, U.S.A.	4786	4872	5657	8392	6474	7809	10241	5921	1858	7637	949	5936	6894	2392	6700	1525	5355	347	6963	7854	1885	5868
Seattle, U.S.A.	5222	4501	5041	7741	6913	7224	10199	5714	1737	7619	1021	5462	6471	2678	6063	899	4782	959	6641	8186	2337	5199
Shanghai, China	5399	7229	5215	3133	12197	2112	8059	8443	7053	3142	6698	6646	772	4934	4959	4869	5710	6477	1152	5005	8039	4235
Singapore, Singapore	5850	8326	6166	2429	9864	1791	6016	8700	9365	2075	9063	7231	1652	6710	5373	7235	6744	8767	1479	3761	10307	5238
Tokyo, Japan	4656	7247	5538	4188	11400	3186	9071	8589	6303	3367	5795	6988	1796	3850	5556	4011	5938	5470	1863	5089	7035	4650
Valparaiso, Chile	6267	5678	7795	10037	761	10993	4998	4649	5268	8961	5452	6408	11607	6793	8172	7271	7263	5527	10930	6998	4053	8792
Washington, D.C., U.S.A.	7066	2667	4167	7988	5216	8088	7894	3486	591	9923	1494	3822	8148	4829	5216	2834	3665	2300	8560	10173	1878	4883
Wellington, New Zealand	2062	11269	11265	7677	6260	7042	7019	10363	8349	3310	7516	12060	5853	4708	10663	7475	11682	6714	5162	1595	6899	10279
Vienna, Austria	10010	2291	328	3718	7368	4259	5671	3147	4694	7974	5383	1386	5429	7626	783	4895	772	6108	6120	9792	6306	1044
Winnipeg, Canada	6283	3389	4286	7644	6297	7424	9054	4556	714	8684	798	4435	7096	3806	5361	1597	3918	1525	7414	9319	2097	4687
Zanzibar, Tanzania	9892	5323	4309	2855	6421	3859	2346	4635	8358	6409	9221	4103	5414	10869	3312	8795	4604	10021	5763	6802	9484	4270

WORLD STEAMSHIP DISTANCE TABLE

	Bombay	Buenos Aires	Cape Town	Colombo	Gibraltar	Halifax	Hamburg	Honolulu	Istanbul	Le Havre	Lisbon	Liverpool	Manila	Melbourne	New Orleans	New York	Panama Roads	Port Said	Rio de Janeiro	San Francisco	Shanghai	Singapore	Valparaiso	Wellington	Yokohama
Bombay, India		9601	5469	1042	5639	8760	7552	9631	4412	7024	6036	7156	4361	6365	10927	9413	14921	3511	8998	11247	5328	2824	11356	7961	6155
Buenos Aires, Argentina	9601		4345	9415	6074	6600	7622	8744	8488	7074	6148	7178	12128	8477	7233	6761	6311	8259	1325	10062	13087	10782	3181	6956	13921
Cape Town, South Africa	5469	4345		5070	5982	7386	7388	11948	7058	6861	5912	7001	7821	6998	9382	7814	7417	6148	3769	11154	8787	6511	6977	7531	9614
Colombo, Ceylon	1042	9415	5070		6227	9278	8090	8594	4920	7563	6577	7717	3399	5380	13919	4010	8839	10289	4370	1825	11073	7058	12847		5151
Gibraltar, Gibraltar	5639	6074	5982	6227		3051	1863	10433	2099	1336	350	1490	9641	11257	5271	3714	4816	2217	4816	8775	10553	8008	9006		11353
Halifax, Canada	8760	6600	7386	9278	3051		3480	8152	5147	3082	2792	2891	12591	11876	2517	686	2718	5257	5332	6456	12707	11047	5731	10196	11592
Hamburg, Germany	7552	7622	7388	8090	1863	3480		11283	3939	573	1543	1083	16678	13066	5935	4166	5888	4058	6354	9625	12349	9838	8900	13758	14734
Honolulu, Hawaii, U.S.A.	9631	8744	11948	8594	10433	8152	11283		12510	10757	10363	10682	5571	5691	7046	7718	5395	12604	9875	2408	4986	6772	6816	4736	3908
Istanbul, Turkey	4412	8488	7058	4920	2099	5147	3939	12510		3421	2430	3543	8245	4708	4701	5788	7115	910	6897	10884	9210	6700	11020	11540	10037
Le Havre, France	7024	7074	6861	7563	1336	3082	573	10757	3421		1017	578	10856	12540	5315	3640	5363	3521	5820	9095	11822	9312	8347	12801	12649
Lisbon, Portugal	6036	6148	5912	6577	350	2792	1543	10363	2430	1017		1148	9867	11551	5377	3403	4968	2532	4858	8737	10833	8323	7975	12459	11660
Liverpool, United Kingdom	7156	7178	7001	7717	1490	2891	1083	10682	3543	578	1148		11111	12764	5266	3539	5287	3652	5932	9024	12201	9490	8299	12778	13399
Manila, Philippines	4361	12128	7821	3399	9641	12591	16678	5571	8245	10856	9867	11111		5214	12414	13086	10764	7335	11524	7164	1338	1578	11967	5647	2023

SHOWING GREAT CIRCLE DISTANCES BETWEEN PRINCIPAL CITIES OF THE WORLD IN STATUTE MILES

City	New Orleans	New York	Nome	Oslo	Panamá	Paris	Peking (Peiping)	Port Said	Quebec	Reykjavik	Rio de Janeiro	Rome	San Francisco	Seattle	Shanghai	Singapore	Tokyo	Valparaiso	Washington, D.C.	Wellington	Vienna	Winnipeg	Zanzibar
Apia	6085	7242	5438	9247	6514	9990	5903	10485	7406	8678	8120	10475	4786	5222	5399	5850	4656	6267	7066	2062	10010	6283	9892
Azores Islands	3524	2422	4954	2234	3778	1659	6565	3391	2240	1777	4428	2125	4872	4501	7229	8326	7247	5678	2667	11269	2291	3389	5323
Berlin	5116	3961	4342	515	5849	542	4567	1747	3583	1479	6114	734	5657	5041	5215	6166	5538	7795	4167	11265	328	4286	4309
Bombay	8865	7794	5901	4130	9742	4359	2964	2659	7371	5191	8257	3843	8392	7741	3133	2429	4188	10037	8095	7672	3718	7411	2855
Buenos Aires	4916	5297	8848	7613	3381	6877	11974	7362	5680	7099	1218	6929	6474	6913	12197	9864	11400	761	5216	6260	7368	6297	6421
Calcutta	8803	7921	5271	4459	10114	4889	2024	3506	7481	5409	9376	4496	7809	7224	2112	1791	3186	10993	8088	7042	4259	7424	3859
Cape Town	8316	7801	10107	6494	7014	5841	8045	4590	7857	7111	3769	5249	10241	10199	8059	6016	9071	4998	7894	7019	5671	9054	2346
Cape Verde Islands	4194	3355	6438	3444	3734	2666	7763	3672	3355	3248	3040	2772	5921	5714	8443	8700	8589	4649	3486	10363	3147	4556	4635
Chicago	833	713	3314	4040	2325	4133	6592	6103	878	2954	5296	4808	1858	1737	7053	9365	6303	5268	591	8349	4694	714	8358
Darwin	9545	9959	6235	8022	10352	8575	3728	7159	9724	8631	9960	8190	7637	7619	3142	2075	3367	8961	9923	3310	7974	8684	6409
Denver	1082	1631	2925	4653	2636	4885	6348	6819	1752	3596	5871	5561	949	1021	6698	9063	5795	5452	1494	7516	5383	798	9221
Gibraltar	4757	3627	5398	1791	4926	964	6009	2179	3383	2047	4775	1034	5936	5462	6646	7231	6988	6408	3822	12060	1386	4435	4103
Hong Kong	8480	8051	4547	5337	10084	5956	1226	4975	7650	6031	10995	5768	6894	6471	772	1652	1796	11607	8148	5853	5429	7096	5414
Honolulu	4207	4959	3004	6784	5245	7434	5067	8738	5000	6084	8190	8022	2392	2678	4934	6710	3850	6793	4829	4708	7626	3806	10869
Istanbul	6171	5009	5101	1518	6750	1401	4379	693	4644	2558	6395	854	6700	6063	4959	5373	5556	8172	5216	10663	783	5361	3312
Juneau	2905	2854	1094	4045	4460	4628	4522	6215	2660	3268	7598	5247	1525	899	4869	7235	4011	7271	2834	7475	4895	1597	8795
London	4627	3459	4381	714	5278	213	5054	2154	3101	1171	5772	887	5355	4782	5710	6744	5938	7263	3665	11682	772	3918	4604
Los Angeles	1673	2451	2876	5325	3001	5601	6250	7528	2579	4306	6296	6326	347	959	6477	8767	5470	5527	2300	6714	6108	1525	10021
Manila	8724	8493	4817	6016	10283	6673	1770	5619	8124	6651	11254	6457	6963	6641	1152	1479	1863	10930	8560	5162	6120	7414	5763
Melbourne	9275	10355	7558	9926	9022	10396	5667	8658	10497	10544	8186	9934	7854	8186	5005	3761	5089	6998	10173	1595	9792	9319	6802
Mexico City	934	2085	4309	5706	1495	5706	7733	7671	2454	4622	4770	6353	1885	2337	8039	10307	7035	4053	1878	6899	6306	2097	9484
Moscow	5756	4662	4036	1016	6711	1541	3597	1710	4242	2056	7179	1474	5868	5199	4235	5238	4650	8792	4883	10279	1044	4687	4270
New Orleans		1171	3937	4795	1603	4788	7314	6756	1534	3711	4796	5439	1926	2101	7720	10082	6858	4514	966	7794	5385	1418	8754
New York	1171		3769	3672	2231	3622	6823	5590	439	2576	4820	4273	2571	2408	7357	9630	6735	5094	205	8946	4224	1281	7698
Nome	3937	3769		3836		4574	3428	5745	3489	3366	8586	5082	2547	1976	3784	6148	2983	8360	3792	7383	4657	2599	8209
Oslo	4795	3672	3836		5691	832	4360	2211	3263	1083	6482	1243	5181	4591	5020	6246	5221	7914	3870	10974	850	3854	4803
Panamá	1603	2231		5691		5382	8906	7146	2659	4706	3294	5903	3322	3651	9324	11687	8423	2943	2080	7433	6026	2998	8245
Paris	4788	3622	4574	832	5382		5101	1975	3235	1380	5703	682	5441	4993	5752	6671	6033	7251	3828	11791	644	4118	4396
Peking (Peiping)	7314	6823	3428	4360	8906	5101		4584	6423	4903	10768	5047	5902	5396	662	2774	1307	11774	6922	6698	4639	5907	5803
Port Said	6756	5590	5745	2211	7146	1975	4584		5250	3227	6244	1317	7394	6759	5132	5088	5842	8088	5796	10249	1429	6032	2729
Quebec	1534	439	3489	3263	2659	3235	6423	5250		2189	5125	3943	2642	2353	6981	9097	6417	5504	610	9228	3858	1199	7443
Reykjavík	3711	2576	3366	1083	4706	1380	4903	3227	2189		6118	2044	4199	3614	5559	7160	5472	7225	2800	10724	1805	2804	5757
Rio de Janeiro	4796	4820	8586	6482	3294	5703	10768	6244	5125	6118		5684	6619	6891	11340	9774	11535	1855	4797	7349	6136	6010	5589
Rome	5439	4273	5082	1243	5903	682	5047	1317	3943	2044	5684		6240	5659	5677	6232	6124	7420	4435	11524	463	4803	3712
San Francisco	1926	2571	2547	5181	3322	5441	5902	7394	2642	4199	6619	6240		678	6132	8479	5131	5876	2442	6739	5988	1504	9958
Seattle	2101	2408	1976	4591	3651	4993	5396	6759	2353	3614	6891	5659	678		5703	8057	4777	6230	2329	7242	5376	1150	9359
Shanghai	7720	7357	3784	5020	9324	5752	662	5132	6981	5559	11340	5677	6132	5703		2377	1094	11650	7242	6054	5270	6350	5971
Tokyo	6858	6735	2983	5221	8423	6033	1307	5842	6417	5472	11535	6124	5131	4777	1094	3304		10635	6769	5760	5679	5575	7040
Valparaiso	4514	5094	8360	7914	2943	7251	11774	8088	5504	7225	1855	7420	5876	6230	11650	10226	10635		4977	5785	7783	5931	7184
Washington, D.C.	966	205	3792	3870	2080	3828	6922	5796	610	2800	4797	4435	2442	2329	7242	9834	6769	4977		8745	4429	1243	7884
Wellington	7794	8946	7383	10974	7433	11791	6698	10249	9228	10724	7349	11524	6739	7242	6054	5292	5760	5785	8745		11278	8230	8122
Vienna	5385	4224	4657	850	6026	644	4639	1429	3858	1805	6136	463	5988	5376	5270	6036	5679	7783	4429	11278		4604	3983
Winnipeg	1418	1281	2599	3854	2998	4118	5907	6032	1199	2804	6010	4803	1504	1150	6350	8685	5575	5931	1243	8230	4604		8416
Zanzibar	8754	7698	8209	4803	8245	4396	5803	2729	7443	5757	5589	3712	9958	9359	5971	4480	7040	7184	7884	8122	3983	8416	

SHOWING STEAMSHIP DISTANCES BETWEEN PRINCIPAL PORTS OF THE WORLD IN STATUTE MILES

Port	Bombay	Buenos Aires	Cape Town	Colombo	Gibraltar	Halifax	Hamburg	Honolulu	Istanbul	Le Havre	Lisbon	Liverpool	Manila	Melbourne	New Orleans	New York	Panama Roads	Port Said	Rio de Janeiro	San Francisco	Shanghai	Singapore	Valparaiso	Wellington	Yokohama
Melbourne, Australia	6365	8477	6998	5380	11257	11876	13066	5691	9928	12540	11551	12764	5214		10780	11452	9130	9040	9416	8011	6012	4396	7222	1737	5606
New Orleans, U.S.A.	10927	7233	9382	11489	5271	2517	5935	7046	7384	5315	5377	5266	12414	10780		1970	1650	7498	5965	5287	11495	13207	4663	9133	10489
New York, U.S.A.	9413	6761	7814	9941	3714	686	4166	7718	5788	3640	3403	3539	13086	11452	1970		2323	5895	5493	6059	12176	11693	5335	9814	11169
Panama Roads, Canal Zone	14921	6311	7417	13919	5038	2718	5888	5395	7115	5363	4968	5287	10764	9130	1650	2323		7217	5058	3737	9853	12097	3013	7491	8846
Port Said, U.A.R.	3511	8259	6148	4010	2217	5257	4058	12604	910	3521	2532	3652	7335	9040	7498	5895	7217		7006	10986	8301	5791	10225	10630	
Rio de Janeiro, Brazil	8998	1325	3769	8839	4816	5332	6354	9875	6897	5820	4858	5932	11524	9416	5965	5493	5058	7006		8794	12490	10179	4191	7915	13317
San Francisco, U.S.A.	11247	10062	11154	10289	8775	6456	9625	2408	10884	9095	8737	9024	7164	8011	5287	6059	3737	10986	8794		6339	8467	5919	6800	5223
Shanghai, China	5328	13087	8787	4370	10553	12707	12349	4986	9210	11822	10833	12201	1338	6012	12176	11693	9853	8301	12490	6339		2545	11806	6184	1199
Singapore, Singapore	2824	10782	6511	1825	8008	11047	9838	6772	6700	9312	8323	9490	1578	4396	13207	11693	12097	5791	10179	8467	2545		12534	5992	3345
Valparaiso, Chile	11356	3181	6977	11073	9006	5731	8900	6816	11020	8347	7975	8299	11967	7222	4663	5335	3013	10225	4191	5919	11806	12534		5799	10740
Wellington, New Zealand	7961	6956	7531	7058	12847	10196	13758	4736	11540	12801	12459	12778	5647	1737	9133	9814	7491	10630	7915	6800	6184	5992	5799		5736
Yokohama, Japan	6155	13921	9614	5151	11353	11592	14734	3908	10037	12649	11660	13399	2023	5606	10489	11169	8846		13317	5223	1199	3345	10740	5736	

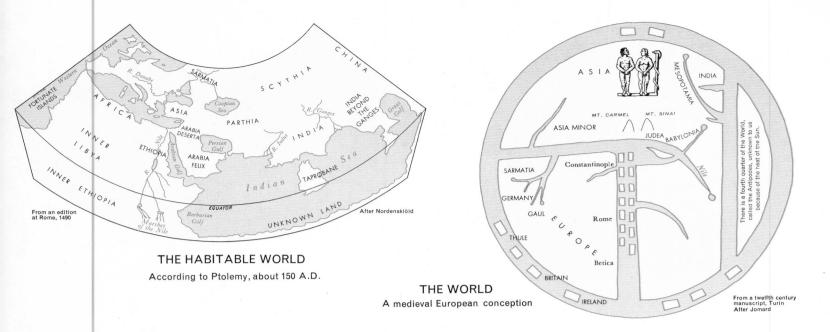

THE HABITABLE WORLD

According to Ptolemy, about 150 A.D.

From an edition at Rome, 1490

After Nordenskiöld

THE WORLD

A medieval European conception

There is a fourth quarter of the World, called the Antipodes, unknown to us because of the heat of the Sun.

From a twelfth century manuscript, Turin
After Jomard

WORLD HISTORY IN MAPS

This world history section of twenty-seven pages is a collection of modern maps illustrating past periods of time, not a collection of old maps made in times past. The maps on this page, however, are drawings of old maps, reproduced here only to show how men at three points in history conceived the world in which they lived.

Centuries of Greek and Near Eastern thought are summarized in the map made by Ptolemy at Alexandria about 150 A.D. He knew that the Earth is a sphere, but he believed about only one-third of the Northern Hemisphere was habitable. His map represents this portion of the globe. He understood the principles of map projection, that is of representing a curved surface on a flat page, and he located places according to longitude and latitude, defining longitude by distance east of the Fortunate Islands (now the Canaries) and latitude by the length of the longest day of the year. His map was defective not in conception but by lack of information.

The sample of a medieval map represents a common form of map in use at this period of time—a diagram rather than a true map. The outer circle represents the ocean, the vertical radius containing oblong islands in the Mediterranean Sea. The East is at the top and the Holy Land is in the center. A person using this map could get a rough idea of direction, but he would have no idea of distance, size, or proportion.

The Behaim globe, below, represents man's conception of the world at the time of Columbus.

There are forty-eight maps in this section, including insets. Asia is represented at successive periods of its history, and we have given attention to Africa and Latin America, but since this book is mainly for American use, the treatment of North American and European history is given better coverage. The maps both illustrate general ideas and supply particular information. Modern maps differ from old maps in being more exact in projection and in scale.

THE WORLD

According to Behaim, 1492

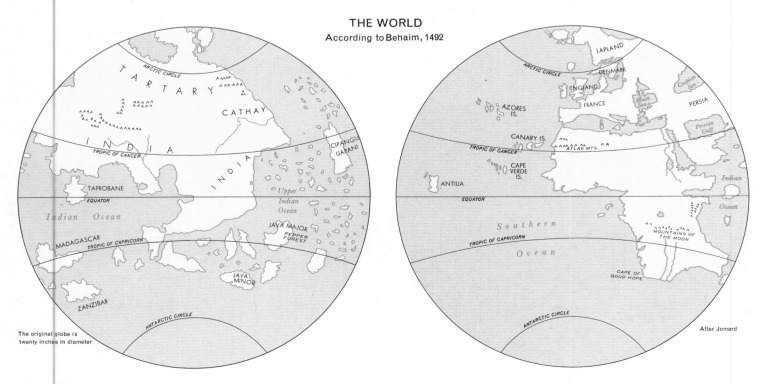

The original globe is twenty inches in diameter

After Jomard

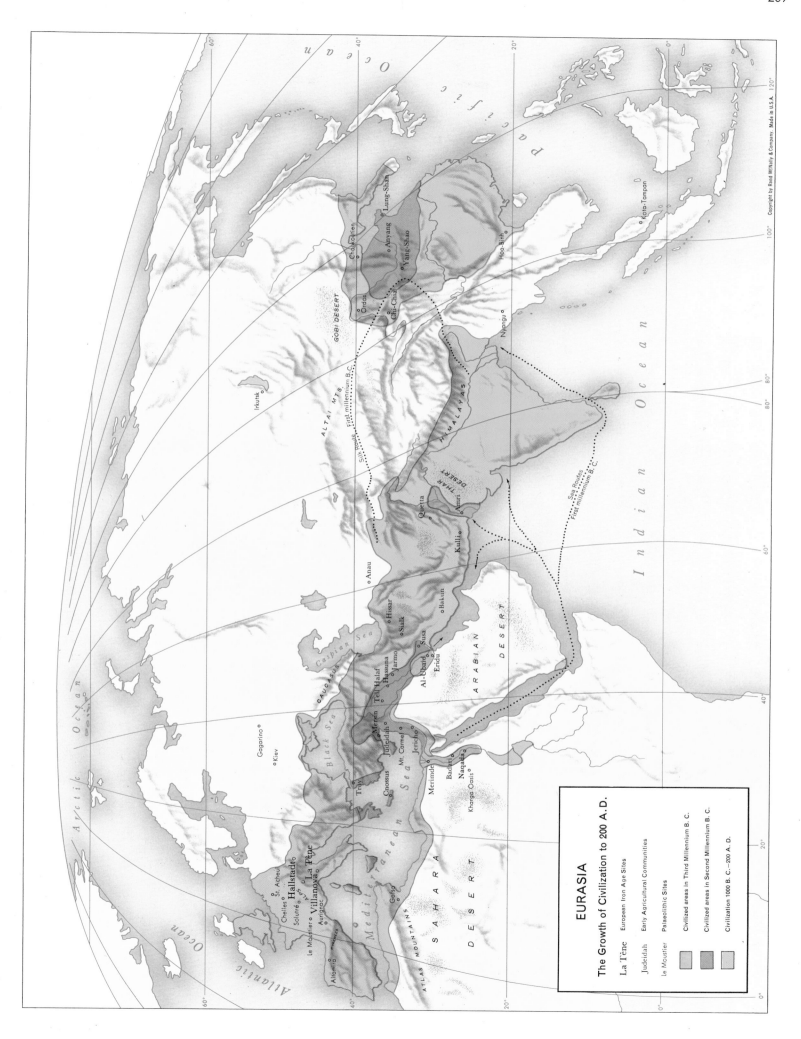

Copyright by Rand McNally & Company Made in U.S.A.

Pacific Ocean

Indian Ocean

Atlantic Ocean

Arctic Ocean

Lung-Shan
Anyang
Yang-Shao
Chou-Kou-tien
Ordos
Chi-Chia
Hoa-Binh

Kota-Tampan

GOBI DESERT

Njangu

ALTAI MTS.

First millennium B.C.

Silk Route

Irkutsk

HIMALAYAS

THAR
DESERT

Quetta
Amri
Kullio

Sea Routes
First millennium B.C.

Anau

ARABIAN

DESERT

Hissar
Sialk
Bakun

Caspian Sea

Merzin
Susa
Jarmo
Eridu
Hassuna
Al-'Ubaid
Tell Halaf

Gagarino
Kiev

CAUCASUS

Black Sea

Judeidah
Mt. Carmel
Jericho

Troy
Knossos
Merimde
Badari
Naqada
Kharga Oasis

Mediterranean Sea

SAHARA   DESERT

Chelles
St. Acheul
Solutré
Le Moustier
Altamira
Aurignac

Hallstadt
La Tène
Villanova

ATLAS MOUNTAINS

Gafsa

EURASIA
The Growth of Civilization to 200 A.D.

La Tène   European Iron Age Sites

Judeidah   Early Agricultural Communities

Le Moustier   Palaeolithic Sites

☐ Civilized areas in Third Millennium B. C.

☐ Civilized areas in Second Millennium B. C.

☐ Civilization 1000 B. C.—200 A. D.

210

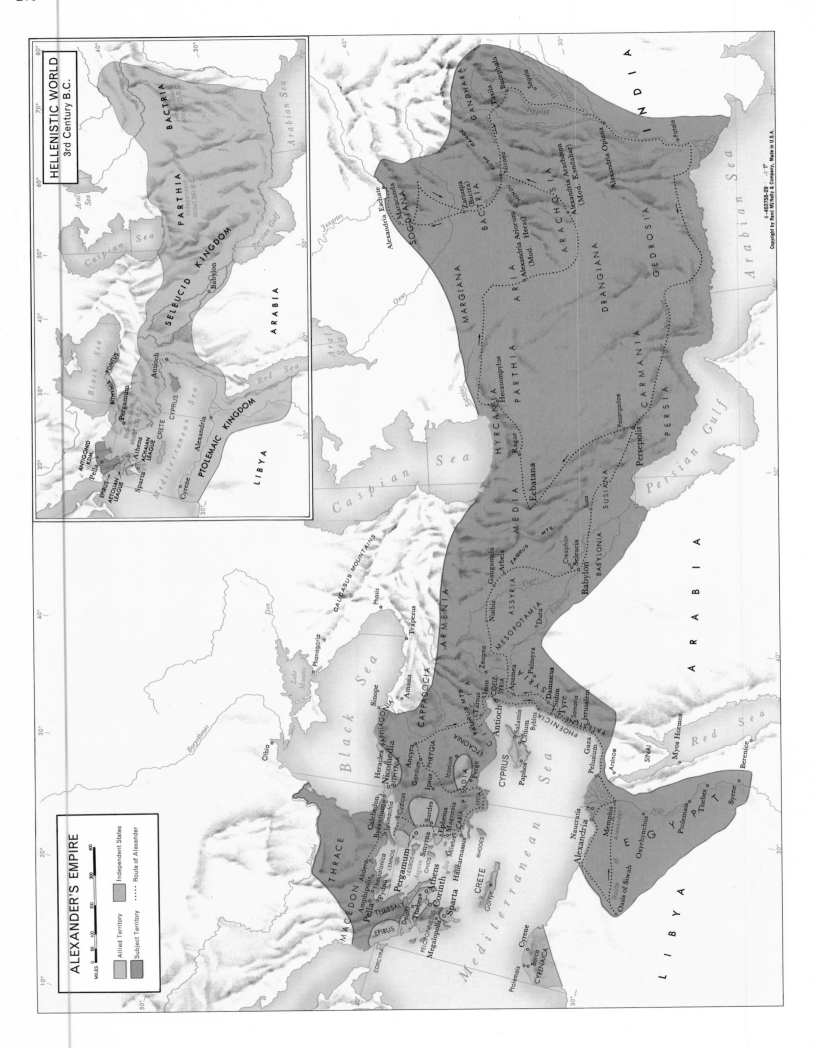

ALEXANDER'S EMPIRE

MILES
0 50 100 200 300 400

Subject Territory

Allied Territory

Independent States

Route of Alexander

HELLENISTIC WORLD
3rd Century B.C.

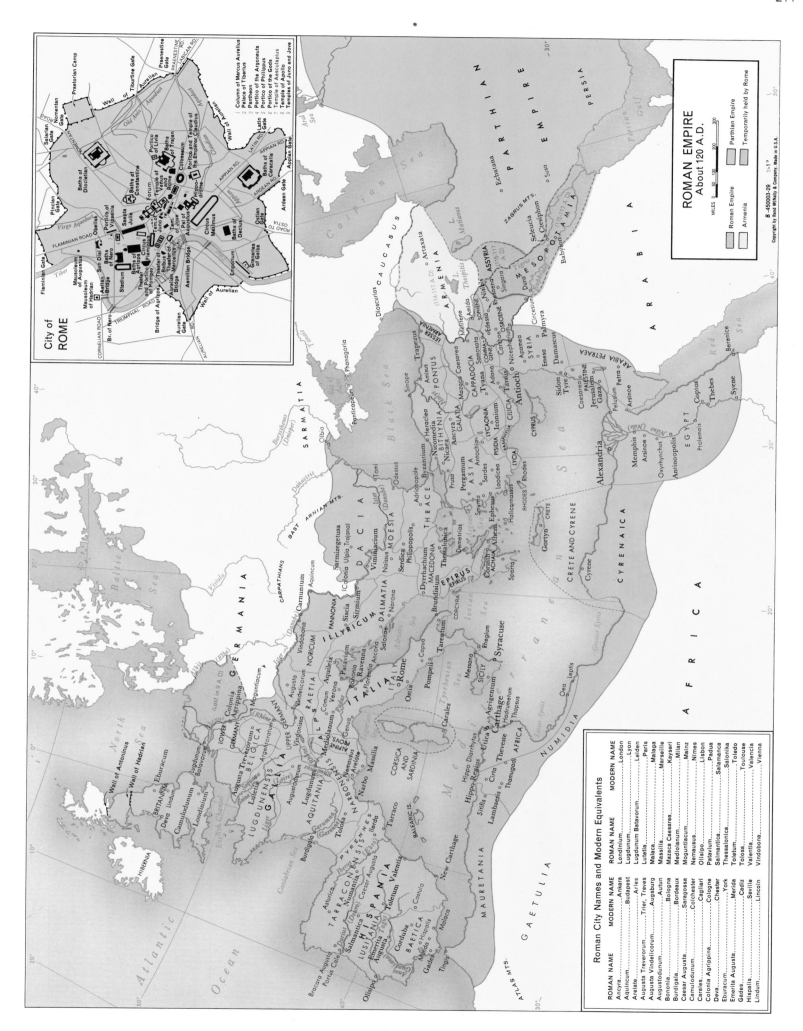

212

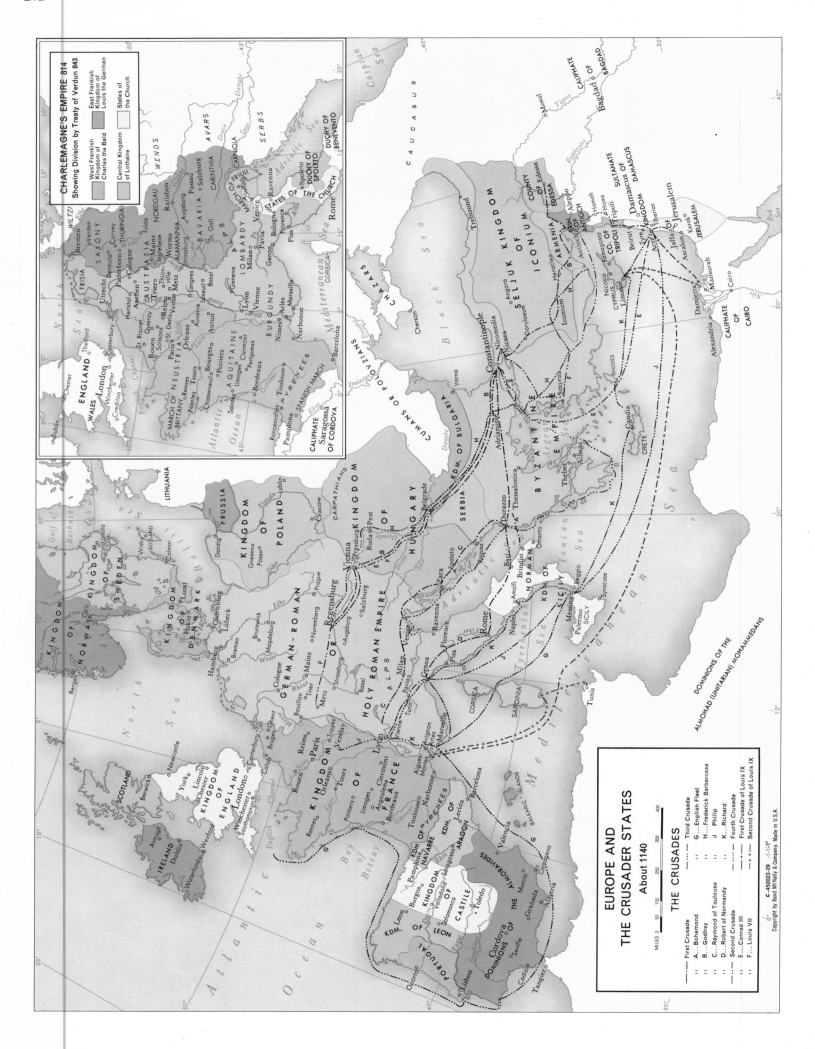

CHARLEMAGNE'S EMPIRE 814
Showing Division by Treaty of Verdun 843

West Frankish Kingdom of Charles the Bald

East Frankish Kingdom of Louis the German

Central Kingdom of Lothaire

States of the Church

EUROPE AND
THE CRUSADER STATES
About 1140

THE CRUSADES

MILES 0 50 100   200   300   400

First Crusade
  A...Bohemond
  B...Godfrey
  C...Raymond of Toulouse
  D...Robert of Normandy
Second Crusade
  E...Conrad III
  F...Louis VII

Third Crusade
  G...English Fleet
  H...Frederick Barbarossa
  J...Philip
  K...Richard
Fourth Crusade
First Crusade of Louis IX
Second Crusade of Louis IX

C-450023-29   -1-11ª
Copyright by Rand McNally & Company. Made in U.S.A.

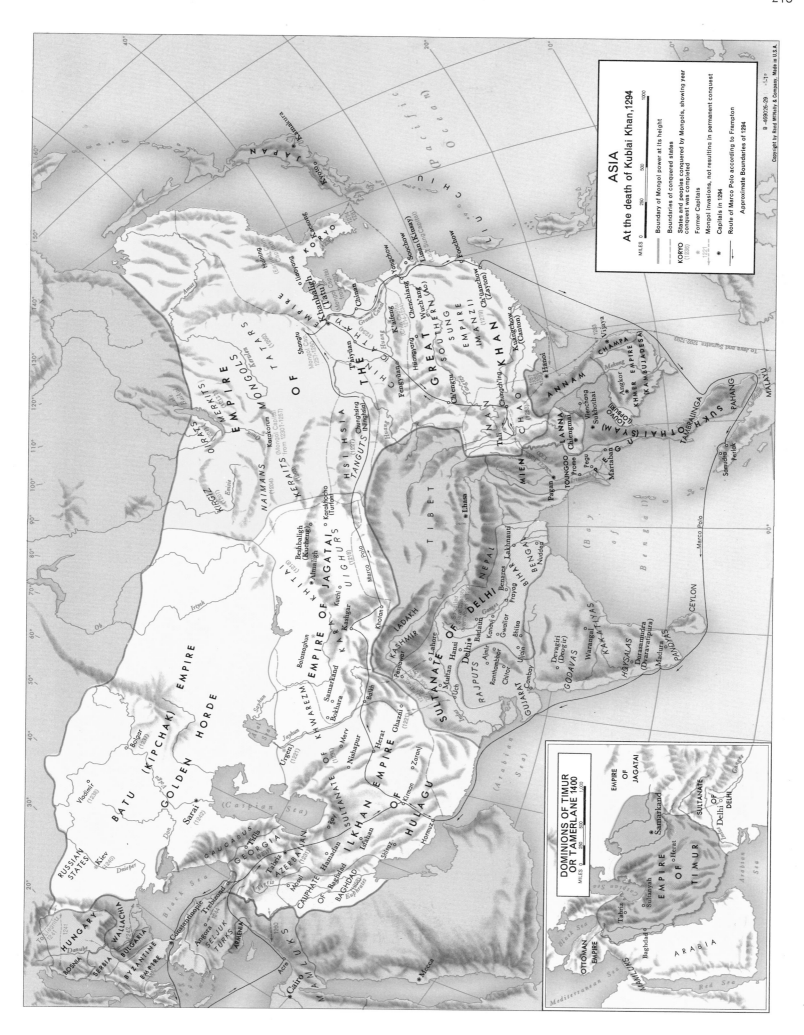

ASIA

At the death of Kublai Khan, 1294

MILES 0   250   500   1000

Boundary of Mongol power at its height

Boundaries of conquered states

States and peoples conquered by Mongols, showing year conquest was completed

KORYO   Former Capitals
(1330)

★   Capitals in 1294

→   Mongol invasions, not resulting in permanent conquest

       Route of Marco Polo according to Frampton

       Approximate Boundaries of 1294

Copyright by Rand McNally & Company, Made in U.S.A.

B -469026-29   -L1ᵇ

DOMINIONS OF TIMUR
OR TAMERLANE 1400

MILES 0   250   500   1000

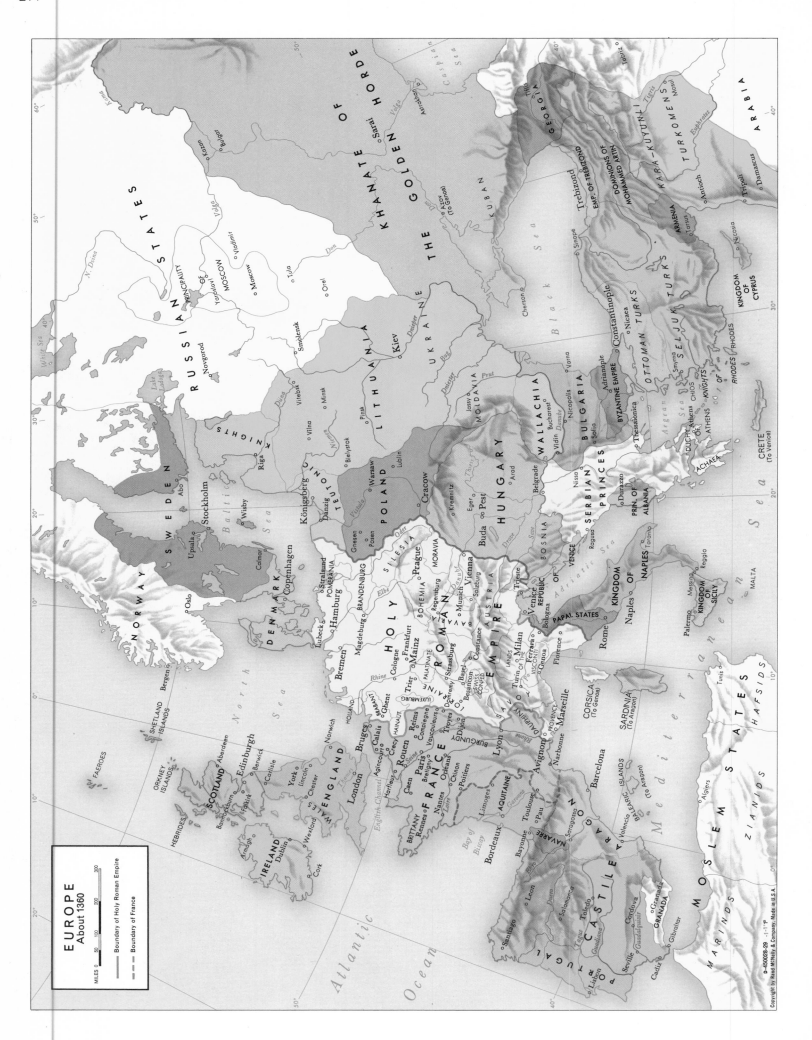

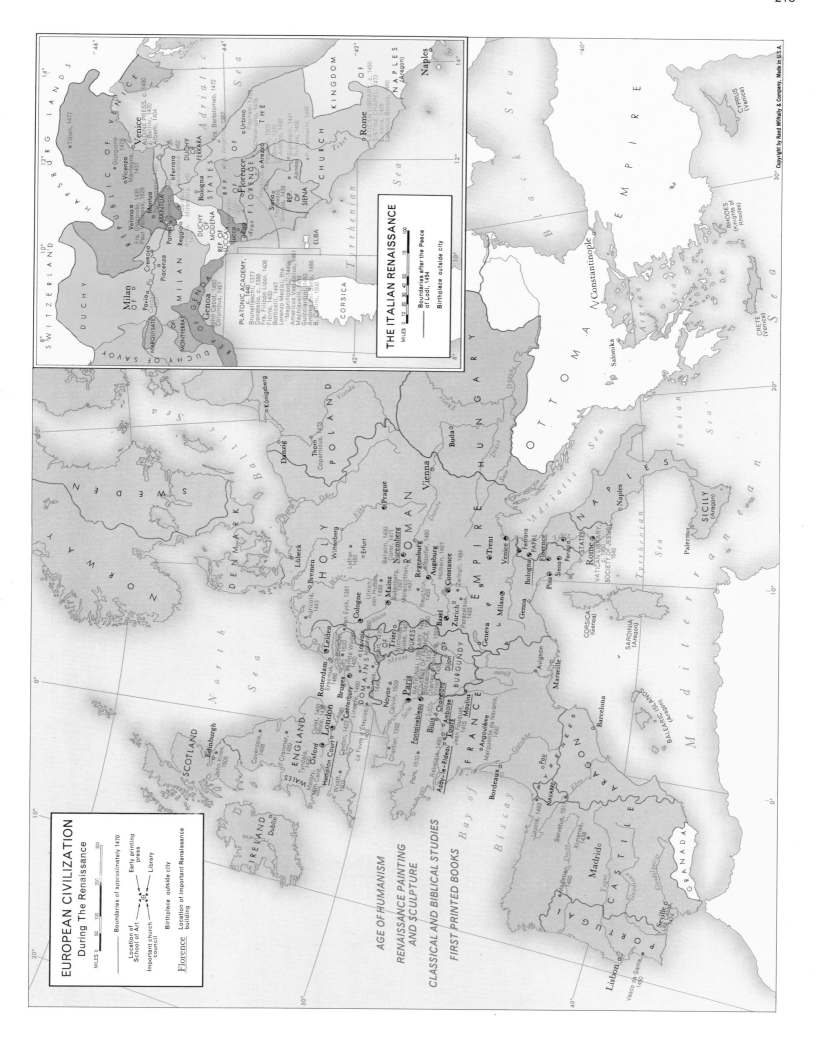

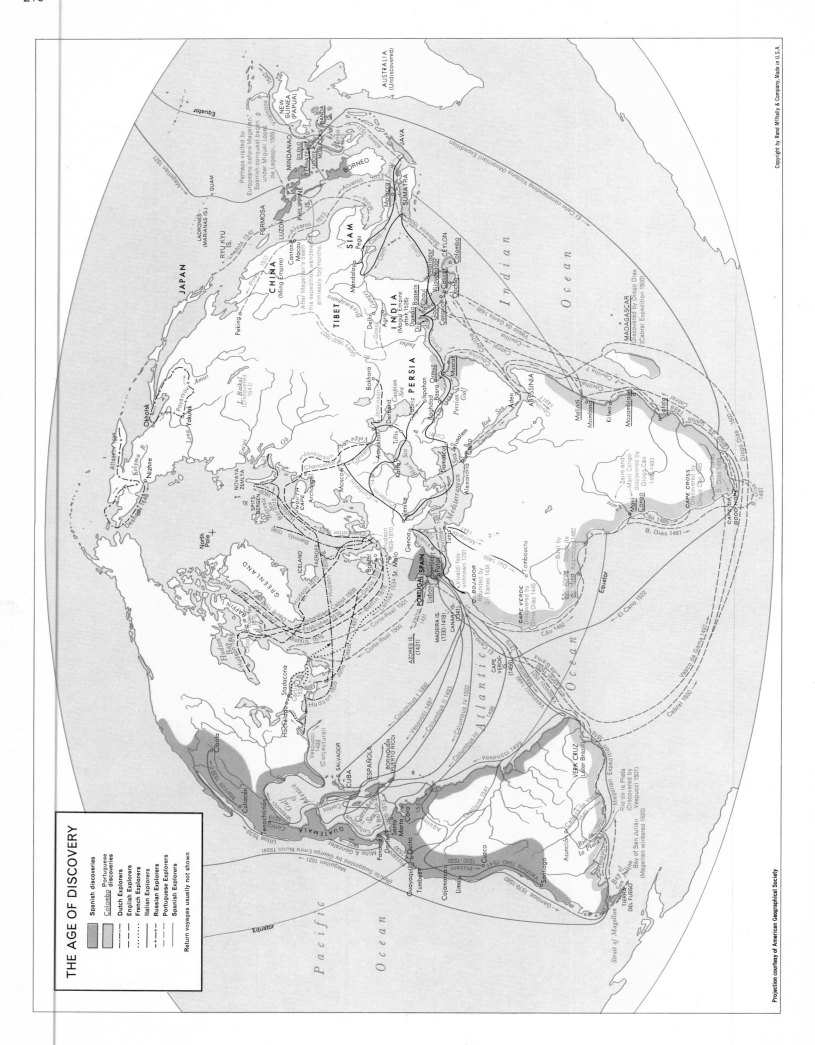

217

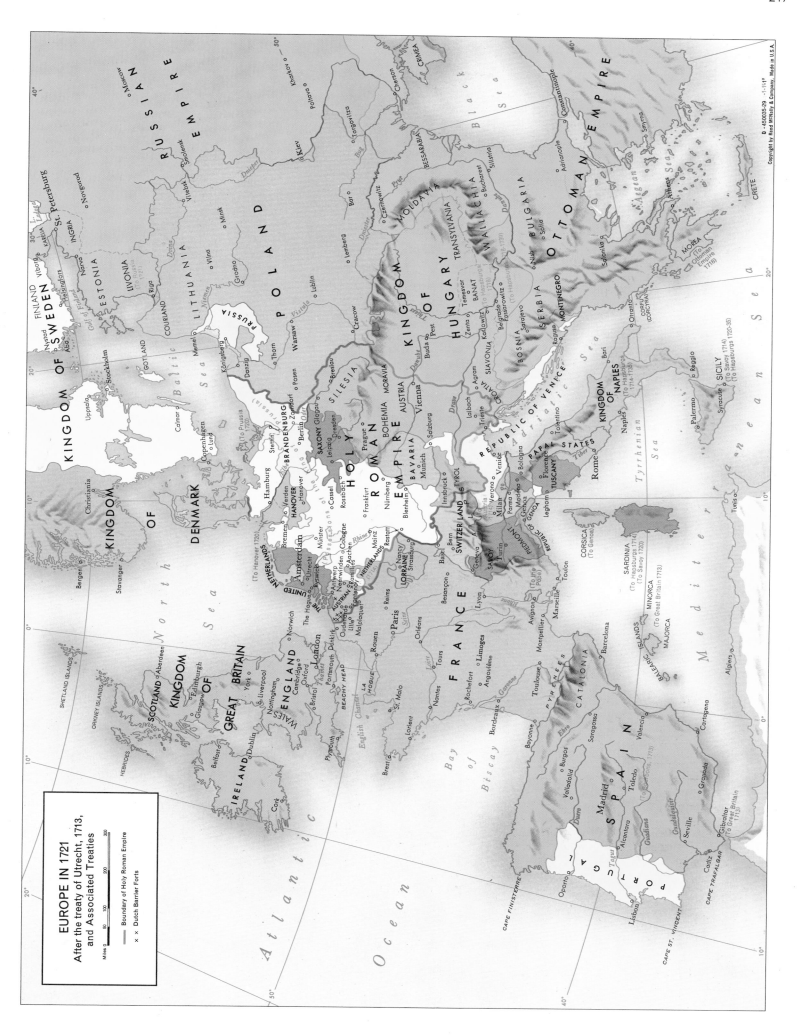

EUROPE IN 1721
After the treaty of Utrecht, 1713,
and Associated Treaties

Boundary of Holy Roman Empire
x x Dutch Barrier Forts

Miles 0 50 100 200 300

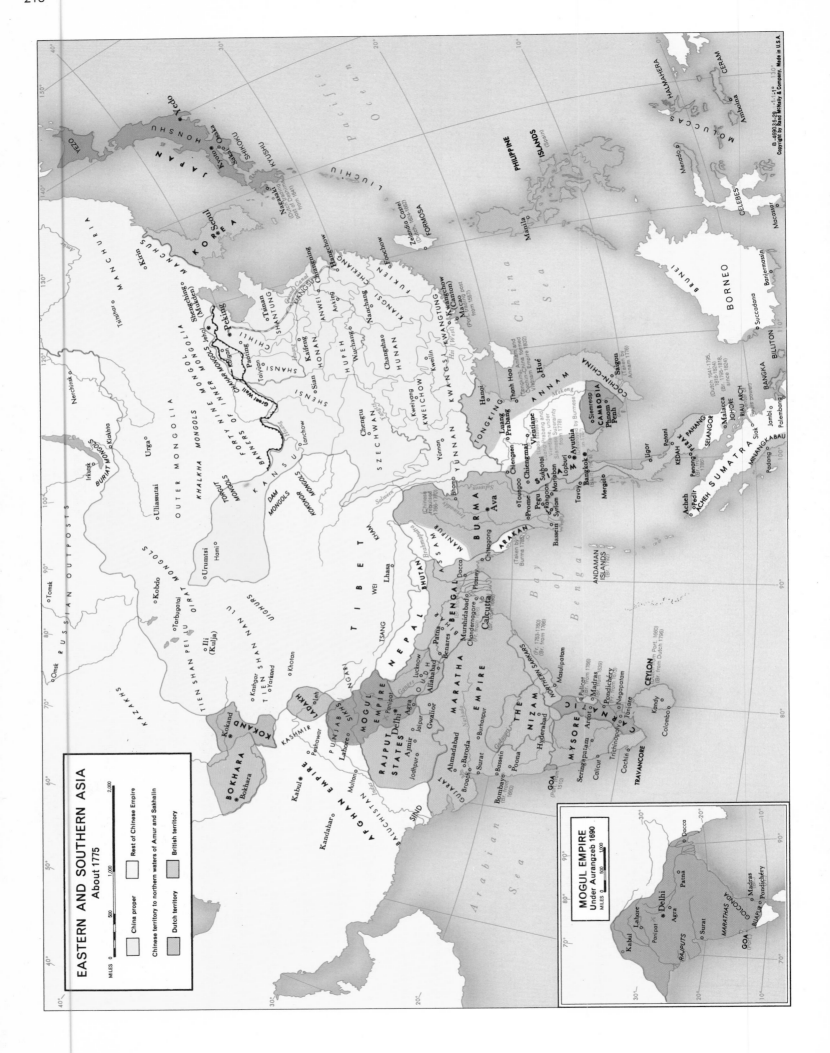

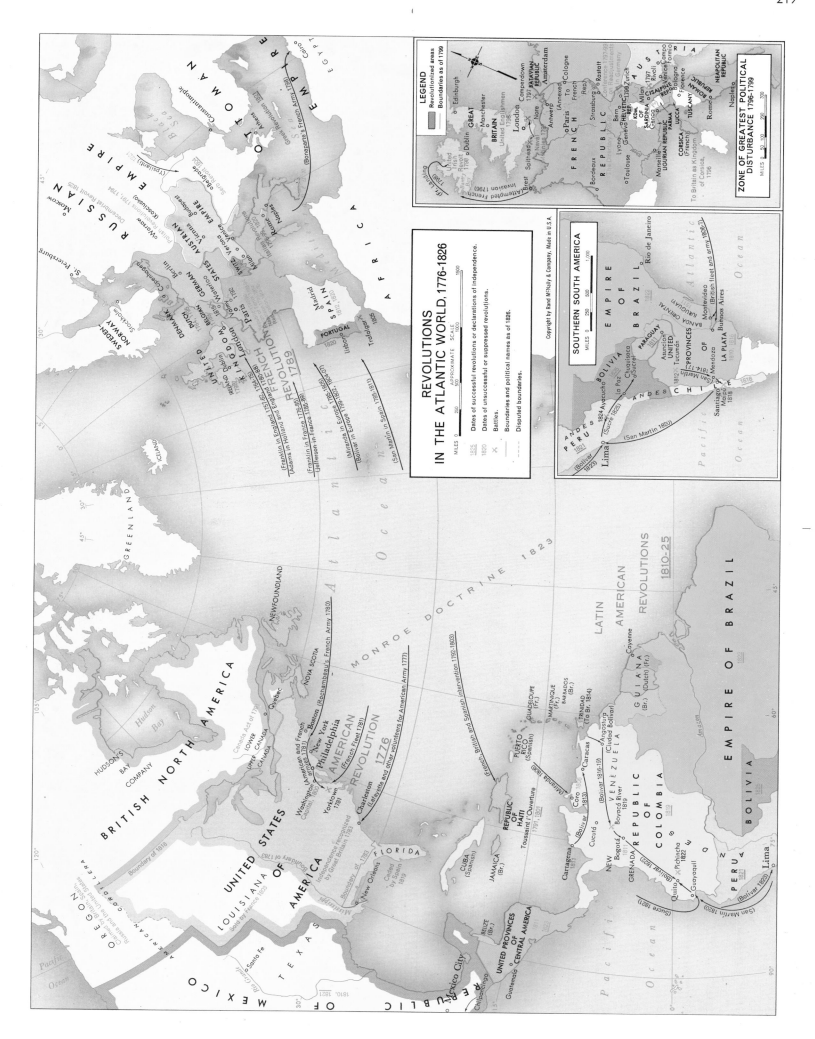

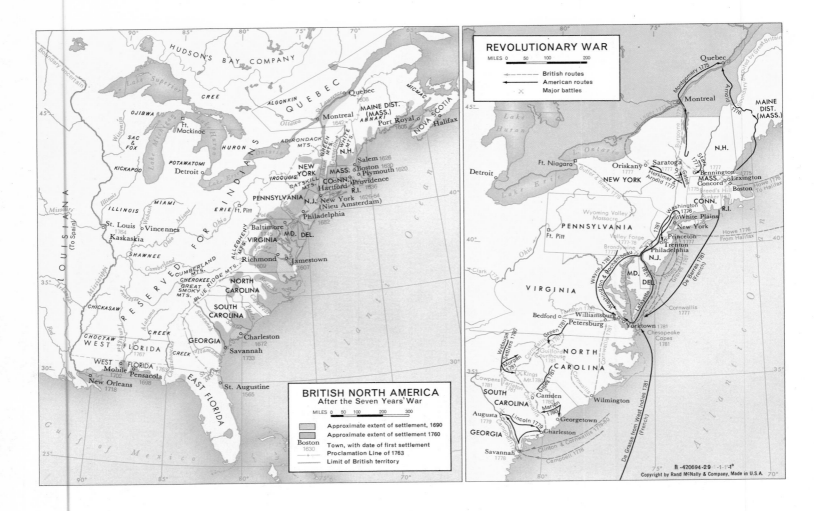

BRITISH NORTH AMERICA
After the Seven Years' War

MILES 0 50 100 200 300

Approximate extent of settlement, 1690
Approximate extent of settlement 1760
Boston 1630   Town, with date of first settlement
Proclamation Line of 1763
Limit of British territory

REVOLUTIONARY WAR

MILES 0 50 100 200

British routes
American routes
×   Major battles

B -420694-29 -1-1'4°
Copyright by Rand McNally & Company, Made in U.S.A.

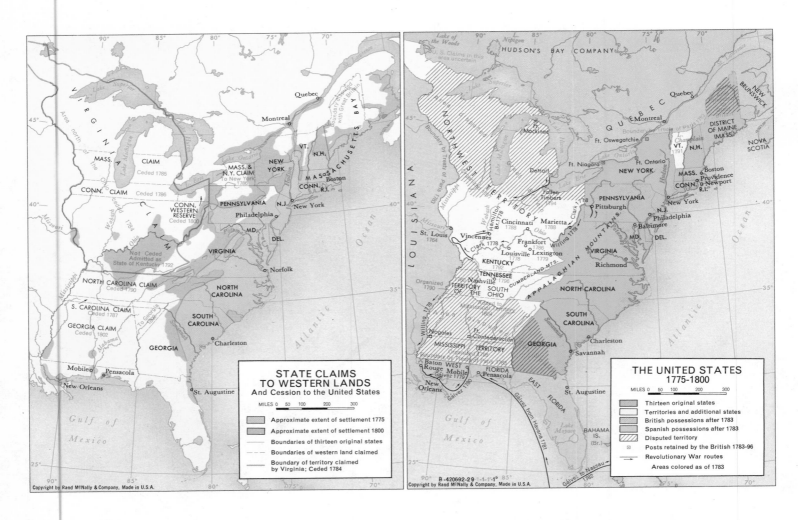

STATE CLAIMS
TO WESTERN LANDS
And Cession to the United States

MILES 0 50 100 200 300

Approximate extent of settlement 1775
Approximate extent of settlement 1800
Boundaries of thirteen original states
Boundaries of western land claimed
Boundary of territory claimed
by Virginia; Ceded 1784

Copyright by Rand McNally & Company, Made in U.S.A.

THE UNITED STATES
1775-1800

MILES 0 50 100 200 300

Thirteen original states
Territories and additional states
British possessions after 1783
Spanish possessions after 1783
Disputed territory
Posts retained by the British 1783-96
Revolutionary War routes

Areas colored as of 1783

B -420692-29 -1-1'-1°
Copyright by Rand McNally & Company, Made in U.S.A.

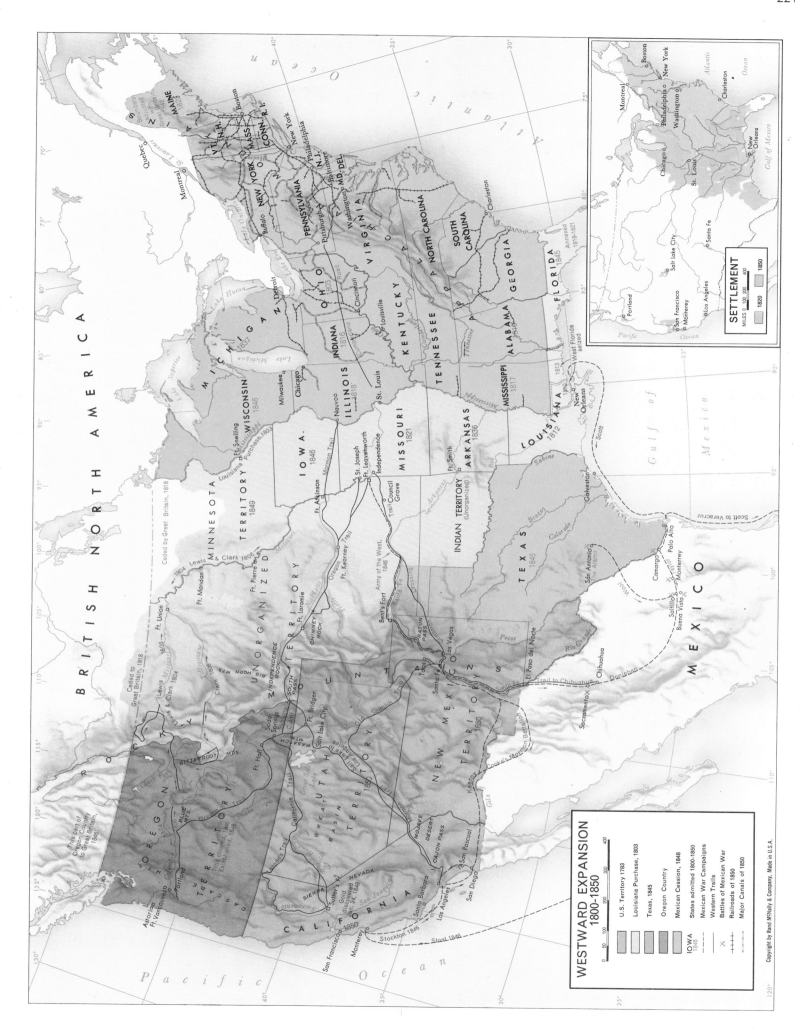

WESTWARD EXPANSION
1800-1850

U.S. Territory 1783
Louisiana Purchase, 1803
Texas, 1845
Oregon Country
Mexican Cession, 1848
States admitted 1800-1850
Mexican War Campaigns
Western Trails
Battles of Mexican War
Railroads of 1850
Major Canals of 1850

IOWA
1846

Copyright by Rand McNally & Company. Made in U.S.A.

SETTLEMENT
MILES 0 100 200 400
1820 1850

222

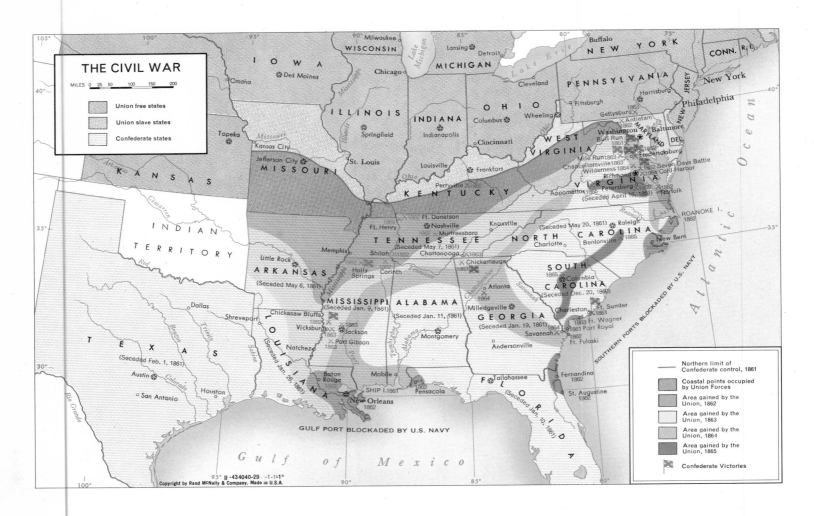

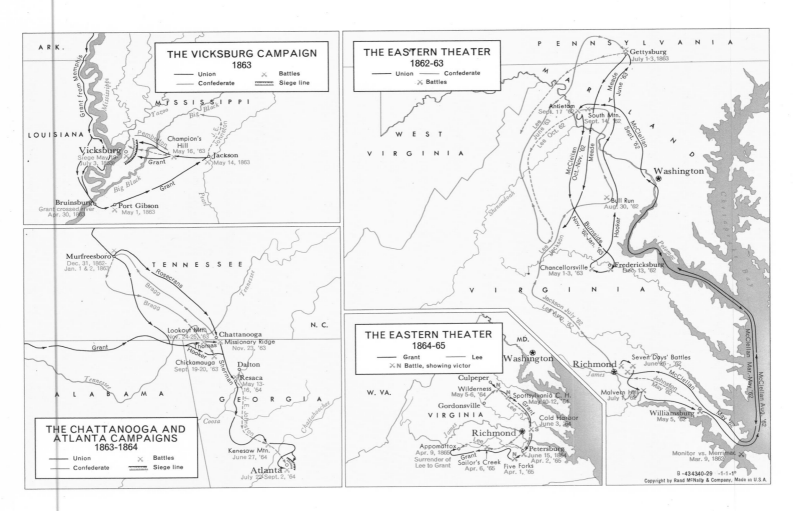

BRITISH NORTH AMERICA

UNITED STATES OF AMERICA

Disputed with
U.S. 1783-1795

Atlantic

Tropic of Cancer

CAPTAINCY-GENERAL OF LOUISIANA

St. Louis

INTENDANCY OF NUEVA CALIFORNIA
San Francisco 1776
Monterey 1770
Santa Barbara 1782
San Luis Obispo 1772
Los Angeles 1781
San Juan Capestrano
San Diego 1769
VICEROYALTY OF VIEJA CALIFORNIA
La Paz 1535

INTENDANCY OF NUEVO MEXICO
Santa Fé 1609
El Paso
INTENDANCY del Norte
PRESIDENCY OF SONORA
Chihuahua
INTENDANCY OF DURANGO
INTENDANCY OF GUADALAJARA
Culiacán 1531
San Antonio 1718
Laredo 1764
INTENDANCY OF SAN LUIS POTOSI
INTENDANCY OF ZACATECAS
Saltillo 1575
Querétaro 1550
Guadalajara
INTENDANCY OF MEXICO
Vera Cruz 1519
Vera Cruz
Mexico City 1325
INTENDANCY OF VALLADOLID
INTENDANCY OF PUEBLA
INTENDANCY OF OAXACA
CHIAPAS

INTENDANCY OF YUCATAN
Belice
CAPTAINCY GENERAL (AUDIENCIA) OF GUATEMALA
Guatemala
San Salvador 1525
León
Granada 1524
San José 1736
Cartago 1564
Portobelo 1584
Panama 1519

Gulf of Mexico

New Orleans 1718
Pensacola 1698
WEST FLORIDA
EAST FLORIDA
St. Augustine 1565

Habana 1519
CAPTAINCY-GENERAL OF CUBA
Santiago 1514
JAMAICA Br. 1655
Port-au-Prince 1749
Santo Domingo 1496
San Juan 1511
PUERTO RICO

CAPTAINCY-GENERAL OF SANTO DOMINGO
Ceded to France 1795

Caribbean Sea

Santa Marta 1525
Cartagena 1533
La Guaira 1588
Caracas
TRINIDAD
Ceded to Great Britain, 1802

CAPTAINCY-GENERAL OF CARACAS
VICEROYALTY OF NEW GRANADA
Established 1717, Refounded 1739
AUDIENCIA OF Bogotá
SANTA FÉ

Stabroek (Georgetown) Approx. 1740
Paramaribo 1640
DUTCH GUIANA
Dutch in 1790
Cayenne 1664
FRENCH GUIANA

GALAPAGOS IS.
Claimed by Spain, but unoccupied

Quito
PRESIDENCY (AUDIENCIA) OF QUITO
Guayaquil 1535

Barcelos 1658
CAPTAINCY OF RIO NEGRO
Barra do Rio Negro 1660
Tabatinga 1780
CAPTAINCY OF PARA
Belem 1616
São Luís 1612
Fortaleza 1609

Trujillo 1535
AUDIENCIA OF LIMA
VICEROYALTY OF PERU
Callao 1537
Lima 1537
Cuzco 1534
PRESIDENCY (AUDIENCIA) OF CUZCO
PRESIDENCY (AUDIENCIA) OF CHARCAS
La Paz
Chuquisaca 1538
Potosí

Príncipe de Beira 1780
CAPTAINCY OF MATO GROSSO
Villa Bella (Mato Grosso) 1752
CAPTAINCY OF GOIAZ
Santa Anna (Goiaz) 1736

VICEROYALTY OF BRAZIL
Definitively established 1714
CAPTAINCY OF MARANHÃO
CAPTAINCY OF PIAUI
Recife (Pernambuco) 1561
CAPTAINCY OF PERNAMBUCO
CAPTAINCY OF SERGIPE
CAPTAINCY OF BAÍA
Salvador (Baía) 1549

Tijuco (Diamantina)
CAPTAINCY OF MINAS GERAIS
Ouro Preto
CAPTAINCY OF ESPIRITO SANTO

Tropic of Capricorn

Ocean

VICEROYALTY OF LA PLATA
Salta
Tucumán 1585
La Serena 1544
Mendoza 1561
Córdoba
AUDIENCIA OF Santa Fé
BUENOS AIRES
Buenos Aires 1580
BANDA ORIENTAL
Colonia 1680
Montevideo 1724

PARAGUAY
Asunción 1537
CAPTAINCY OF SÃO PAULO
São Paulo 1554
Santos 1536
Rio de Janeiro 1567
CAPTAINCY OF RIO DE JANEIRO
CAPTAINCY OF SANTA CATARINA
CAPTAINCY OF RIO GRANDE DO SUL
Porto Alegre 1743
Rio Grande 1737

Loosely Joined to Peru
CAPTAINCY-GENERAL (AUDIENCIA) OF CHILE
Valparaíso 1544
Santiago 1541
Concepción 1550
Valdivia 1552
CHILOÉ

PATAGONIA

TIERRA DEL FUEGO
MALVINAS (FALKLAND ISLANDS)

CAPE HORN

Drake Passage

LATIN AMERICA ABOUT 1790

MILES 0   250   500   1,000

European Colonies

Spain
Great Britain
Netherlands

Portugal
France
* Seat of Government

1535 Lima Dates indicate year of founding

B -440037-29 -1-1-1° 10°
Copyright by Rand McNally & Company, Made in U.S.A.

224

UNITED STATES

Columbia

42nd Parallel

Ceded to U.S. 1818

San Francisco
Monterey

San Diego

LOWER

CALIFORNIA

Chihuahua

Mesilla Strip
Sold to U.S.
1853

Santa Fé

TEXAS
Independent 1836
Annexed to U.S. 1845

New Orleans

Atlantic

Tropic of Cancer

Monterrey

Gulf of Mexico

MEXICO
Independent 1821
Monarchy 1822-23
Republic 1824

Tampico

Jalapa

Mexico City

Puebla

Acapulco

Vera Cruz

YUCATAN
Independent
1839-48

Habana

CUBA
Sp. until 1898

Santiago

JAMAICA
(British)

HAITI

Port au
Prince

DOMINICAN REPUBLIC
United with Haiti
until 1844

Santo
Domingo

PUERTO
RICO
Sp. until 1898

VIRGIN
ISLANDS
(Den.)

BRITISH
HONDURAS

Belice

Caribbean   Sea

CURACAO (Dutch)

TRINIDAD
(British)

(CHIAPAS)
To Mexico 1822

Guatemala

GUATEMALA

San Salvador
SALVADOR

HONDURAS

Tegucigalpa

NICARAGUA

Managua

Ocean

CENTRAL AMERICA
Independent 1821
United with Mexico 1821
Independent Confederation 1823
Divided into five states 1838

San José
COSTA RICA

PANAMA ISTHMUS
To Colombia 1821-1903

Panama

La Guaira

Caracas

VENEZUELA

GREAT
COLOMBIA
(1819-1830)

BRITISH
GUIANA

DUTCH
GUIANA

FRENCH
GUIANA

Bogotá

New Granada 1831
Granadine Confederation 1858
United States of Colombia 1863
Republic of Colombia 1886

Ceded by
Venezuela to
Brazil 1859

GALAPAGOS IS
Ecuador since 1832

Quito
ECUADOR
State of the Equator 1830
Rep. of the Equator 1835

Guayaquil

Paita

Ceded by
Colombia to
Brazil 1907

Ceded by Ecuador
to Brazil 1904

Amazon

MARAJO I.

Belem

São Luiz

Fortaleza

Pacific

Trujillo

PERU
(1821)

Callao
Lima

CHINCHA IS.
(Peru)

Ceded by Bol. to Braz. 1867
Claim relinquished
by Peru 1909

To Peru
1909

Peru and Bolivia
Cuzco
Confederated 1836-1839

BRAZIL
Empire of Brazil, Monarchy 1822-1889
United States of Brazil since 1889

Recife
(Pernambuco)

Arequipa
Mollendo

To Chile 1883
To Peru 1929
TACNA
To Chile 1883
ARICA
TARAPACÁ
To Chile 1883

ATACAMA
To Chile 1884

Antofagasta

Arica

Iquique

Republic of
Bolivar 1825,
Later Bolivia

La Paz

BOLIVIA

Sucre

Ceded to
Brazil 1907

São Salvador
(Baia)

Belo
Horizonte

Tropic of Capricorn

CHACO
Claimed by
Bolivia and
Paraguay

Ceded to
Brazil
1870

Salta

Tucumán

PARAGUAY

Asunción

São Paulo
To Brazil
1895

Santos

Rio de Janeiro

To Brazil
1851

JUAN FERNANDEZ
ISLANDS
Chile since 1818

Valparaíso

Córdoba

Santa Fé

Mendoza

Rosario

ARGENTINA
United Provinces of
Rio de la Plata 1816
Argentine Confederation
1825
Argentine Republic 1853

URUGUAY
Cisplatine Province
Spanish expelled 1814
To Portugal 1817
To Brazil 1822
Republic of Uruguay 1828

Santiago

CHILE
Original Republic of Chile 1818

Buenos Aires

Federal District
since 1880

Montevideo

Argentine
Nation
1860

PAMPAS

PROVINCE OF
BUENOS AIRES
Independent
1853-1859

Bahia Blanca

CHILOÉ

PATAGONIA
Boundary adjusted by treaty 1881
Conquered by Argentina 1876-1879

Strait of
Magellan

FALKLAND IS.
Held by Great Britain
since 1833
Claimed by Argentina

LATIN AMERICA AFTER
INDEPENDENCE

MILES 0   250   500   1,000

TIERRA DEL FUEGO
Disputed between
Argentina and Chile
Divided 1902

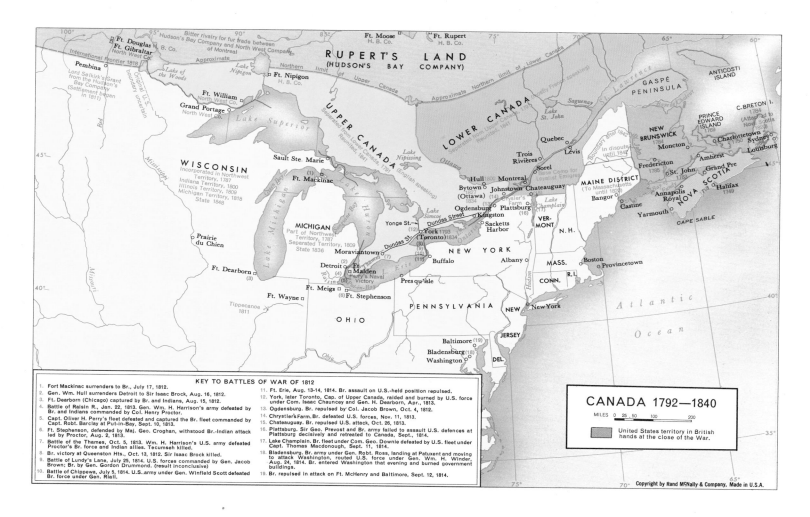

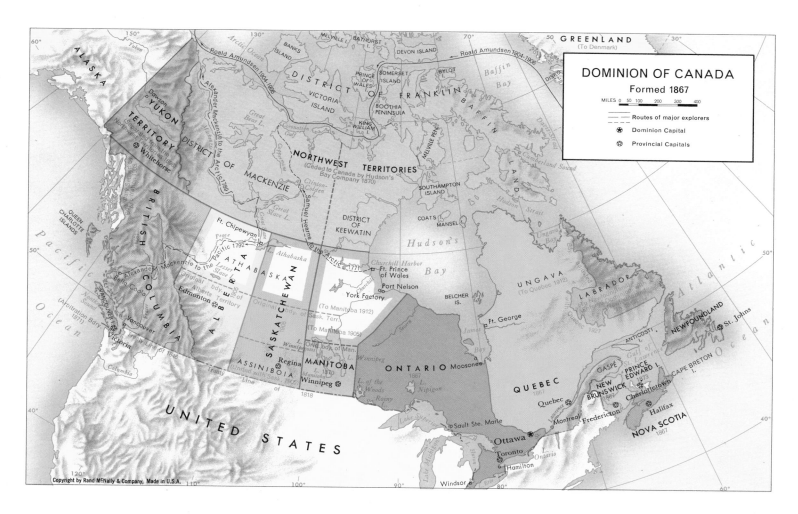

CANADA 1792—1840

MILES 0 25 50 100 200

United States territory in British hands at the close of the War.

KEY TO BATTLES OF WAR OF 1812

1. Fort Mackinac surrenders to Br., July 17, 1812.
2. Gen. Wm. Hull surrenders Detroit to Sir Isaac Brock, Aug. 16, 1812.
3. Ft. Dearborn (Chicago) captured by Br. and Indians, Aug. 15, 1812.
4. Battle of Raisin R., Jan. 22, 1813. Gen. Wm. H. Harrison's army defeated by Br. and Indians commanded by Col. Henry Proctor.
5. Capt. Oliver H. Perry's fleet defeated and captured the Br. fleet commanded by Capt. Robt. Barclay at Put-in-Bay, Sept. 10, 1813.
6. Ft. Stephenson, defended by Maj. Geo. Croghan, withstood Br.-Indian attack led by Proctor, Aug. 2, 1813.
7. Battle of the Thames, Oct. 5, 1813. Wm. H. Harrison's U.S. army defeated Proctor's Br. force and Indian allies. Tecumseh killed.
8. Br. victory at Queenston Hts., Oct. 13, 1812. Sir Isaac Brock killed.
9. Battle of Lundy's Lane, July 25, 1814. U.S. forces commanded by Gen. Jacob Brown; Br. by Gen. Gordon Drummond. (result inconclusive)
10. Battle of Chippewa, July 5, 1814. U.S. army under Gen. Winfield Scott defeated Br. force under Gen. Riall.
11. Ft. Erie, Aug. 13-14, 1814. Br. assault on U.S.-held position repulsed.
12. York, later Toronto, Cap. of Upper Canada, raided and burned by U.S. force under Com. Isaac Chauncey and Gen. H. Dearborn, Apr., 1813.
13. Ogdensburg. Br. repulsed by Col. Jacob Brown, Oct. 4, 1812.
14. Chrystler's Farm. Br. defeated U.S. forces, Nov. 11, 1813.
15. Chateauguay. Br. repulsed U.S. attack, Oct. 26, 1813.
16. Plattsburg. Sir Geo. Prevost and Br. army failed to assault U.S. defences at Plattsburg decisively and retreated to Canada, Sept., 1814.
17. Lake Champlain. Br. fleet under Com. Geo. Downie defeated by U.S. fleet under Capt. Thomas Macdonough, Sept. 11, 1814.
18. Bladensburg. Br. army under Gen. Robt. Ross, landing at Patuxent and moving to attack Washington, routed U.S. force under Gen. Wm. H. Winder, Aug. 24, 1814. Br. entered Washington that evening and burned government buildings.
19. Br. repulsed in attack on Ft. McHenry and Baltimore, Sept. 12, 1814.

Copyright by Rand McNally & Company, Made in U.S.A.

DOMINION OF CANADA
Formed 1867

MILES 0 50 100 200 300 400

— — — Routes of major explorers
✴ Dominion Capital
⊛ Provincial Capitals

Copyright by Rand McNally & Company, Made in U.S.A.

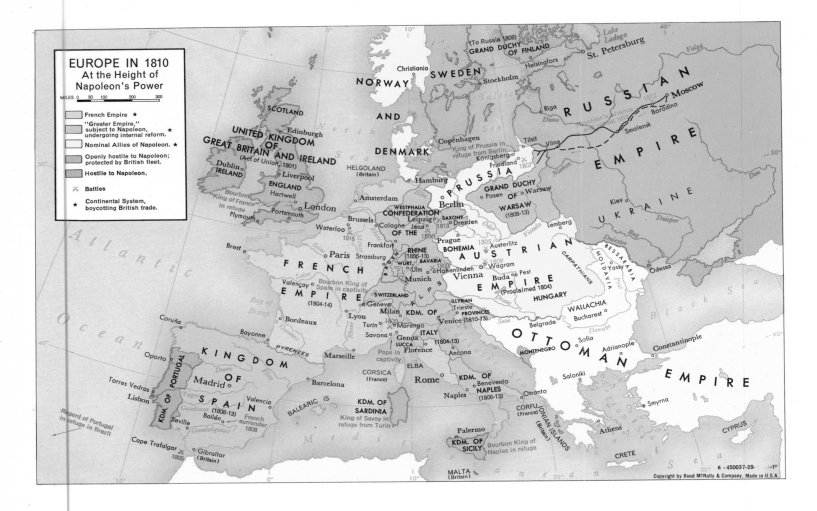

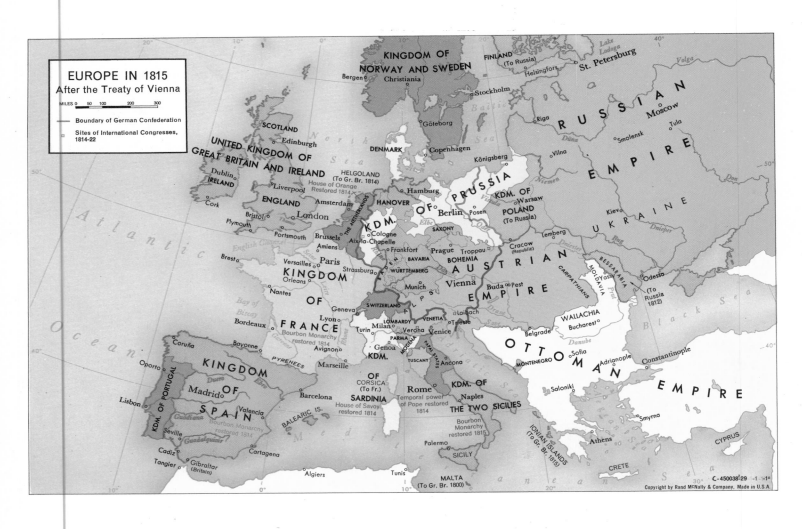

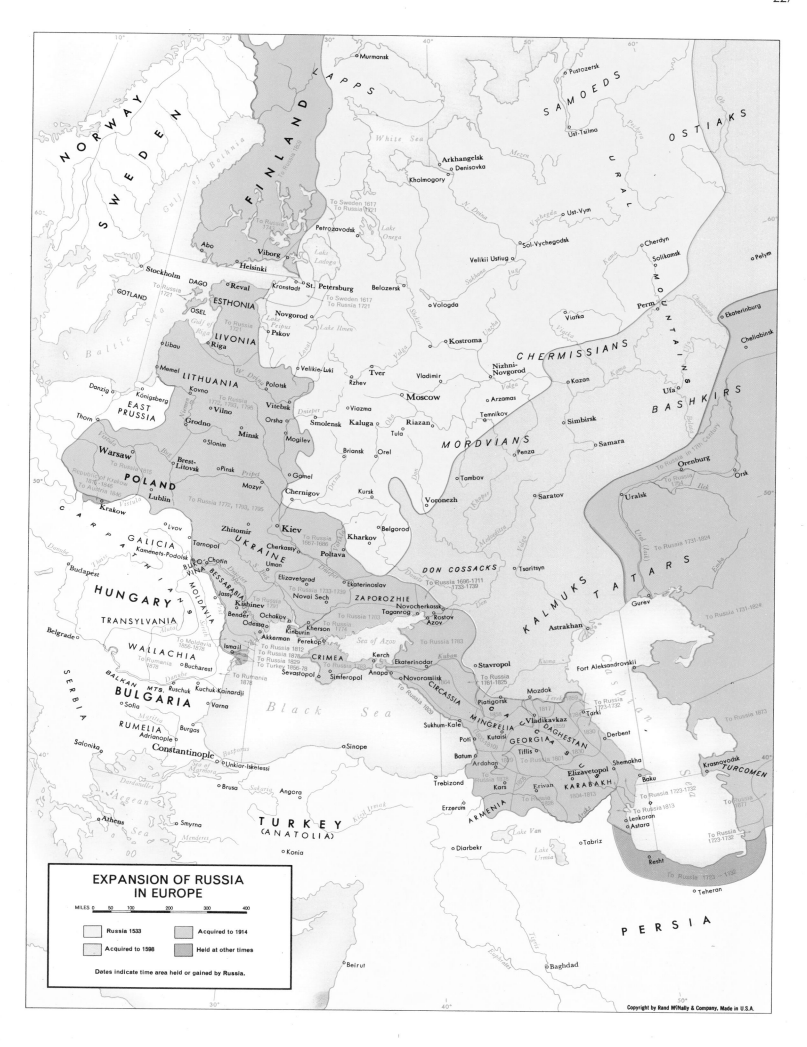

EXPANSION OF RUSSIA IN EUROPE

MILES 0   50   100   200   300   400

Russia 1533

Acquired to 1598

Acquired to 1914

Held at other times

Dates indicate time area held or gained by Russia.

Copyright by Rand McNally & Company. Made in U.S.A.

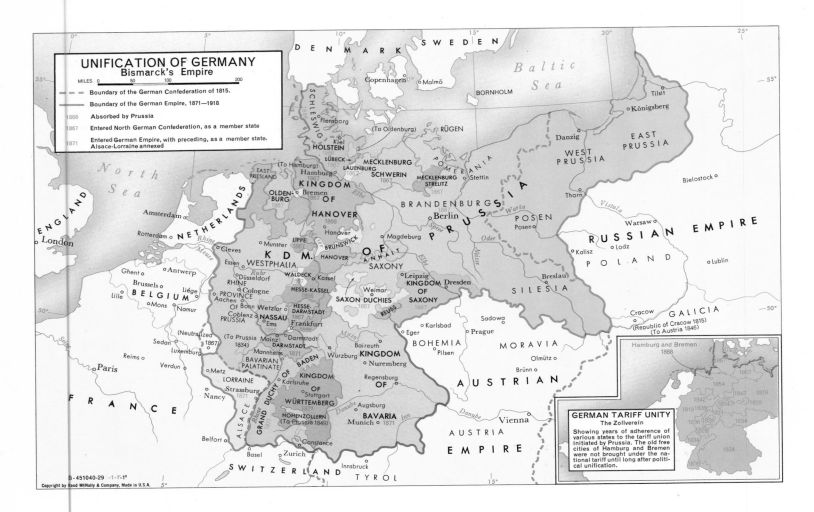

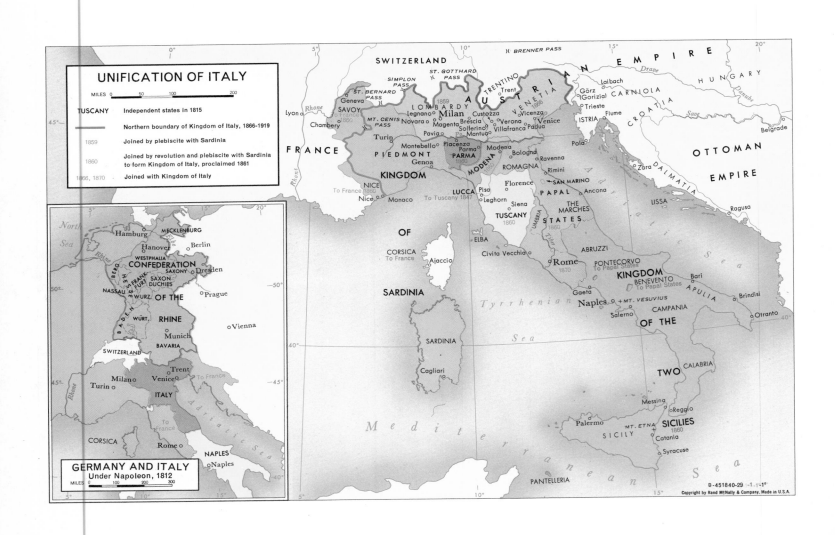

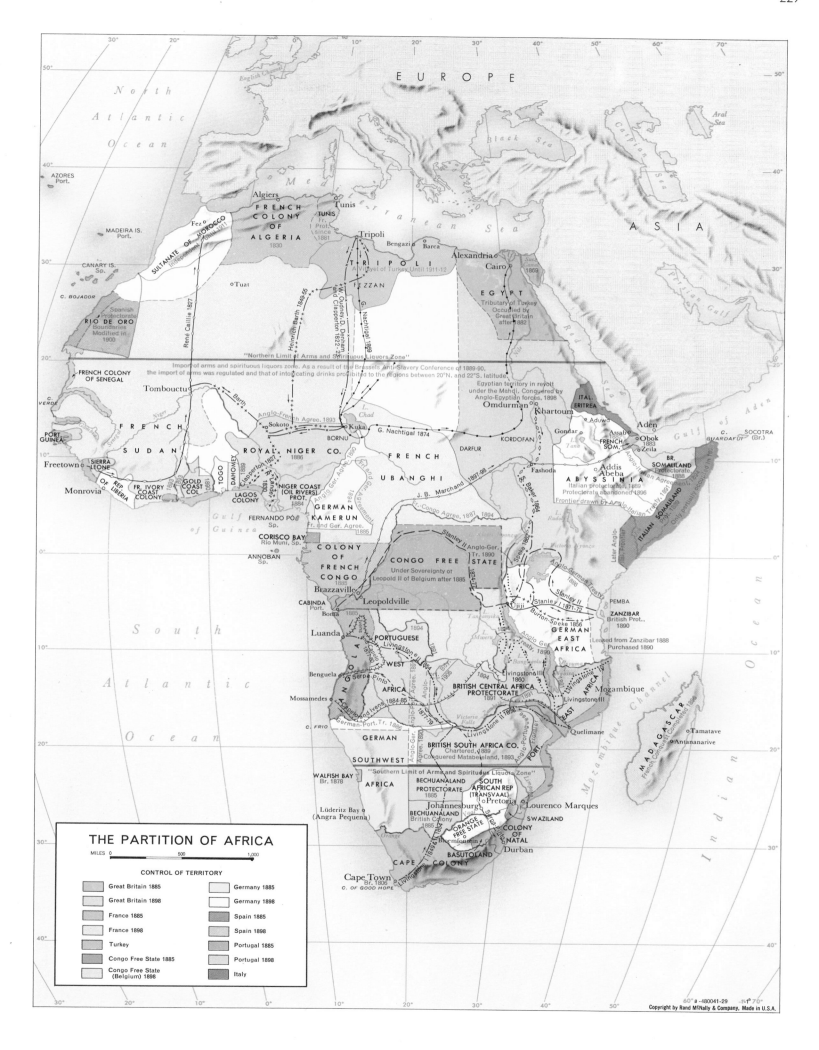

EUROPE

ASIA

North Atlantic Ocean

AZORES
Port.

MADEIRA IS.
Port.

CANARY IS.
Sp.

C. BOJADOR

RIO DE ORO
Spanish
Protectorate
Boundaries
Modified in
1900

SULTANATE OF MOROCCO
Independent until 1911

Fez

Algiers

FRENCH
COLONY
OF
ALGERIA
1830

TUNIS
Fr.
Prot.
since
1881

Tunis

Tripoli

Benghazi

Barca

TRIPOLI
A Vilayet of Turkey Until 1911-12

FEZZAN

Tuat

Alexandria

Cairo
1869

EGYPT
Tributary of Turkey
Occupied by
Great Britain
after 1882

"Northern Limit of Arms and Spirituous Liquors Zone"

Import of arms and spirituous liquors zone. As a result of the Brussels Anti-Slavery Conference of 1889-90,
the import of arms was regulated and that of intoxicating drinks prohibited to the regions between 20°N. and 22°S. latitude.

FRENCH COLONY
OF SENEGAL

Tombouctou

PORT.
GUINEA

C. VERDE

FRENCH

SUDAN

SIERRA
LEONE

Freetown

Monrovia

REP.
OF
LIBERIA

FR. IVORY
COAST
COLONY

GOLD
COAST
COL.

TOGO

DAHOMEY

ROYAL NIGER CO.
1886

Sokoto

BORNU

Kuka

NIGER COAST
(OIL RIVERS)
PROT.

LAGOS
COLONY

FERNANDO PÓ
Sp.

CORISCO BAY
Rio Muni, Sp.

ANNOBAN
Sp.

GERMAN
KAMERUN
Fr. and Ger. Agree.
1885

Egyptian territory in revolt
under the Mahdi. Conquered by
Anglo-Egyptian forces, 1898

Omdurman

Khartoum

KORDOFAN

DARFUR

FRENCH

UBANGHI

G. Nachtigal 1874

ITAL.
ERITREA

Aduwa

Gondar

Assab
FRENCH
SOM.
Obok
1883
Zeila

Aden

BR.
SOMALILAND
Protectorate,
1884

ABYSSINIA
Italian protectorate, 1889
Protectorate abandoned 1896
Frontier drawn by Anglo-Italian

Addis
Abeba

Fashoda

J. B. Marchand

COLONY
OF
FRENCH
CONGO
1885

Brazzaville

CABINDA
Port.

Leopoldville

Boma

CONGO FREE
STATE
Under Sovereignty of
Leopold II of Belgium after 1885

Stanley II Anglo-Ger.
Tr. 1890

Ujiji

Stanley I 1871-72

Stanley II

Burton-Speke 1856

ZANZIBAR
British Prot.,
1890

PEMBA

Leased from Zanzibar 1888
Purchased 1890

GERMAN
EAST
AFRICA

Luanda

ANGOLA

Benguela

Mossamedes

PORTUGUESE

WEST

AFRICA

BRITISH CENTRAL AFRICA
PROTECTORATE
1891

Livingstone III
1860

Mozambique

Livingstone III

Quelimane

MADAGASCAR
French Conquest Completed 1896

Tamatave

Antananarive

Walfish Bay
Br. 1878

GERMAN

SOUTHWEST

AFRICA

Lüderitz Bay
(Angra Pequena)

"Southern Limit of Arms and Spirituous Liquors Zone"

BECHUANALAND
PROTECTORATE
1885

BRITISH SOUTH AFRICA CO.
Chartered, 1889
Conquered Matabeleland, 1893

BECHUANALAND
British Colony
1885

SOUTH
AFRICAN REP
(TRANSVAAL)

Johannesburg

Pretoria

Lourenco Marques

SWAZILAND

ORANGE
FREE
STATE

Bloemfontein

COLONY
OF
NATAL

Durban

BASUTOLAND

Cape Town
Br. 1806
C. OF GOOD HOPE

CAPE COLONY

South Atlantic Ocean

Indian Ocean

Mozambique Channel

THE PARTITION OF AFRICA

MILES 0 — 500 — 1,000

CONTROL OF TERRITORY

Great Britain 1885	Germany 1885
Great Britain 1898	Germany 1898
France 1885	Spain 1885
France 1898	Spain 1898
Turkey	Portugal 1885
Congo Free State 1885	Portugal 1898
Congo Free State (Belgium) 1898	Italy

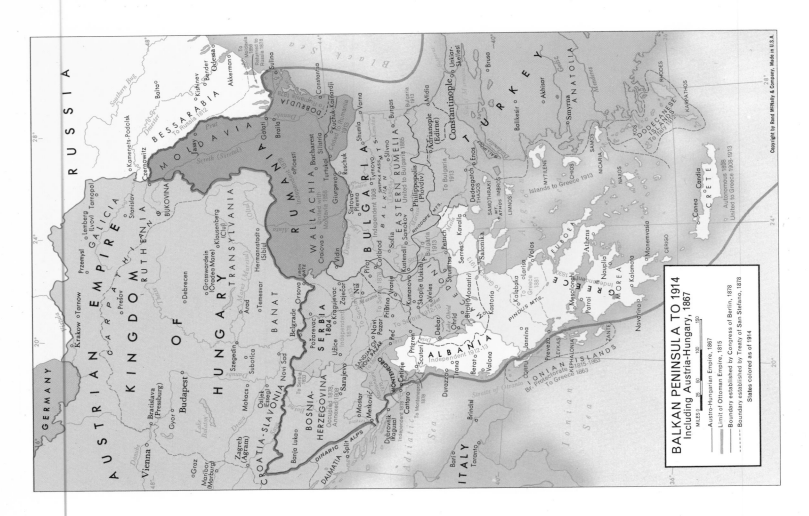

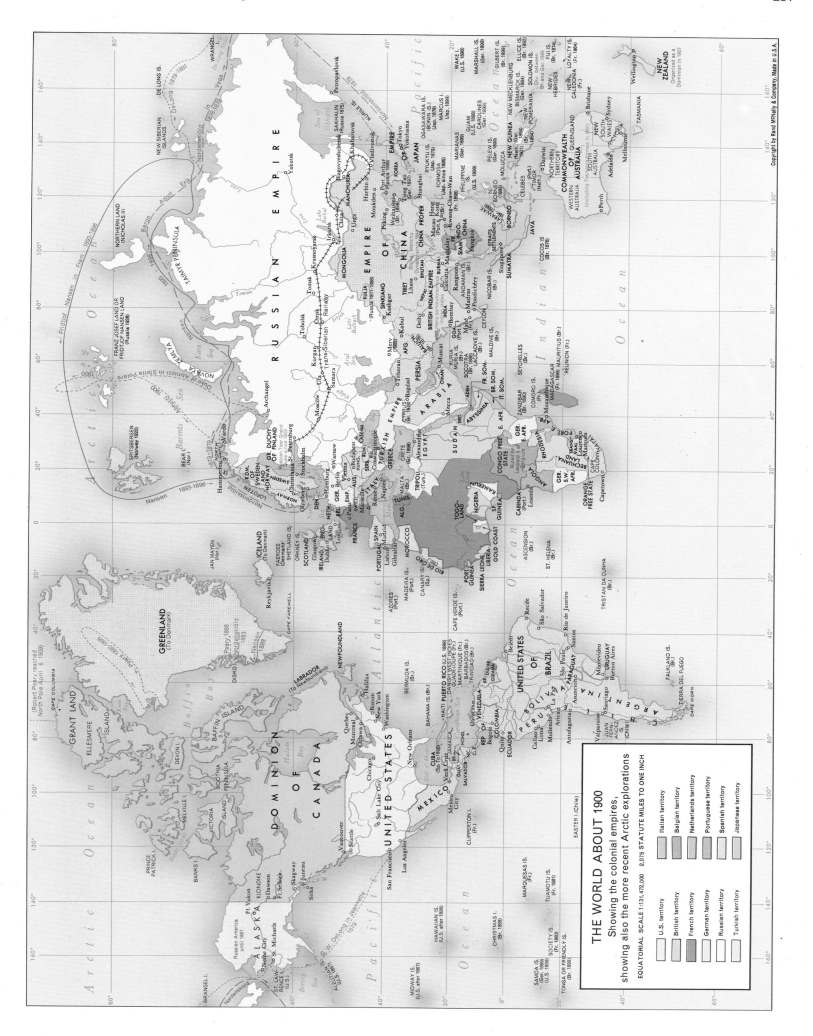

THE WORLD ABOUT 1900

Showing the colonial empires,
showing also the more recent Arctic explorations

EQUATORIAL SCALE 1:131,472,000   2,075 STATUTE MILES TO ONE INCH

U.S. territory	Italian territory
British territory	Belgian territory
French territory	Netherlands territory
German territory	Portuguese territory
Russian territory	Spanish territory
Turkish territory	Japanese territory

Copyright by Rand McNally & Company. Made in U.S.A.

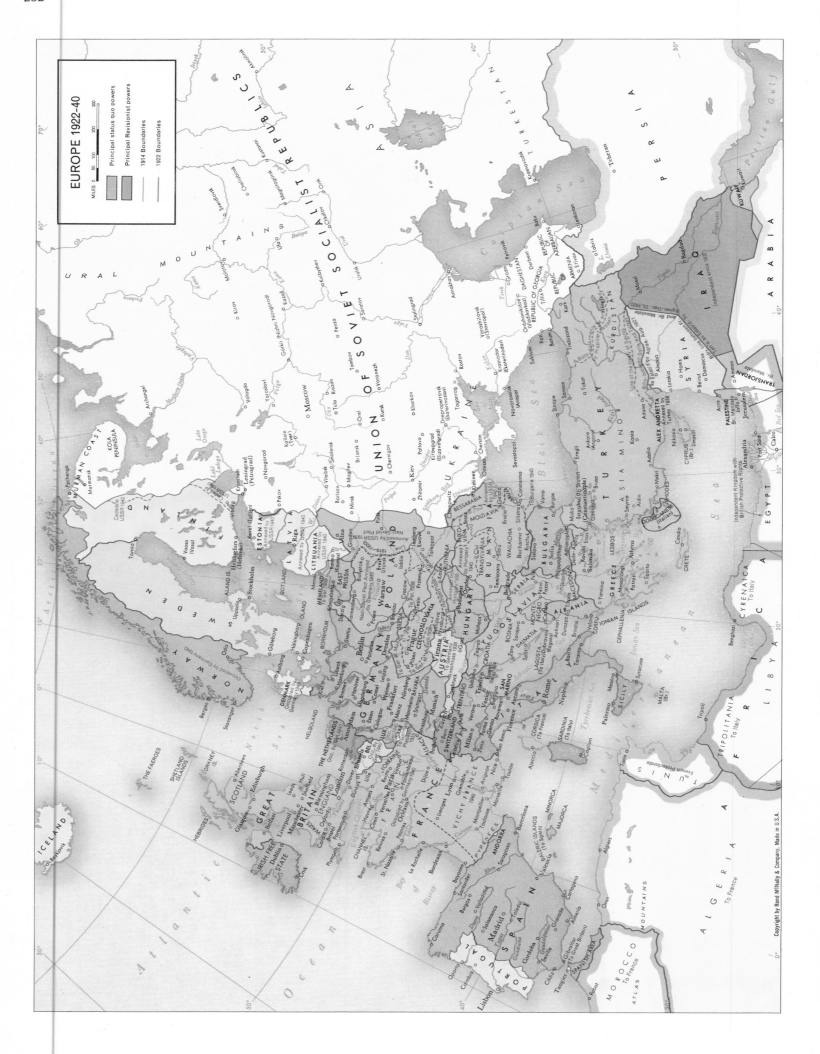

EUROPE
AFTER WORLD WAR II
Showing changes to 1950

MILES 0 50 100   200   300   400   500

North Atlantic Treaty Organization (NATO)

Soviet Russia and People's Democracies.

Major Neutral Powers

Yugoslavia—Communist State but Neutral

Copyright by Rand McNally & Company, Made in U.S.A.

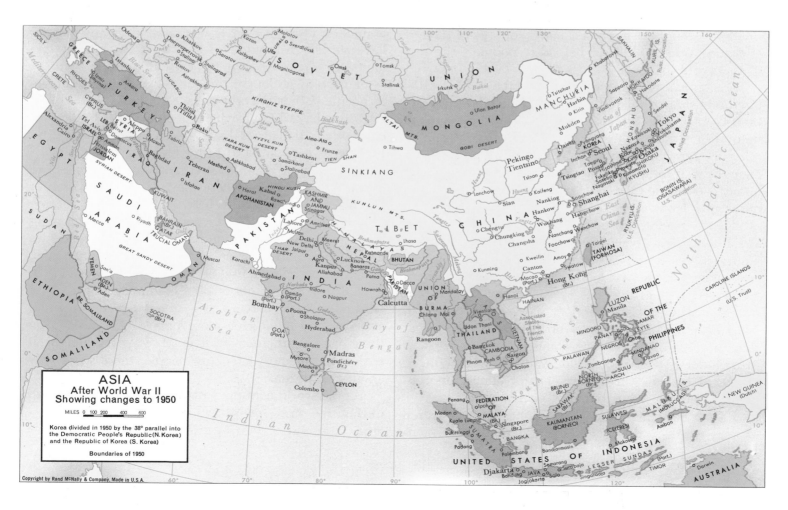

ASIA
After World War II
Showing changes to 1950

MILES 0 100 200   400   600

Korea divided in 1950 by the 38° parallel into
the Democratic People's Republic (N. Korea)
and the Republic of Korea (S. Korea)

Boundaries of 1950

Copyright by Rand McNally & Company, Made in U.S.A.

WORLD POPULATION

The most important thing in the world is its people. Many live crowded together; others live miles apart. Belgium has more than 700 people for every square mile of its land, and Brazil has fewer than 25. In Belgium, the people are dispersed evenly over the land. Brazil has more than 250 people for each square mile of land around its big cities, but in its vast interior there are thousands of square miles with scarcely any people at all.

The population of the earth is now somewhat over three billion; exactly how much it is impossible to say. No one knows exactly how many people there were in the world 500 years ago, but it was certainly only a small fraction of the numbers that inhabit the earth today. Then, as now, Europe contained a large population. Since the great age of exploration and discovery which began in the fifteenth century, the population of Europe has increased many fold, even though migrating Europeans have helped to populate the rest of the world.

The spread of Europeans around the world, without diminishing the numbers in the homeland, suggests the two means by which population can grow. One is natural increase, the excess of births over deaths. The other is migration. Natural increase in Europe has been enough to produce an evergrowing population at home, even while thousands of emigrants were moving out to new lands.

The most crowded large areas of the world are in India and China. They have grown almost entirely by natural increase, and comparatively few of their people have moved out to new lands. Neither have many people moved in since the last great invasions several centuries ago. Both China and India are overcrowded. They have too many people for their resources unless they can find a way to bring about great improvement in their method of production. India has no room to expand. China has great stretches of almost unoccupied land in the west, but it is nearly useless.

People have migrated all over the earth in search of land worth settling. It is thought that many thousands of years ago the first human beings lived in one region of the earth. There is reason to believe that man's homeland may have been Africa, although some evidence seems to indicate that it was Asia. From somewhere on this earth then, people moved out into all habitable lands long before they had learned to leave written records.

Wherever people went in the first few thousands of years of their migrations, they were looking for a place where they could find food. When they found such a place some of them would stay. In the beginning they were looking for good hunting grounds and for beaches where fish and shellfish were abundant. When, a long time later, some had learned to farm, they looked for land they could cultivate.

Wherever people have migrated in the world, they have been looking for something of value. Where abundant resources have been found, many people have settled. Although food will always be a prime factor in man's continuing existence, its immediate availability is no longer the only reason large numbers of people gather in certain places to live.

Cities have grown where people could trade with each other. Industries have grown where transportation made it possible to bring together raw materials and to distribute manufactured goods, and people have gone to live in places where they could find work.

In the modern world, urban centers have become larger and larger, until in some places the growing circles of heavy population have met and merged into great urban belts. In one way or another, iron and coal, oil, and the availability of sources of power are as powerful determinants of population concentration as food once was. There are now about 135 metropolitan areas of one million or more people. A century ago there were only four or five. Sixty years ago, well within the memory of many people, there were only about two dozen.

As the world continues its rapid population growth during the next few decades, the number of large cities is almost certain to grow even more rapidly.

The flea market in Madrid, Spain, one of the world's one hundred-odd cities with a population over a million. Although crowded cities seem to be a symbol of our crowded world, only 10 per cent of the world's people live in cities as large as Madrid or larger.

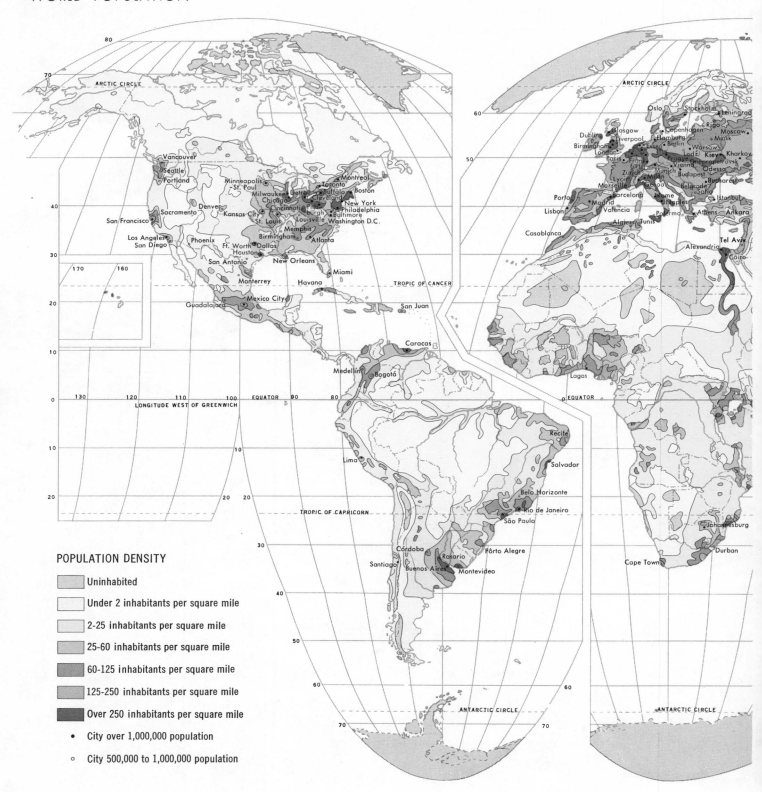

POPULATION DENSITY

- Uninhabited
- Under 2 inhabitants per square mile
- 2-25 inhabitants per square mile
- 25-60 inhabitants per square mile
- 60-125 inhabitants per square mile
- 125-250 inhabitants per square mile
- Over 250 inhabitants per square mile
- • City over 1,000,000 population
- ◦ City 500,000 to 1,000,000 population

POPULATION
OF THE WORLD

The colors on the map show the pattern of population on the earth. Despite the fact that the world seems so crowded, the areas of dense population are considerably smaller than those that are unpopulated or very sparsely populated. Some of the reasons that people live where they do and not elsewhere can be found on the world vegetation, climate, and landform maps. Human life depends on the things that support it, and until comparatively recent times these were largely the gifts of nature. As man gains increasing control over his environment the pattern on a population map may be greatly altered.

Sometimes there are very obvious reasons for details of the population pattern. In northeast Africa, what seems to be a red snake with a purple head follows the irrigated Nile Valley. The scanty population on either side of the Nile occupies the Sahara region. The scattered spots of red and orange are oases in the desert.

The wide, dark band across northern India represents the close-packed cities and farm villages of the Ganges Valley. Gray regions at the far north and far south indicate lands where no one lives because they are perpetually buried under ice and snow. Other patches of gray

clearly mean the most forbidding depths of the world's great deserts, where there is not even scattered grass for grazing or dry shrubs that camels and goats might eat. The city symbols and names on the map explain some of the small spots of red and purple. In contrast to Asia and Africa, where density seems directly related to fertility of the soil, in North America all the areas of heaviest population are urban—cities or clusters of cities, where industry and commerce have caused people to congregate. Western Europe shows relatively even distribution of heavy population over both rural and urban areas.

In so small a space,

                    so many . . . .

The skyscrapers of New York City are one solution to the problem of finding living and working space for millions of people on a small area of land. In general, they indicate a standard of living for most of New York's people that is as high as any other in the world.

Frankfurt, Germany, is in one of the most densely populated regions of western Europe. A flourishing industrial economy creates such problems as rush-hour traffic, but it also creates a prosperous middle class, as can be seen from this well-fed, well-dressed crowd.

Kowloon, on the mainland of the colony of Hong Kong. People living on boats on the rivers and in the harbors is one example of overcrowding along the coast of eastern Asia. Where every scrap of earth is used, there are people who literally cannot find a place on the land for themselves and their families. Here dense population means poverty and a low standard of living.

The Bedouins of Arabia must move constantly from place to place over the bare and empty desert to find what little grass there is to feed their sheep, goats, and camels. Somewhere beyond the horizon the young men of the tribe are watching the herds. When the sparse grass is gone, or when the people hear that rain has fallen elsewhere, they will pack up their tents and travel on.

In so vast a space, so few ....

Although the Andes Valley in Peru (right) seems populous, with its cultivated fields and numerous houses, it is surrounded by rugged mountains where no human being could make a home, so the region as a whole has a small population. Ushuaia, Argentina (below), is the southernmost town in the world, far from all areas of heavy population on the dry, cold, windswept island of Tierra del Fuego. The region around it suffers the same harsh climate. These towns, in their different but equally difficult environments, show two of the reasons why South America has great expanses of sparsely populated land.

Since man first learned to float down a river on a log, water has carried him and his goods from one place to another. In the highly industrialized modern world, many great metropolitan areas, such as Tokyo, served by its own port and that of Yokohama (shown here), receive most of the food for their millions of people and raw materials for their industries by way of the sea. By sea they send their manufactured goods to all parts of the world. Goods are still carried more cheaply by water than any other way.

WORLD TRANSPORTATION

Transportation maps reflect population density almost as well as a population map does. Railways and highways connect cities and penetrate all areas where there is any significant degree of economic development. The principal continental and international airline routes link the principal metropolitan centers of the world. Heavily laden ocean vessels travel frequented sea routes from busy industrial regions. Furthermore, nowhere in the world is there a cluster, no matter how small, of civilized people without some form of transportation providing them with contact, no matter how infrequent, with the rest of the civilized world.

The modern world could not exist without transportation. Modern transportation routes are man-made, created for the convenience of man. Nearly everywhere in the world people, industries, and transportation routes go together.

Both people and goods travel by land, water, and air. The more complex, the more highly industrialized, and the more densely populated a region is, the more it needs good transportation. Transportation of one kind or another has carried people to every corner of the world. Where large settlements have grown, more transportation has been provided. Where transportation is good, more industries have been started and more people have come.

The development of transportation facilities since the industrial revolution has been incomparably greater and more rapid than any change in either method of travel or extension of routes of travel that preceded it. A few hundred years ago, a community with 20,000 people was considered a large city. Most people produced their own food and probably the materials for their own clothing. The small cities were supplied by the surrounding countryside. Only a few types of goods were carried any distance—salt, dried or salted fish, metal articles, and such luxuries as spices, furs, jewels, and knickknacks. Traffic by water was slow, and ships and river boats too small to carry any but light cargoes. On land, goods were carried by long trains of pack animals over roads that were often mere ruts.

As population increased, and people gathered in cities, the need for trade increased. A vast area of farms would be required to feed a city of a million people. Food and raw materials for manufacturing must be brought into densely populated industrial regions, such as western Europe and Japan. Even in the United States, the great cities along the Atlantic Coast depend upon other parts of the country for food supplies. As industrial regions grow, the industries themselves make more and more use of transportation. Raw materials and fuels are brought from greater distances, and the products go to markets that may become worldwide.

Western Europe is the most highly industrialized region in the world. European farmers produce huge crops, but still they cannot feed all the people of their own countries. Nor can the natural resources of Europe supply all the needs of its industries. It depends on imports from less densely populated lands.

In China, alone, the relationship between transportation patterns and dense population seems to break down. It is a huge area teeming with a multitude of people, but it is poorly supplied with transportation routes. Unlike Europe or North America, most of the people of China live on tiny farms, and each family eats what can be grown on their own acre or two of land. If the crops fail in one area, there is likely to be famine, and people may die by the thousands because it is so difficult to bring them food from elsewhere.

Nearly everywhere else in the world, however, dense population and a dense transportation network go together. In India a tight pattern of roads and railways falls across the Ganges Valley, the most heavily populated part of the country. In Mexico, railways and highways meet near Mexico City. In South America, railways fan out from the ports through the regions that have the most people. In the places where the hoot of a train whistle or the roar of a motor are never heard, there are probably few people to listen for them. Transportation routes go where there are people and industry; and where there is transportation, there people and industry will be found.

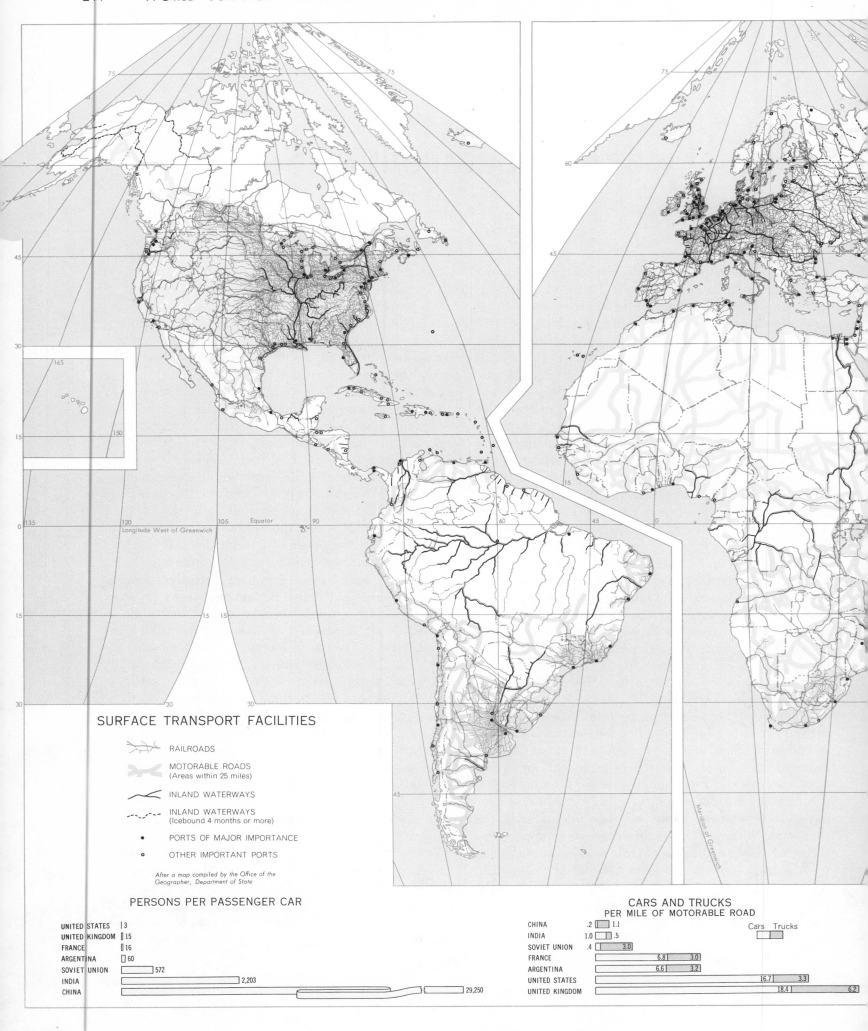

SURFACE TRANSPORT FACILITIES

RAILROADS

MOTORABLE ROADS
(Areas within 25 miles)

INLAND WATERWAYS

INLAND WATERWAYS
(Icebound 4 months or more)

• PORTS OF MAJOR IMPORTANCE

○ OTHER IMPORTANT PORTS

*After a map compiled by the Office of the
Geographer, Department of State*

PERSONS PER PASSENGER CAR

UNITED STATES	3
UNITED KINGDOM	15
FRANCE	16
ARGENTINA	60
SOVIET UNION	572
INDIA	2,203
CHINA	29,250

CARS AND TRUCKS
PER MILE OF MOTORABLE ROAD

Cars   Trucks

	Cars	Trucks
CHINA	.2	1.1
INDIA	1.0	.5
SOVIET UNION	.4	3.0
FRANCE	6.8	3.0
ARGENTINA	6.6	3.2
UNITED STATES	16.7	3.3
UNITED KINGDOM	18.4	6.2

SINUSOIDAL EQUAL AREA PROJECTION (condensed)

0   500   1000   1500 Miles

0   500   1000   1500   2000 Kilometers

Only distances along all latitudes
and the central meridians are true.

75

60

45

30

Equator   60   75   Longitude East of Greenwich   90   105   135   150   Equator   165

15

30

45

60

RAILROADS AND MOTORABLE ROADS
MILES PER 100 SQUARE MILES

Country	Railroads	Motorable Roads
CHINA	.5	2.6
ARGENTINA	2.5	4.4
SOVIET UNION	.9	9.8
INDIA	2.8	14.3
UNITED STATES	7.1	101
FRANCE	13.6	185
UNITED KINGDOM	20.6	195

Railroads
Motorable Roads
(excluding city streets)

INLAND WATERWAYS
THOUSANDS OF MILES

Country	Miles
UNITED KINGDOM	2.4
ARGENTINA	4.2
INDIA	5.1
FRANCE	8.2
CHINA	19
UNITED STATES	28.6
SOVIET UNION	62.2

Copyright by Rand McNally & Co.
Made in U.S.A.

Man journeys endlessly .... down rivers,

Boats on small waterways are probably the oldest means of transportation. These Vietnamese, making their way home at the end of the day, are poling themselves along a small canal in a homemade boat of a kind that has been used on quiet, shallow waters for hundreds of centuries. The boat moves hardly faster than a man can walk, but it carries more with much less effort, and where the distances are short or the time long, speed is unimportant.

An extensive system of canals and locks have made the Great Lakes, their connecting rivers, and the mighty St. Lawrence into the St. Lawrence Seaway (right). Through it ocean-going vessels can now travel almost to the heart of the United States Middle West. Iron, coal, wheat, and paper are among the many bulky cargoes that are moved across the lakes.

Wherever there is lumbering and a river, logs are floated away from the forests where they are cut. Sometimes they are tumbled into the water and carried by the current down to a sawmill or paper mill. Sometimes, as in the Fraser River in British Columbia, they are fastened together into a raft and pulled by tugboat. Old as this method is, it is still the easiest and safest.

across cities, countries, continents . . . .

This fantastic tangle of concrete ribbons is a highway interchange in San Francisco, similar to hundreds that are carrying streams of automobiles over, across, and under each other in or near almost every large city in the United States. The tremendous number of cars on modern highways, and the speed at which they travel, have created problems in the control of traffic that could not have existed in the age of the horse and buggy. The larger the city, the greater its traffic problem is.

The Trans-Siberian Railway crosses the Soviet Union from Moscow to Vladivostok on the Pacific. The line of its passage can be clearly seen on a population map—a narrow streak of settlement through vast and almost empty lands.

TIME ZONES

The surface of the earth is divided into 24 time zones.. Each zone represents 15° of longitude or one hour of time. The time of the initial, or zero, zone is based on the central meridian of Greenwich and is adopted eastward and westward for a distance of 7½° of longitude. Each of the zones in turn is designated by a number representing the hours (+ or −) by which its standard time differs from Greenwich mean time. These standard time zones are shown by bands of brown and yellow. Orange indicates areas which have a fractional deviation from standard time The irregularities in the zones and the fractional deviations are due to political and economic factors. (Revised to September 1956.)

AIR TRANSPORT

— Principal continental and international airline routes.

▰ Well-developed scheduled airline net; generally, but not always, in areas of high economic development.

▰ Scheduled airlines serving more isolated centers.

☐ Few, if any, scheduled airlines; generally areas of little or no economic development.

AIR TRANSPORT

Copyright by Rand McNally & Co.
Made in U.S.A.

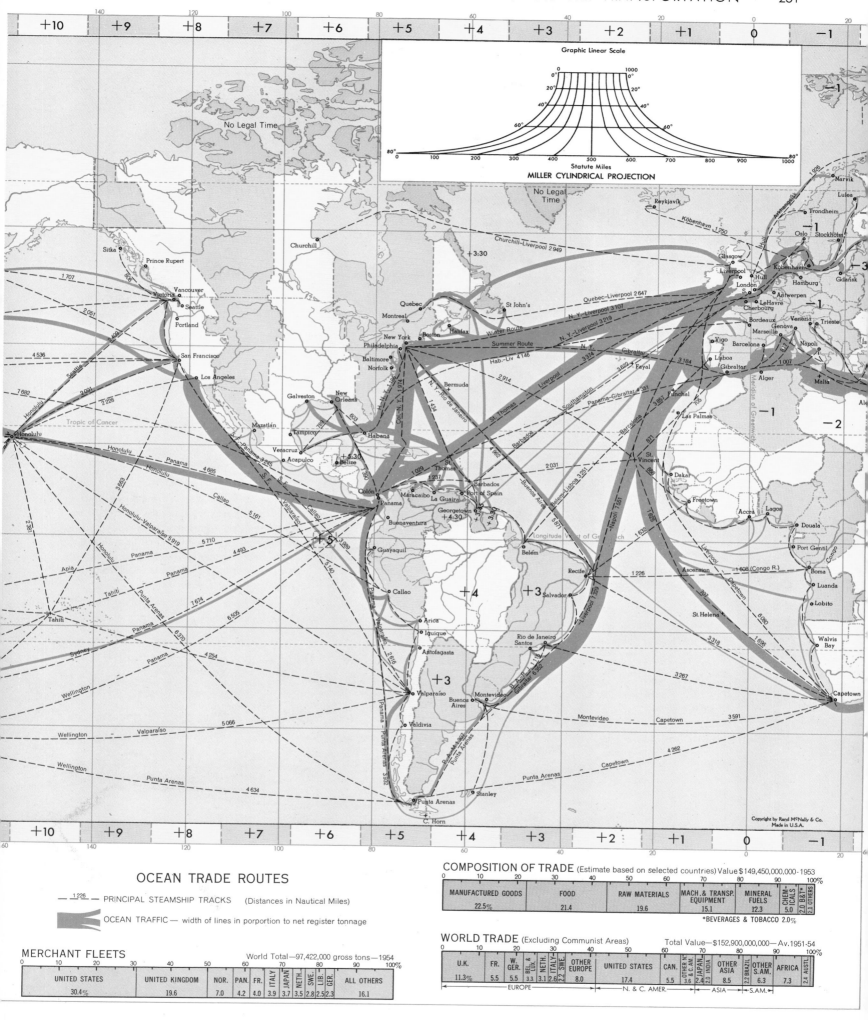

OCEAN TRADE ROUTES

— 1226 — PRINCIPAL STEAMSHIP TRACKS (Distances in Nautical Miles)

OCEAN TRAFFIC — width of lines in porportion to net register tonnage

COMPOSITION OF TRADE (Estimate based on selected countries) Value $149,450,000,000-1953

MANUFACTURED GOODS	FOOD	RAW MATERIALS	MACH. & TRANSP. EQUIPMENT	MINERAL FUELS	CHEM-ICALS	B&T*	OTHERS
22.5%	21.4	19.6	15.1	12.3	5.0	2.0	2.1

*BEVERAGES & TOBACCO 2.0%

WORLD TRADE (Excluding Communist Areas)   Total Value—$152,900,000,000 — Av.1951-54

U.K.	FR.	W. GER.	BEL. & LUX.	NETH.	ITALY	SWE.	OTHER EUROPE	UNITED STATES	CAN.	OTHER N. & C. AM.	JAPAN	INDIA	OTHER ASIA	BRAZIL	OTHER S. AM.	AFRICA	AUSTL.
11.3%	5.5	5.5	3.3	3.1	2.6	2.2	8.0	17.4	5.5	3.6	2.0		8.5	2.2	6.3	7.3	2.4

EUROPE — N. & C. AMER. — ASIA — S.AM.

MERCHANT FLEETS
World Total—97,422,000 gross tons—1954

UNITED STATES	UNITED KINGDOM	NOR.	PAN.	FR.	ITALY	JAPAN	NETH.	SWE.	LIB.	GER.	ALL OTHERS
30.4%	19.6	7.0	4.2	4.0	3.9	3.7	3.5	2.8	2.5	2.3	16.1

*over oceans,
through the air,
beyond all barriers.*

Great northern ports were once shut in by ice for several months of the year. Now the sea lanes are kept open during the winter by ice-breakers like this Russian atomic-powered vessel, crushing its way through the Berents Sea to Arkhangelsk in the Soviet Union.

The world's largest ships, like the *Queen Elizabeth* shown leaving New York Harbor, sail between the world's largest ports.

Only airports as large or larger than the one at Amsterdam, Netherlands, can accommodate today's giant jets.

DIVIETO TRANSITO
DALLE 8 ALLE 21

DIVIETO PERMANENTE
DI TRANSITO

MANENTE
SITO

360

DIVIETO TRANSITO
DALLE 10 ALLE 21

DIVIETO PERMANENTE
TA

DI CARICO E SCARICO
DALLE 8 ALLE 21

BVLGARI

LANGUAGES OF THE WORLD

Language, that set of sounds and symbols by which ideas and feelings are expressed, is a distinctive characteristic of human beings. No people, no matter how primitive, have ever been found who had no language. Man's body is equipped with special mechanisms that make speech possible: an area in the front of the human brain that controls his ability to form and to understand words; muscles in the tongue and throat that he uses to produce the complicated sounds that are spoken language. Not only do all normal human beings have the physical equipment for speech, they are also born with a natural and instinctive desire to talk.

Although speech is instinctive, language is not. Each child must learn a language before he can talk. He learns the one that he hears spoken around him. This language reflects his life and the society in which he lives. It has words for the objects he sees and uses, words for the ceremonies and customs of his people, for the tasks he performs, the games he plays, the food he eats, and words that describe how those foods are prepared. The language he speaks influences the way he thinks. He arranges ideas in his mind as he arranges words in his sentences, and it is almost impossible for him to grasp an abstract thought if his language has no words to express it.

Language is one of the things that binds groups of men together. It is also one of the things that keeps them apart. In the Biblical story of the Tower of Babel, the Lord stopped the descendants of Noah from building their great tower and powerful city by "confounding their speech." When they could no longer understand one another they could no longer work together, and they scattered in all directions over the earth.

Thousands of different languages exist today, and they are so varied that they show no sign of ever having been one common tongue. Most of them, however, belong to one or another of several large language families, and these related languages developed, over the centuries, from the same parent language. English belongs to a family called Indo-European. Languages in this group are spoken from western Europe to India and have been carried to distant parts of the earth. Each Indo-European language has hundreds of words that can be traced to the same origin. The English word *father*, for example, is *fader* in German, *padre* in Spanish, *pater* in Latin, and *pitar* in Sanskrit, an ancient language once spoken in India. Related words in different languages are called "cognate" words, meaning literally "words born together."

Latin, the language of the ancient Romans, is an Indo-European tongue, and although its principal use today is as the official language of the Roman Catholic Church, a family of living languages has descended from it. The Romance languages, French, Italian, Spanish, Portuguese, Romanian, and Romansh, are all spoken in countries that were once part of the Roman Empire.

English belongs to the Germanic group of Indo-European tongues, which includes the Scandinavian languages and Dutch, as well as the various dialects of German. Although English is not a Romance language it has, as an Indo-European tongue, a good many words that are cognates of Latin words, and more important, it has borrowed a great many Latin words. Latin was once the language of government, education, and religion in England; much of it passed from official use into the language spoken by the people.

In time all languages change. They change with changing customs, with the need for new words or because old words are no longer needed, or when any new influence has been exerted on culture. Human languages are the echo of human history.

Some languages are written in words, some in pictures that express ideas. Traffic signs in Rome use both words and pictures, so that he who walks or drives, whether he knows Italian or not, may read and understand. The same kind of sign is used in many places in Europe.

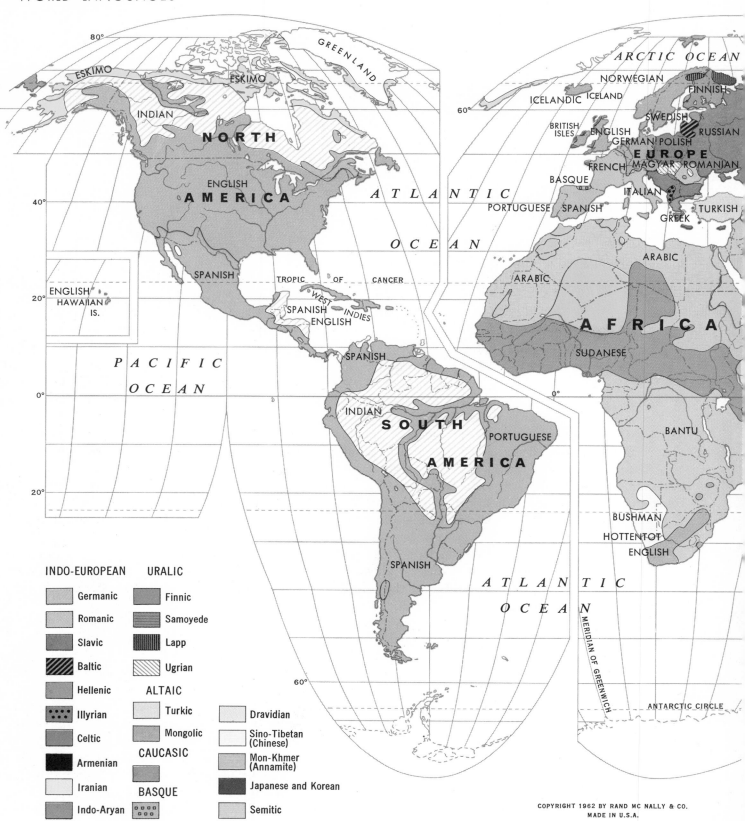

**LANGUAGES
OF THE WORLD**

INDO-EUROPEAN
- Germanic
- Romanic
- Slavic
- Baltic
- Hellenic
- Illyrian
- Celtic
- Armenian
- Iranian
- Indo-Aryan

URALIC
- Finnic
- Samoyede
- Lapp
- Ugrian

ALTAIC
- Turkic
- Mongolic

CAUCASIC

BASQUE

- Dravidian
- Sino-Tibetan (Chinese)
- Mon-Khmer (Annamite)
- Japanese and Korean
- Semitic

Thousands of languages are spoken in the world, and no map can show them all. In many areas where more than one language is in use, an attempt to indicate the mixture would only be confusing. The color on the map shows the language spoken by a majority of the people. Indian languages in the Americas, for example, are shown for large areas in South America, but omitted in continental United States, and Bantu is not shown in the Sudanese area of Africa.

Hamitic

Sudanese

Bantu

Hottentot
(or Bushman)

Tungus

Chukchi (and
other languages)

Eskimo

Indian-language families

Malayo-Polynesian

Papuan and Negrito

Of all the language families, Indo-European is by far the most important. Indo-European tongues are spoken by almost two-thirds of the human race. Next in importance are the Chinese dialects and related languages, called Sino-Tibetan, spoken by almost a fourth of the world's people. In contrast to these two tremendous families some languages are spoken by only a few people. Basque, for example, which is not related to any other language, is spoken only in one small area along the Spanish-French border. It is one of the great language mysteries, and it has always interested language scholars.

Patterns of conquest and migration can be traced on a language map. Latin, from which the Romantic tongues came, was carried to all parts of the Roman Empire. The wide spread of Arabic reflects the sweep of the Moslems across Africa. The English took their language to North America, and the Spanish and Portuguese took theirs to Central and South America.

Recorded language is the enemy of ignorance. . . .
and of the forgetfulness of time.

Egyptian hieroglyphics are symbols that stand for the sound of words. They probably began as picture writing, with drawings standing for the objects they represented. Gradually the drawings came to mean any word that had the same sound as the original object. If this system were used in English, a drawing of the eye, for example, would come in time to mean "I" as well.

The words are Spanish (left), but the same alphabet is used to write English, German, Latin, and a number of other languages. The characters in an alphabet represent sounds. Alphabets are the most highly-developed and convenient form of writing. All the many words in a language can be expressed by combinations of a few interchangeable letters.

In written Chinese (below) the characters stand for ideas or meanings of words and have nothing to do with the sound. Learning to read and write means memorizing thousands of symbols. The Japanese use the same characters although their language is entirely different.

RACES OF THE WORLD

In the largest sense, all human beings belong to the same race: Mankind. We are the speakers of languages, the makers of tools, the shapers and builders, the thinkers of abstract thoughts, the seekers after God. These common qualities transcend all differences and set man apart from all other animals.

Physically, also, all men share certain characteristics. The bodies of men are covered with thin, smooth skin; they have hair, not fur or feathers; human cells are different from the cells of other animals, as is human blood. Large groups of human beings are also distinguished from other large groups by physical characteristics that are determined before birth, by inheritance. On the basis of these traits, mankind has been classified as having three great divisions, the Caucasoid, the Mongoloid, and the Negroid.

The general characteristics that are used to describe these three great divisions are: shape of head; type (straight, wavy, or curly) of hair; color and texture of hair; color of eyes, and presence or absence of a fold in the corners of the eyelids; size and shape of foot; size and shape of hand; skin color; shape of nose; relative proportions of upper and lower leg and upper and lower arm, and many others. No single characteristic is a reliable indication of race, and each characteristic shows great variation within the racial group.

Furthermore, the three principal groups have innumerable subgroups within them, which often differ widely from each other, and some peoples have characteristics of at least two of the three main divisions.

The Caucasoid group includes most Europeans, from the blond northerners to the dark southerners, the peoples of India, the Ainu of northern Japan, and possibly the Polynesians of the western Pacific and some of the aborigines of Australia. The Mongoloid group includes most of the peoples of eastern and central Asia, the Indians of the Americas, and the Eskimos. The Negroid group includes the Negroes of Africa, some of the peoples of the Pacific Islands, and the pygmy peoples of Africa and Malaysia.

There are fascinating groups of people about whom the evidence is not at all clear. For example, the African Bushmen have some characteristics that seem to be Negroid, but there are also many differences between them and other African Negroes. Some scientists think that they may be a remnant of an older race that has disappeared except in a few places. The Melanesians, who live on some of the islands of the southwest Pacific, are classed as Negroid by some scientists and as a separate race by others.

As research yields more knowledge about the world, especially the prehistoric world, the migrations of many racial groups can be traced. Measurement of skeletal remains show that racial groups have wandered over the earth. Some have disappeared from areas where they once lived and been replaced by others. Some have increased in numbers and occupied larger and larger areas. In the course of human history, all groups of people have encountered other groups unlike themselves and have changed them and been changed by them.

The term "race" is often erroneously used with reference to things that have nothing to do with racial characteristics. There is no such thing as racial culture, for example. The customs, language, religion, literature, and art of a people are not inherited characteristics of a racial group. Race has nothing to do with nationality, which is a political division of mankind that was invented by man. People of any race may be a member of any nation, and most nations have had citizens who were members of each of the great races, all of whom help to people Our World.

The population of Hawaii is a happy blend of peoples—European, Asian, and Polynesian—and most racial types and most racial subtypes are represented in it. When Hawaii was discovered by Europeans, it was inhabited by Polynesians.

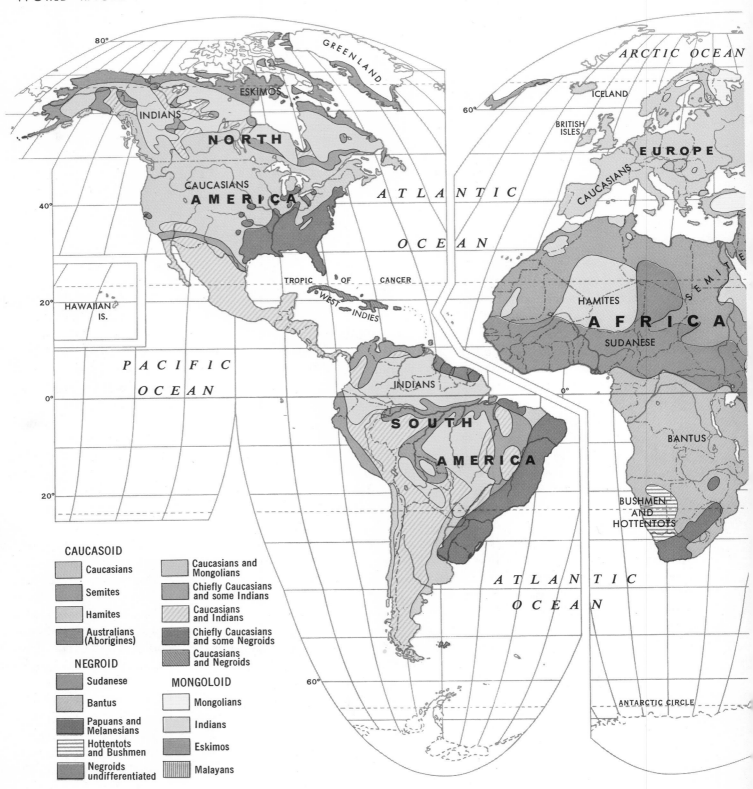

CAUCASOID
- Caucasians
- Semites
- Hamites
- Australians (Aborigines)

Caucasians and Mongolians
Chiefly Caucasians and some Indians
Caucasians and Indians
Chiefly Caucasians and some Negroids
Caucasians and Negroids

NEGROID
- Sudanese
- Bantus
- Papuans and Melanesians
- Hottentots and Bushmen
- Negroids undifferentiated

MONGOLOID
- Mongolians
- Indians
- Eskimos
- Malayans

RACES
OF THE WORLD

No exact diagram of the distribution of the major races of the world is possible since, during the course of history, so many subdivisions have developed that it is almost impossible to distinguish the root stock in many cases. The map shows what scientists consider the predominant racial types in each area.

Some conclusions concerning man's travels across the world can be drawn from the map. The Caucasoids are the only race to spread in large numbers into every inhabited continent. They occupy nearly all of Europe, southwestern Asia, and North Africa. In northern Asia,

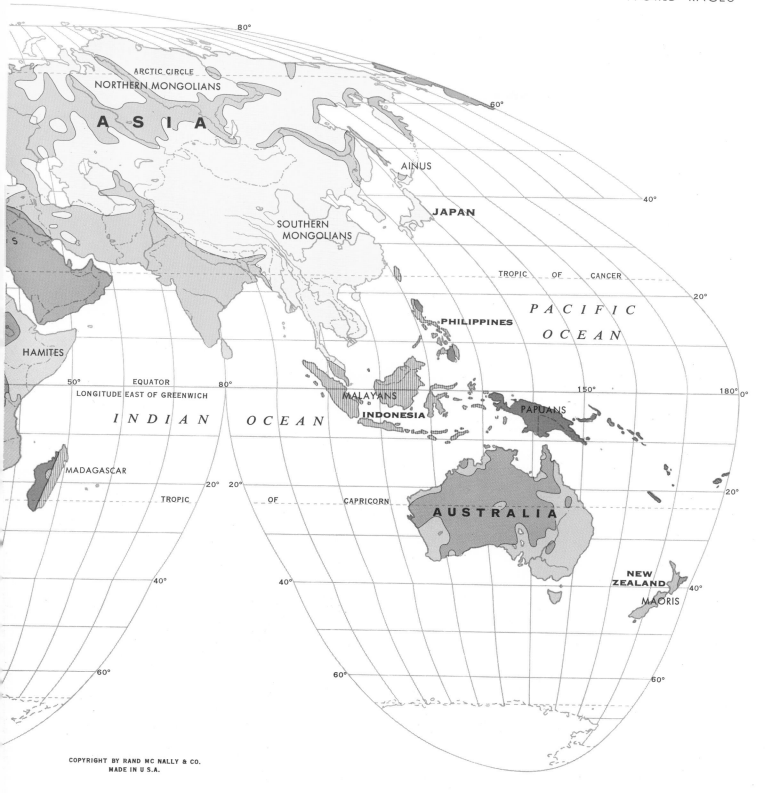

ASIA

NORTHERN MONGOLIANS

ARCTIC CIRCLE

80°

60°

AINUS

JAPAN

40°

SOUTHERN MONGOLIANS

TROPIC   OF   CANCER

20°

PACIFIC

OCEAN

PHILIPPINES

HAMITES

50°   EQUATOR   80°
LONGITUDE EAST OF GREENWICH

150°

180° 0°

INDIAN   OCEAN

MALAYANS

INDONESIA

PAPUANS

MADAGASCAR

20° 20°

TROPIC   OF   CAPRICORN

20°

AUSTRALIA

40°   40°

NEW ZEALAND

40°

MAORIS

60°   60°

60°

COPYRIGHT BY RAND MC NALLY & CO.
MADE IN U.S.A.

Russians have settled all across Siberia. Caucasians from Europe are a great majority in North America and a somewhat smaller percentage of the total population in South America. They occupy all but the great desert of Australia.

The Semitic branch of the Caucasoids are believed to have originated in Arabia, the Hamites probably in Africa.

Mongoloids also have wandered a long way over the earth. They occupy a large part of Asia, including all the most densely populated areas except India. Members of the Malayan subrace people Indonesia and the Philippines and are a majority on Madagascar. The most remarkable Mongoloid migration was into the Americas, probably across the Bering Strait; they gradually occupied the land to the southern tip of South America. The Eskimos are part of a relatively late wave of migration from Europe.

Negroes, the people of Africa south of the Sahara, seldom left Africa of their own volition. During the sixteenth, seventeenth, and eighteenth centuries, thousands of them were taken to the Americas as slaves.

*The differences are great,
the likeness greater....*

These peoples are one race:
CAUCASOID

In spite of the many differences in appearance, and of the widely separated parts of the world in which they live, all of the people shown in the pictures on these two pages are members of the same large racial group, the Caucasoid. Almost all Europeans are Caucasoid, though Norwegians seem very differ-

ent from Spaniards or from Greeks. Left, above, are typical eastern European Caucasians, called Slavs. In general, they have wide faces, and rounder heads and darker hair and eyes than western European peoples. The Norwegian girl (right), has coloring typical of certain peoples of northern Europe.

The Australian native to the left is also a Caucasoid. The predominant features that lead scientists to classify him as such are heavy beard and wavy hair, and measurements of the skull and other bones.

Arabs are Semites, one of the almost infinite number of subdivisions of the Caucasoid family. In body measurements and appearance, Semitic peoples are closer to the European types than other non-European Caucasoid groups.

The Ainu man and wife below belong to a small group of people who now live only on Hokkaido, in northern Japan, but probably they once occupied a much larger area in northern Asia. The Ainu have wavy hair and heavy beards, characteristic of Caucasoids.

The face of man has infinite variety....

NEGROID

Most of the people of Uganda, like the two women above, are Bantus, and are called Baganda. The name Bantu refers to speakers of a large group of related languages, and the people themselves differ considerably from tribe to tribe, but there are enough similarities for them to be considered one group.

The people of Ghana (left) are Sudanese, sometimes called the "true Negroes." The traits that distinguish the Negroids can be seen clearly in them; tightly curled hair, and the shape of the nose, mouth, and jaw are distinctive features. The ancestors of most North American Negroes came from the Sudanese area.

There is some mystery about the tribal origin of the Hottentots (below). They share some traits with the Bushmen. Both groups have hair so tightly curled that it forms separate tufts, usually called peppercorns. Bushmen, however, are very short and Hottentots are considerably taller. Those in the picture are boys. Hottentots are probably a mixture of Bushmen and taller tribes.

And these, the third great race: MONGOLOID

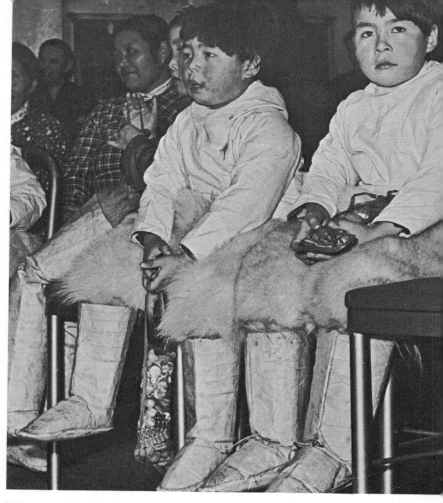

The two Nepalese women in the picture above are quite typical in appearance of the majority of Mongoloids of central and northern Asia. In the more familiar Japanese, Chinese, and Koreans, some of the Mongoloid characteristics are exaggerated. Mongoloids take their name from the Mongols of central Asia.

American Indians are also Mongoloids, although the relationship was not recognized until comparatively recently. The Seminoles (below) belong to the Creek tribe, which has fairly distinct Mongoloid features. Many Indians look even more Mongoloid; in others the only trace is their straight black hair.

Eskimos are Mongoloids, almost exactly like the Mongoloid people of northeastern Siberia. It is thought that they crossed to North America considerably later than the American Indians, and they have few cultural traits in common with any of the Indian groups. They live near Thule, Greenland.

Although the people of the Indonesian Island of Bali take their religion and much of their culture from the Hindus of India, who are Caucasians, they seem to be predominantly of a Mongoloid subgroup. Their ancestry probably includes some mixture of Javanese and Polynesian with the aboriginal inhabitants.

Ritual is a fundamental part of all religions. In the Hindu religion of India, bathing is a symbol of purity and precedes every religious rite and many acts of daily life. Rivers are considered to be sacred and the Ganges the holiest of all, particularly at Banares. Bathing in the waters of the Ganges is one of the most important acts of religious observance in the life of every Hindu.

RELIGIONS OF THE WORLD

Religion is the road man follows in his search for spiritual truth. Through it he seeks knowledge of and oneness with the power of creation and life, the ruling force of the universe. Although there have been, and are, many religions, they all have certain things in common: a belief in a superior being or beings; a set of ritual and ceremony by which the deity is worshiped; a set of rules governing the behavior of men towards each other, called ethics, and the requirement of faith.

Religion has shaped the history of mankind. Wars have been fought, governments overthrown, and journeys made across the known world because of religion. Although at times fanatic believers have sought to spread their own religion by the sword, or to stamp out the religions of others by death and destruction, the noblest thoughts, the highest expressions of unselfishness and love, and the most magnificent works of art have all been inspired by religious feeling.

The major religions of the world today are Christianity, Judaism, Islam, Brahmanism or Hinduism, and Buddhism. Jainism, Confucianism, Taoism, and Shinto also have many followers, primarily in the Far East. Many of these religions are divided into smaller groups whose members differ on various minor points, but the fundamental beliefs of each are shared by all who profess it.

Christianity and Judaism are very closely related. The Old Testament of the Bible is regarded as sacred by both Jews and Christians, both share a belief, called monotheism, in one God; and Jesus, who brought Christianity to the world, was a Jew.

Judaism is the older of the two religions. Like the Jewish people themselves, it is now scattered over most of the world, and only in Israel is it a national religion. It was one of the first great religions to teach that there is only one God, whom the Hebrews called Jehovah, and that He was infinitely just and wise. The Hebrew law was given to the Jews by Moses, the great prophet who led the Israelites out of bondage in Egypt to the Promised Land.

The teachings of Jesus of Nazareth are the law of the Christian religion. He, too, taught that there is but one God. When Jesus came forth as a teacher, his followers accepted him as the Messiah, or Christ, whose coming had been prophesied to the Jews. Although in the end his teachings were rejected by the Jews, and carried by Paul the Apostle to the gentiles, converts to the new religion were called Christians. Christianity gained a firm foothold in southern Europe, and even before it became the official religion of Rome, in the fourth century, had spread to the farthest lands of the Roman Empire. Today Christianity is the predominant religion of the western world.

Islam, founded by Mohammed and also called Mohammadism, is a monotheistic religion. It teaches that "There is no God but Allah, and Mohammed is His Prophet." Its followers are called Moslems. (See page 275.)

Brahmanism is the major religion of India. It is also called Hinduism and its followers are Hindus. The absolute, all-pervading Power of the Hindus is brahman, and it has three aspects, each of which is regarded as a god: Brahma, the Creator, Vishnu the Preserver, and Siva, the Destroyer. Final union of the soul with brahman is believed to be the goal of all life; to achieve this, the soul must have attained perfect purity and freedom from sin, and each soul must be reborn many times in many bodies before this state is reached.

Buddhism, now one of the dominant religions of the Orient, was founded in India by a Brahman, Guatama Siddhartha. After prolonged meditation he had a profound religious experience, called the Enlightenment, in which the meaning of all life seemed to come to him in a single instant. He taught that each soul could reach a state of perfect peace and oneness with god and the universe, called Nirvana.

A recurring theme in all great religions is that of aspiration toward something greater and more beautiful than human experience. In striving toward it, man has achieved some of his finest works.

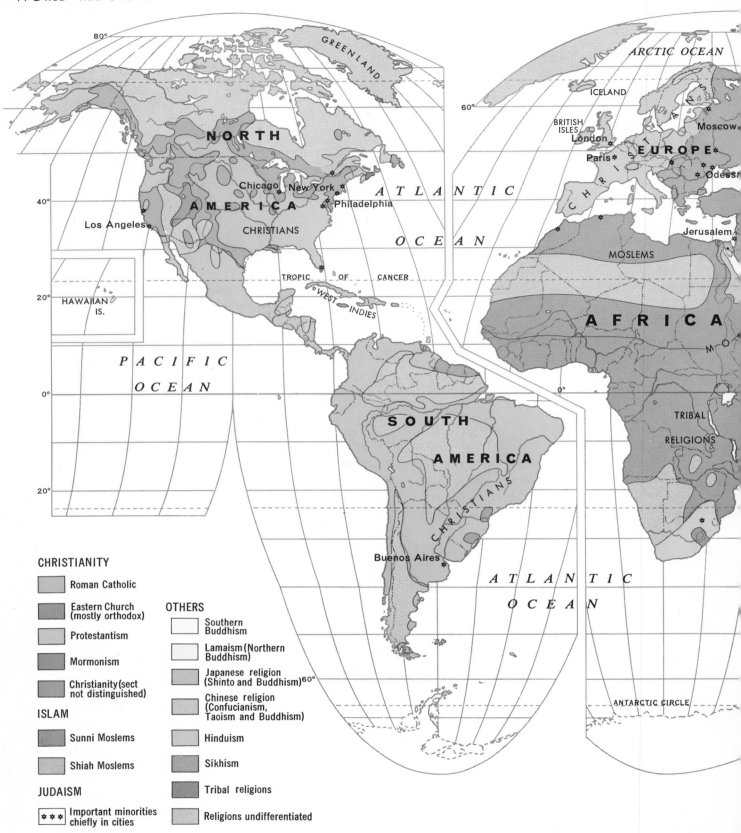

CHRISTIANITY

Roman Catholic

Eastern Church (mostly orthodox)

Protestantism

Mormonism

Christianity (sect not distinguished)

ISLAM

Sunni Moslems

Shiah Moslems

JUDAISM

✸✸✸ Important minorities chiefly in cities

OTHERS

Southern Buddhism

Lamaism (Northern Buddhism)

Japanese religion (Shinto and Buddhism)

Chinese religion (Confucianism, Taoism and Buddhism)

Hinduism

Sikhism

Tribal religions

Religions undifferentiated

PRINCIPAL
RELIGIONS
OF THE WORLD

Certain general conclusions can be drawn concerning the distribution of the principal religions of the world by comparing this map with the language map, although fewer religions than languages are shown.

Christianity, Islam, and Buddhism have been the missionary religions of the world. Western Europe, and those lands settled primarily by European peoples, are overwhelmingly Christian. Christianity was carried throughout the Roman Empire, as was Latin, the source of the Ro-

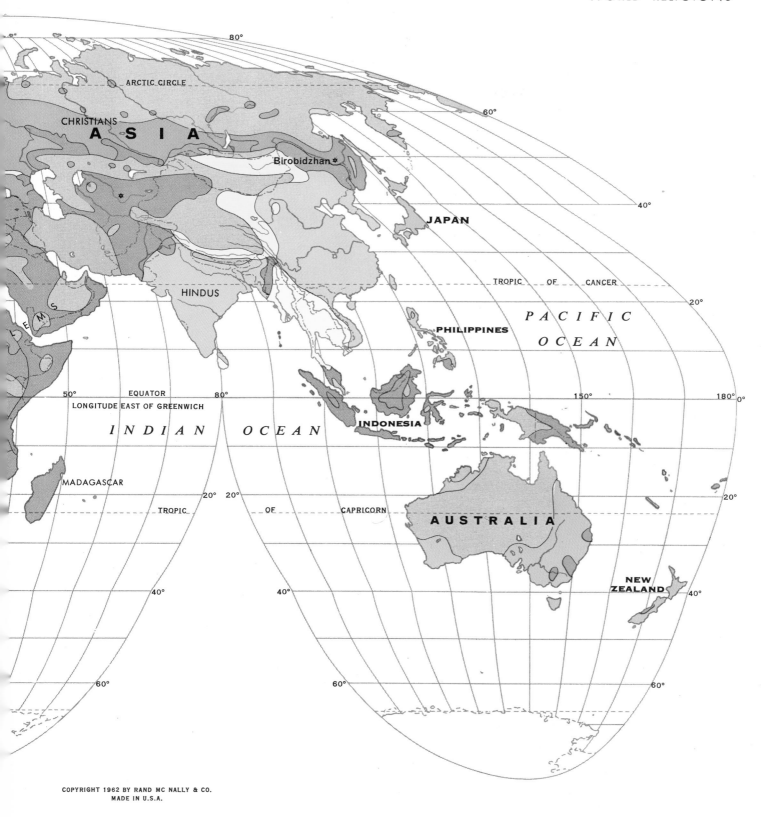

mance languages. The Romance-speaking world, with a few exceptions such as Romania, is Roman Catholic. Protestantism, which sprang from the German Reformation, gained its greatest strength in countries where Germanic tongues were spoken, and was carried to lands settled by Germanic-speaking peoples. The teachings of Mohammed spread rapidly among the Arabs of the Middle East, and his followers carried Islam and the Arabic language throughout what is now the whole Arab world.

Buddhism originated in India, but was carried throughout eastern and southern Asia. Today it is particularly strong in China, although the principal religions of the Chinese-speaking world include not only Buddhism, but also Confucianism and Taoism.

Judaism is shown on the map by a symbol rather than by color because Jews are concentrated in many small areas rather than in one large area. Israel, where Judaism is a national faith, is the sole exception.

*Each in his way,
and in his faith,
serves God. . . .*

The Torah, which is the law of the Hebrews given to them by
the Prophet Moses, is studied by all Jewish men. Many orthodox
Jews, especially in Europe and Israel, wear beards and long
locks of hair. All of them must cover their heads when they are
in the synagogue.

The World Council of Churches stresses Christian unity. Most Protestant denominations and branches of Christianity are represented. Recently the Russian Orthodox Church was admitted. The officers of the Council shown here are from (left to right) Nigeria,
West Germany, the Orthodox Archbishopric of North and South America, England, India, and the United States.

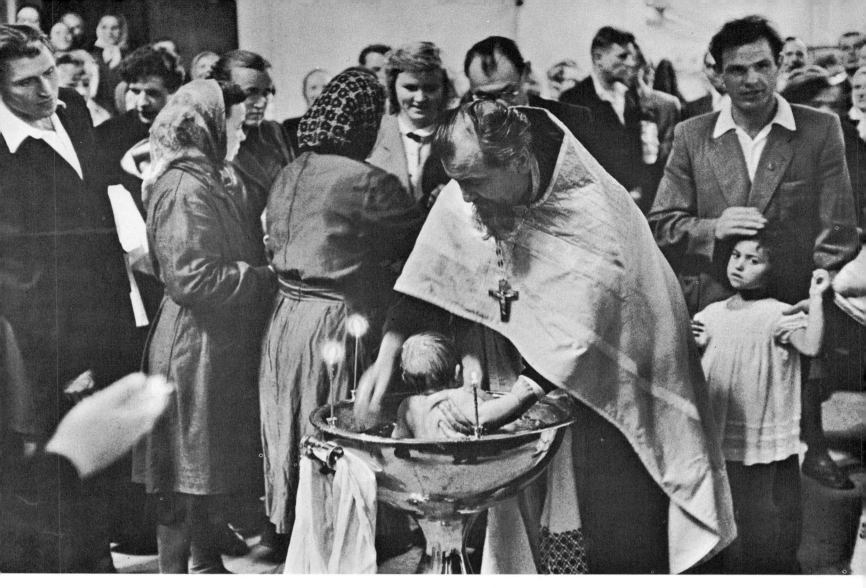

The Russian Orthodox Church is part of the eastern branch of Christianity. It was once the state Church of Russia, and although religion is not encouraged by the Communists, many Russians keep their faith as is shown by this christening in Leningrad.

The College of Cardinals is the supreme Senate of the Roman Catholic Church. Its members elect the Pope, head of the Church, are his immediate assistants and advisors, and head the Curia, the Church's governing body. They are the princes of the Church.

*A shrine is holy
to the one
whose god it holds....*

Above is a traditional portrait of Confucius, the religious leader who taught the Chinese people reverence for the past and for their ancestors. He also taught a code of behavior that for centuries was followed by the majority of Chinese. At the left, two Burmese girls place offerings of flowers and lighted candles before a statue of Buddha in a family shrine. Below are the seated figures of four gods in a temple in Thailand. Each god has his own attributes and his own ceremonies. Among other eastern religions, Shinto, in Japan, is nature worship, based on the belief that a spirit resides in everything in nature. Taoism, found in China, is also a kind of nature worship.

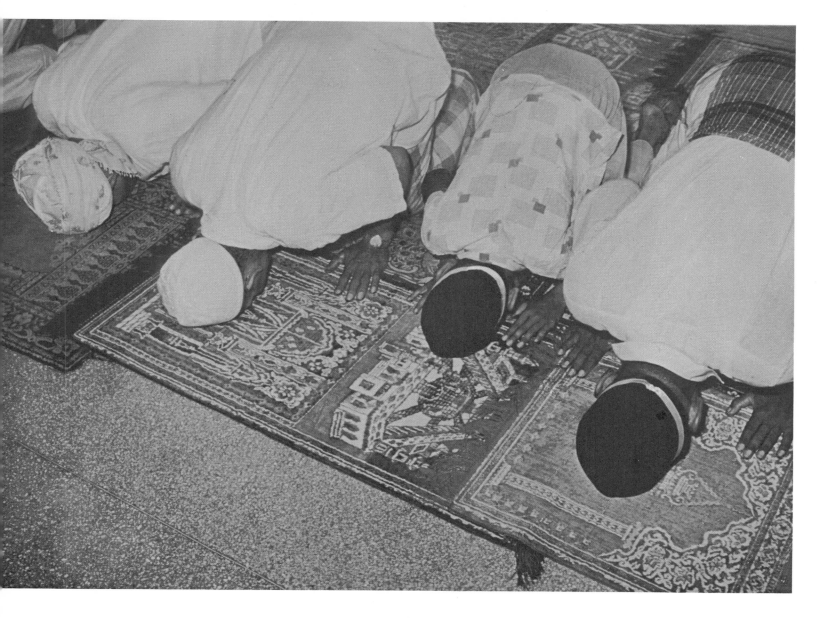

Five times a day, at the call of the *muezzin*, devout Moslems prostrate themselves on their prayer rugs (above), facing Mecca the holy city, and worship Allah. Services of formal worship are held in their mosques. Islam, the name of their religion, means ''Peace and submission'' (to the will of God).

Primitive religions involve the worship of many gods. Each tribe usually has its own gods and sacred objects, and its own rituals, ceremonies, and shrines (such as the grass-thatched hut in the Congo, shown at the right). The forces of nature are considered to be gods in some tribal religions; in others all things, animate and inanimate, are believed to be inhabited by spirits who must be appeased. There is a strong element of magic in all such religions, and ritual actions are more important than doctrine or formal religious belief.

The indescribably beautiful deserts of the southwestern United States are not barren wastes of sand, but teeming communities of plants and animals that have learned, through the ages, to adapt themselves to heat and drouth and scarcity. Many desert plants, such as the cactus, have fleshy stems that store water and small leaves that reduce the moisture lost by evaporation.

NATURAL VEGETATION

Except for ice-covered polar lands and mountain tops and the driest cores of the deserts, plants cover the land. Plants grow luxuriously on deep-soiled plains and in valleys; they climb high mountains until they are stopped by perpetual snow near the summits. They flourish in the shallow margins of lakes and in the water of swamps and marshes. Plants grow where the salt ocean water washes their roots at every tide. They crowd to the foot of glaciers, cling to rocks, and grow out of cracks in city sidewalks.

Without plants, there could be no life of any kind on earth. Only plants can take chemicals from air and water, expose them to sunlight, and turn them into food. All animals, including man, must live by eating food that plants have made. The lion that dines on a zebra or the robin that pulls an earthworm from the ground or the man who enjoys a well-browned steak is merely getting his plant food one step removed. Even the gull snatching a fish from the water is dependent on plant food, for there are plants in the ocean. Fish eat them or eat other sea creatures that have eaten them. Every food chain goes back to plants.

Plants must have water to carry chemicals from the soil up to their leaves and flowers and to carry food down for storage in stems and roots. They must be able to obtain the necessary chemicals from soil or water, and they must have warmth and sunshine in order to manufacture food.

Since plants vary in their requirements, the vegetation of the earth varies from region to region. The wild plants of a region—the natural vegetation—are an excellent clue to climate. Settlers in newly-opened lands have used the plants as an indication of what crops are likely to be successful.

There are four main types of natural land vegetation in the world: forest, grassland, desert, and tundra. Each of these has many subdivisions. The basic division in forest types is between needle-leaved and broad-leaved trees. Well-known examples of needle-leaved trees are pine, spruce, fir, hemlock, cedar, and juniper. Not all have truly needle-shaped leaves, but all are closely related. Popularly, they are often called evergreens because most of them keep their leaves the year round, but there are exceptions. In North America the larch or tamarack and the bald cypress shed their leaves in the fall. Needle-leaved trees are the softwoods of the lumber industry, though by no means all of them have wood that is actually soft.

Broad-leaved trees are the lumberman's hardwoods, though the softest known woods, such as balsa, belong to this group. There is great variety in broad-leaved trees—cottonwoods and aspens with wide leaves, narrow-leaved willows, trees with the saw-edged leaves like the elm and birch, and the deeply indented leaves of the oak and maple.

Where winters are cold, most of the broad-leaved trees are deciduous; that is, they lose their leaves in the fall. (There are exceptions, such as the holly.) Where there is warmth all year, the broad-leaved forest is evergreen. Most trees do shed their leaves briefly at some time during the year, but the forest as a whole remains green.

Next to the forests in area are the grasslands. They vary from the thick sod and tall blades of the prairie grasses to the short, scattered tufts of the near desert. On the whole, they occupy lands with a little less moisture than trees require. Grass of some variety will grow almost everywhere. Grass grows on the floor of forests wherever a little light trickles through the trees. It grows in marshes, it invades the tundra, and grows far above the tree line on mountains. Where winters are long and cold or summers are hot and dry, the green blades turn brown and die, but the roots are still alive, ready to cover the earth with a new blanket of green when the season changes. Where a forest is cut or burned, where a lake is drained, where a river builds new land at its mouth, there the grass soon takes over.

To man, forest and grassland are much the most important vegetation regions. Nearly all the densely populated parts of the earth are in areas where trees or grass were the natural vegetation.

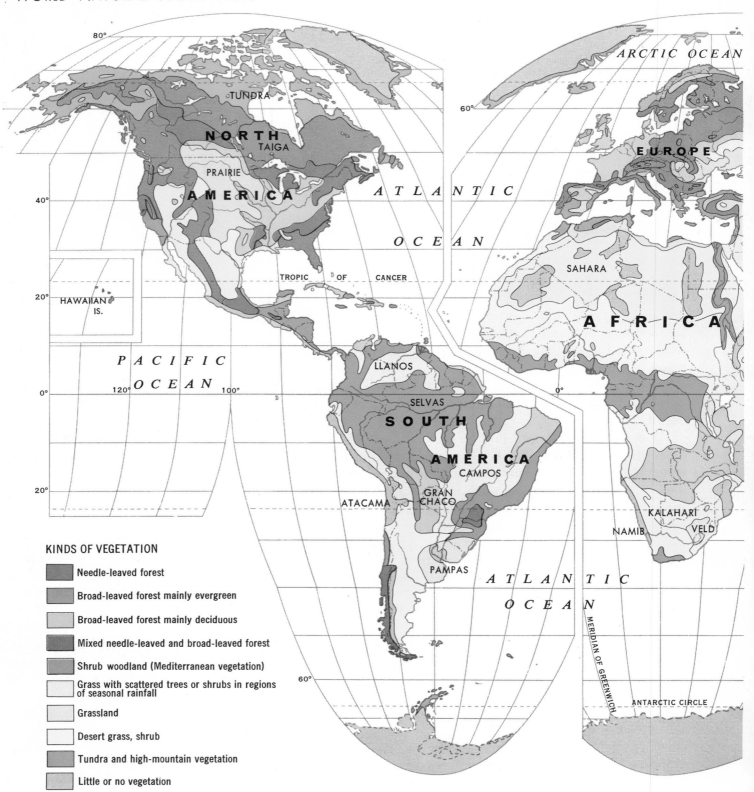

KINDS OF VEGETATION

- Needle-leaved forest
- Broad-leaved forest mainly evergreen
- Broad-leaved forest mainly deciduous
- Mixed needle-leaved and broad-leaved forest
- Shrub woodland (Mediterranean vegetation)
- Grass with scattered trees or shrubs in regions of seasonal rainfall
- Grassland
- Desert grass, shrub
- Tundra and high-mountain vegetation
- Little or no vegetation

NATURAL VEGETATION OF THE WORLD

The pattern on a vegetation map is very similar to the pattern on a world climate map. The most important single factor in the determination of type and extent of vegetation is climate, although soil and altitude also are significant. As vegetation depends on climate, so does population depend on vegetation. Some of the best general-farming land in the world is in broad-leaved forest regions, in North America, western Europe, and eastern Asia, for example, where most forests were cut long ago.

TUNDRA

ARCTIC CIRCLE

TAIGA

A S I A

STEPPE

STEPPE

GOBI

TROPIC   OF   CANCER

P A C I F I C

O C E A N

EQUATOR
LONGITUDE EAST OF GREENWICH

I N D I A N   O C E A N

TROPIC   OF   CAPRICORN

A U S T R A L I A

Grasslands have become the world's producers of bread and meat. All the cereal grains, wheat, rye, barley, oats, millet, rice, and corn (maize), belong to the large botanical family of grasses. These grains are grown in the moister grasslands, and the drier lands retain their indigenous grasses and are used as grazing lands, mainly for cattle and sheep.

Two vegetation classes, "shrub woodland" and "grass with scattered trees," belong to the regions with great seasonal differences in rainfall. They make excellent farmland where they can be irrigated.

Most of the tropical broad-leaved forests have never been cleared. It is too difficult, and when the trees have been cut, the soil loses its fertility.

Needle-leaved trees, in general, will tolerate more severe conditions than broad-leaved. They grow where winters are long and cold, where the soil is acid or sandy and infertile, or in the thin soil of mountain slopes.

Trunk, limb, green leaf....great trees adorn the earth.

Slender, pointed, needle-leafed firs form a dense forest on a mountain slope in the Canadian Rockies near Lake Louise. Above treeline the mountainside is bare rock, too high and cold for any but such primitive plants as lichen and mosses. A grassy mountain meadow lies hidden under the snow. In late spring and summer, a profusion of wildflowers will bloom there.

The glorious flames of autumn burn in the Berkshires of Massachusetts. The foliage of the broad-leaved trees turns from the cool green of summer to fiery orange, red, and gold in the crisp, cold air of fall. As the brilliant colors die, the leaves will drop. This color change occurs in North America, western Europe, small regions in Asia, and a few places in southern South America.

Tropical rain forests, found in the humid low latitudes, are green above, dark and shadowy below. Trees grow so close together that their tops form a solid canopy, and young trees can grow only where an old tree falls and lets in the light. Like this one in Puerto Rico, all tropical forests are made up of broad-leaved trees, and they are always green.

No shield against the wind,
No shelter from the sun
  ....these are the treeless lands.

The desert of Saudi Arabia, the desolate "empty quarter." This is one of the regions of "little or no vegetation." It is a nightmare expanse of blowing sand. The dunes in the background show how the sand has blown away from the windward side and into a slope downwind. At the left a moving dune has killed and half buried a shrub that had managed to find a foothold.

In the high mountains of Wyoming, left, plants like those of the far-northern tundra grow. The ground is covered in a scanty fashion, but the plants are dwarfed and meager. Even the woody bushes that grow here and there are only a few inches high.

CLIMATES OF THE WORLD

A generation or two ago, geography textbooks had a very simple scheme for describing world climates. Along the equator, between the Tropic of Cancer and the Tropic of Capricorn, was the torrid zone, which was always hot. Between the Tropic of Cancer and the Arctic Circle, and between the Tropic of Capricorn and the Antarctic Circle, were the temperate zones, which were neither hot nor very cold. Around both poles were the frigid zones, which were always cold.

The pattern was simple and easy to learn, but it had very little relation to the real earth. The "torrid zone" has regions of perpetual snow on its highlands. The "temperate zone" has extreme temperatures ranging from 50 degrees below zero to more than 130 degrees above. Within the "frigid zone" there may be summer days when the temperature rises above 90 degrees. Evidently a useful classification of climates cannot be quite so simple.

The climate of a region is controlled by a combination of many factors. So many combinations are possible that no two regions of the earth have exactly the same climate. In order to classify climates, they must be grouped and small variations must be disregarded.

Distance from the equator, or latitude, is one factor in climate. It is related, not only to temperature, but also to rainfall, wind direction, hours of daylight, number of storms, and the kind and degree of seasonal differences.

Another factor is elevation, height above sea level. High mountains can make a tropical area as icy as Greenland and bring tundra vegetation to equatorial Africa. The temperature drops, on the average, about 3.3 degrees for every thousand feet of elevation. Highlands can bring rain in a desert or dryness to a lowland on their leeward side, as on the east coast of southern South America.

A region in the center of a continent will have a more severe climate, with hotter summers and colder winters, than a region at the same latitude near the ocean. West coasts, in general, have milder climates than east coasts in the same latitudes. Toward the poles from about 40° of latitude north or south, most west coasts have much more rain than east coasts; but from about 20° to 30° north and south, most west-coast regions are very dry. These variations are caused by the difference in prevailing winds. Ocean currents also have an effect on the climate of coastal regions. Warm currents bring heat and rain to the land. Cold currents chill the air.

Another element in climate is the tilt of the earth's axis in relation to the sun. Because of it, the noonday sun shines directly overhead north of the equator during half the year and south of it during the other half. Because of this shift, the seasons change.

The world wind belts shift north and south with the changing position of the sun's vertical rays, and this change helps give the earth its delightful Mediterranean regions. When the sun is south of the equator, the belt of westerly winds shifts far enough south to blow across the Mediterranean Sea. These are moist winds from the Atlantic, and they bring rain. When the direct rays of the sun fall north of the equator, desert conditions shift north, too, and the Mediterranean lands have no rain. In the same latitude in southern California, there is the same effect. At the same distance south of the equator, there are regions of Mediterranean climate in South America, Africa, and Australia.

Temperature around the year, rainfall, seasonal contrasts, the changeability of the weather from day to day—all these make up the climate of any given place. World patterns of climate are closely related to patterns of vegetation, to population density, and to all human activities.

The warmth and humidity of these terraced rice fields in the Philippines are almost visible. The region is classified as "humid low latitude." Low latitude places the area near the equator, and high temperature and moist air make the climate humid.

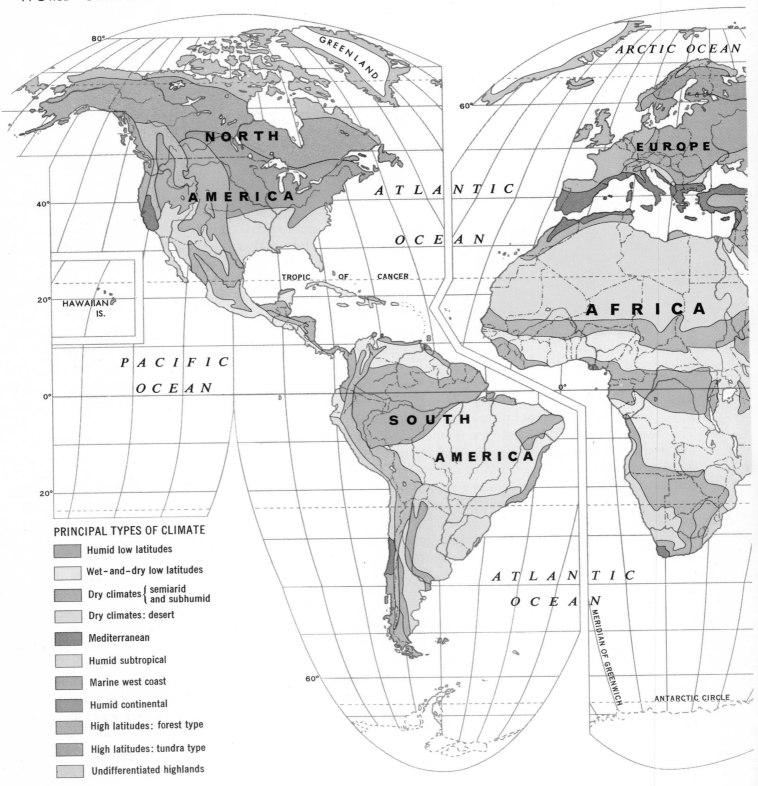

PRINCIPAL TYPES OF CLIMATE

- Humid low latitudes
- Wet-and-dry low latitudes
- Dry climates { semiarid and subhumid
- Dry climates: desert
- Mediterranean
- Humid subtropical
- Marine west coast
- Humid continental
- High latitudes: forest type
- High latitudes: tundra type
- Undifferentiated highlands

CLIMATES OF THE WORLD

Lowlands near the equator are the humid low-latitude regions of the world, warm and wet the year round. The wet-and-dry low latitudes are also near the equator, but they have a distinct dry season during the year. These regions of seasonal rainfall are characteristically grassland with scattered trees or shrubs. Crops must be able to complete their growth during the rainy season unless irrigation is possible. They are also seasonally good pasture lands.

Semiarid and subhumid climates vary from not quite enough moisture for farming to lands that are popularly

ARCTIC CIRCLE

A S I A

TROPIC   OF   CANCER

P A C I F I C

O C E A N

EQUATOR
LONGITUDE EAST OF GREENWICH

I N D I A N   O C E A N

TROPIC   OF   CAPRICORN

AUSTRALIA

called deserts. A little grain may be raised, and usually there is a cover of short grass. Geographers generally restrict the word desert to still drier lands.

Mediterranean climates are well known for their dry summers and humid winters. Except for grain grown in winter, most farm crops require irrigation.

Humid subtropical lands are well supplied with moisture. They have a long growing season, but winter has at least a few cold days. Typical crops are cotton and rice.

Marine west-coast climates have fairly heavy rain and winters made mild by ocean winds.

A humid continental climate means hot summers and cold winters. The natural vegetation may have been either forest or grass.

The term "high latitudes" refers to the high numbers of the parallels—from about 60° to 90°. The high-latitude type of climate in the northern hemisphere may extend south in places beyond 50°. The southern hemisphere has none of this climatic type because only Antarctica lies south of 60°. There are two types of high-latitude climate, the forest and the tundra. The tundra type is a little colder and a little drier.

The most remote and isolated place on earth, Antarctica, is also the coldest. It is cut off from all other continents by hundreds of miles of angry sea and attacked ceaselessly by fierce winds. The frigid temperature of the great icy land mass affects the climate of the entire world.

To the South African Bushmen of the Kalahari Desert, water is almost the most precious thing on earth. Streams flow only after the rare rains. Drinking water may have to be drawn up through hollow reeds from the very little moisture that remains in the sand of the streambeds.

Rain falls or does not ....green land or barren decrees abundance or want.

Winters are long and cold, summers hot and often dry, but this field in North Dakota is part of the great North American wheat belt, which produces food for millions of people. There are also many cattle ranches in this area, which is near the western edge of the humid continental region.

"England's green and lovely land" is, in a sense, a gift of the sea. This beautiful farming country with its many trees, along the southwestern coast of England, is typical of regions with a marine west-coast climate. Winds from the Atlantic Ocean keep the temperatures mild and bring rain and many cloudy days.

Mountains are the most conspicuous landforms on the face of the earth. The top of Mount McKinley is the highest point in North America, almost four miles above sea level. The mountain can be seen from many miles away, and the view from its summit is said to encompass 3,000 square miles of Alaska, with lower mountains, valleys, rolling hills, and tundra-covered plains.

LANDFORMS

Since they first had languages for speaking, people have been naming landforms. They have given individual names to specific features, and they have also created general names for whole classes of features, such as "mountains." The numerousness of these names indicates the importance that people have always attached to the various forms that make up the surface of the earth.

Mount McKinley is not the highest mountain in the world. Mount Aconcagua in South America is almost a half mile higher, and Mount Everest in the Himalayas is more than a mile and a half higher. The summit of Mount Everest is the highest point on earth, but jet airliners on regularly scheduled flights climb nearly a mile higher. Anyone who has flown across a coastline (sea level) at 30,000 feet or more has looked down from a height greater than the elevation of the highest mountain on earth. Within those narrow limits, plus the depth of a few small land areas that are slightly below sea level, lie all the earth's landforms. The range of inhabited land is still less. Very few people live at an elevation of as much as 12,000 feet. At much lower levels, most people are made uncomfortable by the thinness of the air and a lack of oxygen.

A great variety of landforms and landform names are associated with mountains. There are mountain peaks, summits, ridges, and ranges. A line following the highest elevations of a range is its crest. Mountain ranges are part of highland regions. At the edge of a mountain range, there are usually foothills. Included in highlands are plateaus, high plains, mountain valleys, and many other features.

Lowlands may be plains, valleys, or basins. Plains may be flat, rolling, or hilly. Special types are coastal plains, high plains, and flood plains of rivers.

Another very large group of landforms is associated with coastlines and the relationships between land and water. Land reaches into the water in peninsulas, capes, points, and headlands. Where the land curves inward instead of projecting into the water, there are bays, inlets, fiords, estuaries, gulfs, sounds, and seas.

Straits separate two bodies of land, and isthmuses unite them.

Rivers have sources, channels, and mouths. They cut valleys which may, in special cases, be called ravines, canyons, gulches, and gorges. If a river dries up during part of the year, its valley is an arroyo, or sometimes a draw, in the United States and a wadi in North Africa.

These are only a few of the many landform names commonly used in English. Other languages have their own terms. English has borrowed some of these terms. For instance, fiord is the Norwegian term for a special kind of narrow inlet bordered by mountains. Sierra Nevada Mountains is incorrect usage because "sierra" is Spanish for mountain range.

Another class of names refers to man-made landforms. There are embankments, dikes, levees, mounds, dams, cuts, canals, ditches, polders, and causeways. Other names refer to the use people make of a feature. A valley through mountains is not a pass unless it is used as a transportation route. A bay is not a harbor unless it becomes a shelter for ships.

Geographic terms are hard to define because they have not been applied scientifically. Features were usually named by early explorers and settlers, not by geographers. East and west of India are two extensions of the Indian Ocean of about the same size and general shape. There is no good geographic reason why one should be the Arabian Sea and the other the Bay of Bengal. Hudson Bay is three times as large as the Baltic Sea, and much larger than the Persian Gulf.

There are no definitions that will make sharp distinctions between gulfs, seas, and bays; straits and channels; capes and points. A plateau is almost impossible to define satisfactorily, though many plateaus are named on the map. Features may be called mountains in one place, while very similar features in another place are called hills.

People have invented so many names for landforms because the surface features of the earth are of great importance to human living.

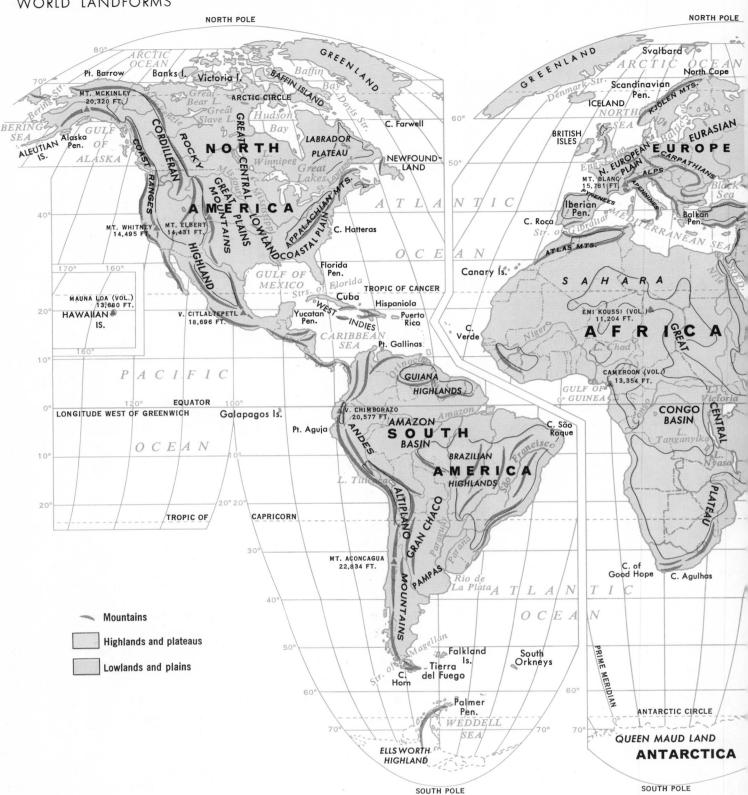

Mountains

Highlands and plateaus

Lowlands and plains

LANDFORMS OF THE WORLD

The map on these pages is a generalized representation of the landforms of the earth. The major mountain ranges, indicated by wide gray lines, appear as parts of great mountain systems, such as the Rockies. Even these systems are not the end of the story of mountain relationships. The western highlands of the Americas sweep on range after range from northwestern North America to the southern tip of South America, but even that is not the end. They appear again in the spine of the Palmer Peninsula of Antarctica.

The Old World has an even more spectacular system of mountains. Starting with the Pyrenees and the Atlas ranges, the mountains curve through the Apennines and Alps to the Carpathians and continue through central Asia. Then the pattern splits up into several branches. One runs through China and southeastern Asia to the islands and continues along the coast of Australia.

Another branch makes a circuit through northeastern Asia, curving back to the south through ranges in Kamchatka, Korea, Japan, the Philippines, and Borneo. At the far northeast of Asia, other ranges link up with those of North America.

Most of the great plateaus of the world are associated with mountains. In western North America, the plateaus lie between two systems of mountains. However, some plateaus have bordering mountains and some do not.

This generalized map does not show details of surface features. Maps on pages 1 to 89 should be used with it. Those maps indicate elevations and surface features by various symbols, as shown on page 90.

The highlands....
thrown up by fire,
rock built on rock....

The most terrifying and dramatic of all nature's great spectacles is the eruption of a volcano. Craters, like that shown at left of a volcano in Peru, are usually formed when the top of the mountain collapses after an explosion. Active volcanoes rise from the great mountain chains that encircle the Pacific.

Peninsulas, capes, isthmuses, bays, and straits—all features associated with shorelines—show in miniature along mountain-bordered Lake Scutari on the boundary between Yugoslavia and Albania. In the far distance a tiny island rises from the water. This part of the lake follows the curve of a narrow valley. The land includes many features characteristic of mountain landscapes.